PIMLICO

17

F . E . SMITH

John Campbell was born in 1947 and took his degree at the University of Edinburgh. In addition to *F. E. Smith*, his other books are *Lloyd George: The Goat in the Wilderness* (1977), *Roy Jenkins* (1983) and *Nye Bevan and the Mirage of British Socialism* (1987). He edited *The Experience of World War II* (1989) and is the General Editor of the Cardinal series *Makers of the Twentieth Century*. He also reviews regularly in *The Times*, *TLS*, and occasionally elsewhere. He is currently writing a biography of Edward Heath. He is happily married with two children, and lives in London.

F. E. SMITH

First Earl of Birkenhead

JOHN CAMPBELL

PIMLICO

PIMLICO

20 Vauxhall Bridge Road, London SW1V 2SA

London Melbourne Sydney Auckland Johannesburg
and agencies throughout the world

First published by Jonathan Cape Ltd 1983
Pimlico edition 1991

© John Campbell 1983

Printed and bound in Great Britain by
Mackays of Chatham PLC, Chatham, Kent

ISBN 0-7126-5117-9

To Alison
in love and gratitude

Contents

Part Three: 1919–1924

Part Four: 1924–1930

Preface

It is customary, when offering to the public a book of this size, to make some apology for its length: particularly when the subject, though at the very front of the second rank, is not in the first rank of public figures – in other words, to put it crudely, he was never Prime Minister.

I make no apology, except for the inevitably high price. But I feel I should offer an explanation of why this book has turned out to be so long.

F.E. (as Birkenhead was universally known by his contemporaries, a habit which I have followed) covered in a relatively short career an extraordinary amount of ground. Quite apart from his legal achievements, he played a prominent part in all the main controversies of an exceptionally turbulent period of political history, before, during and after the First World War: more important, he had fresh and penetrating things to say about every one of them. If there is any point in writing about F.E. at all, it seems to me essential not merely to repeat the well-known stories but to examine what he actually did and said, and on what his formidable reputation rested. This necessarily involves some explanation of the often complex issues in contention. But the effort is, I believe, worth while; because F.E., through the force of an outstanding intellect allied to a merciless debating technique and a taste for arguing from fundamentals, sheds more illumination on what these issues were ultimately about than any other controversialist of his day – or many subsequent books. No one, to my knowledge, deployed the Tory case for Ulster or the House of Lords or preparedness for war, against women's suffrage, trade union privileges or Indian nationalism – all unpopular causes today, more often dismissed as 'reactionary' than squarely answered – more seriously or with more intellectual power than did F.E. He was a supreme advocate, and a devastating debater. I hope and believe that this book, in fully examining his arguments, justifies itself not only as biography but as history too.

There are so many episodes that could not be treated usefully at all, except at some length. What would be the point of simply echoing the conventional judgment that F.E.'s was the most brilliant maiden speech in parliamentary history? I wanted to dissect it, gibe by gibe, and explain its obscurities. Similarly the notorious 'Glittering Prizes' speech, which put a phrase into the language but is invariably taken out of context and misunderstood. If F.E. was a 'great' Lord Chancellor, I wanted to see in what greatness on the Woolsack consists. He is commonly accused of hanging Casement and unscrupulously blackening his name; I wanted to look at the evidence. And so on. In particular, I have treated F.E.'s Oxford years at what may seem disproportionate length. I do so on the grounds, first, that it was to an unusual extent at Oxford that F.E. made his reputation, which preceded him into the wider world; and second, that F.E. is so much the epitome of the Oxford (and particularly the Oxford Union) swell, that if the species is not studied in a life of F.E. it never will be.

I wanted also to see his career, not in isolation, but in the context of his friends, rivals and colleagues, so that his fluctuating relationships over thirty years with Churchill and Beaverbrook, with John Simon and Austen Chamberlain, with Archibald Salvidge and Leslie Scott, would recur as continuing themes throughout the book; for so much of the special character of politics in this period is contained in such relationships.

But the single fundamental reason why this book is so long is that I believed substantial quotation to be essential to the purposes of both history and biography. Essential to history, if F.E.'s lucid Toryism was to be fully developed. Essential to biography, since I hold strongly that only a man's words can adequately convey the man. F.E. was in the class of Churchill and Lloyd George as a master of vivid and individual language. Not to quote extensively from his speeches, books and private letters would be to present a mere shadow – F.E. through the glass of my prose darkly, instead of face to face.

For these reasons I make no apology. Neither in point of form nor of content do I believe that F.E. could be encompassed in a shorter book.

JOHN CAMPBELL

Acknowledgments

From the moment I first conceived this book – back in 1975 – I have had nothing but help from the Birkenhead family. I was fortunate to see the second Lord Birkenhead shortly before he died in 1975, and although he clearly realized that my book was intended to supplant his own life of his father, he was kindness itself and gave me every encouragement. His sister, F.E.'s younger daughter, Lady Hartwell, was similarly most helpful in supplying me with the addresses of friends I should speak to and prompting me with other leads and suggestions: I greatly regret that she should have died, in 1982, before she could read the finished book. My most continuous debt has been to the present Lord Birkenhead and to his mother, the Countess of Birkenhead. They have welcomed me (and on occasion my wife) several times to Charlton and, most important, gave me exclusive use of F.E.'s papers there. Most unfortunately, a fire destroyed a considerable part of what was anyway a fairly small collection between my first visit and my second; but I am very grateful for the use of what was saved. I am grateful, too, for their help with illustrations: by allowing me to use a large number of previously unpublished family photographs they greatly reduced my dependence on the expensive commercial picture agencies. Finally I am indebted to Lord Hartwell, first for allowing me access to the minutes of the Other Club; then for generously photocopying the entire typescript for me at the *Daily Telegraph*.

No less valuable has been the help I have received from F.E.'s more distant family: in particular from Hugh Spencer (F.E.'s cousin, the grandson of his uncle E.P. Smith), who at the time I first met him was still a partner in Smith & Sons in Birkenhead. He had in his possession and freely lent me a large collection of family correspondence (extensively quoted in Chapters 2 to 4), plus books of press cuttings relating to F.E., his father and his uncle. As well as himself giving me a great deal of insight into F.E.'s Birkenhead roots, he also introduced me to other cousins and descendants whose recollections of F.E., his mother and his brothers were equally fascinating: Miss Elaine Smith (cousin), Miss

Marjorie Hodgson (cousin) and Mrs Joyce Dangerfield (F.E.'s niece, the daughter of his sister Clara Thompson). I am also grateful to Mr Frederick Thompson (F.E.'s nephew) for sending me his memories.

I cannot thank individually those – more than eighty – who wrote to me in response to letters placed in the *Daily Telegraph* and *Liverpool Post* in 1976. I will only pick out Mrs Enid Kohler (the daughter of F.E.'s clerk J.E. Peteil) who contacted me in this way and sent me the most vivid recollections of a childhood 'dominated by the magical initials F.E.' But I should also like to thank Sir Nigel Fisher, M.P., for sending me, and Sir Herbert Marchant for telling me, one good story each.

Sadly, several of those who gave me valuable interviews have died before the book could come out: Lieutenant-Colonel G.H.M. ('Buns') Cartwright; the Marquesa de Casa Moury (Mrs Freda Dudley Ward); Viscount Gage; Sir John Masterman; and Lord Selwyn-Lloyd. Others to whom I am indebted, and who I hope will be able to read the book, include Lord Boothby; Sir Thomas Harley; Miss Alannah Harper; Dr H. Montgomery Hyde; Mr Kenneth Lindsay; Lord Longford; Mr Bill Rogers; Mr Fletcher Rogers; and Mr Wrayford Willmer. I think particularly fondly of a convivial afternoon with Mr Cyril Burt (F.E.'s one-time secretary) and friends at the Garrick Club, in whose company I felt closer to the spirit of F.E. than at any other time in my researches.

I am indebted for their help to a large number of librarians and archivists – among them Mrs G.J. Smith, the archivist (in 1976) of Liverpool University; Dr Roger Highfield, Librarian of Merton College, Oxford; Mr P.C. Beddingham, Librarian of Gray's Inn; Mr R.A. Storey, of the Modern Records Centre, the University of Warwick; the indispensable Mr Walters, Senior Librarian of the Oxford Union; Jim Schoff, of the Centre for the Study of Cartoons and Caricature at the University of Kent; and Liz Moore of the *Illustrated London News* Picture Library; also the archivist (in 1976–7) of Wadham College, Oxford, whose name has unfortunately slipped my notes. I am grateful, in addition, to the Headmaster of Birkenhead School, Mr J.A. Gwilliam; the Hon. Secretary of Birkenhead Park Rugby Club, Mr Graeme Marrs; the chairman of the Oxford University Faculty of Law, Mr J.W. Davies; and the Assistant Regional Director (South-West) of the Midland Bank, Mr J.K. Lander, whose offices now occupy 32 Grosvenor Gardens. If I have omitted others whose help exceeded the call of duty, I can only ask them to forgive me: there have been so many.

Many friends have helped me: first and foremost Paul Addison, who certainly encouraged me to take up the subject and may even have been the first to suggest it – since when, over a distance of 400 miles, he has been an unfailing source of inspiration, example and advice. Kathleen Burk, Philip Williamson, John Ramsden, Gerard Douds, John Brown and Owen Dudley Edwards all allowed me to transplant fruitful clippings from their own scholarship. Richard Dawkins got up at an early hour to take a photograph of 32 Grosvenor Gardens for me. To John and Janet Betts I am eternally grateful for having happened to be living in Birkenhead at just the time I needed them there, and for having generously put me up on several visits.

David Machin was the publisher who first believed in the book and originally commissioned it for Jonathan Cape. Unfortunately he subsequently moved on and is now at the Bodley Head, so it was not to him that I eventually delivered the finished typescript; but I am grateful to Liz Calder and Graham C. Greene for taking the project over and publishing it nearly complete despite its length – also to Liz Cowen, who had the mammoth job of editing it. I should also like to mention my agent, Bruce Hunter, for his continuous encouragement over a long haul.

I am grateful to the Twenty-Seven Foundation for some financial help in the early stages; and to the Fellows of St Antony's College, for electing me to an Alistair Horne Fellowship in 1980–1 which was both immensely pleasurable in itself and a great financial help towards the end. I should also record my gratitude to the Trustees of the London Library for enabling me to afford continued membership of their indispensable institution.

Finally, my wife Alison. It was she who was the family breadwinner during the whole time that I was writing the book, and without her it could not have been written. I am enormously grateful to her for her faith, love, support and encouragement (not to mention proof-reading); and it is only proper that the book should be dedicated to her.

Credits

I should like to thank the following individuals and institutions for permission to quote from material of which they own the copyright: Rt Hon. Julian Amery, for Leo Amery papers; the Beaverbrook Foundation, for Beaverbrook, Lloyd George and Bonar Law papers; Mrs Mary Bennett, for H.A.L. Fisher's diaries; the Earl of Birkenhead, for Birkenhead papers; the University of Birmingham, for Austen and Neville Chamberlain papers; Hon. Mark Bonham Carter, for Asquith papers; the British Library, for Balfour papers; Cambridge University Library, for Baldwin papers; Hon. Edward Carson, for Carson papers;

Miss D.E. Collins, for G.K. Chesterton's *AntiChrist*; Edward Colman, for Lord Alfred Douglas's *The Rhyme of F Double E*; Sir Matthew Farrer, for Hanworth papers; William Heinemann Ltd, for Churchill papers; Hodder & Stoughton Ltd, for excerpts from Stanley Salvidge, *Salvidge of Liverpool*; Mrs Maxse, for Maxse papers.

The author and publishers are also grateful to the following for permission to reproduce copyright illustrations: Beaverbrook Foundation; the Earl of Birkenhead; William Collins Ltd; Express Newspapers Ltd and the Centre for the Study of Cartoons and Caricature, the University of Kent; *Illustrated London News;* Keystone Press Agency; The Oxford Union Society; Oxford University Press; *Punch;* BBC Hulton Picture Library.

He was tall, dark, slender and a little over-dressed. His eyes and hair were lustrous; the first from nature, the second from too much oil. His mouth had always a slightly contemptuous droop, his voice was a beautiful drawl. He had acquired, not diligently but with too much ease, the airs of a fox-hunting man who could swear elegantly in Greek. Many people loved him, most distrusted him, some despised him, and he despised almost everybody. In his later career as Earl of Birkenhead he served himself more faithfully than his God or his country, and has been left naked to his biographers; who, when they come to dealing with him, will discover among other less creditable attributes that he was without question the most fascinating creature of his times.

George Dangerfield, *The Strange Death of Liberal England*

PART ONE
1872–1906

1

The Smiths of Birkenhead

Fifty years before F.E. Smith was born, the town from which he took his title did not exist.

Birkenhead appeared very late on the map of industrial England. For centuries there was nothing on the west bank of the Mersey but a few small villages – a map of 1777 shows Walizey, Bidston, Tranmere and Upper Bevington[1] – and, at the mouth of the Birket stream, the ruins of a Benedictine priory dissolved by Henry VIII. The monks had operated, by licence of Edward I, a ferry to Liverpool, the Woodside Ferry, which still runs today; but it carried no great traffic until 1824. In that year an enterprising Scot, William Laird, recently arrived from Greenock, saw the possibilities of the deserted shore for shipbuilding. He bought land there, built dockyards – from which he and his son were soon turning out some of the earliest iron ships – and founded, with high ambition, a new town. That he had in mind no less a model than the elegant expansion of his native Edinburgh is demonstrated by his employment of a Scottish architect, James Gillespie Graham, to design a similar rectangular street plan for Birkenhead, with a handsome central forum, Hamilton Square, corresponding to Robert Adam's Charlotte Square. In the same spirit he engaged Joseph Paxton, from Chatsworth, to lay out a magnificent public park – the first in any town in Britain to be provided at public expense. Birkenhead also boasted, some years later, the country's first trams. The town grew rapidly. Where in 1821 there had lived a bare 200 souls, the census of 1841 counted over 8,000. Five years later the population was estimated at 40,000, but a sharp recession in 1847 temporarily checked this furious expansion, so that in 1851 the official figure was only 24,000, from which, however, it continued to increase steadily throughout the century. In the middle of that booming decade, Birkenhead's explosion excited the attention of the whole country. Disraeli, in *Tancred*, cited the town satirically as the very embodiment of deluded progress. *Chambers' Edinburgh Journal* hailed its sudden rise as 'one of the greatest wonders of the age'; while the *Illustrated London News* sang its praise in verse.

Another glory on the Mersey's side:
   A town springs up as from a magic wand.
Behold these noble docks – the merchants' pride,
   And the fair park extending o'er the strand.
The gallant bark that often had defied
   The wild Atlantic, may no longer dread
The treacherous shore; in safety, now 'twill ride
   Within the waters of fair Birkenhead.[2]

In 1877 Birkenhead came of age. Tranmere and the growing suburbs of Oxton and Claughton were incorporated with it to form a new borough with a combined population of around 80,000. F.E. Smith was then aged five. His father was one of the borough's first Councillors. His grandfather had been one of the original immigrants to the town in the 1830s.

The Smiths came originally from Yorkshire. F.E.'s great-grandfather, Thomas, was a pit-worker of some sort – possibly a fan minder – in the mining village of Allerton Bywater in the West Riding, between Leeds and Pontefract, though he lived a few miles away at Rothwell, whence he rode to work, it is said, on a mule. He is reputed to have been the champion runner and bare-knuckle fighter of the north of England; but these are so clearly the attributes with which his great-grandson would have chosen to credit his ancestor that this claim must be treated with some caution. Thomas Smith, at any rate, managed to keep one of his sons out of the pit. It was this son, also called Thomas, who can most truly be said to have founded the family fortunes.

F.E. liked to portray himself as a self-made man. On his elevation to the peerage he took as his motto the characteristically defiant Latin pun *Faber Meae Fortunae* – Smith of My Own Fortune. Politically this may have been legitimate; F.E. undoubtedly scaled the heights of power and fame by his own unaided efforts. But he did not start his ascent from a base of poverty or even mean gentility, but from a home life of considerable comfort, in which, moreover, the seed of ambition was planted early and deliberately cultivated. His father and grandfather were at least as much 'self-made' as he – perhaps more, since it was they who struggled up the lower rungs of social advancement. The career of each was, in its own sphere, no less remarkable than F.E.'s own; that of his father was a powerful example to him. In truth, the whole line of Smiths, rather than any one of them, should be called self-made; for their history furnishes a model of that Victorian ideal of improvement celebrated by Samuel Smiles – the eldest of each generation raising himself on the shoulders of his father and passing on to his son the opportunity and the ability to rise higher. F.E.'s proud motto fits them all, back to old Thomas. Each played his part equally in the family's progress. Each contributed something to the making of the Lord Chancellor.

F.E.'s grandfather made the critical break from manual to mental work. The younger Thomas, though he was entirely self-taught, somehow acquired sufficient classical education to become a schoolmaster and Wesleyan lay preacher, first in Wakefield, then for a time in Anglesey, and finally in Birkenhead, where he settled some time between 1836 and 1840. There, summing up the need of the expanding town with the sharp business eye of the devout puritan, he soon abandoned teaching and established himself more profitably as an estate agent. Scholarship, the *Birkenhead News* recorded shortly after his death, remained his first love, 'He devoted the whole of his spare time to reading, and it was no uncommon thing for him to read eight hours a day.'[3] Nevertheless the business prospered. He had married Bathsheba Green, a fellow schoolteacher from Wigan,* who bore him five sons and three daughters; three of the former, Frederick, Alfred and Edward, in due course joined him as partners, so that by the time he retired in 1877, the firm of Smith & Sons was solidly established all over Merseyside and the Wirral. To this day its placards still proclaim the name of Smith in every street.

The eldest son Frederick, however, was a boy of too much spirit to enter immediately into such safe employment. After a good education at the High School of the Liverpool Institute which naturally pointed him in that direction, he left home abruptly at the age of sixteen to join the army. Whether he ran away or was ordered out is not certain. The family tradition is that he was ordered from the house by his pious father for the sin of skating on a Sunday. But the *Birkenhead News*, in a tribute published in his lifetime, says that 'his heart was stirred by a love of adventure, and the thought of sitting on a four-legged stool over a ledger was hateful to him'.[3] For whatever reason, he left in January 1861 and enlisted in the Royal Regiment of Artillery, whence he transferred almost at once to the Royal Horse Brigade and was sent to India. If half the stories of his four years there are true, he had a remarkable military career – remarkable not so much for its actual soldiering (though he saw

* This is the grandmother to whom F.E.'s daughter Eleanor romantically attributed gypsy blood, a fantasy which her brother incautiously repeated in the first edition of his life of their father, stating that her past was 'full of mystery'. According to the more prosaic testimony of the *Birkenhead News*, Miss Green was merely the daughter of the foreman of the Phoenix Ironworks in Wigan. Late in life, however, she was remembered in Birkenhead as a 'bespectacled old lady with ways and will and mind of her own'. (J. R. Kaighin, *Bygone Birkenhead*, p. 313). There survives in the possession of Mrs Joyce Dangerfield a letter she wrote to her son Frederick, then aged eight, in 1852, signed 'Mother B. Smith'.

rough service against the hill tribes on the North-West Frontier, and was promoted Sergeant and acting Sergeant-Major before he was twenty-one), as for the commercial enterprise with which he supplemented his army pay. He ran a canteen and a theatre, acted as regimental auctioneer, taught French to the officers' children and was secretary (paid) of the Punjab Auxiliary Committee of the Bengal Asiatic Society. As the *News* commented, he returned to Birkenhead 'a first-class all-round man'.[3] In 1866 his father suffered a serious illness, so Frederick bought himself out of the army and came home to join Smith & Sons. For some years he devoted himself energetically to the expansion of the firm adding, with the benefit of his Indian experience, auctioneering to its activities, and taught in Sunday School, with an originality never forgotten by at least one of his pupils.[4] He married, about 1869, Elizabeth, the daughter of a local rate collector (also reputedly of Yorkshire origin), Mr Edwin Taylor. The couple lived at first in Pilgrim Street, a short street of very modest houses between Hamilton Square and the Mersey; and it was here that their first daughter, Clara, and their first son, Frederick Edwin, were born. The young F.E. was still a baby, however, when they moved a mile and a half out of town to a new house in Green Lawn, Tranmere. By 1875 Frederick Smith, at the age of thirty, was a businessman of some independent substance, and ready to turn his energies to politics. He stood, as a Liberal, for the Tranmere Local Board, and was elected.

His political views at this date were scarcely pronounced. He was a Liberal for no better reason than that his father was a Liberal. In 1876 he was approached by the local Conservatives with an invitation, or a veiled threat, that he should join them if he wished to retain his seat. He refused, but left the Liberals and stood for re-election as an Independent. Defeated, he duly threw in his lot with the Tories, marking his conversion with 'a strong speech' in the Birkenhead Debating Society in favour of the foreign policy of Disraeli's Government.[3] His timing was impeccable. With the incorporation in 1877 of Tranmere into Birkenhead, he was elected one of six Conservative Councillors for the Egerton Ward. Only two Liberals were returned for the whole borough, and they succeeded 'in spite of their politics and not on account of them'.[3] A Tory was the thing to be in Birkenhead in the 1870s.

These were also good years to be a Councillor. The borough was just entering on its second great period of growth. Under the continuing leadership of the Laird family – John Laird, son of the original William, was the town's first M.P., and his sons John and William were its first two mayors – Birkenhead still had pretensions to rival Liverpool. In 1887 an imposing town hall was completed in Hamilton Square 'such as would do no discredit to the largest of our cities';[5] while in the previous year the Prince of Wales had opened the Mersey railway tunnel. This achievement, intended to guarantee the town's bright future, in reality doomed it. The replacement of the old ferry by a rapid rail link reduced independent Birkenhead to a mere dormitory of Liverpool. Of course, the inevitability of decline was not immediately apparent. But as early as 1893 the signs were clear to the visitor who could read them.

> The town of Birkenhead is well planned, the principal streets crossing each other at right angles, and about twenty yards wide; but the streets are chiefly lined with cottage property, with unsightly gaps occurring at short intervals, giving an air of over-growth and too sudden expansion, and showing that the dreams of its founders have not yet been fulfilled.[5]

They never were. Today the centre of 'fair Birkenhead', surrounding the elegant quadrangle of Hamilton Square, is a wasteland of inner city decay.

In the years of its confident heyday, however, Frederick Smith was one of Birkenhead's leading citizens. As such, much can be learned of his character from lengthy 'appreciations' in the local press – for this was an age when local newspapers reported local politics at greater length and with greater seriousness than any paper today devotes to national politics. The special interest of these 'appreciations' for the biographer of F.E. Smith lies in the quite extraordinary likeness that they reveal between father and son. In deference to the legend that F.E. was a phenomenon *sui generis*, too little attention has been paid in the past to the extent to which he actually modelled himself, or was modelled by heredity, on his father. Justice must now be done to a man who, though he trod a narrower stage than his son, trod it so commandingly that by the time of his early death he had opened up for himself those wider horizons which F.E. would conquer.

His career was founded on his gift of public speaking. In an article published in February 1880, rather over two years after his election to the borough council, the *Birkenhead Advertiser* commented somewhat acidly on his record.

> He has taken an active part in the public business of the Council, but has attended indifferently the committees of which he is a member. It would appear that he works best when he is under the stimulating influence resulting from the presence of the representatives of the 'fourth estate', and when there is a probability of the smart things said and done by him being recorded, or when he is face to face with a mob who may be trusted to cheer him if he makes good points.

Condoning this tendency on the ground of youth, however – Frederick
was then thirty-five – the paper expressed the hope that time would
'break him in to work and render him somewhat less of a free lance than
he is at present'. There followed a vivid evocation of his power on the
platform which demands comprehensive quotation:

> He has in him the makings of an orator of the first rank . . . He is
> gifted with fluency, a commanding presence, a rich, sonorous
> voice, and an abundance of energy and confidence in himself. He
> looks like a man calculated to bear down opposition simply by the
> exercise of his own strong will and the thrusting into prominence
> of his own virile personality. Seeing him in one of his rhetorical
> whirlwinds you might fancy that there was in him a turbulent
> spirit to whom strife was as necessary as sunlight is to the flowers.
> He lays about him with a fierceness which has something imposing
> about it. An average meeting is quick to recognize his potentiality.
> People feel that he is able to put into tangible shape the dislike and
> the longing to visit terrible consequences on the heads of their
> opponents of which they are the victims and which are struggling
> to find expression. So when he is at his bitterest – occasionally he is
> unreasonably bitter, fairness towards those against whom he
> arrays himself not being one of his characteristics – they cheer him
> to the echo . . .
>
> Opposition only seems to add fuel to the passion which is
> seemingly raging within him. He will deal with an interruption in
> a savage, summary way, bringing to the front his own virile
> personality, and, in nine cases out of ten, the interrupter will
> inwardly quail before his flashing eyes, scornful tones and defiant
> manner, and regret that the interruption was ventured on. The
> force of the gentleman's oratory lies more in how he delivers
> himself than in what he says, though he makes many good points,
> displays considerable power in the construction of glowing sen-
> tences, indicates that he is a master of the art of derision, shows
> that he knows how to handle facts, and, lastly, demonstrates that
> no-one in the borough is better able to twist an argument to suit his
> purpose of the moment or to tell half a truth in a manner altogether
> damaging to his opponents. But even these decided gifts pale
> before that of his manner . . .
>
> It is, to some extent, theatrical, melodramatic indeed, no doubt.
> But it is, in most of its phases, decidedly effective. Who can help
> being moved when he defends a maligned colleague in tones of
> indignant, highly-wrung pathos which seem to rumble up from
> the pit of his stomach? Who can be emotionless as, when he

reaches the climax of one of the subjects of a speech, he claps his hand on his breast, throws his head back and his chest forward, advances a step or two, speaks at the top of his resonant voice, his ringing tones having risen, in well-arranged order, until they have attained their highest pitch, and, finally, ere the gathering storm of applause breaks over his head, strikes a defiant attitude, which seems to say, 'Here I am; come on, all who like; I am ready for you'?

Again, who can avoid being uncomfortable, if against him – or comfortable, if with him – as he sneers at some poor being whom he has taken upon himself to deride? You have an unpleasant consciousness that the jeers seem to derive additional force as they fall from his tongue and are illuminated by the sarcastic expression of his face . . . Under these circumstances it is not surprising that he is able to carry an audience along with him, though many of it will not approve of the line of action which he is pursuing, and would not like to endorse all the allegations which he makes.

Frederick Smith was clearly not a steady man. 'His enemies maintain that his career will be meteoric . . . His popularity is not commensurate with his talents and he is regarded with distrust by a considerable section of the community.' The *Advertiser* clearly shared a good deal of this mistrust; yet it declined to judge him, concluding that his destiny was in his own hands. 'He has talents much above the average, he has ample opportunity of distinguishing himself ready to his hand, and if, at any time, he makes complete shipwreck of his reputation as a public man he will have only himself to blame.'[6]

He made no shipwreck. In 1881 he was 'broken in to work' as Chairman of the Health, Baths and Parks Committee. His area of responsibility included much that was unglamorous. He risked the loss of his seat by proposing to site a large refuse destructor in Tranmere; and he was 'more than once . . . savagely called to task in connection with the bestowal of the contract for the removal of nightsoil'. His powers of persuasion proved equal to both challenges; but easier popularity was to be won in the Park. Into Paxton's design he introduced cricket and football pitches, bowling greens and a quoiting ground.

He also brought about the erection of lavatories and other conveniences, and earnestly and triumphantly advocated the building of the bandstand, from which such acceptable music has been discoursed on weekday evenings and Saturday afternoons during the past summer or two under the direction of the Ladies' Park Music Committee.[3]

By such achievements are local reputations made. In 1886 Councillor Smith was elected an Alderman.

His eyes were not fixed on the parish pump, however. He had wider political ambitions and, more immediately, a higher professional ambition. At the end of 1883 he resigned from Smith & Sons* and set himself (at the age of thirty-eight) to read for the Bar, undertaking to eat the necessary number of dinners in the Middle Temple. For a couple of years his occupation is listed in the Birkenhead municipal handbook as 'Gentleman'. Then in July 1886 he was called to the Bar; taking chambers in Liverpool, he joined the Northern Circuit, specializing successfully in licensing cases. But Frederick Smith practised as a barrister for only two years: he was given no time to prove his quality on any really important case. His three years of training, however, and his determination to exchange the comfortable security of real estate for the risky glamour of the Law, must have made a profound impression on his son. Not many thirteen-year-olds see their fathers reading for examinations. It was surely from this age that F.E. knew that he must follow his father to the Bar.

Nor was Frederick content with the politics of refuse collection. He became known as a political lecturer throughout Cheshire and Lancashire, and was a valued platform speaker for the Conservatives in national politics: at the General Election of 1885 he spoke in at least three constituencies besides Birkenhead. He was the most vigorous member of the Executive Committee of the local Conservative Association, and by the time of his death was being spoken of as a possible M.P. for the borough in the near future. (A newspaper popularity poll placed him fourth: first and second, inevitably, were the Laird brothers.) As to his political philosophy, the *Birkenhead News* – defiantly Liberal amid the encircling Toryism – judged him a Conservative of a distinctly modern stamp:

> Probably we are not mistaken when we say that he is keenly in sympathy with Lord Randolph Churchill, whose Conservatism, however unsightly it may be in the eyes of a thorough-going Liberal, has very little in common with the Toryism of a quarter of a century ago.[3]

---

* Frederick's resignation left his brother Edward (the third son) in control of the firm. The second son, Alfred, had gone to New Mexico in 1878 and died there from drinking bad water. The fourth son, William, became an estate agent with another firm, and the fifth, Arthur, became a solicitor. Edward Smith's grandson, Mr W.H. Spencer, was the last family partner, until his retirement in 1976.

The positive side of this Conservatism was that concern for the condition of the people which became known as Tory Democracy: Frederick would rhapsodize about 'the glorious rule which characterised the government of Beaconsfield from 1874 to 1880, when more was done for the working classes by broad and wise legislation than had been accomplished in twenty-five years by agitators'. The negative side, which provided the muscle of all Merseyside Toryism for the next thirty-five years, was absolute opposition to Irish Home Rule. With the rise of Parnell's party to the point where it held the balance in the House of Commons, and Gladstone's subsequent conversion to the Irish cause, the latter was the emotive theme which tended to dominate Frederick's speeches. He made great play with the iniquity of Parnell's hold over the Liberal leader, and could always rouse an audience with a ringing patriotic peroration, 'Englishmen may be dull, but they are not, as yet, absolute fools . . . Though there may be dangers around us, naught can make us rue if England to herself but proves true.' (Loud and long continued applause.)*

At a Council meeting on 9 November 1888 Frederick Smith was unanimously elected Mayor of Birkenhead. The *News* gleefully hailed the event as a significant defeat for the older Tories:

> It is an open secret that a certain section of the Conservative Party
> . . . do not like it. Perhaps it would be difficult for them to put their
> antagonism into words, because many of their objections are of
> such a character that sensible persons would only laugh at them if
> they were firmly stated. Still, there is a mass of discontent under
> the surface to be dealt with . . . The power is plainly slipping out of
> the hands of the local Conservatives of the antique type, who used
> to exercise such a despotic sway . . . Clearly, Birkenhead Con-
> servatism is becoming democratised . . . and there are appearances
> that it will not much longer be prepared to elect as member for the
> borough any superannuated soldier, innocent of a knowledge of
> local requirements, whom the Carlton Club may see fit to send
> down here . . .†

The new Mayor was to be welcomed, even by Liberals, as a symbol of this process. He was 'essentially a worker', who had made his own way by his own efforts, not another ornamental drone.

* Speech at a Conservative demonstration at the Theatre Royal, Birkenhead, 12 September 1887. (*Birkenhead News*, 14 September 1887.)

† Lieutenant-General Sir E.B. Hamley, M.P. for Birkenhead 1885–92, was the particular *bête noir* of the *Birkenhead News*.

F.E. Smith, First Earl of Birkenhead

Without endorsing all that he has done, indeed with a disposition
to strongly condemn many of his past speeches and actions, we say
that this is a matter for great satisfaction . . . Liberals may be
excused if they decline to regard Mr. Smith's public life with
approval . . . But they will, we are sure, be prepared to give him a
fair trial and return a true verdict on the evidence which he may
himself supply during the next twelve months.[7]

Alas, his only public act as Mayor was to preside at the opening of
the Birkenhead and Wirral Horticultural Show. In the last week of
November he travelled to London to attend a civic banquet, and caught
a cold on the way back – as a result, it was said, of changing at Crewe
from a warm to an unheated railway carriage. He ignored the symptoms
and returned to work, insisting on chairing a long committee meeting
when already seriously ill. The following day, 29 November, acute
bronchitis set in; he lay unconscious for ten days, and died early on
Sunday morning, 9 December, exactly one month after his election. He
was forty-three.

Reporting the event, the newspapers indulged in an excess of mawkish
melodrama. ('The Mayor is dead! These words fell with a dull, heavy
thud on many a heart last Sunday morning.')[8] Sickly poems by various
hands ('Not dead but gone before')[9] flowed into their offices and were
duly printed, along with sentimental anecdotes and the inevitable story
that his pocket watch had stopped at the precise hour of his death. One
columnist reflected sombrely on the irony that what men most desire
destroys them, while the clergy could not resist the opportunity to
emphasize from every pulpit the vanity of earthly ambition. Yet through
the pieties can be discerned a real sense of shock and a sincere admiration for the dead man; while in the obituaries one has once again the
startling impression that it could as easily be F.E. as Frederick Smith
who is being described.

Forgiven now, if not forgotten, were the extravagant invective and
early indiscretions of Frederick's political career, revealed in death as
meteoric after all. The emphasis was all on the 'bold and adventurous
spirit', the 'keen sensibility and ardent temperament' that had prompted
his occasional excesses. The *Birkenhead News* now had 'no hesitation in
stating that Mr. Smith owed not a little of his popularity to his habit of
trenchant speech and his audacity in political warfare'.

Yet, withal, true to type, he had a large and tender heart. He
would go through fire and water for a friend; he loved to do a
kindly action for anybody; and he liked not to be at enmity with
his neighbour, so that over and over again was he the first to make

overtures for peace when there had been a quarrel. Besides, time was softening him in many ways, and when death claimed him for its own he had, in consequence, fewer personal antagonists than had been the case at any other stage of his public career.[8]

A pseudonymous commentator in the same paper made the same point, 'Fred Smith always struck me as being a man who could not bear anyone a grudge very long . . . He was a man with a big heart, and those who knew him best loved him best.' The writer went on to wonder how he had found time to do so much with his life, since 'he was not one of those who took life sadly, but believed in giving himself a fair amount of recreation and pleasure. Indeed I have seldom met a man who could throw himself more thoroughly into pastimes of a light and momentary character'.*[9]

'This private soldier, estate agent, auctioneer, barrister, and mayor,' concluded the *Advertiser*, 'has a monument to his public worth and achievements in all men's hearts.'[10] An appeal to raise a more lasting memorial to him produced £268, in contributions ranging from £15 to 6d each from eighty-four of Messrs Laird's workmen. Frederick Smith was buried on the Wednesday following his death at Flaybrick Hill Cemetery. Fifty-four carriages followed his body, and there was a crowd of some eight thousand mourners. 'Such manifestations of grief and sorrow . . . had never before been witnessed at any public funeral in the borough.'[8] More than a year later, a granite monument, sixteen feet high, was erected over the grave, bearing the Shakespearean inscription, 'After life's fitful fever he sleeps well.'

Frederick Edwin was sixteen at the time of his father's death.

---

* The secret of this energy was perhaps contained in the *News* profile of the previous year (now conveniently available to be reprinted as an obituary), 'He possesses a constitution tough as wire, and a precious ability for sleeping long periods – he can, we believe, sleep as much as sixteen hours at a stretch – when his system has become exhausted by inordinate demands having been made upon it. This . . . enables him to accomplish what it would be futile for other men to attempt.'[3] Like his son, Frederick Smith relied too heavily on the capacity of a superb constitution to absorb punishment.

2

Young Fred

Frederick Edwin was born on 12 July 1872, the second of seven children born to Frederick and Elizabeth Smith in the space of seven years, of whom five survived infancy. The eldest was a daughter, Clara, born in 1870; there followed Fred (so named after his father: Edwin after his maternal grandfather), and another boy, Sidney; then came the two who did not live long enough to be christened; a third son, Harold, born in 1876; and another daughter, Louie. The growing family moved twice during F.E.'s childhood: from his birthplace in Pilgrim Street, Birkenhead, to 4 Green Lawn, Tranmere, around 1875, and from there to an extra-ordinary house, named 'Roslyn', in Clifton Park, Upper Tranmere. These moves reflected Frederick's rapid progress up the Birkenhead social ladder. Clifton Park was a fashionable suburb built in the 1840s and still in the 1870s partly surrounded by open fields. The houses were large and exotic – none more so than 42 Clifton Road.

> An irregular, gabled composition with traceried windows and heavily moulded doorway . . . Fluted chimney with spiral enrich-ment. Despite a certain heaviness, Georgian picturesque eclec-ticism is closer than Victorian seriousness.[1]

In plain language, it is a Gothic monstrosity. The house still stands today, though in a poor state of repair and stripped of the fine railings which formerly encircled it. Even before 1914, Clifton Park – reflecting the decline of Birkenhead itself – had fallen from fashion into seedy multi-occupied decay.

In the 1880s, however, the Smith family evidently lived there in considerable affluence. The recollections of childhood poverty which F.E. liked to indulge in later life were entirely fictitious. They actually possessed a washing machine – a man came once a week to turn the handle – and one of the first two telephones in Birkenhead. There may possibly have been some small household economies – one servant fewer, perhaps – after Frederick resigned from Smith & Sons in 1883 to read for the Bar, but the fact that he could support his family without difficulty through these years of apprenticeship indicates substantial means. He continued to draw a good income from the profits of the firm; while his knowledge of the property market enabled him to speculate successfully on his own account. The truth must be emphasized that Frederick, while he lived, was able to afford his children every advantage in life: a comfortable home; a good education; holidays in Scotland, Ireland and the Isle of Man; possibly even foreign travel. He himself, for the relief of a throat complaint, 'wintered no fewer than four times in Egypt' (a mark of wealth which greatly impressed the *Birkenhead News*).[2] There is some question whether or not he ever took his sons with him on these trips. F.E. used to recall sailing through the Mediterranean and staying at Shepheard's Hotel in Cairo, and even claimed to have astonished the Egyptians by riding a primitive bicycle ('a boneshaker') from the city to the Pyramids. His niece maintains that this is pure fiction. If she is correct, and F.E. never went to Egypt as a boy at all, but imagined all the colourful details faithfully repeated by his son, then he was reversing his usual tendency to exaggerate the deprivation of his childhood, exaggerating its excitement instead. It seems most probable and characteristic, in fact, that his recollections of the exotic and of the penurious were equally imaginary – romantic backcloths dreamed up to compensate for the dull suburban comfort of the truth.*

Frederick seems to have been an indulgent father, not at all the remote Victorian paterfamilias. 'My ambition', he is said to have declared, 'is to be the friend of my children, and when the last grows up, I mean to be Fred to them.'[3] His own father's devout faith was much diluted in him; he still paid five guineas a year for a family pew in the Wesleyan chapel, but his attendance was no more than conventional: he did not lead his household morning and evening in family prayers. Of his children, only Clara could in later life have been called religious. Nevertheless he took his children's secular education very seriously, and demanded high standards of them. His 'most persistent and unconquerable desire', according to the *News*, 'was to mould the minds and careers of his boys'.[2] (It should be said that he did not neglect the girls: both Clara and Louie were sent as weekly boarders to good Birkenhead schools, and he used to take Clara around with him to political meetings. But inevitably the boys were his main concern.) He encouraged them in the habit of reading widely, set them essays out of school, and awarded prizes which it is likely that F.E., if only on the ground of age, became accustomed to winning. It was certainly in his eldest son that Frederick most successfully stoked the fire of ambition.

* It should be said, however, that his more direct descendants insist that F.E. did go to Egypt.

Sidney and Harold may perhaps have felt overshadowed or unfairly disadvantaged; at any rate neither responded so well to their father's competitive methods. It was perhaps significantly Sidney, who achieved the least in life, who was their mother's favourite.

Compared with her husband, Elizabeth Smith remains a somewhat perplexing personality, whose influence upon F.E. it is harder to assess. The outline is clear enough. 'She was a very shrewd woman with great force of character,' a contemporary biographer quotes F.E. as saying. 'No children ever had a better or more affectionate mother. I cannot myself recall an angry word from her since I was a schoolboy, and I cannot doubt that I deserved many.'[4] This might be mere filial piety, but it coincides closely with her granddaughter's memory of her, 'a forceful little woman', but 'one of the kindest . . . a very good grand-mother to all of us'. She was 'iron-willed', but 'completely uninhibited, she didn't mind what anybody said or thought about her'.[5] These, and not least the latter, were all characteristics that she passed on to her eldest son.

In matters of discipline, as in her religion, she was probably stricter than her husband: she used to send the boys out to buy a switch when she needed to beat one of them, and such was their respect for her authority that the culprit always came back with one. She was self-disciplined, too: when Frederick died, she gave up her lunchtime bottle of stout, not as an economy but as an example to the children. Yet her grandson, describing her as 'kindly but dominating' and asserting that 'every member of the household was under her thumb', also refers to her 'almost Oriental sense of priority for the dominant male', which would appal her future daughter-in-law, raised in gentler surroundings.[6] In the true northern manner, F.E. and his brothers were brought up expecting to be waited on and to have chairs vacated for them by their mother and sisters. It can have done F.E.'s character no good that he was the senior male in the household from the age of sixteen; no wonder he could not remember an angry word from his mother 'since he was a schoolboy'. Strong personality though she was, Elizabeth Smith knew her place in a male world, and after her husband's death dedicated herself to furthering the careers of her sons, particularly that of her precocious eldest. F.E. in the years of his success paid handsome tribute to her role in keeping his feet on the ladder after 1888; he was notably attentive to her needs and cared for her with the genuine devotion of a model son. Yet he was primarily his father's boy.

It was clearly Frederick who implanted in F.E.'s young mind the unusual idea for a small boy that the goal of his life should be the Woolsack. There is no certain record of his earliest schooling. At some time he attended a dame school in Birkenhead run by a Mrs Kate

Lewis. But at the age of ten he was sent away to a preparatory school at Southport – a surprising distance, remembering that the Mersey rail tunnel was not yet built. Arriving with a cocky sense of his own destiny, he was not received with the admiration that he expected. A grandson of the headmaster, Mr R.A. Chadwick, has recalled:

> My grandmother found F.E. Smith . . . crying in a corner of a class room, and when she asked him why he was crying, he replied, 'I have been kicked by the other boys because I said that when I grew up I was going to be the Lord Chancellor.'[7]

Thirty-five years later more than one of those boys remembered F.E.'s boast, and wrote to congratulate him on its fulfilment.

F.E. stayed at Sandringham school for three years, from 1883 to 1886. Much later, as is the way of politicians, he recalled this connection in a speech at Southport, claiming somewhat improbably to have got to know every street in the town. In 1930 a local newspaper looked back through the records to discover that 'he studied the classics, with French as an extra, and also took lessons on the piano'. The latter were certainly wasted: F.E. was entirely unmusical, indeed tone deaf – he once stood up for Annie Laurie, thinking it was 'God Save The King', and thereafter would only stand when he saw other people doing so. The paper unearthed further titbits:

> An amusing item in his first term's account of 7s. 6d. for 'glazier's charge' suggests that he had the normal boy's proclivity for breaking windows, while his well-known generosity is possibly foreshadowed by a recurring item of 5s. for the Poor Box.[8]

Inevitably he also carved his name on a desk top, where it remained visible for many years.

In 1886, F.E.'s ambitions – and his father's – suffered a setback. After Sandringham, it had been hoped to send him to Harrow. But the leap from Southport proved too great: Mr Chadwick's classics teaching was not up to the required level. He travelled down with his mother to sit the entrance scholarship, but failed it dismally: he was weeded out on the first day. Among the other so-called 'half-wits' thus ignominiously rejected was a future Cabinet colleague, L.S. Amery, who later wrote of his own experience, 'It was a complete surprise to me that candidates were supposed to be able to translate whole passages of English into Latin prose and even to write Latin verses.' It is likely that F.E. was

similarly out of his depth.* But Mrs Smith and Mrs Amery made
friends. 'We all had tea together and shared our disappointment when
we went up to the school board to look at the list of those required to
stay, and found our names not there.'⁹ F.E. and Amery were to meet
again in happier circumstances at Oxford. Meanwhile Mrs Smith and
her son returned chastened to Birkenhead – his mother (so F.E. later
claimed) buying the thirteen-year-old as consolation a half-bottle of
'unspeakable railway claret'. Instead of Harrow, F.E. was sent for a
term to a local school in Clifton Road run by a Mr Galloway and his son,
before he was accepted in January 1887 into Birkenhead School.

This rare failure in a conspicuously successful academic career never
ceased to rankle with F.E. In 1919, newly appointed Lord Chancellor,
he happened to meet the unfortunate headmaster, the Rev. Dr Welldon
(by then Dean of Durham) at dinner at Lady Londonderry's, and
'attacked him about it across the table, declaring that he had succeeded
in everything that he had undertaken in life except on this one occasion.
It was his only failure.'

> 'It was rather *my* failure', said the Dean politely. He remembered
> the occasion. Mrs. Amery had come to him and told him how
> clever her son was, but all mothers did that. 'Oh', said F.E., not
> yet mollified, 'there was no need for my mother to tell you the
> same thing about me as she felt certain you would have discovered
> it for yourself'. F.E. said to me [Col. Repington] that thirty-three
> years was a long time to wait, but that one always got one's own
> back in time.¹⁰

The blow to his pride apart, it is possible that F.E. might have
conceded on reflection that his failure to get into Harrow did him more
good than harm. By making plain the educational gulf he had to bridge
to reach equality with his more privileged peers, the rebuff gave him the
necessary incentive to develop his full capacity. Industry and indolence
always wrestled in his nature. At Harrow he might well have relaxed too
early, thinking that he had gained the charmed circle already. As it was
he had to struggle to get to Oxford, so that he arrived there a still rough
provincial boy, awed by his opportunity and burning to prove himself.
Easy success from Harrow onwards might have smoothed away that
undisguised lust for success that made him the force, and the individual, that he was.

---

* It was two years later that Winston Churchill sat the same examination, of which
he wrote a memorably imaginative account in *My Early Life*. Lord Randolph's son
however had the social pull to be admitted in spite of failing the exam. Stanley Baldwin
had just left the school.

Birkenhead School was only twenty years old when F.E. went there in January 1887 – a day Public School of rather under a hundred boys, expensive by local standards. The headmaster was Canon Arthur Sloman, a good classicist (he had edited Terence) and President of the Oxford Union in 1875. In both respects he exerted an important influence on F.E. Certainly, under Sloman's instruction, F.E. began to shine as a classical scholar in his own right: not only was he placed fourth in all England in the Cambridge Local Examinations in Latin in April 1888, but within a year of leaving school he was able to collaborate with a fellow student at Liverpool on a published translation of Plautus's *Mostellaria*. Nevertheless he was not the sole nor even the outstanding star in Sloman's constellation, but only one of five members of a remarkable Upper Sixth who between them took first as well as fourth place in Latin, and second and third in Greek, in the Cambridge examinations, and eventually four Oxford or Cambridge fellowships. Birkenhead at this time must have rivalled any school in the country in the quality of its classical education.

The curriculum was not entirely classical, however, and F.E. also carried off prizes in English Literature, English Essay, History and even French. A contemporary remembered him 'leaving the rostrum on Speech Day staggering under a load of prizes'.[11] Sloman also encouraged debating and acting. There are numerous stories of F.E.'s precocity as a public speaker, both formal – offering a wedding present on behalf of the boys of Clifton Park School to the younger Mr Galloway – or informal: haranguing the other boys in the school yard, arguing with a master ('I decline to accept the view you have taken, sir, and I offer you an open challenge to demonstrate before the form that I am wrong'),[12] or retorting insolently to a Liverpool auctioneer. No doubt his father's example served him well in the school debating society.

Similarly, a talent for the stage ran (and still runs) in the Smith family. Frederick had acted in India; F.E.'s brother Harold was an amateur whose performance as Svengali so impressed Beerbohm Tree that he urged him to turn professional; and his younger sister Louie actually became for a brief period a professional actress. During their childhood the family had a private box at the Birkenhead theatre, and Frederick used to hold a children's party at which they would run through the annual pantomine. F.E. was later to devote his histrionic talents to politics and the law; but as a boy he used to write plays for himself and the other children to act, and he took a prominent part in French and Latin plays at school. His last prizegiving in August 1889 was preceded by a performance of Terence in which F.E. aptly took the title role of 'Phormio, an adventurer'.

On that occasion he received from the Bishop of Chester, among his other trophies, a silver medal and certificate 'presented by the Liverpool Shipwreck and Humane Society for exercises in saving life from drowning';[11] a reminder that F.E. was no bookworm but an enthusiastic games-player and all-round athlete. Birkenhead is traditionally a strong rugby school, enjoying close links with the Birkenhead Park Club. F.E. is said to have captained the school XV and played for the Club too, as 'a good rough forward with a strong hand-off',[13] 'fairly skilful, quite fearless and a trifle ruthless'.[14] It may be so. But one cannot help feeling that these attributes have been read back into his schooldays from his Oxford career when one looks at a school photograph showing F.E., aged fifteen or sixteen, as an astonishingly small boy, wiry perhaps, but distinctly smaller than his contemporaries. He grew relatively late. At school he may have been better cut out for the more solitary sports – swimming, running, sailing and cycling. He was certainly a great cyclist (whatever the truth of his Cairo escapade): he and his brother Sidney once rode to Edinburgh and back, and he once rode from Birkenhead to Oxford on a penny-farthing. He liked walking prodigious distances as well: in one of his Oxford vacations he walked some fifty miles non-stop, from Birkenhead to Llandudno, in fourteen hours – characteristically for a £50 bet, the incentive often needed to impel him to some special feat. In fact, F.E. always relished sheer physical exercise for its own sake, in any form, regarding games very seriously as valuable training and a revealing testing ground of character.

It seems likely that he was a popular boy at school: those who are good at both work and games usually are, especially if they display a streak of the daredevil as well. It would be surprising if his self-confidence, easily verging on arrogance, did not make him some enemies among his contemporaries. ('Robson', he swore to one friend, 'before I die I mean to be either Prime Minister or Lord Chancellor of England'; his ambition was widening).[15] But he was usually generous in the exercise of authority over the younger boys – he was a prefect for his last two terms – and more admired than feared, though 'he could tease rather unmercifully'.[16] His son elicited from one of those juniors a warm recollection which rings true, allowing for exaggeration:

> I was a small boy. He was one of the Seniors. He was very kind to me, and did most of my Greek and Latin translations. I thought he was splendid, the best fellow in the school, but my knowledge of Greek and Latin suffered in consequence.[17]

F.E. was actually at Birkenhead School for only two and a half years – eight terms. He left just after his seventeenth birthday, in August 1889, having won a Ranger Scholarship to University College, Liverpool. This was eight months after his father's death. There is no reason to think that he might have stayed on longer: his brother Sidney left a year later, after precisely the same length of stay. But of course Frederick Smith's death did leave his widow with a problem in finishing the education of five children. It is said that she was left an income of £500 a year, presumably derived from Smith & Sons' investments. This may be an underestimate. By way of comparison, her brother-in-law Edward derived an income in 1897 of £800 from rents and £257 from dividends, in addition to the profit of Smith & Sons (£875), and it seems that the brothers used to buy property jointly.[18] Whatever the figures, however, the loss of Frederick's earnings at the Bar inevitably left his family in reduced circumstances.

Help came from Uncle Edward (always known by his initials as E.P.). Seven years younger than his dead brother, and a much less colourful personality, E.P. was nevertheless a scarcely less formidable character. He was, for one thing, a staunch member of the minority Liberal party in Birkenhead. He did not stand for the Council while his Tory brother sat on it, but he was successfully elected two years after Frederick's death and served until his own sudden death in 1899, when the local obituaries mourned another admired Councillor cut off in his prime. He was, it was said, 'one of the best known men in the peninsula of Wirral, and . . . a universal favourite'. 'At all times a trenchant and unrelenting hitter, he none the less had the happy knack of avoiding any pretence of bitterness, and probably for that reason was as popular with his political opponents as with his colleagues.' Outside politics he was respected as a prosperous businessman, and famous for his charity. 'Quietly, for many, many years', the *Birkenhead News* recorded,

> Mr. E.P. Smith played the part of Father Christmas to the street Arabs of Liverpool. With pockets filled with newest coinage he after nightfall regularly traversed the poorest quarters of the great city, brightening the hearts of the little ones by the distribution of the shining latest products of the mint, and tenderly helping the 'guttersnipes' to tide over their misery . . . Never was made a deserving call that did not meet with ready and hearty response.[19]

His charity began at home. It had to. As head of the family firm, E.P. found himself responsible for a lot of troublesome relations – a mad sister Polly, who died in a Shaftesbury home in Formby, leaving a young daughter; a devious brother-in-law (the husband of his other sister Amelia) who, as his fellow-executor, involved him in tiresome wrangles over Polly's will; and a feckless brother, Arthur, who was a

solicitor but not apparently a successful one, since he seems to have
been dependent on subventions from E.P. to keep him (at least metaphorically) from the poorhouse. E.P. shouldered these burdens dutifully, but not without flashes of fierce exasperation:

> You ought, with your abilities [he wrote to Arthur], to be making
> at least £1000 a year, but you are so infernally indolent that you
> have made an absolute wreck of your career and apparently hate
> nothing so much as work and application. Ponder these points in
> your mind and pester me with no more of your foolish letters,
> which will only be put at the back of the fire.[20]

He was cut to the quick when the ungrateful Arthur suggested that he
was 'the fortunate heritor of a business that my brother Fred con-
structed'; he had been in Smith & Sons from the age of seventeen and he
claimed, probably justly, to have played an equal part with Frederick in
building it up.[21]

On Frederick's death it was natural that his widow should become
the first charge on E.P.'s charity. He supported her to the tune of £400 a
year, and placed himself *in loco patris* to her children, though he had five
of his own of similar age and younger. First Sidney and later Harold
were taken, with differing degrees of success, into Smith & Sons; while
E.P. certainly helped to pay for F.E. and his elder sister to go to
university. He took the closest interest in F.E.'s career, probably
thinking that F.E. was the one member of the family who might be
expected to show some return on his investment. Sending him £50 in
1894, he warned quite explicitly, 'I trust it is casting bread upon the
waters to be gathered (for the benefit of your mother, brothers and
sisters) after many [?] days. The fewer the better let us hope.'[22] F.E.
evidently received more than his share of E.P.'s bounty, but if any of the
relatives showed their jealousy they received short shrift. To Arthur,
E.P. wrote sharply in 1897,

> In reference to your remarks about what I have done for F.E.S.,
> they are uncalled-for and grossly impertinent. I know my duty and
> have done and will continue to do it . . . If I wanted advice you are
> about the last man in England I should go to ask for it.[21]

It was his second nephew, Sidney, who caused E.P. most anxiety.
Sidney joined Smith & Sons on leaving school in 1890, but he devoted
his energies less to the firm than to a succession of unlikely enterprises of
his own – a cab business, dog kennels, a smart property deal with a
client arranged privately behind his uncle's back – letting slide the

auctioneering side of Smith's with which he had been entrusted. Repeated avuncular demands that he take a grip on himself produced contrite promises of reform, immediately broken. After eight years, E.P.'s patience was exhausted and Sidney was sacked, owing the firm £60. He still had the cheek to ask for compensation (while accusing his uncle of trying to reserve the business for his own sons); long-suffering as ever, 'because you are the son of my brother', E.P. advanced him £100 'to give you a chance in starting some business'.[23] To Elizabeth Smith, E.P. wrote apologetically,

> He is only 25 years of age and in my opinion his being cast upon his own resources to try and found a business of his own will do him all the good in the world. If he were an absolute duffer, he would go to the wall, but if he has the pluck and go of a Smith in him he will realize his position, buckle down to work and make a living, leaving his dogs and his pleasures alone until he has made a business which I know he is well capable of doing if he will only throw his heart into it.[24]

Sidney was a grave disappointment to his uncle. He never settled to anything in his life. But he was not altogether the bad egg that might be imagined from the complete silence with which he is passed over by previous biographers of F.E. He was the black sheep of the family only to the extent that he left behind him no worldly achievements to rank with those of his two brothers; but he left the bright memory of a favourite uncle. He was, in the recollection of his niece, 'quite the nicest of the brothers' – not given, as were both F.E. and Harold, to cutting sarcasm, but always kind, 'he never wanted to hurt anyone's feelings'. Clara's children looked forward to his visits. He inherited his full share of both charm and talent, but very little of his father's drive or E.P.'s application – rather his Uncle Arthur's irresponsibility. He was 'a real rolling stone'.[5] Since he scarcely obtrudes again into F.E.'s story, it may be as well to follow his life here to its sad conclusion. He married a girl called Madeleine (or Bessie) Jones, the daughter of a wealthy Birkenhead family; but she was as extravagant as he was and they quickly exhausted their inheritance. She stayed with him, however, as he continued to drift from business to business. Among other ventures, he ran a riding school in Ireland for a time. The outbreak of war in 1914 at last gave a purpose to his life. He lied about his age (he was over forty), joined up as a private and rose to be a Captain; but guarding an ammunition dump in France he received head wounds from which he never fully recovered. He lived on until 1924 in an Officers' home at Midhurst in Sussex, where he died leaving a widow and a son, Leslie, who was as shiftless as his father. Visiting Sidney in these years was a distressing experience; F.E., who was squeamish about illness, did so no more often than he could help. He did, however, use his influence to arrange for Sidney to be looked after by his former batman. Could he have done more? Famous men often seem to have brothers of whom they are slightly ashamed, and there is a contrast between the lengths to which F.E. went to advance Harold's career and his apparent neglect of Sidney. On the other hand, it is clear from E.P.'s experience that Sidney was not easy to help. He was indeed a rolling stone, and he went his own way – not, it would appear, unhappily.

Their father's death must have precipitated a critical time for all the Smith children: adolescence is often the most damaging age at which to lose a parent. There is no way of knowing how hard it hit any of the others; but F.E. reacted with an elaborate display of filial piety and, one may surmise, a redoubled pledge to fulfil his father's ambitions in his own career. There survives in the family a book of press cuttings, reverently inscribed in black ink by a careful hand:

> Extracts dealing with or bearing upon the life, character and work of the late Mr. Frederick Smith, barrister-at-law, together with some account of his illness, death and burial inserted in loving memory by his eldest son Frederick Edwin Smith, December 14th 1888.

Interspersed among the cuttings there are lines of Greek, and between the pages pressed flowers and rose petals. There are also three pages of 'Favourite Poems', cut from books – Tennyson's 'Home they brought the warrior dead'; Byron's 'They mourn, but smile at length'; Thomas Moore's 'There's a bower of roses by Bendemeer's stream'; and this gem:

> All Nature smiles to meet the coming spring
> But I am sad: my heart alone is sore.
> I cannot take delight in anything
> Because my darling Chloris is no more.

This seems not quite appropriate to the loss of a father; one takes from these pages an impression of the young F.E. plundering the anthologies for suitably mournful quotations in a slightly exaggerated mood of self-conscious tragedy – genuine, yet at the same time something of a posture.

The bereaved family moved, in the course of 1889, from Clifton Road to another house, no smaller but less pretentious, in Lorne Road, very near Birkenhead School, where all three boys were now going – though F.E. had only two terms left. Thanks to his Uncle Edward, F.E. was relieved of the responsibility of regarding himself, at sixteen, as the head of the family, which might have necessitated his giving up the idea of university and going out to work. F.E. gave credit to his mother too:

> The greatest debt of the many which I owe to my mother is that she steadfastly encouraged me to attempt [the] hazardous path to a fuller education. Some women, more prudent perhaps but more short-sighted, would have warned me that it was my duty to leave school, to abandon all hopes of the University, and to enter a local firm as a clerk . . . But that was not her advice. With the aid of my schoolmaster and one of my father's brothers, we mapped out a career of scholarships for which I should strive. It was hard work, but ambition made it worth while.[25]

F.E. went back to Birkenhead School and won his £20 scholarship to University College, Liverpool. It seems unlikely that he really could not have gone without a scholarship: his sister Clara was able to go too, with no such assistance. The two of them made the symbolic crossing of the Mersey in October 1889. Clara was allowed to attend for only one year (reading languages) before her mother insisted that she must have her eldest daughter at home. But for F.E. this was the first short step in his emancipation from Birkenhead.

3

From Liverpool to Oxford

The fact that F.E. spent two years at Liverpool University is not well known. Those years are not part of the legend of his life. He himself, and his biographers after him, found it more romantic to forget them, lest they spoil a good story. Yet Liverpool was clearly an important intermediate stage in his educational ascent, without which he must have arrived at Oxford a great deal rawer and less mature than he actually did. Aged seventeen, he would surely have been too young to have made the impact at Oxford that he made at nineteen. The Liverpool interlude, then, probably made his Oxford career possible.

Fortunately, some impression of the life of a Liverpool student in those years can be gained from the unfinished autobiography of the historian and prolific Liberal publicist, Ramsay Muir. Muir was F.E.'s almost exact contemporary, brought up in the same town but without F.E.'s advantages. His father was a Scottish presbyterian minister who had received a 'call' to Birkenhead: Birkenhead School was beyond his means, and when he died still more beyond his widow's, so the young Muir was educated entirely at a small school run by a single Scotsman, which left him ill-equipped to compete with the likes of F.E. for a single scholarship to Liverpool. However, he secured instead another award open to prospective ministers (which he later repaid), and so went up in the same term as F.E.

University College, Liverpool, had been founded only seven years earlier, in 1882; it was one of the first of the 'redbrick' universities established mainly by the benefactions of northern businessmen to offer further education to those to whom for reasons of class, wealth or religion Oxford and Cambridge were closed. It was still in 1889 struggling to find an identity, poorly endowed and poorly housed.

> When I entered it, the main part of the college was housed in a disused lunatic asylum, in a slum district, with a huge workhouse on one side, and on the other the Royal Infirmary with its medical school, which became the Medical Faculty. Across a corner of the

derelict quadrangle ran a deep railway cutting, which belched forth clouds of smoke. The street which climbed the hill from the city to the college – about a quarter of a mile long – contained twenty-two public houses and a number of sordid shops; the pavements were haunted by slatternly women and barefoot street Arabs. The city abattoirs lay just behind and diffused a smell of blood. These were sorry surroundings for the education of aspiring youth.[1]

Muir and F.E. were among only about a dozen undergraduates entering on an Arts degree in 1889; but they do not seem to have got to know one another at all well. They were quite a talented group, including a future Keeper of Oriental Manuscripts at the British Museum (L.D. Barnett), and a future Senior Wrangler at Cambridge: their quality, Muir wrote, 'showed that the new college was giving opportunity to men of real ability'. But they were given little encouragement to mix.

As yet the college was no more than a mere knowledge-shop. It had not begun to be a focus of intellectual life. There were almost no opportunities for the students to meet one another or carry on the vital, if often shallow, talk which is the most valuable element in university life. They all lived at home, and scattered to every part of a wide area when lectures were over. There was indeed a common-room, but it was a dark, comfortless cellar which few ever entered; there was a Refectory, but it was only another cellar where you could buy poached eggs and meat pies and cups of coffee. There was a debating-society, but scarcely anybody ever joined it. There were no cricket or football teams, for all the good players played for their local clubs. The college had not begun to become a living society.[2]

If F.E. did not join the debating society it must have been moribund indeed. On the other hand he probably did take part in performances of plays, since it was with L.D. Barnett that he collaborated to produce the acting translation of Plautus already mentioned. How much strictly academic benefit he derived from his time at Liverpool is uncertain; but the only glimpse Muir gives of F.E. suggests that he had already acquired that contemptuous self-assurance for which he would soon be famous. The Professor of History was a mystical fraud named John Macdonald Mackay who greatly impressed his more gullible students (like Muir) while teaching them (as Muir later realized) nothing at all. Once, in a lecture on Roman history, he read some hundreds of lines of Vergil, in the Latin, in a strange sing-song voice. F.E. Smith . . . ostentatiously read a newspaper; and when Mackay rebuked him, said that he knew the passage by heart, and proceeded to go on where Mackay had broken off. Smith had no patience at all with Mackay: I don't blame him.[3]

At least this story indicates that F.E.'s academic self-confidence was not unjustified. But at Liverpool its basis was not very severely tested. He sat no external degree exam there, but instead, in his fourth term, attempted the next hurdle in his obstacle course of scholarships: the Oxford Entrance Scholarship. 'I yield to no one in my admiration for our modern Universities,' he wrote in a fragment of autobiography published in 1927, which omits any mention of his experience of one of them. 'But I shall give offence to no one if I make it plain that . . . the cleverest boys at all our great schools will always try, to the best of their powers, to go either to Oxford or to Cambridge.'[4]

If F.E. was not already intent on trying to get to Oxford, his resolve was sharpened by a young schoolteacher named John Thompson whom his mother had met at the Wesleyan chapel in Birkenhead and befriended. Thompson had been a scholar of Wadham College in 1884, had taken a Second in 'Greats' four years later, and was now in his first job at the Birkenhead Institute; knowing no one else in the town, he was glad to be invited to Lorne Road, where he soon became a regular visitor and a close friend of the family. In 1891 he became engaged to Clara, though they were not married for several years – her guardian uncle thought that he had not yet the means to support Clara in the manner to which she was accustomed. (As a matter of fact he never did have an income that E.P. would have considered adequate, but that did not stop them being very happy.) Appreciating her brother's exceptional promise, Thompson encouraged his ambition and allayed his mother's doubts; in particular he naturally directed F.E.'s aspiration towards his own old college, Wadham.

The Oxford colleges in those days held their scholarship examinations in a staggered sequence at the end of the year. F.E. travelled down in December 1890, probably ready to try for as many as was necessary. He is said to have missed the first college, Balliol, through an attack of flu; but the second pair, which held a joint exam, were Trinity and Wadham. Candidates were required to state their preference. F.E.'s account of why he chose Wadham is famous: it is one of the finest passages in all his writings. It is undoubtedly a heartfelt piece of nostalgia; but it is essentially another romantic fiction. F.E. first describes how he had put up, with a modesty suited to his means, at the Wilberforce Temperance Hotel – an establishment at which, he noted ironically, he 'never happened to stay' again.

> After dinner on the night of my arrival I proceeded to survey the
> *terrain.* Trinity College was rather fashionable, Wadham not at all
> so. But I looked at the two colleges on a brilliant moonlight night,
> when the beauty of Oxford was rendered even more exquisite, and
> if possible purer, by a dazzling mantle of snow. I saw Trinity first,
> and then I passed along the Broad Street to that grey and perfect
> façade which has remained unaltered since the enlightened and
> splendid bounty of Nicholas and Dorothy Wadham dedicated a
> noble building for the education of students from the West of
> England. I passed into that quadrangle which has undergone no
> change, save where time has mellowed it, since a divine architect
> gave expression to his genius in terms of stone; and advancing
> through the quadrangle towards the chapel, I turned, left-handed,
> into the most beautiful garden in Oxford, walked to the old cedar
> tree, which, alas! has since perished, then turned round and saw,
> radiant in the moonlight, the grey, almost white outlines of the
> chapel and the long line of ancient gables which make, whether
> you see it by day or whether you see it by night, the most
> enchanting spectacle which Oxford can afford. The haunting
> beauty of that winter scene determined my choice in one swift
> moment. I cared then, I am glad to recall, little for fashion; I cared
> intensely for beauty.[5]

Humbug apart, this vision of Wadham by night might well have made a
profound effect on a boy brought up in Birkenhead and used to the
sordid surroundings of Liverpool. He may also have calculated that one
of his background stood a better chance of success at a less fashionable
college. But to a boy knowing little of Oxford, the advice of a friend
would surely be the decisive factor; it should be no cause for surprise
that F.E. placed as his first choice the only college he knew anything
about.*

So F.E. sat for Wadham. The papers, spread over five days, were
predominantly on the classics, but there was also an English essay on
the subject of 'Conventions: Their Use and Abuse'; F.E.'s answer to
this, had it survived, would make good reading. The examination
included an interview, in the course of which – if his own account can be
believed – F.E. was asked by the Warden whether he would accept an
exhibition if he was not offered a scholarship. He replied, shrewdly, that

---

* F.E. probably admitted this in private. At least Sir John Simon, in an obituary
tribute published in the *Sunday Times* on 5 October 1930, suggested that he reserved the
moonlight version for College Gaudies and similar reunions.

he could not afford to go to Oxford except as a scholar; he was later inclined to attribute his success to this answer. At one point he nearly gave up hope and would have returned, on the advice of his former headmaster, empty-handed to make sure of his Liverpool degree, but for a resolute telegram from his mother, stiffened by Thompson. To have thus fled the battlefield, however, would have made a nonsense of his whole enterprise. F.E., in his own words, 'lingered on, anxiously but temperately, in my Temperance Hotel', preparing to sit another group of scholarships if he should fail at Wadham.

And then it became known that the list would be published at the Porter's Lodge at 11 o'clock on Monday morning. Five minutes before that hour a young man – almost a boy – feeling extremely unsuccessful, remembering (how vividly!) all the mistakes he had made, was waiting in the Porter's Lodge . . .

I can still see the old Porter, a veteran, I believe, of the Indian Mutiny, coming from the Warden's lodging – how slow he was! – with a sheet of paper. He opened a glass case – again how slowly! – produced four brass pins, and proceeded to pin up an announcement written in the scholarly hand of Warden Thorley . . . to the effect that the scholars elected at Wadham College as a result of the examination were, in the following order:

> C.B. Fry
> A.B. Willimot
> W.H. Anstie
> F.E. Smith.

Preceded by a jubilant telegram, F.E. took the first train back to Birkenhead. Whether he allowed himself a full bottle of railway claret, or indeed railway champagne, on this occasion is not recorded; perhaps the prospect before him was sufficiently intoxicating already.

The Great Western express (it was called, I still remember, the Zulu) was fast enough, but I was travelling in my mind faster far. For I knew perfectly well, that though in the last place on the list, I had been afforded an opportunity which might be decisive of my whole future career. I was to be educated side by side with those who were to be my rivals and competitors for the rest of my life. They would enjoy no advantage, social or educational, which was denied to me. The field thereafter was open to competition; and I felt confident that I was able to compete.[6]

Nowhere is the Smith philosophy of life more clearly expressed.

Wadham is indeed a beautiful college. It is one of the smallest and youngest of Oxford colleges, founded in 1613 in memory of her husband by Dorothy, widow of Nicholas Wadham of Somerset, and built (in C.B. Fry's words) 'with enthusiasm, grey Cumnor stone, and the advice of no architect'[7] in an arrested gothic style a hundred years out of date but perfect in its simplicity. Sir John Betjeman has deemed it, 'far the most satisfying of seventeenth-century colleges in Oxford . . . It is complete in itself and is remarkable as having [in 1938] not a single ugly or modern building in its make-up.'[8] Wadham could boast no more than a handful of great men in the seventeenth and eighteenth centuries – only Sir Christopher Wren, flanked by Admiral Blake and Mr Speaker Onslow; but a strong legal tradition had in 1861 achieved the college's first Lord Chancellor in Richard Bethell (Lord Westbury), while in the middle of the nineteenth century the name of Wadham was synonymous with the British school of positivism led by Richard Congreve and Frederic Harrison. As that light faded, however, the college had passed into a period of eclipse. It was financially hard hit by the agricultural depression of the 1870s, and there was trouble with a long-lived Evangelical Dean. By the 1880s Wadham was known (prophetically) as 'the Nazareth of Oxford, from which no good thing can come', famous in undergraduate humour only for the slowness of its rowing eight ('Why is the Wadham Boat like Noah's Ark?' 'Because it moves slowly upon the face of the waters and is filled with all manner of beasts'), and for a juvenile prank which is supposed to have resulted in the whole college being sent down. The moment was ripe for a renaissance.

The accident of going to Wadham at the particular time he did was one of the most fortunate in F.E.'s career. Well might he write later of his scholarship as one of the milestones of his life. For it was not simply the entrée to Oxford that mattered; it was specifically Wadham that shaped his development. He was lucky, first of all, to go to a small and hitherto disregarded college where the light of his personality could shine more brightly than it might have done at Balliol or Christ Church. But he was especially lucky in the contemporaries with whom he coincided there. For within a period of two years there converged on Wadham as remarkable a constellation of exceptional talent as has ever been seen at a single college in the whole history of Oxford. In F.E.'s year the top scholar was the legendary all-round athlete C.B. Fry; the year before, there had come up A.A. Roche, destined for the Judicial Bench; and the following year these three were joined by John Simon, another future Lord Chancellor (as well as Home Secretary, Foreign

Secretary and Chancellor of the Exchequer – an unparalleled 'bag' of the top offices of state); and by Francis Hirst, who became a distinguished Liberal writer and editor for ten years of *The Economist*. If F.E. came to Oxford to compete with the best of his generation, he was extraordinarily privileged in being able to do so within his own college.

The early 1890s were the golden age of Wadham. It would perhaps be too much to claim that the quintet of Roche, Fry, Simon, Hirst and Smith dominated the university; but in every sphere of university life – academically and athletically, and in the Union – they certainly far surpassed their contemporaries of any other college, raising the reputation of Wadham to unheard-of heights while laying the foundations of their own. Naturally there had been some able men in the college in the previous generation, and there were as many more in the 1890s who would make successful careers as barristers and bishops, civil servants, colonial governors and dons. It is in the nature of the English education system that the roll-call of most colleges at most times has abounded in such worthies; they must not be allowed by their numbers and solid attainments to disguise the fact that there were simultaneously in the one college five men of an altogether different quality. It is worth pointing out that they were all scholars; all (except Fry) from fairly modest backgrounds; and all (except Roche, who had not even that advantage) from minor public schools. From the perspective of the 1980s, Roche and Hirst may appear lesser figures than the other three; they did not appear so to those who knew them all. Fry may seem a mere cricketer in the company of judges and statesmen; he was not so in the 1890s. All in their day were equally admired. Though not an exclusive 'set', they were close companions; each stimulated the others to develop their full potential, and all, despite political and temperamental differences, felt a special bond for life. F.E. never ceased to acknowledge his debt to Wadham and to these special comrades of his youth. As Francis Hirst justly pointed out at the memorial dinner held for F.E. at the college in 1930, it could be said of him, as it was (in Latin) on the monument to Lord Westbury in the chapel, 'He used to trace the beginning of his fortunes from the day on which . . . he was elected a scholar of Wadham College.' F.E. gave all his loyalty and a lot of his life to Wadham; but, Hirst claimed, looking around him, Wadham had given as much to him.

It was Fry who first set the university ringing with his name. Charles Fry was a phenomenon – the greatest all-round athlete in the history of British sport. As a schoolboy at Repton he had already played football for the Corinthian Casuals; on arrival at Oxford he went straight into the university team in his first term, and that winter played once for England; the following summer he added Blues for cricket and athletics, scoring a century against Somerset and setting a new English amateur record in the long jump against Cambridge. Pausing from these sporting triumphs just long enough to justify his top scholarship at Wadham by picking up a First in Mods, he went on in his second year to captain the university at both football and cricket, and equalled the world record in the long jump – 23 feet 6½ inches. With all this, he was considered into the bargain 'the handsomest man of his day . . . with his beautiful figure . . . the broad shoulders, the slim hips, looking as though he might have stepped from a Grecian frieze'.[9] In an adolescent society much given to hero worship, Fry was a hero indeed: one whose achievements the *Boy's Own Paper* might have hesitated to invent. Dons were said to bow to him in the street. He went on to represent England once more at football in 1901, and played for Southampton in the F.A. Cup Final of that year; thereafter he concentrated on cricket, forming a magical partnership for Sussex and England with Prince Ranjitsinjhi, topping the national batting averages six times, scoring ninety-four centuries (including six in a row in his *annus mirabilis*, 1901), and captaining England six times before retiring in 1912. Off the field, his life declined into a somewhat disappointed middle age, marred by jealousy of the political success of his Wadham contemporaries; despite his name, which he continued to exploit profitably in sporting journalism, he failed three times to get into Parliament as a Liberal in the 1920s. In his prime he had surpassed them all in sheer virile glamour; but unlike Wilde's Dorian Gray, he could not stay young for ever and was overtaken by maturer men.

In their first year together at Wadham, F.E. could not match Fry's instant stardom. Reputations take longer to win at the Union than on the football field, and F.E., though the same age as Fry, was a good deal less polished; fresh from the very different life of Liverpool, he needed a term or two to look around and take the measure of Oxford life before plunging in. Many years later Fry recalled his first impression of a striking but oddly immature young man:

> He had a long back, and sat like a tall man; a lean, almost hard-bitten face, which but for youth and brown health would have been hollow-cheeked, not however a young face; and noticeably two wide open eyes, full of a deep brown light such as one sees in pools of a moorland peat stream, fringed with very long dark eye-lashes; Ouida-esque eyelashes, the fortune of any tall brunette, soft, with a caressing upward curve.[10]

In his less flattering published version of this first meeting, Fry made a point of emphasizing the lack of polish. 'His hair was rather untidy, being of the kind that stands upright unless prevented'; more seriously, 'the moment he opened his mouth he betrayed a Lancashire accent that would rival Gracie Fields'. The first of these flaws was easily remedied by sufficient quantities of hair oil: Simon, coming up a year later, was met by 'a surprising youth, of olive complexion and glossy hair'.[11] As to the second, Fry probably exaggerated, though F.E. undoubtedly did have some accent; he was certainly being malicious when he went on:

> The first indication of his being an uncommon intelligence was that, discovering with characteristic promptness that no sort of provincial accent was an advantage at Oxford, this perceptive youth entirely cured himself of it in about six weeks, and indeed developed a tendency to preciosity.[12]

This is not strictly true; more than two years later, at the height of his fame at the Union, F.E. could still be chided by *Isis* for the sin of betraying his northern origins. Valuably, for once, the writer is specific as to precisely where F.E.'s native Cheshire showed through: it was 'heard in every final "r", and he still retains the north-country fashion of pronouncing quadrisyllables like "circumstances" and "interesting" rather as a double trochee than as a modified dactyl' – that is with the stress on the third syllable, which today sounds more Belfast than Liverpool.[13] This is confirmation that F.E. did go up to Oxford with a noticeable accent, but at the same time an indication that it was worn away gradually by daily contact with Oxford speech, rather than by deliberate and hasty re-education.*

It cannot anyway have been a crippling social handicap, and it certainly did not prevent him quickly forming a close and lifelong friendship with his fellow-scholar. After this first term they had rooms on the same stair, and regularly breakfasted together. F.E. and Fry recognized one another at once as kindred spirits, being both not only scholars and good athletes, but in addition game for anything. F.E. was at this age an astute practical joker. 'He had a talent amounting to genius for landing his friends in situations he regarded as humorous.'[14] On their very first Sunday he dared Fry to climb up and kiss the statue of Dorothy Wadham over the entrance to the Hall, then retired to a safe distance leaving Fry to complete the exploit under the disapproving eye of the sub-Warden. On another occasion he bet Fry that he could not scale a lamp-post in the High Street, extinguish the gas and relight it with a match; this time Fry was interrupted by a policeman and fined £2 7s 6d. The pair of them also founded a society of like-minded dare-

---

* E.C. Bentley, however, tends to confirm Fry's view, 'All I can say is that the speech of F.E., when I first heard him [in 1894] was what it always remained: a rather extreme example of what is known as the Oxford accent.' (*Those Days*, p. 77.)

devils known as the Wadham Cat Club, membership of which entailed climbing in and out of several adjoining colleges before returning undetected to Wadham; there was a dinner at the Clarendon as prize for any member who, on completing the course, could steal the keys of the college from the sleeping porter – F.E. is reputed to have won four such feasts. At more conventional games, too, they formed an excellent partnership, neither having previously played the other's code of football. F.E. introduced Fry to rugby, at which his speed made him a natural wing three-quarter in the Wadham fifteen (and very nearly won him a fourth Blue), while Fry found room for F.E. in the college soccer team, with the remark that 'he could not be worse than some of our eleven, and would in any case be useful to argue with the referee and to draft protests'.

For his first year, F.E. confined most of his energies to these relatively inexpensive pursuits. Not the least important thing that he and Fry had in common was a lack of means to supplement their scholarships. These were worth £80 a year, but it cost around £250 a year to live comfortably in the Oxford of those days, and most undergraduates of good family enjoyed considerably more. F.E. had an allowance from home (probably topped up by his uncle) but an income that was ample in Birkenhead did not go far in Oxford. Fry's family, though formerly landed, was not now much wealthier than F.E.'s; if he had any pecuniary advantage it was quickly eroded by the lavish expenditure expected of a Blue, while F.E. did not immediately incur the comparably ruinous obligations of holding office at the Union. The smart dining clubs and the heavy debts belong to his later Oxford career, when he was an established 'swell' and had to keep up the position – though it did not take him very long to discover the possibilities of the traditionally easy credit system by which generations of young men used to be tided over their undergraduate embarrassments until the expectations of either their talent or their inheritance were realized.

In his first years it is probable that F.E. actually worked quite hard – if not at the ancient classics which were his prescribed study, then certainly at English literature and history, for it was at this time that he read all the Waverley novels, Stevenson, Thackeray and the Brontës, Macaulay, Lecky, Froude and much else. His son relates the story that F.E. delegated the task of writing his weekly essay to a poor Scottish exhibitioner, whom he paid £5 a term, so that when he came to discuss it with his tutor, 'it was questionable which of them brought to the matter a more open mind'.[15] C.B. Fry, however, carries more conviction.

About the only person in the College upon whom F.E. failed to exercise his peculiar talent with success was our common tutor,

Herbert Richards. In fact he is the only man I remember F.E. to have been afraid of. He feared his tongue, and that, from F.E., was a high compliment.[16]

Richards had a backhanded compliment for F.E. too, however, for he once told Simon that 'he first realized the extent of F.E.'s oratorical powers when he heard him attempt to translate, with more power than precision, a difficult passage of Thucydides'.[17] Fry's estimate of F.E.'s calibre as a classical scholar is also backhanded, rating him well below both Simon and Roche, but adding:

> How the great Lord Birkenhead would have figured in this com-
> petition had he worked as hard at the classics as the other two, I do
> not know, because he did not do it. What F.E. could do was this: if
> he knew a shred about a question, he could write an answer
> imposing enough to render the existing authorities obsolete.[18]

As these passages make clear, F.E. was beginning to discover that his true talents were rhetorical and forensic: he had a golden tongue and a quick brain, the power of persuasion with a gift for improvisation – the ability to make a little knowledge go a long way, or a good case out of a bad brief. His father's example already pointed him towards the law, and a year of Oxford told him that he was bored with the Classics. It is not surprising that after five terms and a Second in Mods – his excuse was an injured arm, but the examiners may not have been wrong – he switched over to read Jurisprudence. There are those who regard this as 'intellectual sacrilege' for an able man. Ivor Thomas, for instance, while allowing that F.E. 'had not the financial resources that would enable him to pursue learning for learning's sake', castigates him for taking the short cut to worldly fame rather than crown his education in the approved manner.

> Had F.E. Smith taken *Lit. Hum.* it cannot be doubted that the
> effect on his character would have been pronounced. Many crooked
> places would have been made straight and many rough places
> plain. Jurisprudence emphasized precisely those points in his
> character which his best friends liked least. The study of law casts
> a man at once into the sordid and harsh, into an atmosphere where
> everybody who is not trying to do down is trying not to be done
> down. If a man takes 'Greats' first and then passes to the study of
> law, as Mr. Asquith did, he has been innoculated against the
> disease and jurisprudence may do little harm to his character.[19]

Be that as it may, F.E. had by the end of his first year extracted all the benefit he wanted from the Classics and knew where his vocation lay. Asquith may have been a finer scholar than F.E., was perhaps a wiser man and a better politician; but F.E. was unquestionably the greater lawyer.

It is clear that F.E. was consciously using his Oxford opportunity to make for himself the sort of career, combining the law and politics, on which his father had just been embarking at the time of his death. 'If I were twenty-one again,' he wrote in the last year of his life, 'I have no doubt that I should do once more exactly what I did a third of a century ago. I should devote myself to the law, well aware that there is no better training for a political career.'[20] His father, of course, had done it the other way round, starting in local politics. F.E. could bypass that rung; he knew that his ladder into politics should be that privileged forcing-house of parliamentarians, the Oxford Union. He joined it immediately in his first term, and probably attended regularly to listen to the Thursday evening debates in order to get the feel of the chamber. But he was wiser than to try to speak too soon. He certainly did not follow the dubious advice he later gave to Oxford freshmen that they should not only join the Union but 'speak at it constantly'.

> Do not be afraid of boring your audience. That, after all, is more their worry than yours . . . The majority of those who are giving you an unwilling audience are desirous of speaking themselves and resent the preference which has been given to you. These deserve no mercy at your hands . . . You have paid your subscription and are entitled to speak whenever the President calls upon you to do so; and it is far better that you should bore a number of young gentlemen at the University of Oxford than that you should bore other people afterwards, whose disapproval might easily prove more serious.[21]

F.E. at the age of nineteen had no intention of earning a reputation as a bore. Before attempting to speak at the Union, he practised his style (already developed at home, under the tuition of his father, at school, and at local discussion societies in Birkenhead) in the smaller forum of the Wadham Debating Society; but even there he did not open his mouth until the sixth meeting of his first term, when he intervened (on the losing side, it is interesting to note) against a motion condemning the easy credit system at Oxford as 'immoral and mischievous'. He spoke once more that term, against a motion advocating the abolition of intoxicating liquors (this one was not carried!); but he declined to join in an argument whether 'Scotch Wit and Whiskey are Superior to

Irish'. The Wadham Debating Society was not a highly political body; indeed its minutes give the impression that it was not very serious at all, much of its proceedings being taken up with the most juvenile interruptions, so that sometimes the subject for debate was not even reached. In February, F.E. did get the opportunity to speak on a political subject close to his father's heart, opposing (and heavily defeating, though only by twelve votes to three, which gives some idea of the size of the society) a motion calling for the immediate evacuation of Egypt. It was not this effort, however, but his flippant speech against prohibition the previous term that led to his making his début at the Union earlier than he had probably planned; for the Secretary of the Union, C.H. Eliot of Merton, happened to be the guest of the Wadham Society that evening. F.E. was never one to miss an opportunity: his flippancy was doubtless carefully rehearsed. But if he intended to impress, he succeeded beyond any reasonable expectation. On Eliot's recommendation, he was invited to speak second, on the same favourite subject of drink, in the main Union debate of the Hilary term.

The normal practice expects that an aspiring orator should make his début, and probably two or three further speeches, from the floor of the house, before he is likely to be asked to speak 'on the paper' – that is, to make one of the four major speeches proposing or rejecting the evening's motion. Moreover distinguished guest speakers were at that period invited only rarely to the Oxford Union, which guarded its undergraduate character more proudly than it does today. It was therefore a doubly unusual honour that the President (Arthur Magee of Merton) accorded F.E. in inviting him, an unknown freshman, not merely to lead the opposition to the motion 'That this House approves of Local Option', but in doing so to oppose the most prominent temperance campaigner of the day, Sir Wilfrid Lawson, second baronet, M.P. for Cockermouth and formerly for Carlisle. This was an extraordinary opportunity, and F.E. seized it with both hands.

The motion was proposed by Lord Balcarres (son of the Earl of Crawford), soon to be one of F.E.'s best friends and in the fulness of time a colleague in the Lloyd George Cabinet, but never henceforward known as a temperance reformer. F.E. rose next, facing a packed house of something near 800 undergraduates and guests – the largest audience seen at the Union for over a year. For several minutes he spoke quite seriously, making a solid but well-worn case against local option, dwelling on the practical difficulties – who should be entitled to speak for the locality? – and the unwarranted interference with individual freedom – why, if A was moderate but the sight of a public house proved fatal to B, should A be denied alcohol because B abused it? He referred to the experience of prohibition in parts of Canada and in certain of the

United States, and to the effects of the dry Sunday in Wales. Then, when he had lectured his audience long enough to demonstrate his grasp of the subject, he suddenly changed his tone and turned to Sir Wilfrid Lawson. It was a convention of the house, he said, and a right convention, that honourable visitors should be treated with respect, and their records and conclusions be challenged only by the courteous denials of debate.

> But tonight I must deviate from that custom. The honourable gentleman inherited a noble cellar, in which the piety of his ancestors had laid to rest noble clarets, sustaining ports, stimulating champagnes, and warm and ancient brandies. What did the honourable gentleman do with his cellar? He destroyed that priceless heritage of the ages, in which was stored the bottled sunshine of the south – he destroyed it under circumstances of such barbarity that even the thirstiest throat in Carlisle was denied participation! I tell you, sir, that if in years to come the honourable gentleman comes to me, when I am nestling in Abraham's bosom, and asks me for a drop of water, I shall say to him: 'No. Not a drop! You dissipated greater liquor!'[22]

Sir Wilfrid was a white-bearded gentleman in his sixties, F.E. still some months off twenty. The absurdity of the vision, as well as the effrontery of the rebuke, convulsed the house. The laughter lasted for five full minutes, and in those five minutes F.E.'s reputation was made. Sir Wilfrid's reply, like the other speeches, was quickly forgotten, though he was allowed, by convention, to carry the debate by 151 votes to 86. The talk afterwards was all of the daring young wit from Wadham who had cheeked the distinguished guest, but so cleverly that no offence could be taken.

That at least is the usually accepted story. But there are grounds for some scepticism. For one thing, there is no agreement among the various chroniclers of F.E.'s life as to his exact words; the one contemporary report of the debate, in the *Oxford Review*, records only the serious part of his speech. Nor, though they had no doubt that they had just heard the best maiden speech at the Union for many years, were the Oxford papers quite so ecstatic as legend might lead one to expect. The *Oxford Magazine* praised the 'power, conciseness and brilliancy' of F.E.'s speech,[23] but the *Oxford Review* deemed it merely 'convincing, clear and logical'. The latter, so far from reckoning that the precocious freshman had wiped the floor with the visitor, gave Sir Wilfrid the palm for 'perhaps the wittiest of all the witty speeches to which the present generation of members of the Union has listened'.[24] F.E. in 1927 quoted

Isis proclaiming that, 'The speech of the evening, with all respect to our guest, was the amazingly vivacious and brilliant performance of Mr. F.E. Smith, the Wadham freshman';[25] but wherever F.E. discovered this remark (if he did not invent it) it was not in *Isis*, for *Isis* was not founded until the following term.

The difficulty of separating the truth from the legend surrounding this speech is best illustrated by considering Simon's account of it in his memoirs, published in 1952. He describes the scene vividly – Sir Wilfrid, stroking his beard, genially indicating his approval of the young man's exposition of the opposition case; the gasps when F.E. changed his tone in order to draw attention to 'a regrettable lapse in the past life of the Rt. Hon. baronet'; then a rival version of his words.

'Some years ago the mistaken benevolence of an aged relative bestowed upon him by his will a priceless cellar of wine.' There followed highly wrought descriptions of the various vintages, the only one of which I now recall being 'the bottled laughter of the peasant girls of Spain'. The stripling orator then proceeded, 'What did the recipient do with this precious gift? Why, he took each bottle in turn, broke its neck, and poured its contents down the drain! And when, Sir, in a future existence, I am lolling on Abraham's bosom, and the cry comes up to me from Another Place, the cry of the Rt. Hon. gentleman praying for a drop of water to cool his parched tongue, I shall reply, "Not a drop. You have squandered more precious liquor!"' There was an uproar of merriment in which, to his credit, Sir Wilfrid Lawson heartily joined.

At the word 'lolling', Simon adds a footnote, 'There is a dispute as to this word. Some who heard him would substitute "lounging": others prefer "nestling". But I say "lolling."'[26] It is unfortunate that in his enthusiasm to correct these details sixty years after the event, Simon forgot that he had not yet gone up to Oxford; he was still at school in Scotland at the time.

Simon's confusion, however, does not deny but rather only goes to prove that F.E.'s speech made an unparalleled impression – so much so that his most famous contemporary in later years could not bear to admit that he had not actually been present, but had to tell again a tale that he had heard so often repeated that it had become part of his own memory. Clearly some of the details were embellished and the phrases polished as the legend gathered strength, but a legend must have some foundation. There can be no doubting that on that March night in 1892 F.E. unveiled for the first time before a large audience at least a prototype of the personality which the British public would soon come to know as F.E. Smith. It was unquestionably a bravura performance: an astonishing feat, if not necessarily of exceptional eloquence or wit, then certainly of nerve and timing; if not quite in his mature style, then at least displaying much of the method that would characterize his maturity – the lucid legal exposition, the powerful argument, and the sudden devastating swoop into glorious fantasy or stinging ridicule, above all the suavely mannered insolence that left his victim helpless and the audience roaring its delight; this was at least a recognizable blueprint. That F.E. dared such a speech on his Union début, before an audience of several hundred, after no more than a handful of trial runs in the intimacy of Wadham, is proof of an extraordinary self-assurance; that he carried it off triumphantly is perhaps still more extraordinary, demonstrating two of the special secrets of his success in law and politics in the years to come – his unfailing ability, under any circumstances, to rise to the big occasion, and a rare sensitivity to the 'feel' of a particular audience. The most astonishing thing of all is that F.E. was able to cap this triumph with an even more famous début in the House of Commons fourteen years later.

F.E.'s reaction to his success confirms the impression that it had come earlier than he had planned. He did not let it go to his head. A letter from his uncle E.P. written only four days after the debate shows that he lost no time in reporting home, but also indicates that he had met the imposter, triumph, with great good sense,

Dear Fred,

Many congratulations on your success, & thanks for your letter & following cutting.

I quite approve of your declining to speak in another debate this session.

Speak seldom, but when you speak, let your speech be *well thought out*, and then it will be with power . . .

I for one have confidence in your ballast.

Your ever affect. uncle
Edward.[27]

Far from rushing to press home his advantage, F.E. almost seems to have lain deliberately low for the remainder of the year, not only at the Union but at the Wadham Society too, though he was elected Secretary of the latter. (Simon's tip to historians that the society's minute book would reveal 'passages of daring humour and scathing invective not unworthy to be compared with Aristophanic comedy'[28] is sadly astray: F.E.'s minutes are not noticeably less juvenile that those of other

Secretaries.) He did, however, speak once more at the Union in the summer term. He was invited – did he have to be pressed to reverse his intention? – to propose that 'This House disapproves of Canvassing in connection with Political Elections'; he accepted, and carried the motion by four votes in a poorly attended house – his name on the paper was not yet enough to fill it – on the argument that the house-to-house solicitation of votes from individuals had been rendered pointless by the secret ballot, since no voter could be bound by any promise to a canvasser. The *Oxford Review* commented that his speech was 'well thought-out and delivered. We certainly think that he made the most of a subject not very promising in itself. Considering the general depression and the unattractive nature of his motion, he fully sustained the favourable impression made by his maiden speech'.[29] This second success led to F.E. being elected to the Standing Committee of the Union for the following autumn. But its wider interest is that it shows F.E. drawing on personal experience of canvassing for the Conservative cause in Birkenhead.

The career of the local boy making good was being closely followed in Birkenhead. His scholarship had been announced with pride in the *Advertiser* ('Success of Late Alderman's Son'), and his triumph at the Union was fully reported, complete with snippets of praise from the Oxford papers, and the comment that his success 'will not be a surprise to members of the Palm Grove Literary Society, who have often had a taste of his quality'.[30] Despite this indication that he was beginning to make a local reputation in his own right, however, he was invariably referred to as his father's son, and it was surely respect for his father's memory that carried him so rapidly into the counsels and even on to the platforms of the local Conservative Party. It is clear from his remarks in the Union that he was already an experienced, if humble, party worker; but by the summer he was being billed as a prominent speaker in the General Election campaign. This precocity did not please his uncle – a Liberal, it will be remembered:

Dear Fred,
    I am grieved – deeply grieved – that you should have allowed the Conservative party to drag you into the present political contest & thus commit you publicly in their cause without ever consulting me or asking my opinion in any way whatever.
    If you had spoken to me I would have strongly advised you to hold aloof from both parties, for the present at any rate, until your judgement was more matured . . .
    They (the Conservatives) do not care one straw about you, except to use you for their own purposes. I do, & always shall, &

therefore feel the more pained at the step you have taken.
Believe me always,

Your affect. uncle & sincere friend,
E.P. Smith[31]

E.P. was wasting his time. Never can a young man have had fewer doubts of his political allegiance than F.E. He was his father's son, and his father's causes – the Union, the Empire, Tory Democracy, the freedom of the drink trade – were his causes, his partisanship reinforced by the true conservative's innate scepticism and stance of philosophic pessimism. As Winston Churchill wrote, F.E. very early in his life 'had reached settled and somewhat sombre conclusions'[32] on the fundamental question of existence and belief; and he never modified them. Oxford only polished up his Conservatism, lending it historical support and a legal perspective; it added little essential beyond a reverence for ancient institutions. His uncle's Liberalism meant nothing to him. His fierce loyalty to his father decreed unquestioning Conservatism, and that was that. He only wanted to be given a chance to join the fray.

At the General Election of 1892, the sitting Conservative member for Birkenhead, General Hamley, retired. Had he lived, Alderman Smith must have succeeded him, for no other local man could be found to serve, and the Executive Committee was obliged to select as its candidate a complete outsider, Viscount Bury, the son of the seventh Earl of Albemarle, who had never made a political speech in his life. In the cause of opposing Home Rule, however, the party rallied round him. The Liberals managed to choose a candidate with more connection with the town in the person of the future Lord Leverhulme, W.H. Lever, the soap manufacturer and the founder of Port Sunlight – ironically a man who would soon play an important part in establishing F.E.'s fortune. On 27 June, just a week before the poll, the Conservatives held a big rally in support of Lord Bury in the Queen's Hall in Claughton Road. After the candidate and a number of other speakers (including a token working man) had addressed the meeting, the chairman rose to call upon

one whose name I am sure you will not hear without emotion – it is that of Mr. Fred Smith (Cheers). He is the worthy son of a father who was once esteemed and beloved by all of you. For his father's sake, and for his own – for he is a credit to the university to which he belongs – I ask you to give an attentive hearing to the few words he will address to you. (Hear, hear.)

The report in what was now the *Birkenhead and Cheshire Advertiser and Wallasey Guardian* continues:

Mr. Fred Smith, who was received with tumultuous applause, said he thanked them for the very kind reception given him. It showed that they cherished in fragrant recollection one who, had he been spared to be with them until that day, would have been in the front of the great contest to be waged next Monday. (Cheers.) It was his son's privilege to speak one or two words in support of the resolution. There were two candidates seeking for their votes. At every meeting of the Liberals they had been told that Mr. Lever was a local man and a shrewd man of business, and therefore the best man they could have for Birkenhead. They all knew what interest he took in Birkenhead, either municipally or parliamentary [sic], until he came here for his own selfish end. (Cheers.) Of course, he would like to write M.P. after his name even as a shrewd man of business. (Laughter.) But what consolation would it be to those of them who were Conservatives if they returned Mr. Lever to Parliament, to know that he was using his business shrewdness to pass measures which were distasteful to them. (Hear, hear.) Mr. Lever promised anything and everything. (Laughter.) But Lord Bury had not given himself over to the universal pledge practice. (Cheers.) He said clearly what he would do and what he would not do, but they might depend upon it that what he said he meant to carry out, and what he promised he meant to perform. Mr. Lever apparently would promise to do anything. He (the speaker) verily believed that if they were to ask Mr. Lever if he was in favour of the repeal of the Ten Commandments, he would reply that he emphatically was. (Cheers, and roars of laughter.) Mr. Lever, at any rate, was emphatically in favour of Home Rule. Mr. Gladstone, not quite a generation ago, had emphatically said that Home Rule was 'a path through crime and bloodshed to the dismemberment of the empire', but though Mr. Gladstone had changed, Home Rule had not in the least degree changed. (Cheers, and some uproar.) He (Mr. Smith) asked them to say on Monday next, in the words on a cartoon which had now become famous . . . that 'A stronger Lever is wanted at Birkenhead to disturb the Conservative majority.' (Laughter and applause.)

The resolution was then put and carried unanimously amid great cheering.[33]

One good quotation, two passable jokes and a characteristic show of disrespect for the opposition: if this was F.E.'s first political speech from a public platform, it was not a bad effort. He was wise enough not to try any Oxford Union fireworks on this audience, but gave it strictly what it wanted to hear. He evidently found the right mixture, for he was invited to repeat the dose three days later at Ellesmere Port in support of the Tory member for the Wirral, Colonel Cotton-Jodrell. On this occasion, in place of his aspersions on Lever, F.E. substituted the equally rude remark that he thought the Wirral Liberal candidate's election address 'would secure that gentleman as many votes as his portrait, which was on the front page';[34] otherwise this speech (described by the *Chester Courant* as 'vigorous') was much the same as his earlier one at Birkenhead. He probably repeated it many times over from different platforms in the next few weeks, for General Elections were then staggered affairs. There survives a poster advertising a meeting in support of the sitting member for Eddisbury, Mr Tollemache, on which it is announced in large print that 'Mr. F.E. Smith and others will address the meeting'. This was on 11 July 1892. F.E. was being billed as a principal speaker at an election meeting some thirty miles from his home town the day before his twentieth birthday. The poster gives vivid expression to the main thrust of the Conservative campaign. On one side of a Union Jack are the slogans 'Unity is Strength! Peace and Prosperity! No Wars! Less Taxes!'; on the other, the exhortation 'Support Your Nonconformist Brethren in Ireland against a Priest-ridden Parliament in Dublin' – a clear attempt to win the Dissenting vote from its traditional Liberal allegiance. In vain. In all these Merseyside seats, the Conservatives hung on with reduced majorities; but nationwide, Lord Salisbury's formerly comfortable ascendancy was annihilated; the swing of the pendulum gave the Liberals and Irish nationalists together a majority of forty. Gladstone became Prime Minister for the fourth time at the age of eighty-three.

The result might have had the compensation for F.E. that when he returned to Oxford in the autumn there would be a Liberal administration against which to carry motions of no confidence. With his increased experience in the country he must have looked forward to resuming the political battle in the Union in October. He was in fact listed 'on the paper' as the first speaker at the first meeting of the new academic year, moving 'That this House considers the prospects of Unionism hopeful, and anticipates the speedy restoration to power of the Unionist Government'. For some reason, however, he was not able to keep the engagement. Nor did he speak at all that term; indeed at the beginning of December he had to be replaced on the Standing Committee to which he had been elected the previous June, though he was almost immediately re-elected for the following term. The suggestion that he was ill or somehow unavoidably absent leads to the speculation that it was at this time that F.E. suffered a serious accident which nearly resulted in the loss of his left arm. In stepping from a moving train, he fell heavily on a cinder-covered station platform and cut his elbow. The wound became poisoned and the infection spread to the bone, threatening the whole arm. 'Several London specialists', his son writes, 'all advised immediate amputation.'[35] This drastic step was averted by a Birkenhead surgeon named Mitchell Banks, a friend of his father, who managed to cleanse the arm of poison by scraping it down to the bone. But it was still useless for some time, as well as very painful. Nevertheless there is no obvious reason why this injury should have prevented him speaking at the Union, especially since with extraordinary courage (and great foolhardiness) he insisted on playing rugby, with his arm encased in a protective leather sheath, jointed at the elbow and packed with cotton wool. The records of the Wadham Debating Society show that he was not prevented from speaking there: indeed only four days after missing his date at the Union, he spoke at Wadham on a very similar motion congratulating the voters of Newcastle on their return to Unionism at a by-election. It may be that there is no mystery: perhaps F.E. was simply working too hard for his Mods to give his time to both Wadham and the Union. If so, his failure to get a First must have come as a disappointment for which his injured arm was not a sufficient alibi.

Whatever the truth, F.E.'s fourth term belongs with his first year as part of his apprenticeship at Oxford. Around the time of his transfer from Classics to Law after Mods, one chapter closes and another opens. The arrival of Hirst and Simon signals the high noon of the Wadham renaissance; and the appearance of Hilaire Belloc at the Union sets the scene for an epic period there too. It is from the spring of 1893 that F.E. is fully in his element as a star performer on an exceptionally glittering Oxford stage.

4

President of the Union

'Any one who attempts to sketch the history of the Oxford Union Society in however brief a form must feel that in a certain sense he is beating the air,' wrote F.E. in 1922.

> The feeling of mutual friendship or even of mutual enmity among the officers and members of the Society – the interchange of free debate – the first vague groping of youth towards power – the gradual building up of a tendency towards a certain form of verbal expression – all these are things which may easily be felt by a Corporate Community, but are not easily translated to paper.[1]

The Union played so important a part in F.E.'s life, however – in developing his style, in forming his values, tastes, friendships and lifelong loyalties, quite apart from establishing his name as one to be looked out for – that the attempt must be made. Other men's Oxford years may be related hastily with their schooling. But it was F.E.'s proudest boast that he was an Oxford man; in particular he was all his life an Oxford Union man.

In December 1892, near the end of F.E.'s silent fourth term, the future historian of the Union, H.A. Morrah, proposed in a debate 'That this Society views its present position with regret and its future with apprehension'; the motion was carried by 55 votes to 39. Morrah could have saved his apprehension, for the Society was actually on the threshold of one of the most distinguished periods in its existence. The member who, more than any other, was to inspire the Union for the next few years came up to Balliol at the beginning of the following term, in January 1893. To arrive thus in the middle of a year was most unusual; but Hilaire Belloc was in every way an unusual undergraduate. Though only twenty-two, he might nowadays be classed as a mature student. He was half-French, and aggressively proud of it; bilingual and immensely well read, he had served a spell as a driver with the French army near the German border; he felt himself superior, not without reason, to the callow young men he met at Oxford and made a point of mocking their complacency and insularity – but so brilliantly that he compelled their admiration. In his oratory at the Union he struck a refreshingly different note. 'He dares to be serious,' wrote *Isis*. 'He loves general principles, has a perfect lust of deduction.'[2] By the commitment and the rare Gallic passion of his speaking, Belloc raised the quality of the Union as a whole for the three years that he frequented it.

For sheer oratory Belloc surpassed even F.E., though F.E. was the more skilful debater. Once again, F.E. was fortunate in the timing that paired him with such an opponent. Paired they were, for each quickly became the most prominent speaker on his side of the House. (Reflecting the heightened conflict outside, the Union had in recent years tended to divide more sharply than formerly on party lines, with the Conservative Strafford Club predominating; in F.E.'s time party feeling remained high, but it so happened that most of the ablest speakers, including Hirst and Simon as well as Belloc, were Liberals, leaving F.E. unrivalled as the champion of the Tory majority.) Their first clash was one of the most memorable. The motion, proposed by F.E. on 9 February 1893, could not have been better calculated to provoke Belloc: 'That at the present juncture the advent of a Dictator would be a blessing to the French people'. Moreover F.E. was seconded by a German, Baron Zedlitz of Trinity. 'The first three speeches', wrote the *Oxford Magazine*, 'were delivered with perhaps more fire and passion than any other consecutive three to which a recent audience at the Union has listened.'[3] F.E. castigated the corruption of French politics, derided the impotence of the Chamber of Deputies and dismissed the constitution as 'neither fish, flesh nor fowl', showing (according to *Isis*) great knowledge of the subject and contriving 'just when he threatened to become dull or prosy, to light it up with some quip or quirk'.[4] 'Mr. Smith', the *Oxford Magazine* judged, 'added by a remarkable speech to a reputation which is already considerable: it was, however, unfortunate that much of what he said was marred by an ineffective delivery, which prevented several of his best sayings being caught by the House.'[3] This was a complaint that would be heard again.

'Mr. Belloc, who followed, made quite the speech of the evening – a *tour de force* that for nervous oratory has seldom been equalled . . . at the Union. It was a lesson in gesticulation even to watch him.'[3] He deplored F.E.'s characteristic flippancy, defended the glory of the French Republic – asserting that if England had secured Catholic Emancipation, Parliamentary Reform and the Repeal of the Corn Laws, it was to the French Revolution that she owed these blessings – and looked forward passionately to the coming war of revenge on Germany, making 'a profound impression on the House'. Zedlitz was caustic and conciliatory by turns, 'rather unequal throughout,'[3] leading up to the statement that a dictator would be a blessing in disguise – 'a paradox which it took the House the rest of the evening to digest'.[4] The motion was eventually lost by 39 votes to 63.

F.E. was too taken up with Mods for the rest of that term to speak again, but in the summer he could not fail to intervene in a major debate, spread over two weeks, on Home Rule. 'Mr. F.E. Smith gave us the one really good speech of the evening',[5] thought *Isis*, and the *Oxford Review* agreed.

His was essentially the speech of the whole debate . . . He proved once more that he is one of the best fighting speakers in the Union. Speaking entirely without notes, he kept his audience attentive, sympathetic and at times enthusiastic for nearly twenty minutes. A very able speech was brought to an end by two fine passages from Tennyson, which were very skilfully worked up to and introduced.[6]

There was also a nice dash of his distinctive impudence in it, when he

proceeded to use the trust existing between Irish and Liberal members as the peg on which to hang various suppositions derogatory to the President's moral character, after each of which he was generous enough to observe, 'This, Sir, is, of course, merely hypothetical.'[5]

The slandered President was Lord Beauchamp, who must have been responsible for setting up the second clash between F.E. and Belloc a fortnight later. Both were again 'on the paper' (with Zedlitz again third), and 'a very full House and a still fuller Gallery' testified to the expectation the juxtaposition of their names aroused.[7] If Belloc had won their previous encounter, this one was made for F.E. The motion, seventy-five years ahead of its time, was specially designed for Eights Week and not intended to be taken very seriously: 'That this House would Approve of any Measure which gave Undergraduates a Share in the Government of the University'. Belloc, proposing, was too serious for the occasion and fell relatively flat: he actually believed in the motion, and cited European and Scottish models for a detailed scheme of student representation, rising to a peroration in which he envisaged the University as 'some lofty and well-proportioned cathedral, in which the representation of undergraduates would be a conduit and a drain for the buoyancy of youth'.[8] F.E.'s reply more successfully matched the mood of the House, keeping it 'in fits of laughter from beginning to end'.[9] He twitted Belloc and Zedlitz on their 'unhallowed alliance', and Belloc on the French penchant for duelling, before turning to demolish the motion, ingeniously sliding out of serious discussion by stressing the words 'This House would approve of *any* scheme': this allowed him to sketch an absurd plan of his own, making Belloc Vice-Chancellor, appointing the Union Library Committee to be the Hebdomadal Council ('it will give its members something to do'), and even – the ultimate absurdity – finding room for delegates from the women's colleges, who would 'brighten, if not accelerate, the proceedings'.[7] He ended with a merciless parody of Belloc ('When I contemplate the scheme of the honourable gentleman from Balliol I see it as a high, vast, lofty, well-proportioned drain!'),[8] finally telling him to stop lecturing Oxford and go home and reform the University of Paris. 'I think I've pricked the Belloc bubble,' he is supposed to have said as he sat down amid cheers,[8] while Zedlitz rose to congratulate him on 'the most amusing, excellently delivered, absolutely pointless and scandalously defamatory speech he had ever heard'.[7]

One of those who witnessed this performance from the gallery was John Simon – now at Wadham but not yet a member of the Union. (It is worth noticing that, recalling the occasion for Morrah in 1922, thirty years before writing his unreliable memoirs, he calls this 'my first experience of the Union'.)[10] Simon suggests, and Christopher Hollis in his history of the Union repeats, that F.E. and Belloc were contesting the Presidency that night, and F.E. won it. This is premature: F.E. had to wait another two terms, Belloc another four, for that honour. But F.E. was elected – indeed nominated unopposed – to be Junior Treasurer for the following year. He was rising through the ranks of the Society rapidly enough. As he did so he was making friends of a very different class from anyone he could have met at Liverpool, or even at Wadham. His two closest friends were Earl Beauchamp (of Christ Church) and Lord Balcarres (of Magdalen). Balcarres had a family seat conveniently near Birkenhead, at Haigh Hall near Wigan, and Beauchamp's stately home, Madresfield Court, near Malvern, was pleasantly close to Oxford; F.E. was soon a regular guest at both houses. His correspondence from these years (at least that which has survived) consists mainly of notes and letters from these two, most of them trivial, many concerned with arrangements for debates; some are amusing, and one or two are tantalizing; all breathe a strong flavour of undergraduate plots, jokes and gossip. One postcard, anonymous but addressed in Balcarres's hand to F.E. at Madresfield Court, says simply, 'What an awful bore you are.' Another, a note from Magdalen signed 'Bal' is addressed to 'You Phat Man'. A third, also from 'Bal', is interesting but unfortunately undated, 'All right Fred I will run you, but I must protest against the frequency with which I have to run you.' A letter, dated Haigh Hall, 20 December 1893, begins, 'Hang your cheek, F.E. Smith; your writing is a bad copy of mine: your signature an impudent plagiarism.' The most amusing of Beauchamp's letters is a scribble, 'Have been sent down, am applying St. Mary Hall'; (this was after some rumpus at Christ Church involving the breaking of the Dean's windows, of which Beauchamp, unjustly he claimed, was held to have been the main culprit). The most intriguing are a number which address F.E. as 'My dear Cousin' and refer to him as a relative! Could he possibly have been pursuing a Lygon girl, or was this just blood-brotherhood? It is difficult not to feel that F.E. was deliberately cultivating the best possible connections – the list of his particular friends at the Union includes, in addition to Beauchamp and Balcarres, Viscount Suirdale (heir to the Earl of Donoughmore) and Viscount Fitz-Harris (heir to the Earl of Malmesbury), and the Earl of Westmeath. By his later years at Oxford F.E. had climbed, socially as well as politically, a very long way from Birkenhead.[11]

If it was at the Union that F.E. dazzled the University, it was in the narrower circle of Wadham, where he did not have to strive so hard to impress, that F.E. exercised most winningly his talent to amuse his friends. He spoke frequently in the college debating society. His line on political motions was unswervingly Conservative, and his attitude to social questions such as women's rights was similarly unbending; there is more interest in his views on personal and moral matters. He rejected the proposition that "'Tis better to have loved and lost than never to have loved at all' – but he was in a minority of one, so he may have taken that line solely to make a debate. He denied that suicide was immoral. On a motion that 'the honest blockhead is a more admirable character than the blackguard of genius', which he might have been expected to reject with contempt, he spoke twice, both for and against; his vote was not recorded. At Michaelmas 1893 he became President of the society, signing his name hugely with a paintbrush; but order continued to decline – one evening the minutes record that 'Private business consisted of a series of sallies from Messrs. Anstie and Fry, who sat together on a window seat and vied with each other in the compilation of wretched, scurrilous witticisms at the expense of the President.'

Possibly more serious was the Wadham Literary Society, of which F.E. was elected a member at the beginning of his second year, (having already attended twice as a guest). But its minutes too are framed with such an eye to cleverness that they are not very informative about what was actually said. When at his first meeting, however, it is recorded that

'The President satisfactorily accounted for the non-appearance of the whisky-punch', it seems a fair bet that it was F.E. who demanded the explanation. In the discussion on Germany which followed, F.E. remarked that he had not been there 'but was in Sweden eighteen months ago', which is biographically interesting – it must have been in the Easter vacation before going to Oxford – but can scarcely have been relevant. A characteristic judgment is recorded in February 1893, dismissing Tom Paine as 'a scatter-brained enthusiast'; but what Ivor Thomas has rightly called 'the real gem of the minutes' relates to a meeting in Simon's rooms the following June.

> Mr. Smith read a cleverish paper entitled 'A Holiday' or 'Political Morality'.
> Its style was noticeably different from that usually adopted by the honourable member.
> 'To say what is not', he explained, 'is the road to success; and the art of politics is that by which one-third cajoles the other two-thirds.'
> The President (Mr. A.B. Willimot) congratulated the essayist on his delicate irony. The honest man should not take part in politics. Mr. Roche thought the keynote of the paper was to be found in its title of 'A Holiday'. Politics should not be regarded by anyone as the business of life.
> Messrs. Fry, Hawke, Urwick, Nixon and the Secretary also spoke, more or less to the point.
> The essayist in reply criticized all the speakers with smartness and without exception.[12]

F.E. appears never to have read another paper after this, but he was not backward in criticizing those of others, and several interesting or revealing opinions are recorded. He came strongly to the defence of the little-known country author John Burroughs (insisting that he *had* read him); gave a long lecture on Burke ('Mr. Smith frankly conceded the President's plea of ignorance and proceeded to remedy it . . . With regard to Burke's style of oratory he pointed out that Burke carried the theatrical element to excess, but had good excuses for doing so, for he had often inappreciative audiences of stupid Tory squires'). He expatiated on the relation of man to monkey; compared de Quincey with Shelley; depreciated Walter Pater; compared Meredith to other modern novelists; defended Thackeray against the charge of cynicism; and felt Kipling overrated ('there was in his works a spurious striving after virility'); he did not even shrink from reading Burns in dialect. The content of these discussions may perhaps have been superficial, but the range of reading that is implied would shame most modern undergraduates.*

F.E. was not a member of the Wadham Book Club (a sort of private circulating library to which both Fry and Simon belonged), but in October 1893 he was elected, along with Anstie and Roche, to the Olympic Dining Club, of which Fry was already Secretary. A year later Fry and F.E. were respectively President and Treasurer, and Simon, Hirst and Willimot were now also members. This small club was surely the quintessence of Wadham in these years, the table around which the whole brilliant group gathered three times a term to eat well, drink well and talk well in each other's stimulating company. There were of course no minutes kept, but F.E.'s influence may be imagined in the practice, adopted the year he joined, of dining in full evening dress with the Olympic Club waistcoat, made of Wadham blue cashmere with three brass buttons engraved with the club monogram. (This was where the Oxford credit system began to come in useful.) All his life, F.E. loved dining clubs: he was to found a famous one with Winston Churchill in 1911. The dressing-up, the conspicuous extravagance, and the slightly heightened, artificial but still private conversation among selected friends – the intimately theatrical atmosphere showed him at his best advantage. No doubt he stole the limelight, hammed outrageously, but in this company his friends only loved him for it. 'If he had not enjoyed his own jokes', wrote Hirst, 'and revelled in the convivial society which it was his pleasure to entertain, he would not have been either so lovable or so popular.' At such tables as that of the Olympic Club F.E. radiated an irresistible warmth of personality that the wider public, unfortunately, rarely glimpsed, but which those who knew him well could never forget. 'With all his faults,' Hirst concluded half a century later, listing them mercilessly, 'I like to think of him at his best, the wittiest of companions in our undergraduate days.'[13]

Part of F.E.'s popularity at Wadham derived from his prowess at rugby. He was always a keen games-player and a good performer at any sport he took up. Practically the only game he never seems to have played was cricket. He became a sturdy centre-half in Fry's college soccer team, 'with a capacity for work that made up for his rugby man's disinclination to treat a ball as spherical and susceptible of accurate treatment'.[14] He was also a good three-mile runner, and later in life a

* Yet another college discussion group, very similar to the Literary Society, was the Wadham U.N.X. Society; its membership and subject-matter were almost identical, and it met on the same day! The programmes of both societies for the winter term of 1894 have survived; they reveal that on Sunday 28 January, C.B. Fry was to read a paper on Zola to the Literary Society in F.E. Smith's rooms, and F.E. Smith was to open a discussion in the U.N.X. on 'Good faith in Politics' in C.H. Ransome's rooms. Sundays were not wasted.

first-class tennis-player. But rugby was his first and at this age his best game: according to his own account he had captained Birkenhead Park, presumably while at Liverpool, 'with two of my brothers in the scrum with me'.[15] Rugby required less finesse and more hard physical courage than other games: F.E. loved the very mud and sweat of it, the masculine exhilaration of sheer exertion. He was a great believer in the maxim *Mens sana in corpore sano*: he both acted on it himself and preached it to others.

> No young man who does not take care to harden his body, to exercise his muscles, to promote by judicious exercise his intestinal and perspiratory functions, can hope to address himself to his work with the keenness and vigour of his more athletic rivals. What is more, even if by sheer force of habit he reaches the age of, say, thirty without taking reasonable exercise, he will certainly find after that age an increasing staleness and liability to illness.[16]

Once, when Sir John Masterman asked F.E. the secret of his success at the Bar, he simply rolled up his sleeve and bared his powerful forearm.

In 1893–4 F.E. captained the Wadham Rugby XV to victory in the inter-college championship – a remarkable achievement for a college of only eighty members. At the end of the season the team, which included Fry, Roche and Simon (but not, to his chagrin, Hirst) travelled through to Cambridge to play the Cambridge champions, Caius, and beat them by a try to nothing. (His son claims that F.E. scored the winning try, but Simon does not confirm this too-perfect detail.) This was the high point of F.E.'s rugby career, marred only by an outbreak on the way home of the sort of vandalism that used to be called youthful high spirits; years later F.E. claimed that he had done his best to dissuade his team from wrecking the railway carriage. 'That journey', he told the Oxford University Athletic Club, 'cost me the most miserable twenty pounds that I have even been compelled to borrow.'[17]

He only narrowly missed winning a Blue that year. He was convinced that he had been denied only by a prejudice in favour either of Fettesians or of beefy forwards possessing more bulk than brain – though *Isis* blamed an ill-timed injury. The evidence of his contemporaries, however, suggests that F.E. had not quite the skill to make up for his relative lack of weight: guts and vigour were his qualities. The disappointment was one of those wounds to his pride that never healed. 'To the end of his life', Sir John Masterman has written, 'his language about the University officials who left him out was a lesson in opprobrium.'[18] And Simon tells of F.E. raging to a friend of his about the 'putrid forward' who had kept him out of the team, before discovering that he was talking to the very man.[19] The lack of a Blue spoiled his record as an all-round man.

F.E. was rare enough, however, in combining membership of the Athletic Club with membership of the Union, bridging the widest gulf in university life. One of Beauchamp's letters to F.E. begs him to persuade Fry to join the Union ('We wd. give him any place he liked, and any night');[20] but Fry, though he debated at Wadham, would not be persuaded. His third year was F.E.'s big year at the Union. Hitherto he had spoken, though always to great effect, only five times in all and only once from the floor. Now, as Junior Treasurer, he began to intervene regularly, clearly with his eye on the Presidency. He usually chose the more political debates, which offered an opportunity to attack the Government; and on 23 November 1893, he returned to the dispatch box to move an outright motion of no confidence in an impressive and powerful speech.

The Second Home Rule Bill, just thrown out by the House of Lords, was as usual at the front of his argument. He had no inhibitions about attacking the aged Prime Minister personally for imposing a guillotine on its discussion in the House of Commons: 'his position on the subject of the gag supplied an instance of tergiversation worthy of his younger and more vigorous days'. (F.E. here quoted an entry from the Union minutes of the 1820s, recording that 'Gladstone, of Christ Church, after speaking for the motion at considerable length, proceeded to register his vote against it'. Truly the boy was father to the man!) He condemned the proposal that the Irish M.P.s should retain their seats at Westminster even though Westminster would have no jurisdiction over Irish affairs with the cuttingly pithy slogan, 'One man, one vote; one Irishman, two votes.' He further mocked Gladstone for objecting to the action of the House of Lords, pointing out that no modern statesman had created more peers than he – if only those sixty-four had supported the Bill it would have gone through. Altogether he cleverly represented the Government as betraying not only national interests but its own Liberal traditions. 'Mr. Smith described himself, perhaps ironically, as studiously moderate,' the *Oxford Magazine* noted. 'We should prefer to call him decidedly bitter, but he made an excellent fighting speech, amusing and carefully prepared.'[21]

A few days after this, F.E. appeared with the past and present Oxford Presidents, Beauchamp and H.W. Liversedge, as the guests of the Cambridge Union, opposing a motion that 'the individual judgement of Members of Parliament is unduly controlled from within the House by considerations of Party, and from without by the Press and the Constituencies'. The local papers wondered at such a motion being proposed by a Cambridge Liberal and opposed by an Oxford Tory, but they were uniformly charmed by the grace and wit with which the visitor defended democratic accountability, damning its detractors (with notable enthusiasm for the cause of progress) as 'political Rip Van Winkles'. Liversedge 'did not rise much above the ordinary undergraduate level'; Beauchamp impressed them rather more; but 'Mr. Smith, of Wadham, in style, language and voice soared far beyond our ordinary aspirations. The rest are good speakers – he is an orator.'[22]

This was a busy week for F.E., for the very next day a man with whom his name would in the future be closely linked, Edward Carson – already one of the leading Irish opponents of Home Rule – came to Oxford as the principal guest at the annual dinner of the Strafford Club, held at the Randolph Hotel. Liversedge proposed the main toast of the evening, to the Unionist cause, to which Carson replied. But F.E. proposed 'in measured terms' one of the lesser toasts, to the Houses (note the plural) of Parliament. 'Lord Zouche, in replying, passed a well-deserved eulogy on the oration'; but he added a mild rebuke: he 'wondered if there was not something bitter underlying the delectable constituents of the speech'.[23] Bitter? This was at least the second and it would not be the last time that the word would be used of F.E.'s tongue. He had no obvious cause for bitterness at this moment; his career could scarcely have been developing better. If he was impatient to get into Parliament, the visitor who replied to him on behalf of the Commons should have been an encouraging example to him. Arthur Griffith-Boscawen (another future colleague in the Lloyd George Cabinet) had been President of the Union five years earlier and was now, at the age of twenty-six, M.P. for Tonbridge.

Griffith-Boscawen's rapid progress testified to the value of the Presidency. F.E. was already seeking out his friends to nominate him for the summer term. Balcarres, himself President-elect for January, was initially committed to Morrah, but on his withdrawal agreed to nominate F.E., 'tho' I must enter a protest against a system which has become too common . . . of the Junior Treasurer curtailing his year of office'.[24] F.E. was now, besides speaking frequently, giving a lot of his time to the Society. Morrah in his history commends him as 'a speaker who could unbend and take his full share both in the administrative work of the Union and in the lighter business which brought men together week by week to exercise themselves in the art of repartee'.[25] Two telling examples of the sort of administrative work that fell to him may be quoted from the minutes. In December 1893, 'The Junior Treasurer obtained the sanction of the Committee for the dismissal of Briggs and Roberson, and the engagement of Wm. Prince and Richard Heaver at a weekly wage of 6/-.' The following term, 'The Committee passed a proposal of the Junior Treasurer to spend some £30 to provide bookshelves, furniture etc. for the room under the billiard room.'[26] The cost of this piece of minor refurnishing was equal to nearly two years' wages! A more controversial question of expenditure, however, cropped up when Belloc proposed that the Union buy the complete works of Zola. F.E. supported him, but a poll of the Society confirmed Belloc's view of its prudish insularity by rejecting the proposal. He eventually got around the decision by buying the volumes singly. Agreed on this, Belloc and F.E. continued to clash periodically across the floor of the debating chamber – once over the study of English Literature, another time (more predictably) over the power of the House of Lords. (Was it on this occasion that F.E., complimenting Belloc on his speech, remarked that the more often he heard it, the more he liked it?) It was a week after the latter debate, on 22 February 1894, that F.E. was nominated unopposed to the Presidency.*

About the same time, Hirst and Simon got their Firsts in Mods. Fry was captain of football, cricket and athletics. Balcarres wrote to F.E. from Haigh Hall during the vacation, 'Really you Wadham men are howling swells.'[27]

The apotheosis of a swell was to be featured as an *Isis* Idol. F.E.'s turn came at the beginning of his Presidency, in April 1894 (nearly a year later than Fry). This anonymous 'profile', generally admiring but slightly satirical in tone, gives an illuminating picture of how F.E. was regarded by his fellows at this stage of his life. Due attention is given to his rugby; but the emphasis of the article is all on his career at the Union. The writer notes that after his sensational début 'he spoke but seldom for several terms'.

> Indeed he limited his utterances so entirely to great occasions that there was beginning to grow up an impression that his speeches, though always admirably put together, and usually very effective, were really wonderful efforts of memory rather than triumphs of debating skill. But with his appearance as Junior Treasurer last October term he entirely changed his tactics. From this time hardly a debate elapsed without his intervening, and it was noticeable that his speeches, while still distinguished by depth of foundation and an over-elaborated sarcasm, were now also marked by a flexibility which adapted them to the needs of the moment.

* Four years later when E.C. Bentley was standing for the Presidency, F.E. advised him not to be shy about voting for himself. 'When I was standing, I voted for myself openly and ostentatiously.' (E.C. Bentley, *Those Days* p. 80). No doubt he would have done, but there was in fact no election for him to vote in.

F.E. was now unquestionably 'the best debater in the Union . . . maintaining an average level that is almost equal to Mr. Belloc at his best'.

His manner is considerably more noticeable for the fortitude of its action than the suavity of its mode. He always seems impressed, when answering official questions, with the idea that his inter-rogator must be 'scored off' if possible, and snubbed any way. He has a belief in himself which is probably the secret of his rapid success, and of which nothing but Time will rob him; – nay there are those who would think twice before betting on Time. His actual style of delivery, though fluent and forcible, is marked by a heedlessness of full-stops and a preference for the middle of a sentence as a halting-place. [There follows the criticism of his northern accent already quoted.] His signature, should it ever be uncovered by some twenty-ninth century antiquary, will probably be mistaken for a pictorial illustration of the story of the Ten Little Niggers.[28]

As President, F.E. could no longer speak often himself (which *Isis* regretted). His job was to decide the motions to be debated and select the principal speakers. His predecessor pretended to think the problem would be too much for him.

Dear Fred Smith,
    I suspect you want bucking hup.
    Have you settled the first debate for next term? If not wire to me at once and I will settle everything for you so that you shant make a mess of the whole show.
    Ha Ha. Funny man.
    Write and tell me all the Birkenhead news.
                                                    Yrs ever
                                                      Bal.[29]

F.E. replied that he had already fixed his first motion – 'That the interests of Great Britain will be best served by a rigid neutrality in continental disputes' – but had so far found no Liberal to propose it, though he soon secured one. For his second week he threw in a non-political motion (proposed by Morrah) – 'That this House deplores the worthlessness of the English novel of today'. Thereafter the debates of his Presidency were all more or less political in character. On 10 May he pitted Simon against Beauchamp on Welsh Disestablishment. The following week the future Tory M.P. Howard Gritten proposed (and carried, with the support of Belloc and a rare speech from Roche) a motion that 'This House views with regret the Revolt of the Daughters'. 17 and 24 May were devoted to a two-part debate on the overriding question of Home Rule, for which F.E. secured two distinguished guest speakers – the Irish Nationalist M.P. John Dillon the first week, and the Ulster leader, Colonel Saunderson, the second. (He originally invited Lord Hugh Cecil to put the Unionist case, but Cecil declined, objecting strongly to the invitation to Dillon.) The chamber and gallery were packed both nights: the second saw the better sport, for Belloc spoke and F.E. left the chair to reply to him. It goes without saying that Home Rule was rejected by a heavy majority, 344 votes to 182. The following Tuesday, F.E. and Belloc took their show to Cambridge, where they debated the question of the House of Lords for the umpteenth time before the amazed Cantabrians. Back in Oxford, the last two debates of F.E.'s presidential term featured the future Permanent Secretary to the Treasury, John Bradbury, proposing that 'the policy of the so-called "Conservative Party" during the last half-century has been such as to render the term "Conservative" a peculiar misnomer'; and a future Secretary of the Society for the Propagation of the Gospel deploring the attitude of the Independent Labour Party, with F.E. once again stepping down to lend his support.

That concluded the year at the Union, but there were still one or two more political functions to be attended before F.E. left Oxford for the summer. He took the chair at the annual dinner of the Canning and Chatham Club at the Clarendon Hotel, at which the guests included Charles Darling, Q.C., then still a barrister-M.P., but soon to be raised to the bench – a useful contact, later a sparring partner and friend. At a more mundane level F.E. also did his bit for the local Tory club (town, not gown) by giving an address, between the songs and comic recitations, at a Smoking Concert. As a former President of the Union, he was now a rising political star of proven pedigree, and consequently in demand.

Back in Birkenhead, his fame now almost equalled his father's. He made a great success in the town's mock Parliament, where he appeared, curiously, as 'the junior member for Cambridge University'. Old men nodded their heads and predicted a great future for him. 'He is "a chip off the old block"', wrote the anonymous 'Silent Member' in the *Birkenhead News*.

> He is a grand young debater – a finer I never heard ... Long life to you, Master Fred. We remember the pleasure we derived from listening to your dear and revered father, and it brought some sorrow with our pleasure when we heard you.[30]

During the summer a big rally of the Working Men's Conservative Association was held in Liverpool at which the main speaker was the 27-year-old Earl of Dudley. 'It is quite too funny!' jeered the *Birkenhead News*. 'I wonder what he knows either of working men or politics.'

> There will be a speaker far more interesting to Birkenhead people than the fashionable Earl. I mean, of course, Mr. F.E. Smith, the clever son of a clever father . . .[31]

In view of these expectations, the *News* headline after the event – 'The Coming Man. Brilliant Success of Mr. F.E. Smith' – is no surprise. But the *Liverpool Courier* took the same view.

> The stripling Mr. Smith, son of a late Mayor of Birkenhead, demonstrated once more the great value of the 'Oxford Union' by making the speech of the evening. We are sure no other speaker present* will feel offended by its being so described. There was naturally in the young orator's style something of 'the magnificent courage of inexperience', but even the most bitter political antagonist would have been ready to admit that this feature was much less marked than those of genuine and brilliant promise.[32]

The Times was there too, and in the course of a full report gave several inches to 'a speech of great eloquence and humour' by Mr F.E. Smith.[33]

E.P. Smith was present at this meeting, showing 'a pardonable pride in the triumph of his young nephew, although it was evident that some of the telling hits at the Liberals made the uncle wince and long to have a "go" on his own account for his pert but brilliant nephew'. E.P. must indeed have had mixed feelings and surely shared the fear of the *Birkenhead News* which now began to worry lest all this praise should go to F.E.'s head, and proceeded to lecture him very much as the *Advertiser* had warned his father fourteen years before,

> He has a nice presence, a flexible and pleasant voice, and a ready wit. For so young a man he has already achieved remarkable prominence, and it is to be hoped his success will not spoil him, and induce him to believe that mere smartness, which always fetches the gallery, will do instead of sound argument and thought. He ought to aim at being something better than a mere tickler of the ears of the groundlings.[34]

---

* The other speakers included Walter Long and J.C. Bigham, Q.C., the future Lord Mersey.

The time had come for Liberal papers to stop treating a promising young Tory with generous encouragement and start subjecting him to the same criticism as any other Tory. By October, when F.E. next addressed a local meeting – at a by-election in Birkenhead which arose, to his chagrin, a year or two too early for him to hope to win the nomination – the Oxford Union style was not so universally admired. At least one of his speeches on this occasion was said to be 'full of trivialities and . . . petty-minded in every respect'.[35]

> Mr. Frederick E. Smith, speaking in Tranmere, in the high-falutin' style, gave vent to the feelings of injured innocence and outraged political virtue. 'The Conservative Party', he said, 'were not so fond as their opponents of hitting under the belt' &c. Of course not; they are the 'gentlemanly party', as everybody knows . . . Mr. Frederick E. Smith, indeed, is a *very* superior person – quite one of the young men, in fact, who are only 'a little lower than the angels'. If one may presume to offer a word of advice to the 'Young Hopeful' of local Toryism, it would be to warn him against the pitfalls of rhetorical dandyism. But perhaps that would be hitting him under the belt. The bother of it is that one never knows where some people wear their belts.[36]

Thrusts like this announce F.E.'s emergence, in the course of 1894, as a fully fledged political personality.

Yet at the same time he was still an undergraduate, with his final examinations – his Schools – still to sit. He had at some point to start reading seriously in the law. The story that he did not so much as buy a book until six months before the exam must be an exaggeration, but there is no reliable evidence either way to suggest how hard F.E. did or did not work in 1893–4. Sir Gervais Rentoul reckoned that 'he studied very hard at night and trained himself to need very little sleep',[37] while Maurice Bowra asserted that he worked secretly at the far end of the Warden's garden.[38] It is indeed usually the case that those who surprise their friends with unexpectedly good degrees have actually been working harder than their friends suspect; nevertheless neither Rentoul, who went up to Christ Church in 1903, nor Bowra, who did not become a Fellow of Wadham until 1922, was remotely a contemporary witness. They may be right; F.E. may have used his time exceptionally well. But remembering the extent of his commitment in his third year to the Union, to rugby, to private societies discussing every subject under the sun except the law, to friendship, and to political speech-making in the country, it seems impossible that he had much time left over for legal textbooks.

The traditional story, related by his son, is that F.E. suddenly woke up, around Christmas 1894, to the fact that his whole future depended on getting a first class degree in June. The reason was not so much legal – one does not need a First in order to go to the Bar – as financial. By stylish dressing and extravagant good living far beyond his allowance, F.E. had run up debts totalling between £300 and £400 with the local tradesmen; he was of course confident that in time he would be able to pay them many times over, but he needed both the assurance of future success and the immediate security of a Fellowship (which a First might be expected to carry) if he was to fend off his creditors in the short term. F.E. was to the end of his life unrepentant about these debts; he regarded easy credit as an essential facility if poorer undergraduates were to be able to enjoy the full benefit of university life, and felt that he himself had perfectly vindicated the system by not merely paying off all he owed within a few years but actually continuing to patronize the same tailor for ever after; he even brought up his children to revere this tailor as the man who had made their father's career possible by inducing his other creditors to be patient with him. What they could have gained by having him declared a bankrupt is not clear, but the story is vividly told how, at a meeting in his rooms, they were persuaded to put their trust in his destiny and agreed to spare him. (Dr Wells, later Warden of Wadham, was required to show the same trust and lend F.E. out of his own pocket the money to pay his college bills.)

Having decided, then, that a First offered the only escape from serious embarrassment, F.E. (in his son's words) 'handled the situation in his own manner'.

He isolated himself from his friends, and took rooms in Wellington Square, a grim quadrangle of yellow brick houses lying little known and seldom visited behind Beaumont Street. He carted a library of law books into his lodgings and began the first great effort of his life. The wonderful concentration which he was so reluctant to employ now came to his aid. For six months, he toiled in these dispiriting rooms for fourteen hours a day. He never left them, shunning the world outside, fearful of a break in his rhythm, and the distraction of his friends. From early morning until late at night, when he crawled into bed and fell into a profound coma, his slippers were on his feet. Once each day, at a regular hour, he would come up for air and exercise, pedalling violently round Wellington Square on a safety bicycle, an outing which was, during this period, his sole and pathetic relaxation. It is remark-able that an effort so sustained and in so complex a subject did not utterly confuse his brain and render him hopelessly stale long before he reached the Examination Hall, but he had a mind of great clarity and enjoyed to the full that power which Napoleon praised: '*de fixer les objets longtemps sans être fatigué*'.[39]

Is this a true account, or one of F.E.'s melodramatic fantasies, elegantly elaborated by his son? There is no reason to doubt its basis of truth. It seems certain that F.E. did not start serious work for his Schools until at least the beginning of his final year, and quite characteristic and probable that he left it later than that. On the other hand, so spectacular an effort would surely have been remembered by Simon or Fry in their recollections of F.E. at Oxford. It is demonstrable that he did not in fact withdraw entirely from other activities, since he did not desert the Union. In the autumn term he spoke twice (on Women and on Drink); then in February he made a major speech in opposition to a motion of confidence in the Government moved by Simon – the only time in their undergraduate careers that these two rivals were paired together 'on the paper'. (Belloc was the President who paired them.) This was a particularly interesting performance, for towards the end of his speech, as the *Isis* reporter commented, he 'let himself go on broad general principles as I have never heard him let himself go before'.

> The title by which a Government governs is its superiority to the governed . . . That title Radicals have formally renounced . . . No man is an honest or courageous politician who will not if necessary assume the same attitude towards triumphant democracy as Eliot, Pym or Cromwell assumed towards triumphant monarchy . . . But where the carcase of sovereignty is, there will members opposite be gathered together.[40]

This was strong stuff, not his usual clever flippancy but deadly serious political philosophy. The attempt thus to define the intellectual foundation of his inherited Conservatism perhaps suggests that his mind was indeed now, as never before, powerfully engaged on the study of constitutional law.

He spoke once more, too, at the very end of May, only days before the beginning of his exams. The fact that he could come down to the Union and intervene in a debate at this stage does imply that his preparation was not quite so intensive as his son suggests. Had he done all he could and now stopped to let his mind clear before he put it to the test? Whatever the truth, whatever his programme of preparation, it was triumphantly successful. The exams over, there followed the usual agonizing wait; then another ordeal, listening to the names of those

awarded Firsts read out slowly in alphabetical order from the steps of
the Examination Schools – until finally he heard his own.

> He hired four punts, stocked them with champagne and food, and
> invited all the friends he could find to join his party. They drifted
> downstream amid leaping corks, clad in evening tails and straw
> boaters, and in these inappropriate garments the party were found
> next morning by an early riser sleeping in a hay field, while the
> punts drifted empty down the river.[41]

One wonders whether Fry was of the party. Distracted by his sporting
exploits, he had achieved the still rarer distinction of a Fourth.

5

Fellow of Merton

His First in Schools in the summer of 1895 did not secure F.E.'s immediate election to a Fellowship. The impression given by his son and other biographers that he passed directly from undergraduate at Wadham in June to don at Merton in October the same year is entirely false. In fact, not four but sixteen months elapsed before F.E. found his niche. The intervening year was a difficult one, during which his self-confidence must at times have drooped. Some writers have expressed surprise that he did not concentrate on reading for the Bar, eating his prescribed number of dinners at Gray's Inn (which he had joined in 1894) as quickly as possible so as to sit his final examination in 1897 and be called to practise without delay. The reason appears to be quite simply that he could not afford to. He needed a salary if he was to pay off his debts. So he returned to Oxford in the autumn of 1895 to work for further academic honours which might serve to secure one. His immediate financial position must have been parlous, for his Wadham Scholarship had expired and his uncle's allowance (supposing that E.P. still kept it up) cannot have been nearly enough to support him. He probably earned a little by that perennial standby of the impoverished graduate, private tutoring, but he must have been more than ever dependent on the patience of his creditors – not that he was ready to let that change his habits.

His main target was the B.C.L. (Bachelor of Civil Law) degree, which was examined in June – a perfectly normal additional qualification for aspiring solicitors and barristers, though more often taken by the ablest students as a legal qualification after Greats than on top of a good B.A. in Jurisprudence. A greater prize to aim for, however, was the Vinerian Law Scholarship, for which at that period a special examination was held in March covering 'Civil Law, International Law, General Jurisprudence and especially the Law of England both public and private'.[1] There is a story that F.E. had already competed once for the Vinerian the previous year: he is said to have missed it only through not knowing Shelley's Case and to have promised the examiners that he would supersede it when he became Lord Chancellor. This may fairly safely be discounted, if only because there was no *proxime accessit* to the winner in 1895. F.E.'s chance of winning in 1896 was threatened by the presence in the field of W.S. Holdsworth – a year older than himself, a Double First, already Barstow Scholar of the Inns of Court and a Lecturer at New College, and destined to become the outstanding academic lawyer of his generation. However, F.E., by concentrating upon Roman Law and allegedly astonishing the examiners by his erudition, narrowly defeated Holdsworth to take the prize.

For ever after F.E. took an immoderate delight in recalling this victory, sometimes claiming it as the achievement of his whole life of which he was most proud. During the Casement trial in 1916 he is supposed to have dismissed Holdsworth's opinion, quoted against him by the defence, with the remark, 'I am aware of the high attainments of Professor Holdsworth, since he was the runner-up to me when I was awarded the Vinerian Law Scholarship at Oxford.'[2] He and Holdsworth actually became good friends. In 1920, as Lord Chancellor, F.E. broke with established precedent to award Holdsworth 'academic silk' – that is, he made him a non-practising K.C.; while two years later Holdsworth returned the compliment by dedicating to F.E. the revised edition of his great *History of English Law*. From their early rivalry, each retained the highest respect for the other's ability.

F.E.'s pride in his victory was thus quite legitimate. The Vinerian was 'the blue riband of Oxford Law',[3] 'the most coveted of all university law prizes'.[4] His winning it is the clearest proof of the real quality of F.E.'s legal mind; he was never just a clever barrister, as those who were surprised by his success as Lord Chancellor should have remembered.* As important to him in 1896 as the prestige, however, were the immediately tangible rewards of victory – the prize money of £80 a year for three years and the probability that his path to a Fellowship would now be clear. With this feather in his cap, it would be understandable if he felt that he could afford to slacken his efforts for the B.C.L. in June. The Vinerian was worth more than another First, and he cannot have been too disappointed when he achieved only a Second, though again he held his failure against the unlucky examiner for ever after. The Vinerian was enough. In June the Fellows of Merton appointed F.E. to a three-year Lectureship in Law; and in October they elected him to a

---

* Curiously, it was just after winning the Vinerian, in April 1896, that F.E. wrote an unusually unconfident letter to Professor Dicey, thanking him for a definition of bankruptcy and admitting that his own had missed the essential point. 'I am very grateful for the help you have given me and only wish I were likely to do it more credit, but I am beginning to fear I have not a very legal mind.' (Birkenhead, *Frederick Edwin, Earl of Birkenhead*, p. 80). Lord Birkenhead omitted this letter from the 1959 revised edition of his father's life.

Fellowship, the first Law Lecturer to be so honoured. This gave him, after an anxious year, the security he needed: as he himself put it, 'the problem of existence was satisfactorily solved'.[5]

F.E.'s reason for seeking a Fellowship was frankly practical, and it may be imagined that he chafed at the enforced distraction from the clear purpose of his life. Yet the prospect of another three years at Oxford cannot have been too distasteful to him; his love of the place never tired, he had not yet had his fill of the Union, and the actor in him must have relished the chance to play the new role of don on the stage he had previously dominated as a student. He may even have appreciated the argument that a short breathing-space need not be a distraction from his chosen career, but rather the most important part of his preparation. To Ivor Thomas, going to Merton was the best thing F.E. could have done – almost making up for his desertion of the classics.

> Exception will probably be taken to my judgement that his Fellowship at Merton in 1895 [actually 1896 – Thomas falls into the universal error] was the most important tide in F.E. Smith's affairs. It will be thought that it was a positive set-back in the career of so active a man. But that is precisely its value. A versatile undergraduate's life is a hustle such as no words can express. If he is plunged straight into the busy world of politics, law or journalism he has no time to find his balance. He is almost certain to have learnt nothing worth retaining in the hothouse atmosphere of undergraduate life. F.E. Smith was given the glorious respite of four years [actually three] as a Fellow of Merton before he was called to the Bar in 1899. It enabled him to find his feet, so that when he went out into the world he knew what he wanted and was able to go hard for it. Those who have been amazed at the legal knowledge of Lord Birkenhead will find the answer to it in those years of comparative quiet as a Fellow.[6]

It hardly needed Merton to show F.E. what he wanted from life; nevertheless there must be a good deal in the view that, just as Liverpool University had allowed him to arrive at Oxford two years older and more experienced than would have been the case had he gone there straight from school, so Merton enabled F.E. to mature his knowledge of the law before he put his precocious talent to the test.

Back in Birkenhead, where every stage in his progress had been closely followed, F.E.'s latest success was celebrated with a most exceptional public tribute. A 'complimentary dinner' 'spontaneously inaugurated by leading gentlemen representative of all classes of the community and responded to' – according to the *Birkenhead Advertiser* –

'with like cordiality by the citizens of the borough, was held in the Music Hall, Claughton', three days before Christmas 1896. John Laird and the current M.P., Elliott Lees, sent their apologies, but most of the town council were present as well as most of F.E.'s male relatives, including his feckless Uncle Arthur and his maternal grandfather Edwin Taylor.

> An excellent dinner was served by Mr. Dan Baker, who was complimented on all sides for the judgement displayed in the arrangement of the *cuisine*. During the progress of the repast the company were entertained by the Probyn Ladies Orchestra, a talented body of musicians, who afforded a rare treat to those having the pleasure of being present.[7]

The toast to the guest of honour was proposed by Councillor Benedict Jones, M.A., J.P., whose academic and legal qualifications probably most nearly approached F.E.'s. His speech, expressing pride in the local boy, the son of a former Mayor ('He thought they had every evidence that his son was showing traces of hereditary ability'), who had stormed the citadel of the southern Establishment, emphasized how rare F.E.'s achievement was. F.E.'s reply, taking this cue, was not only witty and suitably modest but notably democratic. After remarking that one of the most salutary lessons of an Oxford education was that however good one might be at any branch of learning or athletics, there were always many others who were a great deal better, he went on to welcome the opening up of the ancient universities to the middle classes (paying particular tribute to the work of the Liberal Party in removing religious tests and disqualifications) and declared that he would like to see the process carried a step further, 'so that facilities will be given to any boy, however humble, to march up every rung of the ladder which led from the elementary school to the higher school, and from the higher school to the University, and from the University to the highest prizes that the Civil Service could afford'. There is more than a hint here of his famous 'glittering prizes' speech of twenty-seven years later.

F.E. also used the opportunity of this municipal dinner to pay deserved but characteristically cheeky tribute to his beneficent uncle, E.P., to whom, he told his audience, he was 'bound by every tie of affection and gratitude, but to whose political convictions I should feel it impossible in orderly language to do justice'.[7] E.P., in a gracious reply, chose not to remonstrate with his nephew.

More problematic than why F.E. sought a Fellowship is the question why Merton should have wanted to elect a Fellow who clearly had no intention of staying longer than three years. He was undoubtedly a good man to have at a High Table, while his Tory politics and his support of the Established Church would have been marked points in his favour; even so, it might reasonably have been suspected that he would not put his heart into the job of teaching. It seems in fact that Merton gambled deliberately on a glamorous appointment. 'We were aware that he was likely to go off to the Bar,' one of the three-man committee that elected him wrote later to the historian of the Law Faculty, 'but thought rightly that he might before doing so stir up the Law students of Merton.'[8] Their daring was well rewarded, for F.E. turned out an excellent and surprisingly conscientious don. 'In three years he had prepared Merton effectively for the ministry of his successor, J. C. Miles'[9] – a Fellow more in the conventional mould, who stayed for life, and finished up as Warden.

As a tutor, F.E. 'took his duties seriously and made his pupils work';[10] he left behind him a reputation for not tolerating perfunctory essays, though it must be said that his only recorded rebuke to a lazy student – 'This is a very modest contribution to learning, Mr. X'[11] – does not seem particularly withering. As a lecturer he might have been thought somewhat perfunctory himself, were it not for his extraordinary ability to improvise, 'He lectured in Contracts and had a habit of taking a couple of cases into the lecture room and speaking extempore from them with great success.'[12] This training in holding a complex argument in his head and developing it as he went along may be seen as the foundation of those feats of memory and lucid exposition with which at the height of his career F.E. so impressed his colleagues and rivals in Parliament and at the Bar. However unorthodox, his lectures must have been well received, for in the second year at Merton he was appointed a Lecturer at Oriel as well; while in his third year he demonstrated his versatility by taking on the further job of a University Extension Lecturer in Modern History, specializing in the seventeenth and eighteenth centuries. Presumably he needed the money, but he doubtless also enjoyed the opportunity to get away from the law and ride a few historical hobby-horses, just for the change.

There is unfortunately no direct testimony from any of those whom F.E. taught in these years. One whom he did not teach but who later came to him as a student in chambers was Harold Jager who, in his own words, 'wandered down to Merton' with a view to signing on for F.E.'s lectures, 'discovered him in the act of giving a lecture . . . listened for some minutes to a stream of rapid, nay lightning, eloquence which I was entirely unable to grasp', and was relieved to find that his list was full and he could take no more. The witness closest to F.E. at this time is E.C. Bentley (the inventor of the Clerihew), who was in his third year at Merton when F.E. arrived there. Bentley had already admired him at the Union. He has recorded his first sight of F.E. in 1894 arising unexpectedly from amid a crowd of freshmen, to the delight of a House which was wondering whether he was going to turn up, to ask 'a grossly personal question' of the President as a preliminary to 'a coruscation of cross-talk' and 'fantastic chaff'. 'Tall and well-built', he was 'the handsomest youth I had ever seen apart from a Charles Dana Gibson drawing; his raised eyebrows, slightly down-drawn lips and long thrusting chin made a singular impression of aggressive arrogance'.[10] If he had initially felt only awe for this alarming figure, however, Bentley's view soon changed.

> After F.E. Smith was elected to a Fellowship at my own College, I came to know something of that large-heartedness which endeared him to a greater number of friends, perhaps, than any other man of his time possessed. There was no reason why he should have taken any interest in one not of his own academic generation, not one of his law-pupils, and not associated with him in any way save in a common interest in the Union Society. But he often showed me kindness.[11]

He used to give Bentley hints about speaking which Bentley absorbed gratefully.

> It is perhaps a measure of the effect produced by F.E. upon his Oxford contemporaries that it never occurred to me to question the importance of such advice . . . He was already so much more the master of the art of oratory than any of the political veterans to whom I had listened from time to time.[11]

The advice which Bentley most clearly recalled was F.E.'s insistence on the thorough preparation of speeches. Were his lectures then perhaps not quite so impromptu as they seemed? Or did they not count as speeches?

F.E. used to reveal to Bentley glimpses of himself. 'I suppose you will be an adventurer like myself,' he said once, showing that he already welcomed the description that was to be so often pinned on him by his detractors.[12] Another time, as they drove from Merton to the Union in the hansom-cab which it was his habit to take for the distance of a few hundred yards, he sketched out to Bentley his intended career: he meant to try for Parliament as soon as his 'probably very exiguous earnings' at the Bar made it possible and then, once in, to seize the earliest opportunity that presented itself to make a mark.[13] Once, too, Bentley was in F.E.'s rooms and happened to sit down at the desk, where he saw written on the blotter 'along with many examples of his own signature' (clearly something of a fetish) the lines:

> Let the world slide,
> Let the world go.
> A fig for a care;
> A fig for a woe.
> If I can't pay,
> Well, I can owe.

When Bentley asked if he had written them himself, F.E. replied 'with a laugh that he was "not enough poet" even for that: he had forgotten where they came from'.[14] They certainly made an appropriate motto for his Oxford career, indeed for his whole life.

Bentley, however, was no ordinary undergraduate, since he shared digs in 1896–7 with F.E.'s friends Hirst and Simon, who had also stayed up in Oxford after their Schools – Simon to compete for a Fellowship at All Souls, which he duly won. He was once present at a heated argument about the Conservative Government's Chinese policy in F.E.'s rooms which ended 'at midnight with Simon tipping F.E. out of his chair and F.E. squirting soda water at Simon'.[15] In his memoirs Bentley is concerned (as also is Fry) to present a warmer picture of Simon than the chilly image which adhered to him in later life; and he draws a telling contrast between Simon and F.E., particularly in their styles of speaking – not concealing his preference for the former.

> Simon used always to stick to the essence of his argument: he could and did hit hard enough in debate, but he was always earnest, lucid, persuasive, forcible. F.E. on the other hand, though he always knew his case, cultivated a theatrically pugnacious style, making liberal use of ridicule and contempt; he excelled in the 'cheap score', as Simon used to say.[16]

Bentley confirms that though F.E. and Simon were good friends, 'intimacy . . . would hardly be the word for the relationship of such very opposite characters'.[17] Chance having thrown them together at Wadham, they were never thereafter fully able to separate themselves in the public mind; and though it was F.E. who in 1927 exploded when Dingle Foot, speaking at the Union, repeated in his hearing the absurd story that he and Simon at the outset of their careers had tossed a coin to determine which of them should join which party, it was undoubtedly Simon who suffered most by being eternally paired with F.E. Just as gifted academically and even more successful politically and at the Bar,

Simon was never able to match F.E.'s public panache; while for the sake of their shared college days he had to suffer a great deal of private ribbing to which he was ill-equipped to reply from a man with whom he had little else in common and of whom he must often have cordially disapproved. It is difficult to believe that his amusement at F.E.'s more outrageous ribaldries at his expense was not something rather strained. For all their outward fraternity, there was a sharp edge to their rivalry, and little true love was ever lost between them.

F.E., even though a don, was still a great figure at the Union. He was now a legend whose retorts and witticisms, endlessly repeated, had passed into Union folklore, and the impact of his appearances was nowadays enhanced by their rarity. One dramatic intervention described by Bentley can in fact be dated to February 1896, when F.E. was still working for the Vinerian; it may nevertheless be quoted here. The motion under discussion concerned (yet again!) the drink question, 'That this House would view with horror the prospect of a teetotal England'.

> The debate had run for some time, in a full house, when the swing doors flew open and in strode F.E. dressed in the full uniform of a Piccadilly lounger of those days – long frock-coat, sponge-bag trousers, patent-leather button boots, dazzling tall-hat, which he removed as he entered, lavender gloves and a little cane. Such an apparition had not been seen in the Union within living memory, for the time when undergraduates dressed in any serious sense of the word had long gone by ... The idea conveyed by this irruption of F.E.'s was that he had been to London for the day and had driven straight to the Union from the station: be that as it might, he took his seat on the Committee bench amid thunders of applause, and at the first opportunity rose and regaled the House with a fluent speech in which, I remember, the teetotal islanders of Tristan da Cunha came in for withering comment.[18]

And yet the motion was defeated by three votes!

Immediately after his election to Merton, F.E. was invited by Hirst (who had at last reached the Presidency) to speak 'on the paper' in the second debate of the new term, in opposition to the motion 'That this House heartily welcomes and supports Mr. Gladstone's intervention in the Armenian agitation'. F.E. was never slow to seize an opportunity to attack Gladstone; the chamber was accordingly filled to overflowing by a crowd described by *Isis* as 'the multitude who sit at the feet of Mr. F.E. Smith'. His fans were not disappointed.

Mr. F.E. Smith's return to political life was signalized by a very forcible and convincing speech. He was loudly received and it was delightful to observe the House settling down to enjoy itself, very much as a theatrical audience settles down at the first bars of the prelude.

His argument was characteristic.

He considered it the clear object of the debate to discuss the agitation itself, apart from the Armenian question, and proceeded to deliver a sweeping indictment of the whole movement, which he characterised as both dangerous and useless. The spirit of the agitation he also condemned: 'a man with a family has no right to become a knight-errant' was his expression.[18]

This vote he carried by 117 votes to 51.

In February he spoke again, from the floor, in support of Her Majesty's Government. This intervention too 'was as eagerly listened to and as enthusiastically received as his speeches always are'. He was answered by Simon, and between them they roused the House.[19] He spoke once more 'on the paper' in May, on the Eastern Question, and again, by popular demand in rather unusual circumstances, in an end-of-term debate. After that, however, one last exceptional occasion apart, he stayed away from debates, though he still attended social functions such as the dinners given at the beginning of their term of office by newly elected Presidents. At one of these, in October 1897, he disgraced himself with a display of that streak of intolerance which surfaced periodically throughout his life, tipping his usual stylish exuberance over into boorishness. It is E.C. Bentley again who tells the story:

When I was Librarian of the Society a president was elected – F. Lenwood – whose principles and practice as regards alcoholic liquor were exactly opposed to those of F.E. Smith, whom Lenwood invited to his dinner as a matter of course. When the invitations had gone out, I doubt if it occurred to any of the guests – it certainly did not to me – that Lenwood's opinions would stand in the way of his deferring to custom in the matter of wine. However, when we were seated, with F.E. at the new President's right hand as being the most eminent of his predecessors then in residence . . . our host arose and announced that he could not reconcile it with his conscience to offer his guests any intoxicating drink, and that he hoped they would not very much mind. I do not suppose that

most of us did very much mind: to me, and doubtless to others, it
was a declaration that compelled respect, considering what courage was needed to make it. Unfortunately F.E. minded a great
deal, and showed it. He turned his shoulder to his host throughout
the dinner; and he called loudly and repeatedly for glasses of milk.
I repeat that this action, done by a younger man who was
entertaining F.E. as a distinguished guest, and who knew all about
him, his opinions, his tastes, and his capacity for making himself
unpleasant at need, showed moral courage of the highest order.[20]

There are other, funnier, stories of F.E. in these Merton years.
Several concern the dog, an Irish terrier, which, against the rules, he
kept in college. It was named Khama, after an African chief then in the
news for banning alcoholic liquor from his territory; for the animal too
was, unlike its master (and probably not for want of the most pressing
offers) a total abstainer. F.E. defied the regulations for some time, until
the day Khama was persuaded by some undergraduates to attend
vespers in the college chapel, after which he had to go. F.E. used also to
take Khama to the Union, another breach of regulations on which he
was repeatedly heckled, notably on one occasion by Rosslyn Bruce of
Worcester. 'The joke, if joke it be, is very stale,' F.E. replied airily, 'and
even when fresh was never A1.' 'Surely Sir,' Bruce responded, 'the joke
could hardly be A1, when it is quite obviously K9.' 'Even after thirty
years,' wrote H.A. Morrah in 1923,

> it rankles a little with the perpetrator of this verbal atrocity that he
> and Mr. Smith were (quite falsely) accused of collusion. It was
> probably one of the few occasions in his whole career that the
> ex-Lord Chancellor did not have the last word.[21]

The second Lord Birkenhead placed in this period the story of F.E.'s
reputed encounter with Oscar Wilde, fantastically elaborating an
anecdote which he attributes to Edward Marjoribanks's biography of
Carson. But Marjoribanks makes it clear (and the date of Wilde's
downfall – 1895 – makes it certain) that if it has any truth at all the story
belongs to F.E.'s Wadham days. This may nevertheless be the place to
dispose of it. Marjoribanks's account, attributed to F.E. himself (which
makes it inherently suspect), is admirably brief.

> The reverent air with which his fellow-undergraduates treated the
> 'Master' sickened him. 'Tell us a parable, Master,' said one of
> them. A virile British expletive was heard, and the door slammed

loudly, with a scholar of Wadham and a future Lord Chancellor on the right side of it.[22]

The climax of the second Earl's more highly coloured version has F.E., nauseated by Wilde's narcissism, asking sarcastically as he left, 'Before I go, Master, could you not tell us something about yourself?' In the revised (1959) edition of his book, however, he admitted that Lord Alfred Douglas had violently disputed this story when first published, adding that he personally did not believe a word of it either![23] The details are indeed unlikely: F.E. probably never walked out on Wilde, possibly never even met him. Yet the story is worth repeating; for there can be no doubt that it accurately reflects what F.E. would have thought of him if he had.

By comparison with all these doubtful legends, the most celebrated incident of F.E.'s whole Oxford career is exceptionally well documented. The occasion was the visit of the Prince of Wales to Oxford in May 1897 to open the new Town Hall. The authorities unwisely called in extra police from London: thus, according to *Isis* (but not *Isis* alone), 'what was intended to be a harmless "rag" was turned into a riot'. The whole episode sounds extraordinarily modern!

> The disagreeable element did not evidence itself until the misjudged interference of the Metropolitan Police, especially those who were mounted, drove the crowd to exasperation. Then there was a general rush, blows being exchanged on all sides; the police on foot decidedly got the worst of the encounter, but those on horseback, by the help of their truncheons, of which they made brutal use, eventually drove the crowd back, only to return again and again to renew the contest, which by this time had attained a serious aspect.[24]

In the middle of all this, F.E. saw his college 'scout' being manhandled and went to his rescue with the intention of arranging bail for him, only to be arrested himself and charged with assaulting a police officer. At this point he had the remarkable presence of mind to call on those looking down on the *melée* from the surrounding houses to witness that he had submitted quietly. He was then taken off to the new municipal building and there locked up for the night. As he was thrust into the new cell he is reported to have stopped, solemnly raised his hand and announced, 'I declare these cells well and truly opened.'[25]

F.E.'s case immediately became a *cause célèbre*. The unprecedented incarceration of a Fellow aroused official Oxford in defence of its historic independence. Outrage at the behaviour of the police was not confined to the student newspapers. The Professor of Comparative Anatomy, who cannot have known F.E., wrote to him:

> Mr Dear Sir,
>   I hope you are not going to submit to the gross injustice done to you. The whole of this police business is a disgrace to England. There are two points about the Oxford affair.
>
> 1st. Ruffians with bludgeons were specially brought to the town from London by servile corrupt magistrates and called upon to deal with the natural results of their wickedness and brutality. There would have been a bit of horseplay in Oxford, but no heads broken, had not these London police-bullies been brought down.
>
> 2nd. The real point we ought to attack is the training and keeping of a metropolitan reserve force of police who are *taught* and *encouraged* to be unscrupulous both in the brutal use of their bludgeons, and in their perjury . . .
>
> I believe the proper course for you is to get a question asked in the House . . .[26]

The Professor wanted the Metropolitan Police Commissioner impeached.

F.E. also received the less violent support of, among others, Professors Anson and Dicey of the Law Faculty, Dicey urging him to retain a good counsel, from London if need be, and offering £5 towards the cost. That was hardly necessary. But the police found that they had taken on not only a young man exceptionally capable of defending himself (how many other great barristers have made their first appearance in court in their own defence?) but also the whole weight of the Oxford Law School. When the case came to court, *Isis* commented ironically on the contrast between the bench and the interested public.

> The Oxford magistrates are doubtless very worthy persons in their private capacity, but they cannot claim to have more than a rudimentary and empiric acquaintance with the law. Directly facing them, however, were Professor Dicey, the Warden of All Souls, and Sir William Markby, each of whom has more law in his little finger than the whole of the local bench put together. I wonder what these *real* lawyers thought of the implicit confidence which the city magistrates showed in the police evidence.[27]

F.E. disputed it brilliantly. When his denial of the charge against him was held to be an allegation of perjury against the accusing officer he denied that too. Since Simon in his memoirs claims to have been present, his account must be assumed to be the most authentic.

'Perjury?' F.E. indignantly exclaimed. 'I do not accuse him of perjury.'

'Yes you do, sir. He swears that you did kick him. You swear that you didn't kick him. What explanation of that is there except that he has committed perjury?'

'On the contrary', said F.E. sweetly, 'that is one of five possible explanations.'

The prosecutor was bound to ask what they were. Smith replied, with immense volubility, throwing out the fingers of his hand and ticking them off as he spoke:

'One is that *he* is committing perjury; the second is that *I* am committing perjury; the third is that *he* is honestly mistaken; the fourth is that *I* am honestly mistaken; and the fifth is that the two assertions though apparently contradictory can none the less be reconciled.'

The applause from undergraduates in the gallery, of whom I was one [if he was there at all Simon was in fact a graduate] could not be suppressed.[28]

In fact, F.E. did allege perjury on the part of *two* policemen, though not the one in court; for the *Oxford Chronicle* printed his statement of the affair, in which he claimed that '"a policeman, whom he had not seen since, leapt upon him with incredible ferocity and struck him on the shoulder with his staff". He accused another of the London police of striking him with his truncheon, and against this man he had issued a summons.'[25] The last was sheer bravado; but the magistrates prudently dismissed the case. F.E. was more of a hero than ever. From his old benefactor Dr Wells of Wadham he received congratulations and condolences

for the absurdly cavalier way in which your counter-charge was dismissed. You seemed to me to prove your case up to the hilt. You certainly have done Oxford men a service by showing how worthless was the evidence on which men were convicted of being drunk and disorderly.[29]

Then at the Union a week later,

the sensation of the evening . . . arrived when the President prevailed upon Mr. F.E. Smith (ex-President, Merton) to speak

fifth. The hon. ex-President, rising with reluctance, was hailed
with such applause as brought men into the House from all parts
of the Union.[27]

Though it had nothing at all to do with the motion in hand, F.E. obliged
with an account of his experience and its lessons which was heard with
rapturous enthusiasm.

Questions were not asked in Parliament, however, and the Metropolitan Commissioner of Police was not impeached. The only significance of the affair concerns F.E. himself; nothing could better
illustrate his capacity to seize an opportunity and turn to his own
advantage an incident that might have jeopardized another man's
career. It was a fortunate chance that made him a test case for the whole
of Oxford, but he took it superbly, relishing the publicity and adding to
his credit in all men's eyes – and also, it seems, in at least one woman's.
For it is said that it was this incident, and particularly his chivalry in
going to his 'scout's' assistance in the first place, that brought F.E.'s
name for the first time to the attention of the 19-year-old daughter of a
Classics don at Corpus Christi, the Rev. Henry Furneaux.

That may be romance, for Margaret Furneaux had probably met
F.E. already at, of all things, a mixed hockey match ('a barbarous
amusement fashionable at the time,' according to their son).[30] Beforehand, she is said to have queried why 'a frowsty old don' should have
been invited. Afterwards she knew. 'Smith arrived in the prime of his
Romany good looks, and Miss Furneaux saw quickly that he was
neither old nor frowsty. On the field he played a game of extraordinary
roughness, by the evening he was in love.'[31]

Margaret was a lively girl of interesting antecedents. The Furneaux
were a genuinely old family who really did come over with the
Conqueror, and had been settled for several centuries in the manor of
Swilly in south Devon. A Captain Tobias Furneaux commanded the
ship which accompanied Captain Cook on his voyage to Australia.
Margaret's father, rather less adventurous, was a distinguished scholar,
the editor of a once standard edition of Tacitus, who should, according
to his grandson, have been Head of his College had he been less
self-effacing. He combined his teaching duties, as was common at the
time, with the living of Heyford, some ten miles north of Oxford. His
wife, Eleanor, was the daughter of the painter Joseph Severn, in whose
arms Keats had died in Rome in 1821, and the twin sister of Arthur
Severn, who had married Ruskin's cousin Joan Agnew and cared for
Ruskin for the last twenty unhappy years of his life. This remarkable
family has been admirably chronicled by Sheila, Countess of Birkenhead,
in her book *Illustrious Friends*.

Margaret, the second daughter (but fourth child) of this marriage, was no conventional beauty, but darkly handsome, striking, high-spirited and strong-minded, a fine horsewoman possessing also in full measure the artistic and musical accomplishments of her Severn inheritance. Before he met her, there is no record that F.E. had ever looked seriously at any girl. No doubt he had enjoyed, or suffered, the occasional brief amorous adventure, but the impression of his under-graduate life is that of a man at his happiest in male society. That preference never really changed – women always played a firmly secondary role in his view of the world; yet there is no doubt that around the age of twenty-five he fell head over heels for Margaret and deter-mined with all the single-mindedness of a commanding character that she should be his wife. The only account of their courtship is their son's; but family tradition is probably the best source in these matters. This maintains that F.E. 'defied all discretion' in pursuit of his quarry. 'Whenever Miss Furneaux appeared at a dance or a party Smith was there too.' Her parents grew alarmed that her suitor was making their daughter 'conspicuous', and doubted whether F.E.'s intentions were truly serious. Her father liked F.E. well enough, but was not sure he was a sound proposition as a son-in-law. 'I know these rising young men,' he complained. 'They never seem to rise.'[31] It would appear that Margaret felt no such qualms but, young though she was, was eager to become engaged within a few weeks of their first meeting. There was no pos-sibility of an early marriage, however. It was a condition of F.E.'s Fellowship that he should remain unmarried and live in college (though rumours of an attachment had reached Merton before he left); while his earnings in the world outside were likely, as he told Bentley, to be 'exiguous' for some time to come.

If his resources were not yet equal to the expense of marriage, however, they could always be stretched to cover the lesser costs of congenial male companionship. In the spring of 1898 F.E. made a memorable journey to the eastern Mediterranean with a new friend, his fellow-reject from Harrow and future Cabinet colleague, Leopold Amery. Amery was a year younger than F.E., a Balliol man who had just been elected (simultaneously with Simon) to a Fellowship at All Souls. He was a brilliant linguist and a great traveller and mountaineer. He so fired F.E. with his talk of a trip he had made the previous year to the Balkans that they determined to make a similar expedition together, to Greece and on to Asia Minor if their money held out. They each raised £100 and in March they set out on what Amery later recalled as 'a joyous wandering'.[32]

It is difficult to be certain how experienced a traveller F.E. was at this age. There is some doubt about the trips to Egypt on which he claimed to have accompanied his father as a boy. It is similarly asserted that he used to spend his long vacations as an undergraduate working his passage to Spain and Scandinavia, and even round Cape Horn *en route* for Vancouver. But there is contemporary confirmation only of the fact that he had visited Sweden before going up to Wadham. His son suggests that he too had been on his own to 'the Levant' in 1897 before teaming up with Amery the following year; but that is not Amery's recollection. It seems likely that F.E. had actually travelled rather less widely than he later imagined, and certainly much less than Amery.

F.E. was a great pretender. He loved to enliven dull reality with fantasy, and on this trip (though the reality might have been thought adequately romantic) the actor in his heredity was given full rein in a series of preposterous impersonations, in which Amery was forced to join. Their first adventure additionally illustrates F.E.'s lifelong inability to manage money. They were in Venice, where in Amery's words, 'F.E. revelled in the canals and buildings but firmly refused to be bored with picture galleries.'[32] While his friend was doing the rounds of the Accademia and the Scuola di San Rocco, F.E. was, as he thought, more profitably employed. Amery emerged to find him congratulating himself on the purchase, for £70, of a massive inlaid-ivory oak four-poster bed with pink brocade hangings and a wardrobe and several chairs to match. Liking the set, he had bought it, with no thought to the fact that he had no house in England to put it into supposing he had ever got it back there, and cheerfully unaware that his bargain had left him a mere £20 with which to continue their journey. Amery had to pose as F.E.'s tutor to persuade the dealer to cancel the sale; after which he took charge of F.E.'s money, permitting him a small daily allowance.

From Venice they crossed to Trieste and then sailed down the Adriatic coast to Corfu. On this voyage they met a girl whose heart F.E. proceeded to win by posing as a wealthy philanthropist who made a practice of rescuing poor boys from the gutter and setting them up as schoolmasters or clergymen after first showing them a little of the world: Amery he presented as one of his most successful protégés. Amery quickly spiked this ploy by telling the mother that F.E. was in fact a mental patient for whom he was responsible; F.E. lost the girl.

In a café in Athens F.E. pretended to be the Lord Mayor of Liverpool (the youngest in England), introducing Amery as the even younger Regius Professor of Greek at Oxford: they had to leave hastily to evade pressing invitations to dinner. Then, travelling by train from Smyrna to Ephesus, they fell into conversation with an English clergyman whom F.E. immediately provoked by making a violent attack on the Church of England from the standpoint of a Roman Catholic. Unable to keep this up for long, however, he recanted and declared himself an agnostic –

but added that if he were to adhere to any faith it would be Buddhism, of which his friend Professor Amery was a famous exponent! Before Amery could get too deeply embroiled in this new imposture, the clergyman mercifully revealed that he had spent fourteen years as a missionary in Japan, so he too was obliged to come clean – having, it must be said, kept up valiantly with F.E.'s testing idea of a practical joke.

At Ephesus the two wanderers explored the ancient sites, then turned inland and penetrated high into the icy mountains of central Turkey – too high for F.E.'s enjoyment, for he had had his coat stolen while bathing and had to go on inadequately dressed in a pyjama jacket of purple flannel, which created some amusement when they got back to civilization. They came down again to Constantinople, and parted at Budapest, where Amery stayed while F.E. left to return to Merton. It had been an experience which neither of them ever forgot – 'a storehouse of happy memories and a bond of understanding'.[32] Amery recalled in particular one night in the Piraeus at Athens, 'a night of magical beauty, a night for young men to muse over all the storied past around them, to confide in each other their dreams and ambitions for the future, and to grow together in friendship'.[32] In fact their paths diverged for the next ten years, as F.E. went to the Bar and Amery to South Africa, and even when they met again in Parliament they were never such close colleagues. Nevertheless a bond had been forged.

It was not long after his return from this adventure that chance, or his lucky star, put in F.E.'s way another extraordinary opportunity to enhance his already brilliant reputation. It so happened that he and Simon, as distinguished ex-Presidents still resident in Oxford, had both been invited to speak at the Union in the traditionally frivolous Eights Week debate on 19 May. But the motion advertised for discussion had to be set aside; for that morning came the news, long expected, of the death of Gladstone. There was irony in the accident that dictated that the Oxford Union's tribute should be paid by one who had so consistently attacked the great man: Simon might more suitably have been promoted to first place in the order, but it is perhaps symbolic of their relationship that he had to follow F.E. Nor was F.E. noted for the gravity of his speeches. But he rose, as always, superbly to the need of the occasion with a perfectly judged brief eulogy which demonstrates that his command of oratory was now (though he was not yet twenty-six) attaining its full maturity.

I rise to move the following motion: 'That in view of Mr. Gladstone's death, this House do now adjourn'.

When I look round, Sir, at this House – at those benches crowded on every side, at the gallery full of our friends and guests – I am conscious of one feeling, and one only, a feeling of profound satisfaction that chance has put it in our power tonight to make a sacrifice – not the small sacrifice of our own, but the great sacrifice of our friends' pleasure – to prove the sincerity of our sorrow for Mr. Gladstone's death.

The circumstances of our assemblage tonight are not wanting in the elements of dramatic contrast. Out of courtesy to our guests, who, by a curious convention, are supposed to be averse from serious discussion; out of concession to a week almost wholly given over to lightness, the subject of our debate tonight was of an altogether trivial character. We came here with jests upon our lips, but they have been frozen before they could find expression by these tidings of death. Certainly I shall utter the feelings of this House, when I say that we must all be acutely conscious of the impropriety, the impossibility, at such a time of such a debate.

Within the walls of this assembly, more than of any other, with the single exception of Westminster, is the rare tribute we shall pay tonight an appropriate one; and in one sense we shall not even yield up our claim to the House of Commons. We cannot forget that if the splendid maturity of his life was theirs – ours, and ours only, was its brilliant dawn, and our claim to mourn over its pathetic end is not less.

Nearly seventy years, Sir, have passed since Mr. Gladstone sat in the chair you fill tonight. He enjoyed, in the discharge of your office, a wealth of contemporary reputation to which I conceive that none of his successors has even approximately attained, and during those seventy years all parties in this House have admitted him with ready assent the most illustrious ornament in the annals of the Society. Other great statesmen, Sir, have sat since Mr. Gladstone in your chair; there have debated within the walls of this Society poets like Swinburne, known wherever the English language is known, men of letters like Ruskin, and a long roll of prelates and judges, the mere recital of whose names would exhaust the patience of this House – yet I think it was said of none of these, as it was said of Gladstone the undergraduate, 'A man is risen in Israel this day.'

In public some of us have exercised, from time to time, our wit and rhetoric against him, but in private, when we would give a high impression of this Society to those unfamiliar with its history, it was the name of Gladstone which rose first to our lips. There are

times, and I think this is one, when we who have busied ourselves
in however inconsiderable a degree in party politics, are glad to
say with Mercutio – 'A plague on both your houses' – when the
desire is strong within us to express sorrow with more than the
perfunctory courtesy of political opponents. We remember that
the last seventy years have been pregnant with changes in our
national life – social changes – political changes – economic
changes. Of these Mr. Gladstone '*pars magna fuit*', and the part he
played was always distinguished, always strenuous, always single-
hearted. When we think that after the stress of these anxious years
the tired body and the busy brain are still, we can think of no better
epitaph for him than the words: 'After life's fitful fever he sleeps
well.'*

We are all proud that so distinguished a personage should have
gone forth from our midst, but we are prouder far of the public
high-mindedness and private conscientiousness, which the wearer
of it never lost. And we are proud, too, not only of the composure
with which Mr. Gladstone met death – for the nature of his
religious convictions made that composure certain – but of the
dignity and fortitude with which he supported the tortures of acute
physical pain. All of us were glad to associate ourselves with the
letter of sympathy which the Vice-Chancellor, the mouthpiece of
this University, wrote to Mr. Gladstone. I am sure that all of us
read the reply with feelings of profound emotion. I remember the
words of it: 'There is no expression of Christian sympathy that I
value more that that of the University of Oxford, the God-fearing
and God-sustaining University of Oxford. I have served her
perhaps mistakenly to the best of my ability. My most earnest
prayers are hers to the uttermost and the last.'

I think there is no-one in this House, whatever his own religious
belief, whatever his view of the efficacy of prayer, who will not be
moved by the thought that the prayers of such a man at such a
moment were given to this University. Sir, I beg leave formally to
move the motion, 'that in view of Mr. Gladstone's death, this
House do now adjourn'.[33]

Simon seconded; the President, C.F. Garbett, a future Archbishop of
York, said a few words; and the House adjourned. This uncharacteristic
but long-remembered tribute was F.E.'s farewell to the Union where he
had served his political apprenticeship. He did not speak there again for

---

* Was it supreme piety, or merely lack of imagination, that led F.E. to apply to
Gladstone the same Shakespearean epitaph that was engraved on his own father's
memorial? The latter, unfortunately: he marked with the same line every death that
punctuated his life.

nearly a decade. When he returned, in 1907, it was as a Member of Parliament.

During these later years at Oxford, F.E. had been preparing himself for the next stage of his progress by reading for the Bar. It was suggested earlier that, having joined Gray's Inn in 1894, he did not hurry to eat his prescribed number of dinners as quickly as he might have done. In fact the record shows that from Michaelmas 1894 to Easter 1896 he kept his terms regularly (that is, he ate three dinners a term in Hall). It was only after he had secured his immediate future by winning the Vinerian and his Merton Fellowship that he relaxed his rate of attendance, knowing that now he had no need to complete the required total of ten terms before 1899.

But he had already given his heart to Gray's Inn. It is said that he chose Gray's Inn rather than the more fashionable Inner or Middle Temple for the same reasons that he had chosen Wadham, for its size and its beauty. 'It was the smallest of the Inns of Court; it was the most intimate and it breathed to F.E. from its beautiful timbered hall the mellow enchantment of Elizabethan England.'[34] Moreover, as Wadham had been among Oxford colleges, Gray's Inn was in 1894 the least regarded of the four Inns. Going to Wadham had in reality been a lucky chance, but his experience there had convinced F.E. of the advantage of belonging to a small and relatively modest community. 'Why do you choose the Inner Temple?' he asked Simon as they travelled to London together. 'I am joining Gray's Inn, and I shall be Treasurer of my Inn before you are Treasurer of yours.'[35] He was, by ten years. Yet such crude ambition as this remark suggests was not the real reason for F.E.'s choice. For one thing, Gray's Inn had a traditional connection with the Northern Circuit, where F.E. intended to begin his practice; more important, F.E. genuinely loved the greater comradeship of a more intimate institution. A deep attachment to the institutions that had moulded him was one of the strongest features of his character; he gave the same lifelong loyalty to Gray's Inn and its members that he gave to Wadham. It was this close sense of personal identification that naturally made him ambitious to be Treasurer. As a member of the Inn, he set out deliberately to raise its standing in the legal world, initially by the reflected glory of his own career, later by urging every able young man he met to join it. He bought pictures for it; he endowed a scholarship; and in 1917 he brought the Prime Minister to dine in Hall and make a major speech on the conduct of the war. In 1922 he entered his 14-year-old son for the Inn, though his inclinations were literary rather than legal, and seven years later held his coming-of-age dinner there. Gray's Inn to F.E. was a part of his extended family. The only slightly surprising thing, in view of his family loyalty, is that he did not follow his own father to the Middle Temple.

In his last year as an academic lawyer at Merton F.E. proved his credentials by writing one specialist article and a short book, both of which were published soon after he left. Of the former, which appeared in the *Law Quarterly Review* in July 1900 under the title 'The Rule in *Hadley* v. *Baxendale*', R.F.V. Heuston has commented, 'No other Lord Chancellor, or indeed Law Lord, is known to have contributed to this scholarly quarterly at such a youthful age.'[36] It dealt with a tricky question of the law of contract, posed in the opening paragraph:

How far . . . can A by informing B of special circumstances connected with a contract between them recover from B, if the latter break it, compensation for damages, the probable occurrence of which without such disclosure B could not have foreseen but with it should not have overlooked?[37]

Twenty years later the *Law Quarterly Review* proudly recalled this article while pointing out that no one had any reason to be surprised at the quality of F.E.'s judgments on the Woolsack.

The book was an elementary introduction to international law, first published in Dent's Temple Primer series in 1900 (price 1s) but regularly reissued in enlarged editions, revised by other editors as its original author became too busy. To the fifth edition, published in 1918, F.E. contributed a new preface luridly stressing the Kaiser's blatant assault on the very concept of international law and calling for legal action to be taken against him. From its steady sales – a sixth edition came out in 1927 – he must eventually have derived a tidy income.

His immediate horizon, however, was the Bar examination in June 1899, which he passed with distinction: he was placed equal first, a fact that Heuston notes with surprise, 'for it was not at that time an examination which Oxford candidates took very seriously'.[38] He ate his last three prescribed dinners at Gray's Inn in the Trinity term; and on 14 June he was formally called to the Bar. At the same time his tenure at Merton expired. After nearly eight extraordinary years in residence in Oxford he left the dreaming spires behind and returned home to Birkenhead – a highly polished man of the world, of great self-confidence, limitless ambition and expensive tastes, but possessing no money – to set about trying to earn his living on the Northern Circuit.

6

Liverpool and the Northern Circuit

It was home to Birkenhead that F.E. initially returned. But though its population was still growing and its shipyards still thriving, the relative decline of Birkenhead from its High Victorian heyday was gathering pace. Though administratively it was still an independent borough, and part of Cheshire not Lancashire, economically and socially it was becoming, since the opening of the railway tunnel in 1885, a suburb of Liverpool. It was to Liverpool that F.E. had to look for his career, both legal and political, and it is only in the context of Liverpool that the mature F.E. can properly be understood.

Liverpool in 1900 was at its zenith, a busy Atlantic seaport and prosperous commercial city, with a population of 147,000. Like most seaports it was a tough mixed society, with large Welsh, Scots and particularly Irish communities disputing primacy with the native northern English. Ethnic differences expressed themselves primarily as religious differences, covering the whole spectrum between Roman Catholics, predominantly Irish, through the loyal upholders of the Established Church, to every variety of Nonconformist. In Liverpool, as in Belfast just over the water, the fundamental rift was between Protestant and Catholic; this old quarrel flared regularly into violent rioting and street battles, fanned by the Orange Lodges in one camp and the Irish Clubs in the other. 'Almost nightly throughout the summer', the Watch Committee reported in 1904, 'the sound of a drum from one side or the other brought out two angry crowds,'[1] adding that such disorders had been chronic for the last several years. But there were also deep divisions within the Protestant side, and not least within the Church of England itself.

The religious divide was reflected in the city's politics – indeed religious questions were in Liverpool the whole substance of political controversy, almost to the exclusion of the issues that agitated the rest of the country. The supreme Protestant party was the Conservative Party, which in 1900 held eight of the city's nine parliamentary seats; the last, the Scotland division, in the Irish quarter, had been held since 1885 by the Irish Nationalist, T.P. O'Connor – who retained this anomalous foothold on the mainland right up to 1929. The Liberals, broadly speaking the Nonconformist party, though they also offered a home to High Anglicans and non-Irish Catholics, provided a strong opposition on the city council and also in the press, where they had the support of the city's leading daily paper, the *Liverpool Daily Post*, but they had not won a parliamentary seat since 1892. The Labour Party had not yet arisen to challenge the Tory hold on the working-class Protestant vote.

The Tories, then, were the popular party in Liverpool. It is of the greatest importance to realize that the Conservatism in which F.E. Smith's political career was rooted and by which it was sustained was a very unusual, populist and democratic brand, quite different from the landed, parson-and-squire image of the party in most of the rest of the country, but comparable only with the Liberal Unionist citadel established by Joseph Chamberlain in Birmingham. The democratic strength of Liverpool Toryism was embodied in the Liverpool Working Men's Conservative Association, a formidable body boasting some 8,000 members, organized in twenty-six separate branches throughout the city and dominated by its powerful boss Archibald Salvidge, its chairman from 1892 to 1927. The official organization of Liverpool Conservatism was the Constitutional Association (whose chairman at this period was Sir Thomas Royden); but the Working Men's Association was affiliated to it and fully represented on its committees and too powerful to be ignored. Doubt has recently been cast on whether the L.W.M.C.A. was quite as democratic a body as it pretended; it has been suggested that it was as much under the control of the local Tory magnate, Lord Derby, and a few rich paymasters, principally brewers, as every other local Tory party at that time; and that Salvidge was not really so powerful as he appeared. In fact, the Association's large, active, subscription-paying membership (branch meetings were held weekly, central committee meetings monthly, and there were frequent debates and other fund-raising functions to supplement the annual one-shilling subscription) did give it exceptional muscle in the counsels of Liverpool Conservatism. It was a force which not even Salvidge was always able to control, and it could be said of both him and Derby that they often found it prudent to follow the Association rather than try to lead it against its inclinations.

The causes for which the Working Men's Association stood were the popular ones of crude Protestantism. The over-riding issue for the past twenty years, somewhat in abeyance now, since the death of Gladstone, the cooling of Liberal enthusiasm and the secure existence of a Tory Government, but ever capable of arousing the fiercest passions if the threat was renewed, was resistance to Irish Home Rule. This was in

Liverpool, even more than in Belfast itself, essentially a religious question, an expression of violent anti-Catholicism and the defence of the Established Church, rather than, as it appeared in most of the rest of the country, an imperial question concerning the integrity of the kingdom. The Orange Lodges were among the most active component bodies of Liverpool Conservatism: Liverpool was in this respect simply a colony of Belfast. This needs to be remembered by those who criticize F.E.'s espousal of the cause of Ulster in 1912–14 as mere opportunism. Politically speaking, Ulster was in his blood at least as much as it was in Bonar Law's or Carson's. The defence of the Union had been his father's cause at the time of his death, and it was a standard which F.E. could not easily have avoided picking up.

But the defence of the Established Church against Catholicism was not limited to resisting the direct onslaught of the Irish; it also involved continual watchfulness against more insidious Roman influence within the Church. Catholicism was on the march, at the rate of nearly a thousand conversions nationally a month; the converts included several disturbingly prominent figures, even one of the sons of the Primate, Archbishop Benson. A Catholic cathedral was being built within a mile of Westminster Abbey. In 1894 there had been revealed a plan for Anglican-Catholic reunion. Within the Church, the 'High' party seemed everywhere to be gaining ground on the 'Low'. Ritualism, sacramentalism, incense and confession were all on the increase. Liverpool Toryism was in the van of the reaction. The Orange Lodges were reinforced in this agitation by the Laymen's League, whose leaders George Wise and Austin Taylor became powerful figures in the L.W.M.C.A., with whom Salvidge had to reckon seriously, as violent demonstrations were organized outside churches alleged to practise Romanish tendencies. The movement centred on the demand for a Church Discipline Bill which could outlaw such practices, or rather 'discipline' those clergy deemed guilty of practising them, since they were already illegal. Support for this Bill became the shibboleth of Liverpool Toryism; no candidate suspected of softness on this question could expect the backing of the Association. In 1900 no less a figure than Walter Long, then President of the Board of Agriculture in Salisbury's Cabinet, was forced to withdraw from the West Derby seat under threat from Salvidge's Protestant zealots.

The cause of the Established Church, however, was not at an emotional level primarily doctrinal at all, but for most of its members more simply and fundamentally patriotic. The Church of England came into being as a doctrinal compromise to cover the nakedness of Henry VIII's assertion of national independence. Through the succeeding reigns and the power struggles of the seventeenth century, the supremacy of the

Church was placed at the very heart of the evolving Constitution. In 1900, despite the gradual removal of many of the disabilities previously imposed on Catholics and Dissenters, the primacy and integrity of the Church could still be seen – as Protestantism is to this day in Northern Ireland – as the symbol and guarantee of the continuity, independence and superiority of the British nation. Thus support for the Church could not be separated from loyalty to the Crown – the Protestant succession was of central importance and the purity of the Coronation Oath was continually under scrutiny – and even extended to the House of Lords (though not necessarily to the Bishops, always suspected of sacerdotalism and priestly ambition). Liverpool Toryism was authentically Disraelian in its peculiar combination of veneration for the most ancient English institutions – Crown, Church and Parliament, to which was now added the Empire – with faith in the democratic wisdom and sovereignty of the English people.

If the defence of Protestantism against the recrudescence of Rome was the overriding priority, however, the Tory Church had battles to fight also on its other flank, against the Nonconformists: first over education, where Balfour's 1902 Bill granting State support for the first time to Church of England schools ran into outraged Liberal opposition, especially in Wales; and second over the rising demand by the chapels for the disestablishment of the 'alien' English Church in Wales. Both these issues aroused strong reactions along the political/sectarian divide in nearby Liverpool.

The real running battle with Nonconformity in Liverpool, however, was not a strictly religious controversy at all, but concerned the emotive question of drink. The demarcation between the overwhelmingly Tory brewers and the Liberal/Nonconformist temperance reformers was an established feature of late Victorian politics, dating from the Liberal Licensing Act of 1871: Gladstone ascribed his Government's defeat in 1874 to the influence of the drink interest, saying that he had been 'borne down in a torrent of gin and beer', and ever since it had been said that every public house was a Conservative committee room and every publican a Conservative agent. The demarcation was nationwide, but feelings ran highest in seaports like Liverpool, where hard drinking was a way of life. Liberal identification with the temperance lobby, increasingly inclined to actual teetotalism, was easily represented as the dogmatic imposition of the tenets of a canting clique of Nonconformist bigots, interfering with the rightful pleasures of freeborn Englishmen (to say nothing of Irish and Scots); here was a further fruitful source of working-class support for Liverpool Toryism. The annual Licensing Sessions became a regular battle ground between the parties, as the city magistrates, under pressure from not only the temperance lobby but also the police, and supported by the Liberals, continually tried to reduce the number of public houses, while the brewers and licensed victuallers, backed by the Tories, fought vigorously for each licence. This was a battle into which F.E., like his father, was inevitably quickly drawn, and one in which political conviction and professional opportunity were powerfully reinforced by his own strong partiality for alcohol in all its forms.

Finally, over and above these sectarian controversies, Liverpool's popular Toryism was also characterized by a robust and raucous patriotism, verging on music hall jingoism, which manifested itself in aggressive pride in the Empire and the armed forces in general and vigorous support for the Boer War in particular, accompanied by a thorough contempt for Liberal pacifists, little Englanders, cosmopolitans, foreigners of all sorts and Jews.

All this comprised the political heritage to which F.E. had been brought up by a father who was, in his brief day, as vociferous an opponent of Home Rule and temperance reform as any on Merseyside, and as a lapsed Methodist had had no difficulty in according primacy to the Established Church as the pillar of the English State, even though he was indifferent to the doctrinal disputes that so excited the zealots. His son took his basic political attitudes unaltered from him, and though Oxford refined and deepened them, it did no more: his undergraduate speeches, at the Union and elsewhere, never strayed far from these fundamental themes – Ireland and drink, the House of Lords, drink and Ireland. F.E. is often seen as the epitome of the Oxford politician, yet his politics were always rooted in Merseyside. Oxford gave his style its gloss, but its underlying crudity, aggression and energy owed much more to Liverpool and Birkenhead. In returning, then, to make his political and legal career, F.E. was in the fullest sense returning home.

His prime ambition was to get into Parliament as quickly as possible, but he had first to build himself a secure foundation at the Bar. As a Tory in Liverpool it was conveniently easy to run the two careers together. The links between the Liverpool Bar and the Constitutional Association were very close: there was a good deal of frankly partisan work to be had, and most of the leading barristers had their eye on a seat in Parliament as a natural step in their careers. The ladder was there. The trouble was the competition to scale it. The Northern Circuit at the turn of the century boasted an unusually distinguished fraternity of advocates.* If F.E. imagined when he finally left Oxford that he was leaving the island of all excellence to plunge back, even temporarily, into a sea of provincial mediocrity, he was quite wrong – pleasantly so

---

* The Northern Circuit at this period comprised Liverpool, Manchester, Carlisle, Appleby and Lancaster.

from the point of view of intellectual companionship, less pleasantly if rivals of the calibre of Alfred Tobin, Arthur Greer, Lancelot Sanderson, Rigby Swift and Walter Greaves-Lord (to name only some of the most notable) were to stand in the way of his building up a lucrative practice as rapidly as he hoped, or block his road to Westminster. Of those mentioned Tobin, Greer and Sanderson were all considerably older than F.E. and were already established as the leading local juniors, though none had yet taken silk. Tobin and Sanderson entered Parliament in 1910, and all three ended their careers as judges. Swift was younger than F.E. but had already by 1899 been in practice for four years; he too went into Parliament in 1910 and was made a judge – by F.E. – in 1920. Greaves-Lord was six years younger than F.E. but started in practice only a year later, in 1900, destined also for Westminster and the bench. These were only the most prominent of those whom F.E. set himself in 1899 to match. There were many more established and aspiring practitioners on the circuit. Yet within a very few years F.E. outstripped them all, his elders and his juniors equally, politically as well as legally: he earned more money than any of them, and he got into Parliament first.

Like anyone else, however, he had to begin at the bottom, serving a brief apprenticeship with an established barrister. The man he selected for the privilege of thus initiating him was another with a political career ahead of him: Leslie Scott, who became M.P. for the Exchange Division in 1910, was Solicitor-General for the last eight months of the Lloyd George Coalition in 1922, but lost office with the fall of that Government and never regained it. Scott was not quite thirty in that summer of 1899, less than three years older that F.E., but he had been in practice since 1894. He had happened to dine at Merton the previous year, where F.E. had taken the opportunity to congratulate him on some articles on maritime law in the *Law Quarterly Review* and asked to join his chambers. Scott is said to have been somewhat apprehensive of taking under his wing so alarming a protégé, but he could not easily refuse. So the name of F.E. Smith was first inscribed on a brass plate below that of Leslie Scott in Cook Street in the commercial heart of Liverpool.

Scott was remembered by another of his pupils, Harold Jager, as

a profoundly industrious and very sound lawyer. He took himself very seriously and the law. He used to worry his cases as a terrier does a rat. He dictated reams of opinions and pleadings to Conway, his clerk; but he had no manner of use for 'devils' or pupils, for he did every jot and tittle of work himself.[2]

Just the man for F.E., who would never have had the patience to work for anyone else and did not intend to wait long before setting up on his own. It was through Scott's chambers, however, that he got his first brief, which must be a momentous occasion for any barrister, though the case is bound to be a trivial one. F.E.'s, in August 1899, was a run-of-the-mill licensing application by one Mary McKenny of Wigan, which fell to him in Scott's absence in Switzerland; his fee was six guineas. His son recounts that F.E., already impatient of hanging around in Cook Street, had just arrived in Cornwall for a holiday when a telegram summoned him back to Wigan. It is difficult to believe that even F.E. could have despaired quite so quickly – it was only a very few weeks since he had been called to the Bar – especially when Scott's absence clearly gave him more chance of an opening than he could normally expect. Be that as it may, he got the brief, soon followed by two or three more of the same sort. This was not at all a bad start. In September he was visited by his old Wadham friend Francis Hirst, and they compared notes.

> We discussed our present fortunes and future ambitions. Simon, who was called last January, has not made much at the Bar. F.E. and I were called on the last day in June. He at the local Bar has made £25 and I [in London] £10. We all three want to get into the House of Commons within a few years.[3]

Between August and December 1899, F.E. earned a total of 48 guineas – which, to put it in perspective, was already the equivalent of a very respectable lower-middle-class salary. He did not live like a clerk, though. Rather than stay cheaply with their mother and sisters in Lorne road, F.E. and his youngest brother Harold – now at twenty-three a partner in Smith & Sons – moved away to rent the first floor of a handsome seventeenth-century farmhouse in the village of Bidston, a little outside Birkenhead. It was the architecture of Oxford that F.E. most missed. The mullioned windows and dark wooden panelling of Bidston Hall probably offered the nearest approximation to the style of an Oxford college to be found in the area. From here he would walk in every morning, 'with long loping stride', the two or three miles to the Woodside ferry, 'pausing at some tobacconist's shop to buy the longest cigar he could find'. Nor were cigars his only extravagance.

> His road took him through the somewhat depressing district of north Birkenhead, but there were odd furniture and curiosity shops which hailed his coming with eagerness, for he seldom

passed without acquiring a bit of fine old glass or some other curio for his collection. On the ferry steamer he would continue his walk round and round the deck, inhaling the fine fresh breeze and early morning beauties of the Mersey.[4]

No more at this time than at any other time in his life is there any impression that F.E. ever thought of economizing on his pleasures, though he can still have had very little money. In October 1899, only a few months after his return to Birkenhead, his benevolent uncle E.P. Smith suddenly died, aged forty-eight – the third brother to die absurdly young. How this blow affected F.E. financially it is impossible to say, but it is unlikely that he was left very much, if anything: E.P. had a widow and five children of his own to make provision for, and if his care for his brother's family continued after his death, it must surely have been confined to Elizabeth. E.P. had invested generously in F.E.'s future during his lifetime, but it is too much to expect that he could continue that help on any significant scale after his death. F.E. thus lost a valuable patron before he was quite ready to stand on his own.

Nevertheless he was still courting Margaret Furneaux, and going back to Oxford as often as he could to see her. He was by now getting along excellently with his prospective father-in-law, whom he genuinely admired as the best type of old-fashioned scholar-clergyman while, one suspects, gently flattering his learning. (He described him, many years later, to Frank Pakenham as 'a Tacitean scholar so formidable that Tacitus himself would have hesitated to engage him in controversy on level terms'.)[5] For Margaret, F.E. threw parties at Merton, and to-gether they would go for picnics up the Cherwell, Margaret com-plaining that 'somehow it always works out that I paddle the canoe while he lies back on the cushions making wonderful plans for the future'.[6] Her parents' last doubts about his intentions were dispelled, according to their son, by the touching sight of F.E. trying, 'with incredible clumsiness', to help Margaret hang some pictures.[7] This willing incompetence seemed to them better proof of true love than all his more calculated protestations. The engagement was announced in September.

Marriage, however, was out of the question until F.E. was earning a steady income. While waiting in Scott's chambers for the briefs to come in, he is said to have passed his time in writing – possibly preparing his anthology of Toryism which appeared in 1903, unless it was in these months that he wrote his little book on international law. Seeking an easier way to make some money in his idle hours, he also took on the job of local secretary of Lady Wimborne's Protestant League, one of those fervent bodies dedicated to combating ritualism in the Church of

England. This episode was represented by his son as a humiliating fiasco.

F.E. Smith had met Cornelia Lady Wimborne two years before he began to practise at the Bar. She was aware that he was the son of a Nonconformist, and nourished the pathetic impression that he would be an energetic champion of the Evangelicals. He was invited to express his views at a meeting specially convened of the National Church League. Agreeably remote from any form of doctrinal prejudice, he spoke with a fire and a passion that Savonarola might have envied, and which moved Mr. Joynson-Hicks to propose his appointment as organizing secretary to advance the cause of the League in the north of England. His acceptance of this post was not uninfluenced by the salary of £300 which accompanied it.

Never one for cheese-paring in a good cause, he took offices for the League, and established his headquarters in them. Finding the rooms bare, he embellished them with eight lithographs of the Virgin Mary which he hung thoughtlessly round the walls of the League offices. After putting up a brass plate on the door announcing *Lady Wimborn's League*, spelling her name wrong, he felt that he had done all that a secretary could do.

Lady Wimborne came up to Liverpool to see how the cause was progressing in the north. She looked with disfavour on the misspelling. 'How would you like it, Mr. Smith, if I were to spell your name wrong on a plate?' 'My dear lady', answered F.E., 'there is scarcely any alteration that you could make to it which would not add to its distinction'. Lady Wimborne winced when she saw the Madonnas and discharged Smith the next day.[8]

Told thus, it makes a good story; but it is wholly implausible. The idea that F.E., as an aspiring Liverpool politician, was 'agreeably remote from any form of doctrinal prejudice' is moonshine. Personally indifferent he may have been but he was steeped in the sectarian politics of the city and, even after eight years in Oxford, knew only too well the provocative significance of the Virgin Mary to Low Protestants. It is impossible that he could have so forgotten the nature of the organization he was running. Moreover, his secretaryship cannot have been entirely disastrous, since he was prepared to boast of it to his constituents a few years later as proof of his sound credentials on the religious question. No, the story bears all the marks of one of F.E.'s tall tales, probably first told some years later to Winston Churchill, who was Lady Wimborne's nephew, and subsequently elaborated between their two families. (Randolph Churchill managed to bring it into his life of *his* father, too.) Clearly, F.E. did take Lady Wimborne's shilling for a short period; undoubtedly it was the colour of her money which influenced him; it is very likely that he was not a success. But he also knew that such a connection, however brief, would do him no harm at all with the Working Men's Conservative Association, and this must have been the decisive calculation in his mind.

During 1900, probably in March, F.E. left Leslie Scott and set up chambers of his own, still in Cook Street, taking with him Harold Jager as his first pupil and employing as his clerk a young man (actually a few years older than himself) named J.E. Peteil. Peteil served F.E. devotedly, in Liverpool and in London, until F.E.'s elevation to the Woolsack in 1919, and remained a family friend thereafter; when F.E. died, Peteil followed him to the grave within a year. For his first few months on his own, F.E.'s earnings dipped from their already modest level: five guineas in April; twenty guineas in May; fifteen guineas in June. But in September and October, they rocketed: 135 guineas and 97 guineas. These were the months of the annual Licensing Sessions; F.E. had wasted no time in cornering a share of this lucrative business.

It is by solicitors, and not directly by their clients, that barristers are retained. Thus the most important thing for a young barrister is to cultivate good relations with the right solicitors. In this respect, F.E.'s political connections stood him in good stead. His early breakthrough in the Licensing Sessions was facilitated by the firm of Edwin Berry, through which most of the local licensing work was channelled. F.E. was recommended to Berry by the racehorse-owning M.P. for Widnes, W.H. Walker (later Lord Wavertree), whom he had presumably impressed at some political meeting; and Berry himself was a local Tory of some influence in the L.W.M.C.A., to whom F.E. was later to be indebted politically as well as legally. It was with the help of these two that F.E. made his first real money, and gained his first foothold in the competitive world of the Liverpool Bar.

The work that gained him his foothold is so far removed from the more sensational nature of his more famous cases that it is worth describing one or two of the hearings at the Licensing Sessions that September. The magistrates were making their annual attempt to reduce the number of public houses in the city. They had indeed good ground for arguing that there were more than was either healthy or necessary: in one district it was admitted that there were 129 within a quarter-mile radius.[9] But their case was usually that where demolition had reduced the population of an area, the number of pubs should be similarly reduced; the brewers and licensed victuallers for their part insisted that there must be some specific ground for each closure, and briefed counsel to plead for the livelihood of every threatened licensee. F.E., in his first full year at the Bar, was one of the team, which also included Alfred Tobin, Collingwood Hope and Rigby Swift, recruited for this purpose by the Liverpool Licensed Victuallers' Association.

His business was normally to defend his client against an alleged offence for which the police hoped to have his, or very often her, licence withdrawn. For instance,

> Annie Coates was objected to in regard to her application for renewal of licence for 6 Upper Surrey-street on the ground that it was used as a lodging house for emigrants. Mr. F.E. Smith represented the applicant and, along with the applicant, gave an undertaking that the house should not be used for this purpose in the future. Applicant said that she had lodged emigrants only five times.
>   The renewal was granted.[10]

In another case the ground for closure was that Thomas Chilton had been serving short measures. F.E. submitted that 'the defect in the measure was caused by an unnoticed dent in it'.[11] In a third, the police objected to Ellen White on the ground that her premises were regularly used as a resort for 'loose women'.

> Mr. Smith, remarking upon the police evidence that in the vast majority of cases the women referred to were accompanied by men, said it would be imposing upon a landlady a responsibility and a burden which was too great if she was to detect women of the objectionable class so long as they were respectably dressed and conducted. She would be running too great a risk if she were to ask them insulting questions. He was prepared, however, on behalf of the applicant, that if the licence were renewed, he would give an undertaking that for the future no women should be served.[12]

No immediate decision was given on this discriminatory proposal.

The assumption that it was women who lowered the tone of a decent pub appears again when F.E. crossed the Mersey to plead at the Birkenhead Sessions for thirteen beerhouses which were threatened with closure on the ground that the licensees had taken other jobs and left the pubs to their wives. F.E. argued that it was not in the best interest either of the pub or of the neighbourhood that 'a man who could do other work should be tied to loafing about his own bar'. But the magistrates insisted that the publican must not leave the premises. 'The physical as well as the moral presence of a man was required.'[13]

These few weeks' work raised F.E.'s earnings in his first full year of practice to £529 2s, a sum equalled by Rigby Swift, for instance, only in his *fourth* year; Swift, starting in 1895, had made only 52 guineas in his first year, and 124 guineas in his second.[14] From this promising beginning F.E. never looked back: his earnings from now on increased by about £1,000 each year. The solicitor who had most to do with this phenomenal success was George Harley, of the firm of Simpson, North & Harley. He it was who directed into F.E.'s chambers, among other business, most of the multifarious litigation, first, of the shipowner and M.P. for West Toxteth, Robert Houston, and later, of the soap manufacturer, W.H. Lever (the future Lord Leverhulme). Though he had one other particularly lucrative case, and licensing work continued to provide him with a steady income, it was to a considerable extent by representing the interests of these two acquisitive and compulsively litigious local capitalists that F.E. made his fortune at the Liverpool Bar. Exactly how and when he first met Harley is not clear, for Harley took no part in politics; but F.E. never forgot the debt he owed him. When Harley was dying in 1915, F.E. (then Attorney-General) found time to write regularly to him, once acknowledging: 'No-one contributed so much as you to my legal career or was quite so faithful a friend.'[15]

Through Harley, F.E. also made a friend of Houston, though he was to prove in the end not quite so faithful. Houston – known in Liverpool as 'the Robber Baron' – was the first of a line of adventurous rogues whom the reckless side of F.E.'s nature could never resist: most notably, Horatio Bottomley and Maundy Gregory in later years. The founder of his own line of steamships, trading at first mainly with South America but later forcing his way by questionable means into the South African market against the concerted opposition of the established interests there, Houston enjoyed a reputation as an unscrupulous pirate, although he sat unmoved for more than thirty years as Unionist M.P. for West Toxteth. As a colleague in the House from 1906, F.E. was soon a regular guest on Houston's palatial 1,600-ton yacht *Liberty*, and the friendship flourished into the 1920s. Then, however, F.E. committed an expensive *faux pas*. There are several versions of the story, but it is certain that Houston had intended to leave F.E., in recognition of his past services, a substantial fortune. The expectations of 'a well-known Cabinet Minister' were actually reported in *The Times* on Houston's death in 1926,[16] and F.E. had, needless to say, spent much of the money in advance. Unfortunately, he had somehow deeply offended either Houston himself or his newly married, fortune-hunting second wife. Whether, as his son asserts, he tactlessly declined to hear the story of Lady Houston's life,[17] or whether – the better story – he cast doubt on the colour of Sir Robert's beard; whether he simply suggested that its colour owed more to Stephens's Blue-Black Ink than to nature,[18] or more wittily dubbed him, referring simultaneously to his politics, 'the original Dye-Hard';[19] the result was that he lost the money. Houston's millions were divided in the proportion four to one between his widow (who promptly underwent a mystical conversion and devoted her wealth to fighting the Communist Anti-Christ) and his secretary.[20] F.E. got nothing.

He did very well professionally, however, out of Houston's legal battles twenty-five years earlier. During 1901, he moved beyond licensing to build a reputation in the still richer fields of commercial and maritime law. He was soon able to remove his practice and growing entourage of pupils to larger and more impressive chambers at 25 Lord Street. To Jager, Edward Wooll and Arthur Strong were now added William Dudley Ward, N.B. Goldie (both future M.P.s) and Guy Rutledge, whom F.E. as Lord Chancellor was later to appoint Chief Justice of Burma. Unlike Scott, F.E. knew how to use his 'devils' and get the best out of them.

> Whatever we did in the way of making notes on cases, or settling pleadings, was always most gracefully accepted. F.E. rarely corrected a pleading or even an opinion, if he thought it would just pass muster. And, even if we were wrong, which doubtless was often the case, he never allowed such a trifle to worry him, or anyone else. This great confidence reposed in us, his 'devils' and pupils, confirmed us in our loyalty and our determination to do our utmost and not to let him down. F.E. himself was the most loyal soul alive; he never shirked responsibility for mistakes, and invariably commended us to his clients on every possible occasion. I think he established the general opinion among his clients that he, F.E., could not be wrong, and indeed he very seldom was.[21]

Jager supports the view that F.E.'s immediate success, almost as soon as he went to the Bar, was due to his quiet three years of study at Merton, when he had had the leisure to read more deeply and widely than most barristers, plunging straight into practice, are able to do. He once told Jager that 'he had read all that was necessary and that he did not intend to read any more, except possibly for amusement'.[22] This astonishing claim was probably more nearly true than might be imagined. What F.E. read he retained; more important, he had the power of breaking down what he read, getting at the heart of it, and incorporating that knowledge permanently into his mental armoury. This formidable basis of book-learning, forgotten at their peril by those who took F.E. to be merely a clever word-spinner, gave him an unrivalled grasp of the broad principles as well as the narrow instances of the law, and it was only from this solid foundation that his powers of argument could so confidently take wing.

He was rarely seen to consult an authority, or even study a brief if he could help it. Harley, who instructed him in most of his biggest cases at this time, knew him well enough not to bother to provide him with a proper brief at all; a few statements and letters would be enough. Jager tells of one quite trivial case arising out of a collision in Lime Street. F.E. asked Jager to look at the brief for him, before a consultation at noon.

Accordingly, I arrived at chambers bright and early, and did the best I could to make a note on the facts and such law as seemed to be involved. Twelve o'clock came but no F.E. At ten minutes past the hour, the solicitor and his client arrived and were ushered in by Peteil, and at 12.20, in came F.E., exceedingly well-groomed and in excellent form, as he always was. Obviously there was no time to glance at the brief or my note, so he sat down, at the same time introducing me to the solicitor as 'my friend who has given me the greatest assistance in this case'. Then he got to work, chatting pleasantly all the time. 'Mr So-and-so', to the solicitor, 'Will you tell me what are your impressions on this case?' Mr So-and-so, nothing loth, doubtless glad of the opportunity of airing his legal acumen, obliged at some length. Then F.E. turned to the lay client and asked him what his views were. Thus, in a few minutes, with great tact and skill, F.E. had elicited all he wanted to know; whereupon, for fully twenty minutes, he gave them a masterly exposition of the law of negligence, applying this principle and that to the facts, all in his most fluent and eloquent manner, interspersing delicate comments on Mr So-and-so's erudition. He then shook hands with his clients, who beamed with satisfaction, ushered them out and returned to have a good laugh and pat himself on the back, before going out to lunch.[23]

Lunch would have been long and lavish, the best of everything, at the Adelphi Hotel or the Palatine Club. 'In those days', Jager continues, 'I scarcely ever saw him when he was not in exuberant spirits.'[24] F.E. had the rare gift of spreading his own enjoyment of life to those around him; he involved his pupils so fully in the adventure of his own career that they became devoted to him and ready to do anything for him, sharing in the reflected glory of his unconcealed ambition. 'The world was completely his oyster. He used to chuckle with glee at the consummate ease and perfect assurance that he could do whatever he pleased . . . so boundless was his confidence in his own ability.'[25] Jager's recollections are all of the sheer fun of working with F.E., clearly the high point of his life. He knew that he would never live so intensely again. How many other young barristers could say with him that 'Life in chambers was a continual delight'?[26]

By the spring of 1901, F.E.'s position was secure enough to marry on. He and Margaret had been engaged for more than eighteen months before they were able to tie the knot. One reason for the delay may well have been her father's death, in January 1900, but money was surely the decisive one. F.E. later claimed that the £60 which he was paid for *International Law*, plus a similar sum for an earlier potted history of Newfoundland, 'formed a considerable element in the decision which both my wife and I took as to when we were married'.[27] This is hard to believe. Leaving aside the private income which Margaret brought with her, which cannot have been negligible, it is perfectly clear that they were married just as soon as F.E. had laid the foundation of a practice capable of supporting her in the style to which she was accustomed and which he demanded. They were married, that is, as soon as F.E. could afford to buy a large and fashionable house on the edge of Birkenhead Park – 2 Cavendish Road – for them to return to after their honeymoon. He did not buy that with the proceeds of two shilling potboilers, but on the sure auguries of his rapid success.

The wedding was at Oxford, at St Giles's Church on 9 April. It was a major social occasion which had the 'lady correspondent' of the *Oxford Times* twittering with excitement – especially since she had a most unladylike struggle to get in. 'Fashionable weddings', she complained, 'ought to take place in the Cathedral, for a parish church, especially one the size of St. Giles' is quite inadequate.' The couple were married by the Dean of Durham (presumably a friend of the Furneaux), with a second minister in attendance. Margaret was given away by her elder brother Arthur, with her sisters Agnes and Joan, F.E.'s sisters Clara and Louie and two other friends as bridesmaids. The best man is not recorded, but it was probably Harold Smith; Sidney does not appear to have attended. The guest list, which was reported in full (complete with all the wedding presents), included the Vice-Chancellor of the University, the Warden of Merton and Professor Dicey; Simon, Anstie, Amery and E.G. Hemmerde from among F.E.'s Oxford contemporaries (but neither Hirst nor Fry); Leslie Scott, Harold Jager and William Salvidge from Liverpool. Several titles testified to the social heights F.E. had successfully scaled during his Oxford years; but there were also present the Galloways, father and son, masters of one of F.E.'s earliest schools in Birkenhead. Since it was in offering a wedding present on behalf of the school to the younger Mr Galloway, fifteen years before, that F.E. is supposed to have made his first public speech, there is a pleasing reciprocity in their attending his wedding; but they must have been amazed by the company they found themselves among.

The 'lady correspondent' enthused predictably over Margaret's dress, while her colleague on the fashion page filled another column and a half with further description of the bride's and bridesmaids' gowns than which, she was certain, nothing could be of more interest to her readers that week. Neither remarked upon the bridegroom's pink shirt. The list of wedding presents suggests another oversight on F.E.'s part: while the bride is said to have given her husband the works of Tennyson and Rudyard Kipling (had he revised his estimate of Kipling since Wadham?), the space for his gift to her is a blank.[28] Was it a secret? Or had he forgotten?

After the reception, held in a large marquee 'sufficiently commodious to seat 300 persons' in the garden of the Furneaux house in Banbury Road, F.E. and Margaret left in a heavy rainstorm for a short honeymoon in London and Brighton. Work was not entirely left behind. It was while they were in Brighton that they met Rufus Isaacs (later Lord Reading) who was just then challenging Carson as the most sought-after silk at the Bar. F.E. already had him marked down as a rival. He introduced Isaacs to Margaret with the whispered comment, 'I may say that I consider this man quite as able as I am myself.'[29]

They returned to Birkenhead and settled into their new home in Cavendish Road. It was from the start an exceptionally successful marriage. Margaret was a vivid personality in her own right, not at all eclipsed by her dominating husband, yet at the same time possessed of a gentleness which enabled her to ride the frequent storms of his ebullience and tolerate his excesses. Their son is the best witness to their perfect compatibility, and to the importance of her contribution to his career.

It is impossible to overestimate the influence exerted by Margaret over her husband . . . It is necessary to emphasize the fact that without her he would have been incomplete. Her character was a complement to his. She loved things of which he knew little, such as music and pictures, while her gaiety and powers of droll narration were the equal of his. But he soon became aware that her gaiety concealed a strong character. She exercised her influence with a sparing hand. She seldom stood firm in thwarting him, but when she asserted herself the decision was usually binding.

He was, from first to last, dependent on her, and although it was his nature to sulk after a rebuke, and to deny its validity, he was usually aware of its justice. Throughout the heavy strain which his combined legal and parliamentary work imposed on him, the momentous crises and anxieties of his life, she supported, cheered and encouraged him, and it is no exaggeration to say that her charm and her influence over him contributed almost as much to his success as his own natural advantages.[30]

F.E.'s inability to share in his wife's artistic pleasures was quite genuine, though he characteristically exaggerated his indifference into philistine hostility. 'Secretly', his son reckons, 'he admired this gift in which he himself was so curiously wanting, the power over strange and unintelligible harmonies, but he refused to admit it.'[31] He used to boast that he would pay good money rather than sit through the finest concert. And he would tell with great delight how Margaret had once gone to sing Schumann to the inmates of a local lunatic asylum, and looked up in the middle of a song to see them all holding their hands tightly to their ears. 'Trying to qualify for their release,' he gleefully explained.[32]

There were other pleasures which they could share, most notably riding. Immediately on their marriage F.E. bought his first two horses, and they used to hunt regularly with the Wirral Harriers and the Cheshire Hounds. As his practice increased, so did his stable. But very soon Margaret's exercise was restricted to a gentle drive in the park: for early in 1902 she gave birth to their first child, christened Eleanor after her own mother. Eleanor later asserted in her romantic memoirs that she was born dead. 'Two doctors . . . announced my death before they had the honour of announcing my birth.'[33] Her brother doubts her story that she had actually been put on the ash-heap, but concedes that her life was touch and go. 'Brandy and vigorous smacking were undoubtedly necessary to produce respiration.'[33] Margaret did not have a second child for five years.

Soon after Eleanor's birth F.E. and Margaret moved out of Birkenhead to the smart little village of Thornton Hough (pronounced 'huff') in the middle of the Wirral, where F.E. bought 'The Grove', a rather gaunt but comfortable three-storeyed house with some land of its own stretching down to a cluster of little lakes, and stables for eighteen horses. As a country seat it is quite modest; but as the house of a thirty-year-old barrister in practice for only three years it is astonishing.

Thornton Hough, moreover, was the place to live; in and around it there was developing an important little community of F.E.'s clients, patrons and colleagues. Lever lived there, at Thornton Manor, and George Harley in nearby Upton. Archibald Salvidge, too, lived at the top of the Wirral, at Hoylake. All were within comfortable riding distance. Lever's habits were a bit spartan for F.E.'s taste, but he was a frequent guest of Harley and, a little later on, of Salvidge, riding over for Sunday lunch, as both men's sons recall. Stanley Salvidge remembers having to hold the head of F.E.'s horse, left standing, huge and terrifying, on a narrow garden path;[34] while Sir Thomas Harley retains a vivid mental picture of F.E. at lunch, leaning back nonchalantly, stretching his long legs under the table as he lit a cigar, and breaking, with a sickening crack, the valuable chair he was sitting on; but talking on regardless, while Harley said nothing.[35]

Thornton Hough was the centre of F.E.'s life for the next few years, up to 1906. He lived well and entertained in style, sometimes Salvidge or Harley, or others politically or professionally important to him; sometimes just the little coterie from his chambers.

> He would often say to Rutledge or Wooll: 'I want you to come out to "The Grove" with me tonight; we must go carefully into that Such-and-such case'. They would go out together; a groom and three horses would meet them at Spital station. Arriving at Thornton Hough they would potter about the garden; F.E. and Wooll would practise jumps in the field. I was often one of the party. We would then dine sumptuously, and the rest of the evening would be spent in light and airy persiflage, in chaff, in amusing dissections of various members of the circuit, and in general relaxation. Next morning we would return to chambers, without the important Such-and-such case having once been mentioned.[36]

Yet the important cases did get considered, Jager never knew how. By the end of 1901 F.E.'s earnings were averaging £100 a month: five months later, double that again. '£55 a week', he wrote to Margaret from London, 'keeps even us going.'[37] He had established his professional reputation in Liverpool with extraordinary rapidity; but he had so far had no case that attracted wide public interest. That November, however, he had his first opportunity to show his paces in London, in a case which arose out of Liverpool's religious troubles. ('In those days', R.F.V. Heuston explains, 'the Liverpool solicitors did not employ London agents but went up themselves to the capital bringing with them the barristers whom they had briefed at the local bar. Therefore Liverpool barristers had an exceptional opportunity of appearing in court in London and so becoming known not only to the Bench and Bar but also to the solicitors of the metropolis. This was an opportunity of which F.E. took full advantage.')[38] His client was the militant Protestant leader, George Wise, who had been bound over by the local magistrate to keep the peace after one of his deliberately provocative anti-Catholic demonstrations in May had ended in a riot. Wise appealed against the magistrate's order, and his appeal was heard in the King's Bench Division of the High Court before the Lord Chief Justice (Lord Alverstone), Mr Justice Darling and Mr Justice Channell.

F.E. did not specifically defend his client's conduct on the evening in question, though it was, of course, no accident that found him on Wise's side of the case. But he was able to make out a good legal defence, basing himself on the precedent of *Beatty* v. *Gillbanks* [1882] in which the principle that a man cannot be held responsible for causing, by his lawful action, the unlawful actions of others had been upheld in favour of a Salvation Army leader in Weston-super-Mare, whose marches had been obstructed by a rival group known as the Skeleton Army. F.E. argued similarly that Wise himself had committed no offence.

> The appellant had not personally been guilty of a breach of the peace, and conduct inducing to a breach on the part of other people was not enough . . . It was admitted that the appellant had used insulting language in regard to Roman Catholics, but it was contended on his behalf that this was not a sufficient ground for making the order.

Lord Alverstone congratulated F.E. on the ingenuity of his argument, remarking that 'everything possible to be said had been pressed upon them by the counsel for the appellant'.[39] Nevertheless he and his fellow judges were agreed that Wise *was* responsible, by the violence of his language, for inciting his followers to a breach of the peace, and accordingly dismissed the appeal. The case (*Wise* v. *Dunning*) has subsequently become known to generations of students as embodying an important modification of the law of public meetings.

F.E. did not mind losing the case. When he returned to his chambers he found there a note from the Lord Chief Justice sufficient to salve any disappointment.

> Dear Mr. Smith,
> 	You argued this case admirably. I predict for you a very brilliant future. I trust we shall often see you.
> 	 	 	Faithfully Yours,
> 	 	 	Alverstone[40]

F.E. promptly had the letter framed and hung beneath a portrait of Alverstone in his chambers.

Three months later F.E. was able to turn another unlikely brief to his own advantage. This was indeed a hopeless case, that of an unfortunate clerk with the Bank of Liverpool named Thomas Goudie, who had got drawn into a major fraud ring, far out of his depth. To pay his racing debts, the hitherto blameless Goudie had used his position as a ledger clerk to forge cheques, initially for quite small sums, in the name of one of the bank's largest customers, the soap-maker R.S. Hudson (soon to be taken over by Lever). His secret had been discovered by two other petty criminals named Kelly and Stiles, who blackmailed him, compelling him to make larger and larger bets which, since he was never allowed to win, he had no choice but to continue to finance from the limitless resources of the bank. Finally these two were themselves swallowed up by three bigger fish named Burge, Marks and Mances, who proceeded to wring still larger sums, totalling £160,000, out of the miserable clerk, whose activities were eventually – after three years – uncovered. Goudie, Kelly, Stiles and Burge (who was a former boxer and Marie Lloyd's brother-in-law) were arrested and tried at the Central Criminal Court in February 1902. Mances and Marks were never caught.

This was F.E.'s first appearance at the Old Bailey, and his first trial in the company of barristers of the top flight: Charles Gill, K.C., prosecuted, while Kelly was defended by Rufus Isaacs, Stiles by Marshall Hall, and Burge by Horace Avory – all leading K.C.s. None of these eminent silks could do anything for their clients. Burge was first found guilty, after three days, of forgery and conspiracy, upon which Kelly and Stiles changed their pleas to guilty. Goudie had never attempted to deny his guilt, but had given damaging evidence against the others. The court was 'densely crowded' on Saturday 22 February to hear Mr Justice Bigham pass sentence. F.E. had the opportunity to plead for lenience, and seized it wonderfully. The heart of his speech must be quoted. Notice the art with which, while admitting the facts, F.E. reverses the lighting on them, trying to make the jury see Goudie, not merely as a poor credulous victim, but actually, just for a moment, as an upright and honourable citizen betrayed into foolishness by his very honesty. This is advocacy – making black appear white and white black – at its most brilliantly seductive.

Three years ago Goudie, a young Scotchman who was in the service of the bank, had five years of good employment and good work behind him; he had excellent testimonials. He then most unfortunately contracted the habit of gambling. One would not require to be a very good prophet to predict, when a clerk earning £150 a year contracted that habit, what the sequel would be. The sequel is only too commonly witnessed in this Court. The first cheque he forged was for £100, in the name of Mr. Hudson; and if it had been mercifully ordained that the discovery had then been made, the present case would never have arisen and his previous good character would have been taken as a consideration. Unhappily, the fraud was successful; some time and somehow or other the £100 which he had taken from the bank had to be replaced, and, if not, he would have had to face certain discovery ... It was absolutely necessary for him either to replace the £100 or to meet the consequences of detection. From that period he went on foolishly attempting to make good the shortage resulting from the first cheque. That was Goudie's object throughout the subsequent forgeries. He could, if he had cared, with absolute ease have made his escape. He could have taken advantage of his summer holiday to leave the country with a fortnight's start. His object in the betting transactions he had made was to replace the money in the bank. It was not to enjoy the proceeds of robbery. *In the whole history of crime there is not a case in which a man enjoyed himself so little as the result of his crime as Goudie.* It is not on record that he spent a farthing of the money on personal indulgence; on the contrary, there is the strongest reason for believing he did not do so, as the expenses of his board and lodging only amounted to £1 a week. He never attempted to escape. From the first moment of his detection he gave full information to the police. He never deviated from his statements, which were strongly corroborated by documentary evidence and remained unshaken in cross-examination. He has made what restitution he can. It was also considered necessary by the prosecution to call him as a witness. I plead earnestly to your Lordship to take as lenient a view as you can of Goudie's conduct.[41]

F.E. sat down to the rare tribute in a lawcourt of sustained applause. One senior counsel passed him a note saying, 'You will be the master of us all. No-one I have ever heard has impressed me so much in a hopeless case';[42] while F.E. himself recalled in his *Famous Trials* that another member of the Old Bailey Bar (or was it the same one, differently remembered?) told him that, 'unless the Bar did away with me it was all up with them, for I would get their work'.[43] Mr Justice Bigham, however, was little moved, if at all. Goudie received the same sentence as Burge, ten years; he actually died in prison after serving only six.

Unsuccessful though it was, F.E.'s plea for Goudie was one of the great triumphs of his career. Once again, as at the Oxford Union and as he would do again in the House of Commons, he had contrived to make his début in a new arena a sensation. On none of these occasions was his success due to the inspiration of the moment. At the end of the Goudie case Horace Avory's clerk, having like everyone else present marvelled at the easy eloquence of F.E.'s appeal, returned to the Temple and found that he had carried away with him 'a little black-covered note-book' which he did not recognize as Avory's.

> To obtain some clue as to its ownership I opened it, and to my amazement discovered that it was a verbatim copy of the much-admired speech. The original draft had been carefully and minutely revised, but there it was, in the finished state in which it had been delivered. The youthful Counsel, who pretended to be a dilettante and a trifler, had determined that his first effort before a London judge and jury should be a success, and to that end he had written out, revised and rewritten his maiden forensic speech in the metropolis and had committed every word of it to memory.[44]

The fact that it was actually F.E.'s second appearance in London is beside the point.

In July 1902 at the Liverpool Assizes F.E. undertook, through the good offices of George Harley, his first action for Lever Bros – a quite minor suit involving a claim for £117 in damages from the English-American Shipping Company in respect of some bags of cottonseed which had deteriorated on board ship due, it was alleged, to improper stowing. Success in this case can have owed little to F.E.'s power of advocacy, since it hung entirely on which particular set of expert witnesses the judge chose to believe.[45] Lever, however, must have been satisfied, for F.E. was to get a steady stream of more lucrative work from him in the future.

Meanwhile three more sensational criminal cases came his way, all involving murder and one, mutiny. The first was another product of Liverpool's endemic religious conflict: this time the Protestant agitator John Kensit reaped the violent harvest of his own verbal provocation. On his way from a meeting in Birkenhead back to the Woodside Ferry in September 1902, he was struck over the eye by a piece of iron thrown from an angry Catholic crowd, and subsequently died of septic pneumonia and meningitis. An 18-year-old labourer named John McKeever was arrested and charged with murder. The case turned on two questions: not only whether it could be proved that it was McKeever who had thrown the missile, but also whether Kensit's death was solely the result of his wound. At the end of a four-day trial held in Liverpool in early December, in which F.E. acted as junior to the prosecuting counsel W.S. Pickford, neither point could be established: the evidence of assorted newsboys on the one hand and doctors on the other proved inconclusive. McKeever was acquitted, and was carried shoulder-high through the streets by his cheering supporters, a Catholic hero to set opposite the Protestant martyr Kensit in Liverpool's pantheon of bigots.[46] F.E. kept the rusty iron projectile as a morbid souvenir.

The very next day F.E. was back in court as the defending counsel in another murder trial. He and his pupil Guy Rutledge were asked by Mr Justice Jelf to act, without payment, for two destitute young servant girls, Ethel Rollinson (aged twenty) and Eva Eastwood (aged seventeen), accused of murdering their bedridden alcoholic former employer. At this stage in his progress fees were less necessary to him than publicity; F.E. dropped an important libel case to take up the defence of Miss Rollinson. He evidently enjoyed hopeless cases; for the case against her was strong, and was not helped by her own unrepentant statements as repeated by a third girl, 'The old woman starved me when I was with her. I said I would do it and I have done it.' His approach was to try to riddle the vital evidence of the third servant as a tissue of lies aimed only at saving herself, and to suggest that Rollinson and Eastwood had intended only to rob Miss Marsden, not to kill her – that they had placed pillows on her to keep her quiet or to prevent her seeing them as they sacked the room, and that it was only as a result of her already poor health that she had died. Though they giggled unhelpfully in court, apparently not realizing the seriousness of their position, he tried (as he had with Goudie) to evoke sympathy for them.

> Both of the prisoners were orphans and friendless, and had no-one
> to take an interest in their welfare. They were sent out into the
> world at an early age to make their own living amid all the cruel
> temptations of a large city.

Like Goudie, they had hitherto led blameless lives, and he begged that if they were found guilty of any offence, it should be 'the minor offence of manslaughter'.

Mr Justice Jelf, however, directed the jury that the girls were guilty of murder or of nothing; they took only half an hour to bring in their verdict, but 'on account of their youth, sex and previous good characters, they strongly recommended them to mercy'. The death sentence was passed, but it was commuted after prolonged outcry – there was always a strong public sentiment against the hanging of women – to life imprisonment.[47]

The case brought F.E. another gratifying letter to adorn his wall:

My dear F.E. Smith,

I must send you a few lines to thank you heartily for your admirable defence of Ethel Rollinson. I never heard a hopeless case more brilliantly defended. I shall watch your future career with the deepest interest, and I feel no doubt that you will be one of the leaders of your great circuit.

Yours very truly,

Arthur R. Jelf[48]

One can only comment that Jelf underestimated F.E.'s ambition.

At exactly the time when these two trials were being conducted in Liverpool, dirty deeds were being done far out in the Atlantic which would furnish F.E., five months later, with his next major case. The mutiny on the S.S *Veronica* was the most violent crime with which he was ever concerned. It would make a good film, except that the action of the mutineers, as it was reconstructed in court, appears entirely senseless and unmotivated. The only grievance ever mentioned was that rations were reduced when the ship – a Liverpool-owned wooden barque of 1,000 tons sailing from the Gulf of Mexico to Montevideo with a cargo of timber – became becalmed off the coast of Brazil. There was no known complaint against the British Captain and First Mate; but four of the mixed crew – three Germans and a Dutchman – conspired together to take over the ship, shooting and throwing overboard Captain, both Mates and the remainder of the crew – two Swedes, an Irishman and an Indian: all but the black cook, whom they unwisely trusted to confirm their story, when they were picked up in a small boat, that fire had destroyed the *Veronica* and they were the only survivors. The cook, however, told a different tale, and in May 1903 he told it again in a court in Liverpool, where it was corroborated by one of the younger Germans, who turned King's evidence.

F.E.'s part in the three-day trial was a fairly minor one, acting as junior to the prosecuting counsel Alfred Tobin (newly a K.C.). Tobin himself led the cook through his evidence and cross-examined the three accused, leaving F.E. to examine the young German and a number of secondary witnesses. The jury had no difficulty deciding which story to believe and took no more that fifteen minutes to find all three guilty of murder. All were hanged.[49]

F.E., as was his habit, took away from the *Veronica* trial a memento: in this case the scale model of the fated ship which was used in court to make clearer to the jury the events described. It is said that it was made and presented to him by the black cook – a nice touch, but unfortunately

untrue. The model was actually made by a Liverpool marine artist
named W.H. Yorke. But it did occupy a place of honour in F.E.'s
chambers for years to come, an object of fascination to Peteil's young
daughter.

These were the dramatic highlights of F.E.'s early years at the Bar.
But the case, or the series of cases, which made him the most money and
advanced his career most rapidly was the interminable litigation arising
out of the liquidation of the Liverpool tobacco firm of Ogden Brothers,
makers of the popular 'Guinea Gold' brand of cigarettes. The background is complex but important. Ogden's had been bought up by an
American tobacco combine bidding to break into the British market.
This initiative was strongly resisted by the existing British companies,
which came together in self-defence to form a combine of their own, the
Imperial Tobacco Company. There followed a short, sharp, price-
cutting war in which the two giants fell over themselves to offer direct
bribes to the retailers to stock their particular brands. At first, Ogden's
appeared to win by promising, in March 1902, to distribute to the
retailers their entire net profits and a bonus of £200,000 p.a. for four
years – an offer which very many retailers found too good to refuse.

In July 1902 the first quarterly instalment of £50,000 was duly
distributed; but then the Americans backed down, deciding the battle
was going to prove too costly, and withdrew to defend their home
market instead. Ogden's was transferred to the British company and
liquidated.

At this point the litigation began. Hundreds of retailers up and down
the country reckoned that Ogden's was defaulting on its obligation to
distribute to them their net profits plus £200,000 a year. The company
contended that liquidation cancelled this obligation, that the payments
were dependent on the company continuing to trade. In the first test
case that came to trial, the judge ruled that the retailers had no claim on
the company's putative profits, since there was little likelihood in the
circumstances that there would have been any; but he did allow their
claim to a share of the promised £800,000. This particular retailer's
share was assessed at only £70, but the company's liability had been
established. Actions now multiplied – nearly 800 retailers claimed
about £700,000. The liquidator retained F.E. to fight each claim
individually.

> I was almost overwhelmed by the number of cases in which I had
> to consider what defence the Company should put up [F.E. wrote
> much later]. The claims were similar, but not all alike. Some had
> no case; others but a shadowy one; and there were many dif-
> ferences arising on the facts peculiar to each claim, all of which

had to be considered carefully. As soon as the defences were delivered, there were hundreds of applications made for the purpose of better defining the issues and preparing for trial.[50]

This was a gold mine for F.E. Moreover, in addition to handling all these small claims, he was also involved in the company's successive appeals to higher courts on the question of principle. In 1904 the Court of Appeal, and in 1905 the House of Lords, confirmed the original ruling – even though Ogden's was represented on the latter occasion by the starry team of Asquith and Isaacs leading Hemmerde and F.E. From the company's point of view, however, these defeats merely reduced the amount of assets from which the traders' claims could be paid. Still the individual cases kept coming to court, up to a total of some 1,200 separate actions. Eventually the retailers realized that all these myriad actions were being fought at their own expense, and only profited their lawyers; they finally settled out of court in September 1906, for what was left.

Over four years F.E. made something like £20,000 out of the Ogden's imbroglio, and gained immeasurably in experience, so that by the time it finished he was nearly ready to take silk.

Every young barrister dreams of being engaged in heavy litigation, but few can ever have had the fortune which came to me, at a time when I had only been called for four years, of being retained in an unprecedented series of actions arising out of the same events, and thus of gaining in a short space of time that indispensable knowledge and experience of practice and procedure which can only be acquired by a busy junior.[51]

True enough; but it was not all fortune. What F.E. does not here admit is something suggested by Harold Jager: that F.E. himself manoeuvred discreetly to increase the number of the claims on the company – not merely to create work and income for himself but as a deliberate strategy for the defence, since it was the very multiplicity of the retailers' actions which threatened to make them self-defeating.

I think it was by his contrivance, in consultation with his clients, that literally hundreds of actions claiming rewards under the Ogden's Bonus Scheme were brought against the Company, whose interests he was instructed to defend, and ultimately, by conducting a prolonged guerrilla warfare in what is called interlocutory proceedings, he was successful not only in tiring out his opponents, but in the end, defeating them piecemeal and *en bloc*.[52]

Nothing could better illustrate F.E.'s ingenuity in serving his client's interests and his own at the same time.

In only six years in practice on the Northern Circuit F.E. built a legendary reputation. It was not merely that his earnings in 1905 topped £6,000, though in a profession in which income is a direct index of success this was enough to excite the wonder and admiration of his peers; in a few years he had overtaken and surpassed all the older established juniors on the Circuit and his contemporaries like Scott and Rigby Swift who had started before him. Exact comparisons are difficult to obtain and somewhat questionable, but there is no doubt that F.E. was making more money more quickly than anyone had done before. More remarkable than his sheer income, however, and the extravagant style of life which it supported, was the wealth of stories that began to gather about his name – of his brilliance, and of his impudence, in court. Most of these have been repeated so often that they have become hackneyed, like the case in which F.E. demolished a boy's claim for damages after an accident. Very sympathetically he asked the victim to show the court how high he could lift his injured arm: with an effort the boy raised it to the level of his shoulder. 'Thank you,' said F.E., 'and now will you show us how high you could raise it before the accident?' Innocently, before his counsel could warn him, the boy shot his arm high in the air – and lost the case. Hackneyed, maybe, but still brilliant, and probably true – which is more than can be said with any confidence of many of F.E.'s best-loved retorts to judges. Authentic or not, however, they are all wonderful stories.

To one judge who remarked that he had read the pleadings and did not think much of F.E.'s case he replied, 'I'm sorry to hear that, My Lord, but Your Lordship will find that the more you hear of it the more it will grow on you.' To another who similarly ventured that having read F.E.'s case he was no wiser than when he started, he flashed back, 'Possibly not, My Lord, but far better informed.' To a third who unwisely asked, after a long dispute about procedure, 'What do you suppose I am on the Bench for, Mr Smith?' he suavely replied, 'It is not for me, Your Honour, to attempt to fathom the inscrutable workings of Providence.' It was with this same judge, Judge Willis, that F.E. had his most celebrated altercation. It was another case of damages for injury after an accident. A boy had been blinded. F.E. was defending the tram company. The judge allowed his human sympathy to override his sense of proper procedure, and suggested that the boy be put up on a chair so that the jury could see him clearly.

F.E. Perhaps Your Honour would like to have the boy passed round the jury box.

JUDGE WILLIS. That is a most improper suggestion.

F.E. It was provoked by a most improper suggestion.

JUDGE WILLIS. Mr. Smith, have you ever heard of a saying by Bacon – the great Bacon – that youth and discretion are ill-wed companions?

F.E. Indeed I have, Your Honour; and has Your Honour ever heard of a saying by Bacon – the great Bacon – that a much talking judge is like an ill-tuned cymbal?

JUDGE WILLIS. You are extremely offensive, young man.

F.E. As a matter of fact we both are; the only difference between us is that I am trying to be and you can't help it. I have been listened to with respect by the highest tribunal in the land and I have not come down here to be browbeaten.[53]

How much of this can possibly be believed? One would have to wonder whether the last rejoinder, at least, was not thought up afterwards, rather than spoken to His Honour's face, even were it not for Jager's supporting evidence that these sallies were sometimes improved in the telling.

F.E. would come in after a day's busy fighting in court. He would pace up and down in his room like a caged lion, talking nineteen to the dozen, telling us how he had scored off judge, counsel and witnesses, illustrating with vivid specimens of his speeches, cross-examinations and encounters with the Bench. A good many of these paeans of victory were the figments of his own imagination. He would invent incidents which never occurred, in order to introduce some especially neat repartee which had subsequently flashed into his mind, too late for actual use, but too good not to be retailed to his admiring audience.[54]

Naturally his wide-eyed disciples circulated the best stories around the legal community of Liverpool. The important thing is not whether they were strictly true or accurately repeated, but that they took root and multiplied, growing in elaboration, so that they are still part of the folklore of the Bar to this day. The glamour of F.E.'s name was such that stories accumulated around it, and every witty remark or clever retort, by whomsoever originated, was likely to end up as an F.E. Smith story. This is not to depreciate F.E.: quite the reverse. Such legends do not grow up except in the receptive soil of a real reputation. The most famous stories might all be proved apocryphal, yet still their existence would testify to his contemporaries' conviction that they had among them an exceptional individual, or, to quote Jager again, 'a unique personality'. 'The ordinary appellations, such as brilliant, talented, endowed with genius, great or distinguished, do not quite apply. He is the only one of his type in history.'[55]

What was really extraordinary about F.E. was that his verbal brilliance, his exuberant high spirits and his reckless love of life were combined with a sincere and serious commitment to the profession that made him, beneath all the glitter, a truly great lawyer. His meteoric success was not achieved by glamour, cheek and self-advertisement alone – such qualities do not impress solicitors – but by a real mastery of law and of the art of advocacy equal to the very greatest of that golden age of legal giants, equal to the power of Carson, equal to the subtlety of Isaacs. All his extravagance, his ostentation, his occasional arrogance were solidly justified at this period by his unprecedented professional achievement. The Northern Circuit had never seen anything like it. One day in 1903 – only four years, note, after F.E. had started out as a pupil with Leslie Scott in Cook Street – when the new Royal Insurance Building, a palatial edifice with a golden dome was just rising on the Liverpool skyline, a group of his fellow barristers was looking out from the St George's Hall over the Mersey. 'What's that?' one of them asked. 'Don't you know?' Rigby Swift replied. 'That's F.E. Smith's new chambers.'[56]

7

Into Parliament

All this time, F.E. was simultaneously building up his political career. He had, of course, laid a good foundation while still at Oxford, trading at first on his father's reputation, but quickly gaining credit himself as an accomplished and, most important, an ever-willing speaker. He was always prepared to come up for by-elections and address other meetings in the vacations. And he was popular; at a time when crowds thronged to political meetings as a rare form of cheap entertainment, his hard-hitting, insolent speeches gave excellent value. As early as 1894 F.E. had known how to make himself useful to Salvidge, whom he recognized as the key man to impress; from the time of his return to Merseyside in 1899 he set out to make himself indispensable. Salvidge for his part knew talent when he saw it, and gave F.E. every encouragement and opportunity that he could contrive. Just as George Harley was in the legal sphere, Archibald Salvidge was F.E.'s political godfather – an investment of support, it may be noted, for which he was well repaid in the future, for as F.E. rose into the topmost counsels of the Tory party he carried Salvidge with him as the party organizer most often consulted in Downing Street.

At the General Election of September–October 1900 – the so-called 'khaki' election called by the Salisbury Government to capitalize on apparent victory in the Boer War – F.E. concentrated his efforts on the Cheshire side of the Mersey. There were only two contests in Liverpool, anyway – in the Kirkdale and Exchange Divisions. In Birkenhead too, the Liberals allowed the sitting Conservative member, Sir Elliott Lees, an unopposed return, in deference to his patriotic absence at the war. But speaking at his re-adoption meeting F.E. – described as Hon. Secretary of the Birkenhead Conservative Association – urged Birkenhead Tories to come and help in the adjoining constituency of Wirral, where a new candidate, the Liverpool shipowner and city Councillor, Joseph Hoult, was being opposed by Lever. Here, if the *Birkenhead News* is to be believed, F.E. injected the only life into a dull campaign, rousing great enthusiasm with outraged attacks on the Liberal 'betrayal' of the

Empire. If these were predictable jingo sentiments, his insistence on a generous peace settlement was less so. 'It is a fixed determination', he declared at New Brighton (for all the world as if he were a Cabinet Minister announcing policy, not merely a local branch secretary), 'that in future there will be domination neither of Boer by Briton, nor Briton by Boer. Equality of Government is the proud boast of this Empire from one side of the hemisphere to the other.'[1] Needless to say this dispensation of equality did not extend to the native races of the Empire; but as a statement of policy toward the Boers this was a notably conciliatory line for a Tory at this moment, very characteristic of F.E. in its combination of belligerence with magnanimity.

Shortly after this election – won as comfortably by Hoult in the Wirral as by the Government nationwide – the *Birkenhead News* rightly scouted a suggestion that F.E. was going to stand for the local council; rightly on two counts. Not only was F.E. quite uninterested in the dim arena of municipal government, but his parliamentary ambitions were firmly directed across the Mersey towards the wider range of opportunity offered by Salvidge's Liverpool, with its eight Tory seats. In the next two or three years he became increasingly active on the Liverpool side of the water, most prominently at two by-elections where he can be clearly seen polishing up his credit with Salvidge and the L.W.M.C.A. At East Toxteth in 1902, where Austin Taylor was returned – recognition of his growing power as Chairman of the Laymen's League – F.E. roundly condemned the 'unscrupulous apostasy' of those who threatened party unity by challenging Salvidge's leadership;[2] while at West Derby in 1903, where the candidate Watson Rutherford (Lord Mayor of Liverpool that year) had repeatedly to satisfy the Laymen's League of the full-heartedness of his support for the Church Discipline Bill, just introduced into the House of Commons by Taylor and McIver (the member for Kirkdale), F.E. is found weighing in strongly for 'law and order in the Church'. 'If we had had more men of Mr. Rutherford's type in the House of Commons two years ago,' he declared, 'we would have made a clean sweep of those who support lawlessness in the Church.'[3] He was simultaneously making his name known among the Protestants through his defence of Wise and his prosecution of the alleged murderer of John Kensit.

Some time in 1903 F.E. became the prospective candidate for the Scotland Division, T.P. O'Connor's Irish stronghold. This was a doubtful honour. It could optimistically be seen as a significant elevation over the heads of older rivals, a priceless opportunity to win his spurs, carrying with it the promise of a winnable seat when one fell vacant. Alternatively it might have been a dead end, or a convenient siding into which an impatient young man could be shunted to blow off steam for a few years, enabling the party to claim the maximum benefit from his undoubted speaking ability without having to promote him out of turn to one of its coveted safe seats. The fact that it turned out to be the former does not mean that it was not intended, by some at least in the party hierarchy who resented his pushfulness, to be the latter. F.E. could have been fighting the Scotland Division all his life without so much as denting O'Connor's majority. As it was, he never had to fight it even once. For his early release from this hopeless assignment F.E. had to thank the intervention, direct or indirect, of Joseph Chamberlain.

In October 1903, at the age of sixty-seven, Chamberlain resigned from the Unionist Government (now headed by Balfour) in order to launch a great national campaign for his new panacea, tariff reform, at a series of mass rallies in the industrial centres of Scotland and the north of England. His fourth stop was at Liverpool on 27 October, where he met with a tremendous reception – one which contrasted strikingly with the cool hearing given to Balfour in February. On that occasion Balfour had entirely ignored Salvidge's public and specific appeal to him to back the Church Discipline Bill, which Salvidge proclaimed as the very cornerstone of the city's allegiance to the Government. To the High Church Cecils – Balfour's cousins – the Bill was an abomination, and though it passed its Second Reading in the Commons by fifty-one votes, with some Liberal support, it was subsequently allowed to perish. At this the loyalty of the more militant elements of the L.W.M.C.A. was severely strained, and Salvidge had the greatest difficulty in maintaining unity. At the municipal elections in November meetings were broken up and Salvidge himself shouted down; several Independent Protestants stood against the official Conservatives, and three (including Wise) were elected. In this atmosphere Salvidge was relieved to be able to welcome Chamberlain to Liverpool, bringing with him the hope of an alternative popular cause to reunite the party, less dangerous than the religious bogey which was getting out of his control. Generally, Liverpool Tories responded enthusiastically to Chamberlain's call – except for Austin Taylor, who created further complications for Salvidge by adhering firmly to Free Trade.

No one responded more enthusiastically than F.E. He was, so he claimed many years later, a tariff reformer of much longer standing than Chamberlain, one who had seen through the delusions of Cobdenism at a time when Chamberlain was still loyal to the orthodoxy on which Britain's commercial greatness had been founded.

I had convinced myself, while still a boy at Oxford, that it was not possible for a Free Trade country to compete over an indefinite period of time with those who enjoyed our market and denied us

theirs. I remember well involving myself in considerable discredit
by a paper which I wrote upon the subject in the year 1892.[4]

There is no evidence that F.E. flaunted this precocious heresy in his
Oxford years, if indeed he had truly embraced it. Nevertheless, when
Chamberlain raised his standard in 1903, he was one of the first to rally
to it. The cause of tariff reform became, and remained, one of the most
strongly held and loudly trumpeted of his political convictions, and
Chamberlain his greatest hero, certainly up to 1914 and in theory for
the rest of his life.

Chamberlain's triumphal progress through Liverpool in 1903 offered
F.E. one of those opportunities which at the critical moments of his
career he never failed to grasp. It was actually Salvidge who created the
opening for him. All the leading local Tories, including most of the eight
M.P.s, were going to be on the platform; but Salvidge chose F.E., as the
city's only candidate without a seat, to second the vote of thanks to
Chamberlain after his speech. He rose to the occasion with his usual
unfailing instinct. Harold Jager's account is worth quoting at length for
its vivid evocation, not only of F.E.'s speech, but of the sort of event a
major political speech of that period was and of the excitement which a
leader like Joe Chamberlain could generate.

> A monster demonstration had been organized in the Hippodrome.
> Salvidge was in the chair, and the great hall was packed with the
> Conservative working men of Liverpool. Flags and streamers,
> portraits of Beaconsfield, Salisbury and Chamberlain decorated
> the walls. As was customary on these great occasions, the hour
> or so of waiting was devoted to patriotic songs. By and by
> Chamberlain and his platform party, which included Mrs.
> Chamberlain, arrived and received a tumultuous welcome. The
> huge audience gave him what is technically known as a 'whisper',
> a very effective and organized demonstration of approval and
> welcome. Hands and feet are clapped and stamped in unison, and
> then, like great ocean breakers, the hand-clapping crashes
> on, wave after wave, to be renewed again and again. It is a
> most impressive and spontaneous burst of enthusiasm. When
> Chamberlain rose to speak and the cheering had ceased, you could
> have heard the fall of the proverbial pin. For an hour and forty
> minutes he held us all spellbound . . .
>
> Now the general rule of these occasions, when a huge audience
> is assembled, is a general shuffling for the exits, as soon as the
> principal speaker has finished his speech. Not so, on this occasion;
> for one thing they wanted to hear what Chamberlain would say in
> reply to the vote of thanks, and, for another, they knew what was

coming. Salvidge now called on that tall and commanding figure, so well known and loved in Liverpool, that fine and most handsome Old English gentleman, Sir Thomas Royden, to propose the appreciatory resolution. This he did most adequately in telling and graceful terms. And now F.E. rose to second, and rose to the occasion. There are speeches and speeches, and the essence of oratory is that it should be attuned to the moment. Never in the course of his scintillating career did F.E. excel the superb master-piece of fluent eloquence to which he treated us that night. The great audience responded with cheer after cheer, 'whisper' after 'whisper'. He voiced the admiration which the whole country felt for Chamberlain and then, in the same vein of humour, satire and scorn that he afterwards used in his famous maiden speech in the House of Commons, proceeded to hold up all his opponents to ridicule. His speech was punctuated with roars of laughter as each bolt was shot home, and prolonged cheering as each point was deftly made. In that brief score of minutes, F.E., who was the candidate for the hopeless, because incurably Nationalist, Scotland division of Liverpool, made such a deep impression on Chamberlain that the path to the front bench, and the necessary opportunity for his famous début was clear for him when, a year or so later, he went to Parliament as member for Walton. I watched Chamberlain – he had never seen F.E. before that day. When F.E. began to speak, he was sitting relaxed in his chair after his own great effort. Suddenly he became alert; he turned to Salvidge to ask him, 'Who is this young fellow?' and then, like everyone else, he fell under the magic spell. After the conclusion, as they were leaving the meeting, Chamberlain stopped to congratulate F.E., and I, standing a yard or so away, overheard him saying: 'I hope we shall very soon see you at Westminster.'[5]

'My advice to you', Chamberlain is supposed to have told Salvidge, 'is to get him into a seat which he can win.'[6] Perhaps he did say it, though much of the rest of F.E.'s account, written many years later, is highly questionable;* probably more important was the fact that F.E. had given an irrefutable demonstration of his quality, on a big occasion,

---

* F.E.'s description of his inauspicious first meeting with Chamberlain, at a lunch in the Town Hall just before the Hippodrome rally, at which he begged Chamberlain to postpone the food-taxing part of his programme until the party was stronger, and was thoroughly snubbed, is especially open to doubt. For one thing, the lunch in question took place the day *after* the rally, by which time Chamberlain is supposed to have been taking a close interest in F.E., not before it. Secondly one may question whether F.E. would have been seated near enough to the great man so to engage him. The story bears the hallmark of F.E.'s fanciful imagination, and was probably dreamed up years later to demonstrate his superior political judgment.

before the whole assembled hierarchy of Liverpool Toryism. Salvidge was clearly already on the lookout for opportunities to promote his brilliant protégé; but F.E.'s success at the Hippodrome must have made it easier for him to do so without arousing too much envious opposition. F.E. had by now established a considerable hold over Salvidge. Jager recalls lunching 'almost daily' at the Conservative Club,

> and there F.E. and Salvidge would invariably meet and mutually agree on the course of action. It was noticeable that Salvidge always waited for and seemed to seek F.E.'s advice, and there is no doubt that F.E.'s quick brain was the controlling spirit in the trend of events.[7]

Jager actually claims that F.E. 'now assumed a very definite lead in Liverpool politics'. This is to go too far, except in the sense that his energy and gift for publicity made him disproportionately prominent. It was natural, for instance, that it was he, rather than any other champion, whom Salvidge put up in January 1904 to debate with Lever when the soap magnate deliberately provoked the L.W.M.C.A. by asking how it was possible for a working man to be a Conservative. No other Liverpool Tory had the panache for such stunts, and his name as a result was never for long out of the papers. Even as the candidate for hopeless Scotland he was determined to make a mark.

In January 1905 there arose the first possibility of a move, though not a very promising one. Despite the enthusiasm roused by Chamberlain's visit, the tariff issue had not reunited the L.W.M.C.A. but opened up another rift. Austin Taylor, a key figure as Chairman of the Laymen's League as well as M.P. for East Toxteth, remained a stubborn Free Trader. The most ardent Tariff Reformers proposed that F.E. should be put up to oppose him. F.E., however, was not keen, as he explained to Salvidge.

> I have had a long talk today . . . with Radcliffe Cousins, the Tariff Reform League Secretary. He is very keen (and assured me Chamberlain is equally so) that I should fight Taylor in East Toxteth. I am very doubtful about the matter myself and see very clearly that I should be badly beaten unless the Liberals put a man in the field. I can't see that it would do me anything but harm to be discreditably beaten, and quite candidly I should anticipate nothing else.
>
> To begin with, I think I have spent a lot of money, at least £100, in the Scotland division and it seems a pity to throw this away. We could, I think, get another candidate (I fancy Tobin would stand),

but even so is it a wise step having regard to my future in Liverpool? I am greatly perplexed and shall be very much influenced by your advice.

I have told Radcliffe Cousins that the following are conditions precedent: (1) a request from Chamberlain; (2) your approval; (3) the support of the official organization in East Toxteth; (4) payment of all my expenses. I hope you won't think the latter claim extortionate, but though I was prepared to put down £200 for the Scotland Division with its inscrutable future and dwindling population, I will not pay a farthing for the decidedly unpleasant prospect of being bottom of the poll in East Toxteth. My only reason would be that I am doing a service to the party. Will you think the matter over?

In the same letter, F.E. went on to ask Salvidge another favour. Could he casually mention F.E.'s name to the Town Clerk as possible counsel to oppose on Liverpool's behalf Bootle's Bill for the annexation of Orrell? (This was the great expansion battle then going on on Merseyside, with Liverpool trying to swallow Bootle, and Bootle trying to preserve its independence by itself swallowing Orrell, Litherland, Ford and Fazakerly.) This, F.E. urged, 'would give me a very great opportunity of establishing myself at the Parliamentary Bar'.[8]

Salvidge replied the next day:

I am bearing the matter of the Bootle Bill in mind. As regards East Toxteth I am convinced that it would be a mistake, in present circumstances, for the Tariff Reform League to put you or anyone else up against Austin Taylor . . .

Taylor is regarded as the Leader of the Protestant party in the House of Commons. If the Tariff Reform League raised opposition to him it would have a bad effect in other local constituencies. One has to think not only of a particular seat but of the whole city as one battle front. The rank and file, as matters stand, could not be persuaded that any other candidate would be as good a Protestant as Austin Taylor. Should the Tariff Reform League try to replace the acknowledged leader of the Protestantism in Parliament it might well end in strengthening Taylor's position and rousing hostility to Tariff Reform in quarters where no such hostility exists.

The religious issue, in other words, still came first in Liverpool. When the election came, Taylor was prudently left unopposed.

But Salvidge ended with a dark hint of encouragement for F.E. 'Referring to your own future, I have other plans. Be patient a little longer.'[9]

There was a by-election pending in Everton, but that seat went to Sir John Harmood-Banner. Within a few weeks, however, the meaning of Salvidge's hint became clear when J.H. Stock, the member for Walton, announced that he would not be standing again. The owner of large estates in Wigtownshire, and a more familiar figure in the hunting field than in either Liverpool or the House of Commons, Stock had not been a distinguished M.P. Nevertheless, since winning the seat in 1892 with a comfortable majority, he had been returned unopposed in 1895 and 1900. With the Balfour Government in palpable disarray, however, and the Liberals resurgent, there was no chance of a walkover this time – indeed the Liberals had just adopted a candidate, a hard-hitting New Zealander named Jellicoe. Moreover the electorate had nearly trebled since 1892. It was now the largest constituency in Liverpool, and predominantly working class. A popular fighting candidate was now needed to hold it for the Tories. Stock was accordingly eased out, and Salvidge, Edwin Berry and other friends of F.E. in the L.W.M.C.A. convinced the Association and the local Executive that he was the man.

The announcement was made on 14 February 1905. The *Liverpool Daily Post*'s long-winded gossip columnist commented a couple of days later:

> A sensation has been produced by the announcement that Scotland Division is to have a new Tory candidate, and that the redoubtable young Admirable Crichton Mr. F. E. SMITH is to transfer his wooing from Scotland Division to Walton Division. The talk was that this is an interesting change; that it shows some grit in the Tory party; that one of the best of the Liberal candidates is Mr. JELLICOE who stands for Walton; that Mr. Stock's resignation has made a good vacancy there; that it would not do to have a bad Tory candidate; that Mr. Jellicoe would make mincemeat of any Tory candidate who was not of good solid stuff; that Mr. F.E. Smith will be a good Tory candidate; that the Tory party have great hopes of him; that they are warranted in having great hopes; that undoubtedly as a speaker and as an advocate he has genius; that he has won success at the bar to a phenomenal extent at an unusually early age; that he has shown himself a ready, adroit and forcible politician; that he is AMBITION INCARNATE; that no doubt he desires to go into Parliament; and that unless Mr. Jellicoe reverses the balance hitherto prevailing in Walton, into Parliament Mr. F.E. Smith will go.[10]

In his first speech in his new allegiance F.E. lost no time – after thanking the officers of Scotland Division for their generosity in releasing him (he had no qualms about losing his £100 now) – in pledging himself as an ardent supporter of Chamberlain – though he was careful also to stress his loyalty to Balfour's more cautious policy of fiscal retaliation. He promised to deal exhaustively with the tariff question in a series of meetings; but he emphasized, as he always did, and indeed as he had in his speech at the Hippodrome, the protectionist aspect of the policy, rather than the imperialist – the real domestic benefits for employment and wages, rather than the sentimental appeal of Empire unity. Tariffs were for him a practical policy for the protection, literally, of the working man and his family from 'cruel and oppressive foreign competition'. Now, in his acceptance speech,

> He asked the electors to treat him as a Progressive candidate. The real future of the Conservative party lay in an understanding with those who represented the working men of this country. The legitimate ambitions of the working classes had in the past been satisfied better by the Conservative Party than by the Liberals, and they could be so satisfied in the future. In closing, he said, as long as he lived and in whatever success he met he would never forget that it was the Walton division of Liverpool that gave him the first opportunity of what it had been the hope of his life to do, namely to make a name for himself in the House of Commons.[11]

The last sentence is characteristically candid: there was no false modesty or concealment about F.E.'s ambition. But the preceding sentences are equally characteristic, an early statement of a theme which he never ceased to proclaim through the following decade up to 1914.

He was not formally adopted as prospective candidate until April – and perhaps not even then, if a letter he wrote to Salvidge just before the meeting was acted upon.

> I have been looking into the law and find it would be undesirable to be actually candidate, as the election expenses would run against my meetings. The resolution should therefore run: 'That this meeting, etc., having listened, etc., expresses its hope, etc., that at the next Parliamentary election Mr. F.E. Smith will consent to become the candidate, etc.,' I will then say, in effect, 'Repeat your offer when there is a vacancy and I shall be there, and in the meantime I hope you will let me come among you, etc.,' – practically I shall be adopted, technically the corrupt practices

Act will not touch me. You know what I mean and how to do it.

I am eternally obliged to you for all you have done in the matter.[12]

The Walton constituency in 1905 comprised the whole eastern side of the parliamentary borough of Liverpool, extending some four miles from County Road, Anfield, in the north to Smithdown Road, Wavertree, in the south, but nowhere much more than a mile across, and tapering at each end. Isolated on the map, it has exactly the outline of a leaping salmon or dolphin. The other eight city constituencies, all much smaller, clustered between Walton and the Mersey; on the other side, beyond the parliamentary boundary (the dolphin's back) lay Bootle. The character of the constituency was as tough and as traditionally Tory as any part of Liverpool – it was in many respects quintessential. It contained at its northern end the grounds of both the city's leading football clubs, Liverpool at Anfield and Everton at Goodison Park; while its politics were embedded in the very street names, redolent of Disraeli's Young England – Tancred Road, Coningsby Road, Sybil Road, Lothair Road – and of the Tory Democracy of the 1880s – Randolph Street, Gorst Street, Balfour Street. Walton's fidelity to this political heritage was under attack by the time F.E. came on the scene; at the last municipal elections the wards of which it was composed had elected eight Liberals to ten Conservatives; but he was just the candidate to revive it.

Its Tory Democratic heroes – Disraeli, Churchill and now Chamberlain – were his heroes; and beneath his Oxford gloss and his high living, he had a close affinity with the type of self-reliant working men who crowded its tenements. They responded quickly to his pugnacity, his lack of pomposity and his panache; he gave them no cant or condescension, but warmly admired their patriotism, humour and independence, and particularly relished their capacity to fight hard and drink hard – both activities in which he had a strong hereditary interest. F.E. always prided himself on his virile northern ancestry, scorning the softness of the south even as he succumbed to its embrace. There was a fruitful tension in his nature between north and south, Birkenhead and Oxford, Liverpool and London, his instinct and his education, his animal love of battle and his moderating intellect. When the two elements were in balance they formed an irresistible combination. It is no accident that he began to decline, politically and personally, almost from the moment that his peerage severed his umbilical connection with Merseyside. So long as he was member for Walton, he drew life and strength from his roots there. His real identification with the aspirations and prejudices of his constituents, to whom he immediately gave the same unquestioning allegiance as to Wadham and Gray's Inn, informed all his political attitudes and shaped his philosophy as it developed before the First World War, while giving him a deserved standing as the leading representative of the democratic forces within the party. The import-ance of the Walton constituency, as the soil in which F.E.'s career flourished up to 1914, cannot be exaggerated. He himself never doubted it. He once advised Robert Boothby that the single most essential requisite for a successful political career was a solid regional base; he cited the Chamberlains in Birmingham, Lloyd George's following in Wales, and his own in Liverpool – and Churchill as an example of a politician whose career lacked that strong anchor.

Whatever the technicalities, he was now effectively the candidate for Walton, with an early election in the offing. The first necessity was to satisfy the Orange Lodges and the Laymen's League of his allegiance to Protestantism and the Established Church; the easiest way to lose the seat would be to give the Protestant zealots the least excuse to put up a splinter candidate against him. Accordingly, at the beginning of March he devoted a speech to making clear his position. He said what was required of him; yet it is noticeable that even at this delicate stage of his career he defended establishment with remarkably secular arguments, with characteristically political, legal and constitutional arguments, rather than pretending to religious ones, though he had the gall to claim that his Protestantism was of long standing (even if he could not claim that it went deep).

He said he would attach little importance to crosses, genuflections and such features of Ritualist churches and services, but for the fact that they indicated in a small minority of churches a treason-able conspiracy directed at the very heart of the Church of England by men who were resolved, covertly, to approximate more closely to the Church of Rome. (Applause.) In opposition to that movement he wished to declare himself in the clearest manner a supporter of Protestantism advocated by many prominent men in Liverpool during the past ten years. His Protestantism, how-ever, was not of recent growth. ('Hear, hear.') He had not, like the late Liberal candidate for the Everton division, for example, been seized with a virulent Protestantism on the eve of an election . . . (Laughter.)

As long as the Church of England remained the Established Church, questions of its doctrines must be decided by the courts. (Applause.)

So far from being a Protestant of yesterday, he took the chair three years ago in Oxford at a meeting addressed by Mr. Walsh,

the author of *The Secret History of the Oxford Movement*. Since then he
had supported the Protestant mission identified with the name of
Lady Wimborne, and he would pledge himself to do his utmost to
secure the successful passage through the House of Commons of
the Church Discipline Bill. (Loud applause, and cries of 'Put that
down, poet.')[13]

There followed nine months of hard campaigning – 'nine months of
the most strenuous work of my career', as F.E. later recalled. They were
strenuous, of course, because in addition to fighting Walton, F.E. had
now built up a legal practice unprecedented for a junior on the
Northern Circuit. By 1906 he was earning nearly £6,000 a year.

Much of his work was neatly tied in with his political concerns, and
well calculated to do him no harm with his supporters. While his big
money derived from the interminable Ogden's litigation, his bread and
butter was still provided by licensing work, with some important test
cases arising out of the new Conservative Licensing Act. In March
1905, for instance, he was involved in an appeal by Walker & Sons, the
brewers, against certain conditions imposed by the Liverpool magistrates on a particular licensee. H.H. Asquith led for the magistrates –
probably F.E.'s first encounter with him – and in the High Court
carried the day. In the Appeal Court a few weeks later, however,
Pickford K.C. and Rigby Swift, for the licensee, and Archibald Bodkin
and F.E., for the owners, succeeded in having the verdict reversed.
Later in the year, in the Liverpool County Court in October, F.E.
appeared for another brewer, Glover's, in a question of apportioning
the compensation provided under the Act for the closure of pubs; he
succeeded in winning the lion's share for his client.

On the sectarian front, too, F.E. defended in March 1905 another
violent Protestant 'lecturer', Albert Stones, in a case that lasted over a
fortnight. In the end Stones was persuaded to plead guilty; but he was
only bound over to keep the peace.

From the moment of his adoption, F.E.'s professional work was made
an issue by the Liberals in Walton – tirelessly cited as an example of the
'Tammany Hall' corruption which characterized Salvidge's rule in
Liverpool. F.E., his opponent Jellicoe argued in April, was

the candidate whom the licensed victuallers and Alderman
Salvidge have transferred from Scotland Division because they
looked upon Walton as their own freehold and pocket borough,
and who was also their well-fee'd lawyer in all litigious matters in
the courts of justice.[14]

F.E. replied the next day, indignantly in defence of Salvidge, blandly turning aside the criticism of himself. It was the case, he admitted, that a relatively small proportion of his practice, though a greatly valued one, was derived from licensing work, but he had also appeared on occasion for the magistrates *against* licensed victuallers. It was, he claimed, the glory of his profession – it was also Jellicoe's profession – that they would act in any cause for which they were engaged. 'It is hardly customary among English barristers', he concluded loftily, 'to make public jokes of one another's fees, but I am so attached to everything colonial that even the brusque homeliness of this pleasantry of Mr Jellicoe's is not unattractive to me.' If, he suggested, Jellicoe made a habit of such imputations against individuals, 'I may appear as *his* well-fee'd lawyer in the near future!'[15]

For his own part, Salvidge made the astonishing assertion that he knew nothing at all of F.E.'s transfer from Scotland to Walton until after it had happened! He then issued a challenge to Jellicoe, offering a deposit of £1,000, subscribed by two local Conservatives, with the editor of the *Liverpool Courier* for donation to local charities, if Jellicoe in turn would substantiate his charges or donate £100. Naturally Jellicoe declined, as did F.E. when Jellicoe issued a counter-challenge of £100 that he could not substantiate his contentions about Chinese labour in South Africa. But it all made good copy for them both. Their wrangles, during this phoney war that lasted for months before the General Election was called, were attended by a gratifying level of publicity more suited to a critical by-election.

It must presumably be true that F.E. did occasionally act professionally against the drink trade, though the evidence is hard to find; but given the controversial character of the drink question at the time, particularly in Liverpool, his Liberal opponents cannot be blamed for drawing attention to the regularity and prominence with which he was employed on the publicans' side – especially as over the summer there broke the greatest *cause célèbre* in pre-war Liverpool, a case in which F.E. was closely involved.

The case again concerned the implementation of the 1904 Licensing Act, but this time it went to the very heart of Liverpool politics. The Act's solution to the problem of reducing the number of pubs in areas where there were thought to be too many was to compensate those licensees whose houses were closed, out of a fund to be levied on those that remained. The level of compensation was to be fixed by the Licensing Committee in each locality. If the compensation was fixed at a high level, the rate of the levy would also have to be high, but it was reckoned that more pubs would be closed than if the compensation was less. Thus the level of the compensation was critical, and a more contentious issue could not have been left to the highly political magistrates of Liverpool. Spurning a disingenuous Liberal suggestion that they should appoint a Licensing Committee equally divided on party lines, the Conservative majority appointed a strictly proportional Committee of ten Conservatives and six Liberals. This majority then duly voted for a low level of compensation.

Next day, 13 July 1905, the *Liverpool Daily Post*, in an editorial, specifically attacked the eight magistrates who had insisted on the Tory line, openly accusing them of partiality, if not actual corruption.

> These gentlemen will hardly pretend that they were influenced in the course they took by a desire to diminish the number of licences in the city . . . The effect of the Committee's decision will be to make the rate of reduction actually less than it was under the old order of things, a result which no doubt was shrewdly foreseen. We congratulate 'the Trade' upon the ability and courage of their friends – we had almost said their representatives – on the Licensing Committee.

At this, the eight named members of the Committee took the extra-ordinary step of suing the editor for criminal libel. It fell to F.E. to make the application for a writ and later, when the case came to court, he acted with W.F. Kyffin Taylor, K.C., for the prosecution. His opponents in Walton alleged that it was he who had 'advised' (or, by implication, urged) his clients to prosecute. This was not so. The legal advice came from the firm of Payne & Frodsham – its objectivity perhaps diminished by the fact that Frodsham was one of the eight plaintiffs. There is no reason to think that F.E.'s opinion was sought on the advisability of bringing the case; his job was merely to prosecute it. It would have been a most unusual lapse of judgment on his part if he had encouraged the action, for it was a disaster. The editor, Sir Edward Russell, was a most distinguished and respected figure, the owner as well as editor of the *Daily Post* for thirty-five years past. To induce a Liverpool jury to convict him on a criminal charge would have been difficult under any circumstances, but he retained for his defence the leading silk of the day, Rufus Isaacs at the height of his powers, who gave one of his most brilliant exhibitions of cross-examination. He ran subtle rings round the plaintiffs, leading one of them into a damaging admission of the importance of ensuring a Tory majority on the Committee, and another into a glowing encomium of Sir Edward's honour and high-mindedness. The prosecution found it impossible to deny that the editorial was fair comment. The jury took only eighteen minutes to reject the charge.

The verdict was a resounding vindication of Liverpool Liberalism, and a public humiliation for Salvidge's arrogant Tory machine at the worst possible moment. On 4 December the distracted Balfour Government had resigned. The result of the Russell case coincided with the announcement of Campbell-Bannerman's Liberal Cabinet. The new Government would obviously go to the country in a few weeks; the election was actually announced in late December. Compounding the generally poor condition of the party nationwide, the Conservative party in Liverpool thus went into battle under the handicap of a severe blow to its morale.

F.E. faced a particularly hard fight in Walton though it was eased by the absence for most of the campaign of his opponent. Balfour's resignation had unluckily caught Jellicoe on a foreign tour; the election came too soon for him, and he could not get back to Liverpool until 13 January, only three days before polling. In his absence, however, his supporters made up for him with repeated attacks on F.E.'s connections with the drink trade and the Russell prosecution. F.E. denied them as before, saying that he would have acted for Russell if Russell had briefed him first, and recalled a case in 1902 in which Shrewsbury Liberals had retained him in connection with a petition alleging bribery by the local Tory party. The example suggests that it was sufficiently unusual to be memorable. One of his assailants actually published a handsome retraction after Leslie Scott had written to the *Daily Post* defending F.E.'s professional integrity. But with another, who had also accused him of knowingly using false diagrams to mislead the electorate, F.E. entered upon a virulent exchange of personalities that continued throughout the election and beyond. F.E. first taunted him with letters to the press.

Mr Edward Evans' long leadership of the Liberal party in Liverpool has been generally recognised, even by his friends, as the greatest asset his opponents enjoy, and I for one wish him many years more of pretentious pompousness and fussy failure.[16]

Then at a rally in the Sun Hall on 11 January he produced a memorable rejoinder to Evans's professional insinuations.

Mr Evans, I understand, purveys, among other things, pills, and I have not the slightest doubt that he sells pills to Conservatives and Liberals alike. He sells pills, and I sell brains, and I claim the same right in my profession to choose my customers by the same standards as Mr Evans claims in his.[17]

The point which F.E. evaded was that he so rarely seemed to sell his brains to Liberals; but perhaps only Conservatives wanted to buy them. Strangely, however, his defence on this occasion was a totally false one which contradicted his previous, correct defence that he, as a barrister, did not himself choose his clients at all. Evans failed to pick this up; but, not to be worsted, replied instead that F.E.'s selling his brains was just what he complained of: he did not appear to have any left, and 'empty vessels make the most noise'.[18]

F.E. kept this duel going as good publicity; the more positive side of his campaign was his own personal tariff crusade. But even this resolved itself into a personal wrangle. He opened up, before the election was even officially under way, with a lecture on the state of British trade which he illustrated with diagrams, drawn by Margaret and Ethel Royden (daughter of Sir Thomas), demonstrating declining exports and rising imports, hence unemployment. He invited any Free Trader who could to challenge his figures, and was promptly taken up by a formidable opponent – the Professor of Commercial Law at Liverpool University, shortly to become a county court judge but in 1906 the Liberal candidate for neighbouring Bootle, A.P. Thomas. Thomas first ridiculed F.E.'s figures in a speech at Knotty Ash; F.E. was forced to admit an embarrassing error – his statistics for the boot and shoe industry were exaggerated 100 times! – though he still insisted that his diagrams were right. The two candidates then began an immense correspondence, exchanging letters each several thousand words in length, printed in both the *Daily Post* and the *Courier*. Thomas's letters were cool and weighty, F.E.'s increasingly truculent, falling back on rhetoric and debating points to cover a series of substantial retreats. The dispute carried on uninterrupted over Christmas, up to 6 January, when F.E. brought it to a close with a hollow flourish which can hardly have accorded with most readers' impression of its course, 'I venture to think that very little is left of the case which Mr. Thomas set out to prove.'[19] (F.E.'s persistent references to his opponent as *Mr* Thomas are typical of his taunting and insolent tone throughout.)

> I note his condescending recommendation to myself not to give way to pessimism. The only pessimism of which I am conscious at the moment is that which is occasioned by seeing the blind pretentiously putting themselves forward as guides to the blind.[20]

The *Daily Post*'s comments on this great debate are of course thoroughly biased, but they are not in this instance unfair.

Both sides admit that Dr. Thomas's articles are excellent; that they are full of knowledge; that they are full of figures; that the figures are sanely used; that Dr. Thomas is at once scholarly and popular; that his style is urbane; that the same cannot be said of *Mr. F.E. Smith*, though his articles also have great ability and remarkable dash; that Mr. Smith is doubtless an excellent judge of barristerial etiquette; that he is doubtless an unerring adviser of his clients; but that he does not add to the urbanity of fiscal discussion; that he has a manner of intermittently sneering which renders his arguments rather annoying to those who wish to enjoy them; that he will do well to conquer this frailty; that he has won a very high position; that this ought to give him a sense of responsibility in discussion; that one would like to see Mr. F.E. Smith grow a little older in proportion to his early success; that such a thing as *ballast* is not bad; that though the ability which dazzles the Oxford Union is a very fine thing to start with, the pertness of adolescence may advantageously be parted with in the controversy of actual life.[21]

From this dispute F.E. turned instead to a series of nine fiscal articles in the friendlier columns of the *Liverpool Courier*.

Meanwhile he was also stumping the constituency.

I held two or three meetings a night, and when the indoor meetings were concluded, I made it my invariable practice to go out in a wagonette with a loud-sounding bell, and with Dr. Richardson, my combative and indefatigable chairman, to hold open-air meetings in vacant spaces of the constituency.[22]

He had the enthusiastic support of Jager, Wooll and his other pupils from his chambers, but the help of only one outside 'star' speaker – and that was back in December and not very starry: the former Under-Secretary for War, the young Earl of Donoughmore (F.E.'s old Oxford friend, Viscount Suirdale). Indeed the only major national figure who came to Liverpool at all was Edward Carson, who addressed a rally at the Sun Hall on 11 January at which all the Tory candidates also spoke briefly. F.E. had some help from these colleagues, but he gave more, speaking for Charles McArthur in Exchange and several times for Tobin, who had succeeded to his hopeless task in Scotland. In Walton, F.E. was justified in later claiming, 'I did it myself.' It was an uphill fight: the tide was strongly against the Tories.

We had to fight, in a constituency where there were many Welsh voters, the unpopular but very statesmanlike Education Act. We had to fight the infamous Chinese slavery cry which branded the Liberal Party with so much indelible infamy. We had to fight against the persistent falsehood with which that Party exploited the cry of 'dear Food!'; and, most formidable of all, we had to fight with the fact that the country was thoroughly tired of us, of our policy, and of everything about us, and was irresistibly determined to make a change.[22]

The substance of his campaign was the positive case for tariffs. True to Chamberlain's original vision he always advocated tariffs as an attack on poverty – directly by increasing employment, indirectly as the means of paying for old age pensions. The protection of British industries was the means to protection of the British working class.

Mr. Smith, in the course of his remarks, said that men who wanted to work went to their opponents and asked them for bread, and they were giving them stones. They might talk about growing trade returns, and point to the cheques of the millionaires, but never would they satisfy him that all was well industrially with a country in which one man in every forty was constrained to submit to the stigma of pauperism. The greatest object was to keep the people to the soil, and supply our own nation with as much of the national food as the soil would afford. In the last ten years our manufactured goods which had been exported to the protected markets of the world had been constantly decreasing, while the imports of the foreigners to our shores had constantly increased. Although he stood for everything which made for the extension and consolidation of the Empire, he would belong to no party which in the realms of domestic affairs could be justly described as reactionary or antagonistic to the just claims of the labouring classes.[23]

Tariff reform was a progressive crusade, in which lay the salvation of the Conservative Party.

Today the struggle is only beginning; it will be long and arduous. More clearly than at any other time in its history the Unionist Party is fighting along its extended front for a *progressive* policy, and many a sword is bared today which will never be sheathed till the battle is won.[24]

For the rest, he regretted the necessity which had obliged the South African Government to import Chinese labour but defended it against the Liberals' sham outrage – flippantly suggesting that it was no different from the existence of Chinese laundries in Liverpool; he supported the Education Act and the principle of state support for religious education of *all* denominations; supported the Established Church, and again, more interestingly, the *principle* of Establishment – he would rather see almost any form of state church than an entirely secular state; and, while defending the Conservative Licensing Act as a sincere and successful attempt to control excessive drinking, attacked the hypocrisy of the Liberal temperance lobby which concentrated its attention exclusively on the beer and spirits of the poor. 'He thought it illogical that those who had the key to their own wine cellars should utter such denunciations against those who had no cellars.'[25]

F.E. also made great play with being a local man, by contrast with his New Zealand opponent, who was not even present to answer his critics until the last days of the campaign! One of his posters proclaimed 'Jellicoe for New Zealand: Smith for Walton.' When Jellicoe did at last appear on Saturday 13 January, three days before polling on the Tuesday, F.E. tried to undercut his first meeting by arriving first and speaking himself a hundred yards away. The *Daily Post*, becoming increasingly partisan, derided his effort.

> The Conservative candidate cut rather a comical figure, at whose appearance the Liberals were highly amused. Dressed in a light tweed overcoat and low bowler hat, and perched on the seat of his car, he resembled nothing so much as a vendor of fancy goods at a fair.[26]

The *Post* was now losing no opportunity to criticize F.E. personally, trying to deflate the bubble of his growing reputation, though still with an air of avuncular concern for a promising youngster. (He was actually now thirty-three, but it persisted in tagging him 'a young college politician'.)

> The language Mr. Smith uses is often so tall and extravagant as to obscure what he really does mean. He has burnished his diction overmuch. A little terse and direct Saxon would be more service- able to him than all his polished jingle, and would save him much subsequent explanation.[27]

The Conservative *Courier*, on the other hand, was lavish in its praise of the young Tory Lochinvar.

Night after night Mr. F.E. Smith has thrilled his listeners with his eloquence and delighted them with his witty repartee when any opposition element has presented itself. On at least two occasions he has stood upon a table and spoken for an hour and a half at a rate approaching 200 words a minute.[28]

But sometimes the withering repartee was misdirected. The *Post* related a story that rings true, of an admirer of F.E. who went along one evening to enjoy 'the flow of grandiloquent verbosity', but incautiously said 'hear, hear' at the wrong moment, was crushed by F.E.'s swift retort, couched in 'lofty and contemptuous sarcasm', and went away resolved to vote for Jellicoe.[29]

As the campaign approached its climax, the likelihood of a Liberal landslide became plain. Already confident of winning the business constituencies of Abercromby and Exchange (on the Free Trade vote), the *Daily Post* began to wonder if Walton might not be within the Liberals' grasp. With Jellicoe's return, it reported, F.E. was becoming 'alarmed'. 'His head-swelling has slightly abated and he has ceased to talk of a huge majority. A few hundreds will now suffice him . . . but there may be a surprise in store for him.'[30]

Then came the news from Manchester and Salford, which voted on the 13th, three days before Liverpool: in the heartland of Free Trade, the Tories had been routed. Eight seats changed hands – five to the Liberals and three – a new portent – to Labour. Most dramatically of all, Balfour himself was beaten. To this depressing omen F.E. responded with magnificent impudence, placarding Walton with the poster, 'Is Balfour Out? Then All The More Reason For Putting Smith In.' The *Post* was not amused.

> Sad will it be if Mr. F.E. Smith be defeated. The overthrow of Mr. Balfour, Mr. Smith has been telling the electors of Walton, 'is all the more reason why he should be returned'. The argument may not be clear to the majority of people, so Mr. Smith explains it. It is 'because you want a few good men on the Conservative side'. Return Mr. F.E. Smith and Mr. Balfour will never be missed! Can the electors of Walton dismiss so delightful an appeal? To do so would be cruel. Yet we imagine they will prefer Mr. Jellicoe.[26]

'This young fine-phrase spinner', it gasped incredulously, 'wants to run the Empire!'

Liverpool went to the polls on 16 January in pouring rain, with the Tories very much on the defensive and F.E. needing to get out every vote.

In those days there were few motors, and we were dependent in the main upon horse-drawn vehicles. It was no occasion for half-measures; and I sent from my own stables eight hunters belonging to myself and my wife, hardly one of which had ever been in harness till a week before. Few indeed of the voters could have realized the risks that they were running. But it is a singular coincidence that the vehicles which they erratically propelled conveyed in the aggregate almost the exact number of the majority by which I was elected.[31]

If this can be believed, they carried 709 people. Walton, as the largest constituency, was the last to be announced to an unprecedented crowd of 80–100,000 assembled in front of the St George's Hall, watching the results on an electric scoreboard. As had been predicted, Abercromby and Exchange fell to the Liberals, though only narrowly; Abercromby to Jack Seely, a dashing Boer War hero who had crossed the floor with Winston Churchill on the question of Free Trade and was to become a good friend of F.E.; Exchange to the new Attorney-General for Ireland, R.R. Cherry. Rutherford, Harmood-Banner, McIver and Houston were returned safely but with reduced majorities for West Derby, Everton, Kirkdale and West Toxteth respectively, the last two defeating *Labour* opponents – another portent; O'Connor's Nationalist majority was undented by Tobin. In the ninth seat, East Toxteth, Austin Taylor was returned unopposed as a Conservative Free Trader. Finally, at 10.30, the Walton result was declared.

F.E. Smith	5,862
E.G. Jellicoe	5,153
Conservative majority	709

The *Daily Post*, ecstatic at the gathering national landslide and well pleased with the Liberals' two gains in Liverpool – though Salvidge too could be proud that the L.W.M.C.A. had weathered the storm so much better than any other city Tory party – could afford for the first time to be generous to the victor of Walton and admitted that its earlier hopes had been exaggerated.

Walton Liberals did excellently. Against the strongest local candidate, who is exceedingly popular . . . Mr. Jellicoe, a stranger within our gates, whose campaign owing to well-known circumstances extended over two days, reduced the Tory majority by nearly one-half.[32]

F.E. was inclined to agree. His success, he wrote later, could not be considered dazzling; 'but it must be measured by the conditions of the day, and it sufficed'.[33]

The new M.P. pledged his services to his constituents in a speech at the Junior Liverpool Conservative Club a couple of days later, reported under the headline 'Characteristic Speech by Mr. F.E. Smith'!

> He would do his best to forward, quietly and modestly, and with due deference to those who had longer experience in the House of Commons, the Unionist cause. If he thought that cause could be best served by silence, at whatever cost to himself (laughter), he would be silent; but if he found that cause could be best served by speech, he did not think it would be very easy to persuade him to remain silent. (Laughter.)[34]

Humbly he pledged himself to use his commercial experience (entirely legal though it was) to fill the void left by the defeated businessmen MacArthur and Lawrence.

Privately, he knew he was on his way.

> This election was incomparably the greatest milestone which I ever had passed – or ever was destined to pass – in my career. I was at least to be afforded the chance of measuring myself with those who were to determine the fortunes of the country.[33]

This was precisely as he had felt on winning his scholarship to Oxford. The door was open: it was now up to him.

His duties as an elected member began immediately. As one of the few Tories to survive the Liberal tide – only 157 were returned – he was much in demand to speak in other constituencies in the area which had still to poll. Thus after only a couple of days of rest at 'The Grove', he emerged from his tent again to speak for his old Oxford friend Balcarres at Chorley; at Bootle against his antagonist in the fiscal controversy, Professor Thomas; and against Lever in the Wirral, where Hoult was this time defeated.

Neither had he yet finished with the *Liverpool Daily Post*, which continued to pursue him for his attacks on Evans. On 22 January it publicly declined to print his latest volley.

> We have received from Mr. Smith a letter couched in terms which we could not be expected willingly to publish; and inasmuch as he informs us that 'to ensure the appearance of this letter' he has sent

a copy of it to the *Liverpool Courier* we feel relieved of the necessity of wasting any further space upon it or him.[34]

The letter, printed in the *Courier*, denied that F.E. had been gratuitously offensive to Evans, but insisted that Evans had repeatedly impugned his honour. It then reminded the *Daily Post* of some of its own 'indiscretions' – notably an outrageous libel of Rutherford which it eventually had to retract. (This was presumably the part which the *Post* was not anxious to publish.) It concluded defiantly:

Purge your own columns of indiscretions before you presume to censure mine. I myself detest personalities. Mr. Jellicoe and I parted with mutual compliments on the friendliness of our campaign. I attack no man, but if any man attacks me I shall deal with him according to the measure of my ability.[35]

With that typically aggressive expression of his bursting self-confidence F.E. left to conquer Westminster.

PART TWO

1906–1918

8

Making a Name:
The House of Commons, 1906–9

The new House of Commons met on 13 February. It was one of the most lop-sided of the century. Facing the triumphant army of 400 Liberals, there were only 157 chastened and leaderless Conservatives (including Liberal Unionists). The disparity was increased, first, by the ominous presence of 30 Labour members, elected with Liberal help under the Gladstone–MacDonald compact and generally to be counted with the Liberal majority – though at the same time to be distinguished from the 24 old-style 'Lib-Lab' members who were completely a part of it; and second, by the eternal Irish, 83 of them, committed to Home Rule and therefore bound to the Liberals as the party still theoretically pledged to it – but with no hold over them so long as the Government enjoyed its immense independent majority, and therefore in the short term less than reliable allies. 157 out of a total of 670 – for the Tory rump it was a dispiriting prospect.

But for the new member for Liverpool, Walton, his party's low tide presented a marvellous opportunity. He had obviously far more chance of making his voice heard in a party of 157 M.P.s than he could have had as one of nearly 400 in the previous Parliament. Moreover, after a defeat so crushing as that which the Tories suffered in 1906, those members who were returned naturally came from the safest seats, with a consequent predominance of southern country gentlemen and unambitious backbenchers. The party had been shorn of talent at every level. The most senior of the defeated Ministers – Balfour, Lyttelton, Walter Long – quickly came back at by-elections. But a great swathe had been cut through the middle reaches of the party; it was this that enabled Bonar Law (defeated himself in Glasgow, but lucky to get back quickly for Dulwich) to rise from a junior position in 1905 to the leadership in 1911. Similarly there was a lack of new blood at the bottom. Only two other future Conservative Cabinet Ministers came into the House of Commons for the first time with F.E. in 1906 – Lord Robert Cecil and

William Bridgeman (both eight years older than F.E.). Two or three others – Walter Guinness, Stanley Baldwin and William Joynson-Hicks – got in at by-elections in 1907 and 1908 as the pendulum began to swing back towards the Tories. But the major new intake was in 1910. In 1906 the field was wide open to thrusting young talent that was not afraid to take its chance. No one fitted this description better than F.E. The situation might have been made for him.

There was one other almost new M.P., younger than himself, with whom F.E. immediately made common cause: this was Viscount Turnour, shortly to become the sixth Earl of Winterton, who had entered the House of Commons for Horsham at a by-election in 1904, aged only twenty-one. F.E. and Eddy Winterton met at a Tariff Reform League dinner a week before the new Parliament assembled, and at once became firm friends and allies, the two most dashing young blades on the Tory benches – though Winterton's subsequent career did not fulfil the expectations raised by its beginning. On his own side of the House F.E. was also reunited with one old friend: Balcarres had been M.P. for Chorley since 1895 and was now a whip.* But Leo Amery had fought Wolverhampton East in vain, and was not to find a winnable seat until 1911. The rest of his Oxford contemporaries were mainly Liberals; those that had found constituencies naturally fared well in the Liberal landslide. Belloc won Salford South, and Simon won Walthamstow; Hemmerde was defeated at Shrewsbury, but got in a few months later for Denbigh East. (Hirst alone never got in, but in 1907 became editor of *The Economist* instead.)

There were familiar faces, then, and every prospect of resuming old rivalries. With Belloc this was not to be: the Robespierre of the Oxford Union cut no ice at Westminster and withdrew in 1910 to concentrate on his prolific writing. But the Liberals quickly learned the habit of putting up Simon to reply to F.E., and their running duel became a favourite subject for the cartoonists and commentators.

By far F.E.'s greatest friend in this House of Commons, however, was another Liberal: Winston Churchill. The precise occasion of their first meeting is not known. It might be thought that the two adventurers would be naturally drawn to one another, and lose no time in seeking one another out. In fact Churchill, newly appointed Under-Secretary for the Colonies, was probably too taken up with the excitement of office to have much time for the Smoking Room in the early months of the 1906 Parliament; while F.E., as a keen admirer of Lord Randolph and

---

* Neither Winterton nor Balcarres was debarred by the possession of a title from sitting in the House of Commons. Winterton's was an Irish peerage, and Balcarres's was the courtesy title of the heir to the ancient Earldom of Crawford, which he inherited in 1913.

an ardent tariff reformer, was initially suspicious of the headstrong son who, from devotion to free trade, had deserted Tory Democracy for radical Liberalism. In later years he used to castigate the Tories for having let Churchill go, but in 1906 he himself took a little time to appreciate his unique gifts. 'He did not wish to meet me,' Churchill recorded in *Great Contemporaries*. 'It was only after the Parliament of 1906 had run some months of its course that we were introduced to one another by a common friend as we stood at the bar of the House of Commons before an important division.'[1] That common friend, whoever it was, had much to his credit. For when they did come together they forged at once a bond of friendship, across the party divide, which was the truest and deepest in either of their lives.

For all his impatience, F.E. allowed himself a few weeks to get the feel of the House. The other Tory new boys, William Bridgeman and Robert Cecil, both spoke at the earliest opportunity, in the debate on the Address. F.E. waited a month. For the first fortnight, indeed, he may still have been fully occupied with the business of moving himself, his wife and four-year-old daughter, and eventually his practice, down to London; for he took no part in the first two divisions of the session, on Home Rule and the 'Chinese slavery' issue. He made his first cautious appearance in Hansard on 1 March, not by speaking but by putting down a question for written answer by the Foreign Secretary, Sir Edward Grey, on the extraordinary subject of the obstruction by Japanese troops of British trade in Manchuria. On 7 March he registered his first vote – against the payment of M.P.s, a proposal moved by Lever and seconded by the new Lib–Lab M.P. for Birkenhead, and carried by 348 to 110 – though it was not acted upon until 1912. Four days later he made his maiden speech.

F.E.'s is still the most famous maiden speech ever made in the House of Commons. Its fame is due to its audacity. The convention was, and still is, that maiden speeches should be short, polite, modest and unprovocative. F.E.'s was none of these things. Scorning convention, F.E. set out to do two things: first, to conquer this assembly, as he had the Oxford Union, and make his name resound in London as it did in Liverpool, with a single sensational speech; and second, to put heart into the dejected Opposition with a dauntless show of mockery and defiance of the inflated Liberal majority. Both objects displayed an appalling hubris in a newcomer to the House, a House famously kind to those who treat it with respect but severe on those who try too hard to impress it. F.E. could so easily have made an ass of himself, been laughed at or jeered out of the chamber, setting back his career by two or three years before it had begun. His arrogance invited, perhaps deserved, ignominious nemesis. But he knew quite well the risk he was taking; and he thought he could carry it off. He gambled for the highest stake; and won. He triumphantly achieved both his objects, and in this one dazzling hour wrote his name, more indelibly than by any of his more solemn later actions, into the history of Parliament.

The occasion was an unusual debate on the fiscal question initiated for the Liberals by the Yorkshire baronet Sir James Kitson with the sole intention of rubbing in the rout of tariff reform at the election. *The Times* dismissed Sir James's motion as 'only a crow of triumph',[2] and Balfour, taking his seat for the first time in the new House, called it sarcastically, 'a novel Parliamentary operation . . . a vote of censure upon the Opposition'.[3] The Liberals' mood of self-congratulation was heightened during the debate by Campbell-Bannerman's brisk waving aside of Balfour's procedural casuistry, 'Enough of this foolery . . . Move your amendments, and let us get to business.'[4] The moment to prick the Liberal bubble could not have been better chosen. Of course F.E. was lucky. Neither his intervention nor his speech was spontaneous. Amery had heard a full-dress rehearsal of most of what he intended to say on a walk around Port Meadow in Oxford several days earlier;[5] while his opportunity, at the prime time of ten o'clock in the evening, an hour after the dinner adjournment, was arranged for him by Joseph Chamberlain.

F.E. relates how, on first coming into the House, he had sought out Chamberlain, reminded him of their meeting in Liverpool and asked him to have a word with the Speaker on his behalf: Chamberlain did so, secured for him the ideal moment and told him, 'This is the chance of your life, my friend; see that you use it.'[6] Some scepticism is again in order, though one need not doubt that Chamberlain helped; someone must have done. But Arthur Lee (M.P. for Fareham since 1900) suggests that F.E. was not quite so unknown as he later liked to imagine. 'Expectations had been aroused by a good deal of advance publicity on behalf of the New Member for Walton – then known as "Smith of Liverpool".' The House, or at least parts of it, wanted to hear him. When another Frederick Smith, the member for the Strand, thought he had caught the Speaker's eye, rose and began to speak, the House, not to be denied, 'began shouting "F.E. Smith" so loudly and persistently that the Speaker realized his mistake and called again "Mr. Frederick *Edwin* Smith"'.[7] The House was not completely unprepared for what followed.

The best description of F.E.'s appearance at this moment of truth comes, though the author was not yet born, in his son's biography.

> He was tall and slim, with coal black hair which seemed to emphasize the pallor of his face. The cheek bones were high, the

mouth contemptuous, with that short upper lip which lends venom to the smoothest utterance, the figure lithe and perfectly dressed, the eyes black and tired, the appearance languid. He wore a tail coat, a red carnation and a tall collar . . . He betrayed no nervousness, but thrust his hands into his pockets, and leaned with an easy informality over the heads of the men in front of him, surveying the packed Liberal benches with sneering mouth and an expression of profound distaste.[8]

He began conventionally enough by congratulating the previous speaker, Philip Snowden, who had just made his maiden speech from the Labour benches.* He then departed slightly from his own prepared speech to answer it, seizing on Snowden's admission that 'the result of sixty years of free trade has been an absolute failure to ameliorate the condition of the working classes'. The Opposition entirely agreed with him in deploring this state of affairs, but could not agree that it would be improved 'by loose, mischievous and predatory proposals affecting those who happen to own land'. A great deal of cant was talked on this question, he declared, encouraged by the laughter and cheers which were already greeting his every sentence.

When I hear vague and general proposals put forward at the expense of large incomes, without any precise information as to the principle upon which these incomes are to be appropriated or tapped for the service of those who have them not, I should like to make this reservation, that there are very few members in this House, whether in Opposition or on the benches opposite, or below the gangway, whose principal business occupation it is not to get as large an income as they honestly can.

So far as this thrust was directed at Snowden and his colleagues it was ill-judged; some of the landed gentlemen might have refuted it too. But as a general observation it was very characteristic of F.E.'s style – not so much cynical, as was often alleged, as disarmingly candid and intolerant of humbug.

Having won the attention of the House, he narrowed his aim and moved back to his intended theme. Declaring himself despite the

* There is no reliable text of F.E.'s speech. The version printed by F.E. in his *Speeches, 1906–9* clearly contains additions and improvements on what he actually said; while the Hansard report is also 'revised'. *The Times* report is considerably abbreviated; the fullest is in the *Liverpool Daily Post*, which contains passages included in neither Hansard nor *The Times*, and also gives the reactions ('laughter' etc.) in the House. The following account draws on all four reports in an attempt to get as close as possible to an authentic reconstruction. (Hansard is Parl. Debs, vol. 153, cols 1014–23.)

election an unrepentant member of the Tariff Reform League, he tendentiously contrasted that body with the organization of Liberal Imperialism, the Liberal League, in order to mock the timely infidelity of the latter's principal members, Asquith, Grey and Haldane, to its founder, Rosebery, which had enabled them to accept office under Campbell-Bannerman. The motion was clearly intended to draw attention to the divisions within the Opposition over tariffs; but F.E. thought that the Liberals might have shown more charity, considering the analogous difficulties on their own side over 'Chinese slavery' and religious education.

> The question of when a tariff becomes protective is no doubt difficult, but not more so than the conundrum 'When is a slave not a slave?' . . . All great political parties have skeletons in the cupboard, some with manacles on and some with only their hands behind their backs. [A reference to Liberal election posters.] The quarrel I have with hon. Gentlemen opposite is that they show an astonishing indelicacy in attempting to drag the skeleton of their opponents into the open. Not satisfied with tomahawking our colleagues in the country, they ask the scanty remnant in the House to join in the scalp dance.

After this pleasantry, F.E. abruptly switched his tone again and rounded on Austin Taylor, who, placing Free Trade above even the Church of England, had shocked Liverpool by crossing the floor, within weeks of being re-elected unopposed as a Conservative, to join the Liberals. The Member for East Toxteth, he suggested, 'has entered the House, not like his new colleagues, on the crest of a wave, but rather by means of an opportune dive'. He added, sweetly sarcastic,

> Everyone in the House will appreciate his presence, because there can be no greater compliment paid to the House by a Member than that he should be in their midst when his heart is far away, and it must be clear to all who know the hon. Member's scrupulous sense of honour that his desire must be at the present moment to be amongst his constituents who are understood to be at least as anxious to meet him.

Vicious; perfectly fair comment, politically, but in unfortunately bad taste for a reason that F.E. could not have known. Taylor's wife was at that moment seriously ill in Liverpool; she died two days later. His heart must indeed have been far away, though not with his constituents.

Another sudden swoop, and F.E. left Taylor and seized on the ambiguous wording of Kitson's motion, which celebrated the electorate's 'unqualified' fidelity to Free Trade. With that lawyer's trick of spurious verbal hair-splitting which so infuriated his opponents but delighted his supporters, he proceeded to turn the ill-chosen word inside-out. 'If we say that a man is an unqualified slave we mean that his condition could be honestly described as completely servile and not merely as semi-servile.' This was a dig at Churchill, who had made a valiant attempt to define degrees of 'slavery' in South Africa.

> If, on the other hand, we say that a man is an unqualified medical
> practitioner, or an unqualified Under-Secretary, we mean that he
> is entitled to no particular respect, because he has not passed
> through the normal period of training or preparation.

He admitted that the first meaning was most probably the one intended in this instance. But there was a little more ironic fun yet to be extracted from the distinction.

> When hon. Gentlemen opposite are successful at the polls it is
> probably used in the first sense. In the comparatively few cases in
> which I and my friends were successful, it is used in the second.
> Birmingham, under circumstances which will never be effaced
> from the memory of hon. Gentlemen on whichever side of the
> House they sit, displayed the rare and beautiful quality of political
> constancy, and voted solid for tariff reform. [Liberal laughter.]
> The result is sneered at in the spirit of that laughter which we have
> just heard as a triumph for Tammanyism, or, more profoundly,
> analysed by an eminent Nonconformist divine as an instance of
> that mysterious dispensation which occasionally allows the un-
> godly to triumph.

Now he had his favourite theme, the hypocrisy of Liberal claims to a higher morality, well in his sights. He first held up to ridicule the smug satisfaction of Herbert Paul, the distinguished historian newly elected for Northampton, that the electorate had 'voted to express discontent that certain capitalists were without a God'. This, he suggested, 'illustrates the Christian charity which is produced by the possession of one'. Next, taking Paul again and then Lloyd George as his examples, he paid caustic tribute to Liberal speakers' superior controversial skills.

> It is far easier, if one is a master of scholarly irony and a charming
> literary style, to describe protection as a 'stinking rotten carcase'
> than to discuss scientifically whether certain limited proposals are

likely to prove protective in their incidence. It is far easier, if one has a strong stomach, to suggest to simple rustics, as the President of the Board of Trade did, that, if the Tories came into power, they would introduce slavery on the hills of Wales.

Lloyd George, falling for the bait, indignantly denied the imputation. But F.E., 'anticipating a temporary lapse of memory', produced a cutting from the *Manchester Guardian* of 16 January, reporting his words, 'What would they say to introducing Chinamen at 1/- a day into the Welsh quarries? Slavery on the hills of Wales! Heaven forgive me for the suggestion!' Amid roars of Tory delight, F.E. went on,

> I myself have no means of judging how Heaven will deal with persons who think it decent to make such suggestions. I can only venture to express a doubt whether any honest politician will ever acquit the right hon. Gentleman of having deliberately given the impression to those he thus addressed that if the Conservative Party were returned they were in danger.

'Was even Manchester won on the Free Trade issue?' he challenged. To Liberal cries of 'Yes' he countered that perhaps members opposite would then explain why repeated meetings were held, and specialist speakers brought in, to discourse on the less attractive cry of 'Chinese slavery'. Salford was not quite Manchester, but near enough: Belloc had stated that he came to Westminster from Salford pledged to demand the immediate repatriation of coolies from the Rand. Was he to be told that actually the electors had only given an unqualified verdict for Free Trade? Similarly, he did not think that Thomas Horridge, who had defeated Balfour in East Manchester, would tell the House that the result in his constituency was an unqualified verdict for Free Trade. He quoted from Horridge's eve of poll appeal:

> You are voting, if you vote for Mr. Balfour, for the exclusion of white labour from South Africa ... Let the people of this division show by their votes that they would have none of this wretched coolie labour in South Africa, and strike a blow for freedom tomorrow at the polls.

'It was in this way', F.E. concluded, 'that the poorer districts of Manchester were captured.' The dishonesty of the cry was that responsible Liberals knew perfectly well that imported labour would continue to be required in South Africa and would continue to be obtained under any Government. Again he turned his satire against

Churchill, who had admitted as much in a speech in 1903, when he was still a Tory. 'The House will recognize the peroration,' he mocked. 'I rather think it has been at the disposal of both parties in the House, before undertaking a provincial tour.' (Ending as it does with the hope that South Africa would 'turn her back on the dark shadows of her past, and march steadily and firmly towards the rising sun', one is inclined to feel not only that F.E. was right, but that the formula had another fifty years ahead of it!) It was all very well for Churchill to claim that he had tried to confine the election in North-West Manchester to the single issue of Free Trade, and had no responsibility for the incendiary campaign waged by others. To that F.E. replied with his single Latin tag in this speech, *Proximus Ucalegon ardebat*, from the *Aeneid*, which he proceeded loosely to construe: *Proximus* – 'Very close to him'; *Ucalegon* – 'the hon. and learned member for East Manchester' (Horridge); *ardebat* – 'was letting off Chinese crackers'. Churchill did not go out of his way to dissociate himself from Horridge's coolie processions, or explain until after the election was safely past that 'slavery' was a 'terminological inexactitude'. On the contrary, 'He took what advantage he could get, and thanked God for it.'

Not that the cheap food cry had been everywhere neglected. F.E. now cited the campaign in North Paddington of Chiozza Money, who, he alleged, 'with an infinitely just appreciation of his own controversial limitations, relied chiefly on the intermittent exhibition of horse sausages as a witty, graceful and truthful sally at the expense of the great German nation'. Nor could he forget the Liberals' skilful use of 'garrulous octogenarians, with their tales of the hungry forties – men whose privations have not impaired their controversial vigour or their span of life'. (Sir James Kitson had in fact opened the debate with just such recollections of his own.)

'Then we had those cartoons showing with such precision the effect on the price of the loaf of a 2/- duty on corn,' he continued, striking a more serious note.

> I do not suppose that, now the fight is over, now that their strategy has been so brilliantly successful, away from the licence of the platform and in the House, where their statements can be met and dealt with, hon. Gentlemen would deny that the immediate effect of a 2/- duty on corn would be an illimitable development of colonial acreage suitable for the growth of wheat.

He paused to allow several dissenting Liberals to fall into another well-dug trap: he had been quoting from Rosebery. He had understood, he taunted them, that at the time Rosebery made the prediction (to frighten farmers from demanding tariffs) they had occupied 'the same tabernacle, or furrow, or whatever was the momentary rendez-vous of the party'. No one could doubt that Canada, 'under judicious stimulation' could supply the entire English consumption of wheat: a United States Government report had found that Winnipeg alone could supply the whole world.

> If this is true, or half true, what becomes of the nightmare of apprehension which has made hon. Gentlemen opposite so infinitely tedious for the last few years? If an illimitable supply of Canadian corn is coming in untaxed, what becomes of the little loaf? Once again I recognize in hon. Gentlemen opposite our electioneering masters, and I compliment them, if not on an unqualified verdict, upon an unqualified pictorial inexactitude.

There followed some banter at the expense of those Liberals whose devotion to Free Trade led them to argue that English money was better invested abroad than in English factories at home: if they were consistent they ought to offer a bounty to capitalists who removed their works abroad! Then he returned to his original point about poverty. Liberal and Labour members were free with 'beautiful sentiments about the feeding of starving children'. He shared them, but remained convinced that the existing fiscal system offered no solution to the problem, but was actually its cause. 'I should like to know how hon. Gentlemen opposite explain the growing poverty of the poor.' Answered with cries of 'the War', F.E. replied that they should ask Haldane and their own front bench about that. The situation anyway went back beyond the Boer War. The Liberals had no answer to unemployment but futile palliatives.

> While the only panacea which hon. Gentlemen opposite can suggest is the employment of broken down artisans to plant trees and construct dams against the encroachment of the sea, the Unionist Party need not be discouraged by its reverses at the polls. We will say of the goddess who presides over the polls as Dryden said of Fortune in general:

> > 'I can enjoy her when she's kind;
> > But when she dances in the wind,
> > And shakes her wings and will not stay,
> > I puff the prostitute away.'

A word not often uttered in the Commons chamber (at any rate as a noun); one can imagine the delicate emphasis with which F.E. endowed it.

Now he drew towards his conclusion. Was the verdict of the electorate 'unqualified', he asked finally, if judged by the aggregate of votes? The combined Liberal, Labour and Nationalist candidates polled 3,300,000 votes: Tariff Reformers and other Tory candidates polled 2,500,000. (Again, it was child's play to lure some gullible Liberals into another timeworn little trap. 'I gather that it is suggested that my figures are wrong.' [Cries of 'Yes'.] 'They very probably are. I got them from the *Liberal Magazine*.')

> I venture to suggest to hon. Gentlemen opposite that the figures I have quoted, so far as they are accurate, are not altogether discouraging to those who for the first time in the nation's history challenged the verdict of the country on tariff reform.

Moreover, he pointed out, the Irish component of the 'Free Trade' majority were not Free Traders at all.

> Will one of them get up to say that Cobdenism has brought prosperity or success to Ireland, or to guarantee that a representative Irish Parliament would not introduce a general tariff on manufactured articles? The jury who gave this unqualified verdict is unaccountably silent. The spectacle of the Cobdenite hen cackling over a protectionist duckling of her own hatching in Ireland would add a partially compensating element of humour even to the prospect of Home Rule.*

* In the published version of the speech in his *Speeches 1906–9*, F.E. included at this point a remarkable paragraph which appears in none of the contemporary reports, an extraordinary condemnation of colonial exploitation. Whether it was omitted only in the heat of the moment from the speech as actually delivered, or was a later elaboration, inserted in 1909, it demands to be quoted.

> The Irish and – I may add – the Indian case for tariff reform were both once and for all conceded by the 'infant community' admission of Adam Smith. Why do we force upon India and Ireland alike a system, of which every honest man knows that – whether it be good or bad for us – it denies to them the right to develop and mature their nascent industries upon the lines in which they themselves most earnestly believe, and in which every country in the world except Great Britain believes? The answer is as short as it is discreditable. We perpetuate this tyranny in order that our Indian and Irish fellow-subjects may be forced to buy from our manufacturers articles which they would otherwise attempt to manufacture for themselves. In other words we perpetuate in these two cases a compulsory and unilateral trade preference – demonstrably the fruit of selfishness – at the sacrifice of a voluntary and bilateral preference, based deep and strong upon mutual interest and mutual affection.

He had one last gibe at the legitimacy of the Liberals' triumph.

> I have heard the majority on the other side of the House described as the pure fruit of the Cobdenite tree. I should say they were begotten by Chinese slavery out of passive resistance, [i.e. the Nonconformist campaign against the 1902 Education Act]. I read a short time ago that the Free Church Council claimed among its members as many as 200 of hon. Gentlemen opposite. The Free Church Council gave thanks publicly for the fact that Providence had inspired the electors with the desire and the discrimination to vote on the right side. I do not in the least mind being cheated at cards; but I find it a trifle nauseating [*The Times* has 'exasperating'] if my opponent then proceeds to ascribe his success to the favour of the Most High.

(This was a very old crack, originally used of Gladstone by Henry Labouchere, but not inappropriately plagiarized here.)

At last F.E. reached his defiant peroration. He had heard, he said, that the Government proposed to deny the 1907 Colonial Conference free discussion of tariff reform, 'so as to prevent the statement of unpalatable truths'.

> I know that I am the representative of an insignificant minority in this House, but I venture to warn the Government that the people of this country will never forget or forgive a Party which, in the heyday of its triumph, denied to the infant Parliament of the Empire one jot or tittle of that ancient liberty of speech which our predecessors in this House vindicated for themselves at the point of a sword.

On the printed page, seventy-five years on, it is still a clever and amusing speech; but its effect in the House of Commons at the moment of delivery can only be reconstructed from the accounts of witnesses. Violet Bonham Carter (then still Violet Asquith) was one of those in the gallery, looking down on a chamber swept from start to finish with 'gales of cheers and laughter'.

> The Conservative rank and file shouted and roared in ecstasy, their leaders rolled about on the Front Bench in convulsions of amusement and delight. The speaker alone remained impassive and unmoved. When he sat down amid a great ovation he was overwhelmed with congratulations.[9]

The cheers may have come from the Tory side, but the laughter and the congratulations came from both. Simon recalled that 'the ranks of Tuscany could hardly forbear from joining in the merriment',[10] while another Liberal M.P. actually thought that 'the loudest laughter came from the Liberal benches';[11] Charles Masterman and his neighbour banged their heads together as they rocked in their seats.[11] One or two dull souls were resistant: Arthur Lee thought the speech ' "smarty" and over-redolent of midnight oil', though he admitted its 'coruscating success';[12] and Sir William Robson, the Solicitor-General, speaking later in the debate, while he could not withhold congratulation, called it 'a most brilliant, yet not, I think, a luminous speech,' containing, like Falstaff's tavern bill, 'an intolerable deal of sack to a very small quantity of bread'.[13] But most members were too carried away by the artistry and nerve of the performance to quibble about its contribution to fiscal enlightenment. Snowden wrote next day, 'It was a piece of comedy more admirably acted than can be seen on the stage for many moons'; he too commented on F.E.'s perfect impassivity amid the roars that greeted nearly every sentence.[14] Lloyd George, who immediately followed F.E., complimented him – though he was one of the victims – on his 'very brilliant speech'.[15] And from the Irish benches Tim Healy passed him a famous note, 'I am old and you are young, but you have beaten me at my own game.'[16] As for Churchill, he was not in his place while he himself was under F.E.'s verbal lash; but he came into the chamber towards the end of the speech, and felt at once 'that the crowded House was listening to a new figure of the first rank'.[17]

It was left to the Liberal press to carp. The *Daily Chronicle* could not dispute F.E.'s success, but wrote it down as a cheap effect, owing more to the Tories' juvenile sense of humour than to any real quality.

In sheer brilliance it was probably the most striking maiden speech delivered since Lord Randolph Churchill. Indeed it recalled Lord Randolph in more ways than one. It was most studiously phrased, it was studiously deliberate, it was excessively witty, and it was impertinent beyond description. The delight of the front Opposition bench was pathetic. They rolled about with delight. You could have placed an apple in Mr. Austen Chamberlain's laugh at any moment. Mr. Wyndham jumped with joy; Sir Edward Carson was so happy as to look almost human. Mr. Smith lashed Liberal members, official and unofficial, one after the other, and so cleverly that not a single one could attempt to reply. Without doubt the speech was a great success. But it had two faults which Lord Randolph could never have committed. It was often strained after effect, merely sophomoric in

its diction . . . And it was far, far too long. Many members who
were delighted with twenty minutes of it had walked out before it
had reached forty minutes.[18]

There is no supporting evidence for this last assertion, which conflicts
with every other account of the occasion and is surely no more than
partisan sour grapes. The man – let alone men – who walked out of F.E.
Smith's maiden speech has not been found.

Liberals had good reason to try to denigrate the speech, for it was not
a flash in the pan but gave a lasting fillip to Conservative morale. As
Winterton recalled,

> It marked the end of the period of depression and awe of the huge,
> overbearing Government majority which at first afflicts a party
> that has been in power and then suffered a terrible electoral defeat.
> From then onward the members of the Conservative Opposition
> on the back benches attacked the Government with a vigour that
> has seldom been surpassed. Some of the younger of us, myself
> especially, probably went too far, and were considered by some of
> the staider members of our Party to use methods of delaying
> business, as well as terms of expression, more suited to Irish
> Nationalists than Conservatives. But we did a good deal to re-
> establish outside the House confidence in the fighting powers of
> the Party, and our action was approved by our leader.[19]

F.E. continued to take a leading part in this guerrilla warfare. It was
most important for him, after his dazzling début, which had after all
been hailed more for its comedy than its serious content, to dispel any
impression that he was a mere trifling dilettante by throwing himself
unreservedly into the major parliamentary battles of the session. There
were two of these in prospect in 1906, over the Trade Disputes Bill and
the Education Bill. F.E. made his second speech, of a very different type
from his first, on the Second Reading of the Trade Disputes Bill.

The Bill was an admitted sop to the Government's Labour allies;
indeed it was a Labour Bill. Its purpose was to confirm the legal
immunity of trade unions' benefit funds from actions claiming damages
arising out of strikes, an immunity which had long been assumed to
exist in practice, until it was blown away by the Taff Vale decision in
1901, by which the courts ordered the Amalgamated Society of Railway
Servants to pay £23,000 compensation to the Taff Railway Company.
The Liberal Government took office under heavy pressure to act at once
to restore the situation to the unions' advantage, and on 28 March duly
produced a Bill. It was too cautious, however, to satisfy Labour. There

was wide agreement among all parties on the need to limit union liability to an extent that would safeguard their benefit funds; but when it was proposed to give union assets complete immunity from any action for tort arising out of union activity, the Attorney-General, Sir John Walton, and other lawyers in the Government drew back from creating a specially privileged class before the law, preferring a complicated formula to restrict the application of the law of agency. The Labour members immediately introduced their own short Bill, incorporating the claim to full immunity, which the Government, giving way, unexpectedly accepted – Campbell-Bannerman himself announcing that since he had voted for the principle many times in the past he would not vote against it now. Asquith and Haldane protested, but were overruled by the Cabinet's preference for the simplest method of correcting the grievance and retaining Labour's good will. As lawyers they remained profoundly unhappy with the Bill, but as Liberals they swallowed it. Tory lawyers had no such reason to stifle their genuine outrage. The Opposition attack was led, vehemently, by Carson, with F.E., not for the last time, strong in his support. F.E. in his second speech was as deadly earnest as he had been flippant in his first a fortnight earlier.

The immunity proposal, he declared, was 'monstrous', and he denied that the unions had ever enjoyed such special protection in the past. He rehearsed all the arguments against it, not in his own words, but more damningly out of the mouth of the Attorney-General, the unfortunate Minister now responsible for this Bill which would enact the very privilege he had so comprehensively and correctly condemned only two days earlier, and which Asquith had declared to be 'wholly inadmissible'. He made no criticism of the Labour members, who honestly believed in the principle of the Bill, but sarcastically congratulated them on their capture of the Government – 'the most powerful Government of modern times' – several of whose members were about to vote for what they had repeatedly stated to be wrong, for dishonourable reasons of opportunism and political cowardice.

The most striking part of this speech today, however, is the opening section, in which F.E. focused on the clauses sanctioning picketing in furtherance of disputes. As member for 'a very large working-class constituency', he regarded himself as a representative of *un*organized labour, a group whose interests were expressly *not* served by the representatives of organized labour; who had never asked to be 'peacefully persuaded' by up to a hundred of their organized brothers; and who, should they suffer such unwelcome attentions, had no wish to be 'cut adrift from those forms of effective redress which an equal system of jurisprudence has hitherto enabled parties injured before the law to exact from the persons who have wronged them'. 'In this House trade unions are powerful and articulate. Unorganized labour, on the other hand, is weak, silent and suffering . . . Its very helplessness gives it a special claim to the consideration and protection of the House.'

He went on to expose the true purpose of picketing in a passage which in seventy years of subsequent debate has never been bettered, but which has, on the contrary, become ever more relevant and remains unanswerable.

We are asked to permit a hundred men to go round to the house of a man who wishes to exercise the common law right in this country to sell his labour where and when he chooses, and to 'advise' him or 'peacefully persuade' him not to work. If peaceful persuasion is the real object, why are a hundred men required to do it? . . .

If I were a man who was wishful to dispose of my labour as I chose, although the member for Merthyr [Keir Hardie] might not persuade me to break a contract, still, if the hon. member came with fifty other peaceful persuaders to the house where I and my wife live, I fear I should be much more likely to yield to persuasion than if the hon. gentleman came by himself. We are told that another object of these well-attended deputations is that information may be given. Is it more convenient that information should be given by fifty men, than by one man? Even in this House it is recognized that, as a general principle, it is more convenient that one member should address the House at one time.

Every honest man knows why trade unions insist on the right to a strong numerical picket. It is because they rely for their objects neither on peacefulness nor persuasion. Those whom they picket cannot be peacefully persuaded. They understand with great precision their own objects, and their own interests, and they are not in the least likely to be persuaded by the representatives of trade unions, with different objects and different interests. But, though arguments may never persuade them, numbers may easily intimidate them. And it is just because argument has failed, and intimidation has succeeded, that the Labour Party insists upon its right to a picket unlimited in respect of numbers.[20]

F.E.'s objection was taken up by few other members, however, and it soon became clear that the bulk of the Tory party was not prepared to fight even on the central question of immunity. No more than sixty-six voted against the Second Reading of the Labour Bill, and when the Government came back to the House in April with its own Bill revised to include the disputed principle, Balfour – while still condemning the

Government's surrender and warning that unions protected by this provision might not always be so moderate as they had been in the past – announced that the Opposition would not oppose it further. F.E., Carson, Robert Cecil and a few others kept up their protests through the Committee Stage in July and August, with F.E. particularly strong in seeking amendments to the picketing clauses, and Carson launching a thunderous philippic against Walton's revolutionary constitutional innovation which he formulated memorably as, 'The King can do no wrong; neither can a trade union.'[21] At the Report Stage in November F.E. was still tireless in pursuit of points of detail, to the vocal irritation of the Labour members. But on Third Reading Balfour gave the Bill his blessing, and the House of Lords, which could have killed it, as it was to kill so many other Liberal measures, let it alone. From first to last the issue only really excited the lawyers in both parties: the Tory leadership was as unwilling to antagonize the emerging power of labour as the Liberals were anxious to placate it. F.E. never ceased to believe that the 1906 Act was an indefensible unbalancing of the law in the interest of one section of society, and felt thoroughly vindicated twenty years later when he found himself a Cabinet Minister in a Government confronted by a General Strike. But for the present the issue was dead: he had gained only useful experience in the arts of parliamentary harassment.

The real battle in the 1906 Parliament was over the Education Bill. Another of the contributory causes of the Liberal landslide, as F.E. had indicated in his maiden speech, was Nonconformist opposition to Balfour's Act of 1902, which had sensibly tried to simplify the complex diversity of denominational and State education by placing both the old Board schools and (without affecting their religious character) the Church schools equally under the care of the local authorities, only to arouse howls of furious protest from the Free Churches, particularly in Wales, that this was 'putting the Church of England on the rates'. The Liberals came to power pledged to redress this grievance by establishing 'full public control' over all schools – in other words to extend to the denominational schools the curriculum of basic Bible teaching which had been given in the Board schools since 1870, providing facilities for denominational teaching only outside school hours. This was represented by the incoming President of the Board of Education, Augustine Birrell, introducing his Bill on these lines on 9 April, as a fair compromise between the denominational (i.e. Anglican and Roman Catholic) desire to safeguard the distinctive teaching of their own schools, and the secularist solution advocated by advanced Labour opinion, which would have no religious teaching in the schools at all. To Tory Churchmen, however, (united on this issue with the Catholics, English and Irish), Birrell's compromise was no compromise at all, but a bare-faced

sectarian assault on the Church of England by an overweening minority
out to foist its own narrow fundamentalism on the whole community.

Birrell's Bill was introduced just before the Easter recess. Over the
next fortnight a vigorous extra-parliamentary agitation arose, led by
the Bishops of London and Manchester and Lord Hugh Cecil. F.E.
plunged willingly into the fray. On 19 April he was the main speaker at
a Primrose League demonstration in Preston, where he issued a
characteristically defiant call to arms. 'Never in the history of the
much-vexed educational problem', he told his audience of 5,000, 'has
there been put forward a measure so partisan in conception, narrowly
sectarian in principle or impudently peremptory in its treatment of
voluntary schools.' The Opposition in the House of Commons, he
promised, would contest it 'clause by clause, line by line and word by
word'. If, however, 'by reason of their massive unintelligent battalions'
– those who, he said, had 'floated in like corks at the top of a dirty wave'
– if by sheer numbers the Government were to force the Bill through by
use of the closure, then, he crowed, 'Thank God there is a House of
Lords.' He made no apology for trusting to the Lords to kill the Bill: if
defeated, he hoped the Government would go to the country on it, for it
enjoyed no real popularity beyond 'a noisy section of political Nonconformists' – a section whose disproportionate influence it was more
and more clearly his chief purpose to expose and destroy.[22]

At the beginning of May the Bill came back to the House of
Commons for its Second Reading. The debate extended over four
highly charged days. F.E. spoke on the third day, maintaining the
standard of his two previous efforts with another powerful parliamentary
performance. He managed to be called immediately after his *bête noire* of
the moment, Austin Taylor, who had endeavoured to cover his defection from the Church party to the Nonconformist party by stressing
their common defence of Protestantism. F.E. was not going to let him
get away with this red herring. He was as much concerned as Taylor, he
insisted, to root out ritualism in the Church of England, but the need to
discipline a few Romanish lawbreakers was no reason to support a Bill
which oppressed everyone else in the Church who had no inclination to
exceed the law – especially since there was good reason to believe that
the Government, to appease the Irish, was about to make significant
concessions to the Catholic schools which it refused to Anglicans. There
was no principle, F.E. insisted, on which concessions to Catholics could
be justified which did not extend equally to the Church. Once again the
Government was simply making an exception of one section of its own
supporters for purely political reasons.

The rest of the speech was a lucid indictment of the one-sidedness
of a Bill which, as Joseph Chamberlain had argued earlier, merely

substituted one grievance for another. 'It is not a compromise, nor a concordat, but a brutal dictation of terms.' 'Thus conscience', he reflected, adapting *Macbeth*, 'doth make bullies of us all.' There was only one passage of rhetorical outrage, when he reacted hotly to Lloyd George's assertion that the enemy of democracy was clericalism.

> If you sit in this House, as so many do, as the result of oratorical efforts on the platform by battalions of Nonconformist ministers, it is not wise, it is not decent, and, surely, it is not grateful to tell the House that the enemy democracy has to fear is clericalism.

Once again, it was the double standard which enraged him. For the most part, though, he was persuasive rather than contentious, relying on his favourite technique of damning the Bill out of the mouths of the Government's own supporters. He quoted Haldane – a man who, he said, quite justly, 'has worked for education while others have shrieked about it' – in 1902 on the difficulties a Liberal Government would face in producing a fair scheme. He quoted Charles Masterman, a Liberal High Churchman, on the Government's lack of a mandate to 'load the dice' against denominational teaching; and Philip Snowden, a secularist, warning that 'Nonconformists, in their joy at having Nonconformity established as a State religion, are embracing a measure which will inflict an outrage on the majority of this country.' He quoted Gladstone on 'the popular injustice of undenominational instruction', and both Gladstone and W.E. Forster on the nature of their 1870 Education Act, intended as a permanent settlement between the State and the Churches, which the present Government was betraying. He pointed out the absurdity of Nonconformists' 'conscientious' objection to supporting from the rates schools which they had previously shown no objection to supporting out of taxes.* Finally he quoted Sir William Harcourt on the injustice of denying to any group its own form of religious instruction; and he ended with a reiterated promise:

> I say, speaking for the rank and file of the party to which I belong, that we shall offer to this Bill, at every stage, a sustained resistance, both in principle and in detail. In doing so, we shall have as our hearers a larger audience than that which we address within these walls, and we shall look forward to an ampler division lobby than that which is about to register your fleeting triumph.[23]

---

* On this point *The Times* commented, 'Well may Mr. F.E. Smith observe that, though we may not jest with the Nonconformist conscience, it is quite capable of jesting with itself.' (*The Times*, 10 May 1906.)

Did he mean the country or the House of Lords? The Tories were confident of both. As the Government forced the Bill slowly through Committee to its Third Reading, eventually resorting to a timetable to defeat relentless Opposition obstruction in which F.E. played his promised part, Balfour made no secret of his view that these lengthy proceedings in the Lower House were irrelevant. They were not entirely so, for the Third Reading revealed a significant decline in Liberal and Labour enthusiasm for the Bill since the Second: four Government supporters voted with the Opposition and fifty-six abstained, while several more, like Masterman, voted without conviction. Nor were the Irish satisfied with their special concessions: most still opposed the Bill, while none actually supported it. A majority of only 192 was an added encouragement to the Lords to feel that on this issue – unlike the Trade Disputes Bill – they could safely follow their own inclinations. As Balfour had foreshadowed, they so amended the Bill as to transform its character. The Liberal majority in the Commons rejected their amendments; so on 17 December their Lordships rejected the Bill. The Government huffed and puffed, but this was not a question on which they cared to try the verdict of the people. After months of wasted labour, they simply scrapped the Bill.

F.E. made two other significant parliamentary speeches in this his first session which show how quickly, by his readiness and ability to speak well on any subject, he was coming to the forefront of the depleted Tory ranks. In July he led the party's attack on Haldane's proposals to reduce the size of the army, protesting particularly at the Government's refusal of adequate time to debate them, but at the same time sincerely voicing one of his deepest convictions, his unvarnished Darwinian belief in the absolute necessity of maintaining military superiority over all rivals. 'An Empire which cannot defend its possessions', he declared, quoting Field-Marshal Lord Roberts, 'must inevitably perish.'[24] This was a steadily growing concern of F.E.'s for the next eight years.

Then in December he seconded the Tory amendment to reject the Government's Plural Voting Bill at its Third Reading stage, having taken no part in the previous debates. He did not defend plural voting as such – though he said that, like Gladstone, he regretted the loss of the old principle that it was a locality, rather than a number of voters, which was represented in Parliament. What he attacked was the Government's attempt to rectify this minor electoral anomaly, from whose abolition they expected to benefit, while leaving untouched the far greater anomaly of the gross over-representation of Ireland. If they really wanted to cut plural voting they would simply hold General Elections on a single day. The Bill as it stood was either a petty piece of electoral manipulation or, since the Government knew the Lords would throw it out, part of the process of 'filling up the cup' – manufacturing grievances against the Upper House.[25] This was pretty accurate; but it must be said that the whole question of electoral reform – plural voting, equal constituencies, manhood suffrage, women's suffrage – was treated with complete cynicism as a matter for partisan calculation and open gerrymandering by both parties up to 1914.

These were F.E.'s principal interventions in his first year in the House of Commons – five major speeches on different subjects (not for him the path of cautious specialization in one or two areas), plus a prominent part in Committee on the Trade Disputes and Education Bills, as well as a large number of minor interventions on matters ranging from the appointment of magistrates to a proposed ban on smoking in the chamber; and questions, both written and oral, mainly concerned with trade in Manchuria (which he must have had some constituency reason for pursuing) and the strength of the armed forces. He also made some helpful professional suggestions to improve the Workmen's Compensation Bill, and moved a noteworthy amendment to the Street Betting Bill to omit the section giving power to the police to arrest on suspicion. He had once, he told the House, recalling his famous brush with the Oxford police, been arrested himself on suspicion and imprisoned, albeit briefly, on a charge of which he was acquitted. Herbert Gladstone, the Home Secretary, expressed sympathy but did not think the experience had done him any harm; this curious attempt by a Conservative to liberalize a Liberal measure was defeated by 191 votes to 98.[26]

On another more important vote he was not so liberal as he later made out. One of the Government's first acts was to grant a generous revision of the 1902 treaty settlement with the Boers, conceding a self-governing democratic constitution to the Transvaal: this gratuitous gesture Balfour and the Tory leadership condemned as reckless and premature, though they very soon came to recognize its wisdom when the Boers, under Smuts and Botha, seemed to have been successfully reconciled to the British Empire. Austen Chamberlain, looking back many years later, named this question as the only one in his career on which he would change his vote if he could have his life again. F.E. persuaded himself that he had changed his. He is widely reputed – for instance by Campbell-Bannerman's most recent biographer – to have been the single Conservative to have voted with the Government. But he did not. Despite the generous attitude which he had displayed in the 'khaki' election six years before, the division list shows that F.E. voted with the rest of his party against the Constitution. Another instance of memory improving on the truth.

After less than a year in the House, F.E.'s arrival on the parliamentary scene was signalled in January 1907 by his appearance in *Vanity Fair*'s famous series of caricatures by 'Spy' – the Westminster equivalent of becoming an *Isis* Idol. 'Spy' drew F.E. very tall and thin, standing in a characteristic pose with his legs apart, his left hand in his trouser pocket, his right hand holding a long cigar; on his head a silk hat, in his buttonhole a red carnation, on his lips a sneer. 'This is very like you,' Margaret is supposed to have told her husband, 'but I never realised until this moment how profoundly dissipated your face is.'[27]

The accompanying character sketch – by 'Jehu Junior' – is a useful corrective to the impression that F.E. was already carrying all before him. He was said to be spoken of in the House as 'Single-speech Smith', his subsequent efforts having 'somewhat dulled the brilliance of his first triumph'. Nevertheless, 'he is certain to come again and be heard of in the future. Poems grafted on Law [the writer was somewhat over-impressed by the fact that F.E. had in 1901 published an edition of Dr Johnson's poetry] have promise in them, and Mr Smith is young enough to become a great Parliamentarian . . . He has done much in his thirty-four years and will do more'.[28]

On his election to Parliament, F.E. at once uprooted the comfortable life he had built for himself in Liverpool and the Wirral, sold 'The Grove', and moved lock, stock and barrel – family, stables and chambers – to London. In fact his daughter and his horses came with him at first only as far as Oxford, where Eleanor stayed for a time with her grandmother; F.E. and Margaret rented a small flat near the House of Commons in – suitably enough – Smith Square (23 St Stephen's Mansions), and went to Oxford at weekends to see her and to hunt. Within a few months, however, they moved to 70 Eccleston Square, a tall terraced house near Victoria Station where Eleanor was able to join them, and where in December 1907 Margaret's second child, their only son, was born.

F.E. established his new chambers at 4 Elm Court, in the Inner Temple – not in Gray's Inn, though he resumed his dining rights there and in 1908 became a Bencher. He brought with him from Liverpool his clerk, Peteil, but not his entourage of pupils, Jager and the rest, who were now going into practice on their own. He still used them, however, to devil for him politically: it was they who scanned the speeches of his opponents for him, culling the damaging extracts which he would quote with such telling effect in the House of Commons. It did not take him long to build up in London a practice to equal and surpass that which he had enjoyed in Liverpool. He had appeared often enough in London to be known to the solicitors of the capital, and of course his brilliant reputation had preceded him and was soon enhanced by his rapid parliamentary success. He was quickly in tremendous demand, so that the background to his political career for the next few years was a busy professional round of the High Court and the Old Bailey and of county courts up and down the country. A great deal of his life was spent in trains.

He was also in demand socially. The sensation created in the chamber of the House of Commons by his maiden speech was reflected, Lady Violet Bonham Carter recalled, 'by a flutter of excitement in the Ladies' Gallery above. A very famous hostess confided in me her plans to get an instant introduction to him so that she might secure him for a coming weekend party.'[29] From the moment he sat down the doors of the highest society were open to him: he and Margaret were sought out by all the great Tory hostesses – Lady Londonderry, Lady St Helier, Lady Desborough. There followed a decade of leisurely weekends on the river with the Desboroughs at Taplow, and glittering dinners at Lady St Helier's – at one of which, in March 1908, Winston Churchill first met Clementine Hozier. Above all, there were not only balls and lavish parties at Londonderry House in Park Lane but also, more significantly, more select weeks with the Londonderries at Mountstewart, which served to add a directly personal element to F.E.'s already strong attachment to the cause of Ulster. Lady Londonderry quickly became one of F.E.'s most important patrons: he repaid her fully by placing his powers of advocacy unreservedly at Ulster's disposal in the years to come.

Although Westminster, the Law Courts and the great country houses were the centres of his new life, yet Liverpool remained F.E.'s power-base which he must continue to cultivate. Though M.P.s were not at this period expected to carry out the burdensome range of constituency functions which their modern counterparts are obliged to undertake, F.E. still visited and spoke there frequently, and consulted closely with Salvidge. The extent of the latter's reliance on F.E.'s advice is illustrated by the awkward internal crisis in the local party in May 1906 when Sir Thomas Royden wished to give up the chairmanship of the Constitutional Association. Salvidge himself, already chairman of the Working Men's Association and the party's effective wire-puller, was unfitted for the formal post of leader. He wrote in his perplexity to F.E. in London, who replied, casting a candid eye over the alternatives.

1. Houston and Watson Rutherford are for different reasons *impossible* and . . . the appointment of either would be a disaster to the party.
2. I am *impossible*, having regard to my juniority, to the jealousy

my selection would excite, and to my certain failure to obtain
support and loyalty from the other members.

3. The choice is therefore between MacIver, Hampson and Petrie
. . . I incline to agree that Petrie would be the least objectionable
selection, though his appointment will certainly cause great dissatisfaction.[30]

F.E. wrote also to Royden, begging him to carry on for another two
years to stave off an embarrassing situation (long enough, perhaps, for
F.E. to have sufficiently overcome his 'juniority' to be a possible successor?). But Royden insisted on giving up, and Sir Charles Petrie it was
(the father of the historian) who took his place.

F.E. was also a big draw as a speaker all over the north-west. In
August he went up to speak at Workington in a by-election consequent
on the death of Sir Wilfrid Lawson, the butt of his maiden speech in the
Oxford Union fourteen years before. This flying visit typifies the hectic
pace of F.E.'s life. Combining politics with business, he met Jager on
the steps of the St George's Hall in Liverpool when the courts rose
for the day; in pouring rain they drove up together the 100 miles
through the Lake District in an open hired car with a leaky hood; F.E.
addressed two packed meetings, before rushing on to Carlisle to catch
the night train back to London, in order to speak in the Commons next
day on the Trade Disputes Bill.[31]

The Conservative, Sir John Randles, won the election, but he owed
his victory neither to F.E.'s nor his own oratory, nor to any swing
against the Government, but entirely to the intervention of Labour, in
the person of Robert Smillie, who took enough votes from the Liberal
(Churchill's cousin, Freddy Guest, the son of Lady Wimborne) to lose
him the seat. This was another clear signal that Labour was not content
to remain the Liberals' subordinate partner – a pointer which, when it
was repeated elsewhere, was soon seized on by F.E., who began to argue
at this early date that the Liberals were becoming irrelevant, already
being squeezed between Conservatives and Labour, the two parties
between whom lay the future.[32]

Back at Westminster, the Liberals still dominated the House of
Commons; but their first controversial attempt to translate their
majority into legislation had been thwarted by the House of Lords.
With the rejection of the Education Bill (as well as the Plural Voting Bill
and one or two other minor provocations) the battle lines for the next
few years were clearly drawn up. The power of the Lords was the one
great issue of politics, overriding and subsuming all others. No question
could be debated except in the shadow of the Lords' veto; while the
Government's stiffening resolve to curb the Upper House brought Irish

Home Rule back to the centre of affairs as, for the first time, a really practical possibility and a serious threat. The events of 1906 had brought the issue sharply into focus. After this, 1907 was a relatively quiet year, a year of retrenchment in which the parties took stock of the situation and tested out their arguments for the trial of strength between the two Houses that eventually came in 1910–11. The Government attempted no major legislation in 1907; in 1908 it brought forward a new Education Bill and a Licensing Bill, but in the certainty that the Lords would reject them, more in the spirit of 'filling up the cup' of grievance than in the hope of carrying them. Not until 1909, with Lloyd George's 'People's Budget', did the storm finally break.

F.E. was energetically involved in this battle from the start, rising through the ranks to increasing prominence in the Tory army as it reached its climax. It may be wondered how such a convinced democrat as F.E. was, sitting for a working-class constituency and very conscious of the fact, could rally so enthusiastically to the defence of the House of Lords. Today the justice of the Liberals' case against the Lords is universally conceded: the 'Peers *v.* People' interpretation of the struggle is accepted, and the Lords' defenders written off as obscurantist reactionaries blatantly bolstering the cause of privilege against democracy. Those Tories, like F.E., not born to privilege appear simply as party hacks cynically following their leaders' self-protective line, or social climbers with their eyes on coronets for themselves.

But F.E. did not in the least betray his belief in democracy in fighting for the House of Lords. On the contrary, he opposed the abolition or emasculation of the Lords on specifically democratic grounds, from fear of the unchecked power of a single chamber, however democratically elected, to inflict on the country unwanted, ill-considered and partisan reforms. The function of the Lords, in F.E.'s constitutional thinking, was to act as a legislative sieve, letting through those measures for which the Government had a clear mandate or for which there was an obvious demand, but rejecting those for which there was none, or which were badly framed. Judged from this point of view he held that the Lords had performed their task admirably in 1906 by passing the Trade Disputes Act, which was unquestionably popular, and killing the Education Bill.

In a brilliant exposition of this principle in the Commons in February 1907 he made great play with the disappointment of certain Liberal spokesmen that the Lords had not spoiled their case by rejecting the Trade Disputes Bill as well. He quoted one of them, T.J. Macnamara, who had suggested that they only passed that Bill out of fear – 'Because the foot of Labour is big' – and turned the implication skilfully to his own advantage.

In other and less picturesque language, when there are reasons for thinking that the majority in the constituencies in favour of the measure is large, then the House of Lords pass that Bill, irrespective of their own moral judgement. Does any hon. member suppose that at the time the House of Lords passed the Reform Bill they approved of it? ['No.']. Precisely, that is the position in regard to the Trade Disputes Bill. [Laughter.] Hon. members who laugh do not mark where that admission leads. It leads a little beyond the pleasantry of the moment. It leads to, and renders necessary the conclusion that, if once the Lords are convinced that the people really want a Bill, they will pass that Bill.

If I have established that preliminary ground I ask the House to mark the practical conclusions that flow from it with reference to the Education Bill. I gather that the view of hon. members on the other side is that the House of Lords is a collection of extremely pusillanimous statesmen. What is it in respect of which they are pusillanimous ? It is not the House of Commons. It is the country, and when they have reason to believe that popular feeling has forbidden or would resent the course of rejection, they pass a particular measure.

F.E. then quoted a long extract from a letter of the Duke of Wellington to Lord Derby in 1846, setting out his considered view that it should be the guiding principle of the House of Lords 'to vote that which would tend most to public order', and cited an example of Lord Salisbury following this advice. In the present controversy, there was no national indignation against the action of the Lords at all. It could not be accepted that whatever the Government of the moment put forward by definition represented the will of the people.

If that view had prevailed, the last Home Rule Bill would have been law today, although the country so speedily rejected it, after the House of Lords threw it out on Second Reading. The real truth is that, historically, the efforts of the Liberal party to deal with the constitutional question have been vitiated by a complete disability to distinguish between the Liberal party and the people.

Looking back over 120 years, F.E. asserted that every time the Liberals had raised an outcry against the House of Lords, the people had rejected them. He traced the origin of the 'offensive' phrase 'the People's House' – offensive 'because it is only used in order to induce, in some way, the view that the Liberals are the special and Heaven-appointed guardians of the people' – to the crisis in 1784 over Fox's

India Bill, which the Lords threw out after the Commons had passed it by a majority of 100. 'The action of the House of Lords provoked protests which are exactly paralleled by the protests made today. The outraged Foxites made England noisy with their clamour, but notwithstanding their protests, 160 of 'Fox's Martyrs' lost their seats.' The same thing happened in 1841 with the Irish Municipal Corporation Bill, and again in 1872.

> Then there was the historic case of the Home Rule Bill. I may remind the House of the meetings in Hyde Park and Trafalgar Square, to protest against the action of the House of Lords in throwing out that measure. So great was the bawling and the clamour that England became no fit home for a quiet man. Hon. gentlemen opposite chose their battleground; they came, they saw, and they were conquered. And that was the end of the great outcry against the House of Lords.

He concluded with satisfaction,

> The Liberal Party has drawn too many cheques on the people in the last sixty years – cheques which have been returned marked 'no assets' – for much attention to be paid to the present pretensions. I may recall the repartee of Charles II, when warned by his brother James that the people meant to assassinate him. Charles replied: 'They are hardly likely to assassinate me to make you king.' The people of England are not likely to assassinate the House of Lords to make the Radical party king. I venture to think that they are similarly unlikely to assassinate the House of Lords, in order to make the House of Commons king. Of all the delusions which obsess the minds of hon. gentlemen opposite, there is none more pathetic than that which leads them to the conclusion that the present House of Commons is the idol of the nation. For myself, I believe that the country is watching their proceedings with a mixture of apprehension and contempt, and I am satisfied that thousands of electors voted for hon. gentlemen opposite in the well-founded belief that, having regard to the known prejudices of the Lords, their capacity for mischief would fall far short of their inclinations.[33]

F.E. was congratulated on this performance both by Balfour, who commended its 'clear and acute analysis', and, generously, from the Government Front Bench, by Birrell.[34] But this was only preliminary skirmishing. In June the Government came up with a complicated

proposal for overriding the Lords by means of a series of joint conferences. There was a major debate, extending over three days, during
which Churchill denounced the Upper House as 'one-sided, hereditary,
unpurged, unrepresentative, irresponsible and absentee',[35] and Lloyd
George dubbed it, famously, not the watchdog of the Constitution, but
'Mr. Balfour's poodle'.[36] F.E. in a long and somewhat involved speech
on the third day, answered them both with his usual spirit, poured
scorn on the Government's proposed machinery for resolving deadlocks
as insulting and unworkable, and – following Balfour – professed to
deplore their dissipating their constructive energies, which might have
been devoted to social reform, to fomenting a consitutional crisis. 'For
myself', he concluded prophetically, 'I place on record my conviction
that in the decade of convulsion which the Government invites, the
Liberal party will find its permanent sepulchre.'[37]

Still, however, the Government was not ready to act; these proposals,
carried overwhelmingly through the Commons, were in the nature of a
warning to the Lords to put their own House in order, reform themselves (as some moderate peers were now willing to consider), or at least
refrain from further mutilation of Liberal Bills. Not that the Government was sending up to them any major Bills to mutilate. The question
of what to do about the Lords hung fire for lack of a clearly popular
measure with which to confront them. F.E.'s opportunities for conspicuous opposition in 1907 were therefore limited. He had some fun
probing chinks in the Government's consistency in employing inden-
tured labour in the New Hebrides, and in maintaining – as the party
opposed to food taxes – the duties on tea and sugar. He had a heated little
row with Lloyd George – carried over into *The Times* – over the right of
railway companies to contribute, like any other ratepayer, to political
funds. ('It will be an evil day for the Conservative party when it
abandons to the mercy of Socialist councils those institutions without
whose enterprise there would hardly be a rate to levy.')[38] He kept up his
pressure over defence spending in both services, and pledged his support, both in Parliament and outside, for Lord Roberts's campaign for
compulsory military training, a few weeks a year, for all men between
eighteen and thirty.

He also made one major speech on a subject near his heart when the
Government brought in a Local Option Bill for Scotland. With his
usual debating skill he set out to demonstrate that this Bill would not
have the effects its authors hoped. Forcefully he argued that existing
restrictions on drinking in Scotland – Sunday closing, ten o'clock
closing – had increased drunkenness, not reduced it (an argument
whose obvious truth was not conceded for another seventy years). He
attacked the absurdity of adjacent 'dry' and 'wet' areas, with drinkers

forced to travel from one to the other. He described, with considerable documentation, the failure of local prohibition in the United States, Canada and New Zealand, where the result was only to bring the law into contempt. And he contrasted the relative success of the 1904 English Licensing Act in reducing licences, with compensation, with the failure of the confiscatory Scottish system. He concluded with a characteristic warning to Liberal members to beware of double standards.

> Let me further recommend to hon. gentlemen opposite that they should extend to the judgement of their neighbour's affairs the same standard of conduct which they apply to their own. I have exchanged many cheerful glasses with hon. gentlemen on the other side who are now wearing an unnaturally austere expression, and I would suggest to them that it is unwise for any great party to yield to the temptation of trying to effect moral reforms at the pecuniary charges of other people. I appeal to the House to resist the temptation of laying up for themselves treasure in Heaven by the inexpensive method of confiscating other people's treasure on earth.[39]

F.E.'s amendment was of course rejected; but the Bill, having passed its Second Reading, went to the Scottish Grand Committee and was never seen again.

Some of F.E.'s most interesting interventions in the Commons in 1907–8 were not of this partisan type, but concerned legal questions. In May 1907 he supported the establishment of a Court of Criminal Appeal; and in August he came down specially to London from the north to lend his vigorous support to the Marriage with a Deceased Wife's Sister Bill. There was no real need for him to do so, for the ecclesiastical opposition to this perennial measure – it was a parliamentary joke even in Gilbert and Sullivan's day – though powerfully led by Robert Cecil, was now small, but it is a measure of his strong feeling on humane matters of this sort, and foreshadows his later passionate commitment to divorce law reform. Another instance of this humanity is the interest F.E. took in the case of George Edalji, an unfortunate young man convicted in 1903, on very questionable evidence, of maiming horses and cattle, for whom in July 1907 F.E. made in the House of Commons an appeal as eloquent as any he ever made before a jury.

The case smelled nastily of racial prejudice. Edalji's father was, amazingly, the Anglican vicar of the Staffordshire parish of Great

Wyrley (between Walsall and Cannock), although he was in origin a Parsee. He attracted some lunatic persecution and, ten years before the cattle maiming began, received a series of anonymous letters threatening the life of his son, then in his teens. George was educated at Rugeley Grammar School, won prizes, scholarships and an untarnished reputation, and became a solicitor, until in August 1903, on the basis of some more anonymous letters which he was alleged to have written himself, he was arrested and charged with killing a pony. The trial, at Staffordshire County Session, was exceedingly unsatisfactory: the prosecution completely changed their case as it became clear that their first theory did not fit Edalji's known movements; moreover when the outrages continued after Edalji's arrest they simply submitted that he was not, as they had originally asserted, the sole perpetrator, but was one of a gang. On this shifting charge he was found guilty and sentenced to a savage seven years' imprisonment.

After numerous petitions and a press outcry orchestrated by Henry Labouchere and Sir Arthur Conan Doyle, the Conservative Home Secretary reduced the sentence, in October 1905, from seven years to three. Then the new Liberal Home Secretary, Herbert Gladstone, ordered an inquiry into the case. The three-man committee reported that Edalji should not have been convicted and returned the damning judgment that the police 'carried out their investigations, not for the purpose of finding out who was the guilty party, but for the purpose of finding out evidence against Edalji'. Evidence against another man, and even a confession, were ignored, and that man was never charged. But the committee decided that it could not overturn what it thought to be the finding of the jury that Edalji *did* write the anonymous letters, and concluded that to this extent he had brought his troubles upon himself. Accordingly Gladstone, while granting Edalji a free pardon, refused him any compensation.

F.E. had had no connection with the case up to now, but he had been deeply disturbed by it, and he took the opportunity offered by a debate on Home Office Affairs on 18 July 1907 to rehearse the whole murky story and challenge this last mean decision. Not only was it incredible, on internal evidence, that Edalji could have written the anonymous letters; the jury had not found him guilty of writing them, since he had not been tried for writing them, and no jury could have pronounced on the question of handwriting anyway. 'The man was besmirched with the insinuation that he wrote the letters, and was refused an inquiry as to whether he wrote them or not.' On asking to know whether Gladstone, in making his decision, had had the benefit of any new evidence brought forward since the trial, the elder Edalji had been told that it was not the Department's policy to divulge the contents of police reports in connection with the Home Secretary's prerogative of mercy. F.E. widened the issue.

> What has become of the indignation aroused in this country by the Dreyfus case? I recall a time when we involved ourselves in our own virtue, and talked of the secret *dossier* in France . . . I spoke of the secret *dossier*; we have also the *chose jugée*, and for the 'honour of the army' have only to substitute the 'honour of the police'.

Narrowing it again to the individual victim, he concluded his review of the case with an appeal.

> I do not rest the case of Edalji in the least upon compensation. His career has been destroyed; he has spent in prison three years of a youth that will never return, and his father, from the resources of an indigent clergyman, has spent £600 in legal expenses. The strength of the case does not lie in the claim for monetary compensation, but in the claim of a citizen of this country that his character shall not be destroyed unless by the public act of a competent tribunal. There has been no public inquiry. There has been no competent tribunal. I would abandon, and I believe that Edalji would abandon, the claim to compensation, if the Home Secretary would order a public inquiry at which the police could be examined and cross-examined with the Press present. It is to the House of Commons, and the House of Commons alone, that the right hon. gentleman can be made responsible. It is to the House of Commons that Edalji makes the last appeal which the circumstances of the case permit. I do not believe that this House – the last sanctuary of the persecuted citizen – will, if the case is properly put to them, turn deaf ears to such an appeal. Should they so treat it, it is only left for this unhappy young man, brooding over his ruined career, the long-drawn years of his imprisonment, and his branded name, to draw such conclusions as he can from the reflection, *civis Britannicus sum.*[40]

Unfortunately F.E. had left Gladstone only five minutes to reply; but that was enough. Impatiently, speaking 'with some heat', he reminded the House that it was not a court of appeal. The case had been tried before a jury, had been for years under Home Office review, had been submitted to two Lord Chancellors and the Law Officers of two Governments; every kind of expert advice had been taken. The process could not be carried any further. Slamming the door, Gladstone was

loudly cheered.[41] The House, as firmly as the Home Secretary, rejected
F.E.'s appeal to its compassion. For Edalji, it was the end of the road.

Another legal matter, but this time relating to international law, on
which F.E. made a notable contribution early in 1908, was the question
of the right, vigorously maintained by the British delegates to the
Hague Conference, of belligerents to capture enemy shipping in time of
war. Taking up a Labour amendment on disarmament, F.E. delivered
what *The Times* called 'a long and learned speech',[42] arguing most
lucidly that the immunity conceded under the 1856 Declaration of Paris
to neutral shipping must be extended to enemy ships (unless carrying
contraband of war), if vague talk of disarmament was ever to be given
any substance.

Here F.E. demonstrated again the deep thought and clear sight
which he brought to important issues. His argument went far beyond
the usual blinkered simplicities of the 'great armaments' school of Tories
with whom he often appeared to be linked. With rare perspective, he
refuted as 'profoundly untrue' Campbell-Bannerman's comfortable
view that British naval supremacy was recognized throughout the
world as 'non-aggressive and innocent of design against the commercial
freedom of other States'. The Admiralty, he pointed out, rested its
argument on the persuasive power of the British naval deterrent as a
force for the preservation of peace.

> To say that we cannot agree to a modification of the existing
> practice, because it supplies us with a weapon so powerful that we
> could destroy their commerce, and to say, at the same time, that
> the existence of the Fleet at its present strength supplies no
> menace at all to Continental Powers is a clear contradiction in
> terms.

Of course the Germans resented the British threat pointed permanently
at their merchant shipping, and of course – as a proud and virile nation
– they would build up their own navy to counter it. So long as the
Government insisted on the right of capture, they could expect nothing
else.

F.E. went on to demolish the case, long outdated, for maintaining
that right. In the age of railways, Britain could do no more than cause
temporary disruption to a continental enemy while its imports were
switched to neutral vessels – and less than that to an enemy farther
afield. So much of the world's shipping was British, and Britain was so
much more dependent than any other Power on imported food and
materials, that Britain actually stood to suffer most in the event of war
under the present convention. Moreover most of the rest of the world's

shipping was insured in Britain! When we could seize *all* shipping, neutral as well as hostile, then perhaps we had a weapon worth insisting on, as J.S. Mill had argued in 1856. But the limited right in modern conditions was worthless and only rebounded against Britain herself.

F.E. ended with some pointed criticism of the Admiralty, which anticipates their later obtuseness over convoys during the war. It would be foolish not to treat their opinion with respect; but it could not be accepted as Holy Writ.

> It will be in the recollection of the House that, many years ago, the Sea Lords produced cogent, convincing, and conclusive arguments to show that steam could not be adapted to the use of ships of war. Shortly afterwards they produced another cogent memorandum proving that armour plates could not possibly be used for ships of war. The Admiralty, therefore, having made mistakes in matters of this kind, which are proper subjects for naval experts, must not be supposed immune from the possibility of mistake in a case which, in its legal and commercial aspects, is not a question for naval experts.

Apart from the strategic question, this was a commercial and, above all, a political problem. 'So long as you maintain this right,' he told the Government, 'your disarmament proposals merely expose you to the contempt which hypocrites deserve.' It was not a party question, and he did not intend to divide the House, but he urged the Government to set up a committee of inquiry. From Grey, however, F.E. received only a lengthy recapitulation of the Admiralty view that Britain could not incur the risk without some prior evidence of disarmament on the part of others. With that the matter rested for the time being.[43]

In his professional practise of the law, as opposed to these political excursions into legal territory, F.E. was involved in one noteworthy case in 1907. This was the famous Lever libel action against the Northcliffe press. In 1906 Lever Bros, in common with other soap manufacturers, had been severely hit by an unforeseen rise in the cost of raw materials, due to their alternative use in the making of margarine. Lever could have responded either by increasing the price of a 1lb bar or by reducing the size in order to maintain the price at 3d; he chose the latter course, and reduced the size of his 3d bar to 15oz. At the same time he set about forming a soap trust, to promote economies throughout the industry and eliminate wasteful expenditure by rival manufacturers on advertising. This immediately attracted the attention of the recently ennobled Lord Northcliffe as a good subject for a major campaign of

crusading journalism in the public interest. Without inquiring too
closely into the details of Lever's venture, he launched his newspapers,
the *Daily Mail*, *Daily Mirror* and *Evening News* on a scurrilous vendetta
against Lever and all his works, which lasted all through the autumn of
1906. The proposed trust was denounced in screaming headlines as a
monopolistic manoeuvre to corner the market, reduce employment at
'Port Moonshine' and raise the price of soap; the clearly announced
trimming of an ounce off a bar of Sunlight was 'exposed' as a greedy
fraud on the British public. Never was the power of the popular press
more dramatically demonstrated. By November Lever's sales were
down 60 per cent on the previous year, and he determined to sue. The
first barrister George Harley consulted advised him against this course.
But this was not the answer Lever wanted: seeking a second opinion, he
instructed Harley to consult his young political opponent and former
neighbour in the Wirral, who had acted for him several times in the
past – F.E.

Accounts differ as to whether F.E. was spending the weekend in
Oxford or hunting in Leicestershire. They are all agreed that he
received a telegram from Harley urging him to return to London on
urgent legal business – though none explains why it was to a room at the
Savoy rather than to his house or his chambers that he was summoned,
nor why his opinion was required, on a stack of papers nearly four feet
high, by nine o'clock the following morning. His response, however, is
eternally enshrined in the mythology of the Bar. He ordered a bottle of
champagne and two dozen oysters and settled down to read the papers,
working through the night for eleven hours. At 8.30 next morning he
gave his opinion, in fifteen crisp and uncompromising words, 'There is
no answer to this action for libel, and the damages must be enormous.
F.E. Smith.'

Of course, he was right, though F.E. himself played only a minor role
in vindicating his own judgment. The case came to court, at Liverpool
Assizes, the following July. F.E. was only one of a starry team of counsel
retained by Lever, third in a batting order consisting of Carson and
Horridge, both K.C.s, himself and Hemmerde. Though opposed by a
scarcely less distinguished team led by Rufus Isaacs, Carson wrapped
the case up on his own in two days. After a five-hour opening speech
demolishing Northcliffe's wild allegations, he called as his first witness
Lever himself, the model employer, who acquitted himself immaculately
under Isaacs's cross-examination. Then and there Isaacs withdrew his
client's defence, and offered £15,000 damages. This sum would in itself
have constituted a record, beating the £12,000 paid in the case of *Kitson*
v. *Playfair* in 1896. But Carson, with Lever sitting behind him, scorned
such a sum. Isaacs offered £20,000, £30,000, £40,000, before Lever

accepted £50,000, more than four times the previous record for libel damages. F.E.'s 'enormous' was no exaggeration.[44]

That was not the end of Lever's actions against Northcliffe, however, and the sequel casts F.E. in a less creditable light. He continued, over the next couple of years, to act for Lever in a number of related minor suits, but somewhat less than whole-heartedly. Together with the tea magnate Sir Thomas Lipton, but for his own reasons, F.E. was anxious to arrange a reconciliation between the disputants. Well aware of the political advantage of Northcliffe's friendship, and still more of the threat that might be posed to his ambitions by his hostility, it seems that F.E. was becoming impatient with his millionaire client's refusal to settle for less than his last ounce of flesh, and began secretly to build bridges to the opposition. After one action in which Lever, having refused £20,000 and insisted on £40,000, was awarded by the jury a mere £500, F.E. wrote, most improperly, to Northcliffe, 'Frankly the result was a great triumph for you. This is very private. None was more disgusted than I at another rechauffé, especially after the extraordinarily liberal offer your people had made.' If this was irregular, it may perhaps be justified as a fair comment, after the event, on the merits of his client's case. But how hard did he fight it? Soon he was going further and offering to withdraw his services from Lever if Northcliffe wished. 'If you feel that you have placed yourself at any disadvantage by discussing the case intimately with me, I am quite willing to withdraw from it – if you don't, I hope you will let us meet anyhow, for, God knows, there are many subjects of interest to discuss besides soap.' The message that F.E. was now placing his political prospects above his professional obligations is most crudely spelled out in notes kept by Northcliffe's confidential secretary after an interview. 'He [Northcliffe] can help me greatly. L. of no use to me. I don't want his money. Would much rather never have seen him.'[45] The self-serving ingratitude of this is breathtaking. In these jottings the most unpleasant streak in F.E.'s character, his willingness when necessary to cut corners in the way of his ambition, is starkly exposed. That he had evidently come to dislike Lever's personal parsimony and self-righteous philanthropy is no excuse for betraying his professional confidence to safeguard his own political standing with a powerful patron. F.E. prided himself on his loyalty to his friends and was celebrated, justly, by them for his fidelity. Lever, however – not a friend but merely a major client who had outlived his usefulness – fell outside the ambit of his code of honour.

By the time these later cases between Lever and Northcliffe came on, F.E. had 'taken silk' – in other words, become a senior barrister, a King's Counsel. This is always said to be a risky step for a barrister to take: a successful junior does not always make a successful leader, which involves handling only the more difficult and complex cases, with no easy bread-and-butter cases; the fees are higher, but the work is more demanding. Some good barristers do fail to make the grade. But for one of F.E.'s calibre the risk was minimal, taking silk no more than a natural milestone in his progress. The only question was how quickly he could achieve it. The average time taken by the most distinguished of his contemporaries between first being called to the bar and being called 'within the bar' was sixteen or twenty years. Among the generation slightly older than his own Haldane and Isaacs had achieved it in ten years. Of his own generation Hemmerde, called in 1897, took silk in 1909. No one else came near to matching the speed of F.E.'s elevation – except John Simon. Simon and he had made a pact while they were still at Wadham that neither would take silk before the other. They were called to the bar in the same year, 1899 – Simon in January, F.E. in June. And they did fulfil their pact, by both taking silk on the same day in February 1908 – though Simon somewhat spoiled the front of perfect amity by making his application to the Lord Chancellor on his own, without telling F.E., who felt aggrieved that Simon had tried to steal a march on him. Still, when Lord Loreburn granted both applications, F.E. could congratulate himself that his time of eight years and eight months was five months shorter than his rival's – who, however, soon left him standing in the political stakes by becoming Solicitor-General in 1910, and Attorney-General with a seat in the Cabinet in 1913. Loreburn is said to have predicted that F.E. would some day hold the position which he himself then occupied; he doubtless said the same thing to Simon. If so he was right in both cases: Simon finally attained the Woolsack in 1940, twenty-one years after F.E. But here too he had stolen a march, because he was offered it, and had declined, as early as 1915.

F.E.'s earnings were now pressing towards five figures: he passed the £10,000 a year mark for the first time in 1910. In 1907 he was easily able to buy two cottages in the village of Charlton on the Oxfordshire–Northamptonshire border which, knocked together, expanded and progressively developed over the years, became his country home for the rest of his life, and is still his family's. Originally described as a hunting box, Charlton grew with F.E.'s practice: he would add a new wing or buy another paddock, build a swimming pool or lay down another tennis court whenever he received a lucrative brief, so that the place was gradually transformed into a substantial country seat, though the front door still opens directly on to the village street.

Here he installed his stable, and soon a lavish fleet of motor cars. He brought down from Thornton Hough his former coachman/groom, Jack Rogers, and his young son Bill, who in due course doubled as chauffeur but also played excellent tennis and was often pressed into service on the court. F.E. also took up golf and used to play – erratically – at Tadmaston Heath, ten miles away. But his first love at this date was still hunting – or rather riding, for he was indifferent to the social etiquette of the hunting field and quite uninterested in the fox. He rode fearlessly and recklessly for the sheer love of steeplechasing, jumping the highest gates and suffering frequent falls, trespassing cheerfully on all the wrong fields and repeatedly scandalizing the officials of the snobbish Bicester Hunt, whose pompous displeasure so spoiled his enjoyment that he eventually gave up – though he still kept his beloved horses, which he always preferred to cars as a means of getting about the countryside.

Meanwhile it was at Eccleston Square that Margaret presented F.E. with a son, born on 7 December 1907 and christened Frederick Winston Furneaux: Freddie after his father and grandfather, Furneaux for his mother's family, and Winston after his godfather, now his father's closest friend. Three years later, when Churchill's son Randolph was born, F.E. acted in return as his godfather and the infant Randolph was given Frederick as his second name – a pleasant binding together at birth of two sons who, if they did not fulfil all the extravagant hopes placed in them, did grow up lifelong friends as their fathers hoped. Winston had married Clementine Hozier in September 1908: the previous month F.E. had been the first to hear of their engagement. They were all staying with Winston's Marlborough cousins at Blenheim. Winston proposed to Clemmie in a little ornamental pavilion in the grounds, and they agreed to tell no one until they had told her mother. But on their way back to the house they saw F.E. 'Churchill danced across the grass and, in full view of the servants, flung his arms around his neck and blurted out the news.'[46]

A few days earlier F.E. had witnessed another inimitable piece of Winston, when there was a serious fire in the house they were both staying in with Freddy Guest. F.E. lost everything he had with him. He had recently been ill, most unusually, and was not allowed to help fight the fire, but Winston, in a fireman's helmet, took command and enthusiastically directed operations, afterwards writing to Clemmie, 'The Fire was great fun and we all enjoyed it thoroughly.' Though many treasures were destroyed, the contents of the wine cellar were saved. As the bottles were brought out and laid on the lawn, F.E. inspected them with an expert eye and remarked to Margaret, 'There, I thought the port was not what he said it was.'[47]

In September 1907 F.E. and Winston spent a month together on the continent, first in France where they attended the French military manoeuvres, so that Winston could compare them with the German which he had seen the previous year, and then in Italy. It was from Italy that F.E. was recalled by an urgent telegram from Salvidge. 'Death of MacIver necessitates straight fight with Labour in Kirkdale. Urge you return immediately help defend Liverpool from Socialists. MacDonald and Henderson already here. The fight of your life. Don't fail me.' Reluctantly F.E. returned, saying that it was Winston who had persuaded him that it was his duty to go to the aid of his party. The seat was one which the Liberals had left to Labour in 1906, and they stood aside again now, while the defeated member for the Exchange division stepped across to defend it for the Conservatives. It was no wonder that Salvidge felt the need of F.E.'s assistance: at Kirkdale the ability of his Working Men's Association to hold off the Labour challenge faced its stiffest pre-war test. After a hard-fought campaign, enlivened by torch-light meetings at which F.E. and Salvidge spoke to audiences of several thousand from mobile platforms, MacArthur was returned by 4,000 votes to 3,300, narrowly increasing MacIver's majority of the previous year. But the result was swung by the last-minute distribution of damaging extracts from the atheistic writings of Robert Blatchford in the *Clarion*. Ramsay MacDonald commented ruefully that whatever the issues at the outset, Liverpool elections always seemed in the end to come down to Orangeism.[48] Not until 1923 did Labour win its first Liverpool seat.

The unscrupulous use of Blatchford to tilt the balance was reputedly the idea of F.E.'s younger brother Harold, who emerged at this election into political prominence for the first time. Having been denied by their father's death the educational opportunities which opened so many doors to F.E., Harold was still in 1907 a partner in Smith & Sons; but he was just now setting out to follow in his brother's footsteps. In 1908 he entered Gray's Inn and began to read for the Bar: he was called in 1911, after which his progress was almost as rapid as F.E.'s. He took silk in 1923, after only twelve years. Politically he began by becoming a Birkenhead Councillor in 1904, and set about organizing Birkenhead Toryism very successfully on the popular lines Salvidge had pioneered in Liverpool. At the second attempt in 1910 his Working Men's Conservative Association wrested the seat back from the Liberal who had won it in 1906. Meanwhile Harold himself had transferred his wooing first to Huddersfield, where he was defeated in January 1910, and then to Warrington, which he won in December and held until 1922.

Although he never fully escaped from F.E.'s shadow – indeed was unquestionably assisted in his career by F.E.'s encouragement and contacts – Harold was a good deal more than a pale imitation of his brilliant brother. He was a fluent and forceful speaker in the same caustic style; a much better organizer; and an even better all-round games-player. Moreover he shone in one sphere which F.E. never touched: from their father he inherited an exceptional talent as an amateur actor. After seeing his performance as Svengali in a Birkenhead Dramatic Society production of *Trilby*, Beerbohm Tree urged him to turn professional – the only amateur, he said, whom he had ever so advised. He also wrote plays, one of which, *The March Hare*, described coldly by *The Times* as 'a screaming farce', had a short run at the Ambassador's Theatre in 1913.[49]

Harold and F.E. were very close. They shared chambers for the last few years before the war, and worked together at the Press Bureau in 1914. In July 1914 Harold married Joan Furneaux, Margaret's younger sister, and soon after the war they bought a country house at Middleton Cheney, an easy ride from Charlton on a Sunday morning. When Harold died in 1924, aged forty-eight, F.E. was desolated, and lost much of his own zest for life.

The 1908 Parliament was dominated by the Government's renewed attempts to legislate on education and licensing. Bills were introduced on both questions within a few days of one another in late February. Birrell having been translated to the Irish Secretaryship after the rejection of his solution, the education imbroglio was now the thankless responsibility of Reginald McKenna, who unfolded his proposals to a crowded House of Commons on 24 February. On to the unchanged principle of Birrell's Bill he had grafted a number of anomalous qualifications. As before, only basic Bible teaching was to be given in the local authority 'provided' schools; but denominational schools in urban areas – though not in single-school rural areas – were to be allowed, by 'contracting out' of local authority control, to give denominational instruction in school hours at their own expense; the upkeep of these schools was to be assisted not from local rates but by grants from central government. These concessions conciliated the Conservative Opposition not at all, but seemed to them simply to pile up insulting exceptions to a general rule still unacceptably tailored to the tenets of Nonconformity. Balfour immediately rejected the proffered olive branch, and he was followed from the Tory benches first by Robert Cecil and then by F.E., who was able, in a characteristic speech skilfully combining destructive argument with an appeal to a higher national principle, both to riddle the exceptions and discredit the rule.

As a debater, F.E. loved nothing more than to expose the internal inconsistencies of his opponents' proposals, and there were easy points for him here as he noted the absence from this Bill of items that were said to be matters of principle in 1906 and the inclusion of concessions that were then said to be inadmissible. He had particular fun with the self-contradictory justifications of one junior Government spokesman, T.J. Macnamara, of whom he remarked (in mock admiration of his 'intellectual acrobatics') that he 'deserves something better than an under-secretaryship. He ought to be a law officer.' He also derided again the absurdity of pretending that there was any essential difference between taxes and rates. 'I should like to hear the view of an intelligent foreigner on being told that in the year 1908 it was proposed to divert the educational charges from the rates to the taxes, not for administrative or educational reasons, but merely to relieve a certain type of conscience.'

More seriously he opposed McKenna's Bill, as he had Birrell's, as essentially and in intention a sectarian measure designed to stereotype the teaching of the Nonconformist minority as the norm for the whole nation. But though he had aligned himself with Cecil and the Bishops in their defence of Church schools, he did not rest his opposition simply on preserving the hegemony of one form of teaching over another. As an unbeliever himself, and as a Liverpool M.P. with not only a host of militant Churchmen but also a lot of Catholics in his constituency, he was able to oppose the Bill on the lofty moral ground of equality – 'on the broad and simple ground that no Bill can ever succeed in this country which does not treat Nonconformist, Anglican, Jew and Catholic alike'.[50] Throughout the educational debate that raged through the year – as McKenna's Bill was replaced by a third effort introduced by yet a third Minister, Walter Runciman, which fared no better than the first two despite prior discussions with the Archbishop of Canterbury, and perished before it even reached the House of Lords – throughout these debates F.E. argued consistently from the high-minded premise of 'parental right': the principle that parents of all recognized denominations, as equal contributors to the rates, had an equal right to have their children educated in their own faith. From this high ground of impartiality between the sects, he was able to demolish any scheme the Liberals were likely to produce as falling short of natural justice, while sliding rather quickly over the real administrative difficulties in achieving it in rural areas with a scattered population and a single school. It was a marvellous debating posture; but at the same time it truly reflected F.E.'s genuine and growing concern with the proper role of the State as the impartial and unifying arbiter between the component sections of the community, a concern that was to lead him in the years to come beyond the simple anti-Liberal responses of his inherited Toryism towards a broader vision of class unity, national efficiency and coalitionism.

This development was stimulated in F.E. by seeing the Liberal Government between 1906 and 1910 trying to use its Commons majority

to force through what seemed to the Tories blatantly sectional legislation. It is the mark of his real open-mindedness – behind his front of
undiminished partisanship – that he quickly saw that the Tories had no
right to complain at the Government's attempting to reverse the
educational grievance of Nonconformists, if their own purpose in
opposing was simply to maintain that grievance. The debate had to be
lifted on to a higher level. The Tories must cease simply to fight for their
own corner, defending their own client Church or, on wider social
matters, their own client class. If they were to have a future, they must
distinguish themselves from the politics of sectional self-interest as
practised by the Liberal and Labour parties, by striking out boldly
towards a more generous, even-handed policy based on national
interdependence.

This was the way F.E.'s mind was moving during the long wrangles
over education in 1908. But if consensus was his distant aspiration, that
implied no relaxation of his opposition to the stubborn pretensions of
Nonconformity in the present. So long as the Government insisted on
trying to force the Church of England (and the Catholics and the Jews)
into a position of educational disadvantage, while rejecting the enlightened solution which he and other Conservatives held out, so long
must they be vigorously opposed, and F.E. pursued the various Bills to
their predestined graves with some of his most strident expressions of
partisan defiance. Equally was this so with the Licensing Bill, where the
Nonconformist conscience was seen at its most assertive, without here
the excuse of a grievance to be remedied, but openly on the offensive in
pursuit of its puritan – and party – prejudice.

The Bill, introduced by Asquith on 27 February, proposed to speed
up the reduction in the number of public houses initiated by the Act of
1904 by taking the discretion of suppressing licenses away from the local
magistrates and setting over them a three-man Licensing Commission
empowered to enforce a single uniform ratio of pubs to population
throughout the country; compensation would be paid to deprived
licence-holders up to a maximum of fourteen years, during which time it
was hoped to reduce the number of licences by 32,000, or about one-
third of the total. The Tory objections to this scheme were two: first,
that it was unjust, amounting – since the compensation was quite
unrealistic – to the confiscation of licensees' property; and second, that
it would not work anyway, since the mere reduction of drinking places
had never been shown to reduce drunkenness (though the latter was a
problematic argument for the authors of the 1904 Act, and involved
them in some tortuous reasoning when they wanted to show that the
Act was already achieving the object perfectly well). F.E., in his
speeches against the Bill – and he spoke forcefully at every stage, on

First, Second and Third Readings and repeatedly in Committee – made extensive use of the first argument, producing detailed figures to demonstrate that the proposed compensation would give no return at all to ordinary shareholders (many of whom, naturally, were widows and poor spinsters), and demanding to know on what ground investors in breweries were to be treated differently from investors in, say, railways. He was emotionally less interested, however, in the financial arrangements of the Bill than in the moralizing which accompanied it, and the political hypocrisy with which he thought it riddled. These favourite targets inspired some of his most elaborate flights of sarcasm since his maiden speech.

Drink was, of course, a sharply political question, and the Liberals made little secret of the fact that much of the force behind the Bill was simply the traditional desire to punish the Tory brewers. When the Solicitor-General could repeat in the House of Commons the old assertion that every tied house was a committee room for the Tory party, F.E. was fully justified in remarking that 'The motives of the moral reformers would appear to be not entirely unmixed.'[51] He went further and charged that the Government, while professing to reduce, on public grounds, the facilities for obtaining drink, in fact 'only interfere with those facilities when they are enjoyed by their political opponents. They leave them untouched in the clubs of their political supporters, and they sedulously protect the monopolies of their grocer friends' – (i.e. off-licences: grocers were as traditionally Liberal as publicans were Tory).[52]

F.E. developed this argument about clubs at great length in his Second Reading speech on 29 April, quoting figures to show that, as pubs were closed, clubs (largely unregulated so long as they were not mere drinking shops, but provided food or entertainment) sprang up to replace them. Not only their numbers but their memberships were soaring. He did not object to this, far from it; but he liked to taunt the Government that if they were serious about reducing drinking facilities they must deal equally with pubs *and* clubs – including Liberal clubs, from which he extracted a lot of ironic fun. He cleared himself at the outset by pointing out that the Conservative Working Men's clubs in Liverpool were all teetotal – a surprising rule on which Salvidge had prudently insisted, to disarm his opponents. But many Liberal clubs were not so strict.

I ask hon. gentlemen opposite, who hold strong moral views on this subject, what they think of the position of their colleagues who represent London constituencies. I do not hesitate to say that, sitting cheek by jowl with these moral reformers, are men who owe their seats in this House to the exertions of political clubs, which, although they are not drinking clubs, are places where drink is supplied with greater facilities than those under which it is supplied in public houses, and where it can be obtained at hours when public houses are closed, as well as on Sundays. These deserve careful study.[51]

He detailed particularly the Walthamstow Liberal and Radical Club, in Simon's constituency, and secondly Macnamara's North Camberwell Radical Club, in which the Sunday afternoon entertainment, he discovered, had recently included a musical comedy entitled *The Hypocrites*. He went on:

Hon. gentlemen opposite cannot afford to deal with the clubs. They dare not. Their political lives are not worth a moment's purchase if they do. The explanation is, that, in dealing with the English people, you are dealing with a strong, virile race. The reason why you cannot compel them to reduce their clubs, and why in this Bill you shrink from dealing with them, is that you know that the people in a democratic country will not allow you to do it, and, when you admit that in connection with the clubs, you have driven the last nail into the coffin of the present Bill.[51]

F.E. returned with powerful effect to the simple unpopularity of the Bill when he spoke on the Third Reading in November, following Simon, who had urged that it was not 'the Bill of an Oriental despot' but represented the will of the British people. This claim F.E. contrasted with the results of recent by-elections which, since the introduction of the Bill, had swung sharply against the Government, and satirically made a serious point out of the Liberals' explanation of them.

The Liberal press is obsessed by pictures of inebriated electors carried prone on shutters to vote against the Bill, while the party bands play 'Beer, glorious beer', as the election proceeds. That is the view of recent by-elections put forward with much spirit and humour by the democratic press. We have now a provision in the Bill which is designed to deal with the case of elections, and it is curious to note how it is found necessary to place restrictions on the very people who are said to desire this measure. The view is carried so far that, while the rulers of this country, the electors under a democratic system, pass to the booths with majestic tread to record their votes on the tremendous issues of peace or war, or to pronounce on the economic mysteries of free trade or protection, they are to be muzzled by their admirers opposite, lest they make drunken beasts of themselves on the way. That is the position in which we are left in the case of a Bill, which hon. gentlemen opposite say the people really want. *Vox populi, vox Dei* – but the voice speaks with a hiccough, unless the right hon. gentleman, the member for Spen Valley [the temperance reformer Sir Thomas Whittaker] takes appropriate precautions.[53]

This was the old Liberal attempt to have it both ways at once. Or as he had complained in a previous speech, 'The democratic party, when successful at the polls, praises the people as the supreme repositories of political wisdom. Their lips are full of mandates. When defeated, they point to the crapulous dupes of an odious trade.'[51] F.E. was always confident that popular Conservatism more closely corresponded to the true desires of the people than the Liberals' self-deluding idea of what they *ought* to want.

Reciting the list of the Government's by-election reverses (which included the defeat in North-West Manchester of Churchill, who had had to stand again on his promotion to the Cabinet, but had quickly found sanctuary in Dundee), F.E. skilfully set up another superb retort worthy of his maiden speech. In the face of these results, he asked, how could any member say that the people were in favour of the Bill?

There has been a most pathetic illustration quite recently, one which excites compassion. Many hon. gentlemen opposite are admirably fitted for peerages by aptitude, taste, generosity and party loyalty, and yet the King's birthday list was entirely un-adorned by their names. I would point out that if twenty stalwarts had been created Peers, able to develop their massive eloquence in another place without the restraint which the consciousness of constituents imposes, they might have leavened the whole gilded loaf. But they linger in this House, mere commoners, humble democrats, with no gleam of hope except a paltry baronetcy, simply because no English constituency is safe. Why is it?

The member for Paisley intervened, perfectly on cue, 'The hon. and learned gentleman does not say that applies to Scotland.' 'No; the Bill does not apply to Scotland, because the Government must preserve some cities of refuge for Cabinet Ministers who lose their seats in England.'[53]

This whole speech was another *tour de force* of tendentious and provocative banter which, according to the *Annual Register*, 'gave a good deal of offence' and was no doubt intended to.[54] Exception was certainly taken when F.E. suggested that the Government should, if it were consistent, seek to banish alcohol from the smoking rooms of the House, since one Liberal member had recently told a chapel audience that not a few Members of Parliament were in grave danger of falling victim to the evil. ('I, for one,' F.E. remarked, 'cannot sufficiently thank him for leaving them anonymous.') This was not, of course, seriously meant, but F.E.'s teasing should not disguise the fact that his opposition to the Licensing Bill, though humorously couched and not uninfluenced by personal predilection and professional indebtedness to the brewing interest, had nevertheless as serious a foundation in political philosophy as his opposition to the Education Bills. The improbability of restrictions being placed on drinking within the Palace of Westminster pointed up another injustice in this and similar Bills which F.E., as a democrat with a strong belief in the right of the free Englishman to judge of his own interest, objected. All temperance legislation he characterized as coercion by the 'cellared classes' of the 'uncellared'. Sunday closing only deprived the poor man who kept no liquor in his house, belonged to no club and could not afford to travel. It was no function of the State to compel sobriety, even if it were possible. 'The only sobriety that is worthy of a free and enlightened people', he told a dinner – admittedly a Licensed Victuallers' dinner – in April, 'is not that which springs from tyranny, but that which is the result of education, freedom and self-control.'[55] Or as he put it in a later essay, 'Better England free than England sober'.[56]

He rested his opposition finally on the democratic – though, for a Tory politician, dangerous – ground that the people did not want the Bill, and as with the 1906 Education Bill, he looked with perfect confidence and justification to the House of Lords to earn the nation's thanks by sinking it, looking forward to an election on the subject if the Government dared to challenge one. The Lords did reject the Bill, by 272 votes to 96, on 27 November. But again the Government conceded F.E.'s populist argument and did not try the electorate's verdict – yet.

But the popular policies on which the Cabinet was preparing for a showdown were beginning to take shape. During the 1908 session Asquith had succeeded the dying Campbell-Bannerman as Prime Minister; the consequent reshuffle had raised Lloyd George to the Exchequer and his Radical brother-in-arms, Churchill, to the Board of Trade. The stage was now set, and the principal players in their places, for a far-reaching programme of social reform which the Lords were challenged to obstruct if they dared. The first fruit of this new reforming urgency had already been foreshadowed the previous year, but it was appropriate that it matured only with the change in the premiership; the Old Age Pensions Bill was announced by Asquith in his last Budget,

but was introduced on 28 May by Lloyd George. This was such a
long-canvassed reform, however, that it excited little Tory opposition.
Had not Joe Chamberlain – crippled and speechless since a stroke in
1906, but still a powerful, brooding force in Unionist counsels – been
pressing for legislation on the subject for more than twenty years? The
Bill did not quite pass through the House of Commons on the nod –
indeed it had to be guillotined in the face of a good deal of technical
criticism – but only twenty-nine Tories (including Carson and Robert
Cecil) voted against its Second Reading on 16 June, while forty-two
(including Bonar Law and the newly elected Stanley Baldwin) actually
voted for it. The House of Lords grumbled about the danger of State
charity sapping the nation's moral fibre, but eventually allowed it
through.

F.E.'s attitude to the Bill is not certain, since he spoke in none of the
Commons debates, but it may be guessed at. As a Chamberlainite who
had sought Walton's votes in 1906 as a 'Progressive candidate', he
might have been expected to be one of those Tories who positively
championed pensions. In fact, he never came out specifically in favour
of them. He would, however, almost certainly have included them
among the benefits which the working class could expect to reap from
the passage of tariff reform, and this may be the explanation of his
unusual silence in 1908. That the Liberals could find the money to
introduce pensions without recourse to tariffs deprived Tory Protectionists of one of their favourite arguments. Though he might desire the
end, therefore, F.E. had a political reason for begrudging the means –
reason enough, certainly, to abstain from swelling the Government's
majority on the Second Reading. On the other hand, this consideration
did not inhibit Bonar Law, an equally ardent Tariff Reformer, and it
may be that F.E. was simply absent, whether for professional reasons or
on holiday, for in July he repaired his omission by being one of only
twelve Conservatives to vote for the Third Reading. The division lists
hint faintly at constituency pressure: for F.E. was the only one of
Liverpool's five Tory M.P.s who did not support the Bill on Second
Reading, (which suggests that even such a Diehard as Houston was
influenced by the popular character of Salvidge's organization). It may
perhaps have been politic for F.E. to get his vote in on Third Reading:
none of the others, having given one vote, bothered to vote a second
time.

If he was guardedly in favour of pensions, however, as being a
properly 'national' policy even when introduced by a Liberal Government, F.E. was strongly opposed to another piece of social, or rather
industrial, legislation which the Government brought forward at the
same time, which he regarded as indefensibly sectional. This was the

Coal Mines (Eight Hours) Bill, a measure to limit miners' hours long demanded by the Labour party on behalf of the union which contributed nearly half its parliamentary strength, and finally conceded by the Government after two years' prevarication in the face of strong objections from not only the coal owners but the rest of industry, orchestrated by the Coal Consumers' League. In the Second Reading debate on 6 July, F.E. effectively repeated these economic arguments, drew attention to the variety of conflicting grounds on which the Bill had been advocated – first to restrict output and raise prices, then to reduce unemployment, finally on social and humanitarian grounds – but most characteristically focused on the question of discrimination in favour of one particularly well-organized pressure group. (Herbert Samuel, Under-Secretary at the Home Office, had given the game away by declaring that if the limitation of hours were denied, there would be a coal strike.) F.E., in his capacity as the self-appointed representative of *un*organized labour, demanded to know the principle on which the Government could pretend to justify this transparent concession to the threat of force.

> The question which I venture to ask is, Why are my constituents, many of whom work 10, 12 or even 14 hours a day, to pay a greatly increased price for their coal? Will anyone inform the House why people in this position, with the slenderest possible margin left after making provision for the necessities of life, should pay a higher price for their coal in order to allow a class, who are admittedly more prosperous and more healthy than any other class of manual labourers, to have an eight hours working day?[57]

Pneumoconiosis had not then been identified, and mining was reckoned to be a relatively healthy occupation. F.E. was able to calculate that one miner in seventeen was over sixty-five, a figure which he used, not to clinch the case for pensions, but to disprove the miners' claim for special treatment. The Bill, however, passed easily through the House of Commons, and the Lords – though they managed to have winding-time excluded from the eight hours – accepted the force of Samuel's argument, and let it pass as they had the Trade Disputes Bill. While working up to a constitutional clash with the Government, they had no wish to pick a quarrel with Labour.

By the end of 1908 Lloyd George was planning his Budget for the following year, talking threateningly of robbing hen roosts to find nest eggs and, in a speech in the Sun Hall, Liverpool, hurling deliberately provocative abuse at the Lords, as if to tempt them to overreach themselves. F.E., as the local Tory champion, delivered a scornfully

defiant reply in the same hall three weeks later, admitting the
Chancellor's brilliant qualities but loftily deploring his 'paltry con-
ceptions' as unworthy of his office: he could not imagine Chatham or
Beaconsfield describing themselves as chicken thieves! Ranging over
the whole field of politics, he personalized every issue into an attack on
Lloyd George. Remembering his part in the Welsh campaign of civil
disobedience against the 1902 Education Act, he promised that
'Lancashire will yet teach him something in the way of revolt', if the
Government persisted in oppressing the Church of England; while he
ended by recalling to his fervently patriotic audience Lloyd George's
disloyalty to British interests during the Boer War.[58] Some of this was
rough stuff. But Lloyd George and Churchill were pulling no punches
on the Liberal side, and F.E. – though still a backbencher of only three
years' standing – was the Tory best equipped to answer them in kind. It
was thus that he forced his way to the top. Of the existing leadership
Balfour was too sophistical, Austen Chamberlain too pedestrian,
Lansdowne and Curzon too remote; Bonar Law was gaining a reputation for effective bluntness, but F.E. alone commanded the power of
rhetoric, combining force of argument with vivid extravagance of
phrase, fired by the sheer love of battle, to trade threats and insults
successfully with the enemy on platforms up and down the country. The
fact that his personal relations with Winston, and increasingly with
Lloyd George too, were excellent only added to the cheerful violence
with which he attacked them. The three of them, indeed, were the best
public speakers of the day just because they shared a common recognition that the public part of politics – as opposed to the serious business
of government – was a great game to be played hard and furiously, with
no ill-feeling, for the glory of winning and the applause of the crowd.
Increasingly F.E.'s obvious temperamental affinity with these rootless
Radical adventurers aroused distrust in staider Tory circles – a distrust
which he never fully overcame, even when he was able to demonstrate
that he was much more than just a self-advertising phrasemonger – but
his platform value to a party not overflowing with solid old-school talent
was too great for him to be neglected.

Not only in the country, but in the cockpit of the House of Commons,
F.E. was uniquely capable of rallying a still uncertain party with his
combative wit. He gave another superb exhibition of this on 22 February
1909 when, to a Liberal amendment to the Address calling for an
immediate Bill to curb the House of Lords, he moved a counter-
amendment demanding, on the contrary, an election to test which of the
two Houses had the nation's confidence, taunting the Government with
their reluctance to take their rejected Bills to the electorate, quoting
back at Ministers their own criticism of the Balfour Government for

clinging to office, and their brave talk of a blow against the Lords which they never seemed ready to deliver. One by one he set them up, in order to blow them down in a puff of ridicule. He quoted Asquith, at a National Liberal Club banquet, vowing to end the veto and *The Times*'s report that the audience had at these words stood up and waved their napkins. 'It was, perhaps, a somewhat sinister omen', he jeered, 'that at this early stage they should have inaugurated a desperate adventure under the white flag.' Then McKenna.

> No-one will fail to recollect that it is less than two years since the First Lord of the Admiralty, when he was at the Education Office, announced to the country in measured and resolute language that he was shortly going to the House of Lords with a sword. It was quickly discovered that his only qualifications for the Board of Education were an insubordinate report and a sword, and he was therefore drafted into a belligerent department.

Churchill's unaccountable desire for delay F.E. satirically attributed to his reluctance to tear himself from his important work of elevating the tone of public debate.

> We can ill spare a shining example in high place of that spirit of moral exaltation which many competent observers thought had forsaken English politics with the late Mr. Gladstone. I for one hope that I shall listen to many more of the courteous and conciliatory impromptu speeches, to the preparation of which the right hon. gentleman has devoted the best years of his life.

Burns, Haldane, Birrell, Lloyd George, each in turn was irreverently mocked, before F.E. seized for his crowning irony on some words used by the Lord Chancellor in trying to persuade the House of Lords not to reject the Licensing Bill. 'The Bill may be an unpopular measure,' Loreburn had admitted, 'so much the more reason why this House should pass it.'

> That is the new theory of Liberal democracy. And what did the Chancellor of the Exchequer say about this Bill, for the rejection of which you are asked to pick a quarrel with the Lords? He said, 'It is the greatest opportunity the Lords has had to rise to the dignity of its great profession as an independent institution, far removed from the passion and interest which sways the multitude.' That is modern democracy as understood in Wales. You appeal to the 'multitude' to punish the Lords for throwing out a Bill which the 'multitude' did not want.

The Opposition could not compel the Government to go to the country, he concluded scornfully, because that decision was in their own hands.

But we can at least invite them to drop the banality of this resolution and the Bill which is to follow it, until they have made up their minds to face the electorate on whose support they so arrogantly count. There is no-one in this House who does not know that, if the Government believed that they could have won a majority against the House of Lords when the Licensing Bill was thrown out, they would have appealed to the country. Consider the strength of a Government, returned on a plain issue placed before the democracy of England. If, instead of indulging in vague bombast, the Government had appealed to the country, and had been returned to power, they could have sent across the corridor a message saying, 'You threw out this Bill; we went to the Bar of the people of England, and we return, armed with their mandate, to curb and control your ancient pretensions.' The Government know well that no such consequences would have followed, and, therefore, they adopt the simpler course of indulging in declamation upon provincial platforms. I suggest to Ministers that they should drop the whole farce, until the performance is ready to commence. If they choose rather to conduct their crude and clumsy rehearsals in public, our opinion of their statesmanship may decline, but they are none the less entitled to the gratitude of the country, for a large contribution to the gaiety of nations.[59]

Even as the political temperature hotted up, however, not all of F.E.'s speeches consisted of this sort of knockabout Liberal-bashing. He was concerned also to get across the constructive side of his political faith, and nowhere did he do this more impressively than in a long and serious disquisition on tariff reform to a large working-class audience at Chatham (a Labour seat) on 24 March 1909. He set out to argue the case from scratch, endeavouring to demonstrate, first, that Britain suffered a higher rate of unemployment and consequent misery than any of the leading Protectionist nations; second, that the lack of stable employment was largely attributable to adherence to Free Trade; and third, that much of this evil could be alleviated by tariffs. But he began by spelling out with characteristic clarity the fundamentally nationalist assumptions that dictated his thinking, starting with an apparent paradox.

As between Free Trade and Protection, I am a Free Trader. I am a

Free Trader – presupposing these alternatives – not because I am convinced by the abstract reasonings of Cobden, which pretend to apply, as an economic generalisation, to any community in any stage of its development, but because I am an Englishman, and looking round at the world, and at the relative commercial developments of the nations today, I am satisfied that if foreign nations were misguided enough to accept the same doctrine, English manufacturers, and, consequently, English working men, would gain more by their unrestricted access to foreign markets than they would lose by foreign competition in English markets. But if I were a Russian or a Canadian, or a subject of the Mikado of Japan, then, as between Free Trade and Protection, I should be a Protectionist, because, in my judgement, each of these nations would gain less by their unrestricted access to foreign markets than they would lose by exposing their relatively immature industries to our highly developed competition in their home markets. No nation under modern conditions can become great which does not possess mature and developed industries, and I am unaware of a single case in history in which a nation has created a generous stream of natural industries under a system of free imports. We asserted, as you are aware, our own supremacy, under a protective system. It is hardly, therefore, necessary that I should admit that, if I were a native of India or an Irish politician, I should insist upon a policy of Protection* . . .

But it is, in fact, a waste of time to consider at length where we stand as between the alternatives of Free Trade and Protection. We are offered no such choice. We must choose between Protection and one-sided Free Imports. Confronted with such alternatives, I am conscious of no doubt whatever. If this indeed be the choice, I am a Protectionist.

Turning to his first proposition, F.E. quoted the conclusions reached by Charles Booth and Seebohm Rowntree from their studies of London and York, that no less than one-third of the population of the country lived on or under what Booth called 'the line of poverty'.

Mr. Booth shows that in London alone – the clearing-house of the world, as Free Traders proudly term it – 354,444 men, women,

---

* At this point F.E. revealed the openness of his mind even on such a divisive question as Irish Home Rule. 'Indeed the strongest argument in favour of Home Rule of which I am aware is that the present Government of Ireland imposes upon an unwilling community a fiscal system which Irishmen of all political views unite in condemning.' This was a strong argument indeed to concede publicly to his opponents.

and children live in chronic want on less than 18s. a week per family, while 938,293 persons subsist on less than 21s. a family.

Nearly 60 per cent of this poverty was due, according to Rowntree, to unemployment, irregular employment and ill-paid employment. To these figures F.E. added the rising emigration statistics (in 1900, 71,000; in 1907, 237,204), and the decline of agriculture (the rural population halved in fifty years) to establish the absolute failure of Free Trade to secure a decent living for the British worker, before passing to comparisons with the United States and Germany designed to demonstrate their relative success in maintaining regular employment despite substantial net immigration, a contrast which he underlined with damaging admissions by Lloyd George and Churchill.

Dealing next with the cause of British unemployment, he continued his trick of illustrating his argument by quotation from his opponents – first Asquith, who had admitted that foreign tariffs placed formidable obstacles in the way of British exports, and then, 'as we are always accused of economic heresy', John Stuart Mill, 'one of the founders of English political economy'. In his essay on 'International Commerce', Mill had anticipated the situation in which Britain now found herself.

> A country cannot be expected to renounce the power of taxing foreigners unless the foreigners will in return practise towards itself the same forbearance. The only mode in which a country can save itself from being a loser by the revenue duties imposed by other countries on its commodities is to impose corresponding revenue duties on theirs.

Experience had confirmed Mill's prescience.

> I am almost ashamed to point out so obvious a fact as that a country which enjoys (1) a protected home market, (2) free access to our market, (3) an equal opportunity with ourselves in the remaining markets of the world, tariff or non-tariff, will surpass us in the amount of employment which it provides for the working classes . . .
> We give to our rivals a free market of 43,000,000 persons in the United Kingdom to add to their own free market. Thus the United States possess an open market of 82,000,000 persons in the United States, plus an open market of 43,000,000 persons in Great Britain, making, altogether, 125,000,000. Similarly Germany possesses an open market of 60,000,000 persons in Germany, plus an open market of 43,000,000 persons in Great Britain. As against this, we possess only such residue of our open market of 43,000,000

persons as the unrestricted competition of foreign nations leaves unimpaired. Will anyone pretend that this circumstance is unrelated to the acuteness of poverty and unemployment among our artisans? It comes to this. We call ourselves Free Traders, but we have never secured Free Trade for ourselves; we have merely succeeded in enlarging the area within which our Protectionist competitors enjoy Free Trade.

F.E. next quoted a passage from a speech of the Liberal M.P. Russell Rea to an international Free Trade conference in London – 'a congress', as he called it, 'of amiable foreigners' from predominantly Protectionist countries, selflessly gathered 'to urge us on to greater commercial triumphs by a sustained adherence to the doctrines of Free Trade . . . We may pause to admire their cosmopolitan generosity'. Rea had told this conference how one British manufacturer after another had seen his export market closed by foreign tariffs, and protested that in this way, 'Protectionist Governments . . . not only determined the distribution of capital and the employment of labour in their own country, but in our country too.' Did they use this power, F.E. asked, in the interest of British working people? Of course not; they used it to protect their own. The result was that in good years British exports increased less rapidly than those of other countries, while in the bad years of the trade cycle – such as 1908 – British exports fell more steeply (11 per cent) than those of Germany (1 per cent), Belgium (4 per cent) or France (5 per cent).

This was the case against free imports. The case for tariff reform F.E. divided into three parts, dealing in turn with the home market, the foreign market, and the colonial market, with particular emphasis on the last. In the home market, he advocated a general 10 per cent duty on foreign manufactured goods, dismissing the Liberals' spurious objection that either such a duty *would* effectively exclude imports – in which case there would be no gain to the revenue to spend on social reform – or it would *not* – in which case where was the gain to British employment? – with the reply that of course it would do both in varying proportions. If, for the sake of argument, half of the £5 million worth of motor cars which Britain imported annually were excluded, he calculated that the Exchequer would gain by £250,000 and British wage-earners by at least £1 million. Proposing such a duty across the whole range of manufactured goods, F.E. looked forward confidently to taking the decision of the industrial population at the polls.

In foreign markets F.E. conceded – after some gibes at Churchill's inconsistency on the subject – that tariff retaliation might have little effect in opening up markets at present barred to British exports, but demanded, 'Does this conclusion not make it more than ever necessary

to secure those markets in which we still find goodwill and encouragement?' This brought him to the colonies – by which he really meant the
self-governing Dominions (for, as he had already pointed out, the fiscal
arrangements of the truly dependent colonies were already rigged by
Westminster to suit British interests). Quite rightly, Canada, Australia
and New Zealand were all firmly Protectionist, but they gave to British
goods a preference which the Government admitted – and F.E. further
demonstrated – had been of 'enormous advantage' to British trade.
They offered to increase that advantage, if Britain would in turn give
them privileged access to the British market: but this the Liberal
Government refused, forcing the Dominion Governments to agree
terms instead with other countries (F.E. cited the recent treaty between
Canada and France) which reduced almost to nothing the value of
Britain's advantage.

Why, F.E. asked, when practically every other country in the world
was anxious to enter into reciprocal relations with Canada, was the
British Government 'so mad and wicked' as to reject the Canadian offer
of further preference? The answer – 'Because we will not tax the food of
the poor' – he dismissed as 'inconsistent hypocrisy' on the lips of a
Government which had taxed food to the extent ot £20,000 a year since
coming into power. Exchange one of these taxes for Chamberlain's
proposed duty on foreign corn, F.E. suggested, and in two or three years
the Empire could supply half of Britain's cereal requirement, untaxed;
the duty on the other half he reckoned at one-eighth of a penny on a
four-pound loaf. Moreover the colonial proportion would continue to
rise and the foreign, dutiable, proportion to fall. No wonder the 'dear
food' cry was now being treated at by-elections with contempt.

After a strong denial that tariff reform must involve the taxation of
industrial raw materials, F.E. wound up with an apology to his audience
for having spoken for over an hour and a half, but laid part of the blame
on their 'generous enthusiasm'. He ended,

> I beg of you to think unceasingly of these problems. Discuss them
> with your fellow-workmen. Challenge argument and controversy
> with those who disagree, for truth can only gain by public disputa-
> tion. But remember, above all, that the time presses for decision. It
> is vital that the next election should reanimate the old bonds, and
> create fresh ones suitable to the ever-growing organism of the
> empire. So used, it will indeed 'lead on' to fortune; this chance
> omitted,

> > 'All the voyage of our life
> > Is bound in shallows and in miseries.'[60]

This speech has been worth treating at length because it well represents both F.E.'s considered and unvarying view of the tariff controversy, which remained the foundation of all his economic and social thinking up to the First World War, and the clarity and seriousness with which he was able to expound it, step by step, to a working-class audience without losing its attention. (Who would think of addressing a popular audience in such adult terms today?) The speech is a *tour de force* of responsible, educative democratic oratory, partisan not in the purely adversary sense, but a serious attempt to change minds by persuasion and force of reason. Not many of F.E.'s speeches were so bare of personalities and rhetorical exaggeration; on the other hand not many were without an impressive core of quite sophisticated argument. Edwardian audiences expected both elements from their favourite speakers. F.E. belonged perfectly to his time in being exceptionally well able to combine them.

As a result of such speeches, he had made an extraordinary reputation in just three years in the House of Commons. He had proved his ability. He was now ready to challenge for a place at the very top table of the Tory party just at the moment that the looming constitutional crisis broke at last with the presentation of Lloyd George's Budget for 1909.

———————— 9 ————————

The People's Budget and the
House of Lords Crisis,
1909–11

(i) The Budget and the First General Election
of 1910

In 1909 the constitutional crisis which had been threatening for the past
three years finally broke. Lloyd George's first Budget – the so-called
People's Budget, by far the most famous Budget in British political
history – introduced on 29 April and contested line by line by the
Conservatives in the House of Commons through the summer, was in
November rejected by the House of Lords, in deliberate defiance of the
convention that the Upper House, whatever it might do to other
legislation, did not interfere with Money Bills. With this action the
country was plunged into two years of stark and often bitter confrontation between the parties, unprecedented and unparalleled, which
included two closely fought General Elections and ended only with the
Conservatives' last-minute climb-down on the Parliament Bill in August
1911. These two dramatic years were the making of F.E. By his conspicuous service to the Unionist cause during the two campaigns he
forced his way on to the Front Bench and into the Shadow Cabinet. In
1909 he was still no more than a prominent backbencher, outspoken but
irresponsible, promising but still very junior. By 1911 he had – though
still under forty – broken through, by sheer ability and force of personality in the face of considerable antagonism, to become one of the
leading group within the party.

This is paradoxical, because he was out of step with his party
throughout. In the first place, he thought the rejection of the Budget

lunacy; but in the second, he held that having rejected it the peers must follow the logic of their own action and reject the Parliament Bill as well. Their actual course, of first setting up a confrontation and then backing away from it, he thought the worst of both worlds, a strategy both stupid and cowardly. His own policy recommendations in these years, though often surprising and sometimes contradictory in appearance, were always clearly argued and never unworthy of respect – informed by a consistent philosophy even when he appeared to be looking two ways at once.

The Budget was not framed with the intention of provoking the Lords to overreach themselves, though Lloyd Geoge was certainly happy to goad them along that path once they had set out on it. Rather its purpose was to circumvent the Lords, to recapture the initiative for a demoralized Government by means of a legislative strike in a form which it was imagined that they could not and would not dare to obstruct. But the fact that it did provoke the Tory party to the extremity of opposition was not quite accidental. Faced with a huge budgetary deficit, due on the one hand to the cost of old age pensions, which were proving more expensive than anticipated, and on the other to the Admiralty's demand for increased naval expenditure to match the German building of Dreadnoughts, Lloyd George characteristically resolved to overcome it in a specifically Liberal, indeed Radical, way, conjuring political inspiration for his party from a financial situation that would have thrown any other Chancellor on to the defensive. There was no argument between the parties on the necessity of raising an extra £16 million in revenue in the 1909 Budget: the Tories were no more willing to deny the overdue justice of pensions than the Liberals were ready to concede to Germany the command of the seas. But the Tories were affronted and enraged by what appeared to them the Chancellor's blatantly partisan concentration of his heavy new demands on one or two notoriously Conservative sections of the community.

It was not merely that he concentrated on wealth: that was to be expected, and the increased rate of income tax at the higher levels, the new supertax and the taxes on motor cars and petrol might by themselves have raised no more than ritual cries of pain. The aspect of the Budget which aroused serious resistance was its heavy weighting against two particular forms of wealth – the land and the drink trade. This was evident in a whole range of new duties on unearned increment from land values, on undeveloped land, on mineral values, and on benefits to landlords at the termination of a lease; and in a swingeing 50 per cent tax on the annual value of licensed premises and increased duties on spirits (and tobacco). To Lloyd George and his party, landowners and brewers were the undeserving rich, anti-social parasites whom it was fair and proper for a right-minded Government to penalize for the benefit of society at large. The Tories, on the other hand, could with some justice argue that there was no ground for discriminating between these forms of wealth-creating, employment-giving investment and others, except political prejudice – though of course no one pretended that the force with which this moral case was argued did not derive from the special relationship of both interests with the Tory party. But if the Conservatives rallied to the defence of their clients, they could say that it was only because they were being unfairly attacked by the Government.

There was a further way in which Lloyd George's proposals merged the defence of vested interests with a higher constitutional cause in Tory minds. By providing in the Budget for a comprehensive valuation of the land (as a preliminary to future taxation) and for a new liquor licensing system, Lloyd George was 'tacking' on to a Money Bill schemes which the Lords had specifically rejected when put up to them as ordinary legislation, in a clear attempt to bypass their veto. It was these clauses which brought the Lords and their power to amend the Budget into the argument from the beginning.

As early as 1 May, only two days after the presentation of the Budget, Lloyd George was reporting to his brother in Wales that F.E. had assured him that the Lords were 'not such fools' as to throw the Budget out. While this suggests that there was already speculation that they might, it also reflects F.E.'s clear view that the Budget was not an issue on which the Tories would be wise to pick a major fight. His own opposition was at first confined to a single speech in the House of Commons concentrating predictably upon the licensing proposals, which he condemned as 'merely a vindictive reflection of the Licensing Bill which was destroyed a year ago because it failed to commend itself to the electors of the country'. Of the wider implications of the Budget he said nothing; but then neither did his leaders say very much for some months. The anti-Budget agitation was built up by pressure groups in the country, and in particular by the great landowners, without much reference to Balfour and Lansdowne, who withheld their encouragement until they saw how deep the party's feeling ran. Even on 16 July Lansdowne could tell a party dinner that the Upper House would 'do its duty' (i.e. pass the Budget) though not 'without wincing'. The self-interested squeals of the Dukes, however, which provided such glorious ammunition for Lloyd George in his famous speeches at Limehouse and elsewhere, caused grave embarrassment to thoughtful Conservatives, and above all to the Tariff Reform League, which was most anxious to direct the rising tide of protest into more constructive channels. To the advocates of tariff reform, the Budget offered a threat and an opportunity. If Lloyd George could successfully – that is, without dire economic consequences – raise the revenue necessary for increased social and naval spending simultaneously by means of ordinary taxation, then one of the most powerful arguments for the necessity of tariffs would have been damagingly refuted. On the other hand, tariff reform was the only obvious alternative that the Tories could oppose to the Budget; their dislike of the Budget therefore served to rally to the cause many previously sceptical Free Traders, while the victory of tariff reform seemed suddenly to be temptingly attainable through the defeat of the Budget. Towards the end of the summer, therefore, the tariff reformers, with Joseph Chamberlain signalling his support from Highbury, took up the running from the landlords in pressing the case for rejection, on the ground that the decision between Free Trade and tariffs could not properly be taken except by the people at a General Election, and by the middle of September Balfour had pretty clearly been won over to this course.

F.E. had not. He was as appalled as anyone by the antics of the Dukes, but he did not think that was any reason to risk the cause of tariff reform by throwing it rashly into the balance against a Budget which the trend of by-elections revealed to be distinctly popular. In August Winterton wrote a long cautionary letter to Leo Maxse, editor of the right-wing *National Review* and one of the leading 'whole hog' tariff reformers. There can be no doubt that the friend whose counsel he was repeating was F.E.

A great friend of mine, who is also a rising and prominent member of the House of Commons (and who does not want me to mention his name to anyone in connection with the matter), has recently been on a tour of the principal towns in the Midlands and the North of England, with a view to discovering the feelings of the local party leaders on the question whether or not the House of Lords ought from our point of view to throw out or amend the Budget; my friend, who is, I may say, a convinced Tariff Reformer and has always been in the forward movement, tells me that he finds an almost unanimous consensus of opinion to this effect – 'Choose any battle ground rather than that of coronets and landowners against the Budget'. He further says that his informants are all of opinion that while Tariff Reform is the only possible alternative to put forward to the Budget, and while it ought to have been put forward long ago, and should now be discussed on every Conservative platform more fully than it has ever been before, yet unfortunately even the alternative of Tariff Reform will not render the Budget less popular in the eyes of the working man; indeed, they go further and say that while Tariff Reform is undoubtedly still very popular in the country, though not quite so popular as it was three months ago, the popularity of Tariff Reform itself will suffer, if we choose the Budget as the battle ground. Or, to put it in another way, that once again our cause will not get a fair hearing, or a fair run, if it is mixed up with the question of the Budget, just as it did not get a fair run at the last election, owing to Chinese Labour and Education.

They are therefore of opinion that in the present state of public opinion it is not advisable to force a dissolution; I am aware that this is rather a thunderbolt, but, privately I have from the beginning very much doubted whether we should be justified in forcing a dissolution on the question of the Budget. There is not the faintest doubt the Dukes and Walter Long have 'queered the pitch', and whatever we may say now, the fight in the minds of nine out of ten working men will be, as I say, to use the phrase quoted above, that of 'coronets and landowners against the Budget'. I am afraid that this is just one of those cases where, however strong one's case may be, it is not desirable to try and have a fight on the main issue, you can only get it by a fight on either some side issue, or on the general principle of taxing the foreigner against the taxation of people in these Islands.[1]

Why was F.E. so reluctant to avow these views to Maxse openly? (Even the fact that he was making his little tour was kept secret: he announced instead that he was cancelling all engagements on account of a sprained ankle sustained in a fall while riding.) Evidently he wanted to safeguard his reputation as a firebrand, while counselling moderation in private. Like Winterton, who was afraid of 'appearing rather a mugwump' in Maxse's eyes, and was at pains to remind him that 'no-one dislikes avoiding a fight more than I do', F.E. did not want to be thought faint-hearted. Though he privately agreed with Winterton that the Budget would have little practical effect if the Government could be removed from office at a tariff election in 1910, he was not willing to say so, but, seeing the party moving towards outright rejection in the late summer and carrying Balfour and Lansdowne with it, gave every outward appearance of following it.

His first major speech for three months, to a great Unionist rally near Bicester (also addressed by Tobin and Leslie Scott) on 12 August – a few days before Winterton's letter – betrayed his uncertainty by avoiding mentioning the Budget at all; he seized the opportunity of Lloyd George's Limehouse speech to attack the Chancellor instead.

Was a more degrading performance ever seen? The successor of Peel and Gladstone ranting on a platform with the antics of a pothouse demagogue! A more vulgar farrago of ignorance and misrepresentation was never produced by a Cabinet Minister.

Taking off into an extravagant farrago of his own, he compared Lloyd George and his friend Churchill to Danton and Robespierre. (Asquith was Mirabeau: a decade later he would have said Kerensky.) 'Both these Frenchmen made cheap and frothy speeches and Robespierre, in the true spirit of Mr. Churchill publicly proclaimed himself the High Priest of the new cult of the Supreme Being – meaning himself.'[2]

This was hollow stuff, the purest froth itself. But by the end of the month he was ready to mount, for the benefit of his own L.W.M.C.A. in Liverpool, a serious attack on the Budget itself, aimed at challenging its popularity among his working-class constituents, and particularly its right to be called the 'People's Budget'.

This name is meant to suggest that it will benefit the people, and particularly the poorest classes. If I thought so, I should support it. Much has been done for the working classes, but no-one is more profoundly convinced than I am that much more still cries aloud for remedy. I oppose the Budget because, for reasons which I am about to give, its mischievous consequences will fall mainly upon the working classes, because it will increase unemployment, penalize unduly your harmless relaxations, and aggravate generally the evils with which your class is now afflicted.

He began with his favourite subject, the liquor duties, which he condemned both for raising the price of the working man's 'harmless relaxations' and for piling additional burdens on the declining trade of an already unfairly overtaxed industry, which could only reduce further the employment which it provided. He pointed out that while penalizing whisky and beer, the Budget 'considerately spares the champagne and foreign liqueurs of the rich man'. The tobacco duty was similarly regressive in its incidence:

A 2/6 cigar pays only 5 per cent. A 1/- cigar 10 per cent, a 6d. cigar pays 16 per cent, and a 2d. cigar 36 per cent. Cigarettes pay 36 per cent, and the kind of tobacco most of you smoke 600 per cent.

'The working classes' – he now quoted Ben Tillett, the dockers' leader – 'are going to be fooled and robbed at the rate of 2d. in the shilling on tobacco, beer and spirits, which means 3s. 4d. in the pound.'

Secondly he looked at income tax and death duties. These surely were progressive? On the contrary, he demonstrated – with a wicked quotation from Asquith's Budget speech of 1906 – that their effect was to drive capital, and employment, to less highly taxed countries overseas.

Now, gentlemen, I am not on principle opposed to a super tax. I shall have to pay this, and I hope I shall do so cheerfully. But I am arguing one point, and one point only – are we, or are we not, taking all the new burdens upon capital together, piling them to such a height as must aggravate unemployment? And here let me remind you in passing that already before this Budget, but under this Government, more English capital was invested abroad in one year than in any single previous year in the whole history of British finance. And remember always you suffer from this – not the capitalist.

This was as close as F.E. came in this speech to spelling out the tariff alternative. Indeed, after some detailed examination of the effect of the higher death duties on some typical estates, he produced one of his wittiest phrases to encapsulate his charge against the Budget.

We see, therefore, the danger of loose Socialistic proposals, and how, like a boomerang, they strike, with injurious rebound, the nation which invokes their specious aid. So far we find no justification for the title the 'People's Budget', unless, indeed, it is so called just as a certain powder is called 'insect' powder not because it nourishes insects but because it destroys them.

Thirdly, he moved on to the land taxes and made a number of telling debating points against them, predicting (correctly) that their yield would be negligible while their machinery was 'oppressive' and their morality 'contemptible'. The Budget as a whole, he concluded, was vicious in principle. 'As a nation we are reduced to the diet of the dog who lived upon its own tail. We are to prey, it seems, upon our own capitalists.'

But F.E. was not quite finished. Despite his private opposition to the extreme course, he went on to offer a challenging defence of the Lords' perfect right to refer the Budget to the constituencies for decision, a defence which could only be read as encouragement to them to do so.

This course might be popular or it might be unpopular; it would certainly not be undemocratic. What democrat would complain if the Lords said: 'We will pass the Budget if the people want it, but we will take their decision from them, and not from a gang of interested place-hunters' . . .

If the Lords should insist that the people of England pronounce upon the Bill before it becomes law, they will have the most complete Constitutional justification before their action. The rule – imperfectly established and depending only upon resolutions of the Commons – that the Lords shall not interfere with finance has always been qualified by the condition that the Budget shall provide for the finance of the year, and for nothing else. Here again the Government has broken the golden rule that they should all tell the same lie. The Master of Elibank, an influential Minister [actually a Government Whip] has announced that the Budget is a social programme for twenty years . . . Another Minister says its object is to encourage long leasehold periods instead of short ones; still another that it will close public houses, and a third that it will prevent over-crowding in the slums. If these claims are true the Lords have admittedly the right to deal with it.[3]

Maybe, since Balfour and Lansdowne were by now all but decided to recommend rejection to the Lords, F.E. was simply, as a good barrister, making the best case that he could for his party's impending action, notwithstanding his own view of the strategy. At any rate, from this point on he threw himself fully into the opposition to the Budget, though always from a carefully 'democratic' point of view – democratic both in the sense that it was, contrary to Lloyd George's claim, most damaging to the democracy (i.e. the working class), and that it was democratic of the Lords to refer it to the people.

In the first two weeks of September when the House of Commons, sitting through the summer without a recess as the Government guillotined the Finance Bill clause by clause through the Tories' organized opposition, F.E. did his bit on the licensing clauses, moving amendments and exposing inconsistencies in his usual nagging way. Then he moved out to join the campaign in the country. First at Huddersfield, where his brother Harold had become the Tory candidate, he addressed a rowdy meeting at which a 45-minute speech on the lines of his Liverpool one took nearly two hours to deliver against organized Liberal interruption. The next day, 22 September, he was one of twenty M.P.s on the platform at Birmingham when Balfour made the major attack on the Budget which was generally reckoned to signal his decision that it should be rejected in the House of Lords, especially since Austen Chamberlain read out, to tremendous applause, a letter from his father urging rejection. F.E. and Bonar Law later addressed an enthusiastic overflow meeting.

Then on the 24th F.E. spoke in Manchester and on the 25th he was again in Liverpool, speaking to Conservative workers in the Belmont Hall, where he justified his opposition to the land taxes with a shamelessly local argument: where land value had increased owing to the enterprise of the community, rather than the landowner, as Lloyd George kept saying was the case, the value created should be taken not by the State but by the local community which had created it, the municipality. This was a marvellous way of opposing an aspect of the Budget to which he was clearly not opposed in principle, in such a way as to gain credit as a strong supporter of local interests.

After a few days, he was back on the stump, beginning with characteristic nerve in Limehouse, where he spoke in the same hall, the Edinburgh Castle, which Lloyd George had made famous a few weeks before, attacking the Government's whole record on unemployment and poverty, which they had neglected while they wasted their energy on unwanted partisan reforms, ('Instead of seeing that men got enough to eat, the Government spent the whole session in securing that they should have nothing to drink'), and moving the argument on to the tariff alternative. Free Trade had broken down: it could no longer pay the nation's bills except by destroying the very sources of national wealth. The Tories had the answer, based on the experience of tariffs in the United States and Europe – 'the great lesson upon which Bismarck taught his fellow-countrymen'.[4]

The next day he was at Bedford, the day after at Wolverhampton (where his friend Leo Amery was still the candidate), concentrating in both speeches on tariff reform, arguing that the rise of economic nationalism had made Free Trade a self-defeating ideal to which Britain clung at heavy industrial cost. Then to Sheffield, where he entertained a large meeting in his other style, mocking the eagerness of certain Welsh Liberals to obtain knighthoods and baronetcies while they zealously blackguarded the House of Lords.[5]

F.E. always sought out the part of the political battlefield where the fight was dirtiest; and towards the end of October, when Balfour became involved in an acrimonious dispute with the Lord Advocate, Alexander Ure, he came so strongly to his leader's aid that he practically made the quarrel his own. Ure had suggested that if the Tories were returned to power they would withdraw old age pensions, because their tariff policy would not bring in enough revenue to pay for them. Balfour denounced this as a 'frigid and calculated lie', intended to frighten the old people, by which Ure had dishonoured his office, his profession and even his Scottish ancestry, and denied it utterly. Ure, however, while insisting that he imputed no bad faith to Balfour, refused to withdraw his judgment that the Tories would not be able to afford to continue to pay pensions, and repeated the prediction up and down the country. F.E. now took up the running and, after accusing Ure in a speech at Manchester on 23 October of 'touching depths of impropriety which, fortunately, have been unknown hitherto in our public life', devoted fully half of a powerful Third Reading speech on the Finance Bill in the House of Commons to presenting a massive indictment, complete with cuttings from a wide range of local papers showing that Ure had continued zealously to foster apprehension among the old long after his leaders and all the Liberal press had accepted Balfour's word that pensions would be regarded by a future Tory Government as sacred.

> If I were one of those who believed that some germ of social right underlay the principles of this Budget, if I were a passionate supporter of the principles upon which it purports to be based, I would say more vehemently than I do, *non tali auxilio eget*. I will gladly translate. It means 'The Budget, if it be an honest Budget, needs no such weapons as those which the Lord Advocate has urged'. There is no-one who is sitting on this side of the House who will not gladly, and for all time, if we are allowed to, leave this squalid and discreditable subject – a subject which the *Westminster Gazette* has censured in stronger language than I have just used. If we ever recur to it, it will be because it has been made necessary by the repetition of a statement which is not true, and which is known to be untrue.[6]

With this speech F.E. was drawing attention to himself as a sort of loyal bodyguard, proving himself again the Tory most willing to take the gloves off, where necessary, and go for the opposition's throat.

Nor was he backward at finding other platforms from which to thrust his articulate views before the party and the public. He was increasingly discovering the pleasure of writing long letters, satirical or serious, to *The Times*. In one of the serious ones, published on 14 September, he wrote as a strong tariff reformer to deplore the attempt to deprive Lord Robert Cecil, the most prominent of the reduced band of Tory Free Traders, of his seat in Parliament – a letter which cunningly combines flattery of Balfour's cousin, concern for party unity and magnanimity, with unrelenting insistence on tariff reform as the party's principal platform in the coming fight.

Cecil, F.E. claimed, was 'far the most distinguished man on the Unionist backbenches today. He has shown in this Parliament a devotion, a penetrating grasp of detail and a shining courage which have been an inspiration to all who sit about him'. He had fought to keep the Tories a Free Trade party. 'This attempt has completely failed. The game is up. The party today is saturated with the principles of tariff reform.' On the other hand, the party face 'a fight *à outrance* – one in which quarter will be neither given nor sought; one in which ancient landmarks may well be submerged; one which will almost certainly prove the grave either of the Liberal Party or of the House of Lords'. Only 'poltroons' would recoil, he declared, from this necessary struggle, 'but men who are not poltroons may labour to consolidate our fighting strength'. Cecil was, in these circumstances, bound to accept tariffs rather than Socialism as represented in the Budget. 'To exclude the son of Lord Salisbury from the fighting line at a moment like the present is, in my humble judgement, an act of perverse folly.'[7] Cecil, rejected by his former seat, East St Marylebone, was shortly afterwards adopted by Blackburn, where F.E. was the only leading tariff reformer to speak for him. He failed, however, to win the seat.

In very different style, F.E. two months later treated readers of *The Times* to an elaborate satire at the expense of the Liberal M.P. for Faversham, one Dr Napier, who had demanded that the Liberal party should not take office again without a definite promise by the King to create as many peers as might be necessary to carry a Lords' Amendment Bill. With what F.E. described as 'inimitable humour', Dr Napier had proposed that '500 Liberals could easily be found who would esteem it an honour to sit in the House of Lords for a year for the special purpose in question'.

The conception of Mr. Asquith inviting 500 democratic volunteers for the forlorn hope of as many peerages recalls a well-known scene from the 'Bab Ballads'. We can imagine these gentry, who up to the present have seen nothing to vary the drab monotony of their democratic outlook but a precarious baronetcy, unanimously crying: 'It is our duty, and we will.' Probably Dr. Napier himself (to oblige his party) would pocket his feelings and stoop to conquer. And it may be noted that this could be very conveniently arranged, for Dr. Napier sits for a Kentish seat, which he must be well aware is from its record singularly unlikely to hesitate between the people's Budget and tariff reform.* The doctor continues: '. . . they would think it an honour afterwards, *if thought advisable*, to pass an Act to dispeer themselves'.

The 'if thought advisable' is distinctly happy. These devoted men are content, it would seem, not merely to enter the gilded cage, but to remain there like captive nightingales unless it is 'thought advisable' to dispeer themselves. Thought advisable by whom? it may be asked. By themselves? What guarantee, for

* Dr Napier did indeed lose his seat in January.

instance, have we that Lord Napier of Kent, while 'esteeming it an honour' to sit in the House of Lords upon the Budget, would not oppose it like Lord Joicey? What guarantee have we further that his lordship would 'think it advisable' to dispeer himself? Sir, the aspiring 500 must wait. They must win their peerages not by a political charge of the Light Brigade, but, like so many of their friends, by willing obedience to the party Whip, or by becoming Maecenases of the Liberal press. Thus they can enter the House of Lords unpledged, and cross its floor as quickly as Lord Joicey.[8]

By such means, by loyal rallying cries mingled with cheap party squibs, as well as by colourful speeches to audiences around the country who packed halls to hear the Tories' newest champion, F.E. forced himself to the front of the national campaign as it gathered momentum towards the end of the year. In November he took the cheeky step of publishing a volume of his speeches, from his first *coup de théâtre* in the House of Commons to his recent assault on the Budget in Liverpool, a thing unknown for an M.P. of only four years' standing. He excused his presumption with characteristic mock modesty.

I am well aware that to publish a volume of political speeches is to invite a stream of not unreasonable criticism. This is true, even when the speaker is a person of the highest political pretensions. It is of course much more true when he advances no such claim. My only reply to such criticism is that, after all, England is still a free country. The price of the book is clearly advertised to the world. The buyer knows pretty well what he may expect, and I may be allowed, as a lawyer, to fall back upon the maxim, *caveat emptor*.

My motive in publishing these speeches is, of course, a different matter from my justification. A general Election is approaching. My political opponents in the North of England not infrequently do me the honour of quoting my speeches. Quite recently I was accused of having described the working classes as fools; a view which – had I held it – I should have counted it imprudent to publish. On the whole it is an advantage, if one is to be quoted at all, that the quotations should be accurate. For this reason I am content to give critics the advantage (if anyone thinks it worth while to criticize the book at all) of finding in this volume much material for attack. Good or bad, the speeches make clear the views for which I have contended in the four stormy years which have passed since I entered Parliament, and I am content that my constituents should judge of me and them with the full material before them.[9]

F.E.'s confidence that his speeches had aroused sufficient interest to justify such a volume was astonishingly vindicated. The 'large first edition . . . necessarily published at a price which is at least adequate to their value' sold out within a few weeks. A second edition appeared in January, to which F.E. took the opportunity to add two more speeches and three of his letters to *The Times*.

On 30 November the die was cast: the House of Lords finally threw out the Finance Bill by 350 votes to 75. The Government immediately responded to the challenge in the only way it could and called an election for the middle of January. The pace of campaigning was redoubled. F.E. kicked off the very next day with a major speech in Shoreditch Town Hall, in which he nailed tariff reform firmly to the Tory mast as the positive alternative to 'the Budget of unemployment' which the Lords had courageously given the country the opportunity to reject. He attacked the Labour party for pretending to be concerned about unemployment while supporting a fiscal policy 'which finds work for Germans and Americans and aggravates our own evils'. He had always contended that the Labour party, whose whole *raison d'être* was the protection of the British worker, had no interest in Free Trade and should naturally be a Protectionist party. He ended with an emotional invocation of the crippled leader of the tariff crusade, identifying himself clearly as a claimant for his mantle.

> Only today I had a long conference with Mr. Chamberlain on the subject of his policy. I spent an hour with him discussing the future of tariff reform. With the same clearness with which he has always approached political questions Mr. Chamberlain discussed the final victory which we are about to achieve, and when I told him that I was coming down tonight to address a meeting at Shoreditch he gave me this message: 'Tell them that I count on the democracy of the East End to help me in the great struggle that is before us.' [Cheers][10]

How could the voters of Shoreditch deny such an appeal? But they did. One of the two divisions, which the Tories had won at a by-election in 1908, was regained by the Liberals in January, and the other was captured, in his first campaign, by Christopher Addison, both against the national swing.

During the rest of December F.E. concentrated his efforts on Lancashire and the Midlands, predicting everywhere a great victory for tariff reform, and not afraid to link that cause with the defence of the House of Lords. 'The people have now to decide', he told his constituents in Walton, 'whether they prefer the party of Tariff Reform and two Chambers to a party of Socialism with one Chamber.'[11] He continued to attack Lloyd George and Churchill as dangerous demagogues, though usually in humorous vein, as in a speech at Birmingham where he posed as prosecuting counsel.

What is the indictment in the *cause célèbre* of *R*. v. *George, Churchill and others?* In the list of previous convictions Mr. George was described as found guilty, by a Welsh jury of nonconformists, of obtaining office on the false pretence of being a Welsh Disestablisher, whereas in fact, so far from wishing to disestablish anyone or anything, his single office in political life was to establish himself. Mr. Churchill was described as an extreme Liberal, as extreme as anyone, particularly as extreme as Mr. George, yielding to no man, not even to Mr. Grayson, in his extremeness, and prepared to prove it by showing that even as a Tory he had been extreme.

This speech ended – inevitably in Birmingham – with another emotional tribute to Chamberlain, whose 'brave and wise counsel' still represented 'to many of us . . . the guiding note in politics'.

A stern and disciplined army is marching to break the Chinese rabble – the children of lies – with the message on their lips that what Birmingham did in 1906 England can do in 1910. [Cheers.] The object close to our hearts is to give Mr. Chamberlain, who gave all for us [Cheers], the crowning mercy of knowing that his labours, his sacrifices and his unbroken courage had freed from economic bondage the England that he loved so well, and the Empire in the cause of whose consolidation he staked, without a backward glance, his career, his health and his life. [Cheers][12]

Stern and disciplined the army may have been, but F.E. never attempted in this campaign to argue the tariff case as seriously as he had at Chatham in March. These were strictly electioneering speeches, a lively mix of chauvinism (Britain, he repeated everywhere, must cease to play Cinderella in the world's pantomime), debating points (John Stuart Mill had said it was admissible to retaliate against foreign tariffs, but that was not good enough for Winston Churchill), and barbed jokes, not always in the best of taste (the Government claimed to be free-fooders, but the only people to enjoy free food were the suffragettes!).[13]

In speeches at Alexandra Palace, Salford and Matlock F.E. also thumped the patriotic drum with strong attacks on the Liberal Government's inadequate defence spending, stressing the necessity of maintaining naval supremacy over Germany to protect British imports and British honour.* Then at the very end of the year he ventured into Wales to attack the Budget again in its author's own lair, at Llandudno on the afternoon of 29 December and in the evening at Caernarvon. Here he encountered vocal (and more than vocal) opposition. When he began to speak of tariff reform, 'the interruptions became continuous, and tramping of feet was added to the other noises, while a number of stones were hurled through the glass panel of the roof . . . Eventually Mr. Smith desisted from the attempt to continue his speech.'[14]

The M.P. for Anglesey, Ellis Jones Griffith saw no need to apologize for the protesters. F.E. had continually insulted and abused the Caernarvon Boroughs, their M.P., and the Welsh Members generally. 'There is a point . . . when the limits of human endurance are reached', and F.E. had 'no-one but himself to blame if Welsh audiences did not hear him gladly'.[15] F.E. for his part, when he got back on his own home ground the next day, refused to withdraw a word of his criticism of Lloyd George, who, he said, went about the country insulting the ancestors of Lord Rothschild, and should not be too sensitive about what was said of him. But he had to apologize in *The Times* to Principal Rhys of Jesus College, Cambridge, whom he had mistakenly accused of inciting the Caernarvon audience to shout him down. 'Unfortunately the name of Rhys, like other distinguished names, is somewhat common.'[16]

On 5 January F.E. spoke for Lord Robert Cecil in Blackburn – to no avail, as it turned out, but much to his credit, not only because of Cecil's unrepentant allegiance to Free Trade, but also because the more zealous of his own Protestant constituents could criticize him for truckling to 'Sacerdotalism'. Thereafter he remained in Liverpool until polling on 18 January. He had another tough fight on his hands in Walton; the *Liverpool Daily Post* made it plain that he was the sitting member they hoped above all to see defeated.

> The Conservative champion – Mr. F.E. Smith – is making for himself something of a national reputation with his laboured witticisms, his abuse of greater men than himself and his flippant treatment of grave issues. He is frequently hailed by his admirers as a future Cabinet Minister; but on this occasion, at any rate, Walton has more important considerations before it than the encouragement of personal ambition, and it is possible that the

---

* This was the line strongly taken by Maxse's fire-eating *National Review*, which monthly denounced Lloyd George and Churchill as traitors, and advocated the rejection of the Budget as the only means of getting rid of them before it was too late.

spoiled darling of a hard-up party may have a rude shock in store for him.[17]

F.E.'s task was made easier, however, by the convenient fact that his opponent of 1906, E.G. Jellicoe, aggrieved at having been dropped by Walton Liberals since his defeat that year, decided to stand again as an Independent Liberal, thus splitting the anti-Smith vote. According to Stanley Salvidge it was more than convenient, and it was F.E. himself, having become friendly with Jellicoe at the Bar over the intervening four years, who actually encouraged Jellicoe to stand.[18] Be that as it may, the Liberal assault on his seat was undoubtedly weakened by Jellicoe's candidature; though Jellicoe had not the resources or the support to fight a very visible campaign, his intervention was an embarrassment to the official Liberal, an energetic local self-made businessman and City Councillor named Francis Joseph.

F.E.'s election address survives among his papers. A double sheet of stiff card carrying on its front a solemn portrait of F.E. framed by lions and imperial flags, it is couched in the form of a letter 'to the Electors of Walton Division'.

Gentlemen,
    Four years ago, in a moment of unexampled disaster to the Conservative party, you sent me to Westminster to advocate the principles of Conservatism before a hostile House of Commons.
    After a long and fierce conflict against overwhelming odds, I submit myself again to your judgement . . .

His prospectus followed, under six headings, every item pugnaciously asserted.

1. *National Defence.*
    Great Britain is confronted by a greater crisis than has tested her patriotism since the Napoleonic Wars . . . The coincidence of aggression abroad with maudlin sentimentality at home has undermined the basis of our Imperial security . . . I advocate the building of two British Dreadnoughts to every German one.*

2. *Tariff Reform and Unemployment.*
    Unemployment is worse in Britain than in Germany . . . In order to redress the comparison I propose to treat and tax

* On polling day in Birkenhead he offered the direct local bribe that a Tory Government could mean another Dreadnought built at Laird's.

the foreigner upon the principles which he thinks good enough for us . . . I recommend commercial consideration for the countries which are building Dreadnoughts to protect us rather than for those which are building Dreadnoughts to destroy us. By taxing in moderation those articles of food which we or our colonies can produce; by placing upon the free list those (at present taxed) which we cannot, it is in our power to reduce the total burden of taxation upon articles of ordinary consumption, while stimulating the Colonial demand for our manufactured articles and fostering the dwindling agriculture of these islands.

3. *The House of Lords.*
The House of Lords requires reform, but only because it will be strengthened thereby. The mischievous and meddlesome incompetence of the last House of Commons is the best argument for a stronger Second Chamber . . . The Lords, and the Lords alone, have secured for the democracy the choice between the Budget and Tariff Reform. Let those who object to being consulted support my opponents.

4. *Education.*
I advocate a recognition of the absolute right of the parent to determine the form of religious education which shall be given to his children in the rate provided schools of the country. I assert this right equally on behalf of Anglicans, Nonconformists, Catholics and Jews, at all times and everywhere.

5. *The Land.*
I am in favour of the rating of land values under equitable conditions, where the value has been increased by communal expenditure. I am utterly opposed to the increment tax of the Budget, first, because it exposes land to burdens placed on no other form of ownership; and, secondly, because it is an impudent encroachment upon a fund which, if specially taxable at all, is and ought to be the exclusive property of the ratepayers of Liverpool.

I agree with the object underlying the cry 'Back to the land' . . . Peasant proprietorship, based upon Tariff Reform, will do much to restore our failing agriculture.

6. *Home Rule*.
    I will be no party to placing the Protestant Nonconformists
    of Ulster beneath the heels of a disloyal and Separatist
    majority.

There are two significant subtleties beneath the bombast of this
manifesto: F.E.'s admission that the House of Lords 'requires reform',
albeit only to strengthen it; and the no less pregnant admission that the
'disloyal and Separatist' elements in Ireland did actually constitute the
majority. Both concessions, pondered in cooler circumstances, would
lead to important modifications of F.E.'s fighting posture in the future.
It is worth noting also his emphasis on education, which played a large
part in his campaign, as he strove to appeal to his Catholic constituents
without antagonizing his Protestant patrons; his lack of generalized
criticism of the Budget (merely his ingenious mixture of principle and
parochial appeal in opposing the land clauses); and his surprising
insistence – unusual for an urban M.P. – on the importance of agriculture, a conviction on which he would find common ground with
Lloyd George later in the year. The rest, the linking together of naval
strength with tariffs, and tariffs with Empire, as the triple pillars of
national greatness, together with the maintenance of the Union, form a
familiar Tory vision. The letter ends with a characteristically combative
assertion of F.E.'s robust belief that a politician must make enemies as
well as friends.

I shall have an opportunity before the polling day of amplifying
these views. Here it is sufficient for me to say that I have never
attempted to conciliate my enemies. My appeal is not to them, but
to my friends. To them I say, 'Send me back in the hour of our
triumph to vote for (and, if need be, to fight for) a Budget which
will place upon the Statute Book the principles which Mr.
Chamberlain taught his countrymen.'
    I am, Gentlemen,
        your obedient servant,
            F.E. SMITH[19]

F.E. certainly made no attempt to conciliate the *Liverpool Daily Post*
but kept up a running battle of sneers and counter-sneers throughout
his campaign. The paper's best effort was an ironic headline greeting
his announcement that he was himself ready to do his bit for the
national defence, 'England Safe: Smith Joins the Territorials'.[20]
    The campaign was a rowdy one, and F.E. was followed everywhere
by hecklers. When the *Post* criticized the violence with which they were

ejected from his meetings by bouncers from Salvidge's brewery, F.E. replied that there was an organized attempt to prevent him speaking and interrupters came to his meetings at their own risk. The *Post* asserted hopefully that this policy was counterproductive and that enthusiasm for F.E.'s nightly meetings was falling off, persistently belittled him as 'a pathetic figure in politics' given to abusing others to bolster himself, but conceded that he had 'stamped his flippancy, his rough-and-ready aptitude and his want of scruple on the consciousness of the political community . . . It is undeniable that he is a personage in public opinion.'[21] The Tory organization was said to be pulling out all the stops to save F.E.'s seat. 'Alderman Salvidge is taking an active part in the work-a-day campaign, realizing, as he does, that the defeat of ("F.E.") would be the greatest disaster that could befall the Conservative Party in this part of the country.'[22] But on polling day they gave the Liberals only 'a bare possibility' of winning the seat.[23]

In the final days the eternal character of Liverpool politics came to the fore, making Ireland as ever the overriding issue. The literal subordination of other issues was made clear in a full page advertisement in the local papers on 17 January. Under the heading 'The Real Issues in Liverpool' came the slogan, in heavy black lettering,

NO HOME RULE FOR IRELAND

with a reminder that the threat was an urgent one. 'Mr. Redmond says: "Home Rule is certain if the Liberals come back to power".'

Below this came IMPERIAL DEFENCE, subdivided into INVINCIBLE NAVY ('Without British Supremacy our Food Supply is Endangered') and EFFICIENT ARMY ('To Defend the Dear Old Homeland and Preserve our Colonial Empire'), followed by equal billing for denominational education, tariff reform and the House of Lords. The advertisement tailed away into details about Church property, taxing the foreigner and extending old age pensions, before the electors were urged, 'You will not fail to demonstrate at this grave crisis that your patriotism is undiminished . . . Let your motto be "Empire and Liberty".' But it was Ireland which dominated the page.[24]

F.E. rose to this theme in his last big meeting, an all-ticket occasion for his own constituents in the Sun Hall. Dragging up again his favourite definition (by Gladstone in his Unionist days) of Home Rule as 'marching through rapine and bloodshed to the dismemberment of the Empire', he ended with a rousing exhortation.

It is for you tomorrow in your thousands, and in your hundreds of thousands, to send to Belfast now, in the throes and agony of the crisis, a message fierce and resolute from the working men of Liverpool: 'We will never betray you: we will not have Home Rule.'[25]

There was more of the same next day at a huge open air rally in front of the St George's Hall, at which a crowd of 15,000 was harangued on the imminence of the threat by five of the city's Tory candidates from the backs of taxicabs, a rally which amazingly passed off without disorder.

(ii) The 'Truce of God' and the Second General Election of 1910

If Home Rule rather than the Budget was the overriding issue with which the Unionists tried to scare the electors in 1910, the result was the worst that could have been imagined, though it was entirely predictable. The Tories had an enormous leeway to make up to recover from the landslide of 1906. There was in fact a very considerable swing in their favour. They pulled back more than a hundred of the seats they had lost four years before, enough to bring them back virtually to equality with the Liberals – 273 seats to 275. (In Liverpool F.E. was returned with a comfortably increased majority of 1,100, the Tories recaptured Abercromby and East Toxteth, but Scott failed narrowly to regain Exchange). But the overall consequence was to leave Labour with 40 and, more important, the Irish with 82 seats holding the balance in the House of Commons and the Government's majority dependent on the continued support of its allies. As in Gladstone's day, the Irish party were back in the box seat, with Redmond now in a position to crack the whip over Asquith. Though Ministers had barely mentioned Home Rule during the campaign, they were as a result of the voting obliged to resurrect the mouldering skeleton and put it back in the forefront of their programme as the price for getting the rest of it accepted. The result of the Tories' relative success was to put back on the immediate agenda the very item they had most strenuously fought to keep off it. With the Government's life henceforth dependent on parliamentary deals, while it threatened to pull down the most sacred pillars of the Tory temple, politics now entered a new and more bitter phase.

For some weeks the Cabinet, to whom the result was almost as unwelcome as to the Tories, dithered, unsure how to proceed, while the Tory backbench guerrillas consoled themselves with the hope that they might be able to defeat the Government on a well-chosen vote and force another election – which, with Home Rule this time well to the front, they would expect to win. F.E. wrote optimistically to Salvidge that they might yet see a Tory Government formed soon.[26] In the Commons he endeavoured heroically to deny that the Government had won the election. The issue had been joined on the House of Lords' rejection of the Budget.

> The event has made its answer, and the brutal truth emerges that that bladder of imposture, the People's Budget, has been pricked. [Cheers.] There is not a majority in the House for the Budget. [Cheers.] Is there an Irish member who will dare get up in the House and say 'My constituents want the Budget'? There is not one.

F.E. knew that the Irish were Protectionists to a man. They would only support the Budget as the trade-off for Home Rule. The majority of honest votes in the House would be against the Budget: therefore the House of Lords had been vindicated again (as it had also been on minor issues like Catholic rights in education). The Government, F.E. declared, had 'dug a pit and fallen into it themselves'. Their proper course was plain: drop the controversial parts of the Budget and get on with reforming the Poor Law and clearing up the slums – measures of national urgency which they knew the Lords would not reject.[27] The Liberal benches, Austen Chamberlain wrote to his wife, 'sat dumb and uncomfortable' under this indictment.[28]

The Government, however, made its bargain with the Irish, who promised to pass the Budget in return for the first steps towards abolishing the Lords' veto. Asquith announced the Cabinet's proposals towards the end of March. Immediately F.E. weighed in with another memorable attack on their partial approach to the problem – 'a brilliant speech', wrote Chamberlain, 'quite the best thing he has done'.[29] Instead of grasping the nettle of reforming the Upper House on a new and defensible basis, the Government proposed to do no more for the present than curtail its powers: in order to become law a Bill would in future merely have to pass the Commons three times in a single Parliament. Thus the Lords would be simply bypassed, and the way would be clear for a Home Rule Bill to be carried on to the Statute Book in three years. F.E. was wonderfully scornful of this arrangement.

> The plain proposition is that what the House of Commons says three times is right. The only historical analogy I can recall is that

of the Snark . . . They may be wrong once or twice, they may not be wrong a third time. Is it something like an incantation?

'The real object', he asserted, 'is not to give effect to the will of the people but to give effect to the will of the Radical caucus,' which was not the same thing. Under these resolutions the 1893 Home Rule Bill would have become law, though even Redmond admitted that its rejection by the Lords was endorsed by the people. Again he cited the Education Bills and the Licensing Bill which the public had not wanted. Lacking any sort of constitutional justification for their convenient formula, he mocked, 'the Government is driven to the position . . . that there is some special virtue in repetition, and that if they add obstinacy to error they are entitled to a degree of political success which is refused to error when it stands alone'. (Laughter and cheers.) The Liberals had an admitted grievance that there was rarely an effective Second Chamber when they were in power. 'The Government finds an evil', F.E. summed up, 'and they propose to duplicate it.' Their resolutions were not a serious reform at all, but a shabby device to give the Irish what they wanted.[30]

Once they had squared the Irish – but not before – the Government re-presented the 1909 Budget and carried it again through the Commons, then sent it back to the Lords, who this time preferred discretion to F.E.'s defiant logic and let it through, saving their powder for the constitutional battle to come. F.E. recognized the overriding importance of that battle. But at the same time, as a northern, urban, industrial M.P., he was acutely concerned that the Tory party should not identify itself exclusively with the coronet image. On the very day, symbolically, that the Budget passed the Lords, he made a well-publicized bid to persuade the party to take up the challenge of social reform, which he maintained that the Liberals, in entangling themselves in constitutional questions, were wilfully neglecting. Never, he declared, opening a discussion at the Waldorf Hotel attended by several M.P.s on the subject of 'Social Policy and the Next General Election', never had the field of social reform been so wide open to the Tories; though his prescriptions as to what they could do to fill it were exceedingly cautious.

The area of human suffering is prodigious, and the fraction that can be touched by legislation is relatively insignificant; but it is nonetheless the duty of any party to determine as far as possible what is the small fraction that can be treated by legislative methods, and we must resist the temptation of the cry when we come back to power – a temptation to which the Unionist Party has been prone – that what the country wants is a rest . . . Our duty as a party is

not to persuade the people that we can cure all the evils by which
the socially-diseased are afflicted, but to march some way forward
so that we may convince them that at least we recognize the
existence of the evils, and are animated by a sympathetic desire to
alleviate them.[31]

F.E.'s purpose was clearly to put himself at the head of a social reform
group within the party. He made few definite proposals for the moment
– the reform of the Poor Law, the establishment of peasant proprietors
on the land – but this meeting was the germ from which sprang two years
later the Unionist Social Reform Committee, with F.E. as chairman.

Meanwhile the constitutional struggle was building up inexorably,
with the House of Lords generally expected to throw out the Parliament
Bill when it came up to them, forcing Asquith to ask the King to create
enough new Liberal peers to get it through, when the situation was
suddenly thrown into confusion: Edward VII, worn out – as the Tories
claimed – by anxiety in the painful dilemma in which Asquith placed
him, succumbed unexpectedly to an attack of bronchitis and died. Just
at the moment when the monarch was being called upon to undertake
the most serious and delicate responsibility to keep the peace between
the warring parties, the Crown passed to the inexperienced and politically innocent George V. There was a general feeling that at such a
moment of grief and transition the new King could not be plunged
straight into the crisis that had so troubled his father. Garvin in the
Observer suggested, and the party leaders gratefully took up the idea of a
'Truce of God', a breathing space during which both Government and
Opposition should stand back from their entrenched positions and see if
they could not spare His Majesty by discovering some constitutional
settlement on which they could agree. The truce was regarded with the
greatest suspicion by the militants of both sides who feared any hint of
surrender of their vital principles; but F.E. chose this moment to
distance himself from the Tory Diehards with a long letter to *The Times*
couched in terms of almost exaggerated statesmanship.

In calling a Constitutional Conference, he declared, the Government
had acted with boldness and generosity which could not 'appeal in
vain to the chivalry of the Unionist party', which was under an obligation of both honour and patriotism not to make party capital of the offer.
There had not been 'since the crisis of Napoleon a moment when
Englishmen could less afford to dissipate their strength upon civil
controversies'. There were anxieties in India and Egypt. 'Nearer home',
he warned, 'a calculated policy challenges our naval supremacy, and in
doing so points the road to sacrifices which will test for many years the
moral character and the material resources of a united people.' With a

new Sovereign on the throne there was an added danger. 'Have we not all been drifting in the last few months into a tone and type of controversy which must weaken the monarchy?'

If the Conference were to achieve anything, there would have to be compromise, not on minor points but on some of the fundamental differences between the parties. Both must give ground. 'It is evident', he declared, stating the unvarying Tory position, 'that the Veto proposals of the Government must undergo profound modification before agreement is possible. Is it less obvious', he demanded of his colleagues, 'that the Unionist party ought to be prepared . . . for changes which have hitherto not been dreamed of in their political philosophy?' They must accept the principle that the House of Lords should give a Liberal Government as good a chance as a Tory Government of getting its legislation through Parliament. He therefore proposed two principles which should form the basis of a settlement: first, that the purpose of a second chamber was to ensure that great changes should not be carried through without being submitted to the electorate; second, that an efficient second chamber must exercise this function impartially. The Government's present proposals ignored the first, while the stereotyped Tory defence of the existing Upper House stolidly ignored the second. A conference could only succeed which accepted both.[32]

F.E. was absolutely right, and the Conference failed. F.E.'s abstract constitution-making was bedevilled by the single pressing issue at the forefront of all minds. The Liberals might in other circumstances have accepted the principle of referral to the electorate, but they were bound to the Irish and they knew that Home Rule would never be a winner in the English constituencies. The Tory leaders in the Conference – Balfour, Lansdowne, Austen Chamberlain and Lord Cawdor – did concede, in somewhat undefined form, the principle of a House of Lords so reformed as to give a Liberal Government with a Commons majority of fifty the power to force disputed measures through joint sessions. But they insisted on reserving 'constitutional questions' to be put to a referendum. In going even so far, Balfour and Lansdowne were going further than the most fervent of their supporters would stomach. 'In common with everyone else I have spoken to,' Willoughby de Broke wrote to Maxse, 'I have nothing but indignation and contempt for the letter that F.E. Smith wrote to *The Times* on Wednesday last, which has been received with rapture by *all* the Radical newspapers and no wonder, as it surrenders our whole position.'[33] It did not, of course. It was really beside the point, because the Conference broke down on his first principle which the Government could not concede. It dragged on, nevertheless, for five months, since each party was unwilling to incur the public odium of its failure.

During this period of suspended animation, from May to November, normal political controversy was largely stilled. But one old issue, long-debated but unresolved, suddenly arose with a new urgency in September: the question, first raised by the Chartists in the 1840s, of payment of Members of Parliament. Payment had been a minor item of Liberal policy for years: backbench motions had twice been carried through the Commons since 1906, though the Government had never got to the stage of framing legislation. On neither occasion did a single Conservative support the principle: F.E.'s very first vote in March 1906 had been against payment. But the rigidity of Tory opposition was broken in 1910 by a fresh consideration. A decision of the House of Lords the previous year had upheld the complaint of a Liberal railway-man against the compulsory political levy raised by the trade unions from their members for the benefit of the Labour Party. The effect, until the Osborne Judgment could be reversed, was to cripple Labour's finances and put an end to the sponsorship by the unions of their own M.P.s. Tories were unanimously delighted with the decision: it was a constitutional affront, of growing significance as Labour grew towards power, that trade union members of whatever political persuasion should be compelled, as a condition of membership, to subscribe to one particular political party. They were determined that a decision so clearly in accordance with natural justice should not be reversed in the special interest of that party. But this raised urgently the problem of preserving some means whereby the possibility of some working-class members continuing to be elected to Parliament could be safeguarded, if the trade union avenue were closed. The obvious answer, suddenly canvassed in formerly hostile sections of the Tory press, was the pay-ment of members by the State. The dilemma for those who had always opposed a salaried House of Commons and the creation of a class of professional politicians, was a sharp one; but it was characteristic that F.E., with his clear analytic mind and his commitment to the idea of working-class Conservatism, was the first prominent Tory to announce his change of view. In an impressively reasoned letter to *The Times* and other papers published on 27 September he confessed that he found one conclusion, much as he disliked it, inescapable.

It is that the payment of members is the only alternative to the intolerable system which the Osborne Judgement has ended. There are many and grave objections to the payment of members, but there is, on the other hand, this overwhelming merit, that it safeguards the independence of Parliament by making the repre-sentative the servant of the country, and not that of a caucus or a union . . .

I am myself a reluctant convert to these views, but I contemplate with grave anxiety the prospect of a blunt *non possumus* in Unionist circles to the claim that an unsubsidized working man shall have access to the House of Commons.[34]

Austen Chamberlain had in fact voiced just such a blunt *non possumus* the previous week; but his reaction to F.E.'s letter shows that much of the party leadership was coming round to the view which F.E. had now taken up. They were divided not so much on principle as on the tactical advisability of agreeing to payment. Even Chamberlain, the strongest opponent of payment, conceded that it would be 'infinitely preferable to the reversal of the Osborne Judgement'; still, he wrote to Bonar Law, he did not think that even for that reason they would be wise to advocate it, and was 'very sorry' to see F.E.'s letter.

Balfour, Austen admitted, though he disliked payment as much as anyone, thought that the Tories might have a better chance of upholding the Osborne Judgment if they were to offer to support payment as an alternative to its reversal; 'and this is the view expressed by yourself in your letter and by F.E. to my father on whom he called yesterday when I was unfortunately out'. F.E.'s argument, evidently based on inside information gained from Churchill, was that the Cabinet was divided between reversal and payment, but was nervous of taking on itself the unpopularity of M.P.s voting themselves public money. If the Tories were to share that unpopularity, the Cabinet would be encouraged to risk it and the Osborne Judgment would be safe. But Austen and his father took the opposite view, holding rather that if the Tories offered payment, the Cabinet would feel obliged to cap them with reversal, while if they stood firm, the Government would stop at payment.[35]

Whether F.E. was right it is impossible to say, for it was the Chamberlains' view which prevailed; what is certain is that their calculation was wrong. Balfour eventually refused to give his blessing to the payment of Members and the party remained officially opposed. Nevertheless the Government went ahead the following year and not only awarded M.P.s salaries of £400 a year but restored the trade unions' political levy as well – though with a provision inserted whereby dissidents could contract out. At this, F.E. perfectly consistently withdrew his support for payment, which had been an *alternative* to reversal, and voted with the rest of the party against it. He continued vehemently to denounce the tyranny of the political levy for the next seventeen years, until as a member of the Baldwin Government he was able to see the procedure reversed from 'contracting-out' to 'contracting-in'.

Meanwhile, in the spirit of his earlier letter to *The Times* on the 'Truce of God', F.E. was trying to promote a much wider measure of agreement between the party leaders than on the minor matter of the payment of Members. This was the extraordinary episode of Lloyd George's breathtaking proposal for a national coalition to take not only the House of Lords, but Ireland, education, national insurance, unemployment, agriculture and defence out of politics and treat them on a non-party basis of practical consensus. Bidding to release in fruitful cooperation the energies currently wasted in the party struggle (which he treated characteristically as mere rhetoric getting in the way of action) Lloyd George drew up a memorandum listing possible areas of agreement which he showed first, in September, to Churchill, then, in early October, to F.E. as the best intermediary to Balfour.

F.E. was enthusiastic and willingly set about converting his leaders to Lloyd George's bold initiative. In a series of long letters to Chamberlain, Balfour and Bonar Law he set out with great frankness the advantages, both national and party, which the scheme offered. First of all, as he put it to Chamberlain on 20 October, the party faced the probability of losing ground in another General Election held in the New Year. This would mean

> (a) defeat in the Lords, (b) National Defence neglected, (c) tariff reform beaten three times running and another futile Colonial Conference, (d) generally: a frittering away of national energy over constitutional crises injurious to the State and menacing to the Monarchy.

By contrast Lloyd George offered, as part of 'the big Settlement',

> (a) National Service and adequate Navy, (b) concessions to Colonies on basis of existing duties and *a real and fair enquiry* of which L.G. has said that he will gladly follow it if it recommends change.

In other words, tariff reform. The price was an Irish settlement on the basis of 'Home Rule All Round' – a fully fledged federal system with provincial assemblies for England, Wales and Scotland, as well as Ireland and an Imperial Parliament. This logical solution F.E. was prepared to accept, to be rid of what he airily called 'a dead quarrel for which neither the country nor the party cares a damn outside of Ulster and Liverpool'.

The question was, could Lloyd George deliver? On this point, F.E. was absurdly optimistic, since the plan required the Liberals to embrace at least two of the principles to which they were most passionately opposed – Protection and conscription. But F.E. was fully convinced of Lloyd George's 'honesty and sincerity. He had been taught much by office and is sick of being wagged by a little England tail'. In these circumstances the Tories had nothing to lose. 'If he proved in a year or two *difficile* or turbulent, where is he and where are we? He is done and has sold the pass. We should still be a united party with the exception of our Orangemen: and they can't stay out long.'[36]

As he put it to Bonar Law,

(a) If it succeeds it means a national party & well directed power for ten years
(b) If it fails L.G. & A are ruined; we are not & might have ten years on our own.

There was thus a strong streak of party self-interest in F.E.'s argument for coalition, even as he appealed in the same letter to the higher national interest.

Never in English history has there been a time when there was greater general weariness of the ordinary party ties & I believe that a cry of relief wd go up all over the country if both parties would *do things* instead of discussing constitutions.[37]

Both impulses were equally sincere on F.E.'s part, and his real desire to sink party differences in action should not be disparaged on account of his inability instantly to shake off partisan habits of thought. Lloyd George was the same: he and F.E. were both, while outwardly taking leading roles in the party battle, privately feeling their way at this time towards a similar view of the role of the State in promoting national unity in the cause of national efficiency in international competition, industrial and military. Their attempt to come together in 1910 was premature; but it bore fruit in the Coalition of 1918–22.

There was undeniably another element in F.E.'s enthusiasm for Lloyd George's plan: it appealed to his love of adventure, ambition, mutual flattery and intrigue. It cannot but have been exciting to a man as ambitious as F.E. but still junior in his party, seeing no early prospect of office while his best friend was already in the Cabinet, to be sought out by the Chancellor of the Exchequer with such a prospect of short-circuiting the normal machinery and charged with a principal role in promoting a realignment which might change the face of British politics for a generation. Quite apart from the fact that the proposal tallied with his own developing conception of political priorities it was, simply on a personal level, irresistible. It is not altogether surprising that he overlooked some of the practical – not to say moral – difficulties raised by Lloyd George's offer and exaggerated to his senior colleagues the prize that was in their grasp.

Chamberlain and Bonar Law were more than half persuaded that Home Rule All Round might provide the solution to the Irish problem: 'provincial councils' had once been Joseph Chamberlain's formula, which naturally recommended it to Austen. But Austen could not see that such a settlement might serve to break the deadlock over the House of Lords. He insisted that the constitutional question must be settled first. F.E. argued powerfully, first to Chamberlain, then to Balfour, that on the contrary only an Irish settlement could dissolve the difficulties over the Lords. 'It is evident', he wrote to Balfour, 'that the issues arising at the Conference and upon which it is stated the Conference almost broke down, present themselves in a wholly different perspective if a Coalition be arranged,' incorporating Federal Home Rule. 'If a Coalition be impossible we are probably right in insisting upon a referendum in case of constitutional changes & other matters but if a coalition be otherwise possible such insistence would appear to be unnecessary.' The sole reason, he understood, for the Unionist members of the Conference wanting to reserve constitutional questions was the fear of Home Rule in its unacceptable, Gladstonian form. 'But if the Coalition agrees that the Federal principle is not inadmissible this stipulation becomes superfluous.'[38] It was worth a lot (this was to Chamberlain) to avoid impaling themselves, for the sake of Ireland, on the commitment to refer every disputed issue in the future to the people. 'Personally I hate the Referendum. We should win matters which don't much matter like the Licensing Question or Education on its sectarian side. But if the Referendum once comes it will spread and in the great predatory appeals of the future the Tory Party would always be beaten. Imagine a Referendum upon the last Budget!'[39]

Here F.E. revealingly betrays his vaunted Tory Democratic faith in the supreme wisdom of the people – which a couple of months later he would again be proclaiming loudly from election platforms. Democracy had hitherto been a useful stick with which to beat the Liberals; but in this passage F.E. seems to foresee with the apprehension of a crustier breed of Tory the rise with the Labour party of a more materialistic, acquisitive, egalitarian and redistributive brand of politics which with frequent recourse to referenda might sweep all property before it. It is only a flash, but it foreshadows the transformation of the self-consciously progressive pre-war F.E. into the anti-Socialist Diehard of the post-war years.

Was F.E. also, in his enthusiasm for Lloyd George's plan, betraying the cause of Ulster which had been, and was to be still more in the next few years, central to his political faith? The answer must be yes, that he *was* prepared to trade Ulster for what he saw as a greater gain for the United Kingdom – and the Tory party – as a whole. As he argued to Balfour, the Lloyd George plan (which he believed Asquith, Grey, Haldane, Birrell and Crewe, as well as Churchill, had also accepted) safeguarded so many of the causes which the Tories held most vital that the narrow interest of Ulster could not be allowed to obstruct it.

> I am myself satisfied that the whole party with the exception of Ulster & possibly (but I think not) Liverpool would welcome a settlement of the question on the lines which the Conference has reached as soon as it became known that a larger agreement had been reached. Ulster would undoubtedly say she had been betrayed and I should have difficulties in Liverpool; on the other hand the Labour party & forty extreme radicals would cry out that they were betrayed. The opposition would apparently be jointly led by Keir Hardie and Hugh Cecil, neutralising one another . . .
>
> We should lose for a time Carson Campbell & possibly Long. I should regret it profoundly but I simply cannot believe that such considerations can count in the face of a proposal which in my judgment will give twenty years power & influence to the Tory party under another name. Graecia victorem captivum duxit. WSC and LG cannot go back without ruin. Remaining they will be more influenced by the Tory party than it by them just as Chamberlain was . . .
>
> Today there is a widespread weariness & distrust of party combined with general apprehension of the national dangers into which party extremists are leading us. Moreover the position would develop normally and naturally. The Conference settlement would arouse (conceding as it does Finance to joint session) a howl of rage among Labour & Radicals. Coinciding with a plain refusal to reverse the Osborne Judgement (which wd be forthcoming and which would go far to justify the coalition if it stood alone) the Government would without any concerted arrangements be defeated within a month. A fortnight crisis caused by the inability of either A or yourself to form a Government would prepare public opinion for joint action. I have some knowledge of the party and will pledge my judgment that the whole party will support with enthusiasm the attempt 'to save Asquith from Keir Hardie'. And I further believe that in three years Ulster members will be supporting the Coalition.[40]

Of course F.E., like so many others since, was carried away by the intoxicating vision he had conjured up. This was the purest fantasy.

The party in the country already viewed the Constitutional Conference with the greatest suspicion and would have been incensed if it could have known what its leaders were seriously discussing at Westminster. Balfour, with the responsibility for keeping the party united, was from the beginning solidly sceptical of the possibility or the desirability of coalition, and found no attraction in the proposed federal solution for Ireland. F.E.'s idea that agreement in the Conference was near was equally optimistic. Balfour, Lansdowne, Chamberlain and Cawdor were never prepared to give up the Lords' veto; the Liberals would never concede it. In November the Conference broke up for the last time and the parties took up fighting positions again for a second General Election in December.

'How strange it is', F.E. had written, 'to think that in eight weeks or twelve we may all be at one another's throats again.'[39] He went into the election with a sinking feeling, frustrated by the dashing of the dream he had thought attainable and fearing a worse defeat than in January. The party was in the greatest possible disarray. Much more clearly than in January, the central issue was the House of Lords. But the Unionists had wasted the months of truce and had only very belatedly in November come up with the vaguest proposals to resolve disputed questions – joint sittings, of undefined composition, with the referendum as a last resort: no settled alternative to the Government's Bill at all. Apart from increased naval spending to meet the German challenge – a solid patriotic plank on which they could safely place additional weight – the one positive item in their programme in January had been tariff reform; but this now proved divisive. Half the party – and particularly the party managers, like Salvidge in Liverpool – who had previously gone along with the policy, now feared that it was an electoral handicap which could be decisive in what was clearly going to be another tight election. Pressure built up to extend the referendum principle to tariffs: Balfour should promise that, if elected, the Tories would not impose food taxes without specifically consulting the electorate. It was hoped, naïvely, that Asquith could thus be cornered into having to promise a similar referendum on Home Rule. When Balfour adopted this course, however, he only exposed himself to furious accusations of weakness and betrayal from Austen Chamberlain and the 'whole-hog' tariff reformers, and the party to Liberal ridicule as they tried to explain how a referendum on such a question might actually work. In this embarrassing situation they fell back more heavily than ever on the easy negative cry of opposition to Home Rule, which, with Redmond bragging confidently of the Government's dependence upon Irish votes and the Parliament Bill only needing to be carried to clip the Lords' veto, was now indeed nearer than ever before.

If F.E. was despondent, however, no one could have told it from his speeches. Even in a losing battle he could still win more medals for a defiant fight, so he threw himself back into the fray with rhetoric more extravagant than ever. He opened his campaign several days before Asquith had even announced the dissolution with a rousing call to arms delivered at Brackley – just down the road from Charlton – on 12 November. It is a speech of magnificent emptiness, whose hollow emotionalism and patriotic posturing, with echoes of Henry V at Agincourt, splendidly demonstrates the cheer-leading role which F.E. eagerly took upon himself in the Tories' hour of need.

> The Unionist Party is called upon for a supreme effort, the greatest perhaps in a long history of resolute and brilliant warfare. We should pay no heed to those who come with counsels of gloom. Never was there a time with less excuse for despair. Never was the spirit of the Conservative Party higher.
>
> Never did a great army attack an enemy embarrassed by such open humiliation. At present Mr. Asquith is inarticulate. No Cabinet decision on any point is possible. He can take no decision until the uncrowned King of political mendicants, his pockets bulging with American gold, appears from the sea like Aphrodite, but less lovely, to give insulting directions to the successor of Chatham. [Laughter.]
>
> Is there a child so simple as to be deceived by the brag and bray of the cocoa press? What were these men saying a year ago? They boasted that they were coming back 'on the People's Budget as in 1906'. Fighting against fierce odds, and never counting them, the Unionist Party attacked Liberals, Irish and Socialists alike. With what result? The majority of 1906 melted away like snow before the sun, or like the Tonypandy rioters when their 'best friends' at last sent the soldiers. [Laughter.] Today the Liberals, who a year ago were supreme in the House, are no more than equal with the Unionists. If that was achieved in January, before the Budget was nailed to the counter, what is not possible in December?
>
> We must have no such word as failure in our vocabulary, and there must be no room in our ranks for those who fear or doubt. Only one condition is necessary to success in the coming Unionist Agincourt. It is unity, first, last and all the time. The man who today criticizes his leaders, or refuses to subordinate minor differences, is guilty of treason to the party, the country and the Empire. [Loud cheers.] Not since the days of Pitt has the Tory Party in a grave crisis contended for a cause so high. We contend for the Navy against a party which depends for life upon the

faith-healers of politics [laughter], for the Constitution against those whose avowed ideal is a single Chamber, and for the Empire against those whose tariff education ends in the *cul-de-sac* of cocoa. [Laughter.]

If there were no issue but the Navy, that quarrel would nerve and brace us with the spirit which saved England and inspired Europe in the Napoleonic wars. What is the position? A great nation, virile, organized, resolute, is challenging with stupendous exertions British supremacy of the seas. Maritime strength, to them a luxury, is life to Britain. [Cheers.] Never was it more necessary for every loyal Englishman to recall Chatham's unforgettable cry, 'Be one people: I set you the example'. [Cheers.] Is this a moment when the Prime Minister of England should depend upon Mr. Keir Hardie? Is this the time for plunging into bitter internal dissensions, for perpetuating divisions which the finger of history may well brand in the blood of the Empire? Sorrowing greatly that such issues at such a time should sap the strength of the body politic, should weaken England on the great stage of Europe, the Unionist Party will nevertheless march on with grim determination to fight the concluding stages of the long drawn-out battle which began in January.

Every constituency must be contested. North, south, east and west, in constituencies where victory is certain, but far more in those where resolution can wrest it even from despair, must the banner be carried in unfaltering hands. Well may Mr. Balfour say, 'He today who fights this fight with me shall be my brother'. Let us fight as a band of brothers. Then we will have the happiness once again of saving the Empire by safeguarding the national defences, by meeting the next Colonial Conference with a message of hope, and by saving an ancient constitution from destruction. The night is long and dark, but the dawn will come at last. It is a dawn of splendid promise, of saner national ideals, and of a patriotism more pure and more sustained.[41]

Two days later F.E. was able to give a similar pep talk to a large gathering of Tory M.P.s and peers at a dinner in honour of Bonar Law, who had boldly given up his safe seat at Dulwich to carry the tariff fight into the heart of Free Trade Manchester; he appeared on a platform with his leader at Nottingham on 17 November, and the next day launched the Conservative campaign in London as the principal speaker (billed above Carson, the Duke of Marlborough and six other M.P.s) at a major rally at Battersea Town Hall. After another speech in Islington, he devoted the remainder of his energy to Lancashire, his own home ground and the area universally expected to decide the result; he spoke all over the county – at Bury, Burnley, Birkdale and over the Mersey in Birkenhead, as well as in Walton and other parts of Liverpool and in Warrington, where his brother Harold, defeated in Huddersfield in January, had found a more pregnable Liberal citadel to besiege. It was an exhausting programme, which F.E. carried out with headline-grabbing *élan*. Sandars wrote that, next to Balfour, he had been the 'leading figure' on Tory platforms. 'His speeches, though violent at times, have been brilliant, forceful and popular. In Liverpool he is what Joe used to be in Birmingham.'[42]

He made little further play with the Kaiser, but concentrated on the nearer threat of Redmond and the iniquity of his American fund-raising, which he professed to regard as the hostile intervention in British domestic politics of a foreign power – as though the United States Government was responsible for the donations of the Boston Irish. He revived Liverpool's 'dead quarrel' with a relish which recalled his father's flights of the 1880s, meeting Redmond's claim that he 'stood where Parnell stood' with the blunt response that the Tories stood 'with the men who broke Parnell'.[43] Repeatedly he portrayed Asquith's Government as 'a kept Government and a kept Prime Minister',[44] and delighted to underline the naked expediency of the Government's commitment to Ireland, pointing out that they had still not included Home Rule in their manifesto and would postpone it indefinitely if they were not dependent on Irish votes – though this was a dangerous argument, since its corollary was that the Union could be secured as well by giving the Liberals a clear majority again as by electing the Tories!

The historic safeguard against such horse-trading in the Commons was the House of Lords, in whose defence F.E. now took up the Tory peers' referendum proposal with an outward conviction which totally belied the private dislike of the device he had expressed to Chamberlain. Earnestly he exploited the democratic argument for referenda for all it was worth, and a good deal more, drawing everywhere the contrast between the Liberals' veto Bill, whose effect would be to entrench the power of the party Whips in the House of Commons, denying the people any voice between elections, and the Tories' trust in the people, demonstrated by their readiness to let the Lords refer contentious issues to their vote. Though he did concede, as he had insisted when advocating compromise in June, that the Lords must in future apply this reference to the electorate even-handedly, he offered no suggestions as to how this new impartial Upper House was to be composed, but preferred simply to attack the 'tyranny' of the Commons. 'We will repudiate and betray the fundamental principles of democracy', he declared at Burnley on

26 November, 'if we arm the House of Commons with unlimited and uncontrollable powers.'[45] 'The passing of the veto Bill', he claimed even more implausibly at Openshaw on 10 December, 'would mean the surrender by the democracy for all time of the rights won by generations of political struggle to be the supreme judges of measures to be placed on the Statute Book.'[46] This was spurious nonsense. F.E. might claim that it would be a desirable refinement of British democracy to make it plebiscitary instead of representative, but he could not credibly pretend that it always had been so. It was a very tenuous extrapolation from the defeat of Gladstone's Governments after the rejection of his 1886 and 1893 Home Rule Bills to assert that consultation was an established procedure of the Constitution. With such unhistorical hyperbole F.E. overreached himself.

But the referendum was the Tories' one potential vote-winner at this election, and F.E. should perhaps be allowed some poetic licence, or at the least given credit for the forensic ingenuity with which he attempted to legitimate it on his party's behalf. He even accepted with apparent enthusiasm its application to tariff reform. At the outset of the campaign he declared himself still firmly in favour of the full tariff programme[43] – that is against the dropping of food taxes – but, like Bonar Law in Manchester (and unlike Austen Chamberlain, who would countenance no dilution of his father's pure doctrine), he appreciated only too well the handicap represented by food taxes in the northern towns, and he grasped gratefully, for the sake of maximizing the Tory vote, the opportunity to postpone that awkward issue by subsuming it in the broad theme of 'democracy' offered by the referendum, even though there was in the case of tariff reform no likelihood of deadlock between the two Houses. He argued that he had never believed that the Tories should attempt to introduce tariffs without an overwhelming national mandate;[47] and that he knew they were unlikely to get at this election anyway. Having accepted this qualification, however, he felt free to continue to assert in every speech that the introduction of a tariff Budget (whose principles would then be submitted to the electorate), would be 'the first constructive work' of a Unionist Government – work in which, moreover, he daringly told his constituents, he himself hoped to play a humble part.[48] At the same time he insisted that the condition of Balfour's promised referendum was that the Government should similarly offer a referendum on Home Rule;[48] and in a controversial speech at Leighton Buzzard at the very end of the campaign, when most of the results were in, he followed Chamberlain in limiting the application of Balfour's promise to the election in hand, leaving the party uncommitted in the future[49] – unless, he explained in another letter to *The Times*, the referendum were to be built into the Constitution as a permanent feature.[50]

F.E. did come out of this election with fresh medals. Not only was he conspicuous, but the Tories did conspicuously better where he had spoken. Overall, the results almost duplicated those of January: the Conservatives and Liberals now tied exactly with 272 seats each, while Labour crept up to 42, the Irish to 84. The Government was confirmed in office with its clear Commons majority for the Parliament Bill intact. But within that picture there were marked regional differences which showed that while the Liberals had gained seats in London and southern England, the Tories had made gains in Lancashire/Cheshire (and also in Devon). In Liverpool, Scott swept the last Liberal out of the Exchange division; Harold Smith captured Warrington, Max Aitken won Ashton-under-Lyne, and Henry Vivian was chased out of Birkenhead, while in Wigan, St Helens, South Salford, Altrincham, Darwen and Newton Liberal and Labour members fell before a strong Unionist tide which was just not strong enough to reward Bonar Law's gamble in North West Manchester. (Burnley went the other way, but that may be countered on F.E.'s personal score sheet by the Tories' only gains in London, which were at Islington, where he had spoken, and neighbouring St Pancras.) *The Times* gave credit where it was due. 'Mr. F.E. Smith, a son of whom Liverpool is justly proud, is to be congratulated upon Unionist successes in a district where he has displayed great activity.' And when the tumult and the shouting had died, the party gave a dinner in honour of F.E.'s exceptional services, at which Balfour paid handsome tribute.

> I think I made a great many speeches, but my number sinks into insignificance in comparison with the brilliant efforts of my learned friend. He was here, he was there, he was everywhere – always courageous, always witty, always a master of his audience, always the most effective of political controversialists. He is surely the most worthy representative of the victorious Unionist politicians.[51]

(iii) The Fight against the Parliament Bill; 'Balfour Must Go'

F.E.'s confidence in his own powers was never lacking. But he had been hitherto a very junior backbencher. Now his acknowledged achievements in the election gave him a strong claim to be taken into the Unionist leadership, and he suffered from no false modesty that might hold him back from pressing that claim. Rather he was gripped by the idea that he was called to be a sort of Tory Joan of Arc, the saviour who alone could lead the party out of the shadow of defeat – if its leaders would only give him his head. To Garvin he wrote on 3 January 1911 an extraordinary letter setting out this sense of destiny.*

My dear Garvin,

I do not hesitate to say that the long letter I got from you today is the most gratifying thing that has happened to me in my political career. Whatever comes of your present efforts it will always be a source of profound pride to me that you take the view you have expressed to J.S. [Jack Sandars] of my services to the party. I hated this last fight as you did believing as I still believe that it could have been avoided & ought to have been avoided. But we both of us bore in different parts of the field the brunt of the fighting while those who ordered us to fight (I don't mean A.J.B. but others) were lounging in their tents. Such things ought not to be possible and we must make them impossible for the future to the extent at any rate that those who do no fighting & command no influence shall not decide prodigious issues behind the backs of those who do fight & who have influence.

Under the encouragement of your letter I will write without false modesty. I am conscious of powers which may be made of real service to the Unionist party & I believe further (promising no other than normal political developments) that if the party gives me the artificial position & standing which they alone can give me I can win the next election for them. If they will give me *formal recognition* I am certain that in two years I can undertake a considered campaign in the country which will itself win 30 or 40 seats. I am assuming of course – a point upon which I have no doubt – that I shall maintain & improve my parliamentary position, and that they put me on the front bench. And I add that unless the party creates some one who can do this there is no reason why we should win the next election at all. The other side will have new bribes & baits, & plural voting will probably be dead.

It is curious how exactly your letter to J.S. stated my own conclusion. It is their gain & not mine if I join their shadow cabinet – they clip my wings & make me responsible for their policy. No one would appreciate such promotion except because it assured him he would obtain an office hereafter of which he was before doubtful. That was once but is no longer my case. By

* It is dated 3 January 1910, but this is quite clearly a mistake.

putting me on the front bench they double my parliamentary position; by merely taking me in counsel they reduce it by excluding Randolphian tactics. [A reference to Randolph Churchill's 'Fourth Party' of the 1880s.]

More of this when we meet. I have much to say which cannot be put in writing. More & more I am assured that in the next few years national defence will matter more & more & all the others except social reform less & less.

Yours ever,

F.E.

Despite his words of appreciation of F.E.'s platform services in February, however, it did not occur to Balfour's strong sense of hierarchy to invite so unfledged a parliamentarian on to his front bench, though he does seem to have invited him to some meetings of the Shadow Cabinet. As the Government, now armed with the private guarantees from the King necessary to override the Lords, prepared once again to push the Parliament Bill through the Commons, F.E. remained in the anomalous position of a backbencher half in but effectively outside the charmed circle of the leadership, conducting his own battle with his particular friends against the monstrous assault which they maintained was being inflicted on the Constitution. He was only one Tory opponent of the Bill among 270 in the House of Commons and many thousands in the country. But as always he marshalled the case against it with a rare lucidity and intellectual coherence that makes his presentation of the arguments peculiarly worth exploring. At the end of January he published in *Reynolds' News* an article setting out the view of the crisis which was to guide his actions over the next climactic months. His stance was at the same time conciliatory and defiant, and provides the explanation of what is at first sight difficult to understand, how the compromising coalitionist of 1910 was found fighting in the last ditch when his leaders had surrendered in 1911. On the one hand he adhered to his admission that the House of Lords was indefensible as it was and needed to be reformed; on the other, he insisted, despite the failure of the 1910 Conference, that a lasting settlement could only be achieved by agreement between the parties. The Constitution could not be changed by a simple majority. If the Liberals, driven by nothing more exalted than the expediency of their parliamentary situation were unilaterally to carry a partial reform designed solely to get the Government off its Irish hook, the Tories would not consent to be bound by such a *diktat*.

What good will it do Liberals if their terms of conquest are reversed on the first Unionist success? . . . A Bill which nobody supports on its merits, which gains support from the representatives of half the nation for motives at once ulterior and inconsistent, which is passionately opposed by the representatives of the other half and which embodies a far-reaching Constitutional change, must end in ultimate and disastrous failure.[53]

The constitutional absolute to which F.E. had come was that there must be a Second Chamber of some sort – its composition, whether by election, nomination, succession or a mixture of the three, was a detail, so long as it ensured a rough impartiality – with effective power to restrain a temporary majority (or coalition of minorities) in the Commons, elected on quite a different issue, from imposing some unwanted change to which the electorate had not given its assent. Though the Government's Bill left the Lords considerable powers of delay, it failed F.E.'s test because it would allow the passage into law, despite the opposition of the Lords, of any Bill passed through the Commons in three successive sessions – in other words, any Bill introduced in the first two years of a five-year Parliament. In practice, of course, 'any Bill' would mean first and foremost a Home Rule Bill, but F.E.'s objection in principle went beyond Home Rule: he objected to the establishment (even if only for two years in every five) of single-chamber government – particularly when it was enacted by Ministers almost all of whom had expressed themselves, when their survival was not at stake, strongly in favour of two chambers. More genuinely than many of his party, who would grasp at any device to protect the Lords, F.E. was ready for any equitable *reform* of the Upper House so long as its *powers* were undiminished. (He was no defender of the privileges of the peers as a class, even though in the heat of debate he did sometimes slip into exaggerated praise of their great traditions; it was the theoretical balance of the Constitution that he was concerned to defend.) Accordingly, in a powerful speech on the First Reading of the Bill on 22 February – a speech which, the *Daily Telegraph* reported, had the Government front bench squirming in acute discomfort – he picked unerringly on its bland preamble, which sought to appease the bicameralists by promising a measure of reform at some time in the future but postponed it for the moment – a moment during which Home Rule would be conveniently slipped through. 'If the preamble to your Bill is so seriously and sincerely meant,' he urged, 'why not carry it out now, and on these lines found your reform on the bed-rock of national consent, rather than on the shifting quicksands of party triumph?'

Citing his letter to *The Times* of the previous June, he repeated his personal commitment to reform of the second chamber; but he modulated menacingly from this tone of sweet reason to one of open challenge as he warned of the Tory response if the Government refused the responsible path of compromise.

> If there is to be a preamble, what time could be so fit as the present? You have at your disposal the unexhausted energies of a youthful Parliament fresh from contact with the constituencies, which have given you authority to reform the Upper House. Will it not be said that the Government are guilty of using the chicanery of the preamble as a soporific to moderate men, while they post-pone it at Irish dictation, in order to smuggle through Home Rule? If I were a peer, I might surrender my own quarrel, if it ended there, before two elections. But I would never surrender knowing that my surrender was to be used to place on the Statute Book a Bill which was abhorrent to millions of my fellow-subjects and the right of deciding which had been filched from them by a trick.[54]

Just as he had done on the education question in 1908, F.E. had now perfected for himself an impregnably high-minded debating posture combining statesmanlike moderation in theory with an inescapable obligation to oppose at any cost the only solution the Government could propose in practice. Righteous in his own – and, rather more ques-tionably, his party's – readiness to embrace reform, he could marshal an unanswerable indictment of the Government's cynical postponement of it. Throughout the spring, as the Parliament Bill progressed by time-table through its stages in the Commons, he kept up the attack in the House, in the country and in the press, continually contrasting the Tories' open-minded concern for a balanced and democratic Constitu-tion with the Liberals' stubborn dependence upon allies (Labour as well as Irish) determined for their own ends to see the House of Lords not reformed but permanently emasculated. Then in May, as a mark of qualified recognition, he was given the responsibility of moving, from his back bench, the rejection of the Bill on Third Reading. The front bench had no new arguments to deploy. Neither had F.E., but he seized his opportunity with another powerful and cogent appeal to reason, described by Churchill – significantly – to the King as 'full of a real spirit of reconciliation', another skilful blend of resolute regret at the Government's misguided persistence in courting confrontation at a time when, he declared – and most of his listeners must have been surprised to hear it – 'a larger area of politics has been withdrawn from the party spirit than at any time in recent memory'.[55]

In the middle of the most bitter party fight of the century, this claim must have appeared eccentric in the extreme. But from F.E.'s particular angle of vision it might easily have appeared true. More than anyone else he had been impressed and excited by Lloyd George's coalition initiative the previous October, which had revealed a considerable readiness to compromise on the part of the leaders of both main parties had they only been free to settle matters on their merits without reference to their rank and file; and he had continual proof that party divisions were not an impermeable barrier to civilized understanding between individuals in his close friendship across the great divide with Winston Churchill, which at just this moment bore its most enduring fruit with the foundation of their joint brainchild – the Other Club.

The place for a fuller description of the Other Club and its importance in F.E.'s life will be the next chapter. Here it is sufficient to say that this most famous of political dining clubs brought together in convivial friendship at this moment of intense inter-party antagonism – when normal social relations were under strain and some of the great hostesses were refusing to entertain opponents – a dozen of the most prominent and promising younger M.P.s from either side, including as its most senior members Lloyd George from the Government and Bonar Law from the Opposition. The purpose was not at all to plot coalition. On the contrary, the rules of the Club specifically decreed, in a phrase unmistakably F.E.'s, that 'Nothing in the rules or intercourse of the Club shall interfere with the rancour or asperity of party politics.' At the same time the Club provided both a valuable safety valve and an opportunity for the members to learn from private argument unrestrained by the presence of reporters what was in the other side's mind, how far they might go, on what point they would stick. It served, over the next few years of bitter controversy, first over the Parliament Bill, then over Home Rule and Ulster, as a reminder that beneath the surface of impassioned confrontation they were all ultimately on the same side, guardians of the same traditions, until the war came to subordinate all their domestic disputes to a common over-riding national loyalty.

George V's Coronation in June – four weeks after the inaugural dinner of the Other Club – provided a more public opportunity for the parties to stand back for a moment from the battle and celebrate their common allegiance. The coronation honours list, too, offered a means to sweeten, in little ways to which politicians attach importance, relations between the parties; that is, it allowed Asquith to hold out a friendly bribe to selected leaders of the Opposition. The effect of one of his efforts in this direction, however, was only to sour relations between F.E. and his leader. It seems to have been Churchill who suggested to the Prime Minister that the award of Privy Councillorships not only to Bonar Law, whose rapid rise in the Tory hierarchy demanded one, but also to F.E., would be a shrewd gesture which would do the Government no harm. He also suggested giving the Order of Merit to Joseph Chamberlain. Asquith could not entertain the latter suggestion, but he adopted the former and, somewhat tactlessly, substituted F.E.'s name for one of Balfour's recommendations, a dim but worthy former Whip and junior Minister, Hayes Fisher. There followed an extraordinary little wrangle in which F.E.'s qualities and deserts were bandied about between the party leaders.

Balfour first protested, understandably, that Asquith's proposed substitution placed him in an impossible position *vis-à-vis* Fisher, whom he had presumably tipped off to expect an honour. At the same time he wrote at some length to explain his action to F.E.

My Dear F.E.,
    I hear that in the list of Unionist Honours which the P.M. is recommending to the King, your name has been substituted for Hayes Fisher's for a Privy Councillorship. I have written to Asquith to remonstrate, and as I regard you in the light of a Cabinet colleague, I feel I cannot do so without acquainting you of the circumstances under which I take a step which may seem hostile to your interests. There is, of course, no comparison between your position and that of Hayes Fisher, either in the House or in the country. You have clearly won for yourself a wholly exceptional position, and we all look to you as one who is predestined to a foremost place in party councils, a statesman and a leader. All the substantial influence which a member of the Opposition could have, you already possess. The decoration will come in no long time. I regard the Coronation honour as the reward of past distinction – not a recognition of the present, still less of future distinction, and it is this principle which has guided my advice to Asquith, when he consulted me about the list. H. Fisher has worked for us with ungrudging zeal for many a long year. He has not been over-well treated by fortune, and I feel confident that you would regret as much as I that he should now be disappointed of an honour he has been led to expect. You will at least acquit *me* of being indifferent to your interests, or blind either to your great abilities or your great success.
                Yours sincerely,
                Arthur Balfour[56]

A flattering letter, but rather too flattering – it must have been news to F.E. that his leader regarded him 'in the light of a Cabinet colleague', since he was not yet even on the front bench – and belied by Balfour's curious view of the Privy Council. The extraordinary story that the Leader of the Opposition was trying to deny to one of his most promising lieutenants a coveted honour which the Prime Minister proposed to bestow on him, and give it instead to a man of whom the public had barely heard, spread quickly through the political world. F.E. was in camp at Blenheim with Winston – they had both joined the Oxfordshire Yeomanry – when he received Balfour's letter, but Clementine Churchill had evidently already heard the rumour before her husband wrote to her to confirm it.

> Yes Balfour has written to A protesting agst FE being made a PC & to FE to tell him so.
> There is a lot of soft sawder about his great position and prospects and about Hayes Fisher's long services (as a wretched whips' room hack & county council wirepuller) & his misfortunes (due entirely to AJB); but the main purpose is pretty plain. They want to keep him (FE) back.
> The result is important either way. If FE does not get it, he will not forgive Balfour. If he does, Balfour will not forgive him. But what an insight into the fatuous and arrogant mind of the Hotel Cecil, wh. even at its last gasp would rather inflict any amount of injury upon the Tory party than share power with any able man of provincial origin. So may it long continue.[57]

Churchill also wrote to Bonar Law, enlisting his help for his friend, telling Law that Asquith would never consent to put Fisher's name forward: the question was simply whether or not F.E. should be honoured.[58] Law, accordingly, writing to Balfour, did not mention Fisher, but restricted himself to pressing F.E.'s claim and the undesirability of gratuitously snubbing him. 'If I were in his place', he warned, 'I should think it hard to have my name rejected after it had been proposed by the Prime Minister.'

> It is the fact also that he is the only member of the back benches who has been invited by you to take part in the private consultations of the Party, and I remember that the fact that he did attend these meetings was made public. This seems to me to single him out in the most distinct way, and I cannot help feeling that he is after yourself the most effective platform speaker on our side and that it would be a misfortune if we were for any cause to lose the full effect of his popular gifts.[59]

Asquith, meanwhile, explained his action to Balfour by reference to the precedent of Salisbury appointing Grey and Haldane Privy Councillors in 1902 (though both had been far longer in the House of Commons than F.E. in 1911). He claimed, somewhat implausibly, that Fisher was unacceptable to the Liberals as a result of his partisan activity on the L.C.C., while F.E. – 'though he has been a caustic and not always – as I think – either a fair or well-mannered critic of myself and my friends' – had won a position in the House of Commons and at the Bar which merited recognition.[60]

For his own part F.E. wrote gratefully to Asquith – 'I can only say that it is a paradoxical and singular circumstance that those against whom I have been fighting for fifteen years have paid me the greatest compliment I have ever had in my life; while those on whose behalf I have been fighting did their best to prevent it'[61] – and made no effort to disguise his feelings in an icily ironic reply to his leader.

Dear Mr. Balfour,

Thank you for troubling in your short holiday to write me so long a letter. I am, I need hardly say, greatly obliged to you for the candour with which you inform me of your remonstrance to the Prime Minister, and for the excessively kind manner in which you speak of my position and prospects. I have never sought for any honour, though I should have greatly valued one offered under circumstances so flattering. Any element of personal competition in such a matter is extremely distasteful to me. I am well aware that the services of Hayes Fisher to the party have been prolonged and continuous. Pray believe that I feel it no grievance that they have been pointedly and authoritatively placed before the Prime Minister.

Yours sincerely,
F.E. Smith[62]

So much for Hayes Fisher! To Balfour's secretary, Jack Sandars, who urged with the sort of pious humbug that F.E. could least tolerate that his son would one day be proud of him if he would now stand unselfishly aside, he reputedly exploded with less dignity, 'My little boy is only four years old, but if I thought that he was such a bloody little fool as to be proud of his father for behaving in such an asinine manner, I should indeed despair of him.'[63] It is more than likely that this is one of those retorts that F.E. thought of later; but it accurately expresses his un-ashamed pursuit of those honours and titles which were the prizes of legitimate ambition. To be a Privy Councillor before he was forty would be another notable step in his meteoric progress – even if Churchill had achieved it at thirty-two – and he was damned if he was going to have it snatched away when it had been offered.

Balfour, in reply to Asquith, adhered to his nomination of Hayes Fisher, denying that Fisher had been more 'partisan' than F.E. and remarking pertinently that he did not see how the Opposition could have honours allocated to them at all if partisanship was considered a bar.[64] The solution eventually adopted was that both Fisher and F.E. received the honour in a list which included, in addition to Bonar Law and Rufus Isaacs, so many undistinguished worthies, Liberal and Conservative, that one wonders what all the fuss was about. At the same time the King's favour was extended to three others who recur in F.E.'s story: W.H. Lever became a Baronet; Bonar Law's friend Max Aitken, for no reason at all, received a knighthood; and a knighthood was also conferred on His Majesty's Consul-General in Rio de Janeiro, Roger Casement.

When the list was published, F.E.'s elevation was widely welcomed by his friends in both parties. But the exuberance of Jack Seely (now Under-Secretary for War) – 'Hurrah and Hurroo! I am indeed glad that you are Rt. Honble. F.E. . . . If you reply to this note I will have you removed from the Army'[65] – contrasts strikingly with the coolness with which Balfour accepted his subordinate's unwelcome advancement.

> By the way, are you proposing to sit on our bench? I need not say that you will be most welcome. If there are reasons against it, they are solely connected with your own conveniences, and with your very special position as a quasi-unofficial member, possessed of an authority which a seat on our bench could hardly increase, and an independence which it might do something to diminish.[66]

This was not an encouraging invitation, and F.E. did not take it up. To be out of his leader's favour at this point was in any case no disadvantage to him, for Balfour's leadership was itself in growing disfavour with much of the Conservative party. Tariff reformers who had always viewed Balfour's fiscal equivocations with impatience were now joined by malcontents from the other wing of the party – most notably Balfour's own cousins, Lords Robert and Hugh Cecil – determined to concede no quarter in the fight for the House of Lords. On the latter issue, as he had always been on the former since his father's withdrawal, Austen Chamberlain was emerging, rather despite himself, as a serious challenger to Balfour's dwindling authority. Even before the Privy Council row F.E. had been gravitating – behind his calls for unity – towards Austen. Now the climax of the House of Lords struggle in July and August drove him into open rebellion against his leader.

F.E. was not a natural rebel. He placed loyalty very high in his pantheon of political virtues. Nor, despite his vehemence on the party platform, where he saw his brief to be to put his side's case as powerfully as possible, was he a natural extremist; he was too intelligent to be an emotional Diehard. Five factors, however, combined to push him into the last ditch in defiance of his leader in the summer of 1911. First place must be given to political principle. F.E. did passionately believe that the Parliament Bill was a partisan outrage upon the Constitution. To the end of his life he never wavered from this view, never accepted the emasculation of the Upper House as right or permanent and continued to assert that every subsequent Government, including those of which he was a member, inherited from Asquith's vague preamble an inescapable obligation to restore the proper balance of a bicameral legislature. Secondly, principle was reinforced by political calculation. F.E. had no time for futile gestures in lost causes. He believed at the height of the crisis that the Tory party had actually less to lose by forcing the Government to go to the limit of its constitutional powers to carry the Bill against a united Opposition than by conceding defeat and so conniving at its passage. This was the critical strategic judgment on which the Diehard 'ditchers' differed from the 'hedgers', who preferred to safeguard their delaying power at the price of losing their veto, rather than risk losing both to a massive creation of jumped-up Liberals.

F.E. and those who thought as he did may have been right or wrong in their reckoning of the odds; but they were not merely indulging an emotional spasm. Their calculation was, first, that the Government did not want to have to create peers at all, and certainly not to create many: the idea of devaluing the peerage with a flood of new titles was as repugnant to Asquith as it was to the King. There was therefore a real chance that if the Tories only stood firm against the threat the Government might shrink at the last moment from enforcing it, and be obliged to reconvene the Constitutional Conference instead to try once again to find an agreed settlement. If, on the other hand, they did create peers, they would create as few as they could, perhaps a couple of dozen, just enough to override the opposition to the Parliament Bill, but not enough to overwhelm the normal Tory majority against Home Rule and Welsh Disestablishment. The Tory peers would thus be no worse off by calling the Government's bluff than by caving in – and, what was more, they would keep their hands clean. The 'ditchers' attached the greatest importance to making the Government find its own majority to carry the Bill, for only by accepting no responsibility for its passage, they argued, could the Tories reserve their right to repeal or amend it when they had the chance. Then again, if the Government were not bluffing, F.E. went so far as to argue that even the creation of 500 peers would not be a catastrophe, but would actually pave the way for precisely that sort of impartial reconstitution of the Upper House which he had always advocated. Whatever happened, forcing the Government to create its peers was the way to keep the crisis alive and a thorough, lasting and soundly based reform high on the national agenda. To give any sort of bipartisan approval to the Veto Bill risked closing the issue, thereby leaving the Constitution permanently unbalanced, to the sole benefit of the Irish and other subversive minorities who might in the future gain a temporary hold over the Commons.

Thirdly, at a more personal level, there is no doubt that F.E.'s normal loyalty to a leader whom in many respects he sincerely admired was – understandably – diminished by Balfour's pointed snub in June, making him less inclined to subordinate his own judgment; especially since, fourthly, Austen Chamberlain and Carson, already the leaders to whom he gave his allegiance on the other issues most central to his political faith, tariff reform and Ulster Unionism, were offering a respectable alternative focus of loyalty in line with his own instincts on the constitutional issue, an alternative which promised more decisive leadership all round than the party had ever received from Balfour. Finally there was the pull of friendship and the sheer excitement of conspiracy. Most of those younger Tories to whom F.E. was closest at this time – Paddy Goulding, Leo Amery (successful at last at a by-election), and Eddie Winterton – and those he most admired, notably the Cecils, were in the rebel camp, and in an atmosphere highly charged with military metaphor he was not one to hang back when his friends were going forth to fight. 'Whatever else may be said about me,' he wrote to Goulding in October, 'I am not a bad man to go tiger-hunting with.'[67] It is the heady exhilaration of rebellion, in a lofty cause and in the company of colleagues whom he believed to embody the future of the Tory party – a potent blend of opportunism and principle – which best explains the extravagance of F.E.'s words and actions in these frenzied weeks when the political temperature was reflected and exacerbated by the extreme heat of an exceptional summer.

The most notorious manifestation of the lengths to which the 'Ditchers' were prepared to carry their opposition occurred on 24 July when Asquith was shouted down in the House of Commons. For half an hour the Prime Minister stood patiently at the dispatch box while his attempts to make himself heard were drowned by furious shouts of 'Traitor', 'Redmond first' and – a particularly vicious insinuation – 'Who killed the King?' Different accounts pick out different names from the Tory mob – Carson, Goulding, George Wyndham, Lord Castlereagh, Major Archer-Shee – but all agree that F.E.'s part in the uproar was second only to Hugh Cecil's. 'I could not take my eyes off Lord Hugh

Cecil,' wrote Violet Bonham Carter, who was in the gallery, 'who screamed "The King is in duress" and in his frenzied writhings seemed like one possessed. His transformation, and that of many other personal friends, was terrifying. They behaved, and looked, like mad baboons.'[68]

Balfour, who did nothing to try to restrain the tumult, was heard in stony silence by the Government benches when Asquith finally gave up the attempt to speak. But when, after Grey had been allowed to say a few words, F.E. rose in his place, the provocation was too great, and he was repaid in his own coin – though with remarkable good humour.

> After vainly attempting to utter a sentence amid the din and excitement, the hon. and learned member turned round to the seat occupied by Mr. John Redmond, at whom he pointed his left hand, and with the right hand he pointed angrily, as if associating cause and effect, to the occupants of the Treasury Bench. The dramatic action of the hon. member was received with derisive laughter by the Liberals and the Irish members, while a warm cheer of encouragement came from the Unionist benches.[69]

After several more minutes, with F.E. still on his feet, the Speaker adjourned the debate.

Despite Hugh Cecil's paroxysms, the Tory demonstration was not a spontaneous outburst, but deliberately stage-managed. Wilfred Scawen Blunt happened the next day upon Wyndham (who was his cousin) closeted with F.E. and the young Duke of Westminster in Belgrave Square congratulating themselves on their success. 'They are all in the highest possible spirits and consider that they have forced Balfour's hand.'[70] Cecil, rebuked by *The Times* for his behaviour, explicitly defended it on the ground that the Government's abuse of the royal prerogative to subvert the Constitution released the Opposition from all constitutional restraints and claimed that in earlier days Asquith would have been impeached. F.E., for his part, publicly regretted the 'hateful necessity' of so treating a Minister from whom he personally had just received an exceptional kindness, but justified it with the argument that the House of Commons, confronted with a *coup d'état*, had no other method of protest left to it, and insisted that considerations of friendship were in these circumstances inadmissible.[71] It was in tones of outraged friendship, nevertheless, and with evident touchiness, that he reacted when Leslie Scott joined a number of other embarrassed Tories in sending Asquith a letter of apology.

> Dear Leslie,
>   I confess that I am simply *astounded* that you should have put your name to that circular without coming to me to hear my views

and my justification. I treat it and shall treat it as a gross affront on the part of the others who signed it and I shall cut them when I meet them in the House of Commons. But my only claim on them was membership of a common party. I was simply *staggered* when I saw your name and realized that you had given it without even giving me the chance of putting my case. Carson who was equally responsible with myself and Cecil is as much at a loss as I am. If you thought me hopelessly and even abominably wrong you at least should have held aloof from public censure. You must have been gratified when you saw the use the Liberal press made of your name as against me.

Yours,
F.E. Smith[72]

The Diehards' next step was to give public notice of their organized existence by means of a banquet in honour of the 87-year-old former Lord Chancellor, Lord Halsbury, whom they had adopted as their figurehead. Immediately after the scene in the chamber a letter was circulated to possible supporters which confirms that F.E., as well as acting as unofficial Whip to the group, was now counted among its leaders.

Dear Sir,

Viscount Wolmer M.P. and Mr. Harold Smith M.P. will be at the House of Commons tomorrow, Tuesday, with tickets for the Halsbury Banquet on Wednesday. Tickets can also be obtained by application to Mr. F.E. Smith at Grosvenor House by telegram or letter.

> Austen Chamberlain
> Edward Carson
> F.E. Smith
> George Wyndham[73]

The banquet was attended by over 600 guests, who were addressed in defiant terms by the four organizers plus Milner, Salisbury and Halsbury himself; Lord Selborne from the chair read out a letter from Joseph Chamberlain. Balfour's policy of protesting acquiescence – backed though it was by Lansdowne, Long, Bonar Law and the majority of the Shadow Cabinet – was denounced on all sides as craven surrender. Austen maintained stoutly that the Government's threat to create enough peers to carry the Bill was 'fraudulent bluff'. Such was the enthusiasm that Halsbury would have been drawn in triumph back to his home in Kensington but for anxiety about his health. Wyndham told Blunt hopefully that the country was in revolt; all the best men in the party were with them. 'The only man who has disappointed them has been George Curzon.'[74] As a leading peer, however, Curzon was a most significant absentee. It was the peers themselves whom the Diehards had to rally to defeat the Bill, and no more than fifty of them attended the banquet.

Nevertheless the Tory party was becoming seriously split, with more than a suspicion that some of the rebels were using the House of Lords issue as a good stick with which to beat a leader with whom they were more generally dissatisfied. There were rumours that Balfour was to be overthrown; some even put F.E. in his place; it is difficult to believe that anyone took the latter seriously, but their existence is evidence both of the unreality of the time and of F.E.'s sudden leap into the very centre of affairs. Churchill reported to the King (in one of his regular letters as Home Secretary) a very distinct movement against Balfour, and exercised his historical imagination a little by comparing 'the spectacle of Lord Hugh Cecil, Mr F.E. Smith and Mr Worthington Evans now all concentrated below the gangway' with the old 'Fourth Party' in the 1880s in which his father and Balfour himself had combined to harass Lord Salisbury.[75]

But attacks on the leadership of the Tory party always provoke a counter-demonstration of loyalty. On 1 August a dinner was held at the House of Commons in honour of the retiring Chief Whip, Sir Alexander Acland-Hood, and his predecessor Aretas Akers-Douglas: F.E. and his friends could not but attend, but the occasion was turned into an explicit rebuff to the rebels, as the editor of the *Globe* reported to Lord Stamfordham.

> F.E. Smith came in late and seemed rather surprised when he found he was not put amongst those on the head table. The dinner was largely attended, not because of an intense desire to do honour to the guests, but because of the bitterness of feeling which has been aroused in the party during the last two days and Austen Chamberlain's letter to Willoughby de Broke in which he spoke of Balfour's policy as involving '*disgrace*' – a letter which has done more to rally men to Balfour's standard than anything else could have done. When Balfour stood up, the company cheered and waved their napkins for *five minutes* – an altogether extraordinary demonstration. Austen Chamberlain looked very serious and glanced down his nose. F.E. Smith got up, and *walked out* first – before Balfour even – Hugh Cecil maintained a sickly smile – and George Wyndham looked as if his dinner had disagreed with him! Mark you – do not imagine that this demonstration was due to a

fervid enthusiasm for Lansdowne's policy. It was simply and solely due to a conviction in the minds of those present that we have come to 'the parting of the ways', and that the moment had come for them to show in unmistakable fashion that they were no followers of Austen C., F.E. Smith or Wyndham.[76]

It was now becoming clear from frantic head-counting that the great majority of Tory peers were preparing to follow the Lansdowne–Curzon line and swallow the poisoned chalice by abstaining, rather than risk being swamped by new Liberal creations. This knowledge rendered somewhat pointless the motion of censure on the Government which Balfour proposed in the Commons on 7 August. From his new seat below the gangway F.E. weighed in as soon as Asquith had replied to Balfour's impotent strictures, heaping vituperation almost equally on both, so that the Liberal Ellis Griffith who followed him remarked that he had moved a motion of censure not on the Government but on his own leader. Not that he spared Asquith: with his usual skill he revived damaging quotations from past speeches in which the Prime Minister promised not to take office if dependent on the Irish for survival; showed how for twenty years his commitment to Home Rule had fluctuated in precise correlation with the balance of parties; and repeated the charge of treason, castigating Asquith's readiness to create corrupt peerages – to be paid for not by money but in votes – as simply obedience to his master Redmond. 'It was a well-understood commercial transaction . . . The right hon. gentleman sold the Prerogative of the Crown for a Finance Bill.' ('What does a Privy Councillorship cost?' shouted an Irish member.) But his bitterest taunts were reserved for Lansdowne's sudden popularity with the Liberal press in recognition of his assistance in passing the Government's legislation. In the light of the Opposition's known complicity, he declared, the censure motion was superfluous and the vote on it was irrelevant. It would have been better, he still insisted, to have called the Government's bluff, to have forced the creation of peers; had the Government actually gone ahead, the Committee of Privileges could have been invoked to question the legality of such 'hireling creations'. The Opposition's resources were not exhausted; the leadership was simply giving up the fight. They should not be afraid of forcing a third election; he was confident that the country would respond to a 'declaration of war' against the party which had sold the King 'for thirty pieces of silver'.[77]

This desperate speech was repeatedly interrupted by angry Liberals, but F.E.'s fighting talk was best answered by Churchill, winding up the debate. With a deflating ridicule worthy of F.E. himself, he applauded his friend's courage.

It is that kind of courage which can not only be maintained in the face of danger, but can even shine brightly in its total absence. Mr Jorrocks has described fox-hunting as providing all the glory of war with only 25 per cent of its danger . . . I think no-one has succeeded in manufacturing a greater amount of heroism with a smaller consumption of the raw material of danger than . . . the Member for Walton Division.[78]

This thrust went pretty near the bone; for the Diehards, if they were not exactly reconciled to defeat, knew by now that it was almost certain. They were fighting on less in the real hope of victory than in order to be seen not to have surrendered. They conceived themselves as fighting, not only for their own personal integrity, but for the honour of the Tory party, believing it vital that some Conservatives at least – the 'best' elements in the party – should be seen to have rejected the Liberal settlement in which their leaders had acquiesced and declared their intention to overturn it in the future. After the critical vote on 13 August, in which the Government mustered 131 votes from its own supporters, most of the bishops and 29 renegade Tories to outnumber the 114 last-ditch peers who refused to abstain, F.E. wrote to Austen of the 'staggering calamity' to which 'nerveless leadership' had brought the party and went on darkly:

I am profoundly convinced that things cannot again be as they were, and that the only men who can ever appeal to the Con-stituencies to repeal the Veto Bill are the men whose hands, in your own phrase, are clean.
    I beg of you in the next few weeks to think out clearly and boldly the probable developments (personal and other) of the next two years and then let us meet when we can with Carson and Wyndham.[79]

But Austen, though he agreed with the substance of F.E.'s criticism, held that 'Halsbury's fight has averted the calamity which a total surrender would have been'; he would not lend himself to continued rebellion.

I confess that Balfour's leadership at times makes me nearly despair . . . But I have been very closely and intimately associated with him for the past eight or nine years, I know his strength as well as his weakness, I have received much kindness at his hands as well as some hard knocks, and I am too much attached to him ever to join in any combination against him or his leadership. I took this decision long ago. I have held fast to it in spite of many difficulties and some provocation, and I am going to hold fast by it still.

All I can do to put more fight into our policy and to strengthen the fighting and constructive section within the party I will do, but what I do must be done within the limits set out above, and must not be directed against Balfour personally or against his leadership.

I don't think you will have expected me to act otherwise, but it is better for us both to make the position quite clear.[80]

Austen, as F.E. had further cause to remark a decade later, 'always played the game'.

The anti-Balfour movement was too strong, however, to be turned aside by Austen's gentlemanly scruples. At the beginning of October the nucleus of the 'last-ditch' group – Selborne, Willoughby de Broke, Wyndham, Milner, Carson and F.E. – formed themselves into a permanent ginger group, the Halsbury Club, to keep together the heroes of August and to carry on into wider fields of Conservative policy the energy and sense of direction released in that fight. They were now agreed that the only form of second chamber to which the country would be persuaded to restore effective powers was a wholly elected chamber: even such a Diehard as Willoughby de Broke now preferred this clear democratic solution to 'some "hanky-panky" nomination scheme which Curzon would manipulate'.[81] Secondly they stood for the restoration to the Tory platform of the full tariff programme, and regarded the promise of a referendum as now void. Furthermore, as Wyndham explained to Chamberlain,

They wished to speak more plainly about national dangers and National Defence; to give more definite form to the Unionist programme of Social Reform; and in all things to take a more vigorous fighting line. . . . They had decided to back Carson for all they were worth in his resistance to Home Rule.[82]

Ostensibly the Club was not to be directed against Balfour's leadership; Austen – the honourable Brutus whom the conspirators needed to lend respectability to what was plainly an organized revolt – insisted as the condition of his approval that it should not be. But its inevitable effect was to make Balfour's position impossible and to promote Chamberlain's succession. His brother Neville had no doubt that the leadership would soon be his if he would only give the Halsburyites his support and encouragement, and told him, in order to stiffen him, what he had heard from Amery – 'that FES said after the Halsbury dinner that if he had ever had any doubts about your being the best leader your speech had dispelled them and that he should follow you loyally and whole-heartedly'.[83]

The Halsbury Club certainly represented without reserve the objects to which F.E.'s political life was now devoted – the Union, a balanced Constitution, national defence, tariff reform and – rather vaguely – social reform. He was actually the chairman of a backbench group known as the Unionist Social Reform Committee set up earlier in the year to inject some plausibility into the Tory claim to be more seriously concerned with social amelioration than the Liberals. There was an element of window-dresing about the Committee, and its reports tended to the anodyne and unexceptionable. But it was important to F.E.'s self-identification as a Tory democrat rather than a simple Diehard. In accordance with this conviction he was one of the first Tories, in the middle of the constitutional crisis, to give a clear welcome to Lloyd George's path-breaking National Insurance Bill. He did so in terms which expressed his own strongly held view of society as an interdependent whole. He warmly approved the contributory principle as helping to bind together the employer, the employee and the State in a common obligation and welcomed what he saw as Lloyd George's conversion to the Tory doctrine of national solidarity, as contrasted with his former exploitation of sectional grievance. The Bill, he declared at Birmingham on 12 May, was 'the abnegation of Limehouse and the doctrine of class hatred, the repentance of the Chancellor. Mr Lloyd George parades before us like Lady Macbeth, trying to wash the bloodstains of class hatred from his hands'.[84]

But if his approval of the National Insurance Bill ruled out a vigorous fighting line in that direction, the rest of the Halsbury programme gave F.E. full scope for a series of attacking speeches around the country in October and November. At Manchester and Edinburgh, Stratford and Bristol he returned to the subject of the 1909 Budget, blaming the combination of free imports and higher taxation for dearer food, higher unemployment and labour unrest; he asserted that there was actually a majority in the House of Commons in favour of tariffs if the Irish would vote according to their fiscal convictions instead of their nationalist aspirations, and derided the ramshackle coalition of Liberals, Labour and Irish who combined for their own conflicting purposes against the united Conservatives, now the largest party in the House. Above all, he took up again with renewed strength the fight for Ulster, justifying his longstanding resistance to Home Rule by a new and convenient constitutional doctrine arising out of the events of the summer.

Unless and until the Second Chamber is restored [he declared at Glasgow on 10 October] and unless and until the constituencies are given some means of expressing their opinions on the great controversies of which today they know nothing [by which he meant issues that had not been explicitly put to them at the last election], I will treat every measure which proceeds from the House of Commons as at present constituted as coming from a tainted source, having no Constitutional strength behind it. This conclusion I will make the guide of my political conduct in the House of Commons in the next few years towards any one of the measures with which we are threatened.[85]

At Stratford on 3 November he was more specific.

I say plainly that I utterly decline to be bound, in my resistance to the programme of those who have been guilty of Constitutional outrages, within the straitwaistcoat of Constitutional resistance. [Cheers.] So far as Home Rule is concerned I will shrink from nothing which will ensure that before it becomes law the electors shall be given an opportunity of pronouncing upon it. [Cheers.] If without an appeal to the electors an attempt should be made to drive forth from the body politic and the British Parliament the men of our blood in Ulster, there is no length to which we will not go in our determination to insist that they shall still remain part and parcel of our nation and sharers of our Parliamentary traditions. [Loud cheers.][86]

And again at Bristol on 13 November,

Things and acts which are indefensible under normal conditions may be deemed inevitable by determined men in revolutionary times and, speaking with a deep sense of responsibility – lawyer as I am – I assert that for those who are loyal in Ireland, who ask nothing except that they should not be cast forth, there is no length from which I will shrink in supporting the leader of the Irish Unionists, Sir Edward Carson.[87]

In Ulster the Orange Lodges were beginning to drill; and on 23 September Carson had announced that the Ulster Unionist Council would set up a Provisional Government to resist Home Rule the moment the Bill was passed. But not until April 1912 did Bonar Law pledge his unlimited support for Ulster. F.E. was the first mainland Conservative to revive in such plain terms Lord Randolph Churchill's old cry that Ulster would fight.

With such battles looming, the movement in the Tory party to replace Balfour with a more aggressive leader gathered strength, spearheaded by Leo Maxse's crude 'Balfour Must Go' campaign in the *National Review*. Despite the absence of any obvious successor Balfour had in fact decided in September to throw in the towel, though he did not announce his decision until 9 November. Three days before, the Halsbury Club found it politic to pass, at its first annual meeting, a resolution of confidence in Balfour, in order not to appear to have driven him from office. F.E., who was in the secret, had the greatest difficulty persuading more junior malcontents like Winterton not to oppose this apparently feeble motion. 'If you knew what I know,' he scribbled, 'you would not go on with your amendment.'[88] Winterton reluctantly withdrew it, the Halsbury Club declared its perfect confidence in Balfour's leadership, and his resignation three days later was publicly ascribed to reasons of age and health.

The principal rivals for the succession were Austen Chamberlain, representing the tariff-reforming thrust of Birmingham Unionism, and Walter Long, representing the older squirearchical Tory tradition of the shires. Each was supported by about half the party but was unacceptable to the other half – Chamberlain because of his antecedents (he was still a Liberal Unionist, not strictly a Conservative, and always his father's son) and Long for his hot temper and modest ability. A bruising battle was impending until Chamberlain, honourable as ever, proposed to Long that they should both stand down in favour of a compromise candidate – shrewdly encouraged to run by his friend Max Aitken – Bonar Law, who was thus unanimously elected at a meeting at the Carlton Club on 13 November. F.E. had been a strong Chamberlainite, convinced that Austen would have won on the second ballot if not the first; he repulsed the efforts of Aitken and Goulding to win him to Law so long as Austen was standing. But once Law was elected he cannot have been displeased for his new leader, though he had been a 'hedger' in August, was a man after his own heart on the questions of tariff reform and Ulster – Law was by descent an Ulsterman himself – and though indifferent to wine, women and good living, shared F.E.'s enjoyment of golf, tennis and bridge and many common friends. He was even a member of the Other Club, though as leader he rarely attended and actually attempted to wind it up in the interest of conducting an uncompromised Opposition. F.E. was perfectly sincere when he welcomed his emergence in a by-election speech, at Oldham on 11 November. (He was equally sincere in describing Balfour as 'one of the greatest intellects that has ever devoted itself to the study of politics in this country', a phrase he repeated frequently to the end of his life; intellect, however, was less important at this moment of Conservative

FRANK HOLLAND.   *Reynolds' Newspaper.*

'Balfour's Shoes'
Austen Chamberlain, Walter Long and Bonar Law (all together):
'What luck! Why they'll just fit me splendidly.'

fortunes than clear leadership.) He claimed Bonar Law publicly as a
friend, praised his courage, his lucidity, his forceful speech, his knowledge of business as well as politics, and particularly 'that transparent
simplicity and honesty of character which has endeared him to you and
me, and which will, I believe, rapidly command the confidence of the
party in the country . . . I believe', he concluded, 'that we have touched
low water; I believe that we are marching on now to the success which
has been too long delayed.'[89]

The Conservatives won Oldham, as a result of the intervention of a
Labour candidate, and went on to win two more seats from the
Government in straight fights in the next few weeks. Bonar Law's
accession did indeed give the party's fortunes an immediate fillip. F.E.'s
prospects of promotion improved simultaneously, though the invitation
to sit on the front bench was not automatic. F.E. himself, with his usual
determination to have what he thought his due, set Goulding and
Aitken to work to secure it. Goulding's letter to Law indicates that he
still had enemies who would have liked to see him snubbed again.

FE as you know is a staunch and generous friend but so many grossly unfair things have [been] and are said of him that I am certain he will think it necessary that the Party and the Public should be acquainted with your confidence by this invitation now or he will find it impossible to accept further on during the period of opposition.[90]

Whether or not Bonar Law really needed to be thus discreetly threatened, he duly came up with the desired invitation which was, of course, in effect an invitation to join the Shadow Cabinet. (F.E. was, as a Privy Councillor, already by Asquith's gift entitled to sit on the front bench, but he was determined that he would not do so except at his leader's invitation.) He took his new seat for the first time on 4 December amid the warm congratulations of friends and opponents, the latter including Lloyd George and Rufus Isaacs. *The Times* noted the 'signal tribute' paid to one who had been in the House of Commons so short a time but did not question that the promotion was deserved. 'The incisive brilliance of Mr F.E. Smith', it recorded in a review of the session, 'which has steadily strengthened his influence with the mass of the electorate has been officially recognised by a seat on the Opposition front bench.'[91] He was now, as Bonar Law's reign got under way, formally numbered among the leaders of the Tory party. He had arrived.

10

F.E. at Forty: Fame, Friends, Wine and Women

By the age of forty – which he reached in July 1912 – F.E. had achieved an extraordinary position in English public life. He had succeeded in reproducing on the national stage the same dazzling personal fame, the same buzz of expectation, that he had created around his inherently forgettable name first at Oxford, and then in Liverpool. In every sphere he touched, political, legal and social, he was an unquestioned star. If in the official hierarchy of the Unionist party he was still only the most junior member of the Shadow Cabinet, he had attained that rank, in the face of the prejudice and hostility which brains and pushfulness always attract, by being at the same time one of the most consistently effective, as well as amusing, debaters in the House of Commons – the words 'F.E. is up' were enough to empty the bars and fill the chamber and the public (not least the ladies') galleries – and the party's best speaker, without a rival, in the country: the only Tory to whose speeches, in those days when politics were a keenly followed popular sport, crowds flocked for entertainment and enlightenment in such numbers as they did for Lloyd George and Churchill on the Liberal side. Then, in the courts, he was the very image of the clever barrister, commanding fabulous fees with a reputation for cheeking judges, melting juries' hearts and destroying hostile witnesses with the most insidious cross-examination – this, again, at a period when quite minor trials were reported at enormous length and the leading counsel were invested with the glamour of film idols. Above and beyond these formal arenas where he made his career, however, F.E. enjoyed by 1912 a wider fame simply for being 'F.E.' Around his bare, magical initials stories accumulated and legends grew. 'Who is this Effie Smith?' one old lady is said to have inquired of another. 'I don't think she can be a modest girl to be talked about so much!'[1] He was talked about because no one quite like him had been seen before. A Conservative and a lawyer, from a landless and unmoneyed provincial middle-class background, he yet contrived to be youthful, handsome, dashing and romantic as no Tory had been since Lord Randolph Churchill. Witty, irreverent, flippant and cynical, careless of enemies and recklessly extravagant, determined to assault the very highest pinnacles of power and privilege but to deny himself none of the trappings of wealth and indulgence on the way, he persuaded others to believe in the inevitability of his seemingly effortless success apparently by sheer self-confidence, so that even those who most disliked his insolence and swagger could not help but be astonished at his nerve. 'He is a magnificent bounder', the Prime Minister's daughter, Cynthia Asquith, summed him up in her diary; but added, 'and I can't help liking him'.[2]

Few who came under the influence of his personality could help liking him: his gaiety and sense of fun, even his unconcealed pleasure in his own success, were boyish and irresistible. Nor could anyone who knew him doubt the hard work and the real intellectual quality on which that success was founded. Inevitably, however, there were many, knowing him less well or not at all, who detested the vulgarity of his too-obvious ambition, resented the rapidity of his rise, and thought his talent merely meretricious. 'F.E. Smith – the Boozer Swank' ran a wonderfully pithy scrawl on a wall in his constituency.[3] At rather greater length the Liberal journalist A.G. Gardiner wrote in 1913 a thoroughly sniffy profile of him, seeing in him nothing more than an unprincipled adventurer, pandering to the populace with a mastery of the cheap gibe but possessing no convictions – a mercenary social climber serving the Tory party only as a lawyer serves a wealthy client.[4] There were many more even in his own party who echoed Wilfrid Scawen Blunt's dismissal of F.E., during the Parliament crisis, as a 'whipper-snapper' – a presumptuous upstart too big for his boots. (Blunt thought the *real* leader of the 'ditchers' was his gilded cousin Wyndham.)[5] Gardiner's is an appalling (but characteristic)misjudgment for a supposedly perceptive professional observer. By repeating the old story of F.E. and Simon tossing a coin to decide which party each should join – he assumed that F.E. had lost! – he entirely overlooked the influence of F.E.'s background and missed the essential seriousness which lay not far behind his flamboyant façade, the solid foundation of learning and thought without which F.E. could not possibly have achieved so much as he already had. Gardiner's view was Liberal superciliousness: Blunt's was simple snobbery, an instinctive reflex to which even an extreme radical of ancient landed family was not immune when confronted by ambitious brains lacking either roots or pedigree. Yet F.E. was a phenomenon there was no getting away from: the Tory party could not do without him. In April 1911 the popular magazine *Every-*

body's Weekly devoted an article to explaining his astonishing rise.

> Personality is the thing that counts. Mr F.E. Smith, the apache of
> Conservative orators, has personality . . . He has reached one of
> the pinnacles of popularity, for picture postcards of him appear in
> stationers' shops alongside those of beaming beauties of light
> opera.
>   When Mr F.E. Smith is billed to address a meeting he can fill
> the hall as quickly as Harry Lauder. He is 'great'. The Con-
> servatives have no other speaker of the ring of 'F.E.'[6]

His star quality as a speaker was based partly on his mastery of the
popular presentation of an argument, partly on his armoury of invective,
ridicule and satire, but not least on his commanding physical presence.
He was still, with all his other advantages, strikingly handsome – tall,
athletic and youthful, his hair as black and glossy as ever, his face not
yet lined by responsibility and good living. He countered the effects of
work and drink by taking strenuous exercise and keeping very fit: all his
life he prided himself on his physical strength, to the somewhat embarrassing extent in middle age of inviting younger friends to feel his
muscles! When he visited the United States in 1912, the *New York Post*,
hailing him with premature enthusiasm as 'the leader of the Unionist
Party', described him as 'a big man physically as well as politically', six
foot three and 200 lbs, 'looking in all like an erudite prizefighter'.[7] F.E.,
priding himself on the bare-knuckle exploits of his great-grandfather,
must have been delighted.

But above all what made him popular with audiences was his wit –
the extended flights of sarcasm; the calculated insolence with which he
pricked the pretensions of the Government and mocked their moralizing;
the swift retorts to hecklers, always the mark of a really good popular
speaker, the ability to turn a hostile interruption to his own advantage
and win a lively audience to his side. He was particularly good with Free
Traders. 'You want to tax my food,' came a cry during one of the 1910
elections. 'No, sir,' F.E. replied, peering into the hall. 'There is no
proposal to put a tax on thistles.'[8] 'Rats,' came a bellow of derision
another time, when F.E. was expounding the benefits of tariffs. 'You are
thinking of your larder under free trade,' he swiftly shot back.[8] It is the
speed of response that matters in these situations, not whether it makes
sense. 'Are you going to put a tax on music?' he was asked on another
occasion. 'What kind of music?' he parried. 'Vocal music,' the ques-
tioner responded, thinking to score. 'No, sir,' F.E. replied. 'That is raw
material. Under Mr Chamberlain's pledge it comes in free.'[9]

Sometimes, of course, he played for the audience contribution, which he then capped with a well-rehearsed laugh line. 'Can it now be said that there is anyone better off because of the land taxes?' he demanded in Bradford in 1912. One 'yes' was audible above the shout of 'no'. 'The gentleman who said "yes" must be a solicitor.'[10] But F.E.'s quick-witted ability to handle the unexpected was prodigious. Once, he was condemning the proposal in the 1909 Budget to tax landowners on ungotten minerals. 'You might as well', he suggested, 'put a tax on bachelors for ungotten babies.' 'Introduce them to the suffragettes,' came a voice. F.E. looked shocked for a second. 'No, sir, I disagree with you. On the contrary both these matters should be left to private enterprise.'[11]

He could not only raise a laugh by repartee, but make a serious point. Revisiting the Oxford Union as Lord Chancellor during the Irish war of 1921 he was extolling to a hostile audience the bravery of the Black and Tans. 'For 12/6 a day,' one undergraduate shouted out – a substantial wage at that date. Half a century later the undergraduate still remembered F.E.'s quiet but crushing response, 'Would the hon. member do it for anything less?'[12]

Yet another of his most quicksilver replies may be quoted here, though it belongs to the very end of his life, 1928 or 1929: it demonstrates the same marvellous fluency of his prime. 'And now', he told his audience, 'I shall tell you exactly what the Government has done for all of you.' 'Nothing,' came a woman's voice from the gallery. 'My dear lady,' F.E. replied with the most exaggerated courtesy,

> the light in this hall is so dim as to prevent a clear sight of your undoubted charms, so that I am unable to say with certainty whether you are a virgin, a widow or a matron, but in any case I will guarantee to prove that you are wrong. If you are a virgin flapper, we have given you the vote; if you are a wife, we have increased employment and reduced the cost of living; if you are a widow, we have given you a pension – and if you are none of these, but are foolish enough to be a tea drinker, we have reduced the tax on sugar.[13]

His gift of swift rejoinder was even sharper away from the platform, in private conversation. He once found himself seated at dinner next to a lady who introduced herself rather pompously as 'Mrs Porter-Porter, with a hyphen'; F.E. promptly replied that he was 'Mr Whisky-Whisky, with a syphon'![14] It is not surprising that his almost physical inability to keep such jests to himself made him as many enemies as friends. He had no patience with bores, and had a repertoire of ways of shutting them up abruptly. On one occasion, around 1920, he was attending with the

Prince of Wales a luncheon in Swansea to mark the opening of the new Town Hall.

At the end of the lunch, the Mayor made an interminable speech which no-one seemed capable of stopping. The Prince turned to Lord Birkenhead, who was sitting next to him, and said 'Can't we dry this chap up?' Birkenhead nodded, picked up a menu-card and wrote a few words on the back. He then told the Toastmaster to give it to the speaker. Shortly after this had been done, the Mayor made some very brief closing remarks and sat down. Later, the Prince very intrigued asked Birkenhead what he had written. F.E. replied, 'I told him his fly-buttons were undone.'[15]

The stories are numberless – not all of them so funny on paper as they evidently were at first telling. But the best are imperishable. One of these is his brilliant retort to the railwayman's leader, Jimmy Thomas – a cheerful character, who positively flaunted his dropped 'h's and would not have taken F.E.'s ribbing amiss.* 'Ooh, Fred,' he complained once after a hard night, 'I've got an 'ell of an 'eadache.' F.E.'s recommendation was instant. 'Try a couple of aspirates.'[17]

F.E.'s income by 1912 was fabulous. He could not be called a rich man, because he spent money as fast as he earned it, and stored up trouble for himself in the future by accumulating no capital; but he disposed of enormous wealth. Precisely how much it is impossible to be sure. After the war, when he had gone to the Woolsack he was inclined to pluck wild figures out of the air to emphasize what a sacrifice he had made in giving up the Bar, and doubtless also to allow for wartime inflation of money values. To Arnold Bennett in 1918 he boasted that he had earned £25,000 a year before the war,[18] and later he pushed this fantasy up to £30,000 or even £40,000, which was what he reckoned he might have earned at post-war prices. In fact, his papers show that in 1913–14 he received in fees only £14,195, and in the previous two years substantially less – £9,925 in 1911–12, and £10,810 in 1912–13.[19] But he had no need to exaggerate. These were by the standard of the day sufficiently fantastic figures, when it is remembered that quite prosperous middle-class salaries were measured in hundreds, not thousands, of pounds; that Cabinet Ministers received £5,000 or £2,000; and that even Lloyd George's 'confiscatory' Budget of 1909 raised income tax only to 1s 2d and supertax to 1s 6d in the pound, with the supertax

* Thomas was first returned to the House of Commons in January 1910. One day, soon after the election, before he had learned his way around, he happened to ask F.E. the way to the lavatory. 'Down the corridor, first right, first left and down the stairs,' F.E. told him. 'You'll see a door marked "Gentlemen", but don't let that deter you.'[16]

threshold at £5,000. To be *earning* £10,000–£15,000 in 1912 was an income truly stupendous.

During 1913 F.E. and Margaret moved from Eccleston Square to a London house more expressive of these figures and the style of living they supported – 32 Grosvenor Gardens, just off Buckingham Palace Road, a large corner house in French Empire style with jutting corners and high roofs, described by F.E. with neither modesty nor exaggeration as a 'palace'.[18] It is an astonishing house for a self-made professional man to be able to afford at the age of forty. Almost certainly F.E. could *not* properly afford it, and its upkeep contributed to his money worries for the rest of his life. But in 1913, when such worries were unimaginable, its purchase was an ostentatious public flaunting of his material success. Inside, the rooms are not in fact so large as one would imagine from the street, but very pleasantly proportioned, with several fine moulded ceilings and marble fireplaces. The best feature is the main staircase, extending up the first two storeys around a decorated, subtly convex-sided stairwell. The grand rooms were all on the first floor: the drawing-room and dining-room, the hub of F.E.'s entertaining, with a small ballroom opening from it; also F.E.'s pride and joy, 'immense and magnificent', his library.[2]

From his Oxford days or earlier he had been a serious book-collector, regardless of expense, and by now he had a very fine collection indeed – the ancient classics in the best editions and bindings, first editions of all the English classics, particularly the great novels. Whether he had read many of them since his youth is doubtful, but his memory was prodigious, so that his knowledge of literature was genuinely impressive, even if his judgments were inclined to be somewhat pat. Addressing the members of the Sir Walter Scott Society in Edinburgh in 1924, for instance, he regaled them with a confidently concise survey of their hero's predecessors, each pinioned with a couple of classifying adjectives, 'the long-drawn out and maudlin sentimentality of Richardson . . . the robust humour, the high spirits, the humanity of Fielding . . . the cynical, ironical and coarse brilliancy of Sterne'.[20] Scott he loved deeply and knew minutely, claiming to have read all his novels three times before he went to university, and to re-read them every decade: Stevenson too, whom he regarded as Scott's true heir and the supreme stylist. What he meant by style was narrative clarity; what he most enjoyed was a good adventure story – which is why one doubts whether he went back often to the ancients or read with much pleasure the moderns. 'His classical memory is wonderfully good,' Leo Amery noted in 1922,[21] but the emphasis was on *memory*. He could trade classical tags with anyone, toss off a witty translation of a Greek couplet at the drop of a hat, or even make a good Latin joke – as on one occasion when as Lord

Chancellor he was receiving a deputation of Kentish hop-growers: one of them complained that there were ''ops, 'ops everywhere but never an 'op of Kent' – which F.E., remembering his Horace, instantly rendered in an undertone as '*Magnas inter opes inops*, in fact'.[22] But he was not, like Asquith for instance, a true scholar, finding continual refreshment in his Homer and Horace, even though he did in 1917 refer Beaverbrook to Thucydides as containing 'the whole art of war' and 'the whole art of statecraft'.[23] His library, which he showed off proudly to everyone who came to the house, was in considerable part a status symbol, designed to display simultaneously his wealth and his discrimination, the proof of a truly cultured man. 'The library is even equal to his own boastings about it,' Arnold Bennett noted in 1918, adding with a writer's distaste, 'but he would continually refer to prices.' On the other hand, 'What astonished me was that he does not keep even really valuable books (from £100 to £2,000 a piece) under glass.'[24] Moreover, Bennett noted with gratitude, both F.E. and Margaret '*did* really *know* my books' – unlike, presumably, many others who lionized him.[18] But then *Clayhanger* and *The Old Wives' Tale* were the sort of modern novels F.E. could understand. He had no time for Joyce or Virginia Woolf.

Grosvenor Gardens remained F.E.'s London home for the rest of his life, except for a period during the war when he gave it up to the American Red Cross. Once – it must have been quite soon after they moved there – he and Margaret were booking in together at a hotel when F.E. noticed that the guest immediately before them, who happened to be the clan chief Cameron of Lochiel, had signed the register simply 'Lochiel and Lady Cameron'. Not to be outdone, F.E. promptly wrote on the next line, '32 Grosvenor Gardens and Mrs Smith'.[25] Another time, less credibly, F.E. is said to have been so bored by the long-windedness of the chairman introducing him at some public meeting that when eventually the unfortunate man ended, 'And now Mr Smith will give you his address', he simply announced, 'Ladies and gentlemen – 32 Grosvenor Gardens,' and left to catch his train![26] When F.E. died, Freddie would not have wanted to keep up his father's palace even if he could have afforded to: its grandeur was not his style. Today it is the South-west Regional Headquarters of the Midland Bank; but it bears a blue plaque, which is the only public memorial to F.E. anywhere.

Though Grosvenor Gardens was their principal residence, the whole Smith family, plus servants, would decamp most weekends and for longer periods in the summer to Charlton. The 'cottage', as F.E. called it, had by 1912 become a substantial country house, expanding all the time as he built on additions with the proceeds of every big brief that came his way: there were tennis courts, both hard and grass, a swimming pond, and of course a stable full of horses, requiring a paddock in which to exercise them. Yet it was still not a grand house and F.E. did not at all act the *grand seigneur*. The children were encouraged to play with the local children, and he dropped in freely at the pub, the Rose and Crown, where he was welcomed as a popular and doubtless generous local character and a good sport. Only the clergy did not consider him a good influence: he did not go to church, and in particular they never forgave an incident in which he dared two ladies, for a bet, to ride *astride* through the village on a Sunday morning, which was considered very wicked.[27]

His motor cars created a stir in a quiet village where such things had never been seen before. It was actually Horatio Bottomley who disturbed the peace by bringing the first car to Charlton, but F.E. soon had his own Rolls-Royce and several other cars. He regarded them, however, to the amusement of his groom/chauffeur, like horses, insisting that they must never be allowed to get overtired – hence the need for a whole fleet which could be used in rota.[27] F.E. belonged to the last age of the horse, thought naturally in terms of horse-power and never understood mechanical power at all. Even after the war, when he had given up hunting, horseback remained his normal method of going about the countryside: he rode regularly into Oxford, twenty miles away, or across country to see Harold at Middleton Cheney or Simon at Fritwell. The cars were used primarily for meeting visitors who arrived by train from St Marylebone at Brackley, five miles away.

Winston and Winterton, Max Aitken and Paddy Goulding, Carson and Bonar Law were among the friends and political colleagues who came most frequently for the weekend. There were also younger friends, pupils from his chambers whom, as at Thornton Hough, he would invite for a day's riding or tennis, and he was already developing the practice which he indulged on a greater scale in the 1920s of patronizing promising young men whom he would ask out from Oxford for strenuous relaxation from their books. In the autumn of 1908, for instance, he suggested to Selborne's son and heir, Viscount Wolmer, then at University College, that he should come to Charlton for a week's 'cobbing': Wolmer declined, on the ground that he must start reading for his Schools the next summer – at which F.E. quickly reversed himself and advised Wolmer that he was quite right, and should read solidly eight hours a day from now until June as he himself had done in his final year![28] Wolmer was a special protégé, whom F.E. once took to dine in Wadham, in defiance of the Oxford etiquette that undergraduates did not dine at High Table. Others whom he patronized at this time included some of the most celebrated of the 'lost generation' of gilded young men who were to die a few years later in the war: Edward

Horner, and Lady Desborough's two sons, Julian and Billy Grenfell. It is difficult to deny an element of snobbery and social climbing in the selection of his younger friends: F.E. always liked to feel that he was cultivating the élite, and despite or because of his own background he did have a weakness for historic titles. Yet no one could doubt the genuineness of the friendship he held out to those he chose, and the wide circle of his friends was as far as possible from being exclusively aristocratic. He liked any exceptional quality, whether it was charm, brains, courage, money or athletic prowess, and always loved the company of the gay and gifted young. Only dullness bored him.

A particularly important younger friend from this period was Jack Scott, whom F.E. first met in 1906 as Master of the University Drag-hounds: he described him as the bravest rider at a fence he ever saw. After Oxford, Scott came to study in F.E.'s chambers, but he was not cut out for the law and found his vocation in the war as an intrepid airman. (Shortly after the end of the war he and F.E. happened to be visiting Germany together, when Scott found himself challenged to a duel for paying too extravagant attention to another man's wife. Bewildered, he named as his second F.E., who retrieved the situation with typical quick-wittedness. 'My choice of weapons, I believe. I choose airplanes and machine-guns.')[29] Scott became secretary first to Winston, then to Freddy Guest, when they were successively Secretary of State for Air; but he contracted double pneumonia on a ski-ing holiday in 1922 and died, mourned by all who knew him – not least by Margaret, who had developed a special fondness for him, and may even have been a little in love with him. F.E. wrote a generous and moving tribute in *The Times*, later reprinted in his *Points of View*.[30]

These were just a few of the friends whom F.E. and Margaret entertained at Charlton in the summers before the war. Above all, however, Charlton was a family retreat. Eleanor was ten in 1912, already a romantic tomboy, and Freddie five: Margaret's third child, Pamela, was born (at Charlton) in May 1914. With all his other activities, which took him away from them a lot, F.E. was devoted to his children and spoiled them dreadfully, delighting in showing off their precocity to his friends while at the same time he instilled in them his own competitiveness and love of challenge. To outsiders, the Smith children – particularly the girls – seemed high-spirited but very rough and physical, much given to teasing and practical jokes. They all, but especially Eleanor, grew up with two great loves – on the one hand for books, but on the other for horses; and as soon as they were old enough to stay in the saddle they each had their own pampered ponies filling up the stables and the surrounding fields.*

* The exception was Pamela, who was found to have an allergy to horses.

Though the love of his family was the emotional anchor of F.E.'s life, he was undoubtedly seen at his best and most characteristic with his friends. It was among his contemporaries and equals, in that masculine atmosphere of uninhibited competitive talk, that he was happiest and shone most brightly. Far and away his most intimate, his greatest friend was Winston Churchill. Almost from the moment they met, he and Winston loved one another, as opponents and later as colleagues, through many disagreements great and trivial, for twenty-four years up to F.E.'s death. Temperamentally they were similar, yet subtly different – F.E. more reckless, Winston more volatile; F.E. more intellectual, Winston more emotional and instinctive; F.E.'s sombre realism balanced by Winston's often impetuous romantic optimism. Where F.E. was relentlessly masculine, he found in Winston 'a quality which is almost feminine in its caressing charm';[31] while Winston found in F.E. 'all the canine qualities in a remarkable degree – courage, fidelity, vigilance, love of the chase'.[32] Clementine Churchill, though she came to recognize that F.E. was a true friend of Winston in his time of trouble, never liked him or approved of his influence on her impressionable husband. She feared that F.E. encouraged Winston to drink too much and particularly to gamble. 'F.E.', Winston's daughter, Mary Soames, has written, 'could always recoup his losses by some brilliant brief, but no such means of replenishment was open to Winston.'[33] Clementine did, however, very much like Margaret.

F.E. and Winston had some of their best times together in these pre-war years playing at soldiers in the annual summer camp of the Oxfordshire Yeomanry, usually held in amazing comfort in the grounds of Blenheim. The serious military purpose of these camps was minimal – both simply enjoyed the opportunity to ride around in uniform with their friends. The evenings were given over to conversation and cards. It was at one of these Blenheim camps that F.E., playing with Winston's cousin the Duke of Marlborough, their host, was asked what they should play for. 'Your bloody palace, if you like,' he replied.[34] History does not record that F.E. became the owner of Blenheim, even for an hour.

F.E.'s friendship with Winston was well known, and did them both considerable harm in their parties. 'It is doubtful', *Vanity Fair* noted in 1911 – doing F.E. the honour of a second feature only four years after its first – 'which of the two suffers most in public estimation by the association.'[35] It was not that they held back from attacking one another in public: quite the contrary – F.E. often seemed to make a special point of attacking Winston, sometimes seriously, as on Home Rule, where he constantly pursued his friend with telling reminders of Lord Randolph's championing of Ulster, and often in jest, as when he opened a speech in

Dundee, Winston's constituency, 'I learn from the *Dundee Advertiser* – the journal, not the politician . . .'[36] Rather their Liberal and Unionist colleagues feared that each was suborning the other in private. Doubtless they were doing their best – they must have had the most tremendous arguments over Home Rule, the Budget and the House of Lords – but neither ever seriously converted the other, unless it be that F.E. was able to convince Winston of the reality of Ulster's determination to fight at a time when the majority of the Cabinet still refused to acknowledge the problem. But feeling between the parties was so inflamed, particularly around 1910–11, that the close friendship of two such leading champions across the great divide seemed to many ardent partisans akin to treason. At the least, as Leo Maxse complained to Paddy Goulding in 1910, such undesirable consorting with the enemy might undermine a good young Tory's principles.

> Our friend F.E. Smith has been touring in the Mediterranean in a thoroughly vicious atmosphere, his host being that first-class blackguard the Baron de Forest [a rich young Liberal, M.P. for West Ham 1911–18]* and his friend the unspeakable Home Secretary [Winston] whom however F.E. seems to have made a laudable effort to 'pot'. I always notice that after these associations F.E. unconsciously comes out with some radical nostrum. You may remember some weeks ago his lamentable letter to *The Times*, giving away the Unionist position on the Constitutional question.[37]

There were rumours in some quarters that F.E. might actually follow Winston into the Liberal party. This misconception, wrote the author of the article in *Everybody's Weekly*, 'has its origin in the knowledge [that] he has little sympathy with the old school of Toryism, but . . . is a supporter of some principles hitherto regarded as Radical, such as the payment of MPs, and . . . is an associate of Mr Winston Churchill'. But misconception it was. 'Mr Smith has principles as well as much ambition.' What he was held to lack, at this date, by comparison with Winston, was the vision of constructive statesmanship: his speeches were all destructive, lawyer's speeches directed at proving his own side right and the Government wrong.[6] This of course was true, but inevitable so

---

* F.E. spared his other Liberal friends on the platform no more than he spared Winston. At the January 1910 General Election, de Forest was the Liberal candidate at Southport: F.E.'s attack on him from the Town Hall balcony made such an impression on one young man in the crowd that he remembers his words to this day – 'We want a member, not a money-bag; a politician, not a purse; a candidate, not a cheque-book.'[3] De Forest lost by 400 votes.

RAVEN HILL.   'Punch," 2nd Nov., 1910.

'Students on the Make'
Mr F.E. Smith: 'Master of Epigram – like me!!'
Mr Winston Churchill: 'Wrote a novel in his youth – like me!'
Together: 'Travelled in the East like us. How does it end?'

long as he was confined to opposition: he would display the positive side of his talent well enough when he got the opportunity of government. No one, meanwhile, doubted that F.E., like Winston, was aiming at the topmost rung of the political ladder and was very likely to get there. *Punch* published in November 1910 a cartoon entitled 'Students on the Make', showing the two friends poring over a large 'Life of Disraeli'. 'Master of epigram – like me,' says F.E. 'Wrote a novel in his youth – like me,' says Winston. 'Travelled in the East like us,' they say together. 'How does it end?'[38]

Another friendship formed at this time, but which lasted with numerous ups and downs, estrangements and reconciliations, to the end of F.E.'s life, was with Max Aitken – the future Lord Beaverbrook. Aitken was then a young Tory M.P. (seven years younger than F.E.), a wild colonial boy who had made a fortune by financial dealing in Canada and come to England to make his political fortune, not yet launched as a newspaper baron but intimately attached to his fellow-Canadian Bonar Law, a man of very different tastes and temperament whose confidence he had nevertheless won to the extent that he was widely seen as Law's puppet-master or Svengali. At the time of the Unionist leadership contest in 1911, Aitken played a major role in pushing Law forward as the compromise candidate between Chamberlain and Long. F.E. enshrined Aitken's acute management of his man in a neat verse. (Pembroke Lodge was Law's house in Kensington.)

> Round Pembroke Lodge in Edwardes Square
> Like rooks the claimants caw:
> And Aitken holds with gargoyle stare
> His vigil over Law.[39]

Aitken's intimacy with Bonar Law was of the greatest value to F.E. Through Aitken's hospitality he was able to be more in the company of his new leader than he could possibly have been otherwise, playing tennis, golf and above all bridge. Both the Beaverbrook and the Bonar Law papers are full of little notes from F.E. accompanying cheques for small losses, up to about £20, at any or all of these games, with usually a few words of congratulations and encouragement for 'the big show'. As well as keeping him in with his leader, Aitken also made a habit of buying shares for F.E. (as he did for all his friends), using his knowledge of the stock market simultaneously to enrich his friends and put them in his debt. F.E. in turn performed other services for Aitken, advising him on buying books or helping to get him into a golf club. In August/ September 1912 they travelled together in a parliamentary delegation

to the United States and Canada. F.E.'s need for Aitken's enlivening
company is urgently expressed in a note written from the Ritz-Carlton
Hotel in New York on 17 August.

Dear Max,
    We leave Boston on the Winnipeg train on Friday so for God's
    sake don't go without us & leave us stranded friendless & penniless
    & bridgeless.
                              Yours ever,
                              F.E.[40]

F.E. and Aitken shared the same tastes and pleasures. They both
played the political game with unashamed enjoyment and warmed to
one another's sense of fun and adventure. Yet Aitken lacked F.E.'s
bedrock of essential seriousness; he was always at heart a gnome, an
irresponsible mischief-maker, whose only constant political commitment (other than to Bonar Law) was the dream of imperial preference
to bind the colonies to the Mother Country by differential tariffs. He
wanted no formal power for himself, but aspired only to be a Kingmaker
(and unmaker): F.E: wanted quite straightforwardly to be King, with
both the glory and the responsibility which that involved. It was thus
inevitable that their relationship should come under strain when F.E.
achieved high office. They were never twin souls sharing anything like
the bond of affectionate sympathy which united F.E. and Winston even
when they were in opposite parties. Aitken's relationship with both was
close but more superficial, existing primarily on the level of political
gossip and intrigue. But gossip and intrigue were the stuff of F.E.'s life
between 1910 and 1914, and Aitken was always close at hand supplying
both.
    The most enduring monument to the F.E.–Winston friendship was
their joint foundation, in the summer of 1911, of the Other Club. F.E.
had little time for the traditional London clubs with their deep leather
armchairs, solemn reading rooms and public school food. One of the
most frequently repeated stories about him tells of his alleged habit of
dropping in to the National Liberal Club (or the Athenaeum, or the
Guards' – but a look at a map shows that it could only be the National
Liberal, which of course increases his effrontery) to use the lavatory on
his way from his home or the House of Commons to his chambers; on
being challenged one day he replied airily, 'Oh, is this place a club
then?' Such pompous establishments had no charm for F.E., though he
did necessarily join the Carlton and by 1912 also listed in *Who's Who*
Pratt's, the Marlborough, the 1900 and the R.A.C. What he loved, from
his Wadham days onwards, were intimate, select dining clubs with no

premises of their own, simply a group of friends who would meet at irregular intervals over an excellent dinner, with no ladies present, to indulge the pleasure of one another's conversation over the port and brandy. F.E. belonged to many such congenial coteries in his time; but in 1911 he and Winston decided to found the perfect one.

It is said that the stimulus was that they were both simultaneously blackballed by 'The Club', the impeccably exclusive Establishment dining circle descended from Dr Johnson's literary talking shop of the 1760s. This explanation is very possible: it would account for the name, and F.E. was always easily stung by such rebuffs. On the other hand both would at this period have been most unlikely members of 'The Club', and the company they had in mind for their own table far more accurately reflected their social preferences and heterodox political outlook. The Other Club was not exactly anti-Establishment, but it comprised a sort of counter-Establishment of all the most *interesting* people in public life – mainly younger men – excluding the bores and the stuffed shirts. Members were invited entirely on personality, as amusing and stimulating dinner companions, very much in the image of the founders, but carefully balanced with an equal representation from each party.

Rule 3 laid down that 'The Club shall consist of no more than 50 members, and not more than 24 members of the House of Commons.'[41] The initial membership was actually 41, with 12 from each side of the Commons, 8 peers and 9 'distinguished outsiders' to leaven the parliamentary lump. The biggest catch from the Government side was Lloyd George, from the Opposition Bonar Law, neither of them normally considered 'clubbable' men: Law in fact resigned as soon as he became Tory leader. The other House of Commons members fell into two categories. The largest group was of ambitious 'Young Turks', potential rebels and 'characters' of both parties, who were most clearly the friends and brothers-in-arms of the two founders – Goulding, Winterton, Jack Hills, Waldorf, Astor, Viscount Castlereagh, the Irish K.C. James Campbell and the half-mad Admiral Lord Charles Beresford from the Tory backbenches; Neil Primrose, Dudley Ward, Freddy Guest, Charles Masterman and Jack Seely from the Liberals. But lest this phalanx of clever troublemakers dining together should attract the censure of the Whips, or raise the sinister spectre of coalitionism, several figures of unimpeachable party orthodoxy were invited too – the Tory party chairman, Arthur Steel-Maitland, and the future Chief Whip, Bolton Eyres-Monsell; the Liberal Chief Whip, the Master of Elibank, and his successor, Percy Illingworth, plus another Cabinet Minister in Rufus Isaacs. Respectability was also ensured by the inclusion of both the King's secretaries, Lord Knollys and Lord

Stamfordham, and the ubiquitous courtier, Lord Esher. Other peers included Churchill's cousin Marlborough, F.E.'s Oxford friend the Earl of Malmesbury, the veteran tariff reformer, Lord Ridley, and most incongruously, Kitchener (who, however, was rarely in England). There was another General in the person of Sir John French; a judge – F.E.'s frequent sparring partner Sir Charles Darling; the actor Beerbohm Tree; the novelist Anthony Hope Hawkins; the Portuguese Ambassador; and four newspapermen – Garvin of the *Observer*, H.W. Massingham of the Liberal *Nation*, Sir George Riddell, proprietor of the *News of the World*, and Sir Henry Dalziell, proprietor of *Reynold's News*, who was also a Liberal M.P. There were no Labour members judged worthy of membership, but one Irish Nationalist, the irrepressible T.P. O'Connor – whose presence might have shocked some of F.E.'s constituents.

Analysed thus, the Other Club can be seen as a full cross-section of Edwardian/Georgian political society, in which the Young Turks who have tended to give the club its image were well balanced by figures of considerable solidity and achievement – not all of whom, however, attended regularly. The club itself did not meet quite so regularly as the rules suggested ('The Club shall dine on alternate Thursdays at 8.15 punctually, when Parliament is in Session': the gap was as often one week or three, or longer) but it kept going pretty well until the summer of 1913 when it inexplicably lapsed, until revived by an exceptionally well-attended dinner on the outbreak of the war. Several new members were elected in these three years, including Max Aitken, who was a surprising omission from the original list, and Mark Sykes; Northcliffe attended the second dinner in 1911, but no other.

The later rules bear F.E.'s stamp unmistakably upon them.

8. The Executive Committee shall settle all outstanding questions with plenary powers.
9. There shall be no appeal from the decision of the Executive Committee.
10. The names of the Executive Committee shall be wrapped in impenetrable mystery.
11. The members of the Executive Committee shall nominate the Joint Secretaries, who shall receive no remuneration, and shall be liable for all unforeseen obligations.

The two members who took on this thankless job, and were responsible for arranging the 'pairing' of members of the House of Commons for divisions, were Eyres-Monsell and Freddy Guest. But it was the last rule which most vividly enshrined the spirit of the Club.

> 12. Nothing in the rules or intercourse of the Club shall interfere
>   with the rancour or asperity of party politics.[41]

That is pure F.E.

If the Other Club was a private manifestation of that curious cross-party camaraderie which co-existed with the bitter allegations and treason and revolution in the overheated atmosphere of politics at this hectic period, the same spirit was publicly and controversially demonstrated only six days after the Other Club's inaugural dinner by one of the most extraordinary high society functions of that sweltering Coronation summer of 1911; and again F.E. was a prime mover. The occasion was a lavish fancy-dress ball which he and Eddie Winterton threw, at Claridge's on 24 May, attended by practically the whole political hierarchy of both parties. Leading political figures, from the Prime Minister and the Leader of the Opposition downwards, disported themselves with a frivolity shocking to staid Victorians who could not imagine Gladstone behaving in such a manner and found the proceedings particularly improper at a moment when their newspapers told them that the country was in the throes of revolution and the parties locked in a life or death struggle for the Constitution.

Asquith and Balfour, admittedly, did not dress up, nor did the Speaker; but everyone else did, many extravagantly.

> From soon after 10 o'clock the stream of guests began to pour into the reception room, at the entrance to which stood Lord Winterton dressed as a gendarme and Mr F.E. Smith in a white 18th century Court suit. The party was altogether less stiff and formal than many of the other big entertainments of the season. Everybody knew everybody else, though in some cases recognition was not exactly instantaneous, and from the moment that they entered the room everybody felt at home, thanks to the cordiality with which they were received by their hosts, by whom they were generally greeted in French of the most colloquial. If Englishwomen are shy, as we have lately been told, they certainly did not show it at Claridge's last night.[42]

The Duchess of Marlborough, for instance, with whom F.E. and Margaret dined beforehand, 'looked charming as a Dresden china shepherdess', and other ladies were very much less modest. Churchill went robed resplendently in scarlet, with the cowl of his domino pulled over his head. Most upsetting to the guardians of dignity, the constitutional crisis itself was mocked when Waldorf Astor appeared on the stroke of midnight dressed as a newly created peer with the number 499 on his coronet, with 'Still One More Vacancy' on the reverse.

'A Peer' wrote in anonymous protest to *The Times*.

> Amid the surroundings of a London hotel, two prominent Unionist politicians, one of whom aspires to high Cabinet rank, and, presumably, to the confidence of his fellow-countrymen, gave last night a fancy dress ball which was attended, not only by young people out for a harmless evening's amusement, but by many of those engaged at the present time in what they themselves have chosen to describe as the greatest political crisis since the Great Rebellion. It shows no deficiency of humour, I hope, to note with a sense of painful surprise, among smart ladies arrayed in every variety of costume from Cleopatra to a pink tulle ballet girl, and among elderly peers masquerading as Tudor Kings, the figures of the Prime Minister and the Leader of the Opposition.

Asquith was reported to have been 'much amused' by the '499th peer'.

> A sense of humour is a saving grace, but is it a grace at all if it saves a statesman from realising the gravity of issues which he himself has raised and which he is endeavouring to persuade his own countrymen to believe are vital to the public interest?

The writer concluded that the view that it was a serious crisis 'must appear to be absurdly exaggerated in the eyes of those who can contemplate without amazement the proceedings of last night'.[43]

Surprisingly, it was Winterton, not F.E. (though F.E. may well have had a hand in it) who wrote a stinging reply defending the ball as a private and perfectly proper social occasion, and attacking the cowardly anonymity of the killjoy peer.[44]

There were other glittering social events that summer and every season as the great hostesses – Lady Cunard, Lady Desborough, Lady Londonderry, Lady Jersey – entertained house parties and threw balls in what was to prove the climax and the finale of that astonishing pageant of wealth, class, culture and unashamed display before August 1914 rang down the curtain on that world for ever. F.E. was a part of this world, spending his weekends as often at Blenheim or Taplow or Wargrave as at Charlton, his evenings dining, dancing or at cards till far into the morning. Yet what was always noted of him with amazement, he was invariably in court again the next day none the worse for wear, the master of his brief, ready for the House of Commons in the afternoon, a speech or a dinner in the evening and another night of strenuous amusement which seemed only to refresh him, never to wear him out. He drank a lot, but it did not yet seem to affect his faculties.

There was never, until after the war, any suggestion that F.E. allowed his pleasures to intrude on the serious pursuit of his career – any more than he let his career crowd out his pleasures: he simply had the energy for both, as the Tory M.P. Sir Henry Page Croft, for instance, recalled in his memoirs.

His energy was boundless, and it was a marvel to his friends how he got through such an immense amount of work. I remember one day I had occasion to see him early. I called at 9 a.m. and found him in bed smoking a long cigar. He engaged in animated conversation for twenty minutes on the subject we had to discuss. Within two hours he was making a great speech in the Courts in a famous divorce case; at 3.45 he was leading the attack on the Liberal Government on licensing questions, showing an amazing knowledge of the intricacies of the licence laws; at 10.15 he rose to his feet and made a brilliant defence of the Welsh Church, speaking with the utmost freedom of Welsh Bishops of bygone ages as if they had been his personal friends. That night at an evening party he was still going strong at 2 a.m. Can anyone deny this was an exceptional man![45]

The details may be conflated, but the conclusion cannot be gainsaid.

F.E.'s was a male world. Politics and the law were exclusively male pursuits, and this for him was a large part of their attraction. The communities he loved – Wadham, Gray's Inn, the legal circuits, the House of Commons, the Other Club – were male communities bound together by a masculine ritual from which the exclusion of women was taken for granted. Women had their role on the fringe of politics: the great hostesses had considerable powers of patronage, and their favour was well worth cultivating. But the grandest of them were no more than on the fringe: serious discussion, if it took place at their tables, began only when the ladies left the room.

Women in this world had their 'separate sphere' of motherhood and suitably feminine interests ranging from fashions to philanthropy. Even in the home, F.E. had been brought up on the uncompromising assumption of male domination, which his mother, though a strong personality, imposed with an 'almost Oriental' rigour. 'When F.E., Harold or Sidney came into the house in the evening,' F.E.'s son has written, 'the two daughters were immediately ordered to leave the armchairs.'[46] Margaret swore to herself the first time she visited F.E.'s family that she would never allow such a rule in her house; nor did she. Her marriage to F.E. was, domestically, a very equal partnership.

He had a deep and genuine respect for her, as well as love; she was never eclipsed by him; and they shared not only their children but their love of both riding and tennis. Nevertheless Margaret had her 'separate sphere'. Her interests were artistic and musical – realms which were entirely foreign to F.E. – and she was quite content to leave the public realm of politics to him, warning him only occasionally if she thought that in some personal attack he had overstepped the limits of good taste. She never attempted, like Clementine Churchill, to act as her husband's political conscience. Nor did she often mind, as Clementine was inclined to mind, that F.E. spent so much of his time, with evident enjoyment, away from her in his male world with his male friends. She had even enough confidence in him – and in herself – not to worry about his flirtations and occasional involvement with female friends.

F.E., while he was devoted to his wife, had a ready appreciation of the attractions of other women. He enjoyed – not to the same extent as Lloyd George, but in marked contrast to the exceptionally faithful Winston – quite a reputation as a 'ladies' man'. In its place, that is as a relaxation from the serious business of life, he much enjoyed female company – so long as it was young, pretty and high-spirited. He liked a girl to be clever, so long as she was not earnest. But he abhorred plain women and blue-stockings. It was not in his view the function of women to be serious, but to entertain – to give pleasure to the eye and ear, to tease, to tempt, occasionally to submit to his attentions; not on any account to usurp the man's role in the world for which they were by nature and aptitude both physically and intellectually unfitted. ('How I hate a political woman!' he once exclaimed to Margaret, very early in their marriage, when telling her how he had been caught at dinner by Lady Ilbert on a visit to London in 1902.)[47] Women were made for higher things, and lower.

In male company F.E. had a strong streak of bawdy and a liking for the naughtier bits of Ovid. At the same time he had a Victorian prudishness about what was suitable for the ears of ladies. Once at the Other Club, after the war, he got into a long argument with Arnold Bennett (who had been elected in 1917) on the subject of Marie Stopes and her famous – then notorious – book on birth control, *Married Love*, which he thought 'disgusting'. 'He had no reasonable arguments,' Bennett recorded in his journal, 'and everything (nearly) he said on the subject was either specious or silly; but he phrased his matter well. He never gave in.'[48] Like most men of his generation, F.E. professed an elevated idea of women's innate purity and superior virtue, yet at the same time had no scruples about defeating it where he could. He had no serious affair of the heart before the war; but there were almost certainly snatched adventures of a sort for which the social circuit of that period,

at once sophisticated and somewhat raffish, gave plentiful opportunity
to a man with his appetite for pleasure. Mostly, however, F.E. simply
enjoyed exercising the power of his personality upon pretty and impressionable young women. One such, with whom he pursued a perfectly
chaste flirtation, was the future Freda Dudley Ward, who achieved
celebrity twenty years later as a close friend of the Prince of Wales. In
1912 Freda was a very young girl sailing on the same ship, the
Mauretania, on which F.E., with a parliamentary delegation including
Max Aitken and Philip Sassoon, was returning from the United States
and Canada. One morning she was sitting on deck reading a novel when
F.E. sat down beside her, tossed her book imperiously into the sea, and
told her she should not waste her time on such trash: he would give her a
list of what to read. She knew from the passenger list who he was, and
instead of being furious at his presumption, was utterly bowled over,
and spent much of the remainder of the voyage in his company. 'I have
seen a very beautiful creature on deck with F.E.,' Aitken reported
lasciviously to Bonar Law, 'and I greatly admire his taste in maids.'[49]
F.E., however, had nothing to dissemble when at Southampton they
were met by Margaret, to whom Freda took an immediate liking. F.E.
continued to write her long letters – about books, but enclosing large
photographs of himself! – and she became a lasting friend of the family,
marrying in 1913 William Dudley Ward, a former pupil in F.E.'s
Liverpool chambers, now a junior Liberal whip (and a member of the
Other Club).[50]

An even more innocent example of the gallantry to which young girls
could inspire him is a delightful little poem which he tossed off in the
autograph book of the thirteen-year-old Nancy Cunard at one of those
glittering house parties in 1910, following contributions by the philosopher George Moore and Max Beerbohm, among others.

> The song and the dance and the charm of romance
> Are everywhere found in these pages.
> Conventional scope has been found for the trope
> Which verse gives to youth down the ages.
> Profound Mr Moore has developed a *tour-*
> *de-force* of illegible wisdom!
> The pencil of Max scribbles age on our backs,
> Not even the diplomat is dumb.
> A humbler refrain, very much to my pain,
> Is mine than your sonnets and easels;
> No muses give ear; 'tis contagion they fear
> For poor little Nancy has measles![51]

If the scansion of line eight is not quite right, the rhyme is wonderfully cheeky, and the whole extraordinarily skilful; it must have delighted not only the afflicted Nancy, but the whole company to whom undoubtedly it would have been shown.

F.E.'s double-faced attitude to women was not, of course, simply a private foible. He was in this respect a typical, almost an archetypal Edwardian. The male supremacy which he took for granted, however, was under serious attack in the years before 1914, with the whole debate centring on the symbolic question of women's suffrage. Since 1905, the militant 'suffragettes', led by Mrs Emmeline Pankhurst, had taken up the running from the peaceful Women's Suffrage Union by adopting a mindless strategy of violent demonstrations, the disruption of meetings, attacks on Ministers (often those, like Lloyd George, who supported them) and sabotage of property to press their demand for the right to vote. The political world was divided down the middle, irrespective of party. Broadly speaking, a majority of Liberals were in favour of giving women the vote and a majority of Unionists against. But both party leaders were in the minority within their own parties, and the situation was further complicated by the question of an extension of the male franchise, which many Liberals thought a higher priority than giving it to women. Under the 1884 Reform Act, large sections of the male population were still excluded from the electorate. The conventional view is that these were predominantly the unskilled working class, whose enfranchisement would benefit the Liberals (and Labour). In fact, the tortuous provisions of the Act, which were differently inter-preted in different areas, tended to discriminate just as sharply against unmarried men of all classes – the great army of lodgers and young men who lived with their parents – many of whom might have been expected to vote Tory. The question of enfranchising women was similarly confused by calculations of party advantage. Those Tories, including both Balfour and Bonar Law, who supported women's suffrage sup-ported only a limited extension of the franchise to propertied women. Liberal suffragists naturally rejected this as likely simply to benefit the Tories, and insisted on an extension to women on equal terms with men which, if combined with the enfranchisement of most men, meant universal suffrage and practically a quadrupling of the electorate – an alarming prospect even to many friends of the women's movement. In these circumstances, with the suffragists divided among themselves about the sort of measure they wanted to see carried, the Prime Minister resolutely hostile, and very many waverers antagonised by the violent methods of the suffragettes, the cause of reform made little progress up to 1910.

In that year, however, despite the distractions of the Parliament crisis – assisted in fact by the party truce that summer – an all-party committee produced a compromise measure, known as the Conciliation Bill, embodying the Tory proposal of a restricted extension of the suffrage to women occupiers, and managed to pilot it through its Second Reading in the Commons by 299 votes to 189. Both Lloyd George and Churchill voted against it on the Liberal ground that it did not go far enough. F.E., on the other hand, opposed it root and branch, and led the anti-suffragists' attack with a terrific onslaught piling practical arguments on theoretical and biological on constitutional in a *tour de force* of sexual conservatism under threat.

First he deployed the High Tory constitutional line that *no one*, male or female, had the *right* to a vote. Voting was not a right, but a privilege entrusted by the State to responsible citizens. The idea of 'natural right' was as dead as Rousseau. Moreover 'no taxation without representation' was a mere catchword: the suffragists adopted it in special pleading, but they did not think to apply it to, for instance, India; nor even thoroughly to Britain. 'Is it to be contended', he asked, as though the question were self-evidently absurd, 'that every man who buys an ounce of tobacco or a quart of ale, and thereby contributes indirectly to taxation, is to be entitled to a vote?' For all his commitment to 'democracy', F.E. was not an advocate even of manhood suffrage.

Next, he made some play, for debating purposes, with opinion surveys to show that most women entirely dissociated themselves from the harpies who campaigned on their behalf, and *did not want the vote*. However, he promptly brushed this consideration aside as strictly irrelevant. 'But, Sir, I confess that if I were satisfied that every woman in the world wanted the vote, it would not influence me one bit.' Women, he contended instead, did not *need* the vote. Their interests were more than adequately cared for by male gallantry. 'After centuries of man-made law woman today occupies a position so preferential that no parallel can be discovered in any civilised country in the world.' Every husband was obliged to support his wife and was liable for her debts – which was not so in reverse. The only grievance he admitted lay in the field of divorce, where he agreed that the law should be made equal. The possession of the vote could do nothing to improve women's economic position, over which Parliament had no control. The proof, F.E. proposed, was that working men, even with the vote, still found it necessary to form unions and strike for higher wages!

Women, he next suggested, trying another tack, already had a wide political field open to them in local government, where they were entitled not only to vote but to sit on county councils and boards of guardians and undertake a wide range of social responsibility of the sort that lay in woman's proper sphere. 'Is not the fact that all these areas of activity are open to women today an answer to those who come here and say they are entitled to enter upon wholly different and vaster areas of work?' The parish pump was one thing, F.E. maintained; the government of the Empire quite another. Here he came to the most interesting part of his argument – a defensible theoretical view of the nature of the State which underlay much of the thinking of the anti-suffragists, but which no one formulated more clearly than F.E.

> Why is it that the majority in this country or in any other are allowed to live peaceably? Because in the last resort they can coerce the minority, and because it is known to the minority that in the last resort they can be coerced, and because it is more easy to vote than to fight. In other words, votes are to swords exactly as bank notes are to gold – the one is effective only because the other is believed to lie behind it.

If women were to be given the vote, the currency would be devalued. What would happen if a majority largely composed of women (by definition unable to fight) were to outvote a minority which might yet contain a majority of men – a situation which could easily arise on such an issue as temperance or national service, which principally affected men?

> The result would be that you would be brought to the very verge of anarchy, inasmuch as that numerically the majority were unable to give effect to their decision ... The most characteristic quality in the conception of law is its sanction, or the means by which it is made effective. In making it effective no woman can play the slightest part.

In the last resort the very existence of the State depended on men: it followed that men alone should have the vote. Women were in this view merely the helpless beneficiaries of male strength, unable to contribute to their own protection. 'This fundamental limitation is not confined to the Army: it extends equally to police, governors of gaols, coastguards, and to every person by whom the coercive power of the State is directly exercised.'

This view of the essential precariousness of the political community, as an island of civilization in a sea of natural barbarism always ready to overwhelm it, though probably derived from the classics and founded on the model of the Greek city states, had some plausibility in Edwardian England, which was still in many respects a very rough and brutal society in which women were well aware of their reliance on the physical protection of their men. It had a particular actuality in the context of Ulster, where the men were indeed preparing to defend their community by force in a situation where consent had broken down. Nevertheless it was a view of society already becoming outdated in practice and certainly in aspiration; and it was to be thoroughly discredited in a very few years by the experience of the war, which demonstrated that – even though it was still the men who fought and died – the contribution of the female population to the protection of the realm was no less vital. Modern war – as he himself recognized – destroyed F.E.'s notion of the pretty little woman gathering her children around her skirts while her husband alone discharged his duty to defend them. Modern woman insisted on taking a hand – and was duly rewarded with the vote.

F.E. in 1910 had other arguments, however. He saw the case for women's suffrage getting weaker, not stronger as civilization progressed. He called in aid H.G. Wells – who actually supported the women – quoting his view that women in the more advanced countries were in their social role *more*, not less, clearly differentiated from men.

> The education, the mental disposition of a white or Asiatic woman reeks of sex; her modesty, her decorum, is not to ignore sex but to refine and put a point to it; her costume is clamorous with the distinctive elements of her form. The white woman in the materially prosperous nations is more of a sexual specialist than her sister in the poor and austere peoples, of the prosperous classes more so than of the peasant woman.

If it was true, however, that women were getting more feminine, the argument was undercut by the fact that advancing civilization and technology were having the simultaneous effect of making men less masculine.

F.E. concluded his attack on the Conciliation Bill with some arguments from simple conservatism. There was first, he insisted, no relevant comparison between Britain, the mistress of a worldwide Empire, and lesser states like Norway or Finland, Australia or New Zealand, which had adopted women's suffrage. (He did not meet the argument that these too had to defend themselves.) 'We are', he declared, 'the legatees of the most nicely adjusted political fabric which the world has ever known.' The balance of the Constitution was already under threat from one direction, he warned his Unionist colleagues who were inclined to support the Bill. If the inter-party conference failed,

we are threatened with the risk of being governed not by a
bicameral, but by a unicameral system; and this is the moment
chosen when we are asked to add two million electors as to whose
bearing and trend at the polls no living man could pronounce with
the slightest confidence.

He begged them to recoil from this leap in the dark.

He also tried the 'thin end of the wedge' argument to frighten Tory
suffragists. Logically, he mocked, there was no stopping point between
granting the right to vote and allowing women to stand as candidates,
take their seats in the House of Commons, or even – the ultimate
absurdity! – hold the great offices of state. Had his colleagues considered these logical consequences of their vote? He quoted Gladstone:

If that be recognised, and none vote for this Bill who are not
prepared to face the consequences, then I have no apprehension as
to the result of the Division. I do not believe that a majority in this
House are prepared to face the results.

Even twenty years later, when he came to write a prediction of what the
world might be like another century on, F.E. felt that the arrival of
women – a bare handful of them – in the House of Commons and even in
the Cabinet was one of the most extraordinary occurrences of the last
hundred years, and he still could not conceive of the possibility of a
woman becoming Prime Minister in the next. The belief that a political
woman was simply against nature went very deep.

In his peroration he carried this argument to new heights of blind
perversity.

The hon. gentleman [the Labour member, David Shackleton]
has spoken of many illustrious women writers and of those of
whom the whole sex, and indeed the whole community, irrespective
of sex, are proud. I do not wish to decry the claim of women to
intellectual distinction. I have never in the course of my observations here or elsewhere founded myself on some assumed intellectual inferiority of women. I do not believe it, but I venture to say
that the sum total of human happiness, knowledge and achievement would have been almost unaffected if Sappho had never
sung, if Joan of Arc had never fought, if Siddons had never played,
and if George Eliot had never written. At the same time, without
the true functions of womanhood faithfully discharged throughout
the ages the very existence of the race and the tenderest and most
sacred influences which animate mankind would have disappeared.

Profoundly believing, as I do, that these influences are gravely menaced by the intrusion of women into the field of politics, I move the Amendment which I have on the paper.[52]

To the end of his life, even under the influence of two clever daughters in whose education and achievements he took a proud interest, F.E. never departed from this view that women must be treated as a lump: though *some* women might be better qualified to vote than *some* men, the average must be compared with the average; and 'the average woman's judgements and opinions' – he stooped to the classic argument in a letter to *The Times* in 1913 – 'are more coloured by emotion and by personal considerations than the average man's and might, especially in moments of public excitement, prove a source of instability and disaster to the State'.[53] In 1928, when actually a member of a Government which was extending the franchise to women at the age of twenty-one instead of thirty, he published an article unrepentently reprinting the final sweeping paragraph of his 1910 speech.[54] And in 1930 he expanded on it, still insisting that there had never been – not for social but for biological reasons – a female Michelangelo or Beethoven, and that Jane Austen and George Eliot could not ultimately be compared with the greatest male novelists – he mentioned Fielding, Cervantes, Dostoevsky and Balzac.* The reason was that while a man would let nothing stand in the way of his genius, a woman's instinct would always put her child first. (He ignored the inconvenient but not irrelevant fact that neither Jane Austen nor George Eliot was married.) However much women might expand their sphere in the future, he asserted, 'to the end of history they must rest content with falling just short of the best work done by men'. They would still, as in the past, attain their highest achievements through the men whom they inspired. 'In 2030 women will still use men as the media by which their greatest triumphs are wrought; they will still be able by their wit and charms to direct the activities of the most able men towards heights which they could otherwise never hope to reach.'[56]

He is here back to the vision of women existing on a spiritually higher plane than men, morally superior but for that reason unfitted for the compromising struggle of the real world. It is a hypocritical vision, flattering to women in theory even as it demeans them in practice. It has not survived the wars of the twentieth century, any more than F.E.'s view of women as mothers, pure and simple, has survived the spread of

---

* In an address to the Edinburgh Philosophical Institution in 1925 F.E. asserted that George Eliot's style 'suggested the use of the lipstick in public. The result is not to be despised, but the degree of the contrivance should be more carefully marked.'[55]

effective contraception – an inkling of what birth control portended for sexual equality presumably underlay F.E.'s hostility to Marie Stopes. At bottom, this vision of F.E. and the many who in 1910 felt as he did can only be regarded as wishful thinking of a plainly self-protective sort. Not just the power but the pleasure, the traditions and the whole mystique of his masculine world were threatened by the intrusion of women; also by extension, for a man who so identified himself and his ambitions within that world, his own personal identity, his very self. It is this that explains F.E.'s fervent feeling on the woman question, the unusual lack of rigour and rationality in his speeches on the subject. It was the one public question on which, for deep-seated psychological reasons, he could not think straight.

Aside from his strong personal feeling, however, he did also believe, in the aftermath of the Parliament crisis, that the suffrage issue offered another wonderful stick with which to beat the Government. The 'Conciliation Bill' died with the 1910 Parliament, unmourned by most Liberals who had no wish to enfranchise wealthy women only. In its place the Cabinet brought forward in November 1911 a new Franchise Bill extending the vote in the first instance to virtually all men, but open, Asquith announced (contrary to his own preference in the matter) to amendment by the Commons to embrace women if a majority so wished. Over Christmas, which he spent with Churchill and the Marlboroughs at Blenheim, F.E. wrote his new leader Bonar Law an enormously long letter urging on him the tactical opportunity the Bill offered the Tories.

'I want you to give your most serious attention to the question of female suffrage,' he wrote. The position was that Asquith and the other anti-suffragists in the Cabinet – now, F.E. confided, including Winston, who had actually retracted his former support as a result of the methods of the suffragettes – would join the Tories in voting against any amendment which extended the vote to all women on the same terms as men. But if the Tories were to propose a 'Conciliation' amendment embodying only a limited extension of the franchise to a few women, then the Liberal opponents would feel obliged, for party reasons, to swallow their doubts and vote with the rest of their party for a thorough-going amendment extending it to all women. 'It is therefore vital', he urged, 'that we should no longer fool about with the Conciliation Bill', as Law had proposed. 'Recent events have made it clear that those of us were right who said its proposals were simply a leaping off board for the longer policy. And make no mistake,' he added, 'the whole thing is monstrously unpopular among the electorate. They stood up & cheered the roof off when I said at Barnstaple that I would not give the vote if every woman in England asked for it.'

But I want you to consider your own position. I do not think you can simply repeat a half-hearted allegiance to the cause given under wholly different circumstances. Each member who hates it but has a vague commitment of the same origin will look to you for a dialectical escape & if he doesn't get it will travel down the road of sentimentalism to disaster.

And surely you are bound in elementary consistency to give such a lead for quite other (and more overwhelming) reasons. How can you possibly run in double harness your 'indignant' campaign against using the Parliament Act to pass Home Rule with connivance in the attempt (far more gross, scandalous & revolutionary) to use the P.A. to pass Female Suffrage. You will not retain a rag of consistency or persuasiveness for your H.R. complaints. Surely the obvious line is that

(1) the Constitution is in suspense (2) the question is of immense novelty & importance (3) it has never been as a specific subject before the people (4) that therefore whatever your own views you cd under these circs no more be a party to carrying either the Conciliation or the more extreme proposals by means of the P.A. than you could be a party to carrying H.R.

Forgive this long hurried & dogmatic scrawl but I write quickly as I talk. Take it from me there is a real chance of a split among the Cabinet if we play our cards properly.[57]

But the question of amendments never arose. The Franchise Bill carried its Second Reading in July 1912 and passed into Committee where, in January 1913, it was abruptly torpedoed by, of all people, the Speaker, who ruled, to general bewilderment (but to the secret relief of Asquith and the delight of F.E.) that any amendment introducing women's suffrage would so alter the complexion of the Bill as to be out of order. Though it went against all precedents, there was no appeal against the Speaker's *démarche* and the Bill was withdrawn, to the accompaniment of renewed suffragette violence. There followed all the famous incidents of forced feeding, the 'Cat and Mouse Act', Emily Davidson throwing herself under the King's horse; but the only effect of the feminists' extremism was to swing opinion sharply against the women's cause, so that in May 1913 a private member's Bill to give the vote to all householders and their wives over the age of twenty-five was defeated by 267 votes to 219. In a speech at the Central Hall, Westminster, F.E. duly gave thanks where credit was due, to the suffragettes;[58] and no further attempt was made to solve the problem until 1917, when war and coalition had transformed the entire scene, so that even F.E. bowed to the inevitable.

11

Smith, K.C.

By 1912 F.E. was firmly established in the very front rank of the barristers of the day. With Rufus Isaacs and John Simon in the Government, and Carson increasingly preoccupied with Ireland, he was perhaps actually the leading advocate in regular practice. His earnings, even if they were not as fantastic as he sometimes boasted (£20,000, £30,000, £40,000 . . .) were nevertheless enormous – well into five figures. For a major case he could get £1,000 a day. Simultaneously with his increasingly high-level political career, he was continuously busy in the courts, as the most casual glance through *The Times* Law Reports will show – divorce suits, contested wills, complicated commercial disputes, libel actions, the occasional murder. Most of these cases were not in any way remarkable and will not be discussed here, but it is important to stress the quantity of work that F.E. was getting through. Many cases on which he gave an opinion, of course, never came to court at all. But they all took a part of his time, and swelled his income.

His chambers, 4 Elm Court in the Temple, were a hive of activity, his lunches not so leisurely as in his early days in Liverpool. The flow of business was managed by the faithful Peteil, his clerk who had followed him south from Cook Street and was now run off his feet trying to keep up with F.E.'s frantic timetable. 'My own childhood', Peteil's daughter has written, 'was dominated by the magical initials F.E. & infected by the speed & precision demanded of my father who repeatedly claimed that "the man" had two brains to the normal man's one . . . The tension of such a life often exhibited itself in slammed doors & hasty exits. F.E. demanded & expected the best & in the case of my father . . . got it.' He still gathered around him a cluster of pupils, most of whom (even if they did not become lawyers) became good friends. Most notable from this period were Edward Horner, who was killed in France in 1917 and Jack Scott, who died in 1922.

How high does F.E. really rate as a barrister? As in politics, so in the law, a part of F.E.'s success lay in his physical appearance, the figure he cut in court and the style which he brought to the leading role. On the platform it was the impression of vitality and physical strength: in court it was more his stillness and icy control which compelled attention.

Legend already surrounded this slim dapper figure, hardly recognisable at first glance in wig and gown, since the sleek ebony hair was concealed by the wig, worn a little jauntily. His sombre eyes and clearcut features were lawyer-like enough; only the mouth lacked the set precision of a typical legal face. The lips were slightly ajar, as if about to close on a cigar; at moments shaped to insolence or disdain, sometimes weary.[2]

His second asset was his voice. The same observer described his speaking style as 'trenchant, rapid, authoritative'. The *Daily Telegraph*, reporting a case in 1913 in which F.E. appeared against Sir Edward Marshall Hall, took the opportunity of an instructive comparison to give a fuller account of his delivery.

He speaks deliberately, with studied calmness and so low at times as to strain the ears of the more distant listeners. But when he has a point to make there is a sudden departure from this quiet conversational manner. He then lifts his voice in crescendo passages, and finishes with a blow on the table that startles the unwary. Delivered of his point he subsides at once, as though nothing had happened. Thus his speech suggests the tide, with intermittent long separated waves, as contrasted with the tumultuous current of his predecessor [Marshall Hall].[3]

Voice and appearance are perhaps more important to an advocate than they should be. From the Goudie case onwards, one of F.E.'s greatest strengths was his power of persuasion – particularly over juries: judges tended to be less susceptible. His essential attribute, however, on which his reputation really rested, was his exceptional clarity of mind. He had the capacity of going straight to the heart of a case. 'Disregarding the folly of solicitors,' John Buchan remembered, 'he refused to argue each and every point, but concentrated on the vital ones; wherefore he was beloved by judges, whose time he never wasted.'[4] In this connection Lord Darling, the judge before whom F.E. seemed to appear more often than any other, once remarked ironically that he would rather hear F.E. open a complicated case before him than any other counsel because it was 'so interesting to discover which of two fresh minds would grasp the facts first'[5] – a barbed compliment, but a compliment none the less, for it was never suggested, wherever he had been speaking or dining the night before, however little preparation he seemed to have had time to put in, that F.E. was not very quickly the master of his brief next morning. His extraordinary speed of assimilation did give rise to some professional jealousy as well as admiration, the suspicion that he was merely a quick-witted word juggler. But this overlooked the influence of his Merton years. His secret was that, more than most barristers who go immediately into practice, he had a solid foundation of academic law to which he could quickly relate whatever particular points came up. The depth of his learning was revealed when he was appointed to the Woolsack in 1919. Unsuspected by his detractors because worn so lightly, it was equally the foundation of his fortune at the Bar.

The one quality that perhaps F.E. lacked was tact – in which Isaacs, for example, excelled. He could be impatient with witnesses, was frequently rude to judges and sometimes antagonized juries instead of charming them. R.F.V. Heuston records one civil case in which the Court of Appeal upheld a claim for a re-trial on the ground that the jury had been provoked by F.E. as defending counsel into awarding £1,000 damages where £100 would have been ample.[6] He was not, by the highest standards, a particularly subtle cross-examiner; his career boasts no outstanding interrogation to compare with Carson's in the Archer–Shee case or Isaacs's examination of Sir Edward Russell. On the contrary, two of his most famous cases, as will be seen, involved his humiliation at the hands of exceptionally difficult witnesses. It is in fact a curious feature of F.E.'s legal career altogether that for all his brilliant reputation and enormous earnings he was involved in no really great case – except the Casement prosecution when he was Attorney-General, and controversy surrounds that. His best were early on, in his Liverpool years. His fame in legal circles is undying: to young barristers today his initials have lost none of their glamour; he is one of the legendary models of the profession. And yet as a leading silk he somehow never landed the famous case which would have enshrined him in the substantial history of the Bar as indelibly as his witty rejoinders have enshrined him in its mythology.

One client with whom F.E. was associated more often than was prudent for his own good was the swashbuckling financier, conman and fraud, Horatio Bottomley – Liberal M.P. for South Hackney from 1906 until forced to withdraw as a bankrupt in 1911; patriotic demagogue, fundraiser and recruiting campaigner in the war; M.P. again in 1918 until finally convicted of fraudulent conversion in 1922 and sentenced to seven years' imprisonment. It was characteristic of F.E. that he could not help liking Bottomley, and felt no obligation to disguise the fact.

He probably saw in Bottomley a distorted mirror image of how he himself might have been had he not, by way of Birkenhead School and Oxford, been able to turn his talents into fame and fortune by the legitimate ladder of academic and legal success. F.E. saw and admired in Bottomley an adventurer very much after his own heart, blessed with quick wits, extraordinary legal acumen, a sharp and fearless tongue, a love of gambling and an extravagant enjoyment of the pleasures and opportunities of life far beyond his means. Though the conventional, respectable and public side of his character necessarily deplored Bottomley's frauds when they were eventually exposed, privately he could not help admiring the style, the bravado, the sheer vulgar cheek of the man and this admiration was not affected by the vicissitudes of Bottomley's career. After his enforced withdrawal from the House of Commons in 1911 Bottomley continued to be a welcome guest at Charlton, and in 1912 F.E. paid him handsome public tribute in an essay on parliamentary oratory in the *Oxford and Cambridge Review*, later reprinted in his *Unionist Policy*, rating Bottomley the best all-round speaker, in the different styles demanded by the House of Commons, the law courts and the public platform, that he had ever heard. 'He united to a brilliant native humour a broad range of treatment, nerves of steel, an original outlook upon affairs, and an exact grasp of detail which hardly ever accompanies the other qualities. His removal from the House of Commons has impoverished the public stock of gaiety, of cleverness and of commonsense.'[7] Much later when there was no public credit whatever to be gained by continuing to associate with Bottomley, F.E. remained true to his high conception of friendship and invited him to lunch on his release from prison in 1927. He continued, too, in his writings to refer with high praise to 'the golden-tongued Bottomley'.

F.E. had no illusions about Bottomley's financial ethics. After the war Bottomley congratulated F.E. in the smoking room of the House of Commons on his elevation to the Woolsack. 'Upon my soul, FE, I shouldn't have been surprised to hear that you have been made Archbishop of Canterbury.' 'If I had,' F.E. replied, 'I should have asked you to come to my installation.' 'That's damned nice of you,' Bottomley responded. 'Not at all,' F.E. shot back, 'I should have needed a crook.'[8]

Bottomley in his rumbustious prime kept the courts busy with fraud and libel cases, and though he usually conducted his own defence – always brilliantly, usually brazenly, with a panache which exasperated prosecuting counsel and drew crowds of supporters to the public galleries to cheer his amazing escapes – there were nevertheless lucrative pickings for his favoured counsel. F.E. led the list, but others of the Liverpool fraternity, Hemmerde and sometimes Scott, appeared repeatedly for, or more often alongside, Bottomley in his many cases.

The biggest of those with which F.E. was concerned arose out of a lengthy investigation by Treasury officials of one of Bottomley's numerous and interchangeable enterprises, known as The Joint Stock Trust and Finance Corporation, which some of the shareholders suspected to be bankrupt, oversubscribed and kept fraudulently solvent only by the massive duplication of shares. Bottomley was eventually arraigned before a City magistrate in December 1908, with Horace Avory leading Richard Muir for the prosecution, F.E. leading two lesser lights for the secretary and bookkeeper of the company, Hemmerde and Scott for the auditor, and Bottomley acting for himself. The hearing ran for twenty-eight days, during which Bottomley drove Avory to distraction and two examining aldermen to illness by his methods before a third dismissed a case which had seemed at the outset straightforward but had become horribly confused. F.E.'s principle contribution was to act with Bottomley as the second barrel in a destructive double examination which demolished the credibility of one of the chief prosecution witnesses, a dismissed clerk, by accusing him damagingly of attempted blackmail.[9]

This was one of Bottomley's major escapes, but he had plenty of minor ones, which always seemed to involve several of the most expensive silks. In April 1910 F.E. and Scott defended Bottomley against a claim by the executors of another financier to recover £25,000 allegedly owed him before his death. The latter were represented by Montague Lush and John Simon, but despite some exceedingly hostile evidence given against him by his notorious fellow-swindler Ernest Terah Hooley, the jury found, as usual, in Bottomley's favour. In the course of his examination of Hooley F.E. made one pleasantly dry retort to Mr Justice Darling. Asked by F.E. whether a certain purchase of shares was not 'a speculative transaction', Hooley demurred but admitted that 'they were not Consols'. Darling intervened, 'Are not Consols speculative?' 'No, my Lord,' F.E. instantly corrected him. 'They represent a steady decline.'[10]

Concurrently with this case there came to court another involving an action for libel brought by a director of the National Cash Register Company against Bottomley's muckraking newspaper *John Bull*. The provocation, an allegation that an employee had been sent abroad so that he could not be called as a witness in another case against the company, was only the latest charge in a campaign of vilification which the paper had been waging against N.C.R. for some years. This time the directors thought they could nail Bottomley and silence him. They briefed Lush and Carson, while on the other side F.E. appeared for the proprietors, Hemmerde for the printers and Bottomley, as editor, for himself. After F.E. had cross-examined the plaintiff on the opening day, Bottomley addressed the court on the second in his most robust manner, roundly repeating all his charges, claiming it as a public service to expose so fraudulent a company and even declaring that such a man as the plaintiff was could not be libelled! Once again the jury warmed to his defence and he was acquitted.[11]

Whether it is to F.E.'s credit that he appeared so frequently on behalf of one who was later proved to be an utter rogue, and had never looked anything else even when nothing could be proved against him, is to ask one of those questions which the etiquette of the Bar does not allow. It is true that evil men must have the same right to legal representation as good men to make the best case they can for them and force the prosecution to prove guilt against them; also true that a barrister may not pick and choose his clients but must be available for hire by any who will pay his fee. In these respects F.E.'s association with Bottomley is technically unimpeachable. Yet in reality there must be an ethical question mark against the frequency and evident relish with which he defended Bottomley. The connection highlights simultaneously one of the least admirable but also one of the most attractive sides of his nature. For one who in one of his aspects was a stern upholder of the law and public morality, F.E. was often ready to smudge the boundaries of propriety where his own affairs or the interests of those he liked or admired were involved. Yet at the same time this softness towards attractive villains stemmed from the same recklessness, warmth of heart and love of life that gave him his own unique glamour. It is difficult to imagine Simon defending Bottomley, except perhaps unavoidably once or twice (as F.E. appeared at least once against him). But then Simon was not F.E.

One of the cases in which F.E. appeared for Bottomley, in March 1911, brought him into contact with an extraordinary character with whom he would cross swords again more seriously in 1914. This was the cantankerous bohemian poet T.W.H. Crosland, who reacted to a hostile article in *John Bull* by suing Bottomley for libel. He won, but was awarded only a derisory three farthings damages. Both Bottomley and F.E. sarcastically regretted that Crosland (pleading illness) was not in court for the hearing, as they had some questions,they would have liked to put to him. Crosland replied, as was his habit, with a satirical sonnet in the *Penny Illustrated Paper*, aimed not at Bottomley but at his sleek sidekick.

And you had questions also, had you Smith?
　　You of the waist, the nostril, the new clo'es,
　　The 'ard 'at and the cheerful purple hose,
The speech that is all crackle and no pith . . .

(The second quatrain is impenetrably obscure.)

　　Allez, my gentle climber, born to star
　　　　The King's Courts with your Patron, while the Town
　　Winks, and the sniggers of the Junior Bar
　　　　Flatter the 'combine' – Nay, sweet coz, don't frown:
　　Bot picked you up and put you where you are,
　　　　And Mister Crosland hereby hands you down.[12]

F.E.'s connection with Bottomley did attract some public comment, then; but there is no reason to believe it did him any serious damage in circles less embittered than Crosland's. All that this diatribe really shows is that F.E. was still a snappy dresser. But Crosland had him marked. 'We shall doubtless have the pleasure of talking to Mr Smith out of a witness box before we die', he wrote – a safe bet, given Crosland's record as a litigant – 'and if he will cross-examine us about this sonnet, King's Bench VIII will once again "rock with laughter", though we are open to lay 100 to 7 that the laughter will not be all Mr Smith's.'[12] Three years later Crosland won his bet.

In the autumn of 1910, F.E. was tangentially involved with one of the most sensational murder trials of the century: the Crippen case. He took no part in either the prosecution or the defence of the bloody doctor himself – his Liverpool colleague Tobin drew the short straw of defending him – but he was called in as counsel for Ethel le Neve, Crippen's mistress and the girl for whose love he had killed his wife, who was tried as an accomplice after Crippen had been convicted. This was an assignment which recalled his defence of Goudie and Ethel Rollinson eight years earlier, calling less for legal acuity than for the rhetorical skill to influence a jury in favour of an unfortunate accused – with the difference that in this instance he had some chance of establishing his client's innocence. The case turned on whether or not le Neve had known, when she moved into Crippen's house after the sudden disappearance of his wife and later when she fled with him to Canada, that he had killed her predecessor. The prosecution, led by Richard Muir K.C., sought to suggest, by a damaging interpretation of circumstantial evidence, that she must have known. F.E.'s defence, presented before

Lord Chief Justice Alverstone at the Old Bailey on 25 October, was first to insist that Muir had failed to *prove* anything at all, and second to argue – without putting his client into the box to deny it for herself – the simple human improbability that Crippen would have told her.

Muir's case rested heavily on the evidence of le Neve's landlady, a Mrs Jackson from whom she had rented a room in Constantine Road, just off Hampstead Heath, a kindly but, as F.E. said, somewhat garrulous lady, whom she used to call 'mum' or 'ma' and to whom she had confided her affair with the married Crippen. After the remains of Crippen's wife had been discovered, in July 1910, Mrs Jackson recalled, under police questioning, an evening around the end of January, very close to the time the murder was committed, when le Neve had come in pale and agitated, trembling and unable to eat, and had still been unable to go to work the next day. The only explanation she had given was that it upset her to think of her lover, Crippen, still living with his unloving wife instead of with her. About a week later, by contrast, she came home in unusually high spirits, saying that Mrs Crippen had unexpectedly gone to America. Soon afterwards she moved out of Mrs Jackson's, into Crippen's house in Hilldrop Crescent, a mile away in Kentish Town. To the prosecution, the obvious explanation of these two recollections was that le Neve had first learned with fear and horror of Crippen's murderous intention but had quickly adjusted herself to its successful accomplishment.

To F.E. they proved no such thing. By skilful questioning of Mrs Jackson he fixed the date of the first incident at about 25 January, a full week before the murder, and established that le Neve was never strong but suffered from anaemia and neuralgia which kept her away from work quite frequently; she had been in poor health throughout January. Her situation was bound to be upsetting, he suggested, to such a respectable girl as she undoubtedly was, and her relief and happiness when told by Crippen that his wife had left him for another man, leaving the way clear for his divorce and remarriage, was entirely natural. Her apparently heartless behaviour in immediately moving into her rival's place and openly wearing her clothes and jewellery F.E. presented as the strongest indications of innocence; to the charge that she could not possibly have believed that Mrs Crippen would suddenly go off to America leaving all her things behind, he returned the clever reply that the police inspector, 'with his wide knowledge of the seamy side of life', had sufficiently believed it to circulate her description in the United States; while her flight, dressed in boy's clothes, did not prove complicity in her lover's guilt but only her meek compliance with his wishes. Above all F.E. ridiculed the idea that Crippen would have had any reason to implicate her.

A more monstrous and stupid suggestion was never made in a Court of Justice. It is suggested that Crippen risked his neck in this way. He coolly weighed every chance, doing his terrible work on February 1 with no accomplice, leaving behind him, as he thought, no trace, disposing of the bones, extremities and mutilated flesh, and removing all traces of the blood. It is suggested that the man who had done all this with fiendish and detailed calculation, and had covered up every trace which might betray his hideous secret, had told a nervous young woman that he had committed this murder. What had Crippen to anticipate if he told her? If human psychology is of any value, he would understand that the odds were prodigious that any young woman not belonging to the criminal classes would receive with aversion, revulsion, disgust a proposal that she should become an accomplice in a crime so horrible that it is spoken of throughout the world today almost with bated breath. The suggestion is that Crippen practically told le Neve, 'This is the way I treated the woman who last shared my house and bed and I invite you to come and share it now.' It is a wild and incredible suggestion that no jury will entertain at all.

On the contrary, F.E. painted a touching picture of le Neve eleven years earlier as a poor friendless little girl, aged sixteen or seventeen – 'the age at which young girls in happier circumstances were going to finishing governesses' – forced out into the world to earn her living as a typist and having the extreme misfortune, 'gentle, retiring and sympathetic' as she was, to come under the influence of 'one of the most dangerous and remarkable men of the century, a man who in the whole history of the psychology of crime would rank as a compelling and masterful personality'.
'What were the relations between these two people?' F.E. asked. 'Crippen was the one really important person in her life . . . Very likely', he surmised, 'the mutual position of these two people was like that of the centurion in the Bible who said to his servant, "Do this and he doeth it." That' – he now stated as a fact – 'was the position for the seven years she was under his influence before he seduced her.' She had, he continued, drawing on the favourable parts of Mrs Jackson's evidence, 'no wickedness, no dissolute habits, no levity and no wantonness of conduct with the exception of that with Crippen', which single spark in her dreary life he excused on the ground that Crippen had told her that his wife no longer loved him. 'She was delicate, a little hysterical, and suffered acutely from fits of depression . . . No one', F.E. asserted, 'suddenly becomes very vicious.'
In conclusion, he appealed directly to the jury to take pity on the girl,

and explained why he had determined not to put her in the witness box.

> I ask you to picture what her life has been like for the last six months, disguised, hunted, harassed, and at last brought face to face with the full details of the charge formulated against her. From that day to this has been one long horror, culminating in the knowledge that the man she loved and trusted had been found guilty of one of the most callous and bloody murders in the calendar of crime. I am not bound and I am not prepared in a case like this . . . after all she has gone through and in her state of health to put her in the witness box and subject her to the detailed cross-examination of my learned friend. . . . She has been punished sufficiently already. When she leaves that dock, acquitted by your verdict, the prospect which opens out to her is not one of great happiness. She will be known all over England as one who has been the mistress of a murderer. I do not ask for mercy. I ask only for justice and I will be content if you will judge her in her hour of agony with the same consideration and the same caution with which you would wish your own daughter to be tried if by some inconceivable misfortune she were placed in such a chain of circumstances as that in which this woman has been placed.

The Lord Chief Justice in his summing up endorsed practically every word of F.E.'s 'very able speech' and added that the jury should take it as no reflection on le Neve's case that she had not given evidence in her own defence. Thus guided, they took only twenty minutes to bring in a verdict of 'Not Guilty'.[13] The story goes, however, that afterwards Lord Alverstone told F.E. that he thought he should have put le Neve into the box. F.E.'s reply was ambiguous. 'No,' he said. 'I knew what she would say. You did not.' The implication of this is not merely that he could not trust her to corroborate his touching picture of a helpless waif, but that he knew that she would actually wreck it if he let her open her mouth. Nevertheless he maintained to the end of his life his conviction that she was entirely innocent. 'Frail she was and of submissive temperament,' he wrote in his *Famous Trials*, published in 1926, 'but not an accomplice in murder nor an ally in its concealment.'[14] He nursed a private grievance, however, that she never in any way thanked him or acknowledged his help in securing her life and freedom.

Of all the cases in which F.E. was ever involved as a practising barrister, none was the subject of greater interest or more wide-eyed society gossip than that of the contested will of Sir John Murray Scott in the summer of 1913. Unfortunately it was not one of his triumphs. He was confronted, in the limelight of the fullest press coverage, by the redoubt-able Lady Sackville, and in a personal duel of a type unusual between counsel and a witness, he was decisively worsted.

Victoria, Lady Sackville, was one of the most extraordinary figures of an age not lacking in extravagant personalities. The daughter – one of seven illegitimate children – of the romantic affair between a high-ranking English diplomat, Lionel Sackville-West, and a Spanish dancer, she had been a famous beauty but was still more remarkable for her combination of overpowering charm, steely ambition and a passionate Latin temper. When her father was British Minister in Washington in the 1880s, after her mother's death, she took the town by storm, erasing the scandal of her birth by the grace and glamour which she brought to the role of his official hostess. When he succeeded in 1888 to the Sackville title, she became the lady of Knole, near Sevenoaks, one of the greatest houses in the country, fell violently in love with it and contrived to secure her tenure by the ingenious device of marrying her cousin, her father's legitimate heir. When the time came, however, the inheritance was challenged. Her eldest brother tried unsuccessfully, and, as it turned out, by fraud, to establish that their parents had after all been married, in order to prove his – and incidentally her – legitimacy and thus his own rightful claim to the title, ahead of her husband. This action was the social sensation of 1910. The prurient British public looked on with relish as the scions of an ancient family wrangled with one another in the High Court over intimate questions of marriage, adultery and legitimacy, with a barony and a stately home with several hundred acres as the prize. There was never much doubt of the out-come, which only made the washing of so much exotic linen in public the more astonishing; but the publicity surrounding the case made the new Lady Sackville – to say nothing of her coltish fifteen-year-old daughter, Vita Sackville-West, known to the press as 'Kidlet' – familiar names to the readers of gossip columns well before the second case, in which F.E. was involved, ever started.

This too concerned an inheritance which Lady Sackville was deter-mined not to lose – not a Sackville inheritance this time but a fortune essential to her if she was to keep up both her prodigal style of life and her beloved Knole. It belonged to Sir John Murray Scott, a kindly old connoisseur of enormous girth who had himself inherited it as a result of having been in his youth confidential secretary to Sir Richard Wallace, the founder of the Wallace Collection. From about 1900 until his death in 1912 Lady Sackville befriended Sir John to such good effect that 'Seery' was almost a second father to the young Vita, certainly an ever-present benevolent uncle; when he was not at Knole, they were usually at his palatial house in the Rue Lafitte in Paris. They shared a common love of art and furniture and undoubtedly brightened one another's lives – 'Seery' was a bachelor and she was increasingly estranged from her rather dull husband; despite occasional tiffs caused by her imperious temper, they were genuinely devoted to each other; nevertheless it cannot be doubted that she counted on his generosity to ease her financial problems after his death as he had unstintingly done in life. Nor was she disappointed. When he died he left her £150,000, plus the almost priceless contents of the house in the Rue Lafitte, which he hoped she would add to the Knole collection.

Sir John had relations, however, who had regarded Lady Sackville's powerful hold over him with distrust and dismay, believing that his wealth should properly come to them, although it was in origin no more Scott money than it was Sackville money, but literally his 'fortune'. Armed with a draft codicil which showed that he had at least seriously considered changing his mind, they challenged the will, contending that Lady Sackville had used 'undue influence' to alienate Sir John's affections, and his fortune, from his rightful heirs.

They retained two K.C.s, F.E. and Hemmerde, with three juniors, to argue their case before the President of the Probate, Divorce and Admiralty Division, Sir Samuel Evans, and a special jury. Strictly speaking, the plaintiff was Sir John's solicitor, claiming probate of his will; the Scott family were the defendants; and Lord and Lady Sackville were 'parties cited', opposing F.E. and Hemmerde with the equal forensic firepower of Carson and Norman Craig K.C. The case came to court on 24 June and occupied eight days over the next fortnight, ending on 7 July.

The previous week, however, Lady Sackville made an extraordinary attempt, first to deflect F.E. from taking up the case against her at all, and when that failed, to subvert his conduct of it by appealing to his friendship and code of honour.

> Dear Mr Smith
>
> I hear that Mr Malcolm Scott has approached you on the subject of attacking me and my husband and my daughter in his iniquitous suit, coming next week.
>
> I can't believe that you would let yourself be mixed up in this painful affair when you and I meet among our friends in society and I meet your wife often too.
>
> The whole Defence put forward by Mr Scott is a tissue of falsehoods against a woman who has behaved well all her life and tried to help saving one of the finest places in England.
>
> I do hope you will think over the undeserved pain you will give so unnecessarily.

I don't know if it is professional or not to write to you and I do only write because I can't believe what I hear of you is true.

I have not told anyone I have written to you.

> Yours sincerely,
> V. Sackville

F.E. replied the same day.

Dear Lady Sackville,

I am not in the least annoyed at your writing to me, but I certainly do not think that you would have done so if you had thought more carefully.

Surely you must know that I am an advocate making my living by putting forward cases good or bad in the law courts. I should have been enchanted to take your case had you thought proper to employ me. You did not do so but selected, or your solicitor did, the very able counsel who now represents you. Surely you must see what an impossible position you are trying to put a professional man in. Is he to refuse every case which is offered to him against every agreeable acquaintance he may possess?

I have not read the papers yet. For all I know your description of the merits of the case and the demerits of your opponent may be exactly as you represent. In that case you may await the result with composure.

For myself I shall discharge a disagreeable duty with such consideration as the circumstances render possible.

> I am yours faithfully,
> F.E. Smith

Lady Sackville was unabashed, and merely tried a different approach.

Dear Mr Smith,

Yes, you are right. I wrote on the spur of the moment and I have been thinking a great deal about you and your difficult position since my letter went. With my sunny nature which always finds a silver lining to every cloud, I thought on the contrary that we were lucky to have a man of the world like you are and a man who knows 'what's what' to examine us, if you did not return the Brief.

I hope now that you will not return it, even after reading the twaddle and the shocking unsubstantiated statements that the Scotts will put upon you. I am really sorry for them as they have completely lost their heads; and perhaps they have refused to

realise that Sir John left *us* only about *one third* of what was declared
for Probate by the Executors themselves. He was a bachelor and
the money did not come from his own family and he was very fond
of us all.

I don't mind anything so far as I am concerned, in the witness
box. I have a clean bill. I only hope my poor husband, who is the
soul of honour, will not be tormented. He has such an important
political position in Kent and works so hard. I am awfully sorry for
him and for my child.

Do spare them – and attack *me* as much as you like. I know you
must do your best for your clients now, but *you* will do it, I am sure,
as a gentleman. And I have nothing to fear.

I thank you from my heart for the way you have written. My
letters and yours will be seen by *no-one* and no-one will know
anything about them.

Yrs gratefully,
V. Sackville

F.E. had no choice but to write again.

Dear Lady Sackville,

I tried in my last letter to make it plain to you as considerately as
I could that correspondence between us was under the circumstances irregular and improper.

Surely you must be aware that I should deserve to be disbarred
if my professional conduct were influenced by any circumstances
of private acquaintance. You did not, I am sure, intend it, but you
will perceive upon reflection that the considerations you place
before me are really dishonouring to my duty as an advocate.

That duty is limited by two considerations only: first the
interests of my client: secondly strict observation of professional
propriety.

Yours faithfully,
F.E. Smith[15]

When the trial began, F.E. himself took up the whole of the first day
and part of the second with his opening speech for the defendants,
which lasted nearly nine hours. He set out their case with admirable
clarity at the very beginning of this marathon.

It is alleged by the defendant that Lord and Lady Sackville spent
many years, more than ten years, in obtaining a complete domination and ascendancy over the late Sir John, and it is alleged that

the influence that they obtained over him had as a result that they, wholly unconnected with him by blood, practically induced him to finance them with enormous sums during his lifetime, and after his death to leave out of an estate of about a million sterling by far the greater part to them. The two complaints made against Lord and Lady Sackville are, first, that they acquired such astounding influence over Sir John that his mind ceased to be his own and became Lady Sackville's. There was great difference between his desires and views when under and when free from the domination of Lady Sackville; and secondly, that over a period of years, and particularly at very critical moments of Lord and Lady Sackville's relations with him, she set herself to wean Sir John from his relations by misrepresentation, depreciation and by disparagement of them, although really he entertained tender and constant attachment to them.[16]

It was Lady Sackville, F.E. explained, who was the active agent in this plot; Lord Sackville's part was simply that he allowed his wife more freedom to consort with Sir John for their mercenary end than was proper or normal for any husband, though F.E. was at pains to emphasize that the defence alleged no sexual impropriety between Lady Sackville and Sir John.

He spent most of the first day on a detailed account of the deliberate way in which Lady Sackville had set out to displace his four brothers and two sisters in Sir John's favour; how she had usurped his elder sister's place as hostess in his London house; how she had snobbishly banished them from his dinner parties and continually disparaged and depreciated them in his eyes, detailing countless hurtful little insults which collectively exposed her (whether or not they were relevant to the case) as a posturing *grande dame* consumed by the most callous egotism. Such a damning recital was presumably what she had hoped to deter F.E. from. She wrote afterwards that, 'F.E. Smith prejudiced many minds by his opening speech. I have heard since that the judge . . . thought I was a pretty bad lot until I got into the witness box.'[17] On the second day he turned to the relationship between Lady Sackville and Sir John himself, his will and her admitted expectations from it, and most important, their quite serious quarrel in 1911. He read out a letter in which Sir John definitely informed her that he had lost confidence in her judgment and was going to alter his will in favour of the Wallace Collection, and others in which she reacted alternately in anger and in sorrow to his threat, regretting on the one hand that he should so publicly humiliate her poor Vita, and on the other that he should darken his last years and cloud their friendship with such an unfair act.

All this was very well, and was supported on the second and third days by a procession through the witness box of Sir John's relations, all telling of insults received at Lady Sackville's hand and portraying Sir John as wholly under her spell when he was with her but anxious to escape from her coils when they were apart. They accused her of all manner of skulduggery to make sure of his money: one family friend even told of surprising Lady Sackville and Vita going through his papers, presumably to discover and destroy a revised will. But none of it materially advanced the family's cause. Carson dismissed with contempt the 'vitriolic blackwashing' of his clients and ridiculed the inglorious spectacle of Sir John's relatives – whom he had supported generously in his lifetime – now queueing up to depict him as 'a weak, miserable, wretched, obsequious, cringing creature, a prey to mesmeric and serpent-like fascination which, however, they could not define'. Their evidence was nothing but a series of 'trivialities magnified by my friend' which, he suggested flatteringly, only demonstrated 'Mr Smith's great powers of mesmerism and fascination', but amounted to nothing at all. Indeed the 1911 correspondence upon which F.E. had laid such emphasis actually proved that Sir John was perfectly capable of altering his will if he had so decided. Moreover if he *had* altered it, the alternative beneficiary would not have been his family anyway but the Wallace Collection.[16]

At this point Carson put Lady Sackville in the box. According to her grandson, Nigel Nicolson, this practically decided the case then and there, such was the impression her personality – and her clothes – made upon the jury after the tweedy matrons and stuffed shirts who had preceded her. 'It was quite evident that the only reason Seery had preferred her company to theirs was that they were dull and she was delightful.'[18] This may be an oversimplification, but her performance effectively destroyed the suggestion of some occult force or witchcraft with which the family had been trying to endow her, while making it very understandable that she should have enthralled Sir John simply by being herself – an exceptionally beautiful and, when she wanted, charming woman.

'Her methods as a witness', her daughter Vita wrote, 'were completely irregular. The ingenuity she displayed in evading any question she didn't want to answer was a triumph of femininity at its best and worst. She was disconcerting, maddening, witty.'[19] 'My plan', Lady Sackville herself wrote in her diary, 'was more or less when Mr F.E. Smith asked me some stupid question, to ask him a very embarrassing one.'[17] F.E., not at his best with feminine repartee, was duly disconcerted and maddened. In a courtroom ablaze with fashionable millinery – Mrs Asquith, Mrs McKenna and Clementine Churchill were among the spectators – she quickly had judge and jury eating out of her hand.

When F.E. tried his favourite trick of quoting her own words against her for instance, she laughingly evaded him.

F.E. You have got a 'dreadful temper', haven't you?

LADY SACKVILLE. I do not think so.

F.E. I am using your own expression which you used in a letter to Sir John.

LADY SACKVILLE. Ah, but I had to agree with him sometimes. (*Laughter.*)

At times she grandly rebuked him for being 'childish', or reminded him that Knole was larger than Hampton Court; at others she teased him with their social familiarity. Her finest moment, however, came when she gave a ludicrous imitation of Sir John's brother, Walter Scott, waddling across a room on his knees protesting his love for her (which he utterly denied). Previous published accounts have followed one another in repeating the story that she got down on her knees herself to demonstrate. Newspaper reports make it clear that in fact she merely 'illustrated with her knuckles on the witness box a person walking on his knees'.[20] But the effect – in her elegant yellow gloves – was uproarious.

With the comedy went an unshakable insistence that she alone was speaking the truth, a ringing defiance which was impervious to F.E.'s ironic scepticism.

F.E. Until you came the witness box has been filled by liars?

LADY SACKVILLE. Yes.

F.E. Your presence is the first gleam of truth that we have had?

LADY SACKVILLE. Very nearly, and every one of the lies has been knocked on the head.

When he got her in difficulties, for instance by producing an indiscreet letter to a friend, she broke down in well-timed tears at the wickedness of her friend in revealing it, and retained the sympathy of the jury that way. On the second day of her examination, she announced that she had been very ill in the night, but had come to court against her doctor's orders, thus winning a tribute to her courage from the judge. She was also adept at rattling F.E. into angry exchanges with Carson, who accused him of misrepresenting everything Lady Sackville said: F.E. could only complain peevishly that 'she puts on me every time the answer to a question I have not asked her'. He could never pin her down.

In his closing speech it was he who seemed to be appealing to the jury for sympathy, though of course it suited his case to play up her exceptional powers.

> In all your experience of litigation did you ever see a lady of more arresting and dominating personality? Did you ever see a lady who showed through every stage of her cross-examination that she was more completely mistress of herself, or who displayed more extra-ordinary and almost uncanny cleverness than Lady Sackville? I submit that you saw in the witness box one of the strongest and most striking personalities which any of you have ever met.

With the stage to himself, he recovered his command to the extent of being able to cast satirical doubt on Lady Sackville's evidence about brother Walter.

> If the jury form the conclusion that she is a lady who, snorting under most gross provocation, refrained from telling the truth from generosity to her aggressor, some of the ancient statues of Mercy might be replaced by modern representations of Lady Sackville.

But he was quite unable to prove that she had brought to bear on Sir John any 'undue influence', which the judge ruled could mean nothing less than actual coercion. The jury took only twelve minutes to find in Lady Sackville's favour.[16]

For this they were all invited down to Knole for a day! Lady Sackville was delighted with her victory. She was correspondingly bitter about F.E.'s professional efforts to discredit her, and fired off a characteristic anathema.

> Mr F.E. Smith,
>   Before the case I was mistaken and thought you were a gentle-man. Since then I have discovered more and more that you are a CAD and as you are so fond of letters, it is good for you to know that I have received dozens of letters, from every rank of society, describing you as a CAD.[21]

F.E. was unfortunate to have crossed the path of this fascinating dragon, particularly in a case which he could probably never have hoped to win. Lady Sackville's virtuoso performance in the witness box won her the sympathy of the court and of the press; but on the point of law it would have been very difficult to have proved 'undue influence' even if she had been an utter monster. As it was, her triumph was widely applauded, and the Scotts made to look mean and foolish. In the sequel, however, she did not prove fully worthy of Sir John's confidence. Instead of adding it to the Knole collection, as he intended, she promptly sold the furniture from the Rue Lafitte to pay her debts.

In 1913–14 F.E. found himself drawn into a very different world from that of the Sackvilles when he was briefed in two of the cases which, a dozen years after Oscar Wilde's death, continued to rumble interminably over his reputation, fed by the bitter feud which had developed between his former protégé, Lord Alfred Douglas, and his literary executor, Robert Ross.

Douglas – 'Bosie' to his friends – the third son of the eighth Marquess of Queensberry, had been, as an undergraduate of effeminate beauty and poetic ambition, the disciple and companion of Wilde's glittering prime in the early 1890s. Their love had been primarily aesthetic and ideal, rather than physical – Wilde found his carnal satisfaction more dangerously elsewhere – yet it was Queensberry, enraged by the corruption of his son, who had exposed Wilde's homosexuality and ruined him. All Douglas's subsequent life, since Wilde's death, had been devoted to clearing himself by means of violent counter-attack of the notoriety which clung to him as Wilde's most famous friend. He had married, become a Catholic and turned furiously against Wilde's memory – which his other friend, Robert Ross, on the contrary, was diligently engaged in rehabilitating by the republication of his complete works.

In 1911 the young Arthur Ransome began to write a critical reappraisal of Wilde. Ross encouraged him and lent him material – notably the complete text of Wilde's great prison letter *De Profundis*, which he had published in expurgated form in 1908 as a sentimental apologia but which in its original form contained an embittered and damning portrait of Douglas, to whom indeed it was actually addressed, though Douglas claimed that he never received it. Ransome was very discreet; he never mentioned Douglas by name, but his book carried Wilde's clear implication that Douglas was responsible for his downfall.

Rashly, Douglas sued, citing not only Ransome but also the publishers and *The Times* Book Club for circulating the libel. F.E. was retained for *The Times*, while J.H. Campbell (Unionist M.P. for Dublin University, a member of the Other Club, later as Lord Glenavy to be Lord Chancellor of Ireland) represented Ransome. In his delightful autobiography, Ransome has left a rather hazy recollection of the trial, a nightmare into which he seems to have stumbled in perfect innocence, but he recalls vividly his horror at realizing that his counsel had evidently not read his book.

My proper defence was the character of my book as a piece of non-sensational literary criticism. Of this Campbell soon showed that he was completely ignorant. I had once or twice looked round in astonishment at what seemed to me the dangerous irrelevance of Campbell's remarks when I felt a touch on my shoulder. I heard a whisper and not a very quiet one: 'Never mind that old sheep. I'll put your case for you.'

It was F.E. Smith, who was appearing for *The Times* Book Club and had realised that if I lost my case his clients would lose theirs. He was as good as his word and, saying next to nothing about *The Times* Book Club, did what Campbell should have done and spoke on behalf of the author, or rather of his book.

'Is the standard to be imposed upon *The Times* Book Club', F.E. asked, 'that they are not to have a book on their shelves which is unsuitable for young girls?'

If that were the standard, there would have to be a considerable clearance from all libraries – public and private – of works of great reputation in literature. People as a rule do not read books about Oscar Wilde unless they are already familiar with the main features of his unhappy story. Can it be suggested that no book about Oscar Wilde should contain any reference to the tragedy in his life? From the point of view of history the world is entitled to know what were the main facts in the history, literary or otherwise, of well-known men, and how these facts could be stated less offensively than in Mr Ransome's book I am at a loss to understand.[23]

'I was always very grateful to Lord Birkenhead for this,' Ransome continued, 'but I believe that my case was won for me by Lord Alfred Douglas and the judge.'[22] Certainly Douglas made a bad impression and Mr Justice Darling was unsympathetic; but the case was really won for Ransome by Robert Ross, who allowed his counsel to read out in court the unpublished extracts from *De Profundis* on which Ransome's alleged libels had been based. In these Wilde had written of the 'entire ethical degradation' which Douglas had brought on him; claimed that 'the froth and folly of our life' had made it impossible for him to write; recalled that 'as far as I can make out, I ended my friendship with you every three months regularly, and each time that I did so you managed, by means of entreaties, telegrams, letters . . . to induce me to allow you back'; most damaging of all, claimed that 'the sins of another were . . . placed to my account', that he could at either of his trials have saved himself at Douglas's expense.

But do you really think that you were worthy of the love I was showing you then, or that for a single moment I thought you were? The aim of love is to love, no more and no less. You were my enemy, such an enemy as no man ever had.[23]

With Wilde's ghost thus devastatingly conjured up to condemn him from beyond the grave, Ransome's vague references to Douglas as 'a man whose friendship had already cost Wilde more than it was worth ... a man to whom Wilde felt he owed some, at least, of the circumstances of his public disgrace' were mild indeed. F.E. dealt heavily with Douglas's bitter protests at having this deadly document dragged up against him: he himself, by bringing his unwise action, had invited it.

When Wilde, that unhappy child of genius, is surviving death and conquering the infamy of his career, and at the moment when men are glad to be able to think more of the artist and less of the fallible human being, there is this bitter legacy of infamy resurrected, the hideous revival of all this story which might and ought to have been forgotten, and which, if plaintiff had consulted his own interest, would have been left alone.[23]

Douglas deserved not a farthing of damages to certify his character.

Nor did he get even that. The jury found Ransome's comment justified, and Douglas had the defendants' costs to bear (Campbell's, F.E.'s and three junior counsels' fees) in addition to his own. It is no wonder that his hatred of Ross, and by association F.E., was redoubled, especially when Ross, having allowed the unpublished parts of *De Profundis* to be used to blacken him, then refused to allow Douglas to quote them, in order to answer them, in his indignant reply, *Oscar Wilde and Myself*. In retaliation Douglas now determined to expose Ross publicly as the homosexual he undoubtedly (unlike Douglas himself) still was,* justifying his private desire for revenge by depicting Ross with the self-righteousness of the fanatical convert as the high priest of a 'Wilde cult' dedicated to glorifying Wilde's perversions and corrupting society at large with his degenerate amorality.

In this crusading enterprise he found an enthusiastic ally in the grotesque, shambling figure (so much the physical antithesis of Douglas himself) of the bohemian poet and literary controversialist, T.W.H. Crosland, one of the last of that species of hack, immortalized in Dr

---

* Ross actually boasted to both Ransome and Frank Harris of having been 'the first boy Oscar ever had', and was in truth far more responsible for Wilde's downfall. Dr Montgomery Hyde believes that it was probably with Ross that Wilde 'first deliberately experimented with homosexual practices', around 1886.[24]

Johnson's *Grub Street*, who still eked out a living – describing himself as a 'jobbing poet' – in the luxuriant literary underworld of Edwardian London. His one famous work was a scabrous diatribe, *The Unspeakable Scot*. For three years, from 1907 to 1910, Douglas and Crosland had collaborated as editor and deputy editor respectively of the once-staid journal *The Academy*, turning it into a vehicle for a series of scurrilous vendettas.

Crosland had come up against F.E. before, in 1911, and had dealt with him to his own satisfaction in the sonnet already cited. Together Douglas and his hatchet man now turned on Ross, Crosland declaring war with a characteristically violent assault on Wilde himself in the form of a satirical 'poem' entitled 'The First Stone', which began

> Thou,
> The complete mountebank,
> The scented posturer,
> The flabby Pharisee,
> The King of Life,
> The Lord of Language
> With the bad teeth;
> The whining convict
> And Prince of Hypocrites,
> That slouchest
> Out of the shameless slime,
> Shamelessly . . .

and carried on in this fashion for some 600 lines, ending with a mock epitaph,

> Oscar Fingal
> O'Flahertie Wills Wilde
> Whose Soul Was All a Sin
> Whose Heart Was All a Lust
> Whose Brain Was All a Lie.[25]

Extravagant abuse of the prophet, however, did not touch his high priest, and the next stage was to try to provoke Ross into suing for libel, as Wilde had disastrously sued Queensberry. To this end Douglas – never subtle in his methods – first dispatched to the Prime Minister (Asquith was a particular friend and patron of Ross), to the Archbishop of Canterbury, Mr Justice Darling and a number of other prominent people a circular letter directly accusing Ross of homosexual practices. When this failed to draw Ross they proceeded (as Crosland protested indignantly, expecting to be congratulated) to do the work of the police for them and on their own initiative set about gathering incriminating evidence to set before Scotland Yard. They got hold of a boy named Charles Garrett, aged eighteen, with two convictions for importuning already to his name, who was a friend of Ross's homosexual friend Christopher Millard (who had himself served a prison sentence in 1906 and was the author, under a *nom de plume*, of several books about Wilde). They prevailed upon Garrett, when he came out of prison the second time, to agree to sign a statement accusing Ross of committing 'certain acts'. This plan backfired, however; when Douglas and Crosland took him before a lawyer to swear his testimony the boy took fright and ran away. The police arrested not Ross but Crosland, charged him with conspiring with Douglas to pervert the course of justice by laying false charges, and produced Garrett to testify against them that he had never met Ross in his life and had only agreed to swear otherwise in the hope of a job, which was what he wanted more than anything. Douglas was out of the country, lurking in Boulogne out of reach of another suit which his father-in-law was bringing against him for criminal libel, so the case proceeded against Crosland alone. Douglas offered to come over if he were given safe conduct, but this could not be guaranteed, so he watched intently from across the Channel, paying Crosland's costs. During the lengthy police court hearing, which lasted through the whole of May 1914, the Crown case was handled, without conspicuous success, by the ironically named Ernest Wild K.C.; for the trial proper, which opened at the Old Bailey at the end of June, he was supplemented by F.E. Crosland was represented by the less expensive skills of Douglas's friend Cecil Hayes, who had acted for him against similar odds in the Ransome case.

The situation was still a dangerous one for Ross, however, for Crosland had got a platform from which to repeat his allegations, even if he could not prove them. Moreover, he did not have to prove them: it was enough for his acquittal that he should convince the jury that he had genuinely believed in the charge he and Douglas had tried to bring, and had not knowingly borne false witness. F.E.'s difficulty in proving malice was further compounded by the character of Garrett: if he was so ready to perjure himself against Ross before, why should he now be believed when he accused Crosland? And if the jury was expected to believe him now, why should Crosland have disbelieved him before? It was, despite the apparent collapse of Crosland's position, an impossible case to argue, and F.E. soon found himself confronted from the box by another exceptionally awkward witness.

Crosland was presented by his counsel as a man 'ferocious in his dis-like of vice', a moral crusader selflessly devoted to cleansing literature of the stain of perversion, who regarded the availability of Wilde's books, and Ransome's biography, at a shilling a copy so that any child could buy them, as a public outrage. Throughout the trial there recurred, as a sort of shibboleth, Wilde's famous epigram 'There is no such thing as a moral or an immoral book. Books are well written or badly written. That is all.' Crosland dismissed it as a dishonest half-truth, 'the standby of all people who write dirty books'. (Ross, called as a witness by the prosecution, could not resist departing in this particular from his master's gospel. Asked by the judge whether there could be such a thing as an immoral book, he retorted, to Crosland's fury, 'Yes. I know heaps of them. Lord Alfred Douglas's poems, for instance.') F.E.'s cross-examination sought to establish that Crosland's loathing of Wilde was of recent origin, and he scored a point early on by quoting at him an article from *The Academy* in 1908, signed by 'A.D.', entitled 'The Genius of Oscar Wilde' – 'Anyone who can maintain that *The Picture of Dorian Grey* is not one of the greatest moral books ever written is an ass.' Then, 'I am one of the asses' was all Crosland could reply. 'And you were assistant editor,' F.E. reminded him. He next asked Crosland if he regarded Douglas as a suitable colleague in his campaign. He did. Did he know Douglas's poem *Two Loves*? F.E. read a part of it.

F.E. Have you any doubt that the reference contained in that last verse is to unnatural affection?

CROSLAND. I regret to have to say my answer is 'No'.

F.E. Let me call your attention to another passage.

CROSLAND. I see the obvious meaning, and I am sorry that it is so.

From this point on, however, Crosland increasingly turned the tables on his prosecutor and got the advantage of him, winning the sympathy of both jury and judge by posing as the poor honest man browbeaten by the clever lawyer. When F.E. pressed him – legitimately, since Hayes had made a point of emphasizing that Crosland was a married man with children – on the fact that he did not actually live with his wife but with a certain Mrs Parnell, Crosland raised a laugh by claiming that, 'In a case like this a man need not be ashamed to say that he has a mistress', and went on angrily, 'My answer is that I do, and I think it is very graceful of you to ask, and I hope it will do you good. If you can't get a conviction, you want to ruin me outside. My wife could take divorce proceedings against me. What do you care?' He objected to F.E. referring to Mrs Parnell as 'this woman', 'as if she were something terrible'; and when F.E. mentioned his 'litigious career' protested that a man was not hung for litigation, and pointed out – perfectly correctly – that Ross gave 'litigation' among his favourite pastimes in *Who's Who*!

He raised another laugh when F.E. remarked that the jury could take care of themselves. 'I have no doubt they can,' Crosland replied, 'I want them to take care of me', and carried on defiantly, with deadly flattery, 'I am here to fight with one of the finest intellects in England, and I'm going to fight. Two thousand "quids" worth of counsel against a poor man.' 'You have got Mr Hayes,' F.E. told him, and pressed on, 'Here is a phrase in a letter to Ross: "Your name will go stinking down the ages".' 'So it will,' Crosland retorted with some heat. 'My object is achieved. I have proved there were two men supporting Wilde. Everyone knows that Stuart Mason is Millard. I bet you a dollar they will withdraw Ransome's book. If Scotland Yard do not arrest Millard there is no need for a Criminal Investigation Department.'

When a witness goes on irrelevantly like this, counsel looks to the judge to call him to order. But Mr Justice Avory had taken Crosland's part and except for once objecting to his language (when he called Ross's use of *De Profundis* 'damned treacherous') allowed him unlimited licence. Crosland took advantage of his opportunity with a skill which belied his mock humility. He teased F.E., throwing back at him his connection with Bottomley ('You used to be a great friend of Mr Bottomley, and he issued hundreds of writs'), and he recalled his speech at the Ransome trial saying that a man's works should be remembered and his sins forgotten. 'As a man grows older he will become riper,' he chided patronizingly. 'As you grow older, Mr Smith, even you will grow riper.' And when F.E., inquiring into the inducements which Crosland and Douglas were alleged to have offered Garrett's mother in return for her son's perjury – she mentioned the sum of £1,800 – asked if he was in the habit of buying charwomen drinks, Crosland turned this damagingly against F.E. as an example of the snobbery of social-climbing politicians, and added that one did not bribe people to commit perjury with a drink. 'Lewis and Lewis may, but I don't.' F.E. could not let this slur on his client's solicitors pass, and protested to the bench. Avory was unsympathetic. 'I think you provoked the witness by your line of cross-examination. You invited the witness to argue.' 'I will certainly not appeal to your Lordship again,' F.E. replied sarcastically, still insisting that his question had been a proper one and Crosland's answer grossly improper.

Again and again Crosland blocked F.E.'s interrogation – 'That's the way you try to fog people . . . you go on browbeating me. If you go on for another five hours you will probably get me to say I murdered Queen Anne' – all the while using the privileged opportunity the trial and an indulgent judge gave him to blackguard with impunity Ross, Millard, Sir George Lewis and everyone he regarded as making up the 'Wilde movement'. 'Have you taken it upon yourself to regulate the private life of Mr Ross?' F.E. asked him at one point, only to receive the blistering reply, 'Oh, no! I don't object to Ross making a pig of himself; but what I do mind is his making a sty of the world.'

It was a performance as brilliant, in a different vein, as Lady Sackville's, and F.E. was again discomfited. He blamed Avory, and in his closing speech accused him openly of bias, while inviting the jury to judge for themselves whether they thought it credible that Crosland and Douglas, conducting 'a cruel and vindictive persecution' of Ross in pursuit of a purely private quarrel that had nothing to do with the public interest, could possibly have believed Garrett's story. Avory, summing up, heavily rebuked F.E.'s criticism of himself and directed the jury firmly to ignore most of what he had said.

> Mr Smith has overlooked the important fact that we are not here merely for the purpose of determining the character of Mr Ross. Nor are we here for the purpose of admiring the advocacy of Mr Ross's counsel. And certainly we are not here to convict anyone merely because Mr Ross has secured the services of one of the most eminent and eloquent of the counsel at the English Bar.

Crosland's veracity as a witness was not the issue; the question was solely whether Crosland, in laying his charges, had believed Garrett's story to be true, or rather, had known it to be untrue. To acquit him, Avory emphasized correctly, was to imply no condemnation of Ross; but he added maliciously,

> If a man allows himself to be associated with such a person as Oscar Wilde – I do not care what his literary genius may be – if he chooses to run that risk, can he complain if a person who is not carried away by admiration for the literary genius of Wilde says, 'A man is known by his friends.'[26]

With this encouragement, Douglas and Crosland were entitled to regard the jury's 'Not Guilty' as a positive vindication. Four months later – the outbreak of war did nothing to deflect his vengeful obsession – Douglas was back in court trying again, inconclusively, to prove homosexuality against Ross. In the meantime, however, he celebrated Crosland's acquittal by circulating a lengthy 'satire', as bad as Crosland's own, a childishly scurrilous attack on the 'Wilde movement's' corrupt leading counsel, entitled *The Rhyme of F. Double E.*

The tone was set early on:

> Said Robert Ross to Smith, 'F.E.,
> The "Movement" is in jeopardy.

But you can pull us through, I think,
If Sheeny Lewis tips the wink . . .

I know you feel, as we all do
That what the suffering saint went through
Remains a national disgrace;
We heard you in the Ransome case
And our hearts warmed to you at once;
If Lewis had not been a dunce
He would have briefed you from the first
Instead of Wild . . .

Wild having made a mess of the police court hearing, F.E. must adopt
less squeamish tactics:

But you must try a different plan
And go for Douglas, he's the man.
Wade in, and make a foul attack
He won't be there to hit you back.
Slander and lie, spit out black dung
Vomit red venom, steep your tongue
In gall and bitterness, the Devil
Will help his own, the powers of evil
Will hover round in unseen flight
To fortify their chosen knight.

'Wilde and the Movement' be your cry,
All the dear comrades will stand by
To cheer you on, the Court will be
Packed with our choicest chivalry,
The fairest Gitons of the town
With scented locks, fair, red or brown
Curled à la Garrett, and rouged lips,
And powdered cheeks and rolling hips
And sweet shrill voices, clamant with
The praises of 'dear Mr Smith',
Will rally round your standard daily
And make a sump of the Old Bailey.

In this congenial atmosphere
You'll smash old Crosland, a mere boor,
A 'minor author', ill and poor . . .
A man who's not ashamed, just think,

To stand a charwoman a drink.
How low, *how* common! You and I,
My dear F.E., would rather die
Than so degrade ourselves, but we
Are in the best society.
I'm right in with the Asquith set
In fact I'm Mrs Asquith's pet . . .
And your position is immense
Thanks to George Wyndham's influence.
How kind he was to you, we know;
It's strange that both of us should owe
Our present brilliant social stations
Chiefly to Douglas's relations
But so it is . . .

Why F.E. was supposed to be so indebted to Wyndham is not clear, but this is a marvellous example of Douglas's egocentric vanity. This section ends with Ross and F.E. picturesquely – and in F.E.'s case quite fantastically – united in praise of the satanic Wilde:

We'll raise dear Oscar from his grave
And build a temple to the cult
And you shall sing 'Quicunque vult'
For the new Faith. And now farewell!
Long live the cult, three cheers for hell! . . .
Consign all prudes to shame and sorrow
And up with Sodom and Gomorrah.

The course of the trial is then gloatingly rehearsed. F.E. takes Ross's money; then,

forth from lucre purchased lips
Came sneers and gibes and twisted quips
And ugly lies with fair words drest,
Spawn of the devil in his breast,
Got on low greed and lust for gold
When Faith was dead and Honour sold.
But all in vain, for Truth is great
And shall prevail. The Syndicate
Of perjured Sodomites sat there
And gnashed their teeth and tore their hair
And all their bottle holding crew
Lister and Wild and George the jew

Looked on aghast with grief and pain
(The tears of Millard fell like rain).
Never was such complete disaster
The great F.E. had met his master!
For Crosland tore him limb from limb
And wiped the dusty floor with him.
And Cecil uppercut him sweetly
And the Judge finished him completely.
The Court was full of grins and chuckles
When Avory rapped him on the knuckles
And took him down a score of pegs
Till with his tail between his legs
Like a well-walloped fox-hound pup
He bolted at the summing up.

So much for Smith. He stands revealed:
The 'gentleman' is hairy-heeled.
Under his patent-leather boots
His get-up at the ducal 'shoots'
Of Blenheim's smirking auctioneer
Is just sartorial veneer
To hide a very ugly heart
That's filled up with 'exchange and mart'
His sentiments are so much tripe
And he'll be rotten before he's ripe.

Not quite 'so much for Smith', however. Douglas had one more barrel
to his pop-gun, and a spectacularly cock-eyed prophecy:

Now Freddie Smith, we know you for
A tainted Privy Councillor,
A hireling who will prosecute
For any Sodomitic brute
Who thinks you worth your dirty fee,
Bottomley's boy, the dud K.C.,
Who pawns the honour of the Bar
To pay for a new motor car.
A mixer-up of wrongs and rights
A smiler upon catamites.
A master of low-down decrying
Whom Avory J. pulled up for lying.
A 'moral bankrupt' fine and large
Who cannot hope for his discharge.

> Ah Freddie, Robert Ross's kiss
> Was fatal to your hopes, I wis,
> As gin was fatal to the parrot
> Or Millard's kiss to the boy Garrett!
> Who'll look at you again, dear Fred,
> Lives there a man with soul so dead?
> Even in Ulster they'll eschew you
> And in 'the House' askance they'll view you.
> You'll hear them whisper, 'We can't sit
> Upon this honest floor with *IT*.
> Oh Smith, you've taken Ross's "thou",
> You'll take the Chiltern Hundreds now.'

The amazing thing about this feeble stuff, which can have caused F.E. nothing but amusement, is that Douglas took it perfectly seriously. In 1926 he republished it, along with a number of other similarly puerile verses, in a volume of *Collected Satires*, with a humourlessly self-satisfied introduction comparing himself with Byron.

> My satire on F.E. Smith may be virulent and scurrilous, it may even be unfair, but it only came as an answer – the poet's answer to the lawyer – to an attack that was more virulent and scurrilous and deliberately unfair . . .
> Persons who unfairly attack or ill-treat a man who happens to be a poet and gifted with the power of hitting back poetically, have only themselves to thank for what they get. In the long run, it is well to remember, the poet always gets the last word.[27]

Poor Douglas really thought he was one of the immortals.

One more hugely reported case which involved F.E. simultaneously with the highest and lowest levels of society deserves to be mentioned. This was a libel action brought in the summer of 1913 by the racehorse trainer Richard Wootton against the editor of the popular racing paper the *Winning Post*, Robert Sievier, who had alleged the existence of a trainers' 'ring' to fix races in order to defraud the bookmakers and the public. F.E. and another K.C. led for the plaintiff Wootton against Sievier himself and Marshall Hall, before the inevitable Justice Darling and a special jury. Practically the whole racing world, from Lord Derby downwards, appeared as witnesses – to the extent that racing at Sandown actually had to be cancelled one day, as owners, trainers, jockeys and stable boys testified to the seamier secrets of their trade. In its way it was as extraordinary a case as the Sackville saga. F.E.

eventually secured the verdict for Wootton, but was unable to prove malice on Sievier's part, so that Darling awarded only a nominal farthing damages; Sievier's supporters treated the result as a famous victory and carried him shoulder-high from the court. For F.E.'s biography the case is chiefly memorable, however, for another neat score over Darling. He was examining a witness who admitted that he had scarcely once gone to bed sober in many years, when Darling reminded him of the maxim that drunken men often tell the truth. 'But that', F.E. retorted, 'is only when they are drunk.' The unfortunate man had to confess that at that moment he was perfectly sober, and his evidence was thereby devalued![28]

These are only a very few of the most lucrative and spectacular of the cases which kept F.E. in constant work in the years up to 1914. There were many others, including further actions for Lever, which cannot be pursued here. While he was giving increasing priority to advancing his political career, where the greatest prize of all seemed attainable, the law remained his profession and his livelihood, the only way he could possibly sustain his family's extravagant style of living. When the war temporarily diverted him to other courses in August 1914, just a month after the end of the Crosland trial, he never imagined that its conclusion would translate him to higher spheres altogether, so that he would never practise as a private member of the Bar again.

12

Bonar Law and the Ulster Crisis, 1912–14

The Unionist Shadow Cabinet which F.E. joined at the beginning of 1912 was a predominantly rather elderly body of which he was, at thirty-nine, by far the youngest member. In accordance with the convention of the time it included all those members of the last Unionist Cabinet who were still alive and fit (not even excluding Halsbury) with only five additions. Besides F.E., there were Bonar Law himself (who had been no more than a Parliamentary Secretary in 1905); Carson and Sir Robert Finlay, who had been respectively Attorney-General and Solicitor-General; and Curzon, who had been Viceroy of India during Balfour's premiership. F.E. – who had not even been in Parliament in 1905 – was alone in having no experience of government.

Yet he had the advantage, through their common friendship with Max Aitken, of being in much closer contact and sympathy with his new leader than were most of his seniors. Off duty as well as on, on the tennis court and round the bridge table, F.E. and Law saw a good deal of one another in the next few years. To what extent Law really liked or trusted F.E. must be open to question – he undoubtedly distrusted his friendliness with Churchill and Lloyd George – but he found him both amusing and useful, not least, paradoxically, as a line of unofficial communication with the Liberals. F.E., for his part, was well aware of Law's intellectual limitations. ('I think & have always thought', he wrote many years later to Beaverbrook on the publication of the latter's inside history of the war, 'much though I loved him – that you greatly over-value Bonar.')[1] But his affection for Law was genuine: Law's misanthropic gloom was oddly endearing to his temperamental opposites. If there was occasionally a touch of the sycophant in F.E.'s relation to Law it is not to be wondered at, for he had every reason to hope that, by attaching himself loyally to him, he might in due course appear as Law's successor. There can be no doubt that this was F.E.'s conscious ambition in these pre-war years.

Who were his rivals? Austen Chamberlain, passed over once in 1911, was nearly ten years older than F.E. and had no fire in his belly; Carson was nearly twenty years older and too exclusively preoccupied with Ireland; George Wyndham was the same age as Chamberlain, a romantic figure in whom some saw great gifts, but he lacked application and died anyway in 1913; Curzon's peerage was already, with the curbing of the Lords, a handicap and one which could only grow with time. Looking around him, F.E. had good reason to feel confident that the momentum of his startling rise would carry him to the very top. By 1915, he should have so consolidated his position at Law's right hand that he would have an incontestable claim to high office – not merely legal office – when the electorate at last returned another Unionist Government. When after a few more years Law retired it would be on F.E. that his mantle would most naturally fall. Why not? Who could foresee the future? Even those like F.E. himself who warned of the coming showdown with Germany could not imagine that the cataclysm when it happened would be such as to shake all careers – those that it did not end – into new and strange channels. F.E. in 1912 had the Prime Ministership well in his sights.

F.E.'s loyalty to Bonar Law, or it may be his perception that his career would be best served by loyalty to Law (whereas a year earlier it had been better served by disloyalty to Balfour) was graphically demonstrated in a sharp little crisis which blew up at the end of 1912 when Law tried to break free from the reservations which had hedged tariff policy under Balfour, and strike out cleanly for the undiluted Chamberlain programme, food taxes and all. F.E. was pulled several ways at once by this new departure. On the one hand, he was a convinced believer in the eventual desirability of the full programme; on the other, he had always recognized that food taxes were an electoral handicap to the Tory party, particularly in his own Lancashire, and felt it foolhardy to risk lasting defeat on greater issues, the Union and the Constitution, for the sake of a fiscal policy that could not be carried through without a wider measure of public acceptance than seemed attainable in the near future. Hence he regarded Law's new initiative as ill-advised, and had every sympathy with the threatened revolt, orchestrated by Derby and Salvidge, that arose in Lancashire; but as the junior member of the Shadow Cabinet he acquiesced in Law's clear line and deplored his old mentor's public opposition. He did his best to represent Lancashire to the leadership while at the same time firmly upholding the leadership in Lancashire. To Law he wrote on 18 December (from Blenheim, where he had gone for Christmas) warning that 'things in Lancashire are on the eve of a smash' and urging that 'you, I, Austen, Carson and if he is well enough Long, ought *to meet at once*',[2] evidently concerned to impress on his leader his importance as a Lancashire expert, sensitive to a swell of opinion with which he admitted he was sympathetic. But in public he delivered himself of a ringing call for unity behind the leader. 'Division means disaster', he declared at Dudley.

> If any man wishes a civil war in Ulster, let him divide the party. If any man wishes to consummate the ruin, first of the Church in Wales and then of the Church in England, let him divide the party. If any man wishes to perpetuate, in our constitution, the Parliament Act and all that it stands for, let him divide the party.
>
> For myself, if I disbelieved in tariff reform as profoundly as I believe in it, I would rather withdraw for ever from public life than lift up my voice at this crisis to disintegrate, and it may be to wreck the only party which . . . offers the slightest guarantee for the maintenance of proprietary right, of political principle, or of constitutional freedom.[3]

A few days later he followed this improbable public protestation with a decidedly pompous private homily to Salvidge on the obligations of loyalty, drawing on his new rank in the party hierarchy to browbeat his old boss.

> The passage of any resolution which amounts to a vote of censure upon Law would, I think, be inconsistent with my retention of my membership of a Liverpool seat. I should regret this more than I can say, for though public life has brought me many sacrifices and disappointments, the representation of Liverpool and my share in it has brought me a great source of compensation. I know that Law, Chamberlain, Long and Carson are committed at the moment to the Albert Hall position. I know that they will never yield to threats and abandon their position today. But I believe that by the exercise of private and powerful influence we might produce what your resolution demands. I want this and Carson wants it. Open disaffection accompanied by threats which are nonetheless threats because masked by protestations of loyalty will merely throw the party into twenty years' opposition . . . Diplomacy and tact can even now save the situation. Nothing else can. I have written to you as I have always done with complete frankness. I tell you what I hope you know, that I cherish the recollection of the friendship and help which from boyhood I have

always received from you. But as to my own course I have no doubt. I shall postpone as far as I can a public breach: if a public breach is forced by the Unionist Party in Lancashire I shall regret it profoundly; nor will it prevent me from fighting the battle of Unionism even if it sever my connection with Lancashire.[4]

Lancashire had been F.E.'s political cradle, and Salvidge his admiring tutor; but this letter is his declaration that he had now outgrown dependence on that nursery, and was a full-fledged London politician whose loyalties lay with a more powerful source of patronage, a leader likely to be the next Prime Minister.

For a time it really seemed that F.E. might have to choose between loyalty to Law and loyalty to Lancashire, as the constituencies generally rallied to the Lancashire revolt and Law and Lansdowne insisted that they would both resign if their leadership was rejected. In the end, however, they were prevailed upon by assurances of the full confidence of practically the whole parliamentary party to stay on while postponing the imposition of food taxes once again until after a *second* General Election. This was a serious defeat for Law, diluting the one positive policy with which he hoped to oppose both Free Trade and Socialism in the name of a united Empire. Chamberlain, Amery and the other 'whole hog' tariff reformers were sickened by what they saw not as a prudent tactical retreat in the interest of higher causes but as another surrender of Unionist principle to match that over the House of Lords. F.E., privately relieved by Law's climbdown, disagreed with his former associates' purism. He had always seemed more interested in industrial protection than in the imperial aspect of tariff reform, and he now continued to proclaim the party's commitment to tariffs, but without the incubus of food taxes. 'We shall claim and we shall assert', he insisted at Manchester in November 1913, for instance, 'that the mandate of the country if we win it at the next election has entitled us – without taxing any subject of food – to protect the working class by a tariff of an adequate character.'[5] Through 1914 he repeatedly affirmed his confidence that a Unionist Chancellor would very soon be introducing the first tariff reform budget. Could he possibly have imagined introducing it himself? In the event, of course, war intervened before the election, and Law was not able to form a Conservative administration until the very different circumstances of 1922 – when F.E. was no longer his colleague and he was obliged to bind himself by an even stricter promise to abjure tariffs of any sort.

Bonar Law's accession to the Tory leadership brought a new sense of attack to the conduct of the Opposition. Where Balfour had often conveyed only a weary patrician distaste for the Government's measurés, Law was blunt and forceful. With the battle over the Parliament Act lost, politics entered a fresh phase in which the Unionists set out to prevent its operation by forcing a General Election before Home Rule or any other measure could be passed three times through the House of Commons. To this end they were prepared to harry and obstruct the Government at every turn, even to the point of opposing a measure like the National Insurance Bill which they had hitherto, with varying degrees of enthusiasm, supported. F.E. had been one of those who had most warmly welcomed it, but taking his cue from his new leader he now changed his tune, not indeed on the principle of the Bill but on the convenient constitutional ground – trotted out as part of a generalized attack on the Government's outrages on the Constitution – that it was being pushed through Parliament without adequate discussion. In a by-election speech at Yeovil on 20 November – one of several gains which the resurgent Tories made at this time – F.E. condemned the 'scandal' of the Government's use of the guillotine and asked why they bothered with the House of Commons at all: Lloyd George might as well simply send M.P.s an occasional picture postcard telling them which Bill was going through![6] The point of this line of attack was of course to promise that the Tories, when returned to power, would restore two effective chambers. During such detailed discussion of the Bill as the Government allowed, F.E. proposed a number of narrow but constructive amendments, including one to remove the appointment of the new Insurance Commissioners from political nomination[7] – an early and notably prescient attack on the limitless growth of patronage attendant on the new welfare system, taken up the following year by Bonar Law himself; but during a speaking tour in Devon and Cornwall at the end of the year he so broadened his criticism of the demagogic manner in which Lloyd George was promoting the Bill – 'swaggering about the country like a Father Christmas who is putting presents into the people's stockings'[8] – while trying to claim the credit for the insurance idea for Tory Democracy in general and Lord Randolph Churchill in particular, that it became pretty hollow. He could not disguise the fact that he personally supported the Bill.

The iniquity of the Parliament Act was still the issue which exercised him, and it was on this subject that he made his first speech as a front bench spokesman in the House of Commons, moving the official Opposition amendment to the King's Speech at the opening of the new session on 19 February 1912. His motion 'regretted' the absence from the Speech of any reference to the Government's pledge – in the preamble to the Parliament Act – to the reconstruction of the Second Chamber, and 'humbly represented' to His Majesty that it would be improper to proceed with measures so vitally affecting the safety of the State and the interests of your people as those named in Your Majesty's Speech whilst the Constitution of Parliament is still incomplete and Your Majesty's subjects are deprived of the usual safeguards of Constitutional government.

Though the contentious preamble had been studiously vague about *when* the Government would proceed to restore the House of Lords, and everyone knew that they had no intention of doing so before Home Rule and Welsh Disestablishment were safely through, it was F.E.'s contention, for debating purposes, that they were committed to bring forward an early measure of reform, and his passionate belief that they had no respectable reason for not doing so. He quoted back at him Asquith's past acceptance of the obligation to do so; now, he jeered, Asquith said he would honour it 'when time permits'.

I think it was Becky Sharp who said that she would have been a very honest woman if she had had £5000 a year. The Government may very well say, 'We will be honourable men, if time permits'. I venture to say that in the subtle records of Jesuitry no more flagrant shuffling from a plain and positive undertaking was ever attempted to be justified by a responsible Minister.

From Asquith sitting uncomfortably on the bench opposite he wrung the admission that the Government *was* still pledged to the reform of the Upper House. Since the Prime Minister admitted that the 1911 settlement of the Parliament crisis was not final, he must agree that the Constitution was temporarily in suspense. How then could he justify carrying major constitutional measures during this interval? Because, of course, he was dependent for his majority on the Irish.

The whole pretentious superstructure of this proposed legislation totters uneasily on the subsoil of chicanery and logrolling. Of all the measures on which the Government ought not to use the suspension of the Constitutional powers of the House of Lords Home Rule is the first, but it was in order that Home Rule might be passed that the whole conspiracy was made.

After tracing once again the record of Asquith's expedient tergiversations over Ireland and rejecting with contempt the 'dull and pompous lectures about legality' with which this corrupt administration saw fit to regale Ulster, F.E. ended with a characteristic declaration of war against the Government. Ministers, he asserted, had refused the opportunity of an agreed settlement when the Unionists had offered it.

That page is now closed, and we warn you that your programme planted on the ruins of a Second Chamber will not succeed, nor will a Government visibly declining in prestige, in unity and in popular support be able to rivet these crazy proposals upon an unconsulted electorate.[9]

If not the sensation of his maiden speech from the backbenches, this was a successful and effective front bench début, which earned congratulation and cheers from both sides of the House. The Liberals put up his old rival Simon, now Solicitor-General, to reply, which he did with characteristic suavity, though without attempting to meet any of F.E.'s arguments. Simon characterized F.E., quite correctly, as 'the most remorseless and diligent exhumer of other people's speeches' – not that this denied the pointed accuracy of his quotations – and won at least one little exchange when he taunted F.E. with the Tories' repeated failure at the polls. 'We are a larger party than you are,' F.E. interjected. (As a result of by-elections there were now eight seats between the parties.) 'If the right hon. gentleman is content with the present position,' Simon purred, 'so am I.'[9]

The second most contentious measure which the Government now set about pushing through in defiance of the Lords was the disestablishment of the Welsh Church, or rather the Church of England in Wales, long promised to its Welsh supporters who regarded the Church as a symbol of alien rule, but impossible so long as the Anglican majority in the Lords retained its veto. A token Bill had first been brought forward in 1909, as part of the process of what F.E. called 'filling the cup', but this had not been proceeded with beyond the First Reading. Now in 1912 the way was clear and the Government presented a new Bill which had its Second Reading over four days in May.

The Welsh Church was the political issue on which F.E. came closest to being a mere barrister, mouthing phoney outrage in accordance with a brief handed down to him by his party. He was not a religious man and he did not in the least share the horror genuinely felt by the Cecils, for instance, at the thought of disestablishment. He followed the party line enthusiastically, however, and found good secular reasons in his own political philosophy to justify himself. Along with disestablishment, the Bill provided for the disendowment of the Church of Wales, and it was this which he seized on, as a lawyer and as a defender of the rights of property, as being the true purpose and the iniquity of the whole exercise, outwardly conceived for reasons of conscience but actually the sheer pillage of Church property. From this standpoint his indifference to the religious argument was an asset.

I do not speak in this House [he declared in the debate on the 1909 Bill] as a convinced adherent of the Church of England. I speak as one who was brought up a Nonconformist, and I state from that point of view my impression of the proposal to disendow the Church in Wales. I tell the House plainly that I cannot distinguish this from any other act of common peculation.[10]

In the debates on the 1912 Bill he made himself an expert on the legal intricacies of centuries-old endowments (Queen Anne's Bounty and the like) in order to be able to confound the Bill's supporters with their ignorance of such complexities, portraying them contemptuously as greedy sectarians interested only in laying their hands on the Church's money, and the Bill as no more than another log-rolling exercise by the Government to repay one section of its supporters for their votes. As an unbeliever, he sailed very close to humbug on occasion; but it was a superb debating point to keep insisting that (as a result of the decline of Nonconformity since its heyday in the 1890s) the Church was now actually the largest single denomination in Wales. 'If Welsh Nonconformists desire spiritual and not political advantage,' he suggested innocently, 'it would surely be better for them to unite with the strongest religious institution in their country to resist the advancing forces of indifference rather than crippling it to further the progress of unbelief.'[11] (His own utilitarian view was that established religion was a good thing as a form of social cement, and that it was reasonable – truth having nothing to do with it – that the largest church in any country should enjoy the accolade of establishment.)

A further reason for opposing the Welsh Church Bill was that it was another constitutional outrage, which would be forced through against the wishes of the electorate while the Constitution was in suspense. In these circumstances its opponents would be as entitled to resist it by resorting to unconstitutional methods themselves as were the opponents of Home Rule. 'The methods by which Mr Lloyd George and Mr McKenna rose to notoriety', he urged in an article in Maxse's *National Review* in 1911 (recalling the Welsh campaign of civil disobedience against Balfour's 1902 Education Act), 'are very capable of an extension at once analogous, extensive and infinitely more defensible.'

Let Churchmen make up their minds to confront desperate opponents with extreme methods of resistance; let them, in a word, be ranged with those who allow no moral or constitutional validity to the acts of the Government until the Second Chamber is restored.[12]

The image of prebendaries and rural deans emulating the men of Ulster by drilling to resist disestablishment is delightful! But F.E.'s exaggerated opposition to the Welsh Church Bill is best remembered for the savage riposte it drew from G.K. Chesterton, one of the most celebrated pieces of satirical verse ever penned. It was the last words of F.E.'s speech on the Second Reading in May 1912 – a speech in which F.E. had rebuked Lloyd George for 'overstating his case as usual'! – which raised Chesterton's hackles. 'The Government', F.E. declared, 'will be well-advised, even at the eleventh hour, to withdraw a Bill which has shocked the conscience of every Christian community in Europe.'[13] Chesterton took this hyperbole literally. What did F.E. know about Christian communities?

> Are they clinging to their crosses,
>   F.E. Smith,
> Where the Breton boat-fleet tosses,
>   Are they, Smith?
> Do they, fasting, trembling, bleeding,
>   Wait the news from this our city?
> Groaning 'That's the Second Reading!'
>   Hissing 'There is still Committee!'
> If the voice of Cecil falters,
>   If McKenna's point has pith,
> Do they tremble for their altars?
>   Do they, Smith?
>
> Russian peasants round their pope
>   Huddled, Smith,
> Hear about it all, I hope,
>   Don't they, Smith?
> In the mountain hamlets clothing
>   Peaks beyond Caucasian pales
> Where Establishment means nothing
>   And they never heard of Wales,
> Do they read it all in Hansard
>   With a crib to read it with –
> 'Welsh Tithes: Dr Clifford Answered'.
>   Really, Smith?
>
> In the lands where Christians were,
>   F.E. Smith,
> In the little lands laid bare,
>   Smith, O Smith!

Where the Turkish bands are busy,
  And the Tory name is blessed
Since they hailed the cross of Dizzy
  On the banners from the West!
Men don't think it half so hard if
  Islam burns their kin and kith,
Since a curate lives in Cardiff
  Saved by Smith.

It would greatly, I must own,
  Soothe me, Smith,
If you left this theme alone,
  Holy Smith!
For your legal cause or civil
  You fight well and get your fee;
For your God or dream or devil
  You will answer, not to me.
Talk about the pews and steeples
  And the Cash that goes therewith!
But the souls of Christian peoples . . .
  Chuck it, Smith![14]

Whether F.E. was amused or annoyed is unknown; but he was publicly unabashed and did not in the least abate his criticism of the Bill as it ground its way painfully towards the Statute Book. It passed its Third Reading in February 1913 but was rejected by the Lords the following week. Under the procedure of the Parliament Act it then started again going through the Commons, passed its Third Reading for the second time in July and was thrown out a second time by the Lords. It went through all its stages in the Commons for the third time in 1914, only to be hung up by the outbreak of war. The Church was not finally disestablished until 1919. F.E. was then a member of the Government which disestablished it; but no one raised an eyebrow.

Even in 1912, however, the Welsh Church was a sideshow. The real battle, now coming to its climax, was over Home Rule for Ireland. For thirty years, ever since Gladstone's conversion to the cause, Home Rule had overhung British politics as an ever-present promise, obligation or threat, depending on party – a promise to the Nationalists, an obligation on the Liberals, a threat to the Unionists. While the Tories were in office, Home Rule was shelved; when the Liberals had an independent majority, it remained on the shelf; but as soon as the Liberal Government was dependent on the Irish for its existence, the old Gladstonian debt of honour was remembered and Asquith accepted as the price of the Government's life the obligation to carry Home Rule. To facilitate Home Rule the House of Lords was not reformed on any rational principle but simply stripped of its veto power. The obstacle on which the Unionists and the Protestants of Ulster had relied to prevent the delegation of the least particle of British rule to a Catholic Parliament in Dublin was thus swept away. For the first time the passage of a Home Rule Bill into law was a serious possibility. Gladstone's Home Rule Bills of 1886 and 1892 had been unreal, mere dummy-runs with no chance of reaching the Statute Book; the Ulster demonstrations against them, with Lord Randolph Churchill playing the 'Orange card' and Liverpool alive with Union Jacks and pledges of Protestant support, these too, for all their tribal fervour, were unreal, making faces at a shadow. 1912 was different. No obstacle now stood between Ulster and a determined Government intent upon delivering Home Rule. This time Ulstermen prepared to resist in earnest, under the granite-faced leadership of Sir Edward Carson, who in September 1911 announced the formation of a Provisional Government in Ulster, ready to take power the moment Home Rule was passed, to repel by force if necessary its application at least to the northern counties of the Protestant plantation.

F.E. had in 1911 already gone further than any other leading English Unionist in attaching himself unconditionally to the cause of Ulster. The year before, impatient that Ulster should not be allowed to block the grand ambition of Lloyd George's coalition plan, he had privately written off Home Rule as 'a dead quarrel'. But this was wishful thinking, soon disproved. He might have wished it dead, but now that it was a live issue again, Carson's defiance once more stirred his imagination and his zest for battle.

F.E. has been much criticized for his enthusiastic, apparently reckless, support for illegality and armed resistance in Ulster in 1912–14. He has been accused of mere self-advertising opportunism in taking up a cause to which he had no more real commitment than he had to the Welsh Church, simply to embarrass the Government. This underestimates him. Certainly there was an element of self-advertisement in everything F.E. did and said in these years: he was candidly out to make a reputation for himself. But to suggest that his espousal of Ulster was entirely cynical is to forget, first of all, the powerful influence of his background – his father, the sectarian politics of Liverpool, Salvidge and the Liverpool Working Men's Conservative Association. If Liverpool was politically a colony of Ulster then F.E. was something more than an honorary Ulsterman. Ulster was in his political heritage at least as much as it was in the blood of Bonar Law, a Canadian-Scot of Ulster extraction, or even of Carson, a Dublin Protestant. F.E. could hardly fail to respond to the revival of the passions of his youth: the whole political tradition in which he was proud to stand impelled him to take Ulster's side. He would have been politically dead if he had faltered.

Nevertheless his conduct in 1912–14 cannot be explained solely as a reflex response to old rallying cries. F.E. was too thoughtful a politician for that. At a deeper level, his support for Ulster reflected his most fundamental understanding of the nature of State power. Men could be governed only by consent or by force. If the men of Ulster withheld their consent from being governed from Dublin, then this was a fact which a democratic government must recognize: it could not impose Dublin government on them except by force, which was barbarous, tyrannical and politically unacceptable to the rest of the United Kingdom, even supposing it was possible, which in 1914 became another question. His support for Ulster was not at bottom an emotional loyalty at all, though it was easy to swell those chords when the cause required; it was based on a characteristic realism in the face of hard facts – the fact that, as the slogan put it, Ulster 'would not have' Home Rule. If Ulster would fight, in other words, then Ulster was right, because its very determination to fight was the proof of a coherent political entity self-consciously different from the rest of Ireland which carried its own legitimacy. F.E. was often attacked for it, but he never at any time in his career lost sight of the fact that ultimately, in the parcelling-out of the world into nation-states, might *is* right – might being the armed majority in any one country or part of a country. His serious purpose in taking up the Unionist cause in Ulster was to bring home to a Government determined to treat the resistance movement as bluff that its Home Rule writ simply would not run in Ulster – it should recognize this truth before it provoked inevitable civil war and modify its intentions accordingly.

From this perspective of unsentimental *realpolitik* F.E. was ready to concede, much earlier than most Unionists, the claim of the rest of Ireland to Home Rule if it wanted it and could discover a workable scheme which did not oppress the Ulster Protestants who – this was the inescapable logic of his position which he did not shirk – had as much right to freedom from Dublin as Dublin Catholics had to freedom from London. For many imperially minded Unionists, Ulster's special claim was no more than a convenient argument with which to oppose Home Rule itself; they regarded Ireland as an integral part of the United Kingdom and worried more about the subversive effect of Irish nationalism in India than in Ireland itself. Emotionally, F.E. was a Unionist of this sort: he could reject Irish aspirations with as grand an imperial contempt as any Tory, and in the cause of defending Ulster did so frequently. But intellectually, in serious discussion away from the platform, he knew that Ulster's case conceded Ireland's. He was from the first, long before the rest of the Tory party or even Carson himself, fighting for Ulster alone and ready for any compromise with the Nationalists that would safeguard Ulster. In this he foreshadowed quite consistently his participation in the Irish Treaty of 1921.

During 1912 the distinction between F.E.'s limited concern for Ulster and the wider purpose of the Tory party as a whole to use Ulster to defeat Home Rule altogether was not apparent. The possibility of partition had barely formed itself explicitly even in Carson's mind: Nationalists and Unionists alike were arguing about the whole of Ireland. The Tory leadership was as concerned about the Southern Unionists as it was for Ulster: the party leader in the Lords, Lansdowne, was himself a large landowner in County Kerry. Nevertheless Ulster was where the resistance was concentrated, and in February, at a rally at Balmoral, outside Belfast, attended by seventy M.P.s including F.E., Bonar Law pledged the party to the defence of Ulster, amid scenes of solemn patriotic and religious fervour. As yet, however, Law kept the talk of fighting vague and lofty. F.E. felt under no such constraint. At a large demonstration with Carson in Liverpool in January and in a series of other speeches around England between January and June he repeatedly spelled out the fact that Home Rule could only be imposed on Ulster at the point of a bayonet, that the Government could only get its way by using the army to shoot down loyal Ulstermen, and that there were no lengths, 'however desperate and unconstitutional', to which Ulster would not be entitled to go in resistance.[15] His military enthusiasm naturally raised in sceptical Liberal minds the question whether he intended to take up arms himself. 'What about yourself?', they taunted in the House of Commons in June. With unusual modesty F.E. replied, to Tory cheers, that 'no-one is less fitted to contribute to the military efficiency of any operation that may be contemplated, but neither I nor my colleagues would ever dream of recommending anyone to take risks we are not prepared according to the measure of our capacity to take ourselves'.[16]

F.E.'s birthday, 12 July, happened to be the most honoured date in the calendar of Ulster Protestantism, the anniversary of William of Orange's victory over James II at the Battle of the Boyne in 1690 – a happy coincidence with which he never failed to make full play when speaking to Ulster or Liverpool audiences. In 1912 he displayed his devotion to the Ulster cause by spending his fortieth birthday as the principal speaker at a major Orange Day demonstration in Belfast, or rather just outside, in a muddy field at Cloughfern, whither a large crowd had marched in steady rain from the city centre. He rewarded them with one of his most remarkable speeches, a wonderful example of his ability to mix argument with eloquence, and low gibes at the opposition with high patriotic sentiment.

He began with a celebration of Ulster's allegiance to the Crown since 1690, contrasting it crudely with Fenian atrocities in the South.

> You compose a section of the community of which even your opponents have never denied that it is prosperous, law-abiding and loyal. You have, it is true, avoided the method of calling attention to your grievances which for generations has distinguished your political opponents; you have maimed no dumb animal, you have shot no woman, you have stabbed no Sunday School child. [Cheers.] Your claims, therefore, on the present Government are obviously small in comparison with those of the men who dictate Mr Asquith's policy; and yet, as compared with them, you ask very little. You only ask to be allowed to sit, as heretofore, in a Parliament which, amid all the vicissitudes of party politics, has not failed to retain your confidence.

He proceeded to a familiar recital of Asquith's cynical record on Home Rule down the years, and mocked the Government's pretence, on the Committee Stage of the Bill a few weeks before, of considering an amendment to exclude Ulster. Redmond would never allow them to exclude Ulster. 'What, indeed, has Home Rule to offer to him and his friends, with no-one to tax and no-one to persecute?' The Nationalists he portrayed as no better than a gang of Papist tyrants.

> You are asked why you distrust the Nationalist members, and why you are so convinced that the establishment of a Home Rule Parliament would be disastrous both to Ulster and the Empire. You answer that it is because you know these men; it is because you have studied their history [cheers]; it is because you choose rather to believe them over a sustained period where they had every inducement to speak the truth than over a limited period in which they have every inducement to deceive; it is because you know that the spirit of ascendancy, of sacerdotalism and persecution is as active and virulent in their ranks as it was active and virulent when your forefathers met and drove theirs in rout at the battle of the Boyne. [Cheers.] It is because you know that these men are in their hearts inexorably committed to the policy of complete separation from England.

'If I were an Ulster Protestant,' F.E. elaborated,

> I would rather be ruled from Constantinople by the Sultan of Turkey, than by a politician like Mr Devlin . . . Hatred of Ulster

breathes in every one of Mr Devlin's speeches . . . The inclusion in
an Irish executive of such a man would be a sufficient exposure of
its spirit, its character and its motives.

Then, changing his tone, he challenged Asquith to face the fact of
Ulster's fixed opposition, and say how he proposed to meet it. The onus
was on the Government, faced with an immovable object: Ulster had
only to demonstrate its inflexible will.

Your course, at any rate, is clear, and it becomes you from now
henceforth to prepare silently, steadfastly and constantly for the
gravest crisis which has tested the men of your race for more than
two centuries. [Cheers.] Above all I would most earnestly press
upon every man who listens to me the vital necessity of maintaining that impression of self-restraint and reserve force which
has already so powerfully and so favourably influenced opinion in
the English constituencies. Let there be no premature or isolated
appeal to force . . . You will not lose, you will gain immeasurably,
by the exhibition of a composure which is in harmony with the
example of your forefathers and your own former practice. And
when the hour comes, as it has come to others, when you are called
upon to put everything you hold dear to the hazard, you will go
forward to face that future which the inscrutable purpose of the
Almighty has in store for you with the quiet confidence of men who
have patiently endured until endurance became treason to their
race. [Cheers.] You are sometimes asked whether you propose to
resist the English Army. I reply that even if this Government had
the wickedness (which, on the whole, I believe) it is wholly lacking
in the nerve required to give an order which in my deliberate
judgment would shatter for years the civilisation of these islands.
But I note with satisfaction that you are preparing yourselves by
the practice of exercises, and by the submission to discipline, for
the struggle which is not unlikely to test your determination. The
Nationalists are determined to rule you; you are determined that
you will never be ruled by them. [Loud cheers.] A collision of wills
so sharp may well defy the resources of a peaceful solution. Should
these fail you will, in my judgment, be entitled to forget the
community which has driven you forth, and to combine in opposition to the community which claims your allegiance as the fruit of
a corrupt and abominable bargain. You will have regained the free
discretion of free men.

With this vision of an independent Ulster F.E. soared beyond

Unionism. But in his rousing conclusion, he did not hesitate to invoke the authority of the whole Tory party for this departure.

> I do not underrate the gravity of this statement; still less do I underrate the responsibility which I undertake in making it. I and my friends have considered this matter deeply . . . On this we are all of us agreed: that the crisis has called into existence one of those supreme issues of conscience amid which the ordinary landmarks of permissible resistance to technical law are submerged. [Cheers.] We shall not shrink from the consequences of this view, not though the whole fabric of the Commonwealth be convulsed, and we shall tread with you the path of your destiny, knowing that whether it leads to freedom or disaster, it is the only road which does not lead to dishonour. [Loud cheers.][17]

'Mr F.E. Smith's great speech', *The Times* reported,

> at first seemed to be a little above the heads of the people he was addressing. For a time the Orangemen hung upon his words in silence, but as the speaker shook his subject clear of the petti-fogging chicaneries of Westminster, and clearly showed his audience what he as a spokesman for his party was prepared to do for Ulster, his words were often drowned in applause. When he came down to the hard facts of what it would be possible and impossible for the Government to do, the men of Ulster clearly understood, and they cheered him full-throatedly.[18]

At the end, amid cries of 'Orange Smith', F.E. was ceremoniously presented with an Orange sash.

From now on F.E. was one of the leading figures in the Ulster campaign: he was not, of course, as an Englishman, a member of Carson's Provisional Government in waiting, but he was the most popular platform speaker in Ulster after Carson himself, and the most prominent and outspoken supporter in England of Ulster's stand – excepting only Bonar Law. On 27 July 1912 the British public was, perhaps for the first time, awakened to the real gravity of the situation by hearing the Leader of the Opposition declare, at a great Unionist rally in the grounds of Blenheim Palace, that he could 'imagine no length of resistance to which Ulster can go in which I should not be prepared to support them'. 'There are things', Law warned, 'stronger than Parliamentary majorities.'[19] The Leader of His Majesty's Loyal Opposition was mobilizing his party against the elected Government in contemplation of civil war.

In September the scene shifted back to Ulster itself. F.E. joined Carson in the extraordinary series of meetings all over the Protestant counties which culminated, after ten days of intense political excitement, in the mass signature in Belfast City Hall and elsewhere on 28 September of the solemn Ulster Covenant. Nearly half a million men and women queued up to pledge in writing their determination to resist by all means necessary what they regarded as the subversion of their civil and religious liberty by the revolutionary 'conspiracy to set up a Home Rule Parliament in Ireland'. 'In sure confidence that God will defend the right we hereto subscribe our names.'[20] At all the meetings which preceded the signing – at Londonderry, Coleraine, Portadown and Ballymena – huge Union Jacks were unfurled and 'O God, Our Help in Ages Past' roared out with passionate conviction, and Carson would inspect the ranks of the – still unarmed – volunteers. It was for the dashing figure he cut at these parades, mounted, in constant attendance on his leader but a few respectful steps behind, that F.E. acquired the derisive nickname 'galloper' – a name which to Liberal wits combined the sense of subaltern or errand-boy (a 'galloper' is correctly speaking an aide-de-camp or orderly officer) with a jeer at F.E.'s childish self-importance rushing about on horseback playing soldiers. The Liberals were still determined not to take Ulster's resistance seriously, and they found F.E., as an English interloper given, they knew, to rhetorical exaggeration, an easy target through whom to make fun, most unwisely, of the whole indigenous and deadly serious movement. Frederick Kellaway, for instance, the M.P. for Bedford, seized the opportunity in a letter to *The Times* to mock a curious phrase of F.E.'s in a speech at Belfast on 23 September, when he had declared that 'if the Unionists of Liverpool are told that they have no concern with the quarrel, and that they must stand idly by while the liberties of Ulster are usurped, the rifles will go off of themselves'.[21] Kellaway recalled F.E. indulging in similar threats of 'desperate resistance' before the Parliament Bill was passed. 'What form did that most desperate resistance take?' he jeered. 'It is a fact that the most bloodthirsty expedient adopted by Mr Smith and the other fellows who fought with him was the Die-Hard dinner at the Hotel Cecil. After that', he concluded ironically, 'I think it is safe to say that unless the Liverpool rifles go off by themselves, they will not go off at all.'[22]

The difference was that this time F.E. was expressing the determination, not of politicians to 'fight' but of ordinary people to fight in earnest, as the scenes all over Ulster that September should have convinced the most complacent Liberal. A *Times* correspondent writing of one meeting in Londonderry on the 20th at which Carson and F.E. voiced their usual defiance – 'I clasp your hand tonight', F.E. declared, 'and I say, under God, we are with you in the fight that lies in front of you'[23] – described 'a scene of joy the like of which I have never yet witnessed in a public place . . . Mr Smith achieved an extraordinary success'.[24] Liberals might mock F.E., but the Ulstermen did not.

After the signing of the Covenant Carson, with F.E. still at his side, sailed in triumph from Belfast, seen off aboard the steamer *Patriotic* by tremendous crowds singing 'Rule Britainnia', 'God Save the King' and 'Auld Lang Syne'. He was met at 7.30 the next morning in the port of Liverpool by even larger crowds, 150,000 strong, who conducted him in procession to the Conservative Club. The next night nearly as many gathered in Sheil Park in F.E.'s constituency, with Salvidge in the chair, to hear Carson himself, F.E. and Londonderry: for this audience F.E. raised his rhetoric another notch by asserting that if the Government dared to order the army to march on Ulster, they would be 'lynched from the lamp-posts of London'.[25] Protestant Liverpool amply proved, on these two days, its solidarity with Protestant Ulster. The past fortnight's demonstrations in Belfast and Liverpool alike, F.E. wrote, had been the most remarkable he had ever witnessed. 'They transcended ordinary political meetings, because behind them loomed the possibility of something sterner than politics.'[26]

The Government, however, resolutely refused to be impressed. From these excitements, therefore, F.E. returned to the more conventional paths of opposition in the House of Commons, where the Home Rule Bill was still in Committee. Instead of challenging the Government's physical power to coerce Ulster he now brought his argumentative artillery to bear on the logical anomalies of its legislation, which he had no difficulty demonstrating was unworkable anyway. His arguments were not only the same as those levelled with destructive effect against Gladstone's Home Rule Bills by Joseph Chamberlain; they were the same as those with which Tam Dalyell and Enoch Powell riddled the similarly anomalous efforts of a Labour Government sixty-five years later to give a devolved Parliament to Scotland. The logical absurdity of a half-baked federalism within a unitary state is eternal. F.E.'s remorseless development of them displays a very different side of his versatile talent than his dramatic posturing in Ulster.

The first illogicality – the same which became known in 1977 as the 'West Lothian question', after Tam Dalyell's constituency – concerned the position of the Irish M.P.s who remained at Westminster after the establishment of the Home Rule Parliament in Dublin. Westminster would no longer have any jurisdiction over Irish devolved affairs – licensing, education, roads and the like – but Irish M.P.s would still be able to vote in the House of Commons on English and Scottish licensing, education and roads. More important they would still determine which party formed the Government in London. The Government's solution was to cut the number of Irish members from 101 to 42. This merely reduced the anomaly – it did not end it. The fact remained that in an evenly divided House the Irish would still hold the balance. Yet the Irish were unquestionably still entitled to be represented, for non-devolved questions, in the imperial Parliament. The problem was that there was no principle, so long as Ireland alone had Home Rule, by which the level of her representation could be determined. Paradox, as John Morley had admitted in his life of Gladstone, was inherent in every solution.

Still more ludicrous, F.E. demonstrated, were the contradictions spawned by the Bill's attempt simultaneously to satisfy the Irish and reassure Unionists. The Bill provided, first, that the Irish Parliament would have an entirely free hand except on those questions which were reserved; second, that the imperial Parliament would retain an absolute veto on all Irish legislation; and third, that the Judicial Committee of the Privy Council would rule on any dispute. The last provision, F.E. pointed out, contradicted the other two, which in turn contradicted each other. 'Such a clumsy, botched-up scheme', he concluded in the periodical essay in which he deployed his fullest indictment of the Bill, 'is inevitable . . . in any attempt to set up two diverse Parliamentary authorities, while claiming that one is independent and that the other is supreme.'

Such a system could not last six months.

> If you once establish an Irish Parliament with an executive responsible to it, you have parted with all real control over Ireland short of a repeal of the proposed Bill or a reconquest by arms. The safeguards – the veto and the rest – are worth less than the paper they are written on; because they can never be enforced if the Irish Ministry of the day threatens to resign, and so to leave the unfortunate Lord Lieutenant without an alternative Ministry.

Asquith had *admitted* in October that the safeguards were worthless if the Irish chose to make them so; who could doubt that they would? It would be better to concede independence at once than come to it painfully through the non-working of the Bill.

> The Bill is designed to lose Ireland without conciliating her, and to break up the Empire in order to establish an inveterate enemy on one flank. When Mr Asquith talks about Ireland as a nation he gives his whole case away. If Ireland is a nation apart, she must

have her separate government, and Imperial safeguards are to her
a mere futile insult: if she is not a nation apart, why should her
inhabitants not be content to share the equal rights enjoyed by the
citizens of the United Kingdom? Between separation and Union
there is no middle course.[26]

He went on to expose the 'hellish confusion' of the Bill's financial
clauses which were littered with special provisions relieving Ireland of
paying her fair share for the armed forces and the National Debt, while
she still enjoyed British benefits. Ireland under the Bill would be
reduced to the status of a 'kept island', her standard of living maintained to a level above her own taxable capacity while she contributed
nothing to her own defence, indulging the romantic delights of separation without losing the solid advantages of Union: having her cake, in
short, and eating it.

All these imbalances and anomalies, F.E. insisted, would make the
Home Rule Bill unworkable and unacceptable to England even if
Ireland were a single community: their force was intensified tenfold by
the fact that there were two Irelands. The Bill provided no means of
protecting Ulster from the oppression of the Catholic South. Ulster had
exactly the same claim against the rest of Ireland that Ireland had
against England. Yet Redmond refused to consider excluding Ulster
from the Bill – for the clear mercenary reason that two-thirds of
Ireland's customs revenue came through Belfast. Once again, as F.E.
characterized the Bill, everyone was to pay for Home Rule except those
who wanted it.

Ultimately, however, all his practical objections to Home Rule were
subordinate to the single overwhelming fact that Ulster would not have
it. He always returned to the point that the Government had three
alternatives: to conquer Ulster, to exclude Ulster or to drop the Bill.
Since it could not do the first, he wrote sarcastically to *The Times* on
30 October, 'there would appear to be much convenience in selecting
the present moment to decide between the two remaining'.[27]

'Does the Government suppose the Opposition enjoys talking about
civil war,' he asked in the House of Commons in January 1913, 'or the
prospect of taking part in it, for which obviously many of us are
unsuited?' This was in the debate on the Third Reading of the Bill: F.E.
from the Tory front bench followed Simon at the beginning of the
second day. It was a highly charged occasion; yet F.E., though deadly
serious in his pleading with the Government to recognize Ulster's case,
lightened the atmosphere with some of his best satirical knockabout on
the subject of Asquith's trust in the 'safeguards' Redmond offered
Ulster.

The Prime Minister, on this as on all other points, is an optimist. Some men are born optimists, some are optimists from choice, and some few are optimists from compulsion. [Loud laughter and cheers.] The Prime Minister trusts the Nationalists, and tells the Ulstermen they ought to trust the Nationalists. The Prime Minister is entitled to trust the Nationalists. It is a long time since the political world has witnessed an association so harmonious, so sustained and supported by so mutual a benefit. [Cheers and laughter.] It has ranged with unimpaired integrity over the whole field of politics – involving in its collateral activities even the defeat of the women. [Renewed cheers and Opposition laughter.] The Prime Minister does well to trust the Irish. They give him the Welsh curates; he gives them Ulster. One accommodation deserves another.

Abruptly F.E.'s tone hardened: he moved suddenly for the kill. 'A shifty, groundless and irresponsible hopefulness, exercised at other people's expense, is political cowardice and a public danger.'[28]

At the end of the debate the Bill was approved by 367 votes to 257. Its passage was the signal for wild demonstrations by both Home Rulers and Unionists outside. When he emerged, F.E. was one of several M.P.s swept by the crowd up Whitehall to the Constitutional Club in Northumberland Avenue, where he made an impromptu speech from a balcony. Twenty years before, he said, the House of Lords had referred Gladstone's Home Rule Bill to the people, who rejected it. This time, he promised, if the House of Lords no longer had the power, there was a force in Ulster strong enough to kill the Bill.

In the middle of all this, at the very moment when they were threatening the Government with civil war in Ulster, F.E. and Carson gave another remarkable demonstration of that code of honour which would not allow political differences, even of so grave a nature, to override all other obligations of personal and professional conduct. To the indignation of much of their party, who looked to them as front bench spokesmen to miss no opportunity to embarrass the Government, they both accepted briefs, in their capacity as leaders of the Bar, to defend four Ministers accused of improper dealing in Marconi shares.

The Marconi scandal first broke in the summer of 1912, when the scurrilous gossip-sheet *Eye-Witness*, owned by Cecil Chesterton (G.K.'s brother) alleged that Herbert Samuel (the Postmaster-General), the Master of Elibank (Liberal Chief Whip), Lloyd George, Rufus Isaacs and his brother Godfrey Isaacs had all bought shares in the Marconi Wireless Company at a time when Samuel was awarding the company a major Government contract for an imperial wireless chain, and then sold them at a large profit when the contract was made known. The truth was that their dealing was in the shares of the *American* Marconi Company which had no formal connection with the British company. The four Ministers had acted unwisely but not corruptly. But the case was eagerly taken up by the Tory press in the ill-concealed hope of catching the hated author of the People's Budget and the two most prominent Jewish members of the Government with their hands in the till – there was a strong current of anti-semitism running on the Tory right at this period, to which the whiff of corruption was meat and drink. While the accused Ministers sued for libel, Tory M.P.s pursued the matter in the House of Commons and forced the setting up of a Select Committee; this, however, divided on strict party lines, with the Liberal majority giving the Ministers a clean bill of moral health while the Tory members found them guilty at least of 'grave impropriety'. Harold Smith resigned from the Committee while it was still sitting, denouncing it as a farce.

In the courts, by contrast, F.E. and Carson took the leading parts in clearing the accused Ministers' names, which led to a furious debate in the Tory party and in the columns of *The Times* over where a barrister-M.P.'s first duty lay, to his profession or to his party and constituents. In April 1913, when it was first announced that Godfrey Isaacs had retained F.E., Bonar Law's private secretary reported 'a good deal of indignation' in the party, but added:

> So far as I can see there seems to be no doubt that the etiquette of the Bar makes it impossible for a man to refuse a brief if an adequate remuneration is offered for his services. This is what I told Monsell [the Tory Chief Whip] had better be told to the grumblers.[29]

Discontent was not so easily appeased. 'Legal etiquette may be what it pleases,' George Younger wrote in May, 'but it could never be held right to utilize it in order to close the mouths of prominent politicians whose duty to their constituents is paramount, and who have no business thus to handicap themselves . . . This feeling is very strong amongst our men.'[30] Lord Charles Beresford wrote that feeling against Carson in particular was not only strong but *violent*.[31]

The case ran for ten days at the Old Bailey at the beginning of June, with Carson and F.E. leading Richard Muir for Isaacs, and Rigby Swift leading Ernest Wild for Chesterton, who was found guilty of criminal libel but fined only £100, plus costs. The next day *The Times* devoted an editorial to the case, suggesting that in accepting Isaacs's brief Carson and F.E. had carried the independence and brotherhood of the Bar too far, and that their separation of their legal from their political selves was confusing to the 'ordinary man'. On 17 June F.E. replied to the charge with a long vindication of their action, some 2,000 words in his loftiest manner. His argument was that barristers were obliged to put their services at the disposal of anyone who would pay them, like 'cabmen in the rank'. Did *The Times* seriously propose, he asked, that he and Carson should have refused to appear on behalf of a client who belonged to the opposing party, that in cases with any political content Conservatives should be defended by Conservatives and Liberals by Liberals? The inescapable consequence of such a system would simply be to reproduce in the Law Courts 'the grotesque travesty of judicial procedure which has disfigured the record of the Marconi committee'. *The Times*'s appeal to the 'ordinary man' he rejected with contempt.

> I do not in this connection recognize such a tribunal. May I without incivility add that, if upon a matter requiring some degree of enlightenment and cultivation for its adequate comprehension the 'ordinary man' is uninstructed on the function which every civilised country in the world has assigned to the advocate, *The Times* would be better employed in informing his mind than in appealing to his judgment? The responsibility will be deep and lasting of those who degrade the Bar of England into the parasites of a party.

For himself, he declared proudly, 'I have spent 20 years of my life in strenuous contention on behalf of the Conservative Party. But I have not surrendered to them or any other party, and I never will, my independence of judgement in matters of professional propriety.'[32]

The controversy ran on vigorously for another two weeks, however, with the weight of letters going against F.E. – a striking expression of the party bitterness of the times and of laymen's irritation with lawyers' pious appeals to professional ethics. Technically, to be sure, F.E. was correct: party must be kept out of the law courts. Yet at the same time his and Carson's colleagues in the House of Commons were entitled to feel that a sharp trick had been played by the accused Ministers in engaging for Isaacs's defence two of their most dangerous political opponents, and that the two lawyers had lent themselves rather too easily, with their invocation of professional etiquette, to this Liberal stratagem.

There was in reality, as at least one letter pointed out, more than just professional obligation in their action. 'They espoused the cause of the Ministers', asserted a critical correspondent who signed himself simply

E.M., 'from a chivalrous feeling of personal friendship – creditable to them no doubt, but for this purpose irrelevant.'[33] This was true, particularly of F.E. Lloyd George and Rufus Isaacs, though Liberals and members of the Government that was trying to fix Home Rule on Ulster, were both his friends, both members of the Other Club; Elibank too. Hard though he would fight them in the political arena, he instinctively rallied to their side in a personal challenge to their honour of a sort which he regarded as quite outside the legitimate run of political controversy. At other times he had acted for Churchill as readily as for Amery in libel cases. Loyalty to his friends was the highest virtue in F.E.'s personal code. If legal etiquette, as in this case, could be called in to buttress this priority, so much the better; but it is out of the question to imagine him appearing for the other side in a case that might have wrecked his friends' careers. He would certainly have pleaded the danger of political bias in order to decline the brief.

His friends were duly grateful. Such was the fellowship of the Bar that Isaacs could scarcely tell friendship and duty apart when he wrote to F.E. after the case was over. 'The Bar will ever remember the part Carson and you played in this matter. You have both behaved so generously and even magnificently.'[34] Lloyd George was equally appreciative. F.E.'s 'personal loyalty', he wrote rather pompously to Garvin, had given him 'a higher conception altogether of his character'.[35] Henceforth he was noticeably readier to trust in delicate matters like compromise discussions over Ulster an opponent whom he had probably regarded hitherto as an attractive but unscrupulous partisan. It was a development of the highest importance for F.E.'s future career when he won Lloyd George's confidence in the Marconi case.

In September 1913, around the first anniversary of the signing of the Covenant, F.E. went back to Ulster for another fortnight of meetings, parades and inspections of volunteers with Carson, interrupted by a few days at Blenheim with the Oxfordshire Yeomanry which gave him the chance of talks with Winston. Outwardly the situation remained frozen in a state of suspended confrontation while the Home Rule Bill dragged its way through the Commons for a second time. Behind the scenes, however, both parties now began to consider seriously for the first time the possibility of excluding Ulster from its operation – as F.E. practically alone had been insisting was the only solution. On the Unionist side both Carson and Law were now prepared, reluctantly, to settle for the preservation of Ulster alone if that could be accomplished; but Lansdowne, Long, Curzon and other Tory magnates were still immovably opposed to any 'betrayal' of the South. On the Government side the Cabinet woke up belatedly to the fact that it faced a serious problem and held its first discussions on Ulster since the crisis arose. But still only Lloyd George and Churchill were disposed to give practical consideration to exclusion. It is difficult to avoid the explanation that they more than other Liberals had the benefit of first-hand accounts from F.E. of Ulster's resolution, and trusted his judgment of it; though Churchill was also ever-conscious of the memory of his father. He knew Lord Randolph's Orange speeches by heart, even without F.E. continually quoting them at him: he had the strongest personal reason for wanting somehow to reconcile his new party allegiance to Home Rule with his father's example. Their colleagues, however, were continually assured by the Liberal press that the Ulster resistance was hot air – for instance by the *Daily Chronicle* on 24 September:

> Carsonism is rapidly tottering to its fall. The reckless speeches which the leader of the 'Ulsterettes' has been making in Counties Down and Antrim during the past week or two are . . . a sign of the weakness of his forces . . . If the people of Ulster are so determined to resist the passage of the Home Rule Bill as Sir Edward would like the English people to believe, one would imagine that it would not be necessary for him and Mr F.E. Smith to make so many appeals to them to join the Ulster Volunteer Force. Men who are eager to do their duty do not require to be coaxed to do it.[36]

The Cabinet did discuss exclusion, however. It concluded that Redmond would not stand for it.

F.E.'s position was now a pivotal one, and exceedingly delicate, as he attempted to mediate between his own leaders, Carson and Law, who were getting ahead of their party, on the one hand, and Churchill and Lloyd George, who were ahead of *their* colleagues, on the other. The goal was to achieve some sort of conference at which the exclusion of the predominantly Protestant counties might be exchanged for Tory acquiescence in Home Rule for the rest. Such a deal could only be carried by an agreement between the two English parties to override Redmond. Only by keeping up their unconditional support for Ulster, however, by repeated pledges of their willingness to go to any length in her defence, could the Tories hope to force the Government to the conference, let alone persuade it once there to abandon Redmond and oblige the Nationalists to settle for three-quarters of a cake. Thus F.E. can be found in the space of a few days quite deliberately speaking with different voices to different audiences. For public consumption – for instance in Ballyclare in East Antrim on 20 September – he scaled new heights of hyperbole as he assured Ulster that the Tory party was 'prepared with you to risk the collapse of the whole body politic to prevent this monstrous crime'[37] – language which had even the Southern Unionist leader Lansdowne protesting to Law in alarm. For private Tory consumption F.E. argued for negotiation, though from a position of unshakeable strength; while to his Liberal friends he pictured a conference which might settle Ulster as part of a wider agreement which recalled Lloyd George's coalition plan of 1910.

For Carson's benefit F.E. set out his views in a memorandum which Carson sent on 20 September to Bonar Law in England. Remembering the 1910 conference F.E. accepted that the Tory party, both in Ulster and in the country generally, would be highly suspicious of another conference in the present situation, as being likely only to 'dissipate enthusiasm and perhaps relax preparation'. Nevertheless the party could not refuse to confer, especially if the invitation came not from the Government but from the King. F.E. then offered his idea of the possible lines of discussion in such a conference.

It would appear that the Unionist leaders could only agree to one of two courses.

1. The survival of the present Bill with the modification necessary to exclude Ulster which might
   (a) be constituted a province with powers analogous to those conceded to the rest of Ireland
   (b) retain her direct connection with the Imperial Parliament.

Here the principal questions are
   (1) Wd Ulster agree to such a solution.
   (2) Wd the rest of Unionist Ireland agree.
In my judgement . . . both these questions would ultimately be answered in the affirmative.

But another difficulty primarily affecting the Govt. arises. Could they procure a majority of their party to support such exclusion? Probably not unless Redmond agreed. It is possible therefore & even probable that the Govt. wd insist as conditions precedent
   (a) that the residue of the H.R.B. should be treated as an agreed Bill
   (b) that the Ulster Bill should be treated as an agreed Bill
   (c) that if necessary the Unionist party should carry these proposals by their votes. Are we prepared to do this?

2. The second & perhaps preferable course open to the Unionist leaders is to recommend the simultaneous application of devolutionary principles if there is to be any application of them anywhere.

This course would
(a) postpone everything to the Greek Kalends
(b) thoroughly dishearten the Nationalists
(c) involve the Govt. in a morass which might ultimately destroy them.

Carson, still unhappy to concede separate treatment for Ulster although coming round to it, preferred the latter course; it seems unlikely that F.E. really did, except as a plausible but unreal alternative with which to force the Government to accept exclusion. He concluded with four 'general observations' which underline his conviction that the Unionists must not show the Government the least hint of weakness.

(1) The existing position is the most favourable to us & the most formidable to the Govt.
(2) We have the best cards for the purpose of negotiation.
(3) We should therefore not unless compelled by public considerations alter our position for the worse by negotiation.
(4) We should always remember that we are now for the first time given the chance of resisting the Parliament Act in operation: perhaps we have our one & only chance of destroying it by counter-revolutionary means.[38]

A week later, most of it spent in company with Winston in Oxfordshire, F.E. was writing in rather different terms to Lloyd George. It was not only Winston whom he had seen while in England.

Secret & Confidential
My dear L.G.,
    I have had long & interesting talks with the King & with Winston. The basis W. & I discussed was
(1) Exclusion of Ulster with facilities for later adherence.
(2) Acceptance of an agreed Bill by the Unionists for the rest of Ireland.
(3) A genuine attempt to make the thing work in the South.
(4) A conference to be summoned to discuss matters.
    I am strongly of opinion the conference should be summoned by the King – W. I am sure wrongly – thinks not. Our extremists wd hate a conference – they think they have you beat – so would yours – but neither of them could hold out against the question – 'would you have us refuse the King when he asks us to confer?'
    If a conference is held I agree with W. it might develop. *In the most strict confidence* I inform you that I received this morning a letter

from Steel-Maitland [Chairman of the Tory party] suggesting to me that if a conference was held on H.R. it might & ought to be extended to cover H. of L. reform & the Land.* From such a conference anything could follow.

Under the circumstances while fully *making your case* at Bedford could you not do it in a restrained way & without unfriendliness to landlords as a class? If things fail you can return at any time to a war-basis. I think a 'statesmanlike' speech (odious phrase!) might produce some remarkable consequences.

Do not attach too much importance to our speeches at the moment. You know Ulster well enough to know that on the supreme issue to herself there is no bluff. But if people may have to go into a conference but do not know, there is a tendency to begin negotiations by putting the case high.

Yours ever,
F.E.[39]

Lloyd George was eager to meet F.E. half-way. 'You know how anxious I have been for years to work with you & a few others on your side,' he wrote back. 'I have always realized that our differences have been very artificial & do not reach the "realities". But what is the good of Steel-Maitland talking of a rapprochement when he sends Cave & Maxse to start another campaign of pure scurrility.' (Lloyd George was particularly sensitive about Maxse, who had pursued him mercilessly over the Marconi case). 'That would mean war to the knife. I know enough of Cave to be able to conclude that he would not be a party to this dirty work unless he had been officially asked to do it. This is certainly not the road to conciliation.'[40]

F.E. arranged to call on Lloyd George in Downing Street on Monday evening before the following Tuesday's Budget. But it was true that he was having more difficulty than he hoped in bringing the Tories to accept a conference. Lansdowne and the other uncompromising Unionists were still adamant against sacrificing the rest of Ireland for the sake of Ulster, and Bonar Law found it necessary to backtrack on the conference proposal, telling Lansdowne that 'F.E.'s talk with the King seemed to me just about as unwise as anything could be'.[41] F.E. had given His Majesty a far too rosy picture of the chance of compromise. Rebuked presumably by his leader, F.E. had to tread more carefully. But he continued to prompt his friends to maintain the momentum. 'I think you will agree that I have played up well,' he wrote to Churchill on 5 October. 'I hope you will do the same now . . . I have run no small

---

* Lloyd George was about to launch a new land-reform campaign.

risks and incurred considerable censure.' Churchill was due to speak at Dundee on the 8th. F.E. suggested that he could draw Carson out by asking directly whether he would accept Home Rule if Ulster were excluded.[42] Churchill did so, giving the first – unauthorized – hint that the Government might be willing to consider exclusion. 'Winston's speech was excellent,' F.E. wrote to Lloyd George next day. 'I am speaking tomorrow & shall help but can only do so guardedly so as not to cause jealousy & do no harm.'[43] At West Bromwich he was careful to emphasize that he spoke only for himself in welcoming Churchill's feeler. But he went on to declare in the strongest terms his belief that the Tory party must accept exclusion. Their unshakeable objection was only to Home Rule in the *north*.

> I am convinced of this, that while upon the inclusion of Ulster no compromise has ever been possible, while upon this issue no surrender will ever be made, it is none the less inconceivable that the Unionist Party should be so base as to make Ulster a pawn in the party game instead of using her exceptional position for the legitimate purpose of enforcing exceptional treatment.[44]

In other words Lansdowne and the Southern Unionists should stop using Ulster as a shield to protect their own no longer defensible position. The monthly *Liberal Magazine* so appreciated how far F.E. was sticking his neck out that it highlighted this passage in its next issue.

Over the next couple of months Law and Asquith had three private meetings, arranged by Max Aitken at Cherkley. Between themselves they agreed that they might be prepared to accept Home Rule for Catholic Ireland only, subject to the approval of their respective parties. But there was little enough chance of agreement on the Unionist side; there was none at all on the Government side, since the power of veto extended to Redmond, to whom Asquith now felt committed not only in expediency but in honour, and Redmond would never give up his party's historic claim to the whole of Ireland. The most Asquith could offer, when the Bill came back to the House of Commons for the third time in March 1914, was that Ulster might opt out of Home Rule for six years. This Carson and Law rejected out of hand as a mere stay of execution, even though the breathing space allowed the hope that a Unionist Government might be elected in the interval which would be able to make it permanent. The slim hope of compromise for which F.E. and Lloyd George and Churchill had been working thus faded. Civil war loomed again and even the peacemakers returned to battle-stations. At the end of the debate Churchill scribbled a doom-laden message to F.E.

My dear,

I grieve more than I can say at BL's speech; and if that is the answer to all that we have offered, there is nothing for it but a trial of strength in which believe me I shall enter with the deepest sorrow, but without doubt or fear.

Alas, alas – –
W.⁴⁵

In a resounding speech at Bradford a few days later he condemned the Unionists' intransigence and accepted on the Government's behalf the challenge to the arbitrament of force with the famous words, 'Let us go forward and put these grave matters to the proof.'[46] Military preparations now went ahead in Ireland.

It was time for the Tories to play their last desperate card. The army on which the Government relied to impose its political will on Ulster was, at least in its officer caste, overwhelmingly Unionist in sympathy. It had been F.E.'s argument all along that in the last resort the Government would simply not have the power to coerce Ulster. As he put it in Manchester in November 1913, with a literary flourish:

When the Attorney-General [Simon] says he will meet force with force, what he means is that he and his friends will place at the disposal of the Nationalist Party . . . the forces of the English Crown. That reminds me of the observation in a well-known passage of one of Shakespeare's plays in which one character claims 'I can call spirits from the vasty deep', to which another replies 'Yes, but will they come?'

He made ironic play with a catalogue of insults and abuse heaped by the Irish in the past on the British army – the Ulster Defence League took it up and published it as a pamphlet – and predicted that if the Government tried to use the army on their behalf to shoot down loyal Ulstermen, 'the instrument will break in their hands'.[47] In Liverpool in January 1914 he had again crudely mocked the dependence of the Nationalists on British arms to fight their battles for them. What if the army would not? 'Are the whining advocates of peace at any price going to turn their mittens into gauntlets? Are the Brunner brigade' – the Liberal businessman Sir John Brunner was one of F.E.'s favourite *bêtes noires* – 'going to use their umbrellas for scabbards?'[48]

F.E. of course denied that he was advocating mutiny: he was merely 'prophesying'. But his 'prophesies' and those of Bonar Law and the other Unionist leaders were self-fulfilling, and were intended to be so. The idea was given respectable currency in army circles that it would be

legitimate in the circumstances of Ulster for officers to defy the fundamental code on which military discipline depends and refuse to obey
orders which offended their political conscience; and even in the
Government's mind the seed of doubt was sown. As the need for a show
of military strength became imminent in March 1914 the War Office
(headed since 1912 by Jack Seely) sought to insure itself against the
possibility of such a refusal by giving officers at the Curragh camp
outside Dublin who were actually domiciled in Ulster the extraordinary
option of taking indefinite leave if a move against the north were in
prospect, though any officer who refused to serve would be dismissed
the service. When General Paget, the Commander-in-Chief in Dublin,
tactlessly put this limited offer to his men with the implication that civil
war in the north was about to commence, General Sir Hubert Gough, the
commander of the Cavalry Brigade at the Curragh, and fifty-nine of his
officers chose to resign.

The Government weakly tried to play down the incident, insisting
that there had been a 'misunderstanding' of the purely precautionary
operation envisaged. After threats of mass resignations from the army
in England if he were disciplined, Gough was reinstated in his command. Although Asquith officially repudiated the unauthorized assurance given Gough by Seely that no military action against Ulster
was contemplated, dismissed Seely and took over the War Office himself, the Tory trump card had in fact succeeded. The army had served
notice, as F.E. and Law had 'prophesied', that it would not be used to
coerce Ulster. Their instrument had indeed broken in the Government's hands: Carson's volunteers had proved their point without a
battle. To rub their victory home, 24,000 rifles, imported from Germany,
were on 25 April successfully run into the ports of Larne and Bangor
outside Belfast, so that the men, or some of them, who had drilled with
dummy guns when Carson and F.E. had inspected them in 1912–13,
were now armed.

With the Government's impotence publicly revealed, the situation
was now more deadlocked than ever. Winston and F.E. got together
again to rough out a new plan to subsume an Irish settlement within a
federal constitution as a whole, for which they tried to canvass support
on both sides of the House of Commons;[49] but nothing came of this
initiative. In June the Cabinet reintroduced the proposal to exclude
Ulster from Home Rule for six years, in the form of an Amending Bill.
The House of Lords, however, promptly transformed it by voting to
make the exclusion permanent, so long as Ulster wished it. This F.E.
hailed as the victory which justified the whole struggle: if the Government insisted on restoring the original proposal, he declared, then

Carson's Provisional Government would simply take power in Belfast and there would be nothing Asquith or Redmond could do about it.[50] But the Government had to insist. July found the party leaders locked once again, at the King's request, in abortive conference at Buckingham Palace. From this impasse the European war, when it broke, came as a welcome release.

The war did not solve the Irish problem, however. When the hurricane finally abated, the terms of the eternal riddle were merely found to have been radically reformulated. Redmond's constitutional Home Rulers were swept away by outright republicans – armed rebels claiming legitimacy from the example of the north – while Ulster remained – as it remains still, some sixty years later, in circumstances otherwise utterly transformed – the intractable core of the whole difficulty. There is an alluring argument which blames Carson and his English supporters before 1914 for the persistence of the Ulster problem, as though they had invented it, and attributes solely to their malignity the fact that a united Ireland was not happily reconciled to a quasi-federal Great Britain under the 1912 Home Rule Act. This is the greatest nonsense. The desire of the Protestant north-east of Ireland to hold apart from the entirely distinct Catholic culture of the south and west was, as it still is, a fact founded on a feeling of national identity as deep as any by which nations the world over are distinguished. It is awkward, it is geographically untidy, but it is irreducible except by force. The tragedy of 1912–14 was the blinkered refusal of the Asquith Cabinet to recognize before it was too late the reality of Ulster's resistance to Home Rule. By the time they woke up to it, they could not give in to it without the appearance of capitulation to illegality. Had they only taken it seriously in 1910–11 they would have been in a much stronger position to have faced Redmond with the necessity, and justice, of some concession and imposed some form of compromise protecting Ulster's separateness – Home Rule within Home Rule – on Nationalists and Unionists equally.

F.E.'s role in trying to bring home to the Government the fact of Ulster's existence was not a dishonourable one. Criticism that he as a lawyer should not have espoused rebellion is ludicrously beside the point. When the making and breaking of nation states is in question – as Ulster undoubtedly felt it was, even though the proposal in 1912 was only for Home Rule – a man's profession is hardly relevant. As a lawyer F.E. had no more a special obligation to the Government than a plumber. One might as well condemn the American colonists, many of them lawyers, who declared independence from Britain in 1776. F.E. had no difficulty citing as precedents heroes from the Liberal pantheon

– Pym and Hampden; the rebels of 1688; Gladstone himself – legitimizing the appeal to force where issues of conscience or nationality overrode the normal restraints of political conduct. Earlier and harder than any other leading Tory, he strove to bring the parties together, to induce his own party to compromise on the rest of Ireland so as to get the Liberals to compromise on Ulster. But he could not accept the subordination of the Ulster people against their will, and it would have been craven indeed had he backed their stand without being prepared to fight with them if, despite his efforts, the need arose.

If willingness to join personally in rebellion if forced to it was honourable, however, a question still hangs over the Tories' recourse to subverting the army's duty to serve impartially the elected Government. Unlike lawyers and plumbers, soldiers do have a special obligation, freely undertaken. While it may have been legitimate for an individual to refuse, on his own head, to carry out orders offensive to his conscience, it cannot be right for a political party to try to bend the servants of the Crown to act politically against the King's Ministers. If Ulstermen were entitled in the last resort to fight, they must expect to have to fight the forces of the Government they were defying. Churchill was entitled to jeer at his friend's courage, as F.E. prepared to fight for Ulster having first prudently made sure that the British army would not be in the field against him! All may be fair in war, but in subverting the army F.E. and his party were acting up to their most extreme rhetoric, risking indeed 'the collapse of the whole body politic' for Ulster's sake. It would have been better – as effective and more defensible – to have adhered to the earlier intention of keeping the onus on the Government, passively defying it to give the order to shoot if they dared.

In later years F.E. had no regrets about his support of Ulster. Prosecuting Casement for treason in 1916, he was unapologetic and unabashed when his own record was thrown back against him. In 1921, when he was widely accused, not least by Carson, of having betrayed Ulster by signing the Irish Treaty, he insisted that he stood by every word he had spoken before the war. 'Every word' is putting it a bit strongly, since he had made some very wild statements; but on the essential point he was entitled to claim both that Ulster's stand had been justified in itself and that he had not compromised it in 1921. He had campaigned solely for Ulster's exclusion from Home Rule. The Treaty gave away more to the Free State than F.E. or anyone else had envisaged before the war; but Ulster was excluded. The existence of two Irelands was acknowledged. Since 1920, of course, the Protestant Governments of Stormont have operated a system of sectarian tyranny against the Catholic minority within their territory which has made the cause of Ulster ever harder for liberal democrats to defend. It is grossly unhistorical, however, to blame this on Carson, still less F.E. In 1912, when F.E. rallied to it, Ulster's cause was a good and fair one, unblemished by the later crimes committed in its name; and it was the Asquith Government's intentions towards an outraged minority that were tyrannical.

13

Tory Democracy

Beneath the excitement of Ulster and prospective civil war, ordinary political life went on. When not galloping around Antrim and Armagh, F.E. was giving serious thought to the future of the party battle in England, and particularly to the future direction of the Tory party, its distinctive philosophy and the policies it should be pursuing. During 1912 he contributed a number of serious essays on these questions to several journals – the *Oxford and Cambridge Review*, the *Fortnightly*, the *Nineteenth Century* and the *National Review* – which in February 1913 he collected together in a book authoritatively entitled *Unionist Policy*. Its purpose, transparently, was to promote his claim to be the next leader of the party after Bonar Law, by presenting himself to the political world, which tended to see him as just a sharp-tongued lawyer, as very much more than that – a thoughtful and statesmanlike politician able to range wide and deep over the whole field of government and public controversy, and forge a coherent philosophy for a modern Tory party, fusing on to the basis of traditional Conservatism a new social awareness capable of meeting the emerging challenge of the twentieth century. As such, *Unionist Policy* is an undeniably impressive blueprint, which shows F.E.'s political thought maturing in a most interesting direction, at once unconventional and characteristic of his time.

The title is important. One of the first things F.E. discusses, in the opening essay, is the party's name. Writing immediately after the long-delayed formal assimilation of the Liberal Unionists, F.E. professes to welcome the retention of the name 'Conservative', with its echo of the tradition of cautious scepticism derived from Burke; at the same time he makes it plain that he would have been equally happy with 'Unionist'. He goes on to develop an illuminating distinction between negative Conservatism and positive Unionism, reaching the conclusion that Unionism should be the *policy*, though the *party* be still labelled Conservative – just as, for instance, Socialism was the policy of the Labour party. The concept of Unionism, F.E. explained, was a very important one, involving far more than merely the preservation of the Union with

Ireland. Unionism implied also the unity of the Empire (Joseph Chamberlain's other great cause, significantly, implying in its turn tariff reform and imperial preference); and the essential social unity of Britain itself, what F.E. called 'national solidarity', the absence of class conflict – that enduring Conservative ideal which the post-1945 generation of Tories, echoing Disraeli, called 'One Nation'. Unionism, as F.E. used the word, was a recognition of what in his view the Liberal and Labour parties existed to deny, the wholeness and interdependence of the national community in all its elements – the Crown and the people, the 'classes and masses', the cities, the counties and the colonies, all comprising in their very diversity a single fabric of Britishness.[1]

Of course, all Tories have always claimed to be the patriotic party, the only party with the true interests of the country and all the people at heart, even while in composition, outlook and action they have been in this century at least as much class-based as their opponents. Such pious claims are an inbred component of party rhetoric and indeed of the party's perfectly sincere self-image: many Conservatives are genuinely unable to conceive of any difference between the party and the national interest. F.E. on the platform made as much use as any Tory of the rhetoric; but more than most he could see through the self-deluding cant. Increasingly he longed for a 'national' consensus, transcending the narrow interests which ruled both parties: he was eager for Lloyd George's premature initiative in 1910 and when war had made coalition a reality ten years later he was the Tory keenest to make it permanent. He was always aware, from his Liverpool background and his knowledge of other northern industrial constituencies, of the limitations of the predominantly southern, rural, middle- and upper-class Conservative party. He never imagined that the Tory party *was* the country. But he did think, if coalition was for the moment ruled out, that it should try harder to *become* a more representative embodiment of the country.

In Liverpool F.E. had seen sectarian politics at their sharpest. He had floated to Westminster on the tide of bigotry, cheerfully pledging himself when required to defend the Church of England equally from the ritualistic subversion of closet Papists and from the assaults of arrogant Nonconformity. But as he raged against the pacifist, temperance and educational dictation of the Nonconformist conscience, his concern grew wider with the realization that the proper aim of government should not be to enact sectarian measures imposing the particular prejudice of the governing party, but to reconcile conflicting prejudices within a community of mutually dependent elements. He realized that to offer an honest alternative to the Liberal programme of paying off, one after another, its debts to the various interest groups who composed the Government's majority, the Tories must not simply appeal to the opposite interests, but aspire to raise politics to a higher, 'national' plane. Thus while continuing to attack with undiminished vigour the cynical immorality of Liberal log-rolling in favour of trade unionists, Welsh dissenters and Irish nationalists, he developed to a new level the Tory claim to be above such dirty dealing, in a wonderfully tendentious essay entitled 'The Conservative Party and the Principle of Government'.

Much of it is the greatest humbug – small party points inflated out of all proportion. A large part of the essay comprises a catalogue of cases of 'administrative corruption' committed by Liberal Ministers, bypassing proper constitutional procedures for party advantage. F.E. cites three separate cases in which actions of McKenna, as President of the Board of Education, were quashed by the courts as *ultra vires*. Churchill's record as Home Secretary he criticizes particularly heavily: first for improperly releasing a convicted criminal, for political capital; second (ironically in the light of popular mythology) for withholding troops from the Tonypandy riots, for fear of tarnishing his Liberal name; third, for daring to voice public criticism of judges. In addition F.E. condemns the general policy of the Government to remove jurisdiction from the courts and give it to the departments. All these allegations are the habitual complaints of Tories, particularly of Tory lawyers, against Liberal and more recently Labour Governments which are never, in their view, fit for the responsibility of holding office at all. Most of them are valid so far as they go, but have less to do with the delinquency of a particular party than with the temptations of power itself, to which Conservative Ministers had not always been noticeably immune. F.E., however, having never yet himself held office at all, did not hesitate to draw from the Liberal record a fundamental distinction between the Liberal and the Tory approach to government.

> The Conservative Party has a distinct and urgent mission to re-establish and maintain the art of responsible government. It must eradicate departmental hooliganism; it must punish administrative indecency; it must restore the authority of respectable tradition to the organs of government. The authors of the present mischief are pursuing the same tactics as some of them did when, in Opposition, they slandered British troops during an arduous war, and otherwise aided and comforted the King's enemies. Such tactics are the tactics of anarchy. An anarchist in opposition may occasionally be a necessary evil, but an anarchist in office, wielding as a weapon of sabotage the great and venerable machine of government, and relying upon the respectful obedience of the

people to that machine, is a deadly menace to the vital principle of government.[2]

In so far as this is not humbug it is naïve. Yet it is the expression of a genuine aspiration – from the luxury of opposition – to lift government above the merely partisan, which takes the more practical form in other chapters of *Unionist Policy* of slaughtering, or at least offering for sacrifice, a number of Conservative sacred cows.

First, the Church of England. Support for the Established Church – 'the Conservative Party at prayer' – was one of the central principles of Victorian and Edwardian Conservatism, one that united, albeit uncomfortably, High Church Hatfield with Low Church Liverpool. F.E. did not by any means advocate disestablishment; on the contrary, he thoroughly endorsed the principle of establishment, but for entirely social, not religious, reasons. He admitted no claim to divine truth, but adapted the argument of ecumenical impartiality he had taken up in respect of education.

> Only bores nowadays dogmatize upon religious subjects, but every sensible person agrees that it is a primary duty of sound statesmanship to encourage every variety of religion which bases itself upon the ethical precepts of the Sermon on the Mount. The dogmas of a particular sect may be right or wrong. All the sects alike are warring against indifference and materialism.

Religion, this indifferent materialist argued without a trace of embarrassment, was a Good Thing. One sect or other had to be established: it did not really matter which.

> I am not myself a Churchman, but I realize as profoundly as any member of the Church the importance of associating religion with the State, and I am unaware of any competitive school of religious thought which can at the present time put forward plausible claims to usurp the position of the Church of England.[1]

If any should overtake the Church, he implied, he had no allegiance of principle that would oppose transferring the mantle of establishment to the successful rival. The important thing was that the Government should hold the ring and guarantee the liberties of all sects equally. In high-minded response to the Liberals' narrow identification with Nonconformity, therefore, the Tory party should abandon its special relationship with the Church of England and become the defender of all faiths. Here F.E. achieved a brilliant rationalization which legitimized in 'unionist' theory a policy which remained – since the Church would not in the foreseeable future be disestablished – impeccably conservative in practice.

Second, the House of Lords. F.E. had recognized early in the 1910 crisis – and publicly admitted, to the fury of the Diehards – that the veto powers of the Lords as then constituted were indefensible. He had argued privately against provoking a General Election on such unfavourable ground. But as soon as the Government proceeded to emasculate the Lords without reforming them, he joined the Diehards in last-ditch defence, not of the existing House, but of the principle of a second chamber. After the passage of the Parliament Act, many Tories accepted the *fait accompli*, settled for powers of delay and reverted to defence of the hereditary House. Not so F.E. To him the Tory-dominated House of Lords was another party interest from which the Conservatives should swiftly disengage themselves, in the higher 'national' interest.

> It is a great mistake to suppose that the absurdly partisan constitution of the House of Lords has been a source of strength to the Unionist Party: it has been a source of weakness . . . A control so lop-sided in its exercise was impossible to maintain, and was doomed to succumb when seriously challenged in a popular quarrel. It is essential that Conservatives should clearly realize that it is far less important to maintain a partisan Second Chamber than an efficient Second Chamber . . .
>
> What is essential is that we should be afforded the security of a strong, independent and impartial Second Chamber, possessing that confidence in its own inherent strength which is the condition precedent of stability and security.

How was such a chamber to be constituted? F.E. ducks this question in *Unionist Policy* (and he was to have as much trouble with it as everyone else who wrestled with it after the war). He saw clearly the problem of creating an elected House, answerable by a different system or on a different time-scale to the same electorate as the Commons; he was still inclined to wish that the Liberals had in 1911 been forced to create their new peers, so as to provide an enlarged pool from which an equal number could have been elected from each side as voting peers. But he insisted, in the present situation, that the restoration of an impartially balanced second chamber, however composed, overrode all objections and must be a primary objective of a 'national' Conservative party.

> I myself should contemplate the establishment of an elective Second Chamber with grave feelings of apprehension, as I am

satisfied that the institution of such a body would shift the whole centre of gravity in our Constitution; certainly it would gravely and perhaps permanently impair the authority of the House of Commons, but I would far rather vote tomorrow for an elective Second Chamber, facing boldly the risk of constitutional deadlock and the consequent conflicts of jurisdiction, than I would vote for a Second Chamber which had not behind it the moral force enough, however much it disapproved it, to reject the Trades Disputes Act [which, of course, the Lords had let through, much against its inclinations, in 1907].[1]

Another 'national' reform of which F.E. was an early and convinced supporter was the rationalization of the electoral system, specifically by the introduction of proportional representation. The whole purpose, he argued, of the House of Commons was that it should represent the people: it deserved no public respect if it did not. Again he was prepared to face the practical difficulties which a proportionally elected chamber might throw up for the sake of the principle, which was incontestable. The injustice of the first-past-the-post system was manifest, not so much at that date in the overall representation of the parties at Westminster, as in the complete non-representation of large minorities in important areas – for instance, the many thousands of Liberals in Liverpool who had no Liberal M.P., or the gross under-representation of Scottish Tories. F.E. hailed the concession of proportional representation for the Upper House of the proposed Irish Parliament as a major advance (despite his opposition to the Bill itself) from which the extension of a just system to the mainland would inevitably flow.[3] Before 1914 F.E. was only one of a considerable number of prominent M.P.s of all three parties who were members of the Proportional Representation Society. He would have been amazed that seventy years later the cause which he thought too obvious to need much argument – he made very little of it in his public speeches – is still not won.

Other overdue reforms of the electoral system – including women's suffrage, on which, for reasons discussed earlier, F.E. took a line at variance with his enlightened views on most electoral questions – were blocked by the calculated machinations of the parties. In 1913 the Government introduced another Bill to abolish plural voting (the Lords had thrown out a previous attempt in 1906), for the transparent reason that most plural votes were thought to be Conservative. The Tories opposed it on the perfectly fair ground that the Government refused to deal simultaneously with the redistribution of seats, the most striking effect of which would be to halve from 101 to 51 the number of Irish members, on whom the Government depended for its majority. There were, F.E. loyally insisted in the House of Commons, respectable arguments for plural voting (the representation of *communities*, the representation of commercial interests) which needed to be answered, not simply dismissed; but he implied that he would not press them if the Government for its part would recognize the anomaly that the electorate in Romford (53,000) was *thirty times* that in depopulated Kilkenny (1,742).[4] The Government's blatant determination to tackle only those reforms of the archaic electoral patchwork which would benefit themselves was a further example of what F.E. called their 'administrative hooliganism'; he opposed them on his party's behalf in party terms, but he wanted the Tories to embrace a higher standard of reference and reform the whole system on an impartial basis – as eventually happened by means of a Speaker's Conference during the war. As part of this package F.E. then accepted with a good grace the enfranchisement of women, but saw a unanimous recommendation of proportional representation defeated in the Commons, after it had passed the Lords.[5]

But by far the most important expression of F.E.'s belief in the wider obligations of Toryism is found in his commitment to what is loosely called 'social reform'. In part this was a simple recognition, reflecting his perspective as a Liverpool member, that the Tories could not afford to leave the field of social improvement to the Liberals and Labour. In part also, however, his view of the kind of social reform Tories should go in for derived from his belief that the Liberal approach was divisive and damaging, whereas the Tories alone could bring to the task that healing 'unionist' philosophy to which he was endeavouring to convert them.

In the opening essay of *Unionist Policy*, 'The Future of the Conservative Party', F.E. sympathizes with those (particularly southern) Conservatives who feel that the first aim of a future Tory Government should be to offer a period of tranquillity after the feverish activity of the Liberal years.

> But it would be folly to ignore the plain and evident fact that a large and, I think, growing section of the party finds itself in acute disagreement with these views in their extreme form . . . This younger school of Conservative thought lays stress upon the undoubted fact that the party will never conquer a majority adequate to its purpose until it re-establishes itself in the confidence of the great industrial centres.

F.E. was evidently setting himself up as the spokesman of this 'younger school', a leader from one of those industrial centres vividly aware of the reality and extent of urban misery in the midst of wealth.

What politician is so bold as to dare to talk of the Empire to men who cannot nourish their families, at the price gladly rendered of a life of grinding toil, and who know that its certain conclusion, when they have become the wastage of the industrial scrap heap, is a lonely and dishonourable death in the workhouse? . . .

The growing discontent of the working-classes cannot be dismissed with a few punitive recommendations . . . The truth is, and it may as well be boldly faced, that the working classes are not satisfied with their share of the joint product of capital and labour.

Their discontent could not be ascribed entirely to the activities of class agitators, but rather – listen to who is talking! – to 'the disastrous spread of ostentatious luxury'.

Motor cars have manufactured more socialists than all the eloquence of Mr Keir Hardie and Mr Lansbury; and although in many well-paid trades the attitude of labour is unreasonable and grasping, the wrongs under which so many poor persons labour are so cruel and so undeniable that it is astounding that any school of political thought should conceive a policy of inactivity to be possible.

He would like to inscribe on the walls of every Conservative Club, the finding of the social investigator Charles Booth that one-third of the population live below the line of primary poverty. The alleviation of this situation, and of the social evils it fermented, should be, F.E. argued, the special concern of the Tory party above all others.

Which party in the State stands to lose most by their continuance? Is it not evident that the party to whom stability and content are vital is far more deeply concerned to secure happier conditions than the party which lives upon discontent and the promulgation of class hatred? A contented proletariat should be one of the first objects of enlightened Conservative policy.[1]

In this and another essay, 'State Toryism and Social Policy', F.E. attempts to lay down the philosophical framework for that enlightened but still Conservative policy. First, he makes clear that he entirely accepts the existence of class distinctions and inequality as not merely inescapable facts of life but actually necessary and desirable.

There has always existed in every human society, and there will always exist, great disparity of fortune, a disparity correspondent in the main, at least in the first or second generation, with the disparity of human ability and human character. No society, civilised or uncivilised, has ever completely redressed the inequalities produced by differences of capacity and temperament. It is always easy under these circumstances for mischievous and unscrupulous persons to preach the doctrines of discontent. Nor within limits is it altogether undesirable that persons should be discontented. The very quality of ambition presupposes the existence of discontent with things as they are; Conservative policy, however, requires that while every class and every individual in that class should be encouraged by every means to improve the conditions of their existence in the community, no class should be encouraged to believe that that improvement can be permanently effected by rancorous hatred and jealousy of other classes, whose co-operation and sustained vigour are the first condition of any general improvement.[1]

The stirring up of class hatred, of which he continually accused Lloyd George in the agitation for the People's Budget, was for F.E. the ultimate crime in a politician, 'the parricide of politics'. All classes, he insisted, were interdependent.

Continuing his theoretical exploration of the alternatives, F.E. identified three possible philosophies for the organization of society: the unfettered individualist/Whig (based on the principles of Bentham, Mill and Cobden); the Radical/Socialist (derived from Marx); and the Conservative, which he portrayed as the pragmatic middle way between two impracticable and entirely academic extremes.

The Socialist has rushed to one extreme and the Individualist to the other. The first has built his state on an imaginary man who, like the bee or the ant, possesses nothing but the faculty of organization; the other on an equally vain imagination – a being possessed of nothing but the instinct for self-advancement and self-preservation. The vice of individualism is that it would hamstring man's power for co-ordinate advance and joint sacrifice; the vice of Socialism is that it would cut the other motor-muscle of character, the desire for the struggle, and for the reward the struggle brings. It is impossible to tamper with the principle of private property and with the principle of the family and hereditary succession which depends on it. Both the extremes are indeed so untenable that criticism of them must partake of the nature of platitude.[6]

Neither, of course, had ever been or ever could be systematically applied; which only made their retention as guiding philosophies more ridiculous.

F.E. went out of his way to deny any identification between Conservatism and *laissez-faire* individualism. It was 'only the class-hatred mind' which could not conceive of social legislation except as an attack on one class for the benefit of another. The only true test of any measure of social reform was, 'Does it, or does it not, add to the total productive efficiency and prosperity of the whole people?' Those Tories fell into the class-hatred trap who condemned every reform as an attack on property, and denied the higher unity of the nation.

> Let us not listen to the plea that all such proposals are, in their essence, Socialistic or Radical. On the contrary, any successful proposal of this kind which can stand the test proposed is the antithesis of Socialism and the destruction of Radicalism. It builds up the race and consolidates the country, while it destroys the social garbage on which the carrion crows of politics feed.

Social reform needed to be seen as an investment by the State in its future. 'A little State capital may well be better invested in training men to new trades or in finding them employment, rather than in paying for them, on and off, as more or less permanent paupers to the end of their days.' Struggling individuals were like struggling industries: it was the duty of the wise State to provide a shield for both – Bismarck had shown the way in Germany. Trade protection (tariff reform) and social protection (social reform) went together as complementary expressions of the same, quite consistent, Tory philosophy which F.E. now traced, somewhat romantically, back to Disraeli.

> Disraeli in his youth laid down the principles on which the England of his time ought to have been based, and his comparative failure to convince his contemporaries or to overbear his philosophic opponents left his country the richer by a supreme instance of political genius and the poorer by its slums, its wasted physique and its industrial unrest and class hatred. If Providence could have made Disraeli a dictator in the early 'thirties, there would have been no social problem today. That great man desired to build up the new industrial State on the principles and practice which had animated the older rural and urban dispensations, on the community of interest between master and man, between capitalist and employee, between guild and guild, between agricultural labourer and town workman. What was best in the feudal

conception of the past was to be applied to the new progressive forces of the nineteenth century, and the aristocracy of industry was to follow in the tradition of the aristocracy of feudalism and make itself the guardian, and not the exploiter, of its new retainers. Like the masque in *The Tempest*, the whole vision, or most of it, vanished 'with a heavy sound'. The 'Whig dogs' had the best of it, under the inspiration of their Radical supporters. Half the Conservative Party broke away, with Sir Robert Peel, to represent the new powerful manufacturing class: rural England was ruined in order to create the social abominations of the nineteenth century industrial era. When Disraeli, after a quarter of a century of unceasing Parliamentary labour, brought the real Tory party back to office once more, the time had passed with the energies of the man. 'The altar of Mammon' to adopt his own phrase, had in the interval, 'burned with a triple flare'; the new system had been created by the Manchester School, and the Tory democracy had only just begun to raise its head again under the stimulus of the Reform Bill of 1867.

Absurdly fanciful though it is in its idealization both of the young Disraeli and of the Arcadia of pre-industrial England, this is a remarkable passage of political mythology: and political traditions need myths and heroes as much as they need policies. To Disraeli F.E. added Randolph Churchill (with reservations) and Joseph Chamberlain to form the trinity of heroes in the pantheon of Tory Democracy. 'One may follow, however humbly, in their footsteps, and say that a policy of union or of empire that leaves Social Reform and class unity out of account is built upon sand, and not upon the solid rock of political reality.'

Claiming the inheritance of Disraeli and Chamberlain, F.E. summed up:

> The essence of Tory Social Reform is the study of the real aptitudes of the people. It is precisely here that Individualism and Socialism fail alike. Humanity is composed neither of men struggling to arrive at all costs nor of men ready to sacrifice anything and everything to a common end. Nor to put the matter in a more concrete form, does the race consist entirely of individuals ready to gamble their chances on the wheel of fortune, and to risk all in order to better their conditions and position. On the contrary most individuals tread in the accustomed paths, and demand of life that it shall give them security, and security in the state in which it has pleased God to call them . . .

It is possible to devise a scheme by which nine men out of ten can get the security they want and the tenth man the opportunity he desires.

The only necessity was to accept the reality and variety of human nature, instead of trying to force all men into the single mould of either dogma.

Security of tenure in all classes of life where such tenure is not a national evil: that is the doctrine of Toryism. Opportunity for talent to develop its own potentialities and the resources of the nation where such a development is to the advantage of the State: that is the doctrine of Toryism. Security to those who need it, opportunity to those who desire it, on what better foundation can the state of the future be built?

In all things we stand midway between conflicting extremes. We are not for the classes or the masses, for their interests are one. We are not for Individualism or Socialism, for neither is founded on fact. We stand for the State, and for the unity which, whether in the form of kingdom or empire or class solidarity, the State alone can bring. Above all stands the State, and in this phrase lies the essence of Toryism. Our ancestors left it to us, and not the least potent method of preserving it is to link the conception of State Toryism with the practice of Social Reform.[6]

F.E. in his prime could certainly write. The prescription may seem platitudinous; but Conservatives have traditionally rested their philosophy on common sense rather than on theory. This has been their strength in an imperfect world which never stands still long enough for academic formulae to be consistently applied. F.E.'s is as crisp and compelling an exposition of the 'theory' of pragmatism (the need to work *with* the facts of life and not against them) as one could ever read. What stops one short is the conclusion, 'Above all stands the State.' Since F.E. wrote, the idea of the over-arching, all-providing State to which all personal interests are subordinated has gone out of favour, particularly with Tories. Since Stalin and Hitler it has a totalitarian ring. The Tory party, while accepting the obligation of welfare in practice, has embraced the ideal of individualism in its ideology to an extent that F.E., in 1912, could not have dreamed. The change began with the war, and affected him as much as any other Tory. The impact first of 'Prussianism', then of the Russian Revolution and the serious threat of socialism, combined to make the overweening State an object of fear and loathing. In 1912, as F.E.'s reference to Bismarck implies,

'Prussianism' was still much admired in Britain – in all parties. Had not Lloyd George's National Insurance proposals been formed after a visit to Berlin to study the German system? F.E. and Lloyd George, though in opposite parties, were indeed moving very close together at this time in their thinking on the question of national regeneration and state power. Despite his condemnation of the Chancellor's past rhetoric, what F.E. called Tory Democracy was actually very close in aspiration to what Lloyd George, away from the platform, was hankering to accomplish, if only he could break clear of the crippling restraints of party orthodoxy – as he had tried to do, striking a chord with F.E., in 1910. Lloyd George was himself much more the heir of Joe Chamberlain than of Gladstone, whom he had found himself having to follow in 1886 rather reluctantly: beneath the Liberal colouring which he had been forced to assume as a Welsh radical Nonconformist, his true political personality as it emerged in the war perfectly qualified him to be F.E.'s next hero and leader, a Tory Democrat (in F.E.'s sense) in all but name, the arch-pragmatist with an ambitious vision of national unity and national greatness untrammelled by party divisions. For six years they worked together in the closest harmony of outlook, before events forced them off their 'national' plateau and they drew apart again. By 1922 the ideal of non-party consensus government had had its day.

Before the war it was still the aspiration of an advanced minority. In 1912 Lloyd George and F.E. were both, from their different starting points, representative of a distinctive current of progressive opinion, very characteristic of the Edwardian decade, concerned with the idea of 'national efficiency'. Its origins lay in the failures of the Boer War and the revelation of the poor physical state of so much of the population, confirmed, measured and explained by the researches into urban poverty of Seebohm Rowntree and Charles Booth. Shock at their findings and the desire to do something about them, for a mixture of reasons – humanitarian, military and simply patriotic, reflecting injured national pride – ranged right across the political spectrum embracing all those of what might be termed a 'Prussian' turn of mind, from the socialist Webbs to the imperialist Milner. The amelioration of social conditions was suddenly seen, not as charity, but as necessary for the very survival of the nation in a competitive world in which Britain's lead, so long taken for granted, was being challenged, both commercially and militarily, by other nations who paid a great deal more attention to their populations. The hidden hand of Cobdenite orthodoxy could no longer be relied upon. Involvement of the State in ensuring the physical well-being of its citizens could not any more be regarded as socialistic interference with liberty and personal responsibility; it had become a duty which the prudent State was obliged to assume for its own preservation. In the age of mass conscript armies and complicated modern weaponry, the health and education (and the contentment and loyalty) of its people bore directly on the Government's primary function. Social reform was a part of military preparedness. Its people were a nation's main resource.[7]

This explains the most superficially surprising element of the coalition package which Lloyd George offered the Tories in 1910 – the inclusion of national service, a militaristic intrusion on personal liberty which offended the deepest instincts of orthodox Liberals even in wartime and which few Tories wanted to handicap themselves with in peace. From his side Lloyd George – the famous pro-Boer and 'pacifist' – saw the merit of it; while F.E. had long been an advocate of compulsory training and became a prominent supporter of Lord Roberts's National Service League as soon as it was founded in 1907, principally for reasons of national defence, but also on the 'national efficiency' ground that military training was good for the manhood of the nation, and the 'unionist' ground that it provided a valuable symbol of common and equal citizenship under the State. Social reform was the other side of the same contract: the citizen fought for the State, and the State protected the citizen. Military 'Prussianism' was complemented, in F.E.'s Tory thinking as in Lloyd George's interventionist Liberalism, by social Prussianism – that is by a commitment to a Bismarckian welfare system, plus trade protection. These two practical expressions of paternalistic government, together with the idea that all citizens had a common loyalty beyond class and sectional interests, were what F.E. meant by State Toryism.

Beside his exposition of the necessity and justification of social reform, it must be admitted that F.E.'s definition of its specific content is studiously vague. More than anything else, as a convinced tariff reformer, he relied upon trade protection, when the Tories could finally introduce it, to increase wages, protect employment and tackle the economic basis of poverty. 'You can never get a British standard of living set up in this country so long as you adhere to Free Trade, and no-one but a fool, a Labour member or a Cabinet Minister will pretend that you can.'[8] He could never understand why the Labour party clung to its Cobdenite belief in the free market internationally, when the whole *raison d'être* of the trade union movement at home was the obstruction of the market: tariff reform to him was simply normal trade union practice writ large. He admitted, however, that tariff reform was not enough. There were more direct measures of public assistance which the Government could properly undertake.

He approved of old age pensions. He also approved in principle of Lloyd George's health and unemployment insurance schemes, though he allowed himself, as part of the Opposition's general attack on the Government in the wake of the Parliament Act, to be provoked into attacking them, largely for the 'class-hatred' way in which Lloyd George sold them to the country, but also for their 'wild-cat finance' which, he alleged, 'involved the country in a contingent liability, out of all proportion to any benefits which are likely to follow'.[1] He insisted, however, that his condemnation of this 'ill-considered' expenditure did not imply a condemnation of all expenditure. There *was* a danger that taxation could be pushed so far that it damaged the wealth-producing capacity of the nation; but he did not think that that point would be reached for some time, so long as Chancellors spared the landowners ('among the most deserving and public-spirited, as they are certainly in the main among the least wealthy, of our better-class population') and concentrated instead upon 'that luxurious class living entirely for pleasure which was treated with comparative indulgence by the Budget of 1910'.[1] He approved of expenditure on properly 'national' objects. He had supported the 1906 Workmen's Compensation Act. He had nothing but praise for Churchill's Labour Exchanges and Trade Boards to control sweated labour. On all these matters, indeed, his thinking was very close to Winston's. Had the accidents of politics thrown *him* into alliance with Lloyd George in 1908–14, he would undoubtedly have entered as enthusiastically as did Winston into the Chancellor's reforming spirit, just as Winston, had he been in opposition, would have found things to criticize. Such is political life. F.E.'s criticism of Lloyd George's and Churchill's social innovations in these years rings unusually hollow; it betrayed more frustrated envy than actual disagreement with what they were doing.

To indicate his own commitment to soundly based Tory social reform, F.E. was instrumental in setting up in 1911 a Unionist Social Reform Committee, with himself as chairman and a membership composed mainly of relatively little known backbenchers of progressive leanings – among them several who emerged to prominence in the Conservative Cabinets of the 1920s: Stanley Baldwin, Samuel Hoare, Philip Lloyd-Greame, Montague Barlow, Arthur Griffith-Boscawen, William Ormsby-Gore. The Committee employed a small full-time staff of researchers and drew on the work of 'some of the best experts available'. 'By this means', F.E. wrote in the *Conservative and Unionist* in May 1911, 'we hope to place at the disposal of our party in Parliament and in the country a trained body of fully-formed critics able not only to expose and correct the usual crudities of Radical-Socialist legislation, but to give form to a comprehensive policy of social reform.'[9] A 'comprehensive policy' was putting the claims of the Committee rather too high; but it produced a number of useful reports on specific areas of social concern. Its most important function in the short term was to improve the party's self-image – and more questionably its public image – as a party of progress. A correspondent wrote scathingly to Beatrice Webb in December 1911 of F.E. 'stumping the country boasting about the great social reforms which the Tories are going to bring about'.[10] But none of them was official policy: F.E. was the only member of the Shadow Cabinet involved in the Committee, though Steel-Maitland continued his connection with it after he became party chairman. Much of the party was distinctly suspicious. There is little ground for imagining the Tory party coming to power in 1915 pledged to an advanced social programme. The Committee's greater importance was in the longer term, as providing a seed-bed and testing ground for some of the ideas and attitudes which came to characterize the Baldwin Governments of the 1920s.

In keeping with F.E.'s stated philosophy of social reform, the published reports of the U.S.R.C. were almost defiantly moderate embodiments of common sense, rather than innovatory. One on the reform of the Poor Law, written by Jack Hills and Maurice Woods, with an introduction by F.E., though described by *The Times* as 'a miracle of condensation',[11] was in substance no more than an amalgamation of the famous Majority and Minority Reports of the Royal Commission of 1909; nevertheless F.E. was perfectly correct to predict that it would take a Tory Government (actually Neville Chamberlain in 1928!) to abolish the mixed workhouse. Though 'even lost reactionaries like the President of the Local Government Board' (John Burns) had realized it was 'a mistake', he jeered, the Liberals would never do anything about it.[12]

Another report, by Griffith-Boscawen on working-class housing, which recommended increased powers to assist and compel local authorities to improve housing, provided further ammunition to contrast the Tories' real care for social conditions with the Government's talk. A Bill incorporating Griffith-Boscawen's proposals was introduced into the Commons in March 1912, passed its Second Reading but was then mutilated by the Government majority in committee: Lloyd George was at just that moment launching his noisy land campaign to achieve similar objects by an attack on landlords with which the Tory Bill was not compatible. F.E. was able to make great play throughout 1913 with the Government's destruction of a good practical Bill that would have reduced bad housing in favour of a controversial measure that had no chance of becoming law, but was introduced solely for campaigning purposes. The Government's attitude proved again 'the hostility of Liberalism to any measure of social reform which is not recommended by the spirit of class hatred'.[13]

For what turned out to be its last report before the outbreak of war a large sub-committee of the U.S.R.C. turned its attention in 1914 to one of the most disturbing problems of the previous few years – industrial unrest, which had resulted in an unprecedented wave of major and prolonged strikes, reaching a peak in 1912. Once again the report, *Industrial Unrest: A Practical Solution*, was written by Hills and Woods; once again F.E. contributed a general introduction stressing its common-sense approach. Its proposals were, he wrote, 'almost too sane and too nearly allied to the immediately practical to attract the support of the stern enthusiasts of any school or party'.[14] They were certainly mild. The main recommendation was that a new Labour Department should be set up within the Board of Trade to arbitrate upon disputes, but without any powers of compulsion; public opinion alone, it was hoped, would be strong enough to enforce acceptance of the board's decisions. Schemes of profit-sharing and co-partnership were considered but rejected as too problematical. A minimum wage, however, was approved as an objective to be aimed at in principle – beginning in the public service industries where it was suggested a minimum might be offered in return for the workers giving up the right to strike.

F.E. had already made the latter proposal in *Unionist Policy*, where he had very quickly grasped the entirely new nature of the latest wave of industrial disputes – in the docks, in the mines, on the railways. Quite unlike the nineteenth-century strike these were political, aimed primarily not at the individual employer but at the State; by closing down services or production essential to the daily life of the community, the unions hoped to force the Government to intervene on their side, and ultimately to hand over to them the running of their own industries. No Government, F.E. was clear, could allow this.

> No nation commits suicide readily, and if Syndicalist attempts at a General Strike were pushed to their logical conclusion, only one of two things could happen: either the strikers would become the masters of the nation, or the nation would assert itself in drastic fashion by organizing itself against the dominance of a particular industrial clique.

F.E. felt no differently as a Cabinet Minister in 1926. But in 1913 he thought that, while abdicating no shred of its authority, the Government could afford to guarantee a fixed minimum to those categories of essential worker, in transport and public utilities, who were protected, even under Free Trade, from the competition of the world market. Such a bargain perfectly exemplified his ideal of 'unionism'.

There is no reason why Toryism should not insist on a scheme which is just in essence and which safeguards both the interests of the State and the rights of the worker. Toryism is the party of the State – Radicalism is the party of the sections. Toryism places the good of the nation above all other considerations – Radicalism is always ready to uphold a dissident element against the national interest.[8]

Syndicalism, as the apotheosis of inflated sectionalism, was the very opposite of 'national' Toryism and quite unacceptable. Legitimate trade unionism, on the other hand – the collective pursuit of economic self-interest by legal means under the State – was the true expression of Toryism in practice. 'The saner Trade Unionism and the wiser Conservatism', he wrote in his introduction to the 1914 report, 'are not very far apart.'

Why indeed should there be any opposition? The Conservative Party is the parent of Trade Unionism, just as it is the author of the Factory Acts. At every stage in the history of the nineteenth century it is to Toryism that Trade Unionism has looked for help and support against the oppressions of the Manchester School of Liberalism, which cared nothing for the interests of the State, and regarded men as brute beasts whose labour could be bought and sold at the cheapest price irrespective of all other considerations.[14]

Whatever truth this dubious claim had once had, the rise of the new school of interventionist Liberalism, let alone the Labour party, was making it less and less tenable by 1914. Theoretically F.E. might be right, but since Gladstone's death the Liberals had been progressively abandoning the strict tenets of Manchester *laissez-faire* with which he was so keen to saddle them, while it was the Tories, whatever Disraeli and Chamberlain were supposed to have taught them, whose instincts still recoiled from interference with the market and were gathering in the old Whigs who found Lloyd George's Liberalism too socialistic. To take an objective test, there was never any question that the Labour Members of Parliament would consider supporting the Tories rather than the Liberals. The Tories, for all F.E.'s protestations, were irrevocably cast as the anti-trade union party.

Nor could F.E. be surprised, for while declaring himself the stoutest supporter of their *legitimate* claims, he cast himself in the forefront of the campaign against their political pretensions (the political levy) and above all their legal immunity, which were the things they and the Labour party cared most for. He thought the system of having to 'contract out' of the automatic levy for the Labour party, which obliged Conservative and Liberal trade unionists to subscribe contrary to their beliefs unless they dared to advertise their allegiance at the risk of losing their jobs, an outrage in a democratic country, and the reversal of the Osborne judgment a scandal. (In February 1912 he made a presentation of a gold watch and a silver tea service to the original Mr Osborne, in recognition of his services to freedom.)[15] And he never relaxed his opposition to the 1906 Trade Disputes Act, by which the Liberals had cravenly conceded the unions a privileged position above the law.

> A Liberal Government [he thundered in *Unionist Policy*] consecrated by the solemnity of law the claim, abhorrent to the jurisprudence of any civilised society, that wealthy corporations may deliberately plan and execute illegal acts without thereby rendering their funds liable to compensate in damages the party injured by calculated illegality . . . The Liberal Government, for reasons unexplained and inexplicable, has discovered in the men who control modern Trade Unions virtues so rare as to deserve or require an immunity from the consequences of civil offences which no civilized society has ever conceded to any individual or corporation.

This was the most monstrous of all the Liberals' pieces of sectional legislation against the national interest. Its result was to make the conduct of industrial relations impossibly one-sided.

> One of the fundamental difficulties today in making any arrangement between Capital and Labour is that Labour, while insistently holding Capital to the word and spirit of their mutual compact, holds itself free to break any inconvenient arrangement at any moment it thinks proper; and that it can do so with complete pecuniary impunity.[8]

This is another of those penetrating remarks, like his statement of the paradox of picketing, which is as true, or truer, seventy years later as on the day F.E. first made it; which has never been put better by anyone else in the intervening period; and which goes to the heart of the industrial problems which plague the country to this day. It can be argued – it was at the time and still is – that in 1906 the balance between Capital and organized Labour needed to be tilted in Labour's favour; by that argument F.E.'s protests were exaggerated. But at worst they were premature. Only too clearly he foresaw the disproportionate power – negative power, divorced from responsibility – which this established immunity would confer on the unions as they grew stronger and more assertive. It is a power which has defeated the efforts of successive Governments of both parties in the 1960s and 1970s to regulate it in the national interest. It was not simple anti-unionism that impelled F.E. to oppose legal immunity in 1906, any more than it has been 'union-bashing' that has motivated more recent attempts at reform. It was, once again, his clear view of the proper relation of sectional interests to the wider interest of the community. F.E.'s 'unionism' demanded the subordination of trade unionism, as of every other component pressure group. If he seemed particularly opposed to Labour's minor privileges, this was because Labour, though still relatively weak, made the most arrogant claim, on behalf of one class, to be the single overriding interest when its hour came.

And yet F.E.'s theory did not really relate to the real world. The Platonic vision of free and equal citizens under an impartial State does him credit, but it does not accord with the way people actually see themselves. The paradox of F.E.'s thinking is that he believed in class, but not in classes. He regarded the existence of class differences as a fact of life reflecting a real hierarchy of intelligence, education and ability (cemented admittedly by money). Within this given framework, however, individuals of ambition and energy should be – and in his view were – able to rise from their original level as high as their ability would carry them, as he had done and his father and grandfather before him. As far as individuals were concerned he saw life as a Darwinian struggle for self-improvement in which the cleverest and most energetic rose and the dull and lazy eventually (despite the legitimate efforts of their ancestors to provide for them – he certainly intended to pass on every possible advantage to *his* family) fell back. He did not, however, recognize a similar struggle between classes. The idea that a whole class might aspire to improve its position, collectively, seemed to him self-defeating nonsense, and the tendency of individuals less gifted than himself to see themselves as members of a class was merely feeble. To the Marxist view of history as the history of class conflict, F.E. opposed a static view in which individuals competed against a background of class relationships which remained essentially unchanging and eternal. His idea of social reform was directed at reducing absolute physical deprivation, not inequality. He imagined that equality of opportunity for the able already existed.

F.E. was of course quite right to see the Marxist exaltation of class conflict as inhuman and pernicious; it *is* better to see people as individuals rather than as class units. Yet it was not sensible of him to close his eyes to the fact that individuals do see themselves, at least some of the time, in class terms – and particularly when called upon to vote. The instinct of class solidarity was stronger than he allowed. As a result his ideal of classless 'national' Tory social reform now reads – and did in 1913 to Socialists, Liberals and many Tories – like so much wishful hot air. Though intended idealistically, his talk of a higher national inter-est above class was bound to be derided as the standard cant of a self-serving upper class defending its own dominance, and it is idle to deny that F.E.'s personal class interest 'objectively' dictated his pious anathemas on the principle of conflict. It has been from its beginnings an axiom of the British labour movement that it alone is the only possible vehicle for the improvement of the position of the working class (making little distinction between individual opportunity and benefits to the whole class), and that any opponent of it is a class enemy. By attacking trade union privileges, F.E. put himself irrevocably in this category, whatever protestations he might make that as a democrat, social reformer, tariff reformer and defender of the right to drink he was the true friend of labour. In 1906 it was still a tenable posture. By 1914 Tory Democracy, a construction of fond illusions, was too frail a craft to survive for long against the rising tide of class-conscious neo-Marxist Socialism. Soon after the war it sank, taking F.E.'s last credible pre-tensions to progressivism with it.

F.E. had long been alive to the danger of war with Germany. In his calls for compromise settlements of the House of Lords crisis and the Ulster crisis he had stressed the urgency of national unity in the face of the external challenge. Prominent among the considerations which stimu-lated his advocacy of social reform was the need for 'national efficiency'. For years he had kept himself in the forefront of the Tory chorus perpetually calling for increased naval spending and accusing the Liberal Government, among other crimes, of wantonly lowering the country's military guard. (He liked to portray those 'patriotic' Ministers like Grey, Haldane and Churchill, who did care for defence, as con-tinually undermined in Cabinet by the foolish and irresponsible 'pacifists' and cosmopolitans epitomized respectively by Lloyd George and Alfred Mond.) Instead of the Admiralty's 'two-power standard', by which it was laid down that the Royal Navy should always be equal to the next two largest navies combined, F.E. began in 1912 to call for a two-to-one standard of superiority over the next largest.[16] He was ahead of his party, too, in his declared support from 1907 onwards, for Lord Roberts's National Service League, which proposed three to four months' compulsory military training for all young men between eighteen and twenty-one, refreshed with another fortnight a year for three years, after which they would pass into a reserve until they were thirty.

Most Conservatives were sympathetic to the League's purpose, but thought it politically suicidal for the party to be identified with its demand. F.E. recognized that compulsory training could not be imposed without national consent, which would not be easy to obtain from a nation 'chloroformed', in his view, into a state of false security. He was careful to advocate it only from National Service League platforms, never as party policy. But he declared in *Unionist Policy* his hope that 'in the not far distant future . . . a political party may, with more or less general assent, find itself in a position to cement . . . a very bad fissure in the dyke of Imperial defence'.

His argument was the classic one that if you want peace you must prepare for war.

> Peace, in a word, consists in being strong . . . The business of a nation is to be strong enough to repel all comers with loss: the very existence of that strength is sufficient guarantee that it will not have to be exercised . . .
>
> There would be no war in Europe – and I go further; I say there would be no apprehension of war in Europe – today, if a million English citizens had been trained in those arts of self-defence which have never been forgotten by any great country except in the period of its decay and as an incident in its dissolution.[17]

F.E. had only contempt for 'that curious school of thought . . . which believes that the social, economic and military greatness of Great Britain is proportionate to the cause of righteousness upon earth'. War, he predicted, was inevitable if Britain neglected her strength; moreover defeat in such circumstances would be not only inevitable but deserved. In one of his most powerful and provocative essays, he came to the defence of Roberts, who had been widely attacked for expressing admiration of Germany's grasp for world power. Backing Roberts unreservedly, he expounded a view of international relations in which morality played no part, international law was futile and the only right was might. What moral title had Britain, he asked, having risen to power under Queen Elizabeth by exactly the methods, directed against Spain, which Germany was now directing against her, to preach restraint to Germany?

> Who are we, that we should invite the Germans to acquiesce in the principle of 'Uti Possidetis' at a moment when we possess comparatively everything and they possess comparatively nothing? It is a law as old as the world's history that those who hold valuable possessions coveted by others will hold them so long as, and no longer than, they are able to protect them by the strong arm . . .
>
> Abuse of Germany for doing what we ourselves did, and for

cherishing ambitions which every powerful nation at every stage of the world's history has entertained, is childish, irrelevant and futile. History laughs at such criticisms . . . Every virile nation of every nationality whose judgement is not debauched by a sentimentalism wholly out of contact with facts, will echo Lord Roberts' tribute. Abuse, disapproval and pious exhortations are utterly useless. Only one thing is useful. This country if it means to survive, must develop its preparations upon the same scale and in the same spirit as does the great nation whose ambitions and development we are examining.[18]

This was not an argument likely to commend itself to conventional patriots of either party who, whether they wanted Britain to demonstrate her superiority by arming against Germany or by disarming, took for granted their own country's unique rectitude. F.E. had at this stage, that is before the Germans' assault on Belgium, no such delusions. In the global board game that was Great Power politics in 1914, he wanted Britain to win because he was British. He supported his side. But he did not pretend that Germany had no right to play. Here was his clearest pre-war statement of that bleak Darwinian view of the inevitability of international struggle and the victory of the fittest nation which drew on him so much odium when he repeated it unaltered in the idealistic post-war climate of the 1920s.

F.E. did not look forward to war in 1914, despite his military rhetoric. Here again he was unusually clear-sighted. Unlike many enthusiastic jingos, F.E. had no illusions about the nature of the fighting that it would involve. Out of respect – not, he insisted, disrespect – for the heroic but puny British Expeditionary Force, he did not want to see it pitched helplessly into the slaughter. 'No student of military history', he wrote,

who is familiar with the carnage of modern war and who recollects the lessons of South Africa and the Manchurian battlefields, will contemplate without horror the engagement of English troops amid the vast armies of Europe, knowing that it means the employment of soldiers who cannot be replaced amid an enemy capable of almost infinite replacement.

Whether or not he could seriously call himself a student of military history, he was absolutely right, while most of those who should have known better were tragically unprepared for the reality of what was to come.

F.E. read the diplomatic situation just as clearly. Since Britain could never stand back and see France crushed by Germany, he argued, a formal alliance would be very much more effective than the present vague *entente*. This brought him back to the question of military training. 'Either we must make up our minds that we will not take part in a European war under any circumstances', he insisted, 'or we must have national service.' In his view there was only one honourable choice: Britain could not pursue the first option 'unless we are prepared to do what our ancestors to their eternal glory refused to do in the days of Napoleon, acquiesce in the hegemony of Europe by one titanic Power'.[18]

The Tories were not anti-German; they were not pro-war. War would be a crime against civilization. But the only way to prevent war was to assert Britain's strength and determination to maintain the European balance. Therefore F.E. called for the minor sacrifice of national service to prevent the greater sacrifices that would be entailed in war.

This was written in 1912. National service made no progress. Britain's commitment to France remained uncertain. Yet in 1914 the crisis caught F.E., like everyone, unawares.

14

F.E. at War: The Press Bureau and the Indian Corps, 1914–15

For years F.E. had appeared to regard a trial of strength with the German Empire as inevitable and even desirable. Yet the occurrence of what he had for so long predicted took him completely by surprise. As a strong public advocate of military preparedness, he personally had made no domestic arrangements at all against the possibility that in the event of war a reserve officer in the Yeomanry might expect to be called up. He confessed to Margaret in some agitation that he had never expected it to happen![1]

During July 1914 his life showed no sign of awareness of the impending catastrophe. In the law courts he was preoccupied with the Crosland case and other business; politically he was closely concerned with the threatening deadlock over Ulster; privately he was much taken up with his family – his second daughter Pamela, born in May, was christened on 8 July, and on 29 July, when the drums were already beginning to beat on the continent, his brother Harold completed the union of the Smith and Furneaux families by marrying Margaret's younger sister, Joan. The reception, after the wedding service at St Margaret's, Westminster, was held at Grosvenor Gardens. But the couple were not destined to enjoy a long honeymoon.

Two days later (31 July) F.E. went down to spend the weekend at Paddy Goulding's house at Wargrave, on the Thames near Henley. Bonar Law and Carson were also there, plus Max Aitken; the intention had been to consider the Unionist party's next moves on Ulster. But Ireland was pushed into the background as the likelihood of European war supervened. Austria had already declared war on Serbia, and Russia had mobilized. F.E. met his colleagues with a message from Churchill. The Liberal Cabinet, he reported, was in danger of breaking up on the issue of British assistance to France. If it did so, Churchill wanted to know, would the Unionist leaders be willing to join a coalition for the prosecution of the war, stepping into the places of those Ministers who resigned? F.E. urged that the Tories return a positive answer: here was another opportunity to achieve that national Government which Lloyd George had first proposed in 1910. But Churchill's feeler was entirely unauthorized, and Bonar Law knew it. F.E. and Winston were up to their usual tricks. Quite apart from the merits of coalition, of which he was anyway doubtful, he disapproved of Churchill's backstairs methods. If Asquith wanted a coalition, he should approach the Leader of the Opposition directly and openly.

F.E. could only report to Winston a general statement of support.

I have spoken to my friends of whom you know and I have no doubt that on the facts as we understand them – & more particularly on the assumption (which we understand to be certain) that Germany contemplates a violation of Belgian neutrality – the Government can rely upon the support of the Unionist party in whatever manner that support can be most effectively given.

I shall be in London on Monday.[2]

Winston replied the next day (1 August) exactly as though he were Prime Minister and his friend the Leader of the Opposition.

Very grateful for your letter with its generous and patriotic offer. I read it to the Cabinet where it produced a profound impression. I cannot think war can be averted now. Germany must march through Belgium, and I believe that the bulk of both parties will stand firm against that. I really think you and BL ought to be in London on Sunday . . . I can put you thoroughly *au fait.*[3]

Churchill invited F.E. and Law to come up and dine with himself and Grey that evening. But Law declined, maintaining his proper attitude that he could deal only with Asquith himself, to whom, however, he wrote on the Sunday pledging the Government the Opposition's 'unhesitating support'.[4] Coalition was not required. The nearest F.E. and Aitken could get to the centre of affairs was a distracted game of bridge with Winston at the Admiralty. When the Germans marched into Belgium the next day the Cabinet waverers rallied, with only two exceptions. Only in one respect was the Government broadened. When war was formally declared on 4 August, the country was in the curious position of having no Secretary of State at the War Office: since Seely's resignation after the Curragh incident in March, Asquith had held the portfolio himself. Now Lord Kitchener – Kitchener of Khartoum, former Commander-in-Chief in India, now British representative in Egypt fortuitously on leave in Britain – was dragged off a train at Dover just as he was returning to Cairo, brought back to London and installed in the vacant chair to symbolize and inspire the nation's effort.

Kitchener had been, even though he could rarely attend, a founder member of the Other Club. F.E., rather surprisingly, greatly admired the old soldier and even claimed him as a friend. That association, together with the prompting of Churchill at the Admiralty, is the somewhat inadequate explanation of Kitchener's immediate and start-lingly incongruous appointment of F.E. to practically the first job that came within his gift. There happened to be a dinner of the Other Club on 5 August. During the evening, Kitchener suddenly announced to Lord Riddell, the proprietor of the *News of the World*, that he was going to appoint a Press Censor, and pointed across the table at F.E. 'There he is. Come and see me in the morning and I will tell you all about it.'[5] Presumably F.E. had already accepted the job earlier in the day. Since joining the Government was for the moment ruled out, he was des-perate to get into some sort of war-related office. Churchill was no doubt anxious to find his friend some sort of position where they could work together, and probably attached importance to the demonstration of cross-party co-operation; while Kitchener was too little versed in politics to see the difficulties F.E. would meet. It was not a clever appointment, but typical of the slapdash way that the mobilization of British society was hastily improvised at the outbreak of war. F.E. can have had very little idea of what he was taking on, since Ministers themselves were hopelessly contradictory in their statements of his intended function. At the Other Club he asked Riddell what he thought of his new job. Riddell replied that there was only one person who could fill it. 'Who is that?', asked F.E., taking him to mean himself. 'The Almighty,' answered Riddell, 'and even He would be criticized.'[5]

The trouble with F.E.'s new office – he was officially Director of the Press Bureau – was that it attempted to combine two contradictory functions. What Kitchener had in mind was straight censorship, 'He will see that nothing dangerous gets into the newspapers', he told Riddell. 'We must make the English people understand that we are at war and that war is not pap.'[6] Churchill, rather more positively, envisaged a sort of Central Office of Information, as he told the House of Commons on 7 August.

From that Bureau a steady stream of trustworthy information supplied by both the War Office and the Admiralty can be given to the Press, which, without endangering military or naval interests, will serve to keep the country properly and truthfully informed from day to day of what can be told, and what is fair and reasonable; and thus, by providing as much truth as possible, exclude the growth of irresponsible rumours.[7]

Kitchener's idea of 'as much truth as possible', however, was severely limited. War correspondents were not allowed at the front, and for the first couple of weeks of hostilities the flow of official information was almost non-existent: not even the dispatch of the British Expeditionary Force to France was reported until days after its arrival. As the papers tried to fill the vacuum as best they could, the censorship side of the Press Bureau's duties was very much uppermost. Yet the Bureau did not have this field to itself, for though it had the job of editing and approving articles submitted to it by the domestic press, the censorship of overseas cables was in the hands of retired army officers abruptly planted on the Post Office. A lack of consistency between what was permitted to be printed at home and what was cabled abroad was inevitable. The Press Bureau was in no way to blame, but took most of the criticism.

F.E. opened shop on 10 August in a disused ('rat-infested', according to Riddell)[6] Admiralty building in Charing Cross, with a dozen naval and military men working in rota round the clock to advise him, a scratch team of clerks and typists, and, controversially, his brother Harold as secretary. For the next three weeks the German armies advanced remorselessly towards Paris and the British were obliged by their retreating French allies to fall back rapidly from Mons to Le Cateau. For these three weeks almost nothing was printed in the British papers to tell the public the gravity of what was happening: complaints began to be heard at Westminster that the news famine was foolish and self-defeating. The banning of responsible correspondents from the front line meant that only tit-bits of news smuggled out by enterprising freelances behind the lines ever got back to the public, and these gleanings were shorn of all specific reference to particular regiments or places – shorn, as M.P.s complained, of all 'human interest' – by the censorship. Then, on 30 August, in a special Sunday edition, *The Times* suddenly published a sensational and highly coloured report, much too full of human interest, depicting the British army in full retreat, exhausted, broken and scattered. The impact of this after so much reassuring pap was shattering. The next day, pressed in the Commons by members demanding to know whether the report had passed the censor, Asquith strongly rebuked the paper for its indiscretion. The editor, Geoffrey Robinson, however, promptly issued a statement describing the source of the offending article and asserting that it had been submitted to the Press Bureau in the usual way.

The Press Bureau retained the message for about three hours before returning it. When it again reached the office of *The Times* certain passages, containing references to the correspondent's route, had been deleted. Other passages and embellishments, however, had been added by the head of the Press Bureau who further conveyed an intimation that, in its new form, the dispatch was approved for publication.

In these circumstances, the editorial staff of *The Times*, who were astonished at the decision of the Press Bureau and had made no arrangements for publishing the message, came, not unnaturally, to the conclusion that it was the wish of the Government that it should appear.[8]

This threw the responsibility squarely and damagingly on to F.E.; but he had an opportunity to defend himself in the House that evening, when a Liberal, Sir Albert Markham, raised the whole question of the function and composition of the Bureau on the adjournment. Markham's speech ranged much wider than *The Times* incident, criticized Kitchener more directly than F.E., but did question the appointment of Harold as secretary and referred to complaints from editors that 'the hon. Member for Warrington acts more like one of the Kaiser's staff officers' than was proper in a British official. Though he insisted that he was not attacking F.E. personally, but repeatedly complimented him on his handling of an anomalous and ill-conceived office, the effect of his words was to bring members springing to F.E.'s defence. Harry Lawson (son and heir to the proprietor of the *Daily Telegraph*, Lord Burnham) rejected Markham's 'most unfair and very ill-informed attack', asserting that F.E. had been 'battling with zeal, energy and tact against overwhelming difficulties and obstructions'. 'It is a thankless task,' Lawson continued, 'and I consider that he has put both the House and the country under a great obligation.' Others, including T.P. O'Connor and Robert Cecil, spoke in similar terms, so that F.E. had had a very easy ride by the time he rose to reply. Astonishingly, no one after Markham mentioned *The Times* dispatch at all. He began by capitalizing on this goodwill by claiming credit for his patriotism in undertaking the job in the first place.

I never sought the office which I hold, and which I was not so foolish as not to be well aware would mean many antagonisms, much invidiousness, and much that would involve every day the expenditure of almost more hours than I have worked in the course of a somewhat busy life.

Fourteen or fifteen hours a day, he claimed. He dwelled on the difficulties of establishing a new department from scratch, without precedent and without clear legal powers. He pointed out that the Press Bureau was not responsible for cable censorship, indignantly rebutted the criticism of 'my hon. Relative', who had been working, as a volunteer, the same long hours as himself and by his business ability had been able to systematize the work of the Bureau as no one else available to him at short notice could have done (which was probably true). Turning to specific instances in which the censorship was alleged to have been unnecessarily strict, he revealed his narrow view of his function by washing his hands entirely of the responsibility. In every case, he had simply asked the War Office or the Admiralty for guidance.

> I have only to say that having received instructions on a matter on which I am assured the safety of either the Army or the Navy depends, as to such and such restrictions, I exercise no discretion of any kind. I take it as an order . . .
> We on our own authority have never suppressed anything from first to last except when we were acting on the instructions of persons in high authority. As an office we do not suppress anything.

Whether he really thought it worth his time to act as Lord Kitchener's blue pencil, he did not say; but his answer came in a very few weeks.

At last he reached the question of *The Times* dispatch. Having gained the sympathy of the House, he appeared now to take it into his confidence. The confusion, he explained, arose from the dual nature of the Bureau's work. He had dealt with the dispatch himself, but at a moment of high pressure, when he had only had time to excise those detailed references which violated the positive rules of what might be printed; in returning it to *The Times* he ought, if he had had the time, to have written an accompanying letter indicating his view that, though not expressly forbidden, it was probably not suitable for publication. As it was, unfortunately, *The Times* had taken the fact that he had not actually suppressed it to mean that it was an officially approved statement. Dealing with his supposed 'embellishments', he thought that the only addition he made was to insert a reference, in keeping with Kitchener's known wishes, to the need for more reinforcements.[8]

In saying this, however, he contradicted himself, for there was no point in adding such an appeal if he had not intended that the dispatch be published. Only one member in the subsequent debate (from which F.E. excused himself on the high-handed ground that he had had no dinner) pointed this out. In fact F.E. was in this apology deliberately misleading the House; one has to say, lying. For the covering note with which he returned the article to *The Times*, far from indicating that it had better not be printed, had actually quite specifically urged that it should be. On the top sheet F.E. had written, in his own hand,

> I am sorry to have censored this most able and interesting message so freely but the reasons are obvious. Forgive my clumsy journalistic suggestions but I beg you to use the parts of this article which I have passed to enforce the lesson – reinforcements and reinforcements at once.[9]

What could the paper do on receipt of this but assume the censor to be expressing the will of the Government that the article be published and act accordingly? The revelation of this letter in 1934, four years after F.E.'s death, fully vindicated Robinson's contemporary account and casts F.E.'s conduct in a sharply unflattering light; he had sought to deny responsibility for his own decision by a smokescreen of mock candour and actual untruth which Robinson could, had he wished to pursue the argument, easily have exposed. To his credit, he let it drop; it was F.E. who, knowing the thinness of the ice on which he had skated, continued to nurse a grievance, telling Max Aitken bitterly that Robinson had 'betrayed' him,[10] and still in 1918 regaling Colonel Repington with his version of their quarrel, since when, he boasted, he had 'cut' Robinson whenever they met.[11]

It is a discreditable story. F.E. never found it easy to admit a mistake. There is a breathtaking nerve, therefore, in the closing words of his Commons defence, when he blandly congratulated himself on how few complaints there had been considering the many thousand dispatches his office handled every day, and concluded:

> I do not in the least pretend that mistakes have not been made. I will go further. I will take the House completely into my confidence and say I am quite certain mistakes will continue to be made. But all I can say is we are getting more experienced in the office.[8]

He would admit mistakes in general, with a calculated show of large-mindedness; but he would go to any length to avoid admitting responsibility for a particular lapse. Always generous in success, it has to be said that F.E. could be spitefully unscrupulous when cornered.

F.E.'s first experience of administrative office, then, was not a conspicuous success. The fault was not entirely his. He and Harold did achieve a good deal in setting up and running the Bureau in the chaotic conditions of the first few weeks of the war, even if, on F.E.'s admission, the criteria to which they worked were largely handed down from above. On 10 September McKenna, as Home Secretary, took over formal responsibility for the Bureau, though F.E. continued as Director for another fortnight. Other changes were made at the same time to meet other criticisms: the cable censorship was brought under the control of the Bureau, and trained journalists were at last admitted to have a role to play in the dissemination of official news. The reconstituted structure of the Bureau remained fundamentally unaltered for the remainder of the war, under a succession of Directors.[12] When F.E. resigned, on 26 September, after just seven weeks, he was succeeded by the Solicitor-General, Sir Stanley Buckmaster, who was at least able to give the Bureau some ministerial standing, but only at the cost of totally neglecting his legal duties. Buckmaster was succeeded in 1915 by Sir Frank Swettenham and Sir Edward Cook, the one a diplomat, the other a Liberal editor, who shared the burden between them. F.E. unquestionably had the most difficult task of any of them, having to establish his own guidelines at a time when the press was unaccustomed to restriction and events in France were so delicate and fluid that reliable news was both more sensitive and more scarce than it became when the war settled down to immobility and the Generals had nothing better to do than write dispatches home. In many ways, no doubt, F.E. earned the fulsome praise which he received from several quarters, including some journalists, for his discharge of what was admitted to be a thankless task. Nevertheless the *Manchester Guardian* was expressing a common view when in 1915 it wrote of his time at the Press Bureau as 'a complete and disastrous failure'.[13] He was, it has to be said, a bad appointment: he understood nothing of journalism or the legitimate needs of the press; he was tactless in dealing with editors while too deferential to the military; and he reacted badly to his first taste of criticism. It was an uncongenial and unsuitable role, which he gave up as soon as he decently could, with the excuse that his first duty was to join the Oxfordshire Yeomanry in France.

It was more than an excuse, since there was some murmuring that he, who was so free with stirring calls to the youth of the country to volunteer, seemed reluctant to act on his own advice. He had certainly stuck his neck out in a way that invited awkward questions by contributing a fervent preface to Sir Arthur Conan Doyle's recruiting pamphlet *To Arms*, which was rushed out in scores of editions in the early weeks of the war.

How any able-bodied man [F.E. wondered], unhampered by private obligations which make enlistment impossible, can read the stories printed in the newspapers in the last few days without doing all in his power to join the small British force in France is hard to understand . . . The need is very urgent. The call is loud. None can pretend that he has not heard it. Let every qualified man answer it in the only way that will save his honour, his freedom and his country.[14]

On 11 September F.E. took time off from the Press Bureau to join with Churchill and Labour's Will Crooks in addressing an all-party meeting at the London Opera House in Kingsway, at which he expounded three reasons why Britain had to fight this war: to honour her treaty obligation to Belgium, to defend international law, and to meet in the only possible way the German challenge to British greatness. 'The whole history of virile nations teaches us this profound and unalterable truth – that calculation and cowardice never pay.' He went on to rouse his audience with a phrase which Churchill, sitting beside him, remembered and tucked away for use again twenty-seven years later. The battle of the Marne, he declared, was not the beginning of the end.

It is only the end of the beginning. [Cheers.] This war is going to end either when we break this barbarous system or when this barbarous system breaks us. [Cheers.] There is no other end. It is a fight to the finish. [Cheers.] The terms of peace will be arranged either in London or Berlin. We think, on the whole, that it might be Berlin. [Laughter and Cheers.]

His peroration, too, is today difficult to read in other than a Churchillian accent.

The nation approaches this, the greatest crisis in her history since Napoleon fell, in no boastful spirit, but in a spirit of calmness and resolution. It is hopeful that, if God wills, these ancient realms, purged of unworthiness and disciplined by warlike vicissitudes, may yet see order wrested from chaos, may extort even, from the existing welter of bloodshed, the hope of a permanent peace, and might, in the end, convince the world that a proud nation may passionately love peace and yet be fit for war. [Cheers.] The sword will never be laid aside by this country – in all our long history it never has been – until we have won a lasting and honourable peace.[15]

But was he himself prepared to set the example which his ringing words demanded? There were certainly good reasons why a 42-year-old Member of Parliament, now charged with important national work for the War Office at home, should not have to throw it up to risk his life in France. Yet as a Lieutenant in the Oxfordshire Yeomanry he had a plain duty in time of war and he was sensitive to suspicion that he was shirking it. His appointment to the Press Bureau, the day after he had publicly taken his leave of Bonar Law and Balfour on his departure to the war, occasioned no little ribaldry at Westminster.[16] A year later the charge that he had evaded service at the outbreak of the war was made directly in an anonymous letter in the *Morning Post*, and F.E. had to go to the length of getting his commanding officer to refute it. Colonel Dugdale wrote willingly that F.E. had reported quite properly at Oxford H.Q. at the declaration of war, but had there found a telegram calling him to the Press Bureau; he had asked leave to go and had been granted it, since there was no immediate likelihood of the Oxford Hussars being sent to France anyway.[17]

In September, however, the Oxford Hussars were sent to France and F.E., according to Colonel Dugdale's letter, promptly wired his willingness to join them if required, only to be told that he was not needed for the present. Strictly, then, the *canard* must be admitted to be baseless; but his subsequent conduct continues to lend it plausibility. His work at the Press Bureau was so unrewarding that F.E. was soon anxious to use his duty to the Hussars as an honourable escape route. Yet having determined to go to France, he did not actually join his regiment at the front at all, but managed to secure himself what can only be called a cushy appointment behind the lines as Recording Officer – a sort of regimental historian – to the Indian troops who were just arriving *via* Marseilles.

It was another very odd job for someone of his standing and ability. Max Aitken had got himself appointed to a rather similar position with the Canadian troops; but he was both a master publicist and a Canadian. After the war, indeed, F.E. was to be both a highly paid columnist and Secretary of State for India. But at this point in his career he had no particular experience of journalism – except his recent experience as censor – and no connection at all with India. Kitchener was again responsible for the appointment, acting apparently on the suggestion of the Indian Secretary Lord Crewe.[18] But why on earth did F.E. accept it, when its incongruity was obvious and he must have seen that he would be laying himself wide open to the charge of shirking the role of combatant which he so strenuously pressed on others? The Press Bureau was work of undoubted national importance which arguably needed someone of his prominence at its head; no such case could be made out for the job of writing official dispatches for the Indian press, and anyway F.E. was wildly unqualified for it. *The World* was justified in protesting at the use of non-journalists in such roles,[19] and the whisperers had good cause for cynicism at F.E.'s convenient posting to a ringside seat from which he could experience the suffering of the forces at first hand from a personal position of some comfort.

The Indian troops, suddenly transported from their native climate to the cold damp trenches of northern France to be slaughtered in their thousands, suffered even more than most. They arrived just in time to be flung into the first battle of Ypres. Then through 1915 they held the stretch of the front around Givenchy, taking part in the battles of Festubert, Neuve Chapelle, second Ypres and Loos. By November there were few survivors of the original strength of 24,000; the quality of the replacements was said to be getting low and losses among their British officers too high – one battalion with a normal complement of thirteen officers went through seventy in the year. The remnant was therefore withdrawn and sent home, though Indian soldiers served later in Gallipoli, Salonika, Mesopotamia and Palestine, and Indians continued to be much used as labourers behind the lines on the Western Front. By the ghastly double standard of this war, however, those who had fallen in a cause of which they could have had no conception were held, perhaps rightly, to have helped to raise the status of India within the Empire and thus, indirectly, to have died for India's eventual freedom as well as Belgium's. F.E., in the official history in which he collaborated with his successor, Colonel Merewether, *The Indian Corps in France*, went so far as to claim that the Indians 'saved the Empire' in 1914; if this was an exaggeration, it was not more so than many similar claims at this time. The Indians certainly plugged a critical gap at a critical time.[20]

F.E.'s personal contribution, however, is more uncertain. His precise function, when he was not writing reports, is unclear. He never regarded himself merely as a passive observer, but took every advantage of his temporary rank of Major and his access to General Headquarters to make his presence and his opinions felt. It is scarcely surprising that he encountered jealousy and resentment from the regular officers. He was in the anomalous position of a Staff Officer with no proper military training or experience – far worse placed than Churchill when, later in the war, he came out to command a battalion for a few months. Churchill had been a soldier: F.E. was every inch a politician and not a tactful one. He suffered fools and military etiquette equally badly. 'He was inclined', Max Aitken wrote, 'to talk at St. Omer as if he were at the Carlton Club.'[21] He was bound to put backs up and he did. Yet those who felt the warmth of his friendship – his comradeship, his story-telling and his supply of brandy – loved him for ever.[22]

Characteristically he made a good friend of the one man who really mattered, the Commanding Officer of the Indian Corps, General Sir James Willcocks. Willcocks was an unusual soldier who appreciated the very quality in F.E. which others resented, and backed him against his detractors.

> FE, as he was alone known, was an extraordinarily attractive personage; he could say in one pithy sentence what to others would take pages to describe; and it was perhaps this very gift which secured him some enemies. But big men generally find enemies in plenty, and FE could afford to smile at those he met in France. He is a resolute man who, if he had started as a soldier, would assuredly have risen high, and if he had had the opportunity, would have reached the highest ranks.[23]

To F.E. himself, when he returned to England, Willcocks wrote in the warmest terms.

> As for you, FE, I am glad and proud to have made a friend of you. From the first day I met you in Marseilles I thought you and I would get on well together, for we have one thing in common at least, and that is the saving grace of common sense and human nature. I knew there were some who, in a narrow-minded way, looked on you as the civilian soldier, but the moment I knew it I was drawn closer, for I felt I needed a man of sterling common sense who would trample on red tape and interests in war time, and *you* were the man. I assure you I shall always retain a very happy recollection of our acquaintance.[24]

But what did he *do*? 'There is independent testimony,' the *Times Literary Supplement* conceded, somewhat back-handedly, reviewing his book, 'that he did his work at the Front zealously and well, and that ready help soon made good his lack of knowledge of the Sepoy's peculiarities. He wrote dozens of admirable narratives nearly all of which were ruthlessly suppressed by the censorship.'[25] This irony – the former gamekeeper now prevented from poaching – is confirmed by Willcocks. 'Little of what he related was ever allowed to appear, except in the baldest form. It was undoubtedly this quite unnecessary amount of censorship that long kept India in the dark and most adversely affected recruiting.'[23] Be that as it may – it is difficult to believe that more detailed accounts of the muddy slaughter would really have stirred Indian enthusiasm to join up – F.E. was evidently something more than a reporter. 'I was very sorry when he left the Corps',

Willcocks wrote, 'as he was always a cheery companion and an optimistic coadjutant.'[23] One can only guess that he acted as a sort of informal adviser, the General's extra pair of eyes and ears. No wonder the regular officers disliked him in their midst.

F.E.'s letters home to Margaret shed little light on this mystery, but they give a wonderfully vivid picture of a Staff Officer's life in France, his views on the war – written with a freedom and indiscretion which would have made his successor at the Press Bureau blench and would certainly have been censored in the letters of a private soldier – and above all of F.E. himself, the loving husband and father. As the only regular letters he ever wrote to Margaret they are worth quoting at some length.

First of all they demonstrate his love for his family, an ever-deepening concern throughout his life but especially stimulated at this moment by the shock of temporary, and the fear of permanent, separation.

I have been very gay and happy [he wrote on 15 October 1914] until I got your two letters on my return to the depot here. They make me sad, throwing over me here the atmosphere of home and your affection and the recollection of the darling little children. One's psychology is so odd. There is the constant society of brave and attractive men, and one thinks only of the campaign and the prospects – but there comes a reminder like your letter of all the sweetness of great domestic happiness and one becomes in a flash absurdly effeminate . . .

My dearest I do hope that you are not unhappy or lonely. This fear is far my greatest trouble. I am quite happy except when I think of my many faults of extravagance and remember how well off I could have left you if only we had lived sensibly. But the one thing I never anticipated was what has happened. What twelve happy years we have had together and what successful ones – surely no-one was ever happier or better suited to one another than we have been. Won't it be nice when one comes back with one's duty done according to the highest standards and as we hope with England and the Empire saved for our children and their children after them? What fun we will have and if it is with our last copper you shall come to Paris perhaps bringing Eleanor to meet me. What joy to look forward to.[1]

The money worry was a serious one, absurdly enough. Earning an enormous income, F.E. had always spent recklessly. He never minded accumulating debts, since he always took it for granted that he could easily earn enough to pay them if necessary. But now his earning power was abruptly stopped. Indeed he had several thousand pounds in advance fees to pay back. It is extraordinary that he should never have taken seriously his own warnings about the imminence of war, nor made any provision for the moment when his jolly games with the Oxfordshire Yeomanry should suddenly turn real. But it appears to be so. How were Margaret and the children to live while he was abroad? Max Aitken characteristically came to the rescue with a guarantee of £7,000.[26] A more immediate expedient was to let Grosvenor Gardens to the Red Cross and move into a smaller house near by in Wilton Street. Another was to sell off some of F.E.'s beloved hunters to the Government, which was still at that time thinking in terms of a cavalry war. F.E. himself took three with him to France. Three more – named Ajax, Harkaway and Sultan – were sold. 'If we sell Punch and Exeter that gives you £140 more to be going on with which is better than a poke in the eye with a burned stick . . . I shall never get a stud of hunters again,' he reassured Margaret, 'so that cause of anxiety is removed from you.'[27]

Some luxuries, however, were not to be given up. 'The two grass tennis courts [at Charlton] should be most carefully weeded in order that the dashing young cavalry officer may have good tennis next summer on his return from Berlin.'[27]

F.E. was only half joking. He was at the outset as blithely confident of a quick victory as most other people – excepting Kitchener. 'I should think it will develop into a Crimean winter before the thing is over,'[27] he wrote with what was evidently intended to be gloomy realism. A few weeks later he admitted that 'it is a long way to Berlin'[28] (2 November), but on 21 November he was anticipating with mixed feelings having to leave his comfortable billet in an old rectory to follow the army as it pursued the retreating enemy eastward.[29] Only when the Germans instead dug in did he concede that the war 'looks like a long affair. I expect when I come back Eleanor will have her hair up and Freddy be almost ready to join the Oxfordshire Yeomanry'[30] (25 November). But this joke too was nearer the truth than he probably imagined. Eleanor was in fact sixteen and Freddy eleven by the time the war ended.

If he remained optimistic about the outcome, F.E. had no illusions, from his privileged viewpoint, about the intensity of suffering by which victory was being bought – contrary to the impression being given at home. 'All this talk about the men coming singing out of the trenches is damned nonsense,' he wrote on 1 November. 'They come out dead to the world and some of them gibbering idiots.'[31] 2 November: 'We got yesterday's *Times*. The optimism and the buck nearly make us all sick . . . Don't imagine I have a vestige of doubt as to the ultimate result, but one does get a reaction from the sort of swagger and ignorant optimism which fills the English Press.'[28]

The truth was that the Indians were having a bad time.

> My dear, all these things in the papers about the Indian troops are
> lies. They are not doing very well (rather the contrary) and we are
> very anxious about them. This, of course, is most deeply secret.
> Our line, about 13 miles, is held by Indians alone without any
> reserve (none can be spared) and we are told on the Staff to have
> our motors and horses prepared in case the line is broken.[32]

This was 2 November. Nine days later, however, the crisis was past.
The main German attack was launched, fortunately, at Ypres, fifteen
miles away, and was beaten back. The Indians were now 'behaving
splendidly'.

> They are getting used to it. Poor wretches, they were marched
> straight from motor omnibuses into a style of warfare of which they
> knew nothing, and many of them shoved into trenches too deep for
> them, so that they could not even fire from them, and, so handi-
> capped, they were exposed to the hideous concentration of shell
> fire.[33]

Though they held on heroically when it mattered, F.E. was nevertheless convinced that the Indians, whom he characterized as 'superb
troops',[34] were tragically out of their element and wasted in France. As
the war in the west settled down to deadlock F.E., like Churchill (who at
this time favoured an expedition to Schleswig-Holstein) and Lloyd
George (who favoured Salonika), was beginning to look for alternative
theatres where the war might be won more quickly. F.E.'s idea was to
use the Indian Corps for an attack on Turkey in Smyrna. Soon after
Christmas he was in London for a week's leave and was able to put his
scheme to the Prime Minister.[35] Asquith was initially attracted, but
Kitchener refused to contemplate withdrawing the Indians from France
– the eastern plan that was beginning to take shape was to be a naval
attack on the Dardanelles. Undeterred, F.E. wrote to Winston as soon
as he got back to France, citing Willcocks's support for his project.

> My dear W.
> Our General says that with his A.C. [Army Corps] & 25,000
> Territorials he cd. take Smyrna & hold a wide range of trenches
> around it against 100,000 Turks. He says the morale of his troops
> would be superb in that climate & against that enemy.
> 　　　　　　Yrs
> 　　　　　　　　F.E.[36]

The Indians were eventually redeployed against the Turks, but not so soon as F.E. hoped. He was himself hoping to 'go with them for a couple of months to finish my writing and see if the Turks put up a fight' (29 December).[37] He was getting increasingly bored in France. It was not that his life as a Staff Officer was uncomfortable. One of his Other Club friends, Neil Primrose, who was serving near by with the Buckinghamshire Yeomanry, sent Margaret in October a satirical picture of F.E. at war.

> I am irresistibly tempted to write you a line to describe the appalling hardships which your husband undergoes. They were poignantly brought to my mind tonight, because I was sitting in his bedroom after dinner when he read out from a letter which he had just received from you that your brother thought him an idiot to have come out here. FE was lying in an enormous bed, which looked very comfortable, in the best bedroom in the hotel, after an excellent dinner well tempered with burgundy, with an enormous cigar in his mouth and a glass of rum and hot water by his bedside. I feel that you must give him an appalling time at home if he is not to be considered as living a most luxurious life.[38]

Even when the Corps moved into the thick of the fighting, F.E. did very well for himself.

> We got beautiful rooms here (I a large bed with electric light on each side to read) and that damned fellow Haig the General came and turned us out. Then on a wet morning we searched everywhere in vain for billets and at last found a picturesque old chateau with a moat round it which everyone had rejected as too damp. It isn't really damp as we have got the sole possession of it. We have enormous fires everywhere, including our bedrooms, and on the whole are very comfortable. It is huge and we are waited on by Ward and the two chauffeurs – quite amazing. (29 December)[37]

In the same letter F.E. describes the Indian troops being kept in the trenches 'for ten days without change, standing up to their knees in water'.[37]

One of the necessities of F.E.'s existence was not readily available, however, unless Margaret supplied it, as he carefully instructed her on 21 October.

> Also, my angel, do send me from the Stores every 20 (or perhaps 18) days a box of my cigars. I can live, as I am doing, on bully beef.

I can drink, as I am drinking, cocoa and tea. But I cannot, and I will not, as long as my bank will honour my cheques, wash them down, so to speak, with nothing but a pipe. I can smoke two pipes a day, but not more, which leaves me with a necessity for five cigars, or say seven (two for a friend) and honestly the support of my system requires this. This is most important and quite serious. Tell the Stores not to print any indication that the boxes are cigars. Have printed yourself some gummed labels as follows:

ARMY TEMPERANCE SOCIETY
PUBLICATIONS SERIES 9

and put this and nothing else on the outside. These precautions are very necessary, as cigars are always stolen by the men if they escape the officers.[39]

Presumably Margaret complied, not necessarily to the last detail. Other luxuries were more occasional.

Jimmy Rothschild has sent me six dozen oysters, a hare and two bottles of 1811 brandy: isn't he an angel? Sunny [the Duke of Marlborough] is staying with me. Tomorrow night we are dining with the General so I am sending him the oysters and the hare with my compliments.[40]

F.E. was able to maintain an extraordinary social life in France, with Marlborough coming to stay, friends like Aitken and Primrose and Margaret's brother Claude Furneaux near by, all apparently quite free to move around and dine with one another. F.E. and Aitken spent the New Year together in Paris, staying at the Ritz. Nevertheless there were long intervals of boredom, and by February 1915 F.E.'s requests were increasingly for reading matter.

Will you send me cheap but legible editions that I can destroy of Richardson's *Clarissa Harlowe*, *Tom Jones*, *David Copperfield*, the sequel of *Monsieur Lecocq* by Gaborian, Balzac's *Père Goriot* and any books you think I would like. I am not exactly bored but I live absolutely alone with quite an impossible mess. Except when I go with the General and do messages I ride alone and motor alone to see someone and am always alone 5–7 and 9–12. As you know I am intensely sociable in my habits but I get on wonderfully well . . . (7 February)[41]

Please send me *Anna Karenina* and any other of Tolstoy's novels
quite cheap but they must be legible as my eyes have been giving me
a little difficulty lately. (12 February)[42]

Living his sheltered life amid the slaughter, F.E. was still sensitive to
the charge that he was shirking. 'My dear, the Oxfordshire Yeomanry
are actually in the trenches,' he wrote on 2 November. 'I feel rather a
cad when I think of my comparative safety and comfort.'[28] His safety
was not absolute, for his duties did bring him under fire occasionally. 'I
wasn't in the least afraid,' he wrote when a shell burst within twenty
yards of his car, 'which pleased me';[43] while General Willcocks recalled
a time when F.E. was accompanying him round the trenches and 'a
bullet struck the beam to which he was holding within an ace of his
head; it was very near its mark and somehow I felt it was meant for F.E.
personally'.[23] At other times F.E. was inclined to court danger in
somewhat self-conscious displays of bravado, intended to prove, one
suspects, something to himself as much as to others. On one such
escapade he insisted on accompanying his old friend Jack Seely, now
commanding the Canadian Cavalry Brigade, up the Front Line during
the night bombardment before a German attack. He lent Seely one of
his hunters for the mission, and had his own shot from under him as
they went forward. Half-way up the line, when they paused behind a
bank, F.E. solemnly entrusted to Seely his last greetings to his family in
case he should be killed and Seely survive. 'They were touching, simple
messages to his wife and each of his children; nothing flamboyant, but
just words of love and deep affection.'[44]

It cannot truly be said, as his son suggests, that F.E. was 'indifferent
to fire'[45] – that he believed he bore a charmed life or felt any sort of
fatalism. On the contrary, it is clear that he was very conscious whenever he ran the risk of premature extinction. Admiring courage above
all other qualities, he attached the greatest importance to showing it
unflinchingly as often as was necessary for his self-regard. He was very
pleased when he managed to get himself mentioned in despatches for
his part in the fighting just before Christmas, 'rather a smack in the
teeth for people like that little swine from the *Globe*,' he told Margaret.[46]
Nevertheless he was far from relishing the thrill of battle as Winston
did. F.E., who rode so recklessly at high fences, did not possess a large
stock of that passive courage needed to withstand prolonged gunfire. (It
is typical of him that his most dangerous moment in France occurred
when his horse reared and fell back on top of him.) Certainly he had no
wish to go on risking his life any longer than the minimum requirement
of personal honour dictated.

'He is very human,' was General Willcocks's last word on F.E.[23] And it was perhaps only human to want to get away from France as soon as he could honourably contrive. Personal factors apart, the war was developing into a depressing stalemate. 'Everyone is groping here with no plan & no prospects,' he wrote to Churchill on 15 February.

> I shudder for fear our new million get swallowed up here if the Germans can match them with another million or even (on defensive lines) with 500,000.
>   Why don't you make a deal on any terms with Italy for joint action in the Spring & send the new army to Italy to break through in the North Munichwards? Probably this is impracticable but so apparently is everything. The result is certain but Russia is disappointing. We make no progress here & haven't in the least conquered the offensive.[47]

F.E. could stand anything but inaction. Winston too, increasingly under criticism at the Admiralty, supported the promptings of his friend's growing conviction that he could be better employed at home.

> I wish you could manage to come over here in the near future for a few days. There are many things I want to talk to you about. I am sorry that you are away. In your absence Bonar Law is surrounded only by persons who wish to revive party bitterness at the earliest possible moment. Your influence here in politics would be invaluable and the services you could render to the country would be far greater than you could render in the ungrateful sphere in which you move, but of course there is the difficulty of pulling out of the hunt.

There was indeed. Churchill went on:

> I hope you have seen something of French and got on friendly terms with him. I spoke very earnestly to him when he was here upon the subject of your position. Some of the smaller military people are very short-sighted. I know you do not let these passing irritations distress you . . .[48]

In fact F.E. was far from friendly with Sir John French. His deteriorating relations with G.H.Q. – of which there are teasing but unspecific hints in his letters home ('Brade is being invaluable to me in a further development of the controversy with G.H.Q. in which the Meek Major is just managing [by turning his cheek to the smiter] to keep his end up,' 12 February)[42] – were exacerbated by what F.E. regarded as French's dishonest official account of the fighting just before Christmas, in which he implicitly censured Willcocks for carrying out, with disastrous results, orders which he now denied having given. Willcocks bore the injustice with professional composure, but F.E. was loyally furious on his behalf and vowed to 'make all these things clear' after the war.[40] His view of French as an untrustworthy cad was henceforth unshakeable, and he found ample confirmation a few months later in French's self-serving conduct, going behind the back of Kitchener, during the munitions crisis which brought down the Liberal Government. He soon had more authoritative opportunities than were open to him as Recording Officer of the Indian Corps to publish his criticism.

Meanwhile this quarrel was yet another reason for 'pulling out of the hunt' if he could find a way. He was due for a month's leave at the end of March: Margaret urged him to come home for good. F.E. explained to her the difficulty: if he gave up his position with the Indian Corps, he would still be bound to the Oxford Hussars.

> About staying at home, it isn't quite as simple as it sounds. You see, my regiment is on active service. It is as much under discipline as C's [Claude Furneaux's] company. I needn't go to it as long as I am formally seconded under circumstances of military employment of a nature to earn pay. I could not (I mean literally I would not be allowed to) come back to the Bar and have no genuine military occupations.

But the implication that this is what he would like to do, fairly disgraceful in the light of his fervent recruiting speeches, is clear. 'I am not having fun here,' he added, as if that were the point of the exercise. 'I hate it: it would be different if there was variety and an advance. This sodden immobility is appalling.' Some officers felt an obligation, just because it was so appalling, to stay with their men. F.E. was frankly more worried about restoring his domestic income.

> The money isn't as bad as you think. It is really better than at the outbreak of war for we shall not be *pressed* for our debt but allowed reasonable time. I have no doubt that living at the rate of £5000 a year which we can do we can pay it off in two years . . . Of course we shall have a bit of trouble: but my health never was better – I feel as strong as a bull – Duke I am sure is going soon* and I have

---

* Henry Duke was a leading K.C. who was picking up a lot of the work released by younger counsel who had gone to France.

In one case at this time he was explaining to Mr Justice Darling that he had taken over the brief from 'my friend Mr F.E. Smith K.C., who is now Major F.E. Smith'. 'I

no doubt of my ability to make £12,000 a year at least.[49]

F.E.'s optimism is hard to understand, since it assumed that he would be able to go back to the Bar which, as he had just explained, would not be possible so long as the war lasted. However, he evidently came back to London with the hope of securing some position which would keep him there. In April he got himself appointed to a military court set up to investigate a complaint about the raising of a special battalion of the City of London Regiment, Royal Fusiliers. Then in May he was appointed a member of the Committee of Enquiry into the sinking of the *Lusitania* by a German submarine. Minor tribunals of this sort, however, would not keep a fit and active 42-year-old worthily employed for the remainder of the war – nor would it make him any money. Fortune came to F.E.'s rescue just in time, in the shape of a political crisis.

Although he was now in London, F.E. played little part in the political machinations which, after nine months of war, finally compelled Asquith, reluctantly, to broaden his Liberal Ministry into an all-party coalition – Arthur Henderson was the token Labour member – for they centred on the Conservatives' mounting antagonism to his friend Winston at the Admiralty. The Tory party had always detested Churchill, as a renegade, more than any other Liberal and now distrusted him more than ever as a wild man, consumed by personal ambition, who threatened to lose the war in the vainglorious attempt to win it single-handed. In the spring of 1915 the Opposition's loyal support for the Government, already strained by the months of disillusion and deadlock, was stretched still further by the open row, publicized by Colonel Repington in *The Times*, between French and Kitchener over the supply of shells to the army. But the factor which really forced Asquith to give way was the private quarrel between Churchill and his First Sea Lord, the 74-year-old megalomaniac Admiral Jacky Fisher (whom he himself had recalled from retirement in August) which culminated on 16 May in Fisher's abrupt resignation. Asquith had to act decisively to contain the damage, and Bonar Law's price for joining the Government was Churchill's removal. Churchill was outraged and incredulous. Despite what he had written to F.E. in March, he had not realized the weight of hostility building up against him. F.E. and Aitken, good foul-weather friends, rallied to his side, spending most of the night of 18 May with him at the Admiralty while he clung to office 'as if the salvation of England depended on it'.[51] But Bonar Law and his colleagues were determined that Churchill must go, and F.E.'s influence

should think he's General F.E. Smith by this time,' interjected Darling – exemplifying the common legal view of F.E.'s powers, not shared by the military.[50]

with his leader was diminished by the very fact that he was the scape-goat's closest friend. So, ironically, the coalition which Churchill more than anyone else had advocated since the very first day of the war came about over his own dead body. Haldane, Lord Chancellor since 1912 but now scandalously hounded for his German connections, was the other principal casualty.

F.E. was one of the minor beneficiaries. The Tories in general did very poorly out of the new Government. Asquith was determined to keep the adulteration of his Government to a minimum, and most of the major posts remained in Liberal hands. Balfour – the type of cultured Conservative whom Asquith respected – replaced Churchill at the Admiralty but Bonar Law – whose philistinism Asquith snobbishly despised – was insultingly palmed off with the Colonial Office, which with true self-abnegation he accepted. Carson, who only a few months earlier had been threatening to lead Ulster in open rebellion against the Crown, became Attorney-General in place of Simon, who was promoted to the Home Office. Simon was actually offered and had the distinction of declining, at the exceptionally early age of forty-two, the vacant Woolsack – an elevation which would really have left his old Wadham rival at the mark. Instead, Asquith had to promote Buckmaster from Solicitor-General to be Lord Chancellor, which left an obvious opening for F.E. He was duly offered, and gratefully accepted, the second Law Officer's job on 26 May. The opportunity was taken, with F.E.'s appointment, quietly to terminate the Solicitor-General's responsibility for the Press Bureau.

Quite apart from its fortunate timing, this was a very significant step in F.E.'s career: his first Government office and a promotion from which he would never look back. Of course, it was a relatively humble office. As Austen Chamberlain (who had himself taken the India Office) wrote to him, 'The circumstances have prevented you from reaching at once the position to which in any Unionist Government your ability and your work would naturally have carried you.'[52] But F.E. was in no position to worry about that. He had, it is true, hoped to be Attorney-General with a seat in the Cabinet; but, as Margaret admitted to Aitken, whom she credited with having overcome Law's recent distrust of F.E., there was compensation enough in getting any job.

I must thank you for all I know you have done for Fred – and I know it is not *your* fault he is not in the Cabinet!! Of course it *is* a disappointment, but directly we knew Carson was coming in, we practically lost all hope of the Attorney-Generalship! I do not expect he would have got this, had he not had such a kind friend at court.

This puts our money worries at an end and keeps him in England, and I think I have a *very great deal* to be thankful for.[53]

Temporarily, at least, their money worries were indeed solved, since the Law Officers received salaries larger than those even of the Prime Minister and the Lord Chancellor, justified by the need to tempt the top advocates from the Bar, where they could of course earn far more; not only salaries, either, but their fees for acting for the Government as well. Before the war Isaacs and Simon had cleared something like £12,000 on top of their basic £7,000. By a wartime agreement F.E.'s remuneration was in fact reduced by £5,000 from what he might have expected, but he must still have made well over £10,000 a year, easily enough to pay his debts and restore his credit for some time to come.[54] Nor was this all. As a further sweetener for the material sacrifice of taking office, the Law Officers also traditionally receive knighthoods. Margaret was able, in the letter quoted, to thank Aitken for being the first to address her (prematurely) as Lady Smith; and on 9 June F.E. went to Buckingham Palace and emerged as Sir Frederick. For the next three and a half years he was known to the world, most unfamiliarly, by his christian name instead of by his famous initials.

15

Law Officer in Wartime:
The Casement Trial, 1916

F.E. was Solicitor-General for only six months before Carson's resignation in October 1915 opened his way to the senior post of Attorney-General. Even before that he took on a good deal of Carson's work, as Carson concerned himself predominantly with the prosecution of the war. There is no clear demarcation between the functions of the two offices: the Solicitor-General is simply the Attorney-General's deputy. The difference in their status was temporarily heightened at this period, however, by the fact that since 1912, when Asquith had needed to compensate Rufus Isaacs for denying him the Woolsack in favour of Haldane, successive Attorneys – Isaacs, Simon, now Carson and soon F.E. – were accorded a seat in the Cabinet. The constitutional arguments against this doubling of legal and executive roles were strong, and in 1919 Lloyd George demoted the office again to its traditional rank. In 1915, however, F.E.'s promotion, while it made little difference to his legal work, was another important step in his political progress, though negated in 1916 when the full Cabinet was superseded by a small War Cabinet of only five or six.

The Law Officers have two principal functions, which correspond roughly to the two branches of the law. On the one hand, they are the Crown's legal advisers, in which capacity they are consulted on the drafting of all legislation and advise the Government, like solicitors, on all matters of law. On the other, they act in cases of public importance as counsel for the Crown in the courts. For this reason they are always barristers, but while they hold office the Crown is their only client and they receive a salary to compensate them for the loss of other fees. The Attorney-General (or, in his absence, his deputy) exercises certain of the functions of a Minister of Justice. He controls the office of Public Prosecutions, supervising the work of its Directors; certain classes of offence can only be tried with his consent; and he has the right to stay criminal proceedings in the higher courts. At this period, too, his permission was necessary for appeals to the House of Lords – a provision which was to involve F.E. in controversy in the Casement case.

These were the peacetime duties of the Law Officers. F.E., however, was a Law Officer in war, when these normal functions were almost overwhelmed by additional burdens. On the one hand, there was a mass of special legislation, mainly restrictive, most obviously the Defence of the Realm Act (DORA), to be drafted, piloted through Parliament, defended and continually amended. Secondly, there was a torrent of work connected with that unique wartime institution, the Prize Court, to which (by an extraordinarily civilized rule of international law) captured ships had to be brought to have their cargoes either seized or restored according to whether they were judged to be of 'enemy character' or innocently neutral. There were also a great many prosecutions for breaches of DORA and the occasional espionage or subversion case. Finally, the administration of justice in a war of conscript armies involved some clarification and reform of the antiquated procedures of courts martial. It is not surprising that Carson found the job of a Law Officer in 1915 infinitely more demanding than he had between 1900 and 1905, so that he had to resign to give the attention he wanted to the conduct of the war. It did not leave F.E. much time for politics either.

He was plunged at once into this mass of technical business and disappeared from the public view for most of the war. 'In some ways I miss the big advocacy cases which took up so much of my time before the war,' he wrote to George Harley in 1916. 'But it is interesting work and very important and responsible.'[1] His parliamentary appearances were largely confined to such matters as the temporary restriction of nightclubs (a snare for young officers on the loose in London for the first time 'with cheque-books and the appetites of youth'),[2] the impounding of alien property, the suppression of subversive literature and similar curtailments of the freedom the country was fighting to defend. The index to Hansard for 1916 is by itself enough to convey the type of case for which F.E. had to answer in the House of Commons: 'Cardiff gentleman banished; Squire's daughter arrested and imprisoned; Young man of Dutch-German origin, case of'; and so on.[3] F.E. had no doubts about these measures. 'My hon. friend has delivered a panegyric on British liberty,' he told Charles Trevelyan on one occasion. 'But British liberty will only survive in very exiguous quantities if the war is carried on by the methods he seems to think adequate.'[4] Gradually – as his powers of exposition and defence were for the first time shown to be equal to his power of ridicule and attack – he was entrusted with wider responsibilities beyond the strictly legal sphere: the small print of the

Conscription Bill in committee in January 1916; the Corn Production Bill in July 1917 ('I am one of the few', he admitted in his disarming way, 'who have attempted to take part in this debate wholly uncontaminated by any expert knowledge of agriculture';[5] but that did not stop him putting the case for the Government's emergency response to the U-Boat menace); the Bill setting up the Royal Air Force in November 1917.

In the grey area between politics and law F.E. had also, as Attorney-General, to advise the Government on legal problems thrown up by the war. Did Ministers switched to different offices really need to submit themselves to by-elections? Was it legal to hold conferences with the enemy, as it was alleged the Labour party proposed to do by meeting German socialists in Stockholm? Was the Mesopotamia Commission a properly constituted legal court? Could the Government prosecute Pemberton Billing?

Then there was the administration of military law. The somewhat rough and ready system of courts martial which had served adequately the needs of a professional army in peacetime was unable to cope with a volunteer army at war. F.E. had seen the need for reform at first hand in France; but his attempts as an interfering junior officer to promote it only contributed to his unpopularity at G.H.Q. On becoming Solicitor-General, however, he took over from Kitchener the function of reviewing appeals from courts martial (now running at eighty a month) and won his agreement to reforming the personnel and procedure of the courts: most important was the inclusion of a civilian legal expert where previously there had not necessarily been a trained lawyer at all. At the end of the war he received the formal thanks of the Army Council for what he had achieved. 'Your influence', the letter noted, 'was always exercised on the side of humanity.'[6]

F.E.'s most time-consuming work as a Law Officer was centred on the Prize Court. The function of this remarkable institution, which exists only in war, was classically described by Lord Mersey, speaking for the Judicial Committee of the Privy Council in the case of the *Odessa* in 1915.

All civilised nations up to the present time have recognized the right of a belligerent to seize, with a view to condemnation by a competent Court of Prize, enemy ships found on the high seas or in the belligerents' territorial waters, and enemy cargoes. But such seizure does not, according to British Prize Law, affect the ownership of the thing seized. Before that can happen, the thing seized, be it ship or goods, must be brought into the possession of a lawfully constituted Court of Prize, and the captor must then ask for and obtain its condemnation as prize . . . It is a suit *in rem*, and the function of the court is to enquire into the national character of the thing seized. If it is found to be of enemy character, the duty of the Court is to condemn it; if not, then to restore it to those entitled to its possession.[7]

The Prize Court was automatically constituted by Order in Council on the outbreak of war in August 1914, and the President of the Probate, Divorce and Admiralty Division, Sir Samuel Evans – the same before whom F.E. had fenced with Lady Sackville; an old Welsh colleague of Lloyd George's who had been Solicitor-General himself from 1908 to 1910 – took his seat for the first time on 4 September. To Simon, who was then Attorney-General, fell the duty of opening the first case. But no Prize Court had sat in Britain for sixty years, since the end of the Crimean War. The main principles of Prize Law as it existed in 1914 had been laid down by Lord Stowell during the Napoleonic Wars. Evans and the counsel who appeared before him had therefore an enormous task to revise and apply to the world of steam and Dreadnoughts a body of law evolved in the age of sail. From the moment he became Solicitor-General in May 1915 to the end of the war F.E. undertook the Crown's case in most of the many hundreds of cases of extreme commercial complexity which came before the Court. It was important work, but too tediously technical to bear detailed repetition. F.E. had to cheat slightly to include in the section of his *Famous Trials* devoted to his own cases the only one that makes a good story – the case of the German 'hospital ship' *Ophelia*, captured in October 1914, which turned out not to be a hospital ship at all but to be equipped for spying. It actually came before Sir Samuel Evans, who duly condemned it, three weeks before F.E. took office. Simon and Buckmaster were the prosecuting counsel. F.E. only took over in time to oppose the appeal to the Privy Council – something one might just be able to deduce from a careful reading of *Famous Trials*, but would never guess from his son's stirring account.[8]

F.E. was of course no beginner in the field of international law (as Evans, for instance, admittedly was when suddenly called upon to preside over a tribunal dispensing it). Back in 1899 a short primer on the subject had been his first published book, and he had brought out, with some assistance, revised and expanded editions in 1902, 1906 and 1911, by which time the length of the original text had almost doubled. Now he was able to give his name (*Sir Frederick* Smith) to a fifth edition taking into account Germany's unprovoked aggression, and he preceded this with a shorter volume specifically on the destruction of merchant shipping.[9] As the Germans stepped up their U-Boat campaign and recklessly extended it to neutral, including American, shipping, they gave the Allies priceless opportunities for propaganda, for submarines have no respect for the niceties of Prize Law; and F.E. – who before the war had argued even against the right to search belligerent merchant shipping – was increasingly to the forefront in the legal condemnation of 'German sea-crime'.[10] a counter-offensive especially aimed at bringing the United States into the war.

The most prominent appearances of the Attorney-General in the public eye, however, were still his appearances as counsel for the Crown in the ordinary courts. Most of these were in cases brought under DORA. In one, in November 1915, the former Director of the Press Bureau secured the temporary closure of *The Globe* for speculating prematurely that Kitchener had resigned; in another, in May 1917, charges against eight leaders of an engineers' strike in a munitions factory were withdrawn when the men gave a written undertaking to adhere in future to the agreement between their union and the Ministry. F.E. delivered on behalf of the Government a solemn warning that such strikes endangered British lives and would in future incur the full penalty of the law.[11]

A couple of months earlier F.E. had the remarkable task of prosecuting a group of millenarian Communists charged with the attempted murder of the Prime Minister. A Mrs Wheeldon of Derby and her daughter and son-in-law in Southampton had conceived a wild plot to kill Lloyd George, either with strychnine or with an air-gun bullet dipped in curare; they were discovered only because the chosen instrument to whom Mrs Wheeldon confided her scheme was a police agent introduced into her house as a lodger to watch others suspected of being deserters! With this tip-off from the horse's mouth, the police were able to open her letters and intercepted the parcel containing the poison – the son-in-law in Southampton was a chemist. They were arrested, tried at the Old Bailey and given ten, seven and five years respectively – lenient sentences considering the nature of the crime envisaged, but probably reflecting doubt as to the real seriousness of the conspirators' mad intention.[12]

One other case, unconnected with the war, with which F.E. was concerned in these years is worth mentioning, as it furnishes a curious illustration of the anomalies of trying to apply legal concepts of land ownership to an overseas Empire acquired by settlement and conquest. The question was who owned large unoccupied tracts of Southern Rhodesia: the British South Africa Company, which effectively controlled them for purposes of commercial exploitation; the native Matabele, King Lobengula's people, scattered by the Company's forces in 1893; the white settlers, as an emerging political community; or the British Crown? The situation remained unclear for years: it was finally referred to the Judicial Committee of the Privy Council in 1914, just before the outbreak of war, but then it could not be heard until April 1918. F.E., with his new Solicitor-General Gordon Hewart, led for the Crown. Among the other counsel involved, Leslie Scott represented the natives. Neither the Company nor the settlers were able to show that they had ever been granted title to the lands; and the natives, as F.E. later wrote, 'had a weak case . . . Their claim was inconsistent, not only with the land settlement that had taken place under legislative sanction, but also with European settlement altogether' – which presumably brought with it a higher law.

As a result the Judicial Committee acceded to our argument, that the only satisfactory legal solution, looking at the question both historically and practically, was to hold that the unoccupied lands of Rhodesia were vested in the Crown. We therefore succeeded in preserving for the community of Rhodesia these vast areas with their promise of untold wealth. Existing holdings of settlers, of natives and of the Company were not affected.[13]

At the same time it was conceded that the Company was entitled to some compensation for the money it had spent in developing the disputed lands. A Commission headed by Lord Cave eventually fixed the amount at £4·5 million, a little over half what the Company claimed.

But far and away the biggest case with which F.E. had to deal as Attorney-General, one whose reverberations are still the subject of active controversy even today, was that of the Irish patriot Sir Roger Casement. Such is the power of Irish martyrs, indeed, that F.E.'s conduct at various stages of Casement's road to the gallows has been the subject of more suspicion, accusation and investigation than any other episode in his whole career. Yet much of this literature, partaking more of the nature of hagiography and demonology than of history, has served less to illuminate the events surrounding Casement's death than to obscure them in a poisoned cloud of myth. Committed partisans have not scrupled to build elaborate allegations of legal impropriety and moral infamy on evidence which turns out to be extremely flimsy. The task of F.E.'s biographer in this minefield is, first, to restore some sense of context and proportion to the story and, second, to examine the charges of professional misconduct with a touch of elementary scepticism.

There can be no doubt that from the point of view of the British

Frederick Smith   Elizabeth Smith

'Roslyn', Clifton Park, Birkenhead: the 'Gothic monstrosity' in which F.E. was brought up

Young Fred   a) aged two   b) aged nine

c) at Birkenhead School   d) as a don at Merton

The Standing Committee of the Oxford Union, 1894. F.E., as President, is seated centre, with Hilaire Belloc on his right and Lord Balcarres (holding boater) next to him. Standing behind these three are E.G. Hemmerde (left) and Earl Beauchamp

Wadham College Rugby XV, 1893–4. F.E., as Captain, is seated centre. In the back row are John Simon (top left) and C.B. Fry, with A.A. Roche between them

Electioneering in Walton in 1906

F.E. speaking at an anti-
Home Rule demonstration
in Ulster, September 1912

Carson and 'Galloper' Smith
inspecting Ulster Volunteers
at Dromore, County Down,
in 1913

Austen Chamberlain

Michael Collins as Commander-in-Chief of the Irish Free State Army

The triumvirate: Lloyd George, F.E. and Churchill leaving 10 Downing Street, February 1922

Margaret

Mona Dunn, painted by Sir William Orpen in 1919, about the time she first met F.E.

Tennis at Charlton: Margaret, the Duke of York (later George VI), Mona Dunn on the seat, and F.E.

The sportsman: F.E.'s tennis, 'more vigorous than swift'; his eccentric style of putting; on court with Freddie

Retirement with a book

Crown, whose subject he was, Casement was guilty of treason. For eighteen months from the outbreak of war he had been in Germany, trying – with conspicuous lack of success – to recruit Irish prisoners of war into an Irish Brigade to fight with the Germans for Irish freedom; he was arrested on the west coast of Ireland early on the morning of Good Friday, 1916, three days before the Easter Rising in Dublin, having landed from a German submarine. Even though it transpired that he had actually come to Ireland to try to *stop* the rising, his activities in Germany were more than enough to hang him. Given the fact – even though Casement denied the validity – of Britain's jurisdiction over Ireland, there could be no quarrel with either the charge or the verdict.

But Casement's fate was not the point. He would have gone down to history as just another nationalist executed by the colonial power during the long struggle to end that jurisdiction, had it not been for three particular circumstances which lend his case the special resonance of tragedy. First, there was Casement's public record as a distinguished servant of the British Foreign Office, knighted in 1911 for his humanitarian zeal as Consul in the Congo and Brazil in exposing cruelty and exploitation in the rubber industry: a career as distant as can be imagined from the conventional image of the Irish rebel. Then there was the revelation of his private character by the discovery of his homosexual diaries which besmirched equally – but also to a modern eye deepened – both the previously opposed images of the upright diplomat and the heroic patriot. Third, adding a touch of melodrama, there was the mordant irony that the Attorney-General at the time of Casement's arrest should be not merely a leading English opponent of Home Rule for Ireland but one who had himself been widely charged with treason just a few years earlier for encouraging Ulster's armed defiance of the British Government.

To Casement's apologists it was nothing short of grotesque that he should be prosecuted by a man of F.E.'s antecedents. It was Ulster which had set the example of importing guns from Germany: Ulster whose treasonable sabotage of the Home Rule Act had driven Ireland to desperate measures to secure what Parliament had granted but could not deliver. The first question which hangs over F.E.'s conduct of the trial, then, is whether he should not have acknowledged that his own involvement with the other side of the Irish question should in fairness rule him out and therefore have stood aside, leaving the Crown's case to his Solicitor-General or another counsel.

To pose the possibility is to reject it. It was out of the question for F.E. to have stood aside. To have done so would have been virtually to admit that he had behaved improperly before the war, that he and Bonar Law and Carson and the whole Tory party had been guilty of treason, which he utterly denied: it was the Liberal Government, not the Tories, which had betrayed the Crown, the Union and loyal British subjects. He stood by every word he had spoken in support of Ulster, and recognized no comparison at all between his actions and those of a public servant who in time of war gave aid and comfort to the enemy. Then again, even if he had had the sensitivity to think of standing down, it would have been out of character for him either to shirk the responsibility which his office placed on him for fear of the odium of people he despised, or to surrender what was evidently going to be a leading role in a historic drama. Ambition reinforced his need to prove his conscience clear. Besides, he was not going to sit as judge: to act as prosecutor he was not required to be impartial.

Having decided to prosecute, however, he was at pains that his conduct should be punctilious. He was anxious that the trial should take place as quickly as possible, but he was firm in insisting that it should be in public 'lest in after years we should be reproached with having killed him secretly'.[14] He considered the possibility of a military tribunal if that would be much quicker, but decided that a civil trial for treason would make a better impression in neutral countries. F.E. was from the beginning very conscious of the importance of demonstrating to the neutral world that the British jury system still held up even in wartime: so conscious was he of American opinion, indeed, that he actually cabled the full text of his opening speech at the trial to the United States the night before he delivered it, in order to pre-empt the publication of garbled versions. He was also very anxious that Casement should be seen to have on his side every facility of British justice. When all the leading silks in London refused to touch the case, and Casement's solicitor, Gavan Duffy, had to bring over from Dublin his brother-in-law Serjeant A.M. Sullivan (Serjeant was an archaic Irish legal title), F.E. was worried by the disproportion of legal eminence between the two sides and petitioned the Lord Chancellor, Lord Buckmaster, to appoint Sullivan an English K.C. especially for the trial. But Buckmaster dismissed the suggestion.[15]

F.E.'s concern that Casement be seen to have a fair trial needs to be borne in mind in considering the next contentious aspect of the case – F.E.'s offer to Sullivan of Casement's 'black' diaries. Some days before the trial opened F.E. sent a message to Sullivan suggesting that the diaries – which Sullivan knew all about: the police had already shown extracts to the press – might enable Casement's defence to save his life by entering a plea of 'guilty but insane'.[16] The most sinister motives have been read into this action, which has been widely interpreted as the proof of F.E.'s readiness to stoop to any device to see Casement hanged. The argument is that evidence of homosexuality could never have been adduced as evidence of insanity, so F.E., who must have known this, must have had some other purpose in making this disingenuous suggestion. Either he was so anxious to get his guilty verdict that he thought it worth trying any way to fool Sullivan into pleading guilty from the outset; or, more discreditably, he wanted to have the diaries produced as evidence in court so that their contents could then legitimately be published and Casement's character defamed, whether he was found guilty or not.

But the only scrap of evidence for these theories is an interview that Sullivan gave in 1954 to Réné Macoll, when he was eighty-three, recalling that 'Freddie Smith was savage' because he refused to use the diaries to try to plead insane. If any weight is given to this recollection at all, however, it cuts several ways, since the reason he remembers for F.E. wanting him to plead insane is that 'the Government did not want to hang Casement in view of American feeling', while he goes on to give himself credit for refusing to dishonour Casement by using the diaries, although 'I knew it might save his life'. In other words F.E. did not urge them on him from vindictiveness but the reverse, and their irrrelevance to a plea of insanity was not so obvious as has always been asserted. 'I finally decided', Sullivan says, implying that he had given the matter some thought, 'that death was better than besmirching and dishonour.'[17] Though, as he says, 'a perverted diary would not in itself prove insanity', the obsessive nature of the perversion might have been used, perhaps with other evidence, to argue a mind unhinged, and this might reasonably have been what F.E. was thinking of. At any rate, these forty-year-old recollections prove very little. More to the point is the letter which Sullivan wrote F.E. immediately after the trial, in July 1916, in which he thanked him cordially for having put the diaries at his disposal. 'In view of one defence it was right that they should be available for my information.'[18] In the event this line of defence was not used – Sullivan was determined that Casement should not plead guilty – so he did not read them, though his juniors had done so. Sullivan at that time clearly thought it only proper that F.E. should have offered them to him in case he had intended to plead guilty.

Too much has been made of F.E.'s allegedly sinister intent in this episode. It might well have suited the Government had they, on the one hand, been spared the necessity of proving Casement's guilt and, on the other, been given an excuse for not making a martyr of him. If so, there was nothing machiavellian in F.E. furnishing Sullivan with materials that might have helped achieve such a result, nor even in suggesting that such a conclusion would suit the Government if it had suited Sullivan and his client. Inexperienced in English courts he may have been, but Sullivan was a good enough lawyer to be able to make up his own mind in the interest of his client. There is no evidence that F.E. applied any improper pressure to him. The only impropriety would have been if F.E. had, for reasons of Government policy, withheld from Sullivan any documents he might have wanted to use.

As the preparations for the trial were completed, there developed a serious difference of opinion between Sullivan and his client about what defence he should offer. Casement, knowing that the evidence against him was more than enough to hang him anyway, was anxious to embrace his martyrdom unflinchingly, denying nothing but justifying himself in the sacred cause of Ireland, challenging the British to carry out the inevitable sentence if they were so foolish. He was encouraged in this heroic but realistic stance by Bernard Shaw, among others; but he was eventually persuaded by his few faithful friends and two female cousins, against his inclination, to go along with Sullivan's alternative strategy – the lawyer's low road as opposed to the patriot's high road – and contest the interpretation of the Statute of 1351 under which he was charged. Sullivan proposed to argue that the Statute's unpunctuated definition of treason – 'levying war against the King or being adherent to the King's enemies in his realm giving them aid and comfort in the realm or elsewhere' – was not applicable to what Casement had done, since he had done it outside the realm – an argument of extreme semantic intricacy which depended upon whether the words 'or elsewhere' were deemed to govern only the immediately preceding phrase or the whole sentence. On this ingenious, but from Casement's point of view inglorious, technical loophole Sullivan prepared to rest his case when the trial opened on 26 June before the Lord Chief Justice (Rufus Isaacs, transformed in 1913 into Viscount Reading) and two other judges, Avory (F.E.'s judicial antagonist in the Crosland trial) and Horridge (who ten years before, as the Liberal victor of East Manchester, had been the butt of F.E.'s 'firecracker' joke in his maiden speech). F.E., as Attorney-General, led for the Crown with Sir George Cave (Solicitor-General) and three juniors, A.H. Bodkin, Travers Humphreys and G.A.H. Branson. Casement was represented by Sullivan and Artemus Jones, with the assistance of Professor J.H. Morgan of London University, a constitutional lawyer, and an American barrister, Michael Francis Doyle, who was allowed to sit at the solicitors' table, but did not speak.

Sullivan tried to raise his technical objection at the very outset but was told that the proper time for it was after the prosecution had outlined its case. Thereupon F.E. rose to open the Crown's indictment,[19] beginning with a skilful recitation of Casement's years of honourable and apparently devoted service to the Empire, by which he contrived to cast his subsequent treason into darker shadow.

He is an able and cultivated man, versed in affairs and experienced in political matters. He was not, as you will hear, a lifelong rebel against England, and all that England stood for, as others well known in Irish history have been.

On the contrary, F.E. declared with vicious irony, even as he meant the exact opposite, 'it may be remembered even now to his credit' that Casement boasted 'a career which had not been without public distinction', directed 'not to the destruction of the power of this great Empire, but to its consolidation and development'.

In 1900, for his special service in the South African war, Casement had been awarded the Queen's South African medal, and did not refuse it, though it was, as F.E. pointed out, 'a war of which many Irishmen profoundly disapproved'. The court might therefore reasonably assume, he purred, 'that at the age of thirty-six the crimes and delinquencies of this Empire had not engaged his attention, or at least had not conquered his intelligence'.

Still more damaging was the use F.E. made of Casement's conventionally worded, but if taken literally extravagantly loyal, acceptance of his knighthood in 1911. Casement protested, and his contemporary letters bear him out, that he had not wanted the honour, felt it to be a betrayal of Ireland, but had been unable to refuse it without discourtesy, since it had already been announced before Grey informed him of it. Good manners alone compelled him to accept it.[20] Nevertheless the language of his reply – for all his insistence that it was merely 'perfunctory'[21] – gave a hostage to fortune which F.E. was bound to seize and quote against him.

He wrote, this enemy of England, this friend of Germany, this extreme and irreconcilable patriot, in the following terms:-

Dear Sir Edward Grey,
    I find it very hard to choose the words in which to make acknowledgement of the honour done me by the King. I am much moved at the proof of confidence and appreciation of my service on the Putumayo conveyed to me by your letter, wherein you tell me that the King has been graciously pleased upon your recommendation to confer upon me the honour of knighthood. I am, indeed, grateful to you for this signal assurance of your personal esteem and support. I am very deeply sensible of the honour done to me by His Majesty. I would beg that my humble duty might be presented to His Majesty when you may do me the honour to

convey to him my deep appreciation of the honour he has been so
graciously pleased to confer upon me.

I am, dear Sir Edward,
Yours sincerely,
Roger Casement[22]

Armed with this text, F.E. could condemn Casement's subsequent
conduct out of his own mouth.

Gentlemen, I read that letter because you ought to remember that
those were the feelings on the 19th June 1911, towards the country
which he had served for so long, and towards the sovereign of that
country, of a man of mature years – he was, I think, forty-seven
years old at the time that letter was written – a man who had
nineteen years' experience of the methods of government of this
country, in which indeed he had, and not without credit, borne a
part. Such a man writes in terms of gratitude, a little unusual,
perhaps, in their warmth, and in the language almost of a courtier,
to express his pleasure at the title with which his Sovereign had
rewarded his career. And he presents his humble duty to the King,
and he begs that his deep appreciation of the gracious honour may
be expressed to His Majesty. And this was in 1911.

The history of the relations of England and Ireland up to that
date were as well known as they are today. The controversies,
bitter and protracted, often tragic, springing from those relations
were either the commonplaces of contemporary politics, or they
filled the better known pages of our elementary histories. And well
understanding these controversies, fully versed in the wrongs of
which Irishmen were fruitful in complaint, knowing England's
ideals of government well – for at the outposts of Empire he had
carried them out – he sends his humble duty to his Sovereign.

What occurred between 1911 and 1914 to affect and corrupt the
prisoner's mind I cannot tell you, for I do not know.

(Casement would maintain that F.E. knew better than anyone, because
he played a principal part in it. But F.E. pressed on to the crux of his
indictment.)

I only know of one difference. The Sovereign of the country to
whom his humble duty was sent in 1911 was in that year the ruler
of a great and wealthy nation, unequalled in resources, living at
peace, unassailed, and it almost seemed unassailable. In 1914 this
great nation was struggling for its possessions, for its honour, for
its very existence in the most prodigious war which has ever tested

human fortitude. To the Sovereign of that country in its hour of unchallenged greatness he sends his humble duty. It will be my task now to acquaint you with the method in which he carried out his humble duty in times dark enough to test the value of the unsolicited professions he was so forward in making.

The last sentence is unfair; the whole builds too much on a single polite letter. But it is a brilliant example of destructive advocacy. F.E. went on to give a brief account of Casement's activities in Germany, 'moving with freedom about the country, apparently an honoured guest of the German nation'; described his attempt, and ignominious failure, to seduce Irish prisoners of war from their allegiance to form an Irish Brigade to be convoyed to Ireland to fight the British as soon as Germany controlled the seas, ('Gentlemen, to the honour of Ireland let it be recorded that the vast majority of the Irish prisoners treated the rhetoric, and the persuasions, and the corruptions of the prisoner with contempt'); described as best he could the still somewhat mysterious circumstances of Casement's secret return to Ireland, simultaneous with the sinking off the same Kerry coast of a German ship carrying arms and ammunition; and made a sly point of challenging Casement's 'very experienced counsel' to explain, above everything else, why he went to Germany in the first place.

Piously disdaining histrionics, he nevertheless concluded with studied melodrama:

Such, gentlemen, in general outline, is the case which the Crown undertakes to prove and on which the Crown relies. I have, I hope, outlined these facts without heat and without feeling. Neither in my position would be proper, and fortunately neither is required. Rhetoric would be misplaced, for the proved facts are more eloquent than words. The prisoner, blinded by a hatred to this country as malignant in quality as it was sudden in origin, has played a desperate hazard. He has played it and he has lost it. Today the forfeit is claimed.[19]

F.E. left to Cave, Bodkin and Humphreys the interrogation of most of the witnesses whose evidence added the flesh to the story whose skeleton he had outlined – principally seven Irish soldiers, former prisoners of war whom the Germans, with entire indifference to Casement's safety, had allowed to be exchanged, who told of Casement's visits to the camp in which they were collected and his appeals and inducements to them to volunteer to fight for Ireland. He himself only examined the three Irish peasants who told in their soft Kerry accents

how they had found the boat and seen Casement and his two companions on the morning that they had landed. The succession of policemen and intelligence experts who occupied the second day of the trial he
left to his colleagues.

The prosecution case concluded, Sullivan was allowed to submit his
motion to have the indictment quashed. The legal wrangle which
followed filled the remainder of the second day and much of the third,
and takes up some sixty pages of the trial transcript. First Sullivan,
with expert assistance from Professor Morgan, and continual interruptions and clarification from all three judges and F.E., set out his obscure
contention that Edward III's Statute did not cover actions committed
outside the realm; then F.E. replied, with equal learning, at similar
length and similarly interrupted, quoting authorities and precedents
from treason trials over the past 560 years to support the common-sense
view that treason committed overseas was still treason. Eventually,
after briefly conferring, Reading, Avory and Horridge each in turn
rejected the motion. Reading conceded that for the charge of 'adhering
to the King's enemies' to be valid, the words 'or elsewhere' must be
taken to govern both limbs of the vital sentence, but ruled that the
weight of authority was that they did so. This established that Casement
was indeed on trial for his life: if the facts were proved, his crime was
treason. His semantic escape route blocked, Sullivan now had to try to
contest the facts.

Before he did so, however, Casement was allowed to make a dignified
statement refuting certain allegations for himself. Particularly he denied
what one witness had asserted – but only one: it was never part of the
prosecution case – that he had ever advised Irishmen to fight for
Germany ('I have always claimed that he has no right to fight for any
land but Ireland'), and indignantly denied that he had taken any
money for what he did. 'I trust, gentlemen of the jury, I have made that
statement clearly and emphatically enough for all men, even my most
bitter enemies, to comprehend that a man who in the newspapers is said
to be just another Irish traitor, may be a gentleman.' Truly, a very
English Irishman!

Sullivan began his daunting task with an excessively deferential and
flattering tribute to British justice. It was a matter for congratulation,
he said, 'that such a trial as this at such a time is taking place here in the
capital city of your nation in open Court according to the ordinary
processes of law' – in other words, that Casement had not been summarily court-martialled – and went on to plead for sympathy for his
client as 'a stranger within your gates', a foreigner, indeed, from a
country where the people 'speak differently . . . think differently . . . act
differently' from people in England. 'It is your duty', he told the jury,

to demonstrate in the face of the world, whose attention is challenged, and most properly challenged, by this brave proceeding of open trial in such a case, that old virtue for which you have achieved a reputation the world over, the virtue of the accordance of fair play between man and man. That you will endeavour to do so, I know well, for I am deeply and sincerely and gratefully cognisant from my experience in this Court of the kind of spirit of fair play that is accorded to any stranger who ventures within your precincts.

It is difficult to believe that with this Sullivan was not ingratiating himself with the English Bar, rather than representing what Casement wanted said. But then it was not his part to make a political speech, and there was not much he could do with the admitted facts of the case. The defence he attempted was to claim that Casement's projected Irish Brigade was intended to fight only in Ireland; for Ireland, not for Germany (which was true enough); not even directly against England but only against the Ulster Volunteers who were denying Ireland what England's Parliament had granted her; and only after the German war had ended – which glossed over F.E.'s question why he went to Germany and what benefit the Germans were supposed to get in return for their assistance. The judges grew restless as Sullivan's explanation palpably parted company from the evidence until eventually Reading pulled him up, expressing his astonishment that F.E. had not objected earlier. Sullivan endeavoured to continue, but showed increasing signs of strain until, with the words, 'I regret, my lord, to say that I have completely broken down,' he collapsed.

Next day, the fourth of the trial, Artemus Jones made a much more aggressive job of finishing Sullivan's speech, citing passages of Carson's speeches to answer F.E.'s question 'what changed between 1911 and 1914'; but he was still only able to insist that everything that Casement did was done for love of Ireland and not at all to aid and comfort Germany. Nothing either of them said dented F.E.'s case in any way; and now, as was his right in a Crown prosecution even though Sullivan had called no witnesses, F.E. had the last word.

Scornfully he dismissed the raking up of Irish quarrels as irrelevant to the case. Once the war broke out they were subsumed in a higher struggle; Nationalist and Unionist joined in a truce for the duration. 'From the moment that Germany made her tiger spring at the throat of Europe, I say from that moment the past was the past in the eyes of every man who wished well to England.' That, implicitly, was F.E.'s reply to the comparison of his pre-war support for Ulster with Casement's wartime treason. It was the war that made Casement's

activities unforgivable. He repeated his question 'Why did Casement go
to Germany at all?' and pointed out that it had not been answered.

> His case made before you and through the lips of his counsel is that
> he went there to make sure there would be some men who would
> be strong enough to balance the Volunteers in the north of Ireland
> after the war. Where do you think would be the place in which his
> efforts might be most fruitful if that really was the object? Do not
> you think that if that really was his object he might possibly have
> stayed in Ireland where he would still have been in the King's
> dominions? Why go to Germany?

The failure to answer this question suggested strongly that there was
no admissible answer, and he suspected that if the full story of
Casement's dealings with the Germans were known it would make the
task of the defence even more difficult than it was already. As it was he
brushed aside all Sullivan's talk of fighting the Ulster Volunteers as
'belated after-thoughts and sophistries', and all pretence that whatever
Casement was plotting was to unfold only after the war and would not
serve the military interest of Germany as thoroughly specious. The
critical document, of which he made devastating use and on which,
finally, he rested his case, was a code which Casement had been seen to
drop behind him when he was arrested, which had been picked up by a
boy and was now before the court as Exhibit 18: a code by which
Casement was evidently to communicate to the Germans his instructions regarding future assistance.

> This code, on the submission of the Crown, shows that there is no
> substance at all in the case put forward by the defence. This code,
> on the submission of the Crown, shows that the prisoner Casement,
> who went under circumstances unexplained to us, and which I
> cannot explain, to the enemy country while hostilities were in
> progress, who left that country for Ireland while hostilities were in
> progress, had agreed with the Germans to send them messages
> arranging for a landing, asking for another ship, and asking for
> explosives, for cannons and for ammunition.
>   Gentlemen, if you can reconcile those facts with the duty which
> the prisoner owed to this country, if you can reconcile those facts
> with the submissions which have been made to you on behalf
> of the defence, do so. If those facts taken together, his journey
> to Germany, his speeches when in Germany, the inducements
> he held out to these soldiers, the freedom which he there enjoyed,
> the course which he pursued in Ireland, the messages which he

contemplated as likely to take place between himself and the
Germans, satisfy you of his guilt you must give expression to that
view in your verdict.

While he endorsed Sullivan's hope that they would bring fair and
impartial judgment to bear, the Attorney-General nevertheless firmly
pointed out to the jury where their patriotic duty lay.

You have a duty to discharge as serious and in many ways as
testing as the duties which are discharged by any other men
serving the State in these bloody and critical days. If you should
come to the conclusion that the Crown has proved its case, however painful the duty, it is one from which you cannot and you dare
not shrink. I have discharged my responsibility; do you discharge
yours.[19]

Reading, in his summing-up, made the point that Casement's motiva-
tion was irrelevant. If he knew that what he was doing was calculated to
assist the enemy (and that was the inescapable implication of the
enemy's readiness to assist him), then he was guilty of treason, even
though he had, in his own eyes, quite another purpose in view.

The jury was out for fifty-five minutes, during which they sent out to
see again the code on which F.E. had laid such damning emphasis,
before returning the inevitable verdict. Even Casement's most fervent
apologists have never contended that, on the facts and under the law to
which he was, as a British citizen, subject, he could have been anything
but guilty; nor had Casement himself expected any other verdict. The
speech which he was now permitted to make from the dock before
Reading passed sentence was written, he announced, some three weeks
earlier.

Most of it was aimed squarely at F.E. He began with some conventional Nationalist reflections on the oppressive nature of British rule
in Ireland and complaints of the injustice of trying him in England. But
as soon as he turned to the particular circumstances of his own 'treason'
he dragged clearly into the daylight the bitter – to Irish eyes grotesque –
irony that lay just beneath the legal formality of his confrontation with
an English Attorney-General who by his own treasonable obstruction of
Irish aspirations three years earlier had helped provoke and justify the
patriotic response for which he, Casement, was now to be hanged.

The Irish arming in the South, he claimed, had never had any
quarrel with the Ulster Volunteers.

Our movement was not directed against them, but against the
men who misused and misdirected the courage, the sincerity and

the local patriotism of the men of the north of Ireland. On the contrary, we welcomed the coming of the Ulster Volunteers, even while we deprecated the aims and intentions of those Englishmen who sought to pervert to an English party use – to the mean purposes of their own bid for place and power in England – the armed activities of simple Irishmen.

They aimed, he maintained with wonderfully blinkered faith, at 'winning the Ulster Volunteers to the cause of a united Ireland'.

It was not we, the Irish Volunteers who broke the law, but the British party. The Government had permitted the Ulster Volunteers to be armed by Englishmen, to threaten not merely an English party in its hold on office, but to threaten that party through the blood and lives of Irishmen.

It was all, Casement alleged, pure politics.

The battle was to be fought in Ireland in order that the political 'outs' of today should be the 'ins' of tomorrow in Great Britain. A law designed for the benefit of Ireland was to be met, not on the floor of Parliament, where the fight had indeed been won, but on the field of battle much nearer home, where the armies would be composed of Irishmen slaying each other for some English party again.

'Our choice', Casement declared, 'lay in submitting to foreign law-lessness or resisting it, and we did not hesitate to choose.' The Irish Volunteers were formed in self-defence. But while the Government, the Liberal Government which had carried the Home Rule Bill, made no effort to prevent the running of guns into the north, it went to lengths beyond its legal powers to ban their import into the south. In this situation,

Since arms were so necessary to make our organisation a reality . . . it was our bounden duty to get arms before all else . . . If, as the right honourable gentleman, the present Attorney-General asserted in a speech at Manchester, Nationalists would neither fight for Home Rule nor pay for it, it was our duty to show him that we knew how to do both.

So Casement went to the United States to gather money: not, he insisted, American dollars, but in every case, 'whether it came from the purse of a wealthy man or the still readier pocket of the poor man . . . Irish gold'.

The war, he admitted, changed everything. With Home Rule suspended, he saw no reason why Irishmen should join the British army 'in return for a promissory note, payable after death – a scrap of paper that might or might not be redeemed'.

> I felt over there in America that my first duty was to keep Irishmen at home in the only army that could safeguard our national existence. If small nationalities were to be the pawns in this game of embattled giants, I saw no reason why Ireland should shed her blood in any cause but her own, and if that be treason beyond the seas I am not ashamed to avow it or to answer for it here with my life.

Then, abruptly, Casement returned to his previous theme and from the dock threw back the accusation at his prosecutor, sitting a few feet from him.

> The difference between us was that the Unionist champions chose a path they felt would lead to the woolsack; while I went a road I knew must lead to the dock. And the event proves we were both right. The difference between us was that my 'treason' was based on a ruthless sincerity that forced me to attempt in time and season to carry out in action what I said in word – whereas their treason lay in verbal incitements that they knew need never be made good in their bodies. And so, I am prouder to stand here today in the traitor's dock to answer this impeachment than to fill the place of my right honourable accusers.[19]

F.E. smiled sarcastically and was heard to murmur, 'Change places with him? Nothing doing.' Then he stood up and lounged contemptuously out of the court with his hands in his pockets. This graceless insult to a defeated antagonist whose courage he would in other circumstances have admired stands as a more serious blot on his handling of the case than any of the more sinister allegations made against him. It was coarse, it was crude, it was callous, and it was sadly characteristic of F.E. in one of those recurrent fits of boorishness which call in question the claims made for his great generosity of spirit. It is impossible to imagine Churchill behaving with such a lack of magnanimity. By thus stalking out, F.E. missed the more famous part of Casement's speech, the fervent Nationalist peroration which has echoed, like the words of other executed martyrs, through Irish history to this day. He was also absent from the final scene of the drama, a few moments later, when the Lord Chief Justice pronounced the sentence of death.

Against his own inclination, Casement was persuaded to appeal. After a postponement, Sullivan was sufficiently recovered by 17 July to present again before the higher court his argument that his client's offence did not constitute treason within the definition of the Statute; but Mr Justice Darling and four other judges took the same view as Reading and his colleagues, and did not even require F.E. to repeat his counter-argument before dismissing the appeal. Casement still had one last possible resort: an appeal to the House of Lords, which Gavan Duffy was most anxious to try, believing that there was an important point which Sullivan had failed to argue. But here the recurrent irony of the case once more raised its head. By a curious and in this instance most unfortunate provision of the 1907 Criminal Appeal Act, an appeal to the Lords could only be made with the permission of the Attorney-General.

F.E. was once again placed in a position of great delicacy. In order to decide, in his capacity as principal Law Officer of the Crown, whether a further appeal was in the public interest, he was required to act as though he had not – in the same capacity – been a leading protagonist on one side of the case. Even if he could honestly detach himself from the role he had just played as prosecutor, it would be next to impossible for him to be *seen*, in Ireland and in America, to have detached himself. However he faced the problem with his usual flamboyance.

Gavan Duffy cited four considerations in his application for leave to appeal:

1. The public importance of the case from every point of view.
2. The public importance of obtaining a decision from the Highest Tribunal upon the main point of law involved, since it concerns the gravest crime known to law.
3. The difficulty of interpreting an ancient statute by recondite investigations into the meaning of dicta by legal commentators of other ages.
4. The need, upon the highest ground, of demonstrating to the prisoner's fellow-countrymen and to the world that the prisoner has had the advantage of every possible recourse open to him at law.[23]

The fourth is the ground on which one would expect F.E. to have been most moved, conscious as he had been from the outset of American opinion. Be that as it may, he considered the matter for forty-eight hours and then called in Cave, Humphreys, Bodkin and Branson to give him their views. Why, if he had wanted advice, he should have sought it from the very four lawyers who were as biased as he was is not clear. However, it turned out that he wanted, not their advice, but their concurrence with the decision which he had already taken, quite properly, alone. After each of them had in turn stated his opinion that, eight judges having so far agreed on the case, there was no justification for prolonging it any further, Cave asked if they might hear F.E.'s view. Coolly he told them.

> My clerk has already received my refusal in writing, which would have gone out whatever your views had been. I am gratified to know that you all agree, but I was not going to have it said in the House of Commons that any of you were responsible for the decision. I can now say, as I always intended to say, that the decision was mine alone, but I shall add that having consulted you afterwards you were all of the same mind.[24]

'Loyal to his juniors, as through life he was loyal to his friends,' Humphreys concluded of this episode. 'A very great man.'[25]

This characteristic touch of showmanship apart, there has been no serious legal criticism of F.E.'s decision, though there is a story that he later told Professor Morgan that, had the Law Lords quashed the conviction on a technicality, the Government might have fallen.[26] Were this most improbable consideration a factor, however, it would have been a quite legitimate ground for denying leave to appeal, since the 'public interest' was the criterion informing his decision, and the public interest in wartime arguably demanded a quick resolution, and certainly not a political crisis. More questionable is a line in F.E.'s own later account of the trial, which implies that he could not easily grant leave, since 'I had throughout argued that there was no substance in the point raised by the defence.'[27] The consistency of his own position was the last thing he should have been concerned for in his essentially anomalous situation. But this was written so much later that little importance should be attached to it.

Duffy was furious at F.E.'s refusal. In a statement published in *The Times* on 28 July he protested both at the provision in the law which left such a decision with the leading prosecuting counsel and at the exercise of his prerogative by F.E. of all people, 'whose antecedents in Ulster are well-remembered'.[28] But when Morgan and Jones went to see F.E. to plead with him to reverse his decision, he curtly rejected their objection as 'trivial'. At this point, Morgan sought the opinion of the legal historian Professor Holdworth, whose reputation, he told F.E., 'stands higher than that of any other lawyer in such matters', and who supported him at least to the extent of agreeing that the question was not trivial but 'of great doubt and considerable perplexity'. Having made his decision, however, F.E. was not to be moved, reputedly dismissing the Professor with the superbly crushing compliment, 'I am aware of the high attainments of Mr Holdsworth, since he was runner-up to me when I was awarded the Vinerian Law Scholarship at Oxford.'[29]

With this, Casement was doomed unless the Cabinet decided to advise the King to exercise the royal prerogative in favour of life imprisonment. There were strong political reasons, taking into account American opinion, for showing mercy, and an influential group of Ministers led by Grey and Lansdowne (the Foreign Secretary and his last Tory predecessor in that office) urged this course on an initially sympathetic Prime Minister. Appeals for clemency, including a petition organized by Sir Arthur Conan Doyle and signed by Galsworthy, Chesterton, Arnold Bennett and other Liberal *literati*, flowed in, reinforcing the claims of humanity with that of prudence, and even justice, since it could now be shown that Casement had come to Ireland to try to *stop* the Easter Rising. The scale was finally tipped against him by the discovery among his papers of an agreement with the Germans by which the Irish Brigade, contrary to Casement's insistence at his trial, could have been used outside Ireland to support a revolt against British rule in Egypt. Until this paper came to light, however, the Cabinet was wavering. It was against this background that the campaign to blacken Casement's character by the calculated distribution of his diaries, already begun by the police and Intelligence authorities before the trial, was stepped up.[30]

A greater furore has raged over this admittedly unsavoury campaign than over any other aspect of the trial. Taken in context, however, as a fairly minor piece of black propaganda in the middle of a desperate war in which thousands were dying daily on the Western Front and whose outcome might yet turn on American entry, it must be said that its wickedness has been greatly exaggerated by Irish apologists eager to believe and broadcast anything, including the allegation of forgery, to discredit the British Establishment. The Irish have proved not backward in the black art themselves. For no better reason than that he was Casement's official prosecutor, F.E. has been cast as the leading villain in this campaign, though there is once again *no good evidence at all* to connect him with it.

It is the entirely unsupported assumption of Alfred Noyes, for instance, in *The Accusing Ghost, or Justice for Casement* (published in 1957) that F.E. 'hated Casement as his political enemy' and was therefore determined to see him hang – as though F.E. was in the habit of hating his political enemies! To Noyes, F.E. had 'appointed himself prosecutor' and by refusing leave to appeal had 'personally pronounced sentence of death upon a man more chivalrous than himself'; more, he had actually threatened to resign if the traitor were not executed (a boast put into F.E.'s mouth by the *Boston Post* in 1918). Believing also the fantastic story, now totally discredited, that the diaries were not even authentic, but forged, Noyes professed to believe F.E. to be the moving spirit behind the plot, on the unsubstantiated word of Michael Doyle.[31] Other writers have alleged that F.E. showed the diaries freely around the clubs like dirty postcards.[32] Yet what is this serious charge based on? Upon a single story, told by an old friend of Casement, Bulwer Hobson, in 1956, to the effect that during the trial F.E. showed the diary to the Irish Attorney-General, the Nationalist M.P. James O'Connor. Hobson claimed to have had the story from O'Connor in 1922.

> At the end of the first day after he had left the court F.E. Smith (who he hardly knew) came running down the corridor after him calling out, 'Here, O'Connor, I want to show you something'. He then handed O'Connor a photostat of a page of the indecent diary. O'Connor had no political sympathy with Casement but he was shocked and disgusted at the impropriety of the Attorney-General of England peddling dirty stories in this way about a man he was prosecuting on a charge of treason.[33]

Discounting the hostile gloss – forty years after the event – of the last sentence, all that this amounts to is that F.E. showed parts of the diary to his opposite number, the Irish Attorney-General, a fellow member of the Government, a fellow Law Officer, during the trial, in much the same way he had made it available to Sullivan for the defence. This is the slenderest evidence on which to associate F.E. with the alleged hawking of the diaries around the clubs.

There is no evidence at all that he showed them to anyone else. The only other piece of contemporary evidence, which is as hard and unimpeachable as the O'Connor story is dubious, is a letter from F.E. to Grey on 29 June, the last day of the trial, which points diametrically the other way.

> I am told that the FO is photographing or proposes to photograph portions of Casement's diary with a view to showing them to various persons so as to influence opinion.
>
> It is I think rather a ghoulish proposal & without expressing a final opinion on it I should be glad if you would see me before sanctioning it.[34]

Grey replied that he had not heard of such a proposal, did not approve it and certainly would not sanction it without the authorization of the Cabinet, which he considered improbable. It is now known that agents within the Foreign Office – Lord Hardinge (Permanent Under-Secretary) and Lord Newton (Assistant Under-Secretary) – were indeed conveying copies of the diary to Sir Cecil Spring-Rice in Washington for circulation to the editors of Irish and Catholic newspapers, without Grey's knowledge, indeed in defiance of his instructions.[35] The most machiavellian interpretation of F.E.'s note, suggested by B.L. Reid, is that he was trying to keep the Foreign Office out of the business which he knew was already being undertaken by Scotland Yard and M.I.5; but this is contradicted by the fact that it was the Foreign Office that was doing it.[35] Alternatively, the letter can be dismissed as a simple blind, written deliberately to give F.E. an alibi if ever the truth came out. Such explanations merely impose on the facts ready-made pre-judgments, instead of drawing an interpretation from the evidence. By this method anything can be suggested, and nothing gainsaid. It must be repeated, there is *no* good evidence to connect F.E. with the circulation of the diaries in 1916 at all, and therefore no reason to stand on its head the one strong piece of evidence to the contrary.

Those, such as Paul Johnson writing in the *New Statesman* in 1959, who are determined to accuse F.E. of at the very least gossiping indiscreetly about Casement have been able to fix on only one other shred of evidence, a passage in the diary of Colonel Repington, the military correspondent of *The Times*, describing a dinner party at the house of the actress Maxine Elliott in Bushey Heath on 17 May, the day the magistrates' preliminary hearing of the case ended. The rest of the company comprised F.E., the Duke of Rutland, the actor Sir Forbes Robertson and two other ladies. Repington recorded:

> FE was in great form . . . He had succeeded today in getting Sir Roger Casement sent for trial. He said that he had heard that I knew Casement and did I think him normal? I said that I had only met him once in Brussels before he went off to the Congo, and that he was then apparently normal and very intelligent. He thought Casement would certainly be convicted, but that whether the sentence would take its course would depend upon the Executive.[36]

Johnson thinks this very damaging, and thinks that F.E. would have been bound to deny it when Repington published his book in 1920, if he had been able to. But why should he have denied it? There is no indication that he discussed the case publicly or pruriently over the dinner table – merely that he asked his opinion of Casement of one who knew him (suggesting that the possibility of his pleading insanity was being seriously canvassed), and privately expressed his confidence, as State Prosecutor, that he would get his conviction, while explicitly recognizing that there might be a case for sparing his life. Even allowing for the fact that Repington was a notoriously indiscreet journalist, this scarcely justified Johnson's sweeping claim that F.E. 'used Casement as a society talking point' even once, let alone regularly.[37]

In July the question of clemency came before the Cabinet. As the junior member of that body (one peculiarly interested in the case, admittedly, but for that very reason probably disqualified from a leading part in what was not a legal discussion) F.E. must naturally bear his share of the responsibility for what had evidently become Government policy. The Cabinet was advised on the nature and use of the diaries by the Home Office Legal Adviser, Sir Ernley Blackwell, who counselled most succinctly and explicitly, 'So far as I can judge, it would be far wiser from every point of view to allow the law to take its course, and by judicious means to use these diaries to prevent Casement attaining martyrdom.' The Cabinet by this time clearly knew what was going on: the newspapers were full of hints about Casement's 'depraved' morals and 'degenerate' character. But there were still those who wanted to use the diaries, not as a way of stifling the outcry against Casement's execution but, on the contrary, as a ground for sparing him; and Blackwell's memorandum indicates that F.E. was one of these. Giving his judgment that the diary was not only genuine but accurate, Blackwell went on:

> The point is worth noting, for the Attorney-General had given Sir
> E. Grey the impression that Casement's own account of the fre-
> quency of his performances was incredible and of itself suggested
> that he was labouring under hallucination in this respect. I think
> this idea may be dismissed.[38]

F.E., the implication is, was still inclined – as he had been when offering them to Sullivan – to see the diaries as evidence of insanity. The indications accumulate that far from being, as he has been presented even by B.L. Reid, the member of the Government most determined to see Casement hanged, he was actually one of those most conscious of the effect of his death on neutral opinion and therefore most anxious to evade the necessity if reasonable grounds could be discovered.

Of course, clemency on the ground of insanity would still require some leaking of the evidence to the press, in order to appease the public expectation of the traitor's execution, and this would inevitably have had the effect of preventing Casement's canonization as a holy patriot suffering for Mother Ireland. This interpretation of F.E.'s attitude does not dissociate him from the deliberate dissemination of the diaries by the British Government. But it deserves to be repeated that this was not really so terrible a weapon of war as some politically motivated expressions of horror have claimed. 'It is perfectly obvious', Lord Newton minuted,

> that we shall have to face a huge pro-Casement propaganda, and unless we are prepared to make some use of the material in our possession it will be almost impossible to combat it successfully. Apart from political considerations, it should be borne in mind that large numbers of influential persons in the States and elsewhere honestly believe Casement to be a misguided hero, and it seems only reasonable that they should be enlightened as to his real character.[39]

That a promiscuous homosexual with an obsessive interest in boys' genitals could not be simultaneously a hero seemed in 1916 a matter of simple fact. Within Britain, the Archbishop of Canterbury and the Bishop of Durham were two who withdrew their pleas for Casement on being shown the diaries. The British Government cannot very seriously be blamed, in the middle of a war, for employing their destructive potential discreetly to check the growth of a pro-Casement agitation in the United States as well.

Three further points may perhaps be mentioned which, though minor in themselves, each add their mite against the probability of F.E. having behaved with the scurrilous lack of decency he is accused of. First, when Simon and Haldane were first told of the use the police and Intelligence authorities were making of Casement's diaries before the trial opened, they were shocked and immediately talked of action for contempt of court.[40] F.E. would certainly have had the same lawyer's instinct against anything that might have prejudiced his case. Then there is Sullivan's second letter to F.E., after the trial, in which he went out of his way to praise 'the high plane of thought on which you placed all controversy' and F.E.'s 'profound manifestation of the desire to be chivalrous and generous to the weaker side', which he was glad to find was appreciated in Dublin.[41] This may be humbug congratulating humbug, but it is surely conclusive against any blatant impropriety on F.E.'s part.

Third, on the day after Casement's execution *The Times*, while endorsing the decision to let the sentence take its course, lodged a strongly worded protest against the 'irrelevant, improper and un-

English' campaign of inspired innuendo which had followed him to the gallows. A few days later Professor Morgan wrote to F.E. remarking on the fact that this outspoken criticism of the Government had not been officially contradicted; but he did so only out of a sense of personal justification, since F.E. had told him only a few days earlier that there was 'not a word of truth' in the complaints. He made no suggestion that F.E. was himself especially implicated, but assured him that he wrote 'merely as a public man who is anxious for the good name of his country . . . I do not suppose that anything can now be done, and this letter needs no answer'.[42] This is not the letter of a man with a grievance, even one he cannot spell out, against the recipient, but rather an expression of concern to a highly placed Minister whom he expected to share his disquiet.

The widespread impression of F.E. as the man who, above all, hawked Casement's diaries around London is very largely the much later invention of those who hated him *ex officio* as Casement's prosecutor and either judged him capable of any unscrupulousness or were themselves unscrupulous enough to think that any lie would be believed of him. But it must also owe some of its currency to the fact that F.E. did, more than five years later, in February 1922, show the original diary, at their request and in all solemnity, to Michael Collins and Eamonn Duggan, two of the leaders of the Sinn Fein delegation to the successful negotiations for an Irish settlement the previous autumn. During these negotiations, Collins and F.E. had struck up a relationship of trust and mutual admiration, both within the Conference and outside. Naturally the question of Casement and his notorious diary came up. It seems that Collins remained unconvinced of its genuineness. F.E. offered to satisfy him. On Collins's next visit to London, his diary records an afternoon call at F.E.'s house ('order for inspecting Diary'), followed a few hours later by the entry, '5.30. House of Lords to see Casement Diary'.[43] Clearly there was no hawking around here: F.E. had to place an order for the diary to be made available. Somewhat later, Duggan recorded the occasion:

> Michael Collins and I saw the Casement Diary by arrangement with Birkenhead. We read it. I did not know Casement's handwriting. Collins did. He said it was his . . . It was disgusting . . . Collins was satisfied that it was Casement's. So was Birkenhead.[44]

If F.E. was in this way able to satisfy a leading Irishman that the British Government had not added a most scandalous act of forgery to their accumulated crimes, he was surely right, in the interests of Anglo-Irish relations, to do so.

There is just one further episode in F.E.'s connection with the Casement saga. In 1925 the journalist Peter Singleton-Gates obtained copies of the diaries and attempted to publish them. According to Duggan F.E., who was then Secretary of State for India, intervened with the publishers 'at the request of certain people here who didn't wish the memory of Casement or anyone associated with 1916 reviled', and succeeded in having the book stopped.[44] He may well have intervened also with the Home Secretary, Sir William Joynson-Hicks, whose invoking of the Official Secrets Act was probably the decisive consideration. It does not really matter. It may be said that by this time the diaries had done their damage, that F.E. had now no interest in their publication, that his attitude in 1925 proves nothing about his attitude nine years earlier. It is nevertheless one more example of him acting perfectly honourably and responsibly, to set against the mountain of entirely unfounded allegations on the other side.

There is no evidence of any serious impropriety in F.E.'s conduct of the Casement case from first to last. Collectively, he was a junior member of the Cabinet which sanctioned the leaking of the diaries to counter neutral sympathy for a convicted traitor. Personally, he sent his opening speech for the prosecution to the United States before he had delivered it, and he rudely walked out of court during Casement's speech from the dock. Nothing more heinous than this can be recorded against him.

16

The Politics of War – and Peace, 1915–18

Very fully occupied as he was with his legal duties, F.E. played only a minor role in the politics of the war. Even after he joined the Asquith Coalition Cabinet in November 1915, he was never a member of the inner circle directing operations; nor, despite his friendship with several of the principals, was he at all closely involved in the tortuous power struggle which eventually resulted in the replacement of Asquith by Lloyd George at the end of 1916. The war revealed the extent to which F.E.'s rapid rise in the Tory party had reflected and depended upon his reputation as a parliamentary debater and popular orator. The party truce practically abolished the need for these qualities. The political battle now took place indoors, between a couple of dozen individuals around committee tables at which F.E. did not have the seniority to claim a hearing. His swashbuckling image told against him; the existence of a more judicious side to his nature which gradually emerged to general admiration in the Lloyd George Cabinet was not yet appreciated. Within the Tory party, power was now more than ever concentrated in the hands of a few top magnates of established position: Curzon, Austen Chamberlain, Robert Cecil, Balfour, Long. F.E. was still devoted to Bonar Law, who repaid him by insisting on him being given office; but with the leadership as a whole his standing was seriously compromised by his continued identification with Churchill and, to a lesser extent, Lloyd George.

He was able to put this association to some use in the summer of 1915 when, though still outside the Cabinet as Solicitor-General, he adopted his familiar go-between role on the dominating question of conscription. This was the major ideological divide of the war. Broadly speaking the Liberals – Asquith and his most trusted colleagues Grey, Simon, Runciman, McKenna – adhered to the principle of voluntary recruitment to the forces, disdaining to stoop to Prussian methods to defeat

Prussianism, while the Tories increasingly demanded compulsion, to root out shirkers and symbolize the nation's absolute commitment to the struggle. But it was not so simple. Lloyd George and Churchill, both as determined as any Tory on the vigorous prosecution of the war, were on the side of compulsion: Kitchener, on the other hand, the architect of the great volunteer army, was still opposed to it, and so long as the Secretary of State for War was of opinion that the voluntary system could furnish enough, and better, men to fill the ranks, the conscriptionists had an uphill battle.

One might expect F.E., as a strong believer in the State and a proponent of National Service before the war, to be an unhesitating conscriptionist; by the time he came back from France, in fact, he was, but he had always insisted that compulsion could only be imposed by popular consent, and he seems to have been convinced in 1914 that public opinion was not yet ready. In his post-war writings he repeatedly praised both Asquith and Kitchener for their wisdom in not trying to force the pace too soon. F.E.'s admiration for Kitchener at this time came close to hero-worship, and he had established, during his time at the Press Bureau, a surprising friendship with him. If his own account can be believed, F.E. never came home on leave from France without dining with him, and after he became a Minister 'the intimacy between us continuously strengthened'.[1] Certainly Kitchener, often at sea in the alien world of politics, found F.E. an unusually sympathetic and helpful interpreter in Cabinet. More than any of his other colleagues, then, save Asquith himself, F.E. had the ear of the old soldier. As soon as he was persuaded that the time for compulsion had come, he set himself, and was deliberately used by Lloyd George and the conscriptionist Tories, to win Kitchener over. On 24 August F.E. reported back to Lloyd George the success of his efforts.

> I hear on unimpeachable authority that K is prepared to move within a reasonable time (a month or so) and that both the PM and Arthur Henderson have told him that if he comes to the Cabinet with the statement that the national safety requires it they will neither oppose him.
>   His confidential secretary gave me this information fresh from an interview with him in which considerations with which you are familiar were placed before K at my special instance.[2]

From the other side Margot Asquith desperately urged Kitchener to stand firm against 'Carson, F.E. Smith, Winston & Ll. George' by threatening to resign if the Cabinet insisted on conscription.[3] But the

Tory demand for compulsion was irresistible. Lord Derby's compromise scheme by which men 'attested' their willingness to serve when required failed to produce enough volunteers. By the winter of 1915–16 Kitchener had come down for compulsion and Asquith was obliged, by reluctant stages, to accept it. Only Simon resigned, in a miscalculated gesture of Liberal principle which increased F.E.'s contempt for him. 'It can hardly be supposed', he wrote maliciously, much later, 'that Sir John Simon expected to leave the Cabinet alone.'[4] But he did. The country did not rise in revolt, and though F.E. later liked to give Asquith the credit for giving way at just the strategic moment which would enable compulsion to be carried by public acclaim,[5] the outcome was in reality a clear victory for the Tories (and Lloyd George) from which Asquith's authority never recovered.

F.E.'s personal standing, however, did not much benefit from his contribution to this victory. His name was too insistently linked with Winston's as an ambitious mischief-maker. To his credit, he took no steps to distance himself from his friend at this nadir of his fortunes. On the contrary, in a rare public speech delivered to the Constitutional Association just two days after his promotion to the Cabinet he went out of his way to defend Winston's record on the Dardanelles, going into considerable detail to spread the responsibility for the failure of the combined operation from the Admiralty on to the whole Government, the implication of which can scarcely have been well received by those of F.E.'s new colleagues who preferred to make Churchill the scapegoat for the whole fiasco.

In fact, their friendship only deepened during 1915. The reversal in their fortunes in these few months was ironic. At the beginning of the year F.E. was fretting in France while Winston was still ruler of the Navy; now Winston went off, defeated, to command a battalion at the front just as F.E. was raised to the Cabinet. (Their common friend Paddy Goulding urged Winston not to go. 'To have you and Fred in the Cabinet together is what you both have desired and now there is a chance of its fulfilment. Please let nothing interfere with this.')[6] But Winston was determined not to remain any longer in a Cabinet in which he retained no influence, and resigned to seek honour in uniform instead, hoping to reflate the bubble of his shattered reputation even in the cannon's mouth. While he was away, F.E. was his one important friend in England who sustained him in his bitter exile with letters of encouragement and gossip, visits (bearing, in his turn, brandy and cigars) and his 'active partnership' at home. Clementine, who had not always appreciated F.E. in the past, now wrote generously to Winston that he was, after all, his 'true & faithful friend'.[7]

F.E. first tried to cross over to see Churchill on 19 December, when

Winston was feeling more rejected than ever as a result of Asquith's craven reversal, for fear of political criticism, of his earlier willingness to see him given command of a brigade, which French – now himself replaced by Haig – had approved. 'It is becoming important for me to see you,' Winston wrote on the 18th, 'and I trust you will not fail me. I do not know where I shall be; but a rendez-vous can easily be arranged without exposing your uninsured person to danger.'[8] In the event, the transport arrangements broke down ('a combination of tragic mishaps') and F.E. was unable to come. But he promised faithfully to fly over early in January.

> I have made friends with a great flying man and we will have a long talk then . . . I know all that has happened to you & even if you have to take a battalion at first have no doubts that sufficient pressure can be applied from here to prevent Haig (if he wants to) from leaving you in a backwater . . . You may absolutely rely on seeing me in a fortnight or so and I will make friends with Haig in your interest. BL's [Bonar Law's] star is much in the ascendant & he continues most friendly.

This last bit of information, though reassuring to F.E., can have given little comfort to Churchill. One measure of Law's increasing authority was the end of the Dardanelles adventure, from which he had been the first advocate of withdrawal. 'We fought (Curzon, Selborne, Lansdowne & myself) for the Dardanelles as long as possible,' F.E. reported, '& only gave up when every single soldier abandoned us including K.'[9]

F.E. did not make it to France quite so early in January as he hoped. The conscription question finally came to a head and Simon made his gesture and resigned. F.E. gave Winston the inside story in confused syntax which made very clear his true estimate of his old Wadham 'chum', and went on to reveal Tory hopes of a khaki election to rub in the fainthearts' defeat.

> You will have heard all about our crisis in the papers and there is little to add. I think that our friend Sliman has done himself in. It was a bold & ambitious push & while soapy in form in substance very malicious to the PM who & whose women I am told much resent his speech & contrast its tone unfavourably with that of yours.
>
> It is not yet quite certain that we shall not force an election though the odds are considerably against it . . . It is just conceivable that old Asquith might be gingered up, if enough formidableness developed, to get rid at once (as we easily cd) of the

Pringles & Hogges & Simons. The country is overwhelmingly with us & indeed the Bill has a little restored the prestige of the Government.[10]

Sympathetically and in very much the tone of one writing to keep another's spirits up, F.E. asked his friend to keep him informed how he was getting on and how he liked his fellow-officers. In his next letter words of encouragement almost outweighed the war news.

My dear Winston,

Thanks so much for your letter. I am very busy this week with this compulsory Bill [F.E. had been given the job of piloting the Conscription Bill through Committee] but I will make an effort to come & see you on Friday week if this suits your arrangements . . .

The tonnage question is growing more & more serious. We spent about 1½ hours over it at cabinet today. We seem safe at Salonika now . . .

How sad that your battalion is so young. Tell me more about them. Are any of them nice? What sort of 2nd in command & adjutant have you? I hope you will not be long with them but want you to be happy while you are. I expect you get lonely & hipped at times but I shall be comparatively happy when you get your Brigade for I feel sure that you will not end there when your foot is once on the ladder . . . I am so glad you get on well with your Brigade & Divisional people. I shd like to meet them.

If you write any of your able memoranda send me one & I will circulate it over my august initials to the cabinet.

Goodbye & take as much care of yourself as circumstances allow.

Yours affectionately
F.[11]

A little over a week later, on 28 January, Lloyd George, Bonar Law and F.E. all crossed over to France together, and F.E. went forward alone from St Omer to Churchill's H.Q. at Ploegsteert where there took place one of the most notorious, but in reality ludicrous, incidents of his career. Incautiously, perhaps a little pretentiously – though he *had* recently been promoted to Colonel – he went in uniform; and with typical carelessness of petty regulations which he never imagined applied to him, he omitted to obtain the necessary pass to travel to the forward zone. This oversight should not have mattered. It had been spotted at St Omer and corrected: a telegram was sent on to Ploegsteert instructing the relevant authority there to issue the Attorney-General with the required pass. Someone, however – presumably an officer or a group who had suffered from F.E.'s tongue when he was at G.H.Q. a year earlier and now saw an irresistible opportunity to get back at him – altered the telegram: the instruction as it reached Ploegsteert was to place F.E. under close arrest and return him immediately to St Omer.

While this practical joke was being hatched, its unsuspecting victim was dining happily with Winston in the Hospice where he was to spend the night. 'We had a jolly good meal,' the young officer who supplied Churchill's biographer with the true story of the doctored telegram later recalled, 'and then sat for hours yarning away. Winston and FE had consumed a considerable amount of brandy: Winston seemed all right, but FE was pretty shot when we went to bed.'[12] He was clearly in no state to resist when, at four o'clock in the morning, he was rudely awakened and hauled back to the Hotel du Commerce in St Omer, under arrest. Next morning, however, he was livid. He woke to find two military policemen outside his door who calmly told him that if he tried to leave he would be shot. His furious protests that he was Sir Frederick Smith, His Majesty's Attorney-General and a member of the Cabinet did not impress the Adjutant-General, Sir Nevil Macready. 'If you are a civilian,' he demanded, 'why are you here in uniform? If you are a soldier, why don't you obey regulations?' Without the necessary pass and ignorant of the trick that had been played on him, F.E. was helpless.

Churchill, when he learned what had happened, was incredulous and almost as angry as F.E., interpreting the spiteful pettiness of the military authorities as a further slight upon himself. He wrote at once to Bonar Law in St Omer.

My dear Bonar,
    The arrest of FE in present circumstances seems to be a vy serious event. I received him here in virtue of a telegram from the ADC to the C in C transmitted to me through the HQ of the IXth Division in wh I am serving. Of this I enclose a copy. The act of placing a Cabinet Minister charged with the ultimate appeal in all Court Martial cases in arrest and removing him in conditions of indignity is one wh cannot & will not end here in France. It will become public knowledge and will draw with it many other things. I am of course resolved to take any steps wh the law allows. And I rely on you to give the subject your most earnest & immediate attention as his colleague & friend. You shd show this to Lloyd George.
                                        Yours very sincerely,
                                        Winston S.C.[13]

Churchill was due to meet Law and Lloyd George at Hazebrouck the next morning. All three soon caught up with F.E., now released but still furious, at Max Aitken's Canadian H.Q. in St Omer, 'pacing up and down like a caged lion, in a stinking temper'. Winston, reassured himself by his former colleagues' support, calmed him down and got him to tell the whole story, which he doubtless did with his usual colourful exaggeration. 'Winston sat down in a chair and roared with laughter.' Lloyd George and Law then took F.E., still smouldering, with them to lunch with Haig, during the course of which the incident was quietly closed.[12] F.E., Haig wrote in his diary, 'did himself very well in the way of liquor and ended up with several glasses of old brandy . . . He apologised for having bothered me, and they all agreed it was best to leave the matter as it stood.'[14]

F.E. was in the wrong, of course, and the alteration of the telegram does not alter that. Nevertheless the impulse to alter it, the evident relish with which the authorities from Macready downwards carried out the false instruction, and the glee with which the story was repeated in military circles for years afterwards add up to a striking illustration of the poisoned relations that existed between soldiers and politicians in the First World War. F.E. was a particularly satisfactory politician to humiliate, and he undoubtedly brought his treatment upon himself. Yet the politicians were entitled to feel alarmed at the petty jealousy and lack of proportion which the episode displayed in the military mind. As Churchill wrote to Clementine a couple of days afterwards, 'Some of these potentates get more upset about an "incident" of this kind than about sending 1000 men to their deaths.'[15]

Churchill himself was much heartened by his conversations with Law and Lloyd George, as well as with F.E. He now saw his return to office, and the successful prosecution of the war, as being dependent on the supersession of Asquith. 'The group I want to work with & form into an effective Government instrument', he wrote to Clementine, 'is LG: FE: BL: Carson: & Curzon. Keep that steadily in mind. It is the alternative Government when "wait & see" is over.'[16] From now on Winston was waiting impatiently for Asquith to fall and looking anxiously for the right moment to come home and lead the opposition. In this respect, however, F.E. gave him little encouragement. 'The Government is not popular but indispensable,' he wrote on 25 February, '& I think that the PM is firmer in the saddle than ever.' He thought it would be useful if Winston could come home on leave soon – 'I am sure it is a good thing to turn up at the proper intervals & see people' – but his advocacy was rather concerned with getting him his coveted Brigade than with preparing the ground for his political return.[17]

In March Churchill did come home, but only made himself ridiculous with a wild attack on the conduct of the Admiralty since he had left it, an attack which amply confirmed his enemies' estimate of his judgment and embarrassed his few friends. He returned to France unrepentant, still convinced that the crisis of Asquith's Government was at hand and that Lloyd George would need him as a Liberal colleague in a new administration that was bound to be predominantly Tory. Early in April he wrote to F.E.,

I have a feeling that B.L. and L.G. have a supreme chance now, if they have the resolution to act. It does not seem to me material whether B.L. is first [i.e. Prime Minister] or L.G. War [War Office] or *vice versa*. Either place wd afford the basis of an effective war organisation – compared to wh nothing matters. Munitions will seem to be the easiest opening for me, tho of course you know my wishes, if they are attainable.

The party of the future might be formed. I am sorry the crisis comes now – if it does; but in that case it is to you I must look and do look with entire confidence that you will set my affairs first in yr thoughts. Burn this wh is for your secret eye alone.[18]

F.E., however, did not see the party of the future emerging just yet and was still, in Winston's best interests, concerned that he should stay out of the way in France – as was Clementine. In a letter which must have crossed with Winston's he wrote in evident haste to elaborate a previous letter.

My dear Winston,
When I wrote it seemed that the Tories *might* be driven to form a government which would have left you in a ridiculous position if you had resigned & for a time been compelled to support them.

At present all is *most uncertain* but I am sure that you should not commit yourself until things have been cleared up one way or another which will be in 10 days. Shall I in the meantime try & make sure of your Brigade? I think I can.
Yours,
Fred[19]

The truth is that while Winston was relying (as he told Clemmie) on F.E.'s 'active partisanship' to restore his fortunes, F.E.'s political loyalty to his friend was becoming seriously strained, since he by no means shared Winston's contempt for the existing administration. He was becoming, Clementine warned her husband in January, 'an absolute mandarin & is enamoured of the Government & all its machinery'.[20]

This was perhaps natural in one who was at last tasting the sweet fruits of office which his friend had enjoyed for the previous ten years. It was also characteristic of F.E.'s habitual loyalty to any institution of which he was a member. The filial devotion – 'canine' devotion in Winston's phrase – which he had given in turn to Wadham, Gray's Inn and the Northern Circuit, he now gave whole-heartedly to the Asquith Government and specifically to Asquith himself, the butt of his severest pre-war censure but now the captain of his team, whom he was proud to serve. Not that he was complacent about the progress of the war. Far from it: he was becoming increasingly disillusioned and pessimistic. 'Everybody has been wrong about everything,' he told Repington in May – soldiers, sailors, politicians and financiers equally. But 'for the last six months the soldiers had been running the war' and it was on the soldiers that his criticism was concentrated. From his initial reverence for Kitchener and willingness to give the War Office whatever it wanted, he had come full circle. He foresaw – correctly – only further slaughter from Haig's forthcoming offensive on the Somme ('he thought we should lose 300,000 men and do little good') but thought under-mining the Prime Minister the wrong way to go about putting a civilian brake on the military.[21] Northcliffe's press attacks on the Government he considered 'criminal'.[22]

It was as a loyal member of the Government, therefore, not as a dissident, that he agreed in late July to circulate to the Cabinet over his own initials a memorandum by Churchill challenging the whole strategy of the Somme offensive, which by then had already been going on for a month with no result. He carefully reserved his own position with a covering note stating that he thought the Cabinet should see Winston's critique even though he was himself 'by no means wholly in agreement with his standpoint, thinking, as I do, that he underestimates the importance of our offensive as a contribution to the general strategic situation'.[23] His disclaimer did him little good, however: he was widely assumed – by Sir Maurice Hankey, by Repington, by H.A. Gwynne, by the British Embassy in Paris – to be plotting, either with Winston alone or with Lloyd George and French as well, against not only Haig but also Asquith. But because the former suspicion had some foundation – F.E. told Repington in October that it would be better to bring back French[24] – it did not mean that there was any ground for believing the latter. The revolt was indeed mustering which would topple Asquith, but F.E. played no part in it.

His contemporaries may be forgiven for misunderstanding F.E.'s position, for it is still a puzzle to the historian to find him, in the developing crisis of 1916, separated by a stubborn divide of principle from those who were usually by policy and temperament alike his friends and allies – from Churchill, from Lloyd George, from Carson, from Aitken, even in the end from his leader Bonar Law, all of whom were gradually drawing together, despite deep mutual differences, in the conviction that the effective prosecution of the war depended upon the replacement of Asquith, and might have expected F.E. to be with them, as he had been in the conscription struggle. Only F.E.'s hyper-developed sense of the loyalty due to the man who had given him his first experience of office can explain his refusal to admit any inadequacy in Asquith after he had joined the Government. He was still as anxious as ever to sweep away the Runcimans and McKennas, whom he afterwards blamed for sheltering their leader from the reality of his position and the nation's needs. His faith momentarily wavered when Asquith appointed another Liberal, Edwin Montagu, to the Ministry of Munitions in July (when Lloyd George moved, on Kitchener's death, to the War Office). But he persisted throughout 1916 in believing Asquith to be the sole and indispensable symbol of national unity. Even after the war, when he had successfully transferred his allegiance to Lloyd George, he continued stoutly to defend Asquith's unhurried direction of the first two years' hostilities, when the conventional view with hindsight was to wonder how he had survived so long.* F.E.'s fidelity was more credit to his heart than to his head, which is why his contemporaries, who still generally regarded him as simply an ambitious lawyer on the make, did not believe in it. 'Clever, but with a fatal passion for Churchill and his methods,' was Selborne's typical characterization of F.E. at this time,[26] and in the eyes of his other Tory colleagues, with whom he would have liked to work in support of Asquith, he was similarly damned by past association. The leading Conservative Ministers – Curzon, Austen Chamberlain, Robert Cecil and Walter Long – actually regarded Asquith very much less positively than F.E. did: they were prepared to back him in the December crisis principally out of antipathy to Lloyd George – with whom they lumped Winston and F.E. together as equally irresponsible and self-seeking trouble-makers. F.E. was thus isolated, divided by his loyalty from his friends the rebels, but distrusted as a natural rebel by his fellow-loyalists.

The friend he was most anxious not to be separated from was Bonar Law, to whom also he owed a debt of personal gratitude as well as the loyalty due to his party leader. Law, for his part, was only very slowly driven, by Aitken's coaxing and Asquith's indecisiveness, into joining Lloyd George and Carson in demanding that the coalition he had helped to form in May 1915 should be reconstituted. F.E.'s advocacy,

* 'That old man', F.E. told Salvidge in October 1917, 'has got more brains in his little finger than you and I possess in the whole of our two heads.' It was exceedingly rare for F.E. to praise another man's mental equipment.

according to Aitken, was one of the factors which held him back for so long. But in November a division in the House of Commons on a minor question – the resale of confiscated German property in Nigeria – alerted him to the extent of Tory backbench discontent with the existing Government. That night F.E. dined with Aitken, who found him 'gloomy and despondent', afraid that Law might be shown to have lost the confidence of his party. In the event, the rebellion was contained: a small majority of Conservative members stood by the Government, giving it a large overall majority. One of the rebel tellers, meeting F.E. in the lobby, suggested that Law had only been upheld by the votes of the paid members of the front bench. F.E.'s reply was an enduring piece of political cynicism applicable to many critical divisions down the years. 'We will cross off the votes of the members who are paid,' he offered, 'if you cross off those who want to be paid.'[27] F.E. was right to be despondent, however: the narrow margin helped to steel Bonar Law to the conviction that he must throw his influence behind Lloyd George.

A couple of days later, on 11 November, F.E. and Winston met at Aitken's house near Leatherhead in an unfriendly encounter which, as their host recorded it, dramatically demonstrates F.E.'s isolation. F.E., Beaverbrook wrote in *Politicians and the War* in 1928,

> started with a tremendous attack on Lloyd George for fraternising with the Opposition in the House of Commons and for deliberately abstaining from voting for the Government on the Nigerian debate. He quoted with approval Bonar Law's saying about Lloyd George's dual and ambiguous position – with a foot in both camps. He showed himself an out-and-out supporter of Asquith, believing that the existing administration both could and should be carried on in Lloyd George's despite.

Churchill, on the other hand, passionately took the opposite view.

> So we had the curious spectacle of Churchill attacking the Government while lauding the second most important member of it. Equally strange was it to hear Birkenhead defending the Government while attacking Lloyd George bitterly . . .
>
> Never at any time, I think, have I seen these two friends quite so far apart. My criticism of Birkenhead in the past had often been that though he was naturally sound in counsel he was too easily led astray from his own opinions by his loyalties and friendships. On this occasion he showed an absolute rigidity in holding on to his convictions, from which Churchill could in no way shake him.[28]

In the final crisis of the Asquith Government F.E. played no part at all. He was present at some, but not all, of the meetings of the Conservative leaders in those tense December days and appears to have shared to the end the Curzon–Chamberlain–Cecil belief that Lloyd George could not form a Government without them but, on the contrary, Asquith would emerge strengthened from a showdown with his rival. Once he was used by them as an emissary to Bonar Law. But he was never close to the centre of events. On 2 December Aitken, who was in the thick of them, found him gloomy and incurious – quite unlike Churchill, who was eager for news and convinced that the moment he had been waiting for had come at last. The outcome surprised them both. No sooner had Lloyd George, with the backing of Law and Carson, accepted the King's commission to form a Government and secured the vital support of Labour and nearly half the Parliamentary Liberal Party, than the formerly hostile Tories – first Balfour, then the 'three Cs' – capitulated to the accomplished fact and agreed to join him. Their embargo on Churchill, however, still stood, while the gulf that had separated F.E. from the new Prime Minister was quickly bridged. The night before his summons to the Palace, Lloyd George, with Aitken and Churchill, dined with F.E. in Wilton Street. At this miniature Other Club, Aitken recalled, 'the conversation turned entirely on the personnel of the new Ministry and everyone took a share in it on terms of equality'. But Lloyd George, as he left, charged Aitken with the delicate task of warning Winston that the new Government might have no room for him. The shock to Churchill, who never grasped the depth of the Tories' antipathy to him, was terrible.

> He suddenly felt he had been duped by his invitation to the dinner, and he blazed into righteous anger. I have never known him address his great friend Birkenhead in any other way except as 'Fred' or 'F.E.' On this occasion he said suddenly: 'Smith, this man knows that I am not to be included in the new Government.'[29]

With that he strode out of the house. F.E. followed and tried in vain to bring him back. Once again, however, their situations were ironically opposed. Churchill, who had been working for more than a year to see Asquith replaced, was left empty-handed by the very consummation he had wished; not until the next July did Lloyd George feel strong enough to send him to the Ministry of Munitions. F.E., on the other hand, who had stuck devoutly to Asquith, retained his position as Attorney-General and, though he was theoretically further from the centre of power with the supersession of the old large Cabinet by a small war council, actually began to grow in political stature as one of the new Premier's most trusted colleagues. Without ever retracting his loyalty to Asquith, F.E. rapidly formed a new loyalty to Lloyd George which was to be the lodestar of his next six years.

Not that Lloyd George and Bonar Law did not have to override some strenuous opposition from Tory Diehards in reappointing him. 'Smith is not a serious statesman,' H.A. Gwynne wrote in alarm to Lloyd George on hearing a rumour that F.E. was to become Colonial Secretary;[30] while Leo Maxse raved to Bonar Law, 'We are all terrified of having men like Max Aitken and F.E. Smith thrust upon us, or Winston Churchill. That way disaster lies as you start by chilling public confidence.'[31] When Law protested at the disparagement of Aitken, Maxse fired back:

> I do not know whether your panegyric of Max Aitken likewise covers F.E. Smith but I can only say, if it be true that through the influence of yourself and other friends he is to be appointed Colonial Secretary or to any other great place in the new combination, it would be regarded as a deliberately wicked appointment and its responsible authors would never again pass muster as honest men. Unionist Front Benchers appear to be devoting themselves to wrecking this Cabinet, as they wrecked the Coalition, by insisting upon forcing upon it several of the most incompetent and discredited men in our public life.[32]

In fact it was the likes of Maxse whose violent opinions and prejudices counted for very little.

Whether F.E. was ever seriously considered for Colonial Secretary – which post actually went to Long – there is no record. He was probably more use to the Government where he was. Certainly from the moment of Lloyd George's accession he began to load the Attorney-General with additional responsibilities beyond his purely legal functions.

One important measure which he was partly entrusted with guiding through the Commons, though it was not in fact a Government Bill, raised a muted echo of pre-war controversy. This was the Representation of the People Bill, the result of months of constructive horse-trading by a Speaker's Conference aimed at extending the franchise to virtually the whole male population and settling in a single package the myriad electoral anomalies which had embittered relations between the parties before 1914 – including the question of votes for women. On this F.E. – along with most of the pre-war opponents of women's suffrage – was now, as he explained on 19 June 1917, ready to concede defeat.

> It is not true that I am a convert, but with the experience of the
> war I should modify my argument as to force being in the last
> resort the decisive argument, so that a woman cannot fulfil the
> whole duties of citizenship.

Wars, he was obliged to admit, were no longer fought by male gladiators
alone but by whole nations: the contribution of the nation's women to
this common effort was as vital as that of the men. Nevertheless he
would withdraw his opposition to the female franchise only as part of a
general settlement.

> You must either accept the Report of the Speaker's Conference as
> a whole or reject it. There is no middle course, and it is worth while
> to get a settlement that would secure some degree of leisure for the
> House of Commons to devote to post-war problems . . . But if the
> Bill breaks down I must reserve my liberty as to Woman's
> Suffrage.[33]

In particular, he was prepared to accept women's suffrage as a
trade-off for proportional representation, which he had long favoured
and which had now been unanimously recommended, in one form or
another, by the Conference. The actual proposal was for the Alternative
Vote over the whole country and a proportional system in multi-member
constituencies in the big cities. F.E. would have preferred to extend the
proportional principle to all constituencies, on the simple argument
that the point of a representative system was that it should be representative; but he was ready to settle for the Speaker's package, which
would at least give fair representation to, for instance, the Liberals in
Liverpool, disproportionately crushed by the Salvidge machine. The
1910 House of Commons, however, still thinking narrowly in terms of
party advantage, tore it apart: the Tories would not have the Alternative
Vote, as being likely to promote pacts between Liberals and Labour,
while the Liberals – ironically, could they read the future – went cold on
proportional representation when they realized that it would prevent
any repetition of their swollen majority of 1906.

F.E. considered these self-interested calculations, based on pre-war
arithmetic, short-sighted and irrelevant to the new world that was being
born from the holocaust, and in the debate on 4 July 1917 tried to raise
the horizons of the House, and particularly of his own Conservative
colleagues, with a notable speech whose weight and authority seem to
announce that a new F.E. Smith was also being born from the chrysalis
of his war experience.

Many of my honourable friends, who I think confine their attentions a little too closely to a phase of politics which I believe to be absolutely extinct, are wondering whether the arrangements which will follow upon this Bill are in the interests of the Unionist Party. I greatly doubt whether those who entertain these apprehensions have realized the nature of the resolution which is involved in this Bill. I say plainly that nothing in our politics will ever be the same when once this Bill has become law. Those who are attempting to trim their sails to the wind which died three years ago and will never revive, had better consider the new and real problems of the future, and the party which for many years has justly claimed to have been the party which has stood for the defence of the cause of stability would do well to weigh once, and yet again, the strange seas in which we are to voyage when this war is concluded. There were great reactions after the South African war. Who can measure the reactions which will follow upon the conclusion of this peace? There will be revelations of incompetence, not only in this country, but in every belligerent country. There will be sufferings. There will be immense war indebtedness to be paid, and any man who supposes that elections are going to take place under the old conditions, and with the old controversies, between the two parties, is mad. New issues, new controversies, new parties, are going to determine the future, and I say to those who heretofore in this House have defended the cause of stability, and who think themselves concerned in the future to establish and maintain the centre of gravity of the State, your one chance of salvation is to establish an exact equipoise in the State between the strength of the constituencies and the strength of the House of Commons, and the degree in which you succeed in that object will be the measure of your success in maintaining those causes which minorities will always defend.[34]

Despite F.E.'s earnest eloquence, however, the division which immediately followed his speech rejected the proportional representation clause by 201 votes to 169. Though the Lords, in their greater detachment from the party battle, put it back, the Commons persisted in their refusal to countenance it. For a time the whole Bill hung in the balance, with much tortuous horsetrading between alternative schemes, before the traditional single-member, single-seat system was finally confirmed in February 1918, with only the vague promise of a Royal Commission to look at the matter again.[35]

In other ways, too, F.E. was looking to the post-war future. Only two days after his Commons speech just quoted, he sent out a circular letter to a number of wealthy Conservatives appealing for money to resurrect the Unionist Social Reform Committee, which had run into debt with the outbreak of war.

> Its work and recommendations, published in eight carefully prepared volumes, anticipated much of the constructive work of the last three years and will, I am persuaded, be found most persuasive and valuable in the work of reconstruction which must follow the war.
>
> It is vital that in the immense social upheaval that will come with Peace there should be within the Unionist party a body of men who are attempting to face the problems of the future with prevision and yet who are convinced of the necessity of maintaining the stability and centre of gravity of the State.[36]

He himself was putting down £35, one-tenth of what was required. At least one of those to whom he appealed, however, was unsympathetic. Max Aitken – now translated to his more familiar style of Baron Beaverbrook – wrote back that the U.S.R.C.'s pre-war development 'on Sidney Webb Fabian lines left me decidedly cold'.[37] His attitude is a useful reminder that many Tories had found the Committee's very cautious prescriptions dangerously socialistic.

All this talk of reconstruction in the summer of 1917 reflected a new optimism about the war. This owed nothing at all to Nivelle's latest offensive on the Aisne, which had ground to the same bloody halt as all its predecessors, but everything to the entry into the conflict of the United States, provoked at last beyond endurance by the Germans' reckless declaration of unrestricted submarine warfare. For two and a half years, to British fury, President Wilson had averted his eyes from the loss of American life inflicted by sporadic German U-Boat attacks on unarmed passenger liners, of which the *Lusitania* was only the most famous, attempting to hold a balance between the belligerents by objecting equally to the British insistence on the right to stop and search for contraband all neutral shipping. F.E., closely concerned with the war at sea through his Prize Court work, bitterly expressed his contempt for the American attitude in his letters to Churchill in January 1916. 'The dirty Yanks have decided to do nothing at all about the *Persia*,' he wrote on 11 January. 'What money-grubbing swine.'[38] And a week later, 'The U.S. swine grow more and more truculent & are apparently almost prepared to slobber over Brother Bosch.'[39] Lloyd George encouraged him to speak out publicly. In two speeches in Liverpool and Cardiff in January/February 1917 – the latter the day after the Germans' announcement that they would henceforward sink anything that moved in the eastern Atlantic – F.E. delivered a blunt reply to Wilson's ostensibly even-handed insistence on the 'freedom of the seas'. There would be time for the freedom of the seas, he declared, when Germany had been defeated. Meanwhile Britain was exercising her naval supremacy in strict obedience to international law: Britain had not whined when the Northern States had done the same in the American civil war. Now Britain and her allies would defend their own honour: let the Americans look to theirs. Those who had made the sacrifices, however, would make the decisions later on – a pointed rebuke to Wilson's evident hope of emerging in the end as the peacemaker between the exhausted nations.[40]

Wilson still hesitated; but the Germans forced his hand, in the desperate gamble that by cutting Britain's supply lines they could win the war before the American presence could make itself felt in Europe. They nearly succeeded. Wilson declared war on 6 April, but had neither trained men nor equipment to put into the field. That month the loss of shipping reached a critical level, until Lloyd George single-handedly imposed the introduction of convoys against the entrenched professional advice of the Admiralty. With this, the U-Boat threat immediately receded. Now victory was just a matter of waiting for the Americans to arrive in France in sufficient numbers to break the deadlock.

To encourage this end, the War Cabinet decided at the end of the year to send over to the States a British Minister to help drum up recruitment, and selected F.E. for the mission. He was on the face of it a good choice. As Northcliffe, already in America as head of a permanent mission to co-ordinate the commercial side of the alliance, wrote to Lloyd George on 11 December:

> I think Sir Frederick is the exact man for the task. He has achieved a great position at an early age which Americans much admire. His career can be easily formulated in the Press. I have no doubt whatever that were he to go across the Continent he would have a reception that would greatly surprise our humdrum folk at home.[41]

F.E. had just the combination of youth and energy with an impressive physical appearance – it was the *New York Post* that had once described him as looking like 'an erudite prize-fighter'[42] – and a forceful speaking style which could be expected to go down well in the Midwestern cities which it was intended that he should visit. Despite his earlier strictures on American isolationism, he admired the country and the vitality of its people, and since April had been making enthusiastic speeches about the enduring importance to the world of the great English-speaking alliance. He was the perfect ambassador for the purpose in view – except for three things: he was still deeply distrustful of President Wilson; he was hated by the American Irish as the murderer of Casement; and he was inexperienced in the necessary evasions of diplomacy.

Two days before his departure, Lloyd George did F.E. the signal public honour of attending as his guest a dinner at Gray's Inn. F.E. had just been elected the Treasurer of the Inn, so it was a great coup for him to secure the Prime Minister as his first guest of honour, especially as Lloyd George used the occasion to deliver the Government's considered reply to Lord Lansdowne's letter calling for a negotiated peace. There was, he declared, no half-way house between victory and defeat; and that was the message which F.E. took with him to America. He took with him also a further mark of honour: a baronetcy. This, however, was not achieved without some arm-twisting. Lloyd George, of course, would give a bauble to anyone who wanted one, but Bonar Law – like Balfour in 1911 – made difficulties. F.E.'s characteristic response was a shamelessly direct appeal: he did not believe in humbug where his ambitions were concerned.

> My dear Bonar,
>   I am just off – Freddy [Guest] tells me that you have some feeling that the baronetcy wh I understand the PM is prepared to give me may injure me with the Tory party. Please believe me I have thought the whole thing thoroughly out. I have been Attorney-General for three years [actually a little over two]. Alverstone then A-G was made a Baronet. I greatly desire it – in case anything happens to me as a recognition of my official career and to give my little boy an extra chance in life. You don't agree with me in this but I have thought much about these things & formed my own view.
>   As for the Tory party I don't care a deuce for anyone in it but *you* & I want you to do this for me.
>   Fred[43]

He got his baronetcy. 'Step by step to your appointed Dukedom,' Edwin Montagu wrote in ironic congratulation.[44] He was not far wrong. In another twelve months F.E. acquired a still more glittering advantage to hand on to his son, and for the next four years his steps in the peerage were practically annual. Meanwhile he thanked Beaverbrook for his help in persuading Bonar Law, and added, ever-conscious when he was exposing himself to any risk, 'I am not afraid of not coming back (touching wood) but anyhow remember my dear Max that your friendship has added much to my life & is a thing I greatly prize.'[45] With that he went off to brave the German torpedoes.

Curiously, F.E. asked Arnold Bennett to go with him. They had met on 6 December at the Other Club, to which, at Beaverbrook's instance, Bennett had just been elected. Evidently F.E. liked him (Bennett in turn found F.E. 'a live companion, inclined to recount his achievements, but interesting and informed'), and a week later rang him up to ask him to go with him to America, nominally – 'but only nominally' – as his secretary. Bennett declined. 'Although I like him as a companion,' he wrote in his *Journal*, 'I didn't see myself going to the U.S.A. as F.E.'s secretary and boon companion. Still, he has considerable points.'[46]

Instead, F.E. took Harold, plus another secretary, one Colonel Murray. They sailed from Liverpool on 17 December and arrived in New York, after a tedious voyage, on Christmas Day. After three days of dinners, theatres and informal conversations there, the party moved on to Washington, where they stayed with the British Ambassador, Sir Cecil Spring-Rice, and F.E. met most of the Government and, on 31 December, the President, who only confirmed F.E.'s already dim view of him. Doubtless the feeling was mutual. The story is that F.E., full of the high purpose of his visit, found Wilson unwilling to talk of anything but Oxford; when at length Wilson asked him what was the 'tendency of the modern undergraduate', F.E. answered savagely, 'Steadily to women and drink, Mr President.'[47] Whatever the truth, the interview was not a success.

No matter. F.E. departed next day for Cincinnati on the first leg of a quick swing through the Midwest, taking in St Louis, Chicago, Detroit and Cleveland in nine days, and here he had much greater success at a series of packed public meetings interspersed with legal dinners. His theme was everywhere the same: Britain's undaunted will, America's heroic rallying to the cause, the two countries' combined mission to free the world of German barbarism; the cost of the war, the suffering, the sacrifice, the need for men and money, but equally the nobility of sacrifice, the selfless generosity of the American people, the inspiring idealism of their great President. All in all, the crudest fustian, but shrewd as well, presenting Britain's desperate necessity ('America, we need you, and we need you now')[48] as America's privilege to share in Britain's ennobling crusade. In Chicago again on 14 January, at the start of a second whistlestop tour that took him as far west as Nebraska and as far south as Missouri, he spoke to an enthusiastic audience of 6,000.

Towards the end, when he was speaking of the unity and friendship of the two countries and all it stood for, the U.S. Solicitor-General leaped to his feet and seized the Attorney-General's hand. The audience mounted on chairs and the cheering lasted many minutes.[49]

Similar scenes followed him wherever he spoke. From Detroit, the British Vice-Consul reported to Spring-Rice, 'the unusual and extra-ordinary enthusiasm attending the meetings addressed by Sir Frederick Smith';[50] and when the third leg of his tour took him into Canada, a correspondent wrote to F.E. himself that his visit to Montreal 'made a greater stir before and after than that of almost anyone we have had here since the outbreak of war'.[50] The Canadian Minister of Militia, Sam Hughes, wrote to his friend Beaverbrook, 'I want you to realize what a good impression our mutual friend, dear "young" F.E. Smith has made in Canada & the United States.' Every speech had been perfectly suited to its occasion – broad, non-partisan and tactful.

I wish you would tell Lloyd George and Bonar Law how proud they should be of him and his loyalty to them and to you. He is a great boy, and I hope his health may be spared for a great future. The world needs big men.[51]

These plaudits deserve to be quoted, because they were very soon drowned by the reverberations of one or two unguarded remarks which were rapidly blown up into a diplomatic 'incident'.

'How on earth did F.E. get loose here?' *The Times*'s man in Washington, Arthur Willert, wrote to his editor on 24 January.

In a few short weeks he has exasperated the President by patroniz-ing him publicly and has stirred up such a Hibernian hornets-nest by a Carsonite interview (which he repudiates) that the Boston Bar Association and the Boston Chamber of Commerce have asked to be excused the pleasure of keeping their engagements to hear him speak. It is only fair to say that, if his stay is thus to be cut short, he does seem to have done well in the two tours which we arranged for him in the Middle West.[52]

Evidently F.E.'s public praise of the President lacked the ring of sincerity. Moreover in his most serious speech, to the New York Bar Association on 11 January, he had treated with some Old World scepticism Wilson's lofty scheme for a League of Nations to prevent future wars. As for the Irish interview, F.E. repudiated it strenuously. The *Boston Post* had quoted him supposedly glorying in the death of Casement and boasting of his own part in hanging him.

You will remember that a tremendous effort was made to save Casement, and for a time the Government was wobbling. I gave them the choice of Casement or myself. Nothing has ever given me greater delight than the execution of Casement.[54]

It is largely in the light of this one alleged remark that F.E. has been portrayed as having been determined in 1916 to see Casement hang: there is no other contemporary evidence to substantiate that he either felt or spoke so strongly on the matter. It is possible that he was actually one of those members of the Cabinet who recommended mercy; at any rate the idea that he would have threatened his own resignation, or was in a position to do so with any credibility, is absurd, and the suggestion that he would have talked in these terms to the *Boston Post* scarcely less so. Presumably he was asked about Casement, and doubtless he did express himself somewhat undiplomatically to the effect that the traitor had met his due desert. Equally, however, one can be sure that the *Post* reporter made the most of the opportunity to discredit an enemy of Ireland and twisted whatever F.E. did say into the most damaging form. F.E. immediately dismissed the story as too grotesque for any sensible person to believe – 'The whole tone of this three-column interview, based on a five minutes desultory conversation, was to make mischief with the Irish'[54] – and when he got back to England continued to protest that only in this one interview out of nearly fifty he had given had he been 'abominably' misreported.[55] Spring-Rice, however, writing to Reading on 3 February, suggests that this was not in fact the only occasion on which F.E.'s informality left him open to embarrassment.

F.E. Smith, poor man, fell among reporters who sprang up and choked him. The intention evidently was to make trouble. His speeches as a rule were very successful and effective. But here, it happened that he made an unfortunate speech, without reporters, not knowing that the United States Consul-General was present, in which he made fun of everyone including the United States . . . Two people took it ill and no doubt someone has made mischief over it. It is dangerous for an Englishman to make jokes over here.[56]

F.E. denied that his tour was cut short as a result of these incidents; but he certainly never went to Boston. From Canada he returned at the end of January to New York, where he finished up with several days of purely social entertainment, even including a visit to the Metropolitan Opera to hear Caruso ('I did not stay long'),[57] before he sailed for home in early February. In five weeks he had covered, by rail and mostly in freezing weather, some 15,000 miles and addressed 48 meetings, totalling perhaps 100,000 people. On the boat home he dictated to a typist a diary of his journey, which he then published under the title *My American Visit*. It is a curiously redundant book, though presumably intended to demonstrate the importance of his mission: a compilation of unctuous Anglo-American patriotism and bullying war-fever, lightened with the most banal descriptions of the sights and discomforts of the party's travels and 'impressions' of American life. The most interesting of these are F.E.'s views on prohibition, which by 1917, though not yet universal, was extending its dry hold over most of the continent. To his surprise, he found the absence of alcohol at Rotary Club dinners and the like accepted without resentment. He noted with amazement

> long tables, able, perhaps, to seat eight hundred guests, with hundreds of glasses of water containing lumps of ice. Hundreds of lawyers and businessmen, after long days of hard work, were apparently content to dine without alcohol, and yet exhibited, during and after their meal, great cordiality and enthusiasm.

Before the visit, he continued, 'I should have rejected as utterly incredible the view that the whole of the United States could ever become dry. Today I am less confident.'[58] The prospect was very disturbing to one of F.E.'s partiality for the bottle. The lack of drink also threatened another of his favourite pleasures. 'As a social observer,' he noted with admirable restraint, 'I amused myself by noticing how gravely the drought of these repasts reduces the period in which the men of the party find entertainment in masculine talk.'[59] His scrupulously sober discussion of the pros and cons of this 'great experiment' – in which Lloyd George at home was closely interested – fails, however, to conceal his distaste for the suppression of personal freedom which it involved – to say nothing of the hypocrisy. In one of the fund of stories with which he regaled dinner tables on his return, he gleefully related how 'he and his brother Harold, in one of the dryest states, Nebraska, made the Professor of Rhetoric drunk – although the Professor was the origin of the dryness'.[60]

Most of the fifty-odd speeches that F.E. delivered in America were aimed simply at arousing enthusiasm for the war. But the one which he gave to the New York Bar Association on 11 January was a great deal more weighty, looking forward to the question which, back in England, was going to preoccupy him increasingly in the remaining eighteen months of the war and the first days of the peace: the question of war guilt. Entitled 'Law, War and the Future', it was nothing less than an attempt to formulate the moral and legal case for placing the responsibility of starting the war on Germany and punishing her accordingly, couched in terms of the most polite disbelief in the capacity of President Wilson's high-minded League to do the job.

He began with a quick résumé of the history of international law, back to the earliest rules for the immunity of heralds, but squarely facing the fundamental problem – that international law had never commanded international sanctions to give it effect. Despite this weakness, he asserted, its existence had gained wide respect. He made much of a case which he himself had argued unsuccessfully for the British Government before the Judicial Committee of the Privy Council, in which the Judicial Committee had upheld the duty of the Prize Court to administer, not British law, but international law, which took precedence. By contrast, he described the contempt for international law displayed by Germany since 1914 and further back – since, indeed, the time of Bismarck, even of Frederick the Great. ('Silesia, Poland, Denmark, France and Austria cried aloud through the ages a bloody and plangent admonition to those that had ears to hear.') No British or U.S. statesman, he declared, could have cynically torn up a treaty as Germany had done. The justification that Germany had been denied her rightful place among the nations was without foundation. The Kaiser had simply challenged, without pretext, the very existence of international law with the brutal counterclaim that might is right. As a result, there could be no compromise. Either public law – the plighted word, the sanctity of contract between nations – must be reasserted by force of arms, or anarchy would have triumphed. 'The world has known dynastic wars, it has known territorial wars, but it has never groaned under a war which has so completely challenged and put in issue the whole fundamental basis upon which civilisation, humanity and Christianity depend.'

So far, so conventional. Here, however, as he turned from the past to the present, from the crime itself to the punishment of it and the deterrence of future criminals, F.E. began to distance himself pointedly from Wilson. The sole test of victory, he asserted, lay in the punishment of the defeated.

> Gentlemen, if we win and if we punish those who have broken the public laws of the world, International Law will have received a supreme public vindication. Perhaps no nation, however strong, will ever dare again to dream of aggressive war. Perhaps – I do not know – perhaps the great and splendid dream of an international tribunal, administering a law which would satisfy the analysis I have already examined, may be realized. Perhaps, I say, these things may happen; I do not know.

The scepticism in F.E.'s voice is eloquent even on the printed page. He went on:

> Our examination, as lawyers, of the noble proposals which have been made by your President, and which have been most warmly and sympathetically received in our country, should be reserved, critical, but, as far as may be, helpful. If we do not coolly measure the difficulties which attend these proposals, attractive though they are, it is certain that those difficulties, swiftly and unexpectedly emerging will overwhelm the proposals for – make no mistake – they are stupendous in their aggregate weight . . .
>
> It is not my purpose here tonight to play the pessimist in relation to hopes which may seem to many of us to afford the sole prospect of a happier world as the fruit of this war. My only object, as a lawyer addressing lawyers, is to call attention to the dangers of trusting rhetoric alone, to the immense difficulties which attend in practice the proposal to form an effective League of Nations. When I indicate these difficulties, I do it, not in the spirit of one who wishes to exaggerate their force, but of one who wishes, as far as he can, to suggest any method by which they may be overcome; and I hope it will not be supposed that I am attempting to do anything but assist the proposals of the President when I ask you never to lose sight of the prodigious obstacles which lie in the way of the attainment of the ideal, so eloquently and so persuasively indicated by that great man.

It is no wonder that Wilson felt patronized. F.E. was pointing out, with the shocking cynicism of the wicked Old World, that the American Emperor's clothes were few and transparent. He proceeded to outline some of the problems. How would the proposed League limit the armed forces of each nation? How would it define the freedom of the seas? Would it try to curtail the right of naval powers to police their own sea routes as they saw fit – as, he noted, the United States was now doing just as effectively as Britain had done since 1914? How would it control the secret development of air power? And was the League to fix for all time the frontiers of the world? Empires would continue to wax and wane: F.E. recalled the Spanish-American war of only twenty years earlier, in which Spain had been forcibly relieved by the United States of Cuba and the last vestiges of her American Empire. Was such reconstruction in future to be undertaken by a council of nations? 'If it is, I sincerely trust that it will be unanimous in its decision.' Would proud nations consent to such reconstruction? Would the League have compelled Spain to surrender her colonies? Could the League ever have got agreement among its members to apply compulsion? And, if not, would the Americans have refrained from taking action alone?

Then again, were the Allies' present enemies to be members of the League?

Will a Prussian, crouching for a second spring, be an agreeable bedfellow? Is an unpurged Germany a possible member? Obviously no – only a punished Germany! So, by every route, we are driven back to the one static feature in a dynamic controversy: public law disappears for ever from this world if we are proved powerless in this controversy to castigate the wrongdoer. [Cheers.]

Yet, I agree that it is worth while trying for the ideal.

It is worth while to make the attempt. It is better to harness your wagon to a star than to a machine-gun, though a knowledge of the one may be very useful as a means of attaining to the other. I am not a pessimist in these matters. But I urge upon you, as one cautious by temperament and training, and slow to adopt rhetorical phrases as a substitute for the detailed working out of problems, I urge that it is important, if you cherish, as I know this nation dearly cherishes, these ideals, to prepare now. Get the best minds of your country working now to help this League of Nations to bring to a tortured Humanity the first faint whispers of an imperishable hope. Believe me, it will be far too late when the actual Peace Conference meets.

There is an extraordinary authority in these words from a 45-year-old visiting politician, with less than three years' experience of junior office in his own country, an authority which might have come over simply as cheek but for the gravity and evident realism of his argument. F.E. was not quite finished yet. He went on to doubt the wisdom of Wilson's declared intention that the proceedings of the Peace Conference should be held in public, repeated again that he did not disparage the President's ideals but only, 'as a lawyer addressing lawyers', criticized their application, and concluded with the more positive assertion that whatever else was salvaged from the horror of this war, at least the Anglo-American alliance would endure as a beacon for the future.[61] After prolonged applause, F.E. was unanimously elected an Honorary Member of the New York Bar Association. On his threatening that if he lost his job in England he might take advantage of their kindness by coming to practise in New York, the presiding judge responded with a neat compliment, 'They measure ships by their displacement, and I cannot harbour the thought of the displacement which will be occasioned in the New York Bar if Sir Frederick should come among us; but none the less, we should welcome him then as much as we welcome him here tonight.'[61] President Wilson's retort to F.E.'s speech was more barbed. 'He may as well know that I and the whole country are fed up with lawyers.'[62]

F.E. continued to concern himself with the question of international law and its enforcement after his return to Britain. For an anxious period in the spring and early summer of 1918 it was doubtful whether the Allies would after all be in a position to enforce anything. The second Russian Revolution, the collapse of the eastern front and the Treaty of Brest-Litovsk imposed on the Bolshevik Government in March enabled the Germans for the first time to concentrate all their forces in the west, and at last they broke the stalemate and threatened Paris. It was their last throw, however. The war of movement once having been restored, as soon as the German offensive faltered it turned abruptly into a retreat, as the French and British, now augmented by the Americans and the first intelligent use of tanks, found that they could advance unopposed as the Germans pulled back. With victory suddenly in sight, talk of peace terms became an urgent reality. F.E., though still only Attorney-General, found himself thrust from the periphery where he had languished while military operations were the overriding concern, to the very centre of Government discussions. As soon as the possible punishment of the defeated enemy rose to the top of the agenda, it was to their senior Law Officer that the War Cabinet turned for advice.

F.E.'s view was clear and simple, as foreshadowed in his New York speech: Germany must certainly be punished. But did this mean that the German nation as a whole should be penalized, either territorially or financially? Did it mean rather that the nation's leaders should be arraigned to stand trial for the crime of initiating the war? Or that individual officers and U-Boat commanders should be tried for particularly grave examples of 'frightfulness'? The answer, of course, was all these things; but there was as much confusion in F.E.'s public utterances as in anyone else's between trial and punishment, which were widely assumed to be identical, and also between those penalties which might be imposed as part of the peace settlement and those which would require the establishment of some sort of international court. He strenuously advocated both the punishment of the nation as a whole by the payment of cash indemnities to France and Belgium (for had not Germany herself, in her brief hour of victory, demanded £300 million from Russia?) and the punishment 'in their persons' of guilty individuals both high and low. He denied equally the plea, derived from Clausewitz, of 'military necessity' by which the military leaders might excuse their violation of Belgian neutrality and the precepts of the

Hague Convention; and their followers' anticipated submission that they were only obeying orders. 'An inferior is protected from the consequences of his act', he asserted, 'if it is done under such orders of a superior officer as he is legally entitled to give. If the superior is not and cannot be entitled by law to issue such orders, both he and his inferior are equally guilty.'[63]

No official record of how F.E. advised the Cabinet seems to have been preserved. But it is clear from his anxiety that the armistice terms should provide for the handing over to the Allies of named suspects, and from his appointment on 6 November of a committee of leading silks to inquire into German guilt,[64] that he definitely envisaged the establishment of some sort of international court of the Allies, such as was actually set up at the end of the Second World War, to try and sentence those found guilty of crimes against international order, not in a spirit of revenge but as a deterrent to future aggressors. 'If those who are provably responsible escape, is there any particular reason for supposing that, when this world convulsion is forgotten, others will not be found bold and bloody enough to tread the same guilty road?'[63] If Germany had won the war, he wrote in the preface to the timely new edition of his *International Law*, 'we could have burned our Grotius, our Vattel, our Phillimore, our Wheaton and our Hall'. Germany's defeat must carry with it exemplary retribution.

> The future of civilisation requires that the authority of public law shall be reasserted with as much notoriety as marked the challenge, and it cannot be so reasserted without requiring from those who sought to destroy it, a punishment so memorable, because so dreadful, that the offence will not soon be repeated. For the correction of specific infamies international law does not exclude the castigation of guilty individuals, however highly placed.[65]

The key individual was of course the Kaiser. Dining at Downing Street on Armistice night with Lloyd George, Churchill and Sir Henry Wilson, F.E. was quite bluntly in favour of shooting him. Lloyd George agreed; Churchill and Wilson did not.[66] F.E.'s principal reason for pursuing him as the chief criminal was that the Allies could not, in justice, prosecute lesser villains if their leader were allowed to go free. (A less respectable reason was possibly that his sense of theatre relished the prospect of a symbolic show trial, starring himself as Chief Prosecutor, at which the moustachioed embodiment of German militarism would be ritualistically condemned: a series of minor prosecutions of faceless underlings had not the same attraction.) But the Kaiser did go free, slipping over the border into neutral Holland as the Reich collapsed around him. The Allies were furious, but Holland refused to give the fugitive up. For more than a year the Allies wrangled and cajoled, threatening the Dutch with diplomatic and even economic sanctions for so perversely setting themselves against the justice of the civilized world. Even after they had had to give up the idea of prosecuting him, there was great concern that he should not be allowed to remain in exile so close to Germany. Though the French might not have admitted the comparison, the memory of Napoleon's return from Elba was constantly in the mind of the British Government – F.E. fed Lloyd George with relevant documents from 1814.[67] The British proposed the Falkland Islands as a suitable St Helena for the German Bonaparte. But the Dutch were unmoved; the voluminous indictment which the British prepared against the ex-Kaiser was never brought, and Wilhelm II lived out his days in comfortable, unrepentant seclusion until 1941. As a result, as F.E. had foreseen, it was difficult to proceed against others. Thus the whole project of a Nuremberg Tribunal twenty-four years before its time was quietly abandoned as war hysteria cooled before the problems of peace. All that happened, after three years of high-level legal and political negotiation, was a number of trials in Leipzig in 1921, at which the Germans themselves made a pretence of trying, under German law, certain random individuals accused by the Allies of atrocities. A few light sentences were imposed, but the trials attracted little international interest.

Thus nothing came of all F.E.'s stern rhetoric. His instinctive disbelief in the capacity of any sort of League of Nations to give effective sanction to international law was unhappily vindicated, and he quickly relapsed, after his brief burst of supranational moralism, into the cynical neo-Darwinian view of international rivalry and global order which came most naturally to him and had been his normal stance before 1914. Meanwhile his well-publicized advocacy of hanging (or shooting) the Kaiser and generally making Germany pay did him, as it did other Government candidates, no harm at all in the mundane business of getting re-elected to the House of Commons. As a result of the Representation of the People Bill and the vast expansion of the electorate, the boundaries of the Liverpool constituencies had been redrawn. Most of the voters who had previously made up F.E.'s Walton constituency were now in West Derby: the new Walton lay farther to the north. Reluctant though he was to give up the name with which he had been associated for twelve years in the House of Commons, F.E. was persuaded by Salvidge to switch to West Derby.[68] (His friend Commander Warden Chilcott took over Walton, with the lordly blessing of young Freddie, now aged ten, 'Dear Uncle Chillie, I am glad you are going to annex our old seat in Walton. I think you will represent it quite as well as father did, and he's no slouch.')[69]

Salvidge considered that F.E. made little use, in his campaign, of the call to hang the Kaiser. 'He says that if it really comes off, he is the one who will have to do the hanging – that is to say, conduct the prosecution for the British Government – a task which has more snags than are apparent from the hustings.'[69] But if F.E. was really beginning to have doubts, he did not let them inhibit him to any serious extent; he still boasted of having advised the Cabinet that the Kaiser should be brought to justice,[70] and indulged in similar promises 'as a Minister of the Coalition Government' to 'send back to Germany every Boche in this country'.[71] He did not need to overdo it: his return was assured. He nevertheless enjoyed a lively campaign, thanks to his only opponent, an amiably eccentric Labour Councillor named George Nelson, to whom *The Times* thought that F.E. should propose a vote of thanks, for providing such a perfect foil for his wit.

It happens that for many years Mr Nelson was in the habit of disporting himself in a frock-coat and silk hat, and though he has discarded the latter, he sticks to the coat. It happens also that he makes a practice of putting highly personal questions to the Attorney-General about his 'princely salary', his mission to America, his 'funk-hole' at the Press Bureau and other things. So it comes about that, in the intervals between important announcements of Government policy, Sir F.E. Smith tickles his audiences with picturesque descriptions of his opponent – 'this frock-coated revolutionary', 'this Lenin in a silk hat' and so on – and Liverpool is grateful to them both for enlivening a dull election. Sir Frederick's return is of course a foregone conclusion. If it were ever in doubt, the fact that he, as a Chief Law Officer, advised the War Cabinet that the Kaiser should be brought to justice would ensure his election, for here, as everywhere, the punishment of the guilty is uppermost in the public mind.[72]

F.E. took Nelson's aspersions on his military record seriously enough to read out at a public meeting the letter which he had secured from Colonel Dugdale of the Oxfordshire Yeomanry in 1915, and he challenged Nelson to repeat his slander in print so that he might sue for libel. For the rest, he insisted that his American mission was 'of high national importance. It was no pleasant voyage', and threw back the questions about his income with his usual proud contempt. 'He never tells us whether, if he had had the brains to have earned that income, he would have refused it . . . I did not take it from anybody else. I made it by my own brains.'[73] On wider issues, he pledged himself repeatedly to Lloyd George, that 'stout-hearted and sagacious Welshman', the essential

Prime Minister for the problems of the peace. Would Labour supporters, he asked, rather send Ramsay MacDonald to defend Britain's interests in Paris?[71]

He won, by a two-thirds majority – 11,622 votes to 5,618 (winning, that is, nearly twice the number of votes that he had obtained in Walton, while his opponent got roughly the same number as the Liberal in 1910) while the Unionists made a clean sweep of Liverpool – T.P. O'Connor's Scotland seat always excepted. In Warrington Harold hung on rather more narrowly despite both Liberal and Labour opposition; he was perhaps damaged rather more than F.E. by the persistent allegations that he had gone with his brother to both the Press Bureau and America when he should have been in uniform. Nationwide, the Coalition triumphed irresistibly, the Tories winning 335 seats, Lloyd George's Coalition Liberals (protected by the famous 'coupon') 133, Labour 63 and the shattered rump of Asquithian Liberals only 28. There was danger in such a huge majority; particularly there was danger to Lloyd George in the overwhelmingly Conservative colour of his majority. As soon as the results were declared, F.E. wrote to try to reassure him.

> My dear Prime Minister,
>   I congratulate you most sincerely upon the dimensions of your victory.
>   Do not be alarmed by the size of the Tory vote.
>   In the North they all owe an enormous debt (and they know it) to your own personal prestige.
>   I am a Tory democrat and always have been and I rejoice in the task which awaits us.
>   The Liverpool Workingmen's Conservative Association and Salvidge are *pivotal*. The Tory Party cannot refuse what they endorse. We hold every Liverpool seat and you ought to come and collar them at once.
>   Let me arrange for a meeting at which you get the freedom and then address a non-party meeting in Liverpool.
>   Yours ever,
>   F.E.

This means 30 Tory seats wh will follow *you* anywhere.[74]

F.E. was now on very close terms with Lloyd George. The fact that it was he and Winston, with Sir Henry Wilson, who dined alone with Lloyd George in Downing Street on Armistice night, the climactic evening of the war when the streets outside were filled with dancing, singing crowds, is an indication of the position F.E. had attained in the Prime Minister's inner circle of political friends. A few days earlier he had pledged himself publicly as well as privately to Lloyd George's cause: the public assertion of loyalty drew from Lloyd George a rare letter of gratitude, to which F.E. replied effusively in words that are much warmer than those of a junior colleague.

> My dear P.M.,
>   Thank you for your letter which I greatly value. I only said in public what I have said in private for nearly two years. I think that you and you alone can save this country; and holding that view I sacrifice everything to your support. I need not happily sacrifice the only tie in my own party which goes near my heart for Bonar Law agrees with me. I told him in the morning what I was going to say about you at night and he warmly and most cordially urged me to say it. You have in him a loyal generous and disinterested friend and admirer. He is as incapable of intrigue as of jealousy. Such men are rare in public life. 'Grapple him to your heart'.[75]

F.E. had now definitely thrown in his lot with Lloyd George and with the principle of Coalitionism. He saw a vital role for himself, as a leader of progressive Unionism, in linking the two wings of the Coalition and holding the Tory party loyal to Lloyd George. Writing to Bonar Law at the turn of the year, he made no bones about the power that he felt he commanded in the new political landscape just opening up, nor, characteristically, about the rank to which he felt that power entitled him. There was an alarming rumour that the Attorney-General might not be a member of the new Cabinet. Constitutionally this might be a desirable reversion to traditional practice; but personally it represented a threat to F.E.'s position against which he felt he had to speak out plainly.

> My dear Bonar,
>   The election is now over and we can take stock of the result. We have won by too large a majority and have to make the best of it.
>   The next election will be the critical one and the people who ought, if just methods of appraisement are employed, to be considered are the people who may be able powerfully to contribute to the next election. Unless we get to anarchy in the streets the platform will be decisive in the next four years and no-one knows better than you that I can make a contribution to that controversy.
>   I am writing with the freedom proper in a letter to the only real friend I have on our side of politics. I speak with complete candour. Reading, Simon, Carson and myself – four attorney-

generals in succession have been members of the Cabinet. If as Attorney-General I am left out of the new Cabinet I shall consider that no attempt whatever has been made to arrive at true valuations. I beg you particularly to notice two circumstances both of which seem to me vital.

1. Since you became leader I have shown you more complete loyalty and affection than any man of position in the party. I am the only important man in the party who has an intimate personal feeling for you and who wd sacrifice everything for you.

2. I have a power with the democracy which no-one upon *our* side in politics exceeds. When I say *our* I mean among the Unionists.

3. The large Tory vote will lead to caves. The P.M. must make proposals which will estrange many Unionists. No-one can help you more than I can to avoid and heal these ruptures. No-one has spoken in so many constituencies (or half so many) and can influence so much the candidates for whom he has spoken.

This is an egotistic letter but I fancy it is the first of the kind which you have ever received from me.

I want however to make it plain that the next ten years of my life are the only years which afford me any prospect of making provision for my family: that I could make certainly £5,000 and probably £10,000 a year more in private practice than as Attorney-General: and finally that if I am excluded from the Cabinet now the position of Law Officers has little to recommend it. I have been A-G for nearly all the Great War and I do not seek for judicial promotion. So that I have exhausted all the prestige of the office.

If my friends, on a cool valuation, think that Longs & Chamberlains & others afford a better insurance policy against the next ten years of our politics I shall register a mental (though I agree a partial) dissent from this view. Only events could show who was right.

You will forgive this frankness remembering that I have never been in the habit of importuning you.

But I should not think it right to leave you in ignorance of my views and wishes at a moment so critical to me.

Yours as ever

F.E.[76]

What this amounted to was an ultimatum: F.E. considered that he ought to be a member of the Cabinet and he was not prepared to remain as Attorney-General except as a member of the Cabinet; he would rather go back to realize his full potential income at the Bar. His career was in fact at the crossroads. Politics or the law? Power or money? Of course, what he really wanted was both, but he was always very conscious of his earning power (to say nothing of his earning requirement, the huge income needed to maintain the grand life to which he was committed) and he was not prepared to waste it except in return for advancement to a position of real influence – which meant the Cabinet. It seems that so long as he was in the Cabinet, F.E. had no ambition for the moment beyond the Attorney-Generalship. There is no indication that he had his eye on any of the great offices of State, though he certainly did not see himself confined to the legal departments for ever. The Attorney-Generalship suited him very well, for the very solid reason that as counsel for the Crown he would continue to earn legal fees at least approaching those he could command as an ordinary member of the Bar: far more, anyway, than the salary of any other Cabinet Minister. Moreover, the Attorney-General still seemed likely to have a key role to play in the peace settlement and the judicial punishment of German war criminals. He was afraid that Lloyd George might underestimate this and in his letter of 6 November he wrote at length to emphasize his department's claim to Cabinet rank, first for its past work during the war, but more important, as a major contributor to the peace.

> Let me first remind you that this department – controlled first by me & Cave, then by me & Hewart – is in grave days one of the most anxious in the State. In Napoleonic days Government after Government was involved in disputes which had their origin in the A-G's office. Our difficulties: Prize Law: DORA: the vexed questions of prosecution for sedition etc. have been incomparably greater and more recurrent than any previous Law Officers in the history of the country have had to face. *Yet we have not consumed five minutes of the time of the War Cabinet.* We have never referred a difficulty to them *and no other department has* referred a difficulty which affected us.

> My object in recalling these facts is to remind you officially [the implication is that he had already made his point informally] that in the days which are approaching grave difficulties will arise if the law officers are not kept in touch with events. The argument is already being raised in Germany (& not without plausibility) that the terms of our communication to Wilson dealing specifically with reparations but omitting any mention of punishment make it impossible to import into the peace conditions terms demanding

personal responsibility. One word suggested by any competent lawyer would have avoided all the resultant controversy.

Wherever the Peace Conference is held a law officer should be at hand: *not of course to take part*: but to be ready to advise at any moment. For this purpose it is essential that (i) a house should be taken for the Law Officers, & their staff of secretaries, devils etc. (ii) that arrangements should be made enabling them to take an adequate library, copies of records and so forth.

You may never want them (or their library) but both the Solicitor-General & myself think it necessary to make it quite plain that in our view it is almost certain

   i. That many legal points of great historical and consti-
      tutional complexity will arise requiring immediate advice.
  ii. That we could not undertake the responsibility of giving to
      the Government adequate and immediate advice upon
      such points unless due provision is made for ourselves and
      the necessary secretariat and library.

Forgive this long letter: but you will at least admit that I do not often trouble you.

Yours most sincerely,
F.E.[75]

Lloyd George was probably more sympathetic to F.E.'s personal predicament than impressed by his claims for his department. He would have liked to give F.E. a good job. But he had very little room for manoeuvre. As far as the Attorney-Generalship was concerned, legal opinion was unanimous that the holder of the post should not be in the Cabinet, while like all Prime Ministers he was anxious to keep the size of the Cabinet down to a minimum. (Indeed he was very reluctant, having governed for two years through a War Cabinet of only six or seven, to go back to a full Cabinet at all.) As for promoting F.E. to some other Cabinet office, there were not many vacancies that could easily be created; he needed to reserve as many places as he could for Liberals, which reduced the number available for Conservatives; and he could not afford to offend the Tories by displacing one of their senior figures to make way for F.E. So, despite Churchill's warning that 'his exclusion wd . . . chill a loyal friendship',[77] when he called F.E. to see him on 8 January, he was able to offer him nothing more than that he should continue in his present position, outside the Cabinet.

F.E., true to what he had told Bonar Law, declined.

I made it quite plain, almost in a sentence, that nothing would in-duce me to accept the office of Attorney-General on this condition.

And I added that I was in full sympathy with the Government, but that I was perfectly prepared to resume my practice at the Bar; and that I was sure I would be able to give him independent support from the back benches.

Lloyd George, however, was not unprepared for this reply. 'As quick as lightning the Prime Minister retorted, "How about the Woolsack?" '[78]

This was an astonishingly bold stroke on Lloyd George's part. Quite apart from the objections that would be made to F.E.'s suitability for so dignified an office, he already had a Lord Chancellor, the 76-year-old but well-regarded Lord Finlay, whom he had himself appointed only two years before, and who had agreed (as a wartime economy) to accept the position without the £5,000 a year pension that normally went with it, on the understanding that he would have a reasonable tenure of it. Lloyd George had in fact already contemplated replacing Finlay, for he had – though perhaps half-heartedly – offered the Lord Chancellorship, as a gesture of reconciliation, to Asquith. Had Asquith accepted, Finlay would have been required to make room for a political appointment which would at least have been generally understood and applauded. No such clear national interest would sweeten for Finlay the rebuff of being ousted in favour of F.E.

To F.E., too, Lloyd George's proposal came as a bombshell. 'It is literally true', he wrote some years later, 'that at that time it had never even occurred to me to bring to an end my membership of the House of Commons.'[78] He claimed that he had specifically waived his Attorney-General's traditional option of the Woolsack in 1916 (though whether Lloyd George could have got away with his appointment at that date must be very doubtful); and he told Lord Riddell in July 1918 that he had also refused the Mastership of the Rolls and would refuse the Lord Chancellorship 'if Finlay were to die and I were offered the position', for three clear-cut reasons.

1. Because I could not live on the pension. I have no money and I am extravagant. At the Bar I can make £30,000 per annum. If we went out of office I should be reduced to £5,000.
2. I hate the law. I am successful as a lawyer because I am a very clever man and can therefore grasp legal problems as most others would fail to do. When I became Attorney-General many people said, 'He will fail. He knows no law.' They did not know my educational record in the law and they did not realise that a very clever man can always grapple successfully with a difficult task.
3. I hate dignity. I like to live my life in my own way.[79]

The second reason, if faithfully recorded by Riddell, is evidently a colloquial oversimplification on the part of one who at other times did evince a genuine love of the law as well as that depth of learning in it which surprised so many observers; but it is also a revealing flash of impatience, a frustration which a man of F.E.'s wide interests and unlimited ambition was bound to feel occasionally for the crusty discipline which, while it paid his bills, was also confining his political progress within the legal ghetto. A further reason for looking askance at the Woolsack at this stage of his career was that it would remove him, prematurely and irrevocably, from the cockpit of the political struggle, the chamber of the House of Commons which he had worked so hard to conquer since 1906, and translate him to that dignified mausoleum, stripped in 1911 of the prerogatives of real power, the House of Lords, with the consequent abandonment of his legitimate hope of attaining the very highest office. For all this, the consideration which weighed most heavily against F.E.'s acceptance when the offer was definitely put to him was the financial sacrifice. The salary, so long as he retained the office, would be £10,000 – double that of any other Minister, including the Prime Minister himself. But the pension of £5,000 allowed to ex-Lord Chancellors, though intended to be princely, would be derisory compensation for cutting himself off, for the rest of his life, from the earning power on which his enjoyment of life depended.

Yet against these practical objections, the prize Lloyd George was holding out to him was a glittering one indeed, one of those which at the age of eight he had announced to his schoolfellows it was his ambition to win; one of the most ancient offices in the English State, whose holder ranked second in precedence in the land after the Royal Family, behind only the Archbishop of Canterbury, before the Prime Minister, an office normally reserved for one of the most learned, senior and dignified elder statesmen in the Cabinet. This grand climax to a career he was being offered at the age of forty-six; if he accepted, he would be the youngest holder of the office in modern times, certainly since Lord Cowper in 1707, possibly since Judge Jeffreys in 1685. John Simon would have been the youngest ever had he accepted it in 1915, when he was only forty-two; but he had declined to leave the Commons, and had his reward in the 1930s when he held all the leading offices of state in turn before finally acceding to the Woolsack in 1940. F.E. may have guessed that he did not have so many years in front of him. He was being offered a prize now which, if spurned, might never return. He had always done everything in a hurry, and had already won admiration for the rapidity of his legal and political advancement. To be the youngest Lord Chancellor would be the appropriate crowning glory to his fame. And if his elevation raised an outcry, so much the better: he would ignore it and give his own answer by making his Lord Chancellorship one of the greatest ever.

What was his alternative? To remain a second-ranking Minister outside the Cabinet would be a serious check to his progress, even though he might still restore his fortune at the Bar. Politically, this was the moment he had been waiting and working for, with a Coalition in office with a large majority, the parties in a state of flux, an entirely new political landscape to be charted; a sympathetic Prime Minister, Winston and Bonar Law also in the Cabinet – this was no time to be on the backbenches, but pre-eminently a time to be in Government. Lloyd George was taking a bold risk in making him the offer: it would be churlish, petty, craven to refuse. 'There is a tide in the affairs of men . . .'

Lloyd George wanted F.E.'s answer by ten o'clock the following morning. He had only a few hours to make up his mind whether to divert the whole course of his torrential life into a new, broader but more stately channel. Margaret was at Charlton. He could not send a telegram: he did not think he could safely telephone.

> I had accordingly to take the decision for myself. I promised the Prime Minister to breakfast with him on the following morning, and to give him my answer at this melancholy meal. I spent most of that night in debating the matter in my mind. I had not reached a complete decision when I arrived at No. 10 Downing Street. Winston Churchill was breakfasting there also. He had hitherto shown himself inflexibly opposed to any proposal that I should leave the House of Commons. But after ten minutes' discussion, before our arrival was announced, he greatly weakened. I suppose that I was hardly conscious of having reached a conclusion. I had nevertheless groped my way to one in the long hours of the previous night. At any rate I left the breakfast table on that morning with the knowledge that I was to become Lord Chancellor.[80]

To Margaret and the children he conveyed the news in a brief telegram whose few guarded words encapsulate the agony the decision had cost him. 'I salute my ennobled but impoverished family.' Their reaction is not recorded.[81]

There had already been a premonition of the wider response to F.E.'s elevation in the difficulty Lloyd George had in getting the appointment past the King, who feared (as his secretary delicately put it) that it would 'come as something of a surprise to the legal profession', and asked his Prime Minister to think again.

The King knows that his career both at the Bar and in Parliament has been very successful: but His Majesty does not feel sure that Sir Frederick has established such a reputation-in men's minds as to ensure that the country will welcome him to the second highest position which can be occupied by a subject of the Crown.

His Majesty however only hopes he may be wrong in this forecast.[82]

Lloyd George assured him that he was, claiming, quite erroneously, that 'as His Majesty knows, many of the most distinguished Lord Chancellors in our history attained the office between the age of 30 and 40' – a wonderful example of Lloyd George's way with inconvenient facts. He went on, 'Sir Frederick Smith is, in my opinion, a man of the most brilliant gifts and I shall be surprised if he does not justify the confidence which is being placed in him.'[83]

The same morning, Lord Finlay was abruptly notified that his place on the Woolsack was required for another. 'I did not resign,' he told Haldane, 'and was never more surprised than last Friday when I got my letter of dismissal'[84] – though he could have had an inkling of it if he had read his *Times* that morning. None of the other papers predicted his displacement at all. Several carried lists of the expected new Government, but all listed F.E. still as Attorney-General. Within hours the news was on the streets, with the gloss, presumably supplied by Downing Street, that Finlay was retiring at his own wish. F.E.'s elevation was, as the *Evening Standard* put it, 'easily first in the things the political prophets did not forecast'.[85] The other appointments, with the exception of Churchill's to the War Office, which infuriated the *Morning Post* in particular, were criticized mainly for their dullness, for the automatic confirmation in high office of old party politicians like Chamberlain and Long when the country was felt to be crying out for new men and daring appointments. Of these there were really only two, besides F.E.: Sir Robert Horne, brought in from nowhere to be Minister of Labour, and an Indian barrister, Sir S.P. Sinha, whose appointment as Under-Secretary at the India Office was hailed as a welcome stroke of imagination. Few papers looked so generously on the apotheosis of F.E.

It was not, as has often been written, *The Times* which described his appointment as 'carrying a joke too far', but the *Morning Post*. 'The country was as much amused as affronted when Sir F.E. Smith became Attorney-General. But it is carrying a joke beyond the limits of a pleasantry to make him Lord Chancellor. There are gradations in these matters.'[86] *The Times* merely sniffed and looked the other way, 'Of Sir F.E. Smith's elevation to the Woolsack – the highest judicial post in the

Empire, if not in the world – we prefer to leave the lawyers to speak; but we may be allowed a word of tribute to his predecessor . . .'[87] Northcliffe's other organ, the *Daily Mail*, echoed the King's view that the promotion would 'come as a shock; the public have not been accustomed to regard him as of the weight and calibre associated with that high office'.[88]

The *Birmingham Post* thought the appointment 'laughable and lamentable'.[89] The *Manchester Guardian* thought it 'frivolous', but provided an explanation, 'The mischief was done when he was appointed Attorney-General. There is a sort of trade union rule that the Attorney-General must have the refusal of the Lord Chancellorship if it falls vacant in his time.'[90] The *Guardian* did not know that the Chancellorship had not in fact fallen vacant. The paper's legal correspondent expressed a common Liberal attitude in holding that F.E. was perfectly well qualified legally for the office, but was politically disqualified by his incitement of Ulster to illegality only six years earlier. Tory papers tended to take the opposite point of view, that he was legally unqualified but owed his elevation to purely political considerations. The *Spectator* saw here, as everywhere, the influence of Churchill who, it ludicrously imagined, had the Prime Minister in his pocket.

> Sir F.E. Smith has always had many friends at the Bar, and of course he will have still more now, but there are very few of them, we expect, who in their heart of hearts will say that he is the kind of Lord Chancellor we want to see representing the country when the great judicial points which will have to be settled at the Conference in regard to the League of Nations come up for decision. No, it is impossible to answer the question why Sir F.E. Smith was made Lord Chancellor by saying that he was the best man available. If we are to hazard a guess why he is there, it is because he is Mr Winston Churchill's special friend, and stands in with the group who, in the name of the Prime Minister, have made the Ministry.[91]

Who on earth, with Winston, did the writer think composed this group?

Praise of the appointment was scarce. The *Evening Standard* (not yet owned by Beaverbrook) was one paper which, perceptively, saw merit in precisely those unusual qualities which F.E. would bring to his high position: he possessed, it insisted, 'all the dignity . . . all the nonchalance and all the confidence to carry it off . . . . "F.E." can do the work with ease.'[85] The *Nation*, surprisingly for a Liberal journal, was another which – unless it was being satirical – thought that F.E.'s intellectual calibre would strengthen the Government. 'A little lacking in weight in some Departments, the Government possesses, in the person of Sir F.E. Smith, a *vir pietate gravis* for the Lord Chancellorship.'[92]

The professional press was apprehensive: the *Law Times*, for example, saw the appointment of an underqualified politician to the highest legal office as the inevitable consequence of including the Attorney-General in the Cabinet. 'We can only express the hope', it concluded, reserving judgment, 'that the new Lord Chancellor may disclose on his elevation a legal aptitude equal to the capacity he has shown in other matters.'[93]

Appropriately, it was the legal correspondent of *The Times* which most perfectly summed up the Establishment's view of F.E.'s appointment with a damningly patronizing account of his 'meteoric' career to date. Into his forty-seven years, he was acknowledged to have 'crowded remarkable and promiscuous experiences'. But he had been too frequently the lawyer 'in a hurry'; as Attorney-General he had 'diversified his career by activities which had never been associated with his office'. As a Member of Parliament he had been 'impetuous and intrepid in several causes', including that of Ulster 'of which by training he knew nothing'. He had published books on various subjects 'from the poems of Samuel Johnson to the Licensing Bill of 1908'.

> Indeed a fatal fluency of thought and speech has tended to defeat great natural ability by the production of temporising superficiality. He succeeds a man of wholly different character – a man who was sound in his scholarship, sound in his law, and sound in the manner and tradition of the English Bar.[87]

Whatever else he might be, F.E. was not sound.

One legal voice at least, however, was raised to rebut the stream of depreciation. An old barrister named Arnold Statham wrote to *The Times*, from the Athenaeum, an appreciation of extraordinary sympathy and insight.

> It is the recipient of the honour himself who will suffer by the appointment, rather than the administration of justice or the nation, both of which will be distinct gainers by his phenomenal faculties of penetration and synthesis. On the other hand the meteoric genius who has raced like a thoroughbred to the Chancellorship will doubtless find the gradual petrification of polemic qualities incident to the grave routine of that office painfully destructive of that versatility of talent which made his reputation as a shining light.
>
> His greatest qualification for such appointment is unknown to the general public, consisting neither in brilliant rhetoric nor in fertility of resource in debate, but in a special feature which all those of experience in the practice of the Courts will recognize –

namely a 'transcendentalism', the capacity of taking intuitively a comprehensive view of all sides of any question and of diagnosing correctly the strength or casuistry of any argument. This is a judicial quality that can scarcely be overestimated and in this respect F.E. will display masterly power akin to that which brought such celebrity as a Judge to Jessel, M.R. Master of the Rolls 1873–81. Consequently despite the criticisms which have been made upon the appointment, I confidently predict that he will prove to be one of England's greatest Lord Chancellors.[94]

And so he did.

PART THREE

1919–1924

17

Lord High Chancellor of England, 1919–22

The office of Lord High Chancellor goes back to the very beginnings of the English State, before the Norman Conquest. From at least 1068 he was the keeper of the Great Seal with which royal documents were sealed before being sent out. During the Middle Ages he became the King's first minister and the most powerful subject in the land: Becket was Henry II's Chancellor; Wolsey and More were two of Henry VIII's. Only gradually did the powers of the Chancellor come to concentrate on his role as head of the judiciary, and lawyers to replace clerics in the office. The Chancellorship emerged in its modern form in the nineteenth century through the work of a succession of great jurists: Eldon, Brougham, Lyndhurst, Westbury and Cairns. It is an office unique in the British constitutional system – its uniqueness recognized by its special rank, in precedence after the Archbishop of Canterbury but before the Prime Minister – in that it binds together in the person of one man the three branches of Executive, Legislature and Judiciary.

In the Executive the Lord Chancellor is a Cabinet Minister with his full share of collective responsibility for Government policy and an important Department of his own to run, responsible for the administration of justice. In the Legislature, he is the Speaker of the Upper House of Parliament, presiding from the Woolsack but also intervening as a Government spokesman in debate. At the same time he is the political head of the Judiciary and himself a top judge, presiding over the supreme tribunal of the House of Lords.

It is an anomalous office, but as F.E. had cause to argue during his tenure, one that for that very reason justifies itself in practice. The Lord Chancellor is the licensed exception who serves to soften what might otherwise be the too-rigid application of the separation of powers, interpreting each to the other and smoothing possible conflict. It is, in its triple function, an exceptionally demanding and responsible office.

Its holder is required to be at the same time a party politician of sufficient standing to be an acceptable member of a party Cabinet and a lawyer of sufficient learning to command the respect of the profession; broad-minded enough to be able to transcend his political role as a Minister of the Crown and preside with impartial dignity over the House of Lords in both its legislative and its judicial functions.

It is a tribute to the British genius for tolerant conduct of political controversy that men of the highest ability have always been found to combine these conflicting functions down the years with few allegations of inadequacy, partiality or impropriety. It is not surprising, in view of his partisan and sometimes outrageous past, that F.E.'s elevation to this sensitive and symbolic office, at the apex of the constitutional pyramid, was thought by many to be inappropriate or even dangerous. It is the highest possible tribute to him that he so quickly confounded his critics, and proved himself both in learning and in dignity quite equal to the judicial duties of the Woolsack, while bringing both to the Lords' chamber and to the Lord Chancellor's Department a political vitality often lacking in more elderly Chancellors.

F.E. came to the job with a mixture of reverence, pride and determination. He revered the antiquity of the office and fully appreciated the responsibility it placed upon him to uphold its prestige and tradition; but, never doubting his ability to discharge it, he was justly proud of having attained it at an unprecedented age and in the teeth of prejudice he was determined – while affecting to ignore it – to dispel. 'I have undertaken most arduous and responsible duties,' he told his old constituents in Liverpool, explaining to them on 16 January why he was deserting them for the House of Lords, 'but, while I approach them in a spirit of anxious solicitude, I approach them in no spirit of morbid self-distrust.'[1] He was not afraid to see himself in the succession of his most illustrious predecessors. At a dinner given in his honour by his friends at Gray's Inn in May, he made a gracefully double-edged reply to those who had doubted his essential seriousness.

> I think perhaps I have the advantage – it is the only advantage I claim – over the great Bacon that I excel him in levity. I think in relation to Brougham I may perhaps claim that I excel him in gravity. I desire to push neither comparison further.[2]

If Bacon (1618–21), the quintessential Renaissance man – lawyer, politician, essayist and philosopher, an ambitious adventurer unjustly ruined (as F.E. always contended) by his enemies – was F.E.'s ultimate hero, it was rather on Brougham (1830–4) that he proposed to model his own Chancellorship. The most colourful of the nineteenth-century Lord Chancellors, distrusted alike for his loose living and for his genius by the same sort of 'sound' opinion which frowned on F.E.'s elevation, Brougham nevertheless left behind him a notable achievement as a law reformer. F.E. recognized – as, nervously, did his critics – a predecessor of his own mettle, and set himself deliberately to emulate both the style and the achievement, pinning his hope of posthumous fame specifically on a legacy of law reform and telling Repington – even as he complained, as usual, about the drop in income which the Woolsack cost him – that he intended 'to make his turn at it more memorable than any since Brougham's' – 'and he is quite capable of it,' Repington added.[3]

The desire to be 'memorable', while striking the right balance between gravity and levity, is the key to F.E.'s approach to the office.* The major constitutional and judicial responsibilities of his position he would discharge with a dignity beyond all criticism. As a barrister, he had always abhorred the 'witty' judge (his most famous gibes had been directed at those who, in his view, demeaned their solemn function); while in small matters and in large he was quick to insist on the historic independence of his office, whether this involved rebuking an M.P. (his old protégé Wolmer) who implied a slur on his impartiality as Speaker of the Lords,[5] or resisting the Prime Minister's interference in judicial patronage. At the same time, however, he would not be stuffy. He brought a new informality to the conduct of Lords' debates and, in his political role as a leading Government spokesman in the Upper House he was fully prepared to deploy when necessary the controversial asperities with which he had made his name in the Lower.

Above all he intended to enjoy himself, to indulge the glory and the grandeur of simply being Lord Chancellor in his forty-seventh year, to point the contrast with his elderly predecessors, to make the Lord Chancellorship an active and conspicuous, as well as an honoured and historic, office; in short, since he had given up, he knew, so much, both politically and financially, to accept it, to treat the Woolsack as the great prize it was and live his occupation of it to the full – not moderating but stepping up the extravagance of his pleasures (whatever his loss of income) to suit the magnificence of his new rank.

In this spirit he revelled in being able to entertain the King and sixty exalted guests to a great dinner at the House of Lords in July 1921 (though Lloyd George spoiled it slightly by pleading exhaustion), and enjoyed equally such lesser duties of his office as the opportunity to congratulate his grand old predecessor Halsbury (now ninety-seven) on the seventieth anniversary of his call to the Bar.

* 'Should I be drunk as a lord,' he is supposed to have asked, 'or sober as a judge?'[4]

You were born during the Lord Chancellorship of Lord Eldon; you were called to the Bar in the Chancellorship of Cottenham. You took silk when Westbury was Chancellor; your immediate predecessor on the Woolsack was Selborne; and you had been practising as a leader for eight years when the writer of this letter was born.[6]

So long as he could express it in this sort of resounding rollcall, F.E. delighted in the antiquity of the Chancellorship. On the other hand, some of the minor restrictions which that antiquity imposed on him irked him exceedingly; for instance, he was not supposed to leave the country without the King's permission, which involved putting the Great Seal into commission in his absence and was not granted lightly. Even pettier, he had a running battle with His Majesty over his dislike of wearing a silk hat, which the King regarded as essential to the public appearances of a properly turned-out Lord Chancellor; after several reprimands and one mildly satirical protest which the King considered 'very rude', he gave way with an ill grace.[7] He also hated the constricting formality of the costume – knee-breeches and all – that he was required to wear on the Woolsack, and quickly tired of having to sit long hours listening to other people's speeches, as Repington discovered in February 1919.

He finds the Woolsack a great grind. He sits for ten hours a day, either on appeal cases or while the House of Lords is sitting. He says one can do everything quickly except sit quickly. The Woolsack is a comfortable seat. No-one else is supposed to sit on it unless invited by the Chancellor. But the hours are so long that F.E. thinks of taking a wrinkle from Labour and 'downing wigs'.[8]

And this was scarcely three weeks after taking his seat! Long before 1922 he was thoroughly bored with the formal side of his great office.

The House of Lords in its legislative capacity as a debating chamber, of course, normally sat for only a few hours in the early evening (4.15 till perhaps 7.00), Tuesday to Thursday, and only about half the weeks in the year, unless there was some specially contentious Bill to get through. Nevertheless it was considered the prime duty of the Lord Chancellor to be in his place unless physically prevented – not only to be in it, but to process to and from it with a lot of solemn flummery – and this occupied a sizeable segment of F.E.'s time. Probably more time-consuming overall, however, and intellectually more taxing (though for that reason more interesting) were the judicial sittings of the Lords – that is, of the Lord Chancellor and three or four legal colleagues (the

Law Lords) to hear cases on appeal to the supreme tribunal. These took place, in the Lords' chamber, four days a week during the law term, from 10.30 a.m. to 3.45 or 4.00 p.m. with just half an hour's break for lunch. In addition, there were also occasional sittings, in Downing Street, of the Judicial Committee of the Privy Council to hear imperial appeals. These were the hours regularly taken up of which F.E. complained. Into the time remaining he had to fit Cabinet meetings – theoretically held on Wednesday mornings (the day the Law Lords did not sit) but under Lloyd George much more frequent and irregular – inevitably F.E. missed more than he attended and then had to catch up on what he had missed; numerous Cabinet conferences and Cabinet committees; the writing of his judgments; and the whole administrative business of running his Department, supervising the machinery of justice, and preparing the legal reforms that were to make his name. Doubtless the routine of the Department ran itself to a great extent; F.E.'s active ministerial contribution must have been largely confined to the months when Parliament and the supreme court were not in session. It is small wonder that much older Lord Chancellors have seldom the energy left over for the reforms which they intend.

The smooth running of a Department whose head had so many statutory calls on his time had been since 1915 and would remain until 1944 the responsibility of the Permanent Secretary, Sir Claud Schuster. As with any other department, the political head had to give the political impetus, but the detailed practicalities of the legislation that F.E. presented to Parliament were worked out under the eye of the Permanent Secretary, who gave continuity to the reforming efforts of ten successive Lord Chancellors, from Haldane to Simon. He was already in F.E.'s time a formidable civil servant, agile and diplomatic, an invaluable counsellor and guide. Schuster in his turn formed a high opinion of F.E.'s varied qualities, and wrote an admiring appreciation of him for the *Dictionary of National Biography*, and another, more personal, in a collection published in 1933 entitled *The Post-Victorians*.

In addition to his permanent officials, F.E. had also two private secretaries of his own. One, the more orthodox, was Roland Burrows, a young barrister who had been with F.E. as Solicitor-General and Attorney-General, and went on after 1922 to a varied career on the legal-academic fringes of the civil service, culminating in a knighthood in 1946. His principal function as secretary to the Lord Chancellor was to do the necessary devilling and drafting for F.E.'s judgments – even on occasion to write them where the question at issue did not engage F.E.'s interest. When F.E. left the Woolsack, it was Burrows who edited his judgments for publication.

The other was an extraordinary but shadowy character, Lieutenant-

Colonel G.W.H.M. Cartwright – 'Buns' Cartwright to his friends – who attached himself to F.E. soon after being demobilized in 1919 and stayed with him as a devoted adherent until F.E.'s death. His usefulness to F.E. seems to have been more as a games player than as a conventional secretary.. Through the 1920s he was perpetually at Charlton, always available as a fourth at tennis or golf, ever-present in the background of photographs, in white flannels, racket in hand. F.E.'s children called him the 'Games Master' and loathed him. After F.E.'s death he never saw any of the family again, but devoted himself for forty-odd years to the Eton Ramblers Cricket Club, as player and secretary. (Cricket was just about the only game in which F.E. never took much interest.) He died only in 1977; his obituary in *The Times* and the address at his memorial service in the Guards chapel, delivered by the cricket commentator Brian Johnston to a congregation of several hundred Old Etonian cricketers, spoke of nothing but cricket. How he lived for fifty years is a mystery, but at the very end of his life there was about him a strong whiff of Maundy Gregory, of whom he could proudly display a number of mementoes. He may well have helped F.E. with the murkier aspects of his always chaotic finances: he is thought to have had some connection with stockbroking. It is not impossible that there was even an element of blackmail in his hold over F.E. He certainly spoke darkly in old age of all the things he could reveal if he were so minded; on the other hand those of his recollections that could be checked proved largely false. He was bitter that the second Earl's biography of his father omitted him entirely. He had some cause, since he was undoubtedly a constant companion of the last ten years of F.E.'s life: he gave up his job in the Lord Chancellor's Department in 1924 to follow 'my beloved F.E.'⁹ to the India Office, and then into the City, and he was much more than a secretary. But more than this it is very difficult to add. He was by any standard a very queer fish. He belongs to the shadowy background of F.E.'s life, and whatever it was he might have told, he did not.

Cartwright's job in the Lord Chancellor's Department (he was not strictly F.E.'s private secretary but stayed on for two years under Cave and Haldane until he rejoined F.E.) was ecclesiastical patronage secretary. Until quite recently, the Lord Chancellor was incongruously responsible for the appointment of clergy to an enormous number of livings – three times as many, in fact, as the two Archbishops combined, some 700 in all, mostly the poorer ones. This was one of the more curious unreformed legacies from the medieval Chancellorship. To have such a notorious materialist as F.E. in charge of Church patronage might have been a legitimate reason for raised eyebrows in clerical circles (though in practice F.E., with his Liverpool background and his constitutional reverence for the alliance of Church and State, gave no ground for complaint). To have such a man as 'Buns' Cartwright with day-to-day responsibility for it was even more extraordinary. His criteria for the selection of eligible incumbents were eccentric, even allowing for the traditional affinity between cricket and the cloth. Margaret once asked to see the list of candidates, and was surprised to find their credentials carefully noted against each name: 'good left-hand bowler' or 'right-hand bat'![10]

Another extraneous function of the Lord Chancellor, only marginally legal in character, was responsibility for the welfare of lunatics and others unable to fend for themselves. Until 1959, lunatics had the right to write a daily letter to the Lord Chancellor. One who, according to Cartwright, used to write regularly to F.E., on long sheets of brown lavatory paper, was his own brother Sidney. Sidney Smith was not in the ordinary sense of the word a lunatic; he was rather a war hero. The coming of war in 1914 had at last given him a purpose in life. He had enlisted at once, was promoted from the ranks to a commission in the Royal Fusiliers and transferred in 1915 to the Hampshire Regiment, with whom he went to France. In August 1918 he was commanding an ammunition magazine when it was blown up by aerial bombardment. He suffered severe head wounds and brain damage from which he never properly recovered.[11] F.E. paid much of the cost of seeing him cared for, but the pathetic dependence of this unfortunate brother with whom he had never got along must have been a sore embarrassment to him, particularly when Sidney took to assailing his Department with accusing letters. Mercifully, Sidney died of his wounds in 1924, aged fifty.

The widespread doubts that were expressed about F.E.'s suitability for the Lord Chancellorship did not long survive the day he first took his seat on the Woolsack. He was in point of fact still a commoner, plain Sir Frederick Smith, when he presided over his first judicial hearing in the House of Lords. F.E. sat with his noble and learned colleagues Buckmaster and Finlay (both ex-Lord Chancellors), Atkinson, Dunedin and Shaw (all very much his seniors) in a case in which Friedrich Krupp, the German armaments manufacturers, disputed the breaking at the beginning of the war of their contract with a British iron ore company. He displayed no diffidence and gave a confident judgment, unanimously supported. Five days later, on 4 February, he was formally introduced to their Lordships' House and took the title Baron Birkenhead. In 1910 Mr Justice Bigham, on becoming a Law Lord, had called himself Lord Mersey and joked that he was 'leaving the Atlantic for F.E.'.[12] In the event F.E. was more modest, but he succeeded immediately in investing the name of his decaying industrial birthplace with the same glamour that had for ten years now been conjured by the initials 'F.E.': the name had suddenly as proud a ring to it as Kitchener or Curzon. A week later he sat for the first time as chairman of debates in the new Parliament. Though *Punch* noted that he wore his tricorne hat at a rakish angle,[13] the novelty of the 'Galloper' on the Woolsack quickly faded.

One unseemly row threatened his dignity before it was fully established. During the previous year it had been decided by the House of Lords that the Lord Chancellor, like the Speaker of the Commons, should be provided with an official residence within the Palace of Westminster, and work was put in hand to modernize the accommodation available, in particular by installing a second bathroom and a lift. In the post-war climate of economic stringency, however, the House of Commons refused to sanction the necessary expenditure, which was gleefully represented as a scandalous subsidy from the taxpayer to cushion the notorious extravagance of the new Lord Chancellor. The question of the 'Lord Chancellor's Bath' excited much ribald fun and spurious indignation in the House of Commons and the press. One Liberal M.P. protested that the money could be better spent providing twenty cottages for aged workers, while a Labour member approved the provision of a lift for the servants, but thought it would do F.E. good to have to walk! In vain did Austen Chamberlain, as Chancellor of the Exchequer, and the Financial Secretary to the Treasury, Stanley Baldwin, point out that the initiative to provide him with an official residence was none of F.E.'s idea and that a second bathroom for a house of thirty-three rooms was not excessive luxury.[14] A letter to *The Times* proposed maliciously that since £1,700 had apparently been spent on the 'embellishment' of a private residence, 'not only without authority of the House of Commons, but contrary to its expressed view of the subject, the tenant will surely be disposed to refund the charge out of a Ministerial salary exceptionally munificent'.[15] Eventually F.E. announced that he had never wanted to live in the official residence in the first place, that it would have actually involved him in increased expense (which cannot have been quite true, since he had planned to let Grosvenor Gardens to Winterton while he lived rent free), and that he would now remain in his own house. The renovation was in the end carried out, and his successor Cave was the first Lord Chancellor to move in in 1923. The whole rumpus was directed much more against F.E. than against the principle of a Lord Chancellor's residence. It was an early example of the sort of unbecoming incident with which his ill-wishers expected F.E.'s Chancellorship to be studded; but it was an incident entirely worked up by the ill-wishers themselves, though – like his arrest in France – it continued to spawn stories detrimental to F.E.

Gossip of this sort aside, however, F.E. very quickly impressed his calibre on those who were in a position to judge him in the House of Lords, and his authority on those who sat with him. If his fellow Law Lords had initial doubts – and Dunedin admitted to Lloyd George many years later that they had – they were very soon spreading the word that he was after all a great Lord Chancellor. His academic past was suddenly rediscovered to account for the revelation. The *Law Quarterly Review* claimed never to have forgotten his credentials. Commenting on one of his judgments in July 1920 that 'Lord Birkenhead's judicial utterances in the House of Lords have by this time conclusively disposed of the apprehensions entertained in some quarters that in his period of controversial politics he had forgotten his law', it congratulated itself that 'readers of the Review who are old enough to remember an excellent article on the rule in *Hadley* v. *Baxendale* contributed just twenty years ago by Mr F.E. Smith, then a rising junior . . . have presumably not fallen into any such error'.[16]

The Times, too, in a political profile, conceded that 'he was not a Vinerian scholar for nothing'. He was certainly not a great lawyer – 'one can well imagine', it sniffed, 'that his fondness for short cuts may often have been a trial'. Nevertheless, 'no Lord Chancellor ever had a surer grasp of the main principles of law than he, and, what is not perhaps so well known, no-one ever had a greater power of work – hard, rapid and at the same time sure'.

The writer went on to expand this insight in a paragraph of unusual perception.

Some people do their work, as the Pharisees did their praying, in public, so that all men may see, and they have their reward in being taken very seriously. Mr Smith in this matter of work was – still is as Lord Birkenhead – one of the Sadducees. Work with him is a disagreeable necessity, the mere kitchen and back apartments of the palace that is life . . . But the work gets done . . . and when it is done . . . the real business of a free man, which is to enjoy the phantasmagoria of life and power, begins. Lord Birkenhead has always enjoyed the magnificences, like his distinguished predecessor on the Woolsack, Lord Wolsey . . . Aristotle, it will be remembered, puts magnificence among the virtues.[17]

Nowhere was F.E.'s philosophy of living better or more sympathetically expressed during his lifetime.

A rather less sympathetic commentary on the spectacle of F.E.'s Lord Chancellorship is to be found in the lengthy published correspondence of Harold Laski (from 1920 a young politics lecturer at the London

School of Economics) and his American mentor, the eighty-year-old Supreme Court Justice, Oliver Wendell Holmes. Laski's letters powerfully illustrate the prejudice F.E.'s public persona aroused in those who barely knew him; but a grudging admiration is continually at odds with his determined disapproval. 'The Lord Chancellor . . . his natural blackguardism apart', he confessed in July 1921, 'is the best after-dinner speaker I have ever heard.'[18] Holmes replied to this that he remembered him as 'the most amusing man at dinner when there were no speeches . . . but I shouldn't think he was of the calibre of the great chancellors'.[19] Laski was happy to reassure him of this, 'I agree with you that Birkenhead is far from first-rate. He's exactly the difference between cleverness (which he has in abundance) and ability. He has infinite energy and push, but no natural firmness of mind and no penetration.'[20] This was an extraordinary misjudgment with which no Cabinet colleague or judge who sat with F.E. would have agreed for a moment; but it is significant that Laski wanted to believe it. Again, in February 1922, the denigration is wilful. 'The L.C. is magnificent – first-rate at nothing but invective; but so admirably second-rate in everything that he gives a total impression of quite permanent importance.'[21]

Laski's chagrin is evident. His orderly, puritanical mind, moreover, could not cope with a Lord Chancellor 'whose varied genius enables him to dine one night with the King and on the next with Jimmy Wilde the boxer'.[22] A few weeks later he happened to meet F.E. at lunch at Haldane's in one of his overbearing moods which gratifyingly confirmed his preconception. 'Of his brains there's not a ghost of a doubt,' he now conceded. 'Very clever but an obvious cad. He posed and talked as though he were a revivified Brougham – not a pleasant picture.'[23] Holmes replied that he had found F.E. 'a witty cove, but from reading one or two of his political speeches, I find it hard to believe him profound. Yet' – here was the puzzle again – 'I hear that his decisions show much study and mastery.'[24]

This unpalatable fact F.E.'s detractors were eventually forced by his achievements to admit. In 1925 Laski reported to Holmes another dinner, at which F.E. was not present, with Haldane and 'a galaxy of judges' – Dunedin, Sumner and Shaw, all Law Lords who had sat with five or six Lord Chancellors, plus Schuster, who had now served five. 'You would, I think, have been impressed by the way in which they all spoke of Birkenhead as unquestionably the most successful chancellor of many years.'[25]

One reason for F.E.'s success was that he so thoroughly appreciated the delicate constitutional balancing act which the office demanded. He understood the theoretical anomalies which prompted the recurrent call – dating back to Bentham but most lately revived by Haldane as chairman of an inquiry into the machinery of government – that it should be broken up and its triple functions dispersed between two or three less onerous positions; but he considered them amply justified in practice and determined to defend them both by his actions and in writing. Haldane's principal proposal was for the establishment of a Ministry of Justice on the continental model, headed by an ordinary political Minister who would have no judicial function and need not even be a lawyer, any more than the Minister of Agriculture must be a farmer. F.E. firmly rejected this attack on his historic office, and gave his reasons in two essays published in his collection *Points of View* in 1922.[26] His argument, characteristically practical and founded on his candid understanding of professional ambition as well as his reading of the British Constitution, was that a political Minister, even if he were a lawyer, would not, without the unique prestige conferred by the Woolsack, command the respect from the judiciary and a necessarily aggrandized Attorney-General, to uphold the independence of the judiciary against the continual threat of political interference, of which he gave some examples from quite recent history. It was the fact that he was a judge himself that gave the Lord Chancellor authority over the judges and the fact that he was a Cabinet Minister of special standing that gave him authority in the Government: no Prime Minister could survive the resignation on a point of principle of his Lord Chancellor, whereas a mere Minister of Justice could be dropped or reshuffled at his whim. It was, in short, the anomalous duality of the Lord Chancellor's position, at once 'the buffer and the link' between the otherwise separated branches of the Constitution, which was the guarantee of their separation. He was the licensed exception which sustained the rule. In the last resort, it must be admitted, F.E.'s case came down to simple patriotic conservatism, the preservation of a system that had worked for centuries in preference to a theory, perhaps more logical, that might suit newer nations with written constitutions and Roman systems of administrative law but was inappropriate to Britain's organic constitution and English common law. If the traditional office placed exceptional burdens upon its occupant, he might have added, that was a point in favour of a Lord Chancellor young enough to bear them! It was at this personal aspect, perhaps, that he was hinting, humorously, in his speech at the Lord Mayor's Banquet in November 1921, when he dealt briefly with Haldane's proposal before asserting his outright opposition.

A Ministry of Justice in this country will only be brought into being over my official corpse. [Laughter.] I am in this country the

Minister of Justice [cheers] and having cast my eye, with, I hope, impartial vision, over aspirants to that office, I am unable to discern one who, I think, is likely to discharge the duties better.[27]

Since few Lord Chancellors were ever likely to have his energy, however, F.E. was not the best advertisement for his own argument – especially since even he found the burden of the office too much for his health and twice had to seek periods of rest during his four-year tenure. It was in any case a somewhat surprising argument from one so determined to rationalize other areas of the judicial system; many legal observers felt that a Minister of Justice would be much better able to carry through those reforms than was a Lord Chancellor weighed down with other duties. It was a part of F.E.'s impulse as a reformer, however, to prove that he could fulfil all three roles, combining successfully in his own person both the dignified and the efficient elements of the Constitution. Over the past sixty years, in fact, the burdens of the office have been reduced in certain minor ways; but the essential principle which F.E. sought to uphold remains unaltered. The Lord Chancellor in the 1980s still exercises the triple function – executive, legislative and judicial – which F.E. inherited from Bacon, Brougham and Finlay and passed on intact to Cave.

One of the most responsible functions of the Lord Chancellor as head of the judiciary is the appointment of other judges. F.E. took the bestowal of this patronage very seriously. Undoubtedly he took special pleasure, where he could, in promoting Wadham men and old colleagues from the Liverpool Bar such as Rigby Swift, Arthur Greer and George Branson (who had acted as one of his juniors in the Casement trial). But he was careful to incur no suspicion of favouritism or corruption. He used his own judgment, but his standards were high: he was not prepared to stock the bench with unworthy placemen at anyone's bidding. In appointing Greer, he infuriated Lloyd George, who had wanted the place for one of his old Welsh colleagues, Ellis Griffith, and had probably promised it to him. In 1921 Bonar Law interceded on behalf of the Tory M.P. for Ealing, Sir Herbert Nield, only to receive back two letters – one politely evasive, the other characteristically robust:

The truth is that he is a pompous little ass, who is rewarded beyond his deserts, if foisted onto the County Court Bench, and whose higher promotion would be a blatant public scandal. Should you think it worth while to forward my other letter to the gentleman, it might be well to take care that this is not sent in error.[28]

Harold Laski relayed to Holmes another good story, relating to the legal historian Edward Jenks, who had been examiner in law at Oxford twenty-five years earlier.

> Jenks . . . applied to Birkenhead . . . to be made K.C. In reply he got the following letter: 'My dear Jenks, In 1897 you gave the present Lord Chancellor a second in the B.C.L. In 1898 you gave a second also to the Vinerian Professor [Holdsworth]. These are, I think, sufficient honours for a single lifetime. Yours faithfully, B.'
> A superb letter, I think, which only Birkenhead would have had the intolerable audacity to write.[29]

F.E.'s most important innovation in this area was to promote for the first time a county court judge to the High Court. He had a special reason for doing this. His acceptance of the Woolsack had come as a dreadful shock to Peteil, who was, according to his daughter, 'almost suicidal' at the rupture of their long and lucrative association.[30] To cushion the blow, F.E. raised Edward Acton – incidentally a scholar of Wadham and a member of the Northern Circuit – from the county court and arranged for Peteil to become his Judge's Clerk. The loss of prestige and salary from being clerk to the Attorney-General was compensated by a drop in tension not unwelcome to a prematurely ageing man, whose devotion to F.E. remained unimpaired. Acton proved an excellent judge, and his unprecedented elevation opened the way for similar promotions in the future. Both the innovation itself and the reason for it are highly characteristic of F.E.

The Greer case caused a minor row between F.E. and Lloyd George, but the decision in that instance was F.E.'s. A much more serious dispute arose two years later, when F.E. found himself obliged to resist another political assault on the independence of the judiciary, this time in an area where the prerogative was the Prime Minister's – the appointment of the Lord Chief Justice.

The problem arose because of another of those cherished conventions of the legal pecking order which gave the Attorney-General of the day the right to first refusal of the Chief Justiceship if it fell vacant. It happened that when Lord Reading was appointed to be Viceroy of India in 1921, F.E.'s successor as Attorney-General, Gordon Hewart, was exceedingly anxious to exercise his traditional right; Lloyd George, however, found Hewart too useful as a Liberal spokesman in the House of Commons and refused to let him go. Ever fertile in devices to evade constitutional obstacles, he proposed a compromise: that Hewart should remain in the Commons for the present while an elderly judge was appointed Lord Chief Justice on the understanding that he would retire and make way for Hewart in a year or two. F.E., like Thomas Becket, found it his duty to remonstrate strongly with the chief who had appointed him to his high office. Firmly he drew the Prime Minister's attention to Section 9 of the Judicature Act, which provided 'that all the Judges of the High Court of Justice . . . shall hold office for life subject to a power of removal by Her Majesty on an address presented by both Houses of Parliament'. The appointment of a judge on condition that he should retire when called upon to do so, he asserted, not only breached the letter of the Act but flew in the face of its spirit and actually defeated the object for which the Act was passed, the independence of judges from political control.

> The proposal under contemplation . . . would make the Lord Chief Justice a transient figure, subject to removal at the will of the Government of the day, and the creature of political exigency. I do not think that if such an arrangement were publicly discussed, it would be found capable of reasoned defence.

In other words, he would not be prepared to defend it. In addition – here F.E. diluted his objection of principle with a practical argument – he questioned the fitness of Finlay or any of the other senior judges whose names had been canvassed to discharge the functions of the office for even two or three years. He sympathized with the Prime Minister's difficulty, but did not think that his way to solve it was acceptable.[31]

Lloyd George was not amused by this legalistic pedantry, and returned a stinging reply in his own hand.

> My dear Lord Chancellor,
> I fail to see the point of your lengthy typewritten document with its quotation from the Judicature Act. I never suggested to you the subjects of your elaborate protest. My only proposal to you was that I should appoint a distinguished lawyer on the express understanding that he should retire at 80. If it is contrary to the Judicature Acts to stipulate that high legal functionaries should not cling to their posts into years of decrepitude then it is high time these Acts were amended.
> To take the Attorney-General from his present post under existing conditions would be a national disservice . . .
> As to Finlay's capacity Carson whom you will admit is the most eminent advocate of his day told me the profession would regard his appointment with great satisfaction.[32]

In raising the question of a fixed retiring age, Lloyd George was in fact retreating, behind his bluster, to less objectionable ground. But

F.E. still considered it indefensible to appoint a 78-year-old Chief Justice; nor was he prepared to see the Prime Minister prefer Carson's advice to his own. Tactfully, he wrote his second letter out by hand.

> The question has never arisen whether a judge cd properly be put under a condition to retire at the age of 80 because so far as I know no-one has ever been made a judge at an age which suggested such a stipulation. Campbell was 70 when he became LCJ but his vitality was amazing: he was, I think, a record.
>
> Carson has not practised before Finlay since the latter became Ld Chancellor. I have sat with him continuously. I by no means say that he is unfit for judicial work but he is not the man he was and I do not think that he cd undertake the office of LCJ. The appointment is yours and if you appoint him I will loyally co-operate with him but *I most earnestly hope that if you do you will make him LCJ* without any condition, relying upon his age to terminate his tenure of office within a reasonable time. If any condition is imposed I am sure that we shall find ourselves exposed to the risks and difficulties suggested in my letter the suggestion of which was the object of that letter.[33]

Lloyd George hesitated, but he was not to be deflected from his purpose. F.E. suggested other alternatives. Carson, who was known to be waiting for a vacancy to become a Law Lord, might legitimately become Lord Chief Justice in the interval and then step sideways, making way for Hewart. Or if Hewart became Lord Chief Justice at once, Carson might step back into the breach as Attorney-General – not that this would have suited Lloyd George or, one imagines, have appealed much to Carson.[34] In the end Lloyd George went ahead and appointed, not Finlay, but Mr Justice A.T. Lawrence – one of those whose suitability F.E. had expressly rejected, on grounds equally of ability and age (he was seventy-seven). Presumably Lloyd George secured Lawrence's promise to retire when required, for just a year later he read of his resignation in *The Times* but went without complaint. Hewart (aged only fifty-two) stepped into his coveted inheritance, which he retained despite mounting criticism until 1940 when, his health failing, he was in his turn abruptly sacked by another imperious Prime Minister.[35] F.E. put the best gloss he could on his defeat: at Hewart's swearing-in ceremony he remarked blithely that Lawrence 'warned us . . . that he did not contemplate that his tenure . . . would be of very long duration'.[36]

No such problem arose with the Mastership of the Rolls, the other major judgeship which arose during F.E.'s time on the Woolsack. He concurred fully in Lloyd George's appointment of Lord Sterndale (the former William Pickford K.C.). But the circumstances of Sir Charles Swinfen Eady's retirement from the office through serious illness gave F.E. the opportunity for another characteristic exercise of generosity. Eady's dying wish was for a peerage to bequeath his family: F.E. went out of his way to petition Lloyd George and the King urgently to grant him his desire, and was able personally to convey the news to Eady's deathbed just in time for his fifteen-year-old son to succeed as Baron Swinfen.[37] F.E. always showed great understanding of the concern of distinguished fathers to hand on titles to their sons: such was his own extravagance that he was not able to hand on very much else. When in 1919 the press baron Sir Edward Hulton sought a special stipulation in his peerage to secure the inheritance to his *illegitimate* son, F.E. had no objection; the scheme was vetoed, however, somewhere between Downing Street and the Palace.[38]

There was another sphere in which F.E. had to fight to preserve the independence of the judiciary, though this was not so much a question of political interference with judges as of judges getting drawn into politics. A typical response of the Lloyd George Government to the unprecedented range of post-war problems with which it was faced was to set up an inquiry, often with a judge in the chair. Thus as early as March 1919 F.E., while agreeing to Churchill's request that he release Darling to head an inquiry into court-martial procedure, pointed out that three more of his King's Bench judges, plus three Chancery judges, were already taken up with commissions of one sort and another, in addition to the extended absence of the Lord Chief Justice, Reading, on a special mission to the United States.[39] In June F.E. firmly refused to release another from his judicial duties to chair a Royal Commission on Agriculture.[40]

Even without these distractions from their primary duty, F.E. felt that he had too few judges to cope with the enormous backlog of litigation held up by the war and now overwhelming the courts. He was soon asking Parliament to sanction the appointment of more. The backlog was greatest in the Divorce Court. Before the war, divorce petitions had been running at the rate of about a hundred a month. At the beginning of 1919 the court was faced with 4,201 in two months. In the spring of 1921 F.E. took drastic measures to reduce the arrears. For four weeks he himself sat every morning as an extra judge, with Lord Mersey, three King's Bench and one Chancery judge also called in to assist. In that Easter term they got through 1,261 undefended and 220 defended suits; on the last morning of this blitz, five judges disposed of 142 undefended cases.[41] It was magnificent, F.E. told the House of Lords, but it was war![42] The result, however, was to increase the congestion of cases in the King's Bench division, to meet which a number of expedients were adopted, including Saturday sittings and a curtailment of the Long Vacation.

Among other reforms intended to speed the flow of justice, F.E. successfully pushed through in 1919 the County Courts Act, which extended the Common Law jurisdiction of the county courts to several new areas of litigation (including actions for slander, libel, breach of promise and the like) from which they had previously been excluded, and in 1920 a Bill to establish special children's courts in London. The Administration of Justice Act, 1920, contained a further ragbag of measures relaxing traditional restrictions. The most controversial extended the range of cases which could be tried without a jury; the one nearest F.E.'s heart allowed some divorce cases to be heard by King's Bench judges on circuit, so that poor people would not, as hitherto, be obliged to transport themselves and their witnesses to London in order to present their suit. In December 1920 he foreshadowed in a series of articles in *The Times* (a choice of platform which shocked the professional journals) the further reforms he had in mind, many of which, either procedural – removing the special privileges enjoyed by the Crown as a litigant, for instance – or administrative – dealing with the staffing of courts, judges' salaries and the like – were included in a new Judicature Bill which he left to his successor on leaving office.[43] On one major item of his programme, however, F.E. was defeated: as part of his general rationalization of the judicial system, he proposed to remodel the Assize circuits to take account of shifts in population and the decline in importance of many old county towns which could no longer provide either the business or the facilities to justify their annual visitation by the whole panoply of Bench and Bar on tour. A lot of judicial time and public money were wasted on towns which no longer possessed jails, so that such prisoners as there were had to be transported in specially for trial. But the assize was the social event of the year and a focus of local pride and status. The outcry was too great to be overborne, and F.E. was left reflecting ruefully on the limits of the Lord Chancellor's power.

He amply achieved, however, his ambition to be remembered as a law reformer, as was generally recognized in the legal press when he left office. One measure above all set the seal on his record. This, beyond question the chief legislative monument to his Lord Chancellorship, was the Law of Property Act, 1922. He first conceived it, he told the House of Lords on the day of its final passage, in one of his university vacations thirty years before, when he had taken *Williams on Real Property* on a country walk and concluded that the Statute of Uses was a scholastic anachronism.[44] He was fortunate, nevertheless, that it fell to him to achieve a rationalization which had been the ambition of law reformers for a generation and the active concern of his predecessors on the Woolsack for a decade. For the need had long been recognized to simplify the system of transfer of land which, in the eight centuries since the Norman Conquest had grafted continental feudalism on to Anglo-Saxon custom, had become so encrusted with mediaeval obscurities and piecemeal modernization that it was all but incomprehensible and intolerably expensive.

Part of the answer was thought to lie in the centralized registration of land ownership. To this end Lord Halsbury had in 1897 actually carried a Land Transfer Bill which attempted to establish a system of compulsory registration; but the Act was emasculated by a late amendment sponsored by that ever-powerful trade union, the Law Society, on behalf of the solicitors, anxious then as now to safeguard the profits of their conveyancing monopoly by keeping it as complicated as possible. Compulsory registration was imposed only in London, as an experiment; elsewhere, compulsion was to be enforced only at the specific instance of the County Councils, who nowhere insisted.

One of the solicitors' delaying tactics in resisting registration was to argue that it made no sense to simplify the machinery of transforming title without simultaneously simplifying the concept of title itself, which was an undertaking so enormous that successive Governments quailed before attempting it. But in 1908 a Royal Commission was set up which reported in 1911, and Haldane presented Bills to Parliament in 1913, 1914 and 1915; none, however, made any progress. Still Lloyd George appointed another inquiry in 1917, chaired by F.E.'s old mentor Leslie Scott; and Scott, on his own admission, so packed the committee as to produce a unanimous report and a draft Bill, which F.E., on his accession to the Woolsack, inherited.[45]

Thus the spadework had already been done and the moment was ripe for F.E. to put his name to the comprehensive measure which he had always promised himself would be his first concern if ever he were to become Lord Chancellor. With Schuster's support he set the wheels of his Department in motion within a few weeks of taking office.

Stripped to its essentials, the Bill which F.E. presented to Parliament at the beginning of 1920 had two objects. First, it returned to the question of machinery of transfer and proposed to extend the principle of compulsory registration, county by county, to the whole country over a period of several years. Second, and more fundamentally, it faced up at last to the whole tortuous concept of land ownership and simply abolished the age-old distinction between 'real' property (i.e. land) and 'personal' property (other chattels), so as to make unnecessary most of the arcane and time-consuming document-hunting for which solicitors had hitherto been able to milk their clients. As F.E. himself explained it in *The Times*, 'Its general principle is to assimilate the law of real and personal estate and to free the purchaser from the obligation to enquire into the title of him from whom he purchases, any more than he would have to do if he were buying a share or a parcel of stock.' Such antique curiosities as copyhold tenure and gavelkind were swept into history, where they belonged.[46]

In other important ways, too, the twentieth century was acknowledged: women, for instance, were given an equal right to inherit land in cases of intestacy. For all its simple principle, the Bill required a mass of detailed clauses to stop every gap left by the Statutes it abolished and several hundred technical amendments to the Settled Land Acts, the Conveyancing Acts and the Trustee Acts.[47] The Bill as it eventually emerged to receive the Royal Assent was a monster of 276 pages, 185 clauses and 16 schedules; and even that was only the beginning, requiring another seven consolidating Acts in 1925 to complete the structure of consequent reforms.

The Bill which F.E. initially introduced in 1920 was carried successfully through the Lords and scrutinized by a joint committee of both Houses chaired by Haldane, but had to be withdrawn in the face of generally ignorant professional criticism led by Cave (who ironically had the task, as F.E.'s successor, of crowning the whole work in 1925). Reintroduced the following year, however, it finally reached the Statute Book in June 1922, largely as a result, it was generally acknowledged, of F.E.'s mastery of the House of Lords. Leslie Scott, now Solicitor-General, who bore the brunt of the less troublesome opposition in the Commons, paid generous tribute to him.

> It is to the present Lord Chancellor more than to any one man that the nation is indebted for the Bill as it appears today. It was his great knowledge, his grasp of the essentials of the Bill and, above all, his tact and skill in piloting the Bill through the dangerous shoals of another place, in explaining its provisions, in considering and meeting objections, in assimilating and incorporating suggested improvements – it was these qualities of his which have made it almost an agreed Bill.[48]

A couple of years later, disappointed of the promotion he had expected, Scott was inclined to claim with some bitterness that F.E. 'has had all the credit and I have had none' for what he called 'the biggest legal reform that has ever been put upon the Statute Book of this country'.[45] He had some reason to feel aggrieved: his committee had prepared much of the ground. But the fact remains that it is the political will of the Minister concerned which translates reforming intentions into accomplished Acts, and the undeniable political will which carried the Law of Property Act through the Cabinet and through Parliament was F.E.'s. He saw it as his opportunity to leave a permanent mark on the law, was determined to seize it, and was very proud of his achievement, though he was at pains to stress the co-operative nature of the achievement and the part played by previous Lord Chancellors, by his departmental draftsmen and by Scott. He never pretended to have done more than to provide the political momentum for the work of others. He did not even exaggerate its importance; he knew that his Act was only a beginning. But, as he modestly told a Gray's Inn dinner in honour of its passage, 'We have by the Act established some contact with sanity in dealing with land.'[49]

Only the extension of compulsory registration was a failure. The solicitors continued to resist strongly, and F.E. was forced to promise that no extension would come into force for a transitional ten years after the operation of the rest of the Act; that shelved the question until 1935, and between then and 1939 only Middlesex and Croydon were brought into the scheme. Not until the late 1950s, when the Law Society at last extracted from the Government the principle that solicitors should be paid the same fees for the conveyancing of registered and of unregistered land, did they relax their rearguard action to defeat legislation first mooted in the previous century and actually enacted in 1922. Until that point was gained,

> deeds relating to land normally remained in the hands of the solicitors handling the transaction. The black tin boxes in which they were stored became the mark of a respectable solicitor. They not only protected the documents and represented an important part of the saleable goodwill of a practice, but they also symbolised the profession's monopoly over conveyancing.[50]

F.E. reformed the law, but he could not breach the self-interested conservatism of the lawyers.[51]

It was by his judgments, however, that F.E. as Lord Chancellor most fully established his claim to greatness and revealed his true stature, so often doubted, as a lawyer of the highest accomplishment. Technical as they inevitably are, no account of his career would be complete which did not give some space to considering the most important of them; for more clearly than anything else, they demonstrate the essential seriousness behind his pose of ambition, recklessness and pleasure.

The great majority of them were given in commercial cases – disputes over contracts and the like – and particularly in shipping cases arising from collision or from loss – insurance claims and liability for damages or compensation. These highly specialized questions can hold little interest for the modern reader; but it is worth emphasizing them, for in these even more than in more famous judgments one cannot but be impressed by F.E.'s masterly elucidation of complex issues, his reviewing of precedents, his testing of the arguments against the evidence and his ultimate presentation of his ruling, without pedantry or obfuscation but often with a striking assertion of common sense. The nature of the minefield into which he had suddenly stepped, which constantly required him to chart, as no barrister has to, the judge's narrow path between upholding justice or the letter of the law, may be neatly illustrated by two of these commercial cases, one from 1919, the other from 1920. In the first, *Les Affréteurs Réunis Société Anonyme* v. *Leopold Walford (London) Ltd.*, a question of the commission payable to the brokers who had chartered for clients a ship later requisitioned by the French Government, F.E. rejected the argument that 'custom' legitimized a breach of the strict terms of a contract; in the second, on the other hand, *British and Foreign Insurance Company* v. *Wilson Shipping Company*, he endorsed an established practice of marine underwriters even though it was not explicitly allowed for in the contract. In the first case F.E. was overturning, in the second upholding, the original judgment of Mr Justice Bailhache. On both occasions he was unanimously supported by the colleagues sitting with him.

His remarks in the former provide a good example of his courteously trenchant, just mildly sarcastic manner of expressing disagreement with the finding of a lower court.

My Lords, in contrast with the extreme sanctity which the learned Judge conceded to this custom . . . I confess I am somewhat attracted by the tone of his reference to the deliberate contract entered into between the parties. The custom, the learned Judge says, 'is irrespective of the form in which the commission clause finds its way into the charter-party'. My Lords, in my experience, important clauses do not 'find their way' into important contracts. They are, on the contrary, the fruit of negotiation and consideration. The process is by no means so fortuitous as is supposed. The learned Judge, in my judgement . . . has in effect declared that a custom may be given effect to in commercial matters which is entirely inconsistent with the plain words of an agreement into which commercial men, presumably acquainted with so well-known a custom, have, nevertheless, thought proper to enter. Much evidence would be necessary to convince me of the existence of such a custom, and, if it were forthcoming, I should nevertheless hold the custom to be bad on grounds which seem to me to be both notorious and elementary.[52]

In the insurance case, however, F.E. was prepared to rule the opposite way on what seems to the lay eye a very similar question.

The rule so stated embodies a principle upon which underwriters and merchants have based their practice for upwards of a century, and even if this House were of opinion that the rule did not correctly state the law, it would be a matter for grave consideration whether such a rule, which has been observed for so long, which has been expressly or impliedly incorporated in so many contracts, and which has profoundly influenced the course of dealing between merchants, should be reversed at this period in its history. In my opinion, the question does not arise.[53]

How fine the distinction between differing circumstances!

F.E.'s Liverpool background stood him in good stead in all these shipping cases; much of his early experience at the Bar had been gained arguing similar suits. But of course he did not sit alone. The Lord Chancellor sits as the leader, chairman and chief spokesman of a team of Law Lords, and F.E. was never ashamed, where he did not have the expert knowledge himself, to use the brains of others. One of the most important of his judgments, for instance, that in the case of *Admiralty Commissioners* v. *S.S.* Volute, which was described by Lord Finlay, assenting to it, as 'a great and permanent contribution to our law on the subject of contributory negligence, and to the science of jurisprudence', was largely drafted by Lord Phillimore.[54] This lack of false pride – founded on perfect self-confidence – was one of his strengths. From the very first case on which he sat, F.E. handled his older and legally more eminent colleagues with perfect tact, deferring to their experience where appropriate, but impressing them with his own unsuspected learning and authority. Of the five living ex-Lord Chancellors who might have sat with him, Halsbury and Loreburn never did so; Buckmaster and Finlay, however, sat regularly (in 32 and 34 cases respectively out of a total of 70 hearings over which F.E. presided); Haldane in 15. Of his other possible colleagues, Lords Atkinson (47); Shaw (31) and Dunedin (28) were the most frequent attenders, followed by Lords Parmoor and Wrenbury (19 each), Sumner (16) and Cave (14). Phillimore sat only 6 times, and Moulton (who died in 1921) only 5. Lord Moulton's replacement was Carson, who sat several times under his former 'galloper' when first appointed, but less frequently after their serious quarrel over the Irish Treaty which might have made judicial co-operation difficult. In the only criminal case which came before F.E., Reading sat in as Lord Chief Justice. F.E.'s judgments were almost all unanimously supported by his colleagues: on only five occasions were dissenting judgments offered.

In one case, quite early in his Lord Chancellorship, F.E. showed particularly bold leadership and a readiness to overthrow precedent in an area where he considered the law antiquated and anachronistic. This was in *Bourne* v. *Keane*, a famous case which turned on the legality or otherwise of bequeathing money to certain Roman Catholic communities for the purpose of having masses said for the souls of the dead. The bequest had been declared void in the Chancery Division in accordance with the principle established in *West* v. *Shuttleworth* in 1835, and the decision was upheld by the Master of the Rolls in the Appeal Court. F.E., sitting in the House of Lords with Finlay, Atkinson, Wrenbury and Parmoor, would have none of it. After reviewing at length the history of legal disabilities placed upon Roman Catholics since the Reformation, he concluded that gifts to provide masses for the souls of the dead should have ceased to be deemed superstitious when Catholicism itself ceased to be illegal, and declared eighty-four years of legal authority to the contrary to be wrong.

In my view it is undoubtedly true that ancient decisions are not to be lightly disturbed when men have accepted them and regulated their dispositions in reliance upon them. And this doctrine is especially worthy of respect in cases where title has passed from man to man in reliance upon a sustained trend of judicial opinion.

But this, my Lords, is not the present case. If my view is well founded, citizens of this country have for generations mistakenly held themselves precluded from making these dispositions. I cannot conceive that it is my function as a judge of the Supreme Appellate Court of this country to perpetuate error in a matter of this kind. The proposition crudely stated really amounts to this, that because members of the Roman Catholic faith have wrongly supposed for a long period of time that a certain disposition of their property was unlawful, and have abstained from making it, we, who are empowered and bound to declare the law, refuse to other members of that Church the reassurance and the relief to which our view of the law entitles them. My Lords, I cannot and will not be a party to such a proposal.[55]

This was a fine exercise of 'judicial valour', asserting, as R.F.V. Heuston puts it, 'that the House of Lords is not definitely committed to the view that it is better to be consistently wrong than ultimately right'.[56] Of his colleagues, only Wrenbury was not carried along by F.E.'s boldness. He agreed with F.E.'s interpretation but held, with what can only be called judicial timidity, that 'owing to the length of time the decisions impugned had been in existence and acted upon, it was too late to reverse them'.[57] Finlay, Atkinson and Parmoor, however, were persuaded to follow F.E.'s lead.

F.E. delivered another important judgment in the only criminal appeal which came up to him, *Director of Public Prosecutions* v. *Beard*. In this case, unusually, the appellant was not the prisoner, Beard, who had been convicted at Chester Assizes of murdering a thirteen-year-old girl in the course of raping her, but the Crown; for the Appeal Court had quashed the conviction and substituted one of manslaughter (with a sentence of twenty years' imprisonment instead of death), accepting the argument that he had been too drunk to know what he was doing. If conceded, however, this was a dangerous and important precedent for future murder trials, in which drink was so often a factor; the Crown took the question to the House of Lords where an exceptional sitting of eight judges considered it. The hearing took three days in December 1919; but it was not until 5 March 1920 that F.E. was ready to deliver their Lordships' unanimous judgment. He began by pointing out that the old authorities viewed drunkenness as an aggravation, rather than a mitigation of guilt, but allowed that there had been some relaxation of this attitude in the previous century. He now, however, spelled out the principle clearly: that killing in furtherance of another felony was murder, so that it was necessary for the accused to show not merely that he had not intended to kill but that he had been too drunk even to have formed the intention to commit the lesser crime.

> My Lords, drunkenness in this case could be no defence unless it could be established that Beard at the time of committing the rape was so drunk that he was incapable of forming the intent to commit it, which was not in fact, and manifestly, having regard to the evidence, could not be contended. For in the present case the death resulted from two acts or from a succession of acts, the rape and the act of violence causing suffocation. These acts cannot be regarded separately and independently of each other. The capacity of the mind of the prisoner to form the felonious intent which murder involves is in other words to be explored in relation to the ravishment; and not in relation merely to the violent acts which gave effect to the ravishment.

That was the principle to be applied in future; in Beard's case, their Lordships ultimately decided, the question of his drunkenness was anyway a red herring,

In the present case I doubt, without reaching a conclusion, whether there was any sufficient evidence to go to the jury that the prisoner was, in the only relevant sense, drunk at all. There was certainly no evidence that he was too drunk to form the intent of committing rape. In the circumstances it was proved that death was caused by an act of violence done in furtherance of the felony of rape. Such a killing is by the law of England murder.[58]

Nevertheless the Home Secretary had already indicated that the death sentence would, in the circumstances, be commuted.

Some of the other civil cases which came up to the House of Lords during F.E.'s occupation of the Woolsack are worth noting briefly. There was *Weinberger* v. *Inglis*, in which a stockbroker of Bavarian birth, married and long resident in Britain, who had been a member of the Stock Exchange since 1895, contested the Committee's refusal to re-elect him in 1917. Their Lordships ruled that the Committee, under the rules of the Stock Exchange, was perfectly entitled to refuse anyone on its own discretion. F.E. hoped that with the restoration of peace it would now feel able 'to accept as a satisfactory credential 30 years of British citizenship unimpeached upon the essential point of integrity to the substituted allegiance'; but he would not criticize it for having been 'at a grave moment . . . disinclined . . . to take any risks'.[59]

In *Fitch* v. *Dewes*, (the first case on which Carson sat), F.E. gave an unreserved judgment, unanimously supported, upholding on grounds of public policy the right of an established solicitor to bind his apprentice not to set up in independent practice within seven miles of the same town. His argument was characteristically practical: not only was this limited restraint of trade not contrary to public interest:

I am of opinion that it is in the public interest that a proper restrictive agreement of this kind between an established solicitor, possibly an elderly man, and a younger man, should be allowed. It is in the public interest, because otherwise solicitors, perhaps carrying on their business without a partner, would be extremely chary of admitting competent young men to their offices and to the confidential knowledge to be derived by frequenting those offices.[60]

Sutters v. *Briggs* was one of those instructive cases which reveals an unintended loophole in the law, in this instance the 1835 Gaming Act. Section 2 of the Act, passed to prevent bankruptcy, fraud and other abuses much wider than gaming, was found to have the absurd effect of entitling a person who paid a gaming debt by cheque to recover the amount at a later date. In October 1920 a Mr Briggs placed £50 with a bookmaker, Sutters, on a horse running in the Cesarewitch, which lost; he paid the debt, but afterwards issued a writ to recover his money. The High Court and the Court of Appeal upheld his right, and the House of Lords now agreed that under the Act of 1835 this was correct. F.E. with some embarrassment excused their Lordships from responsibility for this anomaly.

> The consequence of this view will no doubt be extremely inconvenient to many persons. But this is not a matter proper to influence the House unless in a doubtful case affording foothold for balanced speculations as to the probable intentions of the Legislature. Where, as here, the legal issues are not open to serious doubt, our duty is to express a decision and leave the remedy (if one be resolved upon) to others.[61]

In fact, F.E. was able, wearing his other wig, to pilot a short Gaming Act swiftly through Parliament in 1922 to end this absurdity. In the course of the Second Reading debate in the Lords he made the extraordinarily untruthful claim that he 'almost never' risked any money on a bet except on the very rare occasions when he visited a racecourse.[62] The betting book of the Other Club gives him the lie.

Five cases concerned disputed wills. Several more, of greater human interest, which aroused F.E.'s evident compassion, dealt with claims under the Workmen's Compensation Act. In *Innes* v. *Kynoch* F.E. (with the majority of his colleagues but with Atkinson dissenting) reversed the decision of the Scottish Court of Session that a man infected by bacilli while handling artificial manure had not died as a consequence of his employment. In *Lancaster* v. *Blackwell Colliery Company Ltd.* he similarly overturned the Court of Appeal to rule in favour of the widow of a collier who had died as a result of a strangulated hernia caused by heavy work. In *King* v. *Port of London Authority* he took great pleasure in finding against the Authority's callous contention, ingeniously argued by Simon, that a docker's claim for compensation must fail because he had not made it within six months, even though the effects of the injury, which it was admitted arose out of his employment, were not at that time visible. Yet another case in which F.E. overruled the Appeal Court (in this instance the Irish Appeal Court) in favour of a poor applicant, *Manton* v. *Cantwell*, provides a marvellous example of his lucidity in setting out simultaneously the facts, the law and his reasons for ruling as he did. A labourer had been killed as a result of a fall while thatching a farmhouse. F.E. established the farmer's liability in a series of crushing deductions.

It is necessary to observe very closely, that it would not be possible to carry out the business of farming without the provision of either a farmhouse or some substituted premises. However small be the economy of the particular farm, however rudimentary the processes by which the business is conducted, some record at least must be preserved of them; in other words it is hardly possible to conceive of the case of a farm in which at least some office work must not be carried on, and as Mr Scanlan in his very ingenious and very clear argument was driven to admit, the only office which he could suggest in this case would be the farmhouse, the case of which we are now considering.

The result therefore is that we find a man who is earning his living by the process of agriculture finding himself compelled by his own rustic arts to effect a reparation in the roof of the office which is necessary for his business, and without the decent convenience of which he could not carry out his business. He provides the raw material which is required for his premises by using a commodity, itself a subject of barter in agriculture, and which he could dispose of in such a manner if he did not require it for the purpose of restoring his dwelling house. He does not, as he has often done before, and as many of his neighbours the local farmers did, carry out the repairs himself. He employs the deceased man to effect these repairs. I am not able to conceive how the argument can be successfully put forward that a man who employs another in a task of this kind is not employing him for the purposes of his trade or business, and I reach – hesitating to differ from all the Lords Justices in the Irish Court of Appeal but, nevertheless, quite clearly – the conclusion that the deceased man was so engaged, that the decision of the County Court Judge upon this point, amounting as it did to a finding of fact, was right, and that the decision of the Irish Court of Appeal must be reversed.[63]

Two cases in particular of those that came before him aroused a strong personal response in F.E. One of these was the celebrated case of Archdeacon Wakeford, a Canon of Lincoln, who had been convicted under ecclesiastical law by the Consistory Court of the Diocese of Lincoln on a charge of immorality – specifically of spending three nights in a hotel in Peterborough with a woman not his wife. The scandal was tremendous. Wakeford was a highly distinguished Churchman, a well-known preacher and theologian spoken of in Lincoln as the next Bishop, and he vehemently protested his innocence. He was permitted to appeal, not to the House of Lords but to the Judicial Committee of the Privy Council, which on this occasion was composed of F.E. plus three

Law Lords (Buckmaster, Dunedin and Shaw) with the Bishops of London, Gloucester, Rochester and Ely as Ecclesiastical Assessors. Wakeford's solicitors briefed Carson – his last important case before joining their Lordships. The Bishop of Lincoln in reply briefed Douglas Hogg, the most expensive new K.C. to have risen to sudden prominence since the war. The hearing, beginning on 8 April 1921, took the form of a retrial, with the witnesses – the managers of the hotel, waitresses, chambermaids and fellow-guests – all taken through their evidence again, and the press reporting the proceedings at length to an avid nation.

The case turned on a simple – but anything but straightforward – conflict of testimony. The Archdeacon admitted having stayed in the Bull Inn on the nights in question (comprising two separate visits) but denied having been in the company of a woman except briefly a girl to whom he had explained a Latin inscription in the Cathedral. Several witnesses testified that they had indeed seen him dining and breakfasting in the hotel, alone. But the manager and his wife, some of the staff and several guests swore that he had been with a woman aged between twenty-six and thirty (the Archdeacon was sixty-two), and the Visitors' Book contained the damning signature 'J. Wakeford and wife'. F.E., in a long judgment, which took an hour and a half to read, sifted all this evidence minutely: the Archdeacon's was internally quite consistent and complete in itself, his accusers' a fragmentary mosaic made up of scraps of information from many sources, often inconsistent or downright contradictory. Nevertheless the Archdeacon, for all his eminence and blameless record, had reason to lie, while those who claimed to have seen him with a woman could have none. F.E., in the words of Hogg's junior colleague W.N. Stable, 'struggled to the last' to believe Wakeford innocent.[64] Carson had put up a magnificent fight on his behalf, such that it seemed almost that the Bishop was in the dock, facing a hostile court; but then Hogg in his closing speech had brilliantly turned the tables. F.E. and his colleagues were reluctantly convinced. Carson's only explanation of the charge against Wakeford was a conspiracy: it was not possible that so many witnesses could be innocently mistaken. F.E., however, following Hogg, demolished this hypothesis. Granted that his brother-in-law and another clergyman bore him some ill-feeling, it was nevertheless improbable that they could have obtained the co-operation not only of the proprietors of the Bull and of their staff, but of a sergeant in the Peterborough police, in a plot to ruin the Archdeacon. Moreover the dates made it impossible. If a conspiracy had existed, it would have had to be framed before the conspirators even knew that Wakeford would be going to Peterborough or where he would choose to stay if he did.

By what amazing coincidence did it come about that the Appellant should have selected on this occasion the one hotel in Peterborough whose landlord was ready to be corrupted, able to carry with him into this maze of slander and perjury his wife and servants, and zealous to commence a systematic course of forgery in support of the plan?[65]

Convincing evidence that his signature in the Visitors' Book was forged was the last straw that might have saved Wakeford. But he himself admitted that if it were a forgery it was a very skilful one: the handwriting expert called in could not say positively that the writing was the Archdeacon's but agreed that it was very close. F.E. spent several paragraphs of his judgment comparing the exact way in which the letters of the words 'and wife' were formed and where the dot was placed over the 'i'. His son has recorded that, while writing his judgment, he once 'woke his wife at four o'clock in the morning, coming in fully dressed and haggard, with a magnifying glass, a letter with Wakeford's signature, and a photograph of the signature in the book at the Bull Inn. After scrutinizing the two signatures together, they came to the bleak conclusion that there was no difference.'[66] Accordingly F.E. and his fellow judges found, with real reluctance, against the Archdeacon, and the four Bishops could not but concur.

The second case in which F.E. deeply regretted the judgment which he was obliged to pass was a divorce case, at the very end of his Lord Chancellorship. (He had indeed actually left office by the time he delivered judgment.) Divorce was, as will be seen, an area of the law which F.E. had come to regard as desperately in need of reform. He had, by the time this case came up to him, already tried and failed to carry a reform measure through Parliament. *Rutherford* v. *Richardson* powerfully illustrated the cruelty of the law which he wanted to amend. Maude Rutherford's husband had gone out of his mind in 1919, had shot and killed her cousin, and was now confined in Broadmoor. She had petitioned for divorce, claiming adultery allegedly committed with his cousin, Amy Richardson, in 1916. Though there was some supporting evidence from servants, Miss Richardson denied it, and the medical evidence supported her. But with adultery unproven there was no other way, as the law then stood, that Mrs Rutherford – aged only forty – could be freed from her insane and violent husband to begin her life afresh. Her only escape was into adultery herself. F.E.'s ruling was a bleak condemnation of the state of the law.

During many more years, unless death remove him or release her, she must look forward to a loneliness from which she can escape

only by a violation of the moral law. To some this may appear a
harsh, and even an inhumane result; but such, my Lords, is the
Law of England. Your Lordships cannot, because of the sympathy
which you must all feel for this unhappy victim of our marriage
law, impeach the chastity of a woman, equally innocent, who is
also entitled to the sympathy and shelter of the law. The true
remedy lies outside any Court of Law; it lies beyond the scope
of your Lordships' faculties, sitting as the Supreme Appellate
Tribunal. It rests with Parliament (if and when it thinks proper) to
end a state of things which in a civilised community, and in the
name of morality, imposes such an intolerable hardship upon
innocent men and women.[67]

F.E. included with his collected judgments three further divorce suits
which he heard, not as Lord Chancellor sitting in the House of Lords,
but during his emergency stint as an extra judge sitting in the Divorce
division in the spring of 1921. Two of these have a certain prurient
interest. In *C.* v. *C.* (actually Colman v. Colman) a wife of nine years
petitioned for divorce on the ground that the marriage had never been
consummated, alleging impotence on her husband's part. The two told
utterly conflicting stories, he claiming that normal intercourse had
taken place 'when opportunity permitted' throughout the marriage, she
that though 'she was willing to assist . . . by wifely submission . . . he
uniformly failed to procure adequate erection'.[68] The opposing evidence
was necessarily of the most extreme intimacy – carefully distinguishing,
for instance, between manipulation (admissible) and masturbation
(unspeakable) as an aid to sexual arousal. F.E. summarized it all with a
delicacy which is wonderful to read, clothing the most naked of physical
facts with a majestic robe of legal modesty, before choosing to believe
the wife and granting her divorce. The second case, *Gaskill* v. *Gaskill*,
turned on the possible gestation period for a legitimate child. The
husband, serving at Salonika during the war, sued his wife for adultery
on the sole ground that she had produced a son eleven months after the
end of his last leave. She denied it and he furnished no other evidence.
Medical experts testified that pregnancies of this length were rare but
not unknown, and on this basis F.E. concluded that the child must be
assumed to be legitimate and rejected the petition. Closing his judgment on a personal note he begged the young couple to forgive one
another the mistrust which their freakish experience had naturally
engendered.

Both have been the sport of nature. Both are still young. They
were happy together until this suspicion arose. Now that it is

dissipated they should at least consider whether they cannot recapture that which they have lost.[69]

Just two more judgments of a very different order should be mentioned. In *McCawly* v. *The King* before the Judicial Committee of the Privy Council, F.E. enunciated a decision of great importance to the Constitution of Australia concerning the powers of the State Legislature of Queensland. F.E.'s description, in the course of this judgment, of the difference between a 'controlled' constitution (of the colonial type) and an 'uncontrolled' constitution (like the British) is a classic statement, regularly quoted by the writers of textbooks on constitutional law.

The second was not strictly a judgment at all, but a highly technical and learned speech to the House of Lords Committee of Privileges on the question of the right of Lady Rhondda, a peeress in her own right, to take her seat in the House. In part, F.E.'s opposition to Lady Rhondda's petition must be seen as a last instinctive spasm of opposition to the political emancipation of women generally: as he told the Lords during the debate on the Sex Disqualification (Removal) Bill in 1919 – the Government fortunately allowed a free vote on this clause – 'If we are to be abolished, I think that I would rather perish in the exclusive company of members of my own sex.'[70] It was on impeccably legal grounds, however, that he argued in 1922 against Lady Rhondda's admission, holding that the patent creating the peerage (in favour of her father, the wartime Food Controller D.A. Thomas) was issued before the passage of the Act, which expressly did not include the right to sit in the chamber, and that no reading of the patent could be interpreted as giving a woman that right. F.E.'s long speech, delving right back to Stuart times to establish the historic basis of peerages, was a *tour de force* of intricate constitutional law which may perhaps be seen as a last fling of advocacy. No one, anyway, was able to rebut his argument and the Committee, which had previously accepted Lady Rhondda's petition, now rejected it by twenty-two votes to four.

18

The Lord Chancellor As
Cabinet Minister, 1919–22

F.E. did not cease to be an ambitious politician just because he had accepted the Woolsack. On the contrary, he had accepted the Woolsack precisely to make sure of being in the Cabinet. At the same time as being a great Lord Chancellor in his legal capacity, therefore, he intended to be an unusually political Lord Chancellor as well. Some lawyers disapproved of his political prominence, as detracting from his legal dignity; but others welcomed the political weight which he brought to the administration of the law.

In going to the House of Lords at the age of forty-six, F.E. refused to accept that he had entered a mausoleum for politicians with their future behind them, but determined to treat it much like the House of Commons, setting himself by his own brilliance in it to restore its lustre and importance, as he had with Wadham and Gray's Inn. Practically alone, he took seriously the Government's repeated pledges to reform the Lords, as had been promised in 1911. As much as ever, he still regarded the Parliament Act as an abominable unbalancing of the bicameral constitution: now the interest of his own career furnished an additional reason for seeking to re-establish its authority. In his agony of indecision before accepting Lloyd George's offer, there are indications that he sought an assurance that the Prime Minister acknowledged his inheritance of Asquith's obligation – an obligation which a Coalition Government would be far better able than a party one to honour.

For F.E., the post-war Coalition was a dream come true: this was what he and Winston had been working for since 1910. At last he was in high office, with his best friends – Winston, Lloyd George and Bonar Law – in a Government composed of the best men of both main parties, unshackled by pre-war party ties. They had put party behind them, and seemed to have the political world at their feet.

At first, despite his office, F.E. remained relatively junior, still ranking behind Law, Balfour, Long, Chamberlain, Carson and Curzon in the Tory hierarchy. With first Long's retirement, however, then Law's in March 1921; with Carson becoming a Law Lord, Curzon an object of derision to Lloyd George, and Balfour very much the elder statesman, the leadership increasingly devolved on Chamberlain (Law's successor) and F.E., in combination with Lloyd George and Churchill – generals of the stage army of Coalition Liberals. Feeling little sympathy with Chamberlain, Lloyd George came by 1922 to lean more and more heavily on F.E. as his most trusted colleague. The Lord Chancellor was now at the very heart of the administration. But by then the vision of 1919 had faded. Dazzled by their own power and beset by the unprecedented problems of the peace, the Coalition leaders neglected the revival of party and failed to see how dangerously they had cut themselves off from their restless followers. Free of the normal disciplines, they became arrogant and contemptuous of those on whom their power depended. Arrogance bred the nemesis of the Coalition, which fell with a crash from which F.E.'s career never recovered. But it was glorious while it lasted.

(i) The Peace Conference

In fact, F.E. needed a little time to establish his authority in the Coalition Cabinet. The reason was simply that the full Cabinet did not actually meet for eleven months, until November 1919. The Prime Minister was almost permanently in Paris for the Peace Conference, while several other senior Ministers commuted regularly back and forth between Paris and London. In addition, it suited Lloyd George's method of working to govern without a Cabinet for as long as possible: even the old War Cabinet now had little continuous existence – Lloyd George simply dealt with whichever Ministers he needed for any particular purpose. Only reluctantly and under pressure from his colleagues did he finally restore the full Cabinet, when he had no further excuse for postponing it. In the meantime, there had been a serious policy vacuum. Pressed in the Lords in May for some announcement of Government thinking on Ireland, F.E. could only say that this was one of the most urgent matters which the Cabinet would have to consider when it met – after the conclusion of the Peace Conference.

F.E. was particularly frustrated by the delay. It was specifically to be a member of the Cabinet that he had accepted the considerable sacrifice, political and financial, involved in becoming Lord Chancellor; he had also a formal constitutional objection to taking responsibility for things for which he had in fact no shared responsibility. Both his frustration and Lloyd George's peremptory way with his colleagues are well illustrated by a sharp little exchange of letters in March. At the beginning of the month he was appointed chairman of a Cabinet Committee to draft a Land Acquisition Bill designed to take the powers of compulsory purchase necessary to the Government's ambitious housing programme – the fulfilment of the promise to build 'homes for heroes'. Within a fortnight, F.E.'s committee reported to Lloyd George in Paris; but Lloyd George did not like what he read. He complained that instead of a Bill 'to facilitate acquisition of land for most urgent public purposes, speedily and at a fair price', F.E. had recommended one which merely ensured 'that the landlord gets a good price, that the lawyers get their pickings and that there should be no undue hurry in the completion of the transaction'. 'The country', he intoned, 'is in no mood to tolerate reactionaries high or low.'[1]

In reply F.E. pointed out with exemplary restraint that he had been given – over breakfast – a less than adequate brief.

> Had I been present at the original Cabinet, and had the slightest means of understanding what your views were . . . the difficulty, such as it is, would never have arisen. You will, I am sure, agree that in the case of any Bills for which, being technical, I am responsible in the House of Lords I ought to be asked to the War Cabinet in order that I may be familiar with relevant considerations from the outset. It is obvious that otherwise I am wholly in the dark as to policy, and can only advise as a lawyer.[2]

F.E.'s role in Paris was a limited one – much less than he had envisaged when he wrote to Lloyd George in 1918 – but he like other Ministers was back and forth across the Channel fairly frequently. In the huge, drawn-out Conference, with so many conflicting national claims to reconcile, his ability to cut through the complexities of international law was much appreciated by a sorely pressed Prime Minister and no less, on at least one occasion, by Clemenceau. F.E. was called upon to advise at short notice on some thorny issue.

> Without a moment's hesitation [Lloyd George recalled] Lord Birkenhead gave an exposition of his views. The statement lasted ten minutes. At the end of it you felt there was nothing more to be said. M. Clemenceau turned to me and said: 'How wonderfully clear.' I asked him to let us hear what a French jurist – a lawyer of

great distinction – had to say. M. Clemenceau replied: 'It is quite unnecessary. The Lord Chancellor's statement has settled the question.'[3]

There is no record that F.E. met Woodrow Wilson again when he was in Paris. Probably he did not, but the course of the Conference did nothing to modify the estimate he had already formed of the American President. Rather the rest of the British delegation came to share it.

F.E.'s daughter Eleanor happened to be at a finishing school in Paris at the time of the Conference, which was an additional reason for F.E. finding occasion to visit whenever possible. He enjoyed using his position to show Eleanor Paris and to show off his daughter to Parisian society. He enjoyed the night life of Paris, too, liberated from the restraints of war and the threat of occupation. The attractions of Paris, which had no appeal for Lloyd George or Bonar Law or Wilson, were irresistible to F.E., who revelled in the social glitter, both elegant and sleazy, the champagne and the girls. He cut a dashing figure as England's young Lord Chancellor.

The principal question of international law with which F.E. was concerned when he was in Paris was the same which had exercised his last year as Attorney-General – but now in the very different context of actual as opposed to anticipated victory. The Government had promised at the General Election to try the Kaiser for his crimes before an international tribunal; F.E. seems to have advised that this would be possible under international law. In the event, however, the Kaiser having found sanctuary in Holland, the problem before the lawyers changed from the mechanics of trying him to the question of how to persuade, induce or compel the Dutch to surrender him, and whether the Dutch were entitled, under international law, to shield him. Was Wilhelm a political refugee or a criminal? There was serious talk of League of Nations trade sanctions to force Holland to see her duty to humanity. Alternatively it was suggested that the Dutch might satisfy everyone by confining their hospitality to Surinam or some other of their distant colonies. Eventually he was allowed to remain where he was, and was soon forgotten.

The same problem arose on a lesser scale with the minor criminals whom the allies in the first flush of victory had promised to pursue with international retribution. Since Germany had not been physically conquered and occupied, there was no way of actually laying hands on the accused Germans. Extradition proceedings had to be undertaken with the new German Government, which could not afford to be too accommodating to the Allies' demands if it was to retain its already slender hold on authority at home. The great international tribunal which F.E. had envisaged in 1918 handing down exemplary punishments to U-Boat commanders and the perpetrators of atrocities against Belgian nuns dwindled into an interminable series of wrangles between the Allies and Germany on the one hand, but still more between the Allies themselves, over who precisely should be handed over for trial. Right through 1920 and into 1921, F.E. and the new Attorney-General, Gordon Hewart, kept having to return to Paris and elsewhere on the continent to argue with their French and Belgian counterparts over lists of alleged criminals to be demanded, national quotas, who should be included on which list and other points of diminishing interest or relevance to reality. In the end, the solution reached was that the Germans themselves were allowed to conduct trials under German law of certain individuals accused of excesses in the conduct of hostilities. A few trials were held and a few mild sentences passed – enough for F.E. to be able to assure the British public that the mills of international justice were grinding, if exceeding slow. Broadly speaking, however, very little came of these long drawn-out proceedings. International law, in the sense of an international tribunal dispensing justice to individuals who had outraged humanity, remained a myth until the same Allies, faced with a greater assault on human values, made a more determined effort to translate it into reality at Nuremberg twenty-five years later.

F.E. played no important part in negotiating the Peace Treaty. That was principally the work of Lloyd George himself, endeavouring to steer a realistic line between Clemenceau's simple desire for security and revenge and Wilson's high-minded but naïve idealism, under the conflicting pressures from home of Liberals, keen for reconciliation and the League of Nations, and Diehard Conservatives, ardent to extract the full price of the war from the defeated enemy. It seems that in private, in common with most of the rest of the Cabinet, F.E. thought the final Treaty too severe, too much influenced by the French.[4] But in public he struck something very like a Diehard line himself. 'The terms are formidable and even terrible,' he told the Royal Society of St George on the day they were published, 8 May, 'but the Germans have proved themselves a leprous nation.' They had attempted to destroy the moral law, he declared, but 'the moral law has proved stronger than the Prussian'.[5] In a debate in the House of Lords on the repatriation of enemy aliens in April, he rebutted Liberal objections with the contention that the British people were quite right to see a moral line dividing themselves from the Germans – though he accepted that every case should be judged by the Home Secretary on its merits.[6] He continued for some time to speak the strong language of retribution, claiming it in April 1920 as a cause for congratulation that the Government had never faltered on 'the fundamental issue of imposing our will on our enemies', and pledging the Government to keep on 'securing the fruits of victory' for the country.[7]

Gradually, however, his views on the level of reparations Germany could be expected to pay softened as the post-war recession pressed more heavily on Government thinking and the first instinctive impulse to make 'the pips squeak' faded. Following Lloyd George he began, in his public speeches, to educate the public to the truth that if she were to pay anything at all, Germany must be restored to the community of nations, no longer treated as 'leprous'. 'To expect Germany to pay indemnities, and at the same time to refuse to trade with her,' he recognized in 1920, 'is of course absurd.'[8] By 1921 he was telling audiences of businessmen that vindictive reparations impoverished victors and vanquished equally: the prosperity of Europe was indivisible. By the summer of 1922, shortly before the Coalition left office, F.E. had become an eloquent advocate of Lloyd George's efforts, persistently obstructed by the French and still furiously condemned by the Diehards at home, to achieve a generous reconciliation with the former enemy.

> Barren indeed will be the victory and valueless the laurels if by lack of sympathy, understanding and initiative we who won the war fail to take the necessary steps to effect such a reconstruction of Europe as will make trade possible to a Europe that will perish unless trade is restored.[9]

The whole process is a good example of F.E.'s realism, his capacity to adjust his mind – and his rhetoric – in the face of a new recognition of the facts. If he was sometimes slow to reverse strongly held and strongly expressed positions of this sort, many men cannot bring themselves to abandon such positions, however untenable, at all, and cling to them with a proud but hollow consistency. F.E. on the platform sometimes pitched his commitment to a cause which he embraced in over-coloured and combative terms; but it is a mark of his integrity that his mind was not then closed to the changing aspect of the problem. His most powerful convictions remained always open to persuasion by new facts. This flexibility, not trivial or opportunist but the result of serious reconsideration, was most importantly exemplified with regard to Ireland; but the same process, tending to cut him off from the support of that wing of the Tory party which he could on many issues so easily have led, was at work also in relation to Germany and reparations.

One Diehard tenet from which he never deviated, however, was his old belief in a strong national defence. The experience of the war converted him to fashionable internationalism and disarmament not at all. His view of questions of peace and war remained as bleakly realistic as it had always been, firmly rooted in the primacy of the individual nation-state. He placed no faith whatever in the efficacy of Wilson's League of Nations – especially when the American Senate overruled the President and would take no part in it. His idea of a 'sane' foreign policy, which he proposed in a newspaper article in 1920, rested on three planks; but it was clear that he listed them in ascending order of importance. First he placed, but only from obligatory lip-service to convention, the support of the League; second, the maintenance of good relations with the Allies; third, 'last but not least', came 'the main-tenance of a Navy and an Army, which will secure the Empire, should the League of Nations fail'. There was no place in F.E.'s world picture for the idealistic vision of disarmament to which Lloyd George, for instance, though he showed little enough sign of it while in power, was sincerely dedicated. The concept of internationalism was to him an insidious and sentimental illusion. 'There can be no substitute for the national spirit', he insisted after the war as he had before. 'In the last resort the Empire must look to itself and it must never lose the habit of so looking.'[8]

With foreign policy, however, F.E. had little to do until the last months of the Coalition. Departmentally, there was no reason why he should have had. It was traditional, under any Government, that the Foreign Office guarded its province jealously from Cabinet interference; the Cabinet had less of a role to play than ever under a Prime Minister who ran his own foreign policy as Lloyd George did – even the Foreign Secretary, as Curzon repeatedly protested after he succeeded Balfour in that office in October 1919, was frequently in the dark. It is an accurate measure of F.E.'s more intimate association with Lloyd George after the signing of the Irish Treaty in December 1921 that he was drawn so much more into the foreign affairs picture in 1922, at the Genoa Conference in April and in connection with the Chanak crisis in September. For most of the Government's life, his role was in domestic policy – its formulation in Cabinet and Cabinet Committees, and its presentation in the House of Lords and in the country.

(ii) In Cabinet

It was by his contribution in Cabinet that F.E. really won for himself the new respect from which his growing power derived. In tributes after his death, his colleagues all commented that the electorate, used to the dashing public F.E., never saw him at his best – by which they meant giving his opinion in council, where his lucidity, wisdom, seriousness and good sense, his constructiveness, his brevity, his ingenuity in drafting, above all his ability to cut through tangled argument to make starkly clear the issue or alternatives before the Cabinet, aroused their admiration. 'In the Cabinet', Lloyd George wrote,

> he was reserved and generally silent. He was very reluctant to express an opinion on subjects outside his official sphere . . . Unless he had given some previous thought to the subject Lord Birkenhead held back his opinions until he had heard the discussion fully . . . He was cautious as well as sagacious . . . remarkable for his lucidity and brevity . . . a master of words.[3]

To Tom Jones he held up F.E. as a 'strong silent man' – a rare example of a breed of which he was generally sceptical.[10] Lee of Fareham, too – no great friend of F.E. – remembered his 'almost taciturn wisdom in council'.[11] But it was Churchill, characteristically, who best described F.E.'s hold on his colleagues.

> Most of all I liked to hear him in Cabinet . . . He was a singularly silent member. He had acquired in the legal profession the habit of listening mute and motionless hour after hour and he rarely spoke until he was appealed to for his counsel. Then his manner was so quiet and reasonable, so matter-of-fact and sensible that you could feel opinion being changed; and promptly as he warmed to his subject, there grew that glow of conviction and appeal, instinctive and matchless, which constitutes true eloquence.[12]

Despite Lloyd George's introduction of Cabinet minutes, it is difficult to illustrate F.E.'s quality in Cabinet. Indeed without these recollections one might imagine that he never spoke at all, for the practice of the official record is normally to summarize only the arguments of those Ministers – the departmental Ministers concerned – who led the discussion. F.E.'s pithy encapsulations rarely figure – though they may well have been as useful to Hankey and Jones writing the minutes as they were to Lloyd George in the chair. In many ways, in fact, F.E.'s role in Cabinet resembles what is classically regarded as the Prime Minister's function – listening, then summing up. So long as he and Lloyd George were seeing eye to eye, which was most of the time, one can well believe that F.E. was a tower of strength to the Government.

In 1920 and 1921, however, F.E. actually missed more Cabinets than he attended. This at first sight surprising record – he was present at only 24 out of 82 meetings in 1920, 33 out of 92 meetings in 1921, but a much higher proportion, 39 out of 59, in 1922 – is very largely explained by the other duties pressing on the Lord Chancellor, in particular judicial sittings of the House of Lords, exacerbated by Lloyd George's un-businesslike habit of holding Cabinets at irregular hours. During the period April–May 1921 when he was sitting as an emergency judge in the Divorce Court he attended only a single Cabinet, and that was at 7 p.m. His frequent absences, however, also reflect the fact that his health was beginning to show signs of cracking under the strain which he habitually placed on his constitution, once of iron but now betraying signs of wear. His ailments were in themselves minor, but his body seemed to take them hard, as if needing the excuse for a respite.

At the beginning of September 1920, F.E. contracted an ear infection, supposedly from diving off his yacht into very cold water at Cowes. 'I am sorry to say', Margaret reported to Lloyd George on the 22nd,

> that he is suffering from very great neuralgia pain from this ear which is septic. It has now been going on for three weeks and he gets very little sleep. Of course there is always the worry that it may leave him deaf in that ear. He is very depressed and no wonder! and asks me to thank you for your kind messages.[13]

His doctors recommended – as doctors at that period always recommended to wealthy patients – a warm climate, so he and Margaret took off to the south of France. He was still there when the House of Lords reassembled on 20 October: Lord Donoughmore took his place on the Woolsack, informing the House that F.E. was recovering slowly from the painful affliction 'which has caused him a good deal of distress'.[14] A week later *The Times* reported that the 'local malady' was improving, but his doctors forbade him to return to work for some time, so that he might recover his strength and not run the risk of a relapse.[15] Rumours began to appear that he would not in fact be able to resume his duties: the *Law Journal* found it necessary to refute speculation that a new Lord Chancellor was to be appointed.[16] F.E. finally returned to London, and the Woolsack, in the third week of November.

At about this same time, F.E. also underwent a small eye operation which was the first public intimation of another condition which had been worrying him for some while. During 1921 his eyesight continued to give him trouble, so that he had difficulty reading his official papers: for someone so dependent as he was on his ability to absorb large quantities of printed information at great speed, this was a crippling affliction. In March 1922 he had to tell the House of Lords that he had again been ordered to take a month's complete rest. There was, he was assured, no organic weakness, simply overwork.[17] Graphically he described the heavy burdens of the modern Lord Chancellor, with three or four Cabinets a week to attend plus numerous Cabinet conferences and committees – a recital which went somewhat discordantly with his repeated insistence that the diverse functions of the Woolsack should continue to be discharged by a single man. If his health and vigour could not stand it, whose could? A few days later he left London with Margaret and Eleanor to join his yacht at Marseilles. This four-week rest cure in the Mediterranean, however, turned out to be not entirely restful, for the latest in Lloyd George's series of European peace conferences was just assembling at Genoa, and the Prime Minister found it convenient to have the Lord Chancellor unofficially on hand. The cure at any rate was not wholly successful, since F.E. still had trouble reading later in the summer: at times he had actually to have confidential papers read to him by a colleague – presumably Winston.[18]

The notion that the Cabinet delegated much of its detailed work to sub-committees was in 1920 still somewhat heretical to constitutional purists: when Lloyd George in 1921 justified the appointment of Dr Addison as Minister without Portfolio on the ground that he chaired a lot of committees, he provoked an outburst of indignant muttering in the Diehard press. But of course committees are a reality of Cabinet government: both large permanent ones keeping a particular area of policy under continuous review, and a multitude of small *ad hoc* groups of just three or four Ministers charged with considering a particular problem or possibility and advising on the appropriate response. F.E. served on his share of both types and chaired a good many of the latter, a few of which should be briefly mentioned to illustrate the variety of work in which the Lord Chancellor was involved.

He naturally tended to be put on those domestic policy committees on which his legal expertise would be of most value. As Attorney-General before the election he had been a member of the Home Affairs Committee, chaired by the President of the Board of Education H.A.L. Fisher, but he ceased to attend that when it was reconstituted in 1919. He became instead a member of the Government's new emergency committee designed to keep essential services going in the event of a serious strike, the Supply and Transport Committee, chaired by Eric Geddes (Minister of Transport). At the time of the coal strike of 1921 this spawned a sub-committee of its own, of which F.E. was chairman, responsible for 'defence aspects of the industrial situation' – in other words the recruitment of volunteers and special troops for strike-breaking.

In 1922 F.E. served on an important small committee, consisting only of himself, Lord Peel (Secretary of State for India) and Stanley Baldwin (President of the Board of Trade), with Churchill in the chair, to consider economies in the fighting services. A parallel committee under the Chancellor of the Exchequer, Sir Robert Horne, looked at cuts in the Civil Service. Both were set up to meet objections, voiced most strenuously by Churchill but supported by F.E., to the unparliamentary, and therefore strictly irresponsible, Geddes Committee set up somewhat cavalierly by Lloyd George to satisfy the 'Anti-Waste' campaign, which was winning votes at by-elections by alleging excessive Government expenditure. The Cabinet as a whole asserted itself to the extent of forcing Lloyd George to concede that only Cabinet committees should do the actual cutting. The Geddes Committee nevertheless went ahead in a blaze of publicity.

Most of the special purpose committees on which F.E. served were very much less important, many of them dealing with very minor problems of the sort which occupy a disproportionate amount of Government time, like that set up in August 1921 to consider the situation arising from the abandonment of the prosecution of an Indian banker for a munitions fraud. Very many concerned Ireland and particularly the legal difficulties arising from the imposition of martial law over large areas of the country in 1920–1. F.E. chaired a committee in August 1921 to establish the precise legal position of the military governor, and another purely technical one in November to do with the issue of writs of *habeas corpus* by the Master of the Rolls in Ireland for the production of two Irish prisoners.

These, however, were offshoots of perhaps the most important more or less permanent committee of which F.E. was a member, the Irish Situation Committee chaired initially in 1919 by Long, later by Austen Chamberlain. This had the responsibility of keeping the constantly deteriorating Irish situation under practically daily review and involved F.E. inextricably in the developing crisis, the more so since it was he who became the Government's spokesman on Irish policy in the House of Lords, where he had continually to defend and vindicate first the Government's inaction, then its too drastic action, against Diehard dukes on the one hand and anguished archbishops on the other. F.E. could not avoid in these circumstances taking personal responsibility for the twists and turns of Government policy; and it was this which inexorably drew him into the Irish Treaty.

It has to be said, however, that F.E. was remarkably little involved in the actual determination of Government policy in most fields. Outside Ireland and his own departmental responsibility for law reform, there is no area in which it is easy to attribute to him a continuous influence. His value in Cabinet and in Committee lay in his detached intellect and penetrating criticism of whatever problem was put in front of him, rather than in any positive initiative. His wider value lay in his mastery of the House of Lords and of the public platform. In this perspective, the most important standing committee which he chaired was perhaps the Cabinet Publicity Committee, charged with the presentation of the Government's case to the country. He was himself, after the Prime Minister, the Government's most effective and assiduous propagandist. But his prominence in this role meant that it was at his door that much of the blame for the Coalition's increasingly hard-faced public image came to be laid.

(iii) In the House of Lords

From the moment that he became Lord Chancellor F.E. was the Government's principal spokesman on general matters in the Upper House. In terms of age, experience of office and membership of the House, Curzon was the senior figure, and there were other Cabinet Ministers in the Lords as well – Milner (Colonial Secretary) and Lee of Fareham (Agriculture). But Curzon was predominantly a foreign affairs specialist – he succeeded Balfour at the Foreign Office in October 1919 – and it was on F.E., both by virtue of his office and by his aptitude for the job, that most of the burden of the Government's daily domestic business fell. In February 1919 Curzon wrote to Bonar Law that the Lords greatly resented having no Home Office spokesman in their House. 'On Tuesday we have a debate on Industrial Unrest and as there is no-one to answer we have had to impress the Lord Chancellor.'[19] This sort of situation arose frequently; no Home Office spokesman was appointed, and F.E. got used to standing in.

His duties were of two sorts, each demanding different qualities. First, he had to undertake much of the routine work of piloting through their various stages in the Lords a mass of Government legislation – Housing Bills, Electricity Bills, Agriculture Bills, an Aliens Bill, the Sex Disqualification (Removal) Bill (for which he was a somewhat ironic spokesman, though he implemented it loyally as Lord Chancellor). These were all fairly humdrum but complex measures for which he had no particular responsibility and which he had had no hand in drafting. Yet in presenting them to the House, expounding both the principles on which they were based and the details of their application in practice, he was able to give full play to his powers of rapid assimilation and concise and lucid explanation. With this exceptional mastery of material, which had served him so well in the courts, he was able to range over a wider range of subjects than any normal Minister is faced with, re-butting criticisms and trading amendments with the Opposition with perfect confidence and, it should be added, courtesy. His colleague Lord Lee noted with astonishment 'his incredible capacity for mastering an unfamiliar subject, with or without a brief'.[11] The House as a whole greatly appreciated it. This represented, as it were, the neutral side of his barristerial skills.

The positive side was fully exercised by the other facet of his function. This was the duty of replying on the Government's behalf to the innumerable single debates of which so much of the business of the Upper House consisted, debates on motions put down by individual peers to express concern or discontent with some general aspect of Government policy. This role placed F.E. in the forefront of the political battle, for the Government had such a huge majority in the Commons that it was always in greater danger of defeat in the Lords: many of its most influential and dangerous critics sat in the Upper House and there had to be answered. The Liberals, depleted in the Commons and superseded by Labour, were in the Lords the official Opposition, energetically led by Crewe and Buckmaster, with Grey as elder states-man. More numerous and more dangerous, however, to the Coalition were the Diehard Tories, the great magnates led by Salisbury and Northumberland. When these opposing groups combined, as they did for instance in recurrent allegations of Government extravagance – the Liberals' traditional calls for 'economy' being increasingly swallowed up in the Tory 'Anti-Waste' campaign – they could inflict damaging and embarrassing defeats, as in July 1920 when the Government, despite F.E.'s emollient efforts, was overwhelmed by ninety-five votes to twenty-three.

There were other issues on which the Opposition parties made common cause to assail the Government – notably the Honours scandal, which touched the dignity of the House particularly closely and symbolized more than anything else the revulsion which Liberals and Diehards alike came to feel for the whole style and manner of Lloyd George's Government. More often, though, they attacked the Government from opposite directions – for instance over Ireland, where the Liberals and the Bishops denounced the barbarities of the Black and Tans while the Diehards condemned the failure of the Government, by whatever methods, to restore order. On these occasions F.E. was able to play off his critics tellingly against each other. These debates brought out his old combative qualities, undiminished by translation from the Commons to the Lords. He had no hesitation, when the opportunity presented itself, in scoring party points off Buckmaster and Crewe – by rattling again, for instance, the old bones of 'Chinese slavery', or blaming them for the uncompleted Parliament Act. On them, and when necessary on Salisbury, Northumberland and other Tory critics he turned the same weapons of ridicule, heavy irony and destructive logic with which he had made his reputation in opposition in the Commons: counter-attack was always his instinctive form of defence. Yet there was a new note of statesmanship, too: his habitual argument was to contrast the Government's tremendous responsibilities with the irresponsibility of its opponents. At worst, this could shade into cheap taunting of the Opposition: he held office and they did not, so he could treat their naïve alternatives with a lofty contempt. At best, on the other hand, office gave to his speeches a broad-minded understanding of the true complexity of the problems the country faced which did indeed make the carping of the Opposition look partisan and petty. He developed a strain of national idealism in some of these debates which could for a time lift the language of politics on to a new level.

In these ways – by his technical mastery, by his debating vigour and by his eloquence – F.E. immediately stamped his authority on the Upper House. Some thought that he carried it too lightly. *The Times* commented in January 1921 that 'Lord Birkenhead takes dangerous liberties with forms, and he must be the one Lord Chancellor who has dared to be offhand and casual on the Woolsack.'[20] Certainly he was much freer and less concerned with outward dignity when speaking politically (from *beside* the Woolsack) than he ever was in his judicial capacity; he would lounge, too, in his most languid manner with his feet on the bench in front of him. But if some peers felt that he departed too far, both in his informality and in his occasional virulence in debate, from the customary gravity of his office – and even if sometimes they had reason – most respected his abilities too much to want to change him, but positively applauded him for importing a whiff of the House of Commons back into a chamber that was beginning to decline, since 1911, into polite obsolescence. F.E.'s leadership for a time arrested that decline: the galleries used to fill up when he was speaking, just as they had done when he spoke in the Commons before the war, and for some of his major speeches members of the Cabinet from the other place sat on the steps of the Throne to hear him. There was sincerity as well as convention in the tributes paid by his fellow-peers when he was obliged to be absent through ill-health. 'His great abilities, courtesy and industry', Salisbury admitted in October 1920 – though he was by now a stern opponent of the Government over practically the whole field of policy – 'have done an immense deal to improve in every way the efficiency and legislative work of this House.'[21]

The contrary stories, however, tend naturally to be the most vivid and thus the best remembered, though they are not always the most reliable. The memoirs of Lord Lee contain a particularly colourful account of an alleged incident in 1920, during the passage through the Lords of the Agriculture Bill, for which Lee was the responsible Minister. It is, in its tone of moral disapproval combined with grudging admiration, characteristic of so many of the stories that have clustered around F.E.'s reputation that it cannot be ignored; nevertheless, as will be seen, it needs to be taken with a great deal of salt. Lee is describing the Committee Stage of the Bill in November 1920.

The landlord Peers were raining amendments upon me, and, feeling that I could not be expected to maintain the fight for the Bill entirely single-handed . . . I asked the Lord Chancellor to tell off some other Minister (preferably with agricultural knowledge) to give me a hand when necessary. To my astonishment, and I must confess dismay, he said promptly 'I will come and help you myself' and, leaving the Woolsack when the Committee Stage was reached, he came across and plumped himself down beside me on the Government bench. I then realised that, not for the first time, he had been lunching not wisely but too well and I was distinctly startled when he turned to me and said in a highly audible 'sotto voce', 'What *is* this bloody Bill, anyway? Let me see a copy.' I handed him one and he fumbled through its pages for perhaps five minutes; then, looking across the House at the dull but inoffensive Earl of Malmesbury who was delivering a petulant but quite decorous speech against the clause under discussion, FE growled out 'I am tired of that bloody fellow' and started to harry him with rude and irrelevant interruptions. This so put the noble Earl out of his stride that he faltered and sat down prematurely, whereupon FE sprang (somewhat unsteadily) to his feet and launched at his cowering head the most ferocious and unprovoked attack that I had ever heard in the Upper Chamber. It was hardly remotely connected with the Agriculture Bill – about which FE knew nothing and cared less – and took the form mainly of personal reminiscences of alleged indiscretions of Malmesbury when an undergraduate at Oxford. The House listened with amazement, and I feared lest a storm might break which would dispel the whole atmosphere of good-will which I had so laboriously en-gendered, and so jeopardise the passage of the Bill. So intimi-dated, however, were the noble Lords by their experiences of FE's blistering tongue on other occasions, that not a voice was raised in protest and they even listened respectfully to his subsequent interventions on Committee points, some of which amazed me by their erudition and apparent grasp of a highly technical subject. His brain was certainly geared to a pitch which made the rest of us seem pedestrian plodders.[22]

Certain things can be taken from this story which bear out what has already been said. F.E. did on occasion lend other Ministers a hand, even when he knew little about the Bill under discussion, and Lee confesses his amazement at the 'erudition and apparent grasp' which he was rapidly able to bring to bear. Undoubtedly there were occasions when F.E. had visibly had too much to drink, and he was then doubtless less than usually able to suffer fools gladly. The precise incident, as Lee recounts it, however, is impossible to trace in Hansard. The day referred to can only be 17 November, when there was indeed a mild clash between F.E. and Malmesbury on the Committee Stage of the Agriculture Bill. But it was late in the evening, not the afternoon; more important, F.E. had not just come in while Malmesbury was speaking, but had been present for some time, dealing perfectly courteously with a variety of amendments. Malmesbury's intervention was to propose an amendment of his own which it is difficult to blame F.E. for receiving with derision: he suggested that 'interfering busybodies' who alleged that another's land was not being well cultivated should be liable to a £25 fine or three years' imprisonment! F.E.'s reply on this occasion did not pretend to much technical grasp, but he knew a silly idea when he heard one. As an example of his House of Lords manner it is impeccable.

The noble Earl, who is a very old friend of mine and who, if he will allow me to say so, I suspect has pursued his researches into the law as slightly as I have carried mine into the field of agriculture, gratified my curiosity in relation to his Amendment almost in the first sentence of his speech, because he said that this Amendment did not come from a landowner but came from a tenant farmer. If I might give my noble friend some advice which may save him a great deal of money if he lives long enough, it is that if he wants law he should not go to tenant farmers for it. He may reply to me that if I wanted agriculture I should not go to lawyers. If my noble friend Lord Buckmaster were here I should not be disposed to quarrel with that either. But really my noble friend has placed himself in a very high position among the humorists of the House by this Amendment, and I am only sorry that it was not moved at a moment which would have secured for it the degree of publicity that it deserves in this Temple. Although my noble friend appears to be unaware of it, the law, when dealing with defamatory statements,

has already undergone quite a considerable degree of development in the course of the last two or three hundred years, and for
a defamatory statement, whether it deals with a man's skill as a
cultivator or whether it deals with the reputation of his wife, our
law with complete impartiality has already provided tribunals,
and the vigilance of the noble Earl would have possessed the
highest value if it had not been that some three hundred years ago
others devoted their attention to this matter and made alternative
suggestions which, on the whole, I prefer. [Much laughter.]

This ironic rebuke – scarcely a 'ferocious attack' – to an exact
contemporary who had indeed, as Viscount Fitz-Harris, been a friend
of F.E.'s at the Oxford Union thirty years before (it may be that F.E.
recounted some of his 'indiscretions' on another occasion), was received
by the House, not in cowed silence but with 'much laughter'.
Malmesbury's insistence that he stood by his amendment met with
'renewed laughter'. His amendment was then swiftly negatived, and
the House moved on.[23]

The worst that F.E. could be said to have done was to make
Malmesbury look a fool. But there is nothing in the verbatim report to
suggest that he did so offensively or unkindly, or that the House did not
thoroughly enjoy his reply. Lee's story, as a memory of a specific
occasion, holds no water at all. Nevertheless, the way that, twenty years
later, he conflated what must have been a series of impressions into this
particular form must indicate the mixed feelings with which F.E. was
regarded by at least one of his Cabinet colleagues in the Lords. Lee was
an ambitious politician, but an insecure and embittered one, not in his
own view properly rewarded for a career of conscientious public service;
he may well have resented F.E.'s easy brilliance and compared his
dazzling advancement jealously with his own progress. Not too much
need be read into Lee's picture of F.E.; except that this jealousy which
his sometimes arrogant gifts aroused in several of the lesser figures
in the Government had its important consequences in 1922 when the
Tory leaders needed all the support from their juniors that they could
command.

Most of F.E.'s greatest parliamentary speeches in these years were
made in defiance of the right wing of his own party, in defence of
Coalition policies which the hard-line Tories thought excessively per-
meated by 'soft' Liberalism. One of the most notable, which stands
somewhat apart as a rare venture at this period of his career into Indian
affairs, was his speech in July 1920 on the result of the inquiry into the
'massacre' at Amritsar the year before. The events in Amritsar on
13 April 1919 are almost too well known to need repetition. For several

days there had been serious rioting and looting, culminating in a great demonstration in the Jallianwallagh Bagh, an open space no larger than Trafalgar Square. In a premeditated effort to restore order and 'teach a moral lesson to the Punjab', the local commanding officer, Brigadier-General Dyer, ordered his troops to fire, not over the heads of but into the excited crowd, and to keep on firing for several minutes. Nearly 400 unarmed Indians were killed, perhaps 2,000 more wounded. In the subsequent uproar, British and British-Indian opinion was passionately divided between those who demanded that the Government unequivocally condemn Dyer's action and dismiss the General himself, and those who insisted that drastic methods were the only resort available to him in a dangerous situation and maintained that his decisiveness alone had saved India from large-scale disturbances in which many more lives would have been lost than he had been obliged to sacrifice. In India itself and in Conservative and military circles at home the latter view naturally prevailed: Dyer was publicly congratulated by his superiors and promoted. The Government, however, set up a commission of inquiry which returned the verdict that Dyer had committed a serious error of judgment. On 7 July 1920, Churchill announced that Dyer would be suspended from the Army on half-pay. The following day the Diehards, led by Carson, turned and rent the Secretary of State for India, Montagu, in a vicious display of anti-semitic imperial fury. It took a great speech by Churchill, firmly insisting that exemplary terrorism was not the British way of holding an Empire, to swing the debate back the Government's way; but even so 129 members voted for Dyer.

In the country a great storm of indignation arose, whipped up by the Tory press: Dyer was adopted as a maligned hero and no less than £26,000 was raised by public subscription to compensate him for the shameful ingratitude of the cowardly Government. Far more than in the Commons, this outcry found its natural expression in the House of Lords. A motion deploring the Government's treatment of Dyer was set down by F.E.'s predecessor, Finlay, and debated over two days, 19 and 20 July. Midleton, Ampthill, Salisbury and Sumner, among others, spoke vehemently in support of it. For the Government, not only F.E. but those embodiments of Empire, Curzon and Milner, insisted, as Churchill had done in the Commons, that Dyer's action had exceeded the limits of humanity and justice. F.E.'s, however, was the most powerful condemnation: his speech was notable for his authoritative judicial assertion that the principle of equal citizenship must apply throughout the Empire. F.E. was no racial sentimentalist. He believed strongly in competition, economic and political, between individuals and between races, and he believed in the last resort that might secures right. But as a lawyer he believed unshakeably in equality before the law as the fundamental and necessary framework for civilized competition. He was by no stretch of the imagination a progressive in relation to Indian political aspirations: he held like other Imperialists that the Indians must be governed firmly for their own good for as long as was necessary, and took it for granted, like other Tories, that that would be a long time yet. But he could not allow that individual Indians could be treated as inferiors whose lives were of less account than those of other citizens of the Empire, Canadians or native Britons. Would those who defended General Dyer, he asked, use the same arguments if the Canadian Government had used similar methods to quell riots in Winnipeg? Or if the British army had shot strikers in Glasgow? 'The fundamental principle of the Empire', he insisted, 'is that any man who is a citizen, no matter what his colour, creed or geographical location, may appeal with the same equal confidence and certainty to the firmness and justice of this Empire.' General Dyer, gallant soldier though he unquestionably was, had on the fatal afternoon in the Jallianwallagh Bagh, committed an error of judgment which the Empire could not honourably condone.[24]

F.E.'s fine principles raised cheers from both sides of the House. But the peers carried Finlay's motion, against the Government, by 129 votes to 86. The strength of the Diehards had once again been ominously signalled.

(iv) A Private Crusade: Divorce Reform

One cause to which F.E. devoted himself more earnestly than to any other over the last dozen years of his life was the reform of the divorce law. The availability of easier divorce for those trapped in empty marriages to cruel, insane, drunken or simply absent spouses, from which the existing law allowed them no prospect of escape, became for him a passionate crusade, the more so as the hope of reform faded before the entrenched resistance of the Established Church. It was a cause in which his humanity combined with his legal learning and his long experience of the courts in a conviction strong even for him, which he formulated in arguments of unanswerable clarity and power.

It should be stressed that his concern was quite disinterested. Though he was not a strictly faithful husband, and was indeed at the very moment when the divorce controversy was at its height engaged in a serious extra-marital affair, there is no question but that he was very happily married and devoted to his wife. It is inconceivable that he would ever have sought a divorce from Margaret even under the lax divorce law of today; the very limited reform for which he pressed in 1920 would have had no relevance to his situation in any case. There is no evidence that he was worried about the state of the marriage law before he became Lord Chancellor; but his responsibility in that office for legal reform was reason enough to stir himself now.

Reform was on the agenda. It had been so since 1912 when a Royal Commission chaired by Lord Gorell reported. The war had postponed any action on the Commission's recommendations; it had also, as has been seen, increased the pressure on the courts to dissolve a host of unwise marriages. As it stood, the law allowed only one ground of divorce – adultery, which was difficult and expensive to prove and was anyway only one symptom that a marriage might have broken down: neither a necessary accompaniment of breakdown nor, in any but legal terms, a sufficient proof of it. The Gorell Report recommended, by a majority – the minority comprised the Archbishop of York, an ecclesiastical lawyer and the Oxford jurist Sir William Anson – five additional grounds on which divorce should be granted. These were in March 1920 embodied in a Bill introduced into the House of Lords by Lord Buckmaster, to which F.E. gave his strong support. The Government expressed no view on the matter – in matters of faith and conscience their Lordships were allowed a free vote. But speaking purely as a private individual, F.E. delivered on 24 March, on the second day of a Second Reading debate adjourned from a fortnight before, one of the very greatest speeches – perhaps the greatest – of his life.

With his usual lawyer's instinct for the *principle* of an argument, he seized at once on the central inconsistency of the opponents' case. They argued from the absolute sanctity of marriage as a holy sacrament. But if the possibility of divorce were admitted for one cause, adultery, then there was no principle involved in admitting other grounds – it was merely a question of detail. Divorce on the ground of adultery had been admitted since the end of the seventeenth century; it was in practice then obtainable only by private Act of Parliament, which effectively restricted it to the highest in the land, but the principle that marriage, once entered into, was absolutely indissoluble, was from that moment conceded. The only controversy of principle, F.E. insisted, had been settled over three hundred years ago, with practically universal consent. Those who still held to the absolute sanctity of marriage lived in another world: 'their arguments are the whisperings of the abandoned superstitions of the Middle Ages'.

If it was accepted, as he believed it was accepted, by 90 per cent of peers, 90 per cent of the House of Commons and 90 per cent of the public, that marriage was in some circumstances dissoluble, then it only remained to be decided on what grounds marriages should be dissolved. The Royal Commission had laid down the principle, which he accepted, that marriage ought to be dissoluble 'upon any grounds which had frustrated what by universal admission are the fundamental purposes of marriage'. Yet the clergy, acting under the influence of what F.E. called 'an almost unconscious opportunism', claimed a special authority sanctioning their one admitted ground for divorce but no other: 'although marriage is not otherwise dissoluble,' they argued, 'it is nevertheless dissoluble in cases where adultery has been committed.' Against this doctrine, F.E. rebelled with indignant incredulity. 'I, my Lords, can only express my amazement that men of experience, men of affairs, men whose opinion and experience we respect' – he was later to retract some of these tactful compliments – 'should have concentrated upon adultery as the one circumstance which ought to afford relief from the marriage tie.'

> Adultery is a breach of the carnal implications of marriage. Insistence upon the duties of continence and chastity is important. But I have always taken the view that that aspect of marriage was exaggerated, and somewhat crudely exaggerated, in the Marriage Service. I am concerned today to make this point, by which I will stand or fall – that the spiritual and moral sides of marriage are incomparably more important than the physical side.
>
> The question is fundamental, and I invite your Lordships to consider it with the greatest earnestness. It seems indeed to me that there can be no doubt as to which is the higher and the more important side of marriage. If you think of all that marriage represents to most of us – the memories of the world's adventure faced together in youth so heedlessly and yet so confidently, the tender comradeship, the sweet association of parenthood, how much more these count than the bond which nature in its ingenious telepathy has contrived to secure and render agreeable the perpetuation of the species.
>
> I do not know whether there is one in this House who would be bold enough to say that the physical side of marriage is the highest. I greatly doubt it. I do not think that the most reverend Primate the Archbishop of Canterbury, who, I believe, is to follow me in this debate, would for one moment lend the great weight of his authority to the position that the physical side of marriage is the highest. And yet be this observed, that those who oppose this Bill must say so, and for this reason: if they agree that the physical side of marriage is not the highest, they are committed to a

monstrous and mediaeval paradox. They assent to divorce for a breach of the less important obligation, and they deny divorce for a breach of the more important obligations of marriage. I conceive this to be an insult to the spiritual and sacramental conception of marriage, and it is just because I place other elements in the married state far, far higher than I place the physical relationship that I make this fundamental in my argument, and I specially desire that any answer to my argument may deal with this point, that a breach of that which is highest must be treated by the State as not less grave than a breach of that which is lower.

He went on to consider the five additional grounds on which it was proposed that divorce should be available: desertion (after three years); cruelty; incurable lunacy (after five years); habitual drunkenness; and – a rarer case – imprisonment under a commuted death sentence. Under all these circumstances a spouse, usually a wife, might be condemned to live the rest of her life bound in law by a marriage that was no marriage, prevented from marrying again but obliged, if she formed another relationship, to live in sin and dishonour and bring up her children as bastards. He was amazed that those who professed to be concerned for the nation's morals and to be anxious to deter adultery should support a state of law which could only encourage adultery.

What is a young woman of twenty-two to do who is left for the rest of her life, with no hope of alleviation in the future, with a fugitive husband whom she never can identify, while the law says to her plainly, finally and brutally: 'We will do nothing for you'?

It was said that she had open to her a judicial separation. But this did not legalize a future attachment.

Choosing my words advisedly, and being prepared with chapter and verse of a hundred cases even at the date when the Royal Commission reported, and in a thousand cases since, I say that I can prove that the state of judicial separation – admittedly the only alternative – is a hotbed of vice.

The only other alternative, that such a woman remain for ever chaste, was utterly unrealistic.

I have only to observe that for two thousand years, to take the chronology of Christendom alone, human nature has resisted in the warmth of youth these cold admonitions of the cloisters; and I for one take leave to say, with all reverence, that I do not believe that the Supreme Being has set human nature a standard which two thousand years of Christian experience has shown that human nature, in its exuberant prime, cannot support.

At this point F.E. introduced a patriotic argument which seems today somewhat quaint. It was not only the individuals concerned who suffered when a couple were unable to marry because one partner was still tied in law to a drunken, certified or vanished spouse.

There are thousands of English men and women at this moment, in the prime of their lives, who ought to be contributing to the child-strength of the Empire at a moment when the very future of the Empire may depend upon the sufficiency of a virile population. These people are condemned to sterilise their union because they will not bring into the world illegitimate children under the system under which the Legislature has condemned them to live.

The case of the deserted wife was perhaps the clearest injustice. Could it possibly be said to be a less serious violation of the obligations of marriage that a man should wilfully desert his wife for three years than that he should yield momentarily to 'one fleeting physical temptation'? There was social injustice as well as moral: the rich wife could almost certainly trace her husband and probably gather the evidence that would enable her to prove adultery; a poor man could disappear without trace, leaving his wife no legal means of filling his place. The clergy claimed that to allow divorce for desertion would open the door to abuse: but Scotland had admitted desertion as a ground for divorce since 1573 and irrefutable evidence had been produced before the Royal Commission to show that there had been no more divorces for desertion than for adultery. Why should England be different from Scotland in this respect?

The different cases of cruelty, of insanity, and of habitual drunkenness – often associated with cruelty – all rested upon the same argument: that the purposes of true marriage – support, companionship, loving parenthood – were in these circumstances frustrated. For the Church to insist on the enduring sanctity of such marriages was a lie, and for the law to refuse relief from them a barbarity. The fifth just ground proposed in the Bill was an oddity: the situation of a wife whose husband was imprisoned for life under a commuted death sentence. The Archbishop of York had opposed allowing this ground with the argument that it was too exceptional for the law to bother about. F.E. had no time for that excuse. He reckoned that there might be as many as seventy-five women affected. ' "True" ', he imagined the State saying to the wife of a convicted murderer, ' "it is only by the indulgence of the State . . . that you are not discharged from the obligations of matrimony and free to marry again. But, after all, there are so few of you that we do not think it necessary to make any change." Justice, I profoundly believe, is not to be measured in any such detestable scales.'

F.E. concluded with an eloquent appeal, of the sort that he had so often made to juries in court, impressing on the Lords their responsibility for initiating an overdue reform which the Commons might be persuaded to take up if they would approve it.

> It may well be, if your Lordships send down this Bill, that in another place it will meet with a volume of support which will at long last remove this great blot from our civilisation. I would most earnestly implore your Lordships to be the pioneers in this great reform; and if it should prove to be so, I believe that daily and nightly your Lordships' name will be breathed with unspeakable gratitude by thousands of the most unhappy of your fellow-subjects, and, I am sure of this, that by generations yet to be you will be acclaimed for the wisdom of the decision taken tonight.[25]

'The Lord Chancellor's speech', *The Times* enthused next day, 'revealed him as a true modern. He is not by any means, as some affect to believe, a light man but . . . he has sincerity, passion and even a strain of fine democratic idealism.' F.E.'s serious side constantly surprised his critics, who would then fall over themselves to insist that only superficial observers had ever doubted it. 'The Thunderer' tacitly approved, but did not dare fully to endorse, his argument. 'Lord Birkenhead cuts himself adrift from the view of marriage as a religious sacrament. Allow him to do that and the argument of his eloquent speech today seems unanswerable.'[26]

The Archbishop of Canterbury, however, speaking next in the debate, professed himself unable to follow F.E.'s religious argument, and did not attempt to answer it. Lord Parmoor and Lord Salisbury were among others who vigorously opposed the Bill. 'The atmosphere', *The Times* noted, 'was electrical. The cry of "Order, order" was heard at least once' – rare in the Lords – 'and there was much suppressed passion.' At one point, stuck for a better argument, Salisbury asserted that he preferred St Matthew to F.E. 'But I agree with St Matthew,' F.E. expostulated. For once Salisbury had the better of him. 'A compliment, truly, to St Matthew,' he retorted sarcastically.[25]

Despite the Bishops and the High Churchmen, the Bill carried its Second Reading by 93 votes to 45, a margin for which credit must be given to F.E.'s advocacy. In the Commons, however, it was a different story. A resolution moved by a Liberal member in April that legislative effect should be given to the recommendations of the Royal Commission was sharply negatived by 134 to 91, a vote which in *The Times*'s view confirmed the 1918 House as 'the most mediaeval chamber in living memory . . . Nature will out, and nothing could better illustrate the reactionary spirit of the present House'.[27] F.E.'s view, on the other hand, was that the figures did not express the true feeling of the House at all.

> I have little doubt [he wrote a couple of years later] that on a secret vote the majority of the House of Commons would range them-selves in support of Lord Buckmaster's Bill. But the organisation of the Church is very strong in many constituencies: it seems certain to a calculating member that a vote in favour of the Bill will excite many animosities; it is quite uncertain how many friend-ships it will create. And so countless tragedies, easily curable, are made perpetual, in adjustment to the cruellest niceties of the party game.[28]

At the time, F.E. vented his disappointment on a leading Anglo-Catholic divine, Canon Thomas Lacey (author of *Mysteries of Grace, Marriage in Church and State*, and *Nature, Miracle and Sin* among other titles) who wrote to *The Times* the day after the Commons vote to rebut F.E.'s view that the physical side of marriage should be regarded as less important than the moral and spiritual. Replying four days later, F.E. treated the Canon to a full display of that withering contempt with which he not infrequently belaboured in *The Times* and elsewhere those who had the temerity to cross him. He was particularly incensed by Lacey's suggestion that he should confine himself to the law and leave higher mysteries to minds which understood them. With exaggerated mock modesty he countered with a full catalogue of his qualifications to concern himself with divorce.

> I am, Sir, I beg you to believe, genuinely desirous of not overrating either myself or my experience. But I conceive that I am, in all humility, entitled to point out:
>
> 1. That I am a judge.
> 2. That for 20 years I practised at the Bar and always with a considerable experience of the Divorce Court.
> 3. That for four years as Attorney-General I gave directions to the King's Proctor which involved me in an anxious and constant attention to the problems of our Divorce Laws.

4. That I have been a Minister for five years.
5. That I have been a legislator for fourteen years.

Under these circumstances I find the proposal that I should 'leave moral and spiritual and physical questions to other minds' unattractive. To what other minds? To the Canons of Worcester? Or, by an even more laughable reductio ad absurdum, to Canon Lacey?

It may well be doubted whether the arrogance of a minor ecclesiastic has in recent times involved him in a proposal so grotesque.[29]

F.E. was of course right, but such weighty censure of a 'minor ecclesiastic's' absurdity smacks of what is nowadays called overkill. The tone of ironic ridicule which was an admired weapon in the armoury of a young opposition M.P. before the war now seemed inappropriately overbearing in the Lord Chancellor. F.E. was becoming, in the arrogance of power, an intellectual bully.

In May F.E. had to tell Buckmaster that there was no prospect of the Government taking over his Bill to force it through the Commons, but he hoped to persuade the Government's business managers at least to make time for it to be fully debated.[30] He repeated this hope in June, during his speech on the Third Reading in the Lords, which was again carried by a comfortable 154 votes to 107. Privately he was still trying to induce the Cabinet to take it up: he tried, with Winston's support, to have a Divorce Bill included in the King's Speech for the 1921 session.[31] But other Ministers were pressing other Bills and, as H.A.L. Fisher noted, 'We cut all these proposals down ruthlessly.'[32] In March and April 1921 another more limited Bill, allowing divorce for desertion but for none of the other causes proposed in Buckmaster's Bill, went through the Lords. But even this was too problematic for the Commons and was not proceeded with. Not, indeed, until 1935, did the Independent M.P., the humorist A.P. Herbert, succeed in carrying a major relaxation of the law.

Until his death, F.E. carried on the fight in speeches and essays, his tone becoming angrier and less conciliatory as the ecclesiastical veto appeared ever more insurmountable. He treated the whole question again at length in 1927, in an essay in his collection *Law, Life and Letters*. There he rehearsed all his old arguments again but went on to examine, with examples from the Lords' debates, what he saw as the intellectual dishonesty of the Bishops and their allies, who stated their opposition to divorce first on theological grounds but then slid adroitly from there to social arguments which did not follow at all. 'It is curious', he now wrote, 'that no-one either in the Lords or the Commons rose in his place and said: "I disbelieve in divorce on religious grounds, but I recognize that the social argument is against me." It is impossible, I suppose, to expect so much candour.'

F.E. rested his case purely on social and legal grounds. No one, after all, would be obliged to be divorced. There was no question of violating anyone's private beliefs. But there was equally no reason why a minority of strict believers should block a humane reform for the rest of society. F.E. could name several distinguished theologians on the liberal side of the argument. More important, from his essentially secular point of view, the law was becoming increasingly out of touch with public opinion. 'And when this happens', as he went on to illustrate, 'all kinds of undesirable and even dangerous results ensue.'

> Lord Eldon wept on the Woolsack when, because juries would no longer convict, hanging for a forty-shilling theft was abolished. The Duke of Wellington denied to the end of his days that discipline in the Army could be maintained without flogging. What would the law or the Army be like today if the obstructionists had not been compelled to yield to the common sense and common humanity of the nation? In so far as the Bishops are using their public position – not their private right to direct the conscience of their flock – to obstruct Divorce Law Reform they must rank with Eldon and Wellington. That is to say, that if they succeeded, they would damage the institution of marriage in this country as much as Eldon would have brought the law into contempt and Wellington have made the Army impossible.

Public opinion had moved beyond the 1857 Act. The poor – though 'by nature frightfully respectable' – simply ignored it, laying no sense of shame on those who, deserted by their first partners, took a second without benefit of clergy. The rich evaded it by the farcical procedure of feigning adultery in order to meet the sole criterion the law recognized as ground for divorce. The law itself was thus being brought into disrepute by those who persistently and, as F.E. claimed, illegitimately blocked the implementation of the Majority Report of 1912. 'Their moral position', he accused, 'is a curious one.'

> They are not legislating for their own flock. It is open to the Church of England to refuse membership to those who decline to accept its views on divorce. Since the repeal of the Test Acts the Church is a voluntary association with no civic disabilities attaching to a citizen who declines membership. No member of the

Church of England need sue for a divorce nor need re-marry if divorced. All that the Bishops and their lay retainers in the Houses are doing is to compel other people to live up to standards which they do not accept. In this way the Bishops are violently constraining the consciences of people who do not agree with them. In taking up this attitude they are serving no useful purpose whatever. They are merely encouraging the poor to disregard the marriage tie and the rich to laugh at the law.[33]

This was the same F.E. who had ranged himself in 1908 behind the Established Church against the overweening claims of the Nonconformist Education Bills, and with the English drinking man against the killjoy prohibition of Liberal temperance reformers. The argument, now turned against the Church, was the same – against the forcible imposition, in the sphere of private morality, of one section's views upon another section. Logically, perhaps, the corollary of this argument might have led him to Disestablishment; but F.E. never explicitly followed it so far. To have done so would have been to make more problems for himself with the Tory party, the University of Oxford and other institutions which he revered than were worth his while. He noticeably ceased, however, after the war, to insist on the importance of Establishment as he had before.

(v) 'Fusion'

In addition to all his official duties, both judicial and political, in the House of Lords and in the Cabinet, F.E. was also the Government's most active advocate in the country. As a platform speaker he was second only to Lloyd George himself, able to draw large crowds wherever he spoke and keep them enthralled by the power and directness of his words. Churchill could seem contrived, Chamberlain was ponderous, by comparison with F.E.'s easy fluency; and he shared Lloyd George's gift for suiting his words instinctively to the mood of each particular audience. Then again, F.E. was without challenge the supreme after-dinner speaker. This was the ambience, more than any other, in which he shone most brilliantly: a select audience, a good dinner and a sufficiency of drink inside him, and his hearers similarly relaxed. He was top of the list of principal guest speakers sought by every sort of association and society for their annual dinner, and in these four years he attended an unbelievable number – chambers of commerce, tradesmen's guilds, universities, institutes, the Medical-Psychological Association, the Cinematograph Association, the Society of Water-Colourists, the Parliamentary Press Gallery; all these in addition to the annual round of legal dinners – circuit dinners, solicitors' dinners, the Lord Mayor's banquet for judges, the Faculty of Advocates in Edinburgh, dinners for visiting lawyers from overseas. There were dinners at Wadham and Gray's Inn and Liverpool; dinners for actors and dinners for cartoonists and dinners for political agents; to say nothing of major occasions like dinners for visiting Heads of State. It is difficult to see that F.E. ever ate at home, and he never dined out without making a speech. On some of these occasions he made openly political speeches, on others he was strictly humorous; but it was rare that there was not some topical shaft directed at some critic of the Coalition, or a passing remark on the necessity of its continuance in the difficult days through which the country was passing. This was the repeated message, whether earnestly laboured or lightly tossed-off, common to practically all F.E.'s speeches in these years: the country faced problems far too serious to risk going back to party government; only a sustained national effort, embodied in the Coalition, could pull the country through.

F.E. was the best propagandist for the Coalition in the country because he most passionately believed in it. Since 1910, when he had jumped eagerly at Lloyd George's proposal for a coalition to settle the House of Lords crisis, and 1914, when he and Churchill had tried to bring Bonar Law and Asquith into coalition at the outbreak of war, he had been convinced – partly, it may be admitted, through self-interest – that a combination of the best men of both parties was necessary to overcome the institutionalized disagreement that was dividing the nation at a time when it most needed to be united. Now that such a government existed, it was more important than ever, with the whole political world, domestic and international, needing to be built anew after the holocaust of the war, that that unity be not thrown away. Self-interest was, no doubt, again a factor in this conviction, just as it was a factor impelling those outside the Government to attack it; but coalition also embodied his profoundest beliefs about the nature and purpose of government as they had developed since his election as a raw partisan in 1906.

Two distinct strands of thinking co-existed among those who wanted to fuse the two Coalition parties into a single permanent centre party in the years 1919–22. The positive side of coalitionism, which emphasized the spirit of wartime unity, social reconstruction and the obligation to build the promised 'land fit for heroes to live in', was represented inside the Cabinet most insistently by the Liberal Dr Christopher Addison (Minister first of Reconstruction and then of Health, which included

Housing); but outside the Government by a substantial number of idealistic younger M.P.s of both parties, most of whom had fought in the war and returned from it with the war generation's impatience of old men and pre-war loyalties. The negative side, weak in 1919 but growing steadily stronger in the next few years, saw the Coalition primarily as the guarantor of stability, an alliance of the 'constitutional' parties against the new challenge of Labour, with the spectre of Bolshevist revolution and anarchy at its back. F.E. and Churchill and Lloyd George himself – the three leading figures of coalitionism – all became increasingly identified with this negative, defensive aspect, so that the positive, optimistic face tended to be obscured and forgotten. In 1919, however, the positive was definitely uppermost in F.E.'s view of the future, and if it later became overlaid by events it was never entirely swamped.

At the end of the war F.E. still regarded himself, as he had always done, as a progressive Unionist, social reformer and friend of the ordinary un-unionized patriotic working man: a Tory Democrat. It was in these terms that he pledged himself to Lloyd George in December 1918, promising him the enthusiastic support of Liverpool Toryism, and it was in these terms that he continued for some time to present himself to the public. Awarded in April 1919 the freedom of Birkenhead (in recognition, presumably, of the distinction he had brought to the town by taking it as his title), he vigorously rebutted Labour protests that he had never done anything for the working class, citing not only his chairmanship of the Unionist Social Reform Committee but also a list of all the progressive Bills which he had supported or, in one case, even helped Keir Hardie to draft.[34]

His attitude to the Labour party was benevolent, if patronizing – consistent with the attitude he had taken before the war on the payment of M.P.s, that it was important that working men should be directly represented in a democratic Parliament. Faced as the Government was in 1919 with a severe wave of strikes, F.E. expressed understanding and a calm confidence in the fundamental soundness and loyalty of the country. In his very first speech in the House of Lords in February – a maiden speech as unlike as possible his first effort in the Commons, designed to impress the peers with the new Lord Chancellor's sober dignity – he characteristically compared the situation with that at the end of the Napoleonic wars and found the threat of serious disorder very much less. He promised that the Government would act firmly where necessary to stamp out Bolshevism, 'the bitter enemy of democracy'; but promised also that their response would not be merely negative. There were grounds for some unrest: the report of a recent commission on Scottish housing he described as 'one of the most tragic documents ever presented to Parliament. The conditions described in it are a disgrace and a shame to a Christian community.' The Government accepted it as an 'imperative duty' to remedy them.

As for strikes, while pledging the Government to stand firm against 'those who have no concern at this moment except to destroy first one industry and then another', he placed his faith in 'inquiry, publicity, full discussion and complete candour'. No strike could be allowed to succeed against what he called 'the great silent majority of the public'; but he asked the miners and other dissatisfied groups to trust the Government. If they had a remediable wrong, it would be remedied; their claim to a larger share of the product of their labour would be fully examined.[35] Hollow words, perhaps: F.E.'s view of a remediable wrong or the share of the product which capital could afford to pay to labour was always going to be different from that of the Miners' Federation. Nevertheless the important thing was the note of conciliation and good will towards labour which F.E., reflecting the Government as a whole, was determined to strike in these first months of peace, before the Labour party began to disturb the Government's composure by winning by-elections. In 1919 the industrial outlook, riding high on a brief boom, was encouraging. A progressive Coalition dedicated to reconstruction had nothing to fear politically from a sectional party of strictly limited national appeal. It was with an air of paradox that he warned the New Members' Group on 15 July that they should not rule out the possibility of a Labour Government taking office in the next few years. It is evident from the mildness of his remarks, compared with his changed tone a few months later, that he did not appreciate how truly he had spoken.

> He declared that Labour had a great part to play in the future, and he would like to see it educated by a spell of the same responsi-bilities as the other parties had had. By this means alone, in his view, could the Labour party acquire the judgement and balance of the Labour party in Australia.[36]

The occasion of these remarks was a dinner attended by a hundred or so younger M.P.s of both parties (but also both Chief Whips) at the Criterion Restaurant, with the frank purpose of promoting the forma-tion of a permanent Centre party. Primed by Freddy Guest, with Lloyd George's approval, the press reported the evening as 'a political sensa-tion of the first importance'.[37] Churchill was the main speaker, fresh from a weekend with the Prime Minister at Criccieth: during his speech he revealed for the first time in public the story of the 1910 venture. F.E. was not officially present at all. Oswald Mosley, however, then a starry-eyed young Tory member, one of the co-secretaries and leading spirits of the New Members Group, makes a good story of his unexpected appearance. Though doubtless exaggerated by fifty years' maturing in the memory, it is another vivid illustration both of the reputation F.E. had now acquired – he never had it before the war – for drinking too much, and of his extraordinary capacity to rise above it.

> We had no idea that F.E. Smith was in the same building, but a message was brought to Mr Churchill directly after his speech. With gratified surprise [though Mosley speculates that the co-incidence was deliberately contrived between them] he turned to me and said that his old friend was in the restaurant below and it would be a pleasure if he could be invited to our table. This indeed was a coup for the new members, and I hastened to execute my mission. I found the Lord Chancellor seated in a prominent position with the sole company of Lady Birkenhead. He appeared to be in an advanced condition of post-prandial content as he surveyed me indolently through the haze of his cigar-smoke, countenance suffused but genial. I indicated that Mr Churchill would be pleased if he would join our company upstairs, and looked enquiringly at his experienced partner. She said something to the effect that he was quite all right and I should take him along.
>
> He rose with dignity to his feet and, leaning rather heavily on his guide, advanced in stately style to the door, with few words spoken. We proceeded, as the police say, in difficult circumstances to the field of action, where he sat heavily on a chair which was happily near the door. The symptoms were ominous, and I glanced enquiringly at Mr Churchill, as previously at Lady Birkenhead, but his experienced eye immediately reflected an affirmative and he called at once on his old friend to speak, amid our resounding applause. Resting his full weight on his fists clenched on the table, Lord Birkenhead spoke like a bird for twenty minutes with little more than his customary lisp. It was astonishing, but both wife and friend had known the form.[38]

The New Members' Group was the rank and file parliamentary expression of an aspiration to which F.E. and Winston were naturally delighted to give their blessing. More surprisingly Bonar Law, by temperament a much more conventional party man and saddled in addition with the responsibility of the Tory leadership, was coming round to the view – and beginning to voice it in public – that there should be some sort of formal 'fusion' between the wings of the Coalition. In its original and more idealistic form the idea of permanent coalition was an expression of national unity; it was directed against Bolshevism as expressed through strikes, perhaps, but it saw, as F.E.'s speech at the Criterion suggested, no electoral threat from the Labour party. Within a fortnight of that speech, however, that complacent attitude began to be put to the test. On 29 July Labour won its first post-war by-election, capturing a Lanarkshire seat previously held by a Conservative. In August it won another, at Widnes, and in subsequent months it markedly increased its poll in several more, as well as making significant gains in the local elections in November. The climax came at Spen Valley at the turn of the year. For this immemorially Liberal seat the Asquithians put up John Simon (who had lost Walthamstow the previous year) and the Government a Coalition Liberal named Fairfax; but the Labour candidate profited from the split vote to come through and beat them both comfortably. At once the alarm bells were set ringing. Labour was suddenly perceived as an imminent threat – not least by F.E.

F.E.'s reaction to Spen Valley was to write for the *Weekly Dispatch* a series of three articles calling for the immediate fusion of the two parties of the Coalition into a single party which would be able effectively to resist the new challenge from Labour. In pithy form, suitable for a popular paper, they comprise an exceptionally clear and candid account of his view of post-war politics. The first, published on 11 January 1920, created a major sensation in its own right.

It began assertively, with no beating about the bush.

> The recent by-election at Spen Valley has attracted great attention, but not all the comments upon it have been equally intelligent.
> It is acclaimed by one as an immense triumph for Labour, by another as a supreme blow to the Coalition.
> Rightly analysed it is neither . . .

It was not a triumph for Labour, since the two Liberal candidates combined would easily have beaten the Labour candidate. Nor was it a defeat for the Coalition: on the contrary, it marked 'the final decease of the Liberal candidates . . . who withhold allegiance from Mr Lloyd George'. In Sir John Simon they had their strongest candidate, apart from Asquith himself, backed by the official Liberal machine which had held the seat since 1885. Yet Simon lost heavily to Labour and only narrowly beat the Coalition's representative.

> Today this simple truth is unchallengeable. For a year after the election which swept them away not a single one of the leaders of that Party can offer himself for election to one constituency in

these islands with the faintest prospect of success. One and all they must either join the Labour Party or join Mr Lloyd George.

The future, F.E. concluded, lay between Labour and the Coalition. He repeated his prediction that Labour might very well form a Government within a few years. But he suggested that a major reason for Labour's progress had been that the older parties, preoccupied with fighting one another, had never turned the spotlight upon Labour's deficiencies. He now proceeded to remedy this neglect by posing some awkward questions.

> They can, if they choose, call themselves the Labour Party, but who gave them the right to talk as if they and they alone represented Labour?
> Do they represent the millions of unorganised labourers who are not members of any trade union?
> Do they represent the new women voters whom, with almost ill-concealed antagonism, they are attempting to exclude from an equal industrial position with male trade unionists?
> Do they represent the discharged soldiers and sailors to whom today, in hundreds of cases, as an act of deliberate policy, they deny the opportunity of assimilating themselves among many of the most highly-skilled trade unions? . . .
> The first elementary truth which they will do well to grasp is . . . that they do *not* represent Labour as a whole, and that they *never will* represent Labour as a whole.

There were, then, strong arguments to be urged by its opponents against the Labour party's inevitable march to power. 'But' – and here F.E. came to his key point – 'they cannot, in my judgement, be successfully urged by an invertebrate and undefined body such as the present Coalition.' The Coalition was an admirable instrument for winning the war, and had surmounted several dangerous crises since.

> But it is as ineffective an instrument for fighting our English Communists as it was an effective instrument for fighting the Germans.
> The task of meeting the new Party in the political arena cannot be effectively discharged except by a single Party emerging with definite purposes and under one banner.
> For such a task the formation of a National Party is, in my judgement, indispensable . . .

He did not, in this first article, enlarge further, beyond the reflection that 'considerable analogy exists between parties and armies . . . It is not only in war that unity of command counts.'[39] Without further explanation, this blunt declaration, with its dismissal of the present Coalition as 'invertebrate and undefined' exploded on the political scene like a bombshell. It was generally understood as an *attack* on the Coalition, whereas in intention it was quite the opposite. 'What on earth did FE mean by that article of his in the *Dispatch*?' Younger wrote to Guest – evidence in fact that the two halves of the Coalition were already working pretty well together. 'A nice sort of leg-up to our candidates at by-elections to have their party branded as "invertebrate".'[40] *The Times* reported the astonished reaction in the clubs, where F.E.'s article was said two days later to be the single topic of conversation.

> It was difficult to see how the Coalition could stand such a shock to its prestige as that which the Lord Chancellor had given it. Here was one of the half dozen men at the head of the Government, one of the inner ring of Ministers, branding the Coalition as invertebrate and throwing it on one side like an old glove.

In truth it was only F.E.'s language which was stronger than that of his senior colleagues. Not only Churchill but, more significantly, Bonar Law had for some time been floating the idea in public that the two wings of the Coalition should come together in permanent form. In calling for a new party, however, F.E. seemed to be going too far, too fast.

> But where is the LORD CHANCELLOR'S National Party? Who are to be its leaders? What is to be its programme? Nobody knows . . . New parties do not spring up like mushrooms in the night . . . If the LORD CHANCELLOR is speaking any language but that of sheer desperation, he can be contemplating nothing but the Coalition under another name and with a unitary organisation that may for a time pull its loose ends together. Can it be that he is merely clothing the skeleton of 'fusion' which Mr BONAR LAW has cautiously exposed to the view of more than one audience in the country? That would be no new party; it would be the old Coalition writ large.[41]

It is difficult to see the reason for *The Times*'s derision. F.E. was indeed proposing no more than to flesh out, fairly urgently, the bones of Law's tentative skeleton: his new party was not intended to be other than the old Coalition writ large, or rather given formal and permanent existence – as he explained at greater length, answering *The Times*'s criticisms, in his second and third articles. In the meantime, however, he had a somewhat comic exchange with Lord Ampthill, the President of a group of Conservative Diehards who had broken away in 1917 and called themselves the National Party, which title they bitterly resented F.E. stealing for the Coalition. F.E. replied to their pretensions in his most suavely supercilious style. He was, he claimed, 'genuinely un-aware that the "National" Party had survived the General Election'. Even if it had survived, however, 'the fortunes of that party at that Election were hardly crowned with such a degree of success as would obviously entitle its members to the monopoly of a somewhat important English adjective'. He politely declined to answer their questionnaire to determine whether he might be permitted to join Lord Ampthill's party. 'I have other opportunities which I prefer to use of making my views upon public matters plain.'[42]

Why F.E. chose the *Weekly Dispatch* as his favoured platform is not clear, but his second article appeared a fortnight after the first, on 25 January. He began this more extended argument for a united Coalition party with an affectation of surprise at the attention his previous 'somewhat obvious conclusions' had attracted. It was obvious to him that there could be no going back to the pre-war structure of politics.

> Pre-war politics have disappeared. They no longer divide men's minds or afford the material for acute antagonisms . . . For twenty or perhaps fifty years our statesmen must busy themselves with entirely new problems, and the new electors will wave impatiently aside, as if they belonged to the Victorian age, those who try to marshal the dying forces of extinct controversies.

Since he had joined the Government, he declared, there had not been a single question on which Ministers had been divided according to their former political allegiance. That being so it was elementary, indisput-able, axiomatic that if the Coalition wished to remain in being, to remain powerful and to be re-elected 'it must organise itself with a degree of thoroughness comparable to that which is shown by the parties, or the party, which challenge its existence' – in short, Labour.

The opposition Liberals, he repeated, would be forced to make their choice between the two parties. F.E. was obliged, at this point, to qualify the assertion in his previous article that no anti-Government Liberal could get himself elected anywhere in the country, in recogni-tion of the fact that Asquith himself had just been adopted to contest a

promising vacancy in Paisley (which he did in fact win); but he maintained that Asquith's possible return did not affect the general truth of
his proposition. He cited Haldane's move towards Labour with a gentle
joke at the former Lord Chancellor's ample bulk.

> Lord Haldane, looking upon the Labour Party as a tiger, is not
> unwilling to repeat the risk of the young lady of Riga. It may
> indeed be conceded that the tiger which would inconspicuously
> accommodate my distinguished and noble friend would be a very
> large one. But perhaps this one is very large.

'Does anyone think', F.E. resumed, 'that adequate efforts are being
made in constituencies today to defend the causes in which we believe?
If he does, he lives in the clouds.' Labour was being given a free run.
Vividly F.E. pictured the threat.

> At this very moment . . . young, plastic and impressionable minds
> are drinking in false messages because these are the only ones they
> hear . . . In every industrial centre the Socialists are busy. You will
> find them at the street corners of our large towns uttering and
> indeed bellowing economic sophistries. Often you will find at
> these meetings . . . the whole existing basis of society most
> enthusiastically and plausibly assailed. The capitalist system,
> which can be defended by arguments both clear and intelligible,
> goes absolutely by default. Greed, envy and malice are nightly
> inculcated.

The present Government was the strongest, ablest and best-equipped
in sight to tackle the unprecedented problems of the next few years.
Could Asquith, Salisbury, MacDonald or Lord Robert Cecil match
Lloyd George? And yet, he repeated,

> As a fighting force in the constituencies, it is today . . . what every
> Coalition in English history has always been – it is invertebrate. It
> is ineffective in attack; it is unconvincing for the purposes of
> defence. It lets every case go by default . . . No-one is specially
> concerned to defend it and everyone is specially concerned to
> attack it. This state of affairs constitutes a grave menace to the
> State.

Only a united party would be able to arouse the enthusiasm and the
necessary partisanship of workers in the constituencies. They would
have a fine record to defend. The Coalition had won the war, 'gathered

for the Empire the fruits of victory', finally enfranchised the whole nation, and carried the country

> during the twelve months which followed the Armistice, through a period of crisis and unrest . . . comparable in gravity to that which faced us in a critical year of the war. We are now, amid incredible difficulties, addressing ourselves to the work of reconstruction upon lines which are not seriously challenged by any of our political opponents.

F.E. ended with a confident prediction.

> The formation of such a Party may easily be postponed. It may be postponed too long. It may be called a National Party, a Constitutional Party, or a People's Party.
> But even if it be postponed; by whatever name it be called, all those who have criticized me, except those who belong to the Socialist Party, will within five years – in office or in opposition – find themselves, as I shall, among the roll of its members.[43]

In his third article, published on 1 February, F.E. turned to the policies of the projected new party. They are not, of course, at all detailed – no more, he admitted, than 'a series of generalities' – but they do usefully summarize, under five headings, the fundamentals of the faith with which F.E. emerged into the post-war world, and may instructively be compared with the fullest exposition of his pre-war views contained in *Unionist Policy* in 1913.

His view of foreign policy has already been described: lip service to the League of Nations, but maintenance both of wartime alliances and national military strength; Germany to be helped back to prosperity so that she could pay due reparation for her crimes.

The Empire now has two aspects: 'It is, on the one hand, an association of free and equal nations' – the white Dominions, whose equal share in the government of the Empire must be acknowledged – 'and, on the other, the greatest instrument for teaching democracy and progress to the backward millions of mankind that the world has ever seen . . . If we are to deal with the movements of unrest which manifest themselves among the less advanced races of the Empire,' F.E. declared, 'we must encourage a steady development of democracy and responsibility among them.' This was the standard progressive sentiment of the time. What F.E. meant by it was not to be judged during the Coalition, but only five years later when he had responsibility for realizing it under the Baldwin Government.

He repeated, in this 1920 manifesto, but more urgently, his earlier commitment to proportional representation, now essential to defeat the 'direct action' threat to the primacy of Parliament. The House of Commons should mirror as perfectly as possible the expressed desires of the nation. Surprisingly he said nothing of the restoration of the Lords.

The Irish situation had clarified itself into three accepted principles:

- that Southern Ireland must no longer be denied self-government.
- that the solid anti-Home Rule population of Ulster must not be forced under a Dublin Parliament against its will.
- that the secession of Ireland or any part of Ireland from the British Empire must be resisted to the end.

It was on the last that he placed emphasis: 'We shall resist secession as the United States resisted it – that is to say, to the last man and the last sovereign.' The extent of his adherence to this principle will be seen in the next chapter.

Finally, in domestic policy, F.E. enunciated two very vague principles: '"reform" not "revolution" and "individual liberty" rather than "governmental control"'. There was no doubt that 'with goodwill, and good organisation and hard work, we can give everybody a better time than before the war'. Dismissing the superficial attractions of revolution, he made the perceptive prophecy (not at that date a truism) that when the veil was finally lifted from Soviet Russia it would be found that after all the suffering, 'things at the end will not be so different as we should expect from what they were at the beginning'. Dismissing socialism, he admitted that there were – though he did not name them – 'certain national services which can best be nationally owned and run', but ridiculed the Labour party's 'mad desire . . . to convert the whole nation into an army of officials debarred from enterprise, depending for promotion upon higher officials, and controlled and regulated from morning till night'. 'The ideal State', he now asserted, contrasting it with the regulated German state, 'is that in which the individual is so well-educated and so self-sufficient a citizen that the life of the community runs itself with the least possible organization from the top.'[44]

What is striking about this programme is how much more Conservative, in the modern sense of more *laissez-faire*, it is than the distinctly Bismarckian Toryism that F.E. had advocated before the war. The active interest of the State in promoting social reform has dwindled to the hope that it should be possible to 'give everybody a better time'. Under the threat of Bolshevism and with the discrediting of all things German, F.E. has retreated from any detailed talk of social interventionism. The policy of the new National party, in F.E.'s conception, is more liberal than pre-war Toryism on the Empire and Ireland; he has abandoned the dogmatic commitment to tariff reform (on the understanding that the Coalition Liberals have abandoned dogmatic Free Trade). Nevertheless it is, whether 'national' or not, a notably conservative prospectus – very much in line with the development, under the same stimuli, of Churchill's thinking, but scarcely consonant with the still interventionist instincts (when he could tear his mind from foreign preoccupations) of Lloyd George. Their divergent directions after the fall of the Coalition are here foreshadowed. Indeed, what F.E.'s programme really embodies is – ironically – a blueprint for Baldwinism: a benevolent, quietist conservatism, externally liberal, internally *laissez-faire*. His forecast of the evolution of parties, though inaccurate in detail, was in the long run broadly correct. The Liberals *were* to all intents and purposes squeezed out of existence, forced to choose not between Labour and a new National party but between Labour and a moderate Tory party – led, not as he anticipated in 1920 by Lloyd George and himself, but, as he could never have imagined, by the then Financial Secretary to the Treasury, Stanley Baldwin, with F.E. and Winston numbered among his loyal subordinates and Lloyd George in the wilderness.

Going back to February 1920, however, when Lloyd George still bestrode the political world like a colossus and Bonar Law thought he could be Prime Minister for life if he liked, F.E. was not, as *The Times* thought, in front of the band in advocating 'fusion'. The permanent merger of the Coalition parties under Lloyd George's leadership was the agreed policy of the Tory leadership as a whole, though they gravely underestimated the resistance any such move was certain to arouse among their rank and file, who were already beginning to rediscover their old antipathy to Lloyd George and see him no longer as an electoral asset but – as the euphoria of victory gave way to bitter economic reality – as a positive liability. Bonar Law and his senior lieutenants, Balfour, Chamberlain and Long, ignored this persistent flame of primitive party spirit, only temporarily quenched, at their peril. They were saved in 1920 from any action that might have split the party by a quite unexpected veto on 'fusion' by their prospective partners, the Coalition Liberals. It was the Liberal Ministers, Alfred Mond, H.A.L. Fisher, Edwin Montagu and Gordon Hewart, who declined to fuse their party identity in a new structure or, as they doubtless feared, sink their Liberal colours in a sea of Toryism. Of the leading Coalition Liberals, besides Lloyd George himself, only Churchill and Addison were in favour of fusion. The idea was dropped for the moment, to Bonar Law's secret relief but F.E.'s disappointment. In

Liverpool, but in few other places, electoral pacts were arranged that autumn to reverse the local gains made by Labour the previous year. Over most of the country, the coalition idea went into retreat as the Government's popularity declined and the Tories grew more restless. Conservative Ministers found themselves obliged to reflect their followers' anxieties, and the Government began to take on a harder, less Liberal, aspect.

(vi) The 'Plot' against Lloyd George

With the collapse of 'fusion' in 1920, F.E.'s commitment to the Coalition temporarily wavered. The future was suddenly uncertain, and in view of the Coalition Liberal veto on a permanent alliance the Tories were entitled, even bound, to look forward to a purely Conservative Government sooner or later taking over the whole burden of resisting Labour. There was no reason why the Tories should indefinitely accept Lloyd George's leadership and a substantial number of Liberals in the Cabinet – the most unpopular Liberals, associated with the most unpopular policies – if the Coalition Liberals were not willing to accept an ultimate merger. The question of disloyalty to Lloyd George did not arise if Lloyd George was unable to deliver his party to support the new alignment. Accordingly, F.E. started mending his fences with the Tory party. At a dinner for Salvidge in Liverpool in February 1921, for instance (also attended by Bonar Law), he made a thoroughly Tory speech, still defending the Coalition but defending it in thoroughly Tory terms, insisting that the Tory Ministers were betraying none of their Tory principles by adhering to it.[45] Admittedly this was a party occasion; but F.E. would not have spoken in such starkly party terms a few months earlier. Instead of a new party, he was now looking to consolidate his existing party base.

At about the same time, the Government began to run into serious trouble, with mounting evidence that its popularity in the country was exhausted. On the economic front, the brief post-war boom had collapsed and unemployment rose past two million, while strikes multiplied. Addison's ambitious Housing Act ran out of money and its operation had to be curtailed, amid Tory outcry against Government extravagance. The political initiative was seized by a strident 'Anti-Waste' campaign, whose candidates won three by-elections, while from the other flank Labour won several more: even the Independent Liberals won one. Tory discontent with the continuance of the Coalition was fed by rumours of Liberal reunion. On top of everything else, the Government was getting drawn into a bloody civil war in Ireland, and failing to win it. Ministers found themselves under mounting pressure from both wings of their supposed supporters.

In addition to these external pressures, the Government was suddenly shaken by a strange spasm of personal suspicion among its leading members.

F.E. seems to have become temporarily estranged from Lloyd George by their row over Reading's replacement as Lord Chief Justice – Lloyd George was angry with F.E. for obstructing him with legal pedantry, F.E. standing on the dignity of his office and strongly disapproving of the appointment of Lawrence. There is no other visible cause of a quarrel, unless it be F.E.'s impatience with Lloyd George's delay in doing anything about the House of Lords; but this was enough to dent F.E.'s loyalty, at a time when the Coalition was already rocky, the call of party rising, and continued co-operation placed in doubt by the Prime Minister's own colleagues. Moreover he had just lost the other prop of his personal loyalty to the Coalition with the resignation, due to failing health, of Bonar Law, the Tory leader for whom he felt the closest ties of affection and duty. For Austen Chamberlain, his successor, F.E. felt at this period neither the same intimacy nor the same sense of obligation. He regarded himself rather as Austen's equal, with a *greater* position in the country – though nothing came of a move by Joynson-Hicks to run him for the leadership in Austen's place. Lloyd George was similarly deprived by Law's retirement of his closest colleague from the war years: he never achieved the same *rapport* with Austen. Trust was eventually established, but Law's withdrawal removed the lynchpin from the Coalition at a bad moment.

Another source of dissidence within the Government in the months after Law's retirement was Churchill, who was furiously aggrieved that the necessary reshuffle occurred while he was out of the country on Colonial Office business in the Middle East. (He had replaced Milner in the post in February.) Churchill considered that he had the right by seniority to claim the Exchequer when Chamberlain left it to succeed Law as Leader of the House. Lloyd George, however, promoted to the position one of his most successful 'discoveries', Sir Robert Horne (who was both a better financier than Churchill and more likely to be subordinate). Churchill sulked bitterly and refused for some months to have more than formal relations with Lloyd George, addressing him in writing as 'Dear Prime Minister' where previously it had been 'Dear David'.[46]

All this discontent was skilfully played upon and fomented for his own purposes by the ever-scheming Beaverbrook, whose purpose, as soon as Bonar Law was out of it, was to bring down the Coalition. Unscrupulously single-minded in the service of his friend and hero, Beaverbrook disbelieved in the seriousness of Law's illness and calculated that if only the Coalition could be broken up, destroying the credit of both Lloyd George and Chamberlain, Law would be the only possible leader to return and head a new Tory Government – as in fact happened in 1922, though Beaverbrook's triumph then was fleeting. Law gave his designs no encouragement at all; he went to Paris to recover his health, so that he should be seen to be well out of the way, and refused to entertain the suggestion that he might return to office. But Beaverbrook kept him temptingly in touch with the political scene ('Winston is very-very-very-very-angry. FE is as bitter as Winston is angry')[47] and encouraged F.E. to keep in contact with him too, which F.E. did in his most fulsome style.

He had been shocked, he wrote on 5 May, to learn from Max that Law had never received a letter he had written in March at the time of his resignation.

> I cannot my dear Bonar recapture the moment of emotion in which I wrote and to attempt it would now sound extravagant.
>
> But I said and it is permanently true that neither politics generally nor the Unionist party in particular could or would ever be the same to me again. I have now lost a secure and faithful sheetanchor with whom I could discuss everything (the metaphor is mixed) in the most complete candour and friendship. There is no-one who can take your place and as our friendship is nearly fifteen years old it seems very unlikely to me that one will arise. I respect Austin [sic] very much but he is aloof and reserved: I seldom see him and never seem to get to know him any better.

He went on to wonder whether Law was missing 'the great game', reported Winston's disappointment at not getting the Exchequer, but expressed only admiration for Lloyd George's resilience in the face of overwhelming problems: he 'keeps his eye on the Press vigilantly and is not I think quite disinterested in the leadership of the Unionist Party'.[48] Was this intended to stir Law's jealousy? In another letter the following month he explicitly backed Beaverbrook's urging that Law return from Paris soon, implicitly to active politics.

> I am simply delighted to hear such good accounts of your health from Max . . .
>
> But with the restoration of health, new problems will arise. I remember telling you when you spoke to me of resigning that I

doubted whether one who had handled so many immense problems could ever be content, unless health completely failed, with the obscurity of private life, or the substitution of less important employment.

You cannot allow yourself to be permanently exiled in Paris, a place which I should think you would soon come to dislike acutely. You may prolong your stay but you cannot make it indefinite. And as you have to come home I should come whenever you want. Surely it is a misplaced delicacy to think you cannot return without causing embarrassment. You can only avoid this

(i) By a permanent exile

(ii) By dying

As on the whole I suspect that you would think either price too high you will have to come and might as well come now or soon. You need not decide upon any course or policy but be guided by developments and you can remain silent as long as you find it desirable or tolerable. In fact there can be no doubt that it is to the public interest that a man of your experience and ability should be there to give advice, looking at the problems of the day detachedly though with fairly friendly eyes.[49]

Perhaps one should not discount the sincerity of F.E.'s friendship for Law: much of both letters is taken up with talk of tennis, golf and bridge, telling him in the first that he has made £550 at bridge since January ('What cards! you will say. But in fact I am less venturesome'),[48] and in the second that he is troubled with tennis elbow and is playing golf instead ('I am very bad; but we can have some games when you return').[49] Nevertheless the implication of these letters is that F.E. was playing Beaverbrook's game. His reward for encouraging Law's return would presumably have been recognition as heir apparent – to a sick man – over the discarded bodies of Chamberlain and Lloyd George.

But when Law did come over to London for five days in mid-June it was not to gratify Beaverbrook and embarrass Lloyd George but, on the contrary, to promise Lloyd George that he would continue to stay out of the way. Frances Stevenson, who had been deeply suspicious for some weeks, was still not satisfied, fearing that Law was 'entirely in Beaverbrook's hands'.[50] 'It is difficult to believe these things of Bonar, but Beaverbrook seems to be able to make him do anything.'[51] Beaverbrook, she was convinced, was 'engineering for a coup . . . Intrigues are seething everywhere. Winston is very hostile, but D. [Lloyd George] is watching him & FE.'[50] He was indeed. And he moved with devastating effect to scatter the plotters.

Obliged to proceed without any encouragement from Law, Beaverbrook's hope of fomenting a crisis now centred upon the fate of Dr Addison, who had come to symbolize for the Government's opponents the sort of wasteful inefficiency which they alleged characterized it. In March Lloyd George had dismissed him from the Ministry of Health but kept him on, to save his face, as Minister without Portfolio. This apparent sinecure at £5,000 a year was to the Diehards an even more blatant example of Government extravagance, in support of a Minister of proved incompetence. The Tory party was soon up in arms, Addison made matters worse by a defiant interview in which he portrayed himself (not inaccurately) as the focus of a generalized Tory attack on the Liberal component of the Coalition, and Chamberlain had to tell Lloyd George that feeling in his party was such that he could not support Addison's retention.

Beaverbrook and Churchill did their best to ensure that there was no backing down from the crisis which impended by working to stiffen Addison's refusal to resign quietly; there would then have to be a vote in the Commons in which either the Government might be defeated outright, or else Chamberlain might command the support of less than a majority of the Tories, which would have the same result.

How actively F.E. was involved in this design is far from clear. He had no particularly close contact with or liking for Addison. But then neither had Churchill or Beaverbrook. They were using him, quite cynically, to provoke a split in the Government from which they hoped to benefit – though how Winston, as a Coalition Liberal, would benefit from the replacement of Lloyd George by a Tory Government headed by Law – who had no more use for him now than in 1915 – is not obvious. The whole episode appears irrational in the extreme, the expression of childish pique on Churchill's part and mischief-making on Beaverbrook's.

At any rate Lloyd George had no doubt that F.E. was involved. On 23 June the *Manchester Guardian* carried an extraordinary story, directly inspired by Lloyd George through his Press agent Sir William Sutherland (described in the by-line as 'a friend who is a responsible politician and certainly has inside knowledge') which exposed the whole plot – apparently with authority, though actually with remarkably little detail – and named F.E. as its leader, Churchill only as his reluctant lieutenant.

There was an attempted revolt of the Unionist wing, led by Lord Birkenhead, and it broke down because he could get no assured House of Commons backing . . .

The incipient revolt was abandoned mainly on account of Mr Churchill's refusal to go on. There may possibly have been a certain shyness on the part of the Conservatives towards Mr Churchill, but it was nothing compared with Mr Churchill's shyness when it came to taking the plunge. He retired because he was convinced that the time was not yet and that the revolt would have no chance of success.

Lord Beaverbrook was also in the conspiracy. Lord Derby was not . . .

The idea, the paper 'revealed', was 'to establish a provisional Government, only more Conservative in tendency and minus some Liberal Ministers, and, should the opportunity offer, to force a general election on issues of their own choosing'. Lloyd George was to be persuaded 'to go into temporary retirement on the excuse of taking a holiday, which he certainly needs'.

The great difficulty (apart from Mr Lloyd George himself who, though feigning sleep, was watching the thing with one eye open) was that Lord Birkenhead is a peer. Some lieutenant in the House of Commons was needed and Mr Churchill was the obvious man. Mr Chamberlain was not likely to join in, but in any case he was thought to lack the ability to carry the party. Sir Robert Horne was left out and was regarded as certain to stand by the present Prime Minister.

It is far from clear, in fact, apart from F.E., Winston and Beaverbrook, who *was* supposed to be in the plot.

The only motives the *Guardian*'s informant could offer for the alleged conspiracy pointed again to F.E. as the leading spirit.

Political troubles there were, but they were of long standing. Lord Birkenhead is particularly anxious for a reform of the House of Lords, because he fears that with the House of Lords in its present state there is no security if the Labour party came to power . . . He looks to a reformed House of Lords on a more democratic basis as the only guarantee against disaster . . .

In addition the jealousy of the Conservative Coalitionists towards their Liberal friends, the anxiety lest the Prime Minister should go Left, and the very natural and intelligible personal ambition of the conspirators all supplied incentives.

There was no mention of Addison, though it could be assumed that he was one of the Liberal Ministers who would be dropped. But it was suggested that one further ground for the revolt was dissatisfaction with

Lloyd George's Irish policy – not from the Diehard angle (which would be intelligible) but, on the contrary, in support of conciliation.

> Despite the speech of Lord Birkenhead in the Lords it is a fact (so I am assured, though I am still doubtful) that he advocated in the Cabinet the very plan of fiscal autonomy for Southern Ireland which he criticized so severely in the Lords . . .
>
> Strange as it may seem 'Galloper' Birkenhead . . . was disposed to favour some political concession rather than to press the military solution.[52]

Cabinet minutes and Tom Jones's diary reveal this to be nonsense, the reverse of the truth. (The political correspondent's instinct was sounder than his information.) In putting out this story, Lloyd George presumably wished to divert attention from the switch in his own approach to Ireland: it was *he* who was about to initiate talks with de Valera, and F.E., correctly identified as a hawk in regard to Ireland, who had most misgivings. But then it appears from Frances Stevenson's diary that Lloyd George actually believed this story!

> D. did a very skilful thing yesterday. He had heard . . . quite by accident that FE was going to make a sensational statement off his own bat on fiscal autonomy . . . But D. sent for him half an hour before his speech in the Lords, & in the course of conversation asked him what he was going to say in his speech. After that FE could not very well in decency have gone away & said something entirely different. Today however he has been asking *why* the PM sent for him, which shows that he realizes that D. must have guessed something, & FE would doubtless like to know *how much* he had guessed![53]

This glimpse of Lloyd George congratulating himself to Frances for his cunning in preventing F.E. from saying something he was most unlikely to have ever dreamed of saying illustrates the fantasy world Prime Ministers sometimes inhabit. The conclusion of the *Guardian* article, however (which he pretended to know nothing about – 'amazing article . . . we don't know who wrote it or how he got the information, but it is all correct')[54] spelled out the moral which Lloyd George wished the plotters to draw from the episode.

> The position of Mr Lloyd George has been strengthened. He has the overtures of the Wee Frees [Asquithians] to fall back on. In the

meantime the Unionist revolters have advertised their comparative weakness by letting 'I dare not' wait upon 'I would' . . . The election is coming soon. But Mr Lloyd George intends to call the tune himself.[52]

Whatever the true extent of F.E.'s contemplated treachery – it was almost certainly much less planned and perfected than the article implied – Lloyd George's pre-emptive counter-coup had the intended effect of bringing him quickly to heel, denying it utterly and protesting his loyalty in his most effusive manner as of old.

Secret

My dear P.M.
    Winston has just shown me an article in today's *Manchester Guardian*. It is a tissue of lies from beginning to end. You gave me the Woolsack. You made it possible for me to win distinction on it. You have delighted myself and my wife by recommending me for a Viscountcy. There is absolutely no office in the state which at this moment or at any moment which I can foresee I would exchange for mine. When you can find time for a quiet evening I should like a talk with you and I will candidly tell you the only ambition I have left in public life. It is one of which you would not and could not disapprove.
                         Yours ever,
                            F.E.

I am making a public contradiction.[55]

Frances Stevenson thought this letter 'protested too much'. There was no equivalent denial from Churchill, for which Lloyd George had a ready explanation. 'D. says that Winston does not tell actual lies, & that is why he will not deny it. But FE does not care what lies he tells.'[54] This is probably unjust. It is impossible to be sure exactly how much substance the 'plot' had. As with most plots, there was probably little more to it than a certain amount of discontented talk, encouraged by Beaverbrook and later written up by him in his highly coloured history of the period as a more serious revolt than it really was. The effect of the *Manchester Guardian* 'exposure' of these harmless mutterings may nevertheless have been to jolt F.E. into a realization of how much he owed to Lloyd George and how much he had to lose by undermining him. To this extent his indignant letter represented his true feelings to which – if he had deviated from them in recent months – he was now glad to be recalled. If he had been disloyal, he was certainly never so again, during the life of the Government and for some time after. 'F.E. is *most* amiable to D. now,' wrote Frances on 5 July.

> He keeps on denying that he had anything to do with the con-
> spiracy against D. Said it was all Beaverbrook, and that he (F.E.)
> had seen him during the weekend and told him that it was no good
> trying to upset D. That if he did it, there would be no-one to put in
> his place; and that in any case he would not succeed. 'No', was
> Beaverbrook's reply, 'but I can *try*'.[56]

This, for all its tone of self-justification, rings truer than Beaverbrook's subsequent portrayal of a concerted plot.

Some weeks later F.E. was still vigorously protesting to Riddell his devotion to Lloyd George and begging Riddell to pass on what he said.

> I know my powers and I feel I have a right to expect at some
> distant time to be Prime Minister, but this is not my time. If L.G.
> were displaced, Chamberlain would be sent for. He is leader of the
> Tory Party. I am a poor man but I can honestly say I would rather
> pay £20,000, if I had it, than that L.G. should be turned out ... All
> my interest lies in supporting him ... I should like to see him win
> an election and remain in power for three or four years or as long as
> he wanted to remain.

Riddell was instructed to tell Lloyd George that intrigue was foreign to F.E.'s nature. 'What I have to say I say openly. Furthermore I am loyal to my friends and I am loyal to him.' Duly told all this, Lloyd George 'seemed most affected, and said some nice things about Birkenhead'.[57]

If Beaverbrook had briefly tempted F.E. out of his allegiance by playing on passing discontents, Lloyd George pulled him skilfully back into line by a combination of timely patronage (he raised him a step in the peerage to Viscount), embarrassing exposure (the *Guardian* story), and perhaps most decisively, the offer of a more intimate role in the central direction of the Government, particularly in regard to the most pressing and historic crisis now building to its climax – Ireland. His part in the negotiation of the Irish Treaty at the end of the year was to be the high point of F.E.'s career. It was as though he knew it when he wrote to Lloyd George in August (from Warden Chilcott's yacht *Medea*),

> My dear P.M.,
>   Whether the Conference with S.F [Sinn Fein] comes off or not I
> am profoundly grateful to you for having asked me to be a member
> of it.

If it does I will do my best to be helpful, and I shall not in any event forget this mark of your confidence.

Yours ever,

F.E.[58]

Admittedly Lloyd George needed F.E.'s co-operation in his Irish initiative almost more than F.E. needed him. Nevertheless F.E. saw in Lloyd George's invitation an opportunity to take an enduring part in the making of history, and he did do his best – at the risk of his own standing in the Tory party – to be helpful when he could easily have wrecked it. From the summer of 1921, F.E. and Lloyd George established a new relationship out of mutual trust which soon buried the memory of their passing quarrel. With it, F.E. became re-committed to the Coalition, and to ways of achieving 'fusion' in order to perpetuate it. But the crucial purpose for which the Coalition was re-formed and around which its leaders grouped themselves to fight, was the attempt to settle, once for all, the eternal Irish question.

19
Ireland, 1919–22

(i) War

The situation in Ireland had changed – 'changed utterly' – since 1914.

At the beginning of the war F.E. had been optimistic that its effect would be to dissolve the cultural antagonism between North and South and make possible the sort of compromise – Home Rule with Ulster excluded – which had proved unattainable before. He had been deeply impressed by Redmond's patriotic response in the House of Commons to Britain's hour of peril and by the loyalty with which Irishmen, as enthusiastically as Englishmen, Welshmen and Scots, had volunteered for the army. He had refused to join in Bonar Law's indignant protests when in September 1914 the Liberal Government insisted on passing the Home Rule Act (though suspended for the duration) symbolically into law, believing that the whole question would look very different at the end of the war. He was right, but not unfortunately in the way he envisaged. Certainly, on the British side, the leaders of all parties were by 1918 reconciled to compromise – most Tories were now ready to concede the South Home Rule, and most Liberals ready to safeguard Ulster. But in Ireland, opinion had moved on. The Dublin Rising of Easter 1916 – a futile romantic gesture by a tiny minority of Republicans with no popular support – had been transformed by the clumsy response of the Government in executing fifteen of the leaders over a period of several weeks into a propaganda triumph. At the 1918 General Election Redmond's old Nationalist Party, whose parliamentary success in finally getting Home Rule on to the Statute Book had been rendered meaningless by the military veto of Ulster, was swept into oblivion by the spectacular emergence of Arthur Griffith's and Eamon de Valera's Sinn Fein – 'Ourselves Alone' – which captured practically all the constituencies in the Catholic South, then refused to take their seats at Westminster but set up Dail Eirann in Dublin and declared Ireland a Republic.

During 1919 the I.R.A. – the armed wing of Sinn Fein, welded by Michael Collins into a disciplined guerrilla force – established its authority over large areas of the South and West where the British writ simply ceased to run and Republican courts administered a rough but effective justice, enforced by intimidation. Subjected to a calculated campaign of assassination of policemen and soldiers, the British could only impose martial law and pour in more forces from England to assert their rule. The civil war that had threatened in Ulster before 1914 thus actually erupted five years later in the South. The undiminished determination of Ulster that she would not have Home Rule was violently answered by the equal determination of the South to secure, by any means, and for the whole island, not merely Home Rule – now a dead letter – but independence, to which both British parties were as firmly opposed as the Tories had been to Home Rule. The Irish question as it emerged from the European inferno was more tragically, viciously insoluble than ever. It was the greatest achievement of the Lloyd George Coalition that, after three years of bloodshed, it contrived a settlement which at least neutralized the problem for half a century. In this settlement F.E. played, reluctantly at first but in the end heroically, a decisive role. The Irish Treaty eventually signed in December 1921 was the major achievement of his political career; but also, to many old comrades, his greatest betrayal. By either reckoning it was the supreme crisis of his life.

Since he came in the end to feel a very considerable respect, even friendship, for the Sinn Fein leaders, it is worth examining his initial attitude to them in 1919 and the reasons why he, in common with practically all British governing opinion, regarded their claim to an Irish Republic as inadmissible. At first he looked on them quite simply as rebels, a gang of anarchic gunmen, unrepresentative of the over- whelmingly loyal Irish population, despicable and cowardly murderers who must be ruthlessly exterminated. Then as the prosecutor of Casement he had particular reason to remember the German con- nection, to see them as traitors whose hatred of England led them to traffic unforgivably with the enemy in wartime. As for their demand for independence, his grounds for rejecting it were partly the instinctive, emotional reflex of British Imperialism which could not understand how anyone could want not to be British; the conviction that it was simply absurd for self-evidently inferior people to aspire to self- government; perfect confidence in the fact of geography that made Ireland as British as Birmingham; but partly also a more rational calcu- lation of imperial security which dictated, first, that Ireland could not be allowed her freedom without undermining India and the whole Empire, and second, that Ireland occupied too important a strategic position on the Atlantic flank of the defensive unity of the British Isles for Britain ever to be able to permit secession even if she had wanted to. As their prejudices on other points softened during the long negotiations, neither F.E. nor any other British Minister ever budged on the essential defence argument that Britain could not risk Irish ports being used in some future war by enemy submarines. In the last resort, the Union was a military question which concerned the very safety of the British State.

This ultimate argument from *realpolitik* explains the paradox which ran through the whole British attitude to Ireland – the extraordinary two-facedness which resulted in the continual alternation of kicks and kindness, repression and conciliation. Ministers repeatedly insisted that Ireland was British and loyal at heart, an integral part of the Kingdom and the Empire, yet all the time they disparaged the Irish people as essentially un-British and inferior. The language they habitually used about the Irish leads one to wonder why they were so keen to insist that they were British: the answer lies partly in imperial pride, partly in strategic necessity. The Irish must be loyal: if they were not, they must be forced to be loyal, by conquest and occupation. They could never be allowed to go free: therefore for their own sakes they had best be loyal.

There was no distinction between the British parties in 1919–21 in their attitude to an Irish Republic. All were equally adamant that, under whatever form of devolution, Ireland must remain under the British Crown: the most that a few advanced Liberals were beginning to propose in 1919 was Dominion status – independence within the Empire on the Canadian model – but the Cabinet were still solid against any concession to terrorism. Between Conservatives and Liberals in the Coalition there was no disagreement on what they were prepared to offer: Home Rule with guarantees for Ulster. So long as there was no settlement in view, however, each party inevitably spoke still in the accents of its past commitments; and F.E. naturally still reflected a particular solicitude for Ulster.

He insisted, however, that Ulster had nothing to fear. When on 12 July Carson held another threatening parade of the Ulster Volunteers in Belfast, F.E. went out of his way in the House of Lords to condemn it as unhelpful and unnecessary: the Government was pledged absolutely to the integrity of Ulster, and whatever it eventually proposed – when Lloyd George returned from Paris – would respect that pledge.[1] It did. The Government of Ireland Bill which the Prime Minister unveiled to the House of Commons in December – the Government had to act quickly or the 1914 Act would automatically have come into operation on the signing of the last peace treaty – established in Ireland not one but two Home Rule Parliaments, one in Dublin, one in Belfast, with the promise of a third body, a joint Council of all Ireland, gradually to bring them together. For Ulster this was the security that Asquith had never been able to concede. For Sinn Fein, on the other hand, partition was a step backward from what Redmond had secured, on paper, in 1914. But then Sinn Fein were never expected to accept the new Bill anyway. Privately F.E. saw the presentation of the Bill merely as 'an ingenious strengthening of our tactical position before the world'.

I am absolutely satisfied that the Sinn Feiners will refuse it. Otherwise in the present state of Ireland I could not even be a party to making the offer, for I believe that if the Sinn Feiners did accept their parliament they would only use it for the purpose of forwarding separation.[2]

The Government of Ireland Bill gradually wound its way through the House of Commons, however, and by the time it came to the House of Lords towards the end of 1920 F.E. was obliged to put as positive a gloss on it as he could. This he did to such effect that *The Times* remarked in admiration that 'if the Bill had had delivered in its support once a week since its introduction a speech of equal power to the Lord Chancellor's today, the campaign of political peace would by this time have been in proper perspective with the campaign of crime'.[3] Still his main argument for the Bill was that it definitely secured the integrity of Ulster. He pretended to see no reason why Sinn Fein should not accept the Southern Parliament; but in the same breath he warned that if they did so insincerely and then broke their oaths under the new constitution and tried to set up a republic after all 'the existence of that Irish Parliament would be brought to an end by any means that might be appropriate and necessary', not excluding 'the reconquest of the South of Ireland'.

He concluded, by contrast, with a peroration of real beauty – though very little relation, unfortunately, to his realistic expectations – in which he pictured the prize which awaited the Government if only the Irish could be brought to accept and work the Bill. The blithe Anglocentrism of the assumptions here so eloquently expressed goes far to explain why they were bound to refuse.

If we in our day should be so happy as to succeed, History will record of our generation that we inherited indeed a mighty Empire, but that it was menaced abroad by a powerful and most resolute enemy, while at home it was enfeebled at its very heart by a plague-spot of disaffection and sedition. And in such an event the annals of that history will record on a shining page that we – our generation – after five years of martial vicissitude, broke in rout the foreign enemy and, having done so, have at our doors recaptured in a nobler conquest this island of incomparable beauty, and, in doing so, become reconciled to a people so individual in its genius, so tenacious in love or hate, so captivating in its nobler moods.[4]

The very patronizing self-congratulatory British Imperialism against which Sinn Fein were in rebellion could not be better encapsulated in a single passage.

It was not often the velvet glove, however, which F.E. proffered to the Irish in 1920: in most of his speeches he had nothing to offer but the mailed fist, and he was the same in Cabinet, calling with Winston for 'coercion full-blast' and no weakening.[5] His language was uncompromisingly of war. Having seen off the Boers and the Germans, he demanded in May, did anyone imagine the British Empire was going to give in to the Irish? Sinn Fein might hate Britain, but they should not despise her strength or determination. 'Every single motive which led the United States to resist the attempt at secession would, with even greater force, determine this country.'[6] A fortnight later he insisted again that if the existing forces proved insufficient to restore order in Ireland, they would be increased as necessary, as in the war, until the job was done. The Irish could not win.[7]

The trouble was, neither could the British. It was not a war which the I.R.A. was fighting but a sustained campaign of terrorism and assassination, designed to disrupt and demoralize the forces of the Crown and intimidate those members of the Irish population who might give them shelter, information or support. The army and the Royal Irish Constabulary had no way of hitting back except indiscriminately at the civilian population among whom the gunmen moved invisibly. For more than a year the morale and discipline of the Crown forces – predominantly Irish themselves – held up amazingly well in the face of murderous and cowardly attacks. But in the course of 1920, and particularly as the native Irish soldiers and policemen were supplemented by English reinforcements with little training and no feel for the country – the Black and Tans – discipline cracked, and every I.R.A. outrage came to be followed by savage reprisals against the local populations and local property, which played into the I.R.A.'s hands. Whereas before the campaign of murder had been widely condemned, even by nationalists, and denounced from every pulpit, now the British came increasingly to resemble the hostile occupying power of Sinn Fein propaganda and the I.R.A.'s campaign was retrospectively justified.

The Black and Tans ruthlessly destroyed, by their excesses, the substantial fund of good will towards Britain which still existed in Ireland in 1919. By 1921 Sinn Fein had, what it did not have in 1918, real popular backing for independence from Britain.

As reports of the violent methods of the British forces began to appear in the press, accompanied by photographs of refugees fleeing on wagons with their poor belongings from the wrath to come – the wrath of the supposed upholders of law and order – Liberal opinion in Britain was disturbed and was soon in full outcry. Ministers, however, only vied with one another in excusing and justifying the horrors that were being committed in their name. Sir Hamar Greenwood, the new Chief Secretary, and Lloyd George himself led the way; but F.E. was not far behind, defending the indefensible with worldly gusto.

> I agree with the most reverend Primate [he told the Archbishop of Canterbury in the House of Lords on 22 February 1921] that we cannot cast out the devil by calling in devils; it is also unhappily true that we cannot cure the mischiefs existing in Ireland by uttering the sublime admonitions of the Sermon on the Mount. These mischiefs can be cured only by the assertion of force in its most extreme and vigorous form.

F.E. strenuously denied that the Black and Tans were in any way exceeding their duty: such allegations were 'a gross and abominable libel' on brave British soldiers, based on sheer gossip. If there were abuses, faint-hearted critics could not impeach a whole body of loyal and gallant men because one, two or even twenty forgot themselves in a moment of strong excitement under intolerable provocation. Yet at the same time he accepted that outrages were being perpetrated, and winked at them with the true reflex of the embattled Imperialist.

> The Government is now making, has made and will make the strong arm of England respected in Ireland. [Cheers.] I would rather have the Government odious in Ireland than a farce or a sham. [Cheers.] That it is not a farce or a sham is largely due to those devoted men.[8]

Of course F.E. did not know what he was talking about. He was defending British troops on principle, regardless of the rights or wrongs. But how this crude defence contrasts with his brave speech in the Amritsar debate! He was entitled, indeed, to resent the way the weight of denunciation had become transferred from the I.R.A., who had begun and continued to fuel the campaign of terror, on to the British forces who merely responded to it. Critics of the Government, he noted sarcastically, all covered themselves with some perfunctory phrase 'deploring the excesses of the revolutionary movement' before they got on to 'the operative part of the resolution which has really been drafted with resolution and resource', condemning the forces of the Crown.[9] But his indignation overlooked the moral point – that lawlessness on the part of the forces of law *is* more to be condemned than the same crimes committed by declared rebels – and, which might have been expected to make more appeal to him, the political point – that the indiscriminate assertion of force 'in its most extreme and vigorous form' was not winning the war, was not wooing the loyal population from Republicanism but, on the contrary, was driving them over to the I.R.A. for protection. Simultaneously denying and defending the excessive violence of the Black and Tans, F.E. – like Lloyd George, Churchill, Greenwood and every other Government spokesman – was doing the I.R.A.'s work for it with a singular lack, not only of humanity, but of his usual intelligence.

But what other course was there open to the Government but war? Sinn Fein would not retract from its declaration of total independence. Britain, sentiment apart, regarded any Irish claim that involved separate armed forces and a separate foreign policy as a threat to her own security, a military threat that must be defeated by military means, just as over the centuries the occupation of the Low Countries by Germany, France or Spain had represented a challenge which could not be tolerated. 'The view of the Government is plain', F.E. told the Lords in November 1920, 'that in no conceivable circumstances can the control of the Army and Navy be surrendered to an Irish Parliament.'[10] Therefore the existence of a disloyal Irish army – even if it was only a gang of cowardly gunmen – must be terminated. Dominion status for Ireland, which some Liberals were beginning to advocate, was on this analysis as unacceptable as independence.

On 21 June 1921 F.E. delivered his most remorseless declaration yet on the Irish situation. He admitted that what was going on in Ireland was 'a small war', and that the military methods of the Crown forces had, over the previous few months, failed to keep pace with those of the enemy. 'Further sacrifice', he warned, was needed and would be forthcoming. He dismissed as illusion the hopes of those who looked for a settlement to generous fiscal arrangements. 'We are toying with ideals, we are chloroforming ourselves and closing our eyes to the real facts of the situation.' If there were an agreement in sight, he promised, finance would be no problem.

I, for one, can hardly think of any purely financial consideration which would stand in the way if we were offered the prospect of an

Ireland loyal within the Empire, contributing to our Imperial strength, instead of being a source of our Imperial weakness. I can hardly imagine the price which any sensible man would not pay for such a prospect if it were at all compatible with the necessary maintenance of our whole financial structure. [There were qualifications enough here if it ever came to a negotiation.] But the claim of Sinn Fein has never been put upon finance.

Sinn Fein's claim was for independence.

If I am right in saying that those who are carrying on the war in Ireland will be content with nothing less than . . . an independent Republic for Ireland, this is certain, that that is a claim which it will never be possible for this country even to consider, no matter how long the struggle may last [Cheers] . . . if we should be forced to the melancholy conclusion that by force, and force alone, can this mischief be extirpated or prevented, it is a conclusion which, however sorrowfully we accept it, we shall not hesitate logically and completely to act upon.[11]

The bleak prospect held out by this speech appalled the growing host of those in all parties who were coming to realize that the war, as F.E. defined it, could not be won. The Southern Unionist leader, Lord Midleton, now anxious only for some settlement that would restore the unity of Ireland, feared that F.E.'s speech would do more harm than any he had ever made; while *The Times*, now strong for peace, warned gloomily:

If this indeed be the Government's last word, we can but despair of an Irish peace in their lifetime. They hold out naught but a prospect of continued repression and of force warring upon force, until Ireland lies in ruins. This is not statesmanship nor Christianity.[12]

But this was not the Government's last word. Even as F.E. continued to thump the martial drum, Lloyd George had been beginning to put out feelers to Dublin to see if a more constructive alternative might not be found. One go-between who felt himself qualified by his own history of war against the British, followed by reconciliation, to act as peacemaker was the South African, General Smuts. Smuts it was who proposed using the intervention of the King to break the military deadlock and clear the way for a political initiative. The occasion was the opening of the Ulster Parliament at Stormont, now assembling for the first time.

This was the opportunity Lloyd George was looking for to get around a table with the rebel leaders without losing face. The King was sent to Belfast with an emotional speech, drafted by Smuts, appealing to all Irishmen 'to pause, to stretch out the hand of forebearance and conciliation, to forgive and forget, and to join in making for the land they loved a new era of peace, contentment and goodwill'. The King did not insist upon the permanence of partition: on the contrary, he looked forward to the day, to which he hoped his speech might be the prelude, 'in which the Irish people, North and South, under one Parliament or two . . . shall work together in common love for Ireland upon the sure foundation of mutual justice and respect'.[13]

Two days later Lloyd George invited de Valera to a conference in London. There followed several weeks of tortuous semantic haggling about the terms on which the representatives of the Irish Republic were prepared to parley with the oppressor power, and then further bargaining over a military truce, before the principle of a conference in the autumn was eventually agreed.

F.E. was doubtful about this proceeding, but did not oppose it. When the Cabinet debated whether to send the initial invitation to de Valera, he approved it only because he expected nothing to come of it, as is plain from an exchange recorded by Tom Jones.

> LORD BIRKENHEAD. I do not at present find myself in agreement with the broad view Churchill takes of consenting to the financial changes, but to raise these matters at this stage is premature. I cannot say what my decision would be later if I were confident that nothing but finance stood between us and peace but I see no such sign. I am entirely in favour of the proposal made by the PM. It dissipates the apparently harsh disparity between the King's appeal and my speech to the Lords. It was unfortunate they should come on the same day.
>
> THE PM. I think it was helpful they came on the same day. In dealing with the Irish you must show that you mean to go on.
>
> LORD BIRKENHEAD. My speech should be considered as a reply to a two days' debate. I am not sanguine. I do not think de Valera will come . . . If he comes it is a gain. If not, it is to the good. Before we brace ourselves for what is to follow it will be useful to have this.[14]

F.E. calculated that an offer to talk which de Valera rejected could only do Britain good in the eyes of America and the world. But de Valera came to London, and in subsequent discussions F.E. equivocated uncharacteristically between the hard Unionist line, still upheld by Balfour, that one should not talk of truce with murderers at all, and the opposite view to which Churchill was now converted. 'Churchill', wrote Tom Jones, 'has finally acknowledged the failure of the policy of force. Birkenhead wobbles as if unwilling to break either with the PM or with Churchill. Today he was all for meeting de Valera apart from Ulster.'[15]

The talks with de Valera, though very sticky, developed their own slow momentum. Now that they had been begun, neither side wanted the odium of breaking them off. Lloyd George now definitely decided to bend all his arts to achieving a settlement. Just as important, his two principal Conservative colleagues came simultaneously to the conclusion that they should do all in their power to promote rather than to obstruct the cause of peace. Austen Chamberlain recalled some years later how F.E. walked into his room in 11 Downing Street one morning just as he, Austen, was telephoning that he must see F.E.

> 'You and I', he said, 'bear a great load of responsibility. Unless we are agreed, we shall smash the party and destroy any chance of settlement. It is time we each knew exactly where the other stands.'
>
> And he then proceeded to explain his views with that clarity and brevity which always distinguished him in council. I found that he had come to say to me what I had meant to say to him, and thenceforth we co-operated without a shade of difference throughout the long negotiations, the many conferences, and the parliamentary struggle which followed.[16]

The view to which F.E. and Austen found themselves converted, some way ahead of most of their party, was that so long as there was a real chance of its acceptance in good faith the British Government should now be ready to offer Ireland, with certain specified safeguards for British security, the status of a self-governing Dominion. This was for both of them an enormous leap beyond anything they had hitherto thought possible; and though in the course of the subsequent negotiations they were to go farther still in whittling away those safeguards, this was the critical moment at which they resolved to take their political lives in their hands and go all out for peace if it were humanly attainable within the absolute limit of the condition to which they adhered to the end, that Ireland retain some sort of nominal allegiance to the Crown. The moment that he accepted Dominion status for Southern Ireland was the turning point of F.E.'s career. He was by no means certain that it would be accepted by Sinn Fein. The calculation that if they rejected it Britain would stand well in the eyes of the world for having offered it was still at the front of his mind. But he had now committed himself that if they accepted it, so would he; moreover he would strive positively with his leader to induce them to accept.

At Cabinet on 20 July, therefore, he dithered no longer. As soon as Lloyd George's draft offer was read out, he 'weighed in' (H.A.L. Fisher's phrase)[17] – contrary to his usual habit of waiting until everyone else had spoken before intervening – saying that he accepted it. Churchill followed, giving his support and only a few verbal changes were made before the document was presented to de Valera. F.E. was then in the spotlight as he had to justify in the House of Lords his own and the Government's dramatic change of front. He did so with characteristic belligerence, rejecting Diehard talk of the 'shame and dishonour' of negotiating with murderers, distancing himself indignantly from his 21 June speech which he claimed had been wilfully misinterpreted, and from his new conciliatory position condemning the barren criticism of Lord Salisbury, whose only alternative was the resumption of force. He himself still held force in the background, however. This offer was the Government's last word; it was right to make one last attempt at peace – but if the Irish rejected it, the Government would go back to war. He warned against over-optimism, but passionately defended the attempt.[18]

Still insisting on their demand for a Republic, the Irish Cabinet rejected the July offer but, having won so much, were anxious to keep talking, as were the British. The next hurdle to be surmounted, then, was to find a form of words acceptable to both sides by which a formal conference could be established. At the beginning of September Lloyd George was carrying on this game of semantic poker with de Valera from Gairloch, in the north of Scotland, where he was on holiday; and on 7 September he took the unprecedented step – not popular with his colleagues – of summoning them to a Cabinet meeting in Inverness Town Hall. The question was whether or not to insist that discussion could only continue on the basis of explicit Irish recognition of the Empire. F.E., Tom Jones noted, was annoyed at being obliged by the seating arrangement to speak earlier than he liked, and hedged. He was evidently depressed by de Valera's continued intransigence, anxious not to get drawn into his trap, yet still unwilling to take the easy, Tory, way out if there was a real chance of peace. (He had been away cruising on his yacht for the last fortnight and was evidently feeling a little unsure of the position.)

> Two alternatives only before us. (a) To invite them to come to conference saving their face without having put on record that they had accepted discussion on basis of British Empire. (b) The

state which the correspondence has reached makes it extremely difficult for us to write a colourless letter. I do not say it is impossible. It would be a weak stage in this correspondence if we were to invite them in reply to a letter which talks of 'irrevocable proposals'. No-one would like to use this as a ground for a good break if one believes a settlement can be reached but I am apprehensive that the conference may lead to a bad break. We might get to a bad ground, the two counties [Fermanagh and Tyrone: in other words, the size of the area to be excluded]. But if the majority of my colleagues think we can still pluck a good settlement I would run the risk.[19]

The compromise wording eventually hammered out on a basis proposed by Chamberlain, which was neither a surrender nor an ultimatum, asked de Valera for a definite reply as to whether his Government was prepared to enter a conference 'to ascertain how the association of Ireland with the community of nations known as the British Empire can best be reconciled with Irish national aspirations'.[20] This de Valera accepted, but in such truculent terms that Lloyd George, with Chamberlain's and F.E.'s support, immediately withdrew the invitation, so that it was another fortnight before the conference was finally agreed by both sides, and summoned to meet in London on 10 October.

(ii) The Negotiation of the Treaty

The individuals selected by each side to compose the conference were decisive to the outcome. For the British Lloyd George himself naturally led and Austen Chamberlain, both as co-leader of the Coalition and specifically as leader of the Unionist party, was necessarily his deputy. F.E. was included partly for the domestic political reason already described, that Lloyd George wanted to bind him to himself; partly because he would be a skilful negotiator and had a particular contribution to make as a constitutional lawyer; but mainly because he was still seen as the Unionist hard-liner and Diehard defender of Ulster. His reputation cut both ways. On the one hand, in the negotiations themselves, his job was to present to the Irish the face of implacable Unionism, to demonstrate that Lloyd George could offer only so much and no more. On the other, his participation would guarantee Ulster against betrayal by the old Liberal enemy while his agreement would be essential if any settlement were to be sold successfully to the Tories. F.E. and Chamberlain together held the key to the negotiations. There could only be peace with their combined consent and advocacy. But though Chamberlain was the party leader, F.E. had the closer connection with the Irish question and particularly with Ulster, and Lloyd George at least thought his would be the more important voice in carrying the Tories 'as they regarded Chamberlain as a Liberal Unionist'.[21] It was F.E., accordingly, whom he was most anxious to carry with him in the negotiations and F.E. became effectively the second man on the British team.

Formally the delegation was completed by Churchill (for the same reason as F.E., that Lloyd George needed to involve him, but also as a defence expert); Hamar Greenwood (necessary as Irish Secretary, but in practice too much hated by the Irish to be a useful negotiator); Worthington-Evans (another Unionist, also with a departmental interest as Secretary of State for War); and Gordon Hewart (as another lawyer). But as the negotiations developed these played relatively little part.

On the Irish side, confusion was sown by the decision of de Valera to stay behind in Dublin. As a result it was never clear whether the delegation were plenipotentiaries, empowered to reach an agreement on their own authority, or delegates, bound to refer back for authority to Dublin. De Valera's decision to stay behind has been variously interpreted, either as a prudent device to give the delegation an excuse for delay while they referred back, or as a machiavellian insurance policy designed to keep his own hands clean of any compromise signed in London, which he would then be free to accept or disown. Either way the ambiguity had tragic consequences.

In their leader's absence, the Irish team was led by Arthur Griffith, the founder (in 1905) of Sinn Fein, a nationalist of an older generation than Collins and de Valera, much influenced by the example of Hungary and the Dual Monarchy within the Austrian Empire, a gentle man never likely to stake everything on the irreducible demand for a Republic. At his side to strengthen him was Michael Collins, the hard man of the I.R.A., the ruthless gunman who had initiated the policy of terror which had so successfully provoked the reprisals of the Black and Tans (yet who waged his vicious war with such personal bravado that there has always attached to him the romantic aura of an Irish Rupert of Hentzau). Collins, with this background, was supposed to be the voice of extreme Republicanism, the equivalent on the Irish side of F.E. on the British, whose role would be, metaphorically speaking, to lay his gun on the negotiating table, to make sure that there was no sell-out and to bring in the I.R.A. to back a settlement if one were reached. As it happened, however, Collins turned out to be much more flexible than anticipated, willing to compromise on symbolism if he could thereby win the reality of independence. The strong man of the Irish delegation, as Lloyd George quickly sensed, was open to persuasion.

In these circumstances the other members did not much matter. Two of them, Robert Barton and Gavan Duffy, backed by the delegation's Secretary, Erskine Childers, the chilliest non-compromiser of them all, were determined to hold to the strict Republican line laid down by de Valera; but Lloyd George simply froze them out of the negotiations, quickly abandoning the plenary sessions of the conference in favour of small *ad hoc* discussions between the two or three leaders on each side, which enabled him to concentrate his arts on Griffith and Collins, cajoling and threatening by turns until they signed, when Barton and Duffy had little choice but to do likewise.

In this process F.E. played a part second only to Lloyd George's own, practically an equal part, for while Lloyd George got on terms of trust and mutual respect with Griffith, F.E. struck up a surprising but vital bond of understanding with Collins (who distrusted Lloyd George). At this time, Frank Pakenham has written, 'Lord Birkenhead still loomed in Irish Nationalists' imagination as a sinister, even satanic power' – Carson's 'galloper' in 1914, the prosecutor of Casement, more recently the advocate of uncompromising repression, armed with massive legal authority and a destructive intellect, framed in a 'Herculean physique which dwarfed all the Irishmen except Collins'.

> The event proved that his opponents had underestimated, not indeed his gifts, but his humanity. Throughout the two months of negotiations they continued to marvel at his unfailing aptitude for debating retort, for legal exegesis, for instantaneous drafting . . .
> He was nothing if not a British patriot throughout. But he gave them credit for being patriots, too, and as such he always treated them. They were aware of his might but they admired and trusted him.[22]

Collins's respect for F.E. is explicit in his notes and letters written during the conference. In his notes, giving his early impressions of the British delegation, he makes it clear that he distrusts Lloyd George's trickiness and Churchill's overpowering ambition; he is repelled by Chamberlain's public school formality; but he admires F.E.

> If all the British delegation had his capacity for clear thinking, capacity for work and getting ahead, things would be much easier.

Lawyer but with a great difference. Concise. Clearness of ideas a great advantage. Refuses to be drowned by the might of others. A good man.[23]

Several of Collins's letters to his friend and confidant John O'Kane stress this surprising sympathy which he felt with F.E. and the sense that they were increasingly working together to achieve a settlement in the face of common enemies who would thwart them if they could. 'I prefer Birkenhead to anyone else,' he wrote on 15 November. 'He understands and has real insight into our problems – the Dublin one as much as any other.'[24] Expanding on 'the Dublin problem' on 30 November, when the conference looked like breaking down, Collins noted, 'I think also that Birkenhead's integrity of purpose is foiled in other quarters. I can almost see the gloating that is so obvious among some of our opposites.'[25]

At a simply human level too, Collins found F.E. sympathetic. 'I find the strain of looking into Chamberlain's false eye the most nervy of all my experiences,' the intrepid gunman confessed on 29 November. 'Birkenhead sees this – smiles and shrugs his shoulders.'[25]

Outside the conference as well, though the Irish punctiliously refused ever to accept hospitality from their British counterparts, Collins formed what can genuinely be called a friendship with F.E. Closing his eyes to Collins's direct responsibility for the murderous outrages he had so recently and so contemptuously condemned as the work of barbarous anarchists, F.E. found himself irresistibly drawn to Collins as a warm and courageous fellow-creature; he admired his physical courage, increasingly his moral courage, his integrity and his exceptionally quick, untutored intellectual grasp. The gunman and the galloper each found reflected in the other his own qualities – beneath their enormous surface differences, two exceptionally vital and lovable men, with an attitude to life in common.

There is no need here to go into a blow-by-blow account of the conference, which has been fully documented by Pakenham and Tom Jones. F.E.'s role can be brought out by concentration upon certain key points – essentially three – on which the outcome turned.

The first was defence – the British insistence on control of Ireland's ports and dockyards for defence purposes in peace and war. This the Irish at first disputed as infringing their status as an independent power, but the British insisted that this was a geographical fact of life and a strategic necessity. It was F.E., at the seventh and last plenary session on 24 October, who demolished Griffith's counter-argument that benevolent neutrality would protect British interests better. Tom Jones recorded the critical exchange:

LORD BIRKENHEAD. You say that a friendly neutrality would be better, but we are advised that in order to safeguard ourselves we must have the permitted use of your harbours, but if you are neutral you cannot give it us. Therefore it would all go. I should like to know – if it is true as Lord Beatty says he will not be responsible for keeping this people alive unless we have a technical use of your harbours – what would be the use of neutrality? Because in those circumstances no country would recognise it.

MR GRIFFITH. On a point of international law I cannot say. You are an authority. In principle we make no objection to taking those safeguards that are necessary to your security. We agree in principle.

This was the concession which F.E. was looking for. He spelled it out. 'That would entitle other nations with whom we were at war to make you an enemy.' Collins agreed. F.E. then rammed the point home. 'If you are prepared to render un-neutral services is it not a mistake to pin yourselves therefore to a meaningless trophy which angers our people?' Griffith demurred half-heartedly but agreed.[26] Nothing more was heard of 'friendly neutrality'. Britain, in Pakenham's words, had 'won on Defence',[27] and F.E. had gained one of the points on which he had been most insistent, the strategic unity of the British Isles.

The second key issue, really the central turning point of the whole negotiation, was the question of allegiance to the British Crown and the British Empire, on which the British again insisted as an absolute *sine qua non* of an agreement, as opposed to the Irish claim to be a fully independent Republic. This was the critical clash of symbols. The British as they gave away more and more of the reality of unfettered independence would not surrender the mystical bond of union represented by the Crown, while the Irish delegates were bound by instructions from Dublin not to surrender the Republic nor accept any shadow of duty or allegiance to the British King. Their negotiating position, worked out by de Valera in an attempt to reconcile by verbal ingenuity their irreconcilable positions, was 'External Association', by which Ireland would be 'associated', as a free and independent nation, with the British Empire, but not a member of it. This formula the British repeatedly rejected, and throughout Tom Jones's notes, particularly of the British Ministers' discussions among themselves, it was F.E. who was strongest in insisting that the question of the Crown was not negotiable.

On 2 November F.E. had a private session alone with Griffith and Collins at the House of Lords at which he tried, vainly, to get them to agree to 'free partnership', not *with*, but 'within the British Commonwealth'. The same evening, however, he, Lloyd George and Chamberlain together induced the two Irishmen to accept another formula which seemed to the British to secure what they wanted, though Griffith wrote to de Valera that it did not give anything away: 'Free partnership with the other States associated within the British Commonwealth'. That seemed to be another hurdle cleared. The Irish tried again to whittle away any direct allegiance to the King, but F.E. cleverly manoeuvred that question into a legal debate between himself, as the British delegation's constitutional expert, and the Irish delegation's second secretary, John Chartres, who was thrust forward well out of his depth as their constitutional champion. Frank Pakenham's description of this ill-matched confrontation is superbly dramatic. Chartres argued that the British insistence on the Crown was a mere technicality.

> The issue was now at last, perhaps for the first time in the negotiations, fairly stated and fully faced. Chartres had explained that the Irish people insisted on a symbolism tolerable to themselves. Birkenhead had retorted that the British people also had their symbolism which they would never allow Ireland to repudiate.
>
> The moment was ripe for an Irish leader, heavy armed with debating weapons, to push the argument home; to refuse to allow Birkenhead simply to say that the British people would not stand this or that: to make him disclose their reasons for insisting on Allegiance, at least as fully as the Irish had disclosed theirs for resisting it and to make him produce his own justification in logic and morals for the British attitude. Once Birkenhead had been forced to describe his own difficulties, there would have been some chance of proposing alternative schemes to overcome them.
>
> If Griffith had been arguing the Irish case he might have done something to make Birkenhead expose his hand. But in the nature of things such slashing offensive courses were not for Chartres or anyone in his position. He tried instead to interest Birkenhead in a scheme under which the Irish legislature should evidence their acceptance by voting annually a contribution to the King personally, to form part of the Civil List. Birkenhead knew the answer to this: 'It would be a fine gesture and would undoubtedly make a very great impression on the British people, but it would not meet the great difficulty' . . .
>
> Collins argued that Ireland was offering a great concession for the sake of a real peace. Then Griffith took up the tale in a classical statement of the advantages of External Association. Never

afterwards should either Irish party have argued that he failed to devote his energies to pleading it but the moment when he could have caught up Birkenhead had passed; the British position had gone on record, its reasonableness unquestioned.[28]

Finally Griffith and Collins accepted that they would not get the British to budge over the Crown. They were determined – and in this they were in agreement with de Valera in Dublin – that if the negotiations were to break down, it should not be on this mystical question of the Crown but on the third great stumbling block to peace, the unity of the whole of Ireland. They came in the end to a willingness to accept allegiance to the Crown on condition that they were satisfied with regard to the third key issue – Ulster.

Ulster thus became, as always, the nub. The British, and particularly Lloyd George, were as anxious not to break on Ulster, nor to let Ulster alone prevent a settlement, as the Irish were not to break on the Crown. Once they had got the assurances they wanted on the Crown and defence, the British negotiators were actually desperate to satisfy the Irish on Ulster if they could. They were pledged, however, not to force Ulster into any union against her will; and secure behind the rampart of her own Parliament, Ulster was now going to be more difficult than ever to persuade out of it.

F.E., of course, was particularly bound to Ulster by his past actions – which he had made a point, as recently as August, of explicitly vindicating.[29] In line with this past, he took up, in the early stages of the negotiations, a predictably obstructive attitude over Ulster, countering Irish claims on behalf of the Ulster Catholics by repeatedly bringing up the Southern Unionists, and refusing to consider reducing the area of Northern Ireland by local plebiscites. But this was difficult to justify: as Chamberlain admitted, reporting to his colleagues a meeting at which Griffith and Collins had pressed him on *why* the British would not allow county option, 'they could not put a more difficult question'.[30] By this time, 26 October, the British delegates were beginning to find their commitment to the integrity of Ulster (as it had been created in 1920) irksome. As F.E. found himself agreeing with Winston, 'our position re Six Counties is an impossible one if these men want to settle, as they do'.[30]

The Irishmen's wanting to settle was the critical factor. Now that he was convinced of Griffith's and Collins's sincerity, F.E. was ready to believe that Ulster's integrity, for which he had been prepared to fight a mere seven years earlier and to which he was still in honour pledged, could be safeguarded within a Dominion settlement for the whole of Ireland; he therefore saw no betrayal of Ulster or of his previous exertions in working to achieve such a settlement *and persuading Ulster to accept it.* He and the Government were still pledged against coercing Ulster if she would not voluntarily accept it. But he had reached the point where he agreed with Lloyd George that he would 'not be a party to firing another shot in the South of Ireland'.[31]

This was another moment of decision. He and Chamberlain held the future of the negotiations in their hands. Had they chosen to stick their heels in over Ulster, as their past associations might have directed them to do, insisting that they would accept no reduction of the position ceded to Ulster under the 1920 Act, that would have been the end of the conference. The Diehards, among whom they had both been numbered before the war, were restive and increasingly vocal; they had been outraged at the Government's consenting to talk with Irish 'murderers' in the first place, and the longer the conference lasted, the more they scented a sell-out. On 25 October, in a speech to the London Unionist Association at Caxton Hall, F.E. tried to quell their fears, drawing dangerously on past credit in appealing to them to trust their leaders.

> Those who have undertaken this responsibility know the mis-apprehensions our best friends will feel and are entitled to say to you that you must examine our careers and our antecedents before giving rein to apprehension that we shall be prepared to surrender anything of the greatness of this Empire or the fundamental principles on which the whole of this Empire depends.[32]

It would have been the easiest thing to have fallen in with those Tory apprehensions and taken on the mantle of Carson as the leader of last-ditch Unionism, a role for which his 'career and antecedents' amply prepared him. Instead, he and Chamberlain, acting together, threw in their lot with Lloyd George, placed their trust in Collins and Griffith, and resolved to defy the Diehards in the cause of peace, confident that if they could achieve the sort of settlement that was now shaping up, a settlement that kept Ireland at least nominally within the Empire, they could carry the bulk of the party with them in its support. But a major hurdle was looming. The party conference was due to be held on 17 November, in, of all places, Liverpool. There, in Orange Liverpool, just across the water from Belfast itself, the Diehards would have a great chance to drum up all the old Unionist sentiment against the Irish talks and force their leaders to abandon them. If they were to continue, the Government had somehow to win an endorsement of their policy from the conference.

Lloyd George was able to use this threat of a wrecking vote to wring from Griffith a critical letter, which Chamberlain would be able to take to Liverpool, embodying his acceptance of the principle that Ireland should remain within the Empire. Griffith also agreed, under subtle pressure from Tom Jones, not to make difficulties over Ulster, on the understanding that if Ulster ultimately refused to come in under the terms of the eventual settlement, a Commission would be established to redraw the boundary of the excluded area in conformity with the wishes of the local population, which was expected so to reduce the territory of the North as to render it economically unviable and force it to join with the South after all. This promise of Griffith's, exacted under the shadow of Liverpool, was to be crucial in the last decisive hours of the negotiations.

Even with these assurances from Griffith, however, there was no certainty that the Government would get the verdict it needed from Liverpool. The management of the conference would be in the hands of F.E.'s old patron, still the unchallenged boss of Liverpool Unionism, Archibald Salvidge. Salvidge was still a loyal admirer of his old *protégé* and a supporter of the Coalition; he had no wish to see it defeated, yet all his instincts and traditions were on the Irish issue with the Diehards. He had built up his party and his own position in opposition to Home Rule and the defence of Protestant Ulster. If the betrayal of Ulster was in the Government's mind he was bound to mobilize his Orange battalions to prevent it. If, however, he could be persuaded to trust the Government and throw his weight against the Diehards, the Government would be free to continue its efforts, by putting pressure alternately on Griffith and Collins and on Craig, to achieve a peace acceptable to both sides. F.E. was obviously the man to get Salvidge to see where his duty lay. On Friday 11 November, just six days before the conference was due to meet, he summoned Salvidge urgently to London.

> I think it indispensable that you should come to London tonight. Grave issues are impending. If you have been approached from other quarters, please say nothing of this telegram, but come up uncommitted and meet me at my house at twelve o'clock tomorrow morning. I wire imperatively because the matter is imperative.[33]

But Salvidge had a chill and was unfit to travel. Even when Chamberlain urged him again to come down on the Monday he pleaded doctor's orders and refused. On the Sunday, however, after a long talk with Derby, who was strongly in favour of a settlement, and a night's agonizing with his son, he decided to reserve his position: he issued to the press a statement declaring that, while he abated not a whit his support for Ulster, he would not allow the Liverpool conference to be turned into an anti-Coalition rally by the Diehards using the

Ulster issue as a stick with which to beat it. This was all that F.E. and Chamberlain wanted of him. But on the Monday afternoon they did not yet know of his decision. They still felt that they had urgently to see him. The melodramatic episode which followed was, in fact, unnecessary; nevertheless, as recounted by Salvidge in his diary, it vividly expresses F.E.'s commitment at this crisis of his career to achieving a settlement. That evening he travelled up alone and incognito to Liverpool, wiring to Salvidge to come to him in the Adelphi Hotel next morning: if he were still too ill, F.E. would come out to his house at Hoylake, 'though I do not wish to do so'. Salvidge came to the Adelphi.

> As soon as I entered the bedroom, where he had been waiting like a caged lion, Birkenhead swung round and pointing a long finger in my direction, said, 'Give me twenty minutes. Don't interrupt me. Don't argue. Don't raise any point till I have finished. You could not come to the Cabinet, so the Cabinet – or at least its representative – has had to come to you. Under a bond of secrecy, which I ask you to give me, I am going to take you briefly through the inside story of the Irish Conference. When I have finished, if you think I have been false to the things you and I have always stood for in this city, tell me so and adopt what course you like. But you must know the whole position first.'
>
> Obviously under the impression that I was entirely hostile, he put every ounce of his unsurpassed gifts as an advocate into the recital of the Irish negotiations. Gradually from considering the Conference as a waste of time, he had found himself regarding it with increasing interest and hope, till at last he had come to realize it was the biggest thing he had ever had to do with. He now believed that, in spite of their appalling deeds, the Irish representatives were the type of men who, if they once pledged their word to an agreement, would keep it even with their lives. As for Ulster, she had been asked to accept the principle of Dominion Home Rule and discuss the safeguards under which, with advantage to themselves and to fellow Unionists in the South and added strength to the Empire, the people of the six counties could consent to enter a United Irish Parliament. Ten years ago – when he and I had ranged Liverpool behind Carson – a Unionist Party in Ireland, firmly allied with the Unionist Party in this country, presented a formidable opposition to Irish self-government of any kind. Since then Ulster had retreated to the six-county boundary. That was not his fault – or mine. It had been done with Ulster's consent. Could he or I or anyone be blamed for looking at things as they were? Ulster's power of bargaining was probably greater at

that moment than it would ever be again with the future so uncertain. If she declined to co-operate in Dominion Home Rule there would be no coercion. But at least in her own interest she should consider it, and get the best terms possible. He would not agree to any settlement that did not preserve the supremacy of the Crown, that did not keep Ireland within the Empire, that did not leave the British Navy the sole guardian of the shores and seas of Great Britain and Ireland, or that required Ulster's consent by duress. He could assure me such a settlement was almost reached. It only required the impetus of a successful vote at the Liverpool Conference to carry it on to fruition. Would I help to obtain that vote or would I ruin what was undoubtedly the last chance to reconcile the nationalist aspirations of Ireland with loyalty to the Throne and the Empire? I must remember that the alternative was war more bloody and more terrible than anything known previously between the two peoples.

At this point F.E. paused and Salvidge, according to his own account, drily threw him the morning papers which, incredibly, he had not seen. He was delighted with Salvidge's statement but thought his proposed amendment to the Diehard motion did not go far enough. 'The Conservative leaders must have a clear mandate from the party conference for continuing the Irish negotiations.' Neither he nor Chamberlain could be present in person. 'They held other men's secrets as well as their own. It was too dangerous for them to be cross-questioned at such a gathering.' He eventually promised, however, that Worthington-Evans – who knew few secrets – would attend, and with that, Salvidge agreed to try to win a positive endorsement. F.E.'s parting gratitude does him credit.

> He said he realised it was a pretty tough job for me. He was returning to London, but I had to go on living with people who might take years to see that what we were doing was the right thing for all the interests concerned. However, it was destiny. I could not avoid it. It had come to me. And even if it finished us both, it would prove 'not a bad sort of finish'. He had to go then to catch his train. He went straight out into a waiting taxi with his coat collar up and his hat pulled down over his eyes.[34]

Salvidge was as good as his word. Liverpool on the morning of the 17th was covered with *Morning Post* placards screaming betrayal under the headline 'Salvidging Ulster'. The pre-lunch session of the conference was entirely taken up with violent abuse of a treacherous

Government which was sitting down to parley with the 'murder junta', 'men whose proper place is the scaffold or the gaol', when 'another 50,000 troops and a free hand' were all that was needed to restore Ireland to peace and order. In the afternoon, however, Salvidge braved concerted heckling to win the conference back, first to loyalty to the leadership, and then by supreme eloquence to the policy of giving peace a chance. He pledged that if he had to choose between Ulster and the Coalition he would stand by Ulster. But it was 'one thing to be a Diehard in the comfortable security of a conference'.

> It is something quite different to go out – as thousands of young men must go from British homes if these hopes of a settlement are wrecked – and die hard in grim reality in the hideous shambles of an Irish civil war . . .
>
> I beg of you to work for peace whilst peace seems possible, to suspend judgment on those whose lips are sealed by a pledge of silence, and in this, the most critical hour of the Irish negotiations, to uphold and sustain your own men [Cheers] – the men who through you and by you have been called to represent, not only your party, but your native land.[35]

Salvidge was backed by Worthington-Evans and by Derby and his amendment to the Diehard resolution was ultimately carried by an overwhelming majority, expressing the earnest hope that 'consistently with the supremacy of the Crown, the security of the Empire and the pledges given to Ulster and the safeguarding of the interests of the minority in the South of Ireland, a solution to the Irish difficulties may be found in the Conference now in progress'.[35]

Austen Chamberlain, who had been waiting out at Knowsley for the verdict, now had the mandate he needed to deliver, at a mass rally at the Sun Hall that evening, the speech of his life, declaring his hope that an honourable peace was at last within grasp. Whatever else Salvidge had done to deserve the knighthood he had received the previous year, he certainly earned it by his services this day.

It was now very difficult for the Irish delegates to raise further objections to the Crown or Empire without seeming to break faith. When, a few days later, they put up a new draft treaty based on de Valera's formula of External Association, the British could fairly regard it as reneging on Griffith's previous assurances. Chamberlain protested that 'he would not have gone to Liverpool and made the speech he did had he known this was the sort of document they were going to put in'.[36] Through the tactful mediation of Tom Jones a break was averted. Griffith and Collins then had the difficult task of persuading their more unbending colleagues that there really was no more to be gained on this question. In an important speech at Tunbridge Wells on 26 November F.E. publicly underlined that this was so, repeating that 'in no conceivable circumstances, either in substance or in name, would we consent to an arrangement which would produce the secession of Ireland from the commonwealth of nations called the British Empire... In all that concerns themselves they are the absolute masters of their own destinies, but they are united with the citizens of this country by the link of the Crown. The Crown is the simple and necessary symbol of union.' The negotiations swung back to Ulster and the problem of unity. In this connection, too, F.E. did his best at Tunbridge Wells, explaining that while the Government was still irreversibly pledged to reserve to Ulster the powers given by the 1920 Act, they nevertheless hoped 'that in the near future she will realise that her interests will be better served in those matters which concern Ireland as a whole by contributing to an assembly representing Ireland as a whole all she possesses of experience and political and commercial knowledge. No-one can say', he added defensively, 'that in this we derogate any way from the views of the Unionist Party.'[37]

But Craig resolutely refused to have anything to do with an all-Ireland Parliament. Unable to make any progress in that direction, the British had to fall back on the Boundary Commission – a convenient device for postponing a decision which enabled Lloyd George to keep on giving the most favourable assurances as to its outcome to both sides at once. Craig was given the impression that Ulster had nothing to fear, Collins – at a private interview with Lloyd George on the morning of 5 December – the impression that the Free State had everything to gain. To Collins, who was ready to settle for Dominion status and desperate to agree if only he could satisfy himself that 'essential unity' would somehow be preserved, the argument that the Boundary Commission would so truncate Ulster that it would not be able to survive as an autonomous province, was the final consideration that determined him to sign the British terms. Griffith found himself already committed, on paper, by his helpful letter written before the Liverpool Conference.

The last session of the conference lasted through the afternoon and evening of 5 December. F.E. and Collins between them had worked up an Oath of Allegiance, delicately worded so as to inflict as little damage as possible on the Republican conscience while appearing, to a British ear, to make most of the right loyal noises: F.E. is said to have privately described the formula as 'the greatest prevarication in history'. Pakenham insists that the story has been 'authoritatively denied'. But he allows that the careful phrasing 'might well have provoked him, if not to indiscretion, at least to a sardonic smile'.[38] Carson might call it hypocrisy, but to F.E. it was legal ingenuity legitimately exercised to a good end. Unfortunately, however, it did not satisfy de Valera's Republican purists back in Dublin.

Till late in the evening the British thought that only Griffith might sign, though F.E. reckoned that even his signature alone would be worth a lot in America. Barton, Duffy, Duggan and probably Collins would have preferred to refer back to Dublin for instructions. But Lloyd George insisted that it was the delegation's responsibility: they were plenipotentiaries, and he must have their answer that night. By sheer bullying and moral blackmail, threatening the immediate resumption of bloody war for which the Irish delegates, if they refused Great Britain's final generous offer, would be personally responsible, he brought them all – Griffith, Collins and Duggan with conviction, Duffy and Barton against their own judgment – to the point of signing. They signed, in an atmosphere heavy with destiny and tragic foreboding, and pledged themselves to recommend the Treaty to the Dail, though they knew only too well that their surrender of the pure ideal of the Republic might divide Sinn Fein cruelly against itself.

To his friend John O'Kane, Collins expressed both his apprehension and his conviction that, at whatever cost, he had done right to sign.

> Think – what have I got for Ireland? Something which she has wanted these past seven hundred years. Will anyone be satisfied at the bargain? Will anyone? I tell you this – early this morning I signed my death warrant. I thought at the time how odd, how ridiculous – a bullet may just as well have done the job five years ago.
>
> I believe Birkenhead may have said an end to his political life. With him it has been my honour to work.
>
> These signatures are the first real step for Ireland. If people will only remember that – the first real step.[39]

He was right, both about himself and substantially about F.E. Collins was shot dead in an ambush the following August, during the bitter civil war which resulted between the supporters and the opponents of the Treaty. F.E.'s career was not, indeed, at an end; but he never recovered the position that he had hitherto enjoyed in the Conservative party. His influence was fatally undermined.

He thought it worth it. He never ceased to rate his part in securing the Irish Treaty the greatest achievement of his life, nor to proclaim the privilege it had been to work with such men as Collins and Griffith – men of honour and their word. Yet on the question of honour something more needs to be said. It was a curious feature of the talks that the leading negotiators on each side bound themselves in highly charged complicity to agree a settlement in defiance of those who would hold them back. But it was the British Ministers who subtly manoeuvred Griffith and Collins into a position where *they* would be breaking this honourable compact if they did not sign. Then F.E., as Collins's letter makes clear, made a lot of play with the risks he and Chamberlain were running in the cause of peace: but what he was really doing was exploiting his political risk against the Irishmen's political *and physical* risk, and inducing them, in honour, to hazard more than he did – not just their careers, but their lives – on a settlement. The bond of honour was, on examination, cruelly unequal. Third, Collins was brought to the point of signing by an assurance on the border question on the morning of 5 December which turned out to be worthless, if not intentionally misleading. Finally, the 'honourable' agreement that night was ultimately extorted only by some pretty unscrupulous moral pressure by Lloyd George, with the support of his colleagues. There was no good reason why the British had to have an answer that night; there was no reason why the Irish should not have returned to Dublin to confer with de Valera and the rest of the Cabinet before signing; Lloyd George had no reason to insist they were plenipotentiaries, bound to sign then and there or not at all. It was a bravura performance of Welsh wizardry that extracted their signatures despite all these reasons for delay. But its consequence was the Irish civil war and the death of Collins and many more honourable Irishmen. The manner of the Treaty's signing provoked bitter allegations of bad faith – not un-founded – from the unyielding Republicans back in Dublin. What Lloyd George did, in the tense, historically charged atmosphere of Downing Street, was to persuade Griffith and Collins to place the obligations of mutual trust built up over the previous two months in London higher than their obligations to the Prime Minister and Cabinet whom they were in London to represent. It was brilliant; it was successful; perhaps it was the only way to achieve a settlement which got the British out of most of Ireland and in the end, after a further spasm of bloodshed, just about stuck. Yet it was crafty; it was subtle; it was ruthless; it was not quite the triumph of honourable dealing that F.E. liked to pretend.

(iii) Recrimination

The signing of the Treaty came too late for the morning papers. Apart from a brief statement from Downing Street, it fell to F.E. to make the first full announcement of the success of the negotiations. While the other principals met again after a few hours' sleep to hammer out detailed arrangements for implementing the agreement, F.E. was chosen as the Government's advocate to justify the Treaty to the country and the world in two speeches delivered in Birmingham – Joseph Chamberlain's citadel of Unionism – the first to a Conservative Club luncheon, the second, in the evening, to a special meeting of the Birmingham Unionist Association in the Town Hall. In both F.E. painted the Treaty in high historic colours, with much reference to Pitt, Gladstone and Parnell, to the American War of Independence, the creation of the Dominion of South Africa after the Boer War, even to the ancient Kings of Ulster. He spelled out the terms of the Treaty, stressed the perfect right of Ulster to have nothing to do with the all-Ireland Parliament – though in that case there would have to be a Boundary Commission – while expressing again the hope that she would decide to take part in it; but at the same time laid great emphasis on the Irish acceptance of partnership within the Empire and the Oath to the King. 'Bone of our bone, flesh of our flesh', Ireland would be welcomed henceforth at the Cabinet table as an equal with Australia, Canada, South Africa and New Zealand. He recognized that it might not be accepted by the Dail, or even at Westminster; but passionately he expressed his belief that this was an agreement worth fighting for against mean-minded men on both sides of the Irish Sea who refused to accept a compromise honourable to both countries.

> I am one of those who say plainly to you that I care nothing what the result is to myself, I care nothing what the result is to my party. I believe there has come to us in our day and in our generation one of those supreme opportunities which come once and once only. [Loud cheers.] I risk everything on my belief in the good faith of those who have conducted these negotiations with us . . . I am as certain as of my own colleagues who confronted them at the table that they will go back to Ireland taking their lives in their hands to fight their battle as confidently as I and my colleagues go into battle on this side. [Cheers.] . . . In the dark days that lie in front of us, we have made up our minds to the policy, and we intend at all hazards to play the hand out.

Still, however, he expressed the triumph of reconciliation in explicitly imperial terms utterly unacceptable to de Valera and exceedingly unhelpful, one would have thought, to Collins. Admittedly during the negotiations Collins had come to glimpse a vision of an idealized Commonwealth in which Ireland could honourably share, a worldwide league of democracies no longer dominated by Britain. But this was scarcely F.E.'s vision, and it is again difficult to escape the impression that Lloyd George and F.E. allowed Collins to believe what he wanted until he had signed and then held him bound to the same old British Empire as of old. If the Dail confirmed the Treaty, F.E. declared, making a virtue out of what had really been military necessity,

there is a day drawing near for this country and this Empire which will compensate us for the bitter disappointments of the last three years, even for the poignant suffering of the five years that preceded, and that will give us a greater Empire than Chatham ever contrived or than Pitt ever dreamed of. I would rather fail in attempting to translate that dream into reality than I would succeed in carrying out the policy discredited by three hundred years' trial in Ireland, even if it now succeeded – the policy of complete coercion, which would still leave behind it a bitter, an estranged and a hostile Ireland. [Loud cheers.][40]

The forum in which F.E. had to do battle for the Treaty, and vindicate his own honour against those who felt he had betrayed them, was the House of Lords.

The debate on the Treaty opened in both Houses of Parliament on the same day, 14 December. In the Commons Lloyd George expounded its terms amid general congratulation, despite a bitter protest from Craig on the first day and a Diehard amendment moved by John Gretton on the second; the most important speech was that of Bonar Law, sufficiently recovered from his illness of March to make his first public appearance for many months. If there were to be serious opposition to the Treaty in Britain, Bonar Law would have to lead it; reluctantly, however, and not without some criticism of the conduct of the negotiation and the presentation to Ulster of a *fait accompli*, Law gave the settlement his blessing. In the Commons the Treaty was approved by 401 votes to 58; the bulk of the Tory party, taking their lead from Law if not from Chamberlain, toed the Government line.

In the Lords the eventual result was not dissimilar, allowing for the different composition of the House – 119 for the Treaty, 47 against – but the debate was much stiffer. Traditionally, debate in the Upper House is conducted with gentlemanly restraint. This, however, was one of those occasions when restraint broke down; the torrent of bitterness that was unleashed was the more violent and shocking in consequence. Most of it was directed, in the most personal terms, at the Lord Chancellor.

The debate was opened, symbolically, by Lord Morley, Gladstone's last surviving colleague, friend and biographer, who hailed the agreement as the belated fulfilment of his master's great struggle. (King George V recalled to F.E. that Morley had once told him that Home Rule would eventually be enacted by the Conservatives.) Next, Crewe for the Liberal Opposition, and Curzon, for the Government, welcomed the Treaty and urged its approval. Then the mood changed as Carson rose in righteous anger to make his maiden speech in their Lordships' customarily decorous chamber.

Brutally Carson, who had accepted on Ulster's behalf the 1920 Act, denounced the terms of the Treaty as an abject surrender to terrorism, and utter humiliation of the British Empire. It was hypocrisy for the Government to pretend to have agreed these terms on their merits. 'Not at all. They were passed with a revolver pointed at your head. And you know it. You know you passed them because you were beaten.' The implication for the Empire was devastating.

> If you tell your Empire in India, in Egypt and all over the world that you have not got the men, the money, the pluck, the inclination and the backing to restore order in a country within twenty miles of your own shore, you may as well begin to abandon the attempt to make British rule prevail through the Empire at all.

From general condemnation of the Treaty for itself, Carson passed to specific condemnation of those Government Ministers who had until so recently pledged themselves unalterably opposed to ever allowing Ireland control of her own coastline, ports, tariffs and foreign policy, and now defended the concession of all those things. Such a shameless abandonment of all that the Government had claimed to hold most sacred, he asserted, 'will make public life and politics stink in the nostrils of the country for the next twenty years'. The great advocate's solemn tone grew more strident as his grievance became more personal.

> At that time I did not know, as I know now, that I was a mere puppet in a political game. I was in earnest, I was not playing politics. I believed all this. I thought of the last thirty years, during which I was fighting with others whose friendship and comradeship I hope I will lose from tonight, because I do not value any friendship that is not founded upon confidence and trust. I was in earnest. What a fool I was! I was only a puppet, and so was Ulster, and so was Ireland, in the political game that was to get the Conservative Party into power.

Once in power, the party's leaders had trampled on their followers' trust. For Chamberlain, almost universally regarded as the soul of honour, Carson had only furious disgust that he could so betray his father's cause. It was for F.E., his former 'galloper', however, that he reserved his bitterest rebuke.

> Of all the men in my experience that I think are the most loath-some it is those who will sell their friends for the purpose of conciliating their enemies, and, perhaps, still worse, the men who climb up a ladder into power of which even I may have been part of a humble rung, and then, when they have got into power, kick the ladder away without any concern for the pain, or injury, or mischief, or damage that they do to those who have helped them to gain power.[41]

Through this diatribe and several more F.E. sat silent, impassive, stretched upon the Woolsack, eyes closed, biding his time. On the second day Lord Londonderry, the Duke of Northumberland, Lord Finlay, and the Marquess of Dufferin and Ava joined in turn in the condemnation of F.E.'s and the Government's volte-face, countered only by the Archbishop of Canterbury and one or two Liberals. On the third Lord Farnham, a Southern Unionist peer, satirically wondered, if it came to civil war in Ireland, on which side the Lord Chancellor would this time be found.

> Would he be found once more galloping over the plains of Ulster defying arrest? It would be a bold man who would prophesy where he would be found, such an apt pupil of the Prime Minister has he become. Such an unrivalled acrobat has he become that his lightning gyrations and backward somersaults are so rapid that it is impossible even for a normal political eye to follow his move-ments in the air, and no-one could foretell whether he would ultimately land on the stormy plains of Ulster, or in the Sinn Fein saddle as canterer to Michael Collins.[42]

Lord Sumner, too, another of F.E.'s judicial colleagues, focused upon F.E.'s relations with Collins, feeling that 'to rest our relations with Ireland upon the favourable impression which Mr Collins made upon the Lord Chancellor' was 'hardly any wiser than to rest our military preparations in 1912 on the very favourable impression which the German Emperor made upon Lord Haldane'.[42] (One may notice again the paradoxical tendency of Unionists to regard Ireland as an enemy!) F.E. was rather cheekily absent during this and a couple of the other speeches in the debate, declining to cancel a previous engagement to speak to the American Luncheon Club at the Savoy. This was a remarkable way to prepare for one of the great speeches of his life; but he had always seen the Irish question closely in its American context and he gravely thanked his lunchtime audience for sending him strengthened by their good wishes to face his 'Philippi'.[43] He returned to the Woolsack in time to hear Lord Salisbury deliver the Diehards' last denunciation. Then pale, expressionless, speaking at first scarcely above a whisper, he rose to make his reply. Not only were the chamber and the galleries packed; although the same debate was going on simultaneously in the Commons, half the Cabinet including the Prime Minister himself were clustered on the steps of the Throne to hear F.E. scatter his critics.

First he rejected any accusation of inconsistency or betrayal in his own attitude to Ulster since the heady days of 1912–14. He was unmoved by Londonderry quoting back at him his past speeches.

> It may be that they owe something to the atmosphere in which they were uttered, but I say here perfectly plainly that I recede not by one iota from the position which I assumed throughout the whole of those old bitter controversies. I do not recall one act that I would undo here and now if I could, and I only recall one or two incautious expressions which I would have put in another way if I had recollected that when I was Lord Chancellor they would be quoted against me in this House.

Brave words. He insisted that Carson had no cause to feel betrayed.

> Lord Carson has publicly repelled and proscribed me from a friendship which had many memories for me, and which I deeply value. The noble and learned Lord can do that – no-one can prevent him – but he cannot deprive me of memories indissolubly bound up in the past, when we ran common risks and in speech and act I matched and was glad to match the risks that he ran.

Listening to Liberal peers earlier in the debate, he said, still claiming that Ulster should have been coerced before the war, made him feel a partisan again: that course would have meant civil war.

> Having formed that view, I justify myself, even in my present position, for every irregularity I committed, for every advice I gave and for all the steps I took. I stood side by side with Lord Carson at grave and critical moments and neither he nor I knew what advice would be given to His Majesty's Government by those who were then the Law Officers of the Crown.

But this was in the past. The heart of F.E.'s speech lay in the defence of the present Government's solution to the eternal problem. As so often, his chosen method of defence was to ridicule the opposition, taking as his first and easier target 'the self-elected champion of the North and South, Lord Salisbury'. 'In the jaundiced view of Lord Salisbury', he stated gravely, the Government were 'weak puppets, kicked about from one crisis to another in instability of purpose and insecurity of conscience'. He paused.

> We are not indeed supermen, Napoleons; we do not belong to that class to which the noble Marquess in that respect belongs. It is perfectly true that we have changed our minds more than once in the last three years, and we may change them again. Our difficulties lie in attempting to convince the mediaevalists among us that the world has really undergone some very considerable modification in the last few years.

He too would gladly go back to 1905 if that were possible; but it was not.

> We are dealing with a moment in which alternatives, and alternatives only, count . . . Neither Lord Salisbury nor Lord Carson has made any contribution to any alternative policy. Lord Salisbury says he is a Home Ruler, but he does not indicate the particular form of Home Rule he intends to honour with his support and what particular body of people he will succeed in persuading to believe in it.
>
> As for the speech of Lord Carson, his constructive effort at statecraft would be immature on the lips of an hysterical schoolgirl.

At this Carson was on his feet, furiously interjecting that he had accepted the 1920 Act. 'With the single exception of the Boundary Commission,' F.E. told him, 'those for whom the noble Lord stands will retain everything the Bill gave.' Carson denied it. The bitter exchange which followed was imperfectly heard in the gallery, but when F.E. said something about the Government following certain courses, Carson corrected him, 'corpses, not courses'. F.E. affected to ignore the remark but told Carson coldly, 'It is the custom in this House to allow speakers to proceed,' which was not however enough to deter him from further angry interruptions.

Turning to Carson's charge of military humiliation in Ireland, F.E. refuted it by a somewhat irrelevant reference to Britain's material and moral strength as demonstrated in the European War. 'Is not the truth that those who are great can afford to do great things in a great way?' Was he confident that this Treaty was 'a great thing'? Not entirely, but he was hopeful.

> Of this I am certain: that we have given a population which is overwhelmingly homogeneous the opportunity of taking their place side by side with the other communities in the British Empire. That is an immense moment in history. We believe there is a chance that this settlement will satisfy that sentiment of nationhood, and if it does, year by year, the animosities that have poisoned our public life will disappear . . .
>
> Is your alternative any other than this, that we shall now resume the war, that we shall take and break this people, as we can with our military might take and break them? And when we have done that, how shall we be any better off? Shall we be nearer a settlement when Lord Salisbury, if he becomes Prime Minister, has raised the army, carried fire and sword into every village in Ireland, and brought back a new laurel to add to the military standards of the great war? There is no-one listening to me who does not know that on the conclusion of that war, with memories a thousand times more bitterly inflamed, Lord Salisbury would have to do what we have done now, enter into negotiations with these people and define the conditions under which they and we will live our lives.

It was a pity that F.E. and the Lloyd George Government as a whole had not realized a year or two earlier how bitterly their policy of fire and sword was already inflaming Irish feeling against Britain. But for the Black and Tans, the Treaty would have stood a better chance in Dublin. As it was, de Valera had already rejected it and the Dail was very evenly divided. F.E. could only hope that somehow the Irish people would be given a chance to vote their acceptance of it; meanwhile the British Parliament should recommend it to them as wholeheartedly as could be. His conclusion did not disguise how far he had moved from his initial absolute refusal to contemplate Dominion status.

> I would invite your Lordships to vote tonight with a deep sense of responsibility, not confident, but still hoping that we shall see in the future an Ireland which will at last, after centuries, be reconciled to this country; an Ireland to which both the contrasted systems will make each its own splendid and individual contribution,

and an Ireland which, sitting when the Dominions meet at 10
Downing Street to decide, according to the evolutionary organisation of the British Empire, the supreme issues of policy which
affect the fortunes of that Empire, the Prime Minister of Ireland,
an equal by the side of equals, will lift up his voice to support and
give expression to the historic destinies and rightful influence of
that country.[42]

This was a tremendous speech, fully worthy of the occasion. 'A fine
piece of insolent invective,' H.A.L. Fisher called it,[44] but it was much
more than that. 'Cogent in argument, rich in feeling, powerful in
pleading,' *The Times* reported, 'it made a deep impression on the
peers.'[45] Finlay, an opponent who had spoken against the Treaty, told a
friend that he considered F.E.'s speech 'the most wonderful' which he
had ever heard.[46]

It helped to ensure a good majority against the Diehards on the day;
but it did not in any way dispel their bitterness against their leaders,
who had as they thought betrayed them. There were many in the Tory
party in the country who agreed with Carson and regarded F.E. henceforth as an unspeakable turncoat who for personal ambition and love of
Lloyd George had ratted on his old allegiance and was never to be
trusted again. At a dinner at Merchant Taylors' School on 20 December
H.A.L. Fisher was shocked to hear a fellow guest, Mr Justice Eve (who
had actually been a Liberal M.P. before his elevation to the Bench) use
his speech of thanks to deliver 'a violent attack on the Lord Chancellor';[47]
and there were other such incidents. F.E. was unmoved. So long as he
was confident that he was right and had the support of those he
respected, he rather liked having enemies. They added to the excitement of life. The danger was, however, that his studied scorn of those
who attacked him fed his tendency to self-righteous arrogance; his
proud indifference was presently to threaten the Government's survival
almost as seriously as the Treaty itself.

In the New Year the position of the Government, defending the
Treaty, and particularly of F.E. who had staked his reputation on the
good faith of Collins and Griffith, became more difficult. The Dail
passed the Treaty, on 10 January, by the narrowest of margins (64 votes
to 57), and Griffith succeeded de Valera as head of a Provisional
Government to carry it into effect. But the hardline Republicans
refused to accept the decision and within a few months the assassination
squads were back in action and civil war was again rife in the country,
this time between the forces of the new Irish Government and the
'irregulars' – the irreconcilables of the I.R.A. As Craig predictably
rejected the Treaty and stalled over the Boundary Commission, the

I.R.A. stepped up terrorist activity in Ulster and the newly formed 'A' and 'B Specials' retaliated violently against Catholics. Collins was placed in an impossible position, sincerely anxious to impose authority on the rebels in the South but unable with any conviction to restrain them from fighting his old fight in the North; under pressure from the British to take strong action to honour his signature of the Treaty, yet desperate to do nothing to widen the already murderous breach within Sinn Fein. In London F.E. had a tricky task fending off the mounting tide of recrimination voiced with increasing confidence by those who had claimed all along that no good came of making pacts with murderers. In frequent statements in the House of Lords he could only reiterate his faith in the Irish leaders, insist that they were gradually restoring order and stress the importance of giving them all possible help by steadfastly upholding the Treaty from the British side. Even he was shocked, however, in May, when Collins negotiated an electoral pact with de Valera designed – in order to allow elections to be held at all – to take the Treaty out of contention by agreeing to apportion seats in the new Dail in the same pro- and anti-Treaty proportions as in the old. If there were any question, F.E. declared, of including opponents of the Treaty as members of a Coalition Government, that would be ground for re-newing the war. That did not happen – Collins in fact managed to ensure the election of a convincingly pro-Treaty Dail after all – but it continued to look as though Griffith and Collins, with the Four Courts in Dublin occupied and other areas of the country effectively controlled by their opponents, were unable to deliver the terms which they had accepted and still accepted when in London. There were further anguished negotiations about the wording of the new Irish Free State Constitution; further threats of renewed war if the Irish tried to go beyond what had been agreed in December; persistent rioting and sectarian killing in Belfast and armed clashes along the border; and the assassination in London in June of Craig's principal military adviser, Sir Henry Wilson. Eventually, under British pressure for a stern response to this last outrage, the Provisional Government bombarded and reduced to rubble the rebel headquarters in the Four Courts. At this, the war flared up with new virulence, carrying off many of the leaders of both parties. On 12 August, Arthur Griffith died, peacefully but exhausted by the horror of the struggle, as much a victim of the war as if he had been shot. Only ten days later Michael Collins's luck, which had borne him unscathed through many daring escapades against the British, deserted him. He was ambushed on a country road in Cork and shot through the head by a ricochet.

F.E. had not lost his admiration for Collins despite the difficulties of the past nine months. He never ceased to pay tribute to the courage and integrity of both Griffith and Collins: but it was to Collins that he really warmed as a true friend. There is a story that he tried to go to Dublin for Collins's funeral, but was prevented by fog at the airport; it would have been a mad adventure for him to attempt, but the gesture is sufficiently characteristic to be possible: weather reports confirm that there *was* fog in London on that day.[48]

With the death of both Griffith and Collins, the leadership of the pro-Treaty party in Ireland passed to William Cosgrave and Kevin O'Higgins, who proceeded to suppress the Republican opposition with more ruthlessness than Collins had been able to muster against his old comrades, executing by firing squad far more rebels than the British had ever done, including in November Erskine Childers, whom the British delegates to the Treaty negotiations did not mourn. During 1923 they established their authority over the whole of southern Ireland, and the Irish Free State, of twenty-six counties, came officially into being. Not until 1924 did Cosgrave get around to asking the British Government to set up the Boundary Commission promised in the Treaty, and by then Craig had explicitly repudiated it, standing ever more defiantly on the rock of the whole Six County area. The Commission was supposed to consist of one nominee from each part of Ireland with a chairman nominated by Britain, but Craig refused to name a Northern Commissioner. The Labour Government now in power in London, however, appointed a suitable figure on Ulster's behalf, along with a South African judge to act as chairman. But Mr Justice Feetham interpreted the mandate of the Commission very narrowly as allowing no more than minor rectification of the existing border, not the major transfer of population understood by Collins and Griffith in 1921 to have been implicit in the promise to set up a Commission. The Irish representative put up small resistance to the combination of Feetham and the Ulsterman and the Commission duly reported in favour of very little change. This result Cosgrave reluctantly accepted in return for a generous financial settlement, leaving the Catholics in the North feeling cheated and abandoned, a potent source of trouble in the future.

The question remains whether the Irish *were* cheated in 1921, and it is difficult to escape the conclusion that they were. There is no doubt that Collins in particular agreed to leave the territory of Ulster to a Boundary Commission on the verbal assurance of Lloyd George that the Commission would be bound to award the South so much that what was left of the North would be too small to remain viable as an autonomous province and would be obliged in the end to join the Free State after all. 'We would save Tyrone and Fermanagh, parts of Derry, Armagh and Down,' Collins noted after his meeting with Lloyd George on

5 December.[49] But no sooner had the Treaty been signed than the Government was assuring Craig that no major transfer of population or territory was envisaged. In the House of Lords F.E. denied absolutely that assurances of any sort had been given to either Collins or Craig that went beyond a strict wording of the Treaty, which was that the Commission should determine the border 'in accordance with the wishes of the inhabitants, so far as may be compatible with economic and geographic conditions'.[50] Clearly this was wide open to interpretation and F.E. pointed to his Birmingham speech on 6 December, delivered within twelve hours of the signing of the Treaty, as the authoritative proof that the Government's interpretation had always been narrow. His language that afternoon was in fact uncharacteristically obscure, but the crucial sentence appears to be, 'We do not propose to interfere with that which was arranged a year ago in relation to counties.'[51] In other words Tyrone and Fermanagh, despite their Nationalist majorities, would remain part of an essentially unchanged Six County Ulster: 'rectification of frontiers' was only intended to deal with minor anomalies along the border.

The possibility must be considered that Lloyd George contrived to conceal from F.E. and Chamberlain what he was half-promising Collins and Griffith. Certainly it was he who conducted both the critical interviews, with Griffith on 12 November and Collins on 5 December, and he might well have thought it politic not to involve F.E. at this stage if he *were* contemplating the transfer of large areas of Ulster to the South. In practice, however, it is impossible to believe that F.E. did not understand quite well what the Irish hoped to gain from the Commission or fail to appreciate its importance in persuading Collins to sign. In 1925, indeed, he admitted in the House of Lords that the Treaty 'would never have been signed without Article 12'.[52] He cannot have imagined that the possible transfer of a couple of villages made the decisive difference to Collins.

With his clarity of mind F.E. must have seen that there was an irreconcilable contradiction between the hopes that each part of Ireland entertained of the Boundary Commission. Was he then a party to deliberately deceiving Collins? It is more likely that in his anxiety to win the Treaty he allowed himself to hope that the irreconcilable could be reconciled. He would have been as happy as Lloyd George to postpone the resolution of the border issue to another day in order to secure the agreement which he hoped would dispel the poisoned atmosphere and make subsequent settlement easier. Like Collins with his 'first step', he thought the Treaty would create its own momentum, and this justified a degree of ambiguity for the present.

He hoped, in fact, that the question of the Boundary Commission would not arise; he hoped and continued to urge that Ulster would after all see her way to exercise the option the Treaty offered her and, while retaining her own Government at Stormont, send members not to Westminster any longer but to the all-Ireland Parliament. Though Craig rejected this and set about entrenching his Protestant fastness against the world, it remained the assumption of British Ministers in the 1920s that Ulster must sooner or later be absorbed into the Free State. So long as Cosgrave's Government retained the link with the Crown and membership of the British Commonwealth, the question of the border did not seem so important as it has done since de Valera declared the Republic and Ireland became a foreign state. The mistake that F.E. made, in imagining that the Treaty had solved the Irish problem for all time, was to believe that the defiant Ulstermen with whom he had paraded in 1912 would be as impressed as he was by Collins's and Griffith's reasonableness, personal honour and acceptance of the Crown, so that with Ireland at last a settled and satisfied member of the British family their fear of the South would melt away and the border with it, not by coercion but by consent. It did not happen. The Treaty did not command the support of half the governing party in Dublin, who ultimately won the power to overthrow it. For that much of the blame lies with the way Lloyd George and F.E. negotiated it. Their very success bore in it the seeds of failure.

20

The Decline and Fall of the
Coalition, 1922

(i) Coalitionism Defiant

The signature of the Irish Treaty was the high point of the Coalition. The following ten months saw a steady decline in public and political confidence as the Tory party's restlessness to regain its independence became more and more vocal. The party, or most of it, had accepted the Treaty, but with an ill grace; it did not like it, and though it could not use the Treaty openly as a reason to break up the Government, suppressed distaste helped to feed other grievances, many of them of a personal character, against Lloyd George and his leading colleagues – a gang of power-corrupted cronies among whom F.E. ('the boisterous and bumptious Lord Chancellor' as one Irish Diehard dubbed him)[1] was now, to his discredit, prominently numbered. The distrust and even loathing which the Coalition increasingly inspired among its own supporters during 1922 was unprecedented: its downfall could only be a matter of time. Only the lack of an alternative delayed the moment.

In signing the Treaty, F.E. and Chamberlain had thrown in their lot irrevocably with Lloyd George. If he had flirted in 1921 with going back to uncompromised Toryism, F.E. was now committed again, as in 1920, to Coalitionism. His mind therefore reverted to the need to secure the Coalition's future – the necessity of somehow resurrecting the 'fusion' kite which had crashed so ignominiously two years before. Lloyd George was still all in favour, but there was no reason to think that the body of the Coalition Liberals were any keener now than then, and the Conservatives were plainly more hostile. The only solution seemed to be to 'bounce' both parties into renewed marriage by means of a snap election to reap whatever benefit was going from the Irish settlement.

At dinner at Grosvenor Gardens on 19 December, Lloyd George and F.E. overrode the doubts of Chamberlain and Churchill – though Salvidge, who was present, shrewdly urged that what the Coalition most needed was to bring back Bonar Law.[2] Chamberlain knew the likely reaction of the Tory party to being 'bounced', and thought 'fusion' would better precede an election than follow it; but he took the submissive view that the calling of elections was the Prime Minister's prerogative. On Christmas Eve, the party chairman, Sir George Younger, informed him bluntly that the party would not stand another election under Lloyd George's leadership and would regard an early election under any leadership as unduly cynical. He had no hesitation in tracing that cynicism directly to Chamberlain's senior Tory colleague.

> As to FE, he is as usual looking after 'No. 1'. I see his game quite clearly. He would like to keep the Coalition alive to go to the country again as we are. That would give him a better chance in the future than he has at present of securing the leadership.[3]

Two days after the pow-wow at Grosvenor Gardens, F.E. left England with a 'small but congenial' party of friends to spend Christmas at St Moritz; and on Boxing Day Lloyd George travelled to Cannes for a conference with the French. Over the New Year period half the Cabinet seemed to be in France, with Beaverbrook (originally one of F.E.'s party, but depressed by the Alpine snow) moving between St Moritz, Cannes and Paris in his accustomed role as wirepuller. A coded telegram from Churchill conveys the flavour of conspiracy. 'Revered [Lloyd George] proceeds Monday daylight Grasse I go hotel Mon Fleuve Cannes with Freddie [Guest] by same train join me there at earliest if possible bringing plaintiff's counsel [F.E.] who will be needed . . . seasonable greetings to entire troupe.'[4]

Churchill, Horne, Worthington-Evans and Beaverbrook all joined Lloyd George in Cannes, but the 'plaintiff's counsel' could not get away to be with them. 'Regret departmental work takes me back to England,' he telegraphed on 5 January (when he had already been abroad a fortnight) – an irritating instance of government getting in the way of politics. 'I agree on the whole with the course I understand you favour but of course shall support the decision whatever it may be.'[5]

Lloyd George had practically committed his colleagues in Cannes to support the course that he and F.E. favoured – only Churchill remained doubtful – when the ground was cut dramatically from under his feet. Seeing that Chamberlain was too weak to oppose Lloyd George, Younger took matters into his own hands, and leaked to the press the

fact that an election was in contemplation. He thus called down on
Austen's head such an avalanche of Tory hostility that the idea had to
be hurriedly abandoned. Lloyd George was furious. Younger, he raged
to Chamberlain, had 'behaved disgracefully' in disclosing to the press
'secret information which would never have been imparted to him
unless we had depended on his being gentleman enough to keep
counsel'. He utterly denied Younger's suggestion that the proposed
election was 'a Coalition Liberal stunt'. On the contrary, it had been
pressed on him by the Tories, notably by F.E.[6]

Nevertheless both he and F.E. had to admit that Younger had
successfully blocked the election option for the present. On 12 January
F.E. wired Lloyd George his candid view of the position.

> Think that position profoundly modified by Younger's interven-
> tion supported as it evidently is by Chamberlain. In my opinion
> situation now very difficult but not irretrievable. If it comes to a
> row in order to give effect to our view think adhesion Bonar almost
> indispensable. If that adhesion can be secured think that with
> other Unionist colleagues who I believe to be well affected the
> Chamberlain and Younger section can be swept away and dis-
> regarded. Am trying get in touch with Derby, who is making a
> speech on Saturday. I know you will understand my own position
> in one respect namely that I could not contemplate nor indeed
> would it be useful to you that I should contemplate isolation from
> all my Unionist colleagues.[7]

Evidently F.E. did not mind being separated from *some* of his
Unionist colleagues. Forwarding this message on, Lloyd George's Chief
Whip, Charles McCurdy, commented, 'I think Lord Chancellor sincerely desires standing by you.'[7] Freddy Guest, too, thought that
Chamberlain and Younger could be 'swept away', even without the
return of Bonar Law, if only F.E. would seize the moment. On
16 January he wrote Lloyd George an astonishingly optimistic view of
the prospect that fusion might yet be achieved.

> At the risk of appearing importunate, I want to place on record my
> opinion that – given the desire – this is the supreme opportunity
> for the formation of the Central Party and for the establishment of
> the great triumvirate [that is Lloyd George, F.E. and Winston].
>   Of course, it all depends upon whether FE has the courage to
> test his strength with the Tory Party.
>   The events of the last few weeks seem to me to have deliberately
> played into his hands. Younger has joined the Die-Hard
> movement; Chamberlain is discredited for lack of initiative and

leadership; Bonar, in the public mind, has definitely stepped on one side . . .

From my knowledge of the House of Commons and of the Coalition Tory movement, I believe that at least one half of the Tory Members of the House of Commons would listen to a Fusionist appeal against Labour by FE . . . More particularly the Tory electorate are ripe to be captured by a brilliant moderate man.

Is not the Conservative position at the moment rather a counterpart to the one which you tackled so boldly in 1916? FE should do now what you did then. I have spoken to him in this sense, but, if this is to be brought about – and I believe it to be in the National interest – it will require more pressure and more argument than I can produce.[8]

Two weeks later, on 1 February, F.E. did make a major speech, to the New Members' Coalition Group at the Savoy. His theme was the national necessity of keeping the Coalition in being. He denied that the Government was 'decrepit, moribund, decaying or dishonest', stressed the great achievement of the Irish settlement and promised the full implementation of the Geddes Report, but directed most of his effort towards discrediting the available alternatives should the Coalition be defeated. The record of the Labour leaders since the war he dismissed as one of 'consistent and abject poltroonery' in the face of the strikes which had crippled the nation's recovery. 'I am prepared to go to the great centres of population in the country,' he declared, 'in their own strongholds, and brand them with the stigma of men who have not played their part in these three years, and are wholly unworthy to conduct the affairs of a great Empire.'

As for Lord Robert Cecil and Lord Grey, who had been trying to compose a high-minded coalition of 'honest' men to set against the corrupt combination now in power, he derided their pathetic pretensions. They had no support, but merely recommended one another to a country which had no intention of employing either of them in any capacity. Savagely F.E. rejected the 'pontifical and impeccable omniscience' with which Grey attacked the Coalition's foreign policy. Where had *his* diplomacy landed the country? In a war for which his Government had left it unprepared.

The third alternative offered was a return to party strife on the pre-war pattern. Here F.E. made a point of recalling his own lifelong Unionism, going back to the 1892 election. But this, he explained, was overlaid by an obligation of honour to the present Prime Minister and his Liberal colleagues. 'I count myself bound in honour, as long as no great principle manifests itself between myself and them, to march on with them, and as far as I am concerned I shall so march until [here he introduced a curious phrase] a divergence of principle emerges which offers the means of an honourable escape.'

The implication, which was surely not what he intended, was that he was actually looking for 'the means of an honourable escape' from the Coalition; but the rest of his speech was devoted to proving that the Coalition was still indispensable. Its very failure he paraded as grounds for its continuance: Europe was still prostrate, trade depressed, two million good workmen unemployed. This was no moment for a party government. 'If there was any justification five years ago for the formation of a Coalition Government, believe me – who have indeed for eight years lived intimately in the very heart of politics [a characteristic exaggeration of his role in the war] – there is all the same justification today.' Conservative principles themselves, he insisted, demanded continued Coalition for another seven or eight critical years.[9]

Guest was enthusiastic: F.E.'s speech was 'an unqualified success', he told Lloyd George,

> admirably phrased and . . . delivered with great power. The warmth of his defence of the Coalition appeared to come as a surprise to some – proving that it was overdue from some Conservative leader . . . As an ex-whip I recommend that the speech should be circulated . . . to all the Unionist Associations that Younger tampered with. FE is the only leader and speaker that they have got and today finally proved it.[10]

There was little sign over the next few months, however, that F.E.'s words had had the desired effect. As *The Times* stated the next day, the impression given was that the Government had closed its ranks and was preparing to discipline the Tory party into line. 'The Lord Chancellor was dealing with disaffection, but this was not the healing treatment of a physician careful for the closing of a wound, but the stern measure of a surgeon prepared to sacrifice a limb.'[11] F.E.'s approach antagonized, rather than persuaded, those he was attempting to lead.

Three weeks later, F.E. treated the members of the Junior Constitutional Club – this time a specifically Unionist audience – to another hectoring defence of the Coalition and all its works. Again he emphasized that he was a Conservative born and bred, 'I was nurtured in the party and I shall die in that party.' Again he justified the need for continued Coalition by the very size of the problems it still faced, with an utterly incredible pretence that Ministers only continued in office from a sense of reluctant duty.

If there is anybody listening to me today who thinks that there is
one Minister in the Government today who, if he could honourably
escape from his burdens, would not lay them aside with a sigh of
relief, that man is mad. Does anyone suppose that we contemplate
with pleasure the months and years that lie in front of us in dealing
with Ireland, with India, with Egypt, with the financial situation
and with the spectre of two million unemployed in our streets?

A more shameless and transparent piece of humbug was never
uttered by an ambitious politician! But F.E.'s argument that the
Coalition was indispensable whether its leading Ministers liked it or not
was unaffected by the fact that they manifestly liked it very much.
European countries like France and Italy, he declared, with their
succession of short-lived administrations, looked with envy at the
stability of the British Government. The idea that the Conservative
party should withdraw and make an independent appeal to the electors
was 'a counsel of insanity'. 'There is no responsible Unionist leader in
the Government or out of it who takes a different view . . . Mr Bonar
Law, Lord Derby and the Duke of Devonshire are in absolute agreement with the view I have indicated to you.' F.E. omitted Lord
Salisbury from his catalogue of 'responsible' leaders. He went on to coin
an ironic phrase, unmistakably directed at Younger for his recent
exceeding of his authority as party Chairman, which continued to
reverberate through the party for the rest of the year:

> In these circumstances I am not one of those who, when the
> tempest rages and when the captain would naturally be on the
> bridge would give any particular encouragement to the cabin boy
> to seize the helm; and I am more than ever of that opinion when
> the cabin boy has announced that he does not intend to make
> another voyage.

F.E. still insisted that the Government as a Government would have
been absolutely justified in calling an election in the New Year, denying
that there was 'the slightest chance of an independent Unionist Government obtaining an adequate working majority'; while to those who
alleged that the Tory leaders had been 'chloroformed' by Lloyd George,
he retorted that if anyone imagined that men like Balfour, Chamberlain,
Curzon and himself were 'the kind of men who would be chloroformed
by any wizard ever born in Wales', then 'you greatly overrate the Prime
Minister and you greatly underrate your representatives in the
Cabinet'.

The danger to the country, he went on, came from the Labour party, which was winning seats every day and would go on winning unless it was faced by a united front of constitutionalists, loyally supported. Its leaders were no more than figureheads, thrust forward to dole out the soothing syrup for the hard men behind. He challenged Clynes and Henderson to say plainly whether or not they were in favour of the socialization of all the means of production, distribution and exchange, as laid down by the party's 1918 Constitution. 'If they say they are not, they will be swept away like empty corks which have done their work [an extraordinarily compressed metaphor: did he mean the corks of empty bottles? Or had he emptied one too many himself?]; if they say they are, then we shall know where we stand, that battle is declared, and we will undertake that battle and carry it to its conclusion.'

Finally, having tried to frighten his listeners into sticking to the Coalition, he fell back again on the appeal to honour, recalling that the patriotic Liberals who followed Lloyd George had not hesitated to break up their party in 1916 when the country required it; the Tories owed them a debt which he at least would not dishonour. 'So long as these men combine to act straightforwardly and generously with us,' he concluded. 'I shall act, whatever the consequences to myself, straight-forwardly and generously with them.'[12] He met with at least some cheers for this manly declaration. But speeches with this bullying message – 'We are your leaders: you must follow us' – did nothing to allay the rising discontent in the Tory party, but only fuelled it. 'F.E. is a strangely isolated figure,' Edwin Montagu wrote to Reading in India at just this time, 'and very unpopular with the Conservatives.'[13]

If F.E. was not actually 'chloroformed' by Lloyd George in the spring of 1922 he was certainly very strongly under his influence, as was evidenced by the role he played at the Genoa Conference in April, an episode which not only confirmed Diehard suspicions that he had gone culpably soft, but occasioned a temporary but bitter breach with Winston. The question at issue was relations with the Bolsheviks, who by 1920 had clearly consolidated their hold on Russia. With wiser judgment, F.E. had never shared his friend's enthusiasm for military intervention to overthrow the Soviet regime; rather he supported Lloyd George's view that the right policy was to bring Russia back as quickly as possible into the community of nations – partly to moderate the regime's revolutionary excesses, partly in the interest of reopening her market to international trade. In November 1920, when Lloyd George invited a Soviet trade delegation for talks in Downing Street, Winston came close to resignation and was only dissuaded by a strong personal appeal by F.E. 'I am most clearly of opinion', F.E. wrote, 'that . . . you would be making a mistake of a magnitude which shocks me, if you carried out any such intention.'

You would find yourself the hero of the 'Morning Post' and the leader of some thirty Tories in the House of Commons, who would disagree with you on 90% of all the subjects about which you feel really deeply. Moreover, you would cut yourself adrift perhaps permanently, certainly for a very long time, from the Coalition, which on every other point you support, in the necessity of which you believe, and of which in my judgement you are an indispensable member.[14]

He would have no support in Cabinet, and in no way could Russia be seen as the sort of issue of principle which might justify resignation. Winston heeded his friend's advice, but remained deeply suspicious of closer links with Russia.

A year later Lloyd George took another stride down the same road. Desperately seeking a new diplomatic triumph which would distract attention from difficulties at home and restore his image as a great world statesman and the peacemaker of Europe, he pinned his hopes on another top-level conference, held at Genoa in April 1922, at which Russia should be accorded full diplomatic recognition and both Russia and Germany be re-admitted to the concert of peace-loving nations. At once the suggestion ran into strenuous opposition from Tories outside the Government but also, once again, from Churchill inside; this was peculiarly awkward, as Chamberlain explained to Lloyd George on 21 March, given that Churchill was still nominally a Liberal.

The Lord Chancellor and I have done our best to restrain him; but he has said to both of us that he could not remain a member of the Government if *de jure* recognition were granted by this country to the Soviet Government. Putting aside any feelings of our own, you will readily perceive that our position would be impossible if Winston retired because he was more Tory than the Tory Ministers.[15]

At a series of Cabinet meetings and conferences over the next week, Lloyd George was obliged to give ground and agree that he would not recognize Russia at Genoa without definite undertakings that the Soviet Government would, first, accept liability for Tsarist debts, and, second, refrain from hostile propaganda against Britain in India and elsewhere. To further restrict his freedom to negotiate without consultation with a nervous Cabinet, Lloyd George agreed that he should be accompanied to Genoa by the Foreign Secretary, Curzon, and more irregularly by F.E. In the event, Curzon was ill, which left F.E. as the Cabinet's sole brake upon the Prime Minister's impulsiveness.

As a matter of fact F.E. was not at Genoa formally at all, but had been ordered to take a month's rest for the sake of his eyesight and had elected to spend it cruising with his family in the Genoa area, where he could be at hand if Lloyd George needed him. ('Birkenhead's doctor has put the fear of God into his patient,' Warden Chilcott told Riddell;[16] and Lloyd George wrote to Frances Stevenson that F.E.'s eyes were 'very bad').[17] On 24 April he turned up to make a dramatic intervention. Lloyd George was too busy in the conference to speak to the press and asked F.E., who was quite unprepared and dressed in his full yachting rig, to do so for him.

> 'What do you want me to tell them?' he asked L.G. A few minutes' talk and Birkenhead sent for a taxi. Without any preparation he addressed some 700 of the world's newspaper representatives and delivered what the journalists themselves said was the most brilliant and informative speech of the whole conference. And after the speech he invited questions which came at him like shells from a quick firing battery. In his answers he was frank and honest and won the admiration of all who attended.[18]

The burden of his speech was that European recovery depended upon Russian participation, and that it was no business of the rest of Europe to inquire into Russia's domestic arrangements: 'the right of the Russians to choose their own institutions cannot be disputed'. This was perfectly in line with Lloyd George's attitude; but back in London Winston – laid up in bed after a polo accident – was furious. How could F.E. say such a thing, he demanded in a frenzied rebuke which he finally refrained from sending, 'when the whole mass of Russia, whether peasants or intellectuals, is absolutely excluded from the slightest means of representation or freedom of expression? I had your promise', he protested, 'that you would endeavour to see the views which we have represented together . . . given full effect to at the Conference . . . but as far as I can see you have yielded facilely to the influences by which you have been surrounded.'[19]

'Winston is terribly annoyed with FE's attitude,' Philip Sassoon wrote to Lloyd George, 'and considers that he has been nobbled by you!'[20] A few days later he was still more annoyed, when Lloyd George telegraphed to Chamberlain that matters in Genoa were coming to a head and he wanted F.E. (who had moved to Venice) back for the final stages. He was anxious to have F.E., he told Frances, 'to counteract Winston's mischief'.[21] F.E. went. Bitterly Winston railed that he 'could not resist going back . . . for "one final hug" with the Bolshies!'[22] On 6 May Winston poured out in a long personal letter his sense of betrayal at F.E.'s attitude, which threatened a crisis in their political association.

My Dear Fred,

   . . . The absence of Curzon from Genoa altered the balance & doubled your responsibility. But from yr telegram sent after you had been but a few days at Genoa & from yr speech I feared that you had ceased to represent in any way the views wh I thought we shared & wh you certainly undertook to safeguard. This caused me great distress: because all my thoughts in future politics turn on working with you, & all that future will be compromised by a fundamental disagreement. It seemed to me disastrous that you shd weaken yr influence with the Conservative party at this juncture by giving a new cause of reproach to yr enemies. The burden wh you partially assumed abt Ireland was surely enough for you to bear at the present moment. Why shd you go out of yr way to add to it by taking up another policy most bitterly & in my judgement most rightly resented by the bulk of those on whom the strength of Britain depends, & with whom we had hoped to act? Moreover if you were a full plenipotentiary attending continually & every day to the work of the Conference, I shd at least feel that you had a real responsibility. But dropping in now & then you become an easy prey to appeals to yr good nature, & thus run a grave risk of being made use of. However I hoped that the harm, such as it was, was done & that you would return at any rate not particularly compromised with this unhappy policy and episode.

   But now you have been intercepted & summoned to Genoa for the final scene, & of course L.G. wishes to get you in his hand & put the new burden solidly upon you. I know him so well & my dear friend I know so well what an influence he will have upon you by making appeals to yr chivalry & so persuading you to come into the races with him. Once he has got you well compromised he will feel strong enough to run gt risks agst the House or party, & lines of cleavage may be drawn wh will leave you & me again on different sides.

By adhering to fundamental principles, Winston urged, F.E. might yet extricate himself,

   & what is more important this country from the entanglement into wh she has been led by the personal views of one man & may return home with the credit of having stood firm against temptation. In this way you wd restore & regain yr influence with yr own party & greatly promote those future developments abt wh we have so often talked. Everyone wd rejoice to see that you had played a manly part & had stood by those primary Br[itish] national interests to wh you have always been devoted. It is for these reasons as well as on acct of our comradeship that I beg you to reflect on the long consequences that may follow from the steps you take.[23]

Winston's personal pleading with F.E. was reinforced by more formal representations to Lloyd George from Curzon and Chamberlain that recognition would provoke a political crisis; and in the end nothing came of the Genoa Conference at all, except an unexpected and embarrassing alliance secretly patched up between the two pariah nations, Russia and Germany, which was not at all what Lloyd George had been working for. His wider aspiration to include the Russians and Germans in a universal European settlement, however, was vetoed, as usual, by the French. F.E. returned home on 8 May and Lloyd George a week later with very little to show for six weeks of effort on which much of the Coalition's failing credit had been gambled.

But F.E. had bound himself more closely than ever to Lloyd George's destiny.

(ii) Sensibilities Outraged

Another source of Conservative, or at least Diehard, discontent with the Coalition was its failure to do anything about the House of Lords. In theory the Government was pledged to complete the reform begun in 1911 and rebalance the Constitution by restoring some effective power to an Upper House composed on a democratic or otherwise defensible basis. In practice Lloyd George and the Liberal wing of the Coalition had very little wish to undo their 1911 triumph, while no two Conservatives could ever agree on *how* the new House should be constituted. A Cabinet Committee chaired by Curzon and comprising Balfour, Chamberlain, F.E., Churchill, Fisher and Hewart – a pretty high-powered group, especially on the Tory side – sat from November 1920, but made little progress. The King's Speech for 1921 made only the most vague commitment, and Curzon had to confess that there was no hope of a Bill before 1922. Though Lord Selborne raised the spectre that under the existing makeshift arrangement a Labour Government could declare a Republic and abolish private property in two years after gaining power, and insisted that a Government which was three-quarters Conservative must not leave office without safeguarding the fundamental rights of liberty, Milner told him frankly that there was very little interest in reform inside the Cabinet.[24]

This was strange, because at other times the reform of the Lords was an issue on which F.E. placed overwhelming emphasis. Now, though still nominally in favour, he pursued it with little urgency. In the committee, instead of backing the formula on which Curzon and Chamberlain had agreed – roughly the sort of scheme he had supported in 1911, envisaging a House predominantly elected, either directly or indirectly, but including a proportion of hereditary peers, elected by themselves, and a number of Bishops, Law Lords and other *ex officio* nominees – F.E. very curiously reverted to advocating a purely hereditary Chamber. In this he was supported by Churchill and Fisher; but they saw in the hereditary principle a guarantee that the House would be given back no shadow of its former power, whereas F.E. – a measure of his increasing conservatism and the effect of his own peerage – now appeared to want what he had admitted before the war to be indefensible, a hereditary chamber with, if not an outright veto, power at least to refer legislation to a joint sitting.

In the end F.E. agreed to the Curzon–Chamberlain proposal, and a Bill on those lines was actually presented to the Lords in July 1922; but it met with little favour even there, where the peers had since 1911 discovered that the pleasures of dignified impotence were still considerable, and certainly preferable to being replaced by a lot of elected nobodies; and F.E., replying to the debate, had no compunction about confessing his own preference for the hereditary qualification (albeit weeded by a process of self-selection from within the peerage). After the Government's fall, in his *Contemporary Personalities*, F.E. blamed Salisbury for having blocked a reform on which the two wings of the Coalition were agreed and thereby destroyed a chance of bi-partisan reform which would not recur.[25] But this was written under the stimulus of renewed alarm at the formation of a Labour Government. In 1921–2, when he was in a powerful position to press strongly for an agreed and rational reform – no one would ever have been in a better position if he had really taken up the cause – he did no such thing but retreated into a weak and uncharacteristic best-of-both-worlds sentimentalism which carried no conviction. He was himself almost as much responsible as Salisbury for the fact that the Coalition carried no reform. The truth was that nobody had any clear idea how to reform the Lords. The problem recurred under the Baldwin Government, but the outcome was the same.

A question that excited the Lords much more than their powers was the alleged sale of honours. This was the scandal which, more than any other, undermined the reputation of the Coalition, though there was a good deal of hypocrisy in the cries of righteous outrage, since peerages had always been bestowed in recognition of financial contributions to the governing party, and even under Baldwin's sanitized regime in the later 1920s would continue to be awarded on much the same basis. This was the traditional British method of financing politics, and as Lloyd George in his more candid moments used to point out, the giving away of meaningless baubles was a less harmful way of doing it than giving Government appointments or a voice in Government policy – let alone allowing a party to be owned by outside paymasters. Two factors combined to make the established practice embarrassingly conspicuous in 1921–2. First, though Asquith and Gladstone had 'sold' peerages scarcely less freely, Lloyd George was the first Prime Minister who had no respect for what he was selling: now that it was safely emasculated he attached no importance to the House of Lords and did not care who went there – if snobs would part with money in exchange for titles, he was happy to oblige. As a result the trade, managed on the Prime Minister's behalf by Freddy Guest and Sir William Sutherland through the notorious middleman Maundy Gregory, became unpleasantly blatant, with a rumoured tariff of charges beginning at £10,000 for a simple knighthood, and some distinctly unsuitable characters were ennobled, so that the suspicion arose that Lloyd George was seeking deliberately to discredit the peerage. Second, the unusual political circumstances of the time meant that the money paid appeared to go not discreetly into the coffers of an established party – though half of it did go to the Conservative party and no one made a fuss about that – but into the pocket of the Prime Minister himself to build up the Coalition Liberals as his personal following. This looked much more than in Asquith's time as if the Prime Minister was personally selling honours for his own profit, political if not actually financial.

The sale of honours fitted in only too well with the corrupt, cynical image that the Coalition was already projecting, and which was associated as much with F.E. as with Lloyd George himself. Accordingly, F.E. has usually been assumed to have been deeply implicated in Guest's and Gregory's activities. The cap fits very plausibly. For one thing, F.E. did not disguise his enjoyment of his own titles: from knighthood (1915) to baronetcy (1917), to Baron (1919), Viscount (1921) and finally Earl (1922) he valued every step he received and missed no opportunity to flaunt his latest style. At the same time, he was a known cynic who mixed freely and with pleasure in the raffish political underworld peopled by the likes of Gregory and Bottomley, from whom he was happy to take both hospitality and substantial gifts. In reality, too much has been read into these associations. F.E. accepted gifts from all sorts of people, not least Beaverbrook, without any hint of political corruption, just as Lloyd George, for instance, had a house built for him by Lord Riddell. It was quite normal for politicians at that period to be subsidized by wealthy patrons without any eyebrows being raised. These were the legitimate rewards of a public man. Undoubtedly by being seen at Gregory's opulent club, the Ambassador – respectable by day, a distinctly dubious nightspot after dark – F.E. served as a valuable advertisement or endorsement for Gregory's operation; but Gregory's biographer thinks that he, like many others including the Prince of Wales, was used, quite innocently, as a bait to draw lesser fry into the web.[26] Where money and pleasure were concerned, F.E. was extra-ordinarily naïve. His incautious acceptance of both from a man he dubbed 'the cheerful giver' implied no approval of the honours racket.

Quite the contrary: F.E. was not cynical about honours, as his pride in his own titles demonstrates. He had no wish to see the House of Lords diminished by a lot of unsuitable creations. It is easy to believe his son's account that he was as shocked as anyone by the quality of the 1922 honours list, and told Lloyd George that he could not defend it. He could be a stickler in such matters, as he had shown in the case of the Lord Chief Justice. By then, however, the list had already been published and it is equally easy to see Lloyd George persuading him that he had no choice but to defend it or bring down the Government.[27]

Criticism centred on the elevation of an elderly South African diamond magnate of very questionable commercial morals, Sir Joseph Robinson. He had been given a baronetcy in 1908 on the recommenda-tion of Botha, who was said to have recommended him at that time for a peerage; his name had remained on file at Downing Street ever since, despite his conviction in South Africa for fraudulent share dealing, and now surfaced again to receive a barony, allegedly in exchange for £30,000. In the Lords F.E. admitted that the proper procedure of consultation with the Colonial Office had been bypassed in this case and agreed that the award of honours should be more carefully scrutin-ized in the future. But he attempted to deflect criticism, in general by reading a list of the genuinely distinguished peers created in the past four years, and in particular by asserting that he had himself read all the papers in connection with the Robinson litigation in South Africa, implying that they revealed no reason for withholding the honour. (He did not explain how it had happened that the Judicial Committee of the Privy Council had only the previous November dismissed Robinson's appeal.) His trump card was to disclose, for what it was worth, that Robinson had actually declined the honour.[28] Reading out his letter of disclaimer, F.E. naturally did not reveal that the old man had only written it, most unwillingly, at Freddy Guest's dictation, to get the Government off the hook. The story is that when Guest went to see him on this delicate mission, Robinson at first understood that he was simply being asked for more money and pulled out his cheque book asking how much more![29]

If this was a task which F.E. discharged with little conviction, he managed a much more spirited performance three weeks later when he had to announce the Government's decision to appoint a Royal Commission to examine the whole honours system. Much less apologetic this time, he positively defended the award of honours for political service, which in some cases was bound to be financial; made characteristic play with the Labour party's trade union levy; and ended with a ringing celebration of the natural and legitimate desire to acquire a title – a desire least of all to be despised, he reminded their Lordships, by those who possessed them.[30] The next day he came gallantly to the defence of another of the new creations whose elevation had been challenged, Lord Forres, who as Sir Archibald Williamson had been accused – falsely, F.E. maintained – of trading with the enemy during the war.[31] Neither the vindication of individuals nor the defiant justification of the system as a whole, however, dispelled the odour of corruption which surrounded the traffic in titles. Though Lloyd George shrugged off the immediate crisis in June/July, suspicion and rumour continued to damage the Government and contributed to its fall a few months later. It was in this instance undeserved that F.E.'s image, associations and loyalty to Lloyd George tarred him with a share of the blame for one aspect of the Coalition's record for which he had little real responsibility.

F.E.'s behaviour in the last months of the Coalition is the most difficult to explain in his life. He had never suffered fools gladly, he had always been prone to arrogance and outbursts of appalling boorishness when opposed by men he considered inferior to himself; yet normally his impatience was tempered by charm, humour and a saving sense of fun, the driving self-confidence of his ambition restrained by the tact and prudence without which ambition defeats itself. In the summer of 1922 he behaved as though tact and any semblance of respect for others had served their turn and could be discarded. As the Government stumbled to its fall he made no attempt to retain support by argument or persuasion, but tried crudely to command it by a display of contemptuous self-importance breathtaking in its insensitivity and pride. Convinced that he, Lloyd George, Churchill, Chamberlain and Balfour comprised the sum of all the political talent and experience in the country, he dismissed Tory critics as jealous, petty men incapable of understanding the problems of the nation, let alone curing them, and ignored or insultingly rebuffed the anxieties of the party which had raised them up and whose continued support was necessary for their survival. In this suicidal arrogance all the leading Coalitionists shared; but F.E. expressed it most candidly, most provocatively and most frequently, with all the hurtful power of his stinging tongue. It was F.E. who aroused the bitterest resentment in the Tory party, and F.E. therefore who bears most of the responsibility for goading the party to its inevitable revenge. It was almost as if, after the Irish Treaty, he was determined to make himself a martyr to the Diehards.

In mitigation it must be said that he was very overworked, not very well, and as a result tired, strained and irritable. His hours – on the Woolsack, in Cabinet, in committees, travelling and speaking, doing the equivalent of three men's jobs – were enormously long, and he was having trouble with his eyesight. At the same time he insisted on keeping up his strenuous idea of relaxation, cramming an exhausting social life into the hours that were left him, with serious effects on his judgment. Colleagues and observers were always amazed at F.E.'s capacity to burn his candle at both ends without any visible reaction; but in 1922, after seven years in office, three as Lord Chancellor, this resilience on which he relied began for the first time to flag. 'I don't think FE knows where he is at all,' Philip Sassoon wrote to Lloyd George in March.

> It is becoming increasingly difficult to find any sequence in his acts or words. On the other hand his movements are more easy to follow – he and Freddie Guest, Scatters [Sir Matthew Wilson, a wealthy socialite M.P.], Mona Dunn & [illegible] Hart were supping and dancing on the roof garden of the Criterion Restaurant till past 1 o'c this morning![32]

During 1921, to win a bet with Beaverbrook, but presumably also in deference to his doctor (whose advice Beaverbrook was perhaps in his own way trying to reinforce), F.E. either stopped drinking altogether or, more probably, abstained from drinking spirits. It is difficult to believe that his abstinence and consequent sobriety did not contribute to his improved health, to the Law of Property Act and to the Irish Treaty. But it was in celebration of the signing of the Treaty in the early morning of 6 December that he allowed himself a brandy and lost his bet, insisting that the Treaty was worth £1,000 (doubtless never paid). Thereafter he returned rapidly to his former habits. At the beginning of February 1922 he dined with Lloyd George and Winston. 'FE became quite drunk towards the end of dinner,' Lloyd George told Frances Stevenson. 'He was very amusing. He has lately taken to spirits again & says he "means to make up for lost time".'[33] Before the end of the year his colleagues were seriously worried that F.E. was 'poisoning his brain' with excessive drinking.[34]

Drink, eyestrain, tiredness, or just the proud man's contumely – any or all of these factors together must account for one of F.E.'s most graceless and damaging displays of brutal arrogance at a meeting of Conservative Ministers on 3 August. The meeting was arranged as a result of pressure on Chamberlain from the junior Ministers who were still generally in favour of continued coalition but were beginning to insist, in response to constituency pressure, that the party should fight the next election as a separate party, and that if the Coalition were renewed it should only be under Conservative leadership. The case for listening to the constituencies was introduced, according to Leo Amery (then Parliamentary Secretary at the Admiralty), 'quite temperately and fairly' by Sir Robert Sanders, Pike Pease, Sir John Gilmour and Sir Ernest Pollock (respectively Under-Secretary at the War Office, Assistant Postmaster-General, a junior Whip and Attorney-General) – of whom it is worth noting that the last two stuck to the Coalition to the end, despite F.E.'s conduct.

> FE began by rating them for their impertinence in having asked for a meeting at all when they had already been informed of the Cabinet Ministers' views, and then went on in the most astonishingly arrogant and offensive manner to lecture them for their silliness and want of loyalty. I could see them all bristling more and more with every sentence.[35]

> He cross examined Sanders as to his information [this is now Pollock's account] and Willie Bridgeman [Under-Secretary for Mines] upon the deductions to be drawn from it. He poured scorn on both. He derided the reports from the country as mere gossips' tales, unworthy of credit and not representative of the real feeling of the country . . . [His] attitude was unexpected and both hostile and dictatorial as if addressed to inferiors who had no right to express opinions.[36]

He was especially severe on Pollock, who, he thought, as Attorney-General ought to have known better. In vain Pollock protested that they were not disloyal but merely sought a discussion with their leaders. F.E. sent them away with a wigging, while Chamberlain sat by helpless.

> It is idle to pretend [Pollock wrote] that Lord Birkenhead's attitude and language did not create animosity. I have seldom seen men so stirred. They had refrained from words of recrimination, but the very fact that they had done so deepened their feelings of injustice and resentment.[36]

Whatever chances FE may have had of the Unionist leadership in the future [Amery concluded] are not likely to have survived this unfortunate performance.[35]

Whatever had happened to F.E.'s famed power of advocacy and persuasion? This was an important group of responsible fellow-Ministers, not opponents, who held the future of the Government in their hands. Why should he have underestimated them so insultingly and treated them as disobedient children? A few months before, these had been the people he had aspired to lead. Perhaps this was what he understood by leadership. Certainly this was how Chamberlain and Balfour appeared to understand leadership that summer; but they were both withdrawn and formal personalities at the best of times. F.E. of all men should have had the personality, were he not too tired or drunk with the arrogance of office, to lead by persuasion and panache.

Despite the Irish Treaty, there might still have been an opening for him, had he played his cards tactfully, to have supplanted Chamberlain and filled the role actually left to Bonar Law of leading the Tory party out of the Coalition. He would have had to defend the Treaty, as Law did, not as a triumph but as a regrettable necessity. He would have had to make an effort to win the party over to its and his support. Honourably, perhaps, but fatally he made no such effort. On the contrary, he seemed to have determined, with a sort of defiant death-wish, that he would stand or fall by the Treaty and with Lloyd George. He stood by his long and sincerely held belief in a national, centre Government, and a centre party. But his attempts to promote such a party, whose moment had to most observers passed in 1920, were now no more than intellectual bullying. At best, he appeared to think the case for continued coalition too obvious to need serious advocacy. At worst, he seemed simply to believe that so long as he, Chamberlain and Balfour were agreed, no one else in the party mattered.

It was a fatal miscalculation. He had forgotten Bonar Law. It was perhaps true that all the huffing and puffing of Younger and Salisbury and the junior Ministers could be ignored so long as they had no leader capable of forming an alternative Government. But Law's health had now sufficiently recovered for him to think of returning to active politics, as his Svengali Beaverbrook was insistently urging him was his duty. And the crisis was now at hand which would give him the excuse he needed to come out, reluctantly but decisively, against his former colleagues.

Just before events at Chanak rang down the curtain on the greatest Government on earth, there occurred another extraordinary episode which reveals again the incipient megalomania with which Lloyd

George and F.E. were touched at this time. Lord Northcliffe, the genuinely megalomaniac proprietor of *The Times* and the *Daily Mail*, was dying; and the Prime Minister and the Lord Chancellor had the incredible idea of buying *The Times* to provide backing for their proposed new party. 'I have little doubt', F.E. wrote to Lloyd George (who was at Criccieth) on 19 August, 'but that all the money required for the purchases which I recently discussed with you and which are so important in our mutual interest can be obtained from an unimpeachable source (*not* H). What remains is to discover whether there is a willing and *complete* seller. When are you coming South?'[37]

'Thanks,' Lloyd George replied, '– but nothing can happen till N's will is proved. Then we must get busy. It will take at least a fortnight from his death. I assume that the Executors will be in a position to sell but all depends upon the Will. I think I shall be in a position to tell you more about it in another week's time.'[38] At this stage they were still thinking in terms of buying both Northcliffe's papers, which would be a better commercial proposition for their backers than *The Times* alone, but it became clear in September that his brother Rothermere was going to retain the *Daily Mail*. Warden Chilcott was handling the negotiation.

> It is possible [he reported to the two Principals] that a Syndicate could be formed for the acquisition of *The Times* alone, but as the incentive would not be a business proposition but a Political one, the Negotiator would desire further instruction before proceeding with the formation of a Syndicate to purchase same. Without doubt, both Principals would require names of prospective subscribers submitted before they were approached with an invitation to join the undertaking.[39]

Chilcott thought *The Times* would sell for £1 million, of which Lloyd George's millionaire friend and former secretary David Davies was expected to contribute £300,000. Who else might have comprised the Syndicate is uncertain, but both Riddell and Beaverbrook were mentioned in the correspondence. In the event the paper was sold for £3 million to J.J. Astor and its former owners, the Walter family; and Lloyd George and F.E. were saved from a ludicrously impractical and constitutionally dubious enterprise which, if their plans had been known at the time, would have confirmed the darkest suspicions of their enemies.

(iii) Chanak and the Carlton Club Revolt

On 17 September the Cabinet determined to defy the malcontents and fight the General Election as a Coalition. But immediately the decision was taken out of their hands: the Government was plunged into a sudden crisis in the Middle East which proved to be the last straw needed to break its fragile hold on Tory confidence and hence on power. At the end of September the country was alarmed to find itself confronted with the possibility of renewed war with Turkey over the Dardanelles, as Mustapha Kemal's resurgent Nationalists rose against the Treaty of Sèvres imposed by the Allies in 1920. The main provision of the Treaty from the Allied point of view was that the straits were declared a demilitarized zone, to be freely open to the shipping of all nations – a traditional British interest. The offensive aspect from the Turkish point of view was the tactless use of the Greeks to enforce the Treaty – a policy that derived in an unusually personal manner from Lloyd George, who had an irrational obsession with Greece as a small mountainous country akin to Wales and imagined that by backing the Greek against the Turk he was upholding the Gladstonian tradition of kicking the Turks 'bag and baggage' out of Europe. The equally long-standing Tory tradition, up to the war, had been friendship with Turkey; but Lloyd George had his way, despite his colleagues' doubts, until in August 1922 the policy collapsed overnight when the Kemalists drove the Greeks into the sea, reoccupied Smyrna (awarded to Greece by the Treaty) and moved north to threaten the straits, now held by a small British force on behalf of the Allies – the French having refused to help.

For a few days the two sides confronted one another across the barbed wire at Chanak as the British Cabinet, willing to renegotiate the Treaty but determined not to yield to force, demanded that the Turks withdraw out of the neutral zone. Eventually, thanks more to the tactful diplomacy of the British General on the spot than to the orders he was receiving from London, they did so; a new treaty was negotiated at Lausanne in 1923 guaranteeing the freedom of the straits but ceding back to Turkey much of the territory that had been unrealistically given to Greece, and retrospectively the firm handling of the crisis was vindicated as the last time before 1940 that Britain stood up to an aggressor. At the time, however, the Cabinet's brinkmanship – highlighted by Churchill calling publicly for Dominion support in the event of war – aroused a storm of protest. The reckless triumvirate of Lloyd

George, Birkenhead and Churchill was widely accused of warmongering to distract public attention from problems at home. Despite the fact that their policy actually achieved, with the help of General Harington, the desired result without a shot fired, the last shred of trust in their collective judgment was destroyed and their downfall sealed within the month.

The allegations were not without foundation. Winston and F.E. in particular did give even some of their Cabinet colleagues the impression that they wanted war and were disappointed when Kemal climbed down. In F.E. this is further indication that he was in a somewhat overwrought state, for he had no history of hostility to the Turks. In 1921, when the Greek-Turkish problem first blew up, he noted disapprovingly in a letter to Bonar Law that 'Winston seems to have become almost pro-Greek having always hated them. I suspect that the explanation is that the Kemalists are being helped by the Bolshevists & W. will support anyone who attacks them.'[40] He himself shared none of Lloyd George's Greek obsession. But when the Turks advanced on Chanak his position changed. He now took a characteristically strong Imperialist line that Britain's prestige was at stake and there could be no giving in to force. He had not approved the way that the situation had been created, but now that it had, he was adamant against the slightest hint of 'scuttle'. At the Cabinet conference on 29 September which instructed Harington to give the Turks an ultimatum to withdraw he was (exceptionally) recorded in the minutes as making a long speech.

> He would not whittle down the decision which had been taken, and he had no doubt that Parliament and the public would support the Government . . . He was deeply desirous of averting war, and would go to great lengths for this purpose, but he did not think that war would be averted by weakness.[41]

This is fair enough. But off the formal record there is a strong impression that F.E., with Lloyd George and Winston, actually hoped that the ultimatum would not avert war but provoke it. 'What Ll.G., Churchill and Birkenhead dread', Hankey recorded in his diary, 'is that Mustapha Kemal will accept the conference, and we shall have to implement the condition of handing over Eastern Thrace to the Turk, thus bringing him back to Europe with all that that implies for the future.'[42] Churchill frankly confessed to Hankey after the crisis that he regretted its peaceful outcome;[43] and other colleagues did not differentiate between them in being alarmed at 'Winston and FE's warlike policy'.[44] Lee, who was shocked to find Churchill envying his luck in being at the Admiralty 'when there's a show on', had the feeling that

'L.G., Winston, Birkenhead, Horne and even Austen, positively *want* hostilities to break out'.[45] According to both Hankey and Curzon – as Foreign Secretary nominally responsible for the whole situation, but in practice very unhappy about it – the 'warmongers' were furious when they heard that Harington had not delivered their ultimatum, and F.E. wanted him to be formally censured.[46]

The evidence amounts to a serious charge that the leading personalities of the Coalition really did want to involve Britain in renewed war with Turkey. Winston always got excited at the prospect of a fight; Lloyd George was still pursuing his Gladstonian vision, raging to H.A.L. Fisher, for instance, at the 'cynicism with which the French abandon the Christian population in the Near East';[47] but it is out of character for F.E. to have joined so willingly in either of these enthusiasms. Beaverbrook, a strong critic of the Chanak adventure, found his attitude hard to explain. He fell back on the conclusion that though F.E.'s 'reason told him that the Government was taking the wrong course, his loyalty . . . carried him along. Hard-headed, clear-sighted, free from any profound political faith, he was a team man, dazzled by preferment, and influenced by the mistaken belief that Lloyd George could get the votes.'[48] Maybe he did think that a quick police action would restore the Government's popularity; if so he badly misjudged the public mood. It is possible that he hoped to become Foreign Secretary: Lloyd George had certainly lost all confidence in Curzon, who was in addition a sick man, and F.E. had much enjoyed deputizing for him in the summer.[45] It is far from clear that the Government *was* taking the wrong course: what was shocking was the relish with which senior Ministers seemed to anticipate the risk their action ran. The best explanation is simply that they were seized collectively by that summer madness which so often afflicts tired administrations as their term expires.

Before Chanak, mutterings of rebellion had been confined to the lower ranks of the Ministry. Now they reached the Cabinet itself. Arthur Griffith-Boscawen (Agriculture), Lord Peel (India) and Stanley Baldwin (Board of Trade) were sufficiently alarmed by what they had seen to lend their support openly to the disaffected juniors. More important, Bonar Law signalled his re-emergence by writing a studiously moderate but deadly letter to *The Times* on 7 October urging that Britain could not 'act alone as the policeman of the world'.[49] Two days later Beaverbrook made a last effort to win F.E. back to Law and the old tariff reform programme of imperial preference which he hoped Law would bring in. He found F.E. 'tired . . . weary of politics . . . anxious about the future' yet still adamant that he could not desert Lloyd George and clinging to an optimism as unreal as it was unconvincing.

When I tried to persuade him to break with Lloyd George he would reply confidently that though there would of course be a Tory split the great majority would go with Lloyd George and the Conservative Cabinet Ministers. Then a Centre Party would be formed commanding Lloyd George's funds, followers and the *Daily Chronicle* – the Conservative Party funds and organisation and the immense power of patronage. This would secure a triumphant victory at the coming election.

When I spoke of the horrid shock Chanak had been to the country he waved it aside as an episode which would be overwhelmed in the new controversies springing up out of the reconstruction of Parties . . . Lloyd George had learnt his lesson. He would now apply himself to domestic issues. Thus Birkenhead reached his firm decision to march with Lloyd George. It was a fatal error from which he never made a complete recovery.[50]

Fatal it may have been; but if it was founded partly on a politically disastrous misreading of the party feeling against him, it reflected also a highly creditable sense of personal honour. Both are vividly expressed in a letter from Chamberlain to F.E. written on 12 October, after they had determined to drum the party into line by calling the General Election immediately. The two men were acting now in perfect agreement, as in the Irish negotiation. 'I am not sure that it may not now be necessary', Chamberlain wrote, 'to call a Party meeting and to tell them bluntly that they must either follow our advice or do without us in which case they must find their own Chief and form a Government *at once*. They would be in a d——d fix!' Austen had not yet realized the significance of Bonar Law's re-emergence. Even at this stage, though, the rebels would have been satisfied if only Austen had agreed to replace Lloyd George as Prime Minister.

But I am not willing to hand him such an ultimatum from our Party which would make his remaining impossible, and then to step into his shoes . . . The malcontents assume that they can reject our advice and use us for their own purposes. They make a mistake and it may be well to prove it to them.[51]

The party meeting was called for 19 October, the day after a by-election at which it was hoped that a Labour victory would concentrate minds on the threat the Coalition existed to resist. Though fully supporting Austen's strategy, F.E. was in the last days less confident of success, as he warned Lloyd George and Hankey on the 17th.[52] At a meeting with some of the potential rebels on the 16th he was more conciliatory than previously, telling them that there might well be a change of Prime Minister after the election, though he still insisted that it must be for the leadership to decide.[53] Altogether he became more philosophical as defeat approached. On the evening before the decisive meeting he came to Downing Street late after a dinner engagement. 'He had been speaking at some function', Salvidge (who was present) recorded, 'and was resplendent in full dress and Orders. He looked youthful and handsome.' Salvidge had earlier told the company that he had just seen Bonar Law and learned that he *would* be going to the Carlton Club the next day. He now repeated his story, and the roomful of Ministers waited for F.E.'s opinion. 'He sat with his hands thrust deep into his trousers' pockets and his long legs stuck out. "I have always wanted to make a trip round the world," he said. "I think I've got a thousand pounds. I'll be able to go now. The Coalition will not survive tomorrow."'

Generously and characteristically he felt no bitterness against Law. 'Later he remarked that personal ambition had undoubtedly played some part in Bonar's decision, but it had been less of a factor in Bonar's career than in that of any man he knew, and anyhow it was a perfectly laudable ambition.'[54]

The next morning it was learned that the Newport by-election had been won, not by Labour, but by an anti-Coalition Conservative, which was the last spur the rebels needed to go on. At the Carlton Club only Chamberlain (long-windedly) and Balfour (very briefly) spoke for the continuance of the Coalition: F.E. was present, and had rehearsed 'a short but eloquent speech' a couple of days before, but he never made it.[52] Baldwin made the speech of the meeting, damning Lloyd George as a 'dynamic force' who had destroyed the Liberals and would do the same for the Conservatives if not prevented; other moderate Tories spoke for independence; and Bonar Law, kept to his promise by the assiduous Beaverbrook, added his voice decisively in the same sense.[55] The party voted, against the advice of its leaders, by 187 to 87 to end the Coalition.

Lloyd George technically remained Prime Minister for a few more days, while Law went through the formality of getting himself elected Tory leader in Austen's place; and F.E. retained the Great Seal until 25 October. But the great adventure which had been the Coalition was over. The press was almost unanimously jubilant. It deserves to be noted, however, that amid all the rejoicing the legal journals – so affronted at his appointment – paid unstinting tribute to the passing of a great Lord Chancellor.[56]

The rejected Coalitionists were not cast down by their defeat, but still lived in a fantasy world of self-satisfaction. His colleagues assured

Chamberlain that he had spoken 'admirably', while Austen himself said 'he never heard Bonar make a worse speech'.[57] They remained confident that if they only stuck together they were too formidable a combination for any Government to survive for long without them. They were actually sorry for Bonar Law in the situation he had let himself be manoeuvred into, and looked forward with amusement to seeing his efforts to form an administration of inexperienced Under-Secretaries and Diehards. 'There is one man', Austen consoled himself, 'who is sorrier than I, and that is Bonar Law';[52] while Lloyd George cheerfully rebuffed Hankey's suggestion that he might be back as Prime Minister after the election, 'Oh no, nothing will induce me to let Bonar off. Birkenhead and I are determined to keep him to it. Each of us will hold up an arm until sundown.'[58]

Their anger at this stage was directed against Curzon, who had defected to Law at the last moment, having pledged his senior colleagues a few days before that he was with them. Churchill, in bed with appendicitis, conducted a savage exchange of public recrimination. F.E. held back his bile for over a year; but then he delivered his opinion of the noble Marquess's betrayal in a superbly malicious newspaper article, one of his *Contemporary Personalities*, which concluded, 'Of his association with the most recent political developments, I need add little. He was penultimately loyal to the Coalition, and if, when it deliquesced, he found salvation a little quickly, why so, to be sure, did Balaam.'[59] Little love was lost in this quarter for the rest of Curzon's life.

Though they had lost Curzon, as well as Baldwin, Griffith-Boscawen and Peel of the outgoing Cabinet, Chamberlain and F.E. had retained the loyalty of Balfour, Horne, Worthington-Evans, Crawford (F.E.'s old friend Balcarres, now 27th Earl of Crawford) and Lee, as well as the English Law Officers (Scott and Pollock), the Lord Advocate, one Under-Secretary and two Whips. It was a group of thirteen who met at Chamberlain's house at 6 p.m. and put out a dignified statement expressing their refusal summarily to dismiss a Prime Minister from whom they differed neither on principle nor on policy at a time when the country still needed unity, but nevertheless asserting that they remained 'what we have always been, Conservatives and Unionists'.[60] Lloyd George, flattered by their loyalty, congratulated himself that his Tory colleagues were not really Tories at all: Chamberlain had been brought up as a Liberal, Balfour had become a Gladstonian in his old age, F.E. was a 'democrat'.[61] He should have read their statement with more care. Sincere as was their sense of personal obligation to himself, their political preoccupation was with the Tory split and how to recall their insubordinate followers to their duty. Salvidge was taken by surprise by F.E.'s attitude. He had wanted to return to Liverpool after the Carlton Club vote, but F.E. pressed him to stay another night and breakfast with him on the 20th.

> I rather dreaded this breakfast. I had decided that my rightful course was to make some sort of public statement saying that, though to the very last I opposed the break-up of the Coalition, the decision having been made I would faithfully abide by the wishes of the majority of my party, and that in Liverpool we would close up the ranks and work for the triumphant return to power of the Conservative Party under its accredited leader Bonar Law. But to have to tell Birkenhead of my intention was not a pleasant prospect. He had been treated disgracefully the day before, and had even been 'booed' and insulted as he left the Carlton Club. It would sound as though I were one more rat deserting the sinking ship.

But Salvidge had misjudged his F.E.

> As soon as we sat down to breakfast he surprised me by saying that he considered my position in Liverpool required me to make the very sort of announcement I had in mind! My friendship for him must not deter me from maintaining the traditions of Liverpool Conservatism. Austen Chamberlain had gone and Bonar Law had taken his place. For his own part, [he] would pursue an independent course, but our duty in Liverpool was to support Bonar Law just as loyally as we had supported Austen.

Fortunately, this need not involve opposing the dissenters, one of whom, Leslie Scott, still sat for Liverpool Exchange. While Salvidge was at breakfast with F.E., Scott joined them and there was what Salvidge called 'rather a fine meeting between these two friends'.

> The fall of the Coalition was a big blow to Leslie. He had been six months in office as Solicitor-General after twelve years in the House. If he had given the slightest sign of throwing over his colleagues, he could have secured the Attorney-Generalship in the new Administration. Instead he voted with Austen Chamberlain at the Carlton Club. 'Leslie', said Birkenhead, 'that is the sort of thing a man does not forget. Some day there may be a chance to show that I and others remember it.'[62]

Unhappily for Scott, there was not, and he never held office again. Three days later, at a dinner held in his honour by those Tories loyal

to Chamberlain's leadership – attended by some 150 M.P.s and peers –
F.E. held out a similar promise of future reward for his present sacrifice
to Ernest Pollock.

> Birkenhead took me aside in the dining room and said that he fully
> appreciated the sacrifice we were making, but that the new
> Government was for a short time only, that when the Unionist
> Party came to its own again with its proper leaders [F.E. mentioned
> Balfour, himself and Churchill] my conduct would not be for-
> gotten: and he finished by saying – 'It may well be that you will be
> Master of the Rolls.'[63]

Pollock did in fact become Master of the Rolls just a year later; but at
the invitation not of the Tory party's 'proper' leaders – amongst whom
it was decidedly provocative to number Winston – but of Stanley
Baldwin.

If F.E. had seemed at the end reconciled to the Coalition's fall, and
displayed in private a complacent confidence that he and his friends
would soon be in a position again to dispense patronage to their loyal
followers, his public reaction was a sustained spasm of petulant ill-
temper which conveyed quite the opposite impression. While Lloyd
George and Chamberlain, outwardly at least, took their defeat philosophically and with dignity, F.E. chose to unleash on platforms up and
down the country a series of wild attacks on the pigmies who had dared
unseat the most powerful Government of modern times, which only
confirmed in their relief those who thought they were well rid of it. His
tirades contained some splendid rhetoric: but overall this was another
lamentable and seriously misjudged performance, as damaging in the
public arena as his assault on the junior Ministers had been in private.
He appeared to treat the fall of the Government first as a personal
insult; second, as an act of impertinent insubordination by evident
inferiors; third, as an act of treachery; and only fourth as an act of
political unwisdom. The childishness of this tantrum only exposed him
to ridicule. When he boasted, in a speech in London on 4 November,
that though he had lost the Woolsack he was 'still the captain of my own
soul',[64] the cutting reply quickly spread around the clubs that this was
'a small command of which no-one will wish to deprive him'.

At the Tory Coalitionists' dinner on 23 October Chamberlain, Balfour,
Horne and Worthington-Evans all spoke more in regret than in re-
crimination. F.E. alone struck a note of anger and contempt. The cry of
'Judas' which had been levelled at him at the Carlton Club had stung.
'The charge which history has preferred against Judas', he retorted, 'is
that he abandoned his leader. The charge apparently preferred against

me is that I have resolutely refused to abandon mine.' The idea that he could be driven out of the party he dismissed as 'ludicrous if it were not impertinent'; he was not going to be 'the catspaw and the jackal' of the Diehards. The decision at the Carlton Club was irresponsible folly: the need for continued coalition was as great as in the war, to meet the challenge of Labour. He still hoped to forge a united anti-Socialist party – in the meantime he would speak for anyone, Conservative or Liberal (he specifically mentioned Winston) who held to Coalition principles. After the election the same company should meet again to decide what programme to pursue.[65]

The former Coalitionists kept together during the campaign, with Lloyd George allegedly assisting the Tories who supported him with £50,000 from his fund.[66] On 26 October Lloyd George and F.E. accompanied Worthington-Evans to Colchester, his constituency, to attend the annual Oyster Feast. On the 28th they went north with Horne to speak in Glasgow, before all three (Lloyd George, F.E. and Horne) went on to spend a jolly weekend of mutual congratulation with Balfour at Whittingehame. On 2 November, to the fury of the local Tories, F.E. took Lloyd George's place speaking to a Coalition Liberal meeting in Bristol. He also spoke for the Coalition Liberals McCurdy in Northampton and Frederick Kellaway in Bedford, as well as for Scott and his brother Harold in Liverpool (Harold had transferred from Warrington to the safer Wavertree division.) On the 4th F.E. and Chamberlain spoke together at the Stoll Picture House in London, and on the 9th F.E. went up to Dundee to speak for Churchill, who was convalescing after an operation. Finally on the 11th he joined Austen for a mass meeting in his constituency, West Birmingham. Wherever F.E. went, he made aggressively unrepentant, often downright insulting speeches.

Colchester – in deference to a non-political occasion – was one of his more moderate performances. Aside from praising Lloyd George as the man who won the war, a modern Chatham, and 'incomparably the most distinguished living Englishman' (characteristically ignoring the ex-Prime Minister's proud Welshness!), he contented himself with some mild mockery of the exalted composition of Law's Cabinet, in which five of the six Secretaries of State, in addition to the Lord Chancellor and the Lord President, were peers. As a House of Lords man himself, he declared, he was delighted; but he did not think the Commons would like having so much of its business transacted by Under-Secretaries.[67]

At Glasgow, however, he took the gloves off. He had just been elected Rector of the University (by a large majority over his old rival Simon) for which honour – 'at a dark and anxious moment of my career' – he expressed his gratitude. Then he went on, referring to the fall of the Government:

I dearly valued the illustrious office which I held. I would have been well content if I could have honorably clung to it for one more year, as I still had a task which I think would have been useful in the public service to discharge [presumably the consolidation of the Law of Property Act]. Had I possessed the mental agility of others [laughter], I think today I might have still addressed you, or others [laughter], in the capacity of Lord Chancellor, but nature, which gave me some gifts at my birth, denied me others. I never was quick at seeing which way the cat was going to jump. Others of my late colleagues, more happy and more gifted than I, find themselves at this moment in a more favourable position [laughter]. One case history has especially attracted my admiration. It is that of Sir Arthur Griffith-Boscawen, who was down on a menu to respond to a toast of 'His Majesty's Ministers' before the Carlton Club meeting, and found himself still in a position to reply to the toast. I should be slow to despair of a country which possesses statesmen able to adapt themselves so quickly to the new surroundings. [Laughter and cheers.] And there are others who have minds so open that even at the last moment the light of truth sweeps away the cobwebs of doubt.

He picked out for special mention Leslie Wilson, whose transformation from being Chamberlain's Chief Whip to being his executioner was 'swifter than any known in secular or sacred history since Saul of Tarsus changed his name'.

It was Wilson who had betrayed the Conservative party, he asserted, not himself.

I will never cease to be a Conservative. It is in my blood. I was born one, and I shall die one, and the men do not exist who have the power or the ability to drive me out of it. When I criticise this Government, I do it in the interests of Conservatism itself. With the exception of one or two star turns in the House of Lords – and those rather on the wane – it will be a Cabinet of Under-Secretaries promoted to the great office of State. They cannot do it. The government of this country has never been administered on that basis, and never can be. I do not care what the result of this election is. I do not care whether it gives them a majority or not, but I tell you this, that they will not be found, after any considerable distance of time, addressing themselves to the task, because they have not got the heads between them. [Laughter and cheers.]

Bonar Law, he taunted in another phrase that stuck and rankled, was trying to confront 'first-class problems' with a team of 'second-class brains'.[68]

Law lost no time in seeking the material to rebut this sneer, and immediately instructed one of his secretaries to check the academic qualifications of his Cabinet. The reply was telegraphed to him on 4 November.

> Amery double first fellow All Souls. Barlow first law and Senior Whewell Scholar. Boscawen first classics President Oxford Union. Bridgeman scholar Trinity Cambridge. Cave double first scholar and Hon Fellow St John's Oxford. Curzon fellow All Souls President Oxford Union. Hoare double first classics President Oxford Union. Sanders first law. Wood fellow All Souls.[69]

To F.E., however, this sort of head-counting was beside the point. Whatever their paper qualifications, it must be admitted that most of the promoted Under-Secretaries whom he so despised – the likes of Bridgeman, Sanders, Barlow and Lloyd-Greame – *were* politically speaking a dull lot. The fact that several of them, given their chance by the Carlton Club's 'slice off the top', became the mainstays of the Conservative and National Governments of the next two decades does not disprove his point. What is unattractive about his criticism of these worthy figures is not its lack of justice but of modesty: he was so obviously thinking of himself when he lauded the Coalition's first-class brains.

He returned to this theme of thinly veiled self-congratulation when he spoke at Bristol.

> I am not yet convinced that this country, either in business or in politics, has lost the need for the ablest men who are available. To me it is paradoxical that the case is now gravely put forward that the policy which we who were such failures pursued for four years is still to be pursued by our successors, with the apparent recommendation that hitherto they have been accounted less clever.[70]

England, however, and the Tory party in particular, has never been very impressed by brains for their own sake. 'It is better to have second class brains than second class character', Lord Robert Cecil retorted sharply.[71] And when Lloyd George picked up F.E.'s theme by describing Bonar Law as 'honest to the verge of simplicity', Baldwin skilfully responded that the British public would find this exactly the recommendation they were looking for.[72] F.E.'s tirades rebounded to discredit the claims of intellect. As Margot Asquith acidly remarked, 'Lord Birkenhead's brains appear to have gone to his head.'

As the campaign progressed, F.E. indulged more and more in barbed personalities. Leaving Curzon to Churchill, he concentrated on the lesser fry, the 'cabin boys' of the Conservative party, Wilson and Younger – though he did also, while in Liverpool, have an unedifying public row with Derby which only served to emphasize his isolation, since Lancashire rallied inevitably to Derby and even Harold had to dissociate himself from F.E. in order to hold his seat. Wilson he accused directly of having betrayed his leader's trust.

> If Col. Wilson deludes himself by the belief that Mr Chamberlain holds a more favourable view of his conduct than the rest of the world, he is living in a fool's paradise. Mr Chamberlain is far too proud a man to make public complaint in a matter of personal grievance. But I heard his observation when Col. Wilson rose to exhibit his loyalty to one who was still his chief. Col. Wilson did not. I cannot myself discover that even among Col. Wilson's new allies there is any difference of opinion on the part which he has played.[73]

Wilson had left his insecure former constituency at Reading in order to contest the safe Tory seat – unluckily for him, the seat in which Grosvenor Gardens happened to be situated – of St George's, Westminster. This, however, had been captured at a by-election in 1921 by one of Rothermere's Anti-Waste candidates, J.M.M. Erskine, who declined to stand down. Erskine was by any standard a Diehard and a far more pronounced opponent of the Coalition than Wilson. Nevertheless F.E. publicly backed him in his bitter pursuit of Wilson. 'Although I do not agree with all your views,' he wrote in a published letter to Erskine, 'I strongly advise my neighbours and friends to vote for you. You, at least, have neither fled from a constituency nor abandoned a leader.'[74] (Erskine easily retained the seat. Wilson would have done better to have stuck to Reading.)

As for Younger, F.E. saved his latest characterization of the mutinous 'cabin boy' to the very end of the campaign, when he appeared with Chamberlain at Birmingham, and devoted most of his speech to the chairman's treachery in dealing with Bonar Law before the Carlton Club behind his leader's back. Afterwards Younger had said that he would rather lose six leaders than see a split in the party. This, to F.E., was no way for a party functionary to talk. 'When he talks about getting rid of six leaders, my comment is that since the day that the proverbial bullfrog swelled itself up in rivalry with the bull, no man has ever been in such grave physical danger as Sir George Younger is.' This was another sally which only backfired with double effect against F.E. himself.

F.E. alleged that Younger was now trying to do a deal on Bonar Law's behalf with Asquith. 'Having burnt his boats in one direction, [he] is attempting to see whether there is not a new line of rafts somewhere else. Mr Austen Chamberlain and I do not belong to that class of man.' They too, he claimed, could have switched their allegiance, had they wished; but they were not circus artists who could ride with one foot still on the old horse and the other on the new donkey. They were not the sort of men who would abandon their leader at the bidding of a few mediocrities. Again he dismissed the critics of the Coalition with breathtaking arrogance. 'I have worked for the party for thirty years, and when 140 undistinguished members of the Carlton Club tell me to clear out of the party, I say "Clear out yourselves. I have contributed more to the party than all of you put together." '[75]

Chamberlain, who was doing his best to restrain the rancour of the campaign and avoid unnecessarily widening the breach in the Tory party and between the Tory party and the Coalition Liberals, in the hope of renewed co-operation in the event of a stalemate after the election, can only have been embarrassed by these excesses, which did F.E. incalculable damage. At the same time he evidently felt, inside, much of the bitterness which F.E. was openly expressing. He told his Birmingham constituents that at three critical moments in his career – the House of Lords crisis of 1911, the Irish Treaty and now the Carlton Club crisis – he had been fortunate to have F.E. as his friend: he would rather, he declared in the classic phrase, go tiger-shooting with F.E. than partridge-shooting with others he could think of![75] And it was true that in the last stormy months of the Coalition a lasting friendship had been forged between the two very different personalities; it had taken some time for mutual respect and trust to grow between them, but now that circumstances had thrust them so firmly together, their respective qualities complemented one another admirably. If it often seemed over the next two years that F.E. was a cross which Austen had to bear, a colleague whom he would have done well to disown if he wanted a quick return to party favour, it is to Austen's credit that he never thought of doing so; perhaps to F.E.'s too, for Austen appreciated his qualities too much to desert him. As his biographer has written, 'To have gained the friendship of such a man [as F.E.] was for Austen some compensation for the blows which fate was now dealing him.'[76]

F.E.'s still greater friend, Churchill, was in the wars at this time, too. *Hors de combat* at the time of the Carlton Club meeting, Winston felt just as sore as F.E. at the fall of the Government and particularly at the treachery of Curzon. Still convalescent until the very last days of the campaign, he had to leave the defence of his Dundee constituency largely to his wife and friends. Hard though Clementine fought for him, he was heavily defeated (in a two-member seat) by the Labour candidate and a radical prohibitionist – thus being deprived, as he wrote later, within a few weeks of his appendix, his office and his seat. F.E. naturally went up to Dundee to help him; unfortunately he was seen at his worst, devoting much of his speech to a sarcastic attack on the French origins of the Labour candidate, E.D. Morel, and alleging that in a grave international crisis neither he nor the Communist, Willie Gallagher, would be any use to Dundee because they would be in gaol! Clementine was not amused by F.E.'s performance. 'He was no use at all,' she wrote later. 'He was drunk.'[77]

The election result as a whole was a decisive repudiation of Coalitionism. Almost half the Coalition Liberals shared Churchill's fate, as Lloyd George's party was cut from 120 seats to 62. Labour advanced from 76 to 142, surpassing for the first time both Liberal groups combined, while the Conservatives achieved an overall majority of 75 with 345 seats. There was no need for Bonar Law to seek a renewal of cooperation with any other party; no role for the Coalition Liberal fragment, nor for the rump of Tories who still followed Austen and F.E.; nothing to prevent Bonar Law and his new Cabinet governing for the next five years. Lloyd George, Chamberlain, Churchill and F.E. were all equally down and out.

21

The Wilderness – and the Way Back, 1922–4

The next two years were years of frustration, disappointment and prickly self-justification for the Tory Coalitionists as gradually they came to terms with the fact that, right or wrong, they had lost the battle for the leadership of the party. These were the years in which the pattern of British politics for the next half century was determined: the Lloyd George–Birkenhead centre party, whether conceived of ideal-istically as embodying a real vision of classless unity, or cynically as an anti-Labour ramp, was decisively rejected in favour of an essentially two-party system in which a broad-based and moderate Tory party confronted an immature Labour party that was not proscribed but deliberately educated in the responsibilities of occasional power, while the Liberals were squeezed into irrelevance. Lloyd George, still the most creative politician in British public life, was thrown on to the scrap-heap; his Tory partners had no choice but humbly to make their peace with the new Conservatism and the despised rebels of the Carlton Club who were its leaders. This was the outcome: but 1923 and 1924 were years of exceptional fluidity, during which the former Coalitionists had their chances, before the mould had set, to reassert their influence – first when Baldwin succeeded Bonar Law as Prime Minister, then when he called an impetuous General Election, lost it and let Labour in to form a minority Government. Their attempts to take advantage were vitiated, however, by the same pride which had hastened their downfall in 1922 and defeated by the resolution of Baldwin's followers. Through-out, F.E.'s personal unpopularity, greater than ever after his conduct in the 1922 election, was a large factor in ensuring that renewed coalition, even to deny Labour, was an option the party was not prepared to entertain at any price.

(i) Bonar Law to Baldwin

F.E. and Chamberlain were disappointed by Law's absolute majority, which left them no strategy over the next six months but to try to keep together – mainly by means of large dinners organized by F.E. – a body of Tory Coalitionists still loyal to themselves and wait for the weakness of Law's Government to force the party to accept that they were right and indispensable after all. They kept in touch with Lloyd George, but the debt of honour had been paid, and inexorably he was pulled back towards reunion with the Liberals as they reasserted their Conservatism. Churchill, more isolated than anyone, distanced from the Liberals but unacceptable to the Tories, lay low, writing *The World Crisis*. Balfour, too, withdrew into retirement, writing his Gifford Lectures on theology for Edinburgh University and declining invitations to attend F.E.'s dinners. For two months the Chamberlain group maintained an office and a secretariat headed by John Reith – shortly to become the first Director-General of the B.B.C.; but they were not a party. F.E.'s estimate of fifty friendly M.P.s was certainly an overestimate: nearly half of the eighty-six who had voted with Chamberlain at the Carlton Club had resigned or been defeated, and others had accepted the result. F.E.'s devoted supporters as he, Austen, Horne and Worthington-Evans went into the wilderness were really only three lightweight cronies: Warden Chilcott, Oliver Locker-Lampson and Philip Sassoon.

His best remaining platform was the House of Lords, where he immediately tried to appropriate to himself the position of Leader of the Opposition, to the fury of the Liberal peers: to their frustration, he effectively succeeded. In the short autumn session between the election and Christmas he made himself ubiquitously prominent. He tried to be responsible, treating the new Government's attempts to tackle the problems that had plagued the old with a rueful, if somewhat tart, sympathy; but he could rarely resist getting his own back, now that their roles were reversed, on his severest critic, Salisbury, and he missed no opportunity for satire at the expense of Curzon – who, by his timely change of front, had retained under Law the office he had held from Lloyd George, his beloved Foreign Office.

His serious theme, sounded relentlessly through a score of variations, was always the same: that the Coalition should never have been destroyed. In the debate on the Address on 23 November he argued that a strong Government was needed more than ever to fight, on the one hand, unemployment, on the other, the threat of socialism that would undoubtedly rise if unemployment were not reduced. On the first, he was notably prescient: at a time when the economic orthodoxy held that trade must soon recover of its own accord, he took (like Lloyd George) the gloomy view that the depression would be prolonged and could not be relieved by simple reliance on the market.

Our policy must be adjusted to the certainty that not for two, three or four years, but certainly for ten years, perhaps for more, we shall have to continue making these subventions and shall have to continue all these experiments, most of them objectionable in normal circumstances, which we have attempted in the last four years.

On the second he made the mistake, whether genuinely or disingenuously, of taking Labour's newly socialist programme – written into its constitution in 1918 – at face value. A Labour majority next time, he warned, however small, 'could in six months destroy all the results of six hundred years of commercial activity'. Labour had taken four million votes this time, against five million for the Government and another four million for the divided Liberals. 'Is it not obvious that there is the enemy against whom the efforts of every sane politician ought to have been directed in the past, and must be directed now?' Law's Government alone had not the strength to meet the challenge.[1]

In the intervals between these solemn warnings, however, F.E. continued, in every speech, whether on Ireland, on Palestine, on reparations or House of Lords reform, the petty harassment of Curzon.[2] His usual armoury of sly digs and gibes was harmless enough, wounding only to Curzon's pride: but at the beginning of December he thought he had found a means to discredit Curzon seriously, even to force him to resign. In fact he only made himself ridiculous. Somehow Beaverbrook had acquired and published in the *Sunday Express* on 3 December a letter written the previous February by Gounaris, the then Greek Prime Minister (subsequently executed by the Venizelos Government), appealing to Curzon for British arms and money, without which Greece would be defeated in Asia Minor and her army driven into the sea. For some reason not only F.E. but also Lloyd George, Chamberlain and other leading Coalitionists persuaded themselves that they had never seen this important letter; that Curzon had never circulated it to the Cabinet but had replied on his own initiative telling Gounaris to hold on; and that therefore Curzon could be saddled with the whole responsibility for the Greek *débâcle* which had led to Britain's exposed position in the Chanak crisis.

Curzon was abroad, renegotiating the Treaty settlement with Turkey at Lausanne; but F.E. did not scruple to detonate this bombshell under him in his absence. In the House of Lords on 7 December he read out both Gounaris's letter *and* Curzon's reply (which had not been published in the *Express* but which F.E. had also obtained – by a journalist's error, according to Beaverbrook). Neither he nor Lloyd George, he asserted in an angry scene with Salisbury, had seen this critical correspondence.[3] In the Commons, Lloyd George and Chamberlain confirmed his tale.

Four days later, he had to make an abject retraction. Hankey, ever-efficient, had no difficulty in turning up the relevant file to prove that Gounaris's letter had been printed and circulated to the Cabinet in the normal way; not only that, but F.E. had actually initialled it! Without a leg to stand on, F.E. could only repeat the curious circumstance that neither he nor Lloyd George, Chamberlain, Horne, Worthington-Evans, Lee, Mond or Fisher could any of them remember the letter. His apology, to a full House, was 'somewhat frigidly received'.[4] Apart from the evident malice with which he had attempted to use the episode against Curzon, it actually cast retrospective doubt on his own fitness for office in the previous year. For some eighteen months past, he told the House, he had been 'suffering from a growing and anxious affection of my eyes – now I hope happily arrested' which, for the last eight or nine months, had 'made it quite impossible for me to read myself, except on very rare occasions, any written matter at all, and prevented me for the same period from writing anything in my own handwriting'. A colleague, he explained, presumably Winston, had helped him to go through his boxes.[5] But if this method had been efficient, it was no explanation of his having missed the Gounaris letter, while if it were not, it was no excuse for his having remained in office if he could not discharge his responsibilities. He had put himself in a false position in which every defence told against him.

Curzon, at Lausanne, crowed gleefully at the discomfiture of his enemies. In London, his wife took equal pleasure in publicly 'cutting' F.E. With characteristic nerve, he called upon Lady Curzon in Lady Cunard's box at the opera.

> I heard Maud say hallo to FE so I took great care not to look round. He then leant his two arms on the back of my chair and remained there, in full view of the whole theatre (which was crowded with friends) for the entire act . . . I felt he did the whole thing out of bravado.

Lady Cunard consoled her with the usual explanation that he was 'blind drunk'.[6]

In January 1923, Lloyd George took a well-deserved holiday with his wife and daughter Megan at Algeciras. F.E. and Margaret joined them, with Eleanor (now twenty) and Pam (aged eight). They also took with them Eleanor's friend Alannah Harper, and the Lloyd Georges brought a friend of Megan's, the future Conservative M.P. Thelma Cazalet, so they were quite a gay young party, except that F.E. teased Thelma mercilessly, and in Alannah Harper's recollection cruelly, about her appearance. They went for long walks, climbed local hills and attended a bull fight. Because Lloyd George was President of the R.S.P.C.A. it had to be an especially humane fight in which the bull was not killed; F.E., however, was much more worried for the horses.[7]

Lloyd George reported to Frances Stevenson on the 25th:

> FE has arrived but poor fellow he is not in high spirits. Domesticity depresses him and I am afraid his habits are poisoning even his fine constitution. I am unhappy about him. His youngest kiddie – 'the Lady Pam' – is a terror – utterly spoilt. Eleanor is quiet.[8]

Lord Riddell was also there. The day the Birkenheads arrived, Riddell and F.E. had a long talk over a game of golf, which Riddell recorded.

> He did not seem well, and said his eyes were still very bad. He asked my opinion regarding the political situation and dilated at length on the incapacity and inferiority of the present Government. He thought they would prove so ineffective in the difficult times ahead that the country would soon get tired of them and call for abler men. I said one could never tell, but I thought the country was rather tired of clever men and anxious for a little mediocrity. Also that the machine was a powerful thing and that the chances were that if Bonar's health lasted the Government would carry on for a considerable time.[9]

From Algeciras F.E. went on travelling around the continent with Oliver Locker-Lampson and a new ally, Rothermere – the proprietor, since Northcliffe's death, of the *Daily Mail*. Rothermere had done his bit to destroy the Coalition, but was already intent on destroying Bonar Law as well. F.E., who had furiously denounced the pretensions of the press lords only a few months earlier, was now more than happy to accept his aid. 'FE feels', Locker-Lampson reported to Lloyd George, now back in England, 'that under the circumstances it might be better for us to avoid selecting issues for attacking the Government which would not have Rothermere's full support . . . It would in FE's opinion be a mistake to help the Government out of difficulties created by Rothermere.'[10] There was little left of F.E.'s promises of statesmanlike support for the Government in all its troubles.

Locker-Lampson wired simultaneously to Chamberlain, but Austen's heart was not in F.E.'s policy of assailing the Government at every opportunity. On 2 February, he dined with Arthur Lee and his faithful diarist wife. Austen (Ruth Lee recorded)

> is in entire agreement with A[rthur]'s view as to what the retired members of the late Government should do – i.e. 'go away and play' and let the new Government 'stew in its own juice'. No-one wants to hear anything from the late Government – not even the most God-given wisdom – and their best course is to fade out of public recollection as completely as they can. Austen, however, did suggest to A that he should try to curb Birkenhead in the Lords whilst he (Austen) tried to keep L.G. quiet in the Commons, but he realised that both tasks were pretty nearly hopeless.[11]

One subject which F.E. took up in a big way – with Rothermere's support – on his return to England was the state of the country's air defence. He had discovered that Britain's air-force was roughly a quarter of the size of France's, and with Anglo-French relations deteriorating rapidly as a result of failure to agree over the scale of German reparations – a situation which the change of Government in Britain had not at all improved – F.E. found the imbalance 'a most alarming state of affairs'. He did not blame the Bonar Law administration; he specifically blamed the Coalition for having run down the country's defences after the war while France was doing no such thing. 'It had never occurred to me', he admitted, 'that a nation which owed us immense sums of money would find it possible to construct these enormous armaments.'[12] The fact was that today security rested upon the air force exactly as it had rested before the war upon the fleet; and he called for nothing less than a One-Power Standard to guarantee the country's safety. There was nothing hostile or provocative to the French in taking this view. He was all in favour of the best possible relations with France, but history showed that Britain made a habit of being unprepared for wars – that 'enmities are not unappeasable, and that friendships are not unestrangeable'. Britain could not afford to have an air force smaller than her closest neighbour's.[13] F.E. went on pressing the Government on this question, in speeches in the country as well as in the House of Lords, until Baldwin, shortly after succeeding as Prime Minister, announced a doubling of the rate of aircraft building. It was not quite a One-Power Standard, but F.E. was satisfied.

The day after his first strictures on the Government on this question, F.E. launched a more political attack on another topic on which he was scarcely qualified to criticize – the reform of the House of Lords. The purpose of his attack, however, was entirely mischievous, to get his own back for all Salisbury's nagging at the Coalition to take the matter up. Now that he was in office, he was finding it no easier. F.E. expressed ironic amazement at a statement from Curzon announcing further delay on the question. What had Salisbury and his brother-in-law Selborne to say now, he wondered, who had missed no opportunity for attacking the Coalition for neglecting to create a bulwark against socialism? 'I will not say Lord Salisbury and Lord Selborne were the twin brothers of the movement,' he sneered, 'but they were the Dolly Sisters.'[14] This was yet another of those phrases of F.E.'s that gave particular offence, and was never forgiven: to compare two such ornaments of the aristocracy with a pair of popular entertainers was cheap and gratuitously insulting. Even Margaret told F.E. on this occasion that he had gone too far.[15] In the context of his speech, however, this was merely an opening shot: he went on with a bitter indictment of Salisbury's change of front. To concentrate his attack, he for once left Curzon out of it, even going out of his way to praise his late colleague who with him had suffered Salisbury's criticism.

> When I speak of Lord Curzon, I speak of one by whose side I have fought for many years, with great loyalty, many hard fights . . . But when I see Lord Salisbury sitting by him – Lord Salisbury who for four years pursued us with malignant criticism, who impeached us, not merely with criticism as to whether we were right or wrong in our decisions, but who impeached our morality and who, for four years, impeached the honesty of the Government of which Lord Curzon was a member – then I rejoice at the vicissitudes and the paradoxes of politics.[14]

The weight of F.E.'s irony is needed to give this passage the full effect it had on his hearers in the House of Lords.

At the beginning of March the Coalitionists managed to strike one successful blow against the new Government at the polls. Griffith-Boscawen had lost his seat at Taunton at the General Election, but as one of the few ex-Cabinet Ministers available to Bonar Law had been appointed Minister of Health none the less, while he looked for another seat. After no fewer than seventeen rejections, he secured the nomination at Mitcham. Locker-Lampson and Rothermere, however, encouraged a Chamberlainite to stand against him as an Independent Conservative; the spoiler barely saved his deposit, but he took enough votes from Griffith-Boscawen to let Labour slip ahead of him. F.E. and his friends thus had the vengeful satisfaction of bringing Griffith-Boscawen's career to a rude end. He never found a seat or held office again.

The Government lost another by-election to the Liberals on the same day, and Liverpool Edge Hill to Labour three days later. There were some grounds, at that moment, for thinking that the Coalitionists were right and the Government could not long survive. Horne and Worthington-Evans were both approached to take Griffith-Boscawen's place at the Ministry of Health, but both declined. F.E.'s estimate of Law's health, too, which had so angered Beaverbrook in October, was proving sadly accurate. He could barely speak in the House of Commons; cancer of the throat was diagnosed and made rapid progress. His early resignation was rumoured in the press. The Coalitionists now felt that their moment was coming, and stepped up their offensive another notch. Without them, F.E. thundered in the *Sunday Times* on 22 April, the Conservative party was 'being driven swiftly, surely and tragically to a *débâcle* greater than that of 1906'.

We have observed the Government, which we advised not to grasp the reins of power, pass from discredit to discredit. We have seen it undergo the unspeakable humiliation of losing three Ministers in a week at by-elections carefully selected by a grossly incompetent whip because he believed them to be safe . . . We cannot open a Unionist paper without reading pathetic complaints of the in-efficiency and feebleness of the administration.

Personalities and pique apart, however, what was his alternative? To the incompetent Diehards of the Government F.E. opposed, with an echo of 1913 which now rang terribly hollow, the elusive tradition of Tory Democracy. By denying the working man's right to 'a house with the decent amenity of one small parlour' – was this a belated defence of Addison? – the modern Conservative party only invited Bolshevism. 'What Minister ever visits an industrial constituency,' he demanded, 'charged with a high message to the industrial democracy? . . . Until the managers of the Conservative party have relearnt – if ever they knew it – the message of Disraeli, there will be no salvation for that great and noble party.' They must appeal to the youth of England with patriotism and devotion to the Empire, but also with concern for 'the lives of humble men and humble women'. Younger, F.E. claimed, 'a small and very conceited man', had 'recently advised an undergraduate audience not to embrace a career of politics unless they had independent means.

Is this, in these days, to be the lesson taught to Tory democracy by the party of Disraeli?'[16]

The sentiments are fine, but in 1923 they reverberated from a vanished world. What had sounded progressive before the war now sounded – ten years and a holocaust later – no more than empty rhetoric, and F.E.'s social concern a mere wistful paternalism. Despite his devotion to Coalitionism and the Irish Treaty, it was he who, by his attitude to Labour, appeared the Diehard – not Baldwin and Bonar Law. The Tory working class which he had prided himself on representing – the true, patriotic, English drinking class – no longer existed; or rather it still existed, but now voted Labour – not because it was converted to international socialism, but from simple class solidarity. If the Labour party had been the thoroughgoing socialist party of its constitution and his imagination, there would have been room for F.E. to maintain his logically quite consistent posture of being pro-working class but anti-Labour. But in practice, as Baldwin and the Carlton Club rebels more shrewdly realized, Labour had captured the working-class vote precisely by being as patriotic and anti-Communist as any Tory could wish. The Labour party, under moderate leaders like Clynes and Thomas – not, as F.E. pictured them, the tame front men for the extremists behind, but perfectly representative of a tame party – was a far stronger bulwark against revolution than any 'constitutional' coalition could be. All that the Labour party strove for in practice was a better deal from a controlled capitalism; but it wanted also the dignity of equality, the recognition of its aspiration to a new society – it would not be humiliated any more by F.E.'s ideal of a contented proletariat, treated just well enough to keep it in its place. F.E.'s vision was literal and logical as usual: he knew a classless society to be nonsense and socialism, rigidly applied, to be a tyranny. But by saying so and acting as though the threat of Bolshevism were a real one, he was mistaking style for substance, showing no faith in native British pragmatism, and casting himself gratuitously as a selfish capitalist reactionary and class enemy. Baldwin's social and economic beliefs were no different from his; but he found the language for the post-war world that made him acceptable to Labour voters. It was Baldwin, in fact, who picked up and wore the mantle of Disraeli far more successfully than F.E. could now do. In substance it was as threadbare as it had always been; but it served to cloak the harder aspect of the new Conservatism and enabled its wearer to throw back on F.E., not unfairly, the image of the unreconstructed Diehard.

'Insight, imagination and courage' were what F.E. insisted the Government lacked; but assuming that he and Austen embodied these virtues, they were not ready to come to its aid until the Government had learned its lesson. They thus missed their first opportunity. In April Bonar Law, through Beaverbrook, invited Austen to join the Government as Lord Privy Seal (the post was fortuitously vacant), with a strong hint that he would then be in line for the succession on Law's retirement. Still touchy, however, and offended by the use of Beaverbrook as an intermediary, Chamberlain refused. He was proudly unwilling to appear self-seeking or to seem to abandon F.E., who would still have been utterly unacceptable and almost certainly encouraged him to hold on until the party came back to him on its knees.

For the third time in his career, then, Austen by excessive scrupulousness ruled himself out of the chance of being Prime Minister. 'I do not think', F.E. wrote a few months later, 'that, as a young man, Austen Chamberlain saw visions, or that, as an old man, he will dream dreams. He would . . . be a little more formidable if he did.'[17] Around this time, too, F.E. coined the famous remark with which Chamberlain has been cruelly pinned down for all time, 'Austen always played the game, and always lost it.' If it was now, it was particularly ungrateful, though no less true; for it was to a great extent from consideration of F.E. that Austen declined to become Law's heir.

With Austen out of the reckoning, the King's choice lay – when Law resigned in May – between Baldwin and Curzon: the one an obscure, modest figure with much to be modest about, the other the grandest, proudest patrician in the party, an ex-Viceroy with a long and distinguished career of public service but a disdainful manner and a well-earned reputation for trimming. Of the two, F.E. was at first inclined to favour Baldwin, 'This would be a joke but . . . it might be the best way of teaching the Diehards the lesson which they have apparently not yet learned.'[18] But after trying briefly to get Derby to come forward as a reconciling candidate, the Coalitionists decided instead, despite the recriminations of October, to back Curzon, calculating that if Chamberlain, Horne and Worthington-Evans offered to serve under Curzon but not under Baldwin the King would be bound to choose the leader who could unite the party. It was accepted that F.E. had ruled himself out of any new Government for the moment, but Worthington-Evans, who was the keenest of the Chamberlainites to heal the split at once, argued that the others would be able by taking office at once to prepare 'further opportunities . . . for FE later'.[19] Baldwin's friends had been busy too, however, and they succeeded in convincing the King, through his secretary Stamfordham, that Curzon was for personal reasons impossible to contemplate as Prime Minister, while their man was Bonar Law's natural heir; Balfour underlined his separation from the other Coalitionists by offering the same advice. Thus Curzon was summoned to London to receive his crowning disappointment, and Baldwin became Prime Minister.

Apart from the failure of Worthington-Evans's strategy, Curzon's rejection had a special implication for F.E. The excuse given to spare Curzon's feelings was that with the Labour Opposition unrepresented there, it was no longer possible for a Prime Minister to sit in the House of Lords; though this was not the real reason, the precedent was nevertheless established that a peerage must in modern conditions disqualify its holder from the highest office. What remained of F.E.'s hopes – still higher in his own estimation than in anyone else's – received as serious a setback as Curzon's.

With Baldwin's succession, the next question was whether the Chamberlainites should accept office if they were invited. Baldwin himself was anxious to strengthen his Government if he could do so without antagonizing his personal supporters; but he was immediately faced with Leo Amery and others threatening to resign if Austen were brought in, let alone F.E. Going down the line he tried, as Law had tried, to tempt Horne and Worthington-Evans. Horne refused, from a mixture of personal/business reasons and loyalty to his colleagues, even though he could have had the Exchequer. But Worthington-Evans, to Chamberlain's disgust, jumped eagerly at the paltry office – for a man who had been Secretary of State for War – of Postmaster-General. 'It is now or never,' he argued, having lost faith in F.E.'s confidence that they had only to wait for the Government to collapse of its own incompetence. 'There will be no cry for help later on.'[19] He was right; nevertheless 'worthy reasons' became for some time a polite euphemism for self-seeking infidelity.

Chamberlain himself was insulted to be summoned by Baldwin to Chequers to be offered, not office, but the Paris or Washington embassy, which he had already refused from Law; and further outraged by Baldwin's innocent hope that he might be able to offer him office at some time in the future, to which he replied haughtily that he was not prepared to be treated like a small boy on probation. 'To so good and intimate a friend as yourself,' he wrote to F.E., 'I may say . . . that I have been deeply wounded.'[20] Again it was for F.E.'s sake that he suffered. Alone Austen could probably have had any office he wanted, in spite of Amery: it was F.E. who (as Neville Chamberlain wrote to his sister) was 'positively hated and despised'.[21] But Austen would not desert F.E.

F.E. was touched by Austen's loyalty. In a long letter written (or rather dictated, to spare his eyes) on 1 June he was at pains to insist that he did not want to be the reason for Austen holding back if he wanted to join Baldwin; but he went on to argue again the case for remaining aloof. 'The last 12 months, your friendship has been a very precious thing to me,' he wrote. 'It has been the closest political association which I have ever formed. For deep as my affection has always been for W[inston], various circumstances, easily suspected by you, have prevented our political association from being complete.'

> I am concerned in the first place to relieve your mind absolutely from any anxieties in relation to my position. I am not quite in the helpless position of an ordinary Minister who leaves office for an indefinite period. I am the President in the absence of the Lord Chancellor of the Supreme Appellate Court of the British Empire. This position makes it certain that I shall find a field in which industry and ability will meet with their reward, until political changes offer me an opportunity.
>
> And I am able with my pen without any considerable exertion to rely constantly for two or three years upon an additional income of about £10,000 a year.

The idea that matters of political principle might be affected by questions of personal income F.E. would have treated in others as ground for scandalized censure; but he felt no embarrassment in urging Austen that he should feel free to determine his course by political criteria alone. The course he proposed was undeviating, appealing still to Austen's pride.

> What would be your position if you join this Government? Men, hopelessly inferior to yourself and much younger than yourself, will be in control of the Government. Of your new colleagues some are politically your avowed and bitter enemies. As you sit in Cabinet you can look round and identify those who tried to proscribe you from public life, and the mere fact of your joining may perhaps be regarded as an admission that the decision of the Carlton Club was right and that we were wrong.
>
> I could not, myself, make this admission, because I did not believe it then, and I do not believe it now. It is elementary that before forming a grave decision in politics one should project one's mind into the future with such attempt at prevision as is attainable. I have never changed my opinion that the result of the next election must be unfavourable to the Unionist Party. If I am right in that anticipation, there is, in my opinion, complete vindication of our decision at the critical moment and of the course which we have since consistently pursued.
>
> And we should be in an extraordinarily strong position to resume negotiations with others from whom in existing circumstances

we do not disagree upon any important public questions. The history and influence of the Peelites are worth careful study in the light of our present difficulties.[22]

That F.E. should write at such persuasive length is indication that he felt not quite confident that Austen's obstinacy matched his own. His expressions of friendship – to which Austen responded with equal warmth – bound Austen not to abandon him, however, despite his protestations to the contrary; and he kept up the pressure. 'I cannot see any advantage', he repeated on 11 July, 'in joining inferior men who dislike one and who will presently founder under the weight of their own conceit and incompetence.' He regretted that Austen had found it necessary in a speech at Birmingham to pay a polite tribute to Baldwin 'which I fear I could not share'.[23] In August, before Austen spoke again, he wrote to deter him from giving any further hostages to the enemy.

> I do not of course ask, expect, hope or even think it wise that you should imitate what you will probably regard as my habitually impetuous contributions to the general tranquillity of the situation. But I thought very deeply about them, and they were written not on impulse, but as a result of very careful calculation.
>
> I think Baldwin has gone mad. He simply takes one jump in the dark: looks round; and then takes another. And all around him there are yawning pitfalls in which he might find his own destruction, which would matter little, at any time. What is serious is that he takes our fortunes with him. It is not necessary, unless you wish to do so, that you should go an inch further than your really admirable speech in the House of Commons. But I very much hope that you will restate in the same kind of way and with the same kind of atmosphere your apprehensions.

F.E. still placed his confidence in Rothermere, who, he assured Austen, 'has definitely abandoned – 1, the present crowd; 2, the late crowd; and . . . sees in the future a reconstruction of which you are to be the head. This is also my desire.' In the interests of the country, the party and of Austen himself, 'the present situation should be studied most carefully and its opportunities not thrown away'.[24]

His own 'impetuous contributions' to which he referred were, on the domestic front, to keep on blaming the 'Diehards'' complacent failure to counter the appeal of socialism, and on the foreign, to make maximum capital out of the Government's difficulties with France. Losing patience with the Germans' inability to pay the agreed level of reparations, the French had in January taken the matter into their own hands and invaded the Ruhr to collect what was due to them by force, leaving the new British Government calling helplessly for restraint. On 12 July F.E. waded into the imbroglio with a demand that they confront the French with complete candour, tell them that their action damaged Britain's chances of ever receiving *her* share of reparations, and warn that their persistence in unilateral action put the *entente* in doubt. On 2 August he went further and proposed that Britain should actually withdraw her troops from the army of occupation and her delegates from the Reparations Commission, and let France pursue her mis-guided policy alone.[25] He was immediately rebuked by Curzon and other members of the foreign-policy establishment like Grey for his irresponsible intrusion into matters he did not understand; but he undoubtedly expressed a strong (and familiar) popular sentiment of exasperation with France.

Shortly after this, F.E. took himself out of British politics for a couple of months – 'very reluctantly', he wrote to Austen, 'for I feel that great events may be impending'.[24] But what he did and said while he was away made him more unpopular than ever when he returned.

(ii) 'The Glittering Prizes'

On 17 August F.E. embarked on a second speaking tour of North America. He went this time not in any official capacity but as a private individual, making many fewer speeches. It was indeed predominantly a private trip, visiting friends made on his previous tour – leading lawyers, mainly, with whom he had stayed in 1918 and whom he had very often entertained as Lord Chancellor when they visited England. He took with him Eleanor and a friend of hers, plus his latest secretary, the South African Olympic runner Bevil Rudd, a gentle charmer with a heroic war record whom he characteristically engaged more for his athletic than his secretarial ability. In nine weeks they travelled right across the United States and Canada as far west as Vancouver, ending back in New York where they began. Only the Irish Americans, who had not forgotten F.E.'s last visit, gave him a less than friendly welcome. He was delighted to bring home with him a handbill, pub-lished by the Irish-American League of Detroit, colourfully portraying him – not this time as an enemy of Ireland – but as a threat to American isolationism.

AMERICANS BEWARE!
Keep our Soldier Boys from the European Slaughter House.

GALLOPER SMITH (Lord Birkenhead)
Aid to Lloyd George, England's Arch-Conspirator
Is in Detroit.

This accomplished propagandist seeks the
entanglement of the U.S. with Foreign Powers
in the camouflaged League of Nations –
known as the World Court.

Let England Fight Her Own Battles.[26]

If the speeches which F.E. delivered in America had a direct political purpose, it was indeed to counteract isolationism and persuade the Americans that they must not opt out of their part in the multilateral settlement of the reparations muddle. Lloyd George was at the same moment touring the States on the same informal mission. F.E.'s major speeches, however, were not directly political, but rather philosophical/historical/legal, continuing the sombre reflections on international law and morality which he had first tried out in 1918. The same ideas were to cause a sensation when he repeated them to a British audience soon after his return; but all the ground which he covered in his famous Glasgow Rectorial Address in November was previously mapped out in two speeches in America in August and September, the first to the Institute of Politics at Williamstown, Massachusetts, and the second to the Canadian Bar Association in Montreal.

At Williamstown on 24 August – the day after his arrival in New York – he returned to his criticism of President Wilson's naïveté. Wilson, he declared, came to Europe 'with a noble message of hope; but, unhappily, in the sequel, hope proved to be his principal equipment'. Wilson's dream, for all its courage and unselfishness, could never have been realized even if his health had not broken down. 'For the real truth is that while the whole world requires the encouragement and the light of idealism, the whole world would probably not survive if idealism were given a completely free rein.'

F.E.'s world view was still – despite the war – the purest neo-Darwinism. For nations and individuals alike, self-interest was the one eternal and necessary mainspring of existence. The whole biological experience of billions of years, he maintained – for he rested his case on animal and vegetable experience, as well as human – 'entirely unaffected either by Christianity or by civilisation' – all went to give irresistible backing to this 'simple, illuminating, if cynical, truth'.

Wilson, in his idealistic conception of a League of Nations, had made the mistake of neglecting the national self-interest of the United States, of which he was the trustee; and the American people had rejected his policy, dealing a body-blow to the League. 'His judgement of his own countrymen was wrong, and by the error of that judgement he became, paradoxically enough, the agent of all those post-war developments from which his altruistic mind would most specially have recoiled.'[27] Wilson had appealed to American altruism; and on that ground Americans had – quite reasonably and predictably, in F.E.'s view – repudiated him. F.E.'s purpose, on the contrary, was to urge that it was in America's national self-interest to participate in European affairs and in the League. The *New York Times*, dismissing cries of outrage from Wilson's Secretary of War, commended his speech as 'shrewd and able'.[28]

On 3 September, in his address to the Canadian Bar Association, F.E. considered the state of international law as it attempted to recover from the shock of the Great War. In the years before 1914 – the years when the Hague Conference was sitting – there was widespread optimism that the concept of international law was gaining general acceptance. The 'cruel truth', however, was that 1914–18 had 'very nearly demonstrated the moral bankruptcy of that system which had been laboriously and painfully compiled by the humanitarian and intellectual effort of centuries'. From Grotius onwards the international lawyers had skated over the fundamental fact that the rule of law depends on the existence of superior force to make it effective. More-over, international law allowed the arbitration of war as a last resort, and admitted the plea of 'necessity' as sanctioning war. From Bismarck onwards, the Germans had openly scorned the restraints of such a law, conducting their affairs on the principle that victory justified any expedient. And they were right. Had they won the war, they would have dictated peace terms in Buckingham Palace, and the neutrals would have applauded.

> She would have conquered by the agency of poison gas; by sinking hospital ships; by breaking almost every hitherto observed con-vention of war; by converting the sea into a maelstrom of murder; and by a public deification of the doctrine of dreadfulness.

A German victory would have utterly destroyed the concept of inter-national law.

Unfortunately, however, the Allied victory had not fulfilled the hope that it would restore the supremacy of international law. Germany had been branded with infamy for her use of submarines: yet every Admiralty in the world now reckoned on their use in any future war, whether the League were to declare them legal or illegal. The same went for gas, expanding bullets and every other sort of weapon.

> The truth is that when the nations of the world spring to arms, when the glittering counter of world-dominion is placed at the hazard, all the boasted veneer of our civilisation is swiftly dissipated . . . Does any sane person now believe that, if another war should ever emerge, a nation which sees victory or defeat depending almost upon the throw of a coin, will neglect any instrument of destruction, however devastating, the employment of which promises success and all that success brings?

The history of the League of Nations up to the present, F.E. contended, had – unfortunately – vindicated the pessimism of his speech of January 1918 to the New York Bar Association, for which he had been so heavily criticized. He now tried, unconvincingly, to come up with some more optimistic, or at least positive, conclusion to what was still a gloomy prognosis.

> My conclusions, therefore, though sombre, are, I believe, sensible and cautious. Mankind is a combative animal. The world still holds precious and incalculable prizes for those who have the will to conquer and the manhood to die. Nations will still be found willing to put all to the hazard; men will still be found in those nations willing to die. And so the survival of the fit and the elimination of the unfit will still proceed; and all that we, who call ourselves international lawyers, can hope to do is to carry in hands less puissant the torch of Grotius; and preach to an indifferent world the creed that in the long run violence and illegality do not pay; that, to a nation, the white escutcheon of unsullied morality is as priceless as to an individual; and that the Sermon on the Mount was not the idle chatter of a thoughtless Man.[29]

If he had ended his Glasgow address with a few such hypocritical pieties, it might not have attracted such furious attention. This speech in Montreal presented precisely the same diagnosis of the futility of the peace movement, couched in the very same language: 'the glittering counter of world-dominion', 'precious and incalculable prizes'. There is no logical reason why the permutation he happened to hit on in Glasgow – 'glittering prizes' – should have touched off such a furore, unless it was that the Montreal speech was made to a mature and worldly audience of Canadian barristers, whereas the Glasgow one was addressed to an audience of students – young and therefore (by the sentimental definition of the time) impressionable and idealistic. The cry raised against F.E. was the same allegation levelled against Socrates, that of corrupting the nation's youth with his cynicism. (There is no evidence that the young were as shocked by it as their elders on their behalf: he was carried shoulder-high as usual from the ceremony, and the subsequent row did not deter the students of Aberdeen from electing him their Rector in 1927.)

F.E. had been elected Lord Rector of Glasgow University two days after the fall of the Coalition by an absolute majority over Simon and H.G. Wells. At that date the historic function of this ancient position, which exists in all the Scottish universities – of representing the students on the University Court – had fallen into desuetude, not to be revived until the 1960s. The Rector was a purely honorific figure, his election the excuse for the students to have a bunfight, his duties involving no more than a very occasional visit and an inaugural address. F.E. paid a brief visit to Glasgow during the 1922 election. He now went up again almost as soon as he returned from America to give his Rectorial Address on 7 November 1923, on the very suitable subject of 'Idealism in International Politics'. No one would have imagined that a Lord Rector could do other than pay conventional homage to so self-evident a virtue.

F.E. began by defining what he meant by Idealism. He allowed that there was a bland and unexceptional meaning – 'the spirit which impels an individual or group of individuals to a loftier standard of conduct than that which ordinarily prevails around him or them'. This was of course entirely admirable. The sort of idealism with which he was concerned, however, was that which could be distinguished from an alternative way of looking at political problems – realism. To clarify this definition, F.E. tossed his first provocative squib into his audience.

The pre-eminent idealist, he proposed, was Jesus Christ.

> But it would be unreasonable to suppose that when He admonished him who was assaulted to turn the other cheek to the smiter; or him who was rich to sell all his possessions and give them to the poor, He was laying down standards of conduct which He either expected or desired to see generally adopted. He was, on the contrary, diffusing through the medium of metaphor a sweet and beautiful moral atmosphere for the purification of imperfect manhood. Were an autocrat to issue a ukase within his own dominions ordering all rich men to divest themselves of their possessions in favour of the poor, he would be, assuming morality of purpose, an idealist in the narrower sense, but he would also be an idealist in

that more aggressive and dangerous connotation, with which we are principally concerned.

He went on to repeat his familiar antithesis between idealism and self-interest.

And yet nothing is more apparent than that politically, economically and philosophically the motive of self-interest not only is, but must be, and ought to be, the mainspring of human conduct . . . The experience of thousands, perhaps hundreds of thousands of years, has shown that the desire of self-advancement is the only adequate incentive for the standard of labour and achievement which each individual must be encouraged in the common scheme to afford.

The same, F.E. insisted, applied to nations. Many admirable citizens of every country in the world were attracted in a spirit of vague benevolence to a system of world government and the international rule of law. But these were only idealists in the bland sense.

The Idealist in the sense which concerns us is he who believes that these things are in fact attainable; that we ought to take steps and make exertions, and even sacrifices, in order to attain them. And he would indeed, in most cases, actually shape the policy of his country, and even compromise its interests, because he believes in the prospects which he indicates; and in the sanctity and infallibility of international compacts.

Five years after the Tsar of Russia called into being the Hague Conference, Russia and Japan were at war. 'And continuously thereafter the junta of evil and ambitious men, of whom the Kaiser was alike the mouthpiece and the figurehead, was projecting the stupendous tragedy which has almost, in its reactions, destroyed the civilisation of Europe.' Undeterred, the Idealists seized upon the end of the war to try to establish their new international order. F.E. had only scorn for their temerity.

While I thought, and think, that there was, and still is, a modest area within which the League of Nations may make useful contributions to the harmony of the world; the larger claims made on its behalf always seemed to me to be frankly fantastic. Its framers forgot human nature as absurdly as they neglected history.

'What', he asked, 'in the history of the world has ever happened which afforded foothold for expectations so megalomaniac?' There followed a long historical disquisition to demonstrate that man, from the dawn of time to the present, was by nature 'a combative animal'; yet there were always, in every age, men who sincerely but foolishly believed that there would be no war in their day. 'At this point the idealist degenerates into the pacifist; and it is at this point consequently that he becomes a danger to the community of which he is a citizen.' Recalling his own support for Lord Roberts's call for military readiness, F.E. now graphically accused the Liberal Cabinet of 1910–14.

> Even the robust patriotism of my friend Mr Winston Churchill succumbed for a fugitive moment to the miasma; though the lapse in his case was to be nobly retrieved by the demoniac energy elicited by actual contact with the Admiralty. It was . . . in these years that Idealism became rampant with those in power. Notorious and almost vital facts were everywhere ignored. German editors were entertained by English editors in London; and dilated with fluent eloquence upon the pacific intentions of the Fatherland; English editors in their turn visited Berlin to enjoy, in that martial capital, the same agreeable reassurances. And all the time the armies grew. All the time a mighty instrument was being fashioned in the German fleet. All the time Heligoland frowned more impregnably upon the North Sea. All the time those great military railways, unneeded for peaceful traffic, were debouching upon the defenceless Belgian frontier.

Only Haldane belied his reputed partiality for Germany to make the army ready.

Finally, F.E. asked his audience to consider whether it was even *desirable* that war should be abolished.

> Is the ownership of the world to be stereotyped by perpetual tenure in the hands of those who possess its different territories today? If it is, very strange and undesirable consequences will one day follow. For nations wax and wane, so that a Power competent in one age to govern an empire, perhaps remote, in the general interest of the world, will in another abuse a dominion for which it no longer possesses the necessary degree of vigour. The history of Spain supplies a familiar illustration.

In pursuit of this argument, F.E. made explicit an uncompromisingly Darwinian view of Empire.

The general extrusion of savage races from regions . . . to which they had some considerable legal right, shows that, rightly or wrongly, nations of stronger fibre, confronted by indigenous weaklings [a remarkable way to describe the American Indians!], have always asserted the right of forcible expropriation. No-one (to make the argument short) who has studied the history of the world has ever defended the view that the supreme interest of evolutionary humanity can support a definitive delimitation for all time of the surface of the world.

How but by war were necessary adjustments to be made? One can imagine F.E. here adopting his tone of heaviest irony.

Voluntary cessions of territory have not been frequent in the past; and there seems little reason to suppose that they will become more fashionable in the future. For many thousands of years the emergence of new and martial nations has been gradually marked by violent readjustments of national boundaries. It may of course be that human nature has so completely altered that some new method is discoverable. I confess, however, that none has up to the present occurred to my own mind.

It is perhaps a pity that F.E. did not live to see the voluntary liquidation of the British Empire – though that could be explained by his philosophy as a prudent recognition of a shift in the balance of force, once the 'indigenous weaklings' had access to modern weapons. Doubtless, though, he would have deplored the decline in Britain's – and Europe's – imperial vigour, while considering the loss of Empire for that reason both inevitable and well-deserved.

Before he closed, F.E. made a point of denying that he was in any way advocating war. It might be charged, he foresaw, that he and those who thought as he did 'carry in our veins the virus which coloured the sombre and unmoral genius of Treitschke, and which found popular expression in the mosquito propaganda of von Bernhardi'. But that would be unjust.

We neither hold nor have we preached these doctrines. We diagnose certain diseases. We did not create them. A distinction must surely be drawn between him who calls attention to the risk of conflagration and that other who puts his torch to inflammable material.

That said, he moved to his soon notorious peroration.

The purpose and moral of these general observations may be summarized in a few concluding observations. For as long a time as the records of history have been preserved human societies passed through a ceaseless process of evolution and adjustment. This process has been sometimes pacific; but more often it has resulted from warlike disturbance. The strength of different nations, measured in terms of arms, varies from century to century. The world continues to offer glittering prizes to those who have stout hearts and sharp swords; it is therefore extremely improbable that the experience of future ages will differ in any material respect from that which has happened since the twilight of the human race. It is for us, therefore, who in our history have proved ourselves a martial, rather than a military, people to abstain, as has been our habit, from provocation; but to maintain in our own hand the adequate means for our own protection; and, so equipped, to march with heads erect and bright eyes along the road of our Imperial destiny.[30]

The reaction to F.E.'s words was immediate and sustained. To the new orthodoxy of the soft left, to all the *bien pensants* of the League of Nations Union and other bodies which believed, as a fervent act of faith, that all that was necessary to avert war was to talk peace, and held that great armaments by their very existence were the cause of war, F.E.'s blunt scepticism and reiteration that, on the contrary, the only way to preserve peace was to be prepared for war came as a blasphemous affront. For a decade or more after the Treaty of Versailles, even those who had little belief in the efficacy of the League of Nations found it prudent to pay lip-service to its great potential. Alone among leading statesmen, F.E. expressed his doubts; for his effrontery he was reviled as a warmonger for the rest of his life. For daring to suggest that good intentions might not be enough, he was denounced from pulpits and from pacifist platforms up and down the country, and ostracized even by those in his own party who almost certainly, in their hearts, agreed with him.

It was not, in truth, his pessimism that was so shocking, but his cynicism – the apparent pleasure he took in the expectation of being proved right, his derision of the unworldly who clung pathetically to the hope of peace, his evident admiration for the strong and scorn for weaker nations or individuals who would not fight their corner in the struggle for existence and domination. His message in Glasgow was framed as a warning against facile optimism; but the language he habitually used – the language of combat, valour and virility – ensured, not unfairly, that it was taken as a call to arms. The one thing the peace movement thought the war had buried for ever was the glorification of conflict. To a generation that can see, with hindsight, Hitler and Hirohito hovering over F.E.'s shoulder as he spoke, the realism of his diagnosis seems sadly clear-sighted, incontestable. But the tone of relish still shocks.

Reprinting the speech in his *America Revisited*, F.E. was characteristically truculent in the face of criticism. 'It was stupidly, and ignorantly, assailed principally by Bishops who had studied it in headlines. Strangely enough, it was never criticized upon its weakest side; namely that it contributed little to the volume of ascertained and established truth.'[31] He could console himself that the telling of unwelcome truths is never popular. But he was right about the speech being studied in headlines. For much of the criticism, at the time and increasingly later on, took the phrase 'glittering prizes' entirely out of context. Though in fact he was clearly referring to the rewards to powerful nations of military victory in war, he was widely taken to be urging on the students of Glasgow the personal rewards open to competitive ambition in the battle of life – such as, it was suggested, the Woolsack. For ever after, his career was seen, as it still is, as exemplifying the single-minded pursuit of 'glittering prizes', from cups and scholarships to office, wealth and fame. This was not at all the context in which F.E. coined the phrase.* But he never repudiated the interpretation which was put upon it, for it did quite accurately encapsulate his view of life as the field for legitimate ambition and honourable competition, between individuals as between nations. So long as a man did not betray his friends or his principles or breach the fundamental tenets of morality, he believed quite openly in ambition and despised the cant of those who pretended to be above it – particularly when by professing disinterested self-abnegation they somehow rose to be Prime Minister or Foreign Secretary. He felt only pity for those who did not have the necessary ability to aspire to high achievements, and only contempt for those who, having ability, had not the ambition to make the most of it in competition with all comers. This attitude to 'the great game' F.E. never disguised. It was one which earned him, from the outset of his career, as it did his friend and fellow-adventurer Winston Churchill, a great deal of hostility and mistrust in political circles, where ambition was expected to be worn either with a gentlemanly insouciance or beneath a heavy cloak of moral earnestness or social duty. Whether it earned him quite such opprobrium in the country at large as the prigs at Westminster imagined must be a matter of doubt. Henceforth, however, his critics had the phrase

---

* It has been pointed out that there are earlier instances of the phrase, but it seems clear from his Montreal speech that F.E. was neither plagiarizing nor consciously coining an epigram.

with which to damn him out of his own mouth. 'Glittering prizes' became the mocking cry with which he could be pursued and heckled for the remainder of his life. When his judgments as Lord Chancellor were published in 1924 – an unprecedented event about which questions were asked in Parliament – the Liberal Leslie Hore-Belisha suggested that the Board of Education could have the book distributed in the schools as a 'glittering prize'.[32] And so on. Not that F.E. cared. In his Aberdeen Rectorial Address in 1928 (reprinted, appropriately, as the last item in his posthumous *Speeches*) he returned defiantly to the subject of honourable ambition and 'honest opportunism', flaunting the derided phrase before another student audience. 'Each one of you', he told them, contrasting the happy state of Britain with a Communist society, 'is free to create for himself the career he chooses.'

> There is no office in the State, no prize in professional life, no distinction in commercial enterprise, no achievement of scholarship, which does not lie open to the assault of your talents and application . . . The whole world lies before you; you have no 'chains to lose'. I wish each one of you a full measure of success in your attack on the prizes of life. In your hands too may they prove to be glittering.[33]

This was truly F.E.'s philosophy of life.

One other major speech F.E. made while he was in the United States was not on the question of war and peace, but a comparison of the British and American Constitutions, delivered as an address to the American Bar Association in Minneapolis on 29 August. Much of this was fairly conventional, contrasting the written with the unwritten tradition; but his remarks were informed by the challenge which, in his view, was represented to the British Constitution by the rise of Labour – a theme which was to acquire a sudden and unexpected urgency within weeks of his return to England. F.E. saw in the rigidity of the United States Constitution a valuable barrier against revolution: in the flexibility of the British system a dangerous vulnerability. Ironically, he saw no likelihood of a Labour Government in the immediate future. (But then he assumed that Labour would not be in a position to form a Government until it had won a majority of seats.) He was also – in America, where there was no dividend in electoral scaremongering – unusually sanguine about such a Government's likely character.

> I am myself of opinion that a Labour Government would not, if it were afforded an opportunity, prove to be altogether unconservative. It would be very nervous. It would be very anxious to avoid

the obvious criticism that it was destroying the foundations of commerce and industry.

How right he was! Nevertheless, the possibility of a Labour Government still exposed the gap in the Constitution left by the emasculated House of Lords. It was not, however, the danger posed by Labour that he emphasized, but the fact that under a Labour Government, virtually unrepresented in the Lords, the House would become rapidly obsolete.

Reviewing the history of the 1911 crisis for the benefit of his American audience, F.E. repeated his considered view that the Lords had been mad to throw out the Budget in 1909. The nation, though content that the Upper House should be broadly conservative in the non-party sense, was rightly hostile to the attempt to make one limb of the legislature the tool of a single party.

> A fatal mistake was made when that House compromised so many causes upon which the greatness of the country depended in the cause of that which was described in the cant of the moment as the People's Budget.
>
> All that was operative in that Budget was, and has since proved to be, trash. It has been thrown since, with general approval, upon the political dust-heap. But the House of Lords, under bad advice, reasserting a prerogative which unquestionably survived theoretically, but upon which no wise man should have insisted, brought itself into sharp and fatal collision with a powerful, though fugitive, wave of contemporary opinion.

The result was that

> until the House of Lords be reconstituted or reformed Great Britain is the only country in the world which has at once an uncontrolled constitution and an ineffective second chamber . . . We have a Constitution at the mercy of a momentary gust of parliamentary opinion; and secondly . . . we have no second chamber equipped with the political and constitutional power to resist such a gust.

It was only, F.E. concluded, thanks to the character of the British people that so logically indefensible a system had operated tolerably for ten years; but he saw no prospect that the present Government intended any reform. Time alone would show whether the tight constitutional strait-jacket of the Americans or the untrammelled adaptability of the British was the surer salvation for the future.[34]

(iii) Baldwin's Folly

F.E.'s fear, as he left for America in August, lest the political wheel should take another turn in his absence, proved amply justified. For in October, with little consultation with his Cabinet but largely on his own hunch, Baldwin announced in a speech in Plymouth that he had come to the conclusion that the only remedy for unemployment lay in the imposition of a protective tariff for British industry: accordingly he proposed an early General Election in order to honour Law's pledge that the Government would not introduce a tariff without a special mandate. This was a gamble of extraordinary impetuosity. Though Baldwin himself had been a tariff reformer before the war, and was susceptible to the powerful urgings of Leo Amery and Neville Chamberlain among his closest supporters, the senior echelon in his Cabinet (including Devonshire, Salisbury and Lord Robert Cecil) were still committed Free Traders while the great central body of the Tory party was agnostic, not opposed to Protection on principle but electorally apprehensive of a policy which had been a clear handicap to the party before 1914. To risk Bonar Law's safe majority after only one year, without time for the sort of sustained campaign of public education which would be necessary if the electorate's ingrained hostility to tariffs was ever to be overcome, seemed to many Conservatives – afraid above all of letting in Labour – the height of folly. The motive for Baldwin's apparently uncharacteristic action has been endlessly debated. A real desire to tackle unemployment apart, the simplest explanation is probably the truest: that Baldwin, having become Prime Minister somewhat fortuitously, wished to establish his authority in his own right by securing a majority elected to support himself. It never occurred to him that he might lose. There is evidence, however, that he also believed Lloyd George to be about to return from the United States with a Protectionist programme to reunite the Coalition, and wanted to get in first.[35] This was fantasy, even though Beaverbrook *was* trying to lure Lloyd George in that direction: Lloyd George was a better Free Trader than his opponents gave him credit for. More to the point, Protection did offer Baldwin the chance to drive the former Coalitionists finally apart, by drawing Austen and F.E. back to a cause which, however inopportune they thought it, they could not oppose, while forcing Lloyd George back to Asquith and the Liberals. This, intentional or not, was the effect of Baldwin's coup. On 13 November, when both Lloyd George and F.E. were back in England, the four leading

Coalitionists had a last sentimental reunion, arranged by Beaverbrook, and agreed to go their separate ways — Austen and F.E. to join Baldwin's Government if they were invited, Lloyd George and (temporarily at least) Churchill to rejoin Asquith.[36]

There followed another extraordinary few days of negotiation and manoeuvre, at once delicate and clumsy, between Baldwin, Austen and F.E. on the question whether or not Austen and F.E. should join the Government, and if so whether now or later and in what capacity. Baldwin's position was that he needed Austen back to reunite the party, or indeed to balance the possible loss of Salisbury, Cecil and Devonshire. He did not really want F.E. back, but he recognized that he could not get Austen alone; he also needed F.E. if he were not to lose Derby, who disliked Protection and was prepared to back it in Lancashire only if he had the support of F.E. as his leading local speaker. (They had patched up their earlier quarrel.) Accordingly, when he returned to London from Glasgow after delivering his Rectorial Address, F.E. found a note from Baldwin asking him to come and see him for half an hour the next day (Saturday 10 November).[37]

Coolly F.E. replied that he could not spare the time that morning, and suggested the following week.[38] He was not too busy, however, to see Austen, before going off to spend the weekend with Beaverbrook at Cherkley, where Austen later joined him. Their position was that they were prepared to be wooed, but they agreed to pitch their price high, demanding offices commensurate with their status and an element of imperial preference in the programme. Their intention was not, however, to overbid; they did, after all, believe in the policy (though not in the way Baldwin had gone about it); they were seriously afraid of a Labour victory, and did want to reunite the party; moreover they knew that if Baldwin won without them, they would be in the cold for ever. Their calculation was that by coming in, they could not lose: if Baldwin won the election, they would be all right, while if he lost it they would not be responsible, but well-placed to overthrow him for his stupidity.

When they finally met Baldwin on the Monday morning, therefore, though they stood on their dignity as a former leader and Lord Chancellor, they were anxious to join the Government at once — as Ministers without Portfolio if Baldwin did not feel able to displace any of his existing Ministers before the election. Baldwin seemed to accept this, and they went away with the impression that this solution was agreed.[39]

But the rumour that F.E. might be returning to office provoked a wave of outrage in the party which forced Baldwin to have second thoughts. It was said that M.P.s' wives and the all-important new women voters considered F.E. 'morally intolerable';[40] Mrs Davidson (the wife of Baldwin's close friend and right-hand man, J.C.C. Davidson) thought his inclusion would 'offend all decent people',[41] Lord Robert Cecil that it would 'ruin your Government'.[42] Ronald McNeill (a Diehard Ulsterman, Under-Secretary at the Foreign Office) was more specific: F.E.'s 'proceedings *since* Bonar Law took office have alienated people even more than anything that happened during the election, and his abominable Rectoral Address the other day has put the lid on it . . . He is the reverse of an asset to any party, and I earnestly hope he is not to be considered a leader of ours'.[43] At least two junior Ministers threatened to resign if F.E. were brought in: the Ulster members threatened to refuse the Tory Whip. More seriously, F.E.'s return might be the last straw which would drive Salisbury and the other Free Traders in the Cabinet to resign.

The Irish Treaty; his arrogance and bitter language in 1922; his connections with Lloyd George and Churchill; the 'Glittering Prizes' speech: all these played a part in forming the extraordinary hostility which F.E. aroused in 1923. Yet more damning than anything else was his reputation for personal extravagance, ostentatious pleasure-seeking and – increasingly – for excessive drinking. Baldwin's was a distinctly puritanical Government, with a mission to clean up what Baldwin and his supporters felt was a swamp of corruption, both personal and public, left behind by the Coalition. F.E.'s 'moral reputation' was so bad, Neville Chamberlain wrote in his diary,

> and he has so often & so deeply shocked the moral sense of the country by his drunkenness and loose living that our Govt which rests largely on public confidence in our character would be seriously tarnished by association with such a man.[44]

At a deeper level, Maurice Cowling has written, the new Conservatives feared F.E.'s influence

> because corruption in the rectitude of the governing authority, deliberate affronts to the working classes and the philosophy of self-seeking propagated by Birkenhead would stimulate among the working classes a reciprocal hostility to the ruling classes which they already thought was dangerous.[45]

Baldwin was trying to create an image of public service and avuncular benevolence to which F.E., by his contempt for humbug more than for any tangible offence – no one could ever accuse him of actual corruption nor of a lack of rectitude on the Woolsack – was a rude affront.

Nevertheless Baldwin, backed by Amery and – overcoming his distaste – Neville Chamberlain, was disposed to defy the threat of resignations, until the outcry in the country became too strong. There was a curious shift of roles here, for while Davidson told Baldwin that 'the present 2nd Eleven feel exactly the same as the 2nd XI of last Autumn',[46] Neville now felt as stubbornly as Austen the year before that, the offer to F.E. having been made, there could be no going back 'at the dictation of Under-Secretaries', who must be told firmly to put loyalty above their personal feelings.[44] It was not the Under-Secretaries, however, but the Tory ladies in a fit of respectability – 'The women of England', Amery noted cynically, 'want either political or moral respectability (if they can't get both!)'[41] – who forced Baldwin to the embarrassing necessity of summoning F.E. again to tell him that the party would not stand for his return. F.E. and Austen accordingly withdrew with dignity, though not without managing to imply, in a public exchange of civilities, that a Prime Minister who was not sufficiently the master of his own Cabinet to appoint whom he wanted was a poor creature.[47] The episode only confirmed their low opinion of Baldwin's competence. Meanwhile they were still well placed. Baldwin appeared to have recognized his need to bring them back as soon as he was safely re-elected; while if he were not, the party would then be bound to turn back chastened to its 'proper' leaders, who could not be criticized if they had campaigned loyally in the doomed cause. Confident, F.E. for once behaved admirably. 'With great astuteness', Neville noted, he 'took his rebuff with the utmost good humour and has gone off hand-in-hand with Derby to fight for the party in Lancashire'. It was Austen who was still, in his half-brother's words, '*froissé* and stiff'.[44]

On 20 November, as some balm to his pride, F.E. was the principal guest at a luncheon given in his honour at the Constitutional Club. It had been arranged some time before, to balance the dinners already held for Austen Chamberlain and Balfour, by the Coalitionist group; but in the wake of the at least partial reconciliation that had taken place, it was attended by several members of the Government, notably Lloyd-Greame and Joynson-Hicks, as well as his known supporters of the previous few months. Edward Goulding (now Lord Wargrave) took the chair and made the high claim that 'the great cause of democracy owes more to Lord Birkenhead than to any man I can remember since the days of Disraeli'. Chamberlain, Derby and Balfour paid similarly glowing tributes. F.E., in his reply, used the occasion to declare beyond doubt that he would be throwing his full weight behind the Government in the election – though he still regarded Chamberlain and Balfour as his leaders. He claimed to be indifferent to office.

I would like to make it plain to my friends who have had confidence in me in the past, that I am giving up every night and many afternoons in this election to advocating, as I understand it, the case of the Government. If anybody knows me so little as to suppose that any expectations as to the future have entered into my arrangements, then I shall say they are not among those who completely grasp my outlook upon private or public affairs.

Was he being ironic? F.E. was extraordinarily unconvincing whenever he attempted a conventional pose of elevated humbug. But after this astonishing disavowal, he launched into a full exposition of the case for a tariff which was to be the basis of his campaign over the next two weeks. Fundamentally his arguments were the same as fifteen years before. Like Austen, he objected that he would have preferred Joseph Chamberlain's full programme of a general tariff, food taxes and imperial preference; but his argument had always been the practical one of protecting British industries, rather than the visionary one of binding together the Empire, and so it was now. He presented tariff reform still – as Baldwin was doing – in terms of job protection and reducing unemployment. He contrasted the depressed state of Britain with the relative prosperity of France, Italy and the United States behind their tariff walls, citing one new example. Before the war, Britain used to export motor cars to the States; now, he claimed, the Americans had so built up their own industry that they made as many cars in a week as Britain made in a year. British engineering was as good as American; all that was lacking was the tariff. Just as before the war, Britain was hopelessly handicapped by her one-sided adherence to free imports. 'While no other country in the world has any serious unemployment problem, we throw open to the world our markets, and the whole world denies us its markets . . . Is there any other explanation necessary of our 1,300,000 unemployed?'

The Liberals proposed co-operation between employers and employed. Labour proposed a capital levy on the rich. These remedies were beside the point.

There is no use in co-operating when there is no work to be done. There is no use in imposing capital levies upon a capital which every year dwindles and disappears . . . The problem that awaits the people of this country is to increase the markets within which their goods can find employment and you will never increase those markets until you have enabled our working people on equal terms and our manufacturers on equal terms to deal with the working people and manufacturers of the world.[48]

With that message, F.E. plunged into the fray. It was a short campaign, with only ten days between the close of nominations and polling day on 6 December, and for F.E. it was a whirlwind ten days. Having no constituency of his own to defend, he was free to go where he was needed. He began, on the first Monday of the campaign, with a visit to Ramsay MacDonald's constituency, Aberavon, followed by a speech the same evening in Cardiff. He went on to Leeds on the Wednesday, but thereafter, as predicted, concentrated his efforts in Lancashire – despite Salvidge's grip on Liverpool, the traditional heartland of Free Trade – except for a foray on the Saturday to Newcastle, which may well have been a prior engagement. In Lancashire he spoke first at Ashton-under-Lyne and Oldham; then spent a busy day in Liverpool, speaking at a luncheon, three afternoon meetings and an evening meeting; finally he spent the last three days before polling touring the county with Derby, speaking among other places at Eccles, Bolton, Leigh, Blackpool and Preston, as well as Manchester, where they addressed a mass rally on the Monday. In all, he claimed to have addressed forty-seven meetings.

Throughout, he directed his attack far more at the Liberals than at Labour: the overriding issue of the election was fiscal policy, and it was the Liberals – anachronistically, as he contended – who clung to Free Trade. They were the 'Victorian' party who failed to realize that their 'stale and stupid shibboleths'[49] had been swept away a generation ago; Asquith, Runciman and McKenna had themselves accepted the necessity of selected duties in the war. If they advocated removing them now, Lloyd George and Mond would not let them, for no one was keener than Lloyd George on preventing dumping – F.E. claimed him as really a Protectionist. While ostentatiously refusing to say a word against Lloyd George, he did his best to exacerbate the still tender divisions in the hastily reunited Liberal Party by treating Lloyd George as its true leader. At the same time he went out of his way, as so often, to denigrate Simon. (Earlier in the year, when sitting as a Law Lord in the House of Lords, he had had occasion to rebuke Simon for a lapse of legal etiquette, and did so with extraordinary sharpness.)[50] 'I hope I do not need Sir John Simon to teach me elementary economics,' he now remarked at Newcastle,

> any more than Mr Asquith, the leader whom he then abandoned, needed Sir John Simon, in a vital moment in the history of the Empire, when Sir John Simon gave advice to his countrymen which would have lost the war. I have attached little importance to the opinion on any political subject of Sir John Simon since that day.[51]

Though he spent much energy attacking the Liberals as an irrelevance, it was actually Labour whom he treated as irrelevant in this election. Apart from one or two gibes at the capital levy – which he insisted Labour leaders themselves did not really believe in – he sounded no dire warnings about the threat to the life of the country which he had always said Labour posed: it does not seem to have crossed his mind that Labour was a danger in the present contest. He merely reiterated his old contention that Labour ought, logically, to be on the side of tariffs, not Free Trade. Protection was simply the extension to international trade of the basic principle of trade unionism. Labour's Cobdenite tradition, however, rigidly enforced by the party's economic spokesman, Philip Snowden, closed its ears firmly against F.E.'s argument for another fifty years.

Aside from the tariff debate, F.E.'s campaign had one sub-theme – the defence of his Glasgow Rectorial, which he turned into an attack on the Liberals' unpreparedness for war in 1914. When Asquith joined in the criticism of his speech as 'cynical barbarity', F.E. departed from his customary praise of the former Prime Minister's wartime patriotism and blamed him personally.[52] When the Liberal candidate at Ashton criticized it, F.E. retorted characteristically that he either had not read it or was intellectually incapable of understanding it – probably both![53] More positively, he defended his words before the Liverpool Junior Conservative Club as 'a true conception of Tory policy . . . a sane and sound political and international philosophy'.[54] It was madness, he insisted, to think that there would not always be war; the Tory party had preached preparedness before 1914, and they still preached it in 1923, in the face of the same sentimental folly which had deluded the Liberals. Anxiously as Baldwin and his friends tried to dissociate themselves from F.E.'s warlike views, they could not prevent him still proclaiming them as true Toryism. In the climate of the time, they can have done the Government's cause no good.

One other of F.E.'s speeches is of note – at Liverpool, where he faced critics of the Irish Treaty and defended himself again against the charge of betraying Ulster. He was still happy to be called 'Galloper Smith', he declared, and would shrink from no measures to prevent Ulster being forced under a Dublin Government. But the Treaty guaranteed the integrity of Ulster, while ridding Westminster of eighty Nationalist M.P.s; and it placed the task of putting down Irish disorder where it belonged, on Irish shoulders, instead of leaving it to English boys to get killed. He made no apology for this achievement. He would rather, he insisted, never sit in a Cabinet again than not have signed the Treaty[54] – a clear admission, incidentally, that he did expect and hope to return to office before long.

Whether or not he anticipated the Conservative defeat it is difficult to say. Afterwards he lambasted the inexperience and folly which had led

Baldwin to call an unnecessary and disastrous election, and blamed Curzon, Derby and Salisbury bitterly for their failure to exert their combined authority to prevent it.[55] But that was afterwards, when he saw in Baldwin's defeat the vindication of all that he and Austen had been saying since October 1922. During the election, he foresaw that the Tories would lose some seats, but he took it for granted that in a House of Commons divided three ways the older parties would naturally combine against the common enemy, socialism. Hence his lack of alarm at Labour's likely progress: he anticipated the renewal of Coalition over Baldwin's discredited body. He failed to appreciate that the loss of seats in an election called on their own initiative would be universally held to disqualify the Conservatives, as a party – and not merely Baldwin as leader – from any title to share in the next Government. His simplistic anti-socialism blinded him to the reality of three-party politics and the fact that the Liberals still regarded Labour not as a common enemy at all, still less as a mortal danger to themselves, but as their inexperienced protégé and junior partner.[56]

In the event, the Conservatives lost nearly a hundred seats – 47 to Labour, 42 to the Liberals. They remained comfortably the largest party in the House, with 258 seats, but Labour rose to 191 and the Liberals mustered a deceptively healthy 159. Of the smaller Lancashire towns in which F.E. had spoken, only Blackpool was lost, and that had only been held by a whisker in 1922. But in Manchester the Tories lost six seats, while in Liverpool they lost two, both to the Liberals. One of these casualties was Harold Smith in Wavertree, beaten by a Liberal who had not even stood in 1922. The other was West Derby, which F.E. himself had briefly held in 1918. In West Toxteth Houston held on by only 139 votes, and in Exchange Scott survived (against an Irish Nationalist) by 229. Labour retained Edge Hill, captured at a by-election in March. Thus with T.P. O'Connor still unchallenged in Scotland, Salvidge's proud grip on Liverpool was reduced to no more than seven seats out of eleven. Only Birmingham remained unshaken in its Chamberlainite allegiance.

As soon as the result was clear, F.E. – prompted by Derby, who was sick at the Lancashire *débâcle* – took the lead in trying to prevent it leading to a Labour Government. His idea was that when Baldwin resigned – as it was generally assumed he must do immediately – the King should send for Balfour (as the last Conservative Prime Minister still living), who would decline to take office himself but advise him to send for Austen Chamberlain. On the morning of 11 December, he sent his loyal henchman Oliver Locker-Lampson to Buckingham Palace to put this view urgently before Stamfordham. In the afternoon he and Derby were joined by Austen (who believed he had a promise of support from Asquith) and also by Worthington-Evans and Joynson-Hicks, who agreed to go along with this strategy.[57]

The plan miscarried, however, when Baldwin was persuaded by his anti-Coalition supporters that he need not resign at once, but should remain in office to meet Parliament in the New Year; moreover Balfour at once decided that he was right to do so. As soon as they realized that Balfour would not after all play the role assigned to him, but was putting his influence instead behind Baldwin – not the first time that F.E. had entirely misread Balfour's mind – Derby, Worthington-Evans and Joynson-Hicks swung around with him, leaving F.E. and Austen stranded.

In a letter to F.E., Balfour explained his reasoning. He was still, as strongly as F.E., of the opinion that 'it would be a national disaster if Labour came in now, even for a brief period'. He too took it for granted that Labour must be kept out by some sort of arrangement between the Tories and the Liberals. If Coalition were ruled out, it would have to be either 'something less than Coalition, or Coalition called by some other name'. But he considered that it would be unwise to try to replace Baldwin with Chamberlain in mid-crisis. 'In personal claims, in political experience, in debating power,' he admitted, 'Austen seems to me incomparably superior. But I hope his friends will hesitate before they attempt to change horses while crossing the particular stream which threatens to overwhelm us.' Torn, bitter and divided though it was, he thought the party did not want a change of leader at this moment.[58]

Obliged unwillingly to go along with this judgment, F.E. somewhat adapted Balfour's metaphor and took to arguing that the party should not swop *donkeys* in mid-stream. His other rather heavy joke of the moment was to maintain that the only way to avert further disaster was to go for the women's vote by substituting Lucy Baldwin for her husband.[59]

Balfour misjudged the situation as badly as F.E. He assumed that Asquith, even though he had said he would never lift a finger to support Baldwin whereas he might have supported Chamberlain, would in practice be unable to hold to this refusal 'in the face of a grave national danger', and would agree to Baldwin's continuance in office after all, if he only dropped tariffs from his programme. In fact Baldwin had no more intention of attempting to remain in office than Asquith had of supporting him. Both had decided that a minority Labour Government could do little harm but would serve to educate the party's wild men, whereas the attempt to keep it out would only build up sympathy for Labour and make for a bigger victory later on. With the view that the older parties must not be seen to be rigging the Constitution against Labour, the King emphatically agreed. And thus the die was cast.

F.E.'s 'plot' fell to the ground the moment Baldwin decided to meet Parliament and Asquith let it be known that the Liberals were ready to give conditional support to the experiment of Labour rule. But he still struggled against the inevitable, like a boy desperately crying 'wolf' – seeking to awaken the country to the danger it was courting and urging the capitalist parties that there was yet time to avert it. On 16 December he argued his case in a prominent article in the *Sunday Times*, headlined (with provocative echoes of the French Revolution) 'Socialism and the Public Safety'.

> The most amazing element in the situation is that everyone appears to assume that we must inevitably see a Socialist Government in power in four weeks. It is the most astonishing, the most irrational and the most cowardly assumption which experienced politicians have ever made . . .
>
> There is no reason whatever why the Socialist party should be allowed at this moment to take office. There is on the contrary every reason for repelling it. It represents one-third of the House. It is in a far more conspicuous minority in the country than the Conservative Party. The differences in political views which divide it from both the older parties are immeasurably greater than any which separate those two parties.

Standing for a capital levy and the nationalization of the means of production, distribution and exchange, Labour was 'frankly Socialist', affiliated to international bodies to which it had surrendered some degree of independence, and 'committed to a policy of wholesale bribery which would unquestionably effect the financial ruin of the country'. If placed in office, it would put all its bribes in its first Budget, then go to the country when it was defeated with the prestige of a Government seeking a mandate for its programme. History, F.E. was confident, would never forgive the Conservatives and Liberals if, in this crisis, they failed to come together in some combination or another – either Asquith supporting Baldwin or Baldwin supporting Asquith – to save the nation. 'Socialism must be fought, first, last and all the time. It means one thing; we all mean another.'[60]

F.E. was by no means alone in his alarm. The *Sunday Times* printed alongside his article an editorial endorsing it; Rothermere continued to thunder the same message. Derby and Balfour still argued for co-operation to keep Labour out, and Asquith – as he ironically told the House of Commons, describing the contents of his postbag – found himself 'cajoled, wheedled, almost caressed, taunted, threatened, browbeaten and all but blackmailed to step in as the saviour of society'.[61]

But he stood firm in rejecting these appeals, and when Parliament met on 15 January 1924 for a three-day debate on Baldwin's purely notional King's Speech, it was already known that the Government would be defeated and Labour invited to take its place.

In the Lords, F.E. – speaking now from the Government side of the House, but below the gangway – concentrated his irony on the comfortable figure of Haldane, who was to lend his authority to the new Government as the first Labour Lord Chancellor. Haldane, he taunted, spoke with wonderful vagueness of the benefits of a Labour Government, but he never said whether he was actually a member of the Labour party, or whether he was himself in favour of the nationalization of the means of production, distribution and exchange. Lost in his Einstein and Hegel, F.E. alleged, he never came down to such mundane practical matters. But if Haldane alone actually joined the Government, other Liberals were no less to blame for deciding to place in office a destructive administration, opposed by two-thirds of the electorate. It was a historic responsibility. 'They have sounded', he prophesied, 'the knell and doom of the Liberal Party.' In this at least he was not far wrong.[62]

Whether F.E. really believed in the destructive – or, to put it another way, the socialist – intentions of the Labour party in office is difficult to fathom. He could hardly fail to appreciate the concern of MacDonald, Snowden, Clynes and Thomas to present a responsible and moderate front to the electorate; but he insisted either that this was a deliberate smokescreen thrown up for the purpose of achieving office, behind which extreme measures were being prepared which would be offered in tempting form to the voters once the idea of Labour as a governing party was established; or alternatively that MacDonald and his colleagues would be thrust aside as soon as they had, like Kerensky, served their historic purpose as stool-pigeons for the real revolutionaries now sheltering under their protective wing.

Probably he understood perfectly well the true nature of Labour. At the same time he thought it fair game to attack them by taking more literally than they did themselves the professions of thorough-going socialism which formed the party's platform rhetoric and the cold formulations of its Constitution. F.E. was by training and instinct a debater, and his controversial technique had always been to answer and ridicule his opponents' stated arguments. Labour's real appeal, to a sort of soggy humanitarianism, was too nebulous to offer targets to his habitual method of attack. Socialism was to him an inefficient and tyrannical system based on a philosophy and an understanding of human nature self-evidently fallacious. It was natural to F.E. to attack Labour on the one hand for claiming to believe in it, but on the other, if they failed to implement it, for hypocritical betrayal of their own supposed beliefs. This was precisely the technique he had used against the Liberals before the war, painting them as absurdly dogmatic Cobdenites and then damning them for inconsistency if they in any way modified the application of the dogma. The same technique could be applied with equal argumentative effect – but rather reduced political impact – to the first Labour Government.

During the first six months of 1924, F.E. contributed to the *Sunday Times* a series of short sketches of the leading politicians and public figures of the moment, collected together and published in book form in the autumn under the title *Contemporary Personalities*. F.E.'s model may have been A.G. Gardiner's two collections of political portraits, *Pillars of Society* and *Prophets, Priests and Kings*. His example was followed a decade later by his friend Winston, whose *Great Contemporaries* is the classic of the genre. F.E.'s thirty-two articles have none of Churchill's literary quality. They are – as his prose was increasingly becoming as he wrote for money – ponderous, pompous, clichéd and generally lifeless tributes, punctuated only occasionally by a phrase of somewhat feline criticism, exemplified in the thrust at Curzon quoted earlier. Apart from these few shafts of anger or malice, their interest derives from the fact that they were written during this uncertain period after the defeat of Baldwin and before the political mould of the later 1920s had yet set. The articles are full of a rancorous spirit of vindication, asserting again and again that the failure of the Baldwin Government and the criminal incompetence which had now installed a Labour Government ten years ahead of time had utterly justified Chamberlain, Balfour and F.E. himself in the wise advice which the Carlton Club had chosen to ignore in 1922. They breathe, too, a more generalized resentment at the perennial stupidity of the Conservative party, which F.E. paints, in his recollections of 1903 and 1909–11 as much as of more recent years, as a closed, unimaginative circle of old men pursuing their own narrow interest, promoting all the wrong people and mismanaging the affairs of the country by lack of imaginative vision. The impression, accumulated from a multitude of incidental gibes and sneers throughout the book, is extraordinarily contrary to his platform paeons to the traditions of the great Tory party, and demonstrates that, after the rejection he had suffered in 1922–3, F.E. felt as little love for the party of Baldwin – even though he was now officially reconciled to it – as it did for him.

The essay of most interest here is the one on Ramsay MacDonald, which appeared on 20 January, just two days before MacDonald became Prime Minister. In this F.E. displayed a complete misapprehension of that well-meaning but woolly-minded man which is almost a parody of his wider misunderstanding of the muddled but moderate party he led.

Taking MacDonald from his journalistic background to be an intellectual socialist, he emphasized that he should not be seen as 'a kind of
Labour Whig'.

> Mr Ramsay MacDonald is a Socialist of the Chair – as much of a
> doctrinaire as Robespierre or Cobden, both men ready to apply
> cast-iron doctrines of existence to humanity without any immediate
> regard for questions of life and happiness. That his own Socialism
> is growing a trifle *démodé* is nothing but a new proof of the in-
> variable fate which has always overtaken the gentlemen of the Left
> since the Devil, as the first Radical, discovered that 'in the lowest
> depth a lower deep still gaping to devour me opens wide'. It has
> certainly been a thirty years' march from Sidney Webb to Trotsky;
> and Mr MacDonald has not galloped the whole course swiftly
> enough. But what he would of his own volition like to do to the
> suffering people of this country would, I imagine, be quite suf-
> ficiently startling in itself. Those who think the Leader of the
> Opposition a moderate mistake the temperament of their man.
> His very appointment was the triumph of the intellectual extrem-
> ism of the I.L.P. over the plodding moderation of trades unionism.

It did not occur to F.E. that the Independent Labour Party might
have mistaken their man. He found no reassurance in the fact that
MacDonald had declared himself a 'Constitutionalist'; for under the
unwritten British Constitution, with a House of Commons sovereign in
matters of finance, a revolution could be carried through quite constitutionally. 'Private property could practically be wiped out in a Finance
Bill – if a tax of 100% on such property were certified as a purely
financial measure.' F.E. specifically warned against the danger of not
taking Labour declarations of intent literally. Complacent people, he
warned, told themselves that the socialists did not mean what they said,
that the trade unions themselves owned property, that 'the British
working man would never consent to a policy of pure spoliation' and
thought that no harm could come of casting their parliamentary vote for
their respectable trade union secretary. In fact, he pointed out, Governments were elected on the unpopularity of their predecessors. It only
needed some error of judgment on the part of an incumbent Government.

> Before anyone quite knows what has happened Mr Ramsay
> MacDonald, as a type of convinced intellectual Socialist with a
> tame Labour Party, is in power with an instrument to hand, in the
> Budget, more effective than any method of exactions which could
> be wielded by mediaeval kings.

Nobody, F.E. urged, should be deceived by MacDonald's moderation. 'Flexible as a Parliamentarian, he is dogmatic as a schoolmaster.'

> And if the forces which are opposed to Socialism do not forget their other differences and band themselves together in time, this schoolmaster and secretary may be the new, if paler, Cromwell, who will yet give modern England a taste of what the kingdom of the latter-day saints means to life, property and happiness.[63]

(iv) The First Labour Government

As the Conservatives settled into the unfamiliar role of opposition, there were two outstanding problems to be settled: the unity of the party, and how the party now stood in regard to its rejected tariff policy.

On the first Baldwin – the challenge to his leadership passed – moved with unusual decisiveness to bring Austen and F.E. back into the fold. In opposition more than when the party was in Government, they were too dangerous to be allowed to remain outside as a focus of discontent. He did not like the necessity but as leader he accepted it, and was prepared to override the objections of those who still wanted nothing to do with F.E. To Salisbury he wrote firmly on 25 January:

> The House of Commons members of the late Cabinet are unanimous in their opinion that we must have Austen and Horne on the front bench . . . and that it would be foolish to lose this opportunity of healing the breach. Some of us hate the idea of receiving F.E. in full communion, but if it is Austen and F.E. or no Austen, we feel it must be Austen and F.E. . . . . I hope you will say the same.[64]

Salisbury did not say the same. He wrote back to Baldwin next day:

> F.E. is disreputable and has been hitherto unfriendly to your government. I do not imagine he has got many political principles and most of what he has got are wrong . . . Poor devil, he will probably drink himself to death. What however we have to consider is the effect the quasi-public reception of him may have among the leaders of thought in the democracy. They are panting after ideas which they are afraid may be slipping from them. They have no sympathy whatever with the hard-shelled defence of the Haves against the Have-nots. I think F.E. without ideals and with

his crude attachment to the interests of wealth would lose us more than Austen would gain us.[65]

Lord Robert Cecil wrote as strongly, basing his objection on F.E.'s 'hateful' Glasgow speech and arguing that if Baldwin was going to let Chamberlain dictate his colleagues he might as well resign in his favour right away;[66] while Ormsby-Gore declared that he could not support a leader who invited F.E. to join the Shadow Cabinet.[67] Both predicted certain defeat for the party at the next election if F.E. were taken back. But Baldwin, stiffened by Neville Chamberlain, stood firm. Neville brought Baldwin and Austen together over dinner: for once Baldwin handled Austen's prickly self-esteem with tact, while Austen told him frankly how much notice he should take of Cecil, and cordiality was soon established. Baldwin invited Austen and his friends, including F.E., to attend a Shadow Cabinet meeting two days later and sit on the front bench; and Austen, on his own behalf and on F.E.'s, accepted.[68]

At Baldwin's house in Eaton Square, therefore, on 7 February, the Tory party was formally reunited. Austen, F.E., Balfour and Crawford attended as full and equal members of the Shadow Cabinet: only Horne declined, for business reasons, to come in. Those who had objected were assured that there was 'no immediate question of [F.E.] taking office': he was merely being invited 'as an ex-member of the Cabinet'.[69] No one resigned.

The main business was to decide the party's attitude to Protection, now that the country had once again rejected it. Baldwin sat silent and allowed Austen practically to chair the meeting. 'If any outsider had been in the room,' Derby wrote, 'he would have thought that it was Austen Chamberlain and not Baldwin who was leader of the party.'[70] This did not, however, mean a rearguard fight for tariffs. Joseph Chamberlain's son – both his sons, indeed, for Neville was as chastened as Austen – realized as well as anyone that Protection was in the current climate still a loser for the Tory party. He proposed instead to go back to the limited position which Bonar Law had laid down on taking office, involving selective 'safeguarding' of certain vulnerable industries, but dropping the general tariff. Only Amery argued passionately against what he called 'this feeble position' which, in his contention, would only lose the party what was left of its working-class support. A party which stuck to its principles 'would soon have the country begging it to take office on its own terms'. F.E., however, threw his weight – which was always considerable once he was back in counsel, for all the efforts to exclude him – strongly the other way. 'FE followed', Amery recorded, 'and after some complimentary remarks as to how deeply he had been moved and how his soul agreed with me etc., took the line that there were too many great causes beside protection bound up with our Party which would sink with it.'[71] Just so had he argued in 1912: where tariffs were concerned, F.E. was always a politician first and a crusader second.

Amery was disgusted. But, as he sarcastically noted, 'This noble way of stating that it was essential for the existence of the country that we should be in office at the earliest possible moment greatly appealed to everyone.'[72] At the party meeting four days later at which his leadership was confirmed, Baldwin announced the new, unheroic policy of piece-meal 'safeguarding' and devoted most of his speech to ways in which the Tories should work to counter the appeal of Labour in the constituencies – neither by the aggressive populism of pre-war Unionism, nor by negative anti-socialism, but by broadening the class base of the party and presenting a more sympathetic face to the ordinary man. Thus Baldwin set the tone of the 'New Conservatism' for the remainder of the decade.[73]

In this respect, however, though he had outwardly accepted Baldwin's leadership, F.E. declined to follow his lead. While Baldwin was doing his best over the next few months to play down the note of anti-socialist scaremongering, seeking to defuse the Labour challenge by allowing it to learn from the experience of office and the responsi-bility of being the second party of the State, F.E. continued vigorously to pursue the opposite tack.

One of the most lamentable results of the upheaval over the previous eighteen months, from F.E.'s point of view, had been to cut him off once again from Churchill, who as a convinced free trader had been driven by Baldwin's tariff election back to the Liberals. Fortunately for his future, he was defeated at Leicester, and thus escaped any share of the responsibility of installing the Labour Government; now that the Tories had again forsworn Protection, he was once more free to start con-sidering ways of co-operating with them against the common enemy. More than any other leading politician, Winston shared F.E.'s view that the defeat of socialism was the overriding political priority to which all other differences should be subordinated. For his part, since the Liberals' January folly and his own readmission to the Shadow Cabinet, F.E. recognized that the Centre Party dream was dead: the Tory party, as he declared in speeches at Oxford and elsewhere, now constituted 'the only safe and reliable bulwark' against Labour.[74] He had not yet finally accepted Baldwin; almost certainly he hoped that Austen Chamberlain, by sheer weight of experience, would soon again displace him. Even Neville, a loyal Baldwin supporter since 1922, thought this a natural development. Anticipating, therefore, the recovery by the old Coalitionists of their former dominant position in the party, F.E. was anxious, for both political and personal reasons, to see the lost sheep of 1903 restored with them to what he had always believed was his proper party. (Lloyd George, now in the freedom of opposition turning sharply left, was a different case.) Austen shared F.E.'s hope, and pressed it on Baldwin, who was sympathetic so long as Winston did not try to rush his fences, but was prepared to work his passage back by tactful stages.

Winston recognized the feeling against him in the Tory party and took account of it; but he was impatient to be back in the Commons. His idea was not to court unpopularity in both parties by declaring himself outright a double turncoat, but to maximise his support in both by coming out as an Independent Constitutionalist – a Liberal seeking Conservative support on the dominating issue of the day who would be able, if elected, to lead into alliance with the Tories a breakaway group of like-minded Liberals unhappy at being obliged by Asquith and Lloyd George to support Labour. With this in mind, he tried to get himself, not adopted as Conservative candidate in a by-election that arose in the true-blue Abbey division of Westminster in March, but given a clear run by the Conservatives as an anti-socialist. When the local party refused, however, and adopted the nephew of the late member, Churchill determined – against the advice of Chamberlain but almost certainly with F.E.'s encouragement – to stand anyway as an Independent.

This was not the best way to recommend himself to the Tory managers. Had he given the seat to Labour by splitting the Tory vote, his chance of ever being adopted for another seat would have been set back for years to come. By standing, with an impressive number of Conservative endorsements, he advertised the division that still persisted beneath the surface reconciliation of the party. The old Co-alitionists were prepared to flout the official party to back him: he had an M.P. as his campaign manager in *each* of the wards of the constituency! The opponents of the Coalition were equally determined to keep him out. Baldwin tried to keep the Shadow Cabinet neutral; but when Amery insisted on sending a letter of support to the official candidate, he could not prevent Balfour sending another to Churchill. One of the piquant features of the contest was that so many of the leading figures in the wider struggle lived in the constituency. Austen characteristically kept his head down, but voted quietly for Churchill. F.E. made no bones about supporting Winston. He did not go so far as to speak, but he sent a public message to the chairman of the local Constitutional Association contrasting the rival candidates. 'Mr Nicholson is young, and will have many opportunities of acquiring experience. The necessities of the nation demand acquired experience and proved gifts. Mr Churchill possesses both, Mr Nicholson neither.'[74]

He also, with perfect timing, published in the *Sunday Times* at the beginning of the campaign the essay in his biographical series devoted to his friend. As F.E.'s only written appreciation of Winston, it is worth quoting at greater length than its relevance to the Abbey election alone would justify.

Much of it is conventional and familiar – Lord Randolph's disappointment with Winston's lack of promise at Harrow; the soldier of fortune; the war hero escaping from the Boers. But the portrait of the personal qualities of a beloved friend is strikingly sincere, and the analysis of his political career is not only admiring but provocative – not least, one would imagine, to Winston.

The public image of a man 'reserved, insolent and domineering', F.E. insists, is entirely inaccurate, derived from his lack of small talk and his demeanour as a man of destiny. ('He walks through the Lobbies of the House of Commons with an air appropriate to Napoleon Bonaparte on the morning of the crisis of the 18th Brumaire.')

> Only his friends know him well. And they know that there is no man in public life in England with a heart so warm, with a simplicity so complete, with a loyalty so unswerving and so dependable. He has, indeed, in the intimacy of personal friendship a quality which is almost feminine in its caressing charm. And he has never in all his life failed a friend . . .
>
> There is about him a simplicity which no other public man of the highest distinction possesses . . . He is indeed *anima candidissima*. He is almost the only man whom I have ever known who simply could not speak, or acquiesce in, an untruth in a matter great or small, however convenient it might be.

Politically, F.E. had no doubt that Winston should never have left the Tory party.

> Fundamentally he has always been, of our generation, the most sincere and vivid believer in the stately continuity of English life. Like Disraeli, indeed, he believed that this continuity required a restless humanitarian solicitude in the interests of the humbler classes. But he was like a restive young thoroughbred. He had an extraordinarily thick-witted and clumsy rider [the Tory leadership of 1903], and he jibbed tragically. I suspect, without knowing, that he has always regretted it. If he has true perspective he ought to regret it, because he took a sudden, and it may be an irretrievable, step which placed him out of alignment with his natural allies. And his combative qualities being what they are, it was

quite certain that he would be betrayed more and more into extremes of denunciation and invective which would make the breach between himself and the Tory Party more and more difficult to reconcile.

Paradoxically enough, he has always based himself, as a moral justification for his change of party, upon the Tariff Reform controversy. He has clung to this as a moral *tabula in naufragio*. For the new economic proposals enabled him to leave the Conservative Party with the claim that a wholly novel issue justified his defection. Mr Lloyd George is not in the least a Free Trader; he is an opportunist, as every sane man ought to be; for economics are not a static but a dynamic science, and the whole truth of the dismal business is that any man is a fool who dogmatically proclaims himself to be either a Free Trader or a Protectionist. But Winston Churchill is and has to be a dogmatic Free Trader, because, being in the very essence of himself an honest man, he must cling to an honest justification for a change of Party which I cannot doubt that he has always bitterly regretted.

One would love to know Winston's reaction to this. What did he think of the dizzy advancement which F.E. predicted for him, retrospectively, if only he had stayed where he was?

Who can doubt that he would have succeeded to Arthur Balfour's sceptre? In the Parliament of 1906 he would have entered into his kingdom. His audacity, his Parliamentary *flair*, his amazing industry, would have carried him far beyond any of his rivals; and when the Great War began he would, in my judgement, unquestionably have been the leader of the Unionist Party.

Was F.E. trying to re-write history to still the old envy with which, for six years before the war, he had seen his friend sitting in the Cabinet while he remained stranded in opposition? Or was he deliberately exaggerating to emphasize Winston's credentials for readmission and future leadership in 1924? Whatever he was trying to do, it is impossible to take seriously the suggestion that the Tory party, which regarded F.E. with such mistrust as a pushy young adventurer, would in 1911 have offered its leadership to another adventurer two years younger, even if he was the nephew of a Duke.

F.E. pitched his tribute to Winston's war service equally high. His record at the Admiralty was altogether admirable, even in the respect for which he was most criticized.

His conception of the Dardanelles adventure was daring, brilliant and masterly. If successful, the attack, as he conceived it, would have shortened the war by two years; there would probably have been no Revolution in Russia and no Bolshevism, with all which this would have meant to the civilisation of Europe and to the security of the world . . .

Had he only been supreme with the uncontrolled power of appropriating from the Western front what was necessary – and it was so little – to make the Dardenelles campaign a certain success, he would have been acclaimed today by the whole world as the statesman whose brilliant and intuitive genius won the war.

On his friend's contribution to the post-war Coalition, F.E. only commented, 'I was never able to share the sanguineness with which he surveyed each new attempt to dislodge the Soviet murderers. But, at least, his impulses were sound.' He paid somewhat back-handed tribute to Winston's judgment in these years.

In the Cabinet he was always an arresting, original and eloquent adviser. It was not always necessary, or perhaps wise, to adopt his view, but no Cabinet could afford, and ours never did, to decide against him without giving the deepest consideration to the brilliant argument which rendered it so plausible.

The final paragraphs bring the essay down to the reality of the moment – Winston's latest battle in the Abbey division.

An extreme section of the Conservative Party, to whom, paradoxically enough, he bears no small affinity, has definitely repelled him, with others, from the army which must hold the economic fort, upon which the commercial greatness of this country depends, from those who would subvert it. This is the fight – and this is the only fight – of the future.

With characteristic courage and independence he has chosen his side indifferent to the taunt that no man in English politics can change his party twice. Every fibre of his being is individualist; and in office or out of it – in Parliament or out of it – his sword will be flashing in the struggle which awaits us all. And as I survey the combative qualities of those who, equally with himself, are pledged to march in that crusade, I cannot think of one able to bring more decisive qualities to the issues which will so soon determine the genius of our people and the future of our civilisation.[75]

After an exceedingly lively campaign, which attracted nationwide attention, Churchill lost to the official Conservative, Otho Nicholson, by forty-three votes. He was bitterly disappointed, but this was probably the best possible result he could have attained. He had been saved from the sin of defeating the party machine, yet at the same time he had announced himself as a powerful recruit to the Conservative cause who should not be kept out of a seat for very long. The next stage of his rehabilitation was to speak, under Salvidge's auspices, from a Tory platform in Liverpool in May – an arrangement with which, again, F.E. may have had something to do. There was talk of his being the candidate in a by-election at West Toxteth the same month, but a Liverpool constituency was thought to be ruled out by his Home Rule past – which was just as well, since Labour captured the seat. Later in the summer, however, he was adopted, with the approval of Conservative Central Office, for Epping, in time to be returned safely at the General Election which came suddenly in October.

During 1924 both F.E.'s brothers – one year and four years younger than himself – died. Sidney's death, on 17 March, can only have been a relief to him, as it was a mercy to Sidney himself. The black sheep of the family had been in turn a nuisance, an embarrassment and, after the war, a burden to F.E.; his death, of his wartime injuries in a special hospital at Midhurst, held no intimations of mortality for his brothers. Harold's death, however – of cancer at the age of forty-eight – was a blow which hit F.E. hard.

He became ill in the spring, after losing his seat in the General Election the previous November. He underwent a serious operation in June, from which he was stated in August to be making 'a slow but satisfactory recovery' at his home in Middleton Cheney, five miles from Charlton.[76] On 8 September, however, F.E. wrote sadly to Beaverbrook:

> Harold is dying of cancer. He has just been put under intensive morphia which will probably never be relaxed. But don't put anything in the paper [i.e. the *Daily Express*] in case he regains consciousness for he always reads it.
>
> I have had a *terrible* summer; for I loved him.
>
> I want you to get M. Woods [Beaverbrook's faithful research assistant] to prepare something nice for the paper when the news comes. It will comfort his distracted wife and one day will be read with pleasure by his little boy. I really cannot write it; for I am myself too distraught.[77]

Harold died two days later and was buried at Middleton Cheney. At the beginning of the legal term in October there was a memorial service in Gray's Inn chapel, attended by a full turnout of Law Lords, judges and barristers, but – owing to the General Election then in progress – few politicians.

F.E. was saddened, and perhaps a little guilty, at the extent to which the obituaries described Harold 'as if he were some paler phantom of myself, reflecting my views and my personality, rather than possessing his own'. He attempted to do justice to his brother's individual memory by including, as the final essay of his *Contemporary Personalities*, a tribute to Harold.

> No-one [he wrote] would have ridiculed more mercilessly than my brother Harold, at the time of his death, the idea that in the span of years allotted to him he had made good his claim to be included in a series of contemporary personalities. But something must be conceded to fraternal piety . . . I cannot doubt that, with the maturing and strengthening of great natural parts, he would have risen to eminence in his own profession: and possibly to a position of considerable importance in the world of politics, which he very well understood.

There followed a generous appreciation of the early struggles, of a brother who had not had F.E.'s advantages – who, while F.E. was being educated in company with the cleverest young men in England, 'was running uninformed errands from one broker's office to another'. For ten years Harold had devoted himself to Smith & Sons; he had sat for three years on the Birkenhead Town Council and became chairman of the Birkenhead Working Men's Conservative Association, built up in imitation of Salvidge's organization over the Mersey; he played rugby for Birkenhead Park, and developed his acting talent with the Birkenhead Dramatic Society to the point where Beerbohm Tree urged him to turn professional. In his thirties, at F.E.'s prompting, he broke away and read for the Bar; he was called in 1911, and despite the interruption of the war (during which, after his brief spell with F.E. at the Press Bureau, he served, though unfit for active service, with the Royal Navy Reserve) he was in a position to take silk in 1923. From 1910 to 1922 he had been M.P. for Warrington, then for twelve months for Wavertree.

Yet F.E.'s recital of Harold's career does not dispel the impression that he was indeed a shadow of his famous brother, in whose footsteps it was probably a mistake to follow quite so closely. The independent achievement of his short legal career cannot be gainsaid, but he made no impact at all in Parliament – though he was a good speaker and organizer outside. His knighthood in Lloyd George's 1921 Honours List can only have been due to F.E. Harold does not seem to have aroused in anyone the sort of love which his friends felt for F.E. He had if anything an even sharper tongue than his brother's, without the geniality which softened F.E.'s barbs. It is difficult not to feel that he felt simultaneously aggrandized and diminished by F.E.'s fame, so that he had to strain too hard to assert his own personality and knew that whatever success he had would be put down to F.E.'s influence.

F.E. did his best to make amends. His tribute ends with an improbably heroic account of Harold calmly facing death ('I would have liked to have played a longer hand in the game') which is unfortunately contradicted by the letter to Beaverbrook already quoted; but it concludes handsomely.

> To me it has happened in the short period of six months to stand at the graveside of two dear and strong brothers, both younger than myself. Of my brother Captain Sidney Smith I can say nothing in this place; but I have written this of Harold because it grieves me that such an injustice should be done to his memory as to suppose that he was some faint re-echo of myself. He was, on the contrary, a man who gave strength himself; and had need to derive it from no other. My own life is indefinably weakened by his death. I am a poorer man in virtue of it.[78]

He dedicated his book to Harold's memory, 'upon whose judgement of men and affairs I almost always relied; and whose fidelity and devotion never failed me in the anxieties of my life'.[79]

During this 'terrible summer' of 1924, when Harold was dying, F.E. spoke only rarely in the House of Lords – once on 26 June to deplore the Government's abandonment of the limited measures of imperial preference promised the Dominion premiers by the Baldwin Government; once on 30 June to oppose the return of an old bugbear, local option, in the Bishop of Oxford's Liquor Control Bill; and once on 10 July to support the Government's London Traffic Bill as 'the only measure it has yet introduced which possesses the least mark of utility and common sense'.[80] He made few publicly reported speeches in the country: one to the anti-Prohibition League; one to a Canadian luncheon; another – more important – to a dinner of the Liverpool Conservative Club, in which he made clear his interpretation, as a signatory of the Treaty, of the Irish Boundary question.[81] He still sat, with other ex-Lord Chancellors, as a Law Lord when required; he objected, at enormous length in a letter to *The Times*, to a proposal to change the law on insanity as a plea for the defence;[82] and in July he entertained visiting American and Canadian barristers at Gray's Inn with one of his most eloquent eulogies of the Inn and its most famous son, his hero Francis Bacon.[83]

Up until the end of July there continued to appear in the *Sunday Times* his *Contemporary Personalities*, and these convey the best impression of his political frustration and expectations in these months. The accounts of pre-war controversies and of recent events alike are distorted by angry self-justification, colouring his lofty judgments on his rival protagonists in the great game. It is interesting to notice whom he omits from his gallery of thirty-two — Baldwin, most obviously, but also Simon: the minimum politeness due, on the one hand, to his present leader and, on the other, to his oldest friend, was presumably beyond him. Neither Beaverbrook nor Rothermere is included either: these were uncertain friends, quick to take offence, whose backing he was anxious not to alienate. The later essays were mainly devoted to old friends or adversaries, not of the first rank, but men with whose careers F.E.'s own had been significantly entwined at some point in the past – Leverhulme, Seely, Hewart, Darling, O'Connor. In fragmentary form, these were the closest F.E. ever came to his political memoirs.

Apart from MacDonald, F.E. treated two other Labour leaders – Philip Snowden, now Chancellor of the Exchequer, and Jimmy Thomas, Colonial Secretary. Thomas he described with fulsome admiration as a robust patriotic working-class Tory of exactly the type he most admired, caught up as a trade unionist in a party whose socialist principles he abhorred, and clearly a candidate for recruitment at an early date to any new grouping that eventually emerged to fight them. F.E. explicitly compared Thomas to himself.

> He is an adventurer precisely in the sense in which I am myself willing to be called an adventurer. And the great Disraeli did not disdain the name. Life is, in fact, an adventure, and he who (starting from nothing) fights hard, while conceiving ambitiously, must be an adventurer.[84]

F.E.'s *credo* again.

For Snowden – cold, tight-lipped and puritanical – he felt none of the fellow-feeling he felt for the pleasure-loving Thomas, and so utterly misjudged him, as he had MacDonald. His assessment of the man is admirable, 'honest, visionary, implacable, a theorist in his very inconsistencies, he is a man who has fought a hard battle with life and health and won it'. But he insisted on seeing him not as the cautious upholder of financial rectitude he so obviously was, but as a chilly fanatic – 'Robespierre to Mr Ramsay MacDonald's Danton'. His first Budget, received with ironic delight by the Liberals, embodied the purest Gladstonian orthodoxy without a trace of socialism. But F.E. took this welcome moderation to be only tactical. He believed the Budget to have been based on three considerations.

(1) A sound instinct for finance – which Mr Snowden possesses. (2) The necessity of preserving the Government in office. (3) The determination so to heap up the Social Reform expenditure against the Budget of 1925 that the money clearly could not be found without taxation bordering on confiscation.

Then if the Commons throw out the Budget we shall see again the agitation of 1909 back again in an even more violent form. In such a battle, planned largely by his own mind, the Chancellor of the Exchequer would prove no 'moderate' . . .

It is not . . . inconceivable that he may live most grossly to abuse [his] position. For quick parts and madness are still close allies.[85]

This was one of the wildest travesties F.E. ever produced. There were no grounds whatever for thinking that the Labour Government had any plans for a 'People's Budget' in 1925, and if it had Snowden was the very man who would have vetoed such an idea. The last sentence is a monstrous libel. The whole article suggests that F.E.'s conviction that Labour would soon throw off the mask and reveal its true nature was wearing a little thin. But then in August the Government played into its critics' hands by appearing to do just that, not in its domestic finance, but in foreign policy.

One of MacDonald's first acts had been to accord formal recognition to the Soviet Union. This had passed without great protest: Lloyd George had wanted to do the same at Genoa, and the Bolsheviks were now more incontestably than then the established government of Russia. After six months in office, however, he proposed to go further and set Anglo-Soviet relations on a permanent footing by means of a treaty – or rather two treaties – clearing up the outstanding issues between Britain and the Soviets (Tsarist debts and Bolshevik propaganda) in return for a large development loan to assist the reconstruction of Russian industry. The draft treaties were published on 6 August. At once a storm broke. The Labour party appeared to have revealed for the first time in office its partiality for communism and the Soviet Government. The circumstances in which the treaties had been agreed – with the help of four left-wing M.P.s after the Government had announced that negotiations had broken down – seemed to bear out the charge that in the last resort the 'moderate' Ministers would do the bidding of the extremists and kow-tow to Moscow. The Liberals, including Lloyd George, joined the Tories in a chorus of denunciation. F.E., his predictions confirmed at last, joined the hue and cry. 'When the matter is brought before Parliament,' he announced dramatically in September, at a huge outdoor demonstration near Carlisle, 'I am in a position to tell you quite definitely that no legitimate Parliamentary weapon will remain unused which will enable us to destroy proposals so scandalous and so wicked.'[86] This was unnecessary. The Government was evidently doomed by simple arithmetic.

It gave further ammunition to its critics at the end of September, when it was announced that the Attorney-General had abandoned a prosecution for sedition initiated against the editor of *Workers' Weekly* – one John Campbell – who had called upon soldiers, if ever they were deployed against strikers, to refuse to fire on their fellow workers. At once, political influence was again suspected. The Attorney-General, Sir Patrick Hastings, was accused of allowing the course of justice to be deflected by considerations of party. Now, F.E. alleged in the same speech at Carlisle, the socialists were laying hands on 'the ark and the citadel' of British justice.[86]

This was an issue which F.E., as a former Law Officer himself, could make his own. In a long letter to *The Times* on 2 October, he set out the historic constitutional duty of the Attorney-General to allow no interference by his political colleagues in his administration of the law, which was solely his own responsibility, to be discharged solely on legal criteria. He slid over the possibly questionable case, in his own tenure of the office, of the Casement prosecution, but recalled an incident in 1917 to illustrate his punctilious regard for the proper procedure: the War Cabinet, he said, had actually directed him to prosecute a strike leader under DORA, but he had refused to consider it until the unconstitutional instruction had been excised from the minutes. He then asked no fewer than fifteen detailed questions about Hastings's conduct of the Campbell case. 'My hand may have lost its cunning in the framing of interrogatories,' he purred, '(for it is a long time since I have been so engaged) but I suspect that a candid answer to the following questions would supply valuable illumination in a murky atmosphere.'[87]

Hastings refused to answer F.E.'s questions, saying that F.E. would not expect him to answer except in the House of Commons; F.E. replied that he had had his questions down in the House of Lords for ten days without satisfaction, which was why he had written to *The Times*.[88] Tom Jones's diary reveals the Law Officers trying to retaliate by impeaching F.E.'s record. 'About 6 o'clock Patrick Hastings' secretary rang up. Could we find the Minutes of the Ministry of Munitions for May 1920 as it was believed they would reveal material incriminating F.E. Smith.'[89] Presumably Jones could not, or they did not; but the Solicitor-General, Sir Henry Slesser, pressed the allegation that F.E. had in 1917 abandoned a sedition prosecution under DORA in similar circumstances to the Campbell case. F.E.'s answer was emphatic: the circumstances were not similar at all – he had dropped the prosecution of six strikers only on the promise, extracted under dire threat, of good behaviour in the future.

> I was dealing with accused men who were repentant; He [Hastings] was dealing with one who defied him at the moment when he branded him with sedition; and has continued to defy and ridicule him ever since the prosecution was abandoned. No pressure of any colleague was allowed to influence me in my decision which was based solely on my own private conception of the public interest. With no colleague great or small did I ever discuss whether or not I should abandon the prosecution. Nor would I have permitted any political colleague even to enter upon such a discussion with me. Can the Attorney-General say as much?

Having vindicated himself – and incidentally, perhaps, advertised his claim to return to the Woolsack after the expected Conservative victory – F.E.'s wider concern was to use the Campbell scandal to press once again his argument that the old parties must unite to fight socialism.

> I have, Sir, in conclusion, only a word to add. We are dealing, as I understand the facts, with a case in which the left wing of Socialism has been allowed to deflect the arm of justice. We are being treated to menaces as to what will happen if we expel from office a minority Government which ought never to have been allowed to occupy it. Let us treat these menaces with contempt. Even today the Government is the Government of the minority; and had sensible arrangements been made at the last election amongst those who equally detest its principle and its practice it would have been almost a contemptible minority. Let us at least see to it that in the critical struggle which awaits us cut-throat contests are avoided in the constituencies between men who are in fundamental agreement, with the result of handing over constituencies to minority Socialists. Over that road broods suicide; but if we avoid this form of folly there is not the slightest reason why we should not get rid of the nightmare of the last twelve months and begin the new year with a stable and durable Government.[88]

He had made much the same appeal ten days earlier at Carlisle. He had given up blaming the Liberals for having supported Labour in office: he was now trying to woo them.

> Let us on our part make it as easy and as honourable for them to associate with us as any act or word of ours can make it. Do not let us demand that they shall come to us on humiliating terms, making public recantation of things in which they have long believed and which very often resolve themselves into phrases rather than realities when you analyze them.

He proposed Churchill's idea, that Liberals could work with the Conservatives without abandoning their name: no one liked to change his label. 'There is room in the army to which we belong for another wing.' He urged the electors, if faced with a three-cornered contest, to vote for the Liberal or the Conservative according to which had the better chance of beating Labour. The old parties *must* co-operate.

> If we are guilty at a moment so grave of the wickedness and madness of quarrelling among ourselves, we shall have ourselves to blame for the disaster that is certain to come. Whether you have called yourselves Liberals or Conservatives, look at the world in future through wider spectacles, distinguish the false from the real, find out the real enemy, and never be content as a party or a combination of parties until that enemy is destroyed and his madness and badness extirpated.[86]

To a great extent F.E.'s advice was followed in the General Election which MacDonald announced on 7 October, after the Tories and Liberals had voted together for an inquiry into the Campbell prosecution. Partly because of lack of money due to internal quarrels over the Lloyd George fund, the Liberals put up only 340 candidates, giving the Conservatives a clear run in many constituencies where they had been opposed in 1923; in some places – such as Asquith's seat at Paisley – the Tories gave the Liberal a clear run. For the first time the Liberals were seen to be irrelevant to the essential contest of the election: the next Government would be either Conservative or Labour. For the first time the Conservative machine turned its whole attack on Labour.

The result was an exceptionally dirty campaign, in which F.E. joined with crude relish. He spoke up and down the country from Portsmouth to Aberdeen, taking in Horne's constituency in Glasgow; Brentford to speak for Joynson-Hicks; and Epping to champion Churchill's return to the Conservative fold. In *The Times* at least, his speeches were more fully reported than any except those of Baldwin, MacDonald and Asquith.

Predictably he banged away wherever he went at the two easy targets which the Government had offered up: the Russian treaties '"No money for murderers" should be our motto')[90] and the Campbell case ('The whole course of English justice has been deflected and prostituted for political reasons').[91] 'I was never the Prime Minister's Attorney-General,' he avowed in Glasgow; 'I was the King's Attorney-General.'[92] More widely, he mocked the philosophic basis of socialism as contrary to human nature, reliant on the poisonous doctrine of class hatred, inherently bureaucratic and inefficient in practice. It had been a hollow fraud, he alleged, for Labour to claim that they had any remedy for unemployment; the only remedies for unemployment were the return of a Tory Government to restore business confidence and reduce the burdens on manufacturers, and for the workers to work as hard as their overseas competitors. He struck a more personal note, however, in a refrain of savage criticism of MacDonald. First he accused him of 'whimpering and whining' about his opponents[90] – when no Prime Minister had ever been treated so indulgently: MacDonald's 'shifty evasiveness' was unparalleled in F.E.'s political experience.[93] To this he added repeated sneers at MacDonald's unpatriotic – in F.E.'s language, cowardly – opposition to the war which unfitted him to speak for the British Empire, and gibes at his acceptance of a car from the chairman of McVities. 'Dress yourself in your red flag or your yellow flag,' he told MacDonald in his speech for Churchill at Epping. 'Go and attend your board meetings in the McVitie Company. We do not believe in you for this reason – that every speech you make contains some piece of shifty, tricky inventiveness which we have never been used to from the Prime Minister of England.'[94] The next day at Liverpool, MacDonald had become 'the man who vies with Roger Casement in disservice to Britain.'[91]

Neither 'the breezy, expletive personality of Mr Thomas', nor 'the tepid and extremely incompetent personality of Mr Clynes' were at issue in this election, F.E. insisted;[94] not even Sidney Webb, 'the dullest pedant who ever wrote unreadable collections of statistics'.[92] He was not concerned with Haldane, Chelmsford and Parmoor, 'the kid-glove Kerenskys of the movement',[91] but with MacDonald himself and the 'extremist gang'[93] which rode on his back – the Clydesiders (John Wheatley, Jimmy Maxton and so on) and George Lansbury, whom he picked out as 'the admired, the almost subsidised friend of the Soviets'.[91] (The 'almost' was a rare qualification.) Even before the notorious Zinoviev Letter was tossed into the arena by forgers at Conservative Central Office as the *coup de grâce*, F.E. was loudly proclaiming 'Britain for the British, not Britain for the Bolshevists'.[95]

Like every Conservative speaker, F.E. took the authenticity of the letter for granted and fell on it with glee as proving the Labour Government's connivance with Soviet subversion and the fraudulence of the proposed Treaties, which were supposed to put an end to Soviet-subsidized propaganda. It was 'a detestable and treasonable document', he declared at Brentford. Yet the Government 'proposed to lend £40 million to this greatest collective gang of murderers that has never been hanged. I do not think the people of this country will allow it to be made an annexe of Moscow.'[96] Additionally, the confusion about when MacDonald had first received the letter and why he had kept quiet about it until the *Daily Mail* had published it, was another example of MacDonald's characteristic evasiveness. The day before polling, on 28 October at Portsmouth, F.E. pulled together the threads of his whole indictment on the Labour Government in a last personal attack on the Prime Minister.

> Ever since he became Prime Minister, I charge Mr MacDonald with this, that under a mask of moderation, which he is only just beginning to lay aside, he has been in open sympathy with the Russian cause and under the influence of extremists of his own party, most of whom are the tools, whether paid or unpaid, of the Soviet murderers.[97]

Labour was already a minority Government, the Tories already the largest party. Faced with this sort of red scaremongering, to which the Zinoviev Letter gave just the necessary touch of plausibility, plus the Liberal–Conservative pact and the withdrawal of the Liberal candidate in 200 constituencies, the Government had no chance of survival. A Conservative landslide was a practical certainty, and it duly occurred. Labour's aggregate vote and share of the poll actually increased, as the Liberals declined: Labour supporters were not shaken out of their allegiance, but the electorate was polarized, with just the sort of rallying of anti-socialists to the Tories that F.E. had called for. Labour's 193 seats were cut to 151; the Liberal's 158 quartered to only 40; the Conservatives (with various anti-Socialists, 'Constitutionalists' and other hybrid allies of whom Churchill was only the most prominent) won 419. Just a year after his disastrous short-term miscalculation in calling the 1923 election, Baldwin was returned in triumph as Prime Minister at the head of the first independent, united Conservative majority Government since 1905.

'The triumph is stupendous,' F.E. wrote to Sir Robert Houston, who had had to stand down through ill health (he died in 1926).

> If we do not miss our opportunities, we have a chance of rendering the greatest service which the Conservative Party has ever rendered

to the nation. By stable, orderly and resolute government, combining economy with the sympathetic consideration of real grievances, we may at last get over the difficulties and bitterness of the war . . .

The temper of the new elements in the House of Commons is by no means diehard [by 'diehard' he meant Baldwinian] and I think the overwhelming majority is determined that the ablest possible Government should be formed, quite irrespective of the old bitterness.[98]

He therefore confidently expected office.

PART FOUR

1924–1930

22

Cabinet Minister Again: The Indian Summer of Lord Birkenhead

Baldwin's problem, when he came to compose his Cabinet, was an embarrassment of pressing claims to high office. He had somehow to find suitable positions for the returning Chamberlainites, without disappointing those who had stood by him in 1923. Austen himself was relatively easy: he went to the Foreign Office, while Curzon, with only a few months to live, was shuffled off to be Lord President of the Council. F.E. was much harder to place. There was still a strong feeling in the party against bringing him back at all. Baldwin resisted this: F.E. had accepted his leadership with outward loyalty since he had returned to the Shadow Cabinet in February. When *The People* in May published an indiscreet interview in which Baldwin was quoted as deeply distrustful of F.E. intriguing against him, F.E. accepted Baldwin's public denial with a good grace.[1] Since then he had played a prominent part in the election. The difficulty was, however, that Baldwin did not want to displace Cave, who had been Lord Chancellor in 1922–3, to allow F.E. to return to the Woolsack; yet no ex-Lord Chancellor had stepped down to hold a lesser Cabinet post since 1784. F.E. had to be offered a job consistent with his dignity, yet for party reasons it could not be anything too important. If F.E. had insisted, with Austen's support, on the Woolsack or nothing, Baldwin would have had a serious problem. Fortunately F.E. did not insist. He had had his fill of the Woolsack; he had made his mark there and might not be able to repeat his success; the prospect of submitting again to its long hours and formal dress bored him; and he appreciated Baldwin's dilemma. He suggested that he become Lord Privy Seal. There was talk, too, of making him Colonial Secretary or First Lord of the Admiralty. (Amery suggested that he would enjoy the yachting and salutes.)[2] It was Tom Jones who proposed to Baldwin that F.E. should take the India Office. Baldwin had been thinking of giving that to Churchill, but Jones was horrified:

> For heaven's sake do not do that. I have seen him lose his head at critical moments in the Irish business, and but for L.G.'s intervention one would have had bloodshed on the Border more than once . . . I would put Birkenhead in India. He has better judgement than Winston, and it will keep him pretty well occupied.[3]

India suited F.E. very well. Ironically, only a few months earlier he had described it, in his *Contemporary Personalities* essay on Austen Chamberlain, as 'a thankless post, offering in the circumstances of the time [that is, in 1915 when Austen had taken it] no outlet for ambition, and grave risk of personal discredit'.[4] But in 1924 the risk was less, and F.E.'s ambition – now that the highest office was clearly beyond his reach – was much reduced. Though he had never been there, or showed any special interest in the sub-continent, India was a grand enough office for an ex-Lord Chancellor. There was a fine imperial glamour to it; he would have nominal charge of the government of some 270 million souls, while at the same time the Viceroy was responsible for the actual administration of the country on the spot. It would not in practice keep him especially well occupied at all. The job of Secretary of State for India was one of the lightest in the Cabinet: his essential function was to act as the communicating link between the Viceroy and the Cabinet. Moreover – another agreeable factor – the Viceroy at present was his old friend Rufus Isaacs, now Lord Reading. F.E. accepted the India Office with gratitude, as Baldwin told Jones.

> Birkenhead, too, was pleased. He said he had a sharp tongue and had said bitter things about me. He hoped that was past. He would help all he could, and if any action of his hurt me in future, he hoped I would tell him so, have it out, and be done with it.[5]

Churchill's was the appointment which took the Tory party's breath away. As a returning renegade, Winston had not been certain of receiving office at all, and was ready to decline anything unworthy of his great experience. But when Neville Chamberlain did not want the Exchequer, preferring to go back to the Ministry of Health, Baldwin was reluctant to give it to Horne, who had refused it in 1923, and offered it out of the blue to Churchill, on the calculation that more than any other position it would tie him firmly to the Tory party and its leader, if only out of a sense of gratitude, and block any backsliding towards Lloyd George. One would expect F.E. to have been delighted for his friend. Austen, however, was alarmed at the likely shock to the party and (loyal to the colleagues who had stayed loyal to him) annoyed that Baldwin had passed over Horne. 'Beloved,' he wrote to his wife, 'SB is mad! FE is as much disturbed as I am & feels that W's appointment in place of H will rouse great antagonism & is not good for W.'[6] Was F.E. perhaps just a little jealous of the speed and extent of Winston's rehabilitation, after all the fuss made about himself and Austen? If so, the feeling was only momentary. By 3 January he was writing to Reading, 'What an extraordinarily clever thing Winston did in diving from the springboard into a cold and apparently rough sea . . . His career is well in the ascendant and it would not be very easy to assign an end to it.'[7] Austen might continue to resent Horne's exclusion, but Baldwin had in fact done the old Coalitionists proud, without seriously offending the rest of the party, in what was recognized as an extremely skilful exercise in Cabinet making. Only Amery, the arch-Protectionist who alone did not accept the verdict of 1923, was really angry at Churchill's appointment, as he was entitled to be. Baldwin's choice of Chancellor was a public pledge that the Government had learned the lesson of that rebuff. Churchill, for his part, had moderated his Free Trade gospel to the extent of accepting Safeguarding. It was to be a Government of compromise and reconciliation.

One of the most remarkable features, indeed, of the 1924–9 Baldwin Government was the success with which the former Coalitionists were re-assimilated as trusted and equal colleagues. Baldwin nicknamed F.E. and Winston 'our two banditti',[8] but he allowed Winston at the Treasury as free a rein as he did all his Ministers and relied on F.E. when necessary as the colleague best able to restrain him. Though Davidson, Baldwin's faithful watchdog, was always alert for possible trouble, they, Austen and Worthington-Evans formed no cave of dis-affection within the Government, nursed no plots against its leader. If anything F.E. and Winston were rather estranged from Austen for most of the Government's life, irritated by the secretiveness with which he kept Foreign Office business to himself. The scale of the Conservative victory at the election was sufficient to establish Baldwin's authority beyond question; and though F.E. could write privately two days after polling that it was 'a great tragedy that so great an army should have so uninspiring a Commander-in-Chief',[9] he very rapidly came to a more generous appreciation of Baldwin's qualities, which was warmly reciprocated. Like Lloyd George, Baldwin soon came to value the penetration of F.E.'s intellect and sober judgment in Cabinet, and to realize – much as he deplored his extravagance of word and conduct in the public eye – the warmth, generosity and fidelity of his private character. Once in office, F.E.'s natural disposition to loyalty to his leader asserted itself in favour of Baldwin, just as previously he had given his whole-hearted allegiance in turn to Asquith and Lloyd George. By the time he resigned from the Government in 1928, F.E. could write with only mild exaggeration that Baldwin's personality had 'converted a Cabinet, which assembled upon the crater of some bitter and recent memories, into a band of brothers'.[10]

'I suppose one cannot help if Birkenhead and Winston will dine with Beaverbrook,' Baldwin remarked tolerantly to Tom Jones. 'There is no accounting for taste.'[11] With his new self-confidence he no longer felt threatened by them, but looked now with amused indulgence on their liking for high living – a relaxed attitude nicely captured by an undated note among F.E.'s papers passing on with gentle irony a simple message which Winston had asked Baldwin to give F.E., 'The Chancellor of the Exchequer', Baldwin wrote, 'compliments the Secretary of State for India, and if he (the Secretary of State for India) has nothing to do this evening, will he (the Secretary of State for India) come out on the tiles with him (the Chancellor of the Exchequer)?'[12]

In another friendly exchange of notes F.E. scribbled on an envelope during Cabinet (doubtless when Winston or Amery was going on a bit), 'My boy has just been made President of Pop at Eton – F.E.'; to which Baldwin sentimentally replied, 'The proudest position he will ever hold – S.B.'[12] (F.E. might reasonably have retorted, as he had to Sandars in 1911, that if his boy believed that he would despair of him; but now he was more tactful.) Baldwin took his schooldays very seriously. In one of his letters to the Viceroy in India F.E. told how angry he had been one day to discover that the Chief Justice of Bengal was to be made a Privy Councillor, without reference to himself as Secretary of State and in defiance of precedent; he had protested to Baldwin, only to find the Prime Minister disarmingly apologetic. 'He told me that he had been at Harrow with Sanderson, through all his Harrow life. Such an admission, frankly made, explains everything and disables criticism.'[13] F.E. had fallen under Baldwin's comfortable spell.

From the moment the Government was formed he was confident of its prospects. 'If we are sane,' he told a victory dinner at the Constitutional Club on 3 November – that is, barring a repetition of Baldwin's ill-considered folly of 1923 – the Tory party should hold power 'certainly for five years, equally certainly, if we are clever, for nine years.'[14] 'Politically', he wrote to Reading two months into the Government's life, 'we are going strong'.

The Cabinet is both strong and harmonious – the old divisions in the Unionist Party being happily forgotten. The Liberal Party including poor L.G. seem done I think for ever. The Socialists are cowed by the incredible errors of their leaders; the Communists at present discredited and blamed as the authors of the Socialist failure.[15]

'We are not of course popular,' he wrote after a year. 'No Government in these post-war conditions can possibly hope to be.' But he still felt that 'we shall have played our cards very badly if we are not able to go to the country, when our time comes, with a record sufficiently Conservative and yet sufficiently advanced to disincline the constituencies from making an incalculable change'.[16] It was clear that he regarded sheer stability, after the uncertainties of the past few years, as the Government's strongest claim on the confidence of the nation.

F.E.'s role in the Baldwin Cabinet was inevitably much less central than in Lloyd George's. Under Baldwin's easy-going chairmanship – very different from Lloyd George's ubiquitous dynamism – the driving force of the administration was supplied by Neville Chamberlain. F.E. was – in his mid-fifties – in somewhat the position of an elder statesman: a heavyweight whose opinion when he gave it still carried authority, but not an initiator of policy, not one of the Prime Minister's inner circle. His ambition was running down; his mind ran more on when he should bow out of politics than on the hope of conquering fresh peaks. His department did not tax him unduly. Indian interests did dictate that he was a member of most foreign and imperial affairs committees, and his legal expertise also made him a valued member of many *ad hoc* committees on domestic problems both large and trivial. His drafting skill was greatly admired, and he was a good committee chairman, as he proved in the first (and practically the only) crisis which threatened to disrupt the Government's harmony in 1925.

This was the latest round in the perennial battle which faces every Government between the need for economy (represented by the Treasury) and the claims of security (championed by the Admiralty). The 1925 spending review pitted Churchill (unusual in being an ex-First Lord, able to bolster his Treasury arguments from his own experience of the Admiralty before the war) against one of Baldwin's particular friends, William Bridgeman. Bridgeman, dwelling on the threat from Japan, demanded that four new cruisers be laid down in 1925 and three more by 1927; Churchill insisted, in view of the Treasury 'rule' that no war was anticipated in the next ten years, that there was no such urgency. When both threatened resignation, Baldwin appointed F.E. to head a Naval Programme Committee to listen to both sides of the argument and report. Surprisingly for one who never ceased to proclaim his belief in a high level of military preparedness F.E., as he sat in judgment, tended to think that Winston had the better of the argument. Winston was delighted, as he wrote admiringly to Clementine in March.

> The battle with the Admiralty continues ding dong in the Cabinet Committee. FE reveals continually his extraordinary mental powers. He sits like a stuck pig, hardly saying a word for hours, until I wondered whether he was really taking these to him unfamiliar topics in at all. But when the time came for him to draw up a series of questions to be remitted to the Committee of Imperial Defence, he showed a mastery and penetration of the difficulty of the argument, and a power of getting to the root of the matter, most profound and astonishing.[17]

The crisis came to a head and was finally resolved in July. F.E.'s committee reported in favour of reducing the Admiralty's claims – 'almost inevitably', Amery noted sourly, 'with FE in the chair to back up Winston',[18] though this was practically the only time in four years that the Carlton Club Ministers had cause to feel that the former Coalitionists might be ganging up against them. Threats of resignation continued to fly back and forth until Baldwin reluctantly forced his friend the First Lord to compromise. Bridgeman eventually accepted that only two cruisers should be laid down at once: but four more were to be begun in 1926 and another in 1927, so that the Admiralty actually came away with the substance of its programme intact, in return for merely minor economies. In the end it was Churchill whom Baldwin obliged to concede most. When it came to the point, Winston was in no position, politically, to press his resignation.

Away from Whitehall, F.E. quickly slipped back into the role he had found time for even as Lord Chancellor, as the Government's most travelled spokesman in the country, for ever making after-dinner speeches to clubs, societies and institutions – legal, commercial, sporting or show business – from Plymouth to Aberdeen. Avowedly non-political, they invariably incorporated, sometimes humorously, sometimes sententiously, the message that His Majesty's Ministers faced extraordinary, indeed unprecedented difficulties; that they received little support from the supposedly Conservative Rothermere and Beaverbrook newspapers (a repeated and bitter complaint), and could only hope to steer the country to more prosperous times with the hard work, patience and good will of the patriotic British public. As the most sought-after guest speaker on the circuit, seemingly unwilling to refuse any invitation, F.E. must have delivered this message many hundreds of times between

1925 and 1928, to audiences ranging from the Royal Society of Medicine to the Motor Cycle Trades Benevolent Fund dinner.

For the most part he discharged this function responsibly and well: though rumours continually circulated that he had been drunk on this or that occasion, and almost every account begins with the euphemism that 'Lord Birkenhead had dined well', his audiences almost invariably loved him. His ability to strike the right note on the right occasion – the result of thinking on his feet and trusting himself to respond to atmosphere, instead of coming with a preconceived script – was undiminished. Nevertheless he was an incongruous spokesman for the Baldwin Government. Valuable though his services might be in Cabinet, his public reputation was the same as in 1923 when the constituencies and the Tory women were said to be determined not to have him in the Government at any price. His grand manner and shameless hedonism could not have contrasted more sharply with Baldwin's image, carefully cultivated by Central Office, as a tweedy, pipe-smoking countryman whose greatest pleasure was leaning over gates and poking pigs.

F.E.'s public image was cruelly fixed by the cartoonist David Low, who drew him as 'Lord Burstinghead': a pompous figure in evening dress and silk hat, his mouth invariably clamped with a stupefied expression around an immense cigar. (The cigar was a trademark in itself, long before they became associated with Churchill: Winston was at this time famous for his hats.) Satirical squibs which were gleefully repeated at least in political circles played on the same reputation for insufferable pride.

> I cannot help but think it odd
> And jealous, too, of the Lord God
> To go on ruling when, instead,
> He might give way to Birkenhead.[19]

> When Churchill came before the judgement seat,
> No angel sought for mercy to entreat;
> Silent they heard the sentence grim and dread:
> To spend eternity with Birkenhead.[20]

Moreover F.E. absolutely declined to drop from his rhetorical repertoire the 'Glittering Prizes' theme for which he had been practically excommunicated in 1923, but on the contrary missed no opportunity to reiterate and elaborate it. In December 1924, for instance, he found himself in Scotland again to preside at the annual dinner of the Sir Walter Scott Club in Edinburgh. In the course of his eloquent and erudite lecture – during which he apologized as an Englishman for his inability to pay 'even perfunctory tribute to the noble national dish which graced your table', but boasted in mitigation that he had read every one of Scott's novels at least three times before he went to Oxford and re-read them all every five years! – he could not resist characterizing his Glasgow Rectorial as 'an address founded upon the philosophy and teaching of Sir Walter Scott', and went on deliberately to raise the hackles both of those who thought the original speech militaristic and those who thought it an encouragement to youthful ambition, by combining the two interpretations in one.

> I am sure that there has been no poet since Scott who has written so attractively to adventurous youth the story and the gallantry of the past ... I am sufficiently a believer in the teaching of Scott to be sure that neither is this world now, nor hereafter will it be, an easy world to live in. I have never been able to persuade myself that the arms of the strong will not again and again be required by Britain in the years that lie in front of us. Let us by all means devote every influence of which we are masters to avoid war; but do not let us be so blind to the teachings of history as to believe that great possessions will be permitted in the future of the world to soft peoples. They never have been; they never will be.[21]

The repetition of such an uncomfortable message had something of the provocative impact of Enoch Powell's repeated blasphemies on the race question in the 1960s. There were many Conservatives who regarded F.E.'s philosophy as the cynical negation of the spirit of peace and co-operation which the Government was trying to promote both at home and abroad, and considered his unrepentant presence in the Cabinet a standing affront to the idealism with which the post-war generation was supposed to be imbued. But F.E. was untouched by such criticism. Much as some of his younger colleagues might deplore it, nothing could alter the fact that he was in the mid- and later 1920s the most conspicuous and newsworthy member of the Government – Winston not excepted. He was constantly before the public in one guise or another – if not as Secretary of State, then as journalist or playboy, historian, sportsman, sensualist or judge. Not overstretched at the India Office, his political ambition either slaked or realistically abandoned, he was free to expend his still remarkable energy in the untrammelled indulgence of an astonishing range of extra-mural pleasures, both intellectual and athletic, which were all good copy for a popular press increasingly given over to social gossip about the stars of stage, screen and – where they merited it – of politics. With the prestige of a senior Cabinet Minister F.E. simultaneously gave a creditable impersonation of a renaissance prince or an enlightened scholar statesman of his favourite eighteenth century. The fact that he was by the highest standards not outstandingly good at many of the activities to which he turned his hand was beside the point: what mattered was the effortless style, the supreme confidence, with which he dispatched everything he did, whether it was hitting a golf ball or writing a popular history of the world. In this, the high summer of his life, presiding over his little court at Charlton, entertaining his old friends and dispensing generous but searching patronage to young admirers, F.E. was truly – as John Buchan called him – 'Aristotle's Magnificent Man'.[22]

At the heart of F.E.'s life in the 1920s was his family. Through all the adventures of his career his marriage to Margaret had been an exceptionally happy one. Though occasionally worried by their extravagance, she had no more inclination than he to restrain it, but joined fully in his enjoyment of all life had to offer without counting the cost. She was the perfect partner for him, a brilliant hostess in no way overshadowed by her husband, but a powerful and captivating personality in her own right, able to share his love of games and horses but with her own interests – music and painting – to occupy her when he was away. She did not see herself as his puritan conscience, as Clementine rather did with Winston. She rarely reproved him for his excesses either verbal or alcoholic, but seemed on several occasions when others were embarrassed for her only to admire him the more. If he had his lapses from sexual fidelity, she probably compensated with some discreet flirtations of her own; their ultimate devotion to one another was never in doubt. The success of the marriage is nevertheless an extraordinary tribute to her tolerance and strength of character.

It was cemented, of course, by devotion to their children. F.E. was a proud and adoring father, and the two girls in particular were thoroughly spoiled – 'encouraged', as Eleanor wrote in her memoirs, 'to come down after dinner and to be cheeky before solemn statesmen'.[23] By 1925 Eleanor was grown up, a wild girl with F.E.'s love of horses, a romantic hankering for a gipsy life and an ambition to write which very soon she was to turn to popular and profitable account. Pamela was still a child, just moving into her teens in her father's last years, but a strong-willed and impulsive one with a younger daughter's traditional ability to twist F.E. round her little finger. Both girls inherited their full measure of the spirit of adventure from both parents, and it is notable that his pride in their abilities and concern for their futures produced a marked softening of F.E.'s previously contemptuous attitude to women's education and women's role in society and the arts. For he found in them more of the gaiety, recklessness, energy and ambition that he looked for and strove to instil in his only son.

By contrast Freddie, just going on from Eton to Oxford in 1925, was a reserved, somewhat introspective boy, though good at games. He had the misfortune, as the repository of all F.E.'s dynastic hopes, to be brought up with a crushing burden of paternal expectation that he should make precocious use of the advantages which were showered on him: he was expected to follow precisely the sequence of triumphs which F.E. had marked out for him by his own example – the same ladder of advancement which he recommended to all young men of his acquaintance – the Oxford Union, the Bar, then into politics.* Freddie did not positively rebel against this programme: on the contrary, he tried dutifully to do his father's will, and during F.E.'s lifetime was quite successful. He was Captain of his House at Eton, Second Keeper of the Field and President of 'Pop' (the nearest equivalent to Head Boy); when his academic work lagged, and F.E. characteristically offered him a car if he could win the Rosebery History Prize, he duly won it (and kept the car illegally in Slough). At Oxford – Christ Church, not Wadham – he won a half-blue at tennis and blues at squash and fives, hunted with the Heythrop and was President of the Bullingdon, while drawing his friends to an unusual degree from both 'hearties' and intellectuals. Privately, he had many of F.E.'s qualities: 'Chips' Channon found him in 1934 'more charming than any human being I have ever met', and wrote of 'listening entranced to this dark Hermes as he poured forth a torrent of wit'.[25] But he had no appetite for public speaking. For all F.E.'s encouragement, he spoke seldom at the Union; and though he ate his dinners, he never practised at the Bar. Despite a lavish coming-of-age dinner at Gray's Inn in 1928 to which F.E. invited the Prime Minister and half the Cabinet to give him the most spectacular public launch, he had no ambition to cut a figure in the political world. He found his vocation, after F.E.'s death, in writing his biography, and subsequently became a professional biographer of considerable distinction, and a successful and long-serving chairman of the Royal Society of Literature.

He felt no resentment of his demanding parent: his life of F.E. is a model of filial piety, venturing some mild criticism only in a revised version published nearly thirty years after the book's original appearance. F.E.'s early death in fact released him from the appalling difficulty which Winston's fame and long life put in the way of Randolph ever establishing his own identity at all. Freddie was three years older than Randolph, but they were brought up to carry on their fathers' friendship: each had his father's friend as godfather and bore his

---

* 'If you were a Frenchman or a German,' he told Oswald Mosley, 'your profession would clearly be the army, because in those countries it is the great profession. In England it must, of course, be politics or the Bar, or both.'[24]

godfather's name – Frederick *Winston* Furneaux Smith and Randolph *Frederick* Edward Spencer Churchill. If they did not actually become one another's boon companions, they remained bound together in affectionate exasperation by the common problem of escaping from their fathers' shadows – though their friendship may not have helped in this respect for, as Evelyn Waugh discovered when thrown together with them in an extraordinary threesome in Yugoslavia in 1944, their conversation could too easily become dominated by the memorable retorts and sayings of their hero fathers.[26] Thanks to F.E.'s early death, Freddie was able very largely to emancipate himself: Randolph never was, and his failure embittered him. The lives of the sons of other leading politicians of the period – Oliver Baldwin and Richard Lloyd George – were similarly blighted by their fathers' fame. Freddie was by comparison lucky: he might have been the worst case of all, for no one ever set out more deliberately to make his son a little model of himself than did F.E. There is a photograph in the first edition of Freddie's book showing him, as a boy of perhaps ten, standing beside F.E. in precisely the same posture, his hands thrust deep into his trousers' pockets in proud and perfect imitation. In particular F.E. made a point of passing on to his son the habit of strong drink, encouraging him to take it long before he really liked it: the taste for drink and the ability to hold it was always to F.E. a badge of masculinity which he was determined to pin early on his only son, as his admired father had on him. Alcohol was in the family bloodstream. In later life Freddie had a struggle to overcome this part of his inheritance: it was a symbolic achievement of some importance that he did so. Nor is it irrelevant to note that the reaction has lasted into the third generation: the present Earl of Birkenhead is a teetotaller.

Again like his own father, F.E. took the closest interest in the education of all his children, interpreting education in the broadest sense. In the 1920s he took them abroad whenever he could, both singly and together, either on his own or a friend's yacht or travelling on the continent. In 1925, for instance, he took Pamela cruising off the Dalmatian coast; in 1927 he took Freddie on a circuit of tennis tournaments in Germany. At Christmas (when before the war they had usually gone to Blenheim) the whole family went to Cannes or the Canaries. Playboy though he was reputed to be, F.E. took the deepest pleasure in these years on holiday with his family.

Right up to September 1928, F.E.'s mother was still alive. Widowed forty years before, Elizabeth Smith had seen her two younger sons die in 1924 and now lived with her daughter Louie (F.E.'s younger sister, the one-time actress, who never married) in a private hotel in Eastbourne. F.E. visited her dutifully and probably contributed to her support, but she remained by all accounts the one person of whom he was in awe.[27] In August 1927 he wrote to Beaverbrook that she was coming to stay with him. 'My mother aged 85 is arriving at Charlton today against her doctor's orders and my advice – and by motor! I am staying there for a fortnight.'[28] When she died the following year he wrote philosophically, 'I have been deeply but not unreasonably moved. For things become inevitable.'[29]

F.E.'s record as a family man bore the stain of just one serious extra-marital affair. The girl involved was Mona Dunn, the daughter of Beaverbrook's boyhood friend in Canada, fellow-financier and fellow-millionaire, created in 1921 Sir James Dunn. F.E. met her in Paris in 1919, where she was attending the same finishing school as Eleanor. The two girls, aged seventeen, became friends. F.E., when he was over for the Peace Conference, took them out and about together around Paris and Versailles; and sometime in the next year or two he and Mona became lovers.

On her early death, Beaverbrook wrote a remarkable obituary of her.

Mona Dunn was a most unusual girl, cast in her father's image and sharing his love of life and gaiety to a highly unusual degree . . .

The more vivid a personality, the harder it is to put down in words. How then describe Mona's genius? It took the form of an intense originality of view poured out in a rich flow of talk – coruscating, inexhaustible. Yet hers was a mind essentially sympathetic and receptive . . . Like all people of genius she was a stormy little soul. But she was so receptive of love that no-one could help loving her.[30]

As a young girl she was painted by Sir William Orpen: the portrait is reproduced, in colour, in the book Beaverbrook published many years later in memory of his friend Sir James. The vivacity is not shown, but her beauty is indisputable, a serene doll-like beauty framed in a cascade of golden hair falling well below her shoulders, so lit by Orpen that it shines with a wild lustre. This picture was painted a little time before the beginning of her serious involvement with F.E.; but she must always have been an exceptionally pretty girl. In addition to her other attractions, she was devoted, like F.E., to horses and had been an excellent rider from childhood.

F.E. fell in love with Mona, and she with him; the affair seems to have lasted for some years, at what level of intensity it is impossible to say. One friend of hers, thinking back over fifty years, believed that she was more serious than he was – that Mona was utterly besotted with him, while F.E. merely enjoyed having a delightful young thing to go to bed with.[31] This is probably unfair: on the other hand there is no question that F.E. ever thought of leaving Margaret, who remained the unshakeable prop and partner of his life. In the last resort Mona was no more than refreshment on the side. But the affair was serious enough to enrage Eleanor, who understandably took her father's interest in her friend as bitterly as Megan Lloyd George, in somewhat similar circumstances, did her father's love for Frances Stevenson.

Written evidence of the affair is minimal, and all derives from Beaverbrook, who would appear to have acted as protector and go-between of the lovers, very likely providing the necessary opportunities at the Vineyard (his house in Fulham). Whether he told Mona's father what was going on, or whether Sir James knew anyway, must be more doubtful. It was evidently no secret in political circles. In August 1923 Frances Stevenson wrote to Lloyd George, who was in Wales, that she had had a long gossip with Beaverbrook. 'He told me many things about the FE–Mona Dunn affair', she wrote, 'which I will tell you when we meet, though you may have heard them already.'[32] It was presumably to this known liaison, too, that Baldwin referred the same year, when he is said to have remarked piously, as a reason for excluding F.E., then still out of favour, 'We are a Cabinet of faithful husbands, and I think we will remain so.'

In February 1925 Mona broke free of a relationship which could lead her nowhere and married a man nearer her own age: Edmund Tattersall, the scion of a famous racing family, a sportsman with a distinguished war record, invalided out of the army in 1922. Did she marry for love, the affair with F.E. having ended? Or on the rebound, deliberately to get away from F.E.? Or possibly as a cover behind which she might continue the affair? A.J.P. Taylor has written that F.E. was still wrapped up in her in 1925,[33] but there is no evidence for this suggestion: F.E.'s P.P.S. at the India Office, on the contrary, thought that the affair was over before he joined F.E. in 1924.[34] Whatever the truth, F.E. did not attend the wedding, which took place in Paris. Two years later Mona gave birth to a daughter. But then, on 19 December 1928, in Paris again to visit friends, she contracted peritonitis and died, aged twenty-six.*

Though their affair was certainly over by now, F.E. was deeply affected. He had just embarked that day, with his family, on his Christmas cruise to Madeira. 'Do something Dear Mona's funeral,' he cabled urgently to Beaverbrook. 'Am marooned here' – 'here' being the S.S. *Avila* somewhere in the Channel.[35] 'She comes home tonight,' Beaverbrook replied on the 22nd. 'Mona will be buried Monday afternoon at Kingston I will act as you would have done if you had been here.'[36] The same day F.E. wrote again enclosing a poem to Mona's memory.

---

*It has recently come to light that Mona *did* marry 'Bunny' Tattersall as a cover to continue the affair with F.E. Moreover Tattersall, the *mari complaisant*, was paid a fee by F.E. for his co-operation. Soon afterwards she ran off to Paris with another man, where she died 'of appendicitis and drink'.

Dear Max,

If you like and think proper you can publish this – of course unsigned – in next Sunday's Express.

If you do, post the paper to Reid's Hotel, Madeira.

I am deeply upset . . .

Yours as always
F.[37]

Beaverbrook did not publish F.E.'s poem in the *Express*, but he did reprint it thirty years later in his life of her father – attributed this time to F.E., but without explanation of why F.E. should have been so affected by Mona's death.

MONA

OBIIT DECEMBER XIX, MCMXXVIII
ANNO AETATIS SEPTIMO VICESIMO

R.I.P.

How young she lies, five lustres barely past,
    The happy profligate of all she owned;
Who drew on life as on a stuff would last;
    Who laughed, while flinging on the stake, and losing, never
        moaned.

Eyes frosty blue; which still could warmly melt;
    Some Northern legacy of golden hair;
Inapt dissembler of the thing she felt,
    Of gay and reckless temper: yet in reticence how rare.

Loyal in friendship, prodigal in trust;
    Of valiant fibre; over quick to give,
She smiled and loved; and trod the road she must;
    And died as those shall die who dare too vividly to live.[38]

It is a wonderful last line – in fact a fine metrical scheme with its long last line to every verse – which more than makes up for the conventional archness of some of the phrasing. What would the readers of the *Sunday Express* have made of it? It is a heartfelt tribute, which not only shows what the well-educated classicist of those days could turn his hand to with the necessary inspiration, but gives a number of clues to the nature of the relationship F.E. was remembering. Is there not a strong thread of guilt running through it? 'Prodigal in trust . . . over quick to give' suggests that he had abused her love while not prepared to leave his wife for her; 'inapt dissembler . . . in reticence how rare' the secrecy with which their affair had had to be conducted; 'who laughed, while flinging on the stake, and losing, never moaned' surely describes her acceptance of only half his love in return for all of hers. The more one reads it, in fact, the more personal and less conventional an expression of feeling it becomes. There are no grounds at all for the whisper that Mona died in childbirth or as a result of an abortion while carrying F.E.'s child; there was nothing unusual in her being in Paris. But F.E. evidently felt some reason for self-reproach at the sudden eclipse of his bright young lover of five years before. At the very least his poem is a measure of the reality of his love for her.

There was a curious and somewhat farcical sequel to F.E.'s involvement with Mona, when F.E. thought that his secret – so far as it was a secret – had been betrayed to the wide world. In 1926 Arnold Bennett published a novel, *Lord Raingo*, which dealt somewhat sensationally with the politics of the last years of the war. The hero is a millionaire who is raised to the peerage in 1917 by his boyhood friend the Prime Minister in order to become Minister of Records. He is married, unhappily, and keeps a young mistress in London. At the end of the book he dies. Much gleeful speculation went into the question of whom Raingo was intended to represent. Of course the book was a work of fiction, and it was perfectly correct for Bennett to insist that he was based on no single model. Nevertheless the Prime Minister bears certain obvious resemblances to Lloyd George, while another Minister is clearly modelled on Churchill, as Winston himself cheerfully recognized; and advertisements in the *Sunday Express*, which serialized the book, and other papers, did not scruple to suggest that Raingo too was an actual Minister, thinly disguised. Focus centred, naturally, on his double love life – the wife in the country, the mistress in the town. F.E. immediately jumped to the guilty conclusion that Raingo was – or would be taken to be – himself, and made anxious inquiries of Beaverbrook. (So, the old gossip claimed, did two other Cabinet Ministers whom he had never previously suspected of keeping mistresses!) Beaverbrook was able to assure him that the true model was Lord Rhondda, who indeed fitted the external facts – a millionaire, an old friend of Lloyd George who was given a peerage in 1917 in order to become Food Controller but died in 1918. In reality, if the character of Raingo was based on anyone it was on Beaverbrook himself, who had supplied Bennett with most of his political background and checked his facts.[39] But the publication gave F.E. an unpleasant fright.

As soon as he was free of the fear that Raingo could be shown to be himself, F.E. took the offensive, giving an interview to the *Daily Mail* in which he denounced the current pernicious fashion for 'trifling with reputations'. He was given a timely opening by the recent exposure in

the *Mail* of Hesketh Pearson's *The Whispering Gallery*, which had pur-
ported to be the candid memoirs of a distinguished diplomat but turned
out to be a fraud. Using the same arguments as those who fifty years
later objected to the published diaries of Richard Crossman and Cecil
King, F.E. deplored those who since the war had been rushing political
tittle-tattle into print – he mentioned Colonel Repington, Colonel
House and Margot Asquith – and then turned on the novelists who
cheaply caricatured deceased statesmen in the guise of fiction: Bennett
in *Raingo* and H.G. Wells in *The World of William Clissold*. 'What right
has Arnold Bennett,' he demanded, 'whose public services, as opposed
to his literary merits, are unlikely to be celebrated in song or story, to
suggest that his imaginary puppet was modelled from an actual statesman?'[40]

Bennett replied the next day, denying that Raingo was based on
anyone. But F.E. refused to accept his assurance – saying, however, that
he could not disprove it without compounding Bennett's offence by
naming the model.[41] It is difficult to escape the suspicion that F.E., by
repeatedly insisting that the statesman so wickedly traduced was dead
and unable to defend himself – which pointed unmistakeably at
Rhondda – was simply trying to announce to the world that Raingo was
not himself! He had, as usual, a grain of right in his protests, since
Bennett had not disowned his publishers' sensational advertising and if
he was now to be believed the novel could be said to have been sold on
false pretences. But F.E. really seems to have imagined that politicians
– 'statesmen' – were an elite so selfless and so eminent that it was
improper for mere scribblers like Wells and Bennett to criticize them or
even to portray them as ordinary fallible mortals. 'Why do they not
contest a democratic constituency,' he demanded with the most simple-
minded irrelevance, 'and show us how to govern England, instead of
making money by demonstrating our incompetency?'[42]

Bennett closed the correspondence the next day with the observation
that it was not for the author of *Famous Trials* – F.E.'s best-selling
venture into popular criminology, published the same year – to reproach others with caricaturing real people for money.[43] He confessed
in his journal that he had much enjoyed the exchange. 'I love a friendly
scrap in the press.'[44] Besides, he was grateful for the 'vast amount of free
publicity'. Nevertheless, he wrote to his nephew, 'I think that Birk has
an infernal impudence and on Thursday night, if he turns up, I will tell
him so.'[45] Thursday night, by chance, was the next dinner of the Other
Club. F.E. was not one to duck such a meeting, and of course bore no ill
will. 'Birkenhead came in,' Bennett recorded, 'and we were very affable
to one another, and everybody laughed about the just finished scrap
between us in the *Daily Mail*. Afterwards he was most friendly and

asked me to lunch with him alone.' 'There was a great deal of *Raingo* throughout the evening,' he added; 'the dinner was the most agreeable that I remember of the Club.'[46]

Not for the first time, if newspaper controversy displayed F.E. at his hectoring worst, the Other Club saw him at his generous best.

The Other Club had passed through some vicissitudes since its first heyday in 1911–13. The first years of the war had put a damper on its activity, but 1917 had seen an extraordinary revival with no less than eighteen dinners in the year. During the Coalition, inexplicably, the Club went into decline again and in 1923–4, when both its founders were at the nadir of their political fortunes, it appeared to die completely, with not a single meeting. With the return of Winston and F.E. to the Cabinet in late 1924, however, the self-confidence necessary to a good dining club returned as well, and the Club was officially restarted in April 1925 with a free dinner, after which it continued to dine at least four times a year for the rest of the decade. Its membership was considerably altered, compared with pre-war, and its political character still more so. With the eclipse of the Liberals as a party of government and very few Labour members elected – Jimmy Thomas, Josiah Wedgwood and the miners' leader Frank Hodges made up a token representation – there was no longer any attempt to reflect the balance of the House of Commons. With Winston and F.E. now on the same side, as well as fifteen years older, and no great issues of principle like Home Rule and the House of Lords to divide the almost unanimously anti-socialist membership, much of the old needle – the spirit enshrined in F.E.'s 1911 rule about the 'rancour and asperity of party politics' – had inevitably gone out of the Club.

The roll of those who attended the first dinner after F.E.'s death, in October 1930, demonstrates the turnover of members. Though the occasion brought the largest turn-out in the Club's history, thirty-four, death or loss of interest (Lloyd George attended only once in the 1920s) had thinned the number of the founder members to a mere six: Winston, Freddy Guest, Jack Seely, Reading, Dudley Ward and Anthony Hope. Among political members, there had been a reinforcement after the war of Tory Coalitionists – Horne, Worthington-Evans, Locker-Lampson – but by 1930 there was a new generation of M.P.s – Robert Boothby, Duff Cooper, Archie Sinclair. There were many fewer peers, and more non-political outsiders: Keynes was a member, and Professor Lindemann; the architect Edwin Lutyens, the playwright Freddie Lonsdale, the actor Gerald du Maurier; the painters William Orpen and A.J. Munnings, and the critic Desmond MacCarthy: altogether a more catholic, yet at the same time more comfortable, collection than before the war. F.E. was still, however, with Winston, the presiding genius who rarely missed a dinner; and the Club remained a unique forum for some of the cleverest men in public life to meet and match their wits, eat, drink and take wagers on everything from the outcome of the next election to the result of private games of tennis, often handicapped.

F.E. for instance once bet Beaverbrook £50 that he could give him thirty points a game and still beat him over three sets. In another more far-fetched wager – though realistic on F.E.'s part – F.E. bet Seely in 1929 £300 to £10 that he (F.E.) would not be the next Prime Minister! F.E.'s last appearance in the Betting Book also clearly arose from an old argument with Seely: one can imagine the refighting of old battles that prompted it.

> Jack Seely bets £20 to £1 with Lord Birkenhead that there is nothing to be found in Seely's book which gives any colour to the statement that in the spring of 1914 the Cabinet, while not prepared at that moment to crush out Ulster by armed force, might nevertheless have recourse to it later.
>
> Lord Reading to decide after reading the book which Seely undertakes to send to him without charge.

Another page of entries from very much earlier (around 1920) gives a wonderful flavour of the sort of competitive conversation in which F.E. delighted – both self-consciously erudite and self-consciously male. The wager was to see who of those present could produce the best verse translation of a bawdy Greek couplet to the effect that women were good for one thing only. Anthony Hope was appointed arbiter, and F.E. bet £1 that his would be the winner:

> Each daughter of Eve is a curse. But good are two of her hours:
> The first when she offers her nuptial; the second her funeral flowers.

Garvin offered:

> Wild is a woman and strange, but twice has she hours of worth:
> One in the first bed of love; one in the last bed of earth.

While H.A.L. Fisher deserved the palm for brevity:

> Two women only like I well:
> The bride in bed; the corpse in hell.

Hope gave the prize to F.E., though there cannot have been much in it. Not to be outdone, he then offered his own version:

Woman's a Terror – twice, though, she hath charms;
Once in mine own, and once in Pluto's arms![47]

On other occasions the conversation was more masculine than it was erudite. In 1927, a year after the *Raingo* row, Arnold Bennett recorded another evening of 'sparring with Birkenhead, rather loud and abusive, but good-natured', congratulating himself that 'I could be just as abusive as he could'.[48]

One of the attractions of the Other Club to F.E. as he got older was that it provided a link with the past – that gay Edwardian past, before Armageddon, when the world was young, problems seemed soluble and all possibilities seemed open. Of this past his friendship with Winston, enshrined in the Other Club, was the most precious legacy. Another old comrade from the pre-war period was Beaverbrook; but this was always a much more watchful, more ambiguous relationship. There was almost inevitably a touch of jealousy in the early days, as F.E. and Aitken competed for the ear of Bonar Law – a political competition sublimated in bridge and tennis, played for high stakes – and the uncomfortable sense of one-upmanship and of favours asked, given and withheld persisted after the war. Financially Beaverbrook could always wrong-foot F.E. by putting him in his debt through his generous but double-edged habit – which he indulged with all his less wealthy friends – of playing the stock market on their behalf but without their knowledge so as to be able to present them with large profits which they could not refuse. 'The only occasion when I become shy', F.E. wrote to Max after one such windfall in 1919, 'is when I ought to thank a friend for some kindness. But I am under no delusions as to the real nature of this transaction from first to last.'[49]

F.E., in return, used to advise Max on the buying of valuable books. He knew all the dealers, and whenever a book turned up which he thought Beaverbrook ought to have, he let him know: thus in April 1917 he advised that there was a first edition of Boswell's *Life of Johnson* on the market, plus a first edition of Byron's *Don Juan* and Addison's *Bolingbroke* in four volumes, none of which he should miss.[50] The month before he had urged him to buy a *de luxe* edition of Petronius. He recalled also that he had earlier got Jowett's translation of Thucydides for him, and this he urged that Max should actually read. Despite being 'infern-ally busy every day' in court, he had been re-reading Thucydides himself. 'In my view', he wrote, 'the History contains (a) the whole art of war, (b) the whole art of statecraft. You should read it all.'[51] One wonders whether Beaverbrook did! Sometimes F.E.'s recommendations were less improving. In January 1926, for example, he told Max of a new translation of Ovid's love poems, 'faithful and very amusing', which he ought to have. This Beaverbrook ordered the same day.[52]

Among the other services which Beaverbrook used to render to those of his friends whose inclinations lay that way – a number from whom only Winston was certainly excluded – was the procuring of girls for naughty nights at the Vineyard, or weekends at Cherkley. It was one of the least lovable sides of his devious personality, and the source of not a little of his power, that he enjoyed playing Mephistopheles, tempting and testing his friends with the delights which his wealth could put in their way – money, drink or sex – plying each with whichever he could least resist. F.E. unhesitatingly accepted all three, in the same way as he cheerfully took hospitality and gifts from Maundy Gregory and other open-handed millionaires; but while his tastes for drink and for the pleasures of wealth were formed early, it does seem likely that Beaverbrook decisively encouraged his sexual lapses. Certainly he played Pandarus to F.E. and Mona Dunn, and apart from the stories of goings-on at the Vineyard, there are even in their surviving letters hints of more casual liaisons. In August 1919, for instance:

My dear Max,
I hear that you were recently seen on the Terrace with two beautiful ladies. Your old friends do not expect to be excluded from these festivities.
Yours ever,
Fred.[53]

Perfectly innocent, perhaps? But what about a letter dating from July 1927, in which F.E. apologized to Max for the fact that an unnamed lady whom he had been going to bring to Cherkley for the weekend had had to cry off, as her husband was unexpectedly giving a party that day and she had to be there as hostess? 'I cannot think of anyone else I want who could come,' F.E. wrote.[54] One has immediately the suspicion that this might be Mona, and that F.E. was after all still carrying on with her. But this was only a few weeks after the birth of Mona's daughter, which surely rules her out. Whoever the lady was, the implication is fairly inescapable that Beaverbrook was offering a haven for infidelity.

F.E. also counted on Max to do him more conventional favours, in his capacity as newspaper proprietor or, during the war, as Minister of Information. '*I particularly charge your friendship*', he wrote in April 1918, 'with ordering as many copies of My American Visit for propaganda work as you can. After all £100 wouldn't be much and would do my work a lot of good.'[55] During his second tour of the United States in 1923 he cabled from Minneapolis, 'Whole of vast audience stood up and cheered tremendously. Relying on your friendship to make this public through Press Association or any way you think proper.'[56] He regularly asked Max to give a special boost in the *Express* to his books and, when she published her first novel in 1929, to Eleanor's.[57] In return he reckoned to be able to fix Peter Aitken's admission to Christ Church 'which in my judgement is the best college at either university'.[58] (It was there, rather than to Wadham, that he had sent Freddie.) In F.E.'s view, this sort of mutual backscratching was what friends were for.

Despite such exchanges, F.E. and Max seem by the later 1920s to have been seeing less of one another than formerly. Their relationship had always been a prickly one, subject to suspicion and to sudden quarrels. It had evidently suffered such a rift in April 1927, when Max wrote to patch it up and F.E. replied effusively – more than a week later – with a hint that his sharp tongue might have been the cause of the temporary estrangement, but almost an old man's longing to keep the friends of his youth.

> My dearest Max,
> I am so much touched by your letter which nothing but immense occupation and (be it admitted) some slackness have prevented me answering.
> The only two men in England whose company gives me *real pleasure* are you and Winston and at the end of the Budget Cabinet Winston came up to me and said . . . Do get Max to ask you and me for a gossipy talk to the Vineyard.
> Please do this dear Max – you know how slack I am & how I can never resist saying anything if I think it is funny.
> But I have memories which you share, shared by no-one else in England. Life is short, and I have a deep affection for you.
> Even if you quarrelled with me you could not distort that affection.
> > Yours,
> > Fred[59]

It was a continual cause of irritation between F.E. and Max at this time that the latter refused to give loyal – and to F.E.'s way of thinking, patriotic – support to the Government in his newspapers. F.E. had been happy to see Baldwin mocked and pilloried by the Rothermere and Beaverbrook press in 1923, but since the Tory party had been reunited and he himself become a loyal lieutenant of Baldwin, he considered that newspapers which called themselves Conservative had no right to keep on carping at the Government in its difficulties. In particular he was infuriated by Low's cartoons of himself as 'Lord Burstinghead', which Max, showing a lack of proprietorial control inconsistent with F.E.'s idea of friendship, permitted to be published in the *Evening Standard*. In fact Beaverbrook did on occasion try to restrain Low, as F.E. recognized in May 1928 when he thanked him 'for the growing and friendly refinement of your Radical cartoonist'.[60] But F.E.'s grievance on this score was deep and bitter, and though he swallowed his pride for the present, his pent-up feeling boiled over in 1929, after his retirement from politics, when he and Max had their worst quarrel over the result of that year's General Election, which F.E. blamed on the Beaverbrook papers' disloyalty. Part of his past though he was, Beaverbrook was never a friend whom F.E. felt he could entirely trust.

His other most ambiguous relationship continued to be with Simon. On the one hand F.E. and Simon were supposed to be great friends from their Wadham days; but on the other it is little exaggeration to say that at times they seemed to loathe one another. There was certainly always an ironic edge to their friendship, and a special note of bitterness to their political and legal rivalry, until in 1927 F.E.'s appointment of Simon to head the Parliamentary Commission to monitor progress towards Indian self-government brought them for the first time to work together, when F.E. did acquire a new if still somewhat satirical respect for his old sparring partner. Simon's country house, Fritwell Manor, was only a few miles from Charlton, and the two of them began to see more of one another than for many years and to extend their rivalry to games of golf and also billiards. Salvidge happened to witness one of these latter encounters at Simon's house, and left an amusing glimpse of their mutual mistrust.

> I told them that being only an indifferent cueist I preferred to act as marker. Sir John Simon assured me in confidence that this would be a highly valuable service, as Birkenhead, though the most generous of opponents, occasionally needed someone to check his score. As a few moments before Birkenhead had privately confessed to me that Simon, though the best fellow in the world, sometimes thought that his own breaks were rather more than was actually the fact, I felt that I was really being of use. These billiards matches between the two legal luminaries are an important feature of Banbury life and are taken very seriously.[61]

In public, when they appeared together at Wadham dinners and similar Oxford occasions, F.E. could never resist subtly teasing Simon in such a way that Simon felt vaguely humiliated but unable to answer

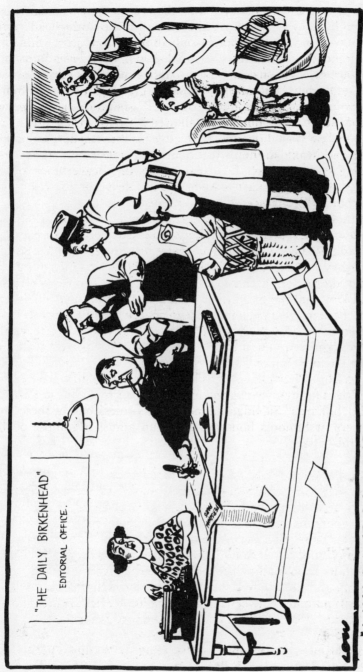

"I MAY ALMOST CLAIM THAT I HAVE FOUNDED A FAMILY OF JOURNALISTS."— *LORD BIRKENHEAD.*

back. 'The law is an arid but remunerative taskmistress,' he announced at one such college reunion, when he was feeling envious of the great earning power which Simon still commanded but which he had sacrificed. 'In me you see an example of its aridity, in Sir John Simon of its remunerativeness.'[62] And he hinted darkly at unrepeatable adventures in their wild youth, most embarrassing to so prim a figure as Simon. Maurice Bowra, who as a young don at Wadham in the 1920s saw a good deal of this teasing, speculated that what provoked F.E. was Simon's 'combination of righteousness and success'. 'He felt', Bowra wrote, 'that there was humbug somewhere, and he took a shot at it.' Simon, for his part,

> accepted it politely, but was not happy. He was not without vanity, and he disliked ridicule. So when Birkenhead made fun of him, he had to pretend to like it and think it characteristic of an old friend, but it took the edge of such pleasure as he hoped to get.[62]

Less important to F.E. at this stage of his life, however, than the old friends of his youth were the younger friends – often originally his children's friends – with whom he filled Charlton at the weekends to play games, to talk, to stimulate him and to keep him young. He had always been good with his children's friends and with young people generally: Oswald Mosley wrote of his 'Pied Piper appeal to the young', attributing it characteristically to 'wit and irreverence, always an irresistible combination to those who themselves combine brains with youth'.[24] F.E. flattered his protégés by never standing on his dignity, but encouraging them to look on him as their contemporary – an affectation ludicrous in many older men that he was able to get away with due to his own lifelong youthfulness of spirit. Ever since leaving Oxford himself he had kept up with the place and taken pleasure in adopting promising young undergraduates to be groomed to follow the *cursus honorum* of his own career; and as soon as Freddie went up to Christ Church in 1926 he made a point of developing this practice on a larger scale in order to surround his son with the sort of competitive excellence he considered good for him. He encouraged Freddie to invite his friends – and younger tutors too – out for days of strenuous physical exertion and mental relaxation. One of those favoured, Frank Pakenham, the present Lord Longford, has described a typical day.

> Selected undergraduates would be expected to play golf before lunch and tennis all the afternoon with riding between tea and dinner. The conversation led by our host was as sparkling as any I

have ever known, the mental brilliance escalating, or seeming to escalate, under the physical exhilaration.[63]

Lord Longford has compared the excitement of Charlton in those days with life in the Kennedy White House in the early 1960s – a comparison which will have baffled most readers of his book on President Kennedy but which vividly conveys – such is the fame of the Kennedy clan – the kind of glamour which F.E. could still command in the late 1920s.

In retrospect Lord Longford feels that the incessant competitiveness, F.E.'s cult of virility and his exaggerated insistence – sometimes pretence – that everyone was superlative in his field – the fastest runner, the most brilliant classicist or whatever – was really rather distasteful. But there is little doubt that he loved and responded to it at the time: his subsequent conversion to socialism and Roman Catholicism can perhaps be seen, at least in part, as a guilty reaction against the pleasures of worldly competition so temptingly laid before him by F.E., for whom personally he retains the most fervent admiration. Others exposed to F.E.'s Kennedy regime did not fulfil his expectations of them either: neither Freddie, who naturally received the most concentrated exposure, nor Randolph Churchill, nor another brilliant young friend of Freddie's, Basil Dufferin, who it was said might have done anything but had not realized his potential before he was killed in action in 1945. There are those, indeed, who consider that F.E.'s effect on Freddie's friends was corrupting rather than stimulating. For all his stress on competition it was his love of pleasure and the philosophy that life is a great game that he passed on, more than the dedication to hard work necessary to win the game which had made possible his own career.

It was perhaps the young dons who came out to Charlton who derived most benefit from F.E.'s patronage without getting their wings singed. Frederick Lindemann was a friend of F.E.'s before he was taken up by Churchill; Roy Harrod was another. Two of the most frequent visitors were Maurice Bowra, a classics don at Wadham since 1922, and John Masterman, then a history don at Christ Church. Both wrote eloquently of him in their memoirs many years later. Bowra's is one of the best portraits of F.E. in his maturity.

My first impression was of someone larger than life, with a tall muscular frame, a rich complexion, and the well-preserved and well-tended hair of a young man. Among his cronies he naturally talked about the past, especially about games, which he had played well and still enjoyed. But there was much more, even at a first meeting. He was then, as always, extremely kind to me, spoke to me as an equal, asked questions about Greek and Latin, and displayed his deep love for the college and for Oxford. In repose his face was meditative, often grave, at times almost sulky, but the moment he spoke it was alive with expression. He spoke with effortless fluency, but always with a literary flavour, which was even more marked when he made a speech. Then the famous voice rolled out the majestic periods, the ironies and the mockeries, the unashamed sentiment and the sheer fun, which made him the delight of every audience . . .

In many ways Birkenhead remained young till his death, and he was always at ease with the young, whom he encouraged and treated as equals. He moved effortlessly from one mood to another, from blithe ribaldry to attentive seriousness, from story telling to easy intimacy. He understood people very well, and though he may not always have managed his own life with prudence, his advice to others was wise and well weighed.[64]

Masterman, a first-class all-round games player who had played tennis and hockey for England and cricket for the M.C.C., had first begun to come to Charlton in the immediate post-war years when F.E. was Lord Chancellor, and it is to this period that his recollection specifically belongs; but there was amazingly little diminution in F.E.'s energy in the following decade.

In the later forties his physical energy was remarkable (he once bared his muscular forearm to explain to me his success at the Bar). When we arrived at lunchtime he would already have ridden or played a round of golf and after lunch tennis went on without interruption till dinner time. As a player he lacked mobility but at the net he was lethal, and his comments on his opponents were worth a few extra points. I used to reckon that partnered by him, we could be pretty sure of beating the Varsity third pair but would probably go down before the first pair. Good though the tennis was the evening talks were even better; his was, I am convinced, the most powerful mind with which I have ever been brought into contact.

Pause at that remark. If any man had by the end of his life met and talked with all the finest intellectuals of the country in this century, that man was Sir John Masterman. From him 'the most powerful mind with which I have ever been brought into contact' is the highest possible tribute. Asked shortly before his death whether he really meant this, Masterman replied impatiently that he did not write what he did not mean.

Nevertheless the emphasis of his memories is not on the mighty intellect, but on the warmth of F.E.'s heart.

> One characteristic of FE's outweighed all others, and that was his loyalty to his friends. Once you were his friend, so you remained. One would go over from Oxford for the day and be greeted as though one was the one person he most wished to see. All very well, a cynic might suggest, he wants to make sure of a good four for tennis. Not at all. One would go again a little later to find the house full of cabinet ministers and suchlike folk, but FE would still treat one as the guest he most gladly welcomed. Could any trait be more endearing in a great man? I never think of him without affection, or without admiration for his great qualities.[65]

That F.E.'s tennis was more vigorous than swift is confirmed by a description in the diary of Cynthia Asquith, who used to play with him at Queen's Club during the war: he played then, as he played all his life, what she called 'an odious man-at-the-net game and pulverised me into sending the ball straight into the lion's mouth time after time – or in trying to avoid him, I sent it gaily out'.[66] Too heavy for speed, he relied upon his long reach, quick reactions and strong wrist: so little did he expect to run about that he often played with a large cigar in his mouth. (The cigar was a fixture: photographs even show him smoking one while swimming!) Yet the standard of tennis played at Charlton was exceedingly high, since F.E. invited not only the best university players but the Wimbledon stars of the day: Bunny Austin, Jean Borotra, Nancy Lyle all played there. At the same time it was very democratic, so that the gardener, an excellent player named Rainbow, frequently made up the four, and even the young son of F.E.'s head chauffeur-*cum*-groom would find himself playing with the Duke of York or the King of Greece. There was usually also on hand, to the children's disgust, the 'games master', 'Buns' Cartwright to organize tournaments. Tennis was a serious business.

Not so golf, which F.E. played purely for fun and with no pretence of being any good. 'His method', one observer noted, 'was to stride up to the ball, slash hastily at it and as briskly follow it up on its erratic path'.[67] Nevertheless he had strength and a good eye, and played to a handicap of eighteen at Tadmarton Heath, near Banbury. Freddie in his biography of his father tells a good story of playing there once with the foreign correspondent Ellis Ashmead-Bartlett just after a violent storm had ripped up several large trees. 'Ah,' said Ashmead-Bartlett, 'I see your father has been playing here.'[68] F.E.'s golf, as is the way with moderate players, was if anything even more competitive than his tennis: he hated to lose, and his mastery of the well-timed, innocently lethal remark was particularly devastating at this, the game in which gamesmanship was invented.

There was one other sport in which F.E. in his later years took a close – though necessarily not an active – interest, and that was athletics, particularly Oxford athletics. When an undergraduate himself he had concentrated on rugby, though he had been not a bad long-distance runner, once finishing third (just behind Lord Alfred Douglas) in the university cross-country trials. After the war, however, runners and running increasingly caught his imagination as the purest alliance of mind and body, of extreme physical exertion with sheer willpower of the sort he most admired in young men, and he became an assiduous patron of the Oxford University Athletic Club, regularly attending the annual Oxford v. Cambridge match and frequently presenting the medals. In March 1920 – the first post-war match – he witnessed the famous dead heat in the quarter-mile between the Oxford South African, Bevill Rudd, and Guy Butler of Cambridge: Rudd actually collapsed at the finish in F.E.'s arms.[69] This effort, plus Rudd's heroic war record in the Tank Corps and his personal charm – 'no-one', it was said, 'ever lost a race against Bevill without feeling that he had won a friend'[70] – so impressed F.E. that he characteristically took him on for a time as his private secretary, though Freddie's account suggests that he was not a great success in that capacity.

It was a natural extension of his patronage of the O.U.A.C. for F.E. to become a prominent supporter of the Olympic Games, for the British Olympic team at that time was dominated by the old universities. At Antwerp in 1920, for instance, Rudd beat Butler by 0·3 seconds to win the gold in the 400 metres and also took the bronze (despite turning his ankle when he might have had the gold) in the 800 metres. The British Olympic Council was so short of money, however, that it was barely able to send a team to Antwerp at all. For Paris in 1924 it determined that adequate funds must be raised well in advance, and established a prestigious Appeals Committee, with F.E. as its Chairman. By public meetings, dinners and patriotic appeals over his name in the newspapers, in which he proclaimed the importance of British participation in the Olympics, both for reasons of national prestige and to uphold before the world the example of British sportsmanship, some £27,000 was raised and a team of nearly 450 sent to Paris.[71] He himself did not go with it. The popular film *Chariots of Fire*, which tells the story of the two British gold medallists in Paris, Harold Abrahams in the 100 metres and Eric Liddell in the 400 metres, recently portrayed F.E. almost as the team manager, travelling with the athletes and attempting in an avuncular manner to dissuade Liddell from his refusal to run in the 100 metres because the heats were to be run on a Sunday. That is certainly cinematic licence: if F.E. was present in Paris at all he can only have paid a flying visit, for he was at a lunch in London on the day of the opening ceremony, 5 July, and spoke in the House of Lords on the Labour Government's London Traffic Bill on 10 July. Abrahams's triumph was on the 7th and Liddell's – in which he knocked a clear two seconds off Rudd's time in Antwerp – on the 11th. Four years later, however, F.E. was unquestionably present at the Amsterdam Games: still Chairman of the Appeals Committee – which this time, however, raised only £18,000 and sent a considerably smaller British team – he travelled not with the athletes but with Freddie on the Duke of Sutherland's yacht (Sutherland was President of the Olympic Council), and made a speech at the closing dinner. The most that can be said is that if he did visit Paris in 1924 he was remarkably inconspicuous about it – which is practically the proof that he did not.

F.E.'s enthusiasm for athletics might have seemed incongruous to many who tended to associate him with less healthy pursuits. Even in the athletic context he was by no means always sober. In 1928 he turned up for the Oxford v. Cambridge match very obviously the worse for drink, wearing the loudest check suit and accompanied by his faithful cairn terrier, Jane, for whom an exception had to be made to the rule that dogs were not admitted; he was propped up for just long enough to deliver his usual sparkling speech, as witty as ever, but then, before the eyes of the delighted undergraduates – still holding a drink in one hand, a cigar in the other and Jane tucked under one arm – slid gently under the table![72] Yet no one in Oxford would have dared challenge his credentials: in the athletic fraternity at least, he was extended infinite licence as a good sport, in honour of one memorable feat, still celebrated in Oxford legend to this day and in the 1920s still fresh in the telling – his great race round Christ Church quad in 1920 with the Olympic miler W.R. Milligan.

During dinner at the High Table F.E. was boasting that at the age of forty-seven he was still pretty fit. To prove it he offered to wager £15 to £5 that he could run four laps of Tom Quad – Oxford's largest, 300 yards round – before Milligan could complete eight. They had both dined well, and were dressed in evening clothes and shoes; F.E. was further encumbered by a large buttonhole. The whole college trooped outside to witness the amazing spectacle of the Lord Chancellor disporting himself with a lack of dignity unheard of and beyond the physical capacity of most holders of his office. Before they began F.E. made one more condition. 'The bets are laid,' the witnesses protested. 'The condition is', F.E. insisted solemnly, 'that I have one more whisky and soda.' He could easily afford it, for he had made his calculations shrewdly: so long as he simply kept going, Milligan would have had to run impossibly fast to maintain twice his speed. Ivor Thomas, reckoning that Milligan might in the circumstances have covered his 2,400 yards in 7½ minutes, has demonstrated that F.E. needed only to manage an average of 5 miles an hour to win. He actually completed his four laps just as Milligan finished six – tribute, as Thomas says, as much to his intelligence as to his wind and limbs, but above all to his superb sense of theatre.[73] No episode in his life better captured the style of the man.

F.E. could dine out in Oxford on this story for the rest of his life. On occasion he offered to improve on it. Some eight years later, dining again at Christ Church, he challenged another noted athlete, R.N. Beaver, to a similar contest: this time he bet that he, now aged fifty-five, could run fifty yards with the lightest man at the table on his back faster than Beaver could run a hundred! The same calculations would have applied as in the Milligan race; but Beaver prudently declined the challenge, fearing either certain defeat or the responsibility for putting a dangerous strain on the Secretary of State for India's heart.[74]

Stories like these kept fresh the lustre of his undergraduate reputation of thirty years before: he was an Oxford character still. But in some quarters there was a feeling that F.E. traded too hard on his status as a legend, and presumed too much. He would still make periodic descents to the Union trailing clouds of glory: usually he was received with rapturous applause, but the interruption was not always welcome to the unfortunate who happened to be speaking at the time, and he could be devastatingly rude if he was not accorded the reverence he expected. When he was invited as a distinguished guest to take part in debates, he had usually drunk too much and was on at least one occasion terribly heavy-handed. This was in 1927 when he came down to pit his authority against the motion – the perennial motion which he himself had so often proposed in the time of Gladstone – that 'this House has no confidence in His Majesty's Government'. The first speaker was Dingle Foot, then a Liberal, who chose to refer to the old story that F.E. and Simon had tossed up at the outset of their careers to decide which of them should join which party. F.E. rose quite unnecessarily to deny it; he required Foot to withdraw it, and later when his turn came to speak he was still angry. 'There is only one thing I have to say about that story,' he hectored (before going on to list three things). 'Firstly, it is not true. Secondly, it is not funny. Thirdly, it is calculated to give offence.' The rest of his speech was in the same vein, sheer browbeating, as he rebuked the undergraduate critics of the Government humourlessly for their impertinence. The whole performance was a grave disappointment to those who had expected to be dazzled by a display of wit, and a sad dent to his Oxford reputation. With young people *en masse* he did not always enjoy the same *rapport* that he showed with his chosen protégés at Charlton. Even so, his ill-tempered retort, 'Firstly, it is not true' etc. lived on for some years as a standby of Union repartee.[75]

Invited to the Cambridge Union the following year he was, by contrast, at his brilliant best. The young Selwyn Lloyd found him charming and courteous, looking suddenly rather older than his age, but showing no mental decline at all. At dinner he drank only one small port; then during the debate he leaned back with his eyes closed – the whole audience thought he was drunk – until it was his turn to speak, when he stood up and replied one by one to every point Lloyd (at that time a Liberal) and his Labour colleague had made against the Government, in a marvellous exhibition of memory and clarity of mind.[76] This was the real F.E.

Lapses into boorishness, however, though they occurred throughout his life, were unquestionably more frequent in his later years. Not only at the Union, but at Wadham too, he was inclined to throw his weight about as though he owned the place. Here again the testimony of Maurice Bowra must be remembered: Bowra saw as much of F.E. at Wadham as anyone, liked him, admired him and received only kindness from him. Nevertheless there were others who felt that he overplayed the old boy act with little sensitivity to the feelings of the new generation now in residence. His visits inevitably recalled the college's golden nineties, with the not always subtle implication that it had reverted to the obscurity from which he, Fry and Simon had rescued it. Their successors would have been poor spirits if they had not sometimes felt their own originality cramped by the illustrious models held up to them, and resented the prescriptive right which he assumed to drop in whenever he felt like it from Charlton.

The sometimes overbearing tone of F.E.'s dealings with his old college may perhaps be gauged from a wonderfully characteristic letter he wrote in January 1927 to the Warden (the same Dr Wells who had helped him with his debts years before). He had been approached by Lady Cunard with the offer of a portrait of another old Wadham man, the conductor Sir Thomas Beecham, which he had duly passed on to the college (together with the offer of a better one of himself than it at present possessed!). Wells was evidently not enthusiastic, so F.E. – who had meanwhile been landed with the portrait himself – put the case to him again, proposing that a party from the college should come to lunch with him to see it.

I am no musician, but I am told by those who understand these matters well, that Beecham is the most brilliant conductor now living in the world. Anyone who does anything non-criminal better than anyone else in the world is evidently remarkable. I have never myself witnessed his efforts and I am sure that if I did they would cause me great inconvenience. The portrait was painted by a very considerable artist, is a marvellous likeness and has a very dramatic appearance, as the musician was depicted – so to speak – in full blast. It cost, I am told, 500 guineas. It is worth considering whether the College should refuse it even if they were not prepared to hang it in the Hall. If they were willing to give it to some other place, not of course a contemptuous one, I should think this would be satisfactory. But I really do not myself care a brass farthing about the matter one way or another.[77]

The lofty disparagement of music; the throw-away encapsulation of his admiration, nevertheless, for anyone who does 'anything non-criminal' superlatively well; and the dismissive last line – all vividly convey the casual, tactless arrogance of F.E.'s habitual manner. The college declined the portrait, on the ground, allegedly, of Beecham's improper relations with Lady Cunard – though seventeen years later, in 1944, it relented and accepted it after all.

F.E. regarded himself with some reason as a great Oxford figure. In 1922 he was proud to accept the office of High Steward of the University, and henceforth gave his new dignity first place in the list of academic honours which he always placed after his name on the title page of his books. (In 1924 the author of *America Revisited* was resoundingly proclaimed as The Rt Hon. The Earl of Birkenhead, P.C., D.L., D.C.L., L.L.D., High Steward of Oxford University, Lord Rector of Glasgow University, Treasurer of Gray's Inn, Honorary Fellow of Wadham College, Honorary Fellow of Merton College. F.E. did like to make sure his prizes glittered.) But the greatest honour that Oxford could confer on its most distinguished sons was the Chancellorship of the University; and this prize eluded him.

Since 1907 the Chancellorship had been held by Curzon. But in March 1925 Curzon died, followed almost at once by Milner, who rather mysteriously had been elected unopposed to the position even though he had tried to decline it. Now there was to be an election, and hats were in the ring.

On paper, by virtue of his academic and political achievements, F.E. should have been a strong candidate, particularly since he was a Conservative and the election was normally contested on unashamedly party lines, with a permanent Tory majority in the electorate. (All members of the university, that is all graduates, had a vote, with the catch that they had to come to Oxford in person to cast them.) But his name encountered strong opposition, partly moral and religious among the powerful clerical element in Oxford, partly political among Diehard Unionists who had not forgiven him for the Irish Treaty or the other iniquities of the Coalition. Only three days after Curzon's death Jack Sandars (Balfour's former but now estranged secretary) was already writing to Leo Maxse, 'An Oxford resident warns me that *Birkenhead* is the danger. We must work overtime against this.'[78] Sandars's friends were entirely successful in stifling any movement for F.E.: at the beginning of May F.E. gave Amery the impression, at a Royal Academy dinner, that he was 'very cross' that he was not being pushed forward.[79] But he cannot have been altogether surprised, and there was another candidate whose credentials he could accept as even better than his own: Asquith, just ennobled as the Earl of Oxford and Asquith. The clumsy title was a concession to the spiteful outcry raised by Tory Oxford against a Liberal Prime Minister adopting the historic Tory title of Oxford. The same hostility was now raised against his becoming Chancellor. To elderly Oxford, Asquith was not an eminent national statesman to be honoured in his old age; he was still the destroyer of the House of Lords, the betrayer of loyal Ireland and the Welsh Church, and most recently the man who had refused to save the country from a Labour Government. To F.E., who had opposed him as strongly as anyone on all these issues, such petty-mindedness was a scandal.

Had the Oxford Tories chosen to run him as their candidate against Asquith, he would no doubt have been happy to pit his qualifications against the Liberal leader. But since they had passed him over in favour of Lord Cave, of whose legal attainments he had no very high opinion, F.E. threw himself strongly into the battle on Asquith's side, against the bigotry of official Oxford. His generosity did him credit, though there were inevitably those in Oxford who suggested that he was only thinking of his own chances in the future, calculating that Cave was younger than Asquith. (In practice, on the contrary, by backing Asquith he can only have further damaged his own chances.) Asquith, he wrote to *The Times* on 19 May, was on any objective reckoning the only possible candidate to follow Curzon and Milner. Hoping that the Oxford electors would not 'choose to make this high office a pawn of politics', he first recalled Asquith's academic career and then, sliding over the years 1906–14, praised his patriotic achievement, first – though 'head of a bewildered and largely pacifist party . . . fed upon fallacious ideals' – in bringing a united nation into the war, and second, in 'enforcing conscription on a nation to whose habits and traditions it was wholly alien'. 'Lord Oxford', he concluded, 'is the greatest living Oxonian. If he were a Conservative he would be elected by acclamation. To reject him because he is a Liberal is to admit partisan prejudices as narrow as they are discreditable.'[80]

Other leading Tories wrote similarly. In June F.E. signed another letter (with the Earl of Middleton, the classicist A.C. Clark and the historian Keith Feiling) avowing the greatest respect for Cave but urging all those Conservatives who thought the election should be non-political to vote for Asquith.[81] Another outraged letter from Sandars to Maxse, however, indicates the depth of prejudice Asquith's supporters were up against.

> It is a strange world. Asquith at the hands of a Conservative Prime Minister has received within a few weeks an Earldom (& such an Earldom!) and the Garter; and now Conservatives of the Cabinet & the House of Commons press his acceptance of the ancient office of Chancellor in succession to Abp. Laud – Grenville – the Duke of Wellington, Lord Derby & Lord Salisbury etc. Where are we?[82]

'In the twentieth century,' one is tempted to reply. But Oxford still lived in the nineteenth, and Cave was elected by a margin of more than two to one, 987 votes to 441. It was a bitter disappointment to Asquith in the difficult evening of his life.

Three years later Cave died. Asquith had predeceased him by a month, and there was now no obvious candidate better qualified than F.E. Never falsely modest, F.E. wrote frankly of his claim and of its predictable rejection in the Secretary of State's weekly letter to the Viceroy in India (Lord Irwin, the future Lord Halifax).

> The Oxford Chancellorship will naturally interest you and me, and you might be glad to have my impressions. I make no secret of the fact that in my humble judgement there is no-one alive who, having regard (1) to his academic career, (2) to his record of achievement in public affairs, (3) to the sustained and constant contact which he has maintained in relation to Oxford, has claims as high as myself. I received an invitation signed by five Heads of Houses and four of the most distinguished Professors in Oxford to stand, whoever the caucus recommended. But I have long since made up my mind that I would never contest the Chancellorship unless there was a sentiment so strong in my favour that one could almost describe it as unanimous. My friends tell me that the clergy were against me. Of this I am the last man in the world to complain. But I feel that I have a small grievance that the clergy should deny me the Chancellorship of Oxford, to which I conceive myself on every ground of merit entitled, whilst by the same post I receive a letter from the Archbishop of Canterbury entreating me as an old friend to support the Revised Prayer Book in the House of Lords.

The candidate who was preferred to F.E. made his grievance the greater.

> The Caucus has selected Salisbury. He is a great gentleman; he is the Leader of the House of Lords; he is a great friend of yourself and myself. But he certainly has an even more surprising claim. He gained a Fourth Class in Science, an academic achievement which, I believe, was not approached by any candidate for that School at that period for five years before or five years after he qualified for a degree. But do not think I am bitter about the business. I think that if I had stood I should have won. Eustace Percy [President of the Board of Education] came up and told me at the Cabinet that he was supporting Salisbury because he heard that I was. The Archbishop of Canterbury made it plain to me that he thought I was the only man for the position. But, as I have said, I love Oxford so much; I conceive myself so much in the debt of Oxford that I would not value the Chancellorship unless it came to me with the general recognition that on all grounds it was desired that I should undertake that office.[83]

'I would rather far be Chancellor of Oxford than Prime Minister,' F.E. wrote with envious regret to Baldwin in 1930, when the latter – without the need of an election – succeeded Balfour as Chancellor of Cambridge.[84] Nevertheless he managed to be philosophical about his disappointment. To John Buchan – who for some reason appears to have been charged with the duty of telling F.E. that the Caucus was not recommending him – he replied cheerfully: 'My dear John, I wholly agree. What Oxford needs in the present crisis of her fortunes is a decorous facade, and that unhappily I cannot provide.'[85] He knew his reputation. What he perhaps did not appreciate was that his 'sustained and constant contact' with Oxford was less of an asset than a liability. Not only were his habits – his performance that very year at the sports, for instance – too well known: had he been elected he would, as Ivor Thomas wrote, 'most probably have taken his duties seriously, and that is a great defect in a University Chancellor'.[86]

Salisbury's candidacy was not persisted with. The honour was bestowed unopposed on Grey – a Liberal more acceptable than Asquith, despite an academic record worse even than Salisbury's. (He was sent down from Balliol for idleness without completing his degree!) Grey's successor in 1933, ironically, was Irwin.

The one thing that, more than anything else – more than his 'betrayal' of Unionism, more than the 'Glittering Prizes' speech or his support for divorce reform – disqualified F.E. from offering Oxford a 'decorous facade' was his reputation for heavy drinking, which by the mid-1920s was threatening to overwhelm the more positive aspects of his fame. It was, to be precise, a reputation not so much for drinking as for drunkenness. He had always drunk a lot, even by the standards of an age whose normal consumption makes strong drinkers blench today. The whole disposition of his family was to heavy drinking, and he deliberately maintained the tradition, from his Oxford days or earlier, as part of his cult of masculinity. It had never, when he was younger, appeared to affect his faculties at all: rather, it had stimulated them. His clerk Peteil used to say that F.E. never spoke better than with his hand around the neck of a bottle of brandy;[87] while he himself once told Robert Boothby that without drink, not only would he have done nothing with his life, he would not have *wanted* to do anything.[88] Alcohol was actually the secret of his stamina and his success. 'At the time and later,' Maurice Bowra wrote, 'some people said that he ruined himself by drink. If it weakened his resistance to illness, as it could have, this may be true, but reliance on it carried him through his career.' Bowra did not know F.E. until 1920, but he is surely right. 'After an evening out, he would work on a brief or a speech for the next day, and in this he needed stimulation. He could not have done so much without it.'[89]

Up to the war, all the stories of F.E.'s drinking are admiring – his exceptional consumption only added to the legend of his achievement. Some time before 1914, for instance, he was in Leeds for an important case, lunching with his clients and their lawyers, and at the end of the meal, which had naturally been accompanied by wine, ordered port. When a glass was brought, F.E. looked at it contemptuously and said that he meant a *bottle*, not a glass, and proceeded to demolish a bottle; after which he returned to court and demolished the opposition![90]

After the war, as a response to the pressures of office, he drank more heavily than ever; and he began to show the effects as he had not before. He was getting older, and even his constitution could not absorb so easily at fifty the punishment it had withstood at forty. More important, however, he no longer cared if he was seen to have had too much. As a young backbencher with the promise of a brilliant career in front of him, he had denied himself nothing, but he was careful never to jeopardize his prospects by making an exhibition of himself; as Lord Chancellor, and still more as Secretary of State for India and a Tory grandee with his future now behind him, he did not have to worry what anyone thought of him. Nobody could take his achievements from him, and he rather gloried in the petty disapproval of the puritanical. Increasingly, therefore, he let himself go.

During 1920, when his health was causing him a lot of worry, F.E.

was for the only time in his life persuaded that he should drink less. For the whole of 1921 he resolved that he would take no spirits. 'He drinks cider & ginger pop,' Winston reported to Clementine in February, '& looks ten years younger. Don't make a mock of this, as he is quite sensitive about it. He looks sad.'[91] A fortnight later Winston was not so sure that abstinence was good for his friend. 'FE dined last night. Only cider! He is becoming vy fierce & calm – a formidable figure – rather morose – vy ambitious. Terrible results of intemperate self-restraint.'[92]

In June Beaverbrook wrote to a friend that F.E., Winston and Lloyd George had all come to his bedside to entertain him when he had been ill. F.E. drank nothing, but on this occasion sparkled without wine. 'He was the gayest guest and talked the most.'[93] Beaverbrook had bet F.E. £1,000 that he could not keep up his resolution to the year's end. F.E. very nearly managed it, giving way only to celebrate the signing of the Irish Treaty in December, and enjoyed an exceptionally strenuous and successful year. But he refused to admit any credit to his self-restraint. In the first few days of 1922, Amery had a long talk with him and found him 'immensely pleased with his recent achievements', particularly with his judgment in the case of *Admiralty* v. *S.S. Volute*; 'but he won't connect these triumphs with his year of sobriety and is, I fear, drinking much more than is good for him – and I noticed a shade of anxiety in Lady F.E.'s reference to the subject'.[94]

Once off the wagon, F.E. quickly regained and surpassed his former levels of intake, to an extent which increasingly alarmed his friends and gave ammunition to his enemies. Frances Stevenson noted in February 1922 that he was 'making up for lost time';[95] and drink undoubtedly contributed to his bullying behaviour that summer and after the fall of the Coalition. His appearance at Dundee to speak on behalf of Winston at the General Election in November was one of the first occasions on which his public performance was seen to be affected. ('He was no use at all,' Clementine wrote angrily. 'He was drunk.')[96] From this time on, there is hardly a story about F.E. that does not begin with the explanation that he had 'dined well', and there are many accounts of him practically helpless. Yet what is striking about these stories is that F.E. was almost always able to pull his faculties together to deliver a dazzling speech in spite of everything. Dundee was an exception, not the rule. He might barely be able to stand up; yet his brain would be unaffected.

In 1926 the Permanent Under-Secretary at the Foreign Office, Sir William Tyrrell, told Neville Chamberlain of an extraordinary demonstration of F.E.'s unimpaired faculties during the Imperial Conference that year. F.E. was frequently absent from the sessions.

On the occasion when the very ticklish question of Status was to be discussed his chair was empty but he came in some twenty minutes after the meeting had begun, looking very red and puffy about the face. Up till then the speeches had all rather shirked the real root of the matter, *viz.* Imperial responsibilities. At last B[irkenhead] asked A.J.B. [Balfour] who was in the chair if he might say a few words and on leave being given he entered into the question of contribution to Imperial defence with such penetration sympathy & tact that Hertzog [the South African Prime Minister] there & then declared that he had been won & wished to thank Lord Birkenhead for his masterly statement of the case.[97]

Two years later Amery described a similar occasion during the complicated wrangling with the Irish Government over the pension rights of civil servants taken over by the Free State. Amery and Douglas Hogg had a meeting with Irish Ministers at the House of Lords.

FE had been asked to come too in view of his friendship with the Irish and previous experience of handling them. He came in looking more hopelessly sodden than I could have imagined possible, a really awful sight, but no sooner had the discussion begun than he took the whole thing in hand and dealt with it with masterly insight, tact and decision, Douglas and I only occasionally interjecting a sentence or two.[98]

When it was a question of speaking to an audience, F.E. had a sort of automatic pilot which seemed to be able to take over and steer him through – but without detracting from the quality of his address. When he was first put on his feet, his eyes would appear glazed and his opening search for words inarticulate and embarrassing. Then suddenly his mind would clear, he would get into his stride, and the wit, the gibes and the arguments would flow as effortlessly as ever. The most extraordinary instance of this unconscious ability is supposed to have occurred during his second speaking tour of the United States in 1923. Before one of his addresses to a large and distinguished legal audience – it must have been the one to the American Bar Association in Minneapolis – his secretaries were at special pains to keep F.E. sober. But a couple of hours before the speech he managed to slip out of his hotel, round the corner to a speakeasy where a little later they discovered him, to their horror, already plastered. It was too late to plead that he was unwell and cancel the meeting. There was nothing for it but to sober him up as best they could and trust to the automatic pilot. It did not fail. After the usual stumbling beginning, F.E. found his subject and proceeded to deliver, apparently from memory, a penetrating and original disquisition on the comparative strengths and weaknesses of the British and American Constitutions. When he had finished, he slumped back in his chair, oblivious to the congratulations pouring in upon him. His secretaries hurried him back to his hotel and put him to bed. The next morning they went in to wake him, and found him sitting up at the desk composing an abject letter of apology for having missed his appointment to speak the previous night. He had no recollection of having done so, and was astonished to be told that he had achieved a triumph![88]

Literally true or not, this story is unquestionably true in spirit: at most an exaggeration of the truth. F.E.'s ability to shine even through a haze of alcohol is remembered by many who heard him speak in these last years. He often seemed to have little idea where he was, yet shrugged aside the handicap as he found his voice, an exercise in sheer mind overcoming matter. The broad-minded marvelled at his enviable capacity; but not all his audiences were so tolerant. In December 1926, for instance, he spoke to the annual conference of the Middlesex Women Unionists – who did not admire drunkenness.

> B. had been dining (and drinking) with J.H. Thomas [this is Sir William Tyrrell again] & when he had arrived at the meeting he was obviously the worse for liquor. He leaned up against the lady next him on the platform & when he spoke his voice was thick & his dress disordered. Davidson . . . who was present, was horrified & said the knowledge of his excesses was getting generally known.[97]

F.E.'s excesses were indeed a worry to Baldwin, who told Neville Chamberlain in 1925 that F.E. had recently been 'three parts drunk' when attending a football match with the Duke and Duchess of York. 'Ramsay MacDonald had to be sent for to sit next to the Duchess & separate her from such an unpleasant neighbour. He was so far gone that he could only speak thickly & forgot to take off his hat when he left.'[99] In 1926 Winston wrote to Clemmie that the King had given him 'a most lurid account' of F.E. dining on the Royal Yacht at Cowes. 'But this is better repeated than written.'[100]

Two years later Baldwin refused to reappoint F.E. Lord Chancellor for fear that he might be seen drunk in the street.[101] He was by then a serious embarrassment to the Government. Yet in 1927, after a long talk with him, Davidson wrote a surprisingly sympathetic account which underlines the personal impression he could still make even on those who most deplored his public degeneration.

> I could not help feeling the tragedy, all the more acute because he was his old sober, charming self, full of fire and wisdom, and

although the ego was over-emphasized he was obviously head and shoulders above the majority of his colleagues in the Cabinet; and then I contrasted the piteous figure on the platform at the Queen's Hall [the Middlesex ladies] or the one which I have seen so often, fuddled, reeling, dragging his dignity and his manhood in the dirt, and I couldn't help feeling deeply sorry, for he was an outstandingly brilliant man.[102]

That 'was' is devastating.

If F.E. seemed able to overcome the effects of alcohol when he wanted to (as opposed to when addressing Tory women, when he could not be bothered), there were nevertheless signs that his habits were undermining him in the later 1920s. Amery noted in 1927 that F.E. expounded the case for the appointment and the composition of the Simon Commission to the Cabinet in 'a second reading speech lasting exactly an hour which could have been done equally well in 20 minutes'.[103] This was very unlike the conciseness of the real F.E. Again, a young Liverpool barrister, who had thought F.E. in 1923 the most wonderful speaker he had ever heard, took his wife to hear him when he spoke at the East Toxteth by-election in 1929 and was sadly disappointed: he was much the worse for drink, had to lean on a table for support, and was a shadow of the speaker he had been six years before. Not having seen him in the interval, this admirer was shocked at the decline he witnessed.[104] On this occasion the automatic pilot evidently failed.

Yet his speeches read well in the papers to the end. Even at half power, F.E. was still an above average performer. He could still go through the motions better than most politicians. Oswald Mosley, in his memoirs, made an acute judgment on the nature of F.E.'s decline. Puritan that he was, Mosley generally had no patience with those who destroyed themselves through self-indulgence; but he almost made an exception for F.E.

Birkenhead was an extraordinary man and his way of life even in that generation was exceptional. He could support it without any apparent impairment of his faculties, but his imitators could not. The wayside became strewn with young men who thought that to be brilliant it was necessary to adopt his fashion.

But even on F.E., he concluded, the pace told in the end.

Even in a man so brilliant as FE I always had the impression that while the performance of youth could be indefinitely repeated, with almost greater effect in age, it was not so easy with such a habit of life to absorb new knowledge or to learn new tricks, equally difficult for old dogs and old drunks.[105]

This was sadly true. F.E. in his mid-fifties was played out, backward-looking, living on his name: his mental arteries had hardened. He could still bring powerful judgment to bear. But he had nothing new to contribute to political debate after about 1926 – possibly even 1922.

His principal preoccupation, indeed, was increasingly not politics at all, but money. Confronted by Lloyd George in 1919 with the choice – money or power – he had chosen the latter. He had enjoyed the power and the pomp of the Woolsack for four years: but since 1922 the power had evaporated and the price had still to be paid. He was debarred from the practice of his profession, and had to find some other means of sustaining the style of life to which he had become accustomed. The Lord Chancellor's pension of £5,000 a year, which was intended to cushion the loss of earning which any Lord Chancellor must suffer, did not begin to meet his debts and obligations. Unlike others, he had left the Bar in the prime of life, with children still to educate as well as two houses to maintain, a fleet of cars, a stableful of horses and a yacht at Cowes; and he had saved nothing. He had never been interested in *having* money: only in spending it. 'After all,' he wrote in his *America Revisited*, expressing incomprehension of American millionaires, 'however much wealth one has, it is as certain as anything can be that at the last dreadful moment it must be left behind.'[106] All his life, he had spent money as he had got it, living from Oxford onwards on his expectations and the confidence that he could always earn as much as necessary, when necessary. He lived with magnificent carelessness from hand to mouth, and gave no thought to the morrow. It is a gay and attractive philosophy while it works, and up to 1918 – apart from a brief alarm in 1914 – it worked very well.

But then he cut himself off from his earning power, and he was in trouble for the rest of his life. He did not in the least cut back on the extravagance of his habits. He assumed more arrogantly than ever that he could draw credit almost infinitely on his name and reputation, and would always be able to hire out his brains to the highest bidder in Fleet Street or the City if no longer at the Bar. But he had to haggle now for what he thought he was worth in a market place less discreet than the Inns of Court; and he was just beginning to realize that there was after all something to be said for laying up a little wealth to take care of his family when his earning power was finally cut off. The growing, guilty recognition that he was likely to leave Margaret and the children nothing but debts injected a note of rancorous urgency into his search for paymasters. As well as by drunkenness, the 'magnificence' of his last years was tarnished by the unedifying combination of conspicuous self-indulgence with repeated pleas of poverty and a succession of undignified public wrangles which eventually obliged him to withdraw from Baldwin's Government before its term was up.

It was between 1924 and 1926 that F.E. lost the fortune which might have eased his problems considerably, that of his old Liverpool colleague and patron, the piratical ship-owner Sir Robert Houston. He is supposed to have lost it by a single tactless joke about the colour of Houston's beard ('the original Dye-hard'); but in reality he was done out of it by the deliberate wiles of a determined woman.

This was Lucy, widow of the ninth Lord Byron, who described herself modestly in *Who's Who* as 'a keen Suffragist . . . donor and administratrix of the first, and for nearly two years the only, Rest Home for tired Nurses during the War'.[107] Her services must have been real enough, for she was created in 1917 one of the first five Dames of the British Empire. By 1924, however, she was after Houston's money and prepared to stoop to any means to divert it from the recipient to whom he had long intended to leave it. F.E., for his part, was not neglecting to cultivate his threatened expectations. Just after the 1924 General Election he wrote Houston a long and effusive letter ('My dear Friend . . . yours very affectionately, F') inquiring after his health and inviting him as an old friend of the Smith family to accompany them on their Christmas cruise to Madeira. He also gave Houston his view of the election result, including the mild comment already quoted that it was 'a great tragedy that so great an army as the Conservative party should have so uninspiring a Commander-in-Chief' as Baldwin.[9] This letter Lady Byron, who had successfully insinuated herself into Houston's confidence, forwarded on to Baldwin, to warn him of the treachery of 'a certain bounder whose name begins with B. – What a false brute he is!'[108] How she imagined this would discredit F.E. with Houston is not clear, but doubtless she was working on his mind with equal resourcefulness.

When Baldwin failed to respond to her solicitude (but instead set the police on to establishing her identity as a known eccentric), she wrote again, this time enclosing a letter from Joan Smith (Harold's widow) quoting F.E. allegedly saying that now 'that dreadful Baldwin must be got rid of'. But this was gratuitous malice; for by now she had made sure of Houston's money by marrying him and now signed herself 'Poppy Houston'.[109]

When Houston died a little over a year later, press reports tipped 'a well-known Cabinet Minister' to do well out of the will. But 'Poppy' had achieved her purpose, and F.E. got nothing. 'What do you think of the papers giving us old H's fortune?' Margaret wrote bitterly to

Beaverbrook. 'We knew only too well that the old B. had done us out of every penny when she married him.'[110]

Denied this help to his finances, F.E. had to seek other means to supplement his ministerial salary – which at £5,000 a year was half what he had received as Lord Chancellor and no more than the Lord Chancellor's pension which it replaced: he could not draw both at once. As Lord Chancellor under Lloyd George he had contributed freely to the newspapers – legal articles, political articles, book reviews – and he counted on being able to continue doing so. In the interval, however, the Bonar Law Cabinet had resolved that Ministers should desist from journalism while in office, and Baldwin had confirmed the ruling. To F.E. this was an unwarrantable curtailment of the income to which he felt – in recognition of the earning potential he had sacrificed in the public service – he was morally entitled. He had more leisure at the India Office than on the Woolsack, and his need for money was greater. He saw no reason why he should be required to give up writing and declined to do so. 'I can earn without the slightest prejudice to my ministerial work £10,000 a year,' he told Winston. If he were not allowed to, he would 'resign & become merely a judge & an author. I have responsibilities to my family which I have too long neglected.'[111]

By June 1925 Baldwin was being given a difficult time in Parliament by members pressing him to say whether the 1923 rule was still in force and what he was going to do about the Secretary of State for India's flagrant breaches of it.[112] F.E. was defiant, choosing to see a large constitutional issue at stake. Ministers had never been required in the past to give up their normal sources of income while holding office, he argued to Baldwin, citing numerous examples including (from the present Cabinet) Joynson-Hicks and Worthington-Evans, who continued to draw thousands from their solicitors' practices, and the great magnates Derby, Salisbury and Devonshire, who never ceased from the active management of their estates. He admitted no difference between their case and his own: he could not return to the Bar – journalism was now his only trade. If Ministers were to have no outside interests, this was a constitutional innovation too important to be determined by a 'haphazard answer' to a parliamentary question. He thanked Baldwin for his patience, offered his resignation if Baldwin wished to accept it, but insisted that 'a privilege conceded to Gladstone, Disraeli, Bolingbroke, Morley and Churchill' could not be withdrawn 'except under the authority of a Cabinet, advised by a Cabinet Committee', to which he expected to be allowed to present his case.[113]

Baldwin had no wish to let F.E. stir this hornets' nest; neither did he want F.E.'s resignation. He preferred to buy his silence. The chairman of the Tory party was discreetly asked to arrange 'that the approximate amount of the Pension which . . . Lord Birkenhead was forgoing . . . be found out of Party funds'.[114] Throughout 1925 articles continued to appear under F.E.'s name – a series on 'Pioneers of Industry', others on such subjects as 'Eloquence' which Baldwin could excuse as being uncontentious; but in 1926 even these ceased as the money began to be paid into F.E.'s bank account in Liverpool. £3,500 was deposited in June, another £6,500 in November, making the equivalent of two years of the pension F.E. had surrendered[115] – after all the political objections to him in 1922–4, a remarkable measure of the value Baldwin placed upon retaining F.E.'s membership of the Cabinet.

Though personally grateful to Baldwin, F.E. nevertheless considered himself hard done by and was not ashamed to complain of the restriction of his liberty to audiences who could not know how he was being compensated. It took some effrontery to suggest, even jokingly, when opening an appeal for a convalescent home for journalists, that he, as an ex-journalist precluded from practising his profession, had an unbeatable claim to the best suite of rooms in the place![116] Moreover he interpreted his bargain with Baldwin very strictly: the moment the two years were up he broke his silence with an outspoken article on the highly contentious subject, which the Cabinet was at that moment considering, of the extension of the franchise to young women. The last public embarrassment had not yet been wrung from F.E.'s financial difficulties.

During the last ten years of his life F.E. collected together the best of his journalism in a steady stream of books. It cannot be pretended that they are any of them of great distinction: they were written – or rather dictated – fast, avowedly for money, and with assistance, certainly in the research and sometimes in the writing, from the prolific journalist and biographer 'Ephesian' – Bechhofer Roberts. Yet they are none of them negligible. They were without exception enthusiastically reviewed and sold well – as is testified by the ease with which they can be picked up in second-hand shops to this day. Undoubtedly they have dated badly. F.E.'s later style was long-winded and flabby in his own day – Arnold Bennett correctly characterized it as 'monotonous, too stately post-Macaulayese'[117] – and it now tends to sound pompous. But behind the overpaid verbiage there was still a powerful mind turning over. There is not one of his books that does not contain passages – sometimes a whole essay – of real quality, while all have a biographical interest, at least, which cannot be ignored.

F.E.'s first collection of general essays, *Points of View*, appeared in two volumes at just about the time he ceased to be Lord Chancellor, in October 1922. They were so well received that a second edition had to be printed within two weeks, and a third only a few weeks after that. A majority – ten out of a total of nineteen – dealt in lucid, popular language with legal questions which had exercised him in his years as Attorney-General and Lord Chancellor: the case against a Ministry of Justice; divorce (a reprint of his great speech in the House of Lords); medical confidentiality; courts martial; plus a tribute to the late President of the Prize Court, Sir Samuel Evans, and a celebration of Wadham's contribution to the law. But he also took up the cudgels on behalf of his great hero Kitchener, reviewing a hostile biography by Lord Esher; and of General Smith-Dorrien, who he believed had been maligned by French after the battle of Le Cateau. He included also a long review from *The Times* of Lady Gwendolen Cecil's *Life of Lord Salisbury*; a strongly autobiographical account of the Oxford Union; fine tributes to three dead friends, Neil Primrose, Jack Scott and Edward Horner; and, somewhat incongruously, his three provocative articles from the *Weekly Dispatch* in 1920 advocating the formation of a new party from the two wings of the 'invertebrate' Coalition.

In 1924, in addition to the book which he contrived from his 1923 tour of America (*America Revisited*), F.E. published his thirty-two biographical sketches from the *Sunday Times* under the title *Contemporary Personalities*. Then in 1925, debarred from writing on political questions, he turned to the law and published in book form a series of essays which had already appeared in the *Empire Review, Fourteen English Judges*. This was a serious book, each essay comprising not only a biographical sketch but 'a technical valuation of each individual subject as an artificer in the Law'. The donkey work was done by Roland Burrows, but the judgments were emphatically F.E.'s own. 'My method differs *toto coelo* from that of Campbell,' he announced, referring to Lord Campbell's classic *Lives of the Lord Chancellors*. 'His technical valuations – on the rare occasions when he attempts them – possess little or no value. I am egotistic enough to believe that mine are, on the whole, just.'[118] His selected fourteen – not, he explained, the greatest: how else could he have omitted Cockburn whom, however, he did not feel up to tackling in the present volume?* – ranged from his beloved Bacon down the intervening centuries to Lord Halsbury, and included the notorious Jeffreys. Nine were Lord Chancellors, and it is difficult not to see the book as a glorification of the office which F.E. himself had so recently adorned. Nevertheless the *Times Literary Supplement* thought he had fulfilled the worthwhile purpose with which he had set out.

This brilliant example of critical biography by Lord Birkenhead

---

* Cockburn should have been excluded quite simply by the title, specifying *English* judges; but F.E. was always impervious to the separateness of Scotland.

on a selected group of his predecessors and other judges is almost
everywhere a model of judicial caution and conservative adoption
of popular judgement, and in this way compares very favourably
with Lord Campbell's caricatures of great lawyers.[119]

This 'stout volume'[120] did not sell very well, however. For his next
collection of legal reappraisals F.E. turned to something more popular:
in *Famous Trials of History* he rehearsed the romantic and macabre
stories of Mary, Queen of Scots, Captain Kidd, Warren Hastings,
Deacon Brodie and a dozen more, to which he added, stretching his title
a little, ten of his own cases including the Goudie case, the *Veronica*
murders, Ethel le Neve, the Marconi scandal and Sir Roger Casement.
The cases in both sections he dissected with a somewhat novelettish
description of the events but a serious discussion of the points of law at
issue. 'Lord Birkenhead takes great pains' – the *Times Literary Supplement*
again – 'to make the legal points and procedure clear, and for that
reason, apart from the intrinsic interest of the stories told, the book will
be of real value to law students.'[121] The *Daily Graphic*, recommending it
to a rather wider audience, pronounced it 'quite astonishingly brilliant'.[122] With this encouragement F.E. produced a second volume,
More Famous Trials, in 1928, which dealt with Joan of Arc, Charles I,
Marie Antoinette, through Burke and Hare and such Victorian villains
as Charles Peace and Madeleine Smith up to the very recent case of
Bywaters and Thompson. 'Rather a mixed assortment of rogues, criminals and victims', *The Times* thought this, but 'a remarkable series of
psychological studies . . . full of living interest'.[123] After F.E.'s death the
two volumes were combined into a single cheap edition which sold so
well that the publishers Hutchinson somewhat questionably prevailed
upon Freddie to edit – not write – a companion volume which appeared
with his name – 'the Rt. Hon. the Earl of Birkenhead' – prominently,
misleadingly and indeed inaccurately (since Freddie was not a Privy
Councillor) on the spine. Apart from a frontispiece showing a young
man very much slighter than his father, there is no indication anywhere
in the book that it was edited by the second Earl, not the first.

Between his two *Trials* collections, F.E. produced another two volumes
of mixed essays, *Law, Life and Letters*. The title accurately describes the
contents. The first volume is predominantly legal – essays on divorce
again, on breach of promise, on the cost of litigation, on the office of
King's Proctor, some miscellaneous reflections entitled 'Leaves from a
Lawyer's Notebook', and a tribute to Edward Marshall Hall. But F.E.
included also his 1924 address to the Scott Society in Edinburgh, an
elaboration of his objections to *Lord Raingo*, *William Clissold* and their
like, and an elegant essay on the decline of letter writing, which leads

into the second volume composed of literary, historical and political essays and one fragment of autobiography, 'Milestones of My Life', from which quotation has been made in earlier chapters. The former include a vivid speculation on the role of accident in history, in 'The 18th Brumaire'; a review of Sir Sidney Lee's life of Edward VII; and what *The Times* called a 'brilliant and moving eulogy of Lord Curzon's work in India'.[124] There are more leisurely reflections on 'Eloquence', 'Patriotism and the Monarchy', 'Reality and Opportunity' – F.E.'s favourite hobby-horse, careers advice for the ambitious young in England and the Empire; but also a sharp rejoinder to the journalistic pinpricks of Margot Asquith, and a wild denunciation of the wicked Bolsheviks which, *The Times*'s reviewer regretted, showed 'that Lord Birkenhead has not yet quite learned to disdain the cheap effect'.[124] Generally, though, reviewers praised both the style and the content of the books, which, despite their somewhat pompous prose, do impressively demonstrate both the depth and the breadth, the generosity and the wisdom of F.E.'s mind when seriously engaged. Like *Points of View, Law, Life and Letters* sold well, going into a second edition within a few weeks. F.E.'s success excited the professional jealousy of a real literary essayist like Augustine Birrell. 'He thinks that if he spits in the street', Birrell complained to Harold Laski, 'men will think it is the waters of heaven. He has satisfied himself that Demosthenes, Cicero and Burke combined to give him birth; and having satisfied himself that this is so, he has compelled every half-wit in London to take him at his own valuation.'[125] Half-wits, unfortunately for Birrell, bought more books than aesthetes.

F.E.'s autumn book for 1928 was *More Famous Trials*. In the spring of 1929 he brought out a selection of his greatest speeches, from his maiden speech in the Commons to the Rectorial Address at Aberdeen the previous autumn, with a preface, rather surprisingly, by Lord Hugh Cecil – an old ally of 1910 but not a recent associate. His next offering was an editing job entitled *The Hundred Best English Essays*, although he specifically declared on the first page that he did *not* put his selection forward as 'the best'.[126] In his introduction he explained too that the original definition of an 'essay' had become widened with the years. This enabled him to include not only examples of the form by Lamb, Bacon and other classic practitioners, but also sermons and letters and any other piece of prose, or indeed extract, short or long, that he wanted, a high proportion of them contemporary: Wells and Bennett, Chesterton and Belloc, Desmond MacCarthy and Lytton Strachey, Philip Guedalla and Neville Cardus. F.E. paid graceful, or flattering, tribute to a number of political friends and colleagues whose writings one would not expect to find in such a collection: Asquith on Alfred

Lyttelton (a brief and banal valediction delivered in the House of Commons); Balfour on science and religion; Hugh Cecil on nationality; even Haldane on the Judicial Committee of the Privy Council. But he also included Churchill's 'Painting as a Pastime', which deserves its place in any anthology.

In the last year of his life F.E. was still, with Bechhofer Roberts's assistance, writing or dictating busily. In April 1930 there appeared his prophetic fantasy *The World in 2030*, his last book published in his lifetime, which will be considered in the final chapter. But no less than four more were published posthumously, of which two may most conveniently be mentioned here.

The first, which appeared just a few weeks after his death, is one of F.E.'s most interesting and successful. In a Hutchinson paperback, *Turning Points in History* sold tens of thousands of copies, quite deservedly. It is popular history, unashamedly so, but none the worse for that: F.E. may have been, as *The World in 2030* embarrassingly showed, unqualified as a popular scientist, but he could survey the sweep of history from the golden age of Greece to the Great War with as much authority as any deeply read layman, and perfect confidence. It is a weakness of more specialized times that so few historians – and those disparaged by the academics as mere journalists – dare to tackle the broad canvas. F.E. dared, and brought off a considerable success. 'The first impression which one gets on looking into this book', wrote Philip Morrell in the *Sunday Times*, 'is one of sheer astonishment at the brilliance and versatility of the man . . . It is an amazing achievement.'[127]

Of course, to modern academic taste F.E. dramatizes his chosen events far too simply into personal conflicts: Napoleon and Nelson, Clive and Dupleix, Kornilov and Kerensky. St Paul is awarded the palm as the individual who changed the course of history more decisively than any other; but the Reformation is Luther assisted by Calvin ('Luther set out to serve God: Calvin to reconcile Luther's God with man'); and the Bolshevik Revolution is entirely attributable to Kerensky's feebleness. ('All this because a foolish opinionated windbag could see no further than his nose, and trusted a half-witted colleague in preference to Kornilov.') Sometimes the book reads like *Famous Trials*, with F.E. as the judge. But to F.E., as to Churchill – as indeed to Macaulay, his evident model – history was a colourful pageant in which giants and pigmies, heroes and villains contended for good and evil against great odds. Such an understanding was the starting-point, not only of his writing, but of his self-conscious living of history in his political career. Where Churchill, however, both in life and on the page, was romantic, positive and optimistic, F.E.'s temperament was generally more sombre – less confident of progress, more conscious of the role of accident in history, the narrow escape or the needless plunge into the abyss.

The book is unbalanced by a concentration of six essays at the end on the Great War, its causes and consequences; and these too are described in highly personal terms. The Kaiser is the sole villain; Kitchener and Asquith are once again lauded for their foresight and timing in bringing Britain into the war united, seeing the need for a mass army and accustoming the country by stages to the necessity for conscription; Lloyd George is strangely neglected; but General Gough is vindicated as the soldier who more than any other brought about the victory of 1918.

It ends, however, with an extraordinarily prescient essay on the misguided creation at Versailles of the Polish Corridor – 'a very real danger to the peace of Europe'. F.E. writes sympathetically of Germany's desire to undo this aspect of the Treaty, but sees Poland now entrenched.

> What can Germany offer to redeem Dantzig, the Corridor and Upper Silesia? What likelihood is there that Poland will give up what she has gained? . . . Will Germany's rancour die down with the flux of time or will some unforeseen and untoward incident upset the balance of power? Then Germany might stretch out a hand to clutch at Poland and all Europe once again be dragged in.[128]

To be able to close a survey of past turning-points with a correct prediction of the next fatal flashpoint of the future is a considerable tribute to the realistic insights of F.E.'s grim world view.

Soon after *Turning Points*, there was published another mixed bag of F.E.'s *Last Essays*. These were predominantly political, but leavened by one historical excursion (on Queen Hortense); one legal (divorce again); one semi-autobiographical ('If I Were Twenty-One'); and one long literary *pot-pourri* ('Reflections in a Library') consisting of a sequence of short reviews – of J.B. Priestley, Harold Nicolson and Lytton Strachey, detective stories, war novels and other genres. The political essays mainly ride again old hobby horses, paying tribute to Lloyd George ('There remains a great role for him to fill . . . I do not observe his equal among the men who deposed him')[129] and to Kitchener, indulging again his contempt for President Wilson on the one hand and the unspeakable Bolsheviks on the other. But there is also a long and devastating dissection of Sir Henry Wilson's published diaries ('The Despised Politician'); and, on more topical concerns, a Diehard account of the General Strike and two newspaper articles on 'The Peril to India' in the aftermath of the Irwin Declaration, of which mention will be made in the following chapters.

'It is a tribute to the force and exuberance of Lord Birkenhead's personality', *The Times* enthused, 'that he can be judged by this sheaf of essays . . . The whole man is in them, with his wide interests, his clear and emphatic mind, and his really magnificent command of his material.' Pointedly, however, the reviewer most admired the literary and biographical essays. 'The volume also includes a group of political papers. For all their forcefulness, they are more indicative of Lord Birkenhead's limitations than his powers.'[130] Is this to be taken as a damning criticism of a lifelong politician? Or is it, on the contrary, a remarkable tribute to the rare breadth of the Secretary of State for India's mind?

23

Secretary of State for India, 1924–8

(i) Reading, 1924–5

'Lord Birkenhead's restoration to the Cabinet', *The Times* opined in a wonderful inversion of its 1919 view of him, 'for any purpose but that of a vacancy on the Woolsack seems to us to be a waste of what was beyond dispute a great judicial reputation.'[1] Nevertheless F.E.'s appointment to the India Office was generally welcomed – not merely as a deft piece of Cabinet making, but as a good choice for the sub-continent as well. Indian opinion was reported by *The Times*'s Delhi correspondent to be agreeably surprised. 'Gratification is expressed that a man of out-standing ability has been entrusted with the Indian portfolio.'[2] All that could be predicted from F.E.'s only previous connections with India seemed favourable: on the one hand his wartime stint with the Indian troops in France, on the other his speech in the Amritsar debate in 1919, which the *Manchester Guardian* thought augured well for the future. 'His speech', it enthused, 'was as soundly Liberal . . . on the essentials of Indian policy as could be desired. If Lord Birkenhead administers the India Office in that spirit, which is the spirit of Burke and of Lawrence, he will not go far wrong.'[3]

But the *Guardian* had mistaken its man. F.E.'s Amritsar speech had concerned justice, humanity and the rule of law: politically he was in no way a Liberal. However conciliatory he had eventually turned out in relation to Irish nationalism in 1921, and despite having been a member of the Government that had granted an important measure of self-government in 1919, F.E. approached India in 1924 as a thorough reactionary. The *Morning Post* came closer to F.E.'s own view of his office in expressing the hope that he might contrive to 'recover a lost Dominion'.[4]

He took office on 7 November. His Under-Secretary was his old comrade in the 1906 Parliament, Eddie Winterton, who had served Lord Peel in the same capacity in the Bonar Law and Baldwin administrations of 1922–3. As his Parliamentary Private Secretary, F.E. selected the 29-year-old Viscount Gage – a large landowner in Sussex more noted for his sporting than his political interests, but a congenial companion. In addition to his official private secretaries (R.H.A. Carter, 1924–7, and D.T. Monteath, 1927–8) F.E. also brought over from the Lord Chancellor's office his old factotum 'Buns' Cartwright. The qualifications of his chosen assistants tell a lot about F.E.'s attitude to his new position. Looking back to his four years with F.E. some half a century later, Lord Gage could only recall, 'We seemed to play an awful lot of golf.'[5] Until his last months in office, however, this did not mean that F.E. neglected his duties. Most of the function of the Secretary of State for India consisted in simply reading the mass of telegrams and memoranda that flowed backward and forward across the five thousand miles between London and Delhi. There is no question that F.E. read and intellectually mastered the detail of Indian administration – perhaps more thoroughly than any other Secretary of State of the period: his comments on memoranda themselves and the grasp of minutiae demonstrated in his letters to the Viceroy are proof of this. But the rapid mastery of complex information was F.E.'s special skill: he could fulfil this aspect of his function more than adequately (now that his eyesight was restored) and still leave himself plenty of time to play golf and pursue his other relaxations – far more than he had had as Lord Chancellor. It was the Government of India that had actually to take the day-to-day decisions – his task merely to supervise, suggest and guide. The questions that came to him for decision were relatively few and never, by definition, urgent. Indians might complain that they never saw pictures of their Secretary of State in their newspapers except 'yachting at Cowes or disporting himself at other centres of pleasure';[6] but this was testimony to the speed of his brain, not – until perhaps the last year of his period in office – to laziness or neglect.

As far as legislation was concerned, the only Bills for which he had to take responsibility during his four years were minor and uncontroversial, the sort of measures which the office was well able to take care of with the minimum of parliamentary assistance from F.E. and Winterton – a Civil Service Bill, an Indian Church Bill, an Indian Navy Bill. F.E.'s only serious parliamentary duty as Secretary of State was to present an annual review of the state of the sub-continent and the Government's thinking towards it. He had a greater role in Cabinet, where he had to fight for India Office interests against other departments – with Churchill at the Treasury over Indian War Pensions, with

Worthington-Evans at the War Office over home leave for the Indian army, with Amery at the Colonial Office over discrimination against Indians in South Africa. As a good departmental Minister he at least twice took up India Office positions contrary to what might in other circumstances have been expected to be his own views. Very early in his term, in the teeth of furious opposition from Winston, he decisively supported a move to allow the autonomous Princes to have their own artillery; and later he insisted on the abolition of the Indian cotton excise duty against the strenuous lobbying of Lancashire to retain it. In none of these functions did F.E.'s fundamental lack of sympathy for those he governed inhibit the conscientious exercise of his responsibility.

It was a different story, however, with some of his informal duties. He was very bad at receiving deputations of visiting Indians, tended to treat them with scant courtesy if not actual rudeness, and often refused to see them at all, on the constitutional ground that Indians should not think they could appeal over the Viceroy's head to London. He particularly ignored and insulted the India Council – a sort of advisory 'quango' of old I.C.S. men and a few Indians in London. Under F.E.'s chairmanship its meetings lasted only a few minutes, and he once showed how much attention he paid it by introducing as a new member an Indian who had actually been a member for five years. Another distinguished Indian assured Wedgwood Benn (F.E.'s Labour successor) that the longest conversation he had ever had with F.E. lasted ten seconds![7] He did enjoy entertaining the grander and more exotic Maharajahs when they came to England, but treated them with amused superiority as picturesque curiosities rather than as leading subjects of the King-Emperor and men of serious political consequence in India. In 1929 Reading's successor as Viceroy wrote to Baldwin that F.E. in this respect 'did an incredible amount of harm'.

Not by policy – for that on the whole was good – but by the impression he produced upon sensitive & self-important Indians visiting England whom either he would not see & so mortified: or saw and produced the impression of one out of sympathy & rather disposed to despise.[8]

The purely administrative side of the work of the India Office F.E. dispatched efficiently and even brilliantly: he understood the constitutional problem which the future of India posed with all his usual grasp and lucidity – on paper. His failing as Secretary of State was that, having never been there, having no understanding of the Indian mind or Indian aspirations but an unshakeable belief in the natural superiority of the British and the beneficence of imperial rule, he had no human understanding of the problem of Indian nationalism as it existed in actuality. Locked in his closed view from London, he soon found himself out of sympathy with both his Viceroys – not only with the Liberal Reading, but with his Conservative successor, and eventually indeed with Baldwin himself.

He was helped at the beginning by his old friendship with Reading, to whose experience of India since 1921 he at first deferred with repeated and uncharacteristic confessions of his own ignorance of the 'immense and novel subject' which he had taken on. 'I can see', he wrote in his first letter to the Viceroy on 13 November, 'that it will take me a long time – though I am, as you know, a fairly rapid worker – to make my opinion of much value.'[9] Two months later he was still 'attempting slowly and with difficulty to master this immense new topic'.[10] He was helped, too, by Curzon, who generously forgave the bitter things said and written by F.E. since October 1922 and until his death in April 1925 made himself tirelessly available to advise him out of his own experience as Viceroy twenty years before. 'He looks upon the Viceroyalty as one of the greatest offices in the world,' F.E. wrote to Reading, 'partly because it is, and partly because he has held it'[11] – a comment, it may be remarked, which could be applied equally to F.E.'s own view of the Lord Chancellorship. F.E.'s letters to India, however, are full of such witty seasoning. They are altogether a wonderful source for the historian. The convention of long-distance government was that the Secretary of State and the Viceroy, in addition to the continuous exchange of official telegrams, each wrote the other a long, semi-private weekly letter in which they could expound their thinking to one another on policies great and small, in a friendly, confidential, almost conversational manner. F.E. used his weekly letter almost as a diary. In it he gave his distant colleague not only his views on India, both general and particular, but also vivid blow-by-blow impressions of political developments and prospects at home, unbuttoned comments upon individuals, and amusing personal vignettes of his own life away from the office (right down to frequent complaints about the English weather). It is unusual to be able to follow a Minister frankly laying bare his thought processes in this way, arguing a case on paper with the colloquial informality of conversation. The biographer can only wish that he could read F.E.'s changing views on Ireland in 1920–1, or his private comments on the House of Lords crisis of 1911, so candidly and so extensively expressed. Thanks to his weekly letter, and to the circumstance that he took office without any opportunity to discuss their mutual responsibility face to face with Reading, so that he had to spell out his approach from scratch, F.E.'s cynical hostility to any further progress towards Indian self-government can be displayed in his own words, not intended for publication but direct and artless.

The European war had given a great boost to Indian demands for self-government. Not only had Britain been fighting ostensibly for the self-determination of all nations; she had not scrupled to throw into the fight scores of thousands of her Indian subjects who not unreasonably hoped that the sacred principle might after the war be extended to themselves. Moreover, in the absence of so much of the peacetime Indian army in France and Mesopotamia, it became particularly important that there should be no civil disorder in India. Military prudence and the demands of wartime propaganda alike, therefore, dictated some concessions to Indian aspirations. While Tory minds were concentrated on the war, Lloyd George's Liberal Secretary of State, Edwin Montagu, made promises which were carried into effect in 1919 through a House of Commons still too preoccupied with post-war troubles to notice the thin end of the wedge that was being inserted into the very core of the Empire. The Montagu–Chelmsford reforms, as they were called (Chelmsford was Reading's predecessor as Viceroy), gave Indians for the first time a share in their own government. The experiment was strictly limited: it applied only to the Provincial Governments, and only in certain 'transferred' fields. Agriculture, transport, postal services and the like were handed over to elected councils, but 'reserved' subjects – finance, trade, law and order – remained the responsibility of British permanent officials. At the centre, a Legislative Assembly of two Houses was set up, but with no more than an advisory function, without power to override the Viceroy's Council which remained the sole executive. Inadequate as this anomalous structure – known as 'dyarchy' – was to meet the expectations aroused by the war and now orchestrated by the eccentric leadership of Gandhi, they were a portentous first step which carried the promise of further concessions and the logical certainty – notwithstanding the stipulation that the end of the road was responsible government *within the Empire* – of ultimate independence. The view even of British Liberals was that advance down that road must be slow and experimental; but the 1919 Act contained the shadow of a timetable in the provision that a Commission should be set up after ten years to examine the working of the reforms and recommend whether there was sufficient progress to justify extension of the principle.

F.E. took office at the midpoint of that ten-year period. It could not be said that by any objective standard 'dyarchy' was working well: in many areas the Indian politicians were refusing to work the new system constructively at all, and the predominant wing of the Congress Party was boycotting the elections and calling for '*swaraj*' – a somewhat mystical, Gandhian conception, crudely translated as 'self-rule' – which was totally unacceptable to the Government in either Delhi or London. The British position was that the Indians must prove their fitness for increased responsibility by operating the existing system effectively before there could be any question of extending it. One part of Congress did try to do this; but their efforts were vitiated by the widespread sense that the system was not permanent anyway, but merely transitional. The whole content of Indian politics revolved around a single question – how soon the Government could be moved on to the next stage.

F.E. believed that the first essential for the British Government was to demonstrate that it would move only in its own good time. 'My reading of Indian history', he wrote in his first letter to Reading, 'has led me to believe that a Government founded so completely as ours is upon prestige can stand almost anything except the suspicion of weakness.'[9] His early letters were therefore full of assurances of support for any firm action that Reading found it necessary to take.

> For your secret information I may say that this Cabinet, as is natural, is, in my analysis, under the influence of a considerable reaction from the Montagu reforms. It has a general impression that under the Coalition, and since, too much has been given away, I will not say through weakness, but through the general malaise which succeeded the war, in India, Ireland and Egypt. On any point, therefore, on which you hold a strong view that the line must be firmly drawn, you are unlikely to lack support either from it or from me.[12]

He was aware that the new spirit in Whitehall ran contrary to Reading's instincts, which were for conciliation wherever possible, rather than repression; he made a point of praising Reading's excellent judgment over the past three years; nevertheless he was determined that the Viceroy should not mistake the new mood.

> What is most important for you to understand is the general atmosphere of this Cabinet. It is one of reaction against weakness and surrender. I think that the influence in it of Austen Winston & myself is very great. You will not fail to meet with full support in any matter which, paying due regard to your own innate prudence, you become satisfied that strong action is necessary, and equally when you think it proper to put the brake on I will see that your reasons are most attentively considered though the tide is now running (and I think rightly) the other way.[13]

In other early letters F.E. set out his own view with characteristic frankness. 'I think you know', he wrote, 'that alone in the Cabinet I distrusted, and indeed to some extent opposed, the Montagu–Chelmsford Report.' This is difficult to substantiate; indeed it *cannot* be strictly true since at the time of the Report F.E. was not a member of the small War Cabinet which considered it. Even in 1919 the Bill implementing the Report went through before the restoration of the full Cabinet, so F.E. had no inside voice to express whatever doubts he may have felt. Unconcerned at that time with India, he may have been reading back from 1924 the opposition he now felt, which was uncompromising.

> To me it is frankly inconceivable that India will ever be fit for Dominion self-government. My present view is that we ought rigidly to adhere to the date proposed in the Act for a re-examination of the situation, and that it is not likely, unless matters greatly change in the interval, that such a re-examination will suggest the slightest extension. In the meantime, little as I have liked dyarchy, obviously it must be given its chance.[14]

In January 1925, commenting on a speech of Reading's, he went further and revealed the deeply cynical basis of his certainty that India would never be fit for self-government.

> In a later passage of your speech, you lamented the recent renewal of outbreaks between Hindu and Mahomedan. Both you and I must of course speak of these outbreaks in the terms you used . . . But surely the complete breakdown of a Hindu–Mahomedan anti-reform unity, looked at very broadly, spells a death blow to Das [leader of the *swaraj* party since 1923] and the whole of his Hindu campaign . . . His task is absolutely hopeless when the fundamental strength of our position is advertised to all India by the resolute determination of the powerful and virile Mahomedan community that they cannot and will not have any form of Home Rule on terms which are acceptable to Das and Nehru.

It was the Ulster situation all over again, with an even better opportunity for the British to exploit it.

> In ultimate analysis the strength of the British position is that we are in India for the good of India. The most striking illustration of the truth of the position is supplied by the infinite variation of nationality, sect, and religion in the sub-continent. The more it is

made obvious that these antagonisms are profound, and affect immense and irreconcilable sections of the population, the more conspicuously is the fact illustrated that we, and we alone, can play the part of composers.[15]

A franker exposition of the old Roman principle of 'Divide and Rule' it would be hard to find.

> I have always placed my highest and most permanent hopes [he wrote again in March] upon the eternity of the Communal situation. The greater the political progress made by the Hindus the greater, in my judgement, will the Moslem distrust and antagonism become. All the conferences in the world cannot bridge over the unbridgeable, and between these two communities lies a chasm which cannot be crossed by the resources of modern political engineering.[11]

As so often with F.E.'s most pessimistic perceptions, he turned out to be perfectly correct, so that when – a mere twenty years later – the principle of independence was conceded to India, there had to be created two separate states, one Hindu and one Moslem, and their birth was attended by appalling bloodshed. It is nevertheless with a sense of shock that one finds the Secretary of State for India explicitly welcoming the recurrence of inter-community violence as a justification for British rule and an excuse for deferring constitutional progress. There was of course nothing unusual in F.E.'s diagnosis of the necessity for British rule to keep the peace in India: most Tories and many Liberals felt, at an instinctive level, much the same way; but few would have had the unshrinking candour, even to themselves, let alone in a semi-official document, to spell it out to the extent of concluding that riots and bloodshed, within reason, should not be regretted but positively served Britain's imperial purpose. In F.E.'s bleakly Bismarckian world view, however, there was no room for self-deception.

Of course, he was not so frank in public. In public he was committed, as the representative of the British Government, to persevere with the 1919 reforms and bound to pay lip-service to the 1917 promise that self-government, however distant, was the ultimate goal. But he was easily able to shelter behind the disunity and obstructiveness, the unrealism and irresponsibility of the Indian politicians, whom he regarded as a small Westernized caste utterly unrepresentative of the numberless peasant masses, clamouring for further advance before they had shown that they could work the present system, as a persuasive reason for moving cautiously. Granted, then, that his lip-service to the ultimate goal was insincere, he was not much less pessimistic in public that he was in his letter to Reading. Thus at a dinner in May 1925 he expressed his adherence to 'the spirit and hope that were translated into statutory terms in the preamble of the famous Act of 1919', but went on to insist that 'we must retain contact with contemporary and immutable facts . . . We are entitled to say to those who are expressing their discontent with the choice already open to them that they must prove their sincerity by a declared willingness to work the present constitution.'[16] Addressing the Central Asian Society the following month he painted a picture of the communal situation in India not very different from that he had given Reading.

> We must never close our eyes to the reality of a situation which might easily be rendered dangerous either by blindness or by the language of optimism. The fundamental fact of the Indian situation is that we went there centuries ago, composing, by the sharp edge of the sword, differences which would have submerged and destroyed Indian civilisation, and it is true that if we were to leave India tomorrow that continent would be submerged by the same anarchical and murderous disturbances which devastated it in the days of Clive and Warren Hastings.[17]

The pretence that the British were in India to save the Indians from themselves was at least half humbug. F.E. was principally concerned to hold India for the glory of the British Crown. At the same time, as he had maintained in his Amritsar speech, there was no glory in an Empire imposed by cruelty and repression upon a hostile population; the glory of Empire lay in governing well, to the clear benefit of a grateful population. From this point of view, while he did not intend to hasten the Empire's demise, F.E. was anxious in some way to add a brick to the edifice of its achievement. He did not wish to preside over five years of purely negative government without leaving some positive mark behind him. In January 1925 he sought Reading's advice.

> Incidentally I should like to have your views as to whether in compensation for the political sterility of our attitude, it is not practicable to conceive of a somewhat ambitious economic or agricultural policy, which would strike the imagination and produce solid results.

He was, he said, 'not so foolish as to imagine that after a few months' office, I can usefully make suggestions myself upon topics so vast, so complicated and so novel'. But he could not help being struck by how little the primitive methods of Indian agriculture, which was still the whole life of 85 per cent of the population, seemed to have changed over the centuries, when there had been such great advances in the application of science to agriculture elsewhere.

> I cannot help wondering whether some further progress in this vitally important matter is not attainable. It would seem a poor record of achievement for four or five years tenure of this office to say simply 'in politics and in the constitution there is nothing doing, and the economic cupboard is equally bare'. You will observe that, as is perhaps inevitable, I am still groping in the dark; perhaps you could supply some ray of illumination.[18]

Reading, when he replied some three weeks later, shared F.E.'s concern but pointed out the ironic difficulty: agriculture was a 'transferred' subject, and thus not the responsibility of the Delhi Government, nor even of British officials in the Provinces, but of the native governments. He had tried calling joint conferences, but these could achieve little. He and F.E. continued, however, to correspond on the necessity of doing something: the next year they had recourse to that tried old standby for expressing unfocused concern and appointed a Royal Commission, chaired by the Marquess of Linlithgow. It reported in April 1928, but predictably achieved little, except perhaps to salve F.E.'s reforming conscience.

A narrower field, in which he could hope to have some effect, was the question of recruitment to the Indian Civil Service. The India Office was alarmed that both the quality and the numbers of candidates for the I.C.S. had fallen in recent years, due, it was assumed, to widespread doubt whether India any longer offered a secure career. F.E. always took a close interest in the opportunities open to bright young men – though his usual advice was unhesitatingly to recommend his own ladder: the Bar and politics, by way of the Oxford Union. Now he threw himself energetically into directing them to India. 'I am sure', he went so far as to tell Reading, 'that my period in office will be largely judged according as I am successful or unsuccessful in keeping up English recruitment for the Civil Service.'[19] In April 1925 he introduced into the House of Lords an Indian Civil Service Bill, embodying the recommendations of a Royal Commission chaired by Lee of Fareham: the idea was to increase to 50 per cent the proportion of Indians employed in the service (the figure was currently 17 per cent). But F.E. warned that it would be difficult to maintain the 50 per cent British component unless home recruitment picked up: the decline was a more disturbing threat to the Empire than all the nationalist movements in India itself.[20]

Accordingly he launched a recruiting drive: he himself, Winterton, Lee and others went round the universities 'in a resolute attempt to beat up enthusiasm . . . among the best class of undergraduate'. He gave Reading a characteristic glimpse of his line of argument.

> With all the political uncertainty of our career, we can at least offer something. The ordinary modern Undergraduate, who has done well at the University, has at present rather a bleak prospect. The Church and teaching are miserably underpaid. There is a famine at the Temple and the number of Calls [to the Bar] since the Armistice have been in ludicrous proportion to the prospects which the Bar affords. Medicine is even more overcrowded, and there must still be many to whom the call of the East, if we can remove prevailing apprehensions, will still make a strong appeal.[21]

There was a need for good British recruits, he asserted tactfully at Glasgow University in May 1925, not because of any innate superiority, but because they contributed something distinctive to India, as in their own way did the Indian recruits.[22] That he was not always so diplomatic off the record is suggested by his account to Reading of a meeting in Oxford in March, when he addressed some 140 undergraduates 'of a very fine athletic type'. Unfortunately he was inhibited in his remarks by the fact that some Indians got to hear of the meeting and came along, which 'made it necessary for me to walk warily and delicately'.[19] One can imagine the line he took when neither reporters nor Indians were present.

F.E. easily convinced himself that his efforts had borne instant fruit. The very next year he was able to tell the Viceroy that the latest I.C.S. examination had produced the best set of men for fifteen years. 'I am told also', he added with satisfaction, 'that a reaction has set in among the undergraduates at Oxford and Cambridge against a business career which seemed after the war to be the premier attraction.'[23] He had no doubt that this was a healthy ordering of priorities. Whether those who were persuaded by his assurances that the I.C.S. offered a career for life were grateful to him when they found themselves, twenty years later, back in England in their mid-forties to begin again, must be – at the least – questionable.

Among the aspects of Indian government in which F.E. took least interest was the problem of the currency. In August 1925 he appointed a Royal Commission to report on ways of stabilizing the rupee: but the extent of his personal understanding of the matter is shown by a teasing note found by Churchill's private secretary in his box after a Cabinet meeting.

FE. What is the value at the present rate of exchange of a lakh of
rupees? W.
Go to hell. B.[24]

A range of questions which did catch F.E.'s interest, however,
concerned relations with the nominally autonomous Princely States of
India. An instructive example of his thoroughness in this connection
was the famous case of the Bhopal succession. It was one of the principal
powers by which the British Government retained the whip hand over
the Princes that it had the authority, as Paramount Power, to determine
disputed successions. In this instance the Begum of Bhopal, a picturesque but formidable old lady, the most important female ruler in
India, wished to pass on her inheritance not to her grandson, as
European primogeniture would dictate, but to her youngest son. The
Government in Delhi refused her petition; whereupon the old lady
appealed to London and came in person to press her case. She made a
thoroughly embarrassing nuisance of herself by importuning everyone
of influence that she could get to see. In October 1925 F.E. satirically
described to Reading her coming to tea a few days earlier with his wife
and family: 'The Begum's tears did not prevent a considerable consumption of hot buttered toast.'[25] On the merits of her case, however,
F.E. instigated researches and came to the conclusion that Delhi had
got the matter wrong. (The reason was not, as was stated, that the India
Office had records going back further than those in India: the officials in
India had simply not looked hard enough.) On the evidence eventually
produced, F.E. ruled in the Begum's favour, on the ground that there
was

> no vestige of evidence that the English system of primogeniture
> had ever been applied or accepted in Bhopal. In these circum-
> stances it seemed to me hardly defensible to apply it for the first
> time in the teeth of many precedents and against the vehemently
> expressed desires of a popular ruler.[26]

Reading was obliged to concur. 'I imagine that the old lady is in the
seventh heaven,' F.E. wrote, 'but I hope that she will spend what
remains of it in her own country.'[26]

The critical factor, however, was that the Begum *was* a popular ruler.
The picture of the Paramount Power impartially applying native law in
the Princely States is somewhat dented by the casual assertion in an
earlier telegram from F.E. to Reading that the decision in such cases
must ultimately be made 'on grounds of policy and not of law'.[27] In
other words, he would have decided differently if it would have suited

British policy better to have put the Begum's grandson rather than her son on the throne. This is the consistent thread running through all F.E.'s dealings with India: that the overriding principle must be to maintain at every level the prestige and the supremacy of the European. This comes through in quite trivial matters. For instance, in 1926 he picked up a report of some of the Nizam of Hyderabad's retainers at the theatre 'leering at inadequately dressed English dancing girls'. 'It is notorious', he wrote at once to the Viceroy, 'that few things are more damaging to our prestige as a people than the exposure of the bodies of white women before Indians.'[28]

A similar racial prudery dictated F.E.'s attitude to the famous 'Mr A.' case, in which the young heir to the throne of Kashmir, on a tour of Europe, was tricked into bed with the wife of an unscrupulous English bookmaker by his own British A.D.C. and blackmailed to the tune of £125,000. F.E. was genuinely sorry for the young man, who, he wrote, 'when little more than a boy, was vilely abused by a gang of English swindlers'. It was, he reflected, 'ironical . . . that the very vastness of the sum which he paid to avoid publicity [was] the very element in the matter which has produced it'.[14] Nevertheless, it was the publicity itself which alarmed him, and the reverberations in India of, first, the sexual involvement of an Indian with a white woman and, second, the fact that it was a British officer, appointed to his staff by the Government of India, who had so scandalously betrayed him. He did all he could to keep these shocking facts, so damaging to British prestige, out of the newspapers. He managed to persuade Lord Darling, the judge before whom the conspiracy ultimately came to trial, to allow the victim's identity to be concealed under the pseudonym 'Mr A.' – a concession which only a Secretary of State of F.E.'s standing at the Bar could have secured – though as always the American papers effectively sabotaged Fleet Street's willingness to maintain this cover. Towards the end of his term of office, when 'Mr A.' came again to Europe, F.E. intervened again with Beaverbrook and Rothermere to try to restrict publicity.[29] He firmly prevented the young man being appointed Indian Ambassador to the League of Nations.

The native Princes – of whom there survived several hundred ranging from the rulers of vast provinces the size of a substantial European country to tinpot local chieftains with no significant territories at all – were an ever-present headache for the Government of India. In one respect their extravagance, sensuality and corruption suited the British book by advertising the undesirable results of Indian self-rule. On the other hand, the native States only survived under the protection of the Paramount Power, so that their often cruel misgovernment resounded to the discredit of their British patrons. During F.E.'s time there was trouble with one of the grandest of the Princes, the Nizam of Hyderabad, who had for some years been allowed a very free rein by a weak British Resident. In December 1925 a new Resident took office and reported a situation in Hyderabad which aroused F.E.'s alarm. 'It would hardly be possible', he wrote, 'to frame a blacker indictment against any Ruler ... A state of gross misrule prevails ... the constitutional machinery has broken down ... the people have almost reached the limits of endurance.' Such a situation could not be tolerated. 'The state of misrule in Hyderabad today reflects grave discredit not only upon the Ruler but upon the British Government which maintains him upon the Masnad.'[30]

The Viceroy was reluctant to interfere, but F.E. was insistent. British prestige was at stake. The Nizam had been shrugging off all warnings since 1918: he must be brought to heel. 'I am sure that you will agree with me', F.E. pressed in September 1926, 'that having once begun we must see the thing through, and insist on prompt and genuine compliance and no eyewash.'[31] 'I do not want to hustle you,' he pressed again in November,

> but the position must be known all over India ... the other Princes look on and wonder *quo usque tandem* ... I do most sincerely trust that you will address yourself energetically and resolutely to this matter. As Arthur Balfour once said, it is better to be odious than ridiculous.[32]

There in a nutshell is F.E.'s understanding of the right way to govern India. In this case he got his way. The Nizam was eventually forced to accept a majority of British officials holding all the principal portfolios in his Council.

In the summer of 1925 Reading came home on leave – an unprecedented departure for a serving Viceroy, which was taken by Indians to indicate important discussions presaging some major announcement. In fact, though he and F.E. did of course have long conversations at the India Office, Reading came home for a badly needed rest as much as anything. F.E. fêted him royally at the India Office and at Gray's Inn, and made a point of introducing him to the Cabinet, 'so many of whose Members', he wrote slyly, 'have emerged since you left these shores'.[33] The result of their discussions was F.E.'s first set-piece speech in the House of Lords, an event which he managed to postpone until July – eight months after taking office. Though it predictably rejected any immediate extension of native responsibility, it was couched in a notably positive and sympathetic tone. Reading's influence was evident, and Indian official opinion was agreeably surprised.[34]

Reviewing the working of the 1919 Constitution, F.E. confessed publicly his initial dislike of the dyarchical principle, while paying tribute to the idealism of its author, Montagu, who had died the year before.

> It seemed to me to savour of the kind of pedantic and hidebound Constitution to which Anglo-Saxon communities have not generally responded, and which in my anticipation was unlikely to make a successful appeal to a community whose political ideas were, thanks in the main to Macaulay, so largely derived from Anglo-Saxon models.

For this reason, however, he felt himself especially bound to give it a fair trial. Had the Montagu–Chelmsford Constitution failed? he therefore asked. 'My Lords, I cannot say that it has failed . . . It has never been given a chance.' The *swarajists* had done their best to wreck it. And yet it had not been wrecked. 'Not all the resources of a very adroit and sophisticated Party have availed to destroy this experimental Constitution.' As a result, 'I who was prepared to curse, upon the balance of the whole matter find myself almost inclined to bless.'

Nevertheless there was nothing sacred about dyarchy; whether it had worked badly or well, it would be reconsidered when the Statutory Commission came to make its report. Nor, F.E. hinted for the first time, was there anything sacred about the date set by Parliament for the Commission to be appointed. 'The door of acceleration is not open to menace,' he warned. 'Still less will it be stormed by violence.' But 'wise men are not the slaves of dates; rather are dates the servants of sagacious men'. The absolute condition that would be insisted on by Parliament before bringing forward the Commission was that Indian leaders should co-operate to work the dyarchical constitution meanwhile. 'The tactics hitherto pursued by the most highly organised Party in India could not have been more happily conceived if they had been subtly intended to forward the cause of reaction.' How different – F.E. almost seemed to enthuse – might it have been if the Indians had set out instead to prove, by their capacity to discharge the limited responsibility placed on them by the latest reforms, their readiness to be trusted with more. 'Does anyone imagine that reactionary critics of those reforms in this country could in that event have retarded the chariot of progress?'

F.E. was speaking from the heart here. It was the tactical stupidity, as he saw it, of the *swarajists* in making it easy for people like himself to argue their unfitness to govern themselves, instead of making it difficult by willing co-operation, that fed his contempt for them and made him confident that they would never accept whatever concessions he might, with apparent generosity, offer them. He saw no prospect of their making out a good case for the acceleration of the Commission. With the same cynical confidence he felt able to make them another fair offer. 'It has been the habit of spokesmen of Swarajist thought to declare in anticipation that no Constitution framed in the West can either be suitable for, or acceptable to, the peoples of India.' (Note the invariable plural, in which lay his whole point.) Very well.

> We do not claim in Great Britain that we alone in the world are able to frame Constitutions, though we are not altogether discontented with the humble constructive efforts which we have made in this field of human ingenuity. But if our critics in India are of opinion that their greater knowledge of Indian conditions qualifies them to succeed, where they tell us that we have failed, let them produce a Constitution which carries behind it a fair measure of general agreement among the great peoples of India.

It would be carefully considered when the time came.

Having thus demonstrated his positive open-mindedness in respect of Indian aspirations, F.E. was able to close his speech with a more characteristic note of warning. While the Government had every hope of ultimately realizing the promise of self-government made in 1919, 'I should be guilty of disingenuousness if I painted at this moment the prospect in colours too vivid or too sanguine.'

> I am not able in any foreseeable future to discern a moment when we may safely, either to ourselves or to India, abandon our trust. There is, my Lords, no 'Lost Dominion'; there will be no 'Lost Dominion' until that moment – if it ever comes – when the whole British Empire, with all that it means for civilisation, is splintered in doom. It is our purpose resolutely, tirelessly and wholeheartedly, to labour for the well-being of India, as our ancestors have laboured throughout the generations. For that purpose we desire and we request goodwill; nor shall we be niggardly bargainers if we meet with the generous friendship which is near and dear to our hearts. We no longer talk of holding 'the gorgeous East in fee'; we invite in a contrary sense the diverse peoples of this continent to march side by side with us in a fruitful and harmonious partnership which may recreate the greatest and proudest days of Indian history.[35]

Like Ireland, therefore, India was to be threatened into friendship. Constitutional advance was limited by the overriding obligation to remain within the British Empire – an eternal junior partner in Britain's imperial destiny.

Soon after this speech, Reading returned to India and F.E. resumed his weekly letters. In November he suddenly struck a new note. In his speech he had carefully opened the door to the possibility of accelerating the Statutory Commission, yet at the same time he had made it clear that if Indian co-operation was to be the criterion he saw little ground for doing so. Now he opened with Reading a more machiavellian line of argument that was in his mind.

When I made my speech in the House of Lords suggesting that it might be possible to accelerate the Commission of 1928, if some measure of co-operation were forthcoming in India, I always had it plainly in mind that we could not afford to run the slightest risk that the nomination of the 1928 Commission should be in the hands of our successors. You can readily imagine what kind of Commission in its personnel would have been appointed by Colonel Wedgwood and his friends. [Wedgwood was a strongly pro-Indian ex-Radical tipped as a possible Secretary of State in a future Labour Government.] I have, therefore, throughout been of the clear opinion that it would be necessary for us, as a matter of elementary prudence, to appoint the Commission not later than the summer of 1927.

If, therefore, we take the view that we are not prepared to run the slightest political risks in a problem so grave and so decisive of the future of India, it becomes evident that we ought to aim for the best possible terms from our opponents in compensation for a concession which, rightly considered, is no concession at all, because our own interests imperatively require that we should make it.

I should therefore like to receive your advice if at any moment you discern an opportunity for making this a useful bargain counter or for further disintegrating the Swarajist Party. If important elements in that party could be disaffected by an assurance discreetly given that a real co-operation would almost certainly result in an acceleration, I invite you to consult me as to the circumstances in which, and the persons to whom, such an assurance could be usefully given, and naturally I invite your advice about the whole matter, though to me it appears plain.[36]

Reading replied that he had always favoured bringing forward the Commission, for exactly the reason that it was a lure with which to tempt the more moderate *swarajists* into co-operation.[37] But F.E. stamped firmly on his wish to hint at an acceleration before he left India in 1926: there was no case for Britain to give away this counter until her own tactical interests dictated the moment.[38] Reading could only acquiesce.

(ii) Irwin, 1926–8

As Reading's five-year term drew to a close, F.E. was closely concerned with the choice of his successor, though the decision was ultimately Baldwin's and the King too took a special interest in the appointment. There had been rumours that F.E. intended to appoint himself, which caused a wave of apprehension in both Britain and India;[39] but Baldwin would never have looked at such an idea. (Other considerations apart, he told Neville Chamberlain, 'it would be murder to send him out there; he would be dead in a year's time.')[40] It was in fact the King who proposed the name of Edward Wood, after the Cabinet had rejected his first suggestion, Lord Haig, as unsuitably military. Wood was the heir to the Viscountcy of Halifax, a large Yorkshire landowner and noted Churchman; he had been one of the most high-minded of the Carlton Club rebels against the Coalition and an opponent of F.E.'s return to favour in 1923; he was one of Baldwin's most trusted friends and Minister of Agriculture in the present Cabinet. If he was scarcely a man after F.E.'s own heart, F.E. probably thought it important to have a Conservative to follow Reading, and Wood appealed strongly to Baldwin as the type of Englishman whom the Indians would most naturally respect; he only wondered whether he could spare so valued a colleague from the Cabinet. When Wood accepted the office in October 1925, F.E. pronounced himself well pleased, 'the best man that we could have got . . . He is a man of the highest character, of very considerable ability, great courtesy of manner, and of distinguished appearance.'[41] Having said this, however, he sounded in his next letter a little put out by the chorus of praise with which the press had hailed the Viceroy-designate.

The reception of Wood's name in the Press has been extraordinarily favourable, even a little surprisingly so. I hardly noted a single discordant word. How much better is life and how much more paying it is to be blameless than to be brilliant; and it certainly pays in such a connection never to have attacked anyone. But as a matter of fact, as I have already told you, I have a real admiration for his character and for his quiet but solid qualities. He is really very intelligent, will count no labour excessive, and will not be easily deflected from any course which he has persuaded himself is right. I am really very happy about the whole business, for though I naturally do not know him anything like as well as I know you, I know enough of him to make it certain that my association with him will be harmonious, and I hope that it may prove useful and fruitful.[42]

A fortnight later F.E. reported:

Wood is now working regularly at the office . . . I have set him a very severe course of reading, the same in fact which I myself pursued in the last 12 months. He is so industrious and capable that I have no doubt he will go to India much more fully equipped than most Viceroys. He enjoys my complete confidence.[43]

To give him the necessary dignity for his new eminence, Wood was created Lord Irwin. (He subsequently became better known, of course, as Neville Chamberlain's Foreign Secretary, as Lord Halifax.) Irwin sailed for India in March 1926, with not only F.E. but Baldwin and the Archbishop of Canterbury at Victoria to see him off. One might have expected that with this new Viceroy F.E. would have been less at ease than with his old friend Reading, his letters less colloquial and indiscreet. If anything, on the contrary, they became more so. For all their different outlooks on life, F.E. assumed – wrongly, as it turned out – an identity of political outlook in a Cabinet colleague which he had not felt with the Liberal Reading. Moreover he was now the senior partner in the Viceroy–Secretary of State duumvirate; there is, with Irwin, no more deference to the Viceroy's longer experience – on the contrary, as his own term of office draws to a close F.E. becomes more assertive in his instructions on Indian affairs, and writes also with increasingly satirical freedom on other matters.

During the first months of Irwin's Viceroyalty, F.E.'s letters, apart from the usual to-and-fro on detailed questions of administration, were largely preoccupied with a blow-by-blow account of the General Strike, during which, he noted, 'India was obliging enough not to obtrude herself upon our attention unduly',[44] and the miners' lock-out which lasted from May to November. India he was pleased to regard as relatively tranquil. There were still outbreaks of Hindu–Moslem violence, but 'an occasional petty eruption can be regarded with calmness, and, after all, it serves as a useful reminder of the indispensability of British control'.[45] In public, in his second annual review in the House of Lords he indignantly denied suggestions that the British welcomed such outbreaks,[46] but otherwise said very little in what he himself described as a 'dull and tiresome' speech; Winterton's in the Commons was even duller. 'It is no disadvantage', he told Irwin, 'that Indian affairs should be debated in Parliament at a low temperature. This condition has been most effectively ensured in both Houses.'[47] He congratulated himself that with the *swarajists* apparently cowed for the moment, confidence in both the India Office and the Government of India was high. He actually proposed that it might be possible for him to pay a purely private visit to India the next year; but Irwin tactfully but firmly discouraged this idea.[48] The thought of the indiscretions which F.E. might commit on the loose in India sent a shock of horror down the collective spine of the Delhi Government. F.E. was not pleased.[49]

With India dull, F.E. began to entertain Irwin with sporting gossip. In one letter, in July 1926, he described the latest Test Match against the visiting Australians, which had 'aroused the greatest public interest, and even overshadowed the series of almost daily sensations provided by the volatile and neurasthenic Lenglen at Wimbledon'. Cricket had always appeared to be the one national sport in which F.E. took no active interest, but here he is found writing knowledgeably of 'Hendren, whom I have long considered the second batsman in England', and weighing up the unusually poor quality of the Australians.* He ended with a comment which more characteristically expresses his impatience with the noblest game, a remark of enduring truth which deserves a place in any anthology of cricketing wit. 'It is a wonder to me that cricket maintains its hold over England. In a three day match, if it happens to be wet, you cannot start the match; if it happens to be fine you cannot finish it!'[50]

The serious question that was concerning F.E. as Secretary of State this summer was not the antics of the Indian politicians but, far more fundamental in his view, the age-old threat to India posed by Russia, through Afghanistan: a tradition now carried on for their own purposes by the Bolsheviks. 'We must realise', he wrote to Irwin in July, 'that we are once again face to face with the ambitions of Czarist Russia in a more dangerous, unscrupulous and poisonous form'.[51] On 31 August a treaty was concluded between the Soviet Union and Afghanistan which underlined his fears. In October he gave the Imperial Conference, gathered in London, a sombre review of the military prospect and India's preparedness to meet it.

> The policy initiated by Peter the Great of penetrating to the warm water has not changed with changing forms of government –

* The first batsman in England was of course Jack Hobbs. In 1925 Reading had had to ask F.E. to convey Moslem outrage to a British cartoonist who had innocently depicted Hobbs among a pantheon of the gods, including Mahomet.

rather, so far as an advance towards India is concerned, has it received an additional incentive from the desire to weaken the great obstacle to the extension of Bolshevik tenets which is presented by the British commonwealth of nations. The fanatical and warlike inhabitants on and across the North-West Frontier of India form an ideal weapon for the purpose; the simple peasantry of India are a fertile soil for the propaganda, and the Bolshevik intention to exploit weapons so suitable was deliberately formed and will be ruthlessly carried out. We must be prepared to meet Russian aggression towards India in a new and far more dangerous form, since it aims at external attack synchronising with, or consequent on, internal disruption. Nor must it be forgotten that we are dealing with a regime far less scrupulous in its diplomatic and propagandist methods than that which it succeeded. There were after all limits to the contrivances conceived and the methods adopted by the older system.[52]

One-third of the Indian army was immobilized, since the recrudescence of communal strife, by the requirements of internal security, and F.E. urged the necessity of building up its strength as a priority of imperial defence. This, he told Irwin, was the overriding issue of his Viceroyalty. Irwin, to F.E.'s exasperation, did not share his sense of urgency, and was even inclined to look for economies in the defence budget. In December 1926 F.E. wrote him a stiff letter which makes clear the gap between them.

I hope that you will not approach me with any proposal of any Military reduction in India. Indeed I must tell you in the friendliest way – and I cannot believe that you will disagree – that so far as my power can be made effective – I could not agree to it. India is at the present time – forgive me for restating the commonplace – the one vulnerable point of the British Empire. You and I are absolutely responsible for rendering it invulnerable. You and I would both be broken – and rightly broken – if we failed in the discharge of this duty. If I were an autocrat like Mussolini, so far from decreasing, I would largely increase, the defensive strength of our Military forces in India. Do not let any Budgetary consideration deflect upon this matter your cool and courageous judgement. For myself, I am quite resolved upon the course which, in this matter, I must pursue, and press upon the Cabinet. I rely upon you to give me advice which will render this necessary task easier and not more difficult.[53]

This was straight talking. But F.E.'s power could *not* be made effective. Irwin was well able to ignore what he wanted to ignore, and the Indian defence budget was reduced in each of the next two years, despite F.E.'s warnings. Fifteen months later the Afghan threat had so far receded that F.E. was found entertaining the King of Afghanistan, on a state visit to Britain, in high splendour at Wadham.

On the one major question of India's political future, however, Secretary of State and Viceroy did have a real dialogue, though here again it was Irwin's view that prevailed. They were agreed, for the party political reason already explained by F.E. to Reading, that the Commission's appointment should be brought forward: in July 1926 F.E. was still thinking of 1928 as the appropriate moment. Where they disagreed initially was over the personnel of the Commission: should it be a mixed body of British and Indians, or exclusively British? It has usually been assumed that it was F.E., with his known disregard for Indian feeling, who insisted on the exclusion of Indians. Irwin himself, in his memoirs, published in 1957, is one of those who attribute the decision unequivocally to the Secretary of State, making no mention of his own part in it at all.[54] In fact, the contemporary correspondence makes it clear that it was Irwin who argued for a purely British Commission, and F.E. who put the counter-arguments until he was persuaded to accede to the Viceroy's judgment. The memoirs of even the most highminded cannot be trusted.

In his letter of 29 July 1926 F.E. happened to mention that he had given no thought as yet to the British members of the Commission.[55] Irwin immediately picked this up. In his reply (19 August) he stated that he had grave doubts about including Indians: the need, if they were admitted at all, to appoint enough to represent each of the major groups within Indian society – Hindus, Moslems and Sikhs; *swarajists* and Liberals; Princes and Untouchables – would make the Commission impossibly unwieldy; while he feared that a mixed Commission would be likely to divide down the middle, producing two or more reports. He favoured a small high-powered Commission of five or so pro-consuls.[56]

F.E. replied in September. 'As to the *personnel* of the Statutory Commission,' he wrote, 'you have persuaded me of the wisdom of your view. I, too, now think that the advantages of having Indians on the Commission are outweighed by the disadvantages.'[57] But he was not fully convinced. Six months later, in March 1927, he was writing that his mind was still 'absolutely open'; 'I am well aware of the arguments in favour of the exclusion of natives . . . but you must remember that [the arguments in favour of inclusion] are *a priori* very strong.'

It will be said that the determination of this constitution, with all that it may mean for India, cannot be settled with the least appearance of authority by a Commission which contains no Indian Member. It will also be pointed out that there are Indians of considerable distinction who have never taken up an irreconcileable attitude in relation to the present constitution, and that to deny the chance of membership to all Indians is to make evident to all the world the 'inferiority complex' with which we choose to brand the peoples of India.

F.E.'s idea was evidently to use membership of the Commission as a mark of favour with which to reward 'good' Indians. He had a more subtle argument, too: that the presence of Indians could actually serve what he took to be Britain's purpose of delaying further advance.

Are you quite certain that the presence on the Commission, both of Hindu and Moslem representatives, that the controversy which would follow, that the probability of divergent Hindu and Moslem reports, might not be of great assistance to you and to us if the Commission took the view that a very considerable advance was not to be recommended at the moment when they report?[58]

Irwin, however, perhaps because unlike F.E. he *did* want to see a constructive, unanimous report which would signpost the next stage in India's constitutional progress, was determined to have an all-British Commission, and decided that the most defensible way of achieving this would be to make it a Parliamentary Commission, composed entirely of M.P.s and peers, on the ground that it was Parliament which would have the responsibility of implementing the Commission's recommendations. F.E. was doubtful about this, too, on the highly revealing ground that it would be difficult to exclude from a Parliamentary Commission certain peers with Indian experience, notably Reading, whose inclusion, F.E. thought, 'would not be an unmixed advantage'.[59] Irwin's answer to this was that, by convention, ex-Viceroys did not revisit India. F.E. finally agreed on 28 April that the Commission should be British and Parliamentary.[60]

Another question that had to be decided in advance was how, if there were to be no Indians on the Commission, Indian opinion was to be consulted. Should an Indian convention be held to draw up its own proposals before the arrival of the Commission? Should the Report be submitted to the Indian Legislature, whose view of it could then be sent on with the Report to Parliament? Or should there be a Round Table Conference, which was what Indians wanted, at which all parties would be represented equally with the Government of India, to consider the

Report? Once again F.E. saw the promise of a Round Table Conference as a carrot in return for which even the most unco-operative Indians might be persuaded to co-operate.

> I have a feeling [he wrote in February] that if you handle the situation with subtlety, a very promising political prospect may now develop. The Swarajists are down. The Hindu–Moslem dissensions have destroyed Gandhi's dream. You may easily be able to negotiate with them in substance – but not of course in manner – *de haut en bas*. I am not opposed to an invitation *from them* to you for an Indian discussion upon the report of the Commission. You say rightly that such an agreement might save their faces if the proposal was known to proceed from their initiative. But my principal preoccupation is not to save their faces; it is to make it certain *beforehand* that a sane and generous proposal would receive *beforehand* the guaranteed support of those who have hitherto been out mad opponents. Otherwise I will not consider it.[61]

The last question to be decided, once it was agreed that they should all be Members of Parliament, was the actual membership of the Commission. The first name that F.E. thought of for chairman was Lord Hewart, the Lord Chief Justice, which shows the sort of eminence he was looking for. There was a precedent in Reading's wartime mission to Washington, but it was not a good principle that the Chief Justice should be sent on extended absences abroad. The second was his old rival and doubtful friend, John Simon, another Liberal lawyer but one with the advantage that he had neither office nor the early prospect of office, to give up: on the contrary, when the offer was made to him he jumped at it as a dignified escape from the squabbling futility to which the Parliamentary Liberal Party had been humiliatingly reduced. Little as he liked him, F.E. well knew Simon's qualifications for the job. 'The work of Chairman', he wrote to Irwin in June 1927, 'requires a man of great subtlety, acuteness, quickness, industry and tact. Simon possesses all these qualities in a remarkable degree. I have every reason, moreover, to believe that his views upon the fundamentals of the matter are very largely in agreement with my own.'[62]

Simon had in fact been to India the previous year and returned, according to Amery (who must have told F.E.), 'very much impressed with the fact that the Oriental is not really adapted to our English scheme of Parliamentary Government'.[63] The 'only objection' F.E. could see to Simon was that he had for so many years been a leading Liberal, 'infected by all the errors of that party'; but evidently he did not feel that Simon's Liberalism was nowadays more than nominal. Apart from the possibility of some Conservative jealousy – 'there is, I am told, a growing impatience amongst our supporters in the House of Commons at the number of posts or functions which have been given in the last year or two to Liberals' – Simon offered all the advantages of appointing a non-Conservative with the confidence that he would take a soundly conservative view. 'His speeches, both on the subject of the General Strike and of China, would', F.E. thought, 'reassure Conservative opinion.' At the same time, 'this selection would . . . make it necessary to have two or three very solid and orthodox Conservatives among those chosen. I have in mind the kind of man who, without being a bigoted Diehard, would command the full confidence of the Right Wing of our Party.'[62]

Irwin agreed readily that Simon be invited to serve as chairman. The biographer Bechhofer Roberts, who wrote lives of both F.E. and Simon and was at this time working with F.E. as a sort of research assistant-cum-literary ghost, gives a most improbable but graphic account of F.E. making the offer to Simon over a game of golf at the course which lay close to both their country houses, Tadmarton Heath near Banbury. Roberts was the third player.

> Lord Birkenhead's golf was unorthodox: his method was to stride up to the ball, slash hastily at it and as briskly follow it up on its erratic course. Simon, on the other hand, has always been a deliberate player: if not a very hard hitter, he is accurate and does not mind taking infinite pains before playing each shot. These different styles meant that, on the day in question, the two men rarely met between the tee and the green, and I found myself sometimes near one and sometimes near the other, alternately in danger from FE's swipes or witnessing from far off his impatient protests at having to wait for Simon to play. After one more than usually maddening wait near a green, we saw Simon skilfully loft his ball out of an awkward bunker to within a few inches of the hole. Lord Birkenhead gave way for a moment to natural and blasphemous indignation, but then allowed broader considerations to widen his view. 'Yes, he's the right man for the Indian job!' he remarked to me, and hit his ball sharply across the green into the bunker which Simon had just vacated. I have always supposed that the earnest manner in which he then engaged Simon in conversation about India was intended as much to put the latter off his game as to clinch the invitation, but Simon did not allow any thought of the future to hasten or impair his shots.[64]

Whether or not this accurately reports the moment of invitation, once the offer had been made and accepted F.E. and Simon did play a lot of golf together ('nearly every day', F.E. told Irwin),[65] and Roberts's description of their respective styles is certainly authentic.

Simon had only one worry: that going to India should not jeopardize his seat in Parliament. F.E. took the view that if he took the chairmanship, the Conservatives would be morally bound to give him a clear run at the next election, and undertook to arrange the matter with the party chairman. Davidson agreed, but had much greater difficulty persuading the local Tories in Spen Valley to be so obliging. In the end, the Tory candidate did stand down; but when the election came, Simon promptly took advantage of being unopposed by speaking all round the country. Churchill considered this 'firing from under a white flag'. But F.E. back-handedly defended his old 'friend'. 'After all, he has been a Liberal all his life since he was a boy at Oxford, and to have left at the last moment of all a sinking ship would have been an act of sacrifice which I should never have thought it right to request at his hands.'[66]

By the end of the summer the personnel of the Commission was completed. First F.E. and Irwin agreed the balance of parties: two Tory peers, two Tory M.P.s and two Labour M.P.s. Then after several refusals and the threat that the Labour party might refuse to allow any Labour members to serve, the names were filled in. The two peers gave most trouble: the heavyweights F.E. first approached, like Crawford and Donoughmore, Bradbury and Beatty, all declined; he eventually fell back on the newspaper proprietor Lord Burnham and the young Strathcona and Mount Royal (who had been an M.P. from 1922 to 1926 and Bridgeman's P.P.S. at the Admiralty). The two Tory M.P.s, picked to reassure the Diehards, were an archetypal squire, George Lane-Fox, and an inoffensive younger son, the Hon. Edward Cadogan. (Lane-Fox was actually Secretary for the Mines, but he had held the position with conspicuous lack of success throughout the coal crisis of the past two years, and it was a kindness to rescue him; he was also married to Irwin's sister.) To fill the Labour places F.E. picked, with MacDonald's help, Stephen Walsh, an old trade unionist who had been Secretary of State for War in 1924, and his little known Under-Secretary in that Government, Major Clement Attlee, under whose Premiership, it would have astonished all concerned to learn, India was to achieve her complete independence just twenty years later! (Walsh had in the event to withdraw almost immediately due to illness; he was replaced by another miners' M.P., Vernon Hartshorn.)

F.E.'s disappointment that he had not assembled a more powerful team was evident in his attempts to assure Irwin that they were 'not . . . unimpressive' nor lacking in considerable ability. At any rate, he wrote, 'We can only now hope for the best and contemplate the constitution-making activities of the Frankenstein – I hope a beneficent one – whom we have jointly called into being.'[67] Irwin pressed for an early announcement of the names. Rumour had already reached India that the Commission was to include no Indian members: there was talk already of a boycott of its investigations if this were indeed the case. Irwin was confident that this would not happen; he was sure that the Moslems would not join in a boycott, and if they co-operated then the Hindus could not afford to let their case go by default. He was anxious to explain the thinking behind a Parliamentary Commission as soon as possible.[68] So in early November 1927 the names were announced.

> I have, of course [F.E. wrote], no delusions as to the howl of rage with which our proposals will be received by the Indian Press. But no-one can charge against us that we had not deeply applied our minds to the problem or that we had not examined every conceivable alternative scheme. Nothing remains but to face such criticism as we shall encounter with coolness and composure.[69]

This was easier for F.E. than for Irwin. F.E. was remote from the furious vituperation which descended on his head when he formally announced the appointment of the Commission in the House of Lords on 24 November. He actually made a strong effort to conciliate Indian outrage, insisting on the one hand on the practical impossibility and constitutional impropriety of a mixed commission, but on the other that the consultation arrangements would amply ensure that all Indian viewpoints were represented. The Commission's report would be submitted for consideration not only to Parliament but to a joint committee of both Houses of the Indian Legislature. 'They are given a function, if they will only understand it, more important than that of the Commission itself.'[70] The Indian press was not convinced. To one Bombay paper his speech was 'a farrago of insolent fallacies . . . To acquiesce in the insult would be to accept the theory of racial despotism.' 'Lord Birkenhead's speech', predicted a Calcutta paper, the *Amrita Bazar Patrika*, 'will only stiffen the boycott movement. Reading his speech as a whole, one does not find any trace of an impartial mind, which could reasonably be expected to do justice to India, or to approach her problems with sympathy.' *The Bengalee*'s response was the more damning for being so moderately expressed, 'We are not prepared to accuse Lord Birkenhead of calculated insult to India, but that his contempt for Indians and their co-operation, though silent, is intense and real, we do not doubt for a moment . . . That silent contempt we feel bitterly.'[71]

The Commission *was* boycotted, on its arrival in India in February 1928, by all the Indian parties, and Gandhi emerged from seclusion to lead a united campaign for fully responsible government at once. F.E. thought to call Gandhi's bluff by once again challenging the Indians to produce their own constitutional solution.

> I am entirely in favour [he wrote to Irwin] of inducing the mal-contents to produce their own proposals, for in the first place I believe them to be quite incapable of surmounting the constitu-tional and constructive difficulties involved; and, in the second, if these were overcome, I believe that a unity which can only survive in an atmosphere of generalisation would disappear at once.[72]

F.E.'s scepticism was as usual sadly justified. When Congress took up the challenge and produced in August 1928 what became known as the Nehru Report, the principal result was to antagonize the Moslems, for whom the proposed Hindu-dominated constitution did not make enough allowance. The largest Moslem party now reversed its boycott of Simon, and began to co-operate with the Commission instead.

Once he had appointed the Commission and seen it off to India in January for the first of two tours, F.E. considered that his responsibility was substantially diminished. For the last nine months of his tenure of the India Office he took a back seat, regarding the whole question of constitutional advance as *sub judice*; in this period he hardly made another speech on India. When Simon and his colleagues returned in April, he was pleased to discover that his confidence in Simon's sound judgment had not been misplaced.

> I may record the impression that, while I think he is still honestly and creditably ambitious of securing a solution which would be a credit to India and the Empire, he is in his heart oppressed without being overwhelmed by the difficulties of the task, and I formed an impression, too, that he has conceived a deep resentment at the antics and demeanour of the Swarajists, and an absolute contempt for their political capacities . . . The talk I had with him confirmed the view I have always held that he has placed us under a deep debt of gratitude, whether he succeeds or whether he fails in undertaking a task which probably no-one in the Empire is more competent to discharge.

He added, for Irwin's amusement, a glimpse of Simon at play, which perfectly corroborates Bechhofer Roberts's description.

> He played the best game of golf with me on Sunday that I have ever seen him play, and in fact himself said that it was the best

game he had ever played in his life. He is as conscientious and laborious in his golf as in everything else, and if he loses a ball, unless you are prepared, which one is not, to insist upon the strict rule, you may sit down, after such perfunctory pretence as one offers of searching for one's opponent's ball, and count upon a steady half hour for reflection.[73]

F.E. was determined that once the Commission's course had been set, there should be no tacking. Irwin, in India, however, was beginning to bend before the wind. In May F.E. wrote to stiffen his resolve, in terms which the Viceroy can hardly have considered anything but patronizing.

The real truth is that if you live your life in an atmosphere in which everyone abuses you and everyone criticizes you, it is difficult to retain a cool perspective. Remember, all of you in the heat of India, that there is a cool and corrective oxygen in this little island. We are solidly behind you: when India confuses you and sometimes angers you, think, my dear Edward, as I know you do, of England.[74]

Three weeks later F.E. gave an explicit warning against what he was increasingly coming to regard as Irwin's softness towards *swarajist* troublemakers, whom he now wished to see formally branded as rebels.

I have been reading . . . of the visit of Motilal Nehru and Srinivasa Iyengar [to the North-West Frontier Province] and notice that during the visit they were the guests of the Government. Both of these politicians, I understand, publicly advocate complete separation from Great Britain as India's ultimate goal. To receive advocates of this policy as guests of the Government cannot fail to give it a sort of recognition as a legitimate policy to pursue. This, in my opinion, it is not.

His reasoning foreshadowed the great divide that was to emerge in British attitudes to India over the next decade. F.E., though sheltering behind Government policy, stated his imperialist position more unflinchingly than he had ever done before.

You will remember that in dealing with the question of the Indianisation of the Indian Army, His Majesty's Government were averse from using the phrase 'Dominion Status' to describe the ultimate and remote goal of Indian political development, because it has been laid down that Dominion status means 'the right to decide their own destinies', and this right we are not prepared to accord to India at present, or in any way to prejudge the question whether it should ever be accorded. I think it fair to infer from this that separatism should be regarded as a hostile movement, and if that is so, its representatives ought not to be treated in the same way as representatives of other political movements, which, though they may be unreasonable or ill-timed, are not illegitimate.

It was a constant complaint, F.E. maintained, of Britain's friends in India that no distinction was made between themselves and the enemies of British rule. The lack of visible reward for co-operation tended – 'Indian human nature being what it is' – to drive them into the hostile camp.

I suggest, therefore, that before the separatist movement develops further, Government should take up a definite attitude towards it, not merely by refusing to accord to its opponents such position as the hospitality of Government implies, but also by not employing them on committees &c., or other forms of work for the Government, and especially by not conferring honours on them. I cannot help thinking that by adopting this line, you would at once clear the air and import a little more reality into Indian political manoeuvres – at all events in Delhi.[75]

F.E. always liked to distinguish his friends from his enemies and to treat the two categories accordingly: in his clear perception of the Indian question it was elementary to apply the same standard. Irwin, on the spot, did not agree, and replied, a month later, to the effect that it was neither wise nor practical to draw so sharp a line – first, because the likes of Nehru were, after all, Assembly members, and second, because to do so would make real separatists of those who at present merely liked to talk of separation.[76] This gave F.E. the excuse for another long theoretical disquisition on how he thought Indians should be handled.

I fully realise the force of all you say. It does not do to take these people too seriously; indeed I find it increasingly difficult to take any Indian politicians very seriously. But granted that you and I and their fellow politicians know that they are talking with their tongues in their cheeks, what about the rest of the world; the failed B.A.'s who edit the newspapers and the thousands of politically-minded students whom the Communists are trying to capture – do they know it? And is not all this loose talk, though it may have no serious thought or even intention behind it, all the time raising the political temperature, and (worse still) blurring the distinction between right and wrong; accustoming the minds of the simple folks to language and ideas which, if they became serious would be highly dangerous, and so heaping up the gunpowder which any spark may kindle?

And though the loyal politicians know that these people are not taken seriously by us, do they like it when they see the Governor at his garden-party giving a great deal more attention to the extremist than to the moderate, and when he is on tour, passing by the loyal but silent landed proprietor (who has his grievances, but cannot get them heard) and spending hours with the vocal agitator? They do not, and I have in the last few months received abundant evidence to that effect . . . I would ask you to consider whether we have not reached the very extreme limits of toleration (if indeed we have not crossed them) and whether India does not now need to be pulled up and pulled together rather sharply.

There is another aspect of the question which I think will appeal to you. You say with great truth that 'to the Indian more than with most human beings there is apt to be a wide gulf between words and thought'. But are we to leave it at that? How are such people ever to govern themselves or even advance to self-government unless they learn to associate closely, not only words and thought, but also action? Is it not for us to teach them, or try to teach them, the difference between appearance and reality, by taking them literally for a time, and treating them as what they publicly profess to be, and not as what we rightly or wrongly believe that in their hearts they are? It seems to me that a consistent course of such treatment might have a very sobering and educative effect. It might no doubt, as you say, drive a few over the brink into serious hostility. But I would be quite logical, and deal with them as the law permits. Such a purging of the body politic might be very wholesome and might stimulate the moderate and loyal elements to healthy thought and action. Do think about this.[77]

Irwin did not think this sort of urging very helpful, but did not bother to argue further. These were problems for the man on the spot. How different, though, is the tone of these letters from F.E.'s early letters to Reading! Forgotten now his initial diffidence in approaching the 'vast and novel' problems of India, forgotten his deference to the Viceroy's local experience. After three years in office F.E. felt qualified to lecture Irwin with unblushing self-confidence that came close at times to being positively peremptory. No wonder Irwin wrote some time later to a friend that serving under F.E. (note the 'under') had been 'bloody'.[78] Where he had the power to overrule the Viceroy, however, F.E. could still do it quite graciously. In June 1928 Irwin suggested that after all it might be a good idea to associate some Indians fully in the deliberations of the Simon Commission on its second tour of the sub-continent. F.E. would have none of it.

> I understand how important it seems at a given moment to make some compromise if even an uncertain hope seems realisable; but I do honestly believe, and I am bound to make it plain, that while we cannot compete with you in actual knowledge of the day-to-day panorama of Indian politics, we possess some small compensating advantage in the detachment which is possible in London and in the India Office. You may perhaps think that while we take these decisions against your advice, you are bearing the heat and burden of the day; and so in a sense you are. But at the same time the ultimate Parliamentary responsibility belongs to me; and the failure, if failure there be, will recoil upon my head.[79]

F.E.'s later letters were by no means all so stern, however. In addition to keeping Irwin briefed on political and other developments at home, he wrote with increasing flippancy of lighter matters, sometimes concerned with the affairs of the Office, sometimes not. On 3 May 1928 he made an unembarrassed joke of his notorious partiality for strong drink.

> You will forgive me for making my letter this week unusually brief, but in five minutes time I am giving a tea-party (of all unsuitable functions for me to preside!) at which Members of the Commission are to be introduced to my Council and the principal members of my Office. A tea-party has never appeared to me a very suitable medium for exciting that generosity of mind which on an occasion like this would certainly have possessed great value. But I have supplemented this inconsiderable meal by some stronger liquors for those who prefer them and by some cigars of unexceptionable quality.[74]

Whether Irwin was amused by this – which might humourlessly have been interpreted as a snub to India's principal export – it is impossible to tell. Did he laugh, one wonders, at F.E. 'making a rush for the Derby' after a Cabinet meeting in June which ended conveniently early? 'I failed', F.E. wrote, 'in common with some millions of other people, to identify the winner' – this although the lift boy at the Savoy had in fact given him the right tip! 'The results, in relation to my modest method of betting, were rather costly.'[80] Did he think quite proper F.E.'s irreverent prediction – inaccurate, as it turned out – that Sir Thomas Inskip was about to exchange the 'very remunerative' office of Attorney-General for the 'barren dignity' of the Speakership? 'I think he will make a better Speaker than Attorney,' F.E. wrote. 'In fact he might become a really great Speaker. He has presence, universally admitted integrity, dignity and patience; moreover *per incredibile*, it appears that he actually enjoys listening to speeches! Not to make such a man Speaker is a waste of an extremely rare aptitude.'[80] (After four years on the Woolsack, F.E. wrote from bitter experience.)

Not long before he left the India Office, F.E. had to deliver another sharp rebuke to his old colleague and patron, Leslie Scott. Early in 1928 F.E. had been persuaded, reluctantly, to appoint a committee to inquire into how the position of the Princely States might be affected by any advance towards self-government in British India. The grounds for his reluctance were characteristic.

Even granted [F.E. wrote] that it may be in the interests of Great Britain (as many people think) no less than of the States themselves that they should be entrenched against an Indianised Government of India, responsible to an Indianised Legislature, the dreaded day is remote, and we cannot afford in the meantime to entrench them against ourselves.[81]

Nevertheless the Committee was appointed, with another name from F.E.'s past, Professor Holdsworth, among its members. Scott, as a leading K.C. not in the Government, accepted the enormously lucrative brief (which had earlier been offered to Simon) to represent the claims of the Princes before the Committee. He grossly exceeded his professional function as their legal representative, however, by simultaneously pressing their interests in his other capacity as a Conservative M.P.; he even entertained the Maharajah of Kashmir to lunch at the House of Commons with other M.P.s so that he might expound to them his grievances. F.E. jumped on this offence with the full authority of his office, invoking the Prime Minister and the Chief Whip to threaten his old friend with dire penalties if he persisted in improperly confusing his roles.[82] A few days later Scott came to see F.E. unrepentant, and succeeded in shaming F.E. off his high horse – as F.E., with good grace, admitted to Irwin.

I suggested that if he had any doubt about what I had said he should consult either the Lord Chancellor, the Lord Chief Justice,

the Master of the Rolls or the Attorney-General. This proposal he
rejected, observing, I thought with a good deal of justice, that if it
had not been for his loyalty to me [that is, at the time of the fall of
the Coalition], he could have held any one of those offices himself.
I thought this was rather good, and contented myself with observing that I had no doubt what advice he would have given to some
other Leslie Scott had he deservedly obtained any of these high
offices.[77]

Thus mollified, Scott had to agree to make no more speeches on the
subject of the Princes while the Butler inquiry lasted.

In October 1928, F.E. resigned from the Government – not as a result of
any disagreement, but for personal reasons.

So far as India was concerned, he undoubtedly felt that, having
appointed Simon and seen his work under way, there was little more for
him to do. It would be another two years before Simon reported. In the
meantime, as he looked back over his four years, he felt more strongly
than ever the impossibility of the task which Simon had taken on and
sincere gratitude to him – allied to the sort of pity one feels for a willing
fool – for having accepted it. In what turned out to be one of his last
letters to Irwin, he reflected with a frankness exceptional even for him
on Simon's undertaking and his own view, formed by four years of
office, of India's future. It is clear that he had still no suspicion how far
Irwin's thinking was beginning to diverge from his own – the revelation
came as a great shock to him the following year.

He described first his usual game of golf with Simon (who was still in
England) and reported him to be 'in very high spirits and very good
health. Indeed the abandonment of his laborious work at the Bar has
rejuvenated everything about him except his hair' – of which he had
little left.

One thing struck me without surprising me. With all his extraordinary ingenuity, cleverness and industry, I believe that he has
as little idea of the constitutional solution as he had on the day
when I first asked him to undertake the duties of Chairman.
Indeed he almost said so in terms. His opinion of the Swarajists is,
I think, at least as unfavourable as yours and mine, and the day to
day association with his native colleagues [the Indians externally
associated with the Commission in its inquiries] is unlikely, I
should imagine, to endear them in any marked degree. I cannot
imagine any more terrible fate in the world in the present situation
in India than to try to hack out a new constitution with such

talkative and incompetent colleagues . . . The more I think of Simon's task the more I marvel at his courage and public spirit in undertaking it.

The matter, of course, would not present the same difficulties to one who holds my own opinons. Those, as you know, are that the Montagu Constitution was a mistake, ill-conceived and potentially extremely mischievous. I should, therefore, if I was dealing with the situation as a Mussolini might, correct the greatest and more obvious defects; give them nothing more, and resolutely face the chatter and abuse, for you get just as much chatter and abuse whatever you do.

I have not in any way indicated my own impression, and perhaps prejudices, to Simon, for I did not think it fair to him to hold any language which might look as if I wished to influence him. I have, therefore, never discussed the merits of the matter with him at all.

I am sending the enclosed observations under separate cover, not because they are particularly important or novel, but because they are expressed with some informality and perhaps too much frankness to go upon an official file.[83]

Simon's labours, when he eventually reported in 1930, turned out to be irrelevant. He proposed, in place of dyarchy, another equally anomalous half-and-half constitution giving wider powers to Indian Governments in the Provinces, but still leaving an absolute veto in the hands of the Governors and the Viceroy. Indian nationalism, however, encouraged by Irwin, had by then less patience than ever with such balancing acts; the Governments of the 1930s had no choice but to scrap Simon and begin again trying to solve what was – in the terms in which the British defined it – an insoluble problem. There *was* no half-way house to independence. That being so, Simon can scarcely be blamed for having failed to find one, nor F.E. for failing to search harder for what he saw perfectly clearly did not exist.

The truth is that the India Office in the 1920s was no place for a logical man. From the moment in the 1890s when Gladstone's last administration had started the process of involving Indians in their own government, British rule in India had been on the slide from one makeshift anomaly to another. There was no stopping the process: it could end only when the last vestige of British supremacy had been eliminated. Historically all the British could do was to prolong the agony, attempting vainly to impose a timetable while they denied the inevitable destination. In the specific period 1924–8 F.E. was placed in an impossible situation, obliged to pretend to believe in a constitution which he privately believed to be unworkable, knowing that retreat was politically impossible but unwilling to concede further advance to the policy of boycott and non-co-operation. Only a woolly-minded man of vaguely benevolent liberal sympathies – like Irwin or Baldwin or MacDonald – could preside over the gradual withdrawal of British rule with the necessary bland indifference to the irrationality and inconsistency of each succeeding constitutional arrangement. F.E. was not such a man. He was always terribly clear-minded. Had his human sympathy been engaged, as it had been by Collins and Griffith in the very similar Irish situation, he might have been able to close his eyes, as he had in 1921, to constitutional anomalies for the sake of progress. But it was not. He surveyed India entirely with his intellect: his only emotions were exasperation and mounting contempt. Logically, as usual, his objections to Indian self-rule in the foreseeable future were sound enough: the nationalists *were* a tiny, unrepresentative, urbanized minority of the Indian population; India *was* composed of a numberless multitude of races, castes, creeds and languages, and the fundamental Hindu–Moslem divide *was* in the end to make a unitary Indian state impossible; there *was* no reason to extend further self-government to those who had abused the responsibility they had been given. But logic has no force against the tide of nationalism; and this his intellect could not grasp. In his last book, *The World in 2030*, written a year and a half after leaving office, he complacently took it for granted that Indians must eventually realize that the government of their vast sub-continent was too complex a task for them, that only the 'benevolent tyranny' of British rule could keep them from each others' throats. 'British rule will endure,' he concluded in a supreme assertion of imperial faith. 'By 2030, whatever means of self-government India has achieved, she will still remain a loyal and integral part of the British Empire.'[84] How could he have ever imagined that in less than half that time the British Empire itself would have ceased to exist?

24

The General Strike, 1926

The single dominating fact of post-war politics was the rise of the Labour party. The Coalition had tried to contain it by combining the older parties against it. The Carlton Club rebels believed that the Tory party could oppose it more effectively alone. In the short run the result had been the experiment of a minority Labour Government. But now, with Labour's defeat, the Liberals' relegation to irrelevance and the overwhelming Conservative victory of October 1924, the initiative lay with the Tories again to come to terms as best they could with the labour movement in all its manifestations, both theoretical – socialism – and practical – the trade unions. Its response to this challenge provided the major theme of the second Baldwin Government: the climax was the defeat of the General Strike in May 1926, but well before that the Government had had to define its attitude to the demands of labour.

There were two possible approaches. One, favoured by probably the majority of the party in the country, called for confrontation and looked to a majority Tory Government – the first, apart from the brief wasted interlude in 1922–3, for twenty years – to legislate at once to take away the unwarranted privileges extended to the trade unions by the Liberals in 1906, now seen as a greater threat than ever to the Tory party and to industry. The other, preferred by Baldwin, proposed on the contrary to disarm Labour by kindness, transforming the socialist bogey by a characteristic British process of assimilation into a sensible party of moderate reform – replacing the Liberals – which might without alarm be accorded the style and dignity of the alternative Government. The two approaches were not entirely mutually exclusive: the Government in fact pursued both at different times, sometimes both together, between 1925 and 1927, attempting to draw a distinction within the labour movement between the moderates, who should be encouraged, and the socialist extremists, who must be confronted and defeated. No one drew this distinction more clearly or pursued both approaches more explicitly than F.E.

In the short run he showed himself surprisingly ready to fall in with Baldwin's emollient approach. The first test of the Government's intentions was the old question of the trade unions' political levy. For years the Tory party had protested – no one more strenuously than F.E. – at the iniquity of this levy, surcharged on the subscriptions of all trade unionists, be they Labour, Liberal or Conservative, for the exclusive benefit of the Labour party: provision for 'contracting out', conceded by the Liberal Government in 1913 in the wake of the Osborne Judgment, made no difference to the principle, since it was often more than a man's job was worth to take advantage of it. The only acceptable procedure would be for those union members who wanted to support the Labour party to 'contract in' to paying the levy. The 1924 Tory Conference had carried an unambiguous motion calling for legislation to embody this reversal. Now, to keep the pressure on the Government, the M.P. for Argyll, Frederick McQuisten, lost no time in introducing in February 1925 a Private Member's Bill which it was generally assumed the Cabinet would have no choice but to support or take over. In fact the unlikely combination of Baldwin and F.E. persuaded their colleagues to oppose it.

F.E. had chaired a committee which lamely recommended promising an inquiry. Reporting this to the Cabinet, however, he added 'his personal conviction that we ought to go straight against the Bill'; but this was at that stage a minority view. The rest of the meeting, Amery noted, 'talked round and about' the various options for some time, until Baldwin asserted his new authority. 'SB summed up with a simple homely eloquence in favour of industrial peace, and what carried no conviction as put by FE carried us all away.'[1]

> When he finished [Edward Wood recalled], no-one said anything, for everybody felt that they had just listened to something of a quite different order from what had gone before. Finally Birkenhead broke the silence to say that if the Prime Minister could say to the House . . . just what he had now said to the Cabinet, he thought that the speech would be made with the unanimous support of the Cabinet, and would carry conviction to the House.[2]

No one disagreed. F.E. also passed Baldwin one of his pencilled notes: 'I think that your action showed enormous courage and for that reason will succeed.'[3]

The Second Reading debate on McQuisten's Bill was held a week later, on 6 March. Baldwin did say to the House of Commons what he had said to the Cabinet, urging that the Conservative party in its moment of victory should hold back from pressing home its political opportunity, and achieved the same overwhelming effect. The Tories were shamed into magnanimity; and years later Labour members still recalled the moral impact of his speech – ending with the famous prayer, 'Give peace in our time, O Lord.'[4] F.E. congratulated himself as well as Baldwin on his triumph.

> You have shown the greatest and rarest form of political courage and I told you it would succeed. I believe this will mean a permanent strengthening of your position in the House *as a whole* which is of immense importance to a Prime Minister.[5]

He was right. Though the Diehards were privately furious, they were thoroughly beaten. For the remainder of the Government's life, there was an end of mutterings against Baldwin's leadership.

The question is, how sincerely was F.E. following his new leader's line? Was his more progressive side reasserting itself, under Baldwin's healing influence? Not really. His speeches over the next few months – all made to strictly Conservative audiences, usually after dinner: it is notable that F.E. now rarely went out into the great cities to make his speeches in the opposition's heartland as he used to, for all his criticism of the 1923 Government on exactly that score – struck a significantly different note from Baldwin's. To Labour's parliamentary leaders he tried – in shocking disavowal of everything he had charged them with at the General Election – to be similarly generous; but such sentiments merely sounded patronizing on his lips. 'Let us do justice', he urged Surrey Conservatives, 'to the leaders of the Government which preceded us.'

> That Government inherited novel and ill-understood responsibilities, and, in my judgement, did their best adequately to the great burdens which were placed on them. We would, indeed, be ill-advised if we branded with the stigma of the Soviet the men who for eight or nine months were responsible for the Government of this country . . .
>
> We acknowledge the debt of gratitude we owe to those who . . . in the face of irresistible temptations to take a course more popular in their own party . . . were not unworthy trustees of the British Empire . . . men of the calibre of Mr MacDonald, Mr Snowden and Mr Thomas.

Has ever a politician more shamelessly branded his own election rhetoric as lies?

On the specific question of the trade union levy, however, F.E. clearly indicated that his own support for Baldwin's policy of restraint was founded upon the more threatening calculation that a showdown with the unions might still be unavoidable in the long run: the weapon of a wider reform of union law was being held in reserve.

> It might conceivably be that still deeper issues will require settlement. If it is necessary for us to attempt to achieve a settlement, as I hope we may achieve a settlement, for the common good, with the trade unions of this country, let us at least not involve ourselves in a dispute upon a point which can be represented as an attempt to do them a mere party hurt. It is upon that ground, and that ground alone, that a unanimous Cabinet will offer advice to the House of Commons in a very difficult and disputable matter next week.[6]

It was F.E.'s understanding, then, that the Tory advantage should not be pressed home on the small point now, only in order that the big question should not be compromised for the future: a tactical retreat significantly less generous than Baldwin's. In other speeches he made it clear that he regarded the restrictive power of the unions as a major problem for the country – an economic, not simply a political problem. In February he attacked the protective exclusivity of the building unions who would not allow unemployed ex-servicemen to take on jobs which they could learn in a few weeks, even though the nation was 'festering' for lack of houses; the Government, he warned, could not submit to this sort of sectional blackmail.[7] On 3 March he sounded the perennial theme that the country must compete or perish; the unions must realize that wage levels were ultimately governed by the wages of their foreign rivals – they might win every battle with their employers yet still be destroyed by foreign competition.[8] He repeated this warning throughout the summer, pointing out that British wages were already high compared with other countries.[9] At the same time as he continued to sing the praises of the parliamentary Labour leadership, he returned increasingly to condemnation of the Moscow-inspired extremists whom he saw stepping up their malign influence in the unions.

All this, of course, was aimed particularly at the miners, the traditional aristocrats of labour, the most tightly unionized group in the country, who since the war had found their industry increasingly hard-pressed by a combination of declining export markets, exhausted pits and inefficient and short-sighted management. Coal was the flagship industry which Labour and the Miners' Federation wanted above all to see nationalized; the majority of the 1919 Sankey Royal Commission had actually recommended the nationalization of at least the mineral royalties, but Lloyd George had shelved the report unimplemented. The miners nursed a bitter sense of betrayal – not least against the comrades in other unions who had let them down on 'Black Friday' 1919 – and the condition of the industry continued to deteriorate. The last straw came with the Bank of England's insistence – against which Churchill as Chancellor had protested in vain – upon putting the pound back on the Gold Standard in April 1925 at its pre-war level against the dollar – thus increasing at a stroke the price of British coal (and other exports) in overseas markets. By July the coal owners claimed to be losing £1 million a month and announced wage cuts. As the miners vowed resistance, a strike loomed.

The Government was not unsympathetic to the miners' plight; but more important, it was not ready for a major strike. On 30 July – 'Red Friday' in Labour mythology – the Cabinet agreed a £10 million subsidy, to last nine months, to maintain wages at their present level while another Royal Commission, to be chaired by Herbert Samuel, reported on the future organization of the industry. Ministers were deeply divided on the morality of this proceeding, which was seen as craven weakness by several hardliners – Cave, Worthington-Evans, Steel-Maitland, Bridgeman, Joynson-Hicks and Hogg. But once again F.E. sided with the heavyweights – Baldwin, both Chamberlains and Churchill – in favour of buying temporary peace. As on McQuisten's Bill, his reasons were tactical. As a principle, he believed that coal, like every other industry, must be made to pay its way without Government assistance, paying whatever wages the market would support. This was a lesson which he believed it to be one of the principal purposes of the Government to teach. Nevertheless he believed that the Government must choose its own moment to confront the miners with this truth, and that the present was not auspicious. 'The mine owners had acted with crude abruptness, as they often do,' he wrote later, 'and it is not an exaggeration to say that, had the quarrel become acute nine months earlier than it did, the great majority of the people of the country would have been with the miners and against the owners.'[10] Moreover the Government's contingency plans for maintaining essential services in the event of a General Strike – threatened by the T.U.C. in support of the miners – were not yet perfected. The wise course was plainly to allow a breathing-space during which the Royal Commission should come up with new proposals on both organization and wages: if the miners rejected these, they would put themselves in the wrong with public opinion, while the public could simultaneously be educated as to the constitutional implications of a General Strike. Whatever Baldwin thought he was doing, F.E. was quite clearly recoiling as a calculated ruse to lure the unions into giving the Government ground for that withdrawal of their 1906 privileges from which it had refrained in March.

For the moment, but at a price [he wrote to Reading in October], we have a truce in the mining industry; but there is considerable risk of fresh trouble in the railway world in November. I am myself of opinion . . . that we shall have no peace until the matter has been fought out to a victory. In my judgement we shall have to set our teeth just as we should have done if six months more war had been necessary, and carry the matter once and for all to a conclusion which will involve a complete reconsideration of the exceptional legal status conceded to the Trades Unions, and which they seem to me, under the influence of extremist elements, to have so grossly abused. I hope that I am wrong, and that we may get into smoother waters by a safer voyage. But I think that I am right.[11]

He began at once preparing the constitutional ground on which the Government would fight if the unions were so foolish, when the subsidy ran out, as to overreach themselves.

'We and we alone [he warned at Dumfries in November], not the Trade Unions, not the Communists, not the employers, are the trustees of the community as a whole, and if and when the threats of industrial anarchy imperil that cause, there is no responsibility of intervention from which we shall shrink, and there will be found little which we have not thought out and prepared beforehand.[12]

Samuel reported in April 1926, recommending the nationalization of the mineral royalties, the reorganization of the industry by substantial closure and amalgamation of uneconomic pits, improved pithead amenities – but also wage cuts. The Government, despite reservations, immediately declared its acceptance of the Report as the basis of a fair settlement, taking up an unassailable public posture as even-handed arbiter; whereupon the miners played into the Diehards' hands by rejecting it. To them, with some reason, Samuel did not seem even-handed at all, demanding wage cuts at once in return for the promise of reorganization later: they had no confidence in the Government's determination to enforce the latter part of the bargain against the owners, once the immediate crisis was past. Nevertheless by reject-ing Samuel out of hand they presented themselves as obstinate and inflexible, while releasing the Government from the obligation of its initial acceptance.

The miners' inflexibility put the T.U.C. on the spot. Having promised a general stoppage in support of the miners, they had to go through with it: they could not afford the humiliation of another 'Black Friday'. Yet they were increasingly embarrassed by the revolutionary implications of a political strike against the elected Government, and aware that they were unprepared for a long struggle. Taking over the negotiations on the miners' behalf, the members of the T.U.C. General Committee were genuinely anxious to find a settlement which would get themselves off the hook, but they had no authority to agree any deal that involved the miners accepting immediate cuts, while they could not be seen to abandon them if they refused to compromise. Their only proposal was that the Government should agree to extend the July subsidy until the promised reorganization could be effected. But this the Cabinet would not consider. They had now got the T.U.C. where they wanted them. For all Baldwin's soft words, he was as determined as any of his colleagues that the time had come for a showdown: the threat of a General Strike had been hanging in the air for too long – either the unions' bluff must be called, and the threat discredited, or the strike must be met and defeated. The Government was now ready. A settlement in the coal fields took second place to this overriding political priority.

F.E. played a principal role in the final talks. As early as 14 April, Tom Jones proposed to Davidson that F.E. would be the best man to bring in to the negotiations on the Government side 'if we could get him sufficiently interested', but Davidson thought him 'too strongly disliked by Labour for this role' and suggested Hogg instead.[13] Jones persisted, however, and a week later pressed Baldwin himself to bring in either F.E. or Worthington-Evans to stiffen Steel-Maitland (Minister of Labour), who was 'ineffective and uncertain'. 'I would rather Birkenhead because he has all the ability required to grasp the situation, he only talks when he has something to say, and when he speaks does so with perfect lucidity.'[14] (A professional's tribute from a Cabinet Secretary.) Evidently Baldwin agreed, and in the last critical discussions between the Government and the T.U.C. negotiating committee on 30 April and 1 and 2 May, it was F.E. with Baldwin and Steel-Maitland who faced Arthur Pugh (of the Iron and Steel Trades Federation), Arthur Swales (of the Engineers) and J.H. Thomas (still, though an M.P. and a Cabinet Minister in 1924, leader of the railwaymen).

F.E. and Thomas were old friends, and F.E.'s introduction to the Government team brought a new tone to the discussions. 'It was a case of "Fred" and "Jimmy"', Walter Citrine (the T.U.C. General Secretary) remembered, 'and we certainly got along much more cordially and less ceremoniously than hitherto.'[15] Tom Jones, in fact, noted at the time that when F.E. first called Thomas 'Jimmy', Thomas quickly slapped back with an ironic 'Frederick', as if determined not to be cajoled by F.E.'s familiarity.[16] Nevertheless it is clear that F.E. did his best to take advantage of the fact that he knew Thomas to be privately opposed to the policy of the General Strike. He also succeeded in getting on friendly terms with Herbert Smith, one of the miners' leaders, when they joined the talks, by mentioning his great-grandfather – the reputed prize-fighter – since Smith had also been a fighter in his day.[15] Such pleasantries were calculated, of course, but they demonstrate the easy informality which F.E. could always deploy, in contrast to the lordly arrogance which was nowadays his public image.

The strategy which F.E., with Baldwin sitting beside him, pursued was to try to divide the T.U.C. leaders from the miners. He could tell that their hearts were not in the threatened strike, that they were only looking for an honourable way to call it off; at the same time he realized that they were not free agents and could not settle on terms which the miners themselves refused to accept; and he was clear that the Government was not prepared to offer terms which the miners *might* accept. He quickly saw that he was not going to succeed. 'I never lost my belief', he wrote in a memorandum a few days later, 'that the limited authority within which the T.U.C. was negotiating disabled them from agreeing to the only basis which we were authorised to discuss . . . My own impression is clear that at no moment in the discussions on Saturday or Sunday (1 or 2 May) were we within reach of any agreement.' Nevertheless, 'the talk was frank and friendly and in view of the gravity of the issues, we were all unwilling to part without an absolute admission of failure'.[17]

What F.E. was trying to do – once he had given up hope of persuading the T.U.C. leaders to abandon the miners – was to keep the talks going so that they should be so compromised by their efforts to get the miners to accept the Samuel terms that if, in the event of failure, they nevertheless felt obliged to go ahead with the General Strike, they would do so on the weakest possible ground and with little conviction. Accordingly, when late on 1 May the T.U.C. representatives asked that the subsidy be extended another fortnight to give them more time to bring the miners round, he and Baldwin were inclined to agree. The two sides took away with them a formula, devised by the Permanent Secretary at the Ministry of Labour, Sir Horace Wilson.

The Prime Minister has satisfied himself as a result of conversations he has had with the representatives of the Trades Union

Congress, that if negotiations are continued ... the representatives of the Trades Union Congress are confident that a settlement can be reached on the lines of the Report within a fortnight.[18]

When Baldwin and F.E. put this proposed extension before the Cabinet next day, however, it met with a uniformly hostile reception.

All who were not present when it was agreed [Tom Jones recorded], reacted in the same way against it, and felt that it would be read by the whole country as a capitulation on the part of the Government to the threat of a general strike. There was nothing on the face of the formula to indicate acceptance of the Report. Birkenhead admitted that it was not ideally drafted but pleaded 1.15 a.m. and the mental exhaustion of everybody.[19]

That evening the representatives of the two sides met again. Before F.E. for the Government could even make clear the Cabinet's doubts about the formula, Pugh confessed that the T.U.C. could not honestly be said to be 'confident' that a settlement could be reached. 'It would be more accurate to say that they had not formed such an opinion.'

In the second place [F.E.'s account continued], they were unable to make the expression 'on the lines of the Report' more definite. They were still unable to substitute the phrase 'accept the Report'. And if the fortnight provisionally allotted to the discussions proved inadequate (and no-one seriously argued on behalf of its adequacy) Mr Thomas frankly stated that they would expect the Government to provide a subsidy for whatever period was in fact occupied by the negotiations on reorganisation. It had by this time become evident that instead of drawing closer together, we were getting further apart.

Instead of agreeing on the very vague formula proposed the night before, both sides were now retreating even from that. F.E. wanted to get clearly on paper how far the T.U.C. was prepared to go.

I informed Mr Thomas very plainly of the general attitude of the Cabinet as disclosed by our discussion in the morning. I told him that further negotiations seemed to me to be useless unless the Trades Unionist leaders were prepared to take the responsibility of advising the Miners that either in the matter of hours or wages there must be a concession whilst the matter of reorganisation was under adjustment. In the conversation that followed he used expressions which indicated that he was going as far as it was in any event possible, then or thereafter, for he and his colleagues to go. I said, 'Well, if that is as far as you feel able to go, it would at least be useful that I should take down your exact words for the consideration of the Cabinet. I make it plain that in my judgement there is no chance whatever that an assurance so vague and so limited will be accepted by them; but you are at least entitled that the words used by you should be placed before them for consideration.'[17]

In the words which F.E. then took down from Thomas's dictation, the T.U.C. undertook to 'urge' the miners to authorize them to carry on negotiations under continued subsidy, 'with the understanding that they and we accept the Report as a basis of settlement and we approach it with the knowledge that it may involve some reduction in wages'.[20] F.E. had said that he had no expectation that the Cabinet would accept this, but at almost eleven o'clock he and Baldwin duly took it through to the assembled Ministers waiting next door in 11 Downing Street. 'Stanley came in very tired' – this is Amery's diary – 'and threw himself into an armchair leaving it to FE to read out as far as they had got with the discussions.' Those who already thought that F.E. had compromised too far the previous night were even less pleased with this latest formula.

> They thought there was no real assurance that it would lead to anything nor did it take any notice of the general strike about which our feelings had stiffened considerably when it was discovered during the course of the day from the Post Office that the actual telegrams to the different Unions telling them to cease work had gone out on Saturday evening.

Yet F.E. still wanted to keep talking. 'FE and Stanley were both inclined to go on with negotiations on that basis, that is to say to wait and hear what the miners who had meanwhile arrived, would say to this formula, but except myself no-one else in the Cabinet was prepared to do so.'[21] Neville Chamberlain recorded that 'warm words' passed between F.E. and Winston, who was characteristically impatient to stop talking and get to war.[22]

F.E. and Baldwin may have been in a minority, but they were the Cabinet's chief negotiators, and Baldwin was Prime Minister: they could not easily be overruled even by their united colleagues. Their desire to wait and at least hear what the miners had to say was overborne, however, by events. It is Neville Chamberlain who gives the most vivid account, which again illustrates the tension to which nerves were stretched.

At this moment [around midnight] Jix came in with a message and dramatically announced 'The Daily Mail has ceased to function. The men have refused to print its leading article entitled "For King and Country"'. 'Thank God' shouted FE & was immediately & hotly attacked by Winston. 'A great organ of the press is muzzled by strikers & you say "Thank God"'. FE said it was only a joke & moreover a joke which Winston himself had made the day before. Thomas had said to him 'There'll be no papers tomorrow' & Winston had replied 'That'll be a comfort anyhow'. 'Yes, but I said that to Thomas', said Winston. 'Well I say it to you', shouted FE.

But Horace Wilson who has a cool head said 'This changes the whole situation & I think it gives you a way out'. FE instantly seized on the idea & reversed his attitude, the PM gave way & in a few minutes we were revising our ultimatum so as to make this 'overt act' the main reason for breaking off . . . About 12.30 the Cabinet intensely relieved at its release from a most awkward situation dispersed.[22]

The T.U.C. were furious at the Government's use of the *Daily Mail* incident, for which they were in no way responsible, to break off negotiations which they afterwards claimed were close to success. They exaggerated, but they were right to feel aggrieved, because they were comprehensively outmanoeuvred. The action by the *Dail Mail* compositors, though unofficial and strictly unconnected with the General Strike threat, gave the Government exactly the sort of dramatic and disturbing pretext it needed to go to the country as the upholder of constitutional government in the face of union anarchy. They seized it adroitly, catching the unions on the wrong foot. Their whole aim, since July 1925, had been to ensure that if there were to be a General Strike it should occur in the circumstances that would attract the least possible public support, so that the spectre might be met and laid. Writing four years later, in one of his *Last Essays*, F.E. recalled the sincere efforts which he, Baldwin and Steel-Maitland had made to ensure that 'the miners, if they refused to accept' the formula which, he too now claimed, the T.U.C. had very nearly accepted, 'must fight their battle alone'. But he thought in retrospect that events had turned out for the best.

I am uncertain whether one ought to shed tears on the failure of that last attempt; for it is probably true that, just as the German war was inevitable, so the General Strike was inevitable; and if it was to come, it could not have been faced at a better moment or in a better cause.[23]

The moment the strike was declared F.E., who had been the moderate in the preceding negotiations, went right over to the side of those most determined to crush it without compunction. In the Supply and Transport Committee – the Cabinet Committee responsible for emergency provision during the stoppage – 'Winston and FE . . . regarded the strikers as an enemy to be destroyed', wanting to see food convoys armed and generally the greatest possible display of force; it was Joynson-Hicks, 'who up till the beginning of the strike had been known as Mussolini Minor', who surprised Davidson by his tact.[24] Winston poured his aggression into the editorship of the Government's emergency newspaper, the *British Gazette*; he and F.E. together repeatedly demanded that the B.B.C. be taken over and run as a Government propaganda agency. Above all, F.E. was keen to lose no time in using the opportunity of the strike to push through the legal reckoning with the unions which he had wanted ever since 1906. This to his mind was what the battle was all about. Hogg prepared for the Cabinet a short Bill making general and sympathetic strikes illegal; F.E. and Winston were enthusiastic to take the Bill through all its stages in both Houses in a single day, so that the Government should then be able to impound the funds of the striking unions and force a quick surrender that way. Sir John Simon, however, confused the issue by giving it as his opinion in a well-publicized speech in the House of Commons that sympathetic strikes were already illegal. Baldwin was made aware by the King, Lord Salisbury and a strong section of Conservative opinion in the country that it would be unwise and unnecessary to do anything so provocative. The General Strike was quietly collapsing anyway from the T.U.C.'s embarrassed lack of belief in the course to which they had been driven. It was better to wait for them to realize their mistake and call it off than to risk raising the temperature by vindictive measures which might appear not strong but panicky.

F.E. was now the principal spokesman in the Lords of the Government's determination to do nothing but wait. 'To whatever unhappy lengths this quarrel may be carried,' he asserted on 5 May, 'it will be ended only with the recognition, alike in fact and in law, that there is one Government and one Government only in this country.'[25] In order to make its point that while the withdrawal of labour was a perfectly legitimate weapon in a pay dispute, the calling of a general strike was an illegitimate use of industrial power against an elected Government, the Government refused absolutely to negotiate under threat. Once it had made that plain and demonstrated that it was well able, by its emergency provision and the help of thousands of middle-class volunteers, to keep essential services going, there was nothing for the T.U.C. to do – since it did *not* have any revolutionary intentions, but had merely wished to show sympathy with the miners' case – but give up after nine days and leave the miners to carry on their struggle alone.

To F.E. the defeat of the General Strike was a famous victory to rank with the roll-call of the British people's victories over successive tyrants. To Irwin in India he wrote in ecstatic celebration when it was all over:

> The result of the General Strike altogether delights one; for it shows that this old England of ours retains its spirit unimpaired. The people tolerate up to a point Russian infiltration, Trades Unionist tyranny, Red Flag demonstrations and Socialist Sunday Schools. But while they say little – rather disappointingly little – they think, intuitively rather than by ratiocination, a great deal. And suddenly they make up their mind. The provocation may be a Pope, a Stuart, a Napoleon, a Prussian or a Trade Union, but once the realisation has gone through the whole country, it is irresistible. It has proved so in this case. The newspapers will have told you of the splendid spirit that animated the whole people. Everyone is asking why this General Strike collapsed so quickly. Fifty contributory explanations are available, but I recall the lines of Edgar Allan Poe:
>
> > 'A wind blew out of the sea,
> > Chilling and killing my Annabel Lee,
> > My beautiful Annabel Lee.'
>
> A wind blew from the whole of England, chilling and killing the spirits and the pretensions of those who were challenging constitutional Government and Parliamentary institutions. More and more they became conscious how numerous were their enemies, how few and in many cases how unwilling were their friends. The collapse was very sudden. I was one of the few Ministers who received the ultimate Trade Unionists' surrender. It was so humiliating that some instinctive breeding made one unwilling even to look at them. I thought of the Burghers of Calais approaching their interview with Edward III, haltered on the neck.[26]

Labour mythology has seized on this unfortunate remark and given it a meaning quite the opposite of what F.E. evidently intended, and quite out of character. F.E. has been represented in a television dramatization, for instance, disdaining to look at the defeated trade unionists out of a grotesque social snobbery – a travesty of what he meant by 'breeding'. Though he undoubtedly felt on public grounds triumphant, it is clear that F.E. felt intensely sorry for the T.U.C. leaders personally – particularly no doubt for Jimmy Thomas, but also for the other leaders with whom he had negotiated ten days before – as they came back to Downing Street to eat humble pie. His human sensitivity to their embarrassment does him only credit.

With the defeat of the General Strike, two problems remained. One, for the longer term, was how to rub home the lesson so that the attempt should never be repeated: although the rush Bill first proposed to make sympathetic strikes illegal had been postponed, the Government remained determined to bring in some such measure in due course, and much of the Tory party – F.E. well to the fore – did not intend to let slip the opportunity to extend it to cover picketing, the political levy and the unions' legal immunity. In the meantime, however, there was the more urgent problem of the continuing coal strike.

Deserted by the T.U.C., the miners fought on alone for another six months, practically to the end of the year, still rejecting absolutely any settlement that involved either lower wages or longer hours. Freed by the miners' rejection of Samuel from the obligation to impose it on the owners, the Government – still refusing to extend the subsidy – sought instead to bridge the gap by legislating to allow longer hours, by suspending for five years the Seven Hours Act passed in 1919. Opposed both by the owners – who still insisted that they must have wage cuts – and by the miners, this could again be presented as a tough but even-handed solution, and F.E. as a member of the Cabinet's Coal Committee supported it. When it had no effect on the miners' intransigence, however, his attitude hardened. Increasingly as the strike dragged on his sympathies turned against the miners, or more particularly against their leaders. In this respect he and Winston changed positions. Up to the outbreak of the General Strike he had worked patiently to avert it, while Winston, frustrated at being excluded from the critical talks, stormed for conflict. During the course of the strike they were at one in demanding a firm response, and in the first weeks after its collapse F.E. was still with Winston in supporting strong action by the Government to impose a solution on the owners. Very quickly, however, as Winston took over the leading role in peace negotiations and strove with a compassion reminiscent of his Liberal days to find ways through the deadlock, F.E. grew bored with the endless attrition, took the owners' part in the struggle and decided that the men must be starved into total defeat.

His letters to Irwin chart in weekly detail the development of his hard line. At the end of May he was still open-minded between the two parties.

The public relief at the crushing of the General Strike is so great that there is a disposition to ignore the formidable fact that a million men are still out of work in the coalfields, and that the very difficult negotiations that remain are not proceeding over smoothly. It would be possible to say without exaggeration of the miners' leaders that they were the stupidest men in England if we had not had frequent occasion to meet the owners. Each party admits that it cannot possibly arrive at a settlement without the others. Unitedly, therefore, they fling at the Government the incredibly difficult task of mastering the details of a complicated and technical matter and proffer the modest request that the Government should supply an adjustment, towards obtaining which neither owners nor men can make the slightest useful suggestion.[26]

By 10 June, though still recognizing the Government's role in facilitating a settlement, he was insistent that the industry must sort out its own financial difficulties.

It looks as if it may be necessary . . . for the Government to intervene. What seems to me quite certain is that, however serious the consequences, we ought not in any event to make ourselves responsible, in the hope of a temporary alleviation, for bringing into existence a state of affairs which is in itself uneconomic and is quite certain to provoke a new disruption in a few months. The matter has to be fought out some time, and in my opinion it must be fought out now.[27]

A fortnight later he had decided to personalize the issue, putting the whole blame for the continuation of the strike on to the most extreme of the miners' leaders, A.J. Cook, a Communist who had provocatively described himself as 'a humble disciple of Lenin'.

My own view has clearly developed that the only way of ending the coal strike is to break the Moscow disciple, Cook, who is directing it. I have, therefore, without much sanction from my colleagues, devoted my public speeches to an attempt to discredit him. As long as he leads the movement, there will be no settlement; it therefore seemed to me, upon a sound and well-established tactical principle, that it was worth while to get rid of him.[28]

Accordingly, in the following months F.E. lost no opportunity to pillory Cook as the dupe or agent of Moscow, who did not want a settlement and was deliberately obstructing all attempts to reach one with the avowed purpose of destroying the economic basis of the coal industry, perpetrating upon the suffering miners a cruel hoax in the interest of an alien dogma.[29] His campaign aroused some response even among Labour people – both MacDonald and Thomas were moved by the obduracy of the miners to suggest that they were being misled by Cook and Smith and should now take the best terms they could get; but in the coalfields the inevitable result of F.E.'s attacks was simply to increase Cook's stature.

In August F.E. wrote scornfully of the clumsy interference of the churches, whose leaders, with 'incredible effrontery', had 'probably prolonged the strike for three weeks' by proposing a further four months' subsidy.

> We have therefore been confronted with the *opéra bouffe* of a consultation of the miners as to whether they will accept terms which no-one in the world except a few half-baked ecclesiastics, most of whom call themselves Christian Socialists, intend to offer them; and even these terms, far exceeding anything within the grasp of the miners, have been rejected.

He still confidently predicted that Cook would soon be swept aside.

> He can, however, at this moment of his existence, make a considerable claim. He has cost the country 150 million pounds; he has entirely depleted the funds of his own Trade Union; and has almost ruined the finances of the other great Trade Unions. The cost has indeed been appalling; but if it has taught the general body of Trade Unions the iron lessons of economic truth, even this gigantic expenditure will not have been thrown away.[30]

In September F.E. went away for a fortnight's holiday with Freddie in Spain and Portugal; Baldwin was simultaneously away at Aix-les-Bains. In their absence, Churchill took charge and made renewed efforts to bring the two sides together. The miners, as significant numbers of men in some areas began to trickle back to work, were becoming more amenable; but the owners, sighting victory, were in no mood to concede an inch. Negotiations now centred on the possibility of arbitration by a national tribunal: the owners insisted that they would only accept local settlements. F.E. did not approve at all of Winston's attempts to put pressure on them. 'Why', he cabled from Biarritz, 'should we impose upon owners national settlement if they are strong enough to obtain district settlements? Why should we enable men's leaders who have done their best to ruin England to escape without the brand of failure?'[31] To compromise now, he thought, was weakness. 'I am not altogether happy', he wrote to Irwin on his return, 'about the attitude adopted by the Government in my absence, although obviously we all have to stand together.'

> I think that Cook and Smith are doing so much mischief and are so hopeless that it would have been better to have faced the economic disadvantages and risks of a fight to a finish, and I think we could have fought and won. Nearly 100,000 men, or ten per cent of the mining community, are now back at work. If we had not resumed discussion with these dangerous and discredited men, I think that the situation might have been carried to a victorious conclusion.[32]

Out of sympathy with the Government's new attitude, F.E. took to staying away from the Coal Committee. On 22 September Tom Jones had the task of summoning F.E. and other Ministers early in the morning to a meeting at eleven o'clock.

> I found Birkenhead was in town, and the clerk spoke to the butler who said his lordship was in the house, and would be told about the meeting. This was between 9.0 and 10.0. Between 10 and 11 Duff [Baldwin's private secretary] was told that Birkenhead had started for Southampton at 9.0 a.m. When I told Churchill he was very angry and mentioned it to the P.M. Churchill was genuinely anxious to get Birkenhead's counsel, and as cross-examiner with the miners he would have been much more helpful than any other Minister on the Committee.[33]

The following week Jones recorded another meeting at six o'clock in the evening. 'Bridgeman was there and Birkenhead, who under private pressure from Winston had been brought back from some club in Kingston; during most of the meeting he was fast asleep.' This did not seem to matter, however. Churchill's desire to put a last generous offer to the miners was severely modified by other Ministers, notably Bridgeman and Lane-Fox (Secretary for Mines).

> Towards the end, Birkenhead woke up and as the discussion was still very much at the point where he had left it when he fell asleep, he had only to listen for a minute, and then join in. 'Cook and Smith', he said, 'have treated us very badly. We ought not to go further than we have gone. Don't let us go to them, let them come to us', and that was the finding of the Committee.
> Birkenhead has been an irregular attender at our meetings, and a few days ago, by way of apology, he explained his absence to the

P.M. in a note in which he said that he felt such contempt for Smith and Cook that if he came to our meetings his presence would make much more for discord than for harmony. With this defence, he managed to escape to his yacht at Southampton.[34]

To Irwin, F.E. explained the thinking behind the offer, against the wishes of the owners, of a national wages tribunal. First, the high price of imported coal was proving very damaging to the rest of industry, so that as winter approached it was becoming important to the Government to get the miners back as early as possible. Secondly, it was argued that a settlement achieved with some degree of willingness, as opposed to utter submission, would create a better political and industrial atmosphere for the future. 'I cannot conceal from you my own view', F.E. confessed, 'that in all the history of the case the owners were entitled to the victory; and that a great economic and industrial lesson would have been taught if they had been allowed to win it.'[35]

When the miners, by ballot, rejected the proposed tribunal, F.E. was relieved. 'Personally,' he wrote, 'I welcome the death of this particular plan,' though he could not blame its defeat on Cook and Smith.[36] Eventually, after another six weeks, he got the result he wanted. The miners were finally forced back on lower pay and longer hours than they could have had in May. 'The discredit of the Miners' Federation', he crowed on 25 November, 'is now complete. Torn by internal dissensions they have been unable to prevent what are practically unfettered separate negotiations in each district.'[37] A week later, however, he had the grace to strike a more sombre note.

You will have seen by now that the strike is officially over. At least 200,000 men will remain without employment, no doubt blessing the inspiring leadership of Cook, who, appropriately enough, leaves tonight for Moscow. So ends the most miserable and futile industrial struggle in our history.[38]

It was not a struggle from which F.E. emerged with much credit in the eye of history. His harsh contempt for the miners' doomed but heroic obduracy is not attractive. But it has to be admitted that, as usual, he was ruthlessly honest according to his understanding of the situation. He had always insisted that the coal industry must pay its way, that there could be no more Government assistance, no subsidizing of one industry, however vital, out of the profits of others. This was the economic orthodoxy of the day and F.E. took it as simple fact, which he believed in spelling out without sentimental pretence that things could be otherwise. On the absolute defeat of the strike came to depend, in his view, 'failure or success in educating the working people of this country into the iron reality of the economic wage'.[39] The critical phrase there, though, is 'working people'; and it reveals the essential limitation of his outlook. He was, in the beginning, as unsympathetic to the coal owners as to the miners. 'It would be possible to say without exaggeration of the miners' leaders that they were the stupidest men in England if we had not had frequent occasion to meet the owners.'[26] He accepted, at this stage, the responsibility of the owners so to reorganize their industry as to enable it to pay, economically, a decent wage. But when battle was joined, and both sides equally defied the Government's half-hearted efforts to mediate, his whole sympathy swung instinctively towards the owners. Churchill, equally belligerent on the constitutional principle of the General Strike, continued to insist that the owners should come half-way and make a settlement. But F.E. narrowed the issue to money and the working man's need to learn the iron law of wages. In the House of Lords he reversed his dictum that the owners were even stupider than the miners;[40] he conceived a personalized contempt for Cook, and in the Coal Committee threw his weight firmly on the side of the unfettered right of capital to exert its might. The fact that Baldwin and most of the rest of the Cabinet found it similarly difficult to imagine compelling the owners to reconstruct their business is no alibi for what must still be interpreted as a naked class instinct. F.E. had always claimed not to be a Diehard. When, before the war and even after it, he had opposed to the challenge of labour a nobler vision of national unity and class interdependence he had posed as a progressive Conservative, a Tory Democrat, the true friend of labour. This benevolence was genuine enough, so long as labour was content to pursue its aspirations within the limits set by a capitalist market economy. His tone changed abruptly, however, as soon as labour presumed to question the 'iron reality' of the marketplace and demanded not just better wages and conditions, but that the laws of economic life should be amended and the basis of society tilted in its favour. At this the limits of his benevolence were reached, the depth of his conservatism revealed, the poverty of his political imagination exposed. Unlike Lloyd George, for instance, or some younger Conservatives, he could see no middle way, was interested in finding no synthesis, between the harsh determinism of the stupidest capitalists and the fallacies of socialism. The coal owners must be supported and that was that. In 1926 F.E. came out in full plumage as a true Diehard.

The outstanding question facing the Government after the ending of the coal strike was to determine its legislative response to the unions' abuse of their power in May. The Tory party was in no doubt that some action, both retributive and deterrent, must be taken; and Baldwin, for

all the conciliatory noises he had made on the collapse of the strike,
made no effort such as he had in 1925, to impose magnanimity in
victory. A Cabinet Committee was set up within a week of the T.U.C.
surrender, chaired by the Diehard Cave and comprising F.E. and
Winston, Joynson-Hicks and Worthington-Evans, Bridgeman, Cunliffe-
Lister, Steel-Maitland and Hogg. F.E. was, at the outset, determined
that the measure which resulted should be far-reaching and made a
point in his public speeches of leaking the deliberations of the Committee to educate public opinion to the view that the privileges granted
the unions in 1906 must be withdrawn.[41] At a quarterly meeting of the
Central Unionist Council on 22 June he made what Amery described as
'a very indiscreet but much approved speech indicating action with
regard to Trade Unions', in which he insisted on the need, not merely
for strike ballots, an end to the closed shop and curbs on picketing, but
also for union funds to be made once again, as the Taff Vale judgment
had declared them to be back in 1901, liable to legal action for damages
arising out of industrial action.[42] To his legal mind, the acquiescence of
lawyers of the standing of Asquith and Haldane in the Campbell-
Bannerman Government's grant of immunity to trade unions in 1906
was the most outrageous violation imaginable of the principle of
equality under the law; and he had campaigned furiously against it ever
since. But – here is the puzzle – now that he had the chance to do
something about it, he put up very little fight for the reversal of 1906 in
the Cabinet Committee.

He was, for one thing, an irregular attender at the Committee's
meetings. When he did attend, the main issue which concerned him was
the control of picketing – particularly making it illegal to picket a man's
home: an old cause, but a relatively minor one. On the question of legal
immunity, Cave and Churchill argued for withdrawal: F.E. was numbered with the majority who opposed it.[43] Writing to Irwin in India in
late November, he did not even mention withdrawal of legal immunity
among the options the Committee was considering.

> You ask me about our Trade Union legislation. Although a great
> deal of work has been done in the matter, the situation is still
> somewhat fluid . . . I think that the Committee will recommend the
> strictest possible control over picketing. It will recommend an
> explicit declaration that a General Strike is illegal. It has found the
> proposal to enforce a compulsory ballot to be beset by grave
> practical difficulties [as F.E. had consistently maintained, against
> a majority who had initially favoured them] . . . It is drafting a
> clause as to the compulsory levy which the Cabinet can adopt or
> not as it likes.[44]

The reversal of the procedure for collecting the political levy, from 'contracting out' to 'contracting in', was in fact the most contentious measure included in the Trade Disputes Bill, published in April 1927 and carried into law in June. For a few years it hit the unions' finances hard, until branch secretaries found ways of circumventing it. Beyond that, as F.E. had foreshadowed, it did no more than declare sympathetic strikes illegal and impose curbs on picketing. Though the Labour party characterized the Bill as a piece of vicious class revenge, it was actually very much milder than it might have been, milder than much of the Tory party wanted and than F.E. had seemed to predict the previous June. And yet he continued to write and speak as though the Bill embodied everything he had ever advocated. 'Claws will have to be clipped', he asserted sternly at the Birkenhead Hippodrome in February; but he made no mention of the sanction which eight months earlier he had considered essential.[45] To Irwin he wrote that the Bill would 'make a great row; and we shall have a very bitter session'.

> But two considerations have made it plain that we must proceed. First, the thing is in itself right and was made inevitable by the industrial disturbances of last year. Secondly, our Party, both in the House of Commons and in the country, is inflexibly determined, whatever the risks may be, that we shall adopt this course.[46]

He relished the fight for the Bill, speaking for it all round the country and giving no hint that it was less sweeping than he had wanted. At a Tory demonstration at the Free Trade Hall, Manchester, on 30 April, he candidly welcomed the renewal of battle on such a clear-cut issue – he described 'contracting in' as the clearest cause he had ever embraced – and defied Labour to do its worst, in quite his old style. 'Hold all your meetings; blow all your trumpets; make all your speeches; unfurl your red flags; and when you have done, the Bill is going through Parliament.'[47] He laughed at MacDonald's promise to repeal it: Labour could not give the Tories a better cry. Did they think the constituencies wanted another General Strike? The whole implication of his speeches was that the Bill would make a repetition of the events of May impossible.

How, then, had he been persuaded that the mere outlawing of sympathy strikes was sufficient sanction, when previously he had insisted that nothing less than the restoration of Taff Vale would be necessary? In one of his *Last Essays*, published in 1930, he gave his answer.[48] He devoted a dozen pages to a generous re-examination of John Simon's important speech during the General Strike, in which Simon had pronounced the strike to be illegal. At the time, F.E. had thought his old rival mistaken: he regarded the strike as the inevitable consequence of the licence granted in 1906, a licence which the unions were bound sooner or later to abuse, and which should, now that they had done so, be withdrawn. This was his position in June 1926. On reflection, however, he appears to have been persuaded that Simon's argument – that the immunity granted in 1906 applied only to actions performed in direct furtherance of a pay dispute, and therefore only to the miners' strike and *not* to the sympathetic action of the T.U.C. – was after all correct. The corollary of this was that from the point of view of preventing future general strikes, all that was required was a clear statement that would put beyond doubt the fact that the funds of unions engaged in sympathy strikes were not covered by the immunity which protected them in pay disputes. This the 1927 Bill provided.

If F.E. had any regrets that the Bill left the narrower immunity conceded in 1906 intact, he never aired them. His objection to the privileged status then accorded to unions was primarily a professional one; and, like Asquith and Haldane all those years ago, he was prepared as a Cabinet Minister, in what the Government perceived as the national interest, to let his legal outrage be stifled by political considerations. The important thing, after 1926, was to concentrate public attention on the inadmissibility of the General Strike: to have pursued the funds of individual unions engaged in pay disputes would have seemed a gratuitous attack on the already beaten miners. (The Bill already hit the unions' pockets through the change in the political levy.) Baldwin's and the Government's line throughout the 1926 crisis had been to draw an absolute distinction between a perfectly legitimate (though misguided) strike by the workers in a single industry against their employers, and the illegitimate use of the strike weapon for political ends against the elected Government. By making explicit the absence of legal protection for the latter while taking no step to inhibit the former, the Trade Disputes Act in its moderate form served to underline that vital distinction. The legal anomaly remained, to become a bone of furious contention again some half a century later; but F.E. was entitled to feel that, for the present, Tory honour was satisfied. He put all his authority into persuading the party that 1906 *had* been repealed.

F.E.'s hard line against the coal strike and against A.J. Cook was part of a wider war against what he and other Tories saw as the subversive influence of Soviet Communism in Britain and the British Empire.

During 1925 F.E. had seemed to acquiesce in Baldwin's attempt to deflect the labour movement from the path of class confrontation by soft words, conciliation and appeasement. The violent denunciations of the

Labour Government's subservience to Moscow with which he had enlivened the 1924 election gave way temporarily to somewhat glutinous tributes to MacDonald and Thomas for not having abused their position, and assurances that Labour could after all be trusted as a majority Government in the future, so long as it represented the whole country and remembered its duty to the Empire. He always made a sharp distinction, however, between 'patriotic' Labour and the 'Moscow-led extremists'. Even during this year of moderation, he never ceased to warn of the malign influence of the latter within the trade unions, regularly entertaining his audiences with contemptuous abuse of the sort of class agitators who, he would allege, had 'never produced anything but treasonable pamphlets without a printer's name and . . . never employed anyone except the police'.[49]

The General Strike brought the Bolshevist bogey back to the forefront of Tory speechmaking. Cook's boasted connections with Moscow were well known, and Russian interference in British domestic affairs seemed to have been made explicit during the coal strike by the revelation of a Soviet fund, supposedly collected by Russian trade unionists, in support of the miners. Since MacDonald's formal recognition of the U.S.S.R. in 1924, the question of how to combat this interference centred on the privileged presence in London of large numbers of Comintern agents in the guise of Soviet diplomats and trade officials. In June 1925 F.E. publicly joined his voice with those who were calling for their expulsion.[9] Austen Chamberlain, however, was clear that such a gesture would do more harm than good, and for the moment he had his way. A year later F.E., at a Conservative fête near Luton, was celebrating in characteristic style the defeat of the General Strike, 'The spirit of old England is stronger than the spirit of new Moscow.' He launched his usual attack on Cook and on the Soviet 'trade unionists'' money for the miners. But on the question of the Soviet agents, he toed the Government line. 'I need not say more than this, that on an evenly-balanced argument the Government decided that since they are here, and since we perfectly understand them, their methods, their purposes and their aims, they can, perhaps, do no more mischief here than they could do elsewhere.'[41] Though he abided by the Cabinet decision, it was evident from this calculated leak which side of the evenly-balanced argument he was on.

A new element was added at the end of the year by the outbreak of serious anti-British disturbances in China, fomented, it was naturally assumed, from Moscow. The Government treated the situation with extreme gravity and sent British troops from India to protect lives and property. Labour criticism of this military response was treated, by F.E. at least, as evidence that Labour was still under the Bolshevik thumb and not yet, after all, fit to govern a great Empire.[50] The next election, he declared dramatically, would be fought (like the last) between England and Moscow, 'between those who believe in the sanity, sobriety and continuity of English life, and those who believe in the fever-stricken and malignant doctrines of Moscow – men who have not hesitated to accept foreign money and foreign dictation'.[51] Increasingly he devoted his public utterances to the solemn denunciation of Moscow and the Communist system. 'I tell you quite plainly', he pledged himself at a meeting at Dulwich Baths in March 1927, 'that in what remains to me in public life I will devote myself in the plainest possible language and by combative methods to defeat this attempt to destroy the British Empire.' Dismissing, amid cheers, an intrepid heckler – not an Englishman, he asserted, but a slave of Moscow, a 'moral and political degenerate' – he launched into a characteristic indictment:

> No language of contempt could do them complete justice, nor would it be worth while to use it. I only attempt a moderate, dispassionate and, on the whole, a rather flattering criticism of the Union of Socialist Republics, because I see there is a maniacal section of our own population who is prepared to imitate them, and desires that we should imitate them. The moment I became convinced that there is a section of my fellow-countrymen that wishes to imitate the Soviet Union, I proposed to ask myself, 'What is this Union? What is its history? What is its record?'
>
> Its murders, assassinations are known to all of us . . . They are not only, as we know, murderers and assassins but the men who authorised the doing to death of the young girls of the Royal House; the men who have justified that ever since; the men who have stolen British property all over Russia; the men who very nearly lost the war to which they were pledged with the Allies. They talk of themselves as establishing the rule of the Proletariat. Do you think the Proletariat rules in Russia? The only right the Proletariat has in Russia is to be shot, and they are shot very freely. The only true Proletariat that exists in Russia is the Proletariat of the peasantry, and they are strongly opposed to the Soviet Government.
>
> We are indebted to them for one thing only. They have made plain in the face of the civilised world the imposture, the cruelty, the severity, the inhumanity and the failure of the Socialist system.[52]

In February 1927, the Cabinet was still divided. The feeling of the Tory party in the country and in the House of Commons, as F.E. wrote to Irwin, was all in favour of the expulsion of the Russians; the Foreign Office was with difficulty holding the Cabinet to the opposite course. F.E. argued, according to Amery, 'at length and with much eloquence' in favour of a breach.[53] 'I suspect that in the end', he told Irwin, 'we shall be kicked into taking this course. If this anticipation is well-founded, we had better do it now.'[54]

In May Joynson-Hicks, another Minister who had made his dissent from the Foreign Office's inaction public, took the matter character-istically into his own hands. Two years before, he had exceeded the proper limits of his departmental authority by rounding up on charges of sedition ten leading homegrown Communists.

> You and I know well enough [F.E. had written satirically to Reading] that the responsibility in such matters belongs to the Attorney-General alone, but our dear friend Jix has been rushing here, there and everywhere – visiting everyone, including the King, and very much the central figure in the picture of justice. I am told that all the cases are very strong; but if the matter happened to go wrong, one doubts whether the Home Office would claim quite so conspicuous a position.[55]

Now the Home Secretary similarly forced the hand of the Foreign Office by ordering a police raid on the premises of the Soviet Trade Delegation, Arcos Ltd, looking for proof of subversive activity. The raid was bungled, and the agents within had time to burn their files. To cover the failure to turn up the expected incriminating evidence, however, the Government released a number of intercepted Comintern telegrams, which Joynson-Hicks and Baldwin solemnly read out in the House of Commons, thus announcing to the Russians that their cypher had been cracked – with the inevitable result that they promptly changed it.[56] Still against Chamberlain's advice, the Cabinet now insisted on breaking off relations. This time F.E. was fully in favour of the Home Secretary's clumsy coup.

> You will have been interested to notice [he wrote to Irwin] that at last we have got rid of the Bolsheviks. Personally I am delighted, though I think that we ought to have done so the moment the General Strike was over; and I have been trying to procure such a decision ever since. I am satisfied that we are absolutely right and shall sustain no injury of any kind in consequence of this step. They never traded with us because they liked us, but only because it suited them. If it continues to suit them, as it must, they will continue to trade with us . . . Materially, therefore . . . we lose

nothing; and upon the other side we have sustained an immense moral gain. We have got rid of the hypocrisy of pretending to have friendly relations with this gang of murderers, revolutionaries and thieves. I breathe quite differently now that we have purged our capital of these unclean and treacherous elements.[57]

Of the ultimate fate that awaited the Bolshevik murderers, revolutionaries and thieves, F.E. had no doubt at all. In one of his *Last Essays*, 'The Future of the Bolshevists', he drew a wonderfully lurid picture of the Soviet leaders, divided, discredited, personally despicable, entirely dependent on the secret police and the army to save them from the vengeance of the hostile population, but unable to trust either – 'caught like rats in a trap', concerned only 'to save their own wretched lives'. The essay is an extraordinary mixture of insight and fantasy. He was correct to perceive so early as 1930 the complete political bankruptcy of the Soviet system; at the same time wisely cautious about predicting its early demise. Yet his interpretation of the Revolution in terms of the crudest racial stereotypes is ludicrous as to be simply hilarious: the Bolsheviks are all Jews and Georgians, the 'torture gangs' are staffed by Letts and Chinamen, all alike preying on the poor, passive Russian people. The end will surely come for the Bolshevik usurpers, F.E. finally assures his readers and himself, 'when at last that sleeping, slow-witted giant awakens'.[58]

It is unusual to find F.E. falling for the consolation of such obvious wishful thinking.

The Baldwin Cabinet,
1926–8

After the General Strike and the defeat of the coal strike, politics moved into a quieter phase in 1927–8, which Labour protests against the Trade Disputes Act did little to disturb. Baldwin had won a great moral victory on top of his party's electoral triumph of 1924, while the effect of the events of 1926 on the Labour movement was to discredit the militant advocates of direct action and restore the authority of the parliamentary leadership. MacDonald and his colleagues now set out deliberately to overcome the extremist image which had done the party so much damage and establish in its place their respectability, moderation and competence as the natural alternative party of government – in perfect fulfilment of Baldwin's strategy of assimilating the Labour challenge peacefully within the parliamentary Constitution. The common aim, henceforth, of both Conservative and Labour leaders, co-operating in unspoken alliance, was to restore the two-party system to the exclusion of Lloyd George, Asquith and the remnant of divided Liberals.

F.E., for all the virulence of his anti-socialism, was now fully in favour of this strategy: the last trace of coalitionism had long since been eliminated from his thinking. Though he would never have admitted that Baldwin and Bonar Law had been right in 1922 and he and Austen Chamberlain wrong, he was in practice a thorough convert to the Carlton Club view that the Tory party alone was the most effective instrument for the defeat, or at least the containment, of socialism, while the Liberal party had become an irrelevance whose members must be painlessly absorbed into one or other of the larger parties between whom the future inevitably lay. It was the Liberals' action in putting Labour into power in 1924 which to him was the unforgivable proof of their spinelessness and folly. Since that date, though he still refused to say a word against Lloyd George, and even expressed some

ironic sympathy for his desperate efforts to flog some flicker of vitality
into a condemned corpse, he had reverted to a public position as
strongly and contemptuously anti-Liberal as he had started out with
back in 1906.

The party's divided counsels during the General Strike amply confirmed him in his view of its 'hopeless and even ludicrous positon',[1] and
exhausted his sympathy for Lloyd George. While Asquith, Grey and
Simon correctly and patriotically condemned the unions and pledged
their support to the Government, Lloyd George, seeking to re-establish
his popular credentials, insisted on condemning equally the Cabinet's
mishandling of the negotiations – for which temerity, though he was
supported by most of the party in the country, Asquith (now ennobled
as the Earl of Oxford) expelled him from the Shadow Cabinet. F.E. saw
this performance as bearing out everything he had ever said about the
Liberals' innate irresponsibility. As he wrote ironically to Irwin in India:

> The odd part about the present situation is that Lloyd George has
> with him every Liberal paper but one in the country. He has also
> nearly all the Liberal agents in the constituencies; and he is not
> lacking in more disinterested support from other Liberal elements.
> The real truth of course is, if one analyses it, that the Liberal party
> has always in all its history, from the days of Charles James Fox
> onwards, been intuitively wrong in every moment of grave national
> crisis. Lloyd George went hopelessly wrong in the strike. He,
> therefore, today, according to the best Liberal tradition, is con-
> sidered right because in fact he was wrong, while Oxford is
> considered wrong because in fact he was right.[2]

From now on his kid-glove treatment of Lloyd George was at an end.
When at the end of 1926 Lloyd George again scandalized Tory opinion
by criticizing the Government's military response to threats to British
property in China, F.E.'s condemnation of his old leader was as severe
as anyone's.

> I am frankly shocked that an ex-Prime Minister, who held with so
> much brilliance and courage the position of great responsibility in
> the war, should condescend now to make a speech wholly irres-
> ponsible, wholly inaccurate, wholly mischievous to the funda-
> mental interests of which he, with every other statesman in the
> country, ought to be the responsible guardian.[3]

During 1927 F.E. did not hesitate to join in the row that broke out
over the source of Lloyd George's famous political fund, pursuing an

extraordinarily petty public squabble in the columns of *The Times* over the number of peers Lloyd George had created by comparison with other Prime Ministers.[4] Since gaining control of the Liberal party after Asquith's retirement following the General Strike fiasco, Lloyd George was now using his fund to finance the development of a novel and far-sighted industrial policy for the party based on the radical but still economically heretical diagnosis of Maynard Keynes. F.E. had only shallow mockery for this distinguished attempt to defy the closing of the two-party trap. 'If 500 Liberal candidates are to be run at the next General Election,' he jeered in a speech at Portsmouth, 'we need no longer argue as to the disposition of those vast funds which Mr Lloyd George controls, because it is quite evident that two elections will dispose of the whole of it in the payment of forfeitures.'[5] To Lloyd George's revival of the old taunt that the Tories were the 'stupid party', F.E. retorted with a characteristic gibe which, though a little premature in 1927, would classically encapsulate the Liberal decline some thirty years later. 'Stupid as we are, our numbers in the House of Commons cannot conveniently be contained in one taxi-cab, or at least' – he realized that he was anticipating slightly – 'in a motor omnibus.'[6] In the face of his brutal conviction that the Liberal party deserved only to be consigned as rapidly as possible to history, his former support for proportional representation – to which he still, though with qualifications, theoretically adhered – wilted in a perfect individual microcosm of the cynicism with which the majority parties, in the arrogance of power, have always regarded the plight of minorities.

The Government's real battle for re-election was with Labour, whom he now again took to praising, after the excitements of 1926, for their moderation and responsibility: the party had shed its alien fringe and was maturing into a true and trustworthy embodiment of the majestic continuity of British history. As such, of course, it posed a greater electoral threat to the Conservatives than a bunch of raw revolutionaries; but by March 1928 he was prepared publicly to admit the possibility that the Government might be defeated – that it must ultimately be defeated – and that this would not be the end of the world. Less than two years before, he had been solemnly declaring that the next election would be between England and Moscow and the survival of free institutions at stake! Now,

Although we have lived dangerously . . . I see signs growing clearer and clearer that not the qualities of the governing class, but the energy, the patience, the generosity and vitality of the British people as a whole are going to carry this country through to the goal to which we are entitled by our exertions in the war.[7]

This, of course, was a perfectly safe line to take between elections, and the impression of a nasty corner turned was intended to redound to the credit of the Government. He considered, mid-way through their term, that they had done pretty well in the face of overwhelming difficulties. 'Since the year 1914,' he reflected to Irwin, as the Chinese crisis followed hard upon the coal dispute, 'there has hardly been a moment in which the Government has been free from the gravest anxieties. Poor Bonar Law's programme of tranquillity will have to wait, it would almost seem, some decades before realization.'[8]

He thought the Government had done all that Government could do to relieve these difficulties. He believed that Neville Chamberlain – 'the able business son of a business father' – had practically solved the housing problem,[9] and enthused annually to Irwin about Churchill's Budgets; he considered his 1928 plan for de-rating industry 'one of the biggest steps taken in recent years to free trade and agriculture from the burden of post-war depression'.[10] No more than any Tory did he imagine that the Government could do more to relieve unemployment than to wait passively for trade to improve.

In his capacity as elder statesman – and only Winston, Austen and Balfour had longer experience of office – F.E. gave Davidson in 1927 a frank assessment of the quality of his Cabinet colleagues in a series of pithy judgments which Davidson considered 'remarkably shrewd'. Several of them were sharply double-edged – particularly those on his closest friends. To Austen, for instance – who was of course Foreign Secretary! – he ascribed 'Very good judgement, generally right on everything except Foreign Affairs'. Churchill, similarly, was 'Often right, "but my God when he's wrong"!!' Leo Amery, most bluntly, was 'Always wrong'. The Lord Chancellor, Cave, F.E. dismissed as 'Very Diehard and unhelpful'; Lord Robert Cecil as simply 'useless'. Neville Chamberlain he thought 'Good' and Samuel Hoare 'Quite sound', while he conceded that he had 'completely underrated' another of Baldwin's closest colleagues, Bridgeman, who 'could always be relied upon to get a common sense view of the man-in-the-street'. The rapidly rising star of the Government – rising very much in F.E.'s own legal footsteps – was the Attorney-General, Sir Douglas Hogg: 'Excellent judgement', F.E. considered, 'except on matters of pure politics when wrong because too diehard.'[11]

Many in the country would have been astonished to hear F.E. still using 'diehard' as a term of censure and would have made precisely the same criticism of F.E. himself. But this points up the difference between his private and his public faces. Diehard though he often appeared on the platform and in print, F.E. was here judging his colleagues on their performance in Cabinet; and there he did not believe in striking postures, but consistently impressed all who saw him in that context by his constructive moderation, flexibility on points of detail and (the word is continually repeated) wisdom.

His surprising capacity for patient and clear-sighted handling of sensitive questions was well demonstrated in the autumn of 1926, when as Secretary of State for India he was centrally involved in the Imperial Conference, held in London through October and November. ('We are living', he wrote to Irwin, 'in a whirl of business . . . There are lunches, and dinners every night, and innumerable speeches.')[12] This was an important gathering, which laid the foundations for the 1931 Statute of Westminster establishing the equality and autonomy within the Empire of the four old white Dominions, plus the Irish Free State. Since the war the Dominions, especially South Africa, had been increasingly anxious to assert their independence of Britain. In fact General Hertzog proved very amenable to British efforts to frame an acceptable constitutional formula embodying complete practical autonomy under the Crown; and this, true to the 1921 Treaty, was willingly accepted by the Irish. F.E. found in Cosgrave's attitude a gratifying vindication of his tortured negotiations of five years before. Inevitably, he wrote to Irwin, having a Republican opposition to appease at home, the Irish had felt obliged to keep making 'tiresome points', but their manner had throughout been 'extremely courteous'.

> They have all expressly recognized the Crown as the common link of Empire, and an Irish Prime Minister is to lay a wreath on the Cenotaph side by side with his colleagues from the other Dominions. When you recall the state of affairs which existed only four years ago, I think you will agree that the Irish settlement is working better than in our most extravagant hopes we could have anticipated.[13]

Alas for those hopes, the replacement of Cosgrave by de Valera was only just around the corner.

The last days of the Conference coincided with the final stages of the coal strike. F.E. was, as he told Irwin, the only Minister who was a member both of the Conference and of the Coal Committee: 'the press of business in the last few days has been almost intolerable'.

> I have been occupied all day in the Committee which has had thrust upon it the task of devising formulae, designed to soothe Dominion susceptibilities, covering almost every conceivable aspect of the relationship of various parts of the Empire both *inter se* and with foreign countries.[14]

One of these *minutiae* was the famous 'O'Higgins comma' conceded in the new form of the King's title: not as the British at first insisted, 'by the Grace of God, of Great Britain *and* Ireland' etc., but 'by the Grace of God, of Great Britain, Ireland, and of British Dominions beyond the Seas'.[15] With such intricacies, F.E.'s legal ingenuity was invaluable; but he was also good on the broader questions of the (white) Empire. At the Cabinet, on 17 November, at which the final Report of the Conference was agreed, the new liberal Constitution came in for heavy criticism, as Amery noted, from Cave – 'a tremendous old Tory' – and from Churchill 'who is really a jingo of the late 19th century and has no sympathy with the idea of Imperial unity by free co-operation'. Balfour and Amery 'waxed eloquent . . . in defence of the modern conception of Empire'; and they were 'usefully helped' by F.E.[16]

The unpredictable way in which F.E. and Winston, sharing a broadly common outlook, differed from day to day on so many topics, one of them at one moment the liberal and the other the reactionary, the next moment the other way round, would make a fascinating separate study in political psychology. In this instance, F.E.'s frequent visits to Canada and his close association with Bonar Law and Beaverbrook perhaps combine with his experience of negotiating the Irish Treaty to explain his more generous appreciation of Dominion aspirations compared with Winston, whose more formative experience was with the Transvaal Constitution when he was at the Colonial Office in 1907. F.E.'s relatively advanced understanding of the meaning of Dominion status, however, only strengthened his determination that that dignity could never in the foreseeable future be conceded to India; and with this Winston was shortly to come out in entire agreement, making the theme his own after F.E.'s death.

During the Baldwin Government the perennial problem of the House of Lords recurred to tease and torment the Cabinet as it had tormented every Cabinet since 1906. The Government came into office in 1924 vaguely pledged to do something about it, but still with no clear idea in any quarter of the party of precisely what. It was generally accepted, even by many Liberals (now that they had shed their Irish blinkers), that the 1911 Act was not a satisfactory or permanent solution. The problem was, as it had been before the war and remains to this day, how to reform the composition of the House in such a way as to make it democratically acceptable to restore to it real powers, without setting up a rival to the Commons and inviting deadlock. Every advocate of reform had his own scheme for the perfect reconstruction of the Lords, but none of them carried conviction or any wide measure of support. F.E. was in this respect no different from every other peer concerned to restore the standing of his House. In principle he was still as anxious as ever for reform; but the experience of the Coalition had made him more cautious in his expectations of what was possible. He had now no wish to try to put the clock back to 1910, and was much less thorough-going than formerly in his arguments for undertaking any reform at all, as he revealed in a major speech in the Upper House in April 1925.

He began by dismissing as 'profoundly stupid and utterly indefensible' Haldane's proposal that the House should be left as it was. The rise of Labour to the position where it was the alternative Government made reform essential, but not so much to provide a safeguard against socialism rushed through by a single chamber – with this bogey F.E. now made very little play – as to avoid the absurdity of Labour Governments being obliged to recruit the likes of Parmoor and Chelmsford to represent it, incongruously, in the Upper House. The need for reform was a simply practical one, if a Second Chamber was to continue to exist at all.

F.E.'s scheme – he stressed that he was speaking solely for himself, not for the Government – was for a much smaller House of about 300 members, perhaps 180 to be chosen by the peers amongst themselves, another 120 or so to be appointed *ex officio* as former holders of certain high positions, with an additional nominated element of life peers which Labour Governments could use to stiffen their debating strength. Like most others, this was a curious hybrid scheme; F.E. rejected as untenable in the post-war world Willoughby de Broke's 'picturesque' defence of the hereditary principle, yet at the same time he rejected all suggestions that the House should be elected. He ended up with a mixture of superannuation, patronage and filtered heredity.

Such a House, he recognized, would not have much democratic authority, and this led him to an important admission.

> I do not think it would be possible, even with a second chamber so reconstituted, to attempt to interfere with the main purpose and effect of the Parliament Act, greatly as I myself detested and resented that Act, and mischievous and artificial as I think its conception was.
>
> But history has moved on, years have passed. We in this House acquiesced, rightly or wrongly, in a conclusion which, at our risk, we could have disputed. We did not dispute it [or rather the peers of 1911 had not disputed it, despite F.E.'s vehement urgings from the Commons] and so far as my individual advice is concerned, I should not advise your Lordships, at this period of our history, and after the political developments which have taken place in the last few years, to re-open this controversy.

He did not therefore propose any restored powers for the reformed House, merely a number of procedural safeguards to guarantee its role.[17]

Moderate and realistic in its acceptance of the Parliament Act, F.E.'s proposal was so modest that it seemed to make no compelling case for reform at all: his Second Chamber would enjoy little more authority, little more public respect and no more power than the existing House. Nevertheless, in another speech the next month F.E. told their Lordships that it was, in his experience of politics, 'inconceivable that the present Government can be so mad or so neglectful of its duty and responsibilities as not to reform the House of Lords before very long'.[18] The main burden of this speech was renewed opposition to the attempt to admit peeresses to the unreformed House – 'mere conduit pipes', he called them, in a wonderfully disparaging phrase, 'established in the hope of making permanent a male succession';[19] but he promised to support their admission on the same terms as men when the House was reformed, which was for him another remarkable concession. Despite all his assertions, however, there was little sign that the Government would ever be ready to act. In June a Cabinet Committee was set up to look into possible schemes, but this failed to reach any sort of agreement for eighteen months. When in late 1926 Cave did begin to push for a thorough-going reform, including increased powers, F.E. was not with him, taking fright, as he wrote to Irwin, 'that we may find ourselves involved in another Peers and People election', which would distract the Government from its more important trade union legislation.[20] In Cabinet he did not after all speak up for early action, but acquiesced in its postponement at least to 1928.[21] To Davidson he 'expressed his firm conviction that any attempt to bring the House of Lords prominently before the electorate would be fatal to our chances at the next election'.[11]

And yet the Government did find itself involved in Lords reform in 1927 – with F.E. to all appearances leading the way. In May the Cabinet gave broad but half-hearted support to Cave's scheme for a House of some 350 peers partly elected from among themselves and partly nominated, but decided not to introduce legislation for the present. In a debate on 22 June, however, F.E. put the cat among the pigeons by emphatically renewing the Government's commitment to legislate in the present session. In an exceptionally aggressive speech, he picked cruelly, not for the first or last time, on poor old Parmoor, taunting him with his 1910 speeches as a Tory in support of the House of Lords. ('If I have discharged no other service to this House since I have been a member,' F.E. crowed over Parmoor's confusion, 'I have done this at least, that I have persuaded, for a brief moment, the noble and learned Lord to silence.') He attacked the Liberals for opposing what was practically the same reform which they had supported under the Coalition; and repeated the Government's obligation in honour to act.[22]

Why did he suddenly take this line, which dismayed the party managers as much as it gratified the Diehards? To Irwin he wrote, rather wearily the next day: 'We are now at the beginning of a House of Lords row. Personally, I should have thought the whole thing a mistake, except for one consideration, that you must allow the Second Chamber to function when a Labour Government is in power.'[23] On his feet, the memory of old battles seems to have carried him away; but his essential argument was much more limited than formerly. The letter to Irwin goes on to imply that what finally weighed with him was a somewhat snobbish anxiety to preserve the quality of the peerage, which could only be done by separating the legislative function from the possession of hereditary rank. Future Labour Prime Ministers, he wrote, would want more representative party and trade union figures in the Upper House.

> Are we then to have a dozen more hereditary peers, very un- suitable in every way for an hereditary rank, and so on *ad infinitum* with the creation of each new Socialist Government? If this is indeed the course to which we are committed, I think that the House of Lords will perish very rapidly amid public contempt.[23]

It is sad to see F.E.'s clearly argued and logically defensible pre-war fighting position – that the Constitution must be re-balanced to restore the safeguard of a democratically accountable Second Chamber against the destructive whim of a temporary majority in the Commons – reduced by 1927 to a merely antiquarian desire to preserve what was left of the traditional character of the old, dignified but toothless House of Lords. This had been the preference of the despised 'hedgers' in 1911. Charitably, his change of front may be adduced as an instance of his post-war realism and moderation, his mature acceptance of the healing spirit of Baldwinism. But really it only represents a slackening of his intellectual rigour. There is no clearer measure of how far the intelligent and intelligible reforming Unionism of his youth had sagged by his last years into lazy conservatism.

Half a century later, when changes in the character of the Labour party again began to raise the spectre of socialism and a single chamber, constitutionally minded Tories like Lord Hailsham began to revive F.E.'s original arguments against unicameralism and to call again in precisely the same terms for a reform of the House of Lords as a bulwark against unrepresentative extremism.[24] In 1927, however, such fears seemed to the rising generation of Tories groundless. Led by John Buchan, in a brilliant maiden speech, they revolted against the Cave formula when the Government brought it forward in the Commons,[25] and the Cabinet was happy to drop the whole subject. F.E. too was content. Yet his former arguments from principle for the honouring of the 1911 commitment somehow to restore a balanced bicameral system remained, as they still remain, unanswered and unanswerable. However elusive the remedy in practice, he was absolutely right in theory, and though the fear which still moved him in 1924 had receded by 1927, the same constitutional flaw survived to be exploited when the Labour party rediscovered primitive socialism in the 1980s. It was only the timetable of his earlier diagnosis that was wrong.

Even after his peerage took him away from the House of Commons and direct dependence upon Liverpool, F.E. maintained his links with the local party and its boss, Salvidge, who had given him his start in politics. It was to Liverpool that he returned more often than anywhere else to make major speeches, and it was in Lancashire and Cheshire that he concentrated his efforts at election time. Though he kept up only the barest connection with his relatives in Birkenhead – still thriving on Smith & Sons – and never went back except for political purposes, he was very conscious, even in the late 1920s, of the strength he drew from his Merseyside roots. He advised the young Robert Boothby that the single most important thing for a politician who was going to make a successful career was a sound geographical base: the Chamberlains had Birmingham, Lloyd George had Wales, he had Lancashire, and in each case they were upheld in their national struggles by the confidence of solid local support. Churchill, by contrast, switching from Manchester to Dundee to Leicester to Epping, had suffered from the lack of such a footing.

For twenty years Salvidge's domination of Liverpool politics – the centralized control of the Liverpool Constitutional Association through the populist manipulation of the Working Men's Conservative Association, and the successful defence of the city as a predominantly Tory stronghold against first Liberal and now Labour attack – had been the subject of continual criticism from the opposition parties alleging corruption, dictatorship and the undue influence of the 'caucus'. Liverpool Conservatives, however, were generally happy with an organization that delivered results, and held it up to the rest of the country as a model.

In 1927 Salvidge suddenly faced a revolt within his own party. Seven of the city's eight Tory M.P.s – the exception was F.E.'s friend Warden Chilcott – made a public bid for independence of his centralized control, raising the demand of the individual constituencies to have separate organizations and separate agents, as elsewhere. They claimed that the unified organization improperly restricted their independence as elected M.P.s, reducing them to the status of delegates. Salvidge strongly denied any such interference with their freedom, but embarrassing accusations and counter-accusations flew back and forth in print between him and the seven M.P.s, who were led by the only one of their number with any claim to national distinction, Leslie Scott. Eventually Salvidge sought a peacemaker in Baldwin. But first he turned to his trusted ally and strong right arm for the past two decades – F.E., who did not fail him. Salvidge's description sounds like consulting a sort of political Sherlock Holmes.

> I arrived at Charlton in time for lunch on the Saturday, and afterwards Birkenhead suggested that he and I should take a cross-country walk in the course of which I could give him the full story of what had been going on. He had seen both Leslie Scott and Chilcott and had of course followed the row in the papers, but so far he had taken no active part. He went striding over half of Oxfordshire while I did my best to keep up with his seven league boots, and beyond a grunt now and then gave not the slightest indication that he was paying any attention to my intricate tale. Yet from past experience I knew that not one word would escape him, and that, when he did at last decide to deliver his opinion and define his own attitude, any weak point or smallest contradiction on my part would be remembered.

> Tea was a family occasion, and then F.E. took Salvidge out to dinner with Simon at Fritwell Manor, where the troubles of the Liverpool Tory party could naturally not be discussed. It was late at night before they got back to Charlton.

> Birkenhead settled me with a cigar and a pile of periodicals and sat himself down at a writing table. After his pen had been going without the slightest hesitation for some time he came over and dropped five sheets of notepaper onto my knee. They took the form of a letter from him to me written for publication. It was about the most scathing thing I ever read in my life. He had covered in concise form the whole of the ground in dispute between Leslie Scott and myself, given his opinion that the charge of interfering with the constitutional rights of Liverpool members was fantastic, and finished off by offering to come down to Liverpool and support the existing organization to the limits of his capacity. Having read

the letter, I said that to publish it would mean the end of his lifelong friendship with Leslie, which would be a tragedy of which I did not wish to be the cause. He replied 'Do not publish unless and until you need to. But you now hold the trump card and can play it if you wish. I still seem to be in request in Liverpool when elections are on, and if you and I held a rally of the whole of the party locally there could only be one termination of the affair. I don't see who could stand against us now any more than in the old days.'[26]

It seems improbable that Scott would have shrivelled under a written diatribe, however withering, but F.E. and Salvidge together undoubtedly remained a powerful combination in Liverpool, even though neither was the force he had been. Salvidge next saw Baldwin and showed the Prime Minister F.E.'s letter. 'When he had read it he gave a long whistle and remarked with a chuckle, "Our mutual friend does not appear to be losing any of his powers of expression."'[27] At Salvidge's suggestion Baldwin made an appeal to both sides in the dispute for harmony, and during the truce which followed Derby managed to arrange an accommodation without any public intervention by F.E.

The centralized structure of the Liverpool party remained outwardly unaltered. But the days of Salvidge's unquestioned control were numbered. His old authority was much diminished, and the following year he died.

At the end of 1927 F.E. could not resist intervening in a famous controversy of the sort he was usually better keeping out of – the great parliamentary row over the Church of England's new revised Prayer Book. Reflecting the sacramental inclinations of the bishops and higher clergy who had laboured for twenty years to produce it, the new Book – though it was only intended to be an alternative, not to supplant Cranmer's hallowed text – was considered by many lay members of the Church to lean too far towards fashionable Anglo-Catholicism; the revolt of outraged Protestantism against 'idolatry' was taken up at Westminster by an incongruous coalition of evangelicals (including several members of the Government, Joynson-Hicks, Hogg and Inskip), nonconformists and unbelievers – including the Communist Parsee, Saklatvala – and on 15 December, after a debate of rare quality and passion, the Book was thrown out by the House of Commons.

F.E., of course, had no doctrinal convictions one way or the other, but he could not see a first-class row without joining in. Twenty years earlier he might well have been obliged by his more fervent Liverpool constituents to join in the outcry against Romanism. (Much of the point of the new Book, indeed, was to give official sanction to some of the very practices which the proponents of the old Church Discipline Bills had been so concerned to ban.) On the other hand, his consistent view of Church–State relations was that the prerogatives of the Established Church should be upheld against all the sectarian jealousies of non-conformity. Forgetting his quarrels with the bishops over divorce and the Oxford Chancellorship, F.E. rallied, militantly, as in the old days of Welsh Disestablishment, to the defence of the hierarchy. The elementary right of the Church of England to formulate its own doctrines, he declared in a letter to *The Times* on 20 December, was not to be denied by a motley majority in the House of Commons – composed to a considerable extent of Irish, Scots and Welsh – under the influence of crude and irrelevant allegations of Popery.

> The Protestantism of these realms was not originally asserted, nor is it in its ultimate destiny to be preserved, by the insistence upon emblems. Vestments and chasubles, albs, copes and genuflexions count in this connection not at all. The Protestant case in these islands depends upon the strong Protestant spirit of the population of these islands; it depends upon an inveterate objection to Papal superstitions, and to the undue and intolerable intrusion of the priest upon the individual conscience. If and when a real menace arises to Protestantism in Great Britain, it will be defeated not by the rhetoric of Parliamentarians (aided by Mr Saklatvala) but by the unchanged and unchangeable spirit of the people of England. England in fact is as unlikely to renounce the fundamental doctrine of Protestantism as the College of cardinals is to elect Sir William Joynson-Hicks to be the next Pope.

The argument that Protestantism, understood as a trait of the national character, was so ingrained as to need no defence, was not one of F.E.'s stronger, despite the scorn which he heaped upon the opposition. 'The speeches which are acclaimed as decisive in that discussion', he wrote of the Commons debate, 'ought not, if competently answered, to have influenced a schoolboys' debating society. For the first time since I left the House of Commons I regretted having done so, for I believe that I could have made an adequate reply to them.' His principal reply, as made in *The Times*, consisted of an assertion that the Church was in no way bound to accept the Commons' decision, which was in reality futile. 'For while it denied to the Church the right to use the amended Prayer Book, it completely deprived the Church of the slightest moral right to correct any incumbent who adopted it.'[28] In other words any clergyman who wished could perfectly safely use the new book without fear of sanction; the Commons' decision, indeed, would merely give it an added vogue. This, like so many of F.E.'s blunt insights, was inconveniently true. He feared that the clash raised the spectre of Disestablishment, but if it came to that he would not be dismayed.

'F.E. Smith has written today a most violent letter to *The Times*, deliberately insulting,' Inskip wrote. 'Jix and Douglas Hogg . . . are furious and I don't wonder. I don't think the Archbishop will like his new ally.'[29] Prompted by Simon, Inskip wrote a reply deploring both the tone and the content of F.E.'s letter. Chesterton's classic 'Chuck it, Smith' might have summed up the enraged evangelicals' reaction to his intemperate meddling in matters he did not understand. F.E. was of course undeterred. On the contrary, during the following year he felt himself vindicated by the bishops' insistence on their new Prayer Book, despite a second defeat in the Commons in October 1928, and wrote triumphantly to Irwin:

> The Bishops have done exactly what I predicted, and what anyone but a congenital idiot ought to have seen that they must do, if Parliament again rejected the measure. Having committed them-selves to the propriety and orthodoxy of the revised edition, they had obviously disabled themselves from interfering with any clergyman who employed it. The result of the rejection, therefore, by the House of Commons has been, as I said would be the case, to make it quite certain that every incumbent who desired to use the revised edition could and would do so with impunity.[30]

A few days later F.E. returned to the public fray. 'Oddly enough', he wrote ironically, 'neither the Archbishops nor the Bishops have asked me to be their champion in the Press. But I confess I was so exasperated by Jix . . . that I could not help intervening.'[31] In *The Times* again, on 9 October, he reiterated his previous warnings.

> These warnings, though their force was evident to any reasonably educated schoolboy, were entirely ignored. Those who chose to ignore them are now 'pained' at the attitude taken up by the Bishops. Very likely they are. So were the Bishops pained by their attitude. But what is it suggested that the Bishops should do? . . . If I were a Bishop, I would a thousand times rather see the Church disestablished than find myself compelled to coerce and bully a subordinate clergyman for doing what I believed to be right; and which I had told the whole world, including himself, that I believed to be right.[32]

The outcome was, just as F.E. predicted, that although the new Book was never approved, many of the forms of worship to which it gave sanction were henceforth tacitly tolerated. Was this, none the less, an argument that F.E. as a non-believer should have kept out of? Surely not. For by his intervention he pointed up the paradox at the very heart of establishment, that the Church places itself, in matters of the most private individual conscience, under the public authority of Parliament, and hence, in the modern world, of infidel parliamentarians like Saklatvala and himself. He was logically quite correct to question the basis of establishment itself if Parliament insisted on outraging the conscience of the Church. As a constitutional lawyer whose grasp of theory was balanced by an equal appreciation of practical reality, his contribution to a somewhat cloudy debate was both pointed and penetrating.

What was objectionable was the truculent manner of his interventions. 'Did you see FE's letter in the *Times* about the Home Secretary today?' Neville Chamberlain wrote to his wife after his last sally. 'His arguments seem to me difficult to controvert but his arrogance and his insolence in expressing his contempt for Jix appear to go far beyond what is decent in speaking of another member of the Cabinet. I don't know what Jix will do, but I should be furious & sorely tempted to send a stinging reply.'[33]

F.E., however, was practically beyond reach of that particular criticism; for within ten days he had ceased to be a member of the Cabinet.

The possibility that F.E. might not see out the Government's life had been common currency almost from the moment of its formation. As early as November 1925, for instance, Hoare had speculated in connection with a crisis over Iraq that F.E. might be looking for an excuse to resign, 'being desperate for want of means, now that journalism is cut off from him'.[34] He was certainly becoming anxious for his family's future and spoke increasingly of leaving politics while he was still young enough to realize his earning potential in some other field; but he was not yet desperate. In April 1927 he wrote specially to Baldwin to dispel rumours that he intended to go soon. It was true, he said, that he had been made 'a very tempting offer of £15,000 a year in gilt-edged surroundings', but he could not dream of abandoning the India Office before the personnel and terms of reference of the Simon Commission were settled,

and by that time we shall be so near a General Election that nothing in the world would induce me to separate myself from my colleagues without playing my part as an official comrade in the

great fight that lies in front of us . . . I should be very unhappy if
you thought so little of my friendship as to imagine that I would
·desert your fortunes as long as my membership of the Government
fortifies it, and will assist you in the troubles that confront us all.[35]

A year later there arose the possibility that F.E. should return to the
Woolsack. In March 1928 Cave was obliged to retire because of illness:
he died within a few weeks. As a former Lord Chancellor who had been
kept out by Cave in 1924, F.E. had a practically irrefutable claim to
resume the position if he wanted, outranking even the Attorney-General,
Hogg. In fact, he had no wish to go back. But Hogg did not welcome the
elevation either. His rise in the party since entering the Commons in
1922 had been meteoric; he was already spoken of as a possible successor to Baldwin's leadership in a few years' time, but this prospect
would be jeopardized by his going to the Lords. Neville Chamberlain,
though a rival heir, was generously anxious to keep Hogg in the
Commons, and pressed Baldwin to persuade F.E. that it was his duty to
take the job. (Besides, he wrote in his diary, 'A change in the India
Office wd have been a good thing. FE never goes there and the officials
are "fed up" with him.')[36] Baldwin, however, replied that though he
thought F.E. could have been persuaded, 'he was afraid to trust him.
He might be seen drunk in the street'.[37] Chamberlain would have taken
the risk, but Baldwin was plainly relieved by F.E.'s reluctance. Moreover since F.E. had already let it be known that he did not intend to
continue in office beyond the election – Baldwin took it for granted that
the Government would be returned – his return to the Woolsack could
only have been a temporary expedient. Hogg was compelled to accept
the inevitable and reluctantly became Lord Hailsham.

His renunciation caused F.E. a passing qualm for, as he wrote to
Irwin, 'it puts me definitely outside the law for the rest of my life'; but he
had no serious regrets. 'As a matter of fact I was rather bored with it.
The ceremonial side depressed me, and the role of a *revenant* is never
very interesting.' As an additional reason for refusing, he repeated that
'having appointed this Commission . . . it was my duty to remain at the
India Office for the next eighteen months'.[38]

Only six months later, however, he had suddenly to ask Baldwin to
release him from this duty. Though there was a lot of malicious
whispering that he was being blackmailed and there was a scandal in
the wind, the reason was quite simply the mounting weight of his debts.
'He *had* to go. His chief backers wouldn't wait', Garvin wrote to Waldorf
Astor after a long 'friendly and affectionate' talk over old times at
Wargrave. Encouraged by Garvin, F.E. did not necessarily see his
withdrawal as permanent, but fantasized a comeback. 'He was very

shrewd, level, clear. Still thinks of being PM when he has put some capital behind him. He has practically none. His children's future disturbs him. He was absolutely confident of making £30,000 a year.'[39]

Baldwin placed no obstacle in F.E.'s way. 'I have thought very carefully about our conversation of yesterday evening,' he wrote on 10 October. 'I am quite clear that for the sake of a few months I ought not to stand in the way of what you propose, and I think, desire to do.' Though their relations had become quite cordial since 1924 – 'You will not misunderstand me when I tell you that we shall part on my side at least with a feeling of personal regret that I could not have believed possible four years ago!'[40] – and he appreciated F.E.'s value in Cabinet, he knew well that F.E.'s reputation was more of a liability than an asset in the country, and he had an obvious replacement at the India Office in Peel, who had served there in 1923. (Peel was in turn replaced as First Commissioner of Works by Lord Londonderry, which gave F.E. the opening for his famous crack that Londonderry – whose mansion in Park Lane was the scene of the most lavish political receptions and entertainments – had 'catered his way to the Cabinet'). The Prime Minister and his retiring colleague published the usual exchange of letters in the press. F.E.'s sheds some discreet light on the circumstances of his withdrawal; is characteristically defiant in the face of criticism of his record; and pays sincere tribute to Baldwin's achievement in winning his loyalty over the past four years.

My dear Prime Minister,

   I am exceedingly grateful to you for having released me from my obligations at an earlier date than we discussed some months ago. I should not have asked you to do so had not some balance of private convenience, which I have explained to you, intervened. Still less should I have done so had there been the slightest prospect that I could have remained long enough at the India Office to take part in the discussions and decisions which the Report of the Simon Commission will require.

   I regret greatly leaving an office where I have spent four of the happiest and most interesting years of my life. The merit or demerit of my work there can at present only be known to the two distinguished Viceroys with whom I have co-operated: to my colleagues in the Cabinet, whom I have kept closely informed of every important decision: to my Council: and to the admirable staff of the India Office, to whose zeal, ability and prudence I have owed so much. For the rest one can only wait for the time one day to come when the India Papers of the last four years will be published.

I do not wish to leave the public stage with anything in the nature of self-praise. I will only therefore say that, after spending four years as a Law Officer and very nearly as long as Lord Chancellor,* I do not believe that the last four years will be ultimately pronounced the most unfruitful of my life.

I am leaving official politics once and for all. But I leave, as you know, in the fullest sympathy with you and your colleagues. I am not without the hope that both in the House of Lords and occasionally in the country I may be permitted to offer some unofficial help.

The moment of parting is always sad. Your own personality has converted a Cabinet, which assembled upon the crater of some bitter and recent memories, into a band of brothers. I leave them and you with emotion and, if I may be allowed to say so, with affection.

Yours very sincerely,

Birkenhead[41]

Baldwin's reply was more conventional, but handsomely expressed – unless a sly irony can be detected in the third sentence.

My dear Birkenhead,

I have received your letter with profound regret, a regret which will be shared by all our colleagues.

For four years your counsel in Cabinet has been invaluable: in dark days, you were a tower of strength, and you have been a generous colleague and a loyal friend. It is too early yet to estimate the value of your work at the India Office, but I am confident that historians of our time will do it justice.

With every good wish for many years of happiness and prosperity in the new sphere of life upon which you are entering,

Believe me to remain,

Yours very sincerely,

Stanley Baldwin[42]

At one of his last attendances at Cabinet, before his resignation was announced, F.E. had a splendid chance to play the elder statesman, when Ministers discussed the parliamentary timetable for the coming session. From the length of his experience he warned against the Chief Whip's optimism that the Government could push through its remaining business in time for an election the following June, and questioned whether it should even want to.

* He was actually Lord Chancellor for longer than he was a Law Officer. F.E. was always vague on such points.

It is thirty-seven years since I spoke daily through the summer as an undergraduate . . . In old days it was a disadvantage to Conservatives to have an election in summer. This has been intensified by increase in the electorate. Street corner speaking is important and a more dominating element than in the vagaries of our English winter. Our enemies are endowed equally with lungs and ignorance to adorn the village rostra. I am, after the Chancellor of the Exchequer, the oldest Cabinet Minister present. [He meant, of course, that he had sat in Cabinets longer than anyone else.] I have never known a case where the estimate of days for Government business was not exceeded. I should be astounded if our difficulties did not prove greater than the Chief Whip estimates.[43]

Despite this sage advice, however, it was decided on 10 October to go for a June election.

F.E. attended his last Cabinet the following week. 'At the end of the meeting', Amery recorded, 'the PM said a few nice words of farewell to F.E., who replied appropriately.'

Whether his going is on balance a loss to the Cabinet or not it will be difficult to say. His judgement has often been very valuable and he gave great help both in the General Strike and with the Irish during the Imperial Conference. On the other hand the wide and naturally exaggerated reports of his manner of living have made him a doubtful asset in the country. From my own point of view I regret the dropping out of a friend.[44]

Among the letters of tribute which F.E. received were generous ones from both the Secretary and the Deputy Secretary to the Cabinet, Maurice Hankey and Tom Jones, who had worked with him at the closest quarters since 1919. F.E. especially valued Hankey's praise, he wrote, because it was a case of *'laudari a viro laudate'* – being praised by a man worthy of the greatest praise himself;[45] while to Jones he replied with greater informality.

Thank you so much for your very friendly letter. I valued it greatly.

We have gone through a good deal together and it was a good combination because my natural cynicism corrected your excessive goodness of heart and vice versa.

Cook's recent disclosures and the speeches of Herbert Smith show that we never had a chance in the coal strike.

Ireland was a triumph and no-one helped more than you.[46]

From the opposite side of the political divide, Ramsay MacDonald wrote a characteristically soggy valediction.

I am so sorry to hear that you are leaving our goodly company of unjust men making other people perfect. May you make money and find peace. If you do, pray let me know, for it is high time that I began the same quest.[47]

Of press comments on F.E.'s departure, *The Times* was the fairest and best-informed, both on his reason for going and on the gap which he would leave.

Lord Birkenhead will be a greater loss to the Cabinet than to his Department, in which he has sat rather loosely for some time past; and, if he were to leave the India Office at all, it is just as well that his successor should take hold of it at the beginning of the main tour of the Simon Commission. But he has always been a valuable counsellor in the general work of the Government. The brilliant invective with which he sometimes delights the House of Lords and reduces a debate to common sense has often been of equal service behind the scenes. Brilliance apart, there is no saner or cooler head in the Cabinet whenever it can be brought to bear upon a difficult problem of administration or politics. The difficulty has always been to keep it concentrated upon public affairs – especially since it became necessary to look outside for a more substantial livelihood than the public service affords.

It is admittedly a matter of money that leads to Lord Birkenhead's resignation; but there is no reason on that account to denounce the 'system' which sometimes induces men of great ability to exchange Downing Street for Lombard Street or Fleet Street, or any of the other thoroughfares where the monetary prizes are largest. It is a commonplace that the business of government cannot enter into competition with these wealthy private concerns; and it is a commonplace also that a highly successful barrister, who joins the Government at the height of his fortunes, may have contracted habits of living which are out of all proportion to his future income.[48]

It was no criticism of the public service, the writer concluded, that it could not keep F.E. in the style to which he had become accustomed; but neither was it a fair criticism of F.E. that he felt unable to continue indefinitely in Government when he could charge more for his brains on the open market. He was not obliged to remain in politics for ever at cost

to himself. Nevertheless the circumstances of his resignation were sufficiently unusual and well-publicized to attract a good deal of less
sympathetic comment, which Edward Hilton Young pithily encapsulated for the benefit of Irwin in India. 'FE's inability to live on ten
thousand a year', he wrote sarcastically, 'has provoked a storm of pity
from press and public.' It was widely thought appropriate that he had
defected at the end openly to the service of Mammon.[49]

Burned Out, 1928–30

'It might have seemed', F.E. had written in his essay on Reginald McKenna in *Contemporary Personalities* in 1924, 'that an ex-Minister in his 54th year was trying destiny rather high when he attempted a career in the City, which lay almost wholly outside anything in his previous experience.'[1] Ironic words, if anyone had recalled them four years later when F.E. himself, in his fifty-seventh year, attempted the same switch of career with a great deal less experience. McKenna, before leaving politics in 1919 to become Chairman of the Midland Bank, had been Chancellor of the Exchequer for eighteen months, and Financial Secretary to the Treasury before that. F.E. had no experience, knowledge or interest in finance or industry at all, except for his considerable experience of commercial law: only a notorious extravagance and inability to handle his own money sensibly. There was not surprisingly a chorus of satirical comment at the ease with which he was able to slip into what were assumed to be highly paid sinecures. *Punch* addressed to him a little guide for the benefit of beginners in the City, stressing the importance of thrift, punctuality and similar virtues of which he knew nothing.[2] Certainly he owed the directorships which he now began to collect more to his friends than to his obvious qualifications. At the same time businessmen at the head of major companies do not pay large salaries even to their friends without some expectation of a return: F.E. was scarcely a confidence-inspiring figurehead, so they must have reckoned to gain some value from his power of analysis, if it could only be engaged upon their problems. Some commentators did see him setting off, with undiminished ambition, having conquered politics and the law, to find fresh fields to conquer, and congratulated the companies that had obtained his services. The truth, however, surely lies with the cynics; his health and his powers palpably declining, he was looking for easy money to pay his debts while he still could.

It was at first assumed that the principal friends who would be coming to his rescue were the Berry brothers, William and Gomer – newspaper magnates who from small beginnings in Wales had built up by 1928 an empire which included the *Sunday Times*, the *Financial Times* and the *Daily Telegraph*; the *Daily Dispatch*, the *Sunday Chronicle*, the *Daily Sketch*, and a whole stable of popular magazines. William had been made a baronet by Lloyd George in 1921, and in 1929 became Lord Camrose in Baldwin's resignation honours; Gomer was made a baronet in 1928 and became Lord Kemsley in 1936. F.E. had known them both for some years; since 1924 much of his journalistic writing had been for the *Sunday Times* which he approved as responsibly Conservative by contrast with the papers of Beaverbrook and Rothermere. It may well have been they who offered him '£15,000 a year in gilt-edged surroundings' in 1927.[3]

In fact, though the family connection between the Smiths and the Berrys was firmly cemented five and six years after F.E.'s death when Freddie and Pam married Camrose's daughter and son, F.E. did not join the Berrys when he left office. 'Apparently Berry Bros are not offering him quite such a fabulous salary as he expected,' Amery gossiped to Irwin, 'and other City firms are said to be similarly narrow-minded. However' – Amery added unsympathetically – 'whatever salary he got he would overspend, so I am not sure that he will be out of his difficulties.'[4] In the event F.E. quickly landed two plum directorships: one on the board of I.C.I., the huge chemicals group founded by Sir Alfred Mond (Lord Melchett) in 1926, and the other with the sugar combine Tate & Lyle. He also joined the board of the General Electric Company, and in February 1929 became chairman of another electrical concern, the Greater London & Counties Trust. The latter, the creation of the Tory M.P. Sir Philip Dawson, paid him a salary of £15,000 a year. Between these four directorships, plus a number of lesser consultancies, he must have very nearly made up the £30,000 he had promised himself.

How much time and energy F.E. gave to his paymasters it is impossible to say. His most visible role was as spokesman and propagandist for the industries with which he became concerned, principally the electricity industry: where before he had made after-dinner speeches to chambers of commerce about the difficulties of the Government, now he regaled them with the benefits of electrification. In September 1929 he paid his last visit to New York, not this time to associate with lawyers and address the Bar Society but as a businessman, to hold talks with leaders of the electricity industry in the United States. On his return he wrote to *The Times* to urge comparable progress in electrical development in Britain, having no patience with the fear that power lines would disfigure the landscape.[5] (He took a similarly philistine view of advertising hoardings, dismissing as contemptible the idea that aesthetic considerations should be allowed to stand in the way of the requirements of business.) In March 1930 he turned up in Bradford, wearing his I.C.I. hat, to lecture the British Research Association for the Woollens and Worsted Industries on the necessity for the textile trades of keeping up with modern methods.[6]

Of the contribution he may have made to I.C.I., G.E.C. or Tate & Lyle in the boardroom there is no record. It can only be concluded that it was not large. F.E. in his last embodiment as industrialist did not begin to make the impact he had done as politician and lawyer, or even as writer, sportsman and wit. In fact he made no significant impact at all. But then it is doubtful whether he tried to.

F.E.'s leaving office was accompanied by another unseemly row about money reminiscent of the trouble over his articles in the press while still in Government. This concerned, not the exchange of the public service for the pursuit of private gain which, as the *Annual Register* fairly commented 'scandalized only the political purists',[7] but the fact, which rapidly became known, that he did not propose to resume what was generally assumed to be his obligation, as an ex-Lord Chancellor, to sit as a Law Lord.

The convention was clear that former Lord Chancellors, so long as they retained their faculties, were expected to sit as Law Lords when required – as Haldane, Buckmaster and Finlay had done under F.E. and as F.E. himself had done in 1923–4 under Cave and Haldane. Having left office with the specific purpose of making money, however, F.E. let it be known in 1928 that he would not be making himself available as a judge, though at the same time he proposed to continue to draw his £5,000 annual pension as an ex-Lord Chancellor. His attitude at once drew down on him a furious outcry.

There was genuine room for dispute whether the 'pension' was indeed a pension, payable under any circumstances to former holders of the office, or was really a payment conditional on the performance of judicial functions. In strictly legal terms, F.E. was on strong ground: it could be clearly shown that Parliament in establishing the Lord Chancellor's pension in 1832 intended it as an unconditional compensation for the earnings which any holder of the office was bound to sacrifice on accepting it. On the other hand, whatever the statute says, the British Constitution grows by convention and precedent, and it was equally clearly the convention that former Lord Chancellors did forgo their pension while not sitting as Law Lords. As recently as 1925 Buckmaster had temporarily surrendered his pension during a brief and unhappy foray into the City, resuming it again when he returned to his judicial function. F.E.'s initial refusal to do the same, which he defended with ill temper on an unconvincing ground of disinterested principle, gave easy ammunition to those who always thought him basely motivated by financial greed.

The attack was led in the House of Commons by the Solicitor-General in the 1924 Labour Government, Sir Henry Slesser, with whom F.E. had already had several sharp exchanges in recent years on trade union law. Now F.E. replied to Slesser in the most personal terms in a letter to *The Times*, sneering at Slesser's rapid rise to office in 1924 and dismissing his advice on proper conduct as 'simply an impertinence'. He defended the wisdom of the Act of 1832 in seeking to make it worthwhile for the highest-paid leaders of the Bar to accept Government office: such financial provision was essential if the Government was to get the best men. 'You can, on the other hand, get cheap men quite cheaply.' He absolutely denied that the Lord Chancellor's pension carried an obligation to serve as a judge: if that were so, £5,000 would be ludicrously inadequate, when a barrister of even the meagre calibre of Slesser could earn three times as much in private practice. The pension was token compensation for the sacrifice of a career.

'Speaking for myself,' he continued, aggressively foreshadowing a retreat, 'if I thought it proper to do so, I should hold myself morally, as I clearly am legally, entitled to retain my pension. On the strength of it I resigned my opportunity to continue my practice at the Bar, in which I should certainly have made eight times the amount. Unlike some Solicitors-General' – he could not resist another *ad hominem* sneer – 'my average earnings for the four years before I became a Law Officer were £4000 a year more than I ever received in that office.' After the loud defiance, however, came the climbdown. 'I do not, however, choose, at a moment of national financial stringency to accept a pension from the State as long as I am able to earn my living in other ways.' He would draw it, he now revealed, only for a brief transitional period.[8]

The controversy continued to excite the letters column of *The Times*. Five days later F.E. returned to the argument with a second defence of his position, citing both reason and three centuries of practice against the views of Halsbury and Haldane raised against him. The relatively low level of the pension was to him the clincher.

For had the purpose of Parliament . . . been to oblige an ex-Lord Chancellor to render judicial services, it could not have determined the scale of remuneration on a lower rate than that assigned to his subordinate colleagues [i.e. the Lords of Appeal in Ordinary, the Law Lords who were not ex-Lord Chancellors]. Upon this point the matter admits of no argument.

The money was unquestionably his to accept or return to the Treasury as he chose. He now saw himself, as over the question of his articles, as the defender of a vital principle.

> My only reason for interposing the delay of a few brief weeks before the abandonment of my pension and the assumption of a commercial life was that I might assert and insist upon the unquestioned rights of my successors in the office of Lord Chancellor. The paltry gain involved never entered my mind. No-one who knows me will doubt this.

He was, he explained, after further swipes at Wedgwood Benn's 'characteristically foolish' speech in the Commons and the 'incredibly inept . . . feeble and pompous' reply of the Attorney-General, Sir Thomas Inskip, considering appointing trustees to administer his pension in favour of certain approved hospitals. 'I shall at least, if I determine upon this course of action, have made it plain that I do not gain one penny of personal advantage from my decision; and that I have protected the rights of my successors from an assault generated in about equal quantities from malice and ignorance.'[9]

F.E. is surely betrayed by the righteous intemperance of these replies to reasonable criticism. The sneers and insults, as so often, spoil his case. His argument was a good one, and if ex-Lord Chancellors had come to be expected to perform judicial functions in return for a payment which was intended, not over-generously, merely as compensation for earnings lost then there was a case for establishing either that they should not be so obliged or that the sum was insufficient. But F.E. would not have shown such temper in defence of a constitutional principle had it not touched his own interest. It is impossible to doubt that, in his admitted need for money, he had intended to continue to draw his pension for his own benefit and that he regarded the sum as far from paltry. It is a pity that he could not argue his entitlement to keep it straightforwardly, with moderation and modesty. He who was in so many respects so free of humbug, however, invariably reacted to personal criticism with angry self-justification like a child accused, guilty but defiant; the very defiance unwittingly proclaims the guilt. At several points in his career, whenever this nerve was touched, F.E. displayed this crude bullying streak; and at this stage in his life he was exceptionally sensitive about money, feeling that for all his achievements he had yet failed his family, and nursing an acute grievance against the system which had required him to choose between political and pecuniary prizes.

In a sense he was still free of humbug; for he made no pretence that he did not feel a grievance and firmly expected the world to sympathize with him in his financial straits. He had no conception of the public judgment that it was his own extravagance that had placed him in difficulties which did not seem to affect other lawyer-politicians in the same way. At a dinner given to mark his retirement on 14 November he referred shamelessly to the impoverishment he had suffered since first joining the Cabinet thirteen years before. 'I do claim the right', he asserted ironically, 'to relieve myself now of the spoils of office for such a period as I may think proper.' But he insisted that he was not leaving politics altogether: he vigorously defended the Government's record and promised, as he had promised Baldwin, that he would continue to play his part in the electoral battles to come.[10]

As the Government neared the end of its term, by-elections were running strongly against it, with the loss of seats to both Labour and the Liberals. The Liberal resurgence in particular was becoming difficult to ignore. Europe might be basking in the false hope of the Locarno Agreement, and a rare peace had descended upon industry; but an intractable million men had remained unemployed since 1920, and it was on the poverty and complacency of the Government's response to this persistent tragedy that Lloyd George concentrated his revived energy and his imagination. In March 1929 he launched a bold programme inspired by Keynes, Seebohm Rowntree and the Liberal Summer Schools to put the unemployed to work on schemes of urgent national regeneration which, he promised, would restimulate the economy at no cost to the taxpayer: all that was needed was an Exchequer loan which would repay itself by the increased revenue derived from the restoration of prosperity.[11] This was a brilliant and far-sighted plan, analogous to the methods by which Roosevelt in the United States and Hitler in Germany were to tackle unemployment in the 1930s, and founded upon the germ of what after the Second World War became the economic orthodoxy of a generation. To the Treasury orthodoxy of 1929, however, to say nothing of the self-evident dictates of good housekeeping, the notion that the country could spend its way out of recession was plain lunacy. The Conservatives determined that their best response – if it was no longer possible to ignore him – was to drown him in ridicule and the allegation that he had now sunk back to his pre-war level of dishonest demagogy.

F.E. joined in this campaign with a will. His economic conservatism was now of the most crusted, and he had only contempt for the Liberals' presumption in imagining that there could be any simple remedy for unemployment which the Government would not have adopted had it been practical. The plan was in fact, he declared at a by-election in Liverpool in March, so ignorant that he did Lloyd George the ambiguous credit of refusing to believe that he had read it! He also indulged his old trick of damning it out of the mouth of one of the Liberal leader's uneasily reunited colleagues, Walter Runciman, who had fulminated against the level of peacetime borrowing. But his sharpest weapon remained ridicule, and in the same speech he produced a memorably dismissive image to disparage his old friend's relentless activity. 'Today', he gibed, Lloyd George 'reminds me very much of a very active wasp under an inverted tumbler. The number of people who can hear him seem to me extremely small and the number to whom his appeal is likely to be successful, if conceivable, is even smaller.'[12]

The by-election at Liverpool, East Toxteth, was one of five held between 19 and 21 March, all in Tory-held seats, making a sort of minor referendum on the Government before the General Election in the summer. The results were ominous. Of the five, Labour won one and the Liberals two, and even where the Conservatives held on, in Toxteth (where F.E. naturally concentrated his effort) and in Bath, they did so with greatly reduced majorities.

Speaking again at Norwich on the 22nd, F.E. put the blame on the Rothermere press and the intervention of bookmakers, but insisted that people used by-elections as a safe opportunity for a protest vote: no Government in modern conditions could expect to be popular, but the electorate would think twice before turning the Conservatives out at a General Election.[13] This has become a familiar refrain of Governments, but in 1929 it was not yet taken for granted that Governments were bound to lose by-elections.

At Norwich he again devoted most of his speech to attacking the Liberals, rather than Labour. Unfortunately he had forgotten that Norwich was a two-member constituency in which the Tories and Liberals still had a reciprocal arrangement – of exactly the sort F.E. had approved in 1924 – to keep out the socialist. Towards the end of his speech he had to be urgently reminded by the chairman of the joint meeting that he was supposed to recommend supporters of the Conservative candidate to give their second vote to the Liberal, Geoffrey Shakespeare. After what had gone before he could hardly turn round and give Shakespeare an enthusiastic endorsement; so, somewhat the worse for drink as he usually was at this stage of his life, he responded with magnificent lack of tact and told the Tories that they had better vote for him anyway on the principle that it was better to vote for a halfwit than for someone who was completely mad! The local Liberals were not amused; but they had the last laugh since at the General Election two months later Shakespeare held his seat while the Conservative lost his to Labour.[14]

That election was called for 30 May. F.E. did his bit, as he had promised, but – as was the privilege of a politician in semi-retirement – only where it suited him. This meant that, apart from a weekend visit to Liverpool, he confined his effort first to seats in convenient reach of Charlton (Northampton, Coventry) and then in the final week to Portsmouth and the Isle of Wight, for the obvious reason that he was then based at Cowes. Nor were his contributions very distinguished. He offered no positive vindication of the Government's achievements, but contented himself with easy gibes and sneers at the opposition parties. Labour he attacked first for their business incompetence – he spoke now as a businessman! – and second (contradicting at election time all the generous things he had said since 1926) for their false front of moderation behind which, he now again alleged, the extremists lurked ready to take over a Labour Government. 'There is not a man in the present Labour Party', he declared at Liverpool, 'whom I would entrust to let out push bicycles.'[15] He dwelt heavily on the absurd idea of Labour leaders trying to run the banks, and suggested that the party always went through mild periods, like measles, just before elections.[16] He voiced none of the extravagant alarm, however, at the prospect of a Labour Government which he had indulged in 1924.

His most vivid language was still reserved for the Liberals, even as he strenuously protested their irrelevance. 'The Liberal Party', he told the Primrose League at the Albert Hall, 'reminds me of a small audience at an unimportant football match who make all the noise but who, by the rules of the game, can not, naturally, score any goals.'[16] On the eve of the poll, at Newport, Isle of Wight, he found a peculiarly offensive metaphor for the Liberals' gallant struggle to survive.

> I do not know whether you have ever inadvertently placed your foot upon a worm or a small snake and observed it, mortal in some point, and yet retaining some rather disgusting symptoms of vitality in another. You did not intend to do it any harm. But you were shocked to observe that, while it seemed at first that a happily conceived destiny had been made uncontemplated and final, yet there were some elements in that strangely constituted organism which still wriggled.[17]

More specifically, he continued to ridicule Lloyd George's unemployment plan, quite deliberately refusing to take it seriously. It was a pity, he thought, that Lloyd George when Prime Minister had 'never found time to mention to the Cabinet that he had tucked away in his drawer this marvellous scheme for ending unemployment';[16] in another speech he wondered why Lloyd George had not produced it when President of the Board of Trade in 1906![17] It did not occur to him that Lloyd George might have used his leisure since 1922 to do some new thinking. He revived his trusty pre-war line that the Liberals never seriously wanted to do anything about unemployment because they needed it for their perorations, and attacked them now for bringing forward at election time loose dishonest proposals which need not be taken seriously since they would never be in a position to implement them. 'It is like a man drawing a cheque for £1,000,000 upon a bank which does not exist. He could just as easily make it £2,000,000. What does it matter?'[17]

He had fun, too, with the unconvincing show of unity with which the former Asquithians belatedly lined up to endorse a party policy which ran directly counter to their traditions and instincts – particularly with Simon, who a year earlier, before finding it opportune to reconcile himself with Lloyd George, had warned the party against the empty promises of 'a cheapjack at the fair'. 'It is an amazing tribute to the Indian climate', F.E. purred in quite his old style, 'and to its soothing and reconciliating qualities that in eight months it should have brought Sir John Simon into the field in support of him whom eight months ago he had described as a cheapjack . . . Now . . . we have two cheapjacks.'[16]

F.E. was not a major figure at this election, though his news value was such that his speeches were still very fully reported. Nothing he said was of any intrinsic importance; yet he does represent, in almost caricature form, a paradigm of the Tory party's whole approach to the electorate. In more sober and homely style, under the slogan 'Safety First', Baldwin offered nothing more than a complacent appeal for renewed trust, patronizing Labour and ridiculing the Liberals. In particular the persistent argument with which F.E. sought to avoid serious considera-tion of the Liberal unemployment plan – intellectually the most dis-tinguished programme put forward by any political party in British politics this century – the cynical argument that it was not worth consideration because the Liberals as a third party were irrelevant, was the same with which the Conservative party as a whole – and Labour too – effectively dismissed the Liberals not only in 1929 but for the following fifty years: the brutal argument of the wasted vote. A vote for the Liberals, F.E. claimed, was a vote for paralysis, endowing Lloyd George with the disruptive and irresponsible power of the old Irish party. The biographer, looking back only a few years to the principled advocate of proportional representation, which he had endorsed as recently as 1921, can only note again the sad decline into arrogance and laziness of F.E.'s middle age.

Baldwin confidently expected to win the election. F.E. too expected the Tories, though they were bound to lose seats compared with the landslide of 1924, to remain the largest party. In the event the Liberals, despite all the derision heaped on them, won nearly a quarter of the total vote, and though their reward for this achievement was only 59 seats, they took enough votes from the Conservatives in many constituencies to let Labour in. The Tories were left with 260 seats: Labour for the first time became the largest party in the House of Commons with 288. (Their progress was measured in Liverpool, where they took their tally of seats in Salvidge's old citadel to four by winning Everton and Kirkdale, and came within a whisker of capturing Walton and Exchange as well.) This time Baldwin resigned at once, and MacDonald formed a second minority Labour Government with Liberal support. At the Carlton Club on election night as the results came in F.E. reacted by getting conspicuously drunk and blaming Baldwin, 'wandering about', according to Samuel Hoare, 'looking much under the weather . . . saying that "You could not win an election with the new electorate with the Sermon on the Mount as an election programme" '[18] – as if his own effort had been so much more constructive.

Later, at a party at Beaverbrook's, F.E. was still 'drunk and bad-tempered' while Max – who ever since 1923 had nursed an implacable grievance against Baldwin – was mischievously and ostentatiously delighted. Even before the election F.E. had been exasperated by Max's refusal to bring his papers out in support of the Government. Now he was so enraged by Max's attitude that at a Derby eve dinner a few days later he publicly shifted on to him the blame for the Conservative defeat.

Beaverbrook responded with a sharp telegram, 'That Jemmy Twitcher should peach me I own surprised me.'[19] The reference was to *The Beggar's Opera*. In 1765 Lord Sandwich, a notorious rake, had rashly attended a performance immediately after denouncing John Wilkes's obscene *Essay on Woman* in the House of Lords; the whole audience had instantly identified him with the character of Jemmy Twitcher, and he became known by that name for the rest of his life. Beaverbrook was charging F.E. with similar hypocrisy.

F.E. was stung into protest, but true to his friendly letter of 1927 he did not want to quarrel. He did not think that Max's wire had been 'entirely friendly', but he insisted that his own speech had been made in a spirit of badinage suitable to the occasion. 'There was nothing of malice; there was nothing of unfriendliness in any observation I made.' At the same time, 'If I take the view that the attitude of the *Daily Mail* and the *Daily Express* has been contributory to the defeat of the Conservative Party I am . . . entitled to say so. Editors are as much in public life as politicians.' He had said nothing that was inconsistent with friendship. The same, he complained (letting his accumulated resentment at Low's cartoons spill over at last without restraint) could not always be said of Max.

While during my political career you have often shown me great friendship and very valuable support, you have very often caused me deep mortification and done me great injury. Your Cartoonist over a long period of time published filthy and disgusting cartoons of me which were intended and calculated to do me great injury. He did not even spare my family after one of the most pleasant weekends which I have ever spent with you as your guest. I liked this very little, but I never made it a breach in a friendship which I greatly value, which is of old standing, and which is filled by unforgettable associations . . .

I should profoundly regret it if you decided to take any real or permanent offence at what I said . . . You will make a profound mistake if you do. For we are all growing older, and it becomes more difficult and more tedious every year to form new friendships.[20]

Beaverbrook replied at once to this strange effusion. He was 'staggered', he said, by F.E.'s letter, and proceeded both to justify his telegram and to dismiss F.E.'s objection to Low.

I rejoiced in Baldwin's downfall. I wanted the defeat of the Government because I believed it was bad.

If I am right in assuming that you did not regret it, then my 'Jemmy Twitcher' was to the point . . .

If I am right in supposing you mentioned to me last Thursday night that you shared with me the view that Baldwin deserved defeat, my telegram is an excellent comment.

You are out of touch with the times and I am too old at fifty. The new generation like the Low caricatures. Ask Eleanor. For my part Low enrages my feelings when he makes me crawl out from under the table or peep through the door. But I hold the view that a caricature cannot give any good ground for complaint. Perhaps I am wrong, but I stick to it.[21]

After a few more days F.E. tacitly conceded the aptness of Max's rejoinder; but his pent-up bitterness against Low was not exhausted. 'I was not unaware of the quotation and its implication', he wrote testily, 'illiterate as I am. But it admitted of two constructions.' (The second was presumably that F.E. was a rake.) 'Anyhow if you are friendly I am.'

As to your filthy cartoonist I care nothing about him now.

But I know all about modern caricature and I never had cause for grievance until you a friend allowed a filthy little Socialist to present me daily as a crapulous and corpulent buffoon.

'Yesterday', he boasted in refutation of these attributes, 'I defeated at tennis the first Cambridge couple which on the eve of 57 is not bad. I should like to see you for we might do some political business.'[22]

In the autumn of 1929 F.E. was drawn back into the centre of politics to take a leading part in what was to prove his last major political controversy. It concerned India, where Irwin's growing sympathy with nationalist aspirations which had become apparent while F.E. was Secretary of State now emerged, with the encouragement of the Labour Government, in a form which threatened all that F.E. thought he had achieved during his time at the India Office. Irwin proposed, without waiting for the Report of the Simon Commission, to announce immediately that the ultimate goal foreshadowed in the 1919 reforms was Dominion status for India. He did not by this intend to suggest that Dominion status would be granted at once, nor that the Simon Commission should be bypassed in its function of advising on the next step towards that goal; he simply judged, as the man on the spot, that Simon's next instalment of constitutional advance would have a better chance of being accepted in India and the advocates of outright independence defeated if it were made explicit that virtual independence within the Empire would be the final consummation of that evolution. F.E., however, and the Tory Right generally, anticipated that if Dominion status were once officially mentioned it would immediately become the nationalists' minimum demand, and the Simon Commission, over which he had taken such pains, would be a dead letter before it had even reported.

On leave in Britain in the summer, Irwin was encouraged by MacDonald and the new Secretary of State, Wedgwood Benn, to go ahead with his projected statement. Baldwin, too, anxious to maintain agreement between the two Front Benches on India, gave his approval, on the condition that Simon had no objection. Simon, however, managed to give the impression that he approved, only to withdraw his approval when it was too late, thus leaving Baldwin embarrassingly exposed. In deference to Tory protests, not least from F.E., who wrote a sharp letter to the *Daily Telegraph* on 14 October insisting that the Statutory Commission representing all parties had been entrusted by Parliament with the responsibility of advising on the next step forward for India and could not be short-circuited, Baldwin tried to get the Declaration abandoned. But when it became clear that Irwin had already too far prepared the ground in India to draw back, he determined to stand by his friend and support the Government, maintaining the bipartisan approach by which he set such store, in defiance of his own Diehards and the Tory press.

On 1 November, the same day that Irwin's announcement was published in India, there appeared in the *Daily Mail* a sensational allegation that Baldwin had secretly committed the Opposition over the summer to supporting the Declaration, but had then been humiliatingly forced by the Shadow Cabinet to repudiate it. 'Mr Baldwin's Crowning Blunder', ran the headline. 'Blind promise to Socialists . . . Rank and File Furious'.[23] Other papers carried a similar story. Baldwin's loyal henchman Davidson immediately assumed this to be the work of F.E. and the former Coalitionists, trying to link up again, as he had been anticipating since 1924, with Lloyd George to get their revenge on Baldwin for 1922.

> Those in our Party who regard SB as an ineffectual, supine Leader [he wrote to Irwin] and whose sympathies are clearly Coalition in character, decided to use the Indian situation to get rid of him for once and for all, and the opportunity was so favourable that there can be no doubt that they believed they would be successful, aided by the *Daily Express*, the *Daily Mail* and Lloyd George. My instinct told me that the centre of this intrigue was not very far removed from Imperial Chemicals. The opening of the attack was the *Daily Mail* article.[24]

Baldwin's biographers and Davidson's editor explain the reference to Imperial Chemicals as meaning Lord Melchett. They forget that F.E. was also a director of I.C.I. It was clearly F.E. whom Davidson meant. He was, however, exhibiting his usual paranoia. There was no Coalitionist plot, seizing on India as a pretext. F.E., and Winston when he returned on 5 November from America, and to a lesser extent Austen Chamberlain and Worthington-Evans (as well as very many other Tories who had been *against* the Coalition in 1922), were all genuinely outraged by the Irwin Declaration and Baldwin's muddled acquiescence in it; while Lloyd George, in joining in the attack, was equally not engaging in any plot but simply, as Liberal leader with no very strong line on India himself, reflecting the views of the two senior members of his party with Indian experience, Reading and Simon. There is no evidence, nor the least likelihood, of the concerted Coalitionist action that Davidson feared. F.E. and Chamberlain had long ago given up any notion of working again with Lloyd George.

If F.E. did inspire the *Daily Mail* story he did so unguardedly, not as the prearranged signal for an intrigue. The very next day he actually helped to draft Baldwin's indignant assertion that 'every statement of fact and every implication of fact contained in that article is untrue'. Davidson feared that this was all part of the plot.

> When SB issued his denial it was so sweeping in character that I was told that both the *Daily Mail* and the *Daily Express* thought that they had got him, and I was not very happy because of the fact that FE had strengthened the original draft of the denial by inserting the phrase 'implication of fact', and the universal implication among our friends in the Lobby Press Gallery definitely favoured FE as the reliable source from which the *Daily Mail* claimed to have obtained the story.[24]

According to Davidson, F.E. was playing a very devious double game. Baldwin, characteristically, had a more amused view of F.E.'s conduct, telling MacDonald a few days later that 'Birkenhead drunk gave information to the *Daily Mail* & Birkenhead sober supplied him (B) with answers to what the *Daily Mail* had published'.[25] This was easily done, since the offending article was filled with minor errors. Presumably in his anger at the sabotaging of the Statutory Commission, F.E. had indeed talked wildly to a reporter; he must have hoped that he could still at that late stage prevent the Declaration being made with the Conservative party's blessing: nevertheless, the fact that he was on hand as a loyal colleague to draft Baldwin's denial indicates that he bore no personal ill will. He was certainly not plotting against Baldwin's leadership.

But he *was* furious at the Declaration itself, partly on Simon's behalf, but also because, more explicitly than he had dared to say publicly while in office, he was still utterly opposed to any suggestion that India would *ever* be fit for self-government. The same day as Baldwin's denial, he fired off another letter to the *Daily Telegraph*. He criticized the vagueness of Irwin's use of the term 'Dominion status'. What did it mean? That India should have control of its own army, navy and police, like Canada and Australia?

> Everyone who knows anything about India plainly realizes that there is no period of time humanly foreseeable in which these changes will be possible without producing in India on an even greater scale the disruptive and anarchical conditions which prevail in China today. The language, therefore, used by the Viceroy, on the authority of the Government, either adds something to the declaration of August 1917 or it does not. If it does, it is mischievous and should be repudiated; if it does not, it is superfluous and should never have been made.[26]

'No honest English statesman', he declared bluntly in another paper, 'will say that Dominion Status for India is attainable in the near future. Why, then, lie about it?'[27]

On 5 November F.E. had the opportunity to repeat his strictures in the House of Lords. It was unfortunate for the Government that the matter was raised first in the Upper House, where Labour was so weakly represented. Reading led off with a powerful but courteous speech demanding answers to three questions: why the statement had been made before Simon reported; whether the conditions for constitutional advance laid down in 1917 and 1919 still applied, and whether the declaration implied any immediate change in policy. To reply, the Government could only wheel on once again poor old Lord Parmoor, now seventy-seven and sadly confused, who stumbled unconvincingly through a tedious brief and showed in what century his mind was stuck by repeatedly referring to 'Her Majesty's Government' and to the Prime Minister as 'Lord MacDonald'. The House of Lords is usually kind to such human weakness. But F.E., who spoke next, was in no mood for chivalry. 'It might have been supposed', thought the *Spectator*, 'that by this time Lord Birkenhead would be weary of hunting Lord Parmoor, but he continued the chase with undiminished zest.'[28] He rose 'with the light of battle in his eye' to inflict what the *Daily Telegraph*, which shared his view of the Declaration, described as 'one of the most memorable castigations suffered by a Government in recent times . . . in terms which exposed without mercy the levity of the whole proceedings'.[29] He took sarcastic exception to Parmoor's tribute to Irwin as the greatest Viceroy of modern times, and angrily rejected his answer to Reading's first question, which was that the Government was bound to follow the advice of the man on the spot. What was the Secretary of State for, if he was bound to subordinate his judgment to the Viceroy? When Parmoor protested that he had not suggested any such thing, F.E. retorted cruelly, 'The noble Lord read so much that I do not think he is quite aware of what he did suggest,' which brought easy laughter from the packed Tory benches and the galleries. (The Government benches, of course, were practically empty.) 'He was asked three questions' – F.E. pressed home his advantage – 'and he came equipped with three long typewritten essays in reply, in which I should conjecture that the typing was bad by the difficulty he had in mastering his suggestions on the spur of the moment.' Taking up Reading's third question, he elicited from Parmoor – whom he treated throughout like a defence witness in the box – the admission he wanted, that Irwin's statement involved no change of policy and no timetable within which Dominion status might be granted. When he tried to press Parmoor futher on whether the Simon Commission had or had not been consulted, the poor intimidated man simply refused to add anything to what he had read out. Banging the table in front of him, F.E. repeated his condemnation of the Government. Never, never, he declared, should Britain yield to threats. Not in a hundred years would the Indians be fit for self-government. The only result of Irwin's rash appeasement would be that the Indians would say they had been cheated. The Government had mishandled the situation totally.[30]

F.E. had gone too far, however. Not only his taunting of Parmoor, which was widely considered to be in deplorable taste, but his violent refusal to admit Dominion status even as a distant objective, was too extreme even for most Diehards, and made it easier for Baldwin, two days later, to rally the party behind his moderate line. *The Times*, worried that F.E. might still be remembered in India as the Secretary of State who had brought forward the Simon Commission, hastened to emphasize that he no longer carried any responsibility.

It was easy work to poke fun at Lord Parmoor, who was there to be offered up as a burnt-sacrifice; but the more serious parts of his attack were frankly those of the free-lance which he has now become, and not of an official leader of his party in Indian affairs.[31]

In the Commons Baldwin, with the help of Simon, who decided that the best way to minimize the damage to his Commission's work was to play down the significance of Irwin's *démarche*, quelled the possibility of a Tory revolt with one of his most high-flown lectures about Britain's mission in India, so that Lloyd George found the mood of the House against him when he tried to keep the pot boiling.[32] Had F.E. in the Lords made the same sort of speech as Reading, Davidson thought that the situation might have been dangerous for Baldwin.[24] As it was, only Churchill among the leading Tories wanted to prolong the issue.

Winston was at one with F.E. on the utter impossibility of India, with its vast diversity of peoples and religions, its tiny political minority and not least it millions of 'untouchables', ever being capable of self-government without the safeguard of British supremacy. More romantically perhaps than F.E., he too saw India as the central jewel in the Imperial Crown, the very core and substance of Britain's greatness, which could never be bartered away. To him, as to F.E., it was culpable, even criminal weakness, on Baldwin's part to be prepared to align the Tory party, against all its traditions, with Labour's readiness to envisage a sequence of concessions leading supposedly to Dominion status but more probably to the gradual but irreversible loss of the entire Empire. In January 1931, three and a half months after F.E.'s death, Winston resigned from the Shadow Cabinet and cast himself again into the wilderness, where he spent the next nine years vehemently but vainly denouncing first the shameful 'surrender' of India to the 'half-naked fakir' Gandhi, then – in language scarcely more extreme – the Allies' feeble 'appeasement' of Hitler's resurgent Germany. F.E., had he lived, would unquestionably have supported his friend strongly on both counts. Whether his intemperate advocacy would have greatly strengthened Winston's efforts to swing the Tory party against the 1935 Government of India Bill must be, on the evidence of 1929, extremely doubtful; but, given health and vigour, he would surely have been a powerful ally in the far more critical campaign to rouse the country against the policy of Munich. Then, like Beaverbrook, Brendan Bracken, Lindemann and other cronies, there can be no doubt at all that F.E. would have been with Winston in his finest hour in 1940, and for the rest of the war. Through his years of isolation and frustration in the 1930s Winston felt the lack of his old friend's encouragement and support: he certainly missed his 'canine qualities' at his side in the supreme challenge of his life. 1940 might have been F.E.'s finest hour too, the appropriately epic climax of that friendship formed behind the Speaker's chair in 1906. But it was not to be. F.E.'s candle had burned out a full ten years before.

The last public utterances of F.E.'s life were all resolutely Diehard. Over Egypt as well as India, and for restoring the diplomatic relations with the Soviet Union broken off by the Baldwin Government after the Arcos raid, he damned the Labour Government for betraying British interests around the world. He took an ill-disguised pleasure in seeing himself thoroughly vindicated in his objections to the Irwin Declaration: the Indians had promptly stepped up their demands, backed by a campaign of civil disobedience, so that Irwin had found himself obliged to put all the principal Congress leaders in jail.[33] His last two major speeches in the House of Lords were both devoted to Russia. On 4 December 1929 he launched what *The Times* considered 'a carefully documented attack, delivered with less than his usual fire'[34] on the folly of trusting a regime which was rightly distrusted by every other Foreign Office in the world; and he repeated the same arguments, 'speaking with great moderation', on 20 February 1930.[35] There was in this speech an unmistakable note of weariness, however, a hint of passion spent, as the elder statesman – aged fifty-seven – denied that he felt any animus against the Government. 'If they will avoid increasing the numbers of the unemployed by 100,000 a week, and leave me something to live on when they come to the next Budget, and leave India, Egypt, the Army and the Navy when they go out of office, I will have nothing against them.'[36]

In April 1930 F.E. published what proved to be the last book to appear from his pen during his lifetime – if it *was* from his pen. *The World in 2030* is reputed to have been largely ghost-written by Bechhofer Roberts: the attribution is generally considered a kindness to F.E.'s reputation, since it cannot be pretended that the book is anything but a potboiler – the lowest expedient to which F.E. ever stooped in the exploitation of his name for money. Amateurish, superficial and opinionated though it is, however, it is not entirely negligible: at the least it has biographical interest, for if Roberts did write it – as opposed to merely doing the research – he reproduced his master's characteristic prejudices, as well as his style, with uncanny skill. Flippant, entertaining and provocative, illuminated by flashes of inimitably sardonic humour, *The World in 2030* reads like genuine F.E. – the relaxation of a powerful but now lazy mind.

The subject, of course, offers a wonderful canvas for F.E. to project his view of past history and of present tendencies into a limitless future. Inevitably, his vision is an incongruous mixture of what is today commonplace and what is still fantastic: futuristic leaps of the imagination shackled by rooted assumptions which were dated even at the time of writing.

A creditable proportion of what F.E. foresaw has either come true or is close to realization half-way to his projected 2030 – the automation of industry; rapid air travel; the development of synthetic foods, synthetic clothing, and all sorts of synthetic substances 'as pleasant and harmless as tobacco'; abundant cheap energy derived from the harnessing of wind and waves; even the atomic bomb which might at any moment reduce the world of the future 'to a flaring vortex of incandescent gas'.

Other elements of F.E.'s future still seem fantastic, thankfully, in 1983: the extension of human longevity to 120 or 150 years; the universal practice of eugenics by which the State – shades of *Brave New World*, published in 1932 – will control the breeding, in laboratories, of babies of predetermined intelligence and aptitudes; most improbable of all, the development of psychology as an exact science by which all human behaviour will be predicted, determined and rationally controlled – to the extent, it would appear, of the actual abolition of free will.

More interesting than these fantasies are the ways in which F.E. used prophecy to enlarge his familiar convictions about the present: for instance to predict that wars, though they might become more humane, will never cease to occur; that in a future in which the nineteenth-century obsession with nationalism will be forgotten, India will remain for ever part of a multinational British Empire; or that women, even though freed from the labour of bearing children to pursue unrestricted careers in equality with men, will nevertheless never challenge men's supremacy in either statesmanship or the arts, to which mysteries the 'feminine genius' is not suited. Above all, while disdaining nationalism and professing to look forward scientifically to a generation of robots, he continually demonstrates how thoroughly his world picture is still rooted in the romantic European past, in such passages as this magnificent assertion:

> So intimately is the history of civilisation bound up with the expression of gigantic personalities, that a single individual may arise in Europe or America to reshape the mould of life before 2030. Another and greater Wesley may call back our grandchildren to fervent emotional Protestantism, and recall the religious wars which racked the seventeenth century. A new and delicious Helen, inflaming the laboratories, may launch a thousand airships and bring to ruin New York's topless towers. A Puritan revulsion may sweep over us, quenching the arts and reconstituting the taboos of the nineteenth century. A mad dictator, jealous of Western progress, may precipitate a war, which will finally burn up and destroy Western civilisation, so that coming generations in China and New Zealand will know it for no more than a memory and a name. But against this peril I pin my faith upon the genius of the Anglo-Saxon race.[37]

The World in 2030 was dedicated to Pamela, and in its quite surprising emphasis on the equality of *opportunity* for women (if only to prove their ultimate inferiority!), it is plainly influenced by F.E.'s hopes for both his daughters. He ends with the characteristic hope that his great-grandchildren will distinguish themselves in the world he has imagined; for himself, however, he finds 'a certain solace in reflecting that my own birthday occurred towards the latter end of the nineteenth century'.[38]

The book had excellent reviews. The *Daily Express* puff, 'An Entertaining and Astonishing Book', may be put down to Beaverbrook; but F.E. had no such influence with the *Manchester Guardian*, which wrote of his 'audacious but uniformly exciting essays . . . as bold as they are terrifying'.[39] Trouble, however, was in store. F.E. had acknowledged in his preface that he followed '– *longum post intervallum* – in the footsteps of Jules Verne, Bellamy, Wells and Haldane'.[40] A few weeks after publication, J.B.S. Haldane alleged that he had done rather more. In a caustic notice in the *Week-End Review*, satirically suggesting that of course F.E. could not possibly be guilty of plagiarism but had evidently been 'psychically inspired', he claimed to have discovered no less than forty-four direct borrowings from his own books, *Daedalus* and *Possible Worlds*, published in 1924.[41] It must be said that the three examples of F.E.'s borrowings which he quoted, presumably the most blatant, are not very impressive and might well be thought to have been covered by F.E.'s acknowledgment: there was some force in F.E.'s reply that they were clichés of popular science for which neither of them could claim much originality. But F.E. could not leave it at this. As usual when accused, he reacted with an ill-temper which spoiled his case. He replied, not in the *Week-End Review* (of which he pretended that he had never previously heard) but in the *Daily Express*, in a tone of sneering contempt for Haldane's absurd impertinence, finally suggesting that he 'mend his manners'.[42]

This time Haldane's comeback in the *Week-End Review*, discarding satire but stating his objections outright, was entirely just. F.E., he said, had had three courses open to him.

He could have maintained his silence.

He could have admitted his failure to acknowledge the exact sources of certain phrases and ideas, pleaded guilty to occasional inaccuracy, and added that ill-health and other occupations had rendered it impossible for him to devote as much care as he would have liked to the revision of the book. Had he done this he would, I think, have earned a good deal of sympathy . . .

He chose a third course. He replied at great length to an audience the vast majority of whom had not read the original criticism. He attempted to defend a number of indefensible statements, and made a series of personal attacks upon me which are irrelevant to the charges made against him.

'His article', Haldane concluded, 'is one of the most comprehensive displays of ignorance which I have read for some years . . . I have no objection to anyone treading in my footsteps. I object to the stealing of my boots to do so, and [the cruellest cut of all] I am amused when they do not know how to put them on. For Lord Birkenhead has taken my wilder speculations seriously.'[43]

To this F.E. had no answer, except privately to beg Beaverbrook to give 'that ass Haldane' no more publicity in his papers and to persuade 'Northcliffe' – by whom in his agitation he clearly meant Rothermere – to do the same:[44] a helpless admission that he knew he was in the wrong. The intellectual bullying to which F.E. always resorted when publicly attacked had this time met its match.

A happier last testament than this inglorious controversy, however, is contained in one of the four posthumously published books on which F.E. was working up to his final illness. *Turning Points in History* and *Last Essays* have been considered in an earlier chapter; the other two were compilations – *500 English Letters* and the splendidly titled *Fifty Famous*

Fights in Fact and Fiction. The latter scrapes the barrel of his literary resourcefulness perhaps even more desperately than *The World in 2030*: it consists simply of favourite excerpts, ranging from David and Goliath from the Book of Samuel to 'The Last Fight of Baron Richthofen', taking in Shakespeare and Cervantes, Scott and Dickens, Rider Haggard and Conan Doyle and – on merit, F.E. insists – his daughter Eleanor. The interest lies in the introduction which F.E. had written before he died. Surprising though it may seem, this was as serious an essay in self-revelation and personal philosophy as he ever wrote. In part of it he simply states his lifelong enjoyment of adventure novels. 'I have never', he begins, 'been able to share the self-satisfaction of those who prefer introspection to action.'

> Nor is my conception of the role and purpose of imaginative prose advanced by pursuing the dreary maunderings of psycho-analysts, still less by following a degenerate's self-denudation, or even a mystic's revelations, when I can gallop along the broad highway in the train of bold narrative and high Romance. No inconsiderable portion of my reading leisure has been spent in the company of swashbucklers and pirates, and I have succumbed deliberately and often to the imposture of the detective tale.*

After justifying his preference for the rattling good yarn and explaining the grounds on which he made his fifty choices, he anticipates the criticism that by glorifying famous fights he was celebrating, even advocating, war; and he tackles it characteristically, head-on, in a fundamental statement of his view of life, as he had lived it and as he thought it should be lived.

> From early boyhood I fell victim to the Great Masters of romantic imagination. It was not that I applauded them or could ever

---

* He took exactly the same attitude to films, as he told a Cinematograph Exhibitors Association dinner in 1922.

> I do not like films which for three hours introduce me to various sentimental passages in the lives of people who at the outset fail to interest me. What I do like to see is somebody dropping, in order to escape justice, from the top of a tree onto an express train. I like to see the fugitive thereupon pursued by several motor cars. If I can not see that, I like above all to see Italian officers going down very steep hills on their horses. That is a great thrill. Otherwise I take little interest in films. When the heroine proceeds for 2½ hours to make devastating love to the hero, I think that the trade is wasting both its opportunities and its resources. The cinema of incident is to me extremely exciting. The cinema of emotion does not interest me nearly so much.[45]

otherwise than deride frothy sentimentalism in life and letters. I have risked some censure elsewhere for reminding adventurous youth of the opportunities which await it. I was blamed, as candid commentators often are, for telling the truth. I do not take naturally to perverted meekness or loose thinking or the shirking of facts, and I resent the exalting of arm-chair theorists into arbiters of conduct in times of crisis. I cannot accept the hypothesis that success awaits the pusillanimous or that nations which bottle up their ambitions will grow to greatness.

War is hateful in its destruction of moral as well as of physical capital. We all know that. The anguish of it has been so branded into recent experience that the world may well refuse to resort again to this backward and inhuman arbitrament, for just long enough, perhaps, to permit the evolution, in the interval, of an enlightened conscience in this respect, reinforced by the development of weapons so lethal that their menace will cow civilisation into better behaviour.

In the interval let us not cultivate sloppy and disingenuous self-satisfaction. All the prattle about peace at international tea-parties before 1914 was ineffective except in leaving Right weaponless – but, thank God, not spiritless – when the challenge came. The blind ostriches of pacifism did not avoid, they merely prolonged the horror.

It is because I deplore war and desire to prevent it and know that violence does not pay in the long run, that I have counselled preparation. It is, however, because I honour decent national pride and legitimate patriotism, and value life at high pressure and would not disdain the title of adventurer myself, that I conceived the notion of a book which, I hope, will not merely prove to be a mirror held up to the flaming faith and gallantry of the past, but which will yield an atmosphere helpful to valiant enterprise in the future.

Before I was of age I had read all Scott's novels more than once. I had galloped as often with the Three Musketeers from Boulogne and dived with the Count of Monte Cristo from the Chateau d'If into the midnight sea; and I cannot but believe, in reference to my own career, that no considerable portion of any success which I may have achieved derives from the impulse of these magicians and the example and emulation of their heroes.[46]

During the winter of 1929–30 it became clear to F.E.'s family and friends that he was not himself. 'His mind', his son wrote, 'was being driven by a flagging willpower and he seemed . . . to have lost his zest for living.'[47] He became withdrawn and depressed, brooding with fear and aversion upon sickness and the possibility that he might be dying; the lingering and painful fate of his brother Harold preyed inescapably on his mind. Yet Harold had died of cancer: there was nothing obviously the matter with F.E. He had suffered an increasing number of minor ailments over the past few years: his eyes, his ears, his bladder and his digestion had all given him trouble, and he had difficulty in sleeping. But now it was as though the frame of his superhuman constitution had suddenly, after years of bearing the terrific strain he habitually imposed on it, cracked – and his physical and mental energy was draining swiftly away.

At the beginning of April he went with his brother-in-law Claude Furneaux and other friends on a golfing holiday to Biarritz. But neither golf nor tennis could stir him from his apathy. On 6 April he burst a blood vessel and suffered a severe haemorrhage. 'Claude,' he announced to Furneaux, who was summoned urgently to his room, 'I think I'm done for.'[47] Margaret flew out to be with him. Within a few days, however, he was out of danger.

> I am glad to say [Margaret was able to write to Lloyd George on the 16th] he is making excellent progress and is now sitting in an armchair having just smoked his first cigar. In a way I am relieved by the whole thing as I have been very worried about him all the winter. The doctors assure me that in four months he will be able to play golf and tennis and be better than he has for years but he will have to be *very* careful always about his diet etc.[48]

By the end of the month he was back at Charlton.

For three months he appeared to be making a good recovery, though it cannot have been helped by the unpleasantness with Haldane. To Baldwin on 8 May he was able to write cheerfully that 'The Doctors, both French and English, give me great encouragement to believe that unless I am unlucky, in three or four months I shall be completely restored to normal health.'[49] But he was not an easy patient. For all that his son describes him at this time as 'quiet and strangely humble',[47] a letter to Maurice Bowra finds him railing against his 'maladroit and expensive medical advisers';[50] and he was still disgusted by his own weakness. Arthur Lee had occasion, during the summer, to see him in connection with a legal battle between the Fox and Gaumont film companies: Lee was acting for Fox, F.E. advising Gaumont. Being unable to go out, he asked Lee to come to him at Grosvenor Gardens. Lee did so, and drew in his memoirs a vivid and terrible picture of F.E.'s broken health.

On going into the library [I] was genuinely shocked by the change in his appearance, although the wreck of his physique, which made his speech almost incoherent at times, had in no way softened his belligerency or weakened his habit of vituperation . . . Eventually I had to tell him that . . . I was not prepared to submit to threats, or legal terrorism. Then the storm subsided, and he became once more an almost speechless and broken man, infinitely pathetic in his realisation of his condition and his essential helplessness. When I got up to go, he insisted on struggling to his feet and on taking my arm to walk with me towards the front door. Opposite to us at the end of the passage was a large mirror in which he caught sight of himself – so terribly changed and broken – and, as if he could not endure the sight, he turned without a word and tottered back to his room silent and bowed.[51]

On 17 July – five days after his fifty-eighth birthday – F.E. spoke for the last time in the House of Lords – appropriately against a renewed attempt to allow peeresses to take their seats.[52] But that evening he was unable to attend the Other Club – the third consecutive dinner he had missed. A little over two weeks later, at the beginning of August, he collapsed again with bronchial pneumonia.

For ten days his doctors issued bulletins every few hours on his condition, which were solemnly reprinted in *The Times*. 'The weakness is very great . . . he had another restless night . . . the fever has subsided . . . the weakness is still very great.' On 14 August he was given a blood transfusion and rallied a little. On the 17th Margaret poured out in a letter to Lloyd George her anxiety and renewal of hope that he would pull through.

It has been *so* kind of you to enquire so often about Fred. He is still terribly ill and of course his weakness is pitiable. It is of course the nervous exhaustion that is so alarming. He was so desperately ill last week and on the point of death twice. He is distinctly stronger since the blood transfusion, and they can go on giving him these. I can never forgive the two doctors who were supposed to be looking after him after he got back from Biarritz – they gave him nothing to take the place of alcohol. His blood pressure was almost alarmingly low. They told him his pain in the shoulder was neuritis when it was arthritis caused by a poisoned tooth. When he couldn't sleep from the pain of this shoulder he took an overdose of bromidium which started the *whole* of this illness. I rang up the doctor and all he said was 'get him out in the fresh air' – when I couldn't even *wake* him – but there I mustn't let my pen run away with me –

thank God we have had a wonderful doctor – Dr Byam and the fact that Fred is alive today is entirely due to the care and trouble and cleverness he has shown.

I fear – if we get him through (and they do believe they will now) that it will be many months before he is well – but what does that matter if he does get well.[53]

A week later the bulletins ceased. F.E.'s heart was said to be 'in an exhausted condition, which will necessitate complete rest and quiet for many weeks'; but he was 'out of any immediate danger'.[54] Another month passed, but progress was slow. During one of his lucid intervals, he asked to see Peteil, his clerk who had served him faithfully for eighteen years at the Bar before he went to the Woolsack. Peteil sat by the bed and held his hand as F.E. whispered simply, 'I'm afraid, Peteil.'[55] On the afternoon of Monday 29 September he suffered a relapse. 'There has been a recurrence of congestion in one lung, accompanied by a considerable rise in temperature.' That evening his temperature was slightly lower, but there had been 'a further extension of trouble in the chest'. The next morning his condition 'continued to cause anxiety': and a little after noon on 30 September it was announced that 'the Earl of Birkenhead passed peacefully away at a quarter past 11 this morning. There had been a further increase in the pneumonic infection, and the heart muscles, feeling the effect of this, dilated and failed.'[56]

Modern antibiotics might have kept him alive. But F.E. was probably luckier to have been allowed to die. For he had lived hard, worked hard, played hard, drunk hard, and his mind and body, to say nothing of his liver, were exhausted. He could not have endured life on a restricted diet and without the full power of his faculties. As Winston wrote, 'Prolonged ill-health and deprivation of all the activities upon which his life was built would have pressed very hard upon him.' An early death fitted the pace at which he had led his life. He had achieved all he was ever likely to. He had already lived longer than either of his brothers, his father or his uncle. So he died. 'Between the setting of the sun and night there was only the briefest twilight. It was better so.'[57]

Yet Winston was desolated. 'Last night', Clementine wrote to Margaret, 'Winston wept for his friend. He said several times "I feel so lonely".'[58]

The obituaries, and innumerable tributes and appreciations by friends, colleagues and opponents from politics and the law, all dwelled on the same extraordinary sense of shock that a personality so vivid and so vigorous could possibly be extinguished. 'No public figure', *The Times* declared in a remarkable leader, 'has been more real to the mass of his contemporaries.'[56] To an exceptional degree, amid the formal celebrations of his career, his achievements and his varied talents, it was the *man*, in all his flawed humanity, whom his colleagues mourned. 'He had qualities of mind and heart which were unique,' wrote Lloyd George. 'His death . . . is an incalculable loss.'[56]

> I can well understand [Austen Chamberlain wrote in a private letter] anyone who had no more than a passing acquaintance with him detesting him cordially, but if you once really got to know him it was impossible not to like and even to love him. It is striking to see how in everything written of him by those who were ever his friends – no matter how great their difference of outlook, character and faith – it is the loyalty and generosity of his friendship that is uppermost in their thoughts. I can well believe that if I had not known him intimately, I should have detested him. As it was, I had a great affection for him, and shall never find a truer or more affectionate friend.[59]

The body was taken from Grosvenor Gardens to lie for two days in state in Gray's Inn chapel, where thousands came to pay their last respects. Then it was removed to Golders Green crematorium, and the ashes taken to Charlton for burial on Saturday 4 October, after a short service at the parish church. Special coaches were attached to the train from London. There was a memorial service in Liverpool Cathedral on the Friday; another in Birkenhead School on the Saturday; and a third in Westminster Abbey on Monday 6th. 'The service in the Abbey today was very wonderful,' Margaret wrote to Beaverbrook, 'and the enormous congregation a very great tribute to *him*.'[60]

The grave in Charlton cemetery, designed by Sir Edwin Lutyens, bears the characteristically proud inscription, leaving nothing out:

> FREDERICK EDWIN SMITH, P.C., G.C.S.I., D.C.L., LL.D.
> FIRST EARL OF BIRKENHEAD
> SOMETIME
> LORD HIGH CHANCELLOR
> SECRETARY OF STATE FOR INDIA
> ATTORNEY GENERAL   SOLICITOR GENERAL
> HIGH STEWARD OF OXFORD UNIVERSITY
> FOUR TIMES TREASURER OF GRAYS INN
> HIS BY SOVEREIGNTY OF NATURE

On 30 October the Other Club drew the largest attendance in its history – thirty-four members, though only six were original members from 1911. In F.E.'s honour, Winston broke one of the unwritten rules of the Club and made a speech, short, simple and moving, which may stand, most appropriately, for all the other tributes of these days.

> For twenty years we have dined together, but tonight there are more round this board than ever before. That is because tonight we have to mark the loss the Club has sustained in the death of one of its founders and its main support – our dear friend FE.
>
> Freddy [Guest] was telling me before dinner that out of seventy-eight dinners which our small Club has held FE attended sixty-eight.* We miss his wisdom, his gaiety, the broad human companionship and comradeship which he always displayed and excited from his friends. We admired his grand intellect and massive good sense. He was a rock; a man one could love, a man one could play with, and have happy jolly times. At this narrow table where he sat so often among us, we feel his loss now. He loved this Club. He was always happy here . . . I do not think anyone knew him better than I did, and he was, after all, my dearest friend.
>
> But there is a wider loss than ours. The country is the poorer. Just at the time when we feel that our public men are lacking in the power to dominate events, he has been taken. This was the occasion and these were the very years for the full fruition of his service to our country. He had the calmness of age while still retaining the force and power of his prime, and the questions which are now most grave and urgentl are the very ones in which|his influence and advice, his experience, his sagacity, his long trained judgement, would have been precious . . .
>
> Let us drink tonight in silence to the memory of a dear and honoured friend whose like we shall never see again.[61]

F.E. left his family only debts. Thirty years later this was still the one thing Freddie found hard to forgive. 'This selfishness and indifference to the interests of his family', he allowed himself to write in the second edition of his life of his father, 'was undoubtedly the least attractive feature of his character.'[62] F.E.'s realization of the need to secure their future by leaving politics came too late – if indeed it was ever more than a gesture. They were saved from serious embarrassment by the generosity of many friends but particularly of Beaverbrook, who even before the funeral wrote to Margaret offering to take over Freddie's and Pamela's education. Margaret accepted his assistance gratefully.

* Guest was wrong. The minute book actually shows that F.E. attended seventy-eight dinners out of ninety-four.

I don't know whether you know what it is to feel a ghastly load on one's mind – which the thought of the children's future *was* – and then to hear what Redmond told me this morning. What would Fred have felt could he have known? As you know he adored the children, and I am sure he never thought he *could* die at such a comparatively early age – or else it would have been a terrible worry to him to think they were not all provided for.[63]

On both Eleanor and Pamela, Beaverbrook settled an allowance of £325 a year for ten years. (After five years Pamela tried to terminate the arrangement when she married; but Max would not hear of it.)[64] And he made similar provision for Freddie.

Margaret sold Grosvenor Gardens at once – including F.E.'s magnificent library, which was sadly broken up – and bought a small house just up the road in Chester Street. She also naturally disposed of F.E.'s yacht and his six expensive motor cars. But she was able, with the help of other wealthy friends, to keep Charlton. After the Second World War, she and her sister Joan, Harold's widow, moved to a smaller house in the village, and it was there that she spent the remainder of her long life, concentrating as she could not during F.E.'s life on her painting, and holding several exhibitions in London. She died only in 1968, aged ninety.

Their futures once secured by Beaverbrook, by writing (in the case of Eleanor and Freddie) and by marriage (in that of Freddie and Pamela), the family flourished in the 1930s with the two girls in particular recreating much of the youthful glamour that had surrounded their father's name before 1914, glinting brilliantly in and out of that rich, indulgent, doomed literary/political society best captured in the diaries of the sybaritic socialite M.P., 'Chips' Channon. 'Untidy, unpunctual and vivacious' was Channon's compressed description of Eleanor in 1937: Pamela was 'pregnant, luscious and original'. Lunching with both girls and Margaret together, he found them all three 'as gay and provocative and quick as ever'.[65]

F.E. lived just long enough to take pride in the considerable success of Eleanor's first picaresque novel of gipsy life, *Red Wagon*. She went on to a highly gratifying career in her chosen genre, turning out a steady stream of best-sellers over the next dozen years with titles like *Flamenco*, *Tzigane* and *Caravan*. Very dated now, they were good rollicking reads in their day, written with powerful conviction, for she believed ardently in the fantasy of her father's gipsy blood, and did her best in her own life to live up to what she imagined to be her inheritance – so far as was compatible with being Lady Eleanor Smith. She even entitled her autobiography (written at the age of thirty-seven) *Life's a Circus*. When she died – yet another Smith to die absurdly young – aged forty-three in 1945, the mourners at her funeral (a Roman Catholic mass conducted by the famous society Jesuit, Father D'Arcy) included Osbert Sitwell, Oliver Messel, Cecil Beaton and a lot of circus proprietors.[66]

Freddie, by contrast, remained all his life a shy, retiring man of letters. He started immediately on F.E.'s death to write his biography, which appeared in two volumes in 1933 and 1935: it is elegant, admiring, more than a little romantic and essentially anecdotal, but a remarkable achievement for a son writing so soon after a dominating father's death. Having thus discovered his vocation, he went on to other subjects – Strafford (1938); Kipling (an authorized life to which Kipling's daughter took exception, and which therefore could not be published until after her death in 1978); 'Prof' Lindemann (1961); Lord Halifax (1965); and Walter Monckton (1969); in addition to a revised and improved version of his '*F.E.*' (1959), and a memoir of Eleanor (1953).

In 1935 he secured the future of the title, Charlton and the family fortunes by marrying Sheila Berry, the younger daughter of Lord Camrose, with whom F.E. had nearly – but not quite – gone into business in 1928. A year later, following the example of F.E. and his brother Harold's double marriage to the Furneaux sisters, Pamela married Sheila's brother, Michael Berry. There is a satisfying symmetry in this alliance between two families which epitomize in their rise to power and rank the mobility of English society and the openness of the English aristocracy to refreshment from below. For the original John Matthias Berry, the father of Camrose and Kemsley, was an estate agent in Merthyr Tydfil at just the time that Frederick Smith was fretting at the same profession in Birkenhead. Both rose through municipal politics to become Mayor of their respective towns, Berry as a Liberal, Smith as a populist Tory. Fifty years later, the marriage of their grandchildren was a major event at the very heart of the Conservative establishment, linking a grand if impoverished and somewhat maverick title with the solid party orthodoxy of the *Daily Telegraph*. The ascent of both families was now complete.

Freddie, though he held minor office as a Lord-in-Waiting in both Neville Chamberlain's pre-war and Churchill's post-war Conservative Governments, remained more of a writer than a politician until his death – at the good age for a male Smith of sixty-seven – in 1975, when he was succeeded by his son Robin, the present Earl of Birkenhead, who has still less political inclination but has followed his father as a biographer. It was Pamela (Lady Hartwell) who revealed herself as the politician *manqué* of the second generation. In 1955 her husband became Chairman and Editor-in-Chief of the *Daily Telegraph* and she a leading and influential hostess, not primarily political so much as artistic and literary, yet fulfilling almost alone in the very different political world of Harold Macmillan, Harold Wilson and Edward Heath the indefinable but vital role discharged in her father's day by Lady Londonderry and her like. It was to 'Lady Pam's', as readers of his diary will remember, that Richard Crossman regularly repaired in the 1960s for good food, good company and good gossip. Lady Hartwell was pre-eminently her father's daughter, keeping his memory vivid for over fifty years, until her own death in 1982.

Winston was of course quite right. The world has not seen F.E.'s like again.

References

1 The Smiths of Birkenhead

1 *The Royal English Atlas* (David & Charles Reprints, 1971).
2 N. Pevsner and E. Hubbard, *Cheshire* (Penguin, 1971), pp. 76, 77.
3 *Birkenhead News* (24 Sept 1887).
4 J.R. Kaighin, *Bygone Birkenhead* (Birkenhead, 1925), p. 313.
5 J.H.F. Brabner (ed.), *The Comprehensive Gazetteer of England and Wales* (London, 1894–5), p. 163.
6 *Birkenhead Advertiser* (14 Feb 1880).
7 *Birkenhead News* (10 Nov 1888).
8 Ibid. (15 Dec 1888).
9 Ibid. (12 Dec 1888).
10 *Birkenhead Advertiser* (15 Dec 1888).

2 Young Fred

1 N. Pevsner and E. Hubbard, *Cheshire* (Penguin, 1971), p. 94.
2 *Birkenhead News* (24 Sept 1887).
3 Birkenhead, *'F.E.'* (Eyre & Spottiswoode, 1959), p. 18.
4 H.A. Taylor, *Smith of Birkenhead* (Stanley Paul, 1931), p. 20.
5 Mrs Joyce Dangerfield, interview.
6 Birkenhead, *'F.E.'*, p. 17.
7 A.J. Hawkins to the author, 13 Feb 1976.
8 *West Lancashire Visiter* [*sic*] (4 Oct 1930).
9 L.S. Amery, *My Political Life*, vol. I (Hutchinson, 1953), p. 33.
10 Col. Repington, *The First World War*, vol. II (Constable, 1920), p. 499.
11 Taylor, *Smith*, p. 33.

12 Ibid., p. 27.
13 Birkenhead, *'F.E.'*, p. 22.
14 Taylor, *Smith*, p. 28.
15 Birkenhead, *'F.E.'*, p. 23.
16 Rev. Percy Robson, quoted in Ivor Thomas, *Our Lord Birkenhead: An Oxford Appreciation* (Putnam, 1930), p. 43.
17 W. Priestley to Lord Birkenhead, quoted in Birkenhead, *'F.E.'*, p. 25.
18 E.P. Smith to his Inspector of Taxes, 16 March 1898.
19 *Birkenhead News* (21 Oct 1899).
20 E.P. Smith to Arthur Smith, 4 Nov 1898.
21 E.P. Smith to Arthur Smith, 29 Jan 1897.
22 E.P. Smith to F.E., 14 Nov 1894.
23 E.P. Smith to Sidney Smith, 23 Feb 1899.
24 E.P. Smith to Elizabeth Smith, 19 March 1899.
25 Birkenhead, *Last Essays* (Cassell, 1930), p. 217.

3 From Liverpool to Oxford

1 Ramsay Muir, *An Autobiography and Some Essays*, ed. Stuart Hodgson (Lund Humphries, 1943), p. 23.
2 Ibid., p. 24.
3 Ibid., p. 27.
4 Birkenhead, *Law, Life and Letters*, vol. II (Hodder & Stoughton, 1927), pp. 184–5.
5 Ibid., pp. 187–8.
6 Ibid., pp. 190–1.
7 C.B. Fry, *Life Worth Living* (Eyre & Spottiswoode, 1939), p. 77.
8 John Betjeman, *An Oxford University Chest* (John Miles, 1938), p. 176.
9 Birkenhead, *Frederick Edwin, Earl of Birkenhead*, vol. I (Thornton Butterworth, 1933), p. 33.
10 Ibid., p. 34.
11 Viscount Simon, *Retrospect* (Hutchinson, 1952), p. 32.
12 Fry, *Life Worth Living*, p. 79.
13 *Isis* (23 April 1894).
14 Fry, *Life Worth Living*, p. 81.
15 Birkenhead, *'F.E.'* (Eyre & Spottiswoode, 1959), p. 33.
16 Fry, *Life Worth Living*, p. 92.

17 Simon, *Retrospect*, p. 33.
18 Fry, *Life Worth Living*, p. 88.
19 Ivor Thomas, *Our Lord Birkenhead: An Oxford Appreciation* (Putnam, 1930), pp. 11–12.
20 Birkenhead, *Last Essays* (Cassell, 1930), p. 218.
21 Birkenhead, *Law, Life and Letters*, vol. II, pp. 197–8.
22 Birkenhead, *Frederick Edwin*, vol. I, p. 52.
23 *Oxford Magazine* (March 1892).
24 *Oxford Review* (19 March 1892).
25 Birkenhead, *Law, Life and Letters*, vol. II, p. 202.
26 Simon, *Retrospect*, pp. 34–5.
27 E.P. Smith to F.E., 21 March 1892.
28 *Sunday Times* (5 Oct 1930).
29 *Oxford Review* (14 May 1892).
30 *Birkenhead Advertiser* (date unknown).
31 E.P. Smith to F.E., 23 June 1892.
32 Winston S. Churchill, *Great Contemporaries* (Thornton Butterworth, 1937), Fontana edn, p. 142.
33 *Birkenhead and Cheshire Advertiser and Wallasey Guardian* (2 July 1892).
34 *Chester Courant* (6 July 1892).
35 Birkenhead, *'F.E.'*, p. 38.

4 President of the Union

1 Birkenhead, 'The Oxford Union Society', in *Points of View*, vol. I (Hodder & Stoughton, 1922), p. 77.
2 *Isis* (date unknown), quoted in R. Speaight, *The Life of Hilaire Belloc* (Hollis & Carter, 1957), p. 89.
3 *Oxford Magazine* (11 Feb 1893).
4 *Isis* (11 Feb 1893).
5 Ibid. (6 May 1893).
6 *Oxford Review* (6 May 1893).
7 *Isis* (20 May 1893).
8 Birkenhead, *'F.E.'* (Eyre & Spottiswoode, 1959), p. 48.
9 *Oxford Magazine* (20 May 1893).
10 H.A. Morrah, *The Oxford Union, 1823–1923* (Cassell, 1923), p. 292.
11 Letters in the possession of Mr Hugh Spencer.
12 Ivor Thomas, *Our Lord Birkenhead: An Oxford Appreciation* (Putnam, 1930), pp. 99–100; Minutes of the Wadham College Literary Society.

13 F.W. Hirst, *In the Golden Days* (Muller, 1948), pp. 105–6.
14 Birkenhead, *Frederick Edwin, Earl of Birkenhead*, vol. I (Thornton Butterworth, 1933), p. 43.
15 Birkenhead, *Last Essays* (Cassell, 1930), p. 223.
16 Ibid., pp. 221–2.
17 Birkenhead, *Frederick Edwin*, vol. I, p. 42.
18 Sir John Masterman, *On the Chariot Wheel* (Oxford University Press, 1976), pp. 166–7.
19 Viscount Simon, *Retrospect* (Hutchinson, 1952), pp. 29–30.
20 Beauchamp to F.E., 5 May 1893.
21 *Oxford Magazine* (29 Nov 1893); for the speech itself, see also *Isis* (25 Nov 1893), and the *Oxford Review* (25 Nov 1893).
22 Unidentified press cutting; but see also the *Cambridge Review* (30 Nov 1893), and *Granta* (2 Dec 1893).
23 *Oxford Magazine* (6 Dec 1893).
24 Balcarres to F.E., 20 Dec 1893.
25 Morrah, *The Oxford Union*, pp. 289–90.
26 Oxford Union Society, Minutes of the Standing Committee, 7 Dec 1893 and 22 Feb 1894.
27 Balcarres to F.E., 14 April 1894.
28 *Isis* (21 April 1894).
29 Balcarres to F.E., 12 April 1894.
30 *Birkenhead News* (date unknown).
31 Ibid.
32 *Liverpool Courier* (10 May 1894).
33 *The Times* (10 May 1894).
34 *Birkenhead News* (12 May 1894).
35 Ibid. (6 Oct 1894).
36 Cutting from unknown paper.
37 Gervais Rentoul, *This Is My Case* (Hutchinson, 1944), p. 50.
38 Maurice Bowra, *Memories, 1898–1939* (Weidenfeld & Nicolson, 1966), p. 146.
39 Birkenhead, *'F.E.'*, p. 54.
40 *Isis* (16 Feb 1895).
41 Birkenhead, *'F.E.'*, p. 56.

5 Fellow of Merton

1 *Oxford University Calendar* (1896).
2 H. Montgomery Hyde, *The Trial of Roger Casement* (William Hodge, 1960), Penguin edn, p. 151.

3 Birkenhead, *'F.E.'* (Eyre & Spottiswoode, 1959), p. 56.

4 H. Montgomery Hyde, *Roger Casement*, p. 151.

5 H.A. Taylor, *Smith of Birkenhead* (Stanley Paul, 1931), p. 53.

6 Ivor Thomas, *Our Lord Birkenhead: An Oxford Appreciation* (Putnam, 1930), pp. 48–9.

7 *Birkenhead Advertiser* (26 Dec 1896).

8 W.W. How to F.H. Lawson, 15 Nov 1930 (Merton College archives).

9 F.H. Lawson, *The Oxford Law School, 1850–1965* (Oxford University Press, 1968), p. 98.

10 E.C. Bentley, *Those Days* (Constable, 1940), pp. 71–2.

11 Ibid., pp. 78–9.

12 Anonymous appreciation in the *Law Quarterly Review*, vol. 47 (Jan 1931), pp. 17–18, said by Lawson to be by Prof. G.C. Cheshire.

13 Bentley, *Those Days*, p. 80.

14 Ibid., p. 76.

15 Ibid., p. 81.

16 Ibid., p. 77.

17 Ibid., p. 73.

18 *Isis* (24 Oct 1896).

19 Ibid. (6 Feb 1897).

20 Bentley, *Those Days*, p. 75.

21 H.A. Morrah, *The Oxford Union, 1823–1923* (Cassell, 1923), p. 290.

22 Edward Marjoribanks, *The Life of Lord Carson*, vol. I (Gollancz, 1932), pp. 193–4.

23 Birkenhead, *'F.E.'*, pp. 67–8.

24 *Isis* (15 May 1897).

25 *Oxford Chronicle* (29 May 1897).

26 Birkenhead, *'F.E.'*, pp. 63–4 (Prof. E.R. Lankester to F.E., 22 May 1897).

27 *Isis* (29 May 1897).

28 Viscount Simon, *Retrospect* (Hutchinson, 1952), p. 36.

29 Dr J. Wells to F.E., 22 May 1897, quoted in Birkenhead, *'F.E.'*, p. 66.

30 Birkenhead, *'F.E.'*, p. 77.

31 Birkenhead, *Frederick Edwin, Earl of Birkenhead*, vol. I (Thornton Butterworth, 1933), p. 87.

32 L.S. Amery, *Days of Fresh Air* (Jarrold, 1939), pp. 74–89.

33 Birkenhead, *Frederick Edwin*, vol. I, pp. 57–8.

34 Ibid., p. 81.

35 Simon, *Retrospect*, p. 44.

36 R.F.V. Heuston, *The Lives of the Lord Chancellors, 1885–1940* (Oxford University Press, 1964), p. 357.

References

37 F.E. Smith, 'The Rule in *Hadley* v. *Baxendale*', *Law Quarterly Review*, vol. 16, pp. 275–87.

38 Heuston, *Lives of the Lord Chancellors*, p. 358.

6 Liverpool and the Northern Circuit

1 Liverpool City Council Watch Committee Proceedings, Dec 1904: quoted in D.A. Roberts, 'Religion and Politics in Liverpool since 1900', (London M.Sc. thesis, 1965).

2 Harold Jager, *Brief Life* (Henry Young, Liverpool, 1934), pp. 57–8.

3 Francis Hirst's diary, 25 Sept 1899, quoted in F.W. Hirst, *In the Golden Days* (Muller, 1948), p. 190.

4 Jager, *Brief Life*, p. 108.

5 Frank Pakenham, *Born to Believe* (Cape, 1953), p. 53.

6 Birkenhead, *'F.E.'* (Eyre & Spottiswoode, 1959), p. 77.

7 Ibid., p. 76.

8 Ibid., pp. 74–5.

9 *Liverpool Daily Post* (13 Sept 1900).

10 Ibid. (12 Sept 1900).

11 Ibid. (22 Sept 1900).

12 Ibid. (13 Sept 1900).

13 Ibid. (27 Sept 1900).

14 E.S. Fay, *The Life of Mr Justice Swift* (Methuen, 1939), p. 12.

15 F.E. to Harley, 4 Nov 1915.

16 *The Times* (16 April 1926).

17 Birkenhead, *'F.E.'*, p. 73.

18 J. Wentworth Day, *Lady Houston, D.B.E.: The Woman Who Won the War* (Allan Wingate, 1958), p. 39.

19 Frank Owen, *Tempestuous Journey: Lloyd George, His Life and Times* (Hutchinson, 1954), p. 191.

20 *The Times* (21 April 1926).

21 Jager, *Brief Life*, pp. 108–9.

22 Ibid., p. 105.

23 Ibid., pp. 106–7.

24 Ibid., p. 107.

25 Ibid., pp. 104–5.

26 Ibid., p. 112.

27 Birkenhead, *'F.E.'*, p. 75.

28 *Oxford Times* (13 April 1901).

29 Birkenhead, *'F.E.'*, p. 77.

30 Ibid., pp. 77–8.
31 Birkenhead, *Frederick Edwin, Earl of Birkenhead*, vol. I (Thornton Butterworth, 1933), p. 89.
32 Birkenhead, *'F.E.'*, p. 78.
33 Ibid., p. 86.
34 Stanley Salvidge, *Salvidge of Liverpool* (Hodder & Stoughton, 1934), p. 62.
35 Sir Thomas Harley, interview 1976.
36 Jager, *Brief Life*, p. 113.
37 F.E. to Margaret, 12 May 1902 (Birkenhead papers).
38 R.F.V. Heuston, *The Lives of the Lord Chancellors, 1885–1940* (Oxford University Press, 1964), pp. 358–9.
39 *The Times* (21 Nov 1901).
40 Birkenhead, *'F.E.'*, p. 80.
41 *The Times* (24 Feb 1902).
42 Birkenhead, *'F.E.'*, p. 84.
43 Birkenhead, *Famous Trials of History* (Hutchinson, 1926), p. 225.
44 F.W. Ashley, *My Sixty Years in the Law* (John Lane/The Bodley Head, 1936), p. 193.
45 *The Times* (4 Aug 1902).
46 *Liverpool Daily Post, The Times* (9–12 Dec 1902).
47 *The Times* (15 Dec 1902).
48 Birkenhead, *Frederick Edwin*, vol. I, p. 100.
49 G.W. Keeton and J. Cameron (eds), *The Trial of the 'Veronica' Mutineers*, (William Hodge, 1952); Birkenhead, *Famous Trials*, pp. 257–67.
50 Birkenhead, *Famous Trials*, p. 294.
51 Ibid., p. 289.
52 Jager, *Brief Life*, p. 110
53 All these stories are in Birkenhead, *'F.E.'*, pp. 98–9.
54 Jager, *Brief Life*, p. 112.
55 Ibid., p. 104.
56 Ibid., p. 164.

7 Into Parliament

1 New Brighton, 25 Sept 1900. *Birkenhead News* (29 Sept 1900).
2 East Toxteth, 1 Nov 1902. *Liverpool Daily Post* (3 Nov 1902).
3 West Derby, 13 Jan 1903. Ibid. (14 Jan 1903).
4 Birkenhead, *Law, Life and Letters*, vol. II (Hodder & Stoughton, 1927), p. 204.

5 Harold Jager, *Brief Life* (Henry Young, Liverpool, 1934), pp. 117–22.
6 Birkenhead, *Law, Life and Letters*, p. 213.
7 Jager, *Brief Life*, p. 123.
8 F.E. to Salvidge, 12 Jan 1905, in Stanley Salvidge, *Salvidge of Liverpool* (Hodder & Stoughton, 1934) pp. 62–3.
9 Salvidge to F.E., 13 Jan 1905. Ibid., pp. 63–4.
10 *Liverpool Daily Post* (18 Feb 1905).
11 Ibid. (15 Feb 1905).
12 F.E. to Salvidge, 3 April 1905, in Salvidge, *Salvidge of Liverpool*, pp. 64–5.
13 *Liverpool Daily Post* (8 March 1905).
14 Ibid. (27 April 1905).
15 Ibid. (28 April 1905).
16 Ibid. (23 Dec 1905).
17 Ibid. (12 Jan 1906).
18 Ibid. (15 Jan 1906).
19 Ibid., and *Liverpool Courier* (6 Jan 1906).
20 *Liverpool Daily Post* (28 Dec 1905).
21 Ibid. (30 Dec 1905).
22 Birkenhead, *Law, Life and Letters*, pp. 222–3.
23 *Liverpool Daily Post* (4 April 1906).
24 *Liverpool Courier* (9 Jan 1906); Jager, *Brief Life*, p. 130.
25 *Liverpool Daily Post* (10 Jan 1906).
26 Ibid. (15 Jan 1906).
27 Ibid. (6 Jan 1906).
28 *Liverpool Courier* (13 Jan 1906).
29 *Liverpool Daily Post* (8 Jan 1906).
30 Ibid. (13 Jan 1906).
31 Birkenhead, *Law, Life and Letters*, p. 224.
32 *Liverpool Daily Post* (17 Jan 1906).
33 Birkenhead, *Law, Life and Letters*, p. 225.
34 *Liverpool Daily Post* (22 Jan 1906).
35 *Liverpool Courier* (22 Jan 1906).

8 Making a Name: The House of Commons, 1906–9

1 Winston S. Churchill, *Great Contemporaries* (Thornton Butterworth, 1937), Fontana edn, p. 141.
2 *The Times* (13 March 1906).

3 House of Commons, 12 March 1906.

4 Ibid.

5 L.S. Amery, *Days of Fresh Air* (Jarrold, 1939), p. 82.

6 Birkenhead, *Law, Life and Letters*, vol. II (Hodder & Stoughton, 1927), p. 236.

7 Viscount Lee of Fareham, *'A Good Innings'*, ed. Alan Clark (John Murray, 1974), pp. 90–1.

8 Birkenhead, *'F.E.'* (Eyre & Spottiswoode, 1959), pp. 126–70.

9 Violet Bonham Carter, *Winston Churchill as I Knew Him* (Eyre & Spottiswoode, 1965), Pan edn, p. 151.

10 Viscount Simon, *Retrospect* (Hutchinson, 1952), p. 73.

11 Lucy Masterman, *C.F.G. Masterman* (Frank Cass, 1939), p.69.

12 Lee of Fareham, *'A Good Innings'*, p. 91.

13 House of Commons, 13 March 1906.

14 Birkenhead, *Frederick Edwin, Earl of Birkenhead*, vol. I (Thornton Butterworth, 1933), p. 155.

15 House of Commons, 12 March 1906.

16 Birkenhead, *Frederick Edwin*, vol. I, p. 157.

17 Churchill, *Great Contemporaries*, p. 141.

18 *Daily Chronicle* (13 March 1906).

19 Lord Winterton, *Orders of the Day* (Cassell, 1953), p. 18.

20 House of Commons, 30 March 1906; *The Speeches of Lord Birkenhead* (Cassell, 1929), pp. 15–22.

21 House of Commons, 3 August 1906.

22 Preston, 19 April 1906. (*The Times*, 20 April 1906.)

23 House of Commons, 9 May 1906.

24 Ibid., 19 July 1906.

25 Ibid., 3 Dec 1906.

26 Ibid., 10 Dec 1906.

27 Recollected by F.E. at a dinner in honour of Sir Leslie Ward ('Spy'), 21 Nov 1921. (*The Times*, 22 Nov 1921.)

28 *Vanity Fair* (16 Jan 1907).

29 Bonham Carter, *Winston Churchill*, p. 152.

30 F.E. to Salvidge, 20 May 1906, in Stanley Salvidge, *Salvidge of Liverpool*, (Hodder & Stoughton, 1934), p. 72.

31 Harold Jager, *Brief Life* (Henry Young, Liverpool, 1934), pp. 199–200.

32 e.g. at Derby, 11 Oct 1907. (*The Times*, 12 Oct 1907.)

33 House of Commons, 18 Feb 1907.

34 Ibid.

35 Ibid., 25 June 1907.

36 Ibid., 26 June 1907.

37 Ibid., 26 June 1907.

38 F.E. to *The Times* (22 March 1907); speeches in the House of Commons, 11 March 1907, 1 May 1907, 9 July 1907, 19 March 1907, 17 April 1907, 17 June 1907; speech at National Service League dinner at the Trocadero, 26 June 1907.

39 House of Commons, 26 April 1907.

40 Ibid., 18 July 1907.

41 *The Times* (19 July 1907).

42 Ibid. (7 Feb 1908).

43 House of Commons, 6 Feb 1908.

44 W.P. Jolly, *Lord Leverhulme* (Constable, 1976), pp. 46–56; E. Marjoribanks, *The Life of Lord Carson*, vol. I (Gollancz, 1932), pp. 402–11.

45 R. Pound and G. Harmsworth, *Northcliffe* (Cassell, 1959), p. 304. The letters are all quoted without date or other reference.

46 Randolph S. Churchill, *Winston S. Churchill: Young Statesman, 1901–1914* (Heinemann, 1967), p. 268.

47 Ibid., p. 267.

48 Salvidge, *Salvidge of Liverpool*, pp. 75–80.

49 *The Times* (11 July 1913). For Harold's political activities in Birkenhead, see Jager, *Brief Life*, pp. 205–11; Jager worked closely with Harold in the Birkenhead W.M.C.A. and succeeded him as chairman. For a general eulogy of Harold's career, see Birkenhead, *Contemporary Personalities*, (Cassell, 1924), pp. 309–17.

50 House of Commons, 24 Feb 1908; F.E.'s other major speeches on the two Education Bills of 1908 were on 19 May and 30 Nov. All three are included in F.E. Smith, *Speeches, 1906–9* (Henry Young, Liverpool, 1909).

51 House of Commons, 29 April 1908.

52 Ibid., 27 Feb 1908.

53 Ibid., 20 Nov 1908.

54 *Annual Register* (1908), p. 223.

55 Licensed Victuallers' Central Protection Society dinner at the Hotel Cecil, 30 April 1908. (*The Times*, 1 May 1908.)

56 F.E. Smith, 'Licensing Policy', in *Unionist Policy* (Williams & Norgate, 1913), pp. 216–33.

57 House of Commons, 6 July 1908.

58 Liverpool, 8 Jan 1909. (*The Times*, 9 Jan 1909.)

59 House of Commons, 22 Feb 1909.

60 Chatham, 24 March 1909. (Smith, *Speeches, 1906–9*, pp. 275–307.)

9 The People's Budget and the House of Lords Crisis, 1909–11

1 Winterton to Maxse, 18 Aug 1909 (Maxse papers 460f. 373).
2 Bicester, 12 Aug 1909.
3 L.W.M.C.A. Central Committee, Liverpool, 27 Aug 1909. (F.E. Smith, *Speeches, 1906–9* (Henry Young, Liverpool, 1909), pp. 330–70).
4 Limehouse, 4 Oct 1909.
5 Bedford, 5 Oct 1909; Wolverhampton, 6 Oct 1909; Sheffield, 8 Oct 1909.
6 House of Commons, 4 Nov 1909. (Smith, *Speeches, 1906–9*, p. 383.)
7 *The Times* (14 Sept 1909).
8 Ibid. (20 Nov 1909). (Smith, *Speeches, 1906–9*, pp. 397–9.)
9 *Speeches Delivered in the House of Commons and Elsewhere, 1906–1909* by F.E. Smith, M.P., One of His Majesty's Counsel, Formerly Fellow of Merton College and Vinerian Scholar in the University of Oxford (Henry Young & Sons, Liverpool, 1909), pp. vii–viii.
10 Shoreditch Town Hall, 1 Dec 1909.
11 Walton, 4 Dec 1909.
12 Inaugural Address as President of the Midland Conservative Club, Birmingham, 9 Dec 1909.
13 e.g. Derby, 10 Dec 1909.
14 *The Times* (30 Dec 1909).
15 Ibid. (31 Dec 1909).
16 Ibid. (4 Jan 1910).
17 *Liverpool Daily Post* (3 Jan 1910).
18 Stanley Salvidge, *Salvidge of Liverpool* (Hodder & Stoughton, 1934), pp. 88–90.
19 Birkenhead papers.
20 *Liverpool Daily Post* (6 Jan 1910).
21 Ibid. (15 Jan 1910).
22 Ibid. (13 Jan 1910).
23 Ibid. (18 Jan 1910).
24 Ibid. (17 Jan 1910).
25 Sun Hall, Liverpool, 14 Jan 1910.
26 F.E. to Salvidge, 4 Feb 1910. (Salvidge, *Salvidge of Liverpool*, pp. 93–4.)
27 House of Commons, 22 Feb 1910.
28 Austen Chamberlain, *Politics from Inside* (Cassell, 1936), pp. 203–4.

29 Ibid., p. 237.
30 House of Commons, 30 March 1910.
31 United Club dinner, 29 April 1910.
32 F.E. to *The Times* (15 June 1910).
33 Willoughby de Broke to Maxse, n.d. June 1910 (Maxse papers).
34 F.E. to *The Times* (27 Sept 1910).
35 Austen Chamberlain to Bonar Law, 29 Sept 1910 (Bonar Law papers, 15/6/85).
36 F.E. to Austen Chamberlain, 20 Oct 1910, in Birkenhead, *Frederick Edwin, Earl of Birkenhead*, vol. I (Thornton Butterworth, 1933), pp. 205–6.
37 F.E. to Bonar Law, 19 Oct 1910 (Bonar Law papers 18/6/126).
38 F.E. to Balfour, 30 Oct 1910 (Sandars papers c761/290).
39 F.E. to Austen Chamberlain, 21 Oct 1910, in Birkenhead, *Frederick Edwin*, pp. 206–8.
40 F.E. to Balfour, 30 Oct 1910 (Sandars papers c761/290).
41 Brackley, 12 Nov 1911.
42 Sandars to Balfour, Dec 1910 (Balfour papers 49767/74–5).
43 Dinner for Bonar Law, Constitutional Club, 14 Nov 1910.
44 Islington, 23 Nov 1910.
45 Burnley, 26 Nov 1910.
46 Openshaw, 10 Dec 1910.
47 Liverpool (Exchange), 28 Nov 1910.
48 Liverpool, 30 Nov 1910.
49 Leighton Buzzard, 15 Dec 1910.
50 F.E. to *The Times* (19 Dec 1910).
51 Unionist dinner, 6 Feb 1911.
52 F.E. to Garvin, 3 Jan 1911, in Birkenhead, *'F.E.'* (Eyre & Spottiswoode, 1959), pp. 150–1, misdated.
53 *Reynolds' News* (20 Jan 1911).
54 House of Commons, 22 Feb 1911.
55 Ibid., 15 May 1911.
56 Balfour to F.E., 3 June 1911 (Balfour papers, 49692/119–22).
57 Churchill to Clementine, 5 June 1911, in Martin Gilbert, *Winston S. Churchill*, Companion Vol. II, ii, p. 1,809.
58 Churchill to Bonar Law, 4 June 1911 (Bonar Law papers, 18/7/174).
59 Bonar Law to Balfour, 6 June 1911 (Balfour papers 49693/12–15).
60 Asquith to Balfour, 7 June 1911 (ibid., 49692/125–6).
61 F.E. to Asquith, June 1911, in Roy Jenkins, *Asquith* (Collins, 1964), Fontana edn, p. 249n.
62 F.E. to Balfour, 6 June 1911, in Birkenhead, *'F.E.'*, p. 163.
63 Ibid.

64 Balfour to Asquith, 14 June 1911 (Balfour papers, 49692/130–7).
65 Birkenhead, *'F.E.'*, p. 164.
66 Balfour to F.E., June 1911. Ibid.
67 F.E. to Goulding, Oct 1911 (Wargrave papers, A/3/2).
68 Violet Bonham Carter, *Winston Churchill as I Knew Him* (Eyre & Spottiswoode, 1965), Pan edn, p. 217.
69 *The Times* (25 July 1911).
70 W.S. Blunt, *My Diaries*, vol. II (Secker, 1921), p. 356.
71 F.E. to the *Observer* (30 July 1911).
72 F.E. to Scott, 26 July 1911 (Scott papers 119/3/P/Gen).
73 Sir C. Petrie, *The Life and Letters of Sir Austen Chamberlain* (Cassell, 1939), p. 279.
74 Blunt, *My Diaries*, p. 356.
75 Churchill to King George V, 26 July 1911, in Gilbert, *Winston S. Churchill*, pp. 1,103–4.
76 Sir George Armstrong to Stamfordham, 2 Aug 1911 (Birkenhead papers).
77 House of Commons, 7 Aug 1911.
78 Ibid.
79 F.E. to Austen Chamberlain, 13 Aug 1911, in Birkenhead, *'F.E.'*, pp. 167–8.
80 Austen Chamberlain to F.E., 20 Aug 1911, in ibid., pp. 169–70.
81 Austen Chamberlain, *Politics from Inside*, p. 358.
82 Ibid.
83 Neville Chamberlain to Austen Chamberlain, 7 Oct 1911 (Austen Chamberlain papers, AC9/3/14).
84 Birmingham, 12 May 1911.
85 Glasgow, 10 Oct 1911.
86 Stratford, 3 Nov 1911.
87 Bristol, 13 Nov 1911.
88 Lord Winterton, *Pre-War* (Macmillan, 1932), p. 231.
89 Oldham, 11 Nov 1911.
90 Goulding to Bonar Law, 18 Nov 1911 (Bonar Law papers 23/3/58).
91 *The Times* (16 Dec 1911).

10 F.E. at Forty: Fame, Friends, Wine and Women

1 'Ephesian' (Bechhofer Roberts), *Lord Birkenhead* (Mills & Boon, 1926), p. 11.
2 Lady Cynthia Asquith, *Diaries, 1915–1918* (Hutchinson, 1968), p. 303 (10 May 1917).

3 Mr O.A. Dod to the author.

4 A.G. Gardiner, *Pillars of Society* (James Nisbet, 1913), pp. 95–103.

5 W.S. Blunt, *My Diaries*, vol. II (Secker, 1921), p. 366.

6 *Everybody's Weekly* (8 April 1911).

7 *New York Post* (16 Aug 1912).

8 Birkenhead, *Frederick Edwin, Earl of Birkenhead*, vol. I (Thornton Butterworth, 1933), p. 265.

9 Traditional.

10 Bradford, 9 Jan 1912.

11 Traditional.

12 Mr D.J. Welch to the author.

13 Birkenhead, *Frederick Edwin*, vol. I, p. 264.

14 Mr C.H. Phillingham to the author.

15 Mr R.P. Garnons-Williams to the author.

16 Traditional.

17 Lady Gaselee to the author.

18 Arnold Bennett, *Journals*, vol. II (Cassell, 1932), p. 229 (2 May 1918).

19 Birkenhead papers.

20 Birkenhead, *Law, Life and Letters*, vol. I (Hodder & Stoughton, 1927), p. 94.

21 L.S. Amery, *The Leo Amery Diaries*, ed. John Barnes and David Nicholson, vol. I (Hutchinson, 1981), p. 276.

22 'Ephesian', *Lord Birkenhead*, p. 207.

23 F.E. to Beaverbrook, 6 March 1917 (Beaverbrook papers C/39).

24 Bennett, *Journals*, vol. II, p. 231 (11 May 1918).

25 Mr Patrick Ennor to the author.

26 Traditional.

27 Mr Bill Rogers.

28 Selborne papers.

29 *The Diaries of Sir Robert Bruce Lockhart*, ed. Kenneth Young, vol. I (Macmillan, 1980), p. 106 (7 Sept 1929).

30 Birkenhead, *Points of View*, vol. II (Hodder & Stoughton, 1922), pp. 136–41.

31 Birkenhead, *Contemporary Personalities* (Cassell, 1924), p. 115.

32 Winston S. Churchill, *Great Contemporaries* (Thornton Butterworth, 1937), Fontana edn, p. 142.

33 Mary Soames, *Clementine Churchill* (Cassell, 1979), Penguin edn, p. 111.

34 Birkenhead, *'F.E.'* (Eyre & Spottiswoode, 1959), p. 175.

35 *Vanity Fair* (9 Aug 1911).

36 Sir Oswald Mosley, *My Life* (Nelson, 1968), p. 169.

37 Maxse to Goulding, 29 Sept 1910 (Wargrave papers A/3/2).

38 *Punch* (2 Nov 1910).
39 F.E. to Aitken, Nov 1911 (Birkenhead/Beaverbrook correspondence).
40 F.E. to Aitken, 17 Aug 1912 (ibid.).
41 Colin R. Coote, *The Other Club* (Sidgwick & Jackson, 1971), pp. 17–20.
42 *The Times* (25 May 1911).
43 Ibid. (26 May 1911).
44 Ibid. (27 May 1911).
45 Lord Croft, *My Life of Strife* (Hutchinson, 1948), pp. 122–3.
46 Birkenhead, *'F.E.'*, p. 17.
47 F.E. to Margaret, n.d. 1902 (Birkenhead papers).
48 Bennett, *Journals*, vol. III, p. 90 (15 May 1925).
49 Aitken to Bonar Law, Sept 1912 (Bonar Law papers 18/7/211).
50 Marquesa de Casa Moury (formerly Mrs Dudley Ward).
51 Anne Chisholm, *Nancy Cunard* (Sidgwick & Jackson, 1979), p. 23.
52 House of Commons, 11 July 1910.
53 *The Times* (23 Jan 1913).
54 *Good Housekeeping* (March 1928).
55 Edinburgh, 3 Nov 1925.
56 Birkenhead, *The World in 2030* (Hodder & Stoughton, 1930), pp. 168–9.
57 F.E. to Bonar Law, 27 Dec 1911 (Bonar Law papers 24/5/153).
58 Central Hall, Westminster, 25 June 1913.

11 Smith, K.C.

1 Enid Kohler to the author.
2 L.E. Jones, *An Edwardian Youth* (Macmillan, 1956), p. 185.
3 *Daily Telegraph* (24 July 1913).
4 John Buchan, *Memory Hold-the-Door* (Hodder & Stoughton, 1940), p. 274.
5 Birkenhead, *Contemporary Personalities* (Cassell, 1924), p. 254.
6 R.F.V. Heuston, *The Lives of the Lord Chancellors, 1885–1940* (Oxford University Press, 1964), p. 365 (*Greenland Ltd.* v. *Wilmhurst* [1913] 3 KB 507 at 532).
7 F.E. Smith, *Unionist Policy* (Williams & Norgate, 1913), p. 296.
8 Birkenhead, *'F.E.'*, (Eyre & Spottiswoode, 1959), p. 457.
9 Alan Hyman, *The Rise and Fall of Horatio Bottomley* (Cassell, 1972), pp. 99–119.

10 *Parker and others* v. *Bottomley* (*The Times*, 10 May 1910); Hyman, *Horatio Bottomley*, pp. 124–5.
11 *Beardall* v. *Bottomley* (*The Times*, 3, 4 May 1910).
12 W. Sorley Brown, *The Life and Genius of T.W.H. Crosland* (Cecil Palmer, 1928), pp. 251–2.
13 *The Times* (26 Oct 1910).
14 Birkenhead, *Famous Trials of History* (Hutchinson, 1926), p. 285.
15 Susan Mary Alsop, *Lady Sackville: A Biography* (Weidenfeld & Nicolson, 1978), pp. 158–60; Birkenhead papers.
16 *Daily Telegraph* (25 June 1913, and following days).
17 Alsop, *Lady Sackville*, p. 181.
18 Nigel Nicolson, *Portrait of a Marriage* (Weidenfeld & Nicolson, 1973), p. 74.
19 Vita Sackville-West, *Pepita* (Hogarth Press, 1937), p. 243.
20 *Daily Telegraph* (4 July 1913).
21 Alsop, *Lady Sackville*, p. 160.
22 *The Autobiography of Arthur Ransome* (Cape, 1976), p. 153.
23 *The Times, Daily Telegraph* (22 April 1913).
24 H. Montgomery Hyde, *Oscar Wilde* (Eyre Methuen, 1976), pp. 185, 120.
25 Brown, *T.W.H. Crosland*, pp. 285–99.
26 *Daily Telegraph* (29 June–7 July 1914).
27 *The Collected Satires of Lord Alfred Douglas* (Fortune Press, 1926).
28 *Daily Telegraph* (24 July 1913).

12 Bonar Law and the Ulster Crisis, 1912–14

1 F.E. to Beaverbrook, 26 May 1928 (F.E.–Beaverbrook correspondence).
2 F.E. to Bonar Law, 18 Dec 1912 (Bonar Law papers 28/1/53).
3 Dudley, 20 Dec 1912.
4 F.E. to Salvidge, 28 Dec 1912, in Stanley Salvidge, *Salvidge of Liverpool* (Hodder & Stoughton, 1934), pp. 128–9.
5 Manchester, 17 Nov 1913.
6 Yeovil, 20 Nov 1911.
7 House of Commons, 29 Nov 1911.
8 Falmouth, 16 Dec 1911.
9 House of Commons, 19 Feb 1912.
10 Ibid., 21 April 1909.

11 F.E. Smith, *Unionist Policy* (Williams & Norgate, 1913), p. 156.

12 Ibid., p. 180.

13 House of Commons, 13 May 1912.

14 G.K. Chesterton, 'AntiChrist, or the Reunion of Christendom: An Ode' in *The Collected Poems of G.K. Chesterton* (Methuen, 1927), pp. 138–9.

15 Liverpool, 22 Jan 1912; see also New Cross, 31 Jan 1912, and Warrington, 10 May 1912.

16 House of Commons, 18 June 1912.

17 Belfast, 12 July 1912. Quoted in Smith, *Unionist Policy*, pp. 115–26.

18 *The Times* (13 July 1912).

19 Blenheim, 27 July 1912.

20 A.T.Q. Stewart, *The Ulster Crisis: Resistance to Home Rule, 1912–1914* (Faber, 1967), p. 62.

21 Belfast, 23 Sept 1912.

22 *The Times* (25 Sept 1912).

23 Londonderry, 20 Sept 1912.

24 *The Times* (21 Sept 1912).

25 Liverpool, 30 Sept 1912.

26 Smith, *Unionist Policy*, pp. 81–115.

27 *The Times* (30 Oct 1912).

28 House of Commons, 16 Jan 1913.

29 John Baird to Bonar Law, 4 April 1913 (Bonar Law papers 29/3/4).

30 Younger to Bonar Law, 25 May 1913 (ibid., 29/4/21).

31 Lord Charles Beresford to Bonar Law, 25 May 1913 (ibid., 29/4/22).

32 *The Times* (17 June 1913).

33 Ibid. (25 June 1913).

34 H. Montgomery Hyde, *Carson* (Heinemann, 1953), p. 333.

35 Lloyd George to Garvin, 31 Dec 1913 (Lloyd George papers C/4/13/1).

36 *Daily Chronicle* (24 Sept 1913).

37 Ballyclare, 20 Sept 1913.

38 Carson to Bonar Law (enclosing F.E.'s memorandum) 20 Sept 1913 (Bonar Law papers 30/2/15).

39 F.E. to Lloyd George, 26 Sept 1913 (Lloyd George papers C/3/7/1).

40 Lloyd George to F.E., 6 Oct 1913 (ibid., C/3/7/2).

41 Robert Blake, *The Unknown Prime Minister* (Eyre & Spottiswoode, 1955), p. 159.

42 F.E. to Churchill, 5 Oct 1913, in Randolph S. Churchill, *Winston S. Churchill: Young Statesman, 1901–1914* (Heinemann, 1967), p. 478.

43 F.E. to Lloyd George, 9 Oct 1913 (Lloyd George papers C/3/7/3).

44 West Bromwich, 10 Oct 1913; *Liberal Magazine* (Nov 1913), p. 618.

45 Churchill to F.E., 9 March 1914 (Birkenhead papers).
46 Bradford, 14 March 1914.
47 Manchester, 17 Nov 1913.
48 Liverpool, 10 Jan 1914.
49 Churchill to Lloyd George, 3 April 1914 (Lloyd George papers C/3/16/11).
50 Bristol, 4 July 1914.

13 Tory Democracy

1 F.E. Smith, 'The Future of the Conservative Party', *Unionist Policy and Other Essays* (Williams & Norgate, 1913), pp. 1–20.
2 'The Conservative Party and the Principle of Government', ibid., pp. 126–56.
3 Proportional Representation Society dinners, 13 May 1912 and 3 Dec 1913.
4 House of Commons, 8 and 30 April 1913.
5 Martin Pugh, *Electoral Reform in War and Peace, 1906–18* (Routledge & Kegan Paul, 1978).
6 Smith, 'State Toryism and Social Reform', *Unionist Policy*, pp. 20–46.
7 See G.R. Searle, *The Quest for National Efficiency* (Blackwell, 1971).
8 Smith, 'Industrial Unrest', *Unionist Policy*, pp. 234–58.
9 John Ramsden, *The Age of Balfour and Baldwin* (Longman, 1978), p. 76.
10 C.M. Lloyd to Beatrice Webb, 11 Dec 1911 (Passfield papers).
11 *The Times* (16 Dec 1912).
12 Ibid. (12 Dec 1912).
13 F.E. to *The Times* (2 July 1912).
14 Introduction to J. Hills and M. Woods, *Industrial Unrest: A Practical Solution* (1914).
15 *The Times* (2 Feb 1912).
16 e.g. Liverpool, 8, 10 Jan 1914.
17 Smith, 'National Service', *Unionist Policy*, pp. 47–63.
18 'Lord Roberts and Germany', ibid., pp. 64–80.

14 F.E. at War: The Press Bureau and the Indian Corps, 1914–15

1 F.E. to Margaret, 15 Oct 1914, in Birkenhead, *'F.E.'* (Eyre & Spottiswoode, 1959), p. 264.
2 F.E. to Churchill, 31 July 1914, in Randolph S. Churchill, *Winston S. Churchill, Young Statesman, 1901–1914* (Heinemann, 1967), Companion Vol. iii, p. 1,990.
3 Churchill to F.E., 1 Aug 1914, in Birkenhead, *'F.E.'*, p. 241.
4 Sir Austen Chamberlain, *Down the Years* (Cassell, 1935), p. 99.
5 *Lord Riddell's War Diary, 1914–1918* (Ivor Nicholson & Watson, 1933), p. 9.
6 Ibid., p. 10.
7 House of Commons, 7 Aug 1914.
8 Ibid., 14 Aug 1914.
9 *The History of 'The Times'*, vol. IV, part 1 (*The Times*, 1952), p. 222.
10 Aitken to Bonar Law, 2 Sept 1914 (Bonar Law papers 34/5/7).
11 Col. Repington, *The First World War*, vol. II (Constable, 1920), p. 245.
12 Sir Edward Cook, *The Press in Wartime* (Macmillan, 1920).
13 *Manchester Guardian* (20 May 1915).
14 Quoted in *The Times* (8 Sept 1914).
15 London, 11 Sept 1914.
16 *The Scotsman* (8 Aug 1914).
17 F.E. to Col. Dugdale, 13 Nov 1915; Col. Dugdale to F.E., 20 Nov 1915 (printed copies in the Beaverbrook papers, C/39).
18 Crewe to Kitchener, 20 Sept 1914 (Kitchener papers 30/57/69/WO/4).
19 *The World*, n.d.
20 Lt-Col. J.W.B. Merewether and Sir Frederick Smith, *The Indian Corps in France* (Murray, 1917).
21 Beaverbrook, *Politicians and the War* (Butterworth, 1928; Collins, 1960 edn), p. 183.
22 H.W. Luttman-Johnson (Indian Army retd) to the author.
23 Birkenhead, *'F.E.'*, pp. 257–8.
24 Ibid., p. 258.
25 *Times Literary Supplement* (13 Dec 1917).
26 A.J.P. Taylor, *Beaverbrook* (Hamish Hamilton, 1972), Penguin edn, p. 125.
27 F.E. to Margaret, 15 Oct 1914, in Birkenhead, *'F.E.'*, p. 263.

28 F.E. to Margaret, 2 Nov 1914, in ibid., p. 267.
29 F.E. to Margaret, 21 Nov 1914, in ibid., p. 269.
30 F.E. to Margaret, 25 Nov 1914, in ibid., p. 270.
31 F.E. to Margaret, 1 Nov 1914, in ibid., p. 266.
32 F.E. to Margaret, 2 Nov 1914, in ibid.
33 F.E. to Margaret, 11 Nov 1914, in ibid., p. 268.
34 F.E. to Margaret, 23 Oct 1914, in ibid., p. 266.
35 Martin Gilbert, *Winston S. Churchill, 1914–1916* (Heinemann, 1971), pp. 237–8.
36 Gilbert, *Churchill*, Companion Vol. iii, pp. 400–1.
37 F.E. to Margaret, 29 Dec 1914, in Birkenhead, *'F.E.'*, p. 271.
38 Neil Primrose to Margaret, 18 Oct 1914, in ibid., pp. 264–5.
39 F.E. to Margaret, 21 Oct 1914, in ibid., p. 265.
40 F.E. to Margaret, 17 Feb 1915, in ibid., p. 272.
41 F.E. to Margaret, 7 Feb 1915, in ibid.
42 F.E. to Margaret, 12 Feb 1915, in ibid.
43 F.E. to Margaret, 3 Nov 1914, in ibid., p. 268.
44 Birkenhead, *'F.E.'*, p. 261.
45 Ibid., p. 262.
46 F.E. to Margaret, 22 Feb 1915, in ibid., p. 273.
47 F.E. to Churchill, 15 Feb 1915, in Gilbert, *Churchill*, Companion Vol. i, pp. 514–15.
48 Churchill to F.E., 7 March 1915, in ibid., pp. 652–3.
49 F.E. to Margaret, 8 March 1915, in Birkenhead, *'F.E.'*, p. 274.
50 *The Times* (17 Oct 1914).
51 Beaverbrook, *Politicians and the War*, p. 118.
52 Austen Chamberlain to F.E., 6 June 1915, in Birkenhead, *'F.E.'*, p 280.
53 Margaret to Aitken, 26 May, 1915 (Beaverbrook papers C/39).
54 House of Commons, 21 July 1915.

15 Law Officer in Wartime:
The Casement Trial, 1916

1 F.E. to Harley, 14 March 1916 (in the possession of Sir Thomas Harley).
2 House of Commons, 21 Oct 1915.
3 Parliamentary Debates, Fifth Ser., vol. 81, p. 478.
4 House of Commons, 23 March 1916.
5 Ibid., 10 July 1917.

6 Birkenhead, *Points of View*, vol. II (Hodder & Stoughton, 1922), p. 28.

7 J.W. Garner, *Prize Law During the World War* (Macmillan, 1927), p. 1.

8 Birkenhead, *Famous Trials* (Hutchinson, 1926), pp. 247–56; Birkenhead, *'F.E.'* (Eyre & Spottiswoode, 1959), pp. 281–3.

9 Sir Frederick Smith, *The Destruction of Merchant Ships under International Law* (Dent, 1917).

10 *Times Literary Supplement* (19 April 1917).

11 *The Times* (23 May 1917).

12 Birkenhead, *Famous Trials*, pp. 207–16.

13 Ibid., pp. 195–206.

14 Sir Basil Thomson, *The Scene Changes* (Collins, 1939), p. 280.

15 H. Montgomery Hyde, *Roger Casement*, Notable British Trials series (William Hodge, 1960), Penguin edn, p. 69.

16 Ibid., pp. 75–6.

17 Birkenhead, *'F.E.'*, pp. 309–10.

18 Ibid., p. 311.

19 *The Trial of Roger Casement*, ed. George H. Knott, Notable British Trials series (William Hodge, 1926) is the full transcript.

20 B.L. Reid, *The Lives of Roger Casement* (Yale, 1976), p. 137.

21 Hyde, *Roger Casement*, p. 71.

22 Ibid., p. 45.

23 Ibid., p. 132.

24 Ibid., p. 133.

25 Birkenhead, *'F.E.'*, p. 314.

26 Hyde, *Roger Casement*, p. 151.

27 Birkenhead, *Famous Trials*, p. 244.

28 Hyde, *Roger Casement*, p. 144.

29 Ibid., pp. 150–1.

30 Ibid., pp. 134–40; Brian Inglis, *Roger Casement* (Hodder & Stoughton, 1973), pp. 352–66.

31 Alfred Noyes, *The Accusing Ghost, or Justice for Casement* (Gollancz, 1957).

32 e.g. Brian Inglis in the *Spectator* (6 March 1959).

33 Hobson to Roger McHugh, 2 Nov 1956, in Reid, *Lives of Roger Casement*, p. 409.

34 F.E. to Grey, 29 June 1916, in ibid., p. 410.

35 Ibid., pp. 411, 420.

36 Col. Repington, *The First World War*, vol. I (Constable, 1920), p. 202.

37 *New Statesman* (19 Dec 1959).

38 Reid, *Lives of Roger Casement*, p. 418.

39 Ibid., p. 420.

40 Hyde, *Roger Casement*, p. 75.
41 Birkenhead, *'F.E.'*, pp. 311–12.
42 Hyde, *Roger Casement*, pp. 163–4.
43 Rex Taylor, *Michael Collins* (Hutchinson, 1968), p. 217.
44 Birkenhead, *'F.E.'*, p. 307.

16 The Politics of War – and Peace, 1915–18

1 Birkenhead, *Points of View* (Hodder & Stoughton, 1922), p. 3.
2 F.E. to Lloyd George, 24 Aug 1915 (Lloyd George papers D/16/4/1).
3 Margot Asquith to Kitchener, 18 Oct 1915, in Martin Gilbert, *Winston S. Churchill, 1914–1916* (Heinemann, 1971), Companion Vol. ii, p. 1,225.
4 Birkenhead, *Points of View*, p. 12.
5 Birkenhead, *Contemporary Personalities* (Cassell, 1924), p. 30.
6 Goulding to Churchill, 24 Oct 1915, in Gilbert, *Churchill, 1914–1916*, p. 1,236.
7 Mary Soames, *Clementine Churchill* (Cassell, 1979), Penguin edn, p. 226.
8 Churchill to F.E., 18 Dec 1915, in Gilbert, *Churchill, 1914–1916*, p. 615.
9 F.E. to Churchill, 19 Dec 1915, in Gilbert, *Churchill, 1914–1916*, Companion Vol. ii, pp. 1,336–7.
10 F.E. to Churchill, 11 Jan 1916, in ibid., pp. 1,366–7.
11 F.E. to Churchill, 18 Jan 1916, in ibid., pp. 1,383.
12 Gilbert, *Churchill, 1914–1916*, pp. 694–7.
13 Churchill to Bonar Law, 31 Jan 1916 (Bonar Law papers 53/5/12).
14 Gilbert, *Churchill, 1914–1916*, p. 697.
15 Churchill to Clementine, 1 Feb 1916, in ibid.
16 Churchill to Clementine, n.d., in ibid.
17 F.E. to Churchill, 25 Feb 1916, in Gilbert, ibid., Companion Vol. ii, p. 1,436.
18 Churchill to F.E., 8 April 1916, in ibid., p. 1,481.
19 F.E. to Churchill, 6 April 1916, in ibid.
20 Clementine to Churchill, Jan 1916, in Gilbert, *Churchill, 1914–1916*, p. 693.
21 Col. Repington, *The First World War*, vol. I (Constable, 1920), p. 203.
22 Stanley Salvidge, *Salvidge of Liverpool* (Hodder & Stoughton, 1934), p. 149.
23 Gilbert, *Churchill, 1914–1916*, Companion Vol. ii, p. 1,534.
24 Repington, *The First World War*, p. 360.

25 Salvidge, *Salvidge of Liverpool*, p. 160.
26 Selborne papers, 80/285–9.
27 Beaverbrook, *Politicians and the War* (Butterworth, 1928; Collins, 1960 edn), p. 294.
28 Ibid., pp. 303–4.
29 Ibid., pp. 489, 492.
30 Gwynne to Lloyd George, 8 Dec 1916 (Lloyd George papers F/22/4/1).
31 Maxse to Bonar Law, 7 Dec 1916 (Bonar Law papers 53/4/34).
32 Maxse to Bonar Law, 8 Dec 1916 (ibid., 81/1/20).
33 House of Commons, 19 June 1917.
34 Ibid., 4 July 1917.
35 Martin Pugh, *Electoral Reform in War and Peace, 1906–18* (Routledge & Kegan Paul, 1978), pp. 155–67.
36 F.E. to Beaverbrook, 6 July 1917 (Beaverbrook papers C/39).
37 Beaverbrook to F.E., 7 July 1917, ibid.
38 F.E. to Churchill, 11 Jan 1916, in Gilbert, *Churchill, 1914–16*, Companion Vol. ii, p. 1,366.
39 F.E. to Churchill, 18 Jan 1916, in ibid., p. 1,382.
40 Liverpool, 27 Jan 1917; Cardiff, 1 Feb 1917.
41 Northcliffe to Lloyd George, 11 Dec 1917 (Lloyd George papers F/41/7/34).
42 Aitken to Bonar Law, 17 Aug 1912 (Bonar Law papers 27/1/45).
43 F.E. to Bonar Law, Dec 1917 (ibid., 84/5/3).
44 Montagu to F.E., 4 Jan 1918 (Birkenhead papers).
45 F.E. to Beaverbrook, Dec 1917.
46 Arnold Bennet, *Journals*, vol. II (Cassell, 1932), pp. 207–8.
47 Birkenhead, *Frederick Edwin, Earl of Birkenhead*, vol. II (Thornton Butterworth, 1935), p. 91.
48 Topeka, 17 Jan 1918 (*The Times*, 19 Jan 1918).
49 *The Times* (17 Jan 1918).
50 Birkenhead, *Frederick Edwin*, vol. II, pp. 93–4.
51 Hughes to Beaverbrook, 25 Jan 1918 (Bonar Law papers 82/8/6).
52 Willert to Robinson, 24 Jan 1918 (*The Times* archive, file 1917–18, p. 4).
53 Birkenhead, *Frederick Edwin*, vol. II, p. 93.
54 *The Times* (16 Feb 1918).
55 Repington, *The First World War*, p. 245.
56 Spring-Rice to Reading, 3 Feb 1918 (Spring-Rice papers, CASR 1/55).
57 Sir Frederick Smith, Bart, *My American Visit* (Hutchinson, 1918), p. 222.
58 Ibid., pp. 26–7.

59 Ibid., p. 211.

60 Bennett, *Journals*, vol. II., p. 231.

61 Smith, *My American Visit*, pp. 118–57.

62 R. Pound and C. Harmsworth, *Northcliffe* (Cassell, 1959), p. 610.

63 *Daily Express* (4 Nov 1918).

64 F.E. to Lloyd George, 6 Nov 1918 (Lloyd George papers F/4/7/4); *The Times* (8 Nov 1918).

65 Sir Frederick Smith, *International Law*, ed. C. Phillipson (Dent, 1918).

66 Sir Henry Wilson's diary, 11 Nov 1918, in Gilbert, *Winston S. Churchill, 1917–1922*, Companion Vol. i, p. 412.

67 F.E. to Lloyd George, 27 and 28 Jan 1918 (Lloyd George papers F/4/7/14–15).

68 Salvidge, *Salvidge of Liverpool*, p. 163.

69 Ibid., p. 169.

70 West Derby, 2 Dec 1918.

71 Bournemouth, 30 Nov 1918.

72 *The Times* (10 Dec 1918).

73 Birkenhead, *Frederick Edwin*, Vol. II, p. 109.

74 F.E. to Lloyd George, 29 Dec 1918 (Lloyd George papers F/4/7/6).

75 F.E. to Lloyd George, 6 Nov 1918 (ibid., F/4/7/4).

76 F.E. to Bonar Law, 30 Dec 1918 (Bonar Law papers 84/4/25).

77 Churchill to Lloyd George, 26 Dec 1918 (Lloyd George papers F/8/2/49).

78 Birkenhead, *Law, Life and Letters*, vol. II (Hodder & Stoughton, 1927), p. 245.

79 *Lord Riddell's War Diary, 1914–1918* (Ivor Nicholson & Watson, 1933), p. 338.

80 Birkenhead, *Law, Life and Letters*, p. 247.

81 Birkenhead, *Frederick Edwin*, vol. II, p. 113.

82 Stamfordham to Lloyd George, 8 Jan 1919 (Lloyd George papers F/29/3/1).

83 Lloyd George to Stamfordham, 10 Jan 1919 (ibid., F/29/3/2).

84 Finlay to Haldane, 14 Jan 1919, in R.F.V. Heuston, *The Lives of the Lord Chancellors, 1885–1940* (Oxford University Press, 1964), p. 340.

85 *Evening Standard* (11 Jan 1919).

86 *Morning Post* (11 Jan 1919).

87 *The Times* (11 Jan 1919).

88 *Daily Mail* (11 Jan 1919).

89 Quoted in the *Leamington, Warwick & County Chronicle* (16 Jan 1919).

90 *Manchester Guardian* (11 Jan 1919).

91 *Spectator* (18 Jan 1919).

92 *Nation* (18 Jan 1919).

93 *Law Times* (18 Jan 1919).
94 *The Times* (13 Jan 1919).

17 Lord High Chancellor of England, 1919–22

1 Liverpool Conservative Club, 16 Jan 1919.
2 Gray's Inn dinner, 9 May 1919.
3 Col. Repington, *The First World War*, vol. II (Constable, 1920), p. 504 (6 March 1919).
4 F.W. Hirst, *In the Golden Days* (Muller, 1948), p. 106.
5 F.E. to Wolmer, 20 Nov 1919 (Selborne papers c. 989/117–86).
6 F.E. to Halsbury, 24 Jan 1920, in *The Times* (26 Jan 1920).
7 Birkenhead, *'F.E.'* (Eyre & Spottiswoode, 1959), p. 395.
8 Repington, *The First World War*, pp. 499–500 (24 Feb 1919).
9 Col. Cartwright to the author.
10 Lord Gage to the author.
11 *The Times* (18 March 1924).
12 Birkenhead, *'F.E.'*, p. 331.
13 *Punch* (12 Feb 1919).
14 House of Commons, 4 June 1919.
15 *The Times* (12 Aug 1919).
16 *Law Quarterly Review* (July 1920), p. 203.
17 *The Times* (3 Jan 1921).
18 Laski to Holmes, 17 July 1921, in *The Holmes–Laski Letters*, ed. M.D. Howe, vol. I (Geoffrey Cumberlege, 1953), p. 351.
19 Holmes to Laski, 30 July 1921, in ibid., p. 354.
20 Laski to Holmes, 14 Aug 1921, in ibid., p. 362.
21 Laski to Holmes, 4 Feb 1921, in ibid., p. 403.
22 Laski to Holmes, 11 March 1922, in ibid., p. 410.
23 Laski to Holmes, 5 April 1922, in ibid., p. 415.
24 Holmes to Laski, 22 April 1922, in ibid., p. 417.
25 Laski to Holmes, 13 July 1925, in ibid., p. 764.
26 Birkenhead, 'A Ministry of Justice' and 'Judges and Politics', *Points of View* (Hodder & Stoughton, 1922), vol. I, pp. 92–139, vol. II, pp. 147–91.
27 Lord Mayor's Banquet, 9 Nov 1921.
28 F.E. to Bonar Law, 10 Feb 1921 (Bonar Law papers 100/2/14).
29 Laski to Holmes, 2 March 1930, in *Holmes–Laski Letters*, p. 1,231.
30 Enid Kohler to the author.
31 F.E. to Lloyd George, 9 Feb 1921 (Lloyd George papers F/4/7/19).

32 Lloyd George to F.E., 11 Feb 1921 (ibid., F/4/7/20).

33 F.E. to Lloyd George, 11 Feb 1921 (ibid., F/4/7/21).

34 F.E. to Lloyd George, 22 March 1921 (ibid., F/4/7/23); Guest to Lloyd George, 12 Jan 1921 (ibid., F/22/3/3).

35 Robert Jackson, *The Chief: The Biography of Gordon Hewart, Lord Chief Justice of England, 1922–1940* (Harrap, 1959), pp. 126–46.

36 *The Times* (9 March 1921).

37 *Lord Riddell's Intimate Diary of the Peace Conference and After* (Gollancz, 1933), p. 402 (15 Jan 1922).

38 Birkenhead papers.

39 F.E. to Churchill, 27 March 1919, in *The Times* (29 March 1919).

40 F.E. to Lord Ernle, 17 June 1919 (Lloyd George papers F/15/8/61).

41 *The Times* (14 May 1921).

42 House of Lords, 2 June 1921.

43 *The Times* (15, 16, 17, 18 Dec 1920).

44 House of Lords, 22 June 1922.

45 Scott's memo of an interview with Baldwin, 12 Nov 1924 (Scott papers 119/3/P/BA).

46 *The Times* (15 Dec 1920); Birkenhead, *Points of View*, vol. II, p. 34.

47 Sir Arthur Underhill, *A Concise Explanation of Lord Birkenhead's Act* (1922).

48 House of Commons, 15 May 1922.

49 Gray's Inn dinner, 17 July 1922.

50 B. Abel-Smith and R. Stevens: *Lawyers and the Courts: A Sociological Study of the English Legal System, 1750–1965* (Heinemann, 1967), p. 202.

51 A. Offer, 'The Origins of the New Law of Property Act, 1910–25', *Modern Law Review* (Sept 1977).

52 *Judgements Delivered by Lord Chancellor Birkenhead*, ed. R. Burrows (H.M.S.O., 1923), pp. 92–3.

53 Ibid., p. 287.

54 R.F.V. Heuston, *The Lives of the Lord Chancellors, 1885–1940* (Oxford University Press, 1964), p. 341.

55 *Judgements*, p. 136.

56 Heuston, *Lives of the Lord Chancellors*, p. 401.

57 *Judgements*, p. 137.

58 Ibid., pp. 237, 239.

59 Ibid., p. 73.

60 Ibid., p. 405.

61 Ibid., p. 426.

62 House of Lords, 2 Nov 1921.

63 *Judgements*, p. 221.

64 Heuston, *Lives of the Lord Chancellors*, p. 457.

65 *Judgements*, p. 379.
66 Birkenhead, *'F.E.'*, p. 401.
67 *Judgements*, p. 515.
68 Ibid., p. 392.
69 Ibid., p. 425.
70 House of Lords, 11 Nov 1919.

18 The Lord Chancellor as Cabinet Minister, 1919–22

1 Lloyd George to F.E., 15 March 1919 (Lloyd George papers F/4/7/9).
2 F.E. to Lloyd George, 17 March 1919 (ibid., F/4/7/10).
3 Lloyd George's Foreword to Birkenhead, *Frederick Edwin, Earl of Birkenhead* vol. II, (Thornton Butterworth, 1935), p. 12.
4 H.A.L. Fisher, diary, 31 May 1919.
5 Connaught Rooms, 8 May 1919.
6 House of Lords, 3 April 1919.
7 Connaught Rooms, 22 April 1920.
8 *Weekly Dispatch* (1 Feb 1920).
9 Australia/New Zealand dinner, 19 July 1922.
10 Thomas Jones, *Whitehall Diary*, ed. K. Middlemas, vol. I (Oxford University Press, 1969), p. 234.
11 Viscount Lee of Fareham, *'A Good Innings'*, ed. Alan Clark (John Murray, 1974), p. 91.
12 Churchill's Foreword to Birkenhead, *Frederick Edwin*, vol. I, p. 14.
13 Margaret to Lloyd George, 22 Sept 1920 (Lloyd George papers F/4/7/44).
14 House of Lords, 21 Oct 1920.
15 *The Times* (27 Oct 1920).
16 *Law Journal* (9, 30 Oct 1920).
17 House of Lords, 30 March 1922.
18 Ibid., 11 Dec 1922.
19 Curzon to Bonar Law, 16 Feb 1919 (Davidson papers).
20 *The Times* (3 Jan 1921).
21 House of Lords, 21 Oct 1920.
22 Lee, *'A Good Innings'*, p. 200–1.
23 House of Lords, 17 Nov 1920.
24 Ibid., 19 July 1920.

25 Ibid., 24 March 1920.
26 *The Times* (25 March 1920).
27 Ibid., 15 April 1920.
28 Birkenhead, *Contemporary Personalities* (Cassell, 1924), p. 160.
29 *The Times* (20 April 1920).
30 *Lord Riddell's Intimate Diary of the Peace Conference and After* (Gollancz, 1933), p. 197 (15 May 1920).
31 Cab. 22/23 (19 Nov 1920).
32 H.A.L. Fisher, diary, 11 Feb 1921.
33 Birkenhead, *Law, Life and Letters*, vol. I (Hodder & Stoughton, 1927), pp. 149–96.
34 Birkenhead, 28 April 1919.
35 House of Lords, 18 Feb 1919.
36 *The Times* (16 July 1919).
37 *Daily Mail* (16 July 1919).
38 Sir Oswald Mosley, *My Life* (Nelson, 1968), p. 103.
39 *Weekly Dispatch* (11 Jan 1920), in Birkenhead, *Points of View*, vol. II (Hodder & Stoughton, 1922), pp. 192–7.
40 Younger to Guest, 16 Jan 1920 (Lloyd George papers F/23/1/5).
41 *The Times* (13 Jan 1920).
42 Ibid. (22 Jan 1920).
43 *Weekly Dispatch* (25 Jan 1920), in Birkenhead, *Points of View*, vol. II, pp. 197–207.
44 *Weekly Dispatch* (1 Feb 1920), in ibid., pp. 207–16.
45 Liverpool, 25 Feb 1921.
46 *Lloyd George: A Diary by Frances Stevenson*, ed. A.J.P. Taylor (Hutchinson, 1971), p. 210 (26 April 1921).
47 Beaverbrook, *The Decline and Fall of Lloyd George* (Collins, 1963), p. 260.
48 F.E. to Bonar Law, 5 May 1921 (Bonar Law papers 107/1/22).
49 F.E. to Bonar Law, 9 June 1921 (ibid., 117/1/33).
50 Frances Stevenson, diary, p. 223 (20 June 1921).
51 Ibid., p. 224 (24 June 1921)
52 *Manchester Guardian* (23 June 1921).
53 Frances Stevenson, diary, p. 223 (22 June 1921).
54 Ibid., p. 223 (24 June 1921).
55 F.E. to Lloyd George, 23 June 1921 (Lloyd George papers F/4/7/26).
56 *Frances Stevenson diary*, p. 226 (5 July 1921).
57 *Lord Riddell's Intimate Diary*, pp. 309–10 (2 Aug 1921).
58 F.E. to Lloyd George, 10 Aug 1921 (Lloyd George papers F/4/7/30).

19 Ireland, 1919–22

1 House of Lords, 15 July 1919.
2 C. Townshend, *The British Campaign in Ireland, 1919–1921* (Oxford University Press, 1975), p. 38.
3 *The Times* (24 Nov 1920).
4 House of Lords, 23 Nov 1920.
5 H.A.L. Fisher, diary, 27 July 1920.
6 House of Lords, 6 May 1920.
7 Ibid., 19 May 1920.
8 Ibid., 22 Feb 1921.
9 D.G. Boyce, *Englishmen and Irish Troubles, 1918–1922* (Cape, 1972), p. 94.
10 House of Lords, 23 Nov 1920.
11 Ibid., 21 June 1921.
12 *The Times* (22 June 1921).
13 Ibid. (23 June 1921).
14 Thomas Jones, *Whitehall Diary*, ed. K. Middlemas, vol. III (Oxford University Press, 1971), pp. 80–1 (24 June 1921).
15 Ibid., p. 85 (6 July 1921).
16 Austen Chamberlain, *Down the Years* (Cassell, 1935), pp. 144–5.
17 H.A.L. Fisher, diary, 20 July 1921.
18 House of Lords, 27 July, 10 and 19 Aug 1921.
19 Jones, *Whitehall Diary*, pp. 108–9 (7 Sept 1921).
20 Frank Pakenham (Lord Longford), *Peace by Ordeal* (Cape, 1935; Sidgwick & Jackson, 1972), paperback edn, p. 77.
21 Jones, *Whitehall Diary*, p. 151 (29 Oct 1921).
22 Pakenham, *Peace by Ordeal*, pp. 106–7.
23 Rex Taylor, *Michael Collins* (Hutchinson, 1958; New English Library, 1970), paperback edn, p. 122.
24 Ibid., p. 133.
25 Ibid., p. 140.
26 Jones, *Whitehall Diary*, pp. 143–4 (24 Oct 1921).
27 Pakenham, *Peace by Ordeal*, p. 148.
28 Ibid., pp. 196–7.
29 Speech at a presentation to James Craig on his leaving the House of Commons, 3 Aug 1921.
30 Jones, *Whitehall Diary*, p. 146 (26 Oct 1921).
31 Ibid., p. 156 (8 Nov 1921).
32 Caxton Hall, 25 Oct 1921.

33 Stanley Salvidge, *Salvidge of Liverpool* (Hodder & Stoughton, 1934), pp. 196–7.
34 Ibid., pp. 202–4.
35 *The Times* (18 Nov 1921).
36 Jones, *Whitehall Diary*, p. 170 (22 Nov 1921).
37 Tunbridge Wells, 26 Nov 1921.
38 Pakenham, *Peace by Ordeal*, p. 233.
39 Taylor, *Michael Collins*, p. 152.
40 Birmingham Town Hall, 6 Dec 1921.
41 House of Lords, 14 Dec 1921.
42 Ibid., 16 Dec 1921.
43 American Luncheon Club, 16 Dec 1921.
44 H.A.L. Fisher, diary, 16 Dec 1921.
45 *The Times* (17 Dec 1921).
46 R.F.V. Heuston, *The Lives of the Lord Chancellors, 1885–1940* (Oxford University Press, 1964), p. 341.
47 H.A.L. Fisher, diary, 20 Dec 1921.
48 *The Times* (29 Aug 1922).
49 Pakenham, *Peace by Ordeal*, p. 221.
50 Ibid., p. 290.
51 Birmingham Conservative Club, 6 Dec 1921.
52 House of Lords, 9 Dec 1925.

20 The Decline and Fall of the Coalition, 1922

1 Ronald McNeill, quoted in Maurice Cowling, *The Impact of Labour, 1920–1924*, (Cambridge University Press, 1971), p. 143.
2 Stanley Salvidge, *Salvidge of Liverpool* (Hodder & Stoughton, 1934), p. 225.
3 Younger to Austen Chamberlain, 24 Dec 1921 (Austen Chamberlain papers 32/2/11).
4 Beaverbrook, *The Decline and Fall of Lloyd George* (Collins, 1963), p. 126.
5 F.E. to Lloyd George, 5 Jan 1922 (Lloyd George papers F/4/7/35).
6 Lloyd George to Austen Chamberlain, 10 Jan 1922 (ibid. F/7/5/3).
7 McCurdy to Lloyd George, 12 Jan 1922 (ibid. F/35/17/1).
8 Guest to Lloyd George, 16 Jan 1922 (ibid. F/22/3/37).
9 Savoy, 1 Feb 1922.
10 Guest to Lloyd George, 1 Feb 1922 (Lloyd George papers F/22/3/40).
11 *The Times* (3 Feb 1922).

12 Junior Constitutional Club, 23 Feb 1922.
13 Montagu to Reading, 23 Feb 1921, in H. Montgomery Hyde, *Lord Reading* (Heinemann, 1967), p. 371.
14 F.E. to Churchill, 17 Nov 1920, in Martin Gilbert, *Winston S. Churchill, 1917–1922* (Heinemann, 1975), pp. 428–9.
15 Austen Chamberlain to Lloyd George, 21 March 1922, in ibid., p. 775.
16 *Lord Riddell's Intimate Diary of the Peace Conference and After* (Gollancz, 1933), p. 368 (4 April 1922).
17 Lloyd George to Frances Stevenson, 4 May 1922, in A.J.P. Taylor (ed.), *My Darling Pussy* (Weidenfeld & Nicolson, 1975), p. 49.
18 A.J. Sylvester, *The Real Lloyd George* (Cassell, 1947), pp. 89–90.
19 Gilbert, *Churchill, 1917–1922*, pp. 782–3.
20 Sassoon to Lloyd George, 28 April 1922 (Lloyd George papers F/45/1/13).
21 Lloyd George to Frances Stevenson, 3 May 1922, in *My Darling Pussy*, p. 48.
22 Sassoon to Lloyd George, 5 May 1922 (Lloyd George papers F/45/1/14).
23 Gilbert, *Churchill, 1917–1922*, pp. 783–4.
24 Milner to Selborne, 6 May 1921 (Selborne papers I/12 f.315).
25 Birkenhead, *Contemporary Personalities* (Cassell, 1924), p. 180.
26 Tom Cullen, *Maundy Gregory, Purveyor of Honours* (Bodley Head, 1974), pp. 133–6.
27 Birkenhead, *'F.E.'* (Eyre & Spottiswoode, 1959), pp. 443–4.
28 House of Lords, 29 June 1922.
29 Cullen, *Maundy Gregory*, p. 116.
30 House of Lords, 17 July 1922.
31 Ibid., 18 July 1922.
32 Sassoon to Lloyd George, 24 March 1922 (Lloyd George papers F/45/1/11).
33 *Lloyd George: A Diary by Frances Stevenson*, ed. A.J.P. Taylor (Hutchinson, 1971), p. 241 (3 Feb 1922).
34 Stephen Roskill, *Hankey: Man of Secrets*, vol. II (Collins, 1972), p. 299.
35 L.S. Amery, *My Political Life*, vol. II (Hutchinson, 1953), pp. 232–3.
36 Hanworth papers, d.432/141–45.
37 F.E. to Lloyd George, enclosed in Chilcott to Lloyd George, 19 Aug 1922 (Lloyd George papers F/4/7/39).
38 Lloyd George to F.E., 20 Aug 1922 (ibid. F/4/7/40).
39 Chilcott memo in F.E. to Lloyd George, 14 Sept 1922 (ibid. F/4/7/41).
40 F.E. to Bonar Law, 9 June 1921 (Bonar Law papers 117/1/33).
41 Cab. 23/31/134–47 (29 Sept 1922).
42 Roskill, *Hankey*, pp. 289–90.

43 Ibid., p. 295.
44 Peel quoted in H.A.L. Fisher, diary, 7 Oct 1922.
45 Viscount Lee of Fareham, *'A Good Innings'*, ed. Alan Clark (John Murray, 1974), p. 229.
46 Roskill, *Hankey*, p. 291; Leonard Mosley, *Curzon* (Longman, 1960), p. 233.
47 H.A.L. Fisher, diary, 4 Oct 1922.
48 Beaverbrook, *Decline and Fall of Lloyd George*, pp. 185, 166.
49 *The Times* (7 Oct 1922).
50 Beaverbrook, *Decline and Fall of Lloyd George*, pp. 183–4.
51 Austen Chamberlain to F.E., 12 Oct 1922 (Chamberlain papers AC/33/2/52).
52 Roskill, *Hankey*, p. 296.
53 Cowling, *Impact of Labour, 1920–1924*, p. 200.
54 Salvidge, *Salvidge of Liverpool*, pp. 239–40.
55 Keith Middlemas and John Barnes, *Baldwin* (Weidenfeld & Nicolson, 1969), pp. 122–4.
56 e.g. *Law Journal* (21 Oct 1922).
57 H.A.L. Fisher, diary, 19 Oct 1922.
58 Roskill, *Hankey*, p. 300.
59 Birkenhead, *Contemporary Personalities*, p. 92.
60 Sir Charles Petrie, *The Life and Letters of the Right Hon. Sir Austen Chamberlain*, vol. II (Cassell, 1940), p. 204.
61 *The Political Diaries of C.P. Scott*, ed. Trevor Wilson (Collins, 1970), p. 430 (23 Oct 1922).
62 Salvidge, *Salvidge of Liverpool*, p. 241.
63 Hanworth papers, d. 432.
64 Stoll Picture House, 4 Nov 1922.
65 *The Times* (24 Oct 1922).
66 Neville Chamberlain, diary, 4 Dec 1927.
67 Colchester, 26 Oct 1922.
68 Glasgow, 28 Oct 1922.
69 Geoffrey Fry to Bonar Law, 4 Nov 1922, in Nourah Waterhouse, *Private and Official* (Cape, 1942), p. 270.
70 Bristol, 2 Nov 1922.
71 Hitchin, 30 Oct 1922.
72 Thomas Jones, *Whitehall Diary*, ed. K. Middlemas, vol. I (Oxford University Press, 1969), p. 241 (9 June 1923).
73 *The Times* (1 Nov 1922).
74 Ibid. (13 Nov 1922).
75 Birmingham, 11 Nov 1922, in *Manchester Guardian* (13 Nov 1922).
76 Petrie, *Life and Letters of Chamberlain*, p. 207.
77 Gilbert, *Churchill, 1917–1922*, p. 880.

21 The Wilderness – and the Way Back, 1922–4

1 House of Lords, 23 Nov 1922.
2 Ibid., 28, 29, 30 Nov, 5, 13 Dec 1922.
3 Ibid., 7 Dec 1922.
4 *The Times* (12 Dec 1922).
5 House of Lords, 11 Dec 1922.
6 Leonard Mosley, *Curzon* (Longman, 1960), pp. 248–9.
7 Alannah Harper.
8 Lloyd George to Frances Stevenson, 25 Jan 1923, in A.J.P. Taylor (ed.), *My Darling Pussy* (Weidenfeld & Nicolson, 1975), pp. 61–2.
9 *Lord Riddell's Intimate Diary of the Peace Conference and After* (Gollancz, 1933), p. 400. Riddell dates this entry 15 Jan, but F.E. did not arrive in Algeciras until 25 Jan.
10 Locker-Lampson to Lloyd George, 17 Feb 1923, from Marseilles (Lloyd George papers G/11/3/1).
11 Viscount Lee of Fareham, *'A Good Innings'*, ed. Alan Clark (John Murray, 1974), p. 236.
12 House of Lords, 21 March 1923.
13 Ibid., 9 May 1923.
14 Ibid., 22 March 1923.
15 Birkenhead, *'F.E.'* (Eyre and Spottiswoode, 1959), p. 480.
16 *Sunday Times* (22 April 1923).
17 Birkenhead, *Contemporary Personalities* (Cassell, 1924), p. 68.
18 Stanley Salvidge, *Salvidge of Liverpool* (Hodder & Stoughton, 1934), p. 252.
19 Worthington-Evans to Austen Chamberlain, 22 May 1923 (Chamberlain papers AC/35/2/2).
20 Austen Chamberlain to F.E., 31 May 1923 (ibid. AC/35/2/18).
21 Neville Chamberlain to Ida Chamberlain, 26 May 1923 (ibid. NC 18/1/396).
22 F.E. to Austen Chamberlain, 1 June 1923 (ibid., AC/35/2/19).
23 F.E. to Austen Chamberlain, 11 July 1923 (ibid., AC/35/2/23).
24 F.E. to Austen Chamberlain, 15 Aug 1923 (ibid. AC/35/2/24).
25 House of Lords, 12 July, 2 Aug 1923.
26 Birkenhead papers.
27 Williamstown, Massachusetts, 24 Aug 1923, in Birkenhead, *America Revisited* (Cassell, 1924), pp. 103–32.
28 *The Times* (29 Aug 1923).
29 Montreal, 3 Sept 1923, in Birkenhead, *America Revisited*, pp. 159–73.

30 Glasgow, 7 Nov 1923, ibid., pp. 177–201.
31 Ibid., p. xix.
32 House of Commons, 6 May 1924.
33 Aberdeen, 16 Nov 1928.
34 Minneapolis, 29 Aug 1923, in Birkenhead, *America Revisited*, pp. 135–56.
35 Robert Rhodes James (ed.), *Memoirs of a Conservative: J.C.C. Davidson's Memoirs and Papers, 1910–1937* (Weidenfeld & Nicolson, 1969), pp. 184–5.
36 Beaverbrook to Rothermere, 14 Nov 1923, in Martin Gilbert, *Winston S. Churchill, 1922–1939* (Heinemann, 1976), Companion Vol. i, p. 67.
37 Baldwin to F.E., 9 Nov 1923 (*The Times*, 17 Nov 1923).
38 F.E. to Baldwin, 9 Nov 1923 (ibid.).
39 Austen Chamberlain memo, 12 Nov 1923 (Chamberlain papers AC/35/3/216).
40 Maurice Cowling, *The Impact of Labour* (Cambridge University Press, 1971), p. 323.
41 Amery, diary, 10 Nov 1923, in *The Leo Amery Diaries*, ed. John Barnes and David Nicholson, vol. I (Hutchinson, 1981), pp. 355–6.
42 Cecil to Baldwin, 14 Nov 1923 (Baldwin papers 42 f.126–7).
43 McNeill to Baldwin, 12 Nov 1923 (ibid. 42 f.133–4).
44 Neville Chamberlain, diary, 18 Nov 1923.
45 Cowling, *The Impact of Labour*, p. 243.
46 Davidson and Sidney Herbert to Baldwin, 14 Nov 1923 (Baldwin papers 42 f.130–1).
47 *The Times* (16 Nov 1923).
48 Constitutional Club, 20 Nov 1923.
49 Blackpool, 5 Dec 1923.
50 *The Times* (4 May 1923).
51 Newcastle, 1 Dec 1923.
52 Manchester, 3 Dec 1923.
53 Ashton-under-Lyne, 29 Nov 1923.
54 Liverpool, 30 Nov 1923.
55 Birkenhead, *Contemporary Personalities* (Cassell, 1924), pp. 131, 183.
56 Ibid., p. 41.
57 Randolph S. Churchill, *Lord Derby, 'King of Lancashire'* (Heinemann, 1959), pp. 553–4.
58 Balfour to F.E., 11 Dec 1923, in ibid., pp. 554–5.
59 F.W. Hirst, *In the Golden Days* (Muller, 1948), p. 106.
60 *Sunday Times* (16 Dec 1923).
61 House of Commons, 17 Jan 1924.
62 House of Lords, 15 Jan 1924.

63 Birkenhead, *Contemporary Personalities*, pp. 43–52.
64 K. Middlemas and J. Barnes, *Baldwin* (Weidenfeld & Nicolson, 1969), p. 261.
65 Salisbury to Baldwin, 26 Jan 1924 (Baldwin papers 159 f. 260).
66 Cecil to Baldwin, 1 Feb 1924 (ibid. 35 f.203–6).
67 Ormsby-Gore to Baldwin, 29 Jan 1924 (ibid. 42 f.182–7).
68 Austen Chamberlain memo (Chamberlain papers AC/35/4/5).
69 Amery, diary, 23 Jan 1924, in *Amery Diaries*, vol. I, p. 365.
70 Churchill, *Lord Derby*, p. 565.
71 L.S. Amery, *My Political Life*, vol. II (Hutchinson, 1955), pp. 289–90.
72 Amery, diary, 7 Feb 1924, in *Amery Diaries*, vol. I, p. 368.
73 John Ramsden, *The Age of Balfour and Baldwin, 1902–1940* (Longman, 1978), p. 190.
74 *The Times* (18 March 1924).
75 *Sunday Times* (3 March 1924); Birkenhead, *Contemporary Personalities*, pp. 113–23.
76 *The Times* (6 Aug 1924).
77 F.E. to Beaverbrook, 8 Sept 1924 (Beaverbrook papers C/40).
78 Birkenhead, *Contemporary Personalities*, pp. 309–17.
79 Ibid., dedication.
80 House of Lords, 10 July 1924.
81 Liverpool, 30 April 1924.
82 *The Times* (26 May 1924).
83 Gray's Inn, 24 July 1924, in *The Speeches of Lord Birkenhead* (Cassell, 1929), pp. 218–24.
84 Birkenhead, *Contemporary Personalities*, p. 192.
85 Ibid., p. 238.
86 Carlisle, 27 Sept 1924.
87 *The Times* (2 Oct 1924).
88 Ibid. (8 Oct 1924).
89 Thomas Jones, *Whitehall Diary*, ed. K. Middlemas, vol. I (Oxford University Press, 1969), p. 294 (7 Oct 1924).
90 Swansea, 15 Oct 1924.
91 Liverpool, 22 Oct 1924.
92 Glasgow, 23 Oct 1924.
93 London, 17 Oct 1924.
94 Epping, 21 Oct 1924.
95 Aberdeen, 24 Oct 1924.
96 Brentford, 25 Oct 1924.
97 Portsmouth, 28 Oct 1924.
98 F.E. to 'My dear Friend' (Houston), 31 Oct 1924 (Baldwin papers 159 f.215).

22 Cabinet Minister Again:
The Indian Summer of Lord Birkenhead

1 Baldwin to F.E., 20 May 1924 (Baldwin papers 56 f.3).
2 Amery to Baldwin, 9 Nov 1923 (ibid. 42 f.112).
3 Thomas Jones, *Whitehall Diary*, ed. K. Middlemas, vol. I (Oxford University Press, 1969), p. 302 (4 Nov 1924).
4 Birkenhead, *Contemporary Personalities* (Cassell, 1924), p. 69.
5 Jones, *Whitehall Diary*, vol. I, p. 304 (8 Nov 1924).
6 Martin Gilbert, *Winston S. Churchill, 1922–1939* (Heinemann, 1976), p. 60.
7 F.E. to Reading, 29 Jan 1925 (India Office – Secretary of State/ Viceroy correspondence).
8 Neville Chamberlain, diary, 7 Oct 1927.
9 F.E. to Houston, 31 Oct 1924 (Baldwin papers 159 f.215).
10 F.E. to Baldwin, 16 Oct 1928, in *The Times* (19 Oct 1928).
11 Jones, *Whitehall Diary*, vol. I, p. 303 (8 Nov 1924).
12 Birkenhead papers.
13 F.E. to Irwin, 24 June 1926 (India Office – Secretary of State/ Viceroy correspondence).
14 Constitutional Club, 3 Nov 1924.
15 F.E. to Reading, 21 Jan 1925 (India Office – Secretary of State/ Viceroy correspondence).
16 F.E. to Reading, 19 Nov 1925 (ibid.).
17 Churchill to Clementine, 15 March 1925, in Gilbert, *Churchill, 1922–1939*, p. 104.
18 Amery, diary, 15 July 1925, in *The Leo Amery Diaries*, ed. John Barnes and David Nicholson, vol. I (Hutchinson, 1981), p. 416.
19 Harold Laski to Oliver Wendell Holmes, 18 July 1927, in *Holmes– Laski Letters*, ed. M.D. Howe, vol. II (Geoffrey Cumberlege, 1953), p. 963.
20 Laski to Holmes, 3 July 1926, in ibid., p. 855.
21 Edinburgh, 5 Dec 1924, in *The Speeches of Lord Birkenhead* (Cassell, 1929), pp. 225–40.
22 John Buchan, *Memory Hold-the-Door* (Hodder & Stoughton, 1940), p. 234.
23 Lady Eleanor Smith, *Life's a Circus* (Longman, Green, 1939), p. 6.
24 Sir Oswald Mosley, *My Life* (Nelson, 1968), p. 31.

25 *'Chips': The Diaries of Sir Henry Channon*, ed. Robert Rhodes James (Weidenfeld & Nicolson, 1967), p. 17 (1 May 1934).
26 Evelyn to Laura Waugh, 24 Oct 1944, in *The Letters of Evelyn Waugh*, ed. Mark Amory (Weidenfeld & Nicolson, 1980), p. 191.
27 Family information.
28 F.E. to Beaverbrook, 9 Aug 1927 (F.E.–Beaverbrook correspondence).
29 F.E. to Beaverbrook, 3 Oct 1928 (Beaverbrook papers C/41).
30 *Sunday Express* (23 Dec 1928); reprinted in Beaverbrook, *Courage: The Story of Sir James Dunn* (Collins, 1961), pp. 108–9.
31 Alannah Harper.
32 Frances Stevenson to Lloyd George, 23 Aug 1923, in A.J.P. Taylor (ed.), *My Darling Pussy* (Weidenfeld & Nicolson, 1975), p. 69.
33 A.J.P. Taylor, *Beaverbrook* (Hamish Hamilton, 1972), Penguin edn, p. 300.
34 Lord Gage.
35 F.E. to Beaverbrook, 20 Dec 1928 (Beaverbrook papers C/41).
36 Beaverbrook to F.E., 22 Dec 1928 (ibid.).
37 F.E. to Beaverbrook, 22 Dec 1928 (ibid.).
38 Beaverbrook, *Courage*, p. 112.
39 Taylor, *Beaverbrook*, p. 316.
40 *Daily Mail* (23 Nov 1926).
41 Ibid. (24, 25 Nov 1926).
42 Ibid. (29 Nov 1926).
43 Ibid. (30 Nov 1926).
44 *The Journals of Arnold Bennett*, vol. III (Cassell, 1932), p. 173.
45 *Arnold Bennett's Letters to his Nephew*, ed. F. Swinnerton (Heinemann, 1936), p. 174.
46 *Journals of Arnold Bennett*, vol. III, p. 175.
47 Other Club Betting Book: see also Colin R. Coote, *The Other Club* (Sidgwick & Jackson 1971), pp. 55–6.
48 *Journals of Arnold Bennett*, vol. III, p. 243.
49 F.E. to Beaverbrook, 1 May 1919 (F.E.–Beaverbrook correspondence).
50 F.E. to Beaverbrook, 26 April 1917 (ibid.).
51 F.E. to Beaverbrook, 6 March 1917 (Beaverbrook papers C/39).
52 F.E. to Beaverbrook, 25 May 1926 (F.E.–Beaverbrook correspondence).
53 F.E. to Beaverbrook, 12 Aug 1919 (ibid.).
54 F.E. to Beaverbrook, 8 July 1927 (ibid.).
55 F.E. to Beaverbrook, 20 April 1918 (ibid.).

56 F.E. to Beaverbrook, 30 Aug 1923 (Beaverbrook papers C/40).
57 F.E. to Beaverbrook, 24 Jan 1930 (F.E.–Beaverbrook correspondence).
58 F.E. to Beaverbrook, 1 Oct 1927 (Beaverbrook papers C/41).
59 F.E. to Beaverbrook, 10 April 1927 (F.E.–Beaverbrook correspondence).
60 F.E. to Beaverbrook, 1 May 1928 (ibid.).
61 Stanley Salvidge, *Salvidge of Liverpool* (Hodder & Stoughton, 1934), pp. 299–300.
62 Maurice Bowra, *Memories, 1898–1939* (Weidenfeld & Nicolson, 1966), pp. 140–1.
63 Longford, *Kennedy* (Weidenfeld & Nicolson, 1976), pp. 63–4.
64 Bowra, *Memories*, pp. 138–9.
65 Sir John Masterman, *On the Chariot Wheel* (Oxford University Press, 1975), pp. 166–7.
66 Lady Cynthia Asquith, *Diaries, 1915–1918* (Hutchinson, 1968), p. 300 (4 May 1917).
67 Bechhofer Roberts, *Sir John Simon* (Robert Hale, 1938), p. 232.
68 Birkenhead, *'F.E.'* (Eyre & Spottiswoode, 1959), p. 475.
69 Ibid., p. 487.
70 Lord Killanin and John Rodda, *The Olympic Games* (MacDonald & Janes, 1976), p. 77.
71 British Olympic Association, *Official Report of the IXth Olympiad, Amsterdam, 1928.*
72 Sir Herbert Marchant.
73 Ivor Thomas, *Our Lord Birkenhead: An Oxford Appreciation* (Putnam, 1930), pp. 127–30.
74 Ibid., pp. 132–4.
75 Ibid., pp. 73–4; H. Justin Evans to the author.
76 Lord Selwyn-Lloyd.
77 F.E. to Warden Wells, 27 Jan 1927 (Wadham College archive).
78 Sandars to Maxse, 23 March 1925 (Maxse papers 479/362).
79 Amery, diary, 2 May 1925, in *Amery Diaries*, vol. I, p. 409.
80 *The Times* (19 May 1925).
81 Ibid. (24 June 1925).
82 Sandars to Maxse, 7 June 1925 (Maxse papers 479/386).
83 F.E. to Irwin, 3 May 1928 (India Office – Secretary of State/ Viceroy correspondence).
84 F.E. to Baldwin, 8 May 1930 (Baldwin papers 165 f.22–3).
85 Buchan, *Memory Hold-the-Door*, p. 236.
86 Thomas, *Our Lord Birkenhead*, p. 66.
87 Enid Kohler to the author.
88 Lord Boothby.

89 Bowra, *Memories*, p. 139.
90 Mr J.W. Denham.
91 Churchill to Clementine, 9 Feb 1921, in Martin Gilbert, *Winston S. Churchill, 1917–22* (Heinemann, 1975), p. 525.
92 Churchill to Clementine, 26 Feb 1921, in ibid., p. 539.
93 Taylor, *Beaverbrook*, p. 260.
94 Amery, diary, 8 Jan 1922, in *Amery Diaries*, vol. I, p. 276.
95 Frances Stevenson, diary, 3 Feb 1922, in *Lloyd George: A Diary by Frances Stevenson*, ed. A.J.P. Taylor (Hutchinson, 1971), p. 241.
96 Gilbert, *Churchill, 1917–1922*, p. 880.
97 Neville Chamberlain, diary, Dec 1926.
98 Amery, diary, 7 May 1928, in *Amery Diaries*, vol. I, p. 543.
99 Neville Chamberlain, diary, 1 May 1925.
100 Churchill to Clementine, 10 Feb 1926, in Gilbert, *Churchill, 1922–1939*, Companion Vol. i, p. 652.
101 Neville Chamberlain, diary, 28 March 1928.
102 Robert Rhodes James (ed.), *Memoirs of a Conservative: J.C.C. Davidson's Memoirs and Papers, 1910–1937* (Weidenfeld & Nicolson, 1969), p. 202.
103 Amery, diary, 20 July 1927, in *Amery Diaries*, vol. I, p. 518.
104 Mr Fletcher Rogers.
105 Mosley, *My Life*, pp. 103–4.
106 The Earl of Birkenhead, *America Revisited* (Cassell, 1924), p. 5.
107 *Who's Who, 1931.*
108 Lady Byron to Baldwin, Nov 1924 (Baldwin papers 159 f.215).
109 Lady Houston to Baldwin, Jan 1925 (ibid. 159 f.213–225).
110 Margaret to Beaverbrook, April 1926 (Beaverbrook papers C/40).
111 F.E. to Churchill, 18 May 1925, in Gilbert, *Churchill, 1922–1939*, Companion Vol. i, p. 487.
112 House of Commons, 9, 11 June 1925.
113 F.E. to Baldwin, 16 June 1925 (Baldwin papers 56 f.8–11).
114 F.S. Jackson memo, n.d., in Rhodes James, *Memoirs of a Conservative*, p. 277.
115 Ibid.
116 *The Times* (14 Dec 1926).
117 *Evening Standard* (9 Dec 1926).
118 Birkenhead, *Fourteen English Judges* (Cassell, 1926), pp. viii–ix.
119 *Times Literary Supplement* (21 Jan 1925).
120 *The Times* (14 Jan 1925).
121 *Times Literary Supplement* (30 Sept 1926).
122 *Daily Graphic* (10 Sept 1926).
123 *The Times* (26 Oct 1928).
124 Ibid. (30 Sept 1927).

125 Laski to Holmes, 21 Jan 1928, in *The Holmes–Laski Letters*, ed. M.A. Howe (Geoffrey Cumberlege, 1953), p. 1,018.
126 Birkenhead (ed.), *The Hundred Best English Essays* (Cassell, 1929), p. v.
127 Quoted on cover of the paperback edition.
128 Birkenhead, *Turning Points in History* (Hutchinson, 1930), paperback edn, pp. 251–2.
129 Birkenhead, *Last Essays* (Cassell, 1930), p. 12.
130 *The Times* (25 Nov 1930).

23 Secretary of State for India, 1924–8

1 *The Times* (7 Nov 1924).
2 Ibid. (8 Nov 1924).
3 Birkenhead, *'F.E.'* (Eyre & Spottiswoode, 1959), p. 505.
4 *Morning Post* (7 Nov 1924).
5 Lord Gage.
6 *The Statesman* (20 Sept 1928), quoted in *The Times* (21 Sept 1928).
7 *Hindustan Review*, vol. 53 (1929), p. 425ff.
8 Irwin to Baldwin, 28 March 1929, in Martin Gilbert, *Winston S. Churchill, 1922–1939* (Heinemann, 1976), p. 322.
9 F.E. to Reading, 13 Nov 1924 (India Office – Secretary of State/Viceroy correspondence).
10 F.E. to Reading, 29 Jan 1925 (ibid.).
11 F.E. to Reading, 5 March 1925 (ibid.).
12 F.E. to Reading, 20 Nov 1925 (ibid.).
13 F.E. to Reading, 21 Jan 1925 (ibid. This letter was not printed).
14 F.E. to Reading, 4 Dec 1924 (ibid.).
15 F.E. to Reading, 22 Jan 1925 (ibid.).
16 Assam dinner, Connaught Rooms, 25 May 1925.
17 Central Asian Society dinner, Hotel Victoria, 30 June 1925.
18 F.E. to Reading, 29 Jan 1925 (India Office).
19 F.E. to Reading, 10 March 1925 (ibid.).
20 House of Lords, 1 April 1925.
21 F.E. to Reading, 12 Feb 1925 (India Office).
22 Glasgow University, 16 May 1925.
23 F.E. to Irwin, 30 Sept 1926 (India Office).
24 P.J. Grigg, *Prejudice and Judgement* (Cape, 1948), p. 211.
25 F.E. to Reading, 22 Oct 1925 (India Office).

26 F.E. to Reading, 4 March 1926 (ibid.).

27 F.E. telegram to Reading, 19 Nov 1925 (India Office, Telegram 262).

28 F.E. to Irwin, 23 Sept 1926 (India Office).

29 F.E. to Beaverbrook, 10 May 1928 (F.E.–Beaverbrook correspondence).

30 F.E. to Irwin, 22 April 1926 (India Office).

31 F.E. to Irwin, 23 Sept 1926 (ibid.).

32 F.E. to Irwin, 5 Nov 1926 (ibid.).

33 F.E. to Reading, 26 Feb 1926 (ibid.).

34 Lytton to Baldwin, 13 July 1925 (Baldwin papers 102 f.34–5).

35 House of Lords, 7 July 1925.

36 F.E. to Reading, 10 Dec 1925 (India Office).

37 Reading to F.E., 31 Dec 1925 (ibid.).

38 F.E. to Reading, 20 Jan 1926 (ibid.).

39 Viscount Lee of Fareham, *'A Good Innings'*, ed. Alan Clark (John Murray, 1974), p. 259; Neville Chamberlain, diary, 1 May 1925, citing Sir Basil Blackett to Baldwin.

40 Neville Chamberlain, diary, 1 May 1925.

41 F.E. to Reading, 29 Oct 1925 (India Office).

42 F.E. to Reading, 5 Nov 1925 (ibid.).

43 F.E. to Reading, 19 Nov 1925 (ibid.).

44 F.E. to Irwin, 3 June 1926 (ibid.).

45 F.E. to Irwin, 8 July 1926 (ibid.).

46 House of Lords, 28 July 1926.

47 F.E. to Irwin, 29 July 1926 (India Office).

48 Irwin to F.E., 19 Aug 1926 (ibid.).

49 Robert Rhodes James (ed.), *Memoirs of a Conservative: J.C.C. Davidson's Memoirs and Papers, 1910–1937* (Weidenfeld & Nicolson, 1969), p. 201.

50 F.E. to Irwin, 8 July 1926 (India Office).

51 F.E. to Irwin, 21 July 1926 (ibid.).

52 Imperial Conference, 26 Oct 1926 (ibid.).

53 F.E. to Irwin, 9 Dec 1926 (ibid.).

54 Earl of Halifax, *Fulness of Days* (Collins, 1957), p. 114.

55 F.E. to Irwin, 29 July 1926 (India Office).

56 Irwin to F.E., 19 Aug 1926 (ibid.).

57 F.E. to Irwin, 23 Sept 1926 (ibid.).

58 F.E. to Irwin, 23 March 1927 (ibid.).

59 F.E. to Irwin, 27 Jan 1927 (ibid.).

60 F.E. to Irwin, 28 April 1928 (ibid.).

61 F.E. to Irwin, 24 Feb 1927 (ibid.).

62 F.E. to Irwin, 16 June 1927 (ibid.).

63 Amery, diary, 5 March 1926, in *The Leo Amery Diaries*, vol. I, ed. John Barnes and David Nicholson (Hutchinson, 1981), p. 445.

64 Bechhofer Roberts, *Sir John Simon*, (Robert Hale, 1938), pp. 232–3.

65 F.E. to Irwin, 18 Aug 1927 (India Office).

66 Liverpool, 13 May 1929.

67 F.E. to Irwin, 3 Nov 1927 (India Office).

68 Irwin to F.E., 5 Oct 1927 (ibid.).

69 F.E. to Irwin, 8 Nov 1927 (ibid.).

70 House of Lords, 24 Nov 1927.

71 *The Times* (28 Nov 1927).

72 F.E. to Irwin, 5 Jan 1928 (India Office).

73 F.E. to Irwin, 26 April 1928 (ibid.).

74 F.E. to Irwin, 3 May 1928 (ibid.).

75 F.E. to Irwin, 24 May 1928 (ibid.).

76 Irwin to F.E., 28 June 1928 (ibid.).

77 F.E. to Irwin, 19 July 1928 (ibid.).

78 Lord Birkenhead, *Halifax* (Hamish Hamilton, 1965), p. 207.

79 F.E. to Irwin, 26 July 1928 (India Office).

80 F.E. to Irwin, 7 June 1928 (ibid.).

81 F.E. to Irwin, 15 Dec 1927 (ibid.).

82 F.E. to Scott, 3 July 1928 (Scott papers MSS 119/3/S/IN).

83 F.E. to Irwin, 18 Sept 1928 (India Office).

84 Birkenhead, *The World in 2030* (Hodder & Stoughton, 1930), p. 155.

24 The General Strike, 1926

1 Amery, diary, 27 Feb 1925, in *The Leo Amery Diaries*, vol. I, ed. John Barnes and David Nicholson (Hutchinson, 1981), p. 398.

2 Earl of Halifax, *Fulness of Days* (Collins, 1957), p. 103.

3 G.M. Young, *Stanley Baldwin* (Hart Davis, 1952), p. 91.

4 House of Commons, 6 March 1925.

5 Young, *Baldwin*, p. 94.

6 Metropole Hotel, 4 March 1925.

7 Savoy Hotel, 17 Feb 1925.

8 Cannon Street Hotel, 3 March 1925.

9 e.g. Loughborough, 27 June 1925.

10 Birkenhead, *Last Essays* (Cassell, 1930), p. 168.

11 F.E. to Reading, 8 Oct 1925 (India Office – Secretary of State/ Viceroy correspondence).

12 Dumfries, 4 Nov 1925.

13 Thomas Jones, *Whitehall Diary*, vol. II, ed. K. Middlemas (Oxford University Press, 1969), p. 15 (14 April 1926).

14 Ibid., p. 17 (21 April 1926).

15 Margaret Morris, *The General Strike* (Penguin, 1976), p. 220.

16 Jones, *Whitehall Diary*, p. 25 (1 May 1926).

17 F.E. memo, 6 May 1926, in Jones, *Whitehall Diary*, pp. 34–6.

18 G.A. Phillips, *The General Strike* (Weidenfeld & Nicolson, 1976), p. 119.

19 Jones, *Whitehall Diary*, pp. 28–9 (2 May 1926).

20 Sir Horace Wilson memo, 2 May 1926, in Jones, *Whitehall Diary*, p. 32.

21 Amery, diary, 2 May 1926, in *Amery Diaries*, vol. I, p. 451.

22 Neville Chamberlain, diary, May 1926.

23 Birkenhead, *Last Essays*, p. 173.

24 Robert Rhodes James (ed.), *Memoirs of a Conservative: J.C.C. Davidson's Memoirs and Papers, 1910–1937* (Weidenfeld & Nicolson, 1969), p. 243. (Davidson to Irwin, 14 June 1926.)

25 House of Lords, 5 May 1926.

26 F.E. to Irwin, 20 May 1926 (India Office).

27 F.E. to Irwin, 10 June 1926 (ibid.).

28 F.E. to Irwin, 24 June 1926 (ibid.).

29 Hotel Victoria, 22 June; Barnsley, 28 Aug; House of Lords, 25 Oct; Carlton Hotel, 3 Nov 1926.

30 F.E. to Irwin, 16 Aug 1926 (India Office).

31 Martin Gilbert, *Winston S. Churchill, 1922–1939* (Heinemann, 1976), p. 203.

32 F.E. to Irwin, 23 Sept 1926 (India Office).

33 Jones, *Whitehall Diary*, pp. 84–5 (22 Sept 1926).

34 Ibid., pp. 89–90 (28 Sept 1926); F.E. to Baldwin, 23 Sept 1926 (Baldwin papers 180 f.5–6),

35 F.E. to Irwin, 30 Sept 1926 (India Office).

36 F.E. to Irwin, 7 Oct 1926 (ibid.).

37 F.E. to Irwin, 25 Nov 1926 (ibid.).

38 F.E. to Irwin, 2 Dec 1926 (ibid.).

39 F.E. to Irwin, 29 July 1926 (ibid.).

40 House of Lords, 25 Oct 1926.

41 e.g. Luton, 19 June 1926.

42 Hotel Cecil, 22 June 1926, in *Amery Diaries*, vol. I, p. 458.

43 A. Anderson, 'The Labour Laws and the Cabinet Legislative Committee of 1926–7', *Bulletin of the Society for the Study of Labour History* (1973).

44 F.E. to Irwin, 25 Nov 1926 (India Office).

45 Birkenhead, 26 Feb 1927.

46 F.E. to Irwin, 3 Feb 1927 (India Office).
47 Manchester, 30 April 1927.
48 Birkenhead, *Last Essays*, pp. 175–87.
49 Edinburgh University, 3 Nov 1925.
50 Cambridge, 8 April 1927.
51 Southampton, 6 May 1927.
52 Dulwich, 16 March 1927.
53 Amery, diary, 16 Feb 1927, in *Amery Diaries*, vol. I, pp. 496–7.
54 F.E. to Irwin, 17 Feb 1927 (India Office).
55 F.E. to Reading, 22 Oct 1925 (ibid.).
56 Dr Christopher Andrew.
57 F.E. to Irwin, 26 May 1927 (India Office).
58 Birkenhead, *Last Essays*, pp. 140–63.

25 The Baldwin Cabinet, 1926–8

1 F.E. to Reading, 4 March 1926 (India Office – Secretary of State/ Viceroy correspondence).
2 F.E. to Irwin, 3 June 1926 (ibid.).
3 Northampton, 6 Dec 1926.
4 *The Times* (25, 30 June, 12 July 1927).
5 Portsmouth, 7 March 1927.
6 Bolton Abbey, 16 July 1927.
7 Chesterfield, 28 March 1928.
8 F.E. to Irwin, 3 Feb 1927 (India Office).
9 Colchester, 29 Sept 1927; Bolton Abbey, 16 July 1927.
10 F.E. to Irwin, 5 April 1928 (India Office).
11 Robert Rhodes James (ed.), *Memoirs of a Conservative: J.C.C. Davidson's Memoirs and Papers, 1910–1937* (Weidenfeld & Nicolson, 1969), pp. 202–3.
12 F.E. to Irwin, 21 Oct 1926 (India Office).
13 F.E. to Irwin, 4 Nov 1926 (ibid.).
14 F.E. to Irwin, 18 Nov 1926 (ibid.).
15 *The Leo Amery Diaries*, vol. I, ed. John Barnes and David Nicholson (Hutchinson, 1981), pp. 469–70.
16 Amery, diary, 17 Nov 1926, in ibid., p. 481.
17 House of Lords, 2 April 1925.
18 Ibid., 21 May 1925.
19 Ibid., 24 June 1926.
20 F.E. to Irwin, 25 Nov 1925 (India Office).

21 Amery, diary, 14 Dec 1926, in *Amery Diaries*, vol. I, p. 486.
22 House of Lords, 22 June 1927.
23 F.E. to Irwin, 23 June 1927 (India Office).
24 See Lord Hailsham, *The Dilemma of Democracy* (Collins, 1978), pp. 149–54.
25 House of Commons, 6 July 1927.
26 Stanley Salvidge, *Salvidge of Liverpool* (Hodder & Stoughton, 1934), pp. 299–300.
27 Ibid., p. 303.
28 *The Times* (20 Dec 1927).
29 R.F.V. Heuston, *The Lives of the Lord Chancellors, 1885–1940* (Oxford University Press, 1964), p. 582.
30 F.E. to Irwin, 3 Oct 1928.
31 F.E. to Irwin, 11 Oct 1928.
32 *The Times* (9 Oct 1928).
33 Neville Chamberlain to his wife, 9 Oct 1928 (Chamberlain papers NC 1/26/390).
34 Amery, diary, 22 Nov 1925, in *Amery Diaries*, vol. I, pp. 426–7.
35 F.E. to Baldwin, 13 April 1927 (Baldwin papers 162 f.31–4).
36 Neville Chamberlain, diary, 30 March 1928.
37 Ibid., 28 March 1928.
38 F.E. to Irwin, 29 March 1928 (India Office).
39 Garvin to Astor, 17 Oct 1928 (Astor papers).
40 Baldwin to F.E., 10 Oct 1928, in Birkenhead, *'F.E.'* (Eyre & Spottiswoode, 1959), p. 545.
41 F.E. to Baldwin, 16 Oct 1928, in *The Times* (19 Oct 1928).
42 Baldwin to F.E., 17 Oct 1928, ibid.
43 Thomas Jones, *Whitehall Diary*, ed. K. Middlemas, vol. II (Oxford University Press, 1969), p. 143 (1 Oct 1928).
44 Amery, diary, 17 Oct 1928, in *Amery Diaries*, vol. I, p. 568.
45 Stephen Roskill, *Hankey, Man of Secrets*, vol. II (Collins, 1972), p. 472.
46 F.E. to Jones, 17 Oct 1928, in Jones, *Whitehall Diary*, p. 150.
47 Ramsay MacDonald to F.E., 22 Oct 1928, in Birkenhead, *'F.E.'*, p. 547.
48 *The Times* (15 Oct 1928).
49 Hilton Young to Irwin, 24 Oct 1928 (India Office – Halifax MSS).

26 Burned Out, 1928–30

1 Birkenhead, *Contemporary Personalities* (Cassell, 1924), p. 220.
2 *Punch* (17 Oct 1928).
3 F.E. to Baldwin, 13 April 1927 (Baldwin papers 162 f.31–4).
4 Amery to Irwin, 1 Nov 1928 (India Office – Halifax MSS).
5 *The Times* (24 Oct 1929).
6 Bradford, 5 March 1930.
7 *Annual Register* (1928), p. 96.
8 *The Times* (22 Nov 1928).
9 Ibid. (27 Nov 1928).
10 1900 Club, 14 Nov 1928.
11 *We Can Conquer Unemployment: Mr Lloyd George's Pledge* (London, 1929).
12 East Toxteth, 18 March 1929.
13 Norwich, 22 March 1929.
14 Sir Geoffrey Shakespeare, *Let Candles Be Brought In* (Macdonald, 1949), pp. 98–9; Sir Nigel Fisher.
15 Liverpool, 23 May 1929.
16 Albert Hall, 3 May 1929.
17 Newport, Isle of Wight, 29 May 1929.
18 Hoare memo in Templewood papers, Cambridge.
19 Beaverbrook telegram to F.E., 6 June 1929 (Beaverbrook papers C/41).
20 F.E. to Beaverbrook, 6 June 1929 (ibid.).
21 Beaverbrook to F.E., 7 June 1929 (ibid.).
22 F.E. to Beaverbrook, 11 June 1929 (ibid.).
23 *Daily Mail* (1 Nov 1929).
24 Davidson to Irwin, 9 Nov 1929, in Robert Rhodes James, *Memoirs of a Conservative: J.C.C. Davidson's Memoirs and Papers, 1910–1937* (Weidenfeld & Nicolson, 1969), p. 308.
25 Ramsay MacDonald, diary, 4 Nov 1929.
26 *Daily Telegraph*, 2 Nov 1929.
27 Birkenhead, *Last Essays* (Cassell, 1930), p. 45.
28 *Spectator* (9 Nov 1929).
29 *Daily Telegraph* (6 Nov 1929).
30 House of Lords, 5 Nov 1929.
31 *The Times* (7 Nov 1929).
32 House of Commons, 7 Nov 1929.
33 Birkenhead, *Last Essays*, pp. 53–4.

34 *The Times* (5 Dec 1929).
35 Ibid. (21 Feb 1930).
36 House of Lords, 20 Feb 1930.
37 Birkenhead, *The World in 2030* (Hodder & Stoughton, 1930), pp. 98–9.
38 Ibid., p. 208.
39 Advertisement in *The Times* (15 April 1930).
40 Birkenhead, *The World in 2030*, p. ix.
41 *Week-End Review* (10 May 1930).
42 *Daily Express* (21 May 1930).
43 *Week-End Review* (31 May 1930).
44 F.E. to Beaverbrook, 29 May 1930 (Beaverbrook papers C/41).
45 Hotel Cecil, 7 Feb 1922.
46 Birkenhead, *Fifty Famous Fights in Fact and Fiction* (Cassell, 1932), pp. vii–ix.
47 Birkenhead, *'F.E.'* (Eyre & Spottiswoode, 1959), p. 550.
48 Margaret to Lloyd George, 16 April 1930 (Lloyd George papers G/3/11/4).
49 F.E. to Baldwin, 8 May 1930 (Baldwin papers 165 f.22–3).
50 Maurice Bowra, *Memories, 1898–1939* (Weidenfeld & Nicolson, 1966), p. 140.
51 Viscount Lee of Fareham, *'A Good Innings'*, ed. Alan Clark (John Murray, 1974), p. 301.
52 House of Lords, 17 July 1930.
53 Margaret to Lloyd George, 17 Aug 1930 (Lloyd George papers G/3/11/5).
54 *The Times* (23 Aug 1930).
55 Mrs Enid Kohler to the author.
56 *The Times* (1 Oct 1930).
57 Winston S. Churchill, *Great Contemporaries* (Thornton Butterworth, 1937), Fontana edn, p. 151.
58 Birkenhead papers.
59 Sir Charles Petrie, *The Life and Letters of Sir Austen Chamberlain*, vol. II (Cassell, 1940), p. 379.
60 Margaret to Beaverbrook, 6 Oct 1930 (Beaverbrook papers).
61 The Other Club, 30 Oct 1930.
62 Birkenhead, *'F.E.'*, p. 476.
63 Margaret to Beaverbrook, 9 Oct 1930 (Beaverbrook papers).
64 Birkenhead papers.
65 *'Chips': The Diaries of Sir Henry Channon*, ed. Robert Rhodes James (Weidenfeld & Nicolson, 1967), p. 127 (19 May 1937).
66 *The Times* (1 Nov 1945).

Bibliography and Sources

Books by Lord Birkenhead

F.E. Smith, *The Story of Newfoundland* (1897).

F.E. Smith, *International Law* (Dent, 1899, 1902, 1906, 1911, 1918, 1927).

F.E. Smith, *Toryism, Illustrated by Extracts from Representative Speeches and Writings* (Harper & Brothers, 1903).

F.E. Smith, *Speeches Delivered in the House of Commons and Elsewhere, 1906–9* (Henry Young & Sons, Liverpool, 1909).

F.E. Smith, *Unionist Policy and Other Essays* (Williams & Norgate, 1913).

Sir Frederick Smith, *The Destruction of Merchant Ships under International Law* (Dent, 1917).

Lt-Col. J. W. B. Merewether and Sir Frederick Smith, *The Indian Corps in France* (Murray, 1917).

Sir Frederick Smith, Bart, *My American Visit* (Hutchinson, 1918).

Viscount Birkenhead, *Points of View*, 2 vols (Hodder & Stoughton, 1922).

Judgements Delivered by Lord Chancellor Birkenhead, ed. R. Burrows (H.M.S.O., 1923).

The Earl of Birkenhead, *America Revisited* (Cassell, 1924).

The Earl of Birkenhead, *Contemporary Personalities* (Cassell, 1924).

The Earl of Birkenhead, *Fourteen English Judges* (Cassell, 1926).

The Earl of Birkenhead, *Famous Trials of History* (Hutchinson, 1926).

The Earl of Birkenhead, *Law, Life and Letters*, 2 vols (Hodder & Stoughton, 1927).

The Earl of Birkenhead, *More Famous Trials* (Hutchinson, 1928).

The Earl of Birkenhead (ed.), *The Hundred Best English Essays* (Cassell, 1929).

The Speeches of Lord Birkenhead, (Cassell, 1929).

The Earl of Birkenhead, *Turning Points in History* (Hutchinson, 1930).

The Earl of Birkenhead (ed.), *500 English Letters* (Cassell, 1930).

The Earl of Birkenhead, *The World in 2030* (Hodder & Stoughton, 1930).

The Earl of Birkenhead, *Last Essays* (Cassell, 1930).
The Earl of Birkenhead, *Fifty Famous Fights in Fact and Fiction* (Cassell, 1932).

Previous Biographies of Lord Birkenhead

'Ephesian' (Bechhofer Roberts), *Lord Birkenhead* (Mills & Boon, 1926).
Ivor Thomas, *Our Lord Birkenhead: An Oxford Appreciation* (Putnam, 1930).
H.A. Taylor, *Smith of Birkenhead* (Stanley Paul, 1931).
The Earl of Birkenhead, *Frederick Edwin, Earl of Birkenhead: The First Phase* (Thornton Butterworth, 1933).
The Earl of Birkenhead, *Frederick Edwin, Earl of Birkenhead: The Last Phase* (Thornton Butterworth, 1935).
The Earl of Birkenhead, *'F.E.': The Life of F.E. Smith, First Earl of Birkenhead* (Eyre & Spottiswoode, 1959).
William Camp, *The Glittering Prizes* (MacGibbon & Kee, 1960).

Private Papers Consulted

Baldwin papers (Cambridge University Library).
Balfour papers (British Library).
Beaverbrook papers (House of Lords Record Office).
Beaverbrook/Birkenhead letters (a private collection, additional to the Beaverbrook papers, sold at Sotheby's in 1980 and bought by the Birkenhead family).
Birkenhead papers (in the possession of the Earl of Birkenhead, but seriously damaged by fire in 1979).
Austen Chamberlain papers (Birmingham University Library).
Neville Chamberlain papers (Birmingham University Library).
H.A.L. Fisher papers (Bodleian Library, Oxford).
Hanworth papers (Sir Ernest Pollock) (Bodleian Library, Oxford).
Bonar Law papers (House of Lords Record Office).
Lloyd George papers (House of Lords Record Office).
Maxse papers (Sussex County Record Office, Chichester).

Other Club records.
Leslie Scott papers (Warwick University Library, Coventry).
Selborne papers (Bodleian Library, Oxford).
Hugh Spencer collection (in the possession of Mr Hugh Spencer).
Wadham College archive.
Wargrave papers (Edward Goulding) (House of Lords Record Office).

Public Collections Consulted

Cabinet papers, 1915–22, 1924–8 (Public Record Office).
Lord Chancellor's Department Papers (Public Record Office).
Secretary of State/Viceroy correspondence, 1924–8 (India Office Library).

Newspapers and Periodicals Used

Birkenhead Advertiser
Birkenhead News
Isis
Liberal magazine
Liverpool Courier
Liverpool Daily Post
Oxford Magazine
Oxford Review
The Times (All references not otherwise credited are from *The Times*)

Unpublished Thesis

D.A. Roberts, 'Religion and Politics in Liverpool since 1900' (London MSc, 1965).

Bibliography

B. Abel-Smith and R. Stevens, *Lawyers and the Courts: A Sociological Study of the English Legal System, 1750–1965* (Heinemann, 1967).

Susan Mary Alsop, *Lady Sackville: A Biography* (Weidenfeld & Nicolson, 1978).

L.S. Amery, *Days of Fresh Air* (Jarrold, 1939).

——, *My Political Life*, 3 vols (Hutchinson, 1953–5).

The Leo Amery Diaries, ed. John Barnes and David Nicholson (Hutchinson, 1981).

F.W. Ashley, *My Sixty Years in the Law* (John Lane/The Bodley Head, 1936).

Lady Cynthia Asquith, *Diaries, 1915–1918* (Hutchinson, 1968).

Lord Beaverbrook, *Courage: The Story of Sir James Dunn* (Collins, 1961).

——, *The Decline and Fall of Lloyd George* (Collins, 1963).

——, *Men and Power, 1917–18* (Hutchinson, 1956).

——, *Politicians and the War* (Butterworth, 1928).

Arnold Bennett, *Journals*, 3 vols (Cassell, 1932–3).

Arnold Bennett's Letters to his Nephew, ed. Frank Swinnerton (Heinemann, 1936).

E.C. Bentley, *Those Days* (Constable, 1940).

Lord Birkenhead, *Lady Eleanor Smith, A Memoir* (Hutchinson, 1953).

——, *Halifax* (Hamish Hamilton, 1965).

Sheila Birkenhead, *Illustrious Friends* (Hamish Hamilton, 1965).

Robert Blake, *The Conservative Party from Peel to Churchill* (Oxford University Press, 1970).

——, *The Unknown Prime Minister* (Eyre & Spottiswoode, 1955).

Neal Blewett, *The Peers, the Parties and the People: The General Elections of 1910* (Macmillan, 1972).

W.S. Blunt, *My Diaries*, 2 vols (Secker, 1919–20).

Violet Bonham Carter, *Winston Churchill as I Knew Him* (Eyre & Spottiswoode, 1965).

Maurice Bowra, *Memories, 1898–1939* (Weidenfeld & Nicolson, 1966).

D.G. Boyce, *Englishmen and Irish Troubles, 1918–1922* (Cape, 1972).

W. Sorley Brown, *The Life and Genius of T.W.H. Crosland* (Cecil Palmer, 1928).

The Diaries of Sir Robert Bruce Lockhart, ed. Kenneth Young, vol. I (Macmillan, 1980).

John Buchan, *Memory Hold-the-Door* (Hodder & Stoughton, 1940).

Austen Chamberlain, *Down the Years* (Cassell, 1935).

——, *Politics from Inside* (Cassell, 1936).

The Collected Poems of G.K. Chesterton (Burns, Oates & Washbourne, 1927).

'Chips': The Diaries of Sir Henry Channon, ed. Robert Rhodes James (Weidenfeld & Nicolson, 1967).

Anne Chisholm, *Nancy Cunard* (Sidgwick & Jackson, 1979).

Randolph S. Churchill, *Lord Derby, 'King of Lancashire'* (Heinemann, 1959).

——, *Winston S. Churchill: Young Statesman, 1901–1914* (Heinemann, 1967).

Winston S. Churchill, *Great Contemporaries* (Thornton Butterworth, 1937).

Sir Edward Cook, *The Press in Wartime* (Macmillan, 1920).

Colin R. Coote, *The Other Club* (Sidgwick & Jackson, 1971).

Maurice Cowling, *The Impact of Labour, 1920–1924* (Cambridge University Press, 1971).

Lord Croft, *My Life of Strife* (Hutchinson, 1948).

Tom Cullen, *Maundy Gregory, Purveyor of Honours* (Bodley Head, 1974).

George Dangerfield, *The Strange Death of Liberal England* (MacGibbon & Kee, 1935).

Memoirs of a Conservative: J.C.C. Davidson's Memoirs and Papers, 1910–1937, ed. Robert Rhodes James (Weidenfeld & Nicolson, 1969).

J. Wentworth Day, *Lady Houston, D.B.E.: The Woman Who Won the War* (Allan Wingate, 1958).

The Collected Satires of Lord Alfred Douglas (Fortune Press, 1926).

E.S. Fay, *The Life of Mr Justice Swift* (Methuen, 1939).

C.B. Fry, *Life Worth Living* (Eyre & Spottiswoode, 1939).

A.G. Gardiner, *Pillars of Society* (James Nisbet, 1913).

Martin Gilbert, *Winston S. Churchill, 1914–1916* (Heinemann, 1971).

——, *Winston S. Churchill, 1917–1922* (Heinemann, 1975).

——, *Winston S. Churchill, 1922–1939* (Heinemann, 1976).

John Grigg, *Lloyd George: The People's Champion, 1902–1911* (Eyre Methuen, 1978).

P.J. Grigg, *Prejudice and Judgement* (Cape, 1948).

The Earl of Halifax, *Fulness of Days* (Collins, 1957).

Brian Harrison, *Separate Spheres* (Oxford University Press, 1978).

R.F.V. Heuston, *The Lives of the Lord Chancellors, 1885–1940* (Oxford University Press, 1964).

J. Hills and M. Woods, *Industrial Unrest: A Practical Solution* (1914).

F.W. Hirst, *In the Golden Days* (Muller, 1948).

Christopher Hollis, *The Oxford Union* (Evans, 1965).

The Holmes–Laski Letters, ed. M.A. Howe (Geoffrey Cumberlege, 1953).

H. Montgomery Hyde, *Carson* (Heinemann, 1953).

——, *Lord Reading* (Heinemann, 1967).

——, *Oscar Wilde* (Eyre Methuen, 1976).

——, *The Trial of Roger Casement* (William Hodge, 1960).

Alan Hyman, *The Rise and Fall of Horatio Bottomley* (Cassell, 1972).

Brian Inglis, *Roger Casement* (Hodder & Stoughton, 1973).

Robert Jackson, *The Chief: The Biography of Gordon Hewart, Lord Chief Justice of England, 1922–1940* (Harrap, 1959).

Harold Jager, *Brief Life* (Henry Young, Liverpool, 1934).

Roy Jenkins, *Asquith* (Collins, 1964).

——, *Mr Balfour's Poodle* (Heinemann, 1954).

W.P. Jolly, *Lord Leverhulme* (Constable, 1976).

L.E. Jones, *An Edwardian Youth* (Macmillan, 1956).

Thomas Jones, *Whitehall Diary*, ed. K. Middlemas, 2 vols (Oxford University Press, 1969–71).

J.R. Kaighin, *Bygone Birkenhead* (Birkenhead, 1925).

Robert Kee, *The Green Flag* (Weidenfeld & Nicolson, 1972).

G.W. Keeton and J. Cameron (ed.), *The Trial of the 'Veronica' Mutineers* (William Hodge, 1952).

G. Knott (ed.), *The Trial of Roger Casement* (William Hodge, 1926).

F.H. Lawson, *The Oxford Law School, 1850–1965* (Oxford University Press, 1968).

Viscount Lee of Fareham, *'A Good Innings': The Private Papers of Viscount Lee of Fareham*, ed. Alan Clark (John Murray, 1974).

Lord Longford, *Kennedy* (Weidenfeld & Nicolson, 1976).

F.S.L. Lyons, *Ireland since the Famine* (Weidenfeld & Nicolson, 1971).

Edward Marjoribanks, *The Life of Lord Carson*, vol. I (Gollancz, 1932).

Sir John Masterman, *On the Chariot Wheel* (Oxford University Press, 1975).

Lucy Masterman, *C.F.G. Masterman* (Frank Cass, 1939).

K. Middlemas and J. Barnes, *Baldwin* (Weidenfeld & Nicolson, 1969).

K.O. Morgan, *Consensus and Disunity: The Lloyd George Coalition Government, 1918–1922* (Oxford University Press, 1979).

H.A. Morrah, *The Oxford Union, 1823–1923* (Cassell, 1923).

Margaret Morris, *The General Strike* (Penguin, 1976).

Leonard Mosley, *Curzon* (Longman, 1960).

Sir Osward Mosley, *My Life* (Nelson, 1968).

Ramsay Muir, *An Autobiography and Some Essays*, ed. Stuart Hodgson (Lund Humphries, 1943).

Bruce K. Murray, *The People's Budget, 1909–10* (Oxford University Press, 1980).

Nigel Nicolson, *Portrait of a Marriage* (Weidenfeld & Nicolson, 1973).

Alfred Noyes, *The Accusing Ghost, or Justice for Casement* (Gollancz, 1957).

Frank Owen, *Tempestuous Journey: Lloyd George, His Life and Times* (Hutchinson, 1954).

Frank Pakenham, *Born to Believe* (Cape, 1953).

——, *Peace By Ordeal* (Cape, 1935).

Lord Eustace Percy, *Some Memories* (Eyre & Spottiswoode, 1958).

Sir Charles Petrie, *The Life and Letters of Sir Austen Chamberlain*, 2 vols (Cassell, 1939–40).

G.A. Phillips, *The General Strike* (Weidenfeld & Nicolson, 1976).

R. Pound and G. Harmsworth, *Northcliffe* (Cassell, 1959).

Martin Pugh, *Electoral Reform in War and Peace, 1906–18* (Routledge & Kegan Paul, 1978).

John Ramsden, *The Age of Balfour and Baldwin, 1902–1940* (Longman, 1978).

The Autobiography of Arthur Ransome (Cape, 1976).

B.L. Reid, *The Lives of Roger Casement* (Yale, 1976).

Col. C. à C. Repington, *The First World War* (Constable, 1920).

Lord Riddell's Intimate Diary of the Peace Conference and After (Gollancz, 1933).

Lord Riddell's War Diary, 1914–1918 (Ivor Nicholson & Watson, 1933).

Bechhofer Roberts, *Sir John Simon* (Robert Hale, 1938).

Stephen Roskill, *Hankey, Man of Secrets*, 3 vols (Collins, 1970–4).

V. Sackville-West, *Pepita* (Hogarth Press, 1937).

Stanley Salvidge, *Salvidge of Liverpool* (Hodder & Stoughton, 1934).

The Political Diaries of C.P. Scott, ed. Trevor Wilson (Collins, 1970).

G.R. Searle, *The Quest for National Efficiency* (Blackwell, 1971).

Sir Geoffrey Shakespeare, *Let Candles Be Brought In* (Macdonald, 1949).

Viscount Simon, *Retrospect* (Hutchinson, 1952).

Lady Eleanor Smith, *Life's a Circus* (Longman, Green, 1939).

Mary Soames, *Clementine Churchill* (Cassell, 1979).

R. Speaight, *The Life of Hilaire Belloc* (Hollis & Carter, 1957).

Lloyd George: A Diary by Frances Stevenson, ed. A.J.P. Taylor (Hutchinson, 1971).

A.T.Q. Stewart, *The Ulster Crisis: Resistance to Home Rule, 1912–14* (Faber, 1967).

Serjeant A.M. Sullivan, *The Last Serjeant* (Macdonald, 1952).

Alan Sykes, *Tariff Reform in British Politics, 1903–1913* (Oxford University Press, 1980).

A.J. Sylvester, *The Real Lloyd George* (Cassell, 1947).

A.J.P. Taylor, *Beaverbrook* (Hamish Hamilton, 1972).

——, *English History, 1914–1945* (Oxford University Press, 1965).

—— (ed.), *My Darling Pussy: The Letters of Lloyd George and Frances Stevenson, 1913–1941* (Weidenfeld & Nicolson, 1975).

Rex Taylor, *Michael Collins* (Hutchinson, 1968).

The History of 'The Times', vol. IV (*The Times*, 1952).

C. Townshend, *The British Campaign in Ireland, 1919–1921* (Oxford University Press, 1975).

Sir Arthur Underhill, *A Concise Explanation of Lord Birkenhead's Act* (1922).

Philip Waller, *Democracy and Sectarianism: A Political and Social History of Liverpool, 1868–1939* (Liverpool University Press, 1981).

Nourah Waterhouse, *Private and Official* (Cape, 1942).

Lord Winterton, *Orders of the Day* (Cassell, 1953).

——, *Pre-War* (Macmillan, 1932).

G.M. Young, *Stanley Baldwin* (Hart Davis, 1952).

Index

PIMLICO

PAUL SCOTT   A Life by Hilary Spurling

'Must rate as one of the best biographies written since the War. It is a brilliant and disturbing study of a gifted writer whose engaging manner and apparent normality concealed a violent and obsessive nature.' Selina Hastings, *Harpers & Queen*

SURVIVING THE HOLOCAUST   The Kovno Ghetto Diary by Avraham Tory; edited and introduced by Martin Gilbert

'We have here a record of what it is like to live through seasons in Hell . . . Remarkable and unforgettable, I cannot commend this book too highly to anyone who seeks to understand these terrible times.' Allan Massie, *Sunday Telegraph*

BATTLES OF THE ENGLISH CIVIL WAR by Austin Woolrych

'An excellent book . . . It covers the three decisive engagements which sealed the fate of King Charles I: Marston Moor [July 1644] which lost him the North, Naseby [June 1645] which lost him most of his army, and Preston [August 1648] which lost him his head . . . It most skilfully indicates all the essential connections between the Civil War's political, social and military aspects.' C.V. Wedgwood, *Daily Telegraph*

THE ENGLISHMAN'S FOOD   Five Centuries of English Diet by J.C. Drummond and Anne Wilbraham; introduction by Tom Jaine

'The achievement of this pioneering book is very great. It remains a remarkable contribution to the study of eating habits and health in society.' Derek Cooper

BADEN-POWELL by Tim Jeal

'In an age of good biographies, here is one that deserves to be called great . . . a magnificent book.' Piers Brendon, *Mail on Sunday*

BRITANNIA A History of Roman Britain by Sheppard Frere

'Brilliant . . . An integrated commentary and comprehensive judgement on the whole Romano-British scene.' *The Times Literary Supplement*

WEEK-END WODEHOUSE Introduction by Hilaire Belloc

'A peerless collection.' Max Hastings, *Sunday Times*

THE FACE OF BATTLE by John Keegan

'This without any doubt is one of the half-dozen best books on warfare to appear in the English language since the end of the Second World War.' Michael Howard, *Sunday Times*

ALAN MOOREHEAD by Tom Pocock

'Pocock's biography is excellent . . . it would be difficult to think of a better guide to the life of a Second World War correspondent.' Frank McLynn, *Sunday Telegraph*

THE CONTROL OF NATURE by John McPhee

'This splendid book describes three monumental acts of defiance against Mother Nature . . . The human drama is almost as breathtaking as the scale of these enterprises.' *Observer*

ARIEL A Shelley Romance by André Maurois

'An historic landmark in modern literary biography, as fine as any miniature produced by Lytton Strachey or Harold Nicolson.' Richard Holmes

COMPLETE VERSE by Hilaire Belloc; introduction by A. N. Wilson

'The verses sing a multitude of memories. The wonder is, in finding them all collected, how profuse and pure a genius is here displayed.' Evelyn Waugh, *Spectator*

CROSSMAN The Pursuit of Power by Anthony Howard

'Written from a background of great political knowledge and with shafts of penetrating insight . . . I doubt if it will be quickly, if ever, superseded.' Roy Jenkins, *Sunday Times*

GEORGIAN LONDON by John Summerson; a new illustrated and revised edition

'The scintillating text of this provocative classic was never matched by worthy pictures. Now, with a complete, handsome revamp, and with an Epilogue bringing the story up to date, the whole fine book at last truly reflects the perfection of the buildings.' Graham Hughes, *Arts Review*

SELF PORTRAIT WITH FRIENDS **The Selected Diaries of Cecil Beaton** Edited by Richard Buckle

'His book shows him to be sharper and more sardonic with his pen than with his camera – no less talented a portraitist, but an exacter and sometimes a crueller one. What this gifted, witty, sensitive creature writes best about is people. This is a minor masterpiece of wit and observation.' Cyril Ray, *Daily Mail*

A VERY CLOSE CONSPIRACY **Vanessa Bell and Virginia Woolf** by Jane Dunn

'This is not only an important book in its own field, the triumphant outcome of years of loving concentration, but a book of rare discernment and imagination. It is one of the few books which allows me to believe that the author actually knew both my mother and my aunt, and I welcome it as deepening my understanding both of them and their relation to Bloomsbury.' Angelica Garnett

THE POUND ERA by Hugh Kenner

'Not so much a book as a library, or better, a new kind of book in which biography, history and the analysis of literature are harmoniously articulated . . . For the student of modern letters it is a treasure, for the general reader it is one of the most interesting books he will ever pick up in a lifetime of reading.' Guy Davenport, *National Review*